International Criminal Law

ROGER O'KEEFE

OXFORD
UNIVERSITY PRESS

OXFORD
UNIVERSITY PRESS

Great Clarendon Street, Oxford, OX2 6DP,
United Kingdom

Oxford University Press is a department of the University of Oxford.
It furthers the University's objective of excellence in research, scholarship,
and education by publishing worldwide. Oxford is a registered trade mark of
Oxford University Press in the UK and in certain other countries

© Roger O'Keefe 2015

The moral rights of the author have been asserted

First published 2015
First published in paperback 2017

All rights reserved. No part of this publication may be reproduced, stored in
a retrieval system, or transmitted, in any form or by any means, without the
prior permission in writing of Oxford University Press, or as expressly permitted
by law, by licence or under terms agreed with the appropriate reprographics
rights organization. Enquiries concerning reproduction outside the scope of the
above should be sent to the Rights Department, Oxford University Press, at the
address above

You must not circulate this work in any other form
and you must impose this same condition on any acquirer

Published in the United States of America by Oxford University Press
198 Madison Avenue, New York, NY 10016, United States of America

British Library Cataloguing in Publication Data
Data available

Library of Congress Cataloging in Publication Data
Data available

ISBN 978–0–19–968904–0 (Hbk.)
ISBN 978–0–19–880620–2 (Pbk.)

Links to third party websites are provided by Oxford in good faith and
for information only. Oxford disclaims any responsibility for the materials
contained in any third party website referenced in this work.

In loving memory of my father

Preface

This book gives an account of international criminal law from the perspective of a formalist, positivist public international lawyer. Obviously this is not the only frame of reference that could be brought to bear on the subject. Nor need it be considered a better frame of reference than others. Much valuable work in the field continues to be done by scholars with a background in criminal law and criminal legal theory, by scholars of a critical-theoretical persuasion, and by scholars of a criminological, sociological or other empirical bent. The present study seeks merely to complement these voices with that of what might, with a degree of trepidation and no necessary claim to greater legitimacy, be called mainstream public international law.

As with any field, where one pegs the limits of international criminal law is to an extent arbitrary. This book conceives of the field broadly, as encompassing not only the international law relating to international crimes and international criminal courts (what in French is referred to as '*droit pénal international*') but also the rules of international law governing states' assertion and exercise of their respective national criminal jurisdictions (what in French has been referred to as '*droit pénal international*'). At the same time, for the sake of manageability and focus, the book is organized around international crimes and their suppression through national and international criminal courts. So, for example, while the Special Tribunal for Lebanon is examined in the contexts of the definition of an international criminal court and of the different ways of establishing such courts, it does not, in contrast to the other current and recent international criminal courts, enjoy a chapter of its own, on the technical ground that its subject-matter jurisdiction comprises solely crimes under Lebanese law (although ultimately more significantly on the collateral practical ground of the paucity of its output so far).

In its treatment of international criminal courts, the book concentrates on the more substantive legal issues. Although any question as to the legal powers of a court is in one sense procedural, the focus here is not on what is sometimes referred to as 'international criminal procedure', meaning the respective bodies of rules, regulations, and other directives governing how pre-trial, trial, appellate, and related proceedings are or were to be conducted in each of the international criminal courts that exist or have existed to date. The detailed, often jurisdiction-specific legal issues pertaining to the collection, disclosure, presentation, and use of evidence, to cross-examination, to rights of appeal, and so on, in the context of proceedings before the different international criminal courts tend to go beyond what is of most concern to the public international lawyer on the Clapham omnibus. They also exceed the expertise of the public international lawyer who penned this volume. As a result, procedural matters are dealt with here only to the extent that they implicate more substantive questions of public international law. The same goes, for the most part, for sentencing and the enforcement of sentences, for the rights of accused and suspects, and for the protection and support of witnesses and victims and the participation in proceedings of the latter. It goes too for non-penal institutional responses to international crimes, such as Rwanda's *gacaca* courts and other alternative justice mechanisms. (The only intended exception to the last was a chapter on non-penal responses by the various organs and subsidiary organs of the United Nations to actual and alleged international crimes—that is, on various measures in the field of international criminal law, broadly conceived, taken by the Security Council, beyond its establishment and its co-operation in the establishment of international criminal courts and its roles in relation to the International Criminal Court, by the General Assembly, and increasingly by the Human Rights Council. But it became clear while writing the chapter that far deeper research and analysis was needed than time permitted. Should there be a second edition of the book, such a chapter will feature.) None of this, it should be stressed, is to downplay the importance of the omitted topics. A contractual delivery date and word limit, however, mean that a line has to be drawn somewhere, and the point of intersection of the likely interest of the bulk of the book's readership and the outer bounds of the author's expertise seemed a sensible place to draw that line.

In keeping with the formalist outlook of the book, readers will find no discussion of the aims of or functions served by international criminal law (congruence between the two not being self-evident, either logically or observably). Again, this is not intended to imply that such questions are unimportant. But to the putative extent that the aims of international criminal law are any different from the aims of criminal law *tout court*, there is little consensus as to what these particular aims might be, while any intellectually serious account of the functions served by international criminal law demands the skills and knowledge of the socio-legal scholar, the political scientist, the historian and contemporary analyst of the Balkans and central and west Africa, and so on. Suffice here to say that many of the claims made on behalf of international criminal law are either unverifiable or await verification.

As far as can be ascertained, the book reflects the law as it stood on 28 November 2014, although some of the suggested reading at the end of several chapters postdates this.

Acknowledgements

Warm thanks are owed to many people: to Merel Alstein for commissioning the book, to Emma Endean for ushering it through production, and to both for their understanding of the difficult circumstances that accompanied the final months of its writing; to John Louth for encouraging my submission of a proposal for the book; to Sir Franklin Berman for including the book in the Oxford International Law Library; to Dhanuj and everyone at Newgen and to the anonymous copy-editor and proofreaders, all of whose professionalism made the production process as painless as possible; to James Russell for his bibliographical and related research and to Magdalene College, Cambridge, for funding James's summer sojourn at the Lauterpacht Centre for International Law; to Helen Worsnop, to call whose astoundingly meticulous, insightful, level-headed, and tactful research assistance and wider support invaluable would be to understate their contribution to the book's realization; to the Newton Trust Small Grants scheme at the University of Cambridge for funding in part Helen's work; to the Lauterpacht Centre for International Law, and especially to its administrator Anita Rutherford, for making bench space and other arrangements for James and Helen, for managing associated monies, and for making both feel welcome; to the decade and a half of LLM students at Cambridge who served as the gifted guinea-pigs on whom I tested most of the material that follows; and to my parents and siblings for everything.

Contents

Table of Cases	xv
Table of Treaties and Other International Instruments	xxxiii
Table of Legislation	lxi
List of Abbreviations	lxvii

PART ONE FOUNDATIONAL CONCEPTS AND PRINCIPLES

1. **The International Rules on National Criminal Jurisdiction** — 3
    - I. Introduction — 3
    - II. The Concept and Distinct Aspects of Jurisdiction — 3
    - III. Jurisdiction to Prescribe — 6
    - IV. Jurisdiction to Enforce — 29
    - V. Conclusion — 45

2. **The Concept of an International Crime** — 47
    - I. Introduction — 47
    - II. The Concept and Definition of an 'International Crime' — 48
    - III. Species of International Crime — 61
    - IV. Crimes under International Law — 67
    - V. Conclusion — 84

3. **The Types of Criminal Court** — 85
    - I. Introduction — 85
    - II. Terminology — 85
    - III. International and Municipal Criminal Courts: A Formal Binarism — 86
    - IV. International and Municipal Criminal Courts: A Descriptive Pluralism — 105
    - V. The Legal Significance of the Distinction Between International and Municipal Criminal Courts — 105
    - VI. The Legal Significance of the Differences among International Criminal Courts — 111
    - VII. Conclusion — 113

PART TWO THE SUBSTANTIVE LAW OF INTERNATIONAL CRIMES

Crimes under Customary International Law

4 The Crimes		119
I.	Introduction	119
II.	Preliminary Matters	120
III.	War Crimes	123
IV.	Crimes Against Humanity	137
V.	The Crime of Genocide	145
VI.	The Crime of Aggression	154
VII.	Other Crimes?	160
VIII.	A Hierarchy of Gravity?	160
IX.	Conclusion	162
5. Modes of Responsibility		166
I.	Introduction	166
II.	Preliminary Matters	167
III.	Commission	169
IV.	Planning	183
V.	Instigation	184
VI.	Ordering	186
VII.	Soliciting or Inducing	188
VIII.	Aiding and Abetting	188
IX.	Contribution to a Crime Committed or Attempted by a Group of Persons Acting with a Common Purpose	193
X.	Specific Modes of Responsibility for the Crime of Genocide	196
XI.	Attempt	200
XII.	Modes of Responsibility and the Crime of Aggression	201
XIII.	Command and Other Superior Responsibility	201
XIV.	Conclusion	207
6. Grounds for Excluding Responsibility		210
I.	Introduction	210
II.	Preliminary Matters	210
III.	Accepted Defences	212
IV.	Rejected Defences	221
V.	Mitigating Circumstances	223
VI.	Conclusion	224

Treaty Crimes

7. The Crimes and Their Modes of Responsibility		229
I.	Introduction	229
II.	Conceptual Issues	230

	III. The Crimes in Outline	240
	IV. Conclusion	308
8.	**The Obligations and Rights of States Parties**	311
	I. Introduction	311
	II. Characteristic Obligations	313
	III. Some Specific Obligations	342
	IV. Conclusion	354

PART THREE THE SUPPRESSION OF INTERNATIONAL CRIMES

Municipal Law and Courts

9.	**Substantive Law, Jurisdiction, Prosecution, and Courts**	361
	I. Introduction	361
	II. Substantive Law and Jurisdiction	362
	III. Prosecution	370
	IV. Adjudication	375
	V. Conclusion	402
10.	**Immunity and Inviolability**	405
	I. Introduction	405
	II. General	406
	III. The Content of Immunity and Inviolability	409
	IV. Immunity *Ratione Personae* and Inviolability	412
	V. Immunity *Ratione Materiae*	425
	VI. Conclusion	458
11.	**Statutory Limitation and Amnesty**	461
	I. Introduction	461
	II. The State Providing for Statutory Limitation or Amnesty	462
	III. Foreign Prosecuting States	477
	IV. Conclusion	478

International Criminal Courts

12.	**The International Criminal Tribunals for the Former Yugoslavia and Rwanda and Their Residual Mechanism**	483
	I. Introduction	483
	II. General	483
	III. Legality of Establishment	491
	IV. Jurisdiction	493
	V. Relationship to National Criminal Jurisdictions	499
	VI. Relationship to the International Court of Justice	503

VII.	Co-operation with the Tribunals	504
VIII.	Conclusion	507

13. The Special Court for Sierra Leone and Residual Special Court for Sierra Leone — 510

I.	Introduction	510
II.	General	511
III.	Legality of Establishment	518
IV.	Jurisdiction	519
V.	Relationship to the Courts of Sierra Leone	526
VI.	Co-operation with the Special Court	527
VII.	Conclusion	528

14. The International Criminal Court — 529

I.	Introduction	529
II.	General	529
III.	Jurisdiction	538
IV.	Applicable Law	551
V.	Relationship with National Jurisdictions	554
VI.	Co-operation with the Court	563
VII.	Conclusion	581

Index — 585

Table of Cases

NATIONAL JURISDICTIONS

Argentina
Chile v Arancibia Clavel, ILDC 1082 (AR 2004) 11.21
Office of the Prosecutor v Priebke, ILDC 1599 (AR 1995) 11.21
Riveros v Office of the Public Prosecutor, ILDC 1084 (AR 2007) 11.21

Australia
Polyukhovich v Commonwealth of Australia, 91 ILR 1 (1991) 9.12, 9.18, 10.73
R v Tang, 43 ILR 76 (2008) 7.36

Belgium
BVD v NV Deutsche Bank, ILDC 373 (BE 2005).................................... 1.72
Castle John and Nederlandse Stichting Sirius v NV Nabeco and NV Parfin,
   77 ILR 537 (1986).. 1.58
Pinochet, 119 ILR 345 (1998) 10.63, 11.14, 11.21
Sharon and Yaron, Re, 127 ILR 110 (2003)....................... 10.36, 10.44, 10.75, 14.47

Bosnia and Herzegovina
Damjanović, Case No AP 325/08, Decision on Admissibility and Merits, Constitutional
   Court of Bosnia and Herzegovina, 27 September 2013 .... 9.61
Đukić, Case No AP 5161/10, Decision on Admissibility and Merits, Constitutional
   Court of Bosnia and Herzegovina, 23 January 2014............................ 9.61

Cambodia
Case File/Dossier No 001/18-07-2007/ECCC/TC ('*Duch*'), ECCC Trial Chamber,
   Trial Judgment, 26 July 2010.. 9.65
Case File/Dossier No 001/18-07-2007-ECCC/SC ('*Duch*'), ECCC Supreme Court
   Chamber, Appeal Judgment, 3 February 2012 .... 7.36, 9.64, 9.65
Case File/Dossier No 002/19-09-2007/ECCC/TC (*Ieng Sary*), ECCC Trial Chamber,
   Termination of the Proceedings against the Accused Ieng Sary,
   14 March 2013 .... 9.65, 11.28, 11.29
Case File/Dossier No 002/19-09-2007-ECCC-SC (16) (*Ieng Thirith*), ECCC Supreme
   Court Chamber, Decision on Immediate Appeal against the Trial Chamber's Order to
   Unconditionally Release the Accused Ieng Thirith, 14 December 2012 .... 9.65
Case File/Dossier No 002/19-09-2007/ECCC/TC (*Nuon Chea and Khieu Samphan*),
   ECCC Trial Chamber, Decision on the Applicability of Joint Criminal Enterprise,
   12 September 2011 .... 5.29
Case File/Dossier No 002/19-09-2007/ECCC/TC (E313) (*Nuon Chea and Khieu Samphan*),
   ECCC Trial Chamber, Judgment, 7 August 2014............................... 9.65
Criminal Case File No 002-19-09-2007-ECCC/OCIJ (PTC 35, 37, 38 & 39)
   (*Ieng Thirith* et al), ECCC Pre-Trial Chamber, Decision on the Appeals Against the
   Co-Investigative Judges' Order on Joint Criminal Enterprise (JCE),
   20 May 2010 .... 5.29, 9.64

Canada
Federal Republic of Germany and Rauca, Re, 88 ILR 277 (1983) 10.73
Jaffe v Miller, 95 ILR 446 (1993) 10.64

Queen, The v Munyaneza (Désiré), ILDC 1339 (CA 2009) 9.6
R v Finta, 82 ILR 424 (1989), 98 ILR 520 (1992) 10.73

Chile
Pinto (Victor Raúl) v Relatives of Tomás Rojas, ILDC 1093 (CL 2007). 11.14, 11.17
Rodríguez (Miguel Ángel Solís), CA Santiago, 5 January 2004 .... 11.9

China
Shantou Municipal People's Prosecutor v Naim (Atan), ILDC 1161 (CN 2003) 9.7

East Timor
Prosecutor v Armando dos Santos, Case No 16/2001, CA East Timor, 15 July 2003 .... 9.45

France
Agent judiciare du Trésor c Malta Maritime Authority et Camel X, Cour de cassation
　(Chambre criminelle), 23 November 2004, no 04-84.265 .... 10.47
Argoud, Re, 45 ILR 90 (1964) 1.109
Barbie, 78 ILR 124 (1983, 1984, and 1985), 100 ILR 330 (1988). 10.73
Association des familles des victimes du 'Joola', Cour de cassation (Chambre criminelle),
　no 09-84818, *Bull crim* (2010), no 9 .... 10.47
Decision No 98-408 DC (Re Treaty Establishing the International Criminal Court),
　125 ILR 475 (1999). 14.75
Gaddafi, 125 ILR 490 (2001). 10.42
Munyeshyaka, 127 ILR 134 (1998). 9.5, 9.7
Ould Dah, Assize Court of Gard, 1 July 2005. . . . . 10.82, 11.33, 11.34

Germany
Bosnia-Herzegovina Genocide case ('Kusljić'), 131 ILR 274 (2001). 9.7
Decision of Federal Constitutional Court of 2 August 1984, [1984] NStZ 563 .... 1.109
Decision of Federal Constitutional Court of 30 May 1985, [1985] NStZ 464 .... 1.109
Decision of Federal Constitutional Court of 5 November 2003, 109 BVerfGE 13,
　ILDC 10 (DE 2003) 1.109
Former Syrian Ambassador to the German Democratic Republic, 115 ILR 595. . . . . 10.60, 10.66,
　　　　　　　　　　　　　　　　　　　　　　　　　　　　　　　　　　　　　　10.89, 10.98
Honecker, Re, 80 ILR 365 (1984) 10.16
Sokolović, ILDC 56 (DE 2001) 9.7
Tabatabai, 80 ILR 388 (1984) 10.29

Greece
Prosecutor v TP, ILDC 1498 (GR 2003). 1.121

Israel
Attorney-General for Israel v Eichmann, 36 ILR 5 (1961 and 1962). 1.61, 1.64,
　　　　　　　　　　　　　　　　　　　　　　　　　　　　　　　　　　　　1.109, 8.40, 10.73
State of Israel v John (Ivan) Demianiuk, (1988) 18 *Israel Ybk HR* 229 (1988) 10.73

Italy
General Prosecutor at the Court of Appeals of Milan v Adler, ILDC 1960 (IT 2012) 10.60, 10.94
Hass and Priebke, Military Court of Rome, 22 July 1997; Military Court of Appeal,
　7 March 1998; Court of Cassation, 16 November 1998. . . . . .10.73, 11.13
Italy v Djukanović, ILDC 74 (IT 2004) 10.36
Lozano (Mario Luiz), ILDC 1085 (IT 2008) 10.47, 10.79
Milde, Military Tribunal of La Spezia, 10 October 2006. . . . . 10.82

Kenya

Attorney General v Hashi and Others, Civil Appeal No 113 of 2011,
  18 October 2012 .... 1.57

Netherlands

'Cygnus' Case (Somali Pirates), 145 ILR 491 (2010). 1.57
Gerbsch, 13 LRTWC 131 (1948). 6.13
Hague City Party, The and others v Netherlands, ILDC 849 (NL 2005) 10.44
Public Prosecutor v F, ILDC 797 (NL 2007). 11.33
*Slobodan Milošević v International Criminal Tribunal for the former Yugoslavia and
  State of the Netherlands*, 41 ILM 1310 (2002). 12.9, 12.13, 12.19
Slobodan Milošević v State of the Netherlands, Hague District Court, 31 August 2001 .... 12.9, 12.13, 12.19
Van Anraat, ILDC 753 (NL 2009). 4.32
Wijngaarde et al v Bouterse, (2000) 3 *YIHL* 677 (2000) 10.75

Peru

Attorney-General, ILDC 1516 (PE 2009) 11.14

Poland

Koch, In Re, 30 ILR 496 (1959) 10.73

Rhodesia

S v 'A' 1979 (4) SA 51 (R) 1.50

Seychelles

Republic of Seychelles v Ahmed and Five Others, Crim Side No 21 of 2011, 14 July 2011 .... 1.58
Republic of Seychelles v Ali and Ten Others, Crim Side No 14 of 2010, 3 November 2010 .... 1.57
Republic of Seychelles v Dahir and Ten Others, Crim Side No 51 of 2009, 26 July 2010 .... 1.58
Republic of Seychelles v Ise and Four Others, Crim Side No 76 of 2010, 30 June 2011 .... 1.57
Republic of Seychelles v Jama and Fourteen Others, Crim Side No 16 of 2012,
  2 November 2012 .... 1.57
Republic of Seychelles v Osman and Ten Others, 152 ILR 513 (2011) 1.57, 1.59

Sierra Leone

Sesay, Kondewa and Fofana v President of the Special Court and Others, SC No 1/2003,
  Supreme Court, 14 October 2005 .... 3.20, 11.24, 13.6

South Africa

Azanian People's Organization (AZAPO) v President of the Republic of South Africa, 131 ILR 492
  (1996) 11.17
South Africa v Basson, ILDC 494 (ZA 2005) 11.33
S v Ebrahim, 95 ILR 417 (1991) 1.109, 1.114

Spain

Castro, Audiencia Nacional (Plenary), 4 March 1999 .... 10.42
Hassan II, Audiencia Nacional (Central Examining Magistrate No 5),
  23 December 1998. .... 10.42
Obiang Nguema et al, Audiencia Nacional (Central Examining Magistrate No 5),
  23 December 1998. .... 10.42
Rwanda, Audiencia Nacional (Central Examining Magistrate No 4),
  6 February 2008. .... 10.44

Switzerland

A v Ministère public de la Confédération, B and C, Swiss Federal Criminal Court, 25 July 2012
  ('*Nezzar*') 10.8, 10.37, 10.38, 10.79, 10.81
Adamov (Evgeny) v Federal Office of Justice, ILDC 339 (CH 2005) 10.47, 10.54
E v Police Inspectorate of Basle, 75 ILR 106 (1980) 1.72
Kroeger v Swiss Federal Prosecutor's Office, 72 ILR 606 (1966) 10.73

Uganda

Thomas Kwoyelo, alias Latoni v Uganda, Constitutional Court of Uganda,
  22 September 2011 ....11.21, 11.28

United Kingdom

Barak, Re, City of Westminster Magistrates' Court, 29 September 2009, ...10.37, 10.44
Bo Xilai, Re, 128 ILR 713 (2005)...10.37, 10.44
Director of Public Prosecutions v Stonehouse, 73 ILR 252 (1977) 1.50
Heyer and Six Others (The Essen Lynching Case), 1 LRTWC 88 (1945) 4.32
Gorbachev, Re, City of Westminster Magistrates' Court (Daphne Wickham, Deputy
  Senior District Judge), 30 March 2011....................................... 10.44
Jones v Ministry of the Interior of the Kingdom of Saudi Arabia, 129 ILR 629 (2006) ... 10.60, 10.64,
  10.74, 10.88, 10.90
Khurts Bat v Investigating Judge of the German Federal Court, 147 ILR 633 (2011) 10.38, 10.70
Meunier, In re [1894] 2 QB 415.. 1.98
Mofaz, Re, 128 ILR 709 (2004) 10.37
P, Re (No 2), 114 ILR 485 (1998)... 10.24
R v Abdul-Hussain (Mustafa Shakir), Court of Appeal (Criminal Division),
  17 December 1998... 9.15
R v Bow Street Metropolitan Stipendiary Magistrate, Ex parte Pinochet Ugarte (No 1),
  119 ILR 50 (1998).................................... 2.12, 10.63, 10.74, 10.77, 11.32
R v Bow Street Metropolitan Stipendiary Magistrate, Ex parte Pinochet Ugarte (No 2),
  119 ILR 112 (1999)..10.63, 11.32
R v Bow Street Metropolitan Stipendiary Magistrate, Ex parte Pinochet Ugarte (No 3),
  119 ILR 135 (1999)..................1.97, 2.12, 10.42, 10.47, 10.64, 10.72, 10.74,
  10.75, 10.77, 10.80, 10.90, 10.91, 10.92, 10.97
R v Horseferry Road Magistrates' Court, Ex parte Bennett, 95 ILR 380 (1993)..........1.109, 1.114
R v Safi (Ali Ahmed) [2003] EWCA Crim 1809.................................... 9.15
R v Sawoniuk (Anthony) [2000] Cr App R 220..................................... 9.7
R v Treacy, 55 ILR 110 (1970) 1.50
Secretary of State for Trade v Markus [1976] AC 35 .... 1.50
R v Zardad (Faryadi), ILDC 95 (UK 2004) 7.121
Tatchell v Mugabe, 136 ILR 572 (2004) 10.44
Tesch and Two Others (The Zyklon B Case), 1 LRTWC 93 (1946) 4.32

United States

Artukovic v Rison, 79 ILR 383 (1985 and 1986)..................................... 10.73
Demjanjuk v Petrovsky, 79 ILR 534 (1985).. 10.73
Flick v Johnson, 174 F 2d 983 (DC Cir 1949) 3.30
Hirota v MacArthur, General of the Army et al, 338 US 197 (1948).................... 3.16
Institute of Cetacean Research v Sea Shepherd Conservation Society, 156 ILR 718 (2013)........ 1.58
Jacobellis v Ohio, 378 US 184 (1964) 2.18
Klein and Six Others (The Hadamar Trial), 1 LRTWC 46 (1945) 4.32
List and others ('Hostages Trial'), 8 LRTWC 34 (1949) 6.37
Tachiona v Mugabe, ILDC 1090 (US 2004) 10.30
United States v Ali, DC Cir No 12-3056, 11 June 2013.............................1.57, 1.59
United States v Noriega, 808 F Supp 791 (SD Fla 1992)............................... 1.83

Table of Cases xix

United States v Alvarez-Machain, 95 ILR 355 (1992) 1.109, 1.111
United States v Rezaq, ILDC 1391 (US 1998) 8.42
United States v von Leeb et al ('High Command case'), 12 LRTWC 72 (1948)............. 5.106
United States v Yamashita, 13 ILR 255 (1945) 5.62, 5.101, 9.43

Zimbabwe

S v Mharapara, 84 ILR 1 (1985) 1.50

INTERNATIONAL JURISDICTIONS

African Court of Human and People's Rights
Yogogombaye v Senegal, Judgment, 15 December 2009 .... 9.72

Court of Justice of the European Union
Spasic, Case C-129/14 PPU, Judgment, 27 May 2014 .... 1.73

Economic Community of West African States (ECOWAS) Community Court of Justice
Habré v Senegal, Case No ECW/CCJ/APP/07/08, Judgment, 18 November 2010....... 3.35, 9.72
Habré c Sénégal, Case No ECW/CCJ/RUL/05/13, Judgment,
  5 November 2013 .... 3.35, 9.76, 11.14
Hadijatou Mani Koraou v Republic of Niger, ECW/CCJ/JUD/06/08, Judgment,
  27 October 2008 .... 7.36

European Commission of Human Rights
Stocké v Federal Republic of Germany, 95 ILR 327 (1989) 1.108

European Court of Human Rights (ECtHR)
Al-Adsani v United Kingdom, 123 ILR 24 (2001)..................................... 10.7
Al-Jedda v United Kingdom, 147 ILR 107 (2011)..................................... 3.27
Blagojević v Netherlands (dec), no 49032/07, ECHR 2009............................ 12.9
Ergin v Turkey (No 6) (2006) 47 EHRR 829 .... 9.35
Galić v Netherlands (dec), no 22617/07, ECHR 2009 .... 12.9
Jorgić v Germany, 148 ILR 234 (2007)... 8.40
Jones et al *v United Kingdom* (Merits and Just Satisfaction), nos 34356/06 & 40528/06,
  ECHR 2014... 2.75, 10.47
Kononov v Latvia [GC] (Merits and Just Satisfaction), no 36376/04,
  ECHR 2010... 4.32, 5.118, 11.5
Maktouf and Damjanović v Bosnia and Herzegovina [GC] (Merits and Just Satisfaction), nos
  2312/08 & 34179/08, ECHR 2013.. 9.61
Marguš v Croatia [GC] (Merits and Just Satisfaction), no 4455/10, ECHR 2014.......... 11.28
Naletilić v Croatia, 121 ILR 209 (2000)....................... 5.86, 12.12, 12.13, 12.53
Öcalan v Turkey, 156 ILR 30 (2005) 1.112
Selmouni v France [GC] (Merits and Just Satisfaction), no 25803/94, ECHR 1999–V....... 7.119
Siliadin v France (Merits and Just Satisfaction), no 73316/01, ECHR 2005–VII 7.36

Inter-American Court of Human Rights
Cantoral Benavides v Peru, Inter-Am Ct HR (Ser C) No 69 (2000) 9.35
Castillo Petruzzi v Peru, Inter-Am Ct HR (Ser C) No 52 (1999)...................... 9.35
Durand and Ugarte v Peru, Inter-Am Ct HR (Ser C) No 68 (2000) 9.35
The Massacres of El Mozote and Nearby Places v El Salvador, Judgment, 25 October 2012,
  Inter-Am Ct HR (Ser C) 11.17
Radilla Pacheco v Mexico (Preliminary Objections, Merits, Reparations and Costs), Inter-Am
  Ct HR (Ser C) No 209.. 9.35

International Court of Justice (ICJ)

Application of the Convention on the Prevention and Punishment of the Crime of Genocide (Bosnia and Herzegovina v Serbia and Montenegro), Merits, Judgment,
ICJ Rep 2007, 43 . . . . 2.7, 4.74, 4.81, 4.83, 5.98, 8.40, 8.45, 8.56, 8.67, 8.69,
8.70, 8.71, 8.72, 8.75, 12.47, 12.48
Armed Activities on the Territory of the Congo (Democratic Republic of the Congo v Uganda),
Judgment, ICJ Rep 2005, 168. . . . . 10.64
Armed Activities on the Territory of the Congo (New Application: 2002) (Democratic Republic of the Congo v Rwanda), Jurisdiction and Admissibility, Judgment, ICJ Rep 2006, 6 . . . .2.78, 10.88
Arrest Warrant of 11 April 2000 (Democratic Republic of the Congo v Belgium),
ICJ Rep 2002, 3. . . . . 1.19, 1.25, 1.30, 1.34, 1.38, 1.54, 1.55, 1.56, 1.60, 1.61,
1.62, 1.67, 1.75, 2.12, 2.22, 2.81, 3.44, 8.20, 8.25, 8.36, 8.42,
8.54, 8.77, 9.31, 9.32, 10.7, 10.12, 10.13, 10.14, 10.20, 10.31,
10.33, 10.34, 10.35, 10.36, 10.37, 10.38, 10.40, 10.42, 10.43, 10.44,
10.54, 10.76, 10.77, 10.78, 10.79, 10.81, 10.88, 11.30, 13.32, 14.91
Barcelona Traction, Light and Power Co (Belgium v Spain), Second Phase, ICJ Rep 1970, 3 . . . . . 1.33
Certain Questions of Mutual Assistance in Criminal Matters (Djibouti v France), Judgment,
ICJ Rep 2008, 177. . . . . .1.105, 8.22, 10.12, 10.13, 10.15, 10.16, 10.31, 10.35, 10.38,
10.40, 10.44, 10.47, 10.54, 10.58, 10.60, 10.64, 10.80, 10.81, 14.46
Difference Relating to Immunity from Legal Process of a Special Rapporteur of the Commission on Human Rights, Advisory Opinion, ICJ Rep 1999, 62. . . . . 10.8
Gabčíkovo-Nagymaros Project (Hungary/Slovakia), Judgment, ICJ Rep 1997, 7 . . . . 7.119
Jurisdictional Immunities of the State (Germany v Italy: Greece intervening), Judgment,
ICJ Rep 2012, 99. . . . . .10.7, 10.8, 10.82, 10.86, 10.88, 11.30
Legal Consequences of the Construction of a Wall in the Occupied Palestinian Territory, Advisory Opinion, ICJ Rep 2004, 136 . . . . 7.109
Military and Paramilitary Activities in and against Nicaragua (Nicaragua v United States of America), Merits, ICJ Rep 1986, 3 . . . . 1.111, 4.26, 14.105
Questions relating to the Obligation to Prosecute or Extradite (Belgium v Senegal), Judgment, ICJ Rep 2012, 422. . . . . .2.12, 8.2, 8.3, 8.36, 8.47, 8.49, 8.51, 8.53, 9.72, 10.82
Reservations to the Convention on the Prevention and Punishment of the Crime of Genocide, Advisory Opinion, ICJ Rep 1951, 15. . . . . .8.5, 14.105
United States Diplomatic and Consular Staff in Tehran (United States of America v Islamic Republic of Iran), Judgment, ICJ Rep 1980, 3 . . . . 10.17, 10.25, 10.96
Whaling in the Antarctic (Australia v Japan: New Zealand intervening), Judgment,
31 March 2014 . . . . 7.119

International Criminal Court (ICC)

Prosecutor v Abu Garda, ICC-02/05-02/09-243-Red, Pre-Trial Chamber, Decision on the Confirmation of Charges, 8 February 2010 . . . . 5.35, 5.37, 5.38, 5.44, 5.46
Prosecutor v Ahmad Muhammad Harun ('Ahmad Harun') and Ali Muhammad Ali Abd-Al-Rahman ('Ali Kushayb'), ICC-02/05-01/07-57, Pre-Trial Chamber, Decision Informing the United Nations Security Council about the Lack of Cooperation by the Republic of the Sudan, 25 May 2010 . . . . 14.86
Prosecutor v Al Bashir, ICC-02/05-01/09-3, Pre-Trial Chamber, Decision on the Prosecution's Application for a Warrant of Arrest against Omar Hassan Ahmad Al Bashir,
4 March 2009 .4.69, 4.74, 4.75, 4.77, 4.79, 4.81, 4.106, 5.35, 5.45,
5.46, 14.45, 14.58, 14.86, 14.94
Prosecutor v Al Bashir, ICC-02/05-01/09-7, Registrar, Request to All States Parties to the Rome Statute for the Arrest and Surrender of Omar Al Bashir, 6 March 2009 . . . . 14.94
Prosecutor v Al Bashir, ICC-02/05-01/09-94, Pre-Trial Chamber, Second Decision on the Prosecution's Application for a Warrant of Arrest against Omar Hassan Ahmad Al Bashir,
12 July 2010. . . . . .4.69, 4.74, 4.75, 4.77, 4.79, 4.81, 4.106, 14.94

Prosecutor v Al Bashir, ICC-02/05-01/09-96, Registrar, Supplementary Request to All
States Parties to the Rome Statute for the Arrest and Surrender of Omar Hassan
Ahmad Al Bashir, 21 July 2010 . . . . 14.94
Prosecutor v Al Bashir, ICC-02/05-01/09-107, Pre-Trial Chamber, Decision informing the
United Nations Security Council and the Assembly of the States Parties to the Rome
Statute about Omar Al-Bashir's presence in the territory of the Republic of Kenya,
27 August 2010 . . . . 14.94
Prosecutor v Al Bashir, ICC-02/05-01/09-109, Pre-Trial Chamber, Decision informing the
United Nations Security Council and the Assembly of the States Parties to the Rome
Statute about Omar Al-Bashir's recent visit to the Republic of Chad,
27 August 2010 . . . . 14.95
Prosecutor v Al Bashir, ICC-02/05-01/09-117, Pre-Trial Chamber, Decision Requesting
Observations from the Republic of Kenya, 25 October 2010 . . . . 14.95
Prosecutor v Al Bashir, ICC-02/05-01/09-121, Pre-Trial Chamber, Demande de coopération
et d'informations adressée à la République Centrafricaine, 1 December 2010. . . . . 14.95
Prosecutor v Al Bashir, ICC-02/05-01/09-129, Pre-Trial Chamber, Decision informing the
United Nations Security Council and the Assembly of the States Parties to the Rome
Statute about Omar Al-Bashir's recent visit to Djibouti, 12 May 2011 . . . . 14.95
Prosecutor v Al Bashir, ICC-02/05-01/09-132, Pre-Trial Chamber, Decision requesting
Observations about Omar Al Bashir's Recent Visit to the Republic of Chad,
18 August 2011 . . . . 14.95
Prosecutor v Al Bashir, ICC-02/05-01/09-137, Pre-Trial Chamber, Decision requesting
Observations about Omar Al Bashir's Recent Visit to Malawi, 19 October 2011 . . . . 14.95
Prosecutor v Al Bashir, ICC-02/05-01/09-139-Corr, Pre-Trial Chamber, Corrigendum to the
Decision pursuant to Article 87(7) of the Rome Statute on the Failure by the Republic of
Malawi to Comply with the Cooperation Requests Issued by the Court with
Respect to the Arrest and Surrender of Omar Hassan Ahmad Al Bashir,
13 December 2011. . . . . 3.38, 3.44, 14.91, 14.96
Prosecutor v Al Bashir, ICC-02/05-01/09-140-tENG, Pre-Trial Chamber, Decision pursuant
to article 87(7) of the Rome Statute on the Refusal of the Republic of Chad to Comply
with the Cooperation Requests Issued by the Court with Respect to the Arrest and
Surrender of Omar Hassan Ahmad Al Bashir, 13 December 2011 . . . . 3.38, 14.91, 14.96
Prosecutor v Al Bashir, ICC-02/05-01/09-145, Pre-Trial Chamber, Order Regarding Omar
Al-Bashir's Potential Visit to the Republic of Chad and to the State of Libya,
15 February 2013. . . . . 14.96
Prosecutor v Al Bashir, ICC-02/05-01/09-147, Pre-Trial Chamber, Decision Requesting
Observations on Omar Al-Bashir's Visit to the Republic of Chad, 22 February 2013 . . . . 14.96
Prosecutor v Al Bashir, ICC-02/05-01/09-151, Pre-Trial Chamber, Decision on the
Non-Compliance of the Republic of Chad with the Cooperation Requests Issued
by the Court Regarding the Arrest and Surrender of Omar Hassan Ahmad Al-Bashir,
26 March 2013 . . . . 14.96
Prosecutor v Al Bashir, ICC-02/05-01/09-157, Pre-Trial Chamber, Decision Regarding Omar
Al-Bashir's Visit to the Federal Republic of Nigeria, 15 July 2013. . . . . 14.96
Prosecutor v Al Bashir, ICC-02/05-01/09-159, Pre-Trial Chamber, Decision on the
Cooperation of the Federal Republic of Nigeria Regarding Omar Al-Bashir's Arrest and
Surrender to the Court, 5 September 2013. . . . . 14.96
Prosecutor v Al Bashir, ICC-02/05-01/09-162, Pre-Trial Chamber, Decision Regarding Omar
Al-Bashir's Potential Travel to the United States of America, 18 September 2013 . . . . . . 14.78
Prosecutor v Al Bashir, ICC-02/05-01/09-164, Pre-Trial Chamber, Decision Regarding Omar
Al-Bashir's Potential Travel to the Federal Republic of Ethiopia and the Kingdom of Saudi
Arabia, 10 October 2013 . . . . 14.78
Prosecutor v Al Bashir, ICC-02/05-01/09-169, Pre-Trial Chamber, Decision Regarding Omar
Al-Bashir's Potential Travel to the State of Kuwait, 18 November 2013 . . . . 14.78

Prosecutor v Al Bashir, I CC-02/05-01/09-180, Pre-Trial Chamber, Decision on the 'Prosecution's Urgent Notification of Travel in the Case of *The Prosecutor v Omar Al Bashir*', 30 January 2014.. 14.78
Prosecutor v Al Bashir, ICC-02/05-01/09-184, Pre-Trial Chamber, Decision on the 'Prosecution's Urgent Notification of Travel in the Case of *The Prosecutor v Omar Al Bashir*', 17 February 2014... 14.78
Prosecutor v Al Bashir, ICC-02/05-01/09-186, Pre-Trial Chamber, Decision Regarding Omar Al-Bashir's Visit to the Democratic Republic of the Congo, 26 February 2014......... 14.96
Prosecutor v Al Bashir, ICC-02/05-01/09-189, Pre-Trial Chamber, Decision Requesting Observations on Omar Al-Bashir's Visit to the Democratic Republic of the Congo, 3 March 2014 .... 14.96
Prosecutor v Al Bashir, ICC-02/05-01/09-192, Pre-Trial Chamber, Decision Regarding Omar Al-Bashir's Potential Travel to the State of Kuwait, 24 March 2014 .... 14.78
Prosecutor v Al Bashir, ICC-02/05-01/09-194, Pre-Trial Chamber, Decision Regarding Omar Al-Bashir's Potential Visit to the Republic of Chad, 25 March 2014................. 14.96
Prosecutor v Al Bashir, ICC-02/05-01/09-195, Pre-Trial Chamber, Decision on the Cooperation of the Democratic Republic of the Congo Regarding Omar Al-Bashir's Arrest and Surrender to the Court, 9 April 2014 ..... 3.43, 10.44, 14.44, 14.96, 14.96, 14.97
Prosecutor v Al Bashir, ICC-02/05-01/09-199, Pre-Trial Chamber, Decision Regarding the Visit of Omar Hassan Ahmad Al Bashir to the Federal Republic of Ethiopia, 29 April 2014.. 14.78
Prosecutor v Al Bashir, ICC-02/05-01/09-204, Pre-Trial Chamber, Decision on the 'Prosecution's Urgent Notification of Travel in the Case of *The Prosecutor v Omar Al Bashir*', 7 July 2014... 14.78
Prosecutor v Banda and Jerbo, ICC-02/05-03/09-121-Corr-Red, Pre-Trial Chamber, Corrigendum of [*sic*] the 'Decision on the Confirmation of Charges', 7 March 2011 .... 5.35, 5.37, 5.39, 5.40, 5.100
Prosecutor v Bemba, ICC-01/05-01/08-424, Pre-Trial Chamber, Decision pursuant to Article 61(7)(*a*) and (*b*) of the Rome Statute on the Charges of the Prosecutor against Jean-Pierre Bemba Gombo, 15 June 2009 .... 4.28, 4.82, 5.35, 5.36, 5.37, 5.39, 5.40, 5.43, 5.108, 5.110, 5.111, 5.113, 5.115, 5.117
Prosecutor v Bemba, ICC-01/05-01/08-962, Appeals Chamber, Judgment on the appeal of Mr Jean-Pierre Bemba Gombo against the decision of Trial Chamber III of 24 June 2010 entitled 'Decision on the Admissibility and Abuse of Process Challenges', 19 October 2010 .... 8.56, 14.64, 14.74
Prosecutor v Gaddafi and Al-Senussi, ICC-01/11-01/11-344-Red, Pre-Trial Chamber, Public Redacted Decision on the Admissibility of the Case against Saif Al-Islam Gaddafi, 31 May 2013.. 14.78
Prosecutor v Gaddafi and Al-Senussi, ICC-01/11-01/11-420, Pre-Trial Chamber, Decision on the Request of the Defence of Abdullah Al-Senussi To Make a Finding of Non-Cooperation by the Islamic Republic of Mauritania and Refer the Matter to the Security Council, 28 August 2013 .... 14.78
Prosecutor v Gaddafi and Al-Senussi, ICC-01/11-01/11-547-Red, Appeals Chamber, Judgment on the Appeal of Libya against the Decision of Pre-Trial Chamber I of 31 May 2013 entitled 'Decision on the admissibility of the case against Saif Al-Islam Gaddafi', 21 May 2014................... 14.64, 14.65, 14.67, 14.68, 14.70, 14.71, 14.73, 14.77
Prosecutor v Gaddafi and Al-Senussi, ICC-01/11-01/11-565, Appeals Chamber, Judgment on the Appeal of Mr Abdullah Al-Senussi against the Decision of Pre-Trial Chamber I of 11 October 2013 entitled 'Decision on the admissibility of the case against Abdullah Al-Senussi', 24 July 2014 .... 14.64, 14.65, 14.67, 14.68, 14.70, 14.71, 14.73
Prosecutor v Gbagbo, ICC-02/11-01/11-656-Red, Pre-Trial Chamber, Decision on the Confirmation of Charges against Laurent Gbagbo, 12 June 2014 ..... 5.55, 5.63, 5.65, 5.66, 5.67

Table of Cases

Prosecutor v Katanga, ICC-01/04-01/07-3436, Trial Chamber, Jugement rendu en
application de l'article 74 du Statut, 7 March 2014 . . . . .5.5, 5.38, 5.42, 5.43, 5.44,
5.45, 5.79, 5.80, 5.81, 5.84, 5.85, 5.86, 6.37, 14.58
Prosecutor v Katanga and Ngudjolo, ICC-01/04-01/07-717, Pre-Trial Chamber, Decision on the
Confirmation of Charges, 30 September 2008 . . . . .4.30, 5.35, 5.36, 5.37, 5.38,
5.39, 5.40, 5.42, 5.44, 5.45, 5.46, 5.100, 14.58, 14.59
Prosecutor v Katanga and Ngudjolo, ICC-01/04-01/07-1497, Appeals Chamber, Judgment
on the Appeal of Mr Germain Katanga against the Oral Decision of Trial Chamber II of
12 June 2009 on the Admissibility of the Case, 25 September 2009. . . . . . .8.56, 14.60, 14.63,
14.64, 14.74
Prosecutor v Kenyatta, ICC-01/09-02/11-830, Trial Chamber, Decision on Defence Request
for Conditional Excusal from Continuous Presence at Trial, 18 October 2013 . . . . 14.41
Prosecutor v Lubanga, ICC-01/04-01/06-803-tEN, Pre-Trial Chamber, Decision on the
Confirmation of Charges, 29 January 2007 . . . . 2.15, 4.18, 5.35, 5.36, 5.37, 5.38,
5.39, 5.40, 5.41, 5.44, 6.28, 14.59
Prosecutor v Lubanga, ICC-01/04-01/06-1432, Appeals Chamber, Judgment on the
Appeals of the Prosecutor and the Defence against Trial Chamber I's Decision on Victims'
Participation of 18 January 2008, 11 July 2008 . . . . 14.17
Prosecutor v Lubanga, ICC-01/04-01/06-2842, Trial Chamber, Judgment pursuant to
Article 74 of the Statute, 14 March 2012 . . . . 4.28, 4.37, 4.82, 5.5, 5.36, 5.39,
5.40, 5.42, 5.47, 5.80
Prosecutor v Lubanga, ICC-01/04-01/06-2904, Trial Chamber, Decision Establishing the
Principles and Procedures To Be Applied to Reparations, 7 August 2012 . . . . 14.17
Prosecutor v Lubanga, ICC-01/04-01/06-2953, Appeals Chamber, Decision on the
Admissibility of the Appeals against Trial Chamber I's 'Decision Establishing the Principles
and Procedures To Be Applied to Reparations' and Directions on the Further Conduct of
Proceedings, 14 December 2012 . . . . 14.17
Prosecutor v Mbarushimana, ICC-01/04-01/10-465-Red, Pre-Trial Chamber,
Decision on the Confirmation of Charges, 16 December 2011 . . .5.74, 5.78, 5.79, 5.80, 5.81,
5.83, 5.84, 5.85, 5.86
Prosecutor v Mudacumura, ICC-01/04-01/12-1-Red, Pre-Trial Chamber, Decision on the
Prosecutor's Application under Article 58, 13 July 2012. . . . . 5.36, 5.63, 5.65
Prosecutor v Muthaura et al, ICC-01/09-02/11-274, Appeals Chamber, Judgment on the Appeal
of the Republic of Kenya against the Decision of Pre-Trial Chamber II of 30 May 2011
entitled 'Decision on the Application by the Government of Kenya Challenging the
Admissibility of the Case Pursuant to Article 19(2)(*b*) of the Statute',
30 August 2011 . . . . 14.63, 14.64, 14.65, 14.66, 14.67, 14.69, 14.71
Prosecutor v Muthaura et al, ICC-01/09-02/11-382-Red, Pre-Trial Chamber, Decision on the
Confirmation of Charges pursuant to Article 61(7)(*a*) and (*b*) of the Rome Statute,
23 January 2012. . . . . .5.36, 5.37, 5.39, 5.40, 5.43, 5.45, 5.78, 5.80
Prosecutor v Ngudjolo, ICC-01/04-02/12-4, Trial Chamber, Judgment pursuant to
Article 74 of the Statute—Concurring Opinion of Judge Christine van den Wyngaert,
18 December 2012. . . . . .5.5
Prosecutor v Ntaganda, ICC-01/04-02/06-309, Pre-Trial Chamber, Decision Pursuant to
Article 61(7)(*a*) and (*b*) of the Rome Statute on the Charges of the Prosecutor
Against Bosco Ntaganda, 9 June 2014 . . . . 5.36, 5.37, 5.39, 5.40, 5.45, 5.55,
5.63, 5.65, 5.66, 5.69, 5.78
Prosecutor v Ruto et al, ICC-01/09-01/11-307, Appeals Chamber, Judgment on the Appeal
of the Republic of Kenya against the Decision of Pre-Trial Chamber II of
30 May 2011 entitled 'Decision on the Application by the Government of
Kenya Challenging the Admissibility of the Case Pursuant to
Article 19(2)(*b*) of the Statute', 30 August 2011 . . . . 14.63, 14.64, 14.65, 14.67, 14.71

Prosecutor v Ruto et al, ICC-01/09-01/11-373, Pre-Trial Chamber, Decision on the
Confirmation of Charges Pursuant to Article 61(7)(*a*) and (*b*) of the Rome Statute,
23 January 2012.. 5.36, 5.39, 5.40, 5.45, 14.58
Prosecutor v Ruto and Sang, ICC-01/09-02/11-777, Trial Chamber, Decision on Mr Ruto's
Request for Excusal from Continuous Presence at Trial, 18 June 2013................ 14.41
Prosecutor v Ruto and Sang, ICC-01/09-02/11-1066, Appeals Chamber, Judgment on the
Appeal of the Prosecutor against the Decision of Trial Chamber V(a) of 18 June 2013... 14.41
Prosecutor v Ruto and Sang, ICC-01/09-01/11-1274-Corr2, Trial Chamber, Decision on
Prosecutor's Application for Witness Summonses and Resulting Request for State Party
Cooperation, 17 April 2014..14.84, 14.87
Prosecutor v Ruto and Sang, ICC-01/09-01/11-1598, Appeals Chamber, Judgment on the
Appeals against the Decision of Trial Chamber V(a) of 17 April 2014 entitled 'Decision
on Prosecutor's Application for Witness Summonses and resulting Request for State Party
Cooperation', 9 October 2014... 14.58
Situation in Darfur, Sudan, ICC-02/05-185, Pre-Trial Chamber, Decision on Application
under Rule 103, 4 February 2009.. 14.45
Situation in the Democratic Republic of the Congo, ICC-01/04-101-tEN-Corr, Pre-Trial Chamber,
Decision on the Applications for Participation in the Proceedings of VPRS 1, VPRS 2,
VPRS 3, VPRS 4, VPRS 5, and VPRS 6, 17 January 2006 .... 14.17
Situation in the Democratic Republic of the Congo, ICC-01/04-168, Appeals Chamber, Judgment
on the Prosecutor's Application for Extraordinary Review of Pre-Trial Chamber I's
31 March 2006 Decision Denying Leave to Appeal, 13 July 2006 .... 14.8
Situation in the Republic of Côte d'Ivoire, ICC-02/11-14, Pre-Trial Chamber, Decision Pursuant
to Article 15 of the Rome Statute on the Authorisation of an Investigation into
the Situation in the Republic of Côte d'Ivoire, 3 October 2011 .... 4.30

International Criminal Tribunal for Rwanda (ICTR)

Prosecutor v Akayesu, ICTR-96-4, Trial Chamber, Judgment,
2 September 1998 .... 4.26, 4.31, 4.32, 4.76, 4.82, 5.99
Prosecutor v Akayesu, ICTR-96-4, Appeals Chamber, Judgment,
1 June 2001 .... 4.30, 4.32, 4.53, 5.91
Prosecutor v Bagaragaza, ICTR-05-86-AR11*bis*, Appeals Chamber Decision on
Rule 11*bis* Appeal, 30 August 2006 .... 12.40
Prosecutor v Bagilishema, ICTR-95-1A-A, Appeals Chamber, Judgment,
3 July 2002.................................... 5.104, 5.105, 5.107, 5.108, 5.114
Prosecutor v Bagosora and Nsengiyumva, ICTR-98-41-A, Appeals Chamber, Judgment,
14 December 2011...................................... 4.83, 5.63, 5.110, 5.116
Prosecutor v Barayagwiza, ICTR-97-19, Appeals Chamber, Decision, 3 November 1999 ..... 12.33
Prosecutor v Bikindi, ICTR-01-72-A, Appeals Chamber, Judgment, 18 March 2010 .... 4.105
Prosecutor v Bizimungu et al, ICTR-99-50-T, Trial Chamber, Judgment and Sentence,
30 September 2011 .... 6.42
Prosecutor v Bizimungu, ICTR-00-56B-A, Appeals Chamber, Judgment,
30 June 2014 ....5.108, 5.112
Prosecutor v Bucyibaruta, ICTR-2005-85-I, Trial Chamber, Decision on Prosecutor's Request
for Referral of Laurent Bucyibaruta's Indictment to France: Rule 11*bis* of the Rules of
Procedure and Evidence, 20 November 2007...................................... 1.63
Prosecutor v Gacumbitsi, ICTR-2001-64-A, Appeals Chamber, Judgment,
7 July 2006.......................... 4.83, 5.31, 5.32, 5.59, 5.105, 5.109, 5.114
Prosecutor v Gatete, ICTR-00-61-A, Appeals Chamber, Judgment, 9 October 2012 .... 5.88
Prosecutor v Hategekimana, ICTR-0-55B-A, Appeals Chamber, Judgment,
8 May 2012 .... 4.83
Prosecutor v Kajelijeli, ICTR-98-44A-A, Appeals Chamber, Judgment,
23 May 2005 .... 5.62, 5.105, 5.107

Prosecutor v Kalimanzira, ICTR-05-98-A, Appeals Chamber, Judgment,
  20 October 2010 .... 5.32, 5.69, 5.71, 5.73, 5.76, 5.90, 5.91
Prosecutor v Kamuhanda, ICTR-99-54A-A, Appeals Chamber, Judgment,
  19 September 2005 .... 5.62, 5.63, 5.65
Prosecutor v Kanyabashi, ICTR-96-15-T, Trial Chamber, Decision on the
  Defence Motion on Jurisdiction, 18 June 1997 .... 3.26, 12.20, 12.37
Prosecutor v Karera, ICTR-01-74-A, Appeals Chamber, Judgment,
  2 February 2009...5.56, 5.59, 5.63, 5.71
Prosecutor v Kayishema and Ruzindana, ICTR-95-1-T, Trial Chamber,
  Judgment and Sentence, 21 May 1999.................... 4.32, 4.80, 4.83, 4.105, 12.23
Prosecutor v Kayishema and Ruzindana, ICTR-95-1-A, Appeals Chamber,
  Judgment (reasons), 1 June 2001 ....5.13, 5.20, 5.65, 5.69
Prosecutor v Mugenzi and Mugiraneza, ICTR-99-50-A, Appeals Chamber, Judgment,
  4 February 2013..4.83, 5.90
Prosecutor v Munyakazi, ICTR-97-36A-A, Appeals Chamber, Judgment,
  28 September 2011 .... 5.17, 5.23, 5.32
Prosecutor v Munyeshyaka, ICTR-2005-87-I, Trial Chamber, Decision on the Prosecutor's
  Request for the Referral of Wenceslas Munyeshyaka's Indictment to France:
  Rule 11*bis* of the Rules of Procedure and Evidence, 20 November 2007..........1.63, 12.39
Prosecutor v Muvunyi, ICTR-2000-55A-A, Appeals Chamber, Judgment, 29 August 2008..... 5.69
Prosecutor v Musema, ICTR-96-13, Trial Chamber, Judgment, 27 January 2000 .... 4.32
Prosecutor v Nahimana et al, ICTR-99- 52-A, Appeals Chamber, Judgment,
  28 November 2007 .... 4.51, 4.55, 4.69, 4.79, 4.83, 4.105, 5.51, 5.52, 5.53, 5.54,
        5.56, 5.57, 5.58, 5.59, 5.60, 5.63, 5.66, 5.69, 5.71, 5.73, 5.75, 5.88, 5.89,
        5.90, 5.91, 5.92, 5.93, 5.103, 5.106, 5.107, 5.108, 5.109, 5.114, 12.27
Prosecutor v Nahimana et al, ICTR-99-52-T, Trial Chamber, Judgment, 3 December 2003 ... 12.27
Prosecutor v Nchamihigo, ICTR-2001-63-A, Appeals Chamber, Judgment,
  18 March 2010 .... 4.72, 5.56, 5.59, 5.60, 5.61
Prosecutor v Ndahimana, ICTR-01-68-A, Appeals Chamber, Judgment,
  16 December 2013..5.69, 5.71
Prosecutor v Ndindabahizi, ICTR-01-71-A, Appeals Chamber, Judgment,
  16 January 2007... 5.56, 5.59, 5.63
Prosecutor v Niyitegeka, ICTR-96-14-A, Appeals Chamber, Judgment, 9 July 2004 .... 4.79
Prosecutor v Ntabukeze, ICTR-98-41A-A, Appeals Chamber, Judgment, 8 May 2012 ....5.106, 5.114
Prosecutor v Ntagerura et al, ICTR-99-46-A, Appeals Chamber, Judgment,
  7 July 2006.................................4.83, 5.66, 5.70, 5.73, 5.89, 5.108
Prosecutor v Ntakirutimana, ICTR-96-10-A & ICTR-96-17-A, Appeals Chamber, Judgment,
  13 December 2004...............3.26, 4.54, 4.80, 5.14, 5.17, 5.20, 5.23, 5.76, 5.97, 12.20
Prosecutor v Ntawukulilyayo, ICTR-05-82-A, Appeals Chamber, Judgment,
  14 December 2011..5.71, 5.76
Prosecutor v Renzaho, ICTR-97- 31-A, Appeals Chamber, Judgment, 1 April 2011 .....5.63, 5.116
Prosecutor v Rukundo, ICTR-2000-70-A, Appeals Chamber, Judgment, 20 October 2010..... 5.71
Prosecutor v Rutaganda, ICTR-96-3-T, Trial Chamber, Judgment, 6 December 1999.......... 5.99
Prosecutor v Rutaganda, ICTR-96-3-A, Appeals Chamber, Judgment, 26 May 2003......4.30, 4.83
Prosecutor v Rutaganda, ICTR-96-03-R68, Appeals Chamber, Decision on Rutaganda's
  Pending Motions, 27 October 2010... 12.25
Prosecutor v Rutaganira, ICTR-95-1C-T, Trial Chamber, Judgment and Sentence,
  14 March 2005 .... 6.42
Prosecutor v Rwamakuba, ICTR-98-44-AR72.4, Appeals Chamber, Decision on Interlocutory
  Appeal regarding Application of Joint Criminal Enterprise to the Crime of Genocide,
  22 October 2004 ....5.16, 5.20
Prosecutor v Semanza, ICTR-97-20-A, Appeals Chamber, Judgment, 31 May 2000 .... 12.47
Prosecutor v Semanza, ICTR-97- 20-T, Trial Chamber, Judgment, 15 May 2003 .... 2.22

Prosecutor v Semanza, ICTR-97-20-A, Appeals Chamber, Judgment,
20 May 2005 .... 4.32, 4.57, 4.58, 4.72, 4.83, 5.63, 5.98
Prosecutor v Seromba, ICTR-2001-66-A, Appeals Chamber, Judgment,
12 March 2008 .... 4.75, 5.32, 5.61, 5.69, 5.71, 5.76, 5.89
Prosecutor v Setako, ICTR-04-81-A, Appeals Chamber, Judgment, 28 September 2011 ... 4.30, 5.63
Prosecutor v Simba, ICTR-01-76-AR72.2, Appeals Chamber, Decision on Interlocutory
Appeal Regarding Temporal Jurisdiction, 29 July 2004......................... 12.27
Prosecutor v Simba, ICTR-01-76-A, Appeals Chamber, Judgment,
27 November 2007 .... 4.72, 4.83, 5.14, 5.20, 5.22

International Criminal Tribunal for the former Yugoslavia (ICTY)

Prosecutor v Ademi and Norac, IT-04-78-PT, Referral Bench, Decision for Referral to the Authorities
of the Republic of Croatia pursuant to Rule 11*bis*, 14 September 2005 .... 9.37
Prosecutor v Aleksovski, IT-95-14/1, Appeals Chamber, Judgment,
24 March 2000 .... 4.35, 5.62, 5.69, 5.71, 5.73, 5.75, 5.104, 5.108, 5.110, 6.24
Prosecutor v Blagojević and Jokić, IT-02- 60-A, Appeals Chamber, Judgment,
9 May 2007................................. 4.74, 5.71, 5.103, 5.114, 5.116, 6.24
Prosecutor v Blaškić, IT-95-14, Appeals Chamber, Judgment on the Request of the Republic of
Croatia for Review of the Decision of Trial Chamber II of 18 July 1997,
29 October 1997 .... 3.48, 10.47, 10.60, 12.49, 12.52
Prosecutor v Blaškić, IT-95-14-T, Trial Chamber, Judgment, 3 March 2000 ...... 5.57, 5.64, 12.23
Prosecutor v Blaškić, IT-95-14-A, Appeals Chamber, Judgment,
29 July 2004........................... 4.7, 4.51, 4.60, 4.61, 4.62, 5.13, 5.62, 5.66,
571, 5.74, 5.75, 5.108, 5.109, 5.110, 5.111, 6.37
Prosecutor v Boškoski and Tarčulovski, IT-04-82-AR72.1, Appeals Chamber, Decision on
Interlocutory Appeal on Jurisdiction, 22 July 2005 .... 12.26, 12.28
Prosecutor v Boškoski and Tarčulovski, IT-04-82-A, Appeals Chamber, Judgment,
19 May 2010 .... 5.51, 5.54, 5.56, 5.59, 5.60, 5.63, 5.110, 6.19, 6.47
Prosecutor v Bralo, IT-95-17-A, Appeals Chamber, Judgment on Sentencing Appeal,
2 April 2007... 6.25
Prosecutor v Brđanin, IT-99-36-A, Appeals Chamber, Decision on Interlocutory Appeal,
19 March 2004 .... 5.9, 5.14, 5.16, 5.17, 5.19, 5.20, 5.21, 5.22, 5.23, 5.26,
5.30, 5.69, 5.73, 5.75
Prosecutor v Brđanin, IT-99-36-T, Trial Chamber, Judgment, 1 September 2004 .... 5.57
Prosecutor v Češić, IT-95-10/1-S, Trial Chamber, Sentencing Judgment, 11 March 2004 ...... 6.42
Prosecutor v Delalić et al ('*Čelebići*'), IT-96-21, Appeals Chamber, Judgment,
20 February 2001.................... 4.35, 4.83, 5.62, 5.69, 5.71, 5.104, 5.105, 5.106,
5.110, 5.114, 6.9, 6.10, 6.13, 6.42, 12.47
Prosecutor v Delić, IT-04-83-A, Appeals Chamber, Decision on the Outcome of the
Proceedings, 29 June 2010... 12.25
Prosecutor v Delić, IT-04-83-R.1, Appeals Chamber, Decision on Defence Motion for
Review, 17 December 2013 .... 12.25
Prosecutor v Đorđević, IT-05-87/1-A, Appeals Chamber, Judgment,
27 January 2014.. 5.25, 5.26, 6.19
Prosecutor v Erdemović, IT-96-22-T, Trial Chamber, Sentencing Judgment (No 1),
29 November 1996 .... 6.22, 6.42
Prosecutor v Erdemović, IT-96-22-A, Appeals Chamber, Judgment, 7 October 1997...... 6.22, 6.25
Prosecutor v Furundžija, IT-95- 17/1, Trial Chamber, Judgment, 10 December 1998......... 2.81,
4.14, 11.30
Prosecutor v Furundžija, IT-95- 17/1-A, Appeals Chamber, Judgment, 21 July 2000 .... 5.17
Prosecutor v Galić, IT-98-29-T, Trial Chamber, Judgment, 5 December 2003............... 5.57
Prosecutor v Galić, IT-98-29-A, Appeals Chamber, Judgment,
30 November 2006 .... 4.51, 5.63, 5.70, 6.37, 12.23

Table of Cases

Prosecutor v Gotovina and Markač, IT-06-90-A, Appeals Chamber, Judgment,
16 November 2012 .... 5.25, 5.69, 5.109
Prosecutor v Hadžihasanović and Kubura, IT-01-47-A, Appeals Chamber, Judgment,
22 April 2008................................... 5.106, 5.110, 5.111, 5.112, 5.117
Prosecutor v Halilović, IT-01-48-A, Appeals Chamber, Judgment, 16 October 2007 . . . 5.105, 5.109,
5.110, 5.112, 5.117
Prosecutor v Janković, IT-96-23/2-AR11bis.2, Appeals Chamber, Decision on Rule 11*bis*
Referral, 15 November 2005 ....1.70, 9.61
Prosecutor v Jelisić, IT-95-10-T, Trial Chamber, Judgment, 14 December 1999.............. 4.82
Prosecutor v Jelisić, IT-95-10-A, Appeals Chamber, Judgment, 5 July 2001 .... 4.9, 4.72, 4.80, 4.82,
4.83, 5.11
Prosecutor v Karadžić, IT-95-5/18-AR72.4, Appeals Chamber, Decision on Prosecution's
Motion Appealing Trial Chamber's Decision on JCE III Foreseeability, 25 June 2009 .... 5.25
Prosecutor v Karadžić, IT-95-5/18-AR98bis.l, Appeals Chamber, Rule 98*bis* Judgment,
11 July 2013..4.75, 4.81, 4.83, 5.21
Prosecutor v Kordić and Čerkez, IT-95-14/2, Trial Chamber, Judgment,
26 February 2001... 5.64, 6.4, 6.17
Prosecutor v Kordić and Čerkez, IT-95-14/2-A, Appeals Chamber, Judgment,
17 December 2004..................4.24, 4.37, 4.51, 4.60, 5.51, 5.53, 5.54, 5.56, 5.59,
5.60, 5.62, 5.63, 5.66, 6.19, 6.37, 6.46, 12.23
Prosecutor v Kordić and Čerkez, IT-95-14/2-A, Appeals Chamber, Corrigendum to Judgment
of 17 December 2004, 26 January 2005... 6.37
Prosecutor v Kovačević, IT-01-42/2-1, Referral Bench, Decision on Referral of Case Pursuant
to Rule 11*bis* with Confidential and Partly *Ex Parte* Annexes, 17 November 2006....... 9.57
Prosecutor v Krajišnik, IT-00-39-A, Appeals Chamber, Judgment, 17 March 2009 ...... 5.14, 5.17,
5.21, 5.22, 5.53, 5.54, 5.59, 5.63
Prosecutor v Krnojelac, IT-97-25-T, Trial Chamber, Judgment, 15 March 2002.............. 5.99
Prosecutor v Krnojelac, IT-97-25-A, Appeals Chamber, Judgment, 17 September 2003.... 4.9, 5.11,
5.14, 5.23, 5.76, 5.114
Prosecutor v Krstić, IT-98-33-T, Trial Chamber Judgment, 2 August 2001 .... 4.74
Prosecutor v Krstić, IT-98-33-A, Appeals Chamber Judgment, 19 April 2004 ......4.74, 4.77, 4.81,
4.83, 5.76, 5.97, 5.98
Prosecutor v Kunarac et al, IT-96-23 & IT-96-23/1, Trial Chamber, Judgment,
22 February 2001.. 5.6
Prosecutor v Kunarac et al, IT-96-23 and IT-96-23/1-A, Appeals Chamber, Judgment,
12 June 2002 .... 4.30, 4.33, 4.51, 4.54, 4.57, 4.58, 4.61, 4.62, 6.39, 7.36, 7.125
Prosecutor v Kupreškić, IT-95-16, Trial Chamber, Judgment, 14 January 2000 .... 6.40
Prosecutor v Kvočka et al, IT-98-30/1, Appeals Chamber, Decision on Interlocutory Appeal
by the Accused Zoran Zigić against the Decision of Trial Chamber I dated
5 December 2000, 25 May 2001 .... 12.47
Prosecutor v Kvočka et al, IT-98-30/1-A, Appeals Chamber, Judgment,
28 February 2005................. 4.9, 4.32, 5.11, 5.14, 5.17, 5.22, 5.23, 5.24, 6.42, 6.44
Prosecutor v Ljubičić, IT-00- 41-AR11*bis*.1, Appeals Chamber, Decision on Appeal against
Decision on Referral under Rule 11*bis*, 4 July 2006.................... 8.56, 9.61, 12.41
Prosecutor v Lukić and Lukić, IT-98-32/1-A, Appeals Chamber, Judgment, 4 December 2012 .... 5.72
Prosecutor v Martić, IT-95-11-A, Appeals Chamber, Judgment, 8 October 2008 .... 4.51, 5.21,
6.19, 6.40
Prosecutor v Mejakić, IT-02-65-AR11*bis*, Appeals Chamber, Decision on Joint Defence Appeal
against Decision on Referral under Rule 11*bis*, 7 April 2006 .... 8.56, 9.61, 12.38, 12.41, 12.53
Prosecutor v Milošević (Dragomir), IT-98-29/1-A, Appeals Chamber Judgment,
12 November 2009 ....5.51, 5.54, 5.63, 6.40
Prosecutor v Milošević (Slobodan), IT-02-54, Trial Chamber, Decision on Preliminary Motions,
8 November 2001 .... 12.19

Prosecutor v Milutinović et al, IT-99-37-AR72, Appeals Chamber, Decision on Dragoljub
  Ojdanić's Motion Challenging Jurisdiction—Joint Criminal Enterprise, 21 May 2003 . . . 5.14
Prosecutor v Milutinović et al, IT-05-87-PT, Trial Chamber, Decision on Ojdanić's Motion
  Challenging Jurisdiction: Indirect Co-perpetration, 22 March 2006 . . . . 5.31
Prosecutor v Milutinović et al, IT-05-87-T, Trial Chamber, Judgment, 26 February 2009 . . . .5.64, 5.65
Prosecutor v Milutinović et al, IT-99-37-AR72.2, Appeals Chamber, Reasons for Decision
  Dismissing Interlocutory Appeal concerning Jurisdiction over the territory of Kosovo,
  8 June 2004 . . . . 12.19, 12.28
Prosecutor v Mrđa, IT-02-59-S, Trial Chamber, Sentencing Judgment, 31 March 2004 . . . . 6.45
Prosecutor v Mrkšić and Šljivančanin, IT-95-13/1-A, Appeals Chamber, Judgment,
  5 May 2009 . . . . .4.51, 4.52, 4.105, 5.69, 5.70, 5.71, 5.72, 5.77
Prosecutor v Naletilić and Martinović, IT-98- 34-A, Appeals Chamber, Judgment, 3 May 2006. . . . . 4.37
Prosecutor v Nikolić (Dragan), IT-94-2-AR73, Appeals Chamber, Decision on Interlocutory
  Appeal considering Legality of Arrest, 5 June 2003. . . . . 12.34
Prosecutor v Orić, IT-03-68-T, Trial Chamber, Judgment, 30 June 2006 . . . . 5.112
Prosecutor v Orić, IT-03-68-A, Appeals Chamber, Judgment, 3 July 2008. . . . 5.70, 5.77, 5.109, 5.110,
  5.112, 5.116
Prosecutor v Perišić, IT-04-81-A, Appeals Chamber, Decision on Motion for Reconsideration,
  20 March 2014 . . . . .5.72, 5.112
Prosecutor v Perišić, IT-04-81-A, Appeals Chamber, Judgment, 28 February 2013 . . . . 5.72
Prosecutor v Popović et al, IT-05-88-T, Trial Chamber, Judgment, 10 June 2010 . . . . 5.89
Prosecutor v Popović et al, IT-05-88-A, Appeals Chamber, Decision Terminating Appellate
  Proceedings in Relation to Milan Gvero, 7 March 2013. . . . . 12.25
Prosecutor v Šainović et al, IT-05-87-A, Appeals Chamber, Judgment, 23 January 2014 . . . . 5.17, 5.19,
  5.22, 5.23, 5.25, 5.70, 5.72, 5.73, 5.75, 6.19
Prosecutor v Šešelj, IT-03-67-PT, Trial Chamber, Decision on Motion of Vojislav Šešelj
  Challenging Jurisdiction and Form of Indictment, 26 May 2004 . . . . .3.26, 12.19
Prosecutor v Simić, IT-95-9-A, Appeals Chamber, Judgment,
  28 November 2006 . . . . .5.31, 5.69, 5.71, 5.75, 576
Prosecutor v Stakić, IT-97-24-T, Trial Chamber, Judgment, 31 July 2003 . . . . 5.31
Prosecutor v Stakić, IT-97-24-A, Appeals Chamber, Judgment,
  22 March 2006 . . . . 4.9, 4.30, 450, 4.69, 4.79, 4.80, 4.83, 4.105, 5.11,
  5.13, 5.16, 5.17, 5.19, 5.23, 5.31
Prosecutor v Stanković, IT-96-23/2-PT, Referrals Bench, Decision on Referral of Case under
  Rule 11*bis*, 17 May 2005 . . . . 3.28, 9.60, 9.61
Prosecutor v Stanković, IT-96-23/2-AR11*bis*.1, Appeals Chamber, Decision on Rule 11*bis*
  Referral, 1 September 2005 . . . . 12.38
Prosecutor v Strugar, IT-01-42-T, Trial Chamber, Judgment, 31 January 2005 . . . . 5.65
Prosecutor v Strugar, IT-01-42-A, Appeals Chamber, Judgment, 17 July 2008. . . . . 6.37
Prosecutor v Tadić, IT-94-1, Appeals Chamber, Decision on the Defence Motion for
  Interlocutory Appeal on Jurisdiction, 2 October 1995 . . . . .1.61, 1.62, 3.26, 4.7, 4.9,
  4.17, 4.18, 4.26, 4.27, 4.30, 4.35, 4.53, 4.60, 4.61, 4.63,
  12.19, 12.23, 12.37, 12.40
Prosecutor v Tadić, IT-94-1-A, Appeals Chamber, Judgment, 15 July 1999 . . . 5.11, 5.14, 5.16, 5.17,
  5.18, 5.19, 5.20, 5.23, 5.28, 5.29, 5.31, 5.69, 5.71, 5.72, 5.73, 12.47, 12.48
Prosecutor v Todorović, IT-95-9/1-S, Trial Chamber, Sentencing Judgment, 31 July 2001 . . . . . . 6.42
Prosecutor v Todović and Rašević, IT-97-25/1. . . . . 9.61
Prosecutor v Tolimir, IT-05-88/2-PT, Trial Chamber, Decision on Preliminary Motions on the
  Indictment pursuant to Rule 72 of the Rules, 14 December 2007 . . . . 12.19
Prosecutor v Tolimir, IT-05-88/2-T, Trial Chamber, Judgment, 12 December 2012. . . . . 5.89
Prosecutor v Trbić, IT-05-88/1. . . . . 9.61
Prosecutor v Vasiljević, IT-98- 32-T, Trial Chamber, Judgment, 29 November 2002 . . . . 6.42
Prosecutor v Vasiljević, IT-98-32-A, Appeals Chamber, Judgment,
  25 February 2004. . . . . .4.83, 5.9, 5.14, 5.17, 5.19, 5.23, 5.69, 5.71, 5.72, 5.74

International Military Tribunal, Nuremberg
Judgment of the International Military Tribunal for the Trial of German Major War Criminals,
  Nuremberg, 30 September and 1 October 1946, Misc No 12 (1946), Cmd 6964, (1947) 41
  AJIL 172 . . . . .2.57, 2.58, 2.61, 2.62, 2.64, 2.70, 2.73, 6.32

International Military Tribunal for the Far East, Tokyo
United States of America and Others v Araki and Others, Judgment of the International Military
  Tribunal for the Far East, Tokyo, 4 November 1948. . . . . 3.15

Mexico–US General Claims Commission
Mallén v United States of America, 4 RIAA 173 (1927) 10.65

Permanent Court of Arbitration
Island of Palmas (Netherlands/United States of America), 2 RIAA 829 (1928) 3.38, 8.21
Savarkar Case, The (France v Great Britain), Hague Court Reports 275 (1911) 1.108, 1.114

Permanent Court of International Justice (PCIJ)
Exchange of Greek and Turkish Populations, Advisory Opinion, PCIJ Rep Ser B No 10 (1925) 8.2
Payment of Various Serbian Loans Issued in France, PCIJ Rep Ser A No 20 (1929) 3.9
Payment in Gold of the Brazilian Federal Loans Issued in France, PCIJ Rep Ser A No 21 (1929) 3.9
SS 'Lotus', The, PCIJ Rep Ser A No 10 (1927) 1.16, 1.17, 1.18, 1.19, 1.20, 1.21, 1.25, 1.28, 1.29,
  1.34, 1.37, 1.49, 1.56, 1.60, 1.66, 1.75, 1.76, 8.36, 9.15

Special Court for Sierra Leone (SCSL)
Independent Counsel v Bangura et al, SCSL-2011-02-T, President, Authorisation pursuant to
  Rule 4, 29 June 2012 . . . . 13.8
Prosecutor v Brima et al, SCSL-2004-16-A, Appeals Chamber, Judgment,
  22 February 2008 4,14, ...4.48, 5.14, 5.17, 5.18, 5.51, 5.73, 5.75, 5.105, 6.28,
  13.17, 13.26, 13.28
Prosecutor v Brima et al, SCSL-04-16-T, Trial Chamber, Sentencing Judgment,
  19 July 2007. . . . . .6.47, 13.17
Prosecutor v Brima, Kamara and Kanu, SCSL-04-16-T, Trial Chamber, Judgment,
  20 June 2007 . . . . 13.17
Prosecutor v Fofana, SCSL-2004-14-AR72(E), Appeals Chamber, Decision on Preliminary
  Motion on Lack of Jurisdiction: Illegal Delegation of Powers by the United Nations,
  25 May 2004 . . . . .3.21, 13.20
Prosecutor v Fofana, SCSL-2004-14-AR72(E), Appeals Chamber, Decision on Preliminary
  Motion on Lack of Jurisdiction Materiae [*sic*]: Nature of the Armed Conflict,
  25 May 2004 . . . . 4.30
Prosecutor v Fofana and Kondewa, SCSL-04-14-A, Appeals Chamber, Judgment,
  28 May 2008 . . . . .5.59, 5.69, 5.71, 5.73, 5.75, 5.105, 5.114,
  6.37, 6.46, 13.17, 13.26
Prosecutor v Fofana and Kondewa, SCSL-04-14-T, Trial Chamber, Judgment, 2 August 2007. . . . 13.17
Prosecutor v Fofana and Kondewa, SCSL-04-14-T, Trial Chamber, Judgment on the Sentencing
  of Moinina Fofana and Allieu Kondewa, 9 October 2007 . . . . 13.17
Prosecutor v Fofana and Kondewa, SCSL-04-14-ES-836, President, Decision of the President
  on Application for Early Release, 11 August 2014 . . . . 13.17
Prosecutor v Gbao, SCSL-2004-15-AR72(E), Appeals Chamber, Decision on Preliminary Motion
  on the Invalidity of the Agreement between the United Nations and the Government of
  Sierra Leone on the Establishment of the Special Court, 25 May 2004 . . . . . 11.34, 13.20, 13.34
Prosecutor v Gbao, SCSL-2004-15-PT, Acting President, Decision on Appeal by the Truth and
  Reconciliation Commission ('TRC') and Accused against the Decision of Judge Bankole
  Thompson delivered on 3 November 2003 to Deny the TRC's Request to Hold a Public
  Hearing with Augustine Gbao, 7 May 2004. . . . . 13.38

Prosecutor v Kallon and Kamara (Fofana and Gbao intervening), SCSL-2004-15-AR72(E) &
SCSL-2004-16-AR72(E), Appeals Chamber, Decision on Challenge to
Jurisdiction: Lomé Accord Amnesty,
13 March 2004 ....3.20, 11.28, 11.34, 13.6, 13.7, 13.34
Prosecutor v Kallon, Norman and Kamara (Fofana intervening), SCSL-2004-15-AR72(E),
SCSL-2004-14-AR72(E) and SCSL-2004-16-AR72(E), Appeals Chamber, Decision on
Constitutionality and Lack of Jurisdiction, 13 March 2004 .... 3.20, 13.6, 13.25
Prosecutor v Kanu, SCSL-2004-16-AR72(E), Appeals Chamber, Decision on Motion
Challenging Jurisdiction and Raising Objections Based on Abuse of Process,
25 May 2004 ....3.19, 13.34
Prosecutor v Kondewa, SCSL-2004-14-AR72(E), Appeals Chamber, Decision on Preliminary
Motion on Lack of Jurisdiction: Establishment of Special Court Violates Constitution
of Sierra Leone, 25 May 2004 .... 3.19, 13.7, 13.34
Prosecutor v Norman et al, SCSL-04- 14-AR72(E), Appeals Chamber, Decision on
Preliminary Motion on Lack of Jurisdiction Ratione Materiae: Nature of the
Armed Conflict, 25 May 2004..4.13, 4.28
Prosecutor v Norman, SCSL-2003-08-PT, President, Decision on Appeal by the Truth and
Reconciliation Commission for Sierra Leone ('TRC' or 'the Commission') and Chief
Samuel Hinga Norman JP against the Decision of His Lordship Mr Justice Bankole
Thompson delivered on 30 October 2003 to Deny the TRC's Request to Hold a Public
Hearing with Chief Samuel Hinga Norman JP, 28 November 2003.................. 13.38
Prosecutor v Norman, Fofana and Kondewa, SCSL-2004-14-T, Appeals Chamber, Decision
on Interlocutory Appeals against Trial Chamber Decision refusing to Subpoena the
President of Sierra Leone, 11 September 2006 .... 13.11
Prosecutor v Norman, Fofana and Kondewa, SCSL-04-14-T, Trial Chamber, Decision on
Registrar's Submission of Evidence of Death of Accused Samuel Hinga Norman and
Consequential Issues, 21 May 2007 .... 13.30
Prosecutor v Norman (Fofana intervening), SCSL-2003-04-14-AR72(E), Appeals Chamber,
Decision on Preliminary Motion Based on Lack of Jurisdiction,
31 May 2004... 4.14, 13.25, 13.26
Prosecutor v Sesay et al, SCSL-04-15-T, Trial Chamber, Judgment, 2 March 2009........7.36, 13.17
Prosecutor v Sesay et al, SCSL-04-15-T, Trial Chamber, Sentencing Judgment,
8 April 2009..6.47, 13.17
Prosecutor v Sesay et al, SCSL-04-15-A, Appeals Chamber, Judgment,
26 October 2009 .... 5.14, 5.17, 5.18, 5.20, 5.21, 5.22, 5.23, 5.53,
5.63, 5.105, 5.114, 5.116, 13.17, 13.25, 13.26
Prosecutor v Taylor, SCSL-03-01-I, Appeals Chamber, Decision on Immunity from
Jurisdiction, 31 May 2004 ....3.20, 3.38, 3.42, 3.44, 13.6, 13.32
Prosecutor v Taylor, SCSL-03-01-T, Trial Chamber, Judgment, 18 May 2012 ......4.30, 5.57, 5.64,
5.65, 13.17
Prosecutor v Taylor, SCSL-03-01-T, Trial Chamber, Sentencing Judgment, 30 May 2012 ..... 13.17
Prosecutor v Taylor, SCSL-03-01-A, Appeals Chamber, Judgment, 26 September 2013.... 5.5, 5.51,
5.54, 5.57, 5.59, 5.60, 5.63, 5.71, 5.72, 5.73, 13.11, 13.17

Special Tribunal for Lebanon (STL)

Prosecutor v Ayyash et al, STL-11-01/I/AC/R176*bis,* Appeals Chamber, Interlocutory Decision
on the Applicable Law: Terrorism, Conspiracy, Homicide, Perpetration, Cumulative
Charging, 16 February 2011 ....2.22, 2.28, 2.31, 3.9, 3.25, 4.4, 4.105, 5.26
Prosecutor v Ayyash et al, STL-11-01/PT/AC/AR90.1, Appeals Chamber, Decision on the
Defence Appeals against the Trial Chamber's 'Decision on the Defence Challenges to the
Jurisdiction and Legality of the Tribunal', 24 October 2012......................... 3.24

Tribunal under the Treaty of Washington 1871
Alabama Claims Arbitration (United States of America/United Kingdom), 1 Moore
  Int Arb 653 (1872)..8.2, 11.32

United Nations Committee against Torture
Elmi v Australia, UN doc CAT/C/22/D/120/1998 (25 May 1999) 7.121
HMHI v Australia, UN doc CAT/C/28/D/177/2001 (22 January 2003) 7.121

Table of Treaties and Other International Instruments

Additional Protocol to the European
  Convention on Extradition 1975
  (*see also* European Convention on
  Extradition 1957)
  art 1 . . . . 1.98
Additional Protocol to the European
  Convention on Mutual Assistance
  in Criminal Matters 1978 (*see also*
  European Convention on Mutual
  Assistance in Criminal
  Matters 1959) 1.105
African Union-Sudan Status of Mission
  Agreement (SOMA) on the
  Establishment and Management of
  the Ceasefire Commission in the
  Darfur Area of The Sudan (CFC) 2004
  art 62(*b*) 14.99
Agreement between the Democratic
  Republic of East Timor and the
  United Nations concerning the Status
  of the United Nations Mission of
  Support in East Timor 2002
  arts 43–44 . . . . 1.81
  art 55(*b*) 14.99
Agreement between the European
  Union and Japan on Mutual Legal
  Assistance in Criminal Matters 2009
  art 11(1)(*a*) 1.106
  art 11(1)(*d*) 1.73
Agreement between the European
  Union and the Islamic Republic of
  Afghanistan on the Status of the
  European Union Police Mission in
  Afghanistan (EUPOL Afghanistan) 2010
  art 8 . . . . 1.81
Agreement between the Government of
  the Kingdom of the Netherlands
  and the Government of the
  United Kingdom of Great
  Britain and Northern Ireland
  concerning a Scottish Trial in The
  Netherlands 1998 . . . . 1.80
Agreement between the Government
  of the Republic of Senegal and the
  African Union on the Creation of
  Extraordinary African Chambers in
  the Senegalese Courts 2014
  preamble (fifth recital) 9.72
  art 1(1) 9.73
  art 1(3) 3.35
  art 1(5) 3.35, 9.72
  art 2 . . . . 9.72
Agreement between the Government
  of the United Kingdom of Great
  Britain and Northern Ireland and
  the Government of New Zealand
  concerning trials under Pitcairn law
  in New Zealand and related matters
  2002 . . . . 1.80
Agreement between the Parties to the
  North Atlantic Treaty regarding the
  Status of their Forces 1951 . . . . 1.81
  art VII 14.99
  art VII(3)(*a*)(ii) 10.64
Agreement between the Republic of
  Bosnia and Herzegovina and the
  North Atlantic Treaty Organisation
  (NATO) Concerning the Status of
  NATO and its Personnel 1995
  arts 6–7 . . . . 14.99
Agreement between the Republic of
  Croatia and the North Atlantic Treaty
  Organisation (NATO) Concerning the
  Status of NATO and its Personnel 1995
  arts 6–7 . . . . 14.99
Agreement between the Special Court for
  Sierra Leone and the Government
  of the United Kingdom of Great
  Britain and Northern Ireland on the
  Enforcement of Sentences of the
  Special Court for Sierra
  Leone 2007 . . . . 13.17
Agreement between the United Nations
  and the Government of Sierra Leone
  on the Establishment of a Residual
  Special Court for Sierra Leone 2010
  ('RSCSL Agreement') 3.19, 13.5,
  13.6, 13.15
  art 1(1) 3.18, 13.5
  art 1(2) 3.18, 13.5, 13.9

xxxiv *Table of Treaties and Other International Instruments*

art 1(3). 3.18, 13.5
art 3 . . . . 13.15
art 6 . . . . 13.14
art 7 . . . . 13.18
art 10 . . . . 13.8
art 11 . . . . 13.7, 13.39
art 11(d). 13.36
art 13 . . . . 13.7
art 16 . . . . 13.9
Agreement between the United Nations
  and the Government of Sierra
  Leone on the Establishment of a
  Special Court for Sierra Leone 2002
  ('SCSL Agreement') 13.4, 13.6,
                                 13.20, 13.22
art 1(1). 3.18, 13.18, 13.21
art 1(2). 3.18, 13.9
art 1(3). 13.22
art 2 . . . . 13.23
art 2(2). 13.7
art 2(3). 13.7
art 3(1). 13.10
arts 4–5 . . . . 13.23
art 6 . . . . 13.15
art 7 . . . . 13.20
art 10 . . . . 13.8
art 17 . . . . 13.39
art 17(1). 3.48, 13.39
art 17(2). 3.48, 13.36, 13.39
arts 22–23 . . . . 13.20
art 23 . . . . 13.5
Agreement between the United Nations
  and the Kingdom of the Netherlands
  concerning the Headquarters
  of the International Tribunal
  for the Prosecution of Persons
  Responsible for Serious Violations
  of International Humanitarian Law
  Committed in the Territory of the
  Former Yugoslavia since 1991 1994
  (as amended) 12.9
Agreement between the United Nations
  and the Lebanese Republic on the
  Establishment of a Special Tribunal
  for Lebanon 2007
  ('STL Agreement') 3.24
preamble (first and second recitals). 3.25
art 1(1). 3.24
art 2 . . . . 3.25
art 15 . . . . 3.48
art 16 . . . . 11.23
Agreement between the United Nations
  and the Royal Government
  of Cambodia concerning the
  Prosecution under Cambodian
  Law of Crimes Committed
  During the Period of Democratic
  Kampuchea 2003 . . . . 3.34
art 1 . . . . 3.34
art 2(1). 3.34
art 2(2). 3.34, 9.63
art 11 . . . . 11.23
art 11(1). 11.23
art 11(2). 11.23
art 12(1). 9.63
Agreement between the United Nations
  and the United Republic of Tanzania
  concerning the headquarters of
  the International Tribunal for
  Rwanda 1995 . . . . 12.10
Agreement by the Government of
  the United Kingdom of Great
  Britain and Northern Ireland,
  the Government of the United
  States of America, the Provisional
  Government of the French Republic,
  and the Government of the Union
  of Soviet Socialist Republics for
  the Prosecution and Punishment
  of the Major War Criminals of
  the European Axis 1945 (*see also*
  Charter of the International Military
  Tribunal, Nuremberg)
  art 1 . . . . 3.13
  art 2 . . . . 3.13
Agreement concerning Cooperation on the
  Civil International Space Station 1998
  art 22(1). 14.99
  art 22(2)(a) 14.99
Agreement on Extradition between the
  European Union and the United
  States of America 2003
  art 3(1). 1.95, 1.105
  art 3(1)(a) 1.97
  art 3(3)(a) 1.105
  art 4 . . . . 1.97
  art 4(1). 1.97
  art 4(3)(a) 1.97
Agreement on Illicit Traffic by Sea,
  implementing article 17 of the
  United Nations Convention against
  Illicit Traffic in Narcotic Drugs
  and Psychotropic Substances 1995
  ('Council of Europe Agreement
  on Illicit Traffic by Sea') (*see also*
  United Nations Convention against

Table of Treaties and Other International Instruments xxxv

Illicit Traffic in Narcotic Drugs and
 Psychotropic Substances 1988)
 art 3(4).......................... 1.69
 arts 7–10 .... 1.119
Agreement on Refugees and Displaced
 Persons annexed to General
 Framework Agreement for Peace in
 Bosnia and Herzegovina 1995 (*see
 also* General Framework Agreement
 for Peace in Bosnia and
 Herzegovina 1995)
 art VI.......................... 11.21
Amendment of 2005 to the Convention
 on the Physical Protection of Nuclear
 Material (*see also* Convention on
 the Physical Protection of Nuclear
 Material 1979; Convention on
 the Physical Protection of Nuclear
 Material and Nuclear
 Facilities 2005)............. 7.13, 7.67
 art 1............................ 7.67
Arab Convention for the Suppression of
 Terrorism 1998
 art 1(2)......................... 7.106
 art 2(*a*)........................ 7.106
Charter of the International Military
 Tribunal for the Far East ('Tokyo
 Charter') 2.11, 3.14, 3.15, 4.4, 6.3
 art 4(*a*)......................... 4.88
 art 5(*b*)......................... 4.13
 art 5(*c*)............. 4.50, 4.53, 4.54, 4.56
 art 6 .... 6.32, 6.41, 6.42
Charter of the International Military
 Tribunal, Nuremberg ('Nuremberg
 Charter') (*see also* Agreement by
 the Government of the United
 Kingdom of Great Britain and
 Northern Ireland, the Government
 of the United States of America,
 the Provisional Government of
 the French Republic, and the
 Government of the Union of
 Soviet Socialist Republics for the
 Prosecution and Punishment of
 the Major War Criminals of the
 European Axis 1945) ... 2.11, 2.57, 2.58,
 2.59, 2.60, 2.64, 2.65, 2.72,
 3.13, 3.40, 4.4, 4.46, 6.3, 12.23
 art 6..................... 2.57, 2.73
 art 6(*a*)......................... 4.88
 art 6(*b*)......................... 4.13
 art 6(*c*) 4.41, 4.42, 4.44, 4.50, 4.51,
 4.53, 4.54, 4.56, 4.64

art 7..................... 2.70, 12.30
art 8................ 6.32, 6.42, 14.42
Charter of the United Nations 1945 ('UN
 Charter') 13.20
 art 1............................ 13.32
 art 1(1)........... 3.27, 3.38, 3.48, 12.31,
 14.34, 14.44
 art 2(4)........ 2.78, 4.97, 4.98, 8.70, 8.83
 art 2(7).................... 3.27, 12.37
 art 17.......................... 12.14
 art 24(1)................... 3.21, 13.20
 art 25 .... 3.38, 3.41, 3.43, 3.48, 12.36,
 12.44, 12.49, 14.44, 14.86
 art 39............. 12.18, 12.19, 13.32
 art 41............................ 13.32
 arts 41–42 .... 12.18
 art 48(1)......................... 3.48
 art 92................... 12.46, 12.47
 art 103.................. 8.70, 14.86
 ch VII................. 3.11, 3.22, 3.23,
 3.24, 3.25, 3.26, 3.27, 3.43, 3.48,
 7.199, 8.45, 12.3, 12.4, 12.5, 12.7,
 12.19, 12.31, 12.37, 12.49, 13.8,
 13.20, 13.32, 14.5, 14.30, 14.34,
 14.45, 14.78, 14.98
Convention against the Recruitment,
 Use, Financing and Training of
 Mercenaries 1989 ('Mercenaries
 Convention') 7.128
 preamble (second recital) 7.128
 art 1(1)................... 7.129, 7.132
 art 1(1)(*a*)–(*e*).................... 7.130
 art 1(1)(*b*) 7.130
 art 1(2)................... 7.129, 7.132
 art 1(2)(*a*)–(*e*).................... 7.131
 art 1(2)(*b*) 7.131
 art 2...................... 7.7, 7.132
 art 3(1)......................... 7.132
 art 4(*a*)–(*b*)...................... 7.133
 art 5(1).................... 7.128, 8.6
 art 5(3)......................... 8.15
 art 6............................ 8.74
 art 9(1)(*a*) 8.25, 8.30
 art 9(1)(*b*) 8.27, 8.33
 art 9(2)..................... 8.34, 8.52
 art 9(3)......................... 8.42
 art 10(1)......................... 8.46
 art 10(2)......................... 8.46
 art 10(3)......................... 8.46
 art 10(5)......................... 8.46
 art 12........................... 8.48
 art 13(1)......................... 8.62
 art 13(2)......................... 8.62

art 15(1)........................8.58
art 15(2)........................8.58
art 15(3)........................8.58
art 15(4)........................8.58
Convention against the Taking of
  Hostages 1979 ('Hostages
  Convention') 2.12, 7.62, 7.63, 7.83
art 1............................2.44
art 1(1)......................7.7, 7.64
art 1(2)(*a*)–(*b*)..................7.65
art 2.......................8.6, 8.15
art 4............................8.74
art 5(1)(*a*)..................8.25, 8.30
art 5(1)(*b*)..................8.27, 8.33
art 5(1)(*c*)......................8.28
art 5(1)(*d*)......................8.29
art 5(2)....................8.34, 8.52
art 5(3)..........................8.42
art 6(1)..........................8.46
art 6(2)..........................8.46
art 6(3)..........................8.46
art 6(6)..........................8.46
art 8............................8.52
art 8(1)..........................8.48
art 10(1)........................8.58
art 10(2)........................8.58
art 10(3)........................8.58
art 10(4)........................8.58
art 11(1)........................8.62
art 11(2)........................8.62
art 12...........................7.63
art 13.....................7.63, 8.83
Convention against Torture and Other
  Cruel, Inhuman or Degrading
  Treatment or Punishment 1984
  ('Torture Convention')........2.10, 2.12,
    2.14, 4.32, 4.103, 7.13, 7.117, 7.123,
    8.2, 8.49, 9.5, 9.7, 9.16, 10.42,
    10.44, 10.80, 10.90, 10.91, 14.5
art 1............................9.16
art 1(1)... 7.13, 7.118, 7.119, 7.120, 7.122,
    8.73, 9.16, 9.74, 10.74, 10.90
art 2(1)..........................8.73
art 2(2)................8.79, 9.45, 11.8
art 2(3).................8.79, 9.16, 9.74
art 3......................2.44, 7.121
art 4(1)............. 2.10, 7.13, 8.6, 9.16
art 4(2)..........................8.15
art 5(1)(*a*)..................8.25, 8.30
art 5(1)(*b*)......................8.27
art 5(1)(*c*)......................8.29
art 5(2)...........8.34, 8.52, 9.72, 10.74
art 5(3)..........................8.42

art 6(1) (2).......................8.46
art 6(2)....................... 8.47, 9.72
art 6(3)–(4).......................8.46
art 7(1)–(2) 8.48, 9.24
art 7(1)................9.16, 9.72, 10.74
art 8............................8.52
art 8(1)..........................8.58
art 8(2)..........................8.58
art 8(3)..........................8.58
art 8(4)..........................8.58
art 9(1)..........................8.62
art 9(2)..........................8.62
Convention between the Government
  of the United Kingdom of Great
  Britain and Northern Ireland and
  the Government of the People's
  Democratic Republic of Algeria on
  Extradition 2006 ....1.95
art 4(1)..........................1.73
Convention concerning the Laws and
  Customs of War on Land 1899
  ('1899 Hague Convention II') (*see
  also* Regulations concerning the
  Laws and Customs of War on Land
  annexed to Convention concerning
  the Laws and Customs of War on
  Land 1899) 2.56
preamble (ninth recital) 4.40
Convention concerning the Laws and
  Customs of War on Land 1907 ('1907
  Hague Convention IV') (*see also*
  Regulations concerning the Laws and
  Customs of War on Land annexed to
  Convention concerning the Laws and
  Customs of War on Land 1907)...4.12
preamble (eighth recital)............4.40
art 3............................2.56
Convention for the Amelioration of the
  Condition of the Wounded in Armies
  in the Field 1864 ....7.21
Convention for the Amelioration of the
  Condition of the Wounded and Sick
  in Armed Forces in the Field 1949
  ('1949 Geneva Convention I') (*see
  also* Geneva Conventions 1949) 7.8
arts 49–50 ....4.20
art 49......4.25, 7.27, 8.6, 8.7, 8.15, 8.34,
    8.38, 8.41, 8.48, 8.52, 8.77
art 50............... 7.8, 7.25, 7.27, 8.9
Convention for the Amelioration of the
  Condition of the Wounded, Sick and
  Shipwrecked Members of the Armed
  Forces at Sea 1949 ('1949 Geneva

Convention II') (*see also* Geneva
 Conventions 1949) 7.8
arts 50–51 .... 4.20
art 50 .... 4.25, 7.8, 7.27, 8.6, 8.7, 8.15,
 8.34, 8.38, 8.41, 8.48, 8.52, 8.77
art 51 .... 7.8, 7.25, 7.27, 8.9
Convention for the Amelioration of the
 Condition of the Wounded and Sick
 in Armies in the Field 1906 .... 7.21
Convention for the Amelioration of the
 Condition of the Wounded and Sick
 in Armies in the Field 1929 .... 7.21
Convention for the Elimination of All
 Forms of Discrimination against
 Women 1979
 art 6 .... 7.148
Convention for the Prevention and
 Punishment of Terrorism
 1937 .... 7.38, 7.39, 7.102
 art 1(2) 7.103
Convention for the Protection of
 Cultural Property in the Event
 of Armed Conflict 1954 ('1954
 Hague Convention') (*see also* Second
 Protocol to the 1954 Convention for
 the Protection of Cultural Property in
 the Event of Armed
 Conflict 1999) 7.8, 7.29, 7.30,
 11.14, 11.23
 art 1 .... 7.31, 7.32
 art 1(*a*) 7.31
 art 1(*b*) 7.31
 art 18 .... 7.30
 art 19(1) 7.30
 art 28 .... 2.65, 7.29, 7.30, 8.41
Convention for the Protection of Human
 Rights and Fundamental Freedoms
 1950 ('European Convention on
 Human Rights') 9.35
 art 1 .... 14.13
 art 5(1) 1.112
 art 7(1) 4.45
 art 7(2) 4.45, 9.12
Convention for the Suppression of Acts
 of Nuclear Terrorism 2005 ('Nuclear
 Terrorism Convention') 7.40, 7.76,
 7.98, 7.99, 7.100, 8.28, 8.80
 preamble (final recital) 7.99
 art 1(6) 7.99
 art 2(1) 7.7, 8.9
 art 2(1)(*a*)–(*b*) 7.100
 art 2(2)–(4) 7.7
 art 2(2)(*a*)–(*b*) 7.100

art 2(2)(*b*) 8.9
art 2(3) 7.101
art 2(4)(*a*)–(*c*) 7.101
art 3 .... 7.99
art 4(2) 7.99
art 5(*a*) 8.6
art 5(*b*) 8.15
art 6 .... 9.16
art 7 .... 8.74
art 9(1)(*a*) 8.25
art 9(1)(*b*) 8.30
art 9(1)(*c*) 8.27
art 9(2)(*a*) 8.29
art 9(2)(*b*) 8.28
art 9(2)(*c*) 8.33
art 9(2)(*d*) 8.28
art 9(2)(*e*) 8.30
art 9(4) 8.34, 8.52
art 9(5) 8.42
art 10(1)–(2) 8.46
art 10(3) 8.46
art 10(6) 8.46
art 11(1) 8.48
art 13(1) 8.58
art 13(2) 8.58
art 13(3) 8.58
art 13(4) 8.58
art 13(5) 8.58
art 14(1) 8.62
art 14(2) 8.62
art 15 .... 8.59, 8.64
art 16 .... 8.61, 8.66
arts 21–22 .... 8.83
Convention for the Suppression
 of the Financing of Terrorism
 1999 ('Financing of Terrorism
 Convention') 7.83, 7.94, 7.95, 7.96,
 7.97, 7.101, 8.28, 8.30, 8.65, 8.80
art 1 .... 7.96
art 2(1) 7.7, 7.96, 8.9
art 2(1)(*a*) 7.96
art 2(1)(*b*) 7.96
art 2(2) 7.96
art 2(3) 7.96
art 2(4) 7.97
art 2(5) 7.7
art 2(5)(*a*)–(*c*) 7.97
art 3 .... 7.95
art 4(*a*) 8.6
art 4(*b*) 8.15
art 5 .... 8.81
art 6 .... 9.16
art 7(1)(*a*) 8.25

art 7(1)(b) ... 8.30
art 7(1)(c) ... 8.27
art 7(2)(a) ... 8.29, 8.32
art 7(2)(b) ... 8.28
art 7(2)(c) ... 8.28
art 7(2)(d) ... 8.33
art 7(2)(e) ... 8.30
art 7(4) ... 8.34, 8.52
art 7(5) ... 1.69, 8.24
art 7(6) ... 8.43
art 9(1)–(2) ... 8.46
art 9(3) ... 8.46
art 9(6) ... 8.46
art 10(1) ... 8.48
art 11(1) ... 8.58
art 11(2) ... 8.58
art 11(3) ... 8.58
art 11(4) ... 8.58
art 11(5) ... 8.58
art 12(1) ... 8.62
art 12(2) ... 8.65
art 12(3) ... 8.63
art 12(5) ... 8.62
art 14 ... 8.59, 8.64
art 15 ... 8.61, 8.66
art 20 ... 8.83
art 22 ... 8.83
Annex ... 7.96
Convention for the Suppression of the Illicit Traffic in Dangerous Drugs 1936 ('Dangerous Drugs Convention')
art 15 ... 8.7, 9.16
Convention for the Suppression of Terrorist Bombings 1997 ('Terrorist Bombings Convention') ... 7.83, 7.90, 7.91, 7.92, 7.93, 8.28, 8.30, 8.80
preamble (final recital) ... 7.91
art 1(4) ... 7.91
art 2(1) ... 7.7, 8.9
art 2(1)(a)–(b) ... 7.92
art 2(1)(a) ... 7.105
art 2(2) ... 7.93
art 2(3)(a)–(c) ... 7.93
art 3 ... 7.91
art 4(a) ... 8.6
art 4(b) ... 8.15
art 5 ... 9.16
art 6(1)(a) ... 8.25
art 6(1)(b) ... 8.30
art 6(1)(c) ... 8.27
art 6(2)(a) ... 8.29
art 6(2)(b) ... 8.28
art 6(2)(c) ... 8.33

art 6(2)(d) ... 8.28
art 6(2)(e) ... 8.30
art 6(4) ... 8.34, 8.52
art 6(5) ... 8.42
art 7(1)–(2) ... 8.46
art 7(3) ... 8.46
art 7(6) ... 8.46
art 8(1) ... 8.48
art 9(1) ... 8.58
art 9(2) ... 7.91, 7.106, 8.58
art 9(3) ... 8.58
art 9(4) ... 8.58
art 9(5) ... 8.58
art 10(1) ... 8.62
art 10(2) ... 8.62
art 11 ... 8.59, 8.64
art 12 ... 8.61, 8.66
art 15 ... 8.74
arts 17–18 ... 8.83
Convention for the Suppression of the Traffic in Persons and of the Exploitation of the Prostitution of Others 1950 ... 7.148
Convention for the Suppression of Unlawful Acts against the Safety of Civilian Aircraft 1971 ('Montreal Convention') (*see also* Convention on the Suppression of Unlawful Acts relating to International Civil Aviation 2010; Protocol for the Suppression of Unlawful Acts of Violence at Airports serving International Civil Aviation 1988; Convention for the Suppression of Unlawful Acts against the Safety of Civilian Aircraft as amended by Protocol for the Suppression of Unlawful Acts of Violence at Airports serving International Civil Aviation 1988) ... 7.49, 7.53, 7.54, 7.55, 7.56, 7.58, 7.83, 10.42, 10.44
art 1 ... 2.44
art 1(1) ... 7.7
art 1(1)(a)–(e) ... 7.54
art 1(1)(d) ... 7.52
art 1(2) ... 7.7
art 1(2)(a) ... 7.57
art 1(2)(b) ... 7.57
art 2(a) ... 7.54
art 3 ... 8.6, 8.15
art 4(1) ... 7.52
art 4(2) ... 7.52
art 4(3) ... 7.52

art 4(5)..........................7.52
art 4(6)..........................7.52
art 5(1)(*a*) 8.25
art 5(1)(*b*) 8.30, 8.31
art 5(1)(*c*)................. 8.30, 8.39
art 5(1)(*d*) 8.30
art 5(2).................... 8.34, 8.52
art 5(3)..........................8.42
art 6(1)–(2) 8.46
art 6(3)–(4) 8.46
art 7............................8.48
art 8............................8.52
art 8(1)..........................8.58
art 8(2)..........................8.58
art 8(3)..........................8.58
art 8(4)..........................8.58
art 10(1).........................8.74
art 11(1).........................8.62
art 11(2).........................8.62
Convention for the Suppression of
 Unlawful Acts against the Safety
 of Civilian Aircraft as amended
 by Protocol for the Suppression of
 Unlawful Acts of Violence at Airports
 serving International Civil Aviation
 1988 ('Montreal Convention as
 amended by Montreal Protocol') (*see
 also* Convention for the Suppression
 of Unlawful Acts against the Safety of
 Civilian Aircraft 1971; Convention
 on the Suppression of Unlawful
 Acts relating to International Civil
 Aviation 2010; Protocol for the
 Suppression of Unlawful Acts
 of Violence at Airports serving
 International Civil Aviation
 1988)........... 7.55, 7.56, 7.58, 7.83
art 1(1)*bis*........................8.9
art 1(1)*bis(a)* 7.55
art 1(1)*bis(b)* 7.55
Convention for the Suppression of
 Unlawful Acts against the Safety
 of Maritime Navigation 1988
 ('SUA Convention') (*see also*
 Convention for the Suppression
 of Unlawful Acts against the
 Safety of Maritime Navigation
 2005; Protocol of 2005 to the
 Convention for the Suppression of
 Unlawful Acts against the Safety of
 Maritime Navigation; Protocol for
 the Suppression of Unlawful Acts
 against the Safety of Fixed Platforms

Located on the Continental Shelf
 1988) .. 7.7, 7.75, 7.78, 7.79, 7.82, 8.31
preamble (twelfth recital) 7.82
art 1............................7.78
art 2(1)..........................7.78
art 2(2)..........................7.78
art 3.................... 7.7, 7.75, 7.82
art 3(1)(*a*) 9.7
art 3(1)(*a*)–(*g*) 7.82
art 3(1)(*g*).......................7.83
art 3(2)(*a*)–(*b*) 7.86
art 3(2)(*c*)........................7.82
art 4(1)..........................7.78
art 4(2)..........................7.78
art 5...................... 8.6, 8.15
art 6(1)(*a*) 8.30, 8.31
art 6(1)(*b*) 8.25
art 6(1)(*c*).......................8.27
art 6(2)(*a*) 8.33
art 6(2)(*b*) 8.29
art 6(2)(*c*)........................8.28
art 6(4)................ 8.34, 8.52, 9.7
art 6(5)..........................8.42
art 7(1)–(2) 8.46
art 7(3)..........................8.46
art 7(5)..........................8.46
art 9............................8.83
art 10(1).........................8.48
art 11(1).........................8.58
art 11(2).........................8.58
art 11(3).........................8.58
art 11(4).........................8.58
art 11(7).........................8.58
art 12(1).........................8.62
art 12(2).........................8.62
art 13(1).........................8.74
Annex............................7.83
Convention for the Suppression of
 Unlawful Acts against the Safety
 of Maritime Navigation 2005
 ('2005 SUA Convention') (*see also*
 Convention for the Suppression of
 Unlawful Acts against the Safety of
 Maritime Navigation 1988; Protocol
 of 2005 to the Convention for the
 Suppression of Unlawful Acts against
 the Safety of Maritime Navigation;
 Protocol for the Suppression of
 Unlawful Acts against the Safety
 of Fixed Platforms Located on
 the Continental
 Shelf 2005)............ 7.7, 7.76, 7.80,
 7.87, 7.91, 7.106, 8.24, 8.31, 8.84

art 2*bis*(2)	7.80, 7.81, 7.106
art 3	7.7
art 3(1)–(2)	7.7
art 3(1)	7.7, 8.9
art 3*bis*(1)	8.9
art 3*bis*(1)(*a*)(i)–(iv)	7.83
art 3*bis*(*b*)	7.83
art 3*bis*(2)	7.83
art 3*quater*(*a*)	7.83, 7.89
art 3*quater*(*b*)–(*e*)	7.87
art 3*ter*	8.9
art 5	8.6, 8.15
art 5*bis*	8.81
art 6(1)(*a*)	8.30, 8.31
art 6(1)(*b*)	8.25
art 6(1)(*c*)	8.27
art 6(2)(*a*)	8.33
art 6(2)(*b*)	8.29
art 6(2)(*c*)	8.28
art 6(4)	8.34, 8.52
art 6(5)	8.42
art 7(1)–(2)	8.46
art 8*bis*	8.74, 8.84
art 8*bis*(5)–(7)	1.119
art 8*bis*(8)	1.69, 8.24, 8.84
art 8*bis*(10)(*c*)(i)	8.84
art 8*bis*(10)(*d*)	8.84
art 8*bis*(11)	8.84
art 9	8.83
art 10(1)	8.48
art 11(1)	8.58
art 11(2)	8.58
art 11(3)	8.58
art 11(4)	8.58
art 11(7)	8.58
art 11*bis*	8.59, 8.64
art 11*ter*	8.61, 8.66
art 12(1)	8.62
art 12(2)	8.62
art 13(1)	8.74
Convention for the Suppression of Unlawful Seizure of Aircraft 1970 ('Hague Convention') (*see also* Convention for the Suppression of Unlawful Seizure of Aircraft as amended by Protocol supplementary to the Convention for the Suppression of Unlawful Seizure of Aircraft 2010; Protocol supplementary to the Convention for the Suppression of Unlawful Seizure of Aircraft 2010)	2.12, 7.41, 7.43, 7.45, 7.49, 7.54, 7.83, 9.15, 14.5
art 1	2.44, 7.7
art 1(*a*)	7.45, 7.47, 8.9
art 1(*b*)	7.47
art 2	8.6, 8.15
art 3(1)	7.45
art 3(2)	7.43
art 3(3)	7.43
art 3(5)	7.43
art 4(1)(*a*)	8.30
art 4(1)(*b*)	8.39
art 4(1)(*b*)–(*c*)	8.30
art 4(2)	8.34, 8.52
art 4(3)	8.42
art 6	7.43
art 6(1)–(2)	8.46
art 6(3)–(4)	8.46
art 7	7.43, 8.48
art 8	7.43, 8.52
art 8(1)	8.58
art 8(2)	8.58
art 8(3)	8.58
art 8(4)	8.58
art 10	7.43
art 10(1)	8.62
art 10(2)	8.62
Convention for the Suppression of Unlawful Seizure of Aircraft as amended by Protocol supplementary to the Convention for the Suppression of Unlawful Seizure of Aircraft 2010 ('Hague Convention as amended by Beijing Protocol') (*see also* Convention for the Suppression of Unlawful Seizure of Aircraft 1970; Protocol supplementary to the Convention for the Suppression of Unlawful Seizure of Aircraft 2010)	7.42, 7.44, 7.46, 8.31
art 1(1)–(3)	7.7
art 1(1)	7.46, 8.9
art 1(2)	7.46
art 1(2)(*a*)	8.9
art 1(3)(*a*)–(*d*)	7.48
art 1(3)(*d*)	8.9
art 1(4)(*a*)	7.48
art 1(4)(*b*)(i)–(ii)	7.48
art 2	8.6, 8.15
art 2*bis*(1)	8.82
art 2*bis*(3)	8.82
art 3(1)	7.46
art 3(5)	7.44
art 4(1)(*a*)	8.25
art 4(1)(*b*)	8.30, 8.31

Table of Treaties and Other International Instruments

art 4(1)(c) 8.39
art 4(1)(e) 8.27
art 4(2) 8.52
art 4(2)(a) 8.29
art 4(2)(b) 8.33
art 4(3) 8.34
art 4(4) 8.42
art 6(1)–(2) 8.46
art 6(3)–(4) 8.46
art 7 . . . . 8.48
art 7*bis* 7.44
art 8 . . . . 8.52
art 8(1) 8.58
art 8(2) 8.58
art 8(3) 8.58
art 8(4) 8.58
art 8*bis* 7.44, 8.59, 8.64
art 8*ter* 7.44, 8.61, 8.66
art 10(1) 8.62
art 10(2) 8.62
Convention implementing the Schengen Agreement of 14 June 1985 between the Governments of the States of the Benelux Economic Union, the Federal Republic of Germany and the French Republic on the gradual abolition of the checks at their common borders 1990 ('Schengen Convention')
art 40 . . . . 1.79
art 54 . . . . 1.73
art 55 . . . . 1.73
Convention of the Organization of the Islamic Conference on Combating International Terrorism 1999 . . . . . . 7.106
art 1(2) 7.106
art 2(a) 7.106
Convention on Combating Bribery of Foreign Public Officials in International Business Transactions 1997 ('OECD Bribery Convention') 7.13, 7.172, 7.173, 7.174, 8.15, 8.16, 8.27, 8.65, 8.87
art 1(1) . . . 7.13, 7.175, 7.176, 7.177, 7.178, 7.182, 7.189, 8.6
art 1(2) 7.179
art 1(3) 7.175
art 1(4) 7.13
art 1(4)(a) 7.175
art 1(4)(b) 7.175
art 1(4)(c) 7.175
art 2 . . . . 8.81
art 3(1) 8.15, 8.16
art 3(2) 8.81

art 3(3) 8.87
art 4(1) 8.25
art 4(2) 8.27
art 4(3) 1.69, 8.24
art 5 . . . . 8.50
art 6 . . . . 11.9
art 8(2) 8.15
art 9(1) 8.62
art 9(3) 8.65
art 10(1) 8.58
art 10(2) 8.58
art 10(3) 8.49, 8.50
art 10(4) 8.58
art 13 . . . . 7.174
Convention on Mutual Assistance in Criminal Matters between the Republic of Djibouti and the French Republic 1986 . . . . 1.105
Convention on the High Seas 1958
art 13 . . . . 1.60
art 15 . . . . 1.58
art 15(3) 1.59
art 19 . . . . 1.56, 1.57
art 21 . . . . 1.116
art 22(1) 1.117
art 22(1)(a) 1.116
art 22(1)(b) 1.117
art 23 . . . . 1.118
art 23(4) 1.118
Convention on Psychotropic Substances 1971 . . . . 7.135
Convention on Special Missions 1969 ('CSM')
art 1(a) 10.29
art 21(2) 10.33
art 29 . . . . 10.29
art 31(1) 10.29, 10.40
art 31(2)(a)–(d) 10.86
art 31(3) 10.29, 10.40
art 41(1)–(2) 10.29, 10.99
art 41(1) 10.29
art 41(2) 10.29, 10.91
art 42(1) 10.29
art 43(1)–(2) 10.29
art 43(2) 10.60, 10.99
Convention on the Elimination of All Forms of Racial Discrimination 1965 . . . . 7.111
Convention on the Non-Applicability of Statutory Limitations to War Crimes and Crimes against Humanity 1968 . . . . 11.13, 11.14
art 1 . . . . 11.6
art 1(b) 7.111

Convention on the Physical Protection
    of Nuclear Material 1979
    ('Nuclear Material Convention')
    (*see also* Amendment of 2005 to
    the Convention on the Physical
    Protection of Nuclear Material;
    Convention on the Physical
    Protection of Nuclear Material and
    Nuclear Facilities 2005) 7.13, 7.66,
        7.67, 7.68, 7.70, 7.72, 7.72, 7.83
art 1 . . . . 7.13
art 1(*a*)–(*b*). 7.68
art 1(*c*) 7.68
art 2(1). 7.68
art 2(2). 7.68
art 7(1). 7.13, 8.6
art 7(1)(*a*)–(*e*). 7.70
art 7(1)(*f*) 7.72
art 7(1)(*g*). 7.72
art 7(2). 8.15
art 8(1)(*a*) 8.25, 8.30
art 8(1)(*b*) 8.27
art 8(2). 8.34, 8.52
art 8(3). 8.42
art 9. . . . . 8.46
art 10. . . . . 8.48
art 11. . . . . 8.52
art 11(1). 8.58
art 11(2). 8.58
art 11(3). 8.58
art 11(4). 8.58
art 13(1). 8.62
art 13(2). 8.62
Convention on the Physical Protection
    of Nuclear Material and Nuclear
    Facilities 2005 ('Nuclear Material
    and Facilities Convention') (*see also*
    Convention on the Physical
    Protection of Nuclear Material
    1979; Amendment of 2005 to
    the Convention on the Physical
    Protection of Nuclear
    Material) 7.13, 7.67, 7.69, 7.71, 7.91
preamble (seventh, eleventh, and twelfth
        recitals). 7.67
art 1 . . . . 7.13
art 1(*d*). 7.69
art 2(1). 7.69
art 2(4)(*b*) 7.69, 7.106
art 2(5). 7.69
art 7(1). 7.13, 8.6
art 7(1)(*a*) 7.71
art 7(1)(*d*) 7.71
art 7(1)(*e*). 7.71
art 7(1)(*g*). 7.71
art 7(1)(*g*)(i). 7.71
art 7(1)(*j*)–(*k*). 7.73
art 7(2). 8.15
art 8(1)(*a*) 8.25, 8.30
art 8(1)(*b*) 8.27
art 8(2). 8.34
art 8(3). 8.42
art 9. . . . . 8.46
art 10. . . . . 8.48
art 11(1). 8.58
art 11(2). 8.58
art 11(3). 8.58
art 11(4). 8.58
art 11A. 8.59, 8.64
art 11B. 8.61, 8.66
art 13(1). 8.62
art 13(2). 8.62
Convention on the Privileges and
    Immunities of the Specialized
    Agencies 1947 ('CPISA')
art V
    s 13(*a*) 10.96
Convention on the Privileges and
    Immunities of the United Nations
    1946 ('CPIUN'). 10.30
art IV
    s 11(*a*) 10.30, 10.40, 10.99
    s 11(*g*) 10.30, 10.40
    s 12 . . . . 10.99
    s 14 . . . . 10.30, 10.99
Convention on the Protection and
    Punishment of Crimes against
    Internationally Protected Persons,
    including Diplomatic Agents 1973
    ('Internationally Protected Persons
    Convention') 7.13, 7.59, 7.60,
        7.61, 7.83, 8.28
art 1(1). 7.13
art 1(1)(*a*) 7.60
art 1(1)(*b*) 7.60
art 2. . . . . 2.44
art 2(1). 7.13, 8.6
art 2(1)(*a*)–(*c*). 7.60
art 2(1)(*d*)–(*e*) 7.61
art 2(2). 8.15
art 3(1)(*a*) 8.25, 8.30
art 3(1)(*b*) 8.27
art 3(1)(*c*). 8.28
art 3(2). 8.34, 8.52
art 3(3). 8.42
art 6(1)–(2) 8.46

art 7 .... 8.48
art 8 .... 8.52
art 8(1) 8.58
art 8(2) 8.58
art 8(3) 8.58
art 8(4) 8.58
art 10(1) 8.62
art 10(2) 8.62
Convention on the Prevention and
  Punishment of the Crime of
  Genocide 1948 ('Genocide
  Convention') 1.98, 2.11, 2.24,
    2.34, 2.61, 2.62, 4.5, 4.65, 7.10, 7.20,
    8.40, 8.45, 8.64, 8.72, 9.53
preamble (first recital) 7.10
art I 4.65, 4.70, 8.5, 8.67, 8.68,
    8.69, 8.70, 8.71, 8.75, 11.29
art II 4.66, 4.67, 4.69, 4.78, 4.79,
    5.92, 9.48
art II(a)–(e) 4.68, 4.73, 4.74, 4.77
art II(b) 4.75
art II(c) 4.74
art II(d) 4.76
art III 5.87, 9.53
art III(b) 5.89
art III(c) 5.90, 5.92, 5.97
art III(d) 5.99
art III(e) 5.97
art V 8.6, 8.7, 8.15
art VI 8.25, 8.40, 8.45, 8.57, 8.75, 14.4
art VII 8.59
art VIII 8.70
art XIII 8.67
Convention on the Rights of the Child
  1989 (*see also* Optional Protocol to
  the Convention on the Rights of
  the Child on the Sale of Children,
  Child Prostitution and Child
  Pornography 2005)
  arts 32–36 .... 7.167
Convention on the Safety of United
  Nations and Associated Personnel
  1994 ('UN and Associated Personnel
  Convention') (*see also* Optional
  Protocol to the Convention on
  the Safety of United Nations and
  Associated Personnel 2005) 7.13, 7.197,
    7.198, 7.202, 7.203
art 1 .... 7.13, 7.199
art 1(a) 7.199
art 1(a)(i)–(ii) 7.199
art 1(b) 7.199
art 1(c) 7.199, 7.201
art 1(c)(i) 7.199
art 2(1) 7.199
art 2(2) 7.199
art 3(c)(ii) 7.200
art 8 .... 8.85
art 9(1) 7.13, 8.6
art 9(1)(a)–(c) 7.202
art 9(1)(d)–(e) 7.203
art 9(2) 8.15
art 10(1)(a) 8.25, 8.30
art 10(1)(b) 8.27
art 10(2)(b) 8.29
art 10(2)(a) 8.33
art 10(2)(c) 8.28
art 10(4) 8.34, 8.52
art 10(5) 8.42
art 11 .... 8.74
art 13(1) 8.46
art 13(2) 8.46
art 14 .... 8.48
art 15 .... 8.52
art 15(1) 8.58
art 15(2) 8.58
art 15(3) 8.58
art 15(4) 8.58
art 16(1) 8.62
art 16(2) 8.62
Convention on the Suppression
  of Unlawful Acts relating to
  International Civil Aviation 2010
  ('Beijing Convention') (*see also*
  Convention for the Suppression of
  Unlawful Acts against the Safety of
  Civilian Aircraft 1971; Convention
  for the Suppression of Unlawful
  Acts against the Safety of Civilian
  Aircraft as amended by Protocol
  for the Suppression of Unlawful
  Acts of Violence at Airports serving
  International Civil Aviation 1988;
  Protocol for the Suppression of
  Unlawful Acts of Violence at Airports
  serving International Civil Aviation
  1988) 7.53, 7.56, 7.58, 7.83, 8.31
preamble (second and third recitals) 7.51
art 1(1) 8.9
art 1(1)(f)–(i) 7.56
art 1(2) 8.9
art 1(3) 7.56
art 1(3)(b) 8.9
art 1(4) 7.58
art 1(4)(d) 8.9
art 1(5) 7.58

art 3 . . . . 8.6, 8.15
art 4(1) 8.82
art 4(3) 8.82
art 5 . . . . 7.53
art 8(1)(a) 8.25
art 8(1)(b) 8.30, 8.31
art 8(1)(c) 8.39
art 8(1)(c)–(d) 8.30
art 8(1)(e) 8.27
art 8(2)(a) 8.29
art 8(2)(b) 8.33
art 8(3) 8.34, 8.52
art 8(4) 8.34
art 9(1)–(2) 8.46
art 9(3)–(4) 8.46
art 10 . . . . 8.48
art 12(1) 8.58
art 12(2) 8.58
art 12(3) 8.58
art 12(4) 8.58
art 12(5) 8.58
art 13 . . . . 8.59, 8.64
art 14 . . . . 8.66
art 16(1) 8.74
art 17(1) 8.62
art 17(2) 8.62
Convention on the Territorial Sea and
  Contiguous Zone 1958
  art 1(1) 1.120
  art 19(1) 1.121
  art 19(5) 1.121
  art 24(1) 1.123
Convention relative to the Protection
  of Civilian Persons in Time of War
  1949 ('1949 Geneva Convention
  IV') (see also Geneva
  Conventions 1949) 2.81, 7.8, 10.44
  art 64 . . . . 1.84
  art 66 . . . . 1.84
  art 68 . . . . 1.84
  art 70 . . . . 1.84
  art 76 . . . . 1.84
  art 77 . . . . 1.84
  art 78 . . . . 1.84
  arts 146–147 . . . . 4.20
  art 146 . . . . 4.25, 7.27, 8.6, 8.7, 8.15,
           8.34, 8.38, 8.41, 8.48, 8.52, 8.77
  art 147 . . . . 7.8, 7.25, 7.27, 8.9
Convention relative to the Treatment of
  Prisoners of War 1929 . . . . 7.21
Convention relative to the Treatment of
  Prisoners of War 1949 ('1949 Geneva
  Convention III') (see also Geneva
  Conventions 1949) 7.8

art 4 . . . . 4.31
art 85 . . . . 1.83
art 118 . . . . 1.83
art 119 . . . . 1.83
arts 129–130 . . . . 4.20
art 129 . . . . 4.25, 7.27, 8.6, 8.7, 8.15,
           8.34, 8.38, 8.41, 8.48, 8.52, 8.77
art 130 . . . . 7.8, 7.25, 7.27, 8.9
Council of Europe Convention on Action
  against Trafficking in Human
  Beings 2005
  art 31(4) 1.69
Council of Europe Convention on
  Laundering, Search, Seizure and
  Confiscation of the Proceeds from
  Crime and on the Financing of
  Terrorism 2005
  art 28(1)(f) 1.73
Council of Europe Convention on the
  Protection of Children against Sexual
  Exploitation and Sexual Abuse 2007
  art 25(8) 1.69
Criminal Law Convention on Corruption
  1999 . . . . 7.180
  arts 2–11 . . . . 7.180
Draft Treaty of Mutual Assistance 1923 . . . 2.64
European Convention on Extradition
  1957 (see also Additional Protocol
  to the European Convention on
  Extradition 1975) 1.95, 1.97
  art 2 . . . . 1.97
  art 2(1) 1.97
  art 2(4) 1.97
  art 3(1) 1.98
  art 3(3) 1.98
  art 6(1)(a) 1.99
  art 6(2) 1.99
  art 9 . . . . 1.73
  art 14(1) 1.100
  art 14(1)(a) 1.100
  art 15 . . . . 1.101
European Convention on Insider Trading
  1989 . . . . 1.95
  art 8(e) 1.73
European Convention on Laundering,
  Search, Seizure and Confiscation of
  the Proceeds from Crime 1990
  art 18(1)(e) 1.73
European Convention on Mutual
  Assistance in Criminal Matters 1959
  (see also Additional Protocol to the
  European Convention on Mutual
  Assistance in Criminal Matters 1978;
  Second Additional Protocol to the

European Convention on Mutual
    Assistance in Criminal
    Matters 2001) 1.105
    art 2(a)....................... 1.106
European Convention on Offences
    relating to Cultural Property 1985
    art 17.......................... 1.73
European Convention on the International
    Validity of Criminal Judgments 1970
    art 6(e)........................ 1.73
    art 53.......................... 1.73
European Convention on the
    Non-Applicability of Statutory
    Limitation to Crimes against
    Humanity and War
    Crimes 1974 .... 11.10, 11.13
    art 1(1)........................ 11.10
    art 1(2)........................ 11.10
    art 1(3)........................ 11.10
    art 6 11.10
European Convention on the Punishment
    of Road Traffic Offences 1964
    art 9(1)(a) 1.73
    art 9(2)(a) 1.73
European Convention on the Supervision
    of Conditionally Sentenced or
    Conditionally Released Offenders 1964
    art 7(1)........................ 1.73
    art 7(2)(a) 1.73
European Convention on the Transfer of
    Proceedings in Criminal Matters 1972
    art 35.......................... 1.73
Extradition Treaty between the
    Government of the United Kingdom
    of Great Britain and Northern
    Ireland and the Government of the
    United States of America 2003...... 1.95
    art 5(1)........................ 1.73
    art 5(2)........................ 1.73
    art 5(3)(a)–(b) 1.73
General Framework Agreement for
    Peace in Bosnia and Herzegovina
    1995 ('Dayton Agreement')
    (see also Agreement on Refugees
    and Displaced Persons annexed to
    General Framework Agreement for
    Peace in Bosnia and
    Herzegovina 1995)
    art IX......................... 12.54
    Annex 1-A 12.55
        art I(1)(a).................. 12.54
        art VI(1).................... 12.54
        art VI(2)(a) 12.54
        art VI(5).................... 12.54
General Treaty for the Renunciation of
    War as an Instrument of National
    Policy 1928 ('Kellogg-Briand
    Pact') 2.64, 2.69, 2.71
Geneva Conventions 1949 (see also
    Convention for the Amelioration
    of the Condition of the Wounded
    and Sick in Armed Forces in the
    Field 1949; Convention for the
    Amelioration of the Condition of
    the Wounded, Sick and Shipwrecked
    Members of the Armed Forces at
    Sea 1949; Convention relative to
    the Protection of Civilian Persons
    in Time of War 1949; Convention
    relative to the Treatment of Prisoners
    of War 1949; Protocol Additional
    to the Geneva Conventions of
    12 August 1949 and relating
    to the Protection of Victims of
    International Armed Conflicts 1977;
    Protocol Additional to the Geneva
    Conventions of 12 August 1949
    and relating to the Protection of
    Victims of Non-International Armed
    Conflicts 1977) 1.63, 2.65, 4.10,
            4.21, 4.22, 4.23, 4.35, 7.8, 7.18, 7.21,
            7.22, 7.23, 7.24, 7.25, 7.63, 8.9, 8.25,
            8.38, 8.54, 8.77, 9.28, 9.32, 9.64, 9.66,
                    9.74, 10.44, 11.10, 11.14,
                    11.23, 12.22, 14.5
    art 2.................... 7.23, 13.23
    art 3......... 4.16, 4.25, 4.26, 4.35, 8.41,
                    9.74, 12.22
Geneva Protocol for the Pacific
    Settlement of International
    Disputes 1924 .... 2.7, 2.64
Headquarters Agreement between the
    Republic of Sierra Leone and the
    Special Court for Sierra
    Leone 2003 .... 13.8
ICC Regulations of the Court
    reg 103(6) 6.12
ICC Rules of Procedure and Evidence
    ('ICC RPE')............. 14.14, 14.17
    rules 16–19 .... 14.17
    rule 44(2) 14.33, 14.78
    rule 46–50..................... 14.20
    rule 67(A)(ii)(b) 6.13
    rule 67(B)(i)(b)................. 6.13
    rule 68........................ 14.17
    rule 80.......................... 6.5
    rule 86........................ 14.17
    rule 87–88..................... 14.17

rules 89–93 . . . . 14.17
rules 94–99 . . . . 14.17
rule 98 . . . . 14.17
rule 100 . . . . 14.13
rules 104–105 . . . . 14.21
rule 106 . . . . 14.22
rule 134*quater* 14.41
rule 145(2)(*a*) 6.42
rule 145(2)(*a*)(i) 6.13
rule 176(2) 14.79, 14.94
ICTR Rules of Procedure and Evidence
  ('ICTR RPE') 12.10
  rule 7*bis* 12.50
  rules 8–13 . . . . 12.36
  rule 11*bis* . . . 12.6, 12.38, 12.39, 12.40, 12.42
  rule 11*bis*(A)(ii)–(iii) 1.63
  rule 13 . . . . 12.45
  rule 34 . . . . 12.13
  rule 42 . . . . 12.12
  rule 43 . . . . 12.12
  rules 54–61 . . . . 12.50
  rule 62(A)(i) 12.12
  rules 66–70 . . . . 12.50
  rule 69 . . . . 12.13
  rule 75 . . . . 12.13
  rule 79(A)(ii) 12.13
  rule 89(C) 12.27
  rule 101(B)(ii) 6.42
ICTY Rules of Procedure and Evidence
  ('ICTY RPE') 12.9
  rule 7*bis* 12.50
  rules 8–13 . . . . 12.34
  rule 11*bis* 9.37, 9.56, 9.57, 9.59, 12.6,
              12.38, 12.39, 12.40, 12.42
  rule 11*bis*(A)(ii)–(iii) 1.63
  rule 13 . . . . 12.45
  rule 34 . . . . 12.13
  rule 42 . . . . 12.12
  rule 43 . . . . 12.12
  rules 54–61 . . . . 12.50
  rule 62(A)(i) 12.12
  rules 66–70 . . . . 12.50
  rule 69 . . . . 12.13
  rule 75 . . . . 12.13
  rule 77 . . . . 12.52
  rule 77(A)(iii) 12.52
  rule 79(A)(ii) 12.13
  rule 101(B)(ii) 6.42
ILC Articles on Responsibility of States for
  Internationally Wrongful Acts (2001)
  ('Articles on Responsibility of States')
  arts 4–11 . . . . 2.8, 10.64, 10.88
  art 4(1) 10.47, 10.60

art 7 . . . . 10.64, 10.88
art 8 . . . . 1.108
art 26 . . . . 2.78
art 27 . . . . 2.81
art 29 . . . . 8.3
art 30 . . . . 2.78, 8.3
art 31 . . . . 1.108, 2.78, 8.3
art 35 . . . . 1.108
art 37 . . . . 2.54, 11.31
art 37(2) 2.54, 11.31
art 40 . . . . 2.7, 2.78, 2.81
art 41 . . . . 2.7, 10.88
art 48(2) 8.3
art 58 . . . . 2.75
Pt One, ch V 6.8
ILC Draft Articles on Consular Relations
  (1961) 10.64
art 43 . . . . 10.94
ILC Draft Articles on Diplomatic
  Intercourse and Immunities
  (1958) 10.14, 10.15, 10.17
ILC Draft Code of Crimes against the
  Peace and Security of Mankind
  (1996) ('ILC Draft Code of
  Crimes') 4.4, 4.47, 4.89, 6.4, 7.103
  art 1(1) 2.41
  art 1(2) 2.34, 2.41
  art 2(1) 2.67
  art 2(2) 2.73
  art 4 . . . . 2.75
  art 7 . . . . 2.73
  art 11 . . . . 6.33
  art 14 . . . . 6.4, 6.21, 6.22
  art 15 . . . . 6.42
  art 16 . . . . 2.73
  art 17 . . . . 4.67
  art 18 . . . . 4.54, 4.56
  art 18(*e*) 4.53
  art 18(*j*) 4.48
  art 18(*k*) 4.50
  Pt II 2.41, 2.42
ILC Draft Statute for an International
  Criminal Court (1994) ('ILC Draft
  Statute') 2.11, 2.16
  preamble 2.43
  art 20 . . . . 2.67
  art 20(*a*)–(*d*) 2.44
  art 20(*e*) 2.11, 2.15, 2.35, 2.44
  art 33 . . . . 2.15
  art 33(*c*) 2.31
  Annex 2.44
ILC Principles of International Law
  Recognized in the Charter of the

Nürnberg Tribunal and in the
Judgment of the Tribunal (1950)
('ILC Nürnberg Principles') ... 2.11, 2.34,
2.60, 2.61, 4.4, 4.46, 4.47, 6.32, 14.4
principles I–III 2.34
principle III 6.41
principles V–VII 2.34
principle VI 2.73, 4.13, 4.88
Inter-American Convention Against
Corruption 1996 . . . . 7.180
arts VI–VII 7.180
Inter-American Convention on Mutual
Assistance in Criminal Matters
1992 . . . . 1.105
art 9(*a*) 1.73, 1.106
International Agreement for the
Suppression of the White Slave
Traffic 1904 . . . . 7.148
International Covenant on Civil and
Political Rights 1966
('ICCPR') 7.111, 9.35
art 7 . . . . 2.78
art 14 . . . . 9.73, 12.12, 12.19, 14.16
art 14(7) 12.43
art 15(2) 9.12
International Covenant on Economic,
Social and Cultural Rights 1966 . . . . 7.111
International Convention for the
Protection of all Persons against
Enforced Disappearance 2006
('Enforced Disappearance
Convention') . . . 4.56, 7.14, 7.124, 7.125,
7.126, 8.18, 8.79, 10.90, 10.91, 11.22
preamble (fifth recital) 4.50
preamble (sixth recital) 7.14
art 1(2) 8.79
art 2 . . . . 7.14, 7.125, 10.90
art 4 . . . . 7.14, 8.6
art 5 . . . . 4.49, 7.14, 7.125, 11.9
art 6(1)(*a*)–(*b*) 7.126
art 6(1)(*b*) 7.127
art 6(1)(*b*)(i)–(iii) 7.127
art 6(1)(*c*) 7.127
art 6(2) 8.79, 9.16
art 7(1) 8.15
art 7(2)(*a*) 8.18
art 7(2)(*b*) 8.18
art 8(1) 11.9
art 9(1)(*a*) 8.25, 8.30
art 9(1)(*b*) 8.27
art 9(1)(*c*) 8.29
art 9(2) 8.34, 8.52
art 9(3) 8.42
art 10(1)–(2) 8.46
art 10(2)–(3) 8.46
art 11 . . . . 8.52
art 11(1)–(2) 8.48
art 11(1) 8.56
art 13(1) 8.59, 8.64
art 13(2) 8.58
art 13(3) 8.58
art 13(4) 8.58
art 13(6) 8.58
art 13(7) 8.61
art 14(1) 8.62
International Convention for the
Suppression of Counterfeiting
Currency 1929 ('Counterfeiting
Convention')
art 18 . . . . 8.7, 8.12, 9.15
International Convention for the
Suppression of Traffic in Women and
Children 1921 . . . . 7.148
International Convention for the
Suppression of the Traffic in Women
of Full Age 1933 . . . . 7.148
International Convention for the
Suppression of the White Slave
Traffic 1910 . . . . 7.148
International Convention on the
Suppression and Punishment of the
Crime of Apartheid 1973 ('Apartheid
Convention') 2.11, 4.56, 7.11,
7.111, 7.112, 8.45, 8.64
preamble (fifth, sixth, and seventh
recitals) 7.11
art I(I) 1.61, 4.47, 4.49, 7.11
art II 2.44, 7.112
art III 2.73, 7.113, 7.114
art IV 8.6
art IV(*a*) 8.76
art V 8.34, 8.57
art XI 8.59
art 2(*a*)–(*f*) 7.115
art 3 . . . . 7.116
League of Nations Assembly Declaration
concerning Wars of Aggression
(1927) 2.7, 2.64
Mechanism for International Criminal
Tribunals Rules of Procedure and
Evidence ('MICT RPE')
rules 8–13 . . . . 12.34
rule 32 . . . . 12.13
rule 40 . . . . 12.12
rule 41 . . . . 12.12
rule 64(A)(i) 12.12

rule 66 ....12.12
rule 75 ....12.13
rule 86 ....12.13
rule 93(A)(ii) 12.13
Memorandum of Understanding between the Special Court for Sierra Leone and Government of the Republic of Sierra Leone 2013 ....13.12
Military Technical Agreement between International Security Assistance Force (ISAF) and the Interim Administration of Afghanistan 2002
  Annex A
    paras 2–3 ....14.99
    para 4......................14.104
Organization of African Unity Convention on the Prevention and Combating of Terrorism 1999 ....7.106
  art 1(3).......................7.106
  art 3(1).......................7.106
  art 8(3)........................1.73
Optional Protocol to the Convention on the Rights of the Child on the Sale of Children, Child Prostitution and Child Pornography 2005 ('Children Protocol') (*see also* Convention on the Rights of the Child 1989) ...7.13, 7.167, 7.168, 8.87
  art 2..........................7.13
  art 2(*a*).....................7.169
  art 2(*b*).....................7.169
  art 3(1)......7.13, 7.169, 7.170, 7.171, 8.6
  art 3(1)(*a*) 7.169
  art 3(1)(*b*) 7.169
  art 3(1)(*c*)...................7.169
  art 3(1)(*a*)(i)................7.169
  art 3(1)(*a*)(ii) 7.169
  art 3(2).......................7.169
  art 3(3)........................8.15
  art 3(4)........................8.81
  art 4(1)..................8.25, 8.30
  art 4(2)(*a*) 8.27
  art 4(2)(*b*) 8.29
  art 3(4)........................8.34
  art 4(4)........................8.42
  art 5(1)........................8.58
  art 5(2)........................8.58
  art 5(3)........................8.58
  art 5(4)........................8.58
  art 5(5)........................8.50
  art 6(1)........................8.62
  art 6(2)........................8.62
  art 7...........................8.87
Optional Protocol to the Convention on the Safety of United Nations and Associated Personnel 2005 ('UN and Associated Personnel Protocol') (*see also* Convention on the Safety of United Nations and Associated Personnel 1995) 7.197, 7.200
  art I 7.197
  art II(1)(*a*)–(*b*).................7.201
  art II(3) 7.201
  art III.........................8.85
Optional Protocol to the International Convention for the Suppression of Counterfeiting Currency 1929.......8.60
Protocol Additional to the Geneva Conventions of 12 August 1949 and relating to the Protection of Victims of International Armed Conflicts 1977 ('Additional Protocol I') (*see also* Geneva Conventions 1949) ...4.21, 4.22, 4.24, 6.19, 7.8, 7.21, 6.22, 7.24, 7.63, 8.9, 8.77, 12.22
  art 1(3).........................7.24
  art 1(4)...............4.31, 7.24, 7.107
  art 11 ....7.8, 7.26
  art 50 ....4.51
  art 85 ....4.20
  art 85(1).........................7.8
  art 85(2)–(4) 7.8
  art 85(2).......................7.26
  art 85(3)...............7.25, 7.26, 8.9
  art 85(3)(*f*)....................7.26
  art 85(4)...............7.25, 7.26, 8.9
  art 85(4)(*d*)....................8.44
  art 85(5).................. 4.20, 7.8
  arts 86–87 ....7.28
  arts 86–89 ....7.22
  art 88(1).......................8.62
  art 88(2).......................8.58
  art 88(3)................. 8.58, 8.62
  art 90 ....7.22
Protocol Additional to the Geneva Conventions of 12 August 1949 and relating to the Protection of Victims of Non-International Armed Conflicts 1977 ('Additional Protocol II') (*see also* Geneva Conventions 1949).... 4.16, 4.25, 4.26, 7.8, 7.22, 7.63, 8.41, 9.74, 13.23
  art 1(1).........................4.25
  art 6(5).......................11.17
Protocol against the Illicit Manufacturing of and Trafficking in Firearms, Their Parts and Components and

Table of Treaties and Other International Instruments

Ammunition 2001, supplementing
  the United Nations Convention
  against Transnational Organized
  Crime ('Firearms Protocol') (*see also*
  United Nations Convention against
  Transnational Organized Crime
  2000) . . . 7.13, 7.161, 7.162, 7.163, 7.164
 art 1 . . . . 7.162
 art 3 . . . . 7.13, 7.163, 7.165
 art 3(*a*)–(*c*) 7.165
 art 3(*d*) 7.165
 art 3(*e*) 2.47, 7.165
 art 4 . . . . 7.163
 art 4(1) 7.163
 art 5(1) 7.13, 7.165, 8.6
 art 5(1)(*a*) 7.165
 art 5(2) 8.6
 art 5(2)(*a*) 8.11
 art 8 . . . . 7.165
 art 5(2)(*a*)–(*b*) 7.166
Protocol against the Smuggling of
  Migrants by Land, Sea and Air 2000,
  supplementing the United Nations
  Convention against Transnational
  Organized Crime ('Smuggling
  of Migrants Protocol') (*see also*
  United Nations Convention against
  Transnational Organized Crime
  2000) 7.13, 7.154, 7.155,
                          7.156, 7.157, 7.160,
                                 7.162, 8.18
 art 1 . . . . 7.155
 art 3 . . . . 7.13, 7.157
 art 3(*a*) 7.158
 art 3(*b*) 7.158
 art 3(*c*) 7.158
 art 4 . . . . 7.157
 art 5(6)(*a*)–(*c*) 7.160
 art 6 . . . . 7.157, 7.158
 art 6(1) 7.13, 7.158, 8.6
 art 6(2) 8.6
 art 6(2)(*a*)–(*b*) 8.11
 art 6(3) 8.11, 8.18
Protocol of 2005 to the Protocol for
  the Suppression of Unlawful Acts
  against the Safety of Fixed Platforms
  Located on the Continental Shelf
  (*see also* Protocol for the Suppression
  of Unlawful Acts against the Safety
  of Fixed Platforms Located on the
  Continental Shelf 1988; Protocol
  for the Suppression of Unlawful Acts
  against the Safety of Fixed Platforms
  Located on the Continental Shelf
  2005) 7.7, 7.77
Protocol of 2005 to the Convention
  for the Suppression of Unlawful
  Acts against the Safety of Maritime
  Navigation (*see also* Convention
  for the Suppression of Unlawful
  Acts against the Safety of Maritime
  Navigation 1988; Convention for the
  Suppression of Unlawful Acts against
  the Safety of Maritime Navigation
  2005) 7.7, 7.76
Protocol for the Prevention and
  Punishment of the Crime of
  Genocide, War Crimes and Crimes
  Against Humanity and All Forms of
  Discrimination 2006
 art 8 . . . . 11.11
 art 11 . . . . 11.11
Protocol for the Suppression of
  Unlawful Acts against the Safety
  of Fixed Platforms Located on the
  Continental Shelf 1988 ('SUA
  Protocol') (*see also* Convention for
  the Suppression of Unlawful Acts
  against the Safety of Maritime
  Navigation 1988; Protocol of 2005
  to the Protocol for the Suppression
  of Unlawful Acts against the Safety
  of Fixed Platforms Located on the
  Continental Shelf; Protocol for the
  Suppression of Unlawful Acts against
  the Safety of Fixed Platforms Located
  on the Continental Shelf
  2005) 7.7, 7.77, 7.79, 7.83, 8.26
 art 1(1)–(2) 7.75, 7.79
 art 1(3) 7.79
 art 2 . . . . 2.44, 7.7
 art 2(1) 8.9
 art 2(1)(*a*)–(*e*) 7.84
 art 2(1)(*e*) 7.85
 art 2(2)(*a*)–(*b*) 7.88
 art 2(2)(*c*) 7.84
 art 3(1)(*a*) 8.26
 art 3(1)(*b*) 8.27
 art 3(2)(*a*) 8.33
 art 3(2)(*b*) 8.29
 art 3(2)(*c*) 8.28
 art 3(4) 8.34, 8.52
 art 3(5) 8.42
Protocol for the Suppression of Unlawful Acts
  against the Safety of Fixed Platforms
  Located on the Continental Shelf 2005

('2005 SUA Protocol') (*see also* Protocol for the Suppression of Unlawful Acts against the Safety of Fixed Platforms Located on the Continental Shelf 1988; Protocol of 2005 to the Protocol for the Suppression of Unlawful Acts against the Safety of Fixed Platforms Located on the Continental Shelf; Convention for the Suppression of Unlawful Acts against the Safety of Maritime Navigation 2005) 7.75, 7.76, 7.80, 7.88, 7.89, 7.91, 8.26
art 1(1). 7.77, 7.81
art 1(2). 7.81
art 1(3). 7.81
art 2(1). 8.9
art 2*bis* 7.7, 7.85, 7.89, 8.9
art 2*ter* 7.7
art 2*ter*(*a*) 7.85, 8.9
art 3(1)(*a*) 8.26
art 3(2)(*a*) 8.33
art 3(2)(*b*) 8.29
art 3(2)(*c*) 8.28
art 3(4). 8.34, 8.52
art 3(5). 8.42
Protocol for the Suppression of Unlawful Acts of Violence at Airports serving International Civil Aviation 1988, supplementary to the Convention for the Suppression of Unlawful Acts against the Safety of Civilian Aircraft ('Montreal Protocol') (*see also* Convention for the Suppression of Unlawful Acts against the Safety of Civilian Aircraft 1971; Convention for the Suppression of Unlawful Acts against the Safety of Civilian Aircraft as amended by Protocol for the Suppression of Unlawful Acts of Violence at Airports serving International Civil Aviation 1988; Convention on the Suppression of Unlawful Acts relating to International Civil Aviation 2010) . . . 7.50
Protocol supplementary to the Convention for the Suppression of Unlawful Seizure of Aircraft 2010 ('Beijing Protocol') (*see also* Convention for the Suppression of Unlawful Seizure of Aircraft 1970; Convention for the Suppression of Unlawful Seizure of Aircraft as amended by Protocol supplementary to the Convention for the Suppression of Unlawful Seizure of Aircraft 2010) 7.7, 7.42, 7.54
preamble (second recital) 7.42
art I 7.42
art IX 7.42
art XX(2)–(3) 7.43
Protocol to Prevent, Suppress and Punish Trafficking in Persons, Especially Women and Children 2000, supplementing the United Nations Convention against Transnational Organized Crime ('Trafficking in Persons Protocol') (*see also* United Nations Convention against Transnational Organized Crime 2000) 7.13, 7.148, 7.149, 7.150, 7.153, 7.158, 7.162
art 1 . . . . 7.149
art 1(2). 7.150
art 3 . . . . 7.13, 7.150, 7.151
art 3(*a*). 7.151, 9.41
art 3(*b*) 7.151
art 3(*c*) 7.151
art 3(*d*). 7.151
art 4 . . . . 7.150
art 5 . . . . 7.150, 7.151, 8.6
art 5(1). 7.13
art 5(2)(*a*)–(*c*). 7.153
Regulations concerning the Laws and Customs of War on Land annexed to Convention concerning the Laws and Customs of War on Land 1899 (*see also* Convention concerning the Laws and Customs of War on Land 1899) 2.56
Regulations concerning the Laws and Customs of War on Land annexed to Convention concerning the Laws and Customs of War on Land 1907 ('1907 Hague Regulations') (*see also* Convention concerning the Laws and Customs of War on Land 1907) 2.56, 4.12, 4.13, 7.21
art 43 . . . . 1.84
art 46 . . . . 4.14
art 56 . . . . 2.56
Residual Special Court for Sierra Leone Rules of Procedure and Evidence ('RSCSL RPE'). 13.9
rule 4(A). 13.8
rule 4(B). 13.8
rule 7*bis* 13.19
rule 13 . . . . 13.37

Table of Treaties and Other International Instruments

rule 26*bis* 13.13
rule 34 . . . . 13.14
rule 42 . . . . 13.14
rule 43 . . . . 13.14
rule 60 . . . . 13.14
rule 61(i) 13.14
rule 63 . . . . 13.14
rule 69 . . . . 13.14
rule 72*bis* 13.24
rule 75 . . . . 13.14
Resolution on Aggression of the Sixth
  International Conference of
  American States (1928) ('Havana
  Resolution on Aggression') 2.7, 2.64
Rome Statute of the International
  Criminal Court 1998 ('Rome
  Statute') 1.63, 2.15, 3.43,
             4.11, 4.18, 7.104, 14.7, 14.8,
             14.9, 14.14, 14.17
  preamble 2.45
  preamble (fourth recital) 2.44, 14.105
  preamble (sixth recital) . . . 2.11, 11.26, 14.105
  preamble (ninth recital) 2.44, 14.11
  art 1 . . . . 3.13, 14.11, 14.14
  art 2 . . . . 14.11
  art 3(1) 14.13
  art 3(3) 14.13
  art 4(1) 14.12
  art 4(2) 14.13
  arts 5–6 . . . . 8.45
  art 5(1) 2.44, 2.45
  art 5(1)(*d*) 4.90
  art 5(2) 4.90, 14.30
  art 5(*a*) 4.77
  art 5(*d*) 2.73, 4.90
  arts 6–8*bis* 4.4, 4.92, 5.8
  art 6 . . . . 4.67, 8.45, 9.45, 14.14, 14.20,
             14.29, 14.59
  art 6(*a*) 6.18
  art 6(*a*)–(*e*) 4.77
  art 7 . . . . 9.45, 14.14, 14.20, 14.29, 14.59
  art 7(1) 4.51, 4.54, 4.56, 4.60, 7.125,
             9.48, 9.74
  art 7(1)(*a*) 6.18
  art 7(1)(*b*) 4.60
  art 7(1)(*c*) 1.60
  art 7(1)(*f*) 4.57, 4.60
  art 7(1)(*g*) 4.48
  art 7(1)(*h*) 4.49, 4.53
  art 7(1)(*i*) 4.49, 4.60, 8.56
  art 7(1)(*j*) 4.49, 8.45
  art 7(1)(*k*) 4.48, 4.50, 4.60, 9.48
  art 7(2) 9.48

art 7(2)(*a*) 4.51, 4.58, 4.59
art 7(2)(*b*) 4.60
art 7(2)(*c*) 1.60
art 7(2)(*e*) 4.57, 4.60
art 7(2)(*f*) 4.48
art 7(2)(*g*) 4.60
art 7(2)(*i*) 4.60
art 8 . . . . . . 4.11, 4.30, 9.45, 14.14, 14.20,
             14.29, 14.59
art 8(1) 4.33
art 8(2) 4.34
art 8(2)(*a*) 4.23, 4.35
art 8(2)(*a*)(ii) 4.32
art 8(2)(*a*)(iv) 6.38
art 8(2)(*b*) 4.34
art 8(2)(*b*)(xviii) 6.18, 6.38
art 8(2)(*b*)(xxvi) 14.59
art 8(2)(*c*) 4.27, 4.38
art 8(2)(*c*)(i)–(iv) 4.27
art 8(2)(*c*)(i) 4.33
art 8(2)(*b*) 4.11, 4.13, 4.15, 4.23
art 8(2)(*b*)(xxii) 4.14
art 8(2)(*b*)(xxvi) 4.14
art 8(2)(*e*) . 4.11, 4.18, 4.19, 4.27, 4.28, 4.34
art 8(2)(*e*)(vi) 4.18
art 8(2)(*e*)(vii) 4.18, 14.59
art 8(2)(*e*)(xiii) 4.18
art 8(2)(*e*)(xiv) 4.18
art 8(2)(*e*)(xv) 4.18
art 8(2)(*f*) 4.28, 4.31
art 8*bis* . . . 2.73, 4.90, 4.91, 4.92, 4.95, 4.97,
             14.14, 14.59
art 8*bis*(1) 4.94, 4.95, 4.96, 4.97, 4.98,
             4.99, 4.100, 5.101
art 8*bis*(2) 4.92, 4.93
art 8*bis*(2)(*a*)–(*g*) 4.99
art 9 . . . . 14.14
art 9(1) 4.4, 14.14
art 9(3) 14.14
art 10 . . . . 4.4, 4.91
art 11(1) 14.36, 14.39
art 11(2) 14.39
art 12(1) 14.28, 14.33
art 12(2) 3.43, 14.32, 14.33, 14.34,
             14.35, 14.59
art 12(2)(*a*) 14.44
art 12(2)(*a*)–(*b*) 14.35, 14.39
art 12(3) . . . 3.43, 14.32, 14.33, 14.34, 14.35,
             14.39, 14.44, 14.59, 14.78
art 13 . . . . 14.20
art 13(*a*) 14.32, 14.61
art 13(*b*) 14.11, 14.20, 14.32, 14.34,
             14.44, 14.61

art 13(c) 14.32	art 25(3)(a) . . . 5.11, 5.33, 5.35, 5.42, 5.47,
art 14 . . . . 14.61	5.48, 5.78, 5.80, 14.59
art 14(1) 14.20	art 25(3)(b) . . . 5.55, 5.62, 5.67, 5.78, 5.85, 5.99
art 14(2) 14.20	art 25(3)(c) 5.68, 5.74, 5.78, 5.84, 5.99
art 15 . . . . 14.20, 14.61	art 25(3)(d) . . . 5.18, 5.33, 5.78, 5.79, 5.80,
art 15(6) 14.21	5.81, 5.83, 5.99
art 15*ter* 14.34	art 25(3)(e) 5.87
art 15*bis*(2) 14.30	art 25(3)(d)(i)–(ii) 5.86
art 15*ter*(2) 14.30	art 25(3)(f) 5.100
art 15*bis*(3) 14.20, 14.30	art 25(4) 2.75
art 15*ter*(3) 14.20, 14.30	art 25(a) 5.105
art 15*bis*(4) 14.30	art 25(b) 5.105
art 15*bis*(5) 14.35	art 26 . . . . 14.38
art 16 . . . . 14.11, 14.52, 14.53, 14.54	art 27 . . . . 14.40, 14.44, 14.25, 14.91
art 17 . . . . 14.21, 14.61, 14.62, 14.63,	art 27(1) 2.73, 6.36, 6.41, 14.42
14.64, 14.105	art 27(2) 3.43, 14.43, 14.46, 14.47
art 17(1) 14.61, 14.66	art 28 . . . . 5.62, 5.87, 5.111, 5.113
art 17(1)(a)–(b) 14.64, 14.66, 14.67, 14.73	art 28(a) 5.102, 5.104, 5.106, 5.111
art 17(1)(b) 14.74, 14.75	art 28(a)(i) 4.8, 5.115
art 17(1)(c) 14.63, 14.76	art 28(a)(ii) 5.109
art 17(1)(d) 4.77, 14.24, 14.61	art 28(b) 4.8, 5.106, 5.111, 7.127
art 17(2)–(3) 14.64, 14.75	art 28(b)(iii) 5.109
art 17(2)(c) 14.73	art 29 . . . . 11.7, 14.48, 14.49, 14.50
art 18 . . . . 14.61, 14.66	art 30 . . . . 4.8
art 18(3) 14.63	art 30(1) 5.10
art 18(7) 14.63	art 30(2)(a) 5.10
art 19 . . . . 14.27, 14.61	art 30(2)(b) 4.82, 5.10, 5.66
art 19(1) 14.27, 14.61	art 30(3) 4.36, 5.10, 5.66, 6.4
art 19(2)–(3) 14.27	art 31 . . . . 6.5, 6.24
art 19(2)(c) 14.73	art 31(1) 6.4
art 19(3) 14.61	art 31(1)(a) 6.10, 6.11, 6.13
art 19(4) 14.63	art 31(1)(b) 6.14
art 19(5) 14.27, 14.65, 14.71	art 31(1)(c) 6.17, 6.19, 6.36
art 20 . . . . 9.74, 14.63	art 31(1)(d) 6.23
art 20(1) 9.74	art 31(1)(d)(i)–(ii) 6.23
art 20(2) 14.76	art 31(1)(d)(ii) 9.18
art 20(3) 9.74, 12.45, 14.59, 14.76	art 31(2) 6.4
art 21 . . . . 7.12, 14.57	art 32 . . . . 6.5, 6.28
art 21(1) 14.46, 14.58	art 32(2) 6.5, 6.28, 6.29, 6.34
art 21(1)(a) 4.18, 4.23, 14.14	art 33 . . . . 6.28, 6.36
art 21(1)(b) 14.57	art 33(1) 4.106, 6.6, 6.34
art 21(1)(c) 14.57	art 33(1)(b) 6.28
art 22 . . . . 14.59	art 33(1)(c) 6.34
art 22(1) 14.59	art 33(2) 4.106, 6.6, 6.34
art 22(3) 14.59	art 34 . . . . 14.15
art 23(3) 5.49	art 36(8)(a) 14.15
art 23(3)(c)–(d) 5.49	art 39(2)(b)(i)–(iii) 14.15
art 24(1) 14.36, 14.59	art 43(6) 14.17
art 25 . . . . 2.2, 2.67, 5.101, 14.25	art 51 . . . . 14.14
art 25(1) 14.37	art 51(1)–(2) 14.14
art 25(2) 2.2, 2.67	art 51(3) 14.14
art 25(3) 2.2, 5.55, 5.87	art 53(1) 14.21
art 25(3)*bis* 5.101	art 53(1)(b) 4.77, 14.24, 14.61

Table of Treaties and Other International Instruments   liii

art 53(1)(c) 14.75	art 93(1)(j) 14.17
art 53(2) 14.22	art 93(1)(l) 14.84
art 53(2)(a) 14.22	art 93(4) 14.84
art 53(2)(b) 4.77, 14.22, 14.61	art 93(5) 14.84
art 53(2)(c) 4.77, 14.22, 14.61, 14.75	art 93(10)(a) 14.77
art 53(3) 14.22	art 97 . . . . 14.84
art 53(3)(a) 14.24	art 98 . . . . . . 14.88, 14.101, 14.102, 14.103,
art 54 . . . . 14.22	14.104, 14.105
art 54(1)(b) 14.17	art 98(1) . . . 14.44, 14.89, 14.91, 14.92, 14.94,
art 55 . . . . 14.16	14.96, 14.97, 14.100, 14.105
art 56 . . . . 14.22	art 98(2) 14.56, 14.89, 14.99, 14.100,
art 57(3)(c) 14.17	14.101, 14.103. 14.104
art 58(4) 14.82	art 102 . . . . 8.56, 14.83
art 59(1) 14.81	art 103(1)(a) 14.13
art 60 . . . . 14.23	art 112 . . . . 14.7
art 61 . . . . 14.23	art 112(2) 14.7
art 61(7)–(10) 14.23	arts 113–118 . . . . 14.18
art 61(11) 14.23	art 121 . . . . 14.30
art 62 . . . . 14.13	art 121(5) 14.30
art 64(6)(b) 14.87	art 123 . . . . 14.30
art 67 . . . . 14.16	art 124 . . . . 14.31
art 68(1)–(2) 14.17	art 126(1) 14.7
art 68(3) 14.17	Pt 3 . . . . 11.7, 14.50
art 68(4)–(5) 14.17	Pt 9 . . . . 3.48, 14.79, 14.86
art 70(1) 7.12, 7.15	Second Additional Protocol to the
art 70(3) 7.12	European Convention on Mutual
art 70(4)(a) 8.13, 8.25, 8.27	Assistance in Criminal Matters
art 72 . . . . `14.84	2001 (*see also* European Convention
art 75 . . . . 14.17	on Mutual Assistance in Criminal
art 75(2) 14.17	Matters 1959) 1.105
art 77 . . . . 14.59	art 17 . . . . 1.79
art 79 . . . . 14.17	Second Protocol to the 1954 Convention
art 86 . . . . 14.79, 14.86, 14.94	for the Protection of Cultural
art 87 . . . . 14.84, 14.86	Property in the Event of Armed
art 87(1) 14.80	Conflict 1999 ('Second Hague
art 87(1)(a) 14.100	Protocol') (*see also* Convention for
art 87(4) 14.17	the Protection of Cultural Property in
art 87(5) 14.97	the Event of Armed Conflict
art 87(5) 14.80	1954) 7.8, 7.29, 7.31, 7.33
art 87(6) 14.80	art 1(h) 7.31
art 87(7) 14.80, 14.86	art 3(1) 7.30
art 89 . . . . 14.83, 14.94	art 11 . . . . 7.31
art 89(1) 14.81, 14.82, 14.92, 14.94,	art 15(1) 7.7
14.102, 14.105	art 15(1)(a)–(e) 7.8, 7.32
art 90 . . . . 14.83	art 15(2) 7.19, 7.33, 8.6
art 90(2)–(3) 14.83	art 16(1)(a) 8.25
art 90(4) 14.83	art 16(1)(b) 8.27
art 90(6) 14.83, 14.103, 14.105	art 16(1)(c) 8.34
art 90(6)(b) 1.39	art 16(2)(a) 8.44
art 90(7) 14.83, 14.103, 14.105	art 16(2)(b) 8.22
art 92 . . . . 14.82	art 17(1) 8.48
art 93 . . . . 14.84	art 18(1) 8.58
art 93(1) 14.100	art 18(2) 8.58

art 18(3)..........................8.58
art 18(4)..........................8.58
art 19(1)..........................8.62
art 19(2)..........................8.62
art 20(1)................... 8.59, 8.64
art 20(2)................... 8.61, 8.66
art 21.............................8.41
art 22(1)..........................7.30
art 27(1)(*b*) 7.31
arts 40–42 ....7.30
ch 3 ....7.31
ch 4 .... 7.29, 7.30, 8.44
Single Convention on Narcotic Drugs 1961 (*see also* Single Convention on Narcotic Drugs as amended by the Protocol amending the Single Convention on Narcotic Drugs 1972).......................7.135
Single Convention on Narcotic Drugs as amended by the Protocol amending the Single Convention on Narcotic Drugs 1972 (*see also* Single Convention on Narcotic Drugs 1961).........................7.135
Slavery Convention 1926 (*see also* Supplementary Convention on the Abolition of Slavery, the Slave Trade, and Institutions and Practices Similar to Slavery 1956)..................7.34
art 1(1)................ 4.103, 7.35, 7.36
art 6..............................7.34
art 6(1)...................... 7.35, 7.36
art 6(2)...........................7.35
Special Court for Sierra Leone Rules of Procedure and Evidence ('SCSL RPE')......... 13.8, 13.9, 13.13, 13.14
rule 4 ....13.8
rule 13 ....13.37
rule 8(*c*) 13.40
rule 26*bis*......................13.13
rule 34 ....13.14
rule 42 ....13.13
rule 43 ....13.13
rule 60 ....13.13
rule 61(i) 13.13
rule 63 ....13.13
rule 69 ....13.14
rule 72*bis*......................13.24
rule 72*bis*(iii) 13.24, 13.25
rule 75 ....13.14
rule 101(B)(ii) 6.42
Special Tribunal for Lebanon Rules of Procedure and Evidence ('STL RPE')

rule 50 ....14.17
rule 51 ....14.17
Statute of the Extraordinary African Chambers in the Senegalese Courts for the Prosecution of International Crimes Committed in Chad During the Period from 7 June 1982 to 1 December 1990 ....9.72
art 2....................... 3.35, 9.73
art 3(1)...........................9.73
art 3(2)...........................9.73
arts 4–8 ....9.74
art 5..............................9.74
art 5(*a*)........................9.74
art 6..............................9.74
art 7..............................9.74
art 8..............................9.74
art 9.............................11.14
art 10(2)–(5) 9.74
art 11(1)..........................9.73
art 11(2)..........................9.73
art 11(3)–(4) 9.73
art 11(5)..........................9.73
art 12(1)..........................9.73
art 12(2)..........................9.73
art 14.............................9.73
art 14(5)..........................9.73
art 16.............................9.74
art 17(1)..........................9.73
art 18(1)..........................9.75
art 18(2)..........................9.75
art 19(1)–(3) 9.74
art 20 .... 9.74, 11.33
art 21.............................9.73
art 27(1)..........................9.73
art 27(2)..........................9.73
art 27(4)..........................9.73
art 28.............................9.73
art 37(1)..........................9.73
Statute of the International Court of Justice
art 7..............................4.47
art 38(1)(*c*).....................5.3
art 38(1)(*d*) 3.45, 4.4
Statute of the International Criminal Tribunal for Rwanda ('ICTR Statute') 2.11, 4.4, 4.8, 5.100, 6.3, 12.10, 12.23
arts 1–7 ....12.21
art 1.............................12.21
art 2.............................12.22
art 2(2)..........................4.67
art 2(3)..........................5.87
art 3 .... 4.47, 4.51, 4.53, 4.54, 4.56, 12.22

art 3(g)	4.48
art 3(i)	4.50
art 4	12.22
art 6	2.2
art 6(1)	2.67, 5.11, 5.14, 5.49, 5.55, 5.62
art 6(2)	2.2, 2.73, 6.41, 12.30, 14.42
art 6(3)	5.62, 5.102, 9.45
art 6(4)	2.2, 6.33, 6.43, 9.45
art 7	12.27, 12.29
art 8(1)	12.34
art 8(2)	12.36
art 9	12.44
art 9(1)	12.44
art 9(2)	12.44
art 9(2)(a)	12.40, 12.45
art 10(a)	12.10
art 14	12.10
art 15	12.10
art 17(3)	12.12
art 19(1)	12.12, 12.13
art 19(2)	12.12
art 19(3)	12.12
art 20	12.12
art 21	12.13
art 23(1)	12.23
art 28	12.44, 12.49, 12.50, 12.51
art 28(1)	12.36, 12.51
art 30	12.14
art 32	12.11

Statute of the International Criminal Tribunal for the former Yugoslavia ('ICTY Statute') 2.11, 4.4, 4.8, 5.100, 6.3, 12.3, 12.4, 12.23

arts 1–8	12.21
art 2	4.22, 12.22
art 3	4.11, 12.22, 12.23
art 4	12.22
art 4(2)	4.67
art 4(3)	5.87
art 5	4.47, 4.51, 4.54, 4.56
art 5(g)	4.48
art 5(h)	4.53
art 5(i)	4.50
art 7	2.2
art 7(1)	2.2, 2.67, 5.11, 5.14, 5.49, 5.55, 5.62
art 7(2)	2.73, 6.41, 12.30, 14.42
art 7(3)	5.62, 5.102, 9.45
art 7(4)	6.33, 6.43, 9.45
art 8	12.26, 12.28
art 9(1)	12.34
art 9(2)	12.36
art 10	12.44

art 10(1)	12.44
art 10(2)	12.44
art 10(2)(a)	12.45
art 11(a)	12.9
art 15	12.9
art 16(2)	12.9
art 18(3)	12.12
art 20(1)	12.12, 12.13
art 20(2)	12.12
art 20(3)	12.12
art 21	12.12
art 22	12.13
art 24(1)	12.23
art 29	3.48, 12.44, 12.49, 12.50, 12.51
art 29(1)	12.36, 12.51
art 31	12.9
art 32	12.14
art 33	12.11

Statute of the International Residual Mechanism for Criminal Tribunals ('MICT Statute')

art 1(1)	12.7, 12.21, 12.22, 12.26, 12.30
art 1(2)–(3)	12.17, 12.42
art 1(4)	12.51
art 2	12.17
art 5(1)	12.34
art 5(2)	12.36
art 6(1)	12.42
art 6(2)–(6)	12.42
art 7	12.44
art 16(3)	12.12
art 18(1)	12.12, 12.13
art 19	12.12
art 20	12.13, 12.17
art 25(2)	12.17
art 28(1)–(2)	12.51
art 28(3)	12.51
art 30	12.14
art 32(1)	12.11
art 32(2)	12.11

Statute of the Residual Special Court for Sierra Leone Statute ('RSCSL Statute') 13.5, 13.6

chapeau provision	13.9
arts 1–6	13.5
art 1(1)	13.14, 13.18
art 1(2)	13.19, 13.21, 13.28
arts 2–5	13.7, 13.23
art 5	13.27
art 6(2)	13.31, 14.42
art 7	13.19
art 7(1)	13.19
art 7(2)	13.19

art 7(3)	13.19
art 8(1)	13.35
art 8(2)	13.36
art 9	13.37
art 10	13.8, 13.33
art 11	13.7
art 11(3)	13.7
art 13	13.7
art 14(1)	13.10
art 16	13.9
art 17	13.13
art 18	13.14, 13.18
art 21(3)	13.11
art 23(1)	13.12

Statute of the Special Court for Sierra Leone Statute ('SCSL Statute') 3.17, 3.19, 4.4, 4.8, 4.11, 5.100, 6.3, 13.4, 13.6, 13.11, 13.13

art 1(1)	13.21, 13.28
art 1(2)	13.21, 13.22
art 1(3)	13.22
arts 2–5	3.20, 13.7
arts 2–4	11.23, 13.24, 13.33
art 2	2.31, 4.51, 4.54, 4.56, 13.23
art 2(*g*)	4.48
art 2(*h*)	4.53
art 2(*i*)	4.48, 4.50
art 3	4.26, 13.23
art 4	4.11, 4.13, 4.18, 13.23, 13.26
art 4(*a*)	4.25, 13.26
art 4(*b*)	13.26
art 4(*c*)	4.14, 13.26
art 5	2.31, 13.23, 13.24, 13.27, 13.33
art 5(*a*)	13.27
art 5(*b*)	13.27
art 6	2.2
art 6(1)	2.67, 5.11, 5.14, 5.55, 5.62
art 6(2)	2.2, 2.73, 6.41, 13.31
art 6(3)	5.62, 5.102
art 6(4)	2.2, 6.33, 6.43
art 7(1)	13.29
art 8(1)	13.35
art 8(2)	13.36
art 9	13.37
art 10	11.23, 13.33
art 12	3.20
art 12(1)	13.7
art 14(1)	13.9
art 14(3)	13.10
art 16(4)	13.14
art 17	13.13
art 20(3)	13.11
art 22	13.12

Statute of the Special Tribunal for Lebanon ('STL Statute') 3.24

art 2	3.25
art 3	2.2, 3.25
arts 8–9	3.25
art 12(4)	14.17
art 17	14.17

Supplementary Agreement between the Special Court for Sierra Leone and the Government of the Republic of Sierra Leone on the Enforcement of Sentences for Contempt of the Special Court for Sierra Leone 2013 .... 13.12

Supplementary Convention on the Abolition of Slavery, the Slave Trade, and Institutions and Practices Similar to Slavery 1956 ('Supplementary Slavery Convention') (*see also* Slavery Convention 1926) 7.13

preamble (sixth recital)	7.34
art 1(*a*)–(*d*)	7.35
art 3(1)	7.13, 7.35, 8.6, 8.7
art 5	7.13, 8.6, 8.7
art 6(1)	4.103, 7.13, 7.35, 8.6, 8.7
art 6(2)	7.35, 8.6, 8.7
art 7	7.13
art 7(1)(*a*)	7.35, 7.36
art 7(1)(*b*)	7.35

Tokyo Convention on Offences and Other Acts Committed on Board Aircraft 1963 ('Tokyo Convention')

art 1(2)	1.47
art 1(3)	1.47
art 3(1)	1.47
art 3(3)	1.47
art 4	1.47

Treaty of Lausanne 1923 .... 11.20

Treaty of Peace between the Allied and Associated Powers and Austria 1919 ('Treaty of St Germain')

arts 173–174	2.56

Treaty of Peace between the Allied and Associated Powers and Hungary 1920 ('Treaty of Trianon')

arts 157–158	2.56

Treaty of Peace between the Principal Allied and Associated Powers and Germany 1919 ('Treaty of Versailles')

art 227	2.56
art 228	2.56
art 229	2.56

Table of Treaties and Other International Instruments

United Nations Convention against
Corruption 2003 ('Corruption
Convention') 7.13, 7.172, 7.186,
7.193, 7.194, 7.195, 8.12, 8.50, 8.60,
8.65, 8.87, 9.15
art 1(1).........................7.189
art 2(*a*).........................7.188
art 2(*b*).........................7.189
art 2(*c*).........................7.189
art 2(*d*).........................7.190
art 2(*e*).........................7.191
art 15..........................7.188
art 15(*a*)–(*b*)...................7.188
arts 15–18 ....8.6
arts 15–25 ....7.13
art 16(1).......................7.189
art 16(2)................. 7.193, 8.14
art 17(1).......................7.190
arts 17–25 ....2.39
arts 18–22 .... 7.193, 8.14
art 20..........................8.11
art 23................... 7.195, 8.6
art 23(1)................ 7.191, 8.11
art 23(1)(*b*)....................8.11
art 23(1)(*b*)(ii)................7.195
art 23(2)(*e*)....................8.11
art 24................... 7.193, 8.14
art 25................... 7.192, 8.6
art 26(1)–(4) 8.81
art 26(1).......................8.11
art 26(2).......................8.11
art 26(4).......................8.15
art 27..........................8.6
art 27(1)................ 7.194, 8.11
art 27(2)................ 7.194, 8.11
art 27(3)................ 7.194, 8.11
art 28.........................7.187
art 29..........................11.9
art 30(1).......................8.15
art 30(2).......................10.4
art 30(3).......................8.50
art 30(5).......................8.19
art 30(9)................. 8.12, 9.15
art 31..........................8.87
art 42(1)(*a*) 8.25
art 42(1)(*b*) 8.30
art 42(2)(*a*) 8.29
art 42(2)(*b*) 8.27, 8.33
art 42(4).......................8.34
art 42(5)................. 1.69, 8.24
art 42(6).......................8.43
art 44(4)................. 8.58, 8.59
art 44(5).......................8.58
art 44(8).......................8.58
art 44(10)......................8.46
art 44(11)................ 8.49, 8.52
art 44(15)......................8.61
art 44(16)......................8.60
art 46(1).......................8.62
art 46(2).......................8.62
art 46(6).......................8.62
art 46(19)......................8.63
art 46(21)......................8.65
art 46(22)......................8.65
art 47..........................8.86
ch III 7.187
United Nations Convention against
Illicit Traffic in Narcotic Drugs
and Psychotropic Substances 1988
('Illicit Traffic Convention') (*see also*
Agreement on Illicit Traffic by Sea,
implementing article 17 of the
United Nations Convention against
Illicit Traffic in Narcotic Drugs
and Psychotropic Substances
1995)............... 7.13, 7.135, 7.136,
7.137, 7.138, 7.139, 7.140, 8.7, 8.12,
8.18, 8.19, 8.65, 8.84, 8.87, 9.15, 14.5
preamble 7.135
art 1(*q*).......................7.137
art 2...........................8.83
art 3(1)................ 2.44, 7.13, 8.6
art 3(1)(*a*)(i)–(v)...............7.137
art 3(1)(*a*)(iv).................7.137
art 3(1)(*b*) 7.136
art 3(1)(*b*)(i).................7.137
art 3(1)(*b*)(ii) 7.137, 7.144
art 3(1)(*c*)....................8.11
art 3(1)(*c*)(i)–(ii)..............7.138
art 3(1)(*c*)(iv)............ 7.195, 8.32
art 3(11)................. 8.7, 8.12
art 3(2).......... 7.13, 7.136, 7.138, 8.11
art 3(3).......................7.136
art 3(4)(*a*) 8.15, 8.16
art 3(5).......................8.18
art 3(6).......................8.50
art 3(7).......................8.11
art 3(8).......................11.9
art 3(9).......................8.19
art 3(10).......... 8.59, 8.60, 8.64, 8.65
art 3(11)......................9.15
art 4(1)(*a*)(i) 8.25
art 4(1)(*a*)(ii) 8.30
art 4(2)(*a*)(ii) 8.27
art 4(2)(*b*) 8.34, 8.52
art 4(3).......................8.42

art 5	8.87	art 3(2)(a)–(d)	7.141
art 6	4.8	art 4(1)–(2)	8.83
art 6(2)	8.58	art 5	2.39, 7.13, 7.141, 7.143, 7.144, 7.146, 7.147, 7.150, 8.6
art 6(3)	8.58		
art 6(4)	8.58	art 5(1)(a)(i)–(ii)	7.144
art 6(5)	8.58	art 5(1)(b)	7.139, 7.144
art 6(6)	8.61	art 5(2)	7.144
art 6(8)	8.46	art 5(3)	7.144
art 6(9)	8.50	art 6	2.39, 7.13, 7.141, 7.143, 7.145, 7.146, 7.147, 7.150, 7.191, 8.6
art 7(1)	8.62		
art 7(5)	8.65	art 6(1)	7.145, 8.11
art 7(6)	8.62	art 6(1)(a)(i)–(ii)	7.145
art 7(12)	8.63	art 6(1)(b)	7.145
art 8	8.86	art 6(1)(b)(ii)	7.147, 7.195
art 12	7.137	art 6(2)(c)	7.145
art 17	8.84	art 6(2)(e)	7.145, 8.11
art 17(3)	1.119	art 6(2)(f)	7.145
art 17(4)	1.119, 8.84	art 8	2.39, 7.13, 7.141, 7.143, 7.146, 7.150, 7.172, 7.180, 7.181, 7.185, 8.6
art 17(6)	1.119		
art 17(7)	1.119	art 8(1)	7.182
art 17(11)	8.84	art 8(1)(a)	7.146, 7.183, 7.188
art 21(e)	7.137	art 8(1)(b)	7.183, 7.188
United Nations Convention against Transnational Organized Crime 2000 ('Transnational Organized Crime Convention') (*see also* Protocol against the Illicit Manufacturing of and Trafficking in Firearms, Their Parts and Components and Ammunition 2001, supplementing the United Nations Convention against Transnational Organized Crime; Protocol against the Smuggling of Migrants by Land, Sea and Air 2000, supplementing the United Nations Convention against Transnational Organized Crime; Protocol to Prevent, Suppress and Punish Trafficking in Persons, Especially Women and Children 2000, supplementing the United Nations Convention against Transnational Organized Crime)	7.13, 7.140, 7.141, 8.12, 8.14, 8.18, 8.19, 8.50, 8.60, 8.87, 9.15	art 8(2)	7.182, 7.183, 7.184
		art 8(3)	7.185
		art 8(4)	7.183
		art 9(2)(a)	8.29
		art 10(1)–(4)	8.81
		art 11(1)	8.15
		art 11(2)	8.50
		art 11(4)	8.19
		art 11(5)	11.9
		art 11(6)	8.7, 8.12, 9.15
		arts 12–13	8.87
		art 15(1)(a)	8.25
		art 15(1)(b)	8.30
		art 15(2)(b)	8.27, 8.33
		art 15(2)(c)	8.32
		art 15(4)	8.34
		art 15(5)	1.69, 8.24
		art 15(6)	8.43
		art 15(16)	8.60
		art 16(3)	8.58
		art 16(4)	8.58
		art 16(7)	8.58
art 2	7.13	art 16(9)	8.46
art 2(a)	7.142	art 16(10)	8.49, 8.52
art 2(b)	7.142	art 16(14)	8.61
art 2(c)	7.142	art 18(1)	8.62
art 2(d)	7.145	art 18(2)	8.62
art 2(e)	7.145	art 18(6)	8.62
art 2(h)	7.145	art 18(19)	8.63
art 3(1)	7.141, 7.150, 7.181	art 18(21)	8.65
		art 18(22)	8.65

art 21 . . . . 8.86
art 23 . . . . 7.13, 7.141, 7.143, 7.146, 7.147,
 7.150, 7.192, 8.6
art 23(*a*) 7.146
art 23(*b*) 7.146
art 34(2) 7.141, 7.150, 7.181
United Nations Convention on
 Jurisdictional Immunities of States
 and Their Property 2004 ('UN
 Convention on State
 Immunity') 10.50, 10.53, 10.92
art 2(1)(*b*)(iv) 10.47, 10.60
art 6(1) 10.58
Pt III 10.54, 10.86
United Nations Convention on the
 Law of the Sea 1982
 ('UNCLOS') 7.20
art 27(1) 1.121
art 33(1) 1.123
art 33(2) 1.123
art 55 . . . . 1.45
art 57 . . . . 1.45
art 60(2) 1.46, 1.125
art 73(1) 1.45, 1.124
art 73(2) 1.124
art 73(3) 1.45
art 73(4) 1.124
art 80 . . . . 1.46, 1.125
art 92(1) 1.44
art 97(1) 1.44
art 97(3) 1.115
art 99 . . . . 1.60
art 101 . . . . 1.58
art 101(*c*) 1.59
art 105 . . . . 1.56, 1.57, 1.116
art 107 . . . . 1.116
art 108(2) 8.84
art 109 . . . . 1.115
art 109(3) 1.44, 1.115
art 109(4) 1.115
art 110(1) 1.117
art 110(1)(*a*) 1.116
art 110(1)(*b*) 1.117
art 110(1)(*c*) 1.115
art 111 . . . . 1.118
art 111(5) 1.118
UN Model Treaty on
 Extradition 1.95, 1.97
art 2 . . . . 1.97
art 2(1) 1.97
art 3(*a*) 1.98
art 3(*d*) 1.73
art 4(*a*) 1.99
art 4(*b*) 1.73
art 14(1)(*a*) 1.100
art 14(1)(*b*) 1.100
UN Model Treaty on Mutual Assistance
 in Criminal Matters 1.105
art 4(1)(*b*) 1.106
US–Uzbekistan Agreement regarding
 the Surrender of Persons to the
 International Criminal Court 2002
 preamble 14.105
art 1 . . . . 14.101
art 2 . . . . 14.101
art 3 . . . . 14.101
art 4 . . . . 14.101
Vienna Convention on Consular Relations
 1963 ('VCCR') 10.10
art 5 . . . . 10.94
art 5(*a*) 10.94
art 41 . . . . 10.95
art 41(1) 10.95
art 41(2) 10.95
art 41(3) 10.95
art 43 . . . . 10.93
art 43(1) 10.60, 10.93, 10.94
art 44(3) 10.60, 10.93
art 45(1) 10.93
art 45(2) 10.91, 10.93
art 53(4) 10.60, 10.94
art 54 . . . . 10.93
art 54(1) 10.93
art 54(2) 10.93
art 54(4) 10.93
art 58(2) 10.93, 10.95
Vienna Convention on Diplomatic
 Relations 1961
 ('VCDR') 9.64, 11.14, 11.23
art 1(*e*) 10.24
art 3 . . . . 10.98
art 5(*m*) 10.60
art 9(1) 10.24
art 22(1) 1.78
art 29 . . . . 10.15, 10.17, 10.25
art 31 . . . . 10.30
art 31(1) 10.15, 10.24, 10.40
art 31(1)(*a*)–(*c*) 10.86
art 31(2) 10.15, 10.24
art 31(3) 10.15, 10.40
art 31(4) 10.15
art 32(1) 10.27, 10.98
art 32(2) 10.91, 10.98
art 39(1) 10.24
art 39(2) 10.24, 10.26, 10.60
art 40(1) 10.24, 10.25, 10.30

Vienna Convention on the Law of Treaties
    1969 ('VCLT') 14.8, 14.58
    art 2(1)(*b*) 3.43, 14.8, 14.44
    art 11 . . . . 3.19
    art 14 . . . . 3.19
    art 16 . . . . 3.19
    art 18 . . . . 3.19
    art 18(*a*) 14.105
    art 19 . . . . 3.19
    art 26 . . . . 7.119, 8.16, 14.105
    art 27 . . . . 8.2
    art 31(1) 14.73
    art 31(1)(*c*) 8.42
    art 31(2)(*a*) 4.90
    art 31(2)(*b*) 4.90
    art 31(3)(*c*) 3.45, 8.22, 8.70, 8.79, 14.46
    art 31(4) 4.98, 7.175
    art 32 . . . . 10.94
    art 34 . . . . 3.38, 3.48, 8.4, 8.21
    art 36(1) 14.8
Vienna Convention on the Representation of States in their Relations with International Organizations of a Universal Character 1975
    ('VCRS') 10.30
    art 29 . . . . 10.30
    art 30(1) 10.30, 10.40
    art 30(1)(*a*)–(*c*) 10.86
    art 30(3) 10.30, 10.40
    art 31(1)–(2) 10.30, 10.99
    art 38(2) 10.99
    art 45(2) 10.91
    art 50(2) 10.33

Table of Legislation

AUSTRALIA

War Crimes Act 1945. . . . . 9.43
War Crimes (Amendment) Act 1995 . . . . . 9.18

BANGLADESH

Criminal Procedure Code 1898 (as
    amended). 9.68
Evidence Act 1872 (as amended) 9.68
International Crimes (Tribunals) Act 1973
    (as amended) 9.68
    ss 3–4. . . . . 9.68
    s 3(1) 9.68
    s 3(2)(*c*) 9.69
    s 3(2)(*f*) 9.68
    s 6(1) 9.68
    s 10A 9.68
    s 19 . . . . 9.69
    s 21(1)–(2). 9.69
    s 22 . . . . 9.69
    s 23 . . . . 9.69
    s 26 . . . . 9.70
International Crimes (Tribunals)
    (Amendment) Act 2009. . . . . 9.68
International Crimes (Tribunals)
    (Amendment) Act 2012. . . . . 9.68
    s 2 . . . . 9.68
International Crimes (Tribunals)
    (Amendment) Act 2013. . . . . 9.68
    s 2 . . . . 9.68

BELGIUM

Code of Criminal Procedure
    art 1*bis*. 10.36
    art 12*bis*. 9.8
Judicial Code
    art 144*ter*. 11.14
Law of 16 June 1993 on the punishment
    of grave breaches of the Geneva
    Conventions of 12 August 1949 and
    their Additional Protocols I and II
    of 18 June 1977, as amended by the
    Law of 10 February 1999. . . . . 10.42
    art 5(3). 10.42
Law of 16 June 1993 on the punishment
    of grave breaches of the Geneva
    Conventions of 12 August 1949 and
    their Additional Protocols I and II
    of 18 June 1977, as amended by the
    Law of 23 April 2003
    art 8 . . . . 11.14

BOSNIA AND HERZEGOVINA

Decision No 97/03 of the High
    Representative enacting the Law
    re-amending the Law on Court of
    Bosnia and Herzegovina (2003)
    art 12. . . . . 9.60
Law on the Court of Bosnia and
    Herzegovina 2000 (as amended)
    art 13. . . . . 9.59
    art 13(3)(*b*) 9.59
    art 19(2). 9.58
    art 24(1). 9.58
    art 65(2). 9.60
    art 65(4). 9.60
Law on the Amendments to the Law on
    the Court of Bosnia and Herzegovina
    2004 (*Official Gazette* No 61/04)
    art 8 . . . . 9.59
Law on the Transfer of Cases from the
    International Criminal Tribunal
    for the former Yugoslavia to the
    Prosecutor's Offices of Bosnia and
    Herzegovina and the Use of Evidence
    Collected by the International
    Criminal Tribunal for the former
    Yugoslavia in Proceedings before the
    Courts of Bosnia and Herzegovina
    2004 (as amended). 9.59

CAMBODIA

Extraordinary Chambers in the Courts of
    Cambodia Internal Rules 9.63
Law on the Establishment of
    Extraordinary Chambers in the

Courts of Cambodia for the
Prosecution of Crimes Committed
during the Period of Democratic
Kampuchea 2001 (as amended
2004) 3.34, 9.62, 9.64
art 2 . . . . 3.34, 9.63
art 3 . . . . 9.64
arts 3–8 . . . . 9.64
art 4 . . . . 9.64, 11.14
art 5 . . . . 9.64, 11.14
art 6 . . . . 9.64
arts 6–8 . . . . 11.14
art 9 . . . . 9.63
art 10 . . . . 9.63
art 11 . . . . 9.63
art 16 . . . . 9.63
art 13 . . . . 9.63
art 18 . . . . 9.63
art 19 . . . . 9.63
art 20 . . . . 9.63
art 22 . . . . 9.63
art 23 . . . . 9.63
arts 23–24 . . . . 9.63
art 25 . . . . 9.63
art 26 . . . . 9.63
art 28 . . . . 9.63
art 29 . . . . 9.64
art 30 . . . . 9.63
art 33 . . . . 9.63
arts 33–39 . . . . 9.63
art 35 . . . . 9.63
art 40 . . . . 9.64
art 43 . . . . 9.63
art 47 . . . . 9.63
art 47*bis* 9.63
Law on the Organization of the Courts
   1993 (repealed) 3.34
Law on the Organization of the Courts
   2014. . . . . 3.34
Penal Code 1956 . . . . 9.64

CANADA

Crimes Against Humanity and War
   Crimes Act 2000
   s 2(1) 9.6
   s 4(1)(*c*) 9.6
   s 4(3) 9.6
   s 6(1)(*c*) 9.6
   s 6(3) 9.6
   s 11 . . . . 9.19
   s 13 . . . . 9.19
   s 14 . . . . 9.19

CHINA

Criminal Code of the People's Republic
   of China
   art 9 . . . . 9.7, 9.8
Law of 24 October 1946 governing the
   Trial of War Criminals 9.43

CROATIA

Law NN175/03 on the Implementation
   of the Statute of the International
   Criminal Court and the Prosecution of
   Crimes against the International Law
   of War and Humanitarian Law (2003)
   art 12 . . . . 9.37
   art 12(2) 9.37
Law NN 55/11 (2011)
   art 1 . . . . 9.37

DENMARK

Criminal Code
   art 8 . . . . 9.8

East Timor (*see also* **Timor-Leste**)
UNTAET regulation 1999/1 (1999)
   s 1.1 . . . . 3.31, 9.44
   s 1.2 . . . . 3.31, 9.44
   s 3.1 . . . . 9.44
UNTAET regulation 2000/11 (2000)
   s 6 . . . . 9.44
   s 7.3 . . . . 9.44
   s 10 . . . . 3.31
   s 10.1 . . . . 9.44
   s 10.2 . . . . 9.44
UNTAET regulation 2000/15
   (2000) 3.31, 11.15
   s 1 . . . . 9.45
   s 2.1 . . . . 1.63
   s 2.2(*c*) 1.39
   ss 4–7 . . . . 9.45
   s 7.3 . . . . 9.45
   ss 14–21 . . . . 9.45
   s 17.1 . . . . 11.15
UNTAET regulation 2000/30 (2000) 9.45
UNTAET regulation 2001/25 (2001)
   s 3.1(*b*) 9.45
   s 9.3 . . . . 9.44
   s 14.2 . . . . 9.44
   s 15.5 . . . . 9.44, 9.45
   s 17.1 . . . . 9.45
   s 22 . . . . 9.45

EL SALVADOR

Penal Code
  art 12 .... 9.8

ETHIOPIA

Criminal Code
  art 17(1)(*a*) 9.8

FRANCE

Code of Criminal Procedure
  art 689-1 .... 9.7, 11.33
  art 689-2 .... 9.7, 11.33
Code Napoléon
  art 421-1 .... 9.7
Ordinance No 1 of the Commander-in-Chief of the French Zone of Germany (1945) 3.30
Ordinance No 36 of the Commander-in-Chief of the French Zone of Germany (1946) 3.30
Penal Code
  art 222-1 .... 9.7

GERMANY

Criminal Code
  s 6(9) 9.7, 9.8
Law No 10 of the Allied Control Council for Germany (1945) ('Control Council Law No 10') ... 2.11, 3.30, 11.13
  art II 4.8
  art II(1)(*c*) 4.50
  art II(4)(*b*) 6.31
  art II(5) 11.20
  art III(2) 3.30

GHANA

Courts Act 1993
  art 56(4)(*n*) 9.8

GUATEMALA

National Reconciliation Law 1996
  s 8 .... 11.23
Penal Code
  art 5(4) 9.8

INDONESIA

Act 26 of 2000 concerning Human Rights Courts 9.47
  art 1(3) 9.47
  art 2 .... 9.47
  art 3 .... 9.47
  art 4 .... 9.47
  art 5 .... 9.48
  art 6 .... 9.48
  art 7(*a*) 9.47
  art 7(*b*) 9.47
  art 8 .... 9.48
  art 9 .... 9.48
  art 10 .... 9.47
  art 27(1) 9.47
  art 27(2) 9.47
  art 28(1) 9.47
  art 29 .... 9.47
  arts 32–33 .... 9.47
  art 35(1) 9.47
  arts 41–42 .... 9.48
  art 43 .... 9.48
  art 43(1) 9.48
  art 43(2) 9.48
  art 43(3) 9.48
  art 44 .... 9.48
  art 45(1) 9.47
  art 47(1) 9.48
  art 46 .... 9.48
Presidential Decree No 53/2001 establishing an Ad Hoc Human Rights Court at the Central Jakarta District Court (2001) 9.49
  art 2 .... 9.49
Presidential Decree No 96/2001 amending Presidential Decree No 53/2001 establishing an Ad Hoc Human Rights Court at the Central Jakarta District Court (2001)
  art 1 .... 9.49

IRAN

Islamic Penal Code
  art 9 .... 9.8

IRAQ

Coalition Provisional Authority Order No 48 (2003) 9.51
  s 1(1) 3.33, 9.51

Law of Administration for the State of Iraq for the Transitional Period 2004
   art 48 . . . . 3.33, 9.51
Law on the Iraqi High Criminal Court 2005
   art 1(2) 9.53
   art 3(5) 9.52
   art 7(2) 9.52
   art 8(9) 9.52
   art 9(7) 9.52
   art 11–14 . . . . 9.53
   art 11(1) 9.52
   art 11(2) 9.53
   art 12 . . . . 9.53
   art 12(1) 9.53
   art 13 . . . . 9.53
   art 15(2) 9.53
   art 15(3) 9.53
   art 16 . . . . 9.52
   art 17(1) 9.53
   art 17(3) 9.53
   art 17(4) 9.53
   art 17(5) 9.53
   art 17(6) 9.53
   art 28 . . . . 9.52
   art 29(1) 9.53
   art 29(2) 9.53
Statute of the Iraqi Special Tribunal
   arts 11–14 . . . . 11.14
   art 17(*d*) 11.14

JAPAN

Penal Code
   art 4-2 . . . . 9.8

KOSOVO

Constitution of the Republic of Kosovo
   arts 102–103 . . . . 3.32
Provisional Criminal Code of Kosovo 9.40
   art 39 . . . . 9.41
Law No 03/L-052 on the Special Prosecution Office in the Republic of Kosovo 2008
   art 16 . . . . 9.41
Law No 03/L-053 on the Jurisdiction, Case Selection and Case Allocation of EULEX Judges and Prosecutors in Kosovo 2008 . . . . 3.32
   arts 2–4 . . . . 3.32, 9.41

art 3.7 . . . . 9.41
art 4.7 . . . . 9.41
UNMIK regulation 1999/1 (1999) (as amended)
   s 1(1) 3.32, 9.40
   s 3 . . . . 3.32, 9.40
UNMIK regulation 1999/25 (1999) 9.40
UNMIK regulation 2000/6 (2000)
   s 1(1) 9.40
   s 1(2)–(3) 9.40
UNMIK regulation 2000/34 (2000)
   s 1 . . . . 9.40
UNMIK regulation 2000/64 (2000) 3.32, 9.40, 9.41
   ss 1–2 . . . . 3.32, 9.40
UNMIK regulation 2003/25 (2003) 9.40

RUSSIAN FEDERATION

Criminal Code
   art 12(3) 9.8

SENEGAL

Constitution of Senegal
   art 96 . . . . 3.35
   art 98 . . . . 9.72
Law No 2012-25 authorizing the President of the Republic to ratify the Agreement between the Government of the Republic of Senegal and the African Union on the Creation of Extraordinary African Chambers in the Senegalese Courts (2012) 9.72

SERBIA

Code of Criminal Procedure
   art 14 . . . . 9.56
Criminal Code of the Socialist Autonomous Province of Kosovo 9.40
Law on the Organisation and Competences of Government Authorities in War Crimes Proceedings 2003 (as amended)
   art 2 . . . . 9.55
   art 3 . . . . 9.55
   art 9 . . . . 9.55
   art 10 . . . . 9.55
   art 10a 9.55
   art 13 . . . . 9.56

SIERRA LEONE

Constitution of Sierra Leone
 s 40(4) 3.19
Malicious Damage Act 1861 . . . . . 2.31, 13.27
Prevention of Cruelty to Children Act
 1926 . . . . 2.31, 13.27
Residual Special Court for Sierra Leone
 Agreement (Ratification) Act 2011 . . . 3.19
Special Court Agreement 2002
 (Ratification) Act 2002 . . . . 3.19
 s 2 . . . . 3.19
 s 7 . . . . 3.19
 s 10 . . . . 3.19
 s 11(1) 3.19, 13.6
 s 13 . . . . 3.19, 13.6
 s 16 . . . . 3.19
 ss 20–21 . . . . 3.19
 ss 37–42 . . . . 3.19
Special Court Agreement 2002
 (Ratification)(Amendment)
 Act 2002 . . . . 3.19

SPAIN

Organic Law 1/2014 of 13 March 2014 . . . 9.33
Organic Law on the Judiciary
 art 23 . . . . 9.33
 art 23(4)(*p*) 9.8

SWITZERLAND

Criminal Code
 art 6(1) 9.8

Timor-Leste (*see also* **East Timor**)

Constitution of the Democratic Republic
 of Timor-Leste
 s 163(1) 3.31, 9.46
 s 165 . . . . 3.31, 9.46

UGANDA

Amnesty Act 2000 . . . . 11.21
Amnesty (Amendment) Act 2006 . . . . 11.21

High Court (International Crimes
 Division) Practice Directions 2011
 para 6(1) 9.66
 para 8(1) 9.66
Penal Code Act 1950 . . . . 9.66

UNITED KINGDOM

Aviation Security Act 1982
 s 1 . . . . 9.15
Criminal Justice Act 1988
 s 134 . . . . 9.24
 s 134(1)–(4) 9.16
 s 135 . . . . 9.24
Geneva Conventions Act 1957 (as amended)
 s 1A(3) 9.24
International Criminal Court (UK) Act 2001
 s 56(1) 9.18
 s 70(2) 9.24
Royal Warrant of 14 June
 1945 . . . . 3.30, 4.45, 9.43
Sex Offenders Act 1997
 s 7 . . . . 1.32
War Crimes Act 1991
 s1(1) 9.7

UNITED STATES

American Servicemembers'
 Protection Act 14.101
Foreign Corrupt Practices Act 7.173
Foreign Operations Appropriations Act
 2006 . . . . 14.101
Foreign Operations Appropriations Act
 2008 . . . . 14.101
Military Commissions Act 2009 . . . . 9.43
Ordinance No 7 of the Military
 Government of the United States
 Zone of Germany (1946) 3.30, 9.43
Uniform Code of Military Justice
 (UCMJ)
 art 2(*a*) 9.6
 art 18 . . . . 9.6
 art 118 . . . . 9.6
 art 119 . . . . 9.6

List of Abbreviations

AFRC	Armed Forces Revolutionary Council
ALRC	Asian Legal Resource Centre
ASP	Assembly of States Parties
AU	African Union
CAR	Central African Republic
CAT	Committee Against Torture
CDF	Civil Defence Forces
CSM	Convention on Special Missions
CPA	Coalition Provisional Authority
CPISA	Convention on the Privileges and Immunities of the Specialized Agencies
CPIUN	Convention on the Privileges and Immunities of the United Nations
DRC	Democratic Republic of the Congo
ECCC	Extraordinary Chambers in the Courts of Cambodia
ECHR	European Convention on Human Rights
ECtHR	European Court of Human Rights
ECOWAS	Economic Community of West African States
EEZ	exclusive economic zone
EULEX	European Rule of Law Mission
FEC	Far Eastern Commission
IAEA	International Atomic Energy Agency
ICAO	International Civil Aviation Organization
ICC	International Criminal Court
ICCPR	International Covenant on Civil and Political Rights
ICJ	International Court of Justice
ICT	International Crimes Tribunal
ICTR	International Criminal Tribunal for Rwanda
ICTY	International Criminal Tribunal for the former Yugoslavia
ILC	International Law Commission
IMO	International Maritime Organization
IMT	International Military Tribunal
INTERFET	International Force for East Timor
ISAF	International Security Assistance Force
JCE	joint criminal enterprise
MICT	Mechanism for International Criminal Tribunals
OECD	Organization for Economic Co-operation and Development
OTP	Office of the Prosecutor
PCIJ	Permanent Court of International Justice
PFLP	Popular Front for the Liberation of Palestine
PFLP-GC	Popular Front for the Liberation of Palestine–General Command
PLF	Palestine Liberation Front
POW	prisoner of war
RPE	Rules of Procedure and Evidence
RPF	Rwandan Patriotic Front

RSCSL	Residual Special Court for Sierra Leone
RUF	Revolutionary United Front
SCAP	Supreme Commander for the Allied Powers
SCSL	Special Court for Sierra Leone
SFRY	Socialist Federal Republic of Yugoslavia
SITF	Special Investigative Task Force
SOFA	status of forces agreement
SOMA	status of mission agreement
STL	Special Tribunal for Lebanon
TFG	Transitional Federal Government
TRC	truth and reconciliation commission
UNCLOS	United Nations Convention on the Law of the Sea
UCMJ	Uniform Code of Military Justice
UNMIK	United Nations Mission in Kosovo
UNMIL	United Nations Mission in Liberia
UNTAET	United Nations Transitional Administration in East Timor
UNWCC	United Nations War Crimes Commission
VCDR	Vienna Convention on Diplomatic Relations
VCLT	Vienna Convention on the Law of Treaties
VCRS	Vienna Convention on the Representation of States in their Relations with International Organizations of a Universal Character
VPD	vessel protection detachment

PART ONE

FOUNDATIONAL CONCEPTS AND PRINCIPLES

1
The International Rules on National Criminal Jurisdiction

I. Introduction

Some of the most venerable rules of public international law, developed with a view to the peaceful coexistence of states, are concerned with delimiting the lawful scope of each state's authority to regulate and to give effect to the regulation of persons and property. These rules, founded on mostly tacit understandings as to what does and does not constitute an unacceptable inroad into the sovereignty of other states, frame what is known as a state's 'jurisdiction'—in simple terms, a state's international legal authority in relation to national law.   1.1

A familiarity with the international rules on jurisdiction in the criminal context is a prerequisite not just to understanding the national implementation of international crimes but also to appreciating the very concept of an international crime, as well as the historical evolution of international crimes, the obligations undertaken by states parties to any of the multilateral treaties in the field of international criminal law, and even aspects of the workings of the International Criminal Court (ICC).   1.2

II. The Concept and Distinct Aspects of Jurisdiction

A state's 'jurisdiction', in the present context, refers to its authority under international law to regulate and to give effect to the regulation of persons and property. More precisely, it is a state's authority, by reference to international law, respectively to prescribe, to adjudicate on, and to enforce legal rules.[1]   1.3

The concept of jurisdiction and the concept of sovereignty are often conflated. They are not synonymous, although the former is an aspect of the latter. For present purposes, sovereignty refers to a state's inherent and supreme rights in territory. It encompasses not only its exclusive jurisdiction to enforce municipal law within given territory (including the authority to permit the enforcement of foreign law,   1.4

---

[1] The term is also commonly used to refer to, *inter alia*, the act of prescription, adjudication or enforcement, without consideration of the international legal authority for such act.

either by its own organs or the organs of a foreign state) but also, for example, the power to regulate the entry of persons into that territory, the power to alienate that territory by way of cession, and so on. The focus here is strictly on jurisdiction.

1.5 Public international law is concerned with the jurisdiction of the international legal person labelled 'the state'. In its quality as an international legal person, this 'state' is no more than a juridical construct, a formal legal concept abstracted from political and other factual reality, even if it is mapped onto that reality; and for most purposes of international law, this fictive 'state' is an internally undifferentiated entity conceptually distinct from the governmental organs and officials (and, indeed, from the society) which in the real world constitute it. Putting it simply, international rights vest in and international obligations bind a notional unit we call 'the state', rather than any of the actual and particular branches of government or individual holders of public office which national constitutional law and political science would conceive of as the state (let alone any private institution or individual). The upshot of this in the present context is that which governmental organ or organs—be it the legislature, executive or judiciary—exercises or exercise the jurisdiction enjoyed by the state as an international legal person is a matter not for international law but for the constitutional, *viz* municipal, law of the state in question. That said, common sense dictates that jurisdiction to adjudicate will be exercised by the courts.

1.6 The conformity with international law of any claim to jurisdiction by a state depends on which of the three distinct aspects of jurisdiction, respectively referred to as jurisdiction to prescribe (or prescriptive jurisdiction), jurisdiction to adjudicate (or adjudicative jurisdiction), and jurisdiction to enforce (or enforcement jurisdiction), is at issue.

1.7 Jurisdiction to prescribe—sometimes called, potentially confusingly, 'legislative' jurisdiction—refers to a state's authority under international law to assert the applicability of its own law to given persons, natural or legal, or to property, whether by means of primary or subordinate legislation, executive decree or judicial action. Questions of jurisdiction to prescribe centre in practice on whether a state may, as a matter of international law, permissibly regulate acts or things outside its territory.

1.8 Jurisdiction to adjudicate—sometimes called 'judicial' or 'curial' jurisdiction—refers to a state's authority under international law to entertain legal proceedings in respect of given persons or property, whether applying its own substantive law or, as is often the case in civil proceedings, the substantive law of another state. A state's jurisdiction to adjudicate, a question of public international law, is not be confused with its courts' competence (or, as legal terminology unfortunately also has it, 'jurisdiction') *ratione loci, ratione personae*, and *ratione materiae* as a matter of municipal law. Questions of jurisdiction to adjudicate centre in practice on whether a state may, as a matter of international law, permissibly assume judicial competence in relation to acts or things outside its territory.

1.9 Jurisdiction to enforce[2]—sometimes called, again possibly confusingly, 'executive' jurisdiction—refers to a state's authority under international law to exercise

---

[2] Note that, in contrast to its usage throughout this book, the term 'jurisdiction to enforce' is sometimes used in relation solely to the imposition of punishment, whether by way of fine, forfeiture or imprisonment.

investigative, coercive or custodial powers in support of law,[3] be its own or another state's, whether through police or other executive action or through its courts.[4] Questions of jurisdiction to enforce centre in practice on whether a state's police and other relevant executive organs may, as a matter of international law, permissibly operate and its courts permissibly sit outside its territory and whether injunctions and subpoenas issued and orders made by those courts may permissibly extend to persons and property outside that territory.

Jurisdiction in the sense used here can be criminal or civil—that is, it can relate, on the one hand, to rules of criminal law or, on the other hand, to non-penal rules of public law and to rules of private law. The focus of this book will obviously be on criminal jurisdiction. 1.10

Separate reference to jurisdiction to adjudicate is unnecessary in the context of criminal law, where the universal practice is that municipal courts will not apply foreign law.[5] That is, in the criminal-law context, it can be assumed that a municipal court is applying the law of the forum state; and the application of a state's law by its courts is simply the exercise or actualization of prescription, amounting as it does to an assertion that the law in question is applicable to the relevant person or property.[6] In this light, the present book adopts a simple binary division between jurisdiction to prescribe and jurisdiction to enforce. 1.11

The distinction between jurisdiction to prescribe and jurisdiction to enforce in the criminal-law context can be described more concretely as follows. Jurisdiction to prescribe is a state's international legal authority to treat given conduct as criminal. Jurisdiction to enforce is a state's international legal authority to arrest and retain custody over persons and vessels, to have a court sit, to incarcerate persons and confiscate property, to undertake surveillance, to stop and search, to take physical measures to prevent or repress the commission of a crime, to investigate and to collect evidence, to issue *subpoenae ad testificandum* and *subpoenae duces tecum*, and so on—in short, to exercise any or all of the usual range of police, prosecutorial, judicial, and related executive powers in relation to criminal justice. 1.12

---

[3] To complicate matters slightly, there are in fact circumstances in which a state may detain persons for security purposes distinct from law enforcement. Examples include the detention of prisoners of war and preventive detention. The meaning of 'jurisdiction' in this context shades into a distinct, broader use of the term, common especially in the older literature and cases, to denote any physical manifestation of state power.

[4] Judicial powers are as much a coercive means of enforcing law as are the actions of the police or the bailiffs.

[5] That said, in specified cases involving the exercise of extraterritorial adjudicative jurisdiction over conduct also criminal in the state where it was committed, the criminal courts of a range of states are obliged to take account of the criminal law of the state of commission at the sentencing stage in the event that the latter is the *lex mitior*.

[6] 'In criminal law legislative jurisdiction and judicial jurisdiction are one and the same', in the words of Akehurst. See M Akehurst, 'Jurisdiction in International Law' (1972–73) 46 *BYIL* 145, 179. Indeed, even as regards civil proceedings, distinct reference to jurisdiction to adjudicate is really necessary only in those cases where the municipal court applies foreign law. In all other instances, a binary division between jurisdiction to prescribe and to enforce is sufficient.

1.13 A state's jurisdiction to prescribe and its jurisdiction to enforce do not necessarily go hand in hand. By way of distinction with the former, the latter does not, at least as a general rule, extend to the territory of another state.[7] As such, it is very often the case that international law permits a state to criminalize given conduct but, because the author of the conduct is abroad, not to arrest him or her, to undertake on-the-ground surveillance of him or her, and so on, and *vice versa*.

1.14 The following account is, unless otherwise stated, limited to the customary international rules on national jurisdiction. States are always free to establish special jurisdictional rules by way of treaty, applicable to the parties *inter se*, and there are many conventions in the field of international criminal law by which the states parties do precisely this.[8]

III. Jurisdiction to Prescribe

1.15 Jurisdiction to prescribe, to reiterate, refers to a state's authority under international law to assert the applicability of its law to given persons or property. In the specifically penal context, the term refers to a state's international legal authority to treat given conduct as criminal, whether by means of primary or subordinate legislation, executive decree or judicial action.

A. The Structure of Prescriptive Criminal Jurisdiction

1.16 The starting point for any discussion of states' jurisdiction to prescribe has traditionally been *The SS 'Lotus'*,[9] with its famous presumption in favour of a state's prescriptive jurisdiction.[10] After discussing the strictly territorial nature of a state's international legal authority to 'exercise' its jurisdiction (that is, in this context, to enforce its municipal law), the Permanent Court of International Justice (PCIJ) continued:

> It does not, however, follow that international law prohibits a State from exercising jurisdiction in its own territory, in respect of any case which relates to acts which have taken place abroad, and in which it cannot rely on some permissive rule of international law. Such a view would only be tenable if international law contained a general prohibition to States to extend the application of their laws and the jurisdiction of their courts to persons, property and acts outside their territory, and if, as an exception to this general prohibition, it allowed States to do so in specific circumstances. But this is certainly not the case under international law as it stands at present. Far from laying down a general prohibition to the effect that States may not extend the application of their laws and the jurisdiction of their courts to persons, property and acts outside their territory, it leaves them in this respect a wide measure of discretion which is only limited in certain cases by prohibitive rules; as

---

[7] See *infra* section III.A(i). [8] See *infra* paras 8.20–8.41.
[9] *The SS 'Lotus'*, PCIJ Rep Ser A No 10 (1927).
[10] But cf ibid, 34 (diss op Loder) and ibid, 60–1 (diss op Nyholm).

regards other cases, every State remains free to adopt the principles which it regards as best and most suitable.[11]

On its own, this statement suggests that, while jurisdiction to enforce does not, as a rule, extend to foreign territory, a state is entitled to assert the applicability of—that is, to prescribe—its municipal law to any and every extraterritorial situation of its choosing.

1.17 But the above passage from *Lotus* did not seem to accord at the time with the practice and *opinio juris* of states in relation to municipal criminal law, as reflected in their responses to such assertions, which appeared to embody a general presumption *against* extraterritorial assertions of jurisdiction overlaid with specific *permissive* rules. That is, there seemed in practice to be a discrete number of specific bases on which state assertions of prescriptive criminal jurisdiction were accepted by other states as a matter of customary international law. As such, eight years after the judgment in *Lotus*, a Harvard Law School research report entitled 'Jurisdiction with Respect to Crime'[12] rejected the so-called *Lotus* presumption as it applied to criminal jurisdiction, positing instead a small and exhaustive range of acceptable heads of jurisdiction to prescribe. The report was highly influential, with its fundamental prohibitive premise and its specific permissive rules being widely considered consonant with customary international law.

1.18 In the context of criminal jurisdiction, debate over the *Lotus* presumption was something of a storm in a teacup, since the PCIJ had qualified its famous statement with a significant rider:

> Nevertheless, it has to be seen whether the foregoing considerations really apply as regards criminal jurisdiction, or whether this jurisdiction is governed by a different principle... According to [this] other principle, the exclusively territorial character of law relating to this domain constitutes a principle which, except as otherwise expressly provided, would, *ipso facto*, prevent States from extending the criminal jurisdiction of their courts beyond their frontiers; the exceptions in question, which include for instance extraterritorial jurisdiction over nationals and over crimes directed against public safety, would therefore rest on special permissive rules forming part of international law.[13]

Nor was the Court required to settle the point. For all the dicta on the general structure of prescriptive criminal jurisdiction, the ratio of *Lotus* turned on a specific rule as to collisions on the high seas.[14]

1.19 The so-called '*Lotus* presumption' was not reconsidered by the PCIJ or by its successor, the International Court of Justice (ICJ), in the specific context of jurisdiction to prescribe criminal laws until *Arrest Warrant of 11 April 2000*[15] in 2002, and even then only by way of obiter dicta in respective judges' separate and dissenting opinions and declarations. In his separate opinion, President

---

[11] Ibid, 19.
[12] Harvard Law School Research in International Law, 'Jurisdiction with Respect to Crime' (1935) 29 *AJIL Supp* 435.
[13] *Lotus* (n 9), 20.   [14] As for the rule itself, see now *infra* n 51.
[15] *Arrest Warrant of 11 April 2000 (Democratic Republic of the Congo v Belgium)*, ICJ Rep 2002, 3.

Guillaume considered an argument for prescriptive jurisdiction based solely on the *Lotus* presumption as 'hardly persuasive', highlighting the unresolved qualifications placed on its general statement by the PCIJ in *Lotus* itself.[16] On the other hand, in her dissenting opinion,[17] Judge ad hoc Van Den Wyngaert applied the *Lotus* presumption to a contemporary question of prescriptive criminal jurisdiction.[18] At the same time, acknowledging that '[i]t has often been argued, not without reason, that the "*Lotus*" test is too liberal',[19] she did not rely on *Lotus* alone, but argued in the alternative on the basis of a positive permissive rule.[20] Judges Higgins, Kooijmans, and Buergenthal, in their joint separate opinion, limited their discussion of the *Lotus* presumption to the particular context of national jurisdiction over international crimes, where, they argued, '[the] vertical notion of the authority of action is significantly different from the horizontal system of international law envisaged in the "*Lotus*" case'.[21] In this context, they described *Lotus* as 'a continuing potential',[22] even if they did not themselves rely on it.

1.20   A way of reconciling formal doctrine and practice in the context of states' jurisdiction to prescribe criminal laws is to distinguish between ultimate and proximate presumptions. One might, in line with the PCIJ's general statement in *Lotus*, say that the ultimate presumption when it comes to prescribing national law, including criminal law, is one of freedom of state action—in other words, that states are free to 'extend the application of their laws and the jurisdiction of their courts to persons, property and acts outside their territory'[23] unless a rule of international law prohibits them from doing so. At the same time, one might plausibly say that overlaid on this presumption there exists a rule of international law—applicable either in respect of all national law or only in respect of criminal law—prohibiting states from extending their laws and the competence of their courts to 'persons, property and acts' in the territory of another state unless a further rule of international law exceptionally permits them to do so. The prohibition on the assertion by a state of prescriptive jurisdiction in respect of another state's territory would then serve as the proximate or practical or working presumption that a positive, permissive rule would be required to displace before such an assertion of prescriptive jurisdiction could be considered internationally lawful. This putative prohibition, seemingly manifest in the practice of states, could be conceived of as the necessary correlate of what might, again plausibly, be considered each state's exclusive right—subject, that is, to permissive exceptions—as a natural function of its sovereignty over its territory to regulate 'persons, property and acts' within

---

[16] Ibid, 43, para 14 (dec Guillaume).
[17] Note that the dissent was on a different point.
[18] See *Arrest Warrant* (n 15), 169–73 and 176–7, paras 51–58 and 67 (diss op Van Den Wyngaert).
[19] Ibid, 169, para 51 (diss op Van Den Wyngaert).
[20] See ibid, 169, 173–5 and 176–7, paras 51, 59–62 and 67 (diss op Van Den Wyngaert).
[21] Ibid, 78, para 51 (joint sep op Higgins, Kooijmans, and Buergenthal).
[22] Ibid, para 50 (joint sep op Higgins, Kooijmans, and Buergenthal). It is not altogether clear what Judges Higgins, Kooijmans, and Buergenthal mean by this.
[23] *Lotus* (n 9), 19.

that territory. In sum, while the *Lotus* presumption would remain unchallenged, any head of prescriptive jurisdiction involving the criminalization of acts taking place in the territory of another state would reflect a specific permissive rule, as the practice of states appears to suggest.

1.21 All this said, the controversy over the *Lotus* presumption is a question more of theory than of practice. In the final analysis, the only effective difference between the competing positions—and this is rarely significant to the outcome in any given instance—is the burden of proof. As it is, moreover, the Court in *Lotus* summarized its position very generally when it said that 'all that can be required of a State is that it should not overstep the limits which international law places upon its jurisdiction; within these limits, its title to exercise jurisdiction rests in its sovereignty'.[24] This simple statement is unimpeachable.

B. The Accepted Bases of Prescriptive Criminal Jurisdiction

1.22 According to the orthodox approach, there exists a number of bases or 'heads' of jurisdiction pursuant to which, as a matter of customary international law, states may criminalize conduct. Each will be examined here in turn.

1.23 Given that there are multiple heads of prescriptive criminal jurisdiction, a state's authority under international law to criminalize conduct is not necessarily exclusive in any given instance. It is very commonly the case that two or more states enjoy concurrent prescriptive criminal jurisdiction over the same conduct. Despite occasional assertions to the contrary, state practice does not indicate any formal legal hierarchy among states enjoying concurrent prescriptive criminal jurisdiction on different bases.[25] Which state ends up enforcing its law will depend on a range of practical factors, chief among these being which state obtains custody over the suspect.

1.24 Under customary international law, jurisdiction to prescribe is permissive, not mandatory. Whether or not a state actually asserts a prescriptive jurisdiction allowed it by customary international law is a matter for that state. Again, however, the many international criminal law conventions oblige states parties to grant their courts procedural competence over the offences in question on a range of specified bases.[26]

(i) Territoriality

1.25 A state enjoys prescriptive criminal jurisdiction over all acts committed within its territory. This jurisdiction is a straightforward function of a state's sovereignty over its territory, and is not dependent on any permissive rule. This most fundamental basis of prescriptive jurisdiction is recognized by all states.[27]

---

[24] Ibid. [25] See *infra* section II.C. [26] See *infra* paras 8.20–8.41.
[27] See eg *Lotus* (n 9), 20. See also *Arrest Warrant* (n 15), 36, para 4 (sep op Guillaume) and 57–8, para 9 (dec Ranjeva).

1.26   Territorial commission is a sufficient criterion for jurisdiction to prescribe criminal laws. A state enjoys prescriptive criminal jurisdiction over all offences committed within its territory regardless of the nationality of the offender and the nature of the offence.

1.27   Under international law, prescriptive jurisdiction on the basis of territoriality extends to a state's internal waters, territorial sea, and superjacent airspace. It does not, contrary to popular misconception, extend to the premises of its embassies and consulates abroad, which remain the territory of the receiving state and subject to that state's jurisdiction on the basis of territoriality.[28]

1.28   The jurisdictional nexus of territoriality must exist at the time of the commission of the offence. Prescriptive jurisdiction on the basis of territoriality does not extend to conduct committed abroad solely on the ground that the perpetrator subsequently sets foot in the prescribing state. As Judge Loder noted in his dissenting opinion in *Lotus*, speaking of jurisdiction to prescribe on the basis of territory alone,

> a law [cannot] extend in the territory of the State enacting it to an offence committed by a foreigner abroad should the foreigner happen to be in this territory after the commission of the offence, because the guilty act has not been committed within the area subject to the jurisdiction of that State and the *subsequent presence of the guilty person* cannot have the effect of *extending the jurisdiction of the State*.[29]

The assertion of prescriptive jurisdiction solely on the basis of the suspect's presence in the territory subsequent to the alleged commission of the offence is really an assertion of universal prescriptive jurisdiction,[30] albeit one selectively enforced. The municipal requirement that a suspect be proceeded against on the basis of universal jurisdiction only if he or she is at some point present in the prescribing state's territory (that is, not *in absentia*) seeks to limit the attractiveness of that state's criminal courts to forum-shoppers,[31] who, often backed by the resources of non-governmental organizations, have the potential—so, the argument goes—to overload the criminal justice system with cases involving allegations of international crimes committed elsewhere in the world by people with no genuine connection to the forum state and to entangle the government of that state in the diplomatic controversy associated with such cases.

1.29   Most states assert and international law permits prescriptive jurisdiction over criminal acts committed partly inside and partly outside their territory.[32] Prescriptive jurisdiction over a criminal act initiated within and completed outside the territory is known as 'subjective' territoriality and the converse 'objective' territoriality.

---

[28] Perhaps needless to say, the usual situation applies as regards concurrent extraterritorial jurisdiction on the basis of nationality, the protective principle, passive personality, and so on.
[29] *Lotus* (n 9), 35 (diss op Loder, original emphasis).
[30] See *infra* paras 1.54–1.55 for the concept and parameters of universal prescriptive jurisdiction.
[31] Note that the majority of attempted prosecutions on the basis of universality have to date been brought by private parties, rather than by a state's prosecuting authority.
[32] See eg *Lotus* (n 9), 23. See also ibid, 73 (diss op Moore).

(ii) Nationality

1.30 A state enjoys prescriptive criminal jurisdiction over the extraterritorial conduct of its nationals, regardless of the nature of the offence. This basis of jurisdiction to prescribe is sometimes called 'active personality'. Jurisdiction to prescribe criminal laws extraterritorially by reason of the nationality of the offender is uncontroversial as a matter of international law.[33]

1.31 As with all heads of jurisdiction to prescribe under international law, whether or not a state asserts jurisdiction on the grounds of nationality is a question of the municipal law of that state. In practice, nationality tends not to constitute a general basis of criminal jurisdiction in common-law countries, although there is a growing list of statutory assertions. By way of contrast, nationality jurisdiction over extraterritorial crimes is commonplace in the civil law.

1.32 As with territoriality, *mutatis mutandis*, the jurisdictional nexus represented by the nationality of the offender must exist at the time of the commission of the offence. Prescriptive jurisdiction on the basis of nationality does not extend to criminal conduct committed before the alleged offender's assumption of the prescribing state's nationality.[34] The assertion of prescriptive jurisdiction on the sole basis of the suspect's assumption of the prescribing state's nationality after the alleged commission of the offence is really an assertion of universal prescriptive jurisdiction, although again one selectively enforced. 'Subsequent nationality jurisdiction', as it were, is another common means by which states asserting universal prescriptive jurisdiction over international crimes attempt to avoid what they see as the prospect of criminal justice logjam and the diplomatic problems frequently created by the exercise of such jurisdiction.[35] Some states further assert subsequent nationality jurisdiction (that is, 'disguised' universal jurisdiction) over certain other serious offences not amounting to international crimes when the conduct in question is also criminal in the state where it took place.[36]

1.33 For the purposes of, *inter alia*,[37] jurisdiction to prescribe, corporations are treated as nationals of the state under whose law they are incorporated.

---

[33] See eg ibid, 20. See also ibid, 35 (diss op Loder), 92 (diss op Moore), and 95 (diss op Altamira); *Arrest Warrant* (n 15), 37, para 4 (sep op Guillaume) and 92, para 5 (sep op Rezek).

[34] See also International Bar Association (Legal Practice Division), *Report of the Task Force on Extraterritorial Jurisdiction* (28 September 2008), 144: 'The active personality principle, also known as the active nationality principle, permits a state to prosecute its nationals for crimes committed anywhere in the world, if, at the time of the offense, they were such nationals.'

[35] As regards the latter, the prescribing state's calculation would seem to be that alleged offenders prosecuted on the basis of subsequent nationality will either have lost their previous nationality on assumption of a new one, leaving (on account of the continuous nationality rule) no state with grounds to protest the exercise of universal jurisdiction, or will, through the taking of a second nationality, have placed legal obstacles (the predominant nationality rule) and/or political obstacles (a visceral sense of a state's legitimate interest in prosecuting any of its nationals accused of international crimes) in the way of the espousal of their claim by the state of their original nationality.

[36] See eg Sex Offenders Act 1997 (UK), s 7.

[37] In the context of diplomatic protection, see *Barcelona Traction, Light and Power Co (Belgium v Spain), Second Phase*, ICJ Rep 1970, 3, 42, para 70. See also the International Law Commission (ILC)'s Articles on Diplomatic Protection, GA res 62/67, 6 December 2007, Annex, art 9.

(iii) The 'protective' principle

1.34 A state may lawfully criminalize the extraterritorial conduct of non-nationals[38] in order to protect fundamental national interests, often but not necessarily related to national security.[39] Extraterritorial prescriptive jurisdiction over crimes by non-nationals on the basis of this so-called 'protective' principle is not, it hardly needs adding, plenary, but by definition pertains only to offences genuinely capable of harming some vital interest of the prescribing state.

1.35 In the past, the protective principle has been less a general rule than the basis on which a handful of specific extraterritorial assertions of prescriptive criminal jurisdiction over non-nationals have traditionally been tolerated by states, among them the criminalization of the counterfeiting of the state's currency by non-nationals operating in a foreign state. It remains to be seen whether the extraterritorial criminalization of more offences by non-nationals becomes permissible under this head. The principle has obvious potential for expansion, especially in relation to terrorist offences.

(iv) Passive personality

1.36 What is referred to as the 'passive personality' principle provides that a state may assert extraterritorial prescriptive jurisdiction over crimes committed by non-nationals if the victim of the crime is one of its nationals. This putative head of prescriptive criminal jurisdiction was in the past sometimes subsumed terminologically into the protective principle, although they have always been and remain conceptually and legally distinct.

1.37 The PCIJ in *Lotus* reserved its opinion on the lawfulness of this head of jurisdiction.[40] But the assertion of extraterritorial prescriptive criminal jurisdiction on the basis of passive personality was in the past controversial.[41]

1.38 Past disapproval notwithstanding, passive personality has continued to be invoked by states, and increasingly so, to justify prescriptive jurisdiction over certain extraterritorial crimes by non-nationals. Judges Higgins, Kooijmans, and Buergenthal noted in their joint separate opinion in *Arrest Warrant*:

> Passive personality jurisdiction, for so long regarded as controversial, is now reflected... in the legislation of various countries... and today meets with relatively little opposition, at least so far as a particular category of offences is concerned.[42]

---

[38] The term 'non-national' is by and large used in this book in preference to the synonymous 'alien' and 'foreigner'.

[39] See eg *Lotus* (n 9), 20. See also ibid, 35–6 (diss op Loder); *Arrest Warrant* (n 15), 37, para 4 (sep op Guillaume) and 92, para 4 (sep op Rezek).

[40] See *Lotus* (n 9), 22–3.

[41] See eg ibid, 36 (diss op Loder), 55–8 (diss op Finlay), 62 (diss op Nyholm), and 91–3 (diss op Moore). See also Harvard Research report (n 12), 445 and 579.

[42] *Arrest Warrant* (n 15), 76–7, para 47 (joint sep op Higgins, Kooijmans, and Buergenthal).

The 'particular category of offences' Judges Higgins, Kooijmans, and Buergenthal seem to have had in mind is serious offences against the person, especially forms of homicide. For his part, Judge Rezek asserted that a 'majority of countries' gave effect to the principle,[43] while President Guillaume went so far as to treat passive personality as part of 'the law as classically formulated'.[44]

By implication, article 90(6)(*b*) of the Rome Statute of the International Criminal Court ('Rome Statute') treats the nationality of the victim as an acceptable basis for national criminal jurisdiction, as do United Nations Security Council resolutions 1816 (2008)[45] and 1846 (2008),[46] along with UNTAET regulation 2000/15[47] promulgated by the United Nations Transitional Administration in East Timor (UNTAET).   1.39

As a matter of treaty law, numerous international criminal conventions permit the assertion of extraterritorial criminal jurisdiction over non-nationals on the basis of passive personality.[48] These conventional embodiments of the principle—while not formally indicative of the position under customary international law, nor formally affecting it—seem in practice to have acclimatized states to the idea of passive personality jurisdiction.   1.40

In light of modern developments, today it is safe to say that passive personality has emerged under customary international law as a permissible basis of extraterritorial prescriptive criminal jurisdiction over the conduct of non-nationals, at least as regards serious offences against the person.   1.41

As with the nationality of the offender, *mutatis mutandis*, the jurisdictional nexus represented by the nationality of the victim must exist at the time of the commission of the offence. Prescriptive jurisdiction on the basis of passive personality does not encompass conduct committed before the victim's assumption of the prescribing state's nationality.[49] The assertion of prescriptive jurisdiction solely on the basis of the victim's assumption of the prescribing state's nationality subsequent to the alleged commission of the offence alone is, once more, really an assertion of universal prescriptive jurisdiction, although again one selectively enforced. 'Subsequent passive personality' jurisdiction is yet another strategy by which states asserting universal jurisdiction over international crimes attempt to prevent their criminal justice systems from becoming overburdened by 'wholly foreign' cases and to head off diplomatic rows by insisting on what the layperson appears to consider a legitimate link between the crime and the forum.   1.42

---

[43] Ibid, 92, para 5 (sep op Rezek).   [44] Ibid, 37, para 4 (sep op Guillaume).
[45] See SC res 1816 (2008), 2 June 2008, para 11.
[46] See SC res 1846 (2008), 2 December 2008, para 14.
[47] See UNTAET reg 2000/15, 6 June 2000, s 2.2(*c*).   [48] See *infra* para 8.29.
[49] See also International Bar Association (n 34), 146: 'The victim must have been a national of the foreign state...at the time of the crime.'

(v) Sui generis bases

(a) At sea

1.43 A coastal state enjoys prescriptive criminal jurisdiction on the basis of territoriality over its territorial sea.[50]

1.44 As a general rule,[51] customary international law, as codified in article 92(1) of the United Nations Convention on the Law of the Sea (UNCLOS), accords the 'flag state'—that is, the state whose flag a ship is entitled to fly—exclusive jurisdiction, both to prescribe and to enforce, over ships on the high seas.[52] In terms of prescription and in the criminal context, this means that as a general rule the flag state alone has authority under international law to criminalize conduct occurring aboard that ship while it is on the high seas. In contrast, when a ship is within the territorial sea of another state, jurisdiction to prescribe criminal laws is concurrent as among the flag state, the coastal state, and any other state with a recognized jurisdictional nexus, such as the state of nationality of the offender.

1.45 A coastal state enjoys jurisdiction to prescribe fisheries offences in relation to its exclusive economic zone (EEZ).[53] In this connection, article 73(3) of UNCLOS provides that 'penalties for violations of fisheries laws and regulations in the

---

[50] Recall *supra* para 1.27. A coastal state has the right to declare as its territorial sea a belt of sea, not exceeding 12 nautical miles, adjacent to its land territory and internal waters and, in the case of an archipelagic state, its archipelagic waters.

[51] See *infra* paras 1.56–1.59 for the customary exception as regards piracy *jure gentium* to exclusive flag-state jurisdiction on the high seas. As for relevant treaty law, art 92(1) of the United Nations Convention on the Law of the Sea 1982 (UNCLOS) specifies that exclusive flag-state jurisdiction on the high seas is subject to any exceptions provided for in other treaties or in UNCLOS itself. Three such exceptions are the universal prescriptive jurisdiction acknowledged in the second sentence of art 105 of UNCLOS over piracy, which by definition occurs on the high seas; the range of concurrent prescriptive jurisdictions over unauthorized broadcasting on the high seas granted by art 109(3) of UNCLOS; and, to the extent that it grants prescriptive jurisdiction to the state of nationality of the master *et al*, the rule laid down in art 97(1) of UNCLOS in relation to collisions and other incidents of navigation occurring on the high seas.

[52] For this purpose, the 'high seas' are all waters seaward of the territorial sea of any coastal state.

[53] As per arts 55 and 57 of UNCLOS, as now consonant with customary international law, the EEZ is an area beyond and adjacent to the territorial sea that shall not extend beyond 200 nautical miles from the baselines from which the breadth of the territorial sea is measured. Article 56(1)(*a*) of UNCLOS provides that, in its EEZ, a coastal state enjoys 'sovereign rights for the purpose of exploring and exploiting, conserving and managing the natural resources', including and in particular the living resources, of the waters superjacent to the seabed and of the seabed and its subsoil; arts 62(4) and 73(1) presuppose, in the words of the latter, that, 'in the exercise of its sovereign rights to explore, exploit, conserve and manage the living resources in the exclusive economic zone', the coastal state may prescribe 'laws and regulations', with art 73(1) expressly permitting recourse to judicial proceedings to ensure compliance with these; and art 73(3) presupposes that violations of such 'fisheries laws and regulations' of the coastal state as are applicable to its EEZ may be subject to penalties. Article 62(4) stipulates, for the avoidance of doubt, that '[n]ationals of other States fishing in the exclusive economic zone shall comply with the conservation measures and with the other terms and conditions established in the laws and regulations of the coastal State'. *A fortiori*, nationals of the coastal state shall do the same. In sum, under UNCLOS, a coastal state enjoys jurisdiction to prescribe fisheries offences in relation to its EEZ. This is now consonant with customary international law. The rule could be viewed in part as an exception to the exclusivity of the flag state's prescriptive criminal jurisdiction over ships on what is otherwise, for penal purposes, the high seas and in part as prescriptive criminal jurisdiction over activities conducted from, rather than aboard, ships on the high seas.

exclusive economic zone may not include imprisonment, in the absence of agreements to the contrary by the States concerned, or any other form of corporal punishment'; but whether this limitation accords with customary international law is open to doubt.

A coastal state enjoys exclusive prescriptive criminal jurisdiction over artificial islands, installations, and structures in its EEZ and on its continental shelf.[54]   1.46

(b) On board aircraft

In what is now almost certainly a customary rule, article 3(1) of the Tokyo Convention on Offences and Other Acts Committed on Board Aircraft 1963 ('Tokyo Convention'), read in the light of article 1(2) of the Convention, accords the state of registration of an aircraft extraterritorial prescriptive jurisdiction over offences committed on board that aircraft while it is in flight or on the surface of the high seas or of any other area outside the territory of another state.[55] This prescriptive jurisdiction is concurrent as between or among the state of registration and any other state or states with an internationally lawful jurisdictional nexus to an offence committed on board, such as the state on whose territory or in whose superjacent airspace the aircraft may be at the time and the states of nationality of the offender and (in at least certain cases) the victim.[56] In addition, in accordance with article 3(3), the Tokyo Convention does not exclude any criminal jurisdiction exercised in accordance with national law.[57]   1.47

(c) Foreign members of armed forces

Non-nationals serving in the prescribing state's armed forces[58] are, in the practice of all states, subject to its criminal law, even when serving in foreign territory, and remain subject to it in respect of acts committed while in armed service. This is unobjectionable as a matter of customary international law.   1.48

(vi) The 'effects' doctrine?

As noted by the PCIJ in *Lotus*,[59] a state sometimes seeks to justify the assertion of extraterritorial criminal jurisdiction over the conduct of non-nationals on the basis solely of the conduct's effects within its territory. This putative 'effects' doctrine, properly so called, is to be distinguished from prescriptive criminal jurisdiction on   1.49

---

[54] See UNCLOS, arts 60(2) and 80, as consonant with customary international law.

[55] According to art 1(3) of the Tokyo Convention, an aircraft is considered to be in flight 'from the moment power is applied for the purpose of take-off until the moment when the landing run ends'.

[56] But note that art 4 of the Tokyo Convention lays down limitations, applicable as a matter of treaty law, on the territorial state's enforcement of its concurrent jurisdiction.

[57] For the two possible interpretations of a jurisdictional provision of this sort, see *infra* paras 8.42–8.43.

[58] Examples include members of the French Foreign Legion, the variety of Commonwealth nationals serving in the UK armed forces, and the Nepalese Gurkhas in, *inter alia*, the UK and Indian armed forces respectively.

[59] See *Lotus* (n 9), 23.

the basis of objective territoriality. We speak of the effects doctrine, rather than objective territoriality, when no constituent element of the offence takes place within the territory of the prescribing state.

1.50 The assertion of extraterritorial prescriptive jurisdiction over non-nationals on the basis of the effects doctrine is rare. It has seemingly been approved, obiter and uncontroversially, by some common-law courts. But closer analysis indicates that the territorial 'effect' referred to has in fact been a constituent element, actual or intended, of the offence or, in the case of the inchoate offences of attempt and conspiracy, the intended predicate offence or a part of it and that the court's allusion was really to prescriptive jurisdiction on the basis of objective territoriality, actual or constructive.[60] The effects doctrine proper has been relied on to ground assertions of criminal and quasi-criminal jurisdiction over the extraterritorial conduct of non-nationals chiefly in the field of antitrust law, where in its most expansive manifestation it proved combustibly controversial.[61]

1.51 As a general observation, the less direct, deleterious, and intended the alleged effects of the conduct and the less universally conceded the national interest sought to be protected by the prohibition, the more disputed the criminal jurisdiction asserted under the effects doctrine. In the final analysis, the doctrine would appear to have achieved international acceptability where the extraterritorial conduct of non-nationals has and is intended to have a direct and substantial harmful effect within the territory of the prescribing state. Beyond these narrow bounds, it remains a highly dubious basis on which to assert prescriptive criminal jurisdiction over the extraterritorial conduct of non-nationals.

(vii) Residency?

1.52 It is not uncommon for a state to assert prescriptive criminal jurisdiction over certain extraterritorial acts of non-nationals habitually resident in that state. Such assertions of jurisdiction have aroused little apparent objection to date, although the associated *opinio juris* is unclear, especially since these assertions tend to be in respect of crimes over which universal jurisdiction is widely considered permissible.

---

[60] See eg the dicta of Lord Diplock in *R v Treacy*, 55 ILR 110, 128 and 130 (UK 1970), cited with approval in *Director of Public Prosecutions v Stonehouse*, 73 ILR 252, 265 (Lord Edmund-Davies) (UK 1977); *R v Libman*, 84 ILR 672, 685 (Canada 1985); *S v Mharapara*, 84 ILR 1, 9–11 (Zimbabwe 1985). The surrounding passages make it clear that, in speaking of the 'consequences' of conduct, Lord Diplock is referring in *Treacy* not to the effects doctrine but to objective territoriality as a possible international legal basis for the UK's exercise of jurisdiction. He states, *Treacy (supra)*, 130 (original emphasis), that 'where the definition of any...offence contains a requirement that the described conduct of the accused should be followed by described consequences the implied [geographical] exclusion is limited to cases where *neither* the conduct *nor* its harmful consequences took place in England or Wales'. See also ibid, 126–7. The import of Lord Diplock's words is even clearer when they are read in the light of the relevant passages of his Lordship's later speeches in *Secretary of State for Trade v Markus* [1976] AC 35, 61 (UK 1975) and *Stonehouse (supra)*, 64–8. See also *S v 'A'* 1979 (4) SA 51 (R) (Rhodesia 1979); but cf *Mharapara (supra)*, 12–17.

[61] For details, see R O'Keefe, 'Domestic Courts as Agents of Development of the International Law of Jurisdiction' (2013) 26 *Leiden JIL* 541, 552–4.

In some cases, states extend residency jurisdiction to persons who become 1.53
residents after the commission of the offence. This again is a manifestation of
selectively-enforced universal jurisdiction.

(viii) Universality

Despite the view expressed by Judge ad hoc Van Den Wyngaert in her dissenting 1.54
opinion in *Arrest Warrant* that '[t]here is no generally accepted definition of universal jurisdiction in conventional or customary law',[62] universal jurisdiction—more precisely, universal prescriptive jurisdiction or jurisdiction to prescribe on the basis of universality—can be defined in the criminal context as prescriptive jurisdiction over offences committed extraterritorially by non-nationals against non-nationals, where the offence constitutes no threat to the fundamental interests of the prescribing state and does not give rise to effects within its territory. Putting it more succinctly, it is prescriptive criminal jurisdiction in the absence of any other internationally-recognized head of prescriptive criminal jurisdiction.

In *Arrest Warrant*, much was made in the separate and dissenting opinions and 1.55
declarations of so-called 'universal jurisdiction *in absentia*'. Insofar as the term is used as shorthand to describe the coming together of two distinct aspects of jurisdiction, *viz* the enforcement *in absentia* (that is, in the absence of the suspect or accused) of universal jurisdiction to prescribe,[63] there is nothing wrong with it as such, even if it is better eschewed for the avoidance of confusion. But insofar as several judges in *Arrest Warrant* referred to 'universal jurisdiction *in absentia*' as if it were a special and especially repugnant form of jurisdiction to prescribe,[64] this mistakenly conflates prescription and enforcement. Correctly analysed, whether the enforcement *in absentia* of universal criminal jurisdiction to prescribe is acceptable under international law implicates two distinct questions, namely whether jurisdiction to prescribe criminal laws on the basis of universality is internationally lawful and whether the enforcement of criminal laws *in absentia* is internationally lawful. The answer to the second question being yes, the upshot is that, if universal jurisdiction to prescribe criminal laws is internationally lawful in any given instance, so too is so-called universal jurisdiction *in absentia*.

(a) Piracy *jure gentium*

Customary international law has long acknowledged that states may lawfully assert 1.56
universal prescriptive jurisdiction over the crime of piracy *jure gentium*—that is, piracy as defined by customary international law. Piracy *jure gentium* takes place by definition on the high seas, beyond the territorial jurisdiction of any state.[65]

---

[62] *Arrest Warrant* (n 15), 165, para 44 (diss op Van Den Wyngaert).
[63] See eg ibid, 80, para 59, read in the light of 79–80, paras 53–58 (sep op Higgins, Kooijmans, and Buergenthal); ibid, 169–73, paras 52–58 (diss op Van Den Wyngaert).
[64] See ibid, 39–45, paras 9–17 (sep op Guillaume) and 55–8, paras 5–12 (dec Ranjeva).
[65] In contrast, acts of maritime depredation which take place not on the high seas but within a state's territorial sea or internal waters (commonly referred to as 'robbery at sea') cannot constitute piracy under international law and are not punishable on the basis of universal prescriptive

As a result, according to the rationalization preferred above,⁶⁶ a state's presumptive freedom to criminalize conduct is not counteracted by the prohibition on its criminalization of conduct which takes place in the territory of another state. The *Lotus* presumption is, nonetheless, overlaid in this context by the prohibition on a state's assertion of prescriptive criminal jurisdiction over conduct which takes place on board a foreign-flagged ship while that ship is on the high seas.⁶⁷ In turn, however, there exists a permissive exception to the prohibition on a state's extension of its prescriptive criminal jurisdiction to acts aboard a foreign-flagged ship on the high seas in specific relation to the offence of piracy.⁶⁸ It is for this last reason, namely that universal jurisdiction over piracy is ultimately based on an exceptional permissive rule of customary international law, that such jurisdiction extends only to piracy as specifically defined by customary international law—that is, to piracy *jure gentium* ('as per the law of nations'). But whatever the formal rationalization, it remains the undoubted case that piracy as defined by international law is subject to universal prescriptive jurisdiction,⁶⁹ as obliquely affirmed in article 105 of UNCLOS.⁷⁰

1.57   Article 105 of UNCLOS⁷¹ provides that '[t]he courts of the State which carried out the seizure [of the pirate ship] may decide upon the penalties to be imposed'. This could be taken to suggest *a contrario* that no state other than the seizing state enjoys universal jurisdiction over piracy *jure gentium*. But any such implication is contradicted by principle. Were a state's authority to punish piracy to arise only on its subsequent capture of the pirates, it would run counter to the fundamental requirement, rooted in the general principle of criminal law expressed in the maxim *nullum crimen sine lege*, that the jurisdictional nexus must exist at the time of the commission of the crime; and if, as article 105 of UNCLOS provides, 'every State may seize a pirate ship', it stands to reason that every state is permitted to criminalize piracy *jure gentium*. That said, article 105 of UNCLOS might nonetheless to be taken to suggest that, without prejudice to every state's authority to criminalize piracy *jure gentium*, it is the state which seizes the pirate ship that alone may proceed to prosecution and judgment of the pirates—in other words, teasing apart jurisdiction to prescribe and jurisdiction to

---

jurisdiction. For the concept of the 'high seas' for the purposes of prescriptive jurisdiction over piracy *jure gentium*, recall *supra* n 52.

⁶⁶ See *supra* para 1.20.   ⁶⁷ See *supra* para 1.44.

⁶⁸ This positive mutual permission was and is doubtless premised on an appreciation among states that piracy represents a common menace. It is only, however, in a rhetorical sense that pirates have ever been '*hostes humani generis*', or 'enemies of the human race', as the redolent but misleading label has it. Neither pirates nor their ships have ever been considered stateless by virtue (if that is the appropriate word) of the former's crimes.

⁶⁹ See eg *Lotus* (n 9), 51 (diss op Finlay), 70–1 (diss op Moore), and 95 (diss op Altamira); *Arrest Warrant* (n 15), 37–8, 42 and 44, paras 5, 12, and 16 (sep op Guillaume), 55–6, para 6 (dec Ranjeva), 61, para 9 (sep op Koroma), and 78, 79, and 81, paras 51, 52, 54, and 61 (joint sep op Higgins, Kooijmans, and Buergenthal).

⁷⁰ Universal prescriptive jurisdiction over piracy *jure gentium* was previously codified in art 19 of the Convention on the High Seas 1958, which, apart from the insertion of two words, art 105 of UNCLOS restates verbatim.

⁷¹ See also, previously, Convention on the High Seas, art 19.

adjudicate, that it is the seizing state alone that enjoys jurisdiction to adjudicate upon piracy. This second possible implication, however, is contradicted by state practice, as manifest in, *inter alia*,[72] the agreed transfer and trial in other states of pirates, in practice all of them Somali nationals, captured by states engaged in armed patrol of the high seas off the coast of Somalia,[73] a practice repeatedly commended by the UN Security Council.[74]

The definition of piracy under modern customary international law is generally considered to accord with the definition in article 101 of UNCLOS,[75] which, extending to aircraft, provides that piracy 'consists of any of the following acts': 1.58

(*a*) any illegal acts of violence or detention, or any act of depredation, committed for private ends by the crew or the passengers of a private ship or a private aircraft, and directed:
   (i) on the high seas, against another ship or aircraft, or against persons or property on board such ship or aircraft;
   (ii) against a ship, aircraft, persons or property in a place outside the jurisdiction of any State;
(*b*) any act of voluntary participation in the operation of a ship or of an aircraft with knowledge of facts making it a pirate ship or aircraft;
(*c*) any act of inciting or of intentionally facilitating an act described in subparagraph (*a*) or (*b*).

---

[72] See also eg *The 'Cygnus' Case (Somali Pirates)*, 145 ILR 491, 494 (Netherlands 2010) and, by implication, *United States v Ali*, DC Cir No 12-3056, 11 June 2013, 14–15 (US 2013).

[73] See Exchange of Letters between the European Union and the Government of Kenya on the conditions and modalities for the transfer of persons suspected of having committed acts of piracy and detained by the European Union-led naval force (EUNAVFOR), and seized property in the possession of EUNAVFOR, from EUNAVFOR to Kenya and for their treatment after such transfer, Nairobi, 6 March 2009, OJ L 79, 25.3.2009, 49 (terminated, with transfers now occurring on an ad hoc basis); Exchange of Letters between the European Union and the Republic of Seychelles on the conditions and modalities for the transfer of suspected pirates and armed robbers from EUNAVFOR to the Republic of Seychelles and for their treatment after such transfer, 26 September 2009, OJ L 315, 2.12.2009, 37; Agreement between the European Union and the Republic of Mauritius on the conditions of transfer of suspected pirates and associated seized property from the European Union-led naval force to the Republic of Mauritius and on the conditions of suspected pirates after transfer, Port Louis, 14 July 2011, OJ L 254, 30.9.2011, 3; Agreement between the European Union and the United Republic of Tanzania on the conditions of transfer of suspected pirates and associated seized property from the European Union-led Naval Force to the United Republic of Tanzania, Brussels, 1 April 2014, OJ L 108, 11.4.2014, 3. See also *Republic of Seychelles v Osman and Ten Others*, 152 ILR 513 (Seychelles 2011), where the fact that the accused had been captured by a Spanish naval helicopter and warship was not even raised before the Supreme Court of the Seychelles, with Gaswaga J simply affirming, 524, para 32, that the crime of piracy is subject to universal jurisdiction; and, similarly, *Republic of Seychelles v Ali and Ten Others*, Crim Side No 14 of 2010, 3 November 2010 (Seychelles 2010), *Republic of Seychelles v Ise and Four Others*, Crim Side No 76 of 2010, 30 June 2011 (Seychelles 2011), and *Republic of Seychelles v Jama and Fourteen Others*, Crim Side No 16 of 2012, 2 November 2012 (Seychelles 2012). See too, to the same effect, *Attorney General v Hashi and Others*, Civil Appeal No 113 of 2011, 18 October 2012 (Kenya 2012).

[74] See SC res 1897 (2009), 30 November 2009, preamble (ninth recital); SC res 1950 (2010), 23 November 2010, preamble (thirteenth recital); SC res 2020 (2011), 22 November 2011, preamble (eighteenth recital); SC res 2077 (2012), 21 November 2012, preamble (eighteenth recital); SC res 2125 (2013), 18 November 2013, preamble (twenty-third recital).

[75] The provision reproduces near-verbatim art 15 of the Convention on the High Seas.

The reference to 'private' ends is to non-state (that is, non-governmental) ends, the distinction being the classic one drawn by public international law between private and public, rather than between, say, personal and political. In other words, an illegal act of violence or detention or an act of depredation need not be for material gain to count as piracy, provided it is for purposes other than those of a state.[76] Even less need piracy involve robbery, the material elements of the offence encompassing as they do not only acts of depredation but also, in the alternative, illegal acts of violence or detention. The word 'illegal' is referable to municipal law, indicating that, in relation to acts of violence or detention, it is for each state to elaborate such basic elements of the offence as are not specified in the international definition.[77]

1.59 There remains a degree of controversy as to whether conduct on land ancillary to piracy *jure gentium*, such as the instigation, organization or financing of piracy, may be criminalized on the basis of universal jurisdiction. For what it is worth, the UN Security Council has implied that it may. In Security Council resolution 1976 (2011) of 11 April 2011, the Council, 'recognizing that individuals and entities who incite or intentionally facilitate an act of piracy are themselves engaging in piracy as defined in international law',[78] '[r]ecognizes that piracy is a crime subject to universal jurisdiction'.[79] The position is plausible at the level of principle, at least to the extent that the specific ancillary conduct can be characterized as a mode of participation in the crime of piracy *jure gentium*, as per article 101(c) of UNCLOS, rather than as a distinct offence.[80] With other customary international crimes such

---

[76] See eg *Castle John and Nederlandse Stichting Sirius v NV Nabeco and NV Parfin*, 77 ILR 537 (Belgium 1986) (direct action by a non-governmental organization capable of constituting piracy under customary international law); *Institute of Cetacean Research v Sea Shepherd Conservation Society*, 156 ILR 718, 756 (US 2013) (ditto), stating that 'piracy law...defines acts taken for private ends as those not taken on behalf of a state'; *Republic of Seychelles v Dahir and Ten Others*, Crim Side No 51 of 2009, 26 July 2010, para 37 (Seychelles 2010), distinguishing in the context of the crime of piracy between acts committed for private ends and 'acts with governmental objectives', and *Republic of Seychelles v Ahmed and Five Others*, Crim Side No 21 of 2011, 14 July 2011, para 21 (Seychelles 2011), noting that 'according to the definition provided in law...piracy is a war-like act committed by non-state actors (private parties not affiliated with any government) against other parties at sea' and that 'piracy is generally understood as violence or depredation or detention on the seas for private ends without authorization by public authority'. See also D Guilfoyle, *Shipping Interdiction and the Law of the Sea* (Cambridge: Cambridge University Press, 2009), 36–7; M Bahar, 'Attaining Optimal Deterrence at Sea: A Legal and Strategic Theory for Naval Anti-Piracy Operations' (2007) 40 *VJTL* 1, 27, 32–4.
[77] See, similarly, *infra* para 7.18.   [78] SC res 1976 (2011), 11 April 2011, para 15.
[79] Ibid, para 14. See also ibid, para 13, where the Security Council '[u]rges all States, including States in the region, to criminalize piracy under their domestic law, emphasizing the importance of criminalizing incitement, facilitation, conspiracy and attempts to commit acts of piracy'.
[80] See also, previously, Convention on the High Seas, art 15(3). Article 101(c) of UNCLOS was relied on by the US Court of Appeals for the District of Columbia Circuit in *United States v Ali* (n 72), 11–16 and 19, to hold that acts of aiding and abetting high-seas piracy were themselves piracy under international law even if not performed on the high seas, with the consequence that states were permitted to criminalize such acts on the basis of universal jurisdiction. By the same token, the Court held, ibid, 21–3, that conspiracy to commit piracy did not constitute piracy under international law, with the consequence that international law did not permit the criminalization of conspiracy to commit piracy on the basis of universality.

The International Rules on National Criminal Jurisdiction 21

as war crimes, crimes against humanity, and genocide,[81] state practice indicates that states may exercise universal jurisdiction not only over the actual commission of the offence but also over other modes of responsibility for it, such as ordering, aiding and abetting, direct and public incitement, and command and other superior responsibility, insofar as these other modes of responsibility are themselves known to customary international law. That said, whereas the rationale for universal jurisdiction over war crimes, crimes against humanity, and genocide is that they are criminal prohibitions embodied in customary international law itself and as such inherently universal,[82] the linchpin of the rationale for universal jurisdiction over piracy *jure gentium*—which, rather than being prohibited by customary international law itself, is simply subject by virtue of it to a special jurisdictional rule—is that the offence takes place on the high seas, beyond the territorial jurisdiction of any state.[83] In the final analysis, whether conduct on land ancillary to piracy *jure gentium* may be criminalized and punished on the basis of universal jurisdiction will ultimately come down, like the answers to all such questions, to state practice and *opinio juris*.[84]

(b) **Slavery and the slave trade?**

It sometimes said that slavery and trading in slaves are subject to universal jurisdiction.[85] But the proposition is not uncontroversial. The assertion stems from the fact that the UK, in its robust and progressively imperialistic nineteenth-century crusade against the slave trade, asserted universal jurisdiction over slave transports on the high seas (and vigorously enforced it by means of visit, search, and seizure), deeming it for the purposes of its municipal law as a form of piracy. Today, article 99 of UNCLOS obliges only flag-state jurisdiction over high-seas transport of slaves.[86] This is without prejudice, however, to what is permitted, as distinct from mandated, by customary international law. Moreover, it would seem to be the case that enslavement, which would comprehend trading in and transporting slaves, is recognized today as a crime against humanity under customary international law when committed as part of a widespread or systematic attack on a civilian population;[87] and if it is accepted that

1.60

---

[81] For the definition of an international crime, and specifically a customary international crime, posited in this book and the related terminological distinction posited between crimes under customary international law and crimes pursuant to customary international law, see *infra* chapter 2.

[82] See *infra* para 1.64.

[83] This rationale would support the availability of universal jurisdiction over the inchoate offence of attempt to commit piracy, as successfully prosecuted on the avowed basis of universal jurisdiction in *Republic of Seychelles v Osman* (n 73).

[84] In this respect, it may or may not be relevant that the Security Council, despite reiterating in subsequent resolutions various other elements of resolution 1976 (2011), has not repeated its statements to the effect that incitement and intentional facilitation of acts of piracy are themselves 'piracy as defined in international law' and subject as such to universal jurisdiction.

[85] See eg *Lotus* (n 9), 95 (diss op Altamira); *Arrest Warrant* (n 15), 62, para 9 (sep op Koroma). See also Princeton Project on Universal Jurisdiction, *The Princeton Principles on Universal Jurisdiction* (2001), 28–9 and 45–6, principles 1(2) and 2(1) and commentary.

[86] See also, previously, Convention on the High Seas, art 13.

[87] See eg, *inter plurima alia*, Rome Statute of the International Criminal Court ('Rome Statute'), art 7(1)(*c*). Article 7(2)(*c*) of the Rome Statute defines 'enslavement' to mean 'the exercise of any or all of the powers attaching to the right of ownership over a person and includes the exercise of such

crimes under customary international law, such as crimes against humanity, give rise as a matter of principle to universal jurisdiction,[88] then slavery and the slave trade would qualify, regardless of whether they occur on the high seas.

(c) Crimes under customary international law

1.61 Since at least around the end of the Second World War, it has widely been considered that war crimes,[89] crimes against humanity, and genocide—all of which are crimes under customary international law, meaning that customary international law itself prohibits such conduct by individuals on pain of punishment[90]—are subject to universal prescriptive jurisdiction. In other words, the predominant view has been that when states proscribe crimes under customary international law at the municipal level they may do so on the basis of universality. In 1961, for example, in *Attorney-General for Israel v Eichmann*, the District Court of Jerusalem justified its exercise of jurisdiction over crimes committed abroad by a foreign national partly by reference to the fact that these crimes were 'grave offences against the law of nations itself' and that '[t]he jurisdiction to try crimes under international law is universal'.[91] This view was endorsed the following year by the Supreme Court of Israel[92] and seemed to find support among states, a not inconsiderable number of which legislated and occasionally prosecuted to this effect.[93] Subsequently, in 1995, the Appeals Chamber of the International Criminal Tribunal for the former Yugoslavia (ICTY) asserted obiter in *Tadić* that 'universal jurisdiction is nowadays acknowledged in the case of international crimes'.[94]

1.62 The apparent consensus was shaken in 2002 by the views expressed by two judges of the ICJ in *Arrest Warrant*. Although the Court was not, in the event, called upon to decide the question in relation to the war crimes and crimes against humanity at issue in the case after the Democratic Republic of the Congo declined to pursue an initial submission along these lines, President Guillaume came to the stark conclusion in his separate opinion that, except in respect of piracy, customary international law did not recognize universal jurisdiction,[95] a view apparently

---

power in the course of trafficking in persons...'. See also Declaration of the World Conference against Racism, Racial Discrimination, Xenophobia and Related Intolerance, Durban, 8 September 2000, A/CONF.189/12, para 13, in which it is 'acknowledge[d] that slavery and the slave trade are a crime against humanity and should always have been so'.

[88] See *infra* paras 1.61–1.64.
[89] The reference here is to those war crimes provided for by customary international law, some of which may also—along with other, wholly separate war crimes—enjoy a formally distinct and parallel existence in treaty.
[90] For the concept of a crime under customary international law, see *infra* chapter 2.
[91] 36 ILR 5, 26, para 12 (Israel (DC Jerusalem) 1961).
[92] See 36 ILR 5, 298–304, para 12 (Israel (SC) 1962).
[93] Additionally, for what it is worth, art V of the International Convention on the Suppression and Punishment of the Crime of Apartheid 1973—art I(1) of which declares apartheid to be a crime against humanity (that is, an existing crime under customary international law)—permits any state party to prosecute the offence.
[94] *Prosecutor v Tadić*, IT-94-1, Appeals Chamber, Decision on the Defence Motion for Interlocutory Appeal on Jurisdiction, 2 October 1995, para 62.
[95] See *Arrest Warrant* (n 15), 44, para 16 (sep op Guillaume).

shared by Judge Rezek.⁹⁶ In contrast, however, and indeed in implicit response, Judges Higgins, Kooijmans, and Buergenthal accepted the international lawfulness of universal jurisdiction in respect of not only piracy but also war crimes and crimes against humanity at least.⁹⁷ Similarly, Judge ad hoc Van Den Wyngaert, in dissent on a different point, stated that '[i]nternational law clearly permits universal jurisdiction for war crimes and crimes against humanity', including among the latter genocide,⁹⁸ while Judge Koroma held that, 'together with piracy, universal jurisdiction is available for certain crimes, such as war crimes and crimes against humanity, including the slave trade and genocide'.⁹⁹ But all these judicial statements were obiter dicta, since the Court was not required to decide, nor did it decide, the issue.

As for the actual position under customary international law, state practice and *opinio juris* indicate sufficiently clearly that states are indeed permitted to assert universal prescriptive jurisdiction over war crimes, crimes against humanity, and genocide, as defined by customary international law. Very many states of nearly all persuasions now provide in their municipal law for universal jurisdiction over all or one or more of these offences,¹⁰⁰ and such provision has not of itself been the subject of protest by other states. Numerous, although far fewer states have opened investigations, issued arrest warrants, and in relatively rare cases proceeded to prosecute persons on the basis of universality, and—while some of this has proved legally and politically controversial to the extent that it has implicated the immunities under international law to which state officials may or may not be entitled in any given case—these exercises of universal jurisdiction have not per se elicited protest. It is notable in this regard that the states of the African Union (AU), vociferously opposed to what they consider the 'abuse' of universal jurisdiction in

1.63

---

⁹⁶ See ibid, 94, para 10 (sep op Rezek).
⁹⁷ See ibid, 81, para 61 and 83, para 65 (joint sep op Higgins, Kooijmans, and Buergenthal).
⁹⁸ Ibid, 173, para 59 (diss op Van Den Wyngaert).
⁹⁹ Ibid, 61–2, para 9 (sep op Koroma).
¹⁰⁰ Four points are worth making in this regard. First, some states rely on their military law for the prosecution of at least certain offences arguably subject to universal jurisdiction. Surveying such a state's ordinary criminal law alone will not reveal provision for this head of jurisdiction. Secondly, many states do not have specific statutes embodying the relevant offences. Rather, they try such offences as common crimes, albeit common crimes which, when also constituting crimes under customary international law, are subject to a universal jurisdiction provided for via the state's code of criminal procedure, the general part of its criminal code or even its constitution. Thirdly, in the case of war crimes, the only assertions of universal jurisdiction relevant to a permissive rule of customary international law to the effect are those pertaining to war crimes not covered by an applicable treaty-based obligation or permission to assert such jurisdiction, chief among these being the obligation found in the grave breaches regime of the 1949 Geneva Conventions (see *infra* chapters 7 and 8). Finally, and although it has no implications for a state's perception of the international legality of its underlying act of prescription, it should be noted (see *infra* para 9.33) that, in an attempt to obviate the diplomatic and other practical difficulties sometimes associated with the exercise of universal jurisdiction, quite a few states which provide for what formally constitutes prescriptive jurisdiction on the basis of universality over war crimes, crimes against humanity, and genocide have imposed limitations as to the enforcement of this jurisdiction, such as requirements of subsequent nationality or subsequent residency in respect of the alleged perpetrator or victim; and that where statute imposes no such requirements, some national courts have nonetheless demanded a sufficient link between the forum and the alleged perpetrator or victim.

criminal cases involving African state officials, have not protested at the exercise of such jurisdiction over private parties or figures of the *ancien régime*, and accept in principle that war crimes, crimes against humanity, and genocide are subject under customary international law to universal prescriptive jurisdiction.[101] State practice and *opinio juris* in favour of universal prescriptive jurisdiction over all three categories of customary international crime can also be gleaned from the *travaux préparatoires* of the Rome Statute, with numerous states on record as stating that universal jurisdiction attached, in their respective views, to the crimes eventually included within the ICC's jurisdiction *ratione materiae*.[102] Next, rule 11*bis*(A)(ii) and (iii) of the respective Rules of Procedure and Evidence (RPE) of the ICTY and the International Criminal Tribunal for Rwanda (ICTR) permit the relevant Tribunal to refer cases for prosecution in national courts on the basis of universal jurisdiction; and while the RPE are drafted by the judges of the Tribunals, rather than by states, the universal jurisdiction they envisage has not been the subject of criticism by any state and has been implicitly endorsed by the members of the UN Security Council, which on numerous occasions has welcomed the so-called 'completion strategies' of the Tribunals, of which rule 11*bis* is a key element. Nor have several referrals by the ICTR pursuant to these provisions[103] elicited complaint. For its part, section 2.1 of UNTAET regulation 2000/15 vested the Special Panels for Serious Crimes in the Dili District Court—a national court, even if its Special Panels were composed of foreign judges—with universal jurisdiction over war crimes, crimes against humanity, and genocide;[104] and while the practice of UNTAET is again not state practice, no state apparently objected to this jurisdiction.

1.64 The formal legal rationalization for universal prescriptive jurisdiction over war crimes, crimes against humanity, and genocide is arguably different from that for universal jurisdiction over piracy *jure gentium*[105] (the latter, although defined by

---

[101] See eg Assembly of the African Union Decision on the Report of the Commission on the Abuse of the Principle of Universal Jurisdiction, AU doc Decision Assembly/AU/Dec 199(XI), 1 July 2008, para 3; *The scope and application of the principle of universal jurisdiction. Report of the Secretary-General*, UN doc A/66/93 (20 June 2011), para 158. To war crimes, crimes against humanity, and genocide the two cited documents add torture, presumably as a putative crime under customary international law, while the second document additionally includes slavery.
[102] See eg UN doc A/AC.249/1998/DP.2 (23 March 1998) (Germany).
[103] See *Prosecutor v Bucyibaruta*, ICTR-2005-85-I, Trial Chamber, Decision on Prosecutor's Request for Referral of Laurent Bucyibaruta's Indictment to France: Rule 11*bis* of the Rules of Procedure and Evidence, 20 November 2007; *Prosecutor v Munyeshyaka*, ICTR-2005-87-I, Trial Chamber, Decision on the Prosecutor's Request for the Referral of Wenceslas Munyeshyaka's Indictment to France: Rule 11*bis* of the Rules of Procedure and Evidence, 20 November 2007.
[104] The list further includes torture, again presumably as a putative crime under customary international law. For details as to UNTAET reg 2000/15, 6 June 2000, see *infra* paras 3.31 and 9.44–9.46.
[105] At the same time, the functional justification for universal jurisdiction over crimes under customary international law and piracy *jure gentium* respectively is essentially the same. The values and policies embodied in customary international law (in this case, in its specification as to criminal conduct, whether the relevant substantive prohibition be under international law itself or solely under municipal law) are those not of any single state but of all states, at least in theory, so that the concern on which the international rules on the permissible limits of national jurisdiction are premised—namely, the perceived need to mediate between the potentially competing values and policies of individual states—is not, again at least in theory, implicated.

customary international law, not amounting to a substantive international prohibition or, as this book terms the species,[106] a crime under customary international law). The prohibitions on war crimes, crimes against humanity, and genocide, even when their breach is punished through the medium of municipal law, have their ultimate source in customary international law, and the substantive ambit of customary international law is universal. That is, a crime under customary international law is a crime under customary international law regardless of where, by whom, and against whom it is committed and regardless of whether it threatens the fundamental interests of or has deleterious effects in any state. It stands to reason, therefore, that a state's international legal authority to punish a crime under customary international law via the medium of its municipal law is equally without reference to the place of commission, the nationalities of the offender and victim, and the character and impact of the crime. In short, prescriptive jurisdiction with respect to crimes under customary international law is by definition universal.[107]

(d) Common crimes in cases of double criminality?

1.65 It is ironic, given the controversy surrounding universal jurisdiction over crimes under customary international law, that a surprising number of states of the civil-law tradition assert universal prescriptive jurisdiction, to little obvious objection, over common crimes such as murder on the proviso that the same conduct would be punishable under the law of the state where it occurred. The *opinio juris* associated with this largely-overlooked state practice is unclear.

C. A Hierarchy of Concurrent Jurisdictions?

1.66 It has sometimes been suggested that a hierarchy exists among states enjoying concurrent prescriptive jurisdiction over an offence. In his dissenting opinion in *Lotus*, for example, Judge Altamira asserted that a state has preferential jurisdiction over its nationals.[108] More common is the argument that the state in whose territory the alleged offence occurred takes legal priority over the state of nationality of the alleged offender or victim and over any other state with an internationally-lawful basis of jurisdiction. What such a hierarchy would mean in practice is that, in the event of competing claims to prosecute a suspect in a given case, the state or states with the hierarchically-inferior head of prescriptive jurisdiction would be obliged by international law to defer to the state with the superior basis of jurisdiction, for example by not pursuing a competing request for the suspect's extradition from a third state or, in the event that the first state enjoyed custody over the suspect, by refraining from prosecuting him or her until it had ascertained whether or not the state with the superior jurisdiction intended to do so.

---

[106] See *infra* chapter 2.
[107] Recall *Eichmann* (n 91), 26, para 12. See also J Crawford, *Brownlie's Principles of Public International Law* (8th edn, Oxford: Oxford University Press, 2012), 467 and 688.
[108] See *Lotus* (n 9), 95 (diss op Altamira).

1.67   More frequent is the more limited claim that a state seeking to prosecute a suspect on the basis of universal prescriptive jurisdiction must first offer the state where the offence took place the opportunity to act on the relevant charges itself, most commonly, in cases where custody has been obtained, by the offer to extradite the suspect to that state. In their joint separate opinion in *Arrest Warrant*, Judges Higgins, Kooijmans, and Buergenthal extended this principle to an offer to the offender's state of nationality.[109] Belgium in fact made such an offer to the DRC prior to the case,[110] although there is no indication that it felt bound by international law to do so.

1.68   But the suggestion of a hierarchy among concurrent heads of prescriptive jurisdiction was rejected in 1935 by the Harvard Law School research report as 'unwarranted by anything in international law and unsupported by the existing practice of States'.[111] Nor has there been any discernible shift in state practice since then. The idea that there exists a hierarchy among the internationally-accepted bases of prescriptive jurisdiction finds no support in the contemporary conduct of states beyond the single, wholly ambivalent example cited. That said, given that an offer by a state to defer to the criminal jurisdiction of another may not be a matter of public record, relevant practice may not always be easy to discern.

1.69   For what it is worth, no provision giving effect to any hierarchy among concurrent heads of jurisdiction to prescribe is to be found anywhere in the raft of modern multilateral treaties which specify crimes and mandate or permit universal and other forms of extraterritorial prescriptive jurisdiction over them.[112] Indeed, the recent tendency in such treaties is to acknowledge by implication that no such hierarchy exists.[113] The same can be said of the series of UN Security Council

---

[109] See *Arrest Warrant* (n 15), 80, para 59 (joint sep op Higgins, Kooijmans, and Buergenthal).
[110] See ibid, 10, para 16.   [111] Harvard Research report (n 12), 583.
[112] According to M Nowak and E McArthur, *The United Nations Convention Against Torture. A Commentary* (Oxford: Oxford University Press, 2008), 317, para 163, the drafters of the Convention against Torture and Other Cruel, Inhuman or Degrading Treatment or Punishment 1984 expressly rejected the imposition of a hierarchy among the concurrent jurisdictions provided for in the Convention.
[113] See Convention on Combating Bribery of Foreign Public Officials in International Business Transactions 1997, art 4(3) ('When more than one Party has jurisdiction over an alleged offence described in this Convention, the Parties involved shall, at the request of one of them, consult with a view to determining the most appropriate jurisdiction for prosecution.'); International Convention for the Suppression of the Financing of Terrorism 1999, art 7(5) ('When more than one State Party claims jurisdiction over the offences set forth in [the Convention], the relevant States Parties shall strive to co-ordinate their actions appropriately...'); United Nations Convention against Transnational Organized Crime 2000, art 15(5) and, identically, United Nations Convention against Corruption 2003, art 42(5) ('If a State Party exercising its jurisdiction under paragraph 1 or 2 of this article has been notified, or has otherwise learned, that any other States Parties are conducting an investigation, prosecution or judicial proceeding in respect of the same conduct, the competent authorities of those States Parties shall, as appropriate, consult one another with a view to coordinating their actions.'); Council of Europe Convention on Action against Trafficking in Human Beings 2005, art 31(4) and, identically, Council of Europe Convention on the Protection of Children against Sexual Exploitation and Sexual Abuse 2007, art 25(8) ('When more than one Party claims jurisdiction over an alleged offence established in accordance with this Convention, the Parties involved shall, where appropriate, consult with a view to determining the most appropriate jurisdiction for prosecution.'). See too EU Council Framework Decision 2008/841/JHA of 24 October 2008 on the fight against organised crime, OJ L 300/42, 11.11.2008, art 7(2) ('When an offence referred to in Article 2 falls within the

resolutions on piracy off the coast of Somalia[114] (although the non-territorial character of the crime of piracy and the fact that Somalia, the state of the pirates' nationality, is logistically ill-equipped to try detained suspects weaken the claim that these resolutions reflect a belief in the absence of any general hierarchy among the accepted heads of prescriptive criminal jurisdiction). On the other hand, provisions in certain bilateral and multilateral treaties concerned with the interdiction of ships on the high seas establish a priority as between the prescriptive criminal jurisdiction of the flag state and any prescriptive jurisdiction potentially enjoyed by a state that arrests the vessel with the flag state's consent.[115]

For its part, the Appeals Chamber of the ICTY noted in *Janković* in 2005 'that attempts among States to establish a hierarchy of criteria for determining the most appropriate jurisdiction for a criminal case, where there are concurrent jurisdictions on a horizontal level (*i.e.* among States), have failed thus far'.[116] Similarly, a report of 2008 by the International Bar Association's Task Force on Extraterritorial Jurisdiction[117] and the 2009 report of the African Union–European Union Technical Ad hoc Expert Group on the Principle of Universal Jurisdiction[118] both came down against the existence as a matter of customary international law of any pecking order among the various internationally lawful bases of prescriptive criminal jurisdiction. As specifically regards universal jurisdiction, the report of the United Nations Fact-Finding Mission on the Gaza Conflict ('Goldstone report') stated that '[t]his form of jurisdiction is concurrent with others based on more traditional principles of territoriality [and] active and passive nationality, and is not subsidiary to them'.[119]

1.70

---

jurisdiction of more than one Member State and when any one of the States concerned can validly prosecute on the basis of the same facts, the Member States concerned shall cooperate in order to decide which of them will prosecute the offenders, with the aim, if possible, of centralising proceedings in a single Member State.').

[114] See eg SC res 1816 (2008), 2 June 2008, para 11, in which the Security Council '[c]alls upon all States, and in particular flag, port and coastal States, States of the nationality of victims and perpetrators of piracy and armed robbery, and other States with relevant jurisdiction under international law and national legislation, to cooperate in determining [which state will exercise] jurisdiction, and in the investigation and prosecution of persons responsible for acts of piracy and armed robbery off the coast of Somalia, consistent with applicable international law'. See also SC res 1897 (2009), 30 November 2009, para 12; SC res 1950 (2010), 23 November 2010, para 12; SC res 2020 (2011), 22 November 2011, para 14; SC res 2077 (2012), 21 November 2012, para 17; and SC res 2125 (2013), 18 November 2013, para 16.
[115] See eg Convention for the Suppression of Unlawful Acts against the Safety of Maritime Navigation 2005 (being the Convention for the Suppression of Unlawful Acts against the Safety of Maritime Navigation 1988 as amended by the Protocol of 2005 to the Convention for the Suppression of Unlawful Acts against the Safety of Maritime Navigation) ('2005 SUA Convention'), art 8*bis*(8); Agreement on Illicit Traffic by Sea, implementing article 17 of the United Nations Convention against Illicit Traffic in Narcotic Drugs and Psychotropic Substances 1995 ('Council of Europe Agreement on Illicit Traffic by Sea'), art 3(4), cross-referenced with art 1(*b*).
[116] *Prosecutor v Janković*, IT-96-23/2-AR11bis.2, Appeals Chamber, Decision on Rule 11*bis* Referral, 15 November 2005, para 34.
[117] See International Bar Association (n 34), 167.
[118] See *AU–EU Technical Ad hoc Expert Group on the Principle of Universal Jurisdiction: Report*, Council of the European Union doc 8671/09 (16 April 2009), Annex, para 14.
[119] *Report of the United Nations Fact-Finding Mission on the Gaza Conflict*, UN doc A/HRC/12/48 (25 September 2009), 397–8, para 1849.

1.71   In the foregoing light, it is perfectly safe to conclude that customary international law presently recognizes no hierarchy among concurrent, internationally-lawful bases of prescriptive criminal jurisdiction.

D. *Ne bis in idem* among Concurrent Jurisdictions?

1.72   Customary international law embodies no rule of *ne bis in idem* as among national criminal justice systems. That is, from the point of view of customary international law, there is nothing to prohibit a state from proceeding to try, pursuant to a head of prescriptive jurisdiction recognized by international law, an individual who has already been convicted or acquitted of the same offence, or convicted or acquitted on the basis of substantially the same facts, in another state pursuant to a concurrent head of prescriptive jurisdiction.[120]

1.73   At the same time, a number of treaties and other legally binding international instruments specify[121] or give indirect effect to[122] a mandatory[123] rule of *ne bis in idem* as among criminal courts in different states.[124] In addition or alternatively,

---

[120] See eg *E v Police Inspectorate of Basle*, 75 ILR 106 (Switzerland 1980); *BVD v NV Deutsche Bank*, ILDC 373 (BE 2005) (Belgium 2005).

[121] See European Convention on the International Validity of Criminal Judgments 1970, art 53; European Convention on the Transfer of Proceedings in Criminal Matters 1972, art 35; European Convention on Offences relating to Cultural Property 1985 (not in force), art 17; Convention implementing the Schengen Agreement of 14 June 1985 between the Governments of the States of the Benelux Economic Union, the Federal Republic of Germany and the French Republic on the gradual abolition of checks at their common borders 1990 ('Schengen Convention'), art 54 (but see also art 55). Some national legal systems provide likewise. As for non-binding international instruments, see UN Model Treaty on Extradition, GA res 45/116, 14 December 1990, Annex, art 3(*d*). As regards the relevant provisions of the Schengen Convention, see *Spasic*, Case C-129/14 PPU, Judgment, CJEU (GC), 27 May 2014.

[122] See European Convention on Extradition 1957, art 9, first sentence; European Convention on the Supervision of Conditionally Sentenced or Conditionally Released Offenders 1964, art 7(1)(*b*); European Convention on the Punishment of Road Traffic Offences 1964, art 9(1)(*a*); Council Framework Decision 2002/584/JHA of 13 June 2002 on the European arrest warrant and the surrender procedures between Member States, OJ L 190, 18.7.2002, 1, art 3(2) (providing also in art 4(5) for a right of refusal in respect of prior conviction or acquittal in a third state); OAU Convention on the Prevention and Combating of Terrorism 1999, art 8(3), first sentence. As for bilateral treaties, see eg Extradition Treaty between the Government of the United Kingdom of Great Britain and Northern Ireland and the Government of the United States of America 2003, art 5(1) (providing also in art 5(2) for a right of refusal in respect of prior conviction or acquittal in a third state); Convention between the Government of the United Kingdom of Great Britain and Northern Ireland and the Government of the People's Democratic Republic of Algeria on Extradition 2006, art 4(1). In terms of non-binding international instruments, see UN Model Treaty on Extradition, art 4(*b*).

[123] But see also Inter-American Convention on Mutual Assistance in Criminal Matters 1992, art 9(*a*), permitting the requested state to refuse assistance when it determines that the request for assistance 'is being used in order to prosecute a person on a charge with respect to which that person has already been sentenced or acquitted in a trial in the requesting or requested state'.

[124] But cf, to the opposite effect, Treaty of Peace between the Principal Allied and Associated Powers and Germany 1919, art 228 (in relevant part): 'The German Government recognises the right of the Allied and Associated Powers to bring before military tribunals persons accused of having committed acts in violation of the laws and customs of war. Such persons shall, if found guilty, be sentenced to punishments laid down by law. This provision will apply notwithstanding any proceedings or prosecution before a tribunal in Germany or in the territory of her allies.'

certain treaties give indirect effect[125] to a permissive rule of *ne bis in idem* in cases where the competent authorities of another state have decided either not to institute or to terminate proceedings in respect of, variously, the same offence or same conduct.

IV. Jurisdiction to Enforce

Jurisdiction to enforce, as previously defined, refers to a state's authority under international law to exercise investigative, coercive or custodial powers in support of law,[126] be its own or another state's, whether through police or other executive action or through its courts. In the specifically penal context, the term refers to a state's international legal authority to arrest and retain custody over persons and vessels, to have a court sit, to incarcerate persons and confiscate property, to undertake surveillance, to stop and search, to take physical measures to prevent the commission of a crime, to investigate and to collect evidence, to issue *subpoenae ad testificandum* and *subpoenae duces tecum*, and so on—in short, to exercise any or all of the usual range of police, prosecutorial, judicial, and related executive powers in relation to criminal justice.   1.74

A. The General Rule and Its Exceptions

(i) *The general rule*

The general rule of customary international law governing jurisdiction to enforce in the criminal context[127] is that a state may not exercise as of right its law-enforcement powers in the territory of another state, which includes that state's territorial sea and superjacent airspace. This axiomatic limitation on national jurisdiction was expressly affirmed by the PCIJ in *Lotus*:   1.75

> [T]he first and foremost restriction imposed by international law upon a State is that—failing the existence of a permissive rule to the contrary—it may not exercise its power in any form in the territory of another State. In this sense jurisdiction is certainly territorial; it cannot

---

[125] See European Convention on Extradition, art 9, second sentence; Agreement between the European Union and Japan on Mutual Legal Assistance in Criminal Matters 2009, art 11(1)(*d*); European Convention on the Supervision of Conditionally Sentenced or Conditionally Released Offenders, art 7(2)(*a*); European Convention on the Punishment of Road Traffic Offences, art 9(2)(*a*); European Convention on the International Validity of Criminal Judgments, art 6(*e*); European Convention on Insider Trading 1989, art 8(*e*); European Convention on Laundering, Search, Seizure and Confiscation of the Proceeds from Crime 1990, art 18(1)(*e*); Council of Europe Convention on Laundering, Search, Seizure and Confiscation of the Proceeds from Crime and on the Financing of Terrorism 2005, art 28(1)(*f*); Council Framework Decision on the European arrest warrant, art 4(3); OAU Convention on the Prevention and Combating of Terrorism, art 8(3), second sentence. But cf, to the opposite effect, UK–USA Extradition Treaty, art 5(3)(*a*) and (*b*).
[126] But recall *supra* n 3.
[127] The same rule applies in the civil, administrative, and regulatory contexts.

be exercised by a State outside its territory except by virtue of a permissive rule derived from international custom or a convention.[128]

The rule, reiterated in the separate and dissenting opinions and declarations in *Arrest Warrant*,[129] remains cardinal.

1.76   It pays to note the PCIJ's careful description of enforcement jurisdiction as '[i]n this sense' territorial. While the label 'territoriality' may be useful shorthand for the fundamental limitation imposed by customary international law on a state's jurisdiction to enforce its criminal laws, it should be used with caution, since it is not wholly accurate. A state is not prohibited by international law from unilaterally exercising its law enforcement powers beyond the confines of its territory. It is simply that any such exercise in the territory of another state represents a violation of the exclusive enforcement jurisdiction accorded by customary international law to that other state within its own territory. In other words, the general rule is not as stated in the second sentence of the above quote from *Lotus* (at least if that sentence is taken out of context), *viz* that powers of law enforcement 'cannot be exercised by a State outside its territory'. Rather, the rule is as stated by the Court in the first sentence of the quote, namely that one state may not exercise its law-enforcement powers in the territory of another. Putting it another way, we can say that, subject to any customary or conventional permissive rule to the contrary, the jurisdiction to enforce enjoyed by a state within its own territory is exclusive.

1.77   The restriction placed by customary international law on national jurisdiction to enforce criminal laws is reflected most patently in the impermissibility of one state's exercise as of right of police powers in the territory of another. But it is also reflected in the judicial sphere. The criminal courts of one state may not, as of right, sit in the territory of another. Nor, perhaps less obviously, may a foreign criminal court, as of right, subpoena witnesses or documents or take sworn affidavit evidence in foreign territory.

(ii) The exceptions

(a) With the consent of the territorial state

1.78   A state is always free, as an expression of its sovereignty, to consent—whether by way of treaty or on an ad hoc, perhaps informal basis—to the exercise in its territory of another state's powers of criminal law enforcement, and this consent renders internationally lawful such exercise by that other state.[130]

---

[128] *Lotus* (n 9), 18–19.
[129] See *Arrest Warrant* (n 15), 37, para 4 (sep op Guillaume), 79, para 54 (joint sep op Higgins, Kooijmans, and Buergenthal), and 168, para 49 (diss op Van Den Wyngaert).
[130] It is worth noting that diplomatic law does not provide for the exercise by the sending state of powers of criminal law enforcement on the premises of its diplomatic mission. At the same time, in accordance with the customary rule reflected in art 22(1) of the Vienna Convention on Diplomatic Relations 1961, the premises of a diplomatic mission are inviolable, meaning that the authorities of the receiving state may not enter them without the consent of the head of the mission. The usual practice in relation to serious criminal conduct on diplomatic premises is for the head of the mission to invite the competent authorities of the receiving state onto the premises.

Examples in the police[131] sphere of consent to this effect can be found in the   1.79
Convention implementing the Schengen Agreement of 14 June 1985 between the
Governments of the States of the Benelux Economic Union, the Federal Republic
of Germany and the French Republic on the gradual abolition of checks at their
common borders 1990 ('Schengen Convention'), article 40 of which provides for
limited and conditional cross-border powers of police investigation, while article
41(1) permits limited and conditional cross-border 'hot pursuit'.[132] Other, less
formalized examples include several states' consent from at least late 2001 to the
exercise on their territory of powers of investigation and in some cases assumption
of custody and detention by US intelligence agents; Indonesia's permission for
UK, Australian, and other detectives to operate on the island of Bali after the terrorist bombings there in 2002; Germany's permission for UK police to operate in
the former's territory during the football World Cup in 2006; the consent given in
2008 by the Transitional Federal Government of Somalia to the capture by French
forces in Somali territory (and the subsequent transfer to Paris for trial) of the
pirates responsible for the seizure of the French vessel the MY *Le Ponant*; and the
consensual deployment in Paris from late 2011 of Romanian police.

In the judicial sphere, a striking example of consent, in this case by way of   1.80
treaty,[133] to one state's enforcement of its criminal law in the territory of another
was the sitting in the Netherlands of the Scottish High Court of Justiciary, a UK
court, for the purpose of trying and hearing the appeals of the two Libyans suspected of bombing Pan-Am flight 103 over Lockerbie, Scotland in 1988. Even
more singular was the sitting in Auckland, pursuant to a treaty between New
Zealand and the UK,[134] of what were nominally the Court of Appeal of the UK
overseas territory of Pitcairn, for the joined appeals of six Pitcairn men convicted
together on the island of sex offences, and the Pitcairn Supreme Court, for the
subsequent trial on sex offence charges of a further Pitcairn man.

A common instance of one state's consensual exercise in the territory of another   1.81
of both police and judicial powers of criminal law enforcement is pursuant to
a 'status of forces' agreement, or 'SOFA', concluded between the two states (or
among a group of states, including the two in question) in order to regulate the

---

[131] The term is used here broadly to refer to the exercise, by whichever element of the executive, of state powers in relation to the investigation of crime, the surveillance, arrest and detention of criminal suspects, and the like.

[132] See also, similarly, Second Additional Protocol to the European Convention on Mutual Assistance in Criminal Matters 2001, art 17.

[133] See Agreement between the Government of the Kingdom of the Netherlands and the Government of the United Kingdom of Great Britain and Northern Ireland concerning a Scottish Trial in The Netherlands 1998. The trial and appeal ran in total from May 2000 to March 2002.

[134] See Agreement between the Government of the United Kingdom of Great Britain and Northern Ireland and the Government of New Zealand concerning trials under Pitcairn law in New Zealand and related matters 2002. The plan had been for all of the trials before the Pitcairn Supreme Court to take place in New Zealand, but the joined trials of the original seven defendants (one of whom was acquitted) took place in the event on Pitcairn. A first and a second appeal, in 2005 and 2006 respectively, were subsequently heard in New Zealand before the Pitcairn Court of Appeal. The trial of the further defendant took place in New Zealand before the Pitcairn Supreme Court in 2007. There was no appeal.

32   *Foundational Concepts and Principles*

conditions under which the former's armed forces are stationed or otherwise present in the territory of the latter. For example, in accordance with article VII of the NATO SOFA,[135] the military police and courts-martial of the 'sending' state—and, as a general rule, they exclusively[136]—may exercise powers of criminal law enforcement over the sending state's military personnel when they are present in another NATO state. Identical in principle to SOFAs are so-called SOMAs, or 'status of mission' agreements, which are limited in their application to specific deployments.[137]

1.82   Consent by one state to the exercise in its territory of another state's powers in relation to criminal law enforcement is relatively uncommon.

(b) By operation of the customary international law of armed conflict

1.83   Customary international law[138] permits the military forces of a state engaged in international armed conflict in the territory of another state to capture or otherwise take into custody and detain until the end of the conflict enemy combatants (along with their so-called 'camp followers')[139] and civilians taking direct part in hostilities when such persons fall into their power in the course of hostilities. It further permits the trial of such persons by a court of the custodial state, sitting in territory under that state's control or sovereignty (that is, not necessarily in the territory in which the detainees are captured), for any crimes over which international law permits that state prescriptive jurisdiction. The latter is the case even as regards prisoners of war (POWs),[140] as intimated in article 85 of the Third Geneva Convention,[141] considered consonant with customary international law,[142] which

---

[135] Agreement between the Parties to the North Atlantic Treaty regarding the Status of their Forces 1951.

[136] Note that it is always open to the sending state to decline to exercise the exclusive enforcement jurisdiction granted it under a SOFA or SOMA and to surrender its personnel for investigation and trial by the receiving state. See eg the 2001 case of Sergeant Timothy Woodland, a US serviceman stationed on the Japanese island of Okinawa, who was handed over to the Japanese police on suspicion of rape.

[137] See eg Agreement between the Democratic Republic of East Timor and the United Nations concerning the Status of the United Nations Mission of Support in East Timor 2002, arts 43 and 44; Agreement between the European Union and the Islamic Republic of Afghanistan on the Status of the European Union Police Mission in Afghanistan (EUPOL Afghanistan) 2010, art 8.

[138] It is true that the binding force of customary international law derives, according to the classical positivist account, from the consent of states as manifest in their practice and *opinio juris*. But any consent by a state to another's exercise in its territory of jurisdiction to enforce as could be said to be reflected in a permissive customary international rule to the effect is of a sufficiently different order of specificity from that conveyed by an explicit grant of permission as to justify the conceptual distinction drawn here.

[139] The term refers to certain accompanying civilians.

[140] The difference in terms of their amenability to trial between POWs—or, more precisely, those POWs who enjoy combatant status under the international law of armed conflict—and civilians taking direct part in hostilities is that the former may not be tried solely for their participation in hostilities. See eg *Public Committee against Torture in Israel and Palestinian Society for the Protection of Human Rights and the Environment v Israel*, ILDC 597 (IL 2006) (Israel 2006), para 23. In other words, it is not to be deemed criminal, in and of itself, for a combatant to take part in the fighting.

[141] Convention relative to the Treatment of Prisoners of War 1949 ('1949 Geneva Convention III').

[142] The provisions of the Geneva Conventions equally manifest the express consent of any territorial state that is party to them.

is applicable seemingly to all '[criminal] acts committed prior to capture' and not just to those committed during the conflict in violation of the international law of armed conflict.[143] Moreover, while in general POWs may be detained only until the cessation of active hostilities,[144] those against whom criminal proceedings for an indictable offence are pending may be detained until the end of the proceedings and, if necessary, until the completion of their punishment, the latter also applying to those already convicted of an indictable offence.[145]

1.84 In addition, a state in belligerent occupation of all or part of the territory of another state is permitted by customary international law to exercise certain powers of criminal law enforcement—and, indeed, of prior prescription—in that territory. The rules regulating this are codified in the Fourth Geneva Convention.[146] There are two notable differences between these rules and those applicable in respect of persons captured in the course of hostilities. First, while it appears that those captured in the course of hostilities may be tried for any crime against the law of the detaining state over which international law accords that state prescriptive jurisdiction, persons protected by the rules applicable to belligerent occupation may not be prosecuted for acts committed prior to the occupation, with the exception of acts contrary to the international law of armed conflict.[147] Secondly, persons protected by the rules on belligerent occupation must, if detained with a view to prosecution, be detained in the occupied territory and must, if convicted, serve their sentences there.[148]

1.85 An occupying power is further permitted, under certain conditions, to resort to preventive detention.[149] But individual or mass forcible transfers of persons protected by the rules on belligerent occupation from the occupied territory to the territory of the Occupying Power or to that of another state, occupied or not, are prohibited, regardless of their motive,[150] and this would render unlawful the transfer of such persons from the occupied territory to a detention facility outside that territory.

---

[143] An example of the prosecution of an enemy combatant, captured during armed conflict, for offences committed prior to and unconnected with the conflict is the case of General Manuel Noriega, who surrendered to US forces during the latter's invasion of Panama in 1989, was detained, and was ultimately tried, convicted, and incarcerated in the US for extraterritorial conspiracy offences related to racketeering and drug trafficking. See *United States v Noriega*, 808 F Supp 791 (SD Fla 1992). The US District Court for the Southern District of Florida subsequently ruled that he was entitled to be treated during his incarceration as a prisoner of war.

[144] 1949 Geneva Convention III, art 118.   [145] Ibid, art 119.

[146] Convention relative to the Protection of Civilian Persons in Time of War 1949 ('1949 Geneva Convention IV'). See, in particular, ibid, art 64 (prescription) and arts 66, 68, 70, 76, and 77 (enforcement). See also the rule of customary international law reflected in art 43 of the Regulations concerning the Laws and Customs of War on Land, annexed to Convention concerning the Laws and Customs of War on Land 1907 ('The authority of the legitimate power having in fact passed into the hands of the occupant, the latter shall take all the measures in his power to restore, and ensure, as far as possible, public order and safety, while respecting, unless absolutely prevented, the laws in force in the country.'), an obligation—not merely a permission—that extends to policing and punishing violations of the local criminal law in the event that the competent authorities of the territory are not in a position to do so.

[147] See 1949 Geneva Convention IV, art 70.   [148] See ibid, art 76.

[149] See ibid, art 78.   [150] See ibid, art 49.

B. Co-operation in Enforcement in Foreign Territory

1.86 The more usual method of obviating the limits placed by customary international law on states' jurisdiction in respect of the investigation of crimes, the arrest of suspects, and the securing of their appearance before a court, the taking of evidence and the execution of punishments is by means of treaties or ad hoc arrangements in accordance with which, on request, the police, judicial, and related administrative authorities of the territorial state co-operate in—in crude terms, do for them—the work of foreign police and judicial authorities by way of extradition and other assistance in criminal matters.

1.87 It is worth recalling that municipal courts do not, in practice, apply foreign criminal law.[151] That is, a state's criminal courts will not try a person for a crime against the law of another state.

(i) Lawfully securing the presence of the suspect

1.88 The procedural competence of the criminal courts in the common-law tradition is, as a rule, strictly *in personam*. That is, the accused's physical presence before the court is generally a precondition to his or her trial. By way of contrast, many civil law states permit trial *in absentia* under certain conditions. But even where trial *in absentia* is permitted, trial *in personam* is generally considered preferable by states, not least to enable imprisonment in the event of conviction, and every effort is usually made to secure the presence of a suspect.

1.89 Given the general impermissibility of one state's exercise of police powers in the territory of another, securing the presence of the suspect obviously presents a challenge when that suspect is outside the territory of the pursuing state.

1.90 To add to the problem, customary international law imposes no obligation on a state in whose territory a suspect is located to surrender that person to the pursuing state.

1.91 Of course, as a matter of international law, a state in whose territory a suspect is found is free to arrest that person and to surrender him or her to the pursuing state. As a matter of the international rules on jurisdiction,[152] there is no requirement as to formalities in the latter regard. All that is required is that the governmental authorities of the territorial state genuinely consent to the suspect's surrender.[153]

1.92 But municipal law frequently prohibits a state's authorities from surrendering a suspect to a foreign state in the absence of formal extradition. It might also be

---

[151] See *supra* para 1.11.
[152] It may be different as a matter of international human rights law, under which deprivation of liberty must be in accordance with a procedure prescribed by municipal law and must not be otherwise arbitrary.
[153] Although the noun 'surrender' is preferred here, 'rendition' could also be used. Contrary to inaccurate journalistic usage, the latter simply means 'handing over'. The use of the term in no way presupposes illegality or irregularity, let alone kidnapping and transport to a secret detention facility. There can be lawful and regular rendition (such as extradition), and there can be unlawful or otherwise irregular or 'extraordinary' rendition.

the case that the courts of the pursuing state do not permit trial when a suspect's surrender by another state, although genuinely consented to, is contrary to that other state's law or in some other municipal sense irregular. As such, extradition is the most common form of consensual surrender of a suspect by one state to another.[154]

Extradition is a municipal legal procedure by which, on request, the criminal justice authorities of one state (the 'requested' state) arrest and surrender to those of another (the 'requesting' state) a suspect present in the territory of the former and wanted by the latter. Extradition usually involves both executive and judicial authorities, although this is a question for the law of each state.

1.93

Since extradition is a municipal legal process, the details of extradition law vary among states. Notably, some states permit extradition only where a treaty of extradition is in force between that state and the requesting state, while others permit ad hoc extradition. In addition, many states do not, as a general rule, permit the extradition of their own nationals, while other states are perfectly amenable to this.

1.94

In order to create an international obligation to extradite *inter se* and to facilitate this within their respective legal systems, states commonly conclude extradition treaties with each other. This is most commonly done on a bilateral basis,[155] although a longstanding multilateral extradition treaty is the European Convention on Extradition 1957, concluded under the aegis of the Council of Europe.[156] For its part, the UN General Assembly adopted in 1990 a so-called Model Treaty on Extradition 'as a useful framework that could be of assistance to States interested in negotiating and concluding bilateral agreements aimed at improving co-operation in matters of crime prevention and criminal justice'.[157]

1.95

It is typical for the obligation to extradite imposed on the requested state by an extradition treaty to be subject to substantive conditions and exceptions. It is also typical for such a treaty to impose restrictions on the conduct of the requesting state in the event of the suspect's extradition.

1.96

A classic condition precedent to the obligation to extradite is the satisfaction of the rule of 'double criminality', by which is meant the stipulation that the conduct for which extradition is requested constitute a crime—or, more precisely, a crime of a certain character—not only in the requesting state but also in the requested. The consideration is one for the requested state. The requirement

1.97

---

[154] Note that extradition generally applies in respect of not only suspects but also fugitive convicts, *viz* persons already convicted in the requesting state who have managed to abscond to another state.

[155] See eg, among countless others, UK–USA Extradition Treaty; UK–Algeria Convention on Extradition. Consider also Agreement on Extradition between the European Union and the United States of America 2003, in accordance with art 3(1) of which the EU and the USA 'shall ensure that the provisions of th[e] Agreement are applied in relation to bilateral extradition treaties between the Member States and the United States of America, in force at the time of the entry into force of th[e] Agreement'.

[156] As among those parties to the European Convention on Extradition which are also member states of the European Union, extradition has been replaced by surrender pursuant to the 'European arrest warrant'. See *supra* n 122 for the Council Framework Decision on the European arrest warrant. The process shares many features with extradition.

[157] GA res 45/116, 14 December 1990, para 1. For the Model Treaty itself, see *supra* n 121.

is typically found in extradition treaties not *sub nom.* 'double criminality' but under the rubric 'Extradition Crimes', 'Extradition Offences' or 'Extraditable Offences'.[158] It can be embodied textually in one of two ways, namely by the enumeration of an exhaustive list of offences in respect of which extradition is mutually available or by reference to a more flexible requirement of minimum sufficient gravity as adjudged by the penalty affixed. The latter is the approach taken in both the European Convention and the UN Model Treaty,[159] although the European Convention makes additional provision for the former.[160] The precise application of the requirement of double criminality is a matter for municipal law. National courts have typically taken the rule to mean that extradition is permissible as long as the conduct in respect of which extradition is requested constitutes *an* extradition offence, even if not necessarily the same offence, in the requested state.[161] But there is a divergence of opinion as to whether the criminality or otherwise of the conduct under the law of the requested state is to be adjudged by reference to the time of the request or to the time of the alleged commission of the offence against the law of the requesting state, a divergence which reflects a difference of opinion over the rationale for the requirement of double criminality.[162]

1.98   A common exception to the treaty-based obligation to extradite is the 'political offence exception', which provides that extradition shall not be granted if the offence in respect of which it is requested is regarded by the requested state as a political offence or as an offence connected with a political offence.[163] This is again a consideration for the requested state. The exception, historically linked to the practice of political asylum, traditionally served as an important safeguard of individual liberties, particularly of freedom of conscience and of expression. That said, the notions of a political offence and of an offence

---

[158] See eg EU–USA Agreement on Extradition, art 4; European Convention on Extradition, art 2; UN Model Treaty on Extradition, art 2.
[159] See European Convention on Extradition, art 2(1); UN Model Treaty on Extradition, art 2(1). See also EU–USA Agreement on Extradition, art 4(1).
[160] See European Convention on Extradition, art 2(4). In contrast, in accordance with art 3(1)(*a*) of the EU–USA Agreement on Extradition, the minimum sufficient gravity approach adopted in art 4 of the Agreement 'shall be applied in place of bilateral treaty provisions [between EU member states and the USA] that authorise extradition exclusively with respect to a list of specified criminal offences'.
[161] See also, explicitly, EU–USA Agreement on Extradition, art 4(3)(*a*).
[162] In the English courts, the restriction was traditionally thought to be rooted in domestic public policy, the gist being that it would be offensive to English notions of justice to surrender a person for possible punishment abroad on account of conduct not punishable in England. The rule was not thought related to the substantive principle of criminal responsibility encapsulated in the maxim *nullum crimen nulla poena sine lege*, any issue as to the rule of law being for the trial court in the requesting state. In this light, it was widely thought that the criminality or otherwise of the conduct as a matter of English law was to be determined by reference to the time of the request for extradition, rather than of the alleged commission of the offence against the law of the requesting state. But the House of Lords turned this traditional understanding on its head in *R v Bow Street Metropolitan Stipendiary Magistrate, Ex parte Pinochet Ugarte (No 3)*, 119 ILR 135, 144–7 (Lord Browne-Wilkinson) (1999), the correctness of which on point remains open to doubt.
[163] See eg European Convention on Extradition, art 3(1); UN Model Treaty on Extradition, art 3(*a*).

connected with a political offence have on occasion proved fertile sources of accommodating municipal jurisprudence.[164] Moreover, certain treaty regimes have long recognized exceptions to the exception.[165] These exceptions to the exception have proliferated in recent decades in response to modern manifestations of terrorism.[166]

1.99 It is not uncommon for states to refuse to surrender their nationals to the authorities of another state and for treaties otherwise imposing an obligation of extradition to make permissive exception in this regard.[167]

1.100 A typical restriction on the conduct of the requesting state in the event of the suspect's extradition is the rule of 'speciality'.[168] This provides that a person who has been extradited shall not be proceeded against[169] for any offence committed prior to his or her extradition other than that for which extradition was granted. Putting it simply, the rule of speciality dictates that a person extradited to answer charges of, for example, murder may not, on his or her return to the requesting state, be put on trial for, say, theft. The main exception to this prohibition is where the requested state consents.[170]

1.101 A further common treaty-based restraint on the requesting state in the event of the extradition to it of a suspect is that that state may not, without the consent of the requested state, surrender the person onward to another state in which that person is wanted in connection with an offence committed or alleged to have been committed prior to extradition.[171]

1.102 It is worth noting that the requested state's extradition or other consensual surrender of a suspect to another state may, in certain circumstances, place the requested state in breach of treaty obligations owed in the field of international human rights law or international refugee law, both of which embody obligations of *non-refoulement*.

---

[164] See eg *In re Meunier* [1894] 2 QB 415, 419, in which an English court held that, by definition, an anarchist could not commit a political offence.
[165] See eg European Convention on Extradition, art 3(3), to the effect that the taking or attempted taking of the life of a head of state or of a member of his or her family is not to be treated as a political offence. See also Additional Protocol to the European Convention on Extradition 1975, art 1, providing that the crime of genocide embodied in the Genocide Convention, as well as grave breaches of the Geneva Conventions and comparable violations of the laws and customs of war, are not to be considered political offences.
[166] See *infra* para 8.59.
[167] See eg European Convention on Extradition, art 6(1)(*a*); UN Model Treaty on Extradition, art 4(*a*). Note also, however, European Convention on Extradition, art 6(2), providing that, '[i]f the requested Party does not extradite its national, it shall at the request of the requesting Party submit the case to its competent authorities in order that proceedings may be taken if they are considered appropriate'; UN Model Treaty on Extradition, art 4(*a*), to the same effect.
[168] See eg European Convention on Extradition, art 14(1); UN Model Treaty on Extradition, art 14(1)(*a*).
[169] Nor, equally typically, may the person be sentenced, or detained with a view to the carrying out of a sentence or detention order, for any offence committed prior to surrender other than that for which he or she was extradited.
[170] See eg European Convention on Extradition, art 14(1)(*a*); UN Model Treaty on Extradition, art 14(1)(*b*).
[171] See eg European Convention on Extradition, art 15.

(ii) Other assistance in criminal matters

1.103 It is not just the presence in another state of the suspect that poses an obstacle to his or her possible trial. Pre-charge and pre-trial investigation and evidence-taking, among other things, are also limited by the impermissibility of one state's exercise of police and judicial powers in another's territory.

1.104 Customary international law imposes no obligation on a state to render assistance to another state in criminal matters of this sort, although a state will often do so on receipt from the other state of a 'letter rogatory' or 'letter of request' to this end.

1.105 As with securing the presence of the accused, so too with securing assistance in other criminal matters—such as the execution of searches and seizures, the taking of witness statements, and the service of judicial documents—have states sought to oblige and otherwise facilitate the practice *inter se* through the conclusion of bilateral[172] and multilateral[173] treaties. Likewise, the UN General Assembly has adopted a Model Treaty on Mutual Assistance in Criminal Matters 'as a useful framework that could be of assistance to States interested in negotiating and concluding bilateral agreements aimed at improving co-operation in matters of crime prevention and criminal justice'.[174]

1.106 A typical exception to the obligation to afford the widest measure of mutual assistance in criminal matters imposed by treaties in this area is, as with extradition, the political offence exception. A request for assistance may typically be refused if it concerns an offence that the requested state considers a political offence or an offence connected with a political offence.[175]

---

[172] See eg Convention on Mutual Assistance in Criminal Matters between the Republic of Djibouti and the French Republic 1986, as was at issue before the ICJ in *Certain Questions of Mutual Assistance in Criminal Matters (Djibouti v France), Judgment*, ICJ Rep 2008, 177. Consider also EU–Japan Agreement on mutual legal assistance in criminal matters, which has effect as between any EU member state, on the one hand, and Japan, on the other. Consider too Agreement on mutual legal assistance between the European Union and the United States of America 2003, in accordance with which the EU and the USA 'shall ensure that the provisions of th[e] Agreement are applied in relation to bilateral mutual legal assistance treaties between the Member States and the United States of America, in force at the time of the entry into force of th[e] Agreement', as per art 3(1), and 'shall also ensure that the provisions of th[e] Agreement are applied in the absence of a bilateral mutual legal assistance treaty in force between a Member State and the United States of America', as per art 3(3)(*a*).

[173] See eg the European Convention on Mutual Assistance in Criminal Matters 1959, along with its First (1978) and Second Additional Protocols; Convention on Mutual Assistance in Criminal Matters between the Member States of the European Union, annexed to Council Act of 29 May 2000 establishing in accordance with Article 34 of the Treaty on European Union the Convention on Mutual Assistance in Criminal Matters between the Member States of the European Union, OJ C 197/1, 12.7.2000; Inter-American Convention on Mutual Assistance in Criminal Matters.

[174] GA res 45/117, 14 December 1990, para 1. The UN Model Treaty on Mutual Assistance in Criminal Matters, annexed to GA res 45/117, was subsequently amended by GA res 53/112, 9 December 1998, Annex I.

[175] See eg EU–Japan Agreement on mutual legal assistance in criminal matters, art 11(1)(*a*); European Convention on Mutual Assistance in Criminal Matters, art 2(*a*); Inter-American Convention on Mutual Assistance in Criminal Matters, art 9(*c*); UN Model Treaty on Mutual Assistance in Criminal Matters, art 4(1)(*b*).

C. International Abduction Without the Consent of the Territorial State and Other Illegally or Irregularly Obtained Custody

It is sometimes the case that a state seeking a suspect present in the territory of a foreign state resorts without the consent of the territorial state to the suspect's abduction either by its own law-enforcement authorities or by private persons acting in collusion with its authorities.[176] The abduction of a suspect from the territory of one state without that state's consent by the authorities of another state or by private persons whose acts are attributable under international law to that other state represents an exercise of criminal enforcement jurisdiction in violation of the exclusive enforcement jurisdiction of the territorial state. As such, it constitutes an internationally wrongful act engaging the responsibility of the abducting state towards the territorial state.

1.107

The international responsibility of the abducting state entails its obligation to make reparation, in accordance with the fundamental rule of customary international law codified in article 31 of the International Law Commission (ILC)'s Articles on Responsibility of States for Internationally Wrongful Acts. Pursuant to this obligation, in accordance with article 35 of the Articles, the abducting state is 'under an obligation to make restitution, that is, to re-establish the situation which existed before the wrongful act was committed,' provided and to the extent that restitution is not materially impossible and does not involve a burden out of all proportion to the benefit deriving from restitution instead of compensation. In a case of international abduction, where the provisos in article 35 are not relevant, it is incumbent on the abducting state to return the suspect to the state from whose territory he or she was abducted should the latter invoke the former's responsibility.[177] But the territorial state need not insist on the abductee's return.

1.108

---

[176] As regards the latter, the European Commission of Human Rights held in *Stocké v Federal Republic of Germany*, 95 ILR 327, 332, para 168 (1989) that '[i]n the case of collusion between State authorities...and a private individual for the purpose of returning against his will a person living abroad, without the consent of his State of residence, to its territory where he is prosecuted, the [colluding State] incurs responsibility for the acts of the private individual who *de facto* acts on its behalf'. This statement should be read as reflecting the rule on the attribution of private conduct to a state codified since *Stocké* in art 8 of the ILC's Articles on Responsibility of States for Internationally Wrongful Acts, GA res 56/83, Annex, 12 December 2001. Article 8 provides: 'The conduct of a person or group of persons shall be considered an act of a State under international law if the person or group of persons is in fact acting on the instructions of, or under the direction or control of, that State in carrying out the conduct.'

[177] See eg, *a contrario*, *The Savarkar Case (France v Great Britain)*, Hague Court Reports 275, 279 (PCA 1911). See also Inter-American Juridical Committee, *Opinion on the international legality of United States Supreme Court case #91-712*, 15 August 1992, OAS doc CJI/res II-15/92, paras 10–12. See too the UK law officers' opinion of 31 May 1860, in A McNair (ed), *International Law Opinions. Volume I. Peace* (Cambridge: Cambridge University Press, 1956), 78–9; Argentina's initial request for the return of Adolf Eichmann as appropriate reparation for his abduction from Argentine territory by agents of the State of Israel, *Ybk UN 1960*, 196; and the position adopted by Canada in *United States v Alvarez-Machain*, Brief of the Government of Canada as *Amicus Curiae* in Support of the Respondent, reproduced 31 ILM 919, 924 (1992), speaking of 'the understanding in international law that abducted persons must be returned to a nation when it protests the infringement of its sovereignty'.

Nor, in the context of the state-to-state rules on jurisdiction,[178] has the abductee an individual right to be returned.

1.109 In the event, however, that the abducting state fails to surrender the abductee and proceeds to prosecute him or her, it may be the case as a matter of the municipal law of the forum state that the court in question is permitted to try the accused, despite the fact that his or her presence was secured in violation of international law, an approach encapsulated in the maxim *male captus bene detentus*. Within the common-law world, the traditional position has been that, as long as the charge is *bona fide*, a criminal court has jurisdiction to try the accused if the accused is present before the court, regardless of how that presence was secured. Moreover, the jurisdiction of the modern criminal courts is established by statute, and most courts of the common-law tradition are obliged to give effect to the unambiguous words of statute even where these conflict with international law. The upshot of these principles is that the criminal courts are permitted, as a matter of municipal law, to try the accused even when his or her presence before the court has been secured contrary to international law.[179] At the same time, it may, depending on the state in question, be open to the court to decline to exercise the jurisdiction it enjoys, in the exercise of its inherent jurisdiction to remedy abuse of its process.[180] Of the civil law states, France, by way of example, similarly adopts the *male captus bene detentus* approach,[181] as has Germany in the past.[182] On the other hand, the position under the Roman–Dutch common law of South Africa, the jurisdictional limitations recognized by which are considered not to have been abrogated by the statutory jurisdiction of the courts, is that the criminal courts lack jurisdiction to try the accused where his or her presence has been secured in violation of international law.[183] As for international law itself, it would appear that prosecution consequent on abduction in violation of another state's exclusive enforcement jurisdiction within its own territory does not constitute a second international wrong on the part of the prosecuting state over and above that constituted by the abduction. That is, international law does not appear to prohibit such prosecution.[184]

---

[178] But cf, as discussed below, international human rights law.
[179] This was famously highlighted in *Eichmann* (n 91), 59–70, paras 41–49 and *Eichmann* (n 92), 306–7, para 13, as well as in *United States v Alvarez-Machain*, 95 ILR 355, 359 (US 1992).
[180] See eg *R v Horseferry Road Magistrates' Court, Ex parte Bennett*, 95 ILR 380 (UK 1993), not itself a case involving abduction, but see dicta by Lord Bridge, ibid, 395 and 398–9, and Lord Lowry, ibid, 408, referring specifically to abduction by the executive in violation of international law. Note, however, that in certain states the exercise of a jurisdiction enjoyed by the criminal courts is mandatory, not discretionary.
[181] See eg *Re Argoud*, 45 ILR 90 (France 1964).
[182] See eg the decisions of the Federal Constitutional Court of 2 August 1984, [1984] NStZ 563, and 30 May 1985, [1985] NStZ 464. More recent dicta suggest, however, that the approach may change in the future. See the decision of the Federal Constitutional Court of 5 November 2003, 109 BVerfGE 13, ILDC 10 (DE 2003), para 54.
[183] See *S v Ebrahim*, 95 ILR 417 (South Africa 1991).
[184] In the great majority of cases, the court's exercise of jurisdiction, based as it is purely on the applicable municipal law, is without regard to any rule of international law for or against. As such, the mere exercise of jurisdiction can provide no evidence one way or the other of an *opinio juris* on the part of the prosecuting state such as might be relevant to the formation of a pertinent customary prohibition. Nor does the reaction to date of other states, be it the state from which the accused was

It is nonetheless crucial to bear in mind that—whatever the municipal or international lawfulness of the trial of an accused brought before the court through the violation of the exclusive enforcement jurisdiction of the territorial state—the abducting state remains bound, as a consequence of that internationally wrongful violation, by the international obligation to return the abductee to the territory from which he or she was abducted. In addition, restitution would seem to imply, in relevant cases, the nullification of the abductee's conviction and consequent criminal record in the abducting state, neither of which would have arisen but for the abduction. 1.110

There is a question as to whether, in addition to being a violation of the exclusive enforcement jurisdiction of the territorial state, abduction without that state's consent constitutes a breach of any extradition treaty as may be in force between the territorial and abducting state. Extradition treaties tend not to state in so many words that action by one party, not consented to by the other, to secure the rendition of a suspect in any manner not in conformity with that treaty amounts to a breach of the treaty. It was on this basis that the US Supreme Court held in 1992 in *United States v Alvarez-Machain* that the US-sponsored abduction of the accused did not constitute a breach of the extant Mexico–United States Extradition Treaty.[185] But the ruling was strenuously protested by Mexico. Moreover, Canada took the view as *amicus curiae* that the abduction of suspects from Canada by US authorities amounted to a breach of the prevailing Canada–United States Extradition Treaty.[186] Either way, it is worth noting that the ICJ held in *Military and Paramilitary Activities in and against Nicaragua* that a state party to a treaty is obliged by customary international law, independently of the terms of the treaty in question, to refrain from acts calculated to defeat the treaty's object and purpose.[187] 1.111

Foreign-state-attributed abduction without the consent of the territorial state has been held additionally to constitute a violation of international human rights law, specifically of the abductee's right to liberty and security of person, insofar as individuals may be deprived of their liberty only in accordance with a procedure prescribed by municipal law, in this case the law not only of the state effecting the deprivation but also of the state in whose territory the initial deprivation occurred,[188] 1.112

---

abducted or, where different, the state of nationality of the accused, point to the existence of a specific customary rule prohibiting, in addition to extraterritorial abduction, the consequent prohibition of the abductee. In the absence of any such prohibition, the prosecuting state is free to exercise within its territory the jurisdiction to enforce otherwise recognized by international law.

[185] See *Alvarez-Machain* (n 179), 363–8.
[186] See *United States v Alvarez-Machain*, Brief of the Government of Canada as *Amicus Curiae* (n 177), 923–4.
[187] *Military and Paramilitary Activities in and against Nicaragua (Nicaragua v United States of America), Merits*, ICJ Rep 1986, 3, 135–8, paras 270–276.
[188] See, in the context of the right to liberty and security of the person embodied in art 5(1) of the European Convention on Human Rights (ECHR), *Stocké* (n 176), 332, para 167: 'Article 5(1) of the Convention requires that any measure depriving a person of his liberty must be in accordance with the domestic law of the High Contracting Party where the deprivation of liberty takes place. Accordingly, a person who is on the territory of a High Contracting Party may only be arrested according to the law of that State. An arrest made by the authorities of one State on the territory of another State, without

and insofar as the security of individuals requires that the deprivation of their liberty not be arbitrary, which it is considered to be in cases where 'the authorities of the State to which the applicant has been transferred have acted extra-territorially in a manner that is inconsistent with the sovereignty of the host State and therefore contrary to international law'.[189]

1.113   The position as regards international abduction without the territorial state's consent is no different in cases where the offence for which the abductee is wanted by the abducting state is one to which the obligation *aut dedere aut judicare* attaches by virtue of a treaty (or, *a fortiori*, where the offence is a customary international crime, in respect of which no such obligation arises).[190] The obligation *aut dedere aut judicare* is without prejudice to, and indeed is premised on, the impermissibility under customary international law of the unilateral exercise of criminal enforcement jurisdiction by one state in the territory of another.

1.114   In cases where an accused's presence is secured through genuinely consensual rendition by the authorities of the territorial state but outside the usual processes of that state's municipal law, no international rule on jurisdiction is violated, so that the detaining state is not obliged, as a function of such a violation, to return the detainee.[191] As for the municipal permissibility of trial in such contexts, the doctrine of *male captus bene detentus* is *a fortiori* applicable to foreign municipal irregularity or illegality.[192]

D. Jurisdiction to Enforce at Sea

(i) High seas

1.115   The flag state's exclusive jurisdiction over ships on the high seas, as recognized by customary international law and codified in article 92(1) of UNCLOS,[193] encompasses criminal enforcement jurisdiction. This means that as a general rule,

---

the prior consent of the State concerned, does not, therefore, only involve the State['s] responsibility vis-à-vis the other State but also affects that person's individual right to security under Article 5(1). The question whether or not the other State claims reparation for violation of its rights under international law is not relevant for the individual right under the Convention.' In the later case of *Öcalan v Turkey*, 156 ILR 30, 65, para 90 (2005), a Grand Chamber of the Court emphasized that the conformity of the deprivation of liberty with the law of the territorial state is a consideration only when that state is a party to the ECHR. The customary international right to liberty and security of the person, in contrast, would recognize no such distinction.

[189] *Öcalan* (n 188), 64, para 85 and 65, para 90, quote at latter.
[190] See eg, by implication from the fact the rule of 'territoriality' of enforcement was applied, *Arrest Warrant* (n 15). But in terms of state practice see the Security Council debates, *Ybk UN 1960*, 196–8, and the resulting SC res 138 (1960), 23 June 1960, in relation to the abduction of Adolf Eichmann, the ambivalence of both of which is explicable in part by reference to Argentina's ultimate non-insistence on its original demand for Eichmann's return. See, in this last regard, the evasive answer of the Argentine representative to the question of the Soviet representative, *Ybk UN 1960*, 197.
[191] See eg *Savarkar* (n 177), 279, although this was a case of *bona fide* mistake.
[192] At the same time, the approach in *Bennett* (n 180) was enunciated by the House of Lords in precisely this context, while the decision of the South African Supreme Court in *Ebrahim* (n 183) was couched in terms applicable to such situations.
[193] Recall *supra* para 1.44.

while a ship is on the high seas, the flag state alone is authorized by international law to stop and board it, to search it, and ultimately to seize it and arrest its crew, including any foreign nationals, with a view to the enforcement of its own or another state's criminal law.[194] This exclusivity of jurisdiction to enforce is subject to the flag state's express consent to the contrary, whether by way of treaty[195] or on an ad hoc basis, as well as to any exceptions provided for by customary international law.

1.116 A longstanding customary exception, now codified in article 105 of UNCLOS, to the flag state's exclusive high-seas criminal enforcement jurisdiction is in relation to the crime of piracy *jure gentium*, in respect of which there exists universal jurisdiction to enforce on the high seas. That is, every state may seize a ship engaged in piracy, arrest its crew, and seize any property on board while that ship is on the high seas.[196] Article 110(1)(*a*) of UNCLOS codifies the further, ancillary right on the part of all states to board any ship on the high seas where there are reasonable grounds to suspect that it is engaged in piracy.[197]

1.117 Article 110(1)(*b*) of UNCLOS, almost certainly reflective of customary international law, embodies a universal high-seas right on the part of states to board a ship where there are reasonable grounds to suspect that the ship is engaged in the slave trade.[198]

1.118 Customary international law, as codified in article 111 of UNCLOS,[199] accords a coastal state a right of 'hot pursuit', which permits the boarding and seizure of a foreign-flagged vessel on the high seas when, in circumstances where the competent authorities of the coastal state have good reason to believe that the vessel has violated that state's laws, the vessel has been pursued without interruption from the coastal state's internal waters or territorial sea.

1.119 In addition to UNCLOS, a variety of other multilateral and bilateral treaties provide for exceptions, usually framed around the explicit consent of the

---

[194] The exclusivity of the flag state's jurisdiction to enforce applies even in respect of collisions and other incidents of navigation, at least as provided for in art 97(3) of UNCLOS and, before it, art 11(3) of the Convention on the High Seas.

[195] In addition to the exceptions discussed in the text, see art 109(4) of UNCLOS, which grants to those states enjoying prescriptive jurisdiction under art 109(3) (recall *supra* n 51) the right to arrest on the high seas a ship, as well as any persons on board, engaged in unauthorized broadcasting and to seize any broadcasting equipment on board. This right is supported by art 110(1)(*c*) of UNCLOS, which grants boarding rights to those states enjoying jurisdiction under art 109 where there are reasonable grounds to suspect that a ship on the high seas is engaged in unauthorized broadcasting.

[196] Article 107 of UNCLOS, restating almost verbatim the rule in art 21 of the Convention on the High Seas, limits the type of ship or aircraft that may be used to effect such seizure, providing that '[a] seizure on account of piracy may be carried out only by warships or military aircraft, or other ships or aircraft clearly marked and identifiable as being on government service and authorized to that effect'. This is consonant with customary international law.

[197] See also Convention on the High Seas, art 22(1)(*a*).

[198] See also ibid, art 22(1)(*b*). Article 110(1) of UNCLOS and art 22(1) of the Convention on the High Seas presuppose that boarding will be carried out by a warship.

[199] See also Convention on the High Seas, art 23. Again, only certain vessels and, in this case, aircraft may be deployed in the exercise of this right, as indicated in UNCLOS, art 111(5) and Convention on the High Seas, art 23(4).

flag state, to the latter's otherwise exclusive high-seas jurisdiction to enforce criminal laws.[200]

(ii) Territorial sea

1.120 Within a coastal state's territorial sea, just as on its *terra firma*, it is the criminal enforcement jurisdiction of that state which—subject to express consent, whether treaty-based or ad hoc, and to any customary exceptions—is exclusive. That is, as a general rule, a coastal state and only that state may stop, board, search, and seize ships and arrest their crew within its territorial sea. This is implicitly recognized in article 2(1) of UNCLOS, which speaks of the 'sovereignty' of a coastal state over its territorial sea.[201]

1.121 An exception to a coastal state's jurisdiction to enforce criminal laws within its territorial sea is specified in article 27(5) of UNCLOS, which provides that 'the coastal State may not take any steps on board a foreign ship passing through the territorial sea to arrest any person or to conduct any investigation in connection with any crime committed before the ship entered the territorial sea, if the ship, proceeding from a foreign port, is only passing through the territorial sea without entering internal waters'.[202]

1.122 An example of an ad hoc exception to the exclusivity of a coastal state's criminal enforcement jurisdiction within its territorial sea is the consent granted by the Transitional Federal Government of Somalia to states co-operating with it, as expressed in, *inter alia*, its letter to the UN Secretary-General referred to in Security Council resolution 1816 (2008),[203] to enter Somali territorial waters for the purpose of repressing acts of piracy and armed robbery at sea.

(iii) Contiguous zone

1.123 Within a band of sea contiguous with its territorial sea known as its 'contiguous zone', extending not more than 24 nautical miles from the baselines from which the breadth of its territorial sea is measured,[204] a coastal state is permitted by customary international law and article 33(1) of UNCLOS to exercise the control necessary to prevent and to punish the commission within its territory or territorial sea of infringements of its customs, fiscal, immigration or sanitary laws and regulations.[205]

---

[200] See eg Convention against Illicit Traffic in Narcotic Drugs and Psychotropic Substances 1988, art 17(3), (4), (6), and (7); 2005 SUA Convention, art 8*bis*(5)–(7); Council of Europe Agreement on Illicit Traffic by Sea, arts 7–10.

[201] See also Convention on the Territorial Sea and Contiguous Zone 1958, art 1(1).

[202] See also ibid, art 19(5). For a range of purely hortatory treaty-based exceptions, see UNCLOS, art 27(1) and Convention on the Territorial Sea and Contiguous Zone, art 19(1). For the strictly hortatory character of art 27(1) of UNCLOS, see eg *Prosecutor v TP*, ILDC 1498 (GR 2003) (Greece).

[203] See SC res 1816 (2008), 2 June 2008, preamble (eleventh recital).

[204] See UNCLOS, art 33(2), as consonant with customary international law. Since the vast majority of states have, as permitted by UNCLOS, declared a 12-nautical-mile territorial sea, the width of the contiguous zone from the outer limit of a state's territorial sea is usually not more than 12 nautical miles.

[205] See also Convention on the Territorial Sea and Contiguous Zone, art 24(1).

(iv) EEZ and continental shelf

In accordance with article 73(1) of UNCLOS and customary international law, a coastal state may take such measures in its exclusive economic zone, 'including boarding, inspection, [and] arrest', as may be necessary to ensure compliance with the fisheries laws and regulations adopted by it in relation to its EEZ.[206] 1.124

The exclusive jurisdiction granted to a coastal state over artificial islands, installations, and structures in its EEZ and on its continental shelf[207] extends to the jurisdiction to enforce criminal law. 1.125

V. Conclusion

The international rules on national criminal jurisdiction are not difficult to grasp, provided that certain distinctions, chief among them the distinction between jurisdiction to prescribe and jurisdiction to enforce, are kept in mind. An appreciation of these rules is an essential element of the conceptual background to the notion of international crimes and the rights and obligations of states in relation to their suppression. 1.126

Further Reading

CRAWFORD, J, *Brownlie's Principles of Public International Law* (8th edn, Oxford: Oxford University Press, 2012), chapter XXI

GRYMANELI, A, 'La compétence des tribunaux internes en matière de piraterie' in ED Papastavridis and KN Trapp (eds), *La criminalité en mer/Crimes at Sea* (Leiden: Martinus Nijhoff, 2014), 199

GUILFOYLE, D, *Shipping Interdiction and the Law of the Sea* (Cambridge: Cambridge University Press, 2009)

HUANG, Y, 'Universal Jurisdiction over Piracy and East Asian Practice' (2012) 11 *Chinese Journal of International Law* 623

INTERNATIONAL BAR ASSOCIATION (LEGAL PRACTICE DIVISION), *Report of the Task Force on Extraterritorial Jurisdiction*, 28 September 2008, 133–99

LIIVOJA, R, 'Service Jurisdiction under International Law' (2010) 11 *Melbourne Journal of International Law* 309

LOWE, AV and STAKER, C, 'Jurisdiction', in MD Evans (ed), *International Law* (3rd edn, Oxford: Oxford University Press, 2010), chapter 11

NICHOLLS, C, MONTGOMERY, C, KNOWLES, JB, DOOBAY, A and SUMMERS, M, *Nicholls, Montgomery, and Knowles on the Law of Extradition and Mutual Assistance* (3rd edn, Oxford: Oxford University Press, 2013)

---

[206] In accordance with art 73(2) of UNCLOS, the coastal state must promptly release arrested vessels and their crews on the posting of a reasonable bond or other security. Article 73(4) specifies as regards the arrest or detention of foreign vessels that the coastal state is promptly to notify the flag state of the action taken and of any penalties imposed.

[207] See UNCLOS, arts 60(2) and 80, as consonant with customary international law.

O'Keefe, R, 'Domestic Courts as Agents of Development of the International Law of Jurisdiction' (2013) 26 *Leiden Journal of International Law* 541

O'Keefe, R, 'Universal Jurisdiction: Clarifying the Basic Concept' (2004) 2 *Journal of International Criminal Justice* 735

Reydams, L, *Universal Jurisdiction. International and Municipal Legal Perspectives* (Oxford: Oxford University Press, 2003)

Ryngaert, C, *Jurisdiction in International Law* (Oxford: Oxford University Press, 2008)

Trapp, KN, 'La criminalité en mer: l'approche du droit international' in ED Papastavridis and KN Trapp (eds), *La criminalité en mer/Crimes at Sea* (Leiden: Martinus Nijhoff, 2014), 53

2
The Concept of an International Crime

I. Introduction

International crimes occupy a central place in international criminal law, yet there is no agreement as to what is meant by an 'international crime'. No common understanding, let alone common definition of the concept exists. Although the practical consequences of the lack of agreement as to the notion of an international crime are not great,[1] it is almost self-evidently in the interests of a discipline to adopt a standard conceptual framework and terminology. This chapter offers such a framework and terminology in respect of international crimes. The concept of an international crime put forward is not unitary. Rather, the genus 'international crime' is divided into species. The nomenclature suggested extends to these taxonomic divisions. 2.1

One of the species of international crime gives rise to the criminal responsibility of the individual perpetrator under international law itself, rather than merely (and even then only indirectly) to the perpetrator's criminal responsibility under national law alone. The phenomenon of individual criminal responsibility under international law[2] sets this subset of international crimes apart from the general 2.2

---

[1] Indeed, international criminal law has muddled through so far with no common understanding to this effect.

[2] It is sometimes mistakenly implied that the term 'individual criminal responsibility' as used in international law refers generically to the various 'modes' of criminal responsibility recognized by customary international law, such as commission, ordering, aiding and abetting, and so on (see *infra* chapter 5), rather than more fundamentally to the conceptual possibility in the first place that individuals, in contradistinction and in addition to states, can bear legal responsibility under public international law (a responsibility conceived of as criminal in the case of individuals). See eg G Werle and F Jessburger, *Principles of International Criminal Law* (3rd edn, Oxford: Oxford University Press, 2014), 32, para 93 note 176, 42, paras 119–120, and 192–220, paras 508–577 and G Werle, 'General Principles of International Criminal Law' in A Cassese (ed), *The Oxford Companion to International Criminal Justice* (Oxford: Oxford University Press, 2009) 54, 58–9; A Cassese, *International Criminal Law* (2nd edn, Oxford: Oxford University Press, 2008), 33–5 (a passage not reproduced in the third edition); G Boas *et al*, *International Criminal Law Practitioner Library, Volume I: Forms of Responsibility in International Criminal Law* (Cambridge: Cambridge University Press, 2007), 4–5. See also the heading of art 3 of the Statute of the Special Tribunal for Lebanon, UN doc S/RES/1757 (30 May 2007), Annex, attachment. The assumption seems to be that the word 'individual' is intended not to counterpose individual criminal responsibility under international law to state responsibility but to stress the focus on the responsibility of the particular individual on trial for his or her discrete role in what is often, criminologically rather juridically speaking, collective criminality. In other words, the expression 'individual criminal responsibility' is confused with the concept of personal culpability. The confusion would appear to stem from

body of public international law, the breach of whose rules gives rise only to the delictual responsibility of any state in breach. This chapter analyses the history of the evolution of individual criminal responsibility under international law before examining both the relationship between such responsibility and state responsibility and the theoretical source of the binding nature for individuals of this species of international crime.

II. The Concept and Definition of an 'International Crime'

A. International 'Crime'

2.3 The 'crime' aspect of an international crime is unproblematic. But it is worth explaining for the avoidance of doubt.

2.4 The term 'crime' (synonymously, 'offence') formally denotes a legal rule the violation of which results in the liability of the violator to punishment, usually but not necessarily by way of imprisonment, fine, forfeiture or a combination of the three.[3] The term is also used in a second, slightly different sense to refer to the conduct violative of the legal rule in question, namely the act of murder, the act of robbery, and so on. In this second way, it is said that people commit the crime of murder, the crime of robbery, etc.

---

the fact that the common first and third paragraphs of art 7 ('Individual criminal responsibility') of the Statute of the International Criminal Tribunal for the former Yugoslavia ('ICTY Statute'), of art 6 ('Individual criminal responsibility') of the Statute of the International Criminal Tribunal for Rwanda ('ICTR Statute'), and of art 6 ('Individual criminal responsibility') of the Statute of the Special Court for Sierra Leone ('SCSL Statute') deal with modes of responsibility, while the same is the case for para 3 of art 25 ('Individual criminal responsibility') of the Rome Statute of the International Criminal Court ('Rome Statute'). The more basic gist, however, of common para 1 of art 7 of the ICTY Statute, of art 6 of the ICTR Statute, and of art 6 of the SCSL Statute is that a person who participates in a crime within the relevant body's jurisdiction 'shall be individually responsible for the crime', the phrase 'individually responsible' being used in implicit contradistinction to the responsibility of any relevant state. The theme is maintained in common para 2 of each article, which provides that '[t]he official position of any accused person, whether as Head of State or Government or as a responsible Government official, shall not relieve such person of criminal responsibility', as well as in common para 4, which provides that '[t]he fact that an accused person acted pursuant to an order of a Government or of a superior shall not relieve him of criminal responsibility'. As for the rubric of art 25 of the Rome Statute, this derives from the statement in art 25(2), again directed towards the contrast with international law's usual provision for state responsibility, that '[a] person who commits a crime within the jurisdiction of the Court shall be individually responsible and liable for [sic] punishment'. Article 25(3), which spells out the various modes of criminal responsibility under the Statute, does not use the term 'individually responsible', since the contrast with state responsibility is not the essence of the paragraph, but simply 'criminally responsible'. For a conceptually sophisticated use of the term 'individual criminal responsibility' that marries the two understandings, see E van Sliedregt, *Individual Criminal Responsibility in International Law* (Oxford: Oxford University Press, 2012).

[3] As a matter of natural English usage, however, not every rule whose breach is punishable is termed a crime. There is a vast array of regulatory provisions in primary and secondary legislation whose breach results in a sanction, most commonly a fine, but we tend to use more neutral terms like 'breach', 'violation' or 'infringement' for such breaches, seemingly as a reflection of their perceived moral neutrality.

A crime amounts in substance to a legal obligation, punishable in the event of its 2.5
breach, in respect of given conduct, whether that obligation be negative (that is, a
prohibition on such conduct) or, in the case of crimes of omission, positive (that is,
a duty to perform that conduct). In practice, however, crimes are rarely phrased as
prohibitions or duties. Instead, formulations commonly found in municipal legislation include '[given conduct] constitutes an offence', '[given conduct] is punishable by [given penalty]',[4] and the like.

Crimes are to be distinguished from delicts (in common-law parlance, torts), 2.6
the commission of which gives rise to a secondary obligation on the part of the
author to make reparation to any injured party, frequently in the form of the payment of compensation.

Positive international law does not recognize the criminal responsibility of 2.7
states.[5] The term 'international crime' is reserved for offences resulting in the criminal responsibility of individuals.[6]

It is the explicit provision for individual criminal responsibility that distin- 2.8
guishes international criminal law from international human rights law and from
the main body of international humanitarian law (or the law of armed conflict).[7]

---

[4] This second formula is not presently found in international law. Neither customary international law nor those treaties providing for international crimes currently lays down specific penalties for such offences.

[5] It was formerly asserted that, in addition to their traditional delictual responsibility, states were capable of criminal responsibility under international law, as distinct from the individual criminal responsibility of their officials. See eg H Lauterpacht, *International Law and Human Rights* (London: Stevens, 1950), 43. The proposition found its most famous expression in draft art 19(2) of the International Law Commission (ILC)'s Draft Articles on State Responsibility, as they then were, as provisionally adopted on first reading in 1996, *Ybk ILC 1996*, vol II/2, 58. But in the ILC's Articles on Responsibility of States for Internationally Wrongful Acts, GA res 56/83, 12 December 2001, Annex ('Articles on Responsibility of States'), as finally adopted on second reading, state criminal responsibility as such has been rejected, even if traces of the idea can be detected in the concept of 'serious breaches of obligations under peremptory norms of general international law' in arts 40 and 41 of the Articles. In *Application of the Convention on the Prevention and Punishment of the Crime of Genocide (Bosnia and Herzegovina v Serbia and Montenegro), Merits, Judgment*, ICJ Rep 2007, 43, 114, para 167 and 115, para 170, the International Court of Justice (ICJ) affirmed that the responsibility of states is not of a criminal character. See J Crawford, 'International Crimes of States' in J Crawford, A Pellet, and S Olleson (eds), *The Law of International Responsibility* (Oxford: Oxford University Press, 2010), 405. In short, state responsibility is for now formally limited to delictual responsibility—that is, to responsibility giving rise to the secondary obligation to make reparation.

[6] But cf 'international crime', referring rhetorically to a particularly grave violation of international law by a state, as used in certain international instruments of the inter-War period. See Draft Treaty of Mutual Assistance, art 1, LNOJ Spec Supp No 16 (1923), 203; Protocol for the Pacific Settlement of International Disputes, Geneva, 2 October 1924, preamble (third recital), LNOJ Spec Supp No 23 (1924), 498; League of Nations Assembly Declaration concerning Wars of Aggression, 24 September 1927, preamble (third recital), LNOJ Spec Supp No 53 (1927), 22; Resolution on Aggression, Sixth International Conference of American States, Havana, 28 February 1928, in J Brown Scott (ed), *The International Conferences of American States 1889–1928* (New York: Oxford University Press, 1931), 441.

[7] Conceptual clarity in this regard is scarcely fostered by much of the academic literature, the language of which consistently blurs the distinctions between these respective bodies of public international law. See eg, as regards international criminal law and international human rights law, the title of SR Ratner, JS Abrams, and JL Bischoff, *Accountability for Human Rights Atrocities in International Law. Beyond the Nuremberg Legacy* (3rd edn, Oxford: Oxford University Press, 2009) and especially the title of its first chapter, namely 'Individual Accountability for Human Rights Abuses…'. See,

50   Foundational Concepts and Principles

While there is obvious factual overlap between international criminal law and international human rights law,[8] conduct by an individual not in accordance with an international human right guaranteed by treaty or customary international law can give rise under international law, if to anything, only to the delictual responsibility of any state to which the conduct of that individual is attributable,[9] not to the criminal responsibility of the individual himself or herself; and to the extent that both bodies of international law may oblige states to criminalize conduct as a matter of municipal law, only international criminal law does so expressly and provides a definition of the offence.[10] As for international humanitarian law, this intersects with international criminal law insofar as certain breaches of its rules, namely war crimes, implicate the individual criminal responsibility of the perpetrator.[11] But not every violation of international humanitarian law is punishable as a war crime. Many implicate only state responsibility.

B. 'International' Crime

2.9   The requisite 'international' element is where the concept of an international crime becomes disputed.

2.10   Consider—by way of more or less random and representative example of candidates for the label 'international crime'—crimes against humanity, the crime of piracy *jure gentium*, and the crime of torture as provided for in the Convention against Torture and Other Cruel, Inhuman or Degrading Treatment or Punishment 1984 ('Torture Convention'). A crime against humanity gives rise to the criminal responsibility of the perpetrator under customary international law. Putting it another way, customary international law itself embodies a prohibition on conduct amounting to a crime against humanity, as customarily defined.[12]

---

similarly, the title of chapter 5 ('Crimes Against Fundamental Human Rights') of MC Bassiouni (ed), *International Criminal Law. Volume I: Sources, Subjects, and Contents* (3rd edn, Leiden: Martinus Nijhoff, 2008).

[8] In addition, to the extent that international criminal law imposes international legal obligations on individuals, both regimes conceive of the individual as an international legal person.

[9] For the international rules on the attribution of conduct to a state, see Articles on Responsibility of States, arts 4–11.

[10] Certain international human rights guarantees effectively oblige states to criminalize certain conduct under their municipal law. For example, the right to life implies that a state will criminalize murder, while the right not to be tortured implies that a state will outlaw torture. See eg A Huneeus, 'International Criminal Law by Other Means: The Quasi-criminal Jurisdiction of the Human Rights Courts' (2013) 107 *AJIL* 1. But the obligation to criminalize such conduct is not evident on the face of the international rule. Nor is the conduct to be criminalized defined under international law.

[11] Note that, despite the full names of the International Criminal Tribunal for the former Yugoslavia ('International Tribunal for the Prosecution of Persons Responsible for Serious Violations of International Humanitarian Law…') and the International Criminal Tribunal for Rwanda ('International Criminal Tribunal for the Prosecution of Persons Responsible for Genocide and Other Serious Violations of International Humanitarian Law…'), genocide and crimes against humanity—both prosecutable before these tribunals—do not, terminologically speaking, form part of international humanitarian law. Of the offences within the jurisdiction of the two tribunals, only war crimes fall under this heading. All three offences, however, form part of international criminal law.

[12] Other examples of this sort of offence include war crimes, genocide, and aggression as crimes under customary international law.

In addition, according to the empirically more persuasive and conceptually more coherent view, customary international law permits states to assert universal prescriptive jurisdiction over crimes against humanity.[13] On the other hand, the crime of piracy *jure gentium* does not give rise to criminal responsibility under customary international law. That is, customary international law does not itself embody a prohibition on piracy.[14] What it posits, rather, is merely a special jurisdictional rule permitting each state to apply its municipal criminal law on the basis of universality to conduct amounting to piracy as defined by customary international law—in other words, to assert universal prescriptive jurisdiction over the crime of piracy *jure gentium*.[15] In the final analysis, the pirate's criminal responsibility is a function of municipal law alone. Nor, thirdly, does the crime of torture provided for by the Torture Convention give rise to criminal responsibility under international law, in this case treaty. The Convention merely obliges each state party, *inter alia*, to 'ensure that all acts of torture [as defined in article 1] are offences under its criminal law' and to 'take such measures as may be necessary to establish its jurisdiction over [such acts]' on a range of specific jurisdictional bases, including universality.[16] In the event, the criminal responsibility of the torturer is embodied solely in the respective bodies of municipal law of the states parties to the Convention.[17] Now, there is a very respectable body of scholarly opinion which restricts the use of the term 'international crime' to the first type of offence, namely to those offences giving rise to criminal responsibility under international law itself.[18] But other,

---

[13] Some scholars further assert, although the assertion is at present unsustainable, that customary international law obliges states to prosecute such crimes or to hand suspects over to a state that will.

[14] See eg Harvard Law School Research in International Law, 'Piracy' (1932) 26 *AJIL Supp* 739, 755–60; I Brownlie, *Principles of Public International Law* (7th edn, Oxford: Oxford University Press, 2008), 306, especially note 47; P Gaeta, 'International Criminalization of Prohibited Conduct' in A Cassese (ed), *The Oxford Companion to International Criminal Justice* (Oxford: Oxford University Press, 2009) 63, 63; Werle and Jessburger (n 2), 49, para 133; K Parlett, *The Individual in the International Legal System: Continuity and Change in International Law* (Cambridge: Cambridge University Press, 2011), 232; A Cassese and P Gaeta, *Cassese's International Criminal Law* (3rd edn, Oxford: Oxford University Press, 2013), 19. But cf H Kelsen, 'Collective and Individual Responsibility in International Law with Particular Regard to the Punishment of War Criminals' (1943) 31 *Cal LR* 530, 534–5.

[15] It is important to appreciate that the question is not whether international law permits states to criminalize certain conduct. Each state, as an inherent incident of its sovereignty, is entitled to criminalize whatever it chooses (within the bounds of international human rights law), as long as it does so pursuant to jurisdictional bases recognized by international law. The question, rather, is whether international law permits states to criminalize given conduct on an extraordinary jurisdictional basis—that is, on a jurisdictional basis not otherwise lawful under customary international law, such as universality, as in the example of piracy *jure gentium*.

[16] See Torture Convention, arts 4(1), 5(1) (various jurisdictional bases), and 5(2) (universality). Allied to these obligations is the obligation undertaken by a state party, in the event that a suspected torturer is found in its territory, to submit the case to its competent authorities for the purpose of prosecution or to extradite the suspect to a state willing to prosecute him or her, as per Torture Convention, art 7(1).

[17] Other crimes of this sort are provided for in a raft of international conventions in the field of international criminal law. See *infra* chapters 7 and 8.

[18] See eg Cassese and Gaeta (n 14), 18–21; R Cryer, 'International Criminal Law' in MD Evans (ed), *International Law* (3rd edn, Oxford: Oxford University Press, 2010) 752, 753 (but see *infra* n 19); Brownlie (n 14), 587–604; H Ascensio, E Decaux, and A Pellet, 'Présentation de la première partie: Essai de classification et principe de légalité' in H Ascensio, E Decaux, and A Pellet (eds), *Droit*

equally eminent scholars include both categories of offence under the rubric 'international crimes', namely those which give rise to criminal responsibility under international law itself and those which do not.[19]

2.11 The major international instruments and documents of relevance provide no real guidance on point,[20] although very tentative support for the inclusive approach to

international pénal (2nd edn, Paris: Pedone, 2012) 93, 94, para 5 and 95, para 7; *Immunity of State officials from foreign criminal jurisdiction. Memorandum by the Secretariat*, UN doc A/CN.4/596 (31 March 2008), 16, para 12.

[19] See eg Y Dinstein, 'International Criminal Law' (1985) 20 *Israel LR* 206, 221–2; EM Wise, 'International Crimes and Domestic Criminal Law' (1989) 38 *DePaul LR* 923, 932; S Rosenne, 'War Crimes and State Responsibility' in Y Dinstein and M Tabory (eds), *War Crimes in International Law* (The Hague: Martinus Nijhoff, 1996) 65, 67–8; B Swart, 'International Crimes: Present Situation and Future Developments' in Association internationale de droit pénal, *International Criminal Law: Quo Vadis?* (Nouvelles études pénales No 19, 2004) 201, 201–2; MC Bassiouni, 'International Crimes: The Ratione Materiae [sic] of International Criminal Law' in MC Bassiouni (ed), *International Criminal Law. Volume I: Sources, Subjects, and Contents* (3rd edn, Leiden: Martinus Nijhoff, 2008) 129; C Van den Wyngaert (ed), *International Criminal Law: A Collection of International and European Instruments* (2nd edn, The Hague: Kluwer Law International, 2000), listing both types of crime under the heading 'International Crimes'; R Cryer, 'The Doctrinal Foundations of International Criminalization' in MC Bassiouni (ed), *International Criminal Law. Volume I: Sources, Subjects, and Contents* (3rd edn, Leiden: Martinus Nijhoff, 2008) 107, 107–8 and 110; Gaeta (n 14), 65–6; Ratner, Abrams, and Bischoff (n 7), 12; Werle and Jessburger (n 2), 45–6, paras 125–126 and 128; I Bantekas, *International Criminal Law* (4th edn, Oxford: Hart Publishing, 2010), 8–9.

[20] The Charter of the International Military Tribunal, Nuremberg ('Nuremberg Charter') (although cf earlier drafts), the Charter of the International Military Tribunal for the Far East ('Tokyo Charter'), and Law No 10 (20 December 1945) of the Allied Control Council for Germany ('Control Council Law No 10') make no reference to international law, let alone to international crimes, whereas General Assembly resolution 95 (I) ('Affirmation of the Principles of International Law recognized by the Charter of the Nürnberg Tribunal'), 11 December 1946, refers only to 'crimes against the peace and security of mankind'. Both the immediately subsequent General Assembly resolution 96 (I) ('The Crime of Genocide'), 11 December 1946, and the ILC's later Principles of International Law Recognized in the Charter of the Nürnberg Tribunal and in the Judgment of the Tribunal, *Ybk ILC 1950*, vol II, 191 ('ILC Nürnberg Principles'), deal only with offences clearly giving rise to individual criminal responsibility under international law itself, for which they use the more precise term 'crimes under international law'. The same goes for the Convention on the Prevention and Punishment of the Crime of Genocide 1948 ('Genocide Convention') and, at least purportedly, the Convention on the Suppression and Punishment of the Crime of Apartheid 1973 ('Apartheid Convention'). As for the numerous other international criminal conventions, none of these uses either 'international crime' or 'crime under international law'. For its part, the ICTY Statute uses only the (inaccurate) phrase 'serious violations of international humanitarian law', as does the ICTR Statute. The preamble to the ILC's Draft Statute for an International Criminal Court, *Ybk ILC 1994*, vol II/2, 26, para 91 ('ILC Draft Statute'), refers to the crimes within the proposed court's jurisdiction as 'crimes of international concern' and as 'the most serious crimes of concern to the international community as a whole', while art 20(*e*) speaks similarly of 'exceptionally serious crimes of international concern'. In turn, the preamble to the Rome Statute speaks twice of the crimes within the Court's jurisdiction as 'the most serious crimes of concern to the international community as a whole', while art 1 refers to 'the most serious crimes of international concern'. The term 'international crimes' does, however, make an appearance in the sixth recital of the preamble to the Statute, which recalls that 'it is the duty of every State to exercise its criminal jurisdiction over those responsible for international crimes'; but the reference merely begs the question, since a state may exercise its criminal jurisdiction as much in respect of crimes which, while defined by international law (eg in the Rome Statute itself), are ultimately prohibited under municipal law alone as in respect of crimes giving rise to criminal responsibility under international law itself and additionally enacted into the state's municipal criminal law. Indeed, it has been suggested that what the drafters of the Rome Statute had in mind in the sixth preambular recital was certain crimes not falling within the jurisdiction of the ICC, chief among them the treaty crime of drug-trafficking and the treaty-based range of what might loosely be called 'terrorist' offences, only

the concept of an international crime can be drawn from the commentary to the International Law Commission (ILC)'s Draft Statute for an International Criminal Court (1994).[21]

The inclusive approach finds a degree of judicial endorsement, both international and national. In *Questions relating to the Obligation to Prosecute or Extradite*, the International Court of Justice (ICJ) speaks of the 'many international conventions for the combating of international crimes',[22] clearly encompassing within the term 'international crimes' a range of offences which do not give rise to criminal responsibility under international law but, rather, which international law, in the form of the 'many international conventions' alluded to, defines and directs states to criminalize and establish jurisdiction over on extraordinary bases. Similarly, in their joint separate opinion in *Arrest Warrant*, Judges Higgins, Kooijmans, and Buergenthal refer to 'international treaty obligations to make certain international crimes offences also in national law'[23] before surveying an extensive range of treaties, many of them establishing offences which do not give rise to criminal responsibility under international law.[24] Judges Higgins, Kooijmans, and Buergenthal also seem, at least by implication, to include piracy within the concept of an international crime.[25] Judge ad hoc Van den Wyngaert, in her dissenting opinion in the same case, gives the Convention for the Suppression of Unlawful Seizure of Aircraft 1970 and the Torture Convention as examples of 'international crimes'.[26] The former may or may not provide for criminal responsibility under international law, while the latter clearly does not. As for the national level, in *Pinochet (No 1)*, for example, Lords Slynn and Steyn include within their respective understandings of the term 'international crimes' the offences specified in the Convention against the Taking of Hostages 1979 and in the Torture

2.12

---

some of which give only possible rise to individual criminal responsibility under international law. See M Bergsmo and O Triffterer, 'Preamble' in O Triffterer (ed), *Commentary on the Rome Statute of the International Criminal Court* (2nd edn, Munich: CH Beck/Hart, 2008) 1, 11, para 17; Werle and Jessburger (n 2), 45, para 125 note 254.

[21] The ILC Draft Statute—which, in addition to the major crimes under customary international law, vested the proposed court with jurisdiction *ratione materiae* over a range of crimes created by multilateral convention—included within the court's jurisdiction offences, such as torture as provided for in the Torture Convention, which clearly do not give rise to criminal responsibility under international law. All these offences are referred to in the draft preamble as 'crimes of international concern'; but the occasional reference in the ILC's commentary to 'international crimes', as distinct from 'crimes under customary international law' as also used in the commentary in specific circumstances, seems to imply that the former label encompasses both those crimes defined by international law which give rise to criminal responsibility under international law itself and those which do not.

[22] *Questions relating to the Obligation to Prosecute or Extradite (Belgium v Senegal), Judgment*, ICJ Rep 2012, 422, 451, para 75. But cf ibid, 477, para 27 (sep op Abraham), where Judge Abraham describes his use of the term 'international crimes' as 'for convenience' and as notwithstanding his doubts as to its legal relevance.

[23] *Arrest Warrant of 11 April 2000 (Democratic Republic of the Congo v Belgium)*, ICJ Rep 2002, 3, 69, para 20 (joint sep op Higgins, Kooijmans, and Buergenthal). See also, similarly, ibid, 76, para 46, 78–9, para 51, 80, para 58, 85, para 73, and 86–7, para 79 (joint sep op Higgins, Kooijmans, and Buergenthal).

[24] Ibid, 71–4, paras 27–39 (joint sep op Higgins, Kooijmans, and Buergenthal).

[25] Ibid, 74, para 39 and 81, para 61 (joint sep op Higgins, Kooijmans, and Buergenthal).

[26] Ibid, 174–5, paras 60–62 (diss op Van den Wyngaert), referring to Convention for the Suppression of Unlawful Seizure of Aircraft 1970 ('Hague Convention') and the Torture Convention.

Convention,[27] while in *Pinochet (No 3)* Lords Browne-Wilkinson and Hutton each refer to both torture under customary international law and torture as provided for in the Torture Convention as 'international crimes',[28] Lords Browne-Wilkinson and Millet each refer to piracy under this rubric,[29] and Lord Phillips recounts how states have, 'on occasion, agreed by conventions, that their national courts should enjoy jurisdiction to prosecute for a particular category of international crime'.[30]

2.13   Nor is the inclusive usage of the term 'international crime' unprincipled or devoid of merit—indeed, quite the opposite.

2.14   First, despite formal distinctions, there is no compelling semantic or logical reason why each of the three offences considered above (*viz* crimes against humanity, piracy *jure gentium*, and torture pursuant to the Torture Convention) should not be termed an 'international' crime in that each is defined by international law.[31]

2.15   Secondly, in practical terms, what unites those offences which give rise to criminal responsibility under international law and those which, while defined by international law, merely implicate national criminalization is as significant as what divides them. Perhaps most importantly, the fact that it gives rise to criminal responsibility under customary international law or treaty is not a prerequisite for the prosecution of an offence before an international criminal court. No international criminal court is possessed of an inherent jurisdiction *ratione materiae* or an inherent applicable law, and even less would either be limited in principle to international law—that is, to crimes in respect of which international law itself embodies a prohibition or, in the case of culpable omissions, imposes a duty. An international criminal court, like any international court, exercises only the subject-matter jurisdiction accorded it by its constituent instrument, and this instrument can vest the court with jurisdiction over whichever offences the states establishing the court so wish. The same goes, *mutatis mutandis*, for the distinct question of the court's applicable law. The states establishing the court can authorize it to apply whichever law they choose.[32] Indeed, the court's applicable law may include, or may in the first instance consist of or even be limited to, its own statute, which will define the relevant crimes. In this way, the court's statute may itself be effectively constitutive, as a substantive matter, of the crimes it has jurisdiction to try, with no recourse to freestanding customary international law

---

[27] *R v Bow Street Metropolitan Stipendiary Magistrate, Ex parte Pinochet Ugarte*, 119 ILR 50, 65 and 70 (Lord Slynn), 105 (Lord Steyn) (UK 1998).

[28] *R v Bow Street Metropolitan Stipendiary Magistrate, Ex parte Pinochet Ugarte (No 3)*, 119 ILR 135, 140, 148–52, and 155–6 (Lord Brown-Wilkinson), 215 and 217 (Lord Hutton) (UK 1999).

[29] Ibid, 148 (Lord Brown-Wilkinson), 230 (Lord Millet).

[30] Ibid, 243 (Lord Phillips).

[31] Each can also be considered a 'crime' in that it makes express provision one way or another for the criminal responsibility of the perpetrator.

[32] The ILC Draft Statute is an unambiguous case in point. Article 20(*e*) of the Draft Statute proposed to grant the court jurisdiction *ratione materiae* not only over offences for which there is clearly individual criminal responsibility under international law but also over a range of treaty offences which states parties to the respective treaties are merely obliged to criminalize under their municipal law, and these treaties formed part of the proposed court's applicable law in accordance with art 33. Nor was it on such grounds that the ILC eventually ruled out vesting the Court with jurisdiction over piracy.

or treaty being necessary.[33] In short, then, whether or not a crime gives rise to criminal responsibility under international law is immaterial to whether it can be tried by an international criminal court.[34] Similarly, in terms of their suppression at the national level, there is little to distinguish a crime defined by international law for which there is criminal responsibility under international law from one for which there is not.[35] Constitutional principle requires most states either to enact legislation when providing in their municipal law for crimes, a requirement that is without regard to the existence of criminal responsibility or otherwise under international law, or, in the absence of specific legislation and where feasible, to prosecute international crimes as existing common crimes such as murder, assault, and robbery, a possibility again independent of criminal responsibility under international law.

Finally, and perhaps most compellingly, what divides as a formal matter those crimes which give rise to criminal responsibility under international law and those crimes defined by international law which merely implicate national criminalization is often extraordinarily difficult to discern. With treaty crimes, it is simply unclear in many cases whether the specified crime results or not in criminal responsibility under international law.[36] This was acknowledged by the ILC in the commentary to its Draft Statute for an International Criminal Court, which explains that the distinction drawn in one report of the Commission's working group between 'conduct specifically defined as a crime independently of any given system of national law' and 'conduct which a treaty requires to be made criminally punishable under national law' was not retained in the finally adopted Draft Statute on account of the fact that the distinction was thought difficult to draw for some treaties.[37] In short, the adoption of criminal responsibility under international law as the definitional criterion of an international crime 'may lead to unhelpful debate' as to which offences do and do not give rise to such responsibility.[38] This being the case, it seems unwise in principle and unfeasible in practice to use criminal responsibility under international law as the hallmark of an international crime.

2.16

---

[33] The Rome Statute of the International Criminal Court has been held to operate this way. See *Prosecutor v Lubanga*, ICC-01/04-01/06-803-tEN, Pre-Trial Chamber, Decision on the Confirmation of Charges, 29 January 2007, paras 302–303 and, more generally, *infra* para 14.59.

[34] The only difference in cases where a crime within the court's jurisdiction is not consonant with a pre-existing customary international criminal prohibition is that the court's jurisdiction must be strictly prospective if it wishes to avoid violating the principle *nullum crimen sine lege*. But even in the event that its jurisdiction is retrospective, the court will still enjoy that jurisdiction.

[35] That said, the difference will or may have implications for the principle *nullum crimen sine lege* where the offence was committed prior to the coming into force of the statute relied on, at least insofar as municipal law mirrors international human rights law in allowing prosecution in cases where at least international law prohibited the relevant conduct. Moreover, it would be rash to discount altogether differences at the municipal level between species of international crime within the expansive understanding of the term. The question is one for municipal constitutional and criminal lawyers in respective countries, as well as for comparativists.

[36] See *infra* paras 7.6–7.8.   [37] See *Ybk ILC 1994*, vol II/2, 37.

[38] R Cryer *et al*, *An Introduction to International Criminal Law and Procedure* (3rd edn, Cambridge: Cambridge University Press, 2014), 8.

2.17 In sum, not only does restricting the term 'international crime' to those offences which give rise to criminal responsibility directly under international law swim against the tide of what appears to be the increasingly predominant usage but there are, additionally, perfectly sensible reasons to consider as international crimes not only offences of this sort but also those offences defined by international law which give rise to criminal responsibility under municipal law alone.

C. Definition Posited

2.18 The approach one adopts to the concept of an international crime is as much a matter of taste as of law. It really does not matter which school of thought one prefers. Moreover, there is limited practical value to be had in any abstract definition of an international crime. You know one when you see it, to paraphrase Justice Stewart:[39] the punishable conduct is specified by customary international law or treaty; some of the offences in question result in criminal responsibility under international law itself, most others are subject to an international obligation of municipal criminalization, and a few straddle both of these categories; and in nearly all cases, at least on the more convincing view, international law lays down rules either permitting or obliging the assertion by states of prescriptive jurisdiction over the crime on an otherwise exorbitant basis. A descriptive range of potential characteristics such as the foregoing is arguably as useful as the prescription of characteristics common to all.

2.19 There is nonetheless an obvious practical benefit in any field in the adoption of a standard conceptual framework and terminology. This militates in favour of the positing and reasoned defence of a definition of an international crime.

2.20 In this light, it is submitted that an international crime is a crime defined by international law, whether customary or conventional.[40] It is its definition either

---

[39] See *Jacobellis v Ohio*, 378 US 184, 197 (1964).
[40] See also Dinstein (n 19), 221–2. For their part, although they reserve the term '*crime international*' for those crimes prohibited by international law itself, Ascensio, Decaux, and Pellet treat as '*infractions internationales*' all crimes defined by international law. See Ascensio, Decaux, and Pellet, 'Présentation de la première partie' (n 18), 95, para 7, as well as title 2 ('*Les autres infractions internationalement définies*') of Part One ('*Les infractions internationales*') of Ascensio, Decaux, and Pellet (eds), *Droit international pénal* (n 18). It is worth elaborating, for the avoidance of doubt, on what is meant by saying that an international crime is a crime defined by international law. All that is meant is that international law, be it custom or treaty, stipulates the material elements of the crime pursuant to its most basic mode of responsibility, *viz* commission (and commission in its most basic form). That is, for present purposes, international law can be taken to define a crime if it specifies what a person must do to be held to have committed the offence, leaving to one side all other possible modes of responsibility (eg ordering, aiding and abetting, and so on) and the requisite mental element. In the case of those crimes giving rise to individual criminal responsibility under customary international law, it was not until relatively recently that efforts were directed towards elaborating in any systematic fashion the general material and mental conditions of such responsibility. These questions were formerly left to the municipal law of those states which chose to enact such crimes into their municipal law or otherwise to try them. Even now, the customary status of this 'general part' of the relevant law is unclear. It still relies heavily on general principles of law recognized by the world's major criminal justice traditions. The situation was and is somewhat clearer with treaty crimes, many of which specify the requisite material and mental elements of the offences they create. But, even then, questions remain over the exhaustiveness of the elements specified, and states tend to flesh these out by reference

by customary international law or by treaty that is the sole characteristic shared by every offence with a claim to the denomination 'international crime'.[41]

D. Definitional Misconceptions

2.21 Three other characteristics are on occasion treated, effectively if not always formally, as constitutive of an international crime. But none of them distinguishes an international crime—whether as defined here or by the opposing school of thought—from a municipal crime in every instance, and it is this distinction that would seem to be the *raison d'être* of any definition of the former. Nor, *a fortiori*, does any of the three characteristics serve to render what would otherwise be a municipal crime an international one. In short, none of them is a definitional criterion of an international crime.

(i) Gravity

2.22 Scholars and judges alike often allude to especial gravity as if it were a defining characteristic of an international crime.[42] But such talk is misleading.

2.23 For a start, many municipal crimes are just as grave as international crimes, if not graver. It may be a facile observation but wilful killing is wilful killing, whether it is committed by a soldier against the wounded in the field or by a husband against a wife in the home; and, by most reckonings, a purely municipal offence of murder is graver than, for example, the unlawful confinement of a civilian in occupied territory, wilfully depriving a prisoner of war of the rights of fair and regular trial, or declaring inadmissible in a court of law the rights and actions of enemy nationals, all of them international crimes by any definition. Furthermore, were one to point to scale as an index of gravity, the random gunning-down in a shopping mall of ten passers-by at the hands of an aggrieved

---

to their respective municipal criminal laws. The point, therefore, is that an international crime is still an international crime even if international law may not lay down clearly its every material and mental parameter. As long as the material elements of the basic offence are defined by international law, it qualifies as an international crime.

[41] In particular, given the continuing controversy over the existence under customary international law of universal jurisdiction over war crimes, crimes against humanity, and genocide, all of which are unquestionably international crimes, it cannot be stated without exception that international law provides for special jurisdictional rules, permissive or mandatory, in respect of international crimes. As a consequence, the attachment of such rules to international crimes cannot be considered a defining characteristic.

[42] See eg *Arrest Warrant* (n 23), 74, para 37, 75, para 43, 76, para 46, and 81, para 60 (joint sep op Higgins, Kooijmans, and Buergenthal); *Prosecutor v Ayyash* et al, STL-11-01/I/AC/R176*bis*, Appeals Chamber, Interlocutory Decision on the Applicable Law: Terrorism, Conspiracy, Homicide, Perpetration, Cumulative Charging, 16 February 2011, para 134; *Prosecutor v Semanza*, ICTR-97-20-T, Trial Chamber, Judgment, 15 May 2003, para 555; *Pinochet (No 3)* (n 28), 243 (Lord Phillips); N Boister, '"Transnational Criminal Law?"' (2003) 14 *EJIL* 953, 963–4 and 965; B Broomhall, *International Justice and the International Criminal Court. Between Sovereignty and the Rule of Law* (Oxford: Oxford University Press, 2003), 10 and 44–51, especially 50; M Drumbl, *Atrocity, Punishment, and International Law* (Cambridge: Cambridge University Press, 2007), 3–4; Ratner, Abrams, and Bischoff (n 7), 14; *Secretariat Memorandum* (n 18), 16, para 12.

customer, punishable under municipal law alone, is considerably more serious than the shooting in cold blood by a military guard of a single prisoner of war, which is punishable as an international crime.[43] In short, gravity is not exclusive to international crimes, and even less does it render an otherwise municipal crime international.[44]

2.24 Moreover, the historical reality is that, with the partial exception of genocide,[45] international crimes have been created over the years not as a way of condemning the impugned conduct over and above the condemnation implied by its existing or possible criminalization and appropriate punishment under municipal law than for the more basic reason that the condemnable conduct might otherwise have escaped punishment altogether—whether generally or in specific historical instances—for want of jurisdiction over it or of an obligation to prosecute or extradite persons suspected of having committed it, as the case may be.[46] That is, with the partial exception of genocide, criminalization under or pursuant to international law has not been motivated by a perception of the added expressive value of international over municipal law.

2.25 In this light, the designation 'international' does not denote a gravity above and beyond that denoted by characterizing the relevant act as criminal. Putting it simply, an act deemed an 'international' crime is not by definition more serious than an act deemed a municipal crime. Indeed, in many cases the same act will be criminal under both international and some applicable corpus of municipal law. All that the adjective 'international' denotes is the body of law by reference to which the act is considered punishable.

2.26 As it is, gravity would be unworkable as a definitional criterion, since there would be no way of specifying *in abstracto* how grave a crime had to be before it was grave enough to be an international crime. Indeed, the only epistemologically compelling index of whether conduct was sufficiently serious to merit criminalization under or pursuant to international law would be whether it was criminalized under or pursuant to international law—that is, whether it was defined as a crime by international law.

---

[43] The same could be said of the household burglary of a priceless family heirloom in peacetime, solely a municipal crime, and the international crime constituted by a soldier's theft of a bottle of beer from a home during belligerent occupation. Countless similar comparisons could be drawn.

[44] See also Dinstein (n 19), 221. Nor, as such, does gravity turn a violation of international humanitarian law or international human rights law into an international crime.

[45] As explained *infra* chapter 4, the conduct constitutive of the crime of genocide was prosecuted in the wake of the Second World War as the crime against humanity of extermination. In other words, conduct that in 1948 would, via the Genocide Convention, be labelled for the first formal juridical time the international crime of 'genocide' was already punishable as an international crime. To the extent, however, that it was designated an international crime in its own right, this was for expressive purposes.

[46] See *infra* chapters 4 and 7. See also Cryer (n 19), 118–27; E David, 'Les valeurs, politiques et objectifs du droit pénal international à l'heure de la mondialisation' in Association internationale de droit pénal, *International Criminal Law: Quo Vadis?* (Nouvelles études pénales No 19, 2004) 157, 157–8; WA Schabas, *The International Criminal Court. A Commentary on the Rome Statute* (Oxford: Oxford University Press, 2010), 40.

The assertion or unwitting implication that particular seriousness is a necessary 2.27
characteristic of an international crime stems for the most part from the fact that
the best-known historical instances of the commission of such crimes have been
extremely grave. The popular imagination associates the term 'international crime'
with Auschwitz, Halabja, Srebrenica, and so on, and 'crime' as deed tends to elide
with 'crime' as legal concept. The association is reinforced by the practice of international criminal courts from Nuremberg onwards, which, as a function of practicability, have tried only the most serious violations of international criminal law.

(ii) Violation of the fundamental values, etc of the international community, etc

It is often said, frequently as part of the 'gravity' argument,[47] that an international 2.28
crime is a crime that violates the fundamental values or the like of the international
community or some such notional collectivity.[48] But again the statement is misleading,[49] for the same reasons, *mutatis mutandis*, as in relation to the purported
definitional criterion of gravity. First, even were one to accept that all international
crimes violate some or other fundamental value of the international community,
this violative quality would not serve to distinguish international crimes from
municipal crimes, unless one were to deny that murder, rape, infliction of grievous
bodily harm, wanton destruction of property, and so on, even where punishable
under municipal law alone, are intrinsically violations of the fundamental values
of the international community. Even less does this quality render a municipal
crime 'international'.[50] Secondly, the historical reality remains that, with the partial exception of genocide, international crimes were recognized as 'international'
crimes for reasons more practical than abstract.[51]

Against this backdrop, the qualifier 'international' does not signal the viola- 2.29
tion of more universal or fundamental values than does the characterization of the
conduct as a crime. Indeed, as previously stated, in many cases the same act will be
criminal under both international and municipal law. The epithet 'international'
denotes, as before, merely the body of law by reference to which the act is considered punishable.

Moreover, again as with gravity, the violation of the fundamental values of the 2.30
international community would be unworkable as a definitional criterion of an
international crime. The only way of telling conclusively whether conduct was
violative of some fundamental value of the international community such as to
merit criminalization under or pursuant to international law would be whether it

---

[47] See eg Boister (n 42), 964 ('of such exceptional gravity that they impinge on international society's fundamental interests').
[48] See eg *Ayyash* et al, Appeals Chamber Decision on Applicable Law (n 42), paras 91 and 134; Bassiouni (n 19), 133; Cassese and Gaeta (n 14), 20; Gaeta (n 14), 66 and 70; Werle and Jessburger (n 2), 33–6, paras 97–99 and 102–105, and 45–9, paras 125, 128, and 132.
[49] See also Cryer *et al* (n 38), 7.   [50] See also Dinstein (n 19), 221.
[51] Recall *supra* para 2.24.

was criminalized under or pursuant to international law—in other words, whether it was defined as a crime by international law.[52]

(iii) Triability by an international criminal tribunal

2.31 It is sometimes said or implied that an international crime is a crime triable by an international criminal tribunal.[53] Although this is not necessarily untrue, it is misleading insofar as international crimes are not the only crimes that can be tried before an international criminal tribunal, as the statement implies. An international criminal tribunal enjoys whatever subject-matter jurisdiction is vested in it by its constituent instrument and applies whatever law its constituent instrument directs it to apply,[54] and there is nothing to prevent the states or international organization which establishes the tribunal from conferring on it jurisdiction *ratione materiae* over specified municipal crimes or from specifying certain municipal law as the tribunal's applicable law. The possibility was foreshadowed by Kelsen.[55] It was later entertained by the ILC in subparagraph (*c*) of article 33 ('Applicable Law') of its Draft Statute for an International Criminal Court. It has since been realized both in article 5 of the Statute of the Special Court for Sierra Leone, which grants the Special Court, an international criminal tribunal, jurisdiction over certain crimes under Sierra Leone's Prevention of Cruelty to Children Act 1926 and its Malicious Damage Act 1861, and in article 2 ('Applicable criminal law') of the Statute of the Special Tribunal for Lebanon, which vests this international criminal tribunal with jurisdiction solely over certain crimes under Lebanese law. In this light, triability by an international criminal tribunal, while often descriptive of an international crime, is manifestly not determinative of it.

E. Recapitulation

2.32 An international crime is a crime defined by international law, whether customary or conventional. Conduct constitutes an international crime if, and only

---

[52] See also Cryer (n 19), 112–13. Consider, in this light, the 'each-way bet' of the Appeals Chamber of the Special Tribunal for Lebanon in *Ayyash* et al, Appeals Chamber Decision on Applicable Law (n 42), para 91: 'To turn into an international crime, a domestic offence needs to be regarded by the world community as an attack on universal values (such as peace or human rights) or on values held to be of paramount importance in that community; in addition, it is necessary that States and intergovernmental organisations, through their acts and pronouncements, sanction this attitude by clearly expressing the view that the world community considers the offence at issue as amounting to an international crime.' See also ibid, para 134.

[53] See K Kittichaisaree, *International Criminal Law* (Oxford: Oxford University Press, 2001), 3; B Simma and A Paulus, 'The Responsibility of Individuals for Human Rights Abuses in Internal Conflicts: A Positivist View' (1999) 93 *AJIL* 302, 308, original emphasis ('Article VI [of the Genocide Convention] allows for trials at both the national and the international levels and thereby establishes the truly *international* legal character of the crime'). Putting it the other way around, it is sometimes implied that an international criminal tribunal can try only international crimes. See eg Schabas (n 46), 46. Neither of these things is what Cryer *et al* are saying at Cryer *et al* (n 38), 4–5.

[54] Recall *supra* para 2.15.

[55] H Kelsen, *Peace Through Law* (Chapel Hill: University of North Carolina Press, 1944), 122.

if, it satisfies the formal legal definition of one of the various crimes defined by international law such as exist and are applicable to the perpetrator at time of commission.

III. Species of International Crime

A. Suggested Taxonomy and Terminology

While similar enough to be considered a single genus, the varieties of international crime[56] considered above are also different enough to be thought of as belonging to distinct species of that genus. Indeed, for certain purposes, these species are more meaningful than the genus. There are two criteria according to which these species might be distinguished, namely whether or not the offence in question gives rise to criminal responsibility under international law and whether the formal source of the offence is customary international law or treaty. In the final analysis, both criteria are pertinent, appropriate, and useful. 2.33

As far as labelling goes, it is suggested that the familiar tag 'crimes under international law' (synonymously, 'crimes against international law') be used to designate, and be reserved for, the first species of international crime—that is, those offences defined by international law which, like crimes against humanity, give rise to the individual criminal responsibility of the perpetrator under international law.[57] As a straightforward matter of language, the label seems natural. In addition, this is the most common and most authoritative way the term 'crimes under international law' has been used to date. It is how the ILC used the term in its Principles of International Law Recognized in the Charter of the Nürnberg Tribunal and in the Judgment of the Tribunal,[58] in its stalled Draft Code of Offences against the Peace and Security of Mankind[59] and eventual Draft Code of Crimes against the Peace and Security of Mankind,[60] and in the commentary to its Draft Statute for an International Criminal Court.[61] The same usage is found in General Assembly resolution 96 (I) and in the subsequent Convention on the Prevention and Punishment of the Crime of Genocide 1948 ('Genocide Convention'). 2.34

There is no obvious name for the other species of international crime—that is, for those offences defined by international law which do not give rise to individual criminal responsibility under international law but which international law permits or obliges states to criminalize on what would otherwise be an exorbitant 2.35

---

[56] In French, the term is '*crime international*'.
[57] See also eg Werle and Jessburger (n 2), 31–3, paras 89–96 and 45–9, paras 125–133; Brownlie (n 14), 306, 308 and 587–604. The French term is '*crime de droit international*', although art I of the Genocide Convention uses the archaic '*crime de droit des gens*'.
[58] ILC Nürnberg Principles, principles I–III and V–VII.
[59] Draft Code of Offences against the Peace and Security of Mankind, art 1, *Ybk ILC 1954*, vol II, 151.
[60] Draft Code of Crimes against the Peace and Security of Mankind, art 1(2), *Ybk ILC 1996*, vol II/2, 17 ('ILC Draft Code of Crimes').
[61] *Ybk ILC 1994*, vol II/2, 36–41.

jurisdictional basis. Reference is not infrequently made to 'transnational crimes', but the label is problematic and undesirable for several reasons.[62] Despite the unavailability of an obvious name, however, and recognizing that the choice of label is a more-or-less arbitrary one, it is suggested that these offences be designated 'crimes pursuant to international law'. There is some slight and mildly persuasive precedent for this in the primary sources, in the form of article 20(e) of the ILC's Draft Statute for an International Criminal Court. The Draft Statute did not limit the proposed court's jurisdiction over offences defined by treaty to those arguably[63] giving rise to criminal responsibility under international law but also included offences merely the subject of obligations of municipal suppression.[64] In an apparent and judicious recognition of this distinction, article 20(e) accorded the court jurisdiction over crimes 'established under or pursuant to the treaty provisions listed in the Annex'.[65] That the reference to crimes 'established under... treaty provisions' is a reference to criminal responsibility under international law (*viz* treaty) itself seems clear from the commentary's consistent designation of genocide, aggression, war crimes, and crimes against humanity as crimes 'under' general (*viz* customary) international law and, more simply, 'crimes under international law'. *A contrario*, the reference to crimes 'established... pursuant to treaty provisions' would appear to be to those conventional international crimes to which individual criminal responsibility attaches ultimately as a matter only of national law.[66]

2.36   Both crimes under international law and crimes pursuant to international law can have their source in either custom or treaty. Borrowing and extrapolating from

---

[62] See *infra* paras 2.47–2.48.   [63] See *infra* paras 7.6–7.8.   [64] Recall *supra* n 21.

[65] To complicate matters, however, the Annex itself is headed simply 'Crimes pursuant to treaties'. The Commission is at pains to point out in its commentary, *Ybk ILC 1994*, vol II/2, 37, that the inclusion of both species of treaty crime in the Annex 'does not suggest that all of the crimes referred to in the annex are of the same character, which is certainly not the case'.

[66] The French text of art 20(e) of the ILC Draft Statute, however, is vaguer, speaking simply of '*les crimes définis ou visés par les dispositions de traités*'. (The final chairman of the working group on a draft statute for an international criminal court, James Crawford, who prepared the ILC Draft Statute for the Commission's forty-sixth session, did so in English.) In the past, the English phrase 'crimes under international law' as it has appeared in ILC texts has been rendered in French as either '*crimes de droit international*' (see 'Principes du droit international consacrés par le statut du Tribunal de Nuremberg et dans le jugement de ce tribunal' (1950), principes I–VII, and 'Projet de codes de crimes contre la paix et la sécurité de l'humanité (1954), article premier, as translated in *La Commission du droit international et son œuvre* (cinquième édition, New York: Nations Unies, 1997), 182–3 and 183–4 respectively, the *Yearbook of the International Law Commission* being published only in English until 1956) or '*crimes au regard du droit international*' (see 'Projet de codes des crimes contre la paix et la sécurité de l'humanité', *Annuaire de la Commission du droit international 1996*, tome II/2, 17, art 1, para 2). In this light, it is unlikely that the expression '*les crimes définis...par les dispositions de traités*' in art 20(e) was intended to refer to crimes 'under' international law in the English-language sense. Rather, it would seem to be used as a synonym for '*les crimes...visés par les dispositions de traités*', as also used in art 20(e); and it may or may not be significant in this regard that the French title of the Annex is '*Crimes définis ou visés par des traités*' (cf the English version, *supra* n 65, speaking only of 'Crimes pursuant to treaties'). Since all treaty crimes, however, are '*crimes définis...par les dispositions de traités*', the words '*visés par...*' would be redundant on this reading. But be all this as it may. In the end, an appropriate francophone equivalent of 'crimes pursuant to' would be '*crimes visés par le droit international*'. For its part, title 2 of Part One of Ascensio, Decaux, and Pellet (eds), *Droit international pénal* (n 18) refers simply to '*les autres infractions internationalement définies*'.

the ILC's Draft Statute, the respective subspecies might be handily referred to, on the one hand, as 'crimes under customary international law'[67] and 'crimes under treaty' and, on the other, as 'crimes pursuant to customary international law' and 'crimes pursuant to treaty'.

Since treaty can provide for either crimes under international law or crimes pursuant to international law, the term 'treaty crime', as is not uncommon and is adopted here, does not necessarily denote criminal responsibility under international law. It simply identifies the formal international legal source of the crime in question. In other words, the label refers generically to both crimes under and pursuant to treaty. The same could in principle be so, *mutatis mutandis*, for the term 'customary international crimes', although the latter tends not to be used. 2.37

B. Other Labels

(i) 'Core crimes'

The term 'core crimes' is frequently found in the literature, the reference being to genocide, crimes against humanity, war crimes, and the crime of aggression.[68] 2.38

The label 'core crimes' is both formally meaningless and factually misleading. As to the former, the adjective 'core' has no legal import, denoting as it does no juridical quality of the crimes in question.[69] As to the latter, it might with reason be asked in what sense the relevant crimes occupy the position of centrality implied by the word 'core'. Other international crimes are seemingly more prevalent, examples being the various offences provided for in the United Nations Convention against Corruption 2003[70] and in the United Nations Convention against Transnational Organized Crime 2000.[71] The same examples might also be considered as significant or grave as the *soi-disant* 'core' crimes, posing as they perhaps ultimately do a comparable threat to human wellbeing, the stability of states, and international peace and security, especially if one compares them to some specific war crimes.[72] 2.39

In the final analysis, the epithet 'core' would appear[73] merely a historically contingent descriptor referable to no more than the twin facts that most of 2.40

---

[67] See also eg J Crawford, *Brownlie's Principles of Public International Law* (8th edn, Oxford: Oxford University Press, 2012), 467 and 688.

[68] See eg Broomhall (n 42); K Ambos, 'Selected Issues Regarding the "Core Crimes" in International Criminal Law' in Association internationale de droit pénal, *International Criminal Law: Quo Vadis?* (Nouvelles études pénales No 19, 2004) 219; R Cryer, *Prosecuting International Crimes. Selectivity and the International Criminal Law Regime* (Cambridge: Cambridge University Press, 2005), 4 and 84, as well as Cryer (n 19) and Cryer *et al* (n 38), 4–5; Werle and Jessburger (n 2), 32, paras 92 and 95; Gaeta (n 14); Schabas (n 46); Bassiouni (n 19).

[69] Contrast the epithet 'core' with, eg, the qualifiers 'customary international' and 'treaty', both of which indicate the crime's formal source as a matter of international law.

[70] United Nations Convention against Corruption 2003, arts 17–25.

[71] United Nations Convention against Transnational Organized Crime 2000, arts 5, 6, and 8.

[72] Recall *supra* para 2.24. See, in this light, *Ybk ILC 1994*, vol II/2, 75, para 98, recounting the view of some ILC members that 'genocide or crimes against humanity...did not come under the peace and security of mankind unless the concept was given a very broad meaning'.

[73] It is not, in fact, clear in what precise sense the crimes in question are considered 'core'.

(ii) 'Crimes against the peace and security of mankind'

2.41   In 1996 the ILC finally adopted on second reading a Draft Code of Crimes against the Peace and Security of Mankind, containing the crimes of aggression, genocide, crimes against humanity, crimes against United Nations and associated personnel, and war crimes, all of which were deemed to be 'crimes against the peace and security of mankind'.[75] Article 1(2) of the Draft Code declares that '[c]rimes against the peace and security of mankind are crimes under international law and punishable as such'.

2.42   The qualifier 'against the peace and security of mankind' is again one without formal legal significance. It indicates no more than the ILC's value judgment that, in light of 'the necessary threat to peace and security required to constitute a crime under the...Code',[76] the crimes included were 'the most serious on the scale of international offences'.[77] (Oddly, however, for something calling itself a code,[78] the Draft Code was not to be taken to 'cover exhaustively all crimes against the peace and security of mankind'.)[79] Even on its own terms, moreover, the ILC's criterion of exceptional seriousness is opaque, at times referring to the threat to international peace and security represented by the impugned conduct,[80] at others to an act's shocking cruelty,[81] while at other times still its meaning can only be guessed at.[82] Indeed, the problem 'whether it would really be possible to find a common denominator for all of the crimes'[83] explains the Commission's decision not to posit a general, conceptual definition of the crimes the subject of the Draft Code.[84] Putting it simply, the Commission never really settled on what made a crime one against the peace and security of mankind.[85]

---

[74] See eg Cryer (n 19), 108 ('What we often call "core" international crimes are traditionally those that have been tried before international criminal tribunals...') and Cryer *et al* (n 38), 5 ('Our approach does not differentiate the core crimes from others as a matter of principle, but only pragmatically, by reason of the fact that no other crimes are currently within the jurisdiction of international courts.')

[75] ILC Draft Code of Crimes, art 1(1) and Part Two.   [76] *Ybk ILC 1996*, vol II/2, 52.

[77] Ibid, 54.

[78] The oddness was not lost on some members of the Commission. See *Ybk ILC 1994*, vol II/2, 75, para 98.

[79] *Ybk ILC 1996*, vol II/2, 17.   [80] See eg ibid, 20, 22–3, 27, 30, and 51–2.

[81] See eg ibid, 23 and 50.

[82] A suggestion to amend the title of Part II of the Code, containing the crimes themselves, to 'Crimes against universal peace and humanity' was ignored. See *Ybk ILC 1995*, vol II/2, 18, para 51.

[83] *Ybk ILC 1994*, vol II/2, 77, para 113. See also *Ybk ILC 1995*, vol II/2, 18, para 47.

[84] For the Commission's decision not to propose a general definition of a crime against the peace and security of mankind, see *Ybk ILC 1996*, vol II/2, 17.

[85] See, especially, *Ybk ILC 1995*, vol II/2, 19, paras 55–8.

2.43 In the end, the saving grace is that the terminology of 'crimes against the peace and security of mankind' adopted in the Draft Code, which represents one of the more ignominious of the ILC's failures, has never caught on.[86]

(iii) 'Crimes of international concern', etc

2.44 In an apparent effort to avoid unnecessary and time-consuming debate over the definition of an 'international crime', the working group responsible for drafting the ILC's Draft Statute for an International Criminal Court opted for preambular reference to 'crimes of international concern' and to the crimes over which the proposed court was to have jurisdiction as 'the most serious crimes of concern to the international community as a whole'.[87] The latter expression was intended to encompass not only the crimes under general (this is, customary) international law listed in subparagraphs (*a*) to (*d*) of article 20 of the Draft Statute (*viz* genocide, aggression, serious violations of the laws and customs applicable in armed conflict, and crimes against humanity) but also article 20(*e*)'s range of crimes 'established under or pursuant to the treaty provisions listed in the Annex, which, having regard to the conduct alleged, constitute exceptionally serious crimes of international concern'.[88] The eventual Rome Statute of the International Criminal Court adopts the terminology of the Draft Statute, with article 1 referring to the crimes within the ICC's jurisdiction as 'the most serious crimes of international concern' and the preamble[89] and chapeau to article 5(1) speaking of 'the most serious crimes of concern to the international community as a whole'.

2.45 It ought to go without saying that the qualifiers 'of international concern' and 'of concern to the international community as a whole' are once more without formal legal significance, being merely descriptive. Nor do they necessarily imply that no other crimes are of international concern or of concern to the international community as a whole.[90]

---

[86] But cf Ascensio, Decaux, and Pellet (eds), *Droit international pénal* (n 18).

[87] ILC Draft Statute, preamble (first and second recitals).

[88] The crimes listed in the Annex comprise grave breaches of the Geneva Conventions; unlawful seizure of aircraft, within the meaning of art 1 of the Hague Convention; the crimes defined in art 1 of the Convention for the Suppression of Unlawful Acts against the Safety of Civilian Aircraft 1971; apartheid and related crimes as defined in art II of the Apartheid Convention; the crimes defined in art 2 of the Convention on the Protection and Punishment of Crimes against Internationally Protected Persons, including Diplomatic Agents 1973; hostage-taking and related crimes as defined in art 1 of the Hostages Convention; torture within the meaning of the Torture Convention; the crimes defined in art 3 of the Convention for the Suppression of Unlawful Acts against the Safety of Maritime Navigation 1988 and in art 2 of the Protocol for the Suppression of Unlawful Acts against the Safety of Fixed Platforms Located on the Continental Shelf 1988; and crimes involving illicit traffic in narcotic drugs and psychotropic substances as envisaged in art 3(1) of the Convention against Illicit Traffic in Narcotic Drugs and Psychotropic Substances 1988.

[89] Rome Statute, preamble (fourth and ninth recitals).

[90] That said, the preamble and art 5(1) assert that the crimes within the Court's jurisdiction are the most serious of such crimes.

(iv) 'Transnational' crimes

2.46 It is not uncommon for those crimes defined by international law which do not give rise to individual criminal responsibility under international law itself—in other words, what this book calls 'crimes pursuant to international law'—to be labelled 'transnational' crimes.[91]

2.47 Insofar as the qualifier 'transnational' is usually taken to refer to conduct (and usually private conduct) which straddles state frontiers, it is misleading. For a start, not all so-called 'transnational' crimes are in fact capable of commission across borders.[92] For example, neither the crime of torture within the meaning of the Torture Convention nor the crimes provided for in the Protocol for the Suppression of Unlawful Acts against the Safety of Fixed Platforms Located on the Continental Shelf 1988, each 'transnational' crimes according to the relevant school of thought, lends itself to transnational commission. Even more to the point, for only a single 'transnational' crime—namely illicit trafficking in firearms, their parts and components, and ammunition, as defined in article 3(*e*) of the Protocol against the Illicit Manufacturing of and Trafficking in Firearms, Their Parts and Components and Ammunition 2001 supplementary to the United Nations Convention against Transnational Organized Crime 2000 ('Firearms Protocol')[93]—is cross-border commission a prerequisite to criminal responsibility. All of the other crimes in question are, taking into account the scope of application of the relevant convention and the definition of the offence, capable of commission either wholly within the territory, including the territorial sea and airspace, of a single state or at least without entering the territory of a second state. Conversely, the crimes under international law (that is, not 'transnational' crimes) of genocide, crimes against humanity, war crimes, and aggression can all be committed across state frontiers, while the last by definition involves cross-border activity. Moreover, many purely municipal crimes can be committed transnationally. As for the fallback argument that what makes such crimes 'transnational' is that they involve 'conduct that has actual or potential trans-boundary effects of national and international concern',[94] the same criticisms apply.[95]

---

[91] See eg Boister (n 42) and N Boister, *An Introduction to Transnational Criminal Law* (Oxford: Oxford University Press, 2012); Cryer (n 18), 753. Boister (n 42), 954, adopting the term *faute de mieux*, concedes that it 'has definitional problems'.

[92] See also C Fijnaut, 'Transnational Crime and the Role of the United Nations' (2000) 8 *Eur J Crim L & Crim J* 119, 120.

[93] Article 3(*e*) of the Firearms Protocol defines the relevant crime as 'the import, export, acquisition, sale, delivery, movement or transfer of firearms, their parts and components and ammunition from or across the territory of one State Party to that of another State Party if any one of the States Parties concerned does not authorize it in accordance with the terms of [the Firearms] Protocol or if the firearms are not marked in accordance with article 8 of [the] Protocol…'.

[94] Boister (n 42), 954.

[95] A further fallback argument sometimes advanced is that a crime such as torture within the meaning of the Torture Convention is 'transnational' in the sense that 'there is a sufficiently influential cosmopolitan belief that this conduct should be outlawed in all states because of its moral repugnance', in the words of Boister (n 42), 967—what is referred to, ibid, as 'a normative transnational element'. See also, similarly, EA Nadelmann, 'Global Prohibition Regimes: The Evolution of Norms in International Society' (1990) 44 *Int Org* 479, 525. The distinction drawn between this 'normative

The Concept of an International Crime

As it is, given that the respective adjectives in the terms 'international crimes' 2.48
and 'municipal crimes' (or 'domestic crimes' or 'national crimes') denote the
body of law by reference to which the impugned conduct is punishable, rather
than the *locus* of that conduct, the adjective 'transnational' in the expression
'transnational crimes' is fundamentally misconceived. Alternatively, were the
qualifier 'transnational' indeed intended to denote the body of law by reference
to which the defined conduct is considered criminal, it would be inadvisable,
in that it could be taken to suggest the existence of a notional body of law
which, as a formal juridical matter, is neither international nor municipal but
'transnational'.[96]

IV. Crimes under International Law

A crime under international law is a crime defined by international law which gives 2.49
rise to the individual criminal responsibility of the perpetrator under international
law itself.[97] It amounts to an obligation, negative or positive, imposed directly on
individuals by international law, the breach of which results under international
law in the liability of the perpetrator to punishment.

It is usually the case that public international law creates obligations for states 2.50
and, to a lesser extent, international organizations. In creating obligations for individuals, crimes under international law represent an anomalous corpus of public
international legal rules.

A. The Development of Individual Criminal Responsibility under International Law

The history of the rise of individual criminal responsibility under international law 2.51
is one of conceptual cross-currents and confusion.

---

transnational element' and the imagined normative basis for crimes under international law is that, as explained by Boister (n 42), 967, '[t]orture may not yet shock the conscience of international society sufficiently for it to take the step of classifying torture as an international crime *stricto sensu*, but it does undoubtedly shock the conscience of sufficient citizens in influential states for a treaty to be adopted to protect the citizens of other states from torture.' The approach poses more questions than it answers.

[96] Boister (n 42), 974, is alive to the problem. To the extent that reference is often made in a juridical sense to 'transnational law', it is to a mixed bag of rules of national (including private international) law, public international law, *lex mercatoria*, and so on, relevant to the legal regulation of activity that takes place in more than one state. See eg P Jessup, *Transnational Law* (New Haven: Yale University Press, 1956), 2 (speaking of 'all law which regulates actions or events that transcend national frontiers'). It is in this sense that Boister uses the term, as he explains at Boister (n 42), 974–5, and it is in this sense—that is, in a frank acknowledgement that the label 'transnational', insofar as it relates to the juridical rather than geographical or broader phenomenological aspect of the crimes in question, refers to the coincidence of what in formal legal terms are rules of public international law and national law respectively—that the use of the term 'transnational crimes' is by no means indefensible.

[97] Recall *supra* para 2.34.

2.52   The threshold question whether individuals can be held criminally responsible under international law at all is often conflated in the earlier literature with the logically subsequent question whether individuals can be held criminally responsible for certain breaches of international law arguably better seen as the state's alone.[98] The two are treated separately here.

(i) In principle

2.53   The crime of piracy *jure gentium* was the first to which the label 'international crime'—or, previously, 'offence against the law of nations'[99]—came to attach. The crime predates international law in its modern form, having its origins in the various bodies of medieval maritime law applied in the different European ports,[100] which eventually coalesced into a general maritime law that ultimately formed part of the seventeenth-century *jus gentium*, or law of nations, known to Grotius. But Grotius's *jus gentium* was not public international law in the way in which the latter came to be conceived from the mid-eighteenth century onwards, bringing together as it did rules on the conduct of states[101] *inter se*, certain rules of what we would now think of as private international law, and certain rules on individual conduct taking place in more than one state or beyond the jurisdiction of any state. After the consolidation in the late eighteenth and early to mid-nineteenth centuries of the classical law of nations, avowedly having as its subjects only states, it was more accurate to say that piracy on the high seas, rather than being prohibited by the law of nations, was an offence which, as defined by the law of nations, every state was permitted to criminalize and prosecute under its municipal law.[102] That said, to the extent that the trial of piracy by an international court applying international law remained inconceivable in the prevailing state of international organization, the distinction was for all intents and purposes meaningless. One could equally have said that the law of nations did indeed outlaw piracy, with the consequence (as it was seen at the time) that each state, in the application of its own law, was permitted to punish the offence as internationally defined.[103]

2.54   The description 'offences against the law of nations' was also often applied to crimes such as attacks on foreign ambassadors and violation of safe-conducts granted to foreign merchants and travellers.[104] In these contexts the term connoted

---

[98] In turn, the second question is sometimes confused with a further question, namely whether state officials, even if they can in principle be held individually criminally responsible under international law for so-called 'acts of state', benefit under international law from procedural immunity in respect of international crimes committed in the exercise of their official functions. For a discussion of this further question, see *infra* chapter 10.

[99] See eg W Blackstone, *Commentaries on the Laws of England*, book IV, chapter 5, 68. The edition cited is the four-volume University of Chicago Press facsimile of the First Edition of 1765–69 (Chicago: University of Chicago Press, 1979).

[100] These were the *Consolato del mare*, the Wisby code, the Lübeck code, the laws of Amalfi, the laws of Trani, the code of Oléron, and so on.

[101] It is perhaps worth noting that Grotius had only a sketchy conception of the state.

[102] Recall *supra* para 2.10.   [103] See eg Kelsen (n 14), 534–5.

[104] See eg Blackstone (n 99), book IV, chapter 5, 68.

something quite different from its import in relation to piracy, at least from the eighteenth century onwards. It referred to the criminalization and ultimately the punishment under national law of acts constituting a breach of the law of nations by the receiving state either because they were performed by a servant of the state or because they resulted from what we would now call the receiving state's failure of due diligence. In this light, the receiving state's prosecution of the persons responsible for the breach amounted to a form of reparation to the victim's state. In modern terms, we would say that such prosecution acquitted the responsible state's obligation to afford satisfaction to the injured state.[105] What the term 'offence against the law of nations' did not in this context mean from the classical era of international law onwards was that international law itself prohibited individuals from committing the impugned acts. Any such prohibition was under national law alone.

2.55 As for the laws and customs of war, although in Grotius's time these were directed as much towards individuals as towards states, and although the jurists of the seventeenth century and earlier envisaged the punishment of individuals who violated these rules, it is simply unclear whether from the late eighteenth century onwards war crimes implicated individual criminal responsibility under international law itself or whether any such responsibility was under national law alone. What was clear was that the law of nations permitted a belligerent state to punish captured enemy servicemen for violations of the laws and customs of war, at the very least when the impugned acts were committed against the punishing state's servicemen or civilians. If a trial took place, it did so before a military tribunal of the custodial state (that is, before a municipal tribunal), and, depending on the tribunal in question, the applicable law was either the laws and customs of war or the military penal code of the custodial state, the latter embodying common crimes such as murder, assault, destruction of property, theft, and so on, with enemy combatants being tried for such offences only if alleged to have committed them in violation of the laws and customs of war. In either case it is impossible to discern whether the relevant national rule—in the former instance an implied secondary rule rendering violation of the laws and customs of war punishable as a crime, in the latter the provisions of the military penal code—complemented individual criminal responsibility under international law or made up for the lack of it. Again, as long as the prosecution of violations of the laws and customs of war before an international court applying international law remained out of the question, it was a distinction without a difference.

2.56 A belligerent state's right to try enemy combatants for war crimes was recognized in the first codification of the customary laws of war, the Instructions for the Government of Armies of the United States in the Field ('Lieber Code') of 1863,[106] article 13 of which spoke of the punishment of military offences by

---

[105] See Articles on Responsibility of States, art 37, especially art 37(2), speaking of 'another appropriate modality', with one such possible modality, as outlined in para 5 of the ILC commentary to art 37, being 'penal action against the individuals whose conduct caused the internationally wrongful act'. See *Ybk ILC 2001*, vol II/2, 106.

[106] Reproduced in D Schindler and J Toman (eds), *The Laws of Armed Conflicts. A Collection of Conventions, Resolutions and Other Documents* (4th edn, Leiden/Boston: Martinus Nijhoff, 2004), 3.

national military courts 'under the common law of war'. The matter was put more directly in the so-called 'Oxford Manual' of the Laws of War on Land prepared in 1880 by the Institut de droit international,[107] article 84 of which provided that '[o]ffenders against the laws of war' were 'liable to the punishments specified in the penal law'. The Institut's commentary explained that, if any of the rules of the laws of war on land were violated, 'the offending parties should be punished, after a judicial hearing, by the belligerent in whose hands they are'. The reference to 'the penal law' in article 84 of the Oxford Manual was to the penal law of the forum state. No analogous reference found its way, however, into the intergovernmental Draft International Regulations on the Laws and Customs of War ('Brussels Declaration') of 1874[108] or, more significantly, into either the Regulations concerning the Laws and Customs of War on Land annexed to the Convention concerning the Laws and Customs of War on Land 1899 or the later Regulations concerning the Laws and Customs of War on Land ('1907 Hague Regulations') annexed to the Convention concerning the Laws and Customs of War on Land 1907 ('1907 Hague Convention IV'), each of these instruments representing an attempt to codify the customary international law of land warfare. Article 3 of 1907 Hague Convention IV provided for state responsibility in respect of breaches of the annexed Regulations committed by persons forming part of the responsible state's armed forces, while article 56 of the Regulations provided that infractions of that particular provision 'should be made the subject of legal proceedings', by which was meant municipal, although not necessarily penal, proceedings. But nowhere did the Convention refer in general terms to the punishment of individual violators of the laws and customs of war, let alone envisage individual criminal responsibility directly under the Convention (that is, under international law), although it ruled neither out. The right of a belligerent state to prosecute enemy combatants for war crimes was, however, reflected after the First World War in articles 228 and 229 of the Treaty of Versailles 1919.[109] Article 228 read:

The German Government recognises the right of the Allied and Associated Powers to bring before military tribunals persons accused of having committed acts in violation of the laws and customs of war. Such persons shall, if found guilty, be sentenced to punishments laid down by law. . . .

Article 229 stated:

Persons guilty of criminal acts against the nationals of one of the Allied and Associated Powers will be brought before the military tribunals of that Power. Persons guilty of criminal acts against the nationals of more than one of the Allied and Associated Powers will be

---

[107] Institut de droit international, 'Les lois de la guerre sur terre. Manuel publié par l'Institut de droit international' (1881–82) 5 *Annuaire de l'IDI* 157. The Institut is a private body of eminent international lawyers acting in a personal capacity.
[108] Brussels, 27 August 1874, reproduced in Schindler and Toman (n 106), 21.
[109] Treaty of Peace between the Allied and Associated Powers and Germany 1919 ('Treaty of Versailles').

brought before military tribunals composed of members of the military tribunals of the Powers concerned....

Identical provisions, *mutatis mutandis*, were found in the Treaty of St Germain 1919[110] and the Treaty of Trianon 1920.[111] More controversially, article 227 of the Treaty of Versailles provided:

The Allied and Associated Powers publicly arraign William II of Hohenzollern, formerly German Emperor, for a supreme offence against international morality and the sanctity of treaties. A special tribunal will be constituted to try the accused... It will be composed of five judges, one appointed by each of the following Powers: namely, the United States of America, Great Britain, France, Italy and Japan. In its decision the tribunal will be guided by the highest motives of international policy, with a view to vindicating the solemn obligations of international undertakings and the validity of international morality. It will be its duty to fix the punishment which it considers should be imposed....

Again, however, none of this answered the question whether individual criminal responsibility under international law itself was conceptually possible—that is, whether an individual could be prosecuted before an international criminal court applying international law as such, without the interposition of primary or secondary rules of national law.[112]

2.57 The question of individual criminal responsibility under international law took centre stage after the Second World War in the context of the International Military Tribunal (IMT) established at Nuremberg, pursuant to the 'Nuremberg Charter' of 8 August 1945,[113] by the four Allied Powers then in occupation of defeated Germany.[114] Article 6 of the Charter provided that crimes against peace, war crimes, and crimes against humanity were 'crimes within the jurisdiction of the Tribunal for which there shall be individual responsibility', and the IMT handed down guilty verdicts in respect of all three categories of crime. Although the Nuremberg Charter was silent as to the IMT's applicable law, the Tribunal applied what the drafters of the Charter asserted to be international law, even if, to obviate challenges to the Tribunal's jurisdiction, the term 'international law' used in earlier drafts was deliberately omitted from the Charter's final text. But

---

[110] Treaty of Peace between the Allied and Associated Powers and Austria 1919 ('Treaty of St Germain'), arts 173 and 174.

[111] Treaty of Peace between the Allied and Associated Powers and Hungary 1920 ('Treaty of Trianon'), arts 157 and 158.

[112] For divergent readings of the post-First World War practice, compare Parlett (n 14), 240–1 ('The Treaty of Versailles implied that individual responsibility could arise directly under international law'; 'the Treaty of Versailles suggested that individuals held direct obligations under international law') and G Manner, 'The Legal Nature and Punishment of Criminal Acts of Violence Contrary to the Laws of War' (1943) 37 *AJIL* 407.

[113] Charter of the International Military Tribunal, annexed to Agreement by the Government of the United Kingdom of Great Britain and Northern Ireland, the Government of the United States of America, the Provisional Government of the French Republic and the Government of the Union of Soviet Socialist Republics for the Prosecution and Punishment of the Major War Criminals of the European Axis 1945 ('Nuremberg Charter').

[114] A further 19 Allied states expressed their adherence to the agreement to which the Charter was annexed.

the omission of all reference to international law did not, in the event, prevent the defence from 'submitt[ing] that international law is concerned with the actions of sovereign States, and provides no punishment for individuals'.[115]

2.58 The Tribunal was not required to respond to the submission, since it was bound to exercise the jurisdiction *ratione materiae* vested in it by its Charter.[116] Nonetheless, it went out of its way to justify the imposition of individual criminal responsibility under what was claimed to be international law. It rejected the defence's submission,[117] holding that 'individuals can be punished for violations of international law'[118] and reasoning as follows:

> That international law imposes duties and liabilities upon individuals as well as upon States has long been recognized. In the recent case of *Ex Parte Quirin* (1942) 317 US 1, before the Supreme Court of the United States, persons were charged during the war with landing in the United States for purposes of spying and sabotage. The late Chief Justice Stone, speaking for the Court, said:
>
> 'From the very beginning of its history this Court has applied the law of war as including that part of the law of nations which prescribes for the conduct of war, the status, rights and duties of enemy nations as well as enemy individuals.'
>
> He went on to give a list of cases tried by the Courts, where individual offenders were charged with offenses against the law of nations, and particularly the laws of war. Many other authorities could be cited, but enough has been said to show that individuals can be punished for violations of international law.[119]

In conclusion, the IMT relied on robustly instrumental reasoning, declaring famously that '[c]rimes against international law are committed by men, not by abstract entities, and only by punishing individuals who commit such crimes can the provisions of international law be enforced'.[120]

2.59 But the character of the law applied by the Tribunal remained ambiguous. On the one hand, as a court whose establishment and powers derived without interposition of municipal law from an agreement between states (*viz* a treaty), the IMT was by definition an international court,[121] and it was to be assumed that any law applied by an international court that was not obviously the law of a specific state was international law. On the other hand, the US, the USSR, the UK, and France—the four Allied powers in occupation of defeated Germany—expressly assumed, in their 'Berlin Declaration' of 5 June 1945, 'supreme authority with respect to Germany, including all the powers possessed by the German Government...and any state, municipal, or local government or authority';[122] and the Tribunal stated in its judgment that '[t]he making of the [Nuremberg] Charter

---

[115] Judgment of the International Military Tribunal for the Trial of German Major War Criminals, Nuremberg, 30 September and 1 October 1946, Misc No 12 (1946), Cmd 6964, reproduced (1947) 41 *AJIL* 172 ('Nuremberg judgment'), 220.
[116] Ibid, 175 and 216–17.   [117] Ibid, 220.   [118] Ibid, 221.
[119] Ibid, 220–1.   [120] Ibid, 221.   [121] See *infra* chapter 3.
[122] Declaration regarding the Defeat of Germany and the Assumption of Supreme Authority with respect to Germany by the Governments of the United States of America, the Union of Soviet Socialist Republics, the United Kingdom and the Provisional Government of the French Republic, Berlin, 5 June 1945 ('Berlin Declaration').

was the exercise of the sovereign legislative power by the countries to which the German Reich unconditionally surrendered', speaking of the 'right of these countries to legislate for the occupied territories'.[123] In short, the Allied powers claimed to wield through the Tribunal the criminal jurisdiction of the subjugated German state.[124] And the point is that Germany could, as a matter of international law, not only try German nationals for any crimes it so wished but could do so even if they were acting on its behalf. That said, the Tribunal was at pains to emphasize that the Charter was 'not an arbitrary exercise of power on the part of the victorious Nations' but was 'the expression of international law existing at the time of its creation'.[125] This, however, was problematic, since serious doubts existed as to whether the concepts of crimes against humanity and crimes against peace really did reflect customary international law as it stood at the time of commission.

2.60   In the light of these lingering questions, the General Assembly of the new United Nations Organization moved quickly to adopt General Assembly resolution 95 (I) of 11 December 1946, in which it '[a]ffirm[ed] the principles of international law recognized by the Charter of the Nürnberg Tribunal and the judgment of the Tribunal', thereby settling, at a formal level, debate over the principles' claims to the status of positive international law—even if doubts persisted in scholarly circles until the acceptance in 1950 by the Sixth (namely, Legal) Committee of the General Assembly of the ILC's Principles of International Law Recognized in the Charter of the Nürnberg Tribunal and in the Judgment of the Tribunal. In addition, General Assembly resolution 96 (I), also of 11 December 1946, '[a]ffirm[ed] that genocide is a crime under international law... for which principals and accomplices... are punishable', a statement confirmed and given effect two years later by the Genocide Convention, especially articles I and IV. Two years later again, Principle I of the ILC's formulation of the Nürnberg Principles declared that '[a]ny person who commits an act which constitutes a crime under international law is responsible therefor and liable to punishment'.

2.61   But, prior to the acceptance in 1950 of the ILC's Nuremberg Principles, the general agreement that 'individuals can be punished for violations of international law'[126] masked a lack of clarity as to the precise juridical basis for this statement. When read as a whole, the Nuremberg judgment, affirmed as good international law in General Assembly resolution 95 (I), gave conflicting signals, and not even the Genocide Convention was explicit enough to settle the issue.

2.62   One possible construction of both the Nuremberg judgment and the Genocide Convention was that international law, or to be precise its specifically penal content, was capable of imposing obligations on individuals directly, as explicitly asserted by the Nuremberg Tribunal when it declared that 'international law imposes

---

[123] Nuremberg judgment (n 115), 216.
[124] See also G Schwarzenberger, 'The Judgment of Nuremberg' (1946–47) 21 *Tulane LR* 329, 339–41; Q Wright, 'The Law of the Nuremberg Trial' (1947) 41 *AJIL* 38, 49–51; JF Murphy, 'International Crimes' in CC Joyner (ed), *The United Nations and International Law* (Cambridge: Cambridge University Press, 1997) 362, 364; Parlett (n 14), 246.
[125] Nuremberg judgment (n 115), 216.   [126] Ibid, 221.

duties and liabilities upon individuals'[127] and, indeed, that 'the very essence of the Charter [was] that individuals have international duties'.[128] The violation by individuals of their international legal obligations naturally resulted in their international legal responsibility, a responsibility deemed criminal, rather than delictual, in nature. This explanation of the underlying principle accorded with one reading of the past practice in relation to war crimes. It also explained the imposition of individual responsibility for crimes against humanity in circumstances where the German state had committed no international wrong (for example, for acts against its own populace).

2.63   A possible competing view, however, of the liability of individuals to punishment for violations of international law was that it was a function of state responsibility—that is, of the breach by the state of which the individual was an official of an obligation owed by it, rather than of the breach by the individual of an obligation owed by him or her. In turn, there were two possible ways of conceiving of the criminal responsibility of individuals for violations of international law as a function of state responsibility.

2.64   First, it could have been argued that certain egregious breaches of international obligations directed towards and binding on states gave rise under international law to a special secondary rule providing, as a function of the state's responsibility, for the individual criminal responsibility under international law itself of the government officials who, as the state's 'controlling mind', procured the breach, at least where the usual reparative mechanisms of state responsibility, namely restitution and compensation, would be materially impossible or unfeasible or would inadequately reflect the moral injury caused. Such an account of the theoretical underpinnings of individual criminal responsibility under international law would explain why, when it came to crimes against peace, the Nuremberg Charter was able to envisage and the Tribunal to conclude that the major German war criminals were personally liable to punishment for Germany's flagrant violations of the Kellogg–Briand Pact 1928,[129] which had outlawed, among the states parties to it, recourse to war as an instrument of national policy; and, to the extent that it could be argued that the defendant willed the breach and that restitution and compensation would be morally inadequate, the same reasoning might be applied to explain how the Tribunal was able to hold that individual criminal responsibility arose under international law itself for violations of the laws and customs of war codified in the 1907 Hague Regulations. Such a view would also square with the Tribunal's dictum that '[c]rimes against international law are committed by men, not by abstract entities, and only by punishing individuals who commit such crimes can the provisions of international law be enforced',[130] as well as with the view expressed by Lauterpacht, who had been instrumental in the inclusion of this passage in the

---

[127] Ibid, 220.   [128] Ibid, 221.
[129] General Treaty for the Renunciation of War as an Instrument of National Policy 1928 ('Kellogg–Briand Pact').
[130] Nuremberg judgment (n 115), 221.

Nuremberg judgment (having written the part of the UK prosecutor's address from which it was drawn), who stated:

In the field of [breach of treaty] and, to some extent, of [breach of customary international law], the requirements of justice and of international peace can be met by making the corporate entity of the State mainly, if not exclusively, the subject of responsibility. This is not so in the sphere of criminal acts performed by the State, *ie* by persons acting on behalf of the State and under the colour of the authority of the State.... The primary subject of the international duty is the human agency which puts in motion the criminal act...[131]

Terminologically, it could even be said in accordance with this way of thinking that the 'crime against international law' or 'crime under international law' referred to was the state's egregious breach of its obligations,[132] for which the individual officials could, *faute de mieux*, be punished as a matter of international law, rather than the individual's breach of an international prohibition directly binding on him or her.

Alternatively, in a variant of the approach founded on state responsibility, one could have argued that specific egregious breaches by a state of its international obligations gave rise, where the secondary obligations of restitution and compensation on their own would not repair the moral injury, to a secondary obligation of satisfaction on the part of the responsible state in the form of an obligation to prosecute the individuals who procured the breach,[133] an obligation delegated, via the concession of a corresponding right to prosecute, to an opposing belligerent in its capacity as an injured state in the event of the responsible state's default. In other words, individual responsibility for a 'crime against international law' or a 'crime under international law' could be characterized as a function of state responsibility and, additionally, as ultimately arising not under international law itself but under national law—or, in the case of a court constituted by more than one state, under a *sui generis* body of law agreed on for the purpose by those states. Such a characterization was made possible by the fact that the Nuremberg Charter, with its absence of any mention of international law, and certain passages of the Nuremberg judgment could together be read as implicating individual criminal responsibility for violations of international law not directly under international law as such but simply under the specific legal framework of the Nuremberg Charter as drafted and agreed on by the four Powers, even if the content of the latter was asserted to be in accordance with the former. Indeed, the Nuremberg IMT itself stated:

2.65

The Signatory Powers created this Tribunal [and] defined the law it was to administer... In doing so, they have done together what any one of them might have done singly...[134]

---

[131] Lauterpacht (n 5), 42–3.

[132] Indeed, this is precisely how the term 'international crime' was used in a range of inter-War international instruments cited by the Tribunal. See Nuremberg judgment (n 115), 219–20, referring to the Draft Treaty of Mutual Assistance 1923, the Geneva Protocol for the Pacific Settlement of International Disputes 1924, the League of Nations Assembly Declaration concerning Wars of Aggression, and the Havana Resolution on Aggression.

[133] Recall *supra* n 105.   [134] Nuremberg judgment (n 115), 216.

This reading, like the first, also accorded with one characterization of the principles underpinning the past trial of enemy soldiers by national military tribunals, and, indeed, the IMT sought support for its conclusion that 'individuals can be punished for violations of international law' in the practice of the US courts.[135] In addition, such a construction was on a par with the past use of the label 'offences against the law of nations' to refer to internationally wrongful acts such as attacks on ambassadors and violations of safe-conducts punishable under national law. Moreover, the grave breaches regime of the four Geneva Conventions of 1949, under which states parties are obliged to prosecute in their national courts the individual authors of specific aggravated breaches of the Conventions, could have been taken to lend support to this third approach.[136]

2.66 In the event, the ILC—as subsequently endorsed by the Sixth Committee of the General Assembly—settled on the first rationale, stating in the second paragraph of the commentary to Principle I of its Nürnberg Principles that '[t]he general rule underlying Principle I is that international law may impose duties on individuals directly without any interposition of internal law'.[137] Even then, however, the Commission voted six to five against inserting in Principle I itself an explicit acknowledgement of the necessary conclusion to be drawn from its commentary, namely that 'the individual is subject to international criminal law'.[138] Additionally, the UK representative to the Sixth Committee fought a rearguard action against the ILC's commentary, arguing instead in favour of viewing individual responsibility for 'crimes against international law' as a function of state responsibility. 'He fully agreed', he explained, 'that individuals who committed crimes under international law should be subject to trial and punishment', but he believed that 'th[is] aim could be achieved without adopting the theory of the responsibility of the individual under international law'.[139] 'All that was in fact necessary', he argued, 'was to establish the position in which the States admitted that the individuals under their jurisdiction would be subject to punishment for certain acts recognized as crimes under international law'.[140]

2.67 Individual criminal responsibility under international law for certain violations of customary international law is now axiomatic.[141] Moreover, it is accepted that the theoretical rationale for such responsibility is that the few penal rules of customary international law bind individuals directly, prohibiting and in some cases positively mandating conduct by them.

---

[135] Ibid, 220–1.
[136] Consider also, subsequently, art 28 of the Convention for the Protection of Cultural Property in the Event of Armed Conflict 1954, which obliges state parties 'to take, within the framework of their ordinary criminal jurisdiction, all necessary steps to prosecute and impose penal or disciplinary sanctions upon those persons, of whatever nationality, who commit or order to be committed a breach of the...Convention'.
[137] *Ybk ILC 1950*, vol II, 374, para 99.   [138] Ibid, vol I, 36.
[139] *Ybk ILC 1951*, vol II, 50, para 63.   [140] Ibid.
[141] See eg ICTY Statute, art 7(1); ICTR Statute, art 6(1); ILC Draft Statute, art 20 (by implication) and commentary; ILC Draft Code of Crimes, art 2(1) and commentary; Rome Statute, art 25, especially art 25(2); SCSL Statute, art 6(1).

2.68 If individual criminal responsibility under international law for the violation of certain rules of customary international law is conceptually possible, individual criminal responsibility under international law for the violation of specific treaty provisions should also be possible, and indeed is so.[142]

(ii) Acts of state

2.69 The acceptance after the Second World War of the possibility in principle of individual criminal responsibility under international law did not necessarily equate with an acceptance of the possibility in respect of all violations of the laws and customs of war, let alone in respect of illegally launching the War in the first place. It was open to argument that individuals who committed violations of the laws and customs of war in their capacity as an organ of state ought not to be responsible for them individually. If any responsibility arose from their conduct in such circumstances, it was properly to be seen as the state's and the state's alone. It was even more arguable that the whole notion of crimes against peace was misconceived in that only states were bound by the Kellogg–Briand Pact, the legal basis for crimes against peace, which outlawed the European Powers' recourse to war as an instrument of national policy.

2.70 In the event, sure enough, the defendants at Nuremberg submitted 'that where the act in question is an act of State, those who carry it out are not personally responsible'.[143] But article 7 of the Nuremberg Charter already provided that '[t]he official position of defendants, whether as Heads of State or responsible officials in Government Departments, shall not be considered as freeing them from responsibility or mitigating punishment'. Moreover, the Tribunal concluded:

> The principle of international law, which under certain circumstances protects the representatives of a state, cannot be applied to acts which are condemned as criminal by international law. The authors of these acts cannot shelter themselves behind their official position in order to be freed from punishment in appropriate proceedings.... [T]he very essence of the Charter is that individuals have international duties... He who violates the laws of war cannot obtain immunity while acting in pursuance of the authority of the state if the state in authorizing action moves outside its competence under international law.[144]

(The Tribunal's reference to 'immunity' is to substantive, and not simply procedural, immunity—that is, to the absence of criminal responsibility.)[145]

---

[142] See eg Kelsen (n 14), 537; Cryer (n 19), 108 and Cryer *et al* (n 38), 9–10; G Mettraux, *International Crimes and the* Ad Hoc *Tribunals* (Oxford: Oxford University Press, 2005), 7; D Akande, 'Sources of International Criminal Law' in A Cassese (ed), *The Oxford Companion to International Criminal Justice* (Oxford: Oxford University Press, 2009) 41, 48–9; M Milanović, 'Is the Rome Statute Binding on Individuals? (And Why We Should Care)' (2011) 9 *JICJ* 25, 38–47, especially 47.

[143] Nuremberg judgment (n 115), 220.   [144] Ibid, 221.

[145] In addition, the Tribunal's characterization of the relevant substantive defence as a principle of international law was mistaken. See R O'Keefe, 'The ILC's Contribution to International Criminal Law' (2006) 49 *GYIL* 201, 207–9.

2.71   The Tribunal's conclusion had its critics. Kelsen, in particular, maintained that, while the laws of war bound both states and individuals, breaches of these rules committed 'under the order or sanction of government' were formally acts of state, not of the individual concerned, and as such gave rise to the responsibility of the state alone.[146] As regards crimes against peace, the Kellogg–Briand Pact bound only states, so that, in Kelsen's view, its breach resulted in only state responsibility.[147]

2.72   The Nuremberg Charter and the judgment of the Tribunal were nonetheless affirmed as correct statements of international law in General Assembly resolution 95 (I), a position reaffirmed in Principle IV of the ILC's Nürnberg Principles. In the specific context of genocide, the Genocide Convention states in article IV that '[p]ersons committing genocide...shall be punished, whether they are constitutionally responsible rulers, public officials or private individuals'; and in *Reservations to the Convention on the Prevention and Punishment of the Crime of Genocide*, the ICJ stated that the Convention enunciates 'principles which are recognized by civilized nations as binding on States, even without any conventional obligation'[148]—in short, that at least what might be called its doctrinal provisions are consonant with customary international law.

2.73   Today there is no doubt that individuals can bear criminal responsibility under international law even in relation to conduct performed as an organ of state. The proposition has been affirmed many times in international instruments and documents.[149] As to crimes against peace specifically, article 6 of the Nuremberg Charter, endorsed in General Assembly resolution 95 (I), had already implemented the concept, and the Tribunal, going out of its way to justify this category of crime under international law,[150] convicted several defendants on this count. It is now formally indisputable that what is today instead called the crime of aggression gives rise to individual criminal responsibility under customary international law,[151] even if since Nuremberg principle has proved difficult to translate into practice.

---

[146] H Kelsen, 'Will the Judgment in the Nuremberg Trial Constitute a Precedent in International Law?' (1947) 1 *ILQ* 153, 161. The argument, as Kelsen saw it, was of a piece with his view that orders issued by a government or at the command or with the authorization of that government constituted a complete defence to individual criminal responsibility for violations of the laws of war.

[147] Ibid, 160–1: 'The military tribunals to whose practice the [Nuremberg] judgments refers tried and punished individuals for acts of illegitimate warfare performed by them as private persons, not as [an] act of State. The acts forbidden by the Hague Convention, it is true, may be acts of State, as well as acts of private persons performed on their own initiative, not at the command or with the authorisation of their government. However, as to its violation by acts of State, the Hague Convention [provides for] only collective responsibility of the States as such [under Article 3]....The differences between the Hague Convention on the rules of warfare and the Briand–Kellogg Pact is that the former can be violated by acts of State as well as by acts of private persons, whereas the latter can be violated only by acts of State. The Briand–Kellogg Pact does not—as does the Hague Convention—forbid acts of private persons.'

[148] *Reservations to the Convention on the Prevention and Punishment of the Crime of Genocide, Advisory Opinion*, ICJ Rep 1951, 15, 23.

[149] See eg ICTY Statute, art 7(2); ICTR Statute, art 6(2); ILC Draft Code of Crimes, art 7; Rome Statute, art 27(1); SCSL Statute, art 6(2). Article III of the Apartheid Convention recognizes the individual criminal responsibility under international law of 'representatives of the State'.

[150] See Nuremberg judgment (n 115), 218–19.

[151] See eg ILC Nürnberg Principles, principle VI; ILC Draft Code of Crimes, arts 2(2) and 16; Rome Statute, arts 5(*d*) and 8*bis*.

B. Individual Criminal Responsibility under International Law and State Responsibility

(i) General

It is now well established that individual criminal responsibility under international law is a function of the violation by an individual of an international legal obligation binding on him or her. This obligation is conceptually distinct from any obligation binding on any state as an organ of which the individual may act.[152] Indeed, the applicability to an individual of any international legal obligation of a penal character is in no way dependent on the applicability to any state whose organ the individual constitutes of any international legal obligation directed towards states[153]—or, for that matter, on the individual's acting as an organ of state in the first place.[154]

2.74

Putting it another way, the criminal responsibility of individuals under international law is not a function of, nor is it in any way formally implicated by, state responsibility for the breach by any relevant state of an international legal obligation binding on that state.[155] Equally, a finding of state responsibility does not relieve individuals of any criminal responsibility that they may bear under international law in respect of acts by them that are attributable to the relevant state. In short, state responsibility is without prejudice to individual criminal responsibility under international law.[156] Conversely, just because an individual whose acts are attributable to a state violates an international legal prohibition binding on that individual does not mean that the state is responsible for an international wrong.[157] Nor does a finding of that individual's criminal responsibility under international law relieve the state to which the acts of the individual are attributable of any responsibility that it may bear. That is, individual criminal responsibility under international law is without prejudice to state responsibility.[158] In sum, each of the two forms of international responsibility is the consequence of the violation of a different rule or, putting it another way, of a rule binding

2.75

---

[152] See also C Dominicé, 'La question de la double responsabilité de l'État et de son agent' in E Yakpo and T Boumedra (eds), *Liber Amicorum Judge Mohammed Bedjaoui* (The Hague: Kluwer, 1999) 143, 152, para 18 and 156, para 27; Werle and Jessburger (n 2), 43–5, paras 122–124. But cf A Bianchi, 'State Responsibility and Criminal Liability of Individuals' in A Cassese (ed), *The Oxford Companion to International Criminal Justice* (Oxford: Oxford University Press, 2009) 16, 19–20.

[153] This is manifest in the criminal responsibility under international law of state officials in circumstances where the state of which they are officials is not in breach of any international legal obligation owed by it.

[154] This is evident from the routine criminal responsibility under international law of private individuals, *viz* individuals who are not, or are not at the relevant time acting in the capacity of, an organ of state.

[155] But cf R Maison, *La responsabilité individuelle pour crime d'État en droit international public* (Bruxelles: Bruylant, 2004).

[156] See eg Articles on Responsibility of States, art 58 and commentary.

[157] In other words, there is no vicarious state responsibility for such internationally criminal acts of individuals as may be attributable to that state.

[158] See eg ILC Draft Code of Crimes, art 4 and commentary; Rome Statute, art 25(4).

80   *Foundational Concepts and Principles*

on a different subject of international law. This 'duality of responsibility' was emphasized by the ICJ in *Application of the Convention on the Prevention and Punishment of the Crime of Genocide*.[159]

2.76   Despite, however, emphasizing the conceptual separateness of individual criminal responsibility under international law and state responsibility, the ICJ in *Application of the Convention on the Prevention and Punishment of the Crime of Genocide* muddies the waters in deriving from article I of the Genocide Convention an implicit prohibition on the commission of genocide by the contracting parties themselves, and not merely by individuals. The Court reasons in part that '[s]uch a prohibition follows... from the fact that the Article categorizes genocide as "a crime under international law"', by which the Court means that, 'by agreeing to such a categorization, the States parties must logically be undertaking not to commit the act so described'.[160] With respect, this is nonsense. If the term 'crime under international law' refers to an international legal prohibition binding on individuals the breach of which gives rise to the individual criminal responsibility of the perpetrator under international law, and if, as the Court underlines,[161] individual criminal responsibility under international law and state responsibility are conceptually distinct, it is impossible to see how by recognizing a crime under international law a state undertakes not to commit the impugned conduct itself. The problem is compounded by the semantic and juridical oddity of the Court's position—a position into which the Court is forced by the fact that international law does not recognize the criminal responsibility of states, as the Court itself stresses[162]—that the commission of something labelled a 'crime' should result in delictual, not criminal, responsibility.[163] The only possible explanation would seem to be that the Court misconstrues the term 'crime under international law' as used in article I of the Convention.

(ii) Crimes under international law and equivalent obligations for states

2.77   Of the four undisputed heads of crime under customary international law, three—war crimes, genocide, and aggression—are paralleled by respective obligations on states not to engage in equivalent conduct. The same would go for the customary international crime putatively constituted by a single act of torture by a state official. That is, independently of the relevant customary international criminal obligations directed towards and binding on individuals, states are the subject of conventional and customary obligations under international

---

[159] *Application of the Genocide Convention* (n 5), 116, para 173. See also, subsequently, *Jones et al v United Kingdom* (Merits and Just Satisfaction), nos 34356/06 & 40528/06, ECHR 2014, para 207.
[160] *Application of the Genocide Convention* (n 5), 113, para 166.   [161] Recall *supra* n 159.
[162] *Application of the Genocide Convention* (n 5), 114, para 167 and 115, para 170.
[163] See also ibid, 371 (dec Skotnikov). It is certainly not the case under the major national legal systems that a criminal prohibition is per se alternatively remediable as a tort. Conduct amounting to a crime often amounts additionally and coincidentally to a tort, but a crime is not *ipso facto* substitutable by a tort.

humanitarian law,[164] of conventional and customary prohibitions on acts of genocide,[165] of a customary prohibition on acts of aggression,[166] and of conventional and customary prohibitions on torture.[167] Breach of these obligations results in state responsibility, which in turn generates for the responsible state secondary obligations of cessation and non-repetition and of reparation.[168]

2.78 In contrast, there is no persuasive evidence for the existence of an obligation on states not to commit crimes against humanity as such.[169] At the same time, many specific acts which, if performed by individuals endowed with the requisite intent and knowledge, would constitute crimes against humanity under customary international law are prohibited by rules directed towards and binding on states as a matter of customary and conventional international human rights law, customary and conventional international humanitarian law, and other customary and conventional rules of international law the breach of which results in state responsibility.

(iii) Crimes under international law and jus cogens

2.79 It is not infrequently asserted that some or all of the crimes under customary international law of genocide, crimes against humanity, war crimes, aggression, and torture as a putative customary crime in its own right enjoy the status of peremptory norms of general (that is, customary) international law or, synonymously,

---

[164] For the relevant conventional obligations on states, see the raft of conventions on international humanitarian law, such as the 1949 Geneva Conventions and their Additional Protocols. For the relevant customary rules, see eg J-M Henckaerts and L Doswald-Beck, *Customary International Humanitarian Law* (Cambridge: Cambridge University Press, 2005), 3 vols.

[165] See *Application of the Genocide Convention* (n 5), 114, para 167 and 118–19, para 179, finding in the Genocide Convention an implied prohibition on the commission of genocide by states parties. The existence of a customary prohibition on the commission of genocide by a state is, *inter alia*, implicit in the repeated characterization of the prohibition on genocide as a rule of the character of *jus cogens*. See eg *Armed Activities on the Territory of the Congo (New Application: 2002) (Democratic Republic of the Congo v Rwanda), Jurisdiction and Admissibility, Judgment*, ICJ Rep 2006, 6, 32, para 64; paras 4 to 6 of the commentary to art 26 and para 4 of the commentary to art 40 of the Articles on Responsibility of States.

[166] See eg para 5 of the commentary to art 26 and para 4 of the commentary to art 40 of the Articles on Responsibility of States, characterizing the prohibition on aggression by a state as one of *jus cogens* and therefore, by implication, customary. Insofar as a flagrant violation of art 2(4) of the UN Charter amounts to an act of aggression, it could also be said that there exists a conventional prohibition on aggression by a UN member state.

[167] For the conventional prohibition on torture by a state, see, *inter alia*, International Covenant on Civil and Political Rights 1966, art 7. It is generally recognized that torture by a state is prohibited by customary international law as well, as implied by, *inter alia*, the frequent characterization of the prohibition as one of *jus cogens*, as per *infra* n 175.

[168] See Articles on Responsibility of States, arts 30 and 31.

[169] In para 4 of its commentary to art 26 of its Articles on Responsibility of States, the ILC refers to 'the prohibition[ ] of...crimes against humanity' as one of the 'peremptory norms that are clearly accepted and recognized'. The characterization is not repeated in the commentary to art 40, and there is little else to suggest that states are prohibited from committing crimes against humanity as such, as formally distinct from any violations of international human rights guarantees, of rules of international humanitarian law, and so on that may overlap factually with acts constituting crimes against humanity on the part of individual perpetrators.

norms of *jus cogens*.¹⁷⁰ The claim would necessarily appear to be that the respective customary international prohibitions on the commission by an individual of the crime of genocide, of crimes against humanity, etc are prohibitions from which no derogation is permitted. Such assertions call for closer analysis.

2.80 As originally and usually conceived, the idea of peremptory norms of international law (*jus cogens*) relates to obligations, negative or positive, directed towards and binding on states. It is by no means evident that the notion does, as a matter of positive law, or could, as a conceptual matter, pertain to those few prohibitions of customary international law directed towards and binding on individuals. As a conceptual matter, the essence of a peremptory norm of international law as classically formulated is that it may not be derogated from by a state—that is, it may not, once applicable, be set aside by a state as inapplicable to it in given circumstances.¹⁷¹ Since it is not apparent that individuals have or could in principle have the capacity to derogate from those prohibitions of customary international law directed towards and binding on them, it is difficult to see how the concept of *jus cogens* could pertain to crimes under customary international law as such.¹⁷²

2.81 When it is said by usually reliable authorities that the prohibitions on, for example, genocide,¹⁷³ aggression,¹⁷⁴ and torture¹⁷⁵ are rules of *jus cogens*, what is being referred to are the separate prohibitions on the commission of such acts by a state, the legal consequence of which would be the state's delictual responsibility. As for the ICJ's description in *Jurisdictional Immunities of the State* of its judgment in *Arrest Warrant* as involving 'a Minister for Foreign Affairs…accused of criminal violations of rules which undoubtedly possess the character of *jus cogens*',¹⁷⁶ the cryptic reference would appear to be to the grave breaches of which the minister was accused of the customary rules embodied as a matter of treaty law in the

---

¹⁷⁰ See eg Bassiouni (n 19), 138 and 172–8; A Nollkaemper, 'Concurrence between Individual Responsibility and State Responsibility in International Law' (2003) 52 *ICLQ* 615, 623.

¹⁷¹ Derogation from a rule is to be distinguished from its violation. Derogation amounts to a claim by a state that a given rule does not apply to it, whether at all or in specified circumstances. It amounts, in short, to opting out of the rule unilaterally. So, eg, states are said to derogate from a rule of customary international law when they enter into a treaty to different effect. Violation, on the other hand, is simply the breach of an applicable rule. A state is not permitted to violate any rule of international law, be it a rule of treaty, of ordinary custom, or of *jus cogens*. But only rules having the character of *jus cogens* are rules from which a state may not derogate.

¹⁷² It may instead be that the envisaged hypothetical derogation is by a state, as regards the application to its nationals and/or within its territory of a particular customary international prohibition on the conduct of individuals. But the convolutedness of, and doubtful conceptual basis for, the scenario speak to its implausibility.

¹⁷³ See *supra* n 165.   ¹⁷⁴ See *supra* n 166.

¹⁷⁵ See eg *Obligation to Prosecute or Extradite* (n 22), 457, para 99; *Prosecutor v Furundžija*, IT-95-17/1, Trial Chamber, Judgment, 10 December 1998, para 144; para 5 of the commentary to art 27 and para 5 of the commentary to art 40 of the Articles on Responsibility of States. Indeed, it is worth noting in *Obligation to Prosecute or Extradite* (n 22), 457, para 99, the ICJ's studious avoidance of the term 'international crime' in its discussion of the prohibition on torture as a peremptory norm of customary international law, despite its recollection, ibid, 456, para 97, of the parties' agreement 'that acts of torture are regarded by customary international law as international crimes, independently of the [Torture] Convention'.

¹⁷⁶ *Jurisdictional Immunities of the State (Germany v Italy: Greece intervening), Merits, Judgment*, ICJ Rep 2012, 99, 141, para 95, referring to *Arrest Warrant* (n 23).

The Concept of an International Crime

Fourth Geneva Convention, breaches for which the individual perpetrators are punishable under international law over and above the delictual responsibility of the state to which their conduct is attributable.[177]

C. The Theoretical Source of the Binding Nature of Criminal Obligations under International Law

The theoretical source of the binding nature for individuals of criminal obligations under international law is simply the sovereign will of the states recognizing, *viz* establishing, such obligations. It is immaterial in this regard that individuals themselves lack the international legal capacity to consent to be bound by rules of customary international law or treaty. States are the sovereign legislators, as it were, in the international legal system. There are no inherent limits on their competence to create obligations under international law for whichever natural[178] or legal[179] persons they please. In short, international law is what states make it, and they can make it bind individuals directly.[180]

2.82

---

[177] The Court's formulation is unfortunate insofar as it could be taken to suggest that this individual criminal responsibility for grave breaches of the rules reflected in the Convention is a legal consequence of the state's, rather than the individual's, breach of those rules.

[178] But cf the outdated statement of the Permanent Court of International Justice in *Jurisdiction of the Courts of Danzig*, PCIJ Ser B No 15 (1928), 17, that, 'according to a well established principle of international law,... an international agreement... cannot, as such, create direct rights and obligations for private individuals'. It is true that the Court immediately qualifies this with the observation, ibid, 17–18, that 'it cannot be disputed that the very object of an international agreement, according to the intention of the contracting Parties, may be the adoption by the Parties of some definite rules creating individual rights and obligations and enforceable by the national courts'. Indeed, it is not uncommon for commentators to rely on the Court's qualification in support of the capacity of states to impose international legal obligations on individuals, in this case by way of treaty. See eg S Sivakumaran, 'Binding Armed Opposition Groups' (2006) 55 *ICLQ* 369, 384; Cryer (n 19), 121 (not, significantly, reproducing the words 'and enforceable by the national courts') and Cryer *et al* (n 38), 10; Milanović (n 142), 45 note 87. The difficulty, however, is that the 'definite rules creating individual rights and obligations' referred to by the Court in the second sentence, although arising without interposition of national legislation from the international agreement in question, were not, in the case before and in the mind of the Court, international legal rights and obligations; rather, applicable as they were intended by the Danzig–Poland *Beamtenabkommen* to be between the Polish Railways Administration and the Danzig officials, workmen, and employees who had passed into the permanent service of the former, they were no more than an internationally-created species of *sui generis* municipal legal right and obligation—in essence, rights and obligations arising from a contract of service, albeit not one concluded under Polish law. As much is clear from the Court's restatement of the question before it, ibid, 17, which paraphrases the Free City of Danzig's submission that 'the *Beamtenabkommen*, though an international agreement in form, was intended by the contracting Parties to constitute part of the "series of provisions which establish the legal relationship between the Railways Administration and its employees" ("contract of service") and that it is the substance rather than the form of the instrument that determines its juridical character'. That said, the Court's second statement at the very least supports the argument that states can, via international law, create legal obligations of some sort for individuals. In the final analysis, moreover, the point is moot, given that it is now accepted beyond doubt that treaties can create international legal rights and obligations for individuals.

[179] Note, however, that—as a function of a rule established by states themselves—states may not impose treaty obligations on an international (that is, intergovernmental) organization without the latter's consent.

[180] See also Kelsen (n 14), 537; Cryer (n 19), 121; Milanović (n 142), 38–47, especially 47.

V. Conclusion

2.83 In the final analysis, what one chooses to call an 'international crime' is largely a matter of taste, provided that the terminological choice is limited to that between all offences defined by international law and those offences defined by international law that give rise to individual criminal responsibility under international law. The first, more inclusive understanding is the one promoted in this book. The second, more restrictive category of offences, referred to throughout this book as 'crimes under international law', is accordingly treated as a species of the first. In creating obligations for individuals, this second category of offences represents an anomalous corpus of public international legal rules which are to be distinguished at all times, conceptually and technically, from rules creating obligations for states.

Further Reading

BIANCHI, A, 'State Responsibility and Criminal Liability of Individuals' in A Cassese (ed), *The Oxford Companion to International Criminal Justice* (Oxford: Oxford University Press, 2009), 16

CRYER, R, 'The Doctrinal Foundations of International Criminalization' in MC Bassiouni (ed), *International Criminal Law. Volume I: Sources, Subjects, and Contents* (3rd edn, Leiden: Martinus Nijhoff, 2008), 107

DAVID, E, 'Les valeurs, politiques et objectifs du droit pénal international à l'heure de la mondialisation' in Association internationale de droit pénal, *International Criminal Law: Quo Vadis?* (Nouvelles études pénales No 19, 2004), 157

DINSTEIN, Y, 'International Criminal Law' (1985) 20 *Israel Law Review* 206

DOMINICÉ, C, 'La question de la double responsabilité de l'État et de son agent' in E Yakpo and T Boumedra (eds), *Liber Amicorum Judge Mohammed Bedjaoui* (The Hague: Kluwer, 1999), 143

METTRAUX, G (ed), *Perspectives on the Nuremberg Trial* (Oxford: Oxford University Press, 2008)

NOLLKAEMPER, A, 'Concurrence between Individual Responsibility and State Responsibility in International Law' (2003) 52 *International and Comparative Law Quarterly* 615

O'KEEFE, R, 'The ILC's Contribution to International Criminal Law' (2006) 49 *German Yearbook of International Law* 201

PARLETT, K, *The Individual in the International Legal System: Continuity and Change in International Law* (Cambridge: Cambridge University Press, 2011), chapter 4

3
The Types of Criminal Court

I. Introduction

The prosecution of international crimes need not take place before international criminal courts. Municipal (synonymously, 'domestic' or 'national') criminal courts also play a role in the adjudication of international crimes. Moreover, for the purposes of international law, not much hangs on the formal juridical distinction between international and national criminal courts. Of greater significance in international legal terms are the different legal bases on which international criminal courts can be established and empowered. More important in practical terms, furthermore, are the differences as to jurisdiction *ratione materiae*, applicable law, rules of procedure and evidence, composition of the bench and its method of appointment, and so on, among international criminal courts and municipal criminal courts respectively. 3.1

After prefatory terminological and conceptual clarifications, this chapter examines the basis for, and the international legal significance of, the distinction between international and municipal criminal courts. It also looks at what, in juridical terms, are the more important differences among international criminal courts when it comes to the legal underpinnings of their establishment and empowerment. 3.2

II. Terminology

Collective reference is commonly made to 'international criminal courts and tribunals', rather than just to 'international criminal courts' or to 'international criminal tribunals'. This is for the straightforward reason that two of the international criminal adjudicative bodies that have existed or do exist have been or are labelled courts,[1] while the rest have been or are labelled tribunals.[2] The conjunctive formulation, while unobjectionable in legal terms, is cumbersome. Since the 3.3

---

[1] These are the Special Court for Sierra Leone and the International Criminal Court.
[2] These are the International Military Tribunal at Nuremberg, the International Military Tribunal for the Far East at Tokyo, the International Criminal Tribunal for the former Yugoslavia, the International Criminal Tribunal for Rwanda, and the Special Tribunal for Lebanon.

difference between a 'court' and a 'tribunal' is of no international legal significance,³ and since a judicial body is more commonly referred to in ordinary usage as a 'court', this book uses 'international criminal courts' as the generic term for those international judicial bodies that adjudicate upon criminal matters. Similarly, generic reference is made throughout the book to 'municipal criminal courts', rather than to 'municipal criminal courts and tribunals'. Although the distinction between courts and tribunals may be of constitutional significance in some municipal legal systems, it is irrelevant for the purposes of international law, and a more concise term is again preferable from the point of view of convenience.

3.4   It is not uncommon for commentators to use the expression 'the ad hoc international criminal tribunals' to refer only to the International Criminal Tribunal for the former Yugoslavia (ICTY) and the International Criminal Tribunal for Rwanda (ICTR). The restriction of the application of the label to these two tribunals has no juridical or logical basis, and it is unlikely that any is intended. Any international criminal adjudicative body established on a temporary basis in response to specific circumstances—in other words, every international criminal adjudicative body seen to date with the exception of the permanent International Criminal Court (ICC)—is by definition an ad hoc international criminal tribunal or, as this book prefers to call them, an ad hoc international criminal court.

III. International and Municipal Criminal Courts: A Formal Binarism

3.5   The basis of the formal legal distinction between international criminal courts and municipal criminal courts is rarely articulated.⁴ Indeed, there seems to be an embarrassed silence over what this basis might be. Nor is conceptual clarity fostered by reference to 'hybrid', 'mixed', and 'internationalized' criminal courts. The following is with a view to such clarity.

A. No Formal Category of 'Hybrid', 'Mixed' or 'Internationalized' Criminal Courts

3.6   As a formal juridical matter, there exist only two species of criminal court, namely international criminal courts and municipal criminal courts. In strict juridical

---

³ As a semantic matter, the term 'tribunal' tends to connote an ad hoc judicial body, although not all such bodies are given this label, the Special Court for Sierra Leone—an ad hoc international criminal court—being a case in point.

⁴ See also KJ Heller, *The Nuremberg Military Tribunals and the Origins of International Criminal Law* (Oxford: Oxford University Press, 2011), 110; A Kjeldgaard-Pedersen, 'What Defines an International Criminal Court? A Critical Assessment of "the Involvement of the International Community" as a Deciding Factor' (2015) 28 *LJIL* 113, 113–14.

terms, there is no third species of criminal court, variously labelled 'hybrid', 'mixed', 'internationalized' or the like. This is not to say that these adjectives are devoid of value. On the contrary, they may usefully describe the judicial composition, jurisdiction *ratione materiae*, and applicable law of a criminal court, whether international or municipal. But they do no more than this. They do not denote a formal legal category of court. If anything, they obscure the formal legal character of any court referred to.

The composition of the court, its jurisdiction *ratione materiae*, and its applicable law have no bearing on its formal legal character. An international criminal court could be staffed by judges, prosecutors, and administrative personnel of a single nationality appointed by the state of nationality; its jurisdiction *ratione materiae* could comprise exclusively municipal crimes; and it could apply exclusively municipal law. None of this would make it, in strict juridical terms, a 'hybrid' or 'mixed' criminal court. Conversely, a municipal criminal court could be staffed exclusively by foreign judges, prosecutors, and administrative personnel appointed by foreign states or by an international organization; its jurisdiction *ratione materiae* could comprise exclusively international crimes; and it could apply exclusively international law. None of this would make it, in strict juridical terms, a 'hybrid', 'mixed', or 'internationalized' criminal court. In the final analysis, whatever its descriptive admixture of 'international' and 'municipal' elements (which is usually one of any number of gradations between the foregoing poles), a criminal court must formally be either international or municipal.   3.7

B. International versus Municipal Criminal Courts: The Distinction

The juridical character of a criminal court as either international or municipal is a function of the legal order on which the court formally[5] depends for its existence and competence.[6] If the court's establishment and judicial powers derive without formal interposition of municipal law from an international legal instrument or act, be it a treaty, a resolution, decision, regulation, proclamation, etc of an organ of an international organization or of a joint organ of two or more states, a joint declaration by two or more states, or the like, the court is international. Conversely, if the court's establishment and judicial powers derive without formal interposition of international law from a municipal legal instrument or act, be it primary legislation, subordinate legislation, executive decree, or the like, the court is municipal.   3.8

Just as a criminal court's composition, jurisdiction *ratione materiae*, and applicable law cannot transform it, in strict juridical terms, into a third category of criminal court, *viz* a 'hybrid' or 'mixed' court,[7] so too are they irrelevant to whether the   3.9

---

[5] For the emphasis on formal dependence, consider *infra* n 28.
[6] See also, in essence, Kjeldgaard-Pedersen (n 4), 131.   [7] Recall *supra* para 3.6.

court is international or municipal. The judges of an international criminal court need not come from more than one state or be appointed by more than one state or by an international body, and an international criminal court can be vested with subject-matter jurisdiction over municipal crimes and can apply municipal law.[8] Conversely, a municipal criminal court can be composed of foreign judges appointed by foreign states or by an international body, it can be vested with jurisdiction over international crimes, and it can apply international law. It all depends on what the court's constituent instrument provides.

C. International Criminal Courts

(i) Definition

3.10 An international criminal court is a criminal court that formally depends for its existence and competence on international law. In other words, an international criminal court is a criminal court whose establishment and judicial powers derive without formal interposition of municipal law from an international legal instrument or act.[9] This will usually mean that the court's constituent instrument—its statute, charter, or the like—is itself an international legal instrument, be it a treaty or annex thereto, an annex to a resolution of the United Nations Security Council, a proclamation or the like by a joint organ of two or more states, or some other international legal instrument. Alternatively, it may mean that the court's constituent instrument takes the form of or is found in some other document on which an international legal instrument or act has conferred the force of international law by means of express incorporation, adoption, or the like. Indeed, it may mean that the court's constituent instrument takes the form of a municipal legal instrument, whether primary or subordinate legislation, executive decree, etc, on which the force of international law has been conferred by an international legal instrument or act.

---

[8] Where an international criminal tribunal is mandated to apply municipal law, the tribunal—which, in contrast to its assumed knowledge of international law, is not deemed to know the municipal law of every state, as made clear in *Payment in Gold of the Brazilian Federal Loans Issued in France*, PCIJ Rep Ser A No 21 (1929), 124—must ascertain the rule to be applied, either by means of evidence furnished by the parties or through research conducted by it or under its aegis, and must seek to apply that rule as it would be applied in the state in question, paying utmost regard to the decisions of that state's courts. If, however, the municipal law is uncertain or divided on a given point, it is up to the international tribunal to choose the interpretation it considers most in conformity with that law. See eg *Payment of Various Serbian Loans Issued in France*, PCIJ Rep Ser A No 20 (1929), 46–7; *Brazilian Loans* (*supra*), 124; *Prosecutor v Ayyash* et al, STL-11-01/I/AC/R176*bis*, Appeals Chamber, Interlocutory Decision on the Applicable Law: Terrorism, Conspiracy, Homicide, Perpetration, Cumulative Charging, 16 February 2011, paras 35 and 40. In such cases, the international tribunal's determination on a point of municipal law has no formal bearing on how that law is to be applied by the courts of the relevant state.

[9] See eg G Schwarzenberger, 'The Judgment of Nuremberg' (1946–47) 21 *Tulane LR* 329, 333; G Dahm, *Zur Problematik des Völkerstrafrechts* (Göttingen: Vandenhoeck & Ruprecht, 1956), 17–18; Kjeldgaard-Pedersen (n 4), 131.

(ii) Legal means of establishment and empowerment

3.11 To date, international criminal courts have been established and empowered by way of four different international legal instruments or acts. The first is by way of a multilateral treaty among states, the second by way of a proclamation of a joint organ of several states, the third by way of a bilateral treaty between a state and an international organization (in this case the United Nations), and the fourth by way of a decision of the UN Security Council under chapter VII of the UN Charter.

(a) Multilateral treaty among states

3.12 The International Military Tribunal at Nuremberg ('Nuremberg IMT')[10] and the ICC[11] are so far the only two international criminal courts to have owed their existence and competence to a multilateral treaty among states.

3.13 The Charter of the Nuremberg IMT ('Nuremberg Charter') was annexed to the Agreement by the Government of the United Kingdom of Great Britain and Northern Ireland, the Government of the United States of America, the Provisional Government of the French Republic and the Government of the Union of Soviet Socialist Republics for the Prosecution and Punishment of the Major War Criminals of the European Axis, concluded in London on 8 August 1945. Article 1 of the UK–US–France–USSR Agreement states that 'there shall be established...an International Military Tribunal', while article 2 specifies that '[t]he constitution, jurisdiction and functions of the International Military Tribunal shall be those set [out] in the Charter annexed to this Agreement, which Charter shall form an integral part of this Agreement'. The Rome Statute of the International Criminal Court ('Rome Statute'), concluded in Rome on 17 July 1998, is itself a multilateral treaty, open to participation by all states. Article 1 of the Rome Statute provides that '[a]n International Criminal Court ('the Court') is hereby established' and that '[t]he jurisdiction and functioning of the Court shall be governed by the provisions of this Statute'. In neither case did or do the court's establishment and judicial powers formally depend on the municipal law of any state. The Nuremberg IMT derived its existence and competence directly from the UK–US–France–USSR Agreement and annexed Charter, while the ICC derives its directly from the Rome Statute.

(b) Proclamation of a joint organ of states

3.14 The International Military Tribunal for the Far East, better known as the Tokyo IMT or Tokyo Tribunal, is the only international criminal court to date to have been established and empowered by means of a proclamation issued by a joint organ of several states.[12]

---

[10] Recall, generally, *supra* paras 2.57–2.65 and 2.70–2.73.
[11] See, generally, *infra* chapter 14.
[12] For the background to the Tokyo Tribunal's establishment, see N Boister and R Cryer, *The Tokyo International Military Tribunal: A Reappraisal* (Oxford: Oxford University Press, 2008), 20–7.

3.15 On 2 September 1945, Japan surrendered unconditionally to the Allied Powers,[13] represented by the Supreme Commander for the Allied Powers (SCAP), General Douglas MacArthur.[14] On 26 December 1945, at the Moscow Conference, the US, UK, and USSR, backed by China, agreed that SCAP would, on their joint behalf, 'issue all orders for the implementation of the Terms of Surrender [and] the occupation and control of Japan'.[15] On 19 January 1946, SCAP took the decision to issue a special proclamation establishing the Tokyo IMT, which provided in relevant part:

Whereas, the Governments of the Allied Powers at war with Japan on the 26th July 1945 at Potsdam, declared as one of the terms of surrender that stern justice shall be meted out to all war criminals including those who have visited cruelties upon our prisoners;...

Whereas, the undersigned has been designated by the Allied Powers as Supreme Commander for the Allied Powers to carry into effect the general surrender of the Japanese armed forces;

Whereas, the Governments of the United States, Great Britain and Russia at the Moscow Conference, 26th December 1945, having considered the effectuation by Japan of the Terms of Surrender, with the concurrence of China have agreed that the Supreme Commander shall issue all Orders for the implementation of the Terms of Surrender.

Now, therefore, I, Douglas MacArthur, as Supreme Commander for the Allied Powers, by virtue of the authority so conferred upon me, in order to implement the Term of Surrender which requires the meting out of stern justice to war criminals, do order and provide as follows:

Article 1. There shall be established an International Military Tribunal for the Far East for the trial of those persons charged individually, or as members of organizations, or in both capacities, with offenses which include crimes against peace.

Article 2. The Constitution, jurisdiction and functions of this Tribunal are those set forth in the Charter of the International Military Tribunal for the Far East, approved by me this day.[16]

The Charter of the International Military Tribunal for the Far East was approved by SCAP the same day and issued by way of general orders.[17] After a subsequent directive to him by the Far Eastern Commission (FEC),[18] a body

---

[13] The Allied Powers in the Far Eastern and Pacific theatres of the Second World War comprised the US, the UK, the USSR, China, Australia, Canada, France, the Netherlands, and New Zealand.

[14] The US was represented by Admiral Nimitz.

[15] *United States of America and Others v Araki and Others*, Judgment of the International Military Tribunal for the Far East, Tokyo, 4 November 1948, in N Boister and R Cryer (eds), *Documents on the Tokyo International Military Tribunal. Charter, Indictment and Judgments* (Oxford: Oxford University Press, 2008), 71, 73 (Transcript, 48,418).

[16] Special Proclamation: Establishment of an International Military Tribunal for the Far East, Tokyo, 19 January 1946, 4 Bevans 20.

[17] General Orders No 1, General Headquarters, SCAP, 19 January 1946, 4 Bevans 21.

[18] The Far Eastern Commission (FEC) was established by the Allied Powers at the Moscow Conference to formulate policy for Japan's fulfilment of the terms of surrender and to 'review...any directive issued by the Supreme Commander for the Allied Powers or any action taken by the Supreme Commander involving policy decisions within the jurisdiction of the Commission'. See Soviet–Anglo–American Communiqué, 27 December 1945 ('Report of the Meeting of the Ministers of Foreign Affairs of the Union of Soviet Socialist Republics, the United States of America and the United Kingdom'), section II.A ('Far Eastern Commission'), para II(A)(2).

comprising representatives of each of the Allied Powers plus India and the Philippines, SCAP issued further general orders amending the Charter of the Tribunal.[19] Neither the Tribunal's existence nor its competence required the formal interposition of municipal law. The Tokyo IMT was established directly under SCAP's special proclamation of 19 January 1946, and it took its judicial powers directly from the Proclamation and Charter, the latter as amended on 26 April 1946.

3.16 That the Tokyo IMT was not a US court or tribunal, and by implication that it was an international one, was accepted by the US Supreme Court in *Hirota v MacArthur, General of the Army*, et al,[20] a challenge by one of the convicted defendants to the constitutionality under US law of the Tribunal's establishment. The Court stated:

We are satisfied that the tribunal sentencing these petitioners is not a tribunal of the United States. The United States and other allied countries conquered and now occupy and control Japan. General Douglas MacArthur has been selected and is acting as the Supreme Commander for the Allied Powers. The military tribunal sentencing these petitioners has been set up by General MacArthur as the agent of the Allied Powers.[21]

It is well accepted that the Tokyo IMT, as a criminal court established and empowered by the act of a joint organ of several states, was an international criminal court.[22]

(c) Bilateral treaty between a state and an international organization

3.17 The Special Court for Sierra Leone (SCSL) and the Residual Special Court for Sierra Leone (RSCSL) are to date the only international criminal courts to have been established and vested with judicial powers via a bilateral treaty between a state and an international organization.[23]

3.18 The Statute of the Special Court for Sierra Leone was annexed to the Agreement between the United Nations and the Government of Sierra Leone on the Establishment of a Special Court for Sierra Leone concluded in Freetown on 16 January 2002 ('SCSL Agreement'), negotiated and concluded on behalf of the UN by the Secretary-General, via his representative, at the request of the Security Council.[24] Article 1(1) of the SCSL Agreement provides that '[t]here is hereby established a Special Court for Sierra Leone', while article 1(2) stipulates that '[t]he Special Court shall function in accordance with the Statute of the Special Court for Sierra Leone…annexed to this Agreement and form[ing] an integral part thereof'. Article 1(1) and (2) of the Agreement between the United Nations and the Government of Sierra Leone on the Establishment of a Residual Special Court for Sierra Leone concluded in Freetown on 11 August

---

[19] General Orders No 20, General Headquarters, SCAP, 26 April 1946, 4 Bevans 27.
[20] 338 US 197 (1948).   [21] Ibid, 198.
[22] See eg, among myriad others, Boister and Cryer (n 12), 31, concluding that 'it can be unequivocally accepted that the Tokyo IMT was an international tribunal'.
[23] See, generally, *infra* chapter 13.   [24] See SC res 1315 (2000), 14 August 2000.

2010 ('RSCSL Agreement') provide and stipulate the same, *mutatis mutandis*, in relation to the RSCSL, with article 1(3) adding that '[t]he Residual Special Court shall continue the jurisdiction, functions, rights and obligations of the Special Court subject to the provisions of this Agreement and the Statute'.

3.19 The SCSL did not formally depend nor does the RSCSL formally depend for its establishment or judicial powers on the municipal law of Sierra Leone or any other state. The SCSL formally derived its existence and competence directly from the SCSL Agreement and annexed SCSL Statute. Although Sierra Leone enacted the Special Court Agreement 2002 (Ratification) Act 2002, as amended by the Special Court Agreement 2002 (Ratification)(Amendment) Act 2002, the SCSL was formally established and empowered not by the Act but by the Agreement and annexed Statute, unmediated by Sierra Leonean law.[25] The purpose and legal effect of the Act[26] were, first, to fulfil the requirement of section 40(4) of the Constitution of Sierra Leone that certain treaties entered into by Sierra Leone through the action of its president be ratified[27] by parliament[28] and, secondly, to provide for the SCSL's legal capacities, the inviolability and immunity from legal process of its property, and so on, as a matter of Sierra Leonean law; to permit it, as a matter of Sierra Leonean law, to sit in Sierra Leone and to exercise there the jurisdiction granted it by its Statute; to stipulate, for the avoidance of doubt, that the SCSL '[did] not form part of the Judiciary of Sierra Leone' and that offences prosecuted before the SCSL '[were] not prosecuted in the name of the Republic of

---

[25] See eg *Prosecutor v Kanu*, SCSL-2004-16-AR72(E), Appeals Chamber, Decision on Motion Challenging Jurisdiction and Raising Objections Based on Abuse of Process, 25 May 2004, para 2, citation omitted: 'The Special Court is vested with its own specific jurisdiction and competence by the constitutive documents establishing it.... [I]t operates outside the legal system of Sierra Leone and does not derive its jurisdiction from or within that system.' See also *Prosecutor v Kondewa*, SCSL-2004-14-AR72(E), Appeals Chamber, Decision on Preliminary Motion on Lack of Jurisdiction: Establishment of Special Court Violates Constitution of Sierra Leone, 25 May 2004, sep op Robertson, paras 15–18, citations omitted, noting, *inter alia*, that the SCSL was 'established by the Agreement itself, and not by the Ratification Act'; that 'the Agreement entered into force, independently of the local ratifying legislation, by virtue of mutual notification by the parties under Article 21, which [was] not preconditioned upon ratification'; that the SCSL 'derives no power from the law of Sierra Leone'; and that the SCSL 'derives no juristic authority from national law'.

[26] See Special Court Agreement 2002 (Ratification) Act 2002, long title and preamble.

[27] The term is used in section 40(4) of the Constitution of Sierra Leone to denote not ratification within the meaning of the international law of treaties (see Vienna Convention on the Law of Treaties 1969, arts 11, 14, 16, 18, and 19) but, rather, parliamentary approval for, *inter alia*, such changes to the law of Sierra Leone as may be effected by those provisions of the treaty deemed self-executing in the Sierra Leonean legal order.

[28] This in turn enabled Sierra Leone to notify the United Nations that the requirements of its municipal law necessary for the giving of domestic legal effect to the Agreement had been complied with, with the consequence that, in accordance with the procedure specified in art 21 for the Agreement's entry into force, the SCSL Agreement duly entered into force. That the Agreement's entry into force was dependent as a practical matter on the enactment by the government of Sierra Leone of 'ratifying' legislation does not mean, however, that the establishment and judicial powers of the SCSL were dependent as a formal legal matter on Sierra Leonean law. It remains the case that the SCSL formally derived its existence and competence directly from the Agreement, making it an international court.

Sierra Leone'; to direct the Attorney-General of Sierra Leone to provide assistance to the SCSL in specified circumstances; to grant force of Sierra Leonean law to orders made by the SCSL; to provide under Sierra Leonean law for offences against the administration of justice by the SCSL; and so on.[29] For its part, the Residual Special Court for Sierra Leone Agreement (Ratification) Act 2011 has the purpose and legal effect merely of ratifying, within the meaning of section 40(4) of the Constitution of Sierra Leone, the president's expression of Sierra Leone's consent to be bound by the RSCSL Agreement. The RSCSL formally owes its establishment and judicial powers directly to the RSCSL Agreement and annexed RSCSL Statute.

3.20 The SCSL is often referred to as a 'hybrid' or 'mixed' court. The labels are apt to mislead. The Special Court's composition and jurisdiction *ratione materiae* could be described as 'mixed',[30] in that its bench comprised both judges appointed by the UN Secretary-General on nominations from states and judges appointed by the government of Sierra Leone,[31] while the crimes within its jurisdiction comprised both international crimes and crimes under the law of Sierra Leone.[32] But as recognized by the Appeals Chamber of the SCSL[33] and by the Supreme Court of Sierra Leone,[34] the SCSL itself was an international criminal court. The same goes for the RSCSL.

3.21 The Security Council's request to the Secretary-General to negotiate an agreement with the government of Sierra Leone for the establishment of an international criminal tribunal was upheld by the Appeals Chamber of the SCSL as a measure lawfully falling within the Council's responsibility under article 24(1) of the UN Charter for the maintenance of international peace and security.[35]

---

[29] Special Court Agreement 2002 (Ratification) Act 2002, ss 2, 7, 10, 11(1), 13, 16, 20–21, and 37–42.

[30] *Report of the Secretary-General on the establishment of a Special Court for Sierra Leone*, UN doc S/2000/915 (4 October 2000), 3, para 9.

[31] SCSL Statute, art 12.   [32] Ibid, arts 2–5.

[33] *Prosecutor v Kallon and Kamara (Fofana and Gbao intervening)*, SCSL-2004-15-AR72(E) & SCSL-2004-16-AR72(E), Appeals Chamber, Decision on Challenge to Jurisdiction: Lomé Accord Amnesty, 13 March 2004, paras 86 and 88; *Prosecutor v Kallon, Norman and Kamara (Fofana intervening)*, SCSL-2004-15-AR72(E), SCSL-2004-14-AR72(E) and SCSL-2004-16-AR72(E), Appeals Chamber, Decision on Constitutionality and Lack of Jurisdiction, 13 March 2004, paras 55 and 71; *Prosecutor* v *Taylor*, SCSL-03-01-I, Appeals Chamber, Decision on Immunity from Jurisdiction, 31 May 2004, para 42. See too *Report of the Secretary-General on the establishment of a Special Court for Sierra Leone* (n 30), 3, para 11, comparing the SCSL to 'other international jurisdictions'.

[34] *Sesay, Kondewa and Fofana v President of the Special Court and Others*, SC No 1/2003, Supreme Court of Sierra Leone, 14 October 2005, 13–16. See also Office of the Attorney General and Ministry of Justice of Sierra Leone, Special Court Task Force, *Briefing Paper on the Relationship between the Special Court and the Truth and Reconciliation Commission* (2002), para 2.1 ('[T]he implementing legislation will not be the legal basis for the Special Court: that legal basis will be the Agreement for the Special Court. Thus the Special Court will be an international institution, despite its national components.') and para 2.3 ('the Special Court will be a treaty-based international judicial institution').

[35] See *Prosecutor v Fofana*, SCSL-2004-14-AR72(E), Appeals Chamber, Decision on Preliminary Motion on Lack of Jurisdiction: Illegal Delegation of Powers by the United Nations, 25 May 2004, paras 18–21.

(d) Decision of the UN Security Council under chapter VII of the UN Charter

3.22 Four international criminal courts to date have been established and empowered by way of a decision of the UN Security Council under chapter VII of the UN Charter. These are the ICTY, the ICTR, the International Residual Mechanism for the International Criminal Tribunals (also known as the Mechanism for International Criminal Tribunals or MICT),[36] and the Special Tribunal for Lebanon (STL).

3.23 In paragraph 2 of Security Council resolution 827 (1993), the Security Council, acting under chapter VII of the UN Charter,[37]

> [d]ecides hereby to establish an international tribunal for the...purpose of prosecuting persons responsible for serious violations of international humanitarian law committed in the territory of the former Yugoslavia between 1 January 1991 and a date to be determined...and to this end to adopt the Statute of the International Tribunal annexed to the...report [of the Secretary General pursuant to paragraph 2 of Security Council resolution 808 (1993).]

The ICTY Statute, while not annexed to the resolution itself, is given force of international law through its adoption by the Council. Not dissimilarly, in paragraph 1 of Security Council resolution 955 (1994), the Security Council, acting again under chapter VII of the Charter,[38]

> [d]ecides hereby...to establish an international tribunal for the...purpose of prosecuting persons responsible for genocide and other serious violations of international humanitarian law committed in the territory of Rwanda...between 1 January 1994 and 31 December 1994 and to this end to adopt the Statute of the International Criminal Tribunal for Rwanda annexed hereto[.]

More recently, in paragraph 1 of Security Council resolution 1966 (2010), the Council, acting once more under chapter VII of the Charter,[39]

> [d]ecides to establish the International Residual Mechanism for Criminal Tribunals ('the Mechanism') with two branches, which shall commence functioning on 1 July 2012 (branch for the ICTR) and 1 July 2013 (branch for the ICTY), respectively ('commencement dates'), and to this end decides to adopt the Statute of the Mechanism in Annex 1 to this resolution[.]

The Council further decides in paragraph 4 of the resolution that, 'as of the commencement date of each branch referred to in paragraph 1, the Mechanism shall continue the jurisdiction, rights and obligations and essential functions of the ICTY and the ICTR, respectively, subject to the provisions of th[e] resolution and the Statute of the Mechanism'. The existence and competence of

---

[36] For these first three, see *infra* chapter 12.
[37] SC res 827 (1993), 25 May 1993, preamble (final recital).
[38] SC res 955 (1994), 8 November 1994, preamble (final recital).
[39] SC res 1966 (2010), 22 December 2010, preamble (final recital).

none of these courts is formally contingent on any municipal legal act. Each was established without interposition of municipal law by decision of the Security Council, and each takes its judicial powers directly from its statute, as adopted by the Council.

3.24 The basis for the establishment and empowerment of the STL is less straightforward, even if in the final analysis it is clear that it too was established by way of a decision of the Security Council under chapter VII of the UN Charter. By letter to the UN Secretary-General dated 13 December 2005, the prime minister of Lebanon requested the Security Council to establish a 'tribunal of an international character' to try persons suspected of involvement in the assassination on 14 February 2005 of former prime minister of Lebanon Rafiq Hariri,[40] who was killed, along with 22 others, when a limousine carrying him was blown up in Beirut. In Security Council resolution 1644 (2005) of 16 December 2005, the Council acknowledged the Lebanese government's request, and in turn requested the Secretary-General 'to help the Lebanese Government identify the nature and scope of the international assistance needed in this regard' and to report back to the Council.[41] The Secretary-General duly reported back,[42] and the Security Council, welcoming his report, requested him 'to negotiate an agreement with the Government of Lebanon aimed at establishing a tribunal of an international character..., taking into account the recommendations of his report'.[43] On 6 February 2007, the Agreement between the United Nations and the Lebanese Republic on the Establishment of a Special Tribunal for Lebanon was concluded, which was to come into force the day after the Lebanese government had notified the UN that the requirements of its municipal law necessary for Lebanon's ratification[44] of the Agreement—namely, a parliamentary vote—had been fulfilled.[45] But the speaker of the Lebanese parliament, a political opponent of the government, refused to convene parliament for the vote. On 14 May 2007, the prime minister of Lebanon wrote to the Secretary-General informing him that 'a parliamentary majority ha[d] expressed its support for the Tribunal and readiness to formally ratify [the Agreement] in parliament if only a session could be convened' and asking him, 'as a matter of urgency, to put before the Security Council [Lebanon's] request that the Special Tribunal be put into effect' by means of '[a] binding decision regarding the Tribunal on the part of the Security Council'.[46] In the event, the Security Council, acceding to Lebanon's request, opted to establish the Tribunal without waiting for the Lebanese parliament to ratify the Agreement. On 30 May 2007,

---

[40] UN doc S/2005/783 (13 December 2005), Annex.
[41] SC res 1644 (2005), 15 December 2005, para 6.
[42] See *Report of the Secretary-General pursuant to paragraph 6 of resolution 1644 (2005)*, UN doc S/2006/176 (21 March 2006).
[43] SC res 1664 (2006), 29 March 2006, para 1.
[44] The term is used here in the sense ascribed to it by the law of treaties.
[45] Agreement between the United Nations and the Lebanese Republic on the Establishment of a Special Tribunal for Lebanon, UN doc S/RES/1757 (2007) (30 May 2007), Annex ('STL Agreement').
[46] UN doc S/2007/281 (16 May 2007), Annex.

in paragraph 1 of resolution 1757 (2007), the Security Council '[d]ecides, acting under Chapter VII of the Charter of the United Nations', that:

(a) The provisions of the annexed document, including its attachment, on the establishment of a Special Tribunal for Lebanon shall enter into force on 10 June 2007...

The 'annexed document' is the text of the STL Agreement, and its attachment is the STL Statute. The legal effect of paragraph 1(*a*) of Security Council resolution 1757 (2001) is not, however, to bring the STL Agreement as such into force.[47] Rather, the legal effect of paragraph 1(*a*) of the resolution is, as the subparagraph itself states, that the provisions of the annex to the resolution, including its attachment, entered into force on 10 June 2007. Article 1(1) of the annex to resolution 1757 (2001), being the text of article 1(1) of the STL Agreement, provides in part:

There is hereby established a Special Tribunal for Lebanon to prosecute persons responsible for the attack of 14 February 2005 resulting in the death of former Lebanese Prime Minister Rafiq Hariri and in the death or injury of other persons.

Article 1(2) of the annex to the resolution, being the text of article 1(2) of the Agreement, provides:

The Special Tribunal shall function in accordance with the Statute of the Special Tribunal for Lebanon. The Statute is attached to this Agreement and forms an integral part thereof.

In short, it is by way of Security Council resolution 1757 (2007), including its annex, that the STL was formally established, and it is from the resolution, including its annex and the STL Statute attached to that annex, that the Tribunal formally derives its judicial powers.[48] Nor does the existence or competence of the STL formally depend on any municipal legal act by Lebanon or any other state.

3.25   Like the SCSL, the STL is often referred to as a 'hybrid' or 'mixed'[49] court, but again the label is prone to confuse. That said, there is nothing wrong with describing the STL's composition and jurisdiction *ratione materiae*, the latter *lato sensu*, as 'mixed'. The Tribunal's bench combines both 'international' judges appointed by the UN Secretary-General, on the nomination of states and 'competent persons', and Lebanese judges appointed by the Secretary-General from a list of persons presented by the government of Lebanon on the proposal of the Lebanese Supreme Council of the Judiciary.[50] As for the Tribunal's jurisdiction *ratione materiae*, for which no explicit provision is made, it is implicit in the applicable law specified in article 2 of the STL Statute that the crimes within the Tribunal's jurisdiction comprise exclusively certain

---

[47] A treaty can enter into force in its quality as a treaty only according to its provision for entry into force.
[48] See also *Prosecutor v Ayyash* et al, STL-11-01/PT/AC/AR90.1, Appeals Chamber, Decision on the Defence Appeals against the Trial Chamber's 'Decision on the Defence Challenges to the Jurisdiction and Legality of the Tribunal', 24 October 2012, paras 2 and 26–31.
[49] See eg *Report of the Secretary-General pursuant to paragraph 6 of resolution 1644 (2005)* (n 42), which, while referring to the proposed tribunal throughout as one of an 'international character', describes it, 2, para 5, as a 'mixed' tribunal in terms of its 'founding instrument [*viz* a treaty between the UN and Lebanon], jurisdiction, applicable law, location, composition and financial arrangements'.
[50] STL Statute, arts 8–9, cross-referenced with STL Agreement, art 2.

crimes under Lebanese law.⁵¹ At the same time, the modes of responsibility for these crimes recognized in the Statute, either implicitly in article 2 or expressly in article 3, combine Lebanese and international legal concepts.⁵² As for the STL's applicable law, it takes the form, 'subject to the provisions of th[e] Statute', of '[t]he provisions of the Lebanese Criminal Code relating to the prosecution and punishment of acts of terrorism, crimes and offences against life and personal integrity, illicit associations and failure to report crimes and offences, including the rules regarding the material elements of a crime, criminal participation and conspiracy', as well as '[a]rticles 6 and 7 of the Lebanese law of 11 January 1958 on "Increasing the penalties for sedition, civil war and interfaith struggle"'.⁵³ But none of this makes the STL itself anything other than an international criminal court, a characterization reiterated in the STL Agreement⁵⁴ and by the Appeals Chamber of the Tribunal itself.⁵⁵

The lawfulness of the Security Council's establishment of an international criminal court as a measure for the maintenance of international peace and security under chapter VII of the UN Charter was upheld by the Appeals Chamber of the ICTY in 1995 in the landmark *Tadić* case,⁵⁶ as affirmed and reaffirmed since by both the ICTY⁵⁷ and ICTR.⁵⁸ 3.26

The Security Council's authority under the UN Charter to decide on 'collective measures for the prevention and removal of threats to the peace' pursuant to its powers under chapter VII is unfettered by customary or treaty-based rules applicable among states, as indicated *a contrario* by the wording of article 1(1) of the Charter. Although the Security Council is bound by article 24(2) of the Charter to act 'in accordance with the Purposes and Principles of the United Nations' as set out in articles 1 and 2 of the Charter respectively, and although article 1(1) of the Charter requires the UN to act 'in conformity with the principles of...international law' when seeking to 'bring about by peaceful means...adjustment or settlement of international disputes or situations which might lead to a breach of the peace', article 1(1) also makes clear that this limitation does not apply when the Organization takes 'collective measures for the prevention and removal of threats to the peace, and for the suppression of acts of aggression or other breaches of the 3.27

---

⁵¹ See STL Statute, art 2. See also *Ayyash*, Appeals Chamber Interlocutory Decision on the Applicable Law (n 8), paras 12–13.
⁵² See, generally, *Ayyash*, Appeals Chamber Interlocutory Decision on the Applicable Law (n 8), paras 204–207 and 210–211. Article 3 of the STL Statute specifies commission, complicity, organization or direction, common purpose, and superior responsibility.
⁵³ STL Statute, art 2   ⁵⁴ STL Agreement, preamble (first and second recitals).
⁵⁵ *Ayyash*, Appeals Chamber Interlocutory Decision on the Applicable Law (n 8), paras 13, 15, 16, 33, and 39.
⁵⁶ *Prosecutor v Tadić*, IT-94-1, Appeals Chamber, Decision on Interlocutory Motion on Jurisdiction, 2 October 1995, paras 28–40. For details, see *infra* paras 12.18–12.19.
⁵⁷ See eg *Prosecutor v Šešelj*, IT-03-67-PT, Trial Chamber, Decision on Motion of Vojislav Šešelj Challenging Jurisdiction and Form of Indictment, 26 May 2004, para 12.
⁵⁸ See *Prosecutor v Kanyabashi*, ICTR-96-15-T, Trial Chamber, Decision on the Defence Motion on Jurisdiction, 18 June 1997, paras 17–29; *Prosecutor v Ntakirutimana*, ICTR-96-10-A & ICTR-96-17-A, Appeals Chamber, Judgment, 13 December 2004, paras 398–399. For its part, the STL held in *Ayyash*, Decision on the Defence Appeals (n 48), paras 2 and 35, that it had no authority to review the legality of the Security Council decision by which it was established.

peace'[59]—that is, when it exercises, via the Security Council, the powers for the maintenance of international peace and security conferred in chapter VII of the Charter. In short, UN member states agree through being parties to the Charter that when acting under chapter VII the Security Council may, without the express consent in any given instance of the member states concerned, take measures in derogation of the rights and obligations of member states under customary[60] and other treaty-based international law.[61] Additionally, article 2(7) of the Charter specifies that measures taken under chapter VII fall outside that provision's prohibition on intervention by the UN in the domestic affairs of member states.

D. Municipal Criminal Courts

(i) Definition

3.28 A municipal criminal court is a criminal court that formally depends for its existence and competence on municipal law. In other words, a municipal criminal court is a criminal court whose establishment and judicial powers derive without formal interposition of international law from a municipal legal instrument or act.[62] This will usually mean that the court's constituent instrument is itself

---

[59] Article 1(1) of the Charter, enunciating the first of the purposes of the United Nations, reads: 'To maintain international peace and security, and to that end: to take effective collective measures for the prevention and removal of threats to the peace, and for the suppression of acts of aggression or other breaches of the peace, and to bring about by peaceful means, and in conformity with the principles of justice and international law, adjustment or settlement of international disputes or situations which might lead to a breach of the peace.' As is clear from the positioning of the parenthetical phrase 'in conformity with the principles of justice and international law', which qualifies only the second limb of the sentence, the UN is not restrained by principles of international law when taking collective measures for the prevention and removal of threats to the peace, *viz* when acting under chapter VII of the Charter. See also eg H Kelsen, *The Law of the United Nations: A Critical Analysis of its Fundamental Problems* (London: Stevens & Sons, 1950), 294–5; L Goodrich, E Hambro, and A Simons, *Charter of the United Nations. Commentary and Documents* (3rd and rev edn, New York: Columbia University Press, 1969), 27–8 ('It is significant that, at San Francisco, the major powers refused to accept an amendment requiring that collective measures be taken in accordance with international law and justice, on the grounds that this would tie the hands of the Security Council to an undesirable extent... However, they were willing to accept an amendment to the Dumbarton Oaks text providing that adjustment or settlement of international disputes or situations should be "in conformity with the principles of international law and justice" [*sic*].'); R Wolfrum, 'Chapter I. Purposes and Principles', in B Simma (ed), *The Charter of the United Nations. A Commentary* (2nd edn, Oxford: Oxford University Press, 2002), vol I, 39, 43.

[60] This is true at least when the customary right or obligation does not have the status of a peremptory norm (*jus cogens*).

[61] The same goes for the non-peremptory rights of individuals under international law. At the same time, consider the interpretative presumption asserted in *Al-Jedda v United Kingdom*, 147 ILR 107, 172, para 102 (ECtHR (GC) 2011).

[62] See eg *Prosecutor v Stanković*, IT-96-23/2-PT, Referrals Bench, Decision on Referral of Case under Rule 11*bis*, 17 May 2005, para 26: 'With regard to the Defence submission that the War Crimes Chamber of the State Court is incapable of characterization as a "national court," it is apparently assumed by the submission that to be a national court it must be composed of judges who are nationals of the State concerned. No authority is offered for this proposition... The State Court of Bosnia and Herzegovina, of which the War Crimes Chamber is a component, is a court which has been established pursuant to the statutory law of Bosnia and Herzegovina. It is thus a court of Bosnia and Herzegovina, a "national court." Bosnia and Herzegovina has chosen to include in the composition of the State Court judges who are not nationals of Bosnia and Herzegovina. That is a

a municipal legal instrument, be it primary legislation, subordinate legislation, executive decree, or the like. Alternatively, it may mean that the court's constituent instrument takes the form of an international legal instrument on which a municipal legal instrument or act has conferred the force of municipal law by means of express ratification,[63] incorporation, or the like. In rare cases it may equally mean that the court's constituent instrument takes the form of an international legal instrument on which the force of municipal law has been conferred by an international legal instrument or act.

(ii) *Legal means of establishment and empowerment*

There is any number of municipal legal means by which a municipal criminal court might be established and empowered. Usually it will be by primary legislation, occasionally it may be by executive decree or the like. Some of the less routine examples, however, bear special mention. **3.29**

It is sometimes mistakenly thought that the military criminal courts established by the US, UK, and France within their respective zones of occupation in Germany at the end of the Second World War were established directly under Law No 10 (20 December 1945) ('Control Council Law No 10') promulgated by the Allied Control Council for Germany, a joint organ of the four states in occupation of Germany through which—having 'assume[d] supreme authority with respect to Germany, including all the powers possessed by the German Government...and any state, municipal, or local government or authority'[64]—they collectively legislated for the territory of the subjugated German state.[65] But Control Council Law No 10 was no more than the legislative means by which the Four Powers jointly asserted the legal authority to prosecute 'war criminals and other similar offenders' in their respective zones for the crimes specified in the Law and, further, 'established a uniform legal basis in Germany for [such] prosecution'.[66] Each of the military courts eventually relied on for this purpose, which in the case of the British and French military courts predated Control Council Law No 10, was the creature of the municipal law, albeit the executive law, of the state in occupation of the relevant zone.[67] That is, Control **3.30**

---

matter determined by the legislative authorities of Bosnia and Herzegovina. The inclusion of some non-nationals among the judges of the State Court does that make that court any less a "national court" of Bosnia and Herzegovina.'

[63] The term is used here in a municipal legal sense, as well as generically (having as it does different precise meanings in different municipal legal systems).

[64] Declaration regarding the Defeat of Germany and the Assumption of Supreme Authority with respect to Germany by the Governments of the United States of America, the Union of Soviet Socialist Republics, the United Kingdom and the Provisional Government of the French Republic, Berlin, 5 June 1945 ('Berlin Declaration').

[65] See Control Council Proclamation No 1, Berlin, 30 August 1945, arts I and II, cross-referable to Berlin Declaration.

[66] Control Council Law No 10, preamble.

[67] Article III of Control Council Proclamation No 1 provided: 'Any military laws, proclamations, orders, ordinances, notices, regulations, and directives issued by or under the authority of the respective Commanders-in-Chief for their respective Zones of Occupation are continued in force in their respective Zones of Occupation.'

Council Law No 10 was not the formal legal source of the existence and competence of the respective zonal military courts in Germany. Indeed, article III(2) of Control Council Law No 10 provided:

> The court by which persons charged with offenses hereunder shall be tried and the rules and procedure thereof shall be determined or designated by each Zone Commander for his respective Zone. Nothing herein is intended to, or shall impair or limit the Jurisdiction or power of any court or court now or hereafter established in any Zone by the Commander thereof.

The military tribunals in the US zone of occupied Germany were established and empowered under Ordinance No 7 (18 October 1946) of the Military Government of the United States Zone of Germany; the military courts in the British zone—set up, prior to Control Council Law No 10, on the same basis as the British military courts in the Far Eastern theatre, and like them not trying crimes against humanity or crimes against peace—were established and empowered under the Royal Warrant of 14 June 1945;[68] and the military courts in the French zone, already existing in the form of military government courts under Ordinance No 1 (28 July 1945) of the French commander-in-chief, were vested with the jurisdiction envisaged by Control Council Law No 10 by Ordinance No 36 (25 July 1946) of the same. In short, all these criminal courts and tribunals were municipal courts or tribunals.[69]

3.31　If any criminal courts had a plausible claim to being 'hybrid' in a formal legal sense, it would be the special panels for serious crimes in the District Court of Dili and the Court of Appeal of East Timor,[70] although in the final analysis they too were formally municipal courts. By way of Security Council resolution 1272 (1999), the UN Security Council, substituting its own governing authority for that previously exercised over the territory of East Timor by Indonesia, established the United Nations Transitional Administration in East Timor (UNTAET), and empowered it to exercise 'all legislative and executive authority, including the administration of justice'.[71] In turn, UNTAET promulgated a regulation by which '[a]ll legislative and executive authority with respect to East Timor, including the administration of the judiciary, [was] vested' in UNTAET and by which it explicitly claimed the power to 'appoint any person to perform functions in the civil administration in East Timor, including the judiciary'.[72]

---

[68] Army Order 81/1945 (18 June 1945).

[69] See also 15 LRTWC 28–48, making it clear that each was a municipal court or tribunal. But cf the conclusion of the US Court of Appeals for the DC Circuit in *Flick v Johnson*, 174 F 2d 983, 986 (DC Cir 1949), endorsed by Heller (n 4), 113, that the US military tribunals established in the US zone of occupation were not 'tribunals of the United States' within the meaning of the US constitution, a conclusion premised on the understanding that—although it was by way of Ordinance No 7 of the US zone commander that the tribunals were formally constituted and empowered—the 'power and jurisdiction' of these tribunals 'stemmed directly from the Control Council,... exercising its authority on behalf of the Four Allied Powers'.

[70] For a fuller account of the special panels, see *infra* paras 9.44–9.46.

[71] SC res 1272 (1999), 25 October 1999, para 1.

[72] UNTAET reg 1999/1, 27 November 1999, ss 1.1 and 1.2. The 'serious crimes' were genocide, war crimes, crimes against humanity, torture, murder, and sexual offences.

Supplemented by UNTAET regulations and their subsidiary instruments, which were declared to form part of the law applicable in East Timor,[73] the law that applied in the territory immediately prior to UNTAET's establishment was declared to remain in force,[74] with the consequence that the existing courts remained vested with judicial authority. In the exercise of its legislative authority in East Timor, UNTAET conferred on the existing District Court of Dili exclusive jurisdiction to try 'serious crimes' committed between 1 January and 25 October 1999,[75] and established special panels within the Court, composed of both East Timorese and 'international' judges appointed by UNTAET, to exercise this exclusive jurisdiction. Appeal from a special panel of the Court continued to lie, as with any appeal from a district court in East Timor, to the existing Court of Appeal of East Timor, although such appeals were to be heard by a special panel again composed of both East Timorese and international judges appointed by UNTAET. The special panels in the District Court of Dili and the Court of Appeal of East Timor continued to operate for a transitional period after the independence of Timor-Leste in 2002, pursuant to its constitution,[76] ceasing their functions in 2005. At all times prior to and after independence, the special panels, being formally dependent for their existence and competence on municipal law, were municipal criminal courts. Although their shared constituent instrument was to be found in a regulation promulgated by UNTAET, a subsidiary organ of the UN Security Council, this instrument exerted its legal effect via the pre-existing Indonesian and subsequent Timor-Leste municipal law by which the District Court of Dili and the Court of Appeal of East Timor were themselves established and empowered, and it was capable of doing so only in its deemed quality as municipal law in East Timor. Put simply, the special panels for serious crimes in the District Court of Dili and in the Court of Appeal of East Timor were no more than special panels of municipal criminal courts, and these municipal criminal courts owed their establishment and judicial powers to municipal law.

3.32 What goes for the special panels in the courts of East Timor goes as well, *mutatis mutandis*, for the 'regulation 64' panels and the European Rule of Law Mission (EULEX) panels in the courts of Kosovo.[77] After the substitution, pursuant to Security Council resolution 1244 (1999), of the governing authority of the Federal Republic of Yugoslavia over its erstwhile province of Kosovo with that of the United Nations Mission in Kosovo (UNMIK),[78] '[a]ll legislative and executive authority with respect to Kosovo, including the administration of the judiciary, [was] vested' in UNMIK.[79] While initially the law that applied in Kosovo immediately prior to 24 March 1999 continued to apply insofar as it did

---

[73] Ibid, s 3.1.   [74] Ibid.
[75] See UNTAET reg 2000/11, s 10 and UNTAET reg 2000/15, 6 June 2000.
[76] Constitution of the Democratic Republic of Timor-Leste, ss 163(1) and 165.
[77] For a fuller account of the 'regulation 64' and EULEX panels, see *infra* paras 9.40–9.41.
[78] See SC res 1244 (1999), 10 June 1999.
[79] UNMIK reg 1999/1, 25 July 1999 (as amended), s 1(1).

not conflict with, *inter alia*, any regulation promulgated by UNMIK,[80] UNMIK later declared that the law applicable in Kosovo comprised—in addition to UNMIK regulations and their subsidiary instruments—the law that applied in Kosovo on 22 March 1989,[81] before the rescission of the province's autonomous status within the Socialist Republic of Serbia, then a constituent republic of the Socialist Federal Republic of Yugoslavia. A consequence of either legal regime, however, was that the existing courts in Kosovo continued to be vested with judicial authority. In December 2000, by way of regulation 2000/64, UNMIK claimed the power, *inter alia*, to constitute for the purpose of specific proceedings in any court in Kosovo a panel (known as a 'regulation 64' panel) of three judges, of which two, including the presiding judge, were to be 'international'.[82] After UNMIK's judicial and prosecutorial mandate was transferred to EULEX in Kosovo, and in accordance with Law No 03/L-053 on the Jurisdiction, Case Selection and Case Allocation of EULEX Judges and Prosecutors in Kosovo enacted on 13 March 2008 by the Assembly of the self-declared Republic of Kosovo,[83] 'regulation 64' panels were replaced by analogous panels of EULEX judges assigned to the proceedings by the President of the Assembly of EULEX judges. Formally dependent for their existence and competence on municipal law, the 'regulation 64' panels were, and the EULEX panels are, municipal criminal courts. Although the former were constituted pursuant to a regulation promulgated by UNMIK, a subsidiary organ of the UN Security Council, they derived their judicial authority and jurisdiction from the pre-existing municipal law by which the courts in Kosovo were established and empowered, and UNMIK regulation 2000/64 was capable of affecting the composition of the bench of a court in Kosovo only by virtue of its deemed quality as municipal law in Kosovo. As for the EULEX panels, they are provided for by the law of the Republic of Kosovo, and derive their judicial authority and jurisdiction from the law of the Republic of Kosovo under which the latter's courts are established and empowered.[84]

3.33 The Iraqi High Criminal Court (also known in English as the Iraqi High Tribunal), established to try the most senior figures of the ousted Baath regime in Iraq, has equally been at all times a municipal criminal court.[85] The 'proposed provisions'[86] of the statute of what was then called the Iraqi Special Tribunal were drafted, in consultation with Iraqi stakeholders, by lawyers from the Coalition Provisional Authority (CPA), the joint organ through which the states in belligerent occupation of Iraq from 2003 to 2004 governed the territory, but by Order

---

[80] Ibid, s 3. Section 3 of UNMIK reg 1999/1 was repealed by UNMIK reg 1999/25, 15 December 1999, consequent upon the promulgation of UNMIK reg 1999/24, 15 December 1999.
[81] UNMIK reg 1999/24, s 1.
[82] UNMIK reg 2000/64, 15 December 2000, ss 1 and 2.
[83] See Law No 03/L-053 on the Jurisdiction, Case Selection and Case Allocation of EULEX Judges and Prosecutors in Kosovo, 13 March 2008, arts 2–4, especially arts 3.7 and 4.7.
[84] See Constitution of the Republic of Kosovo, arts 102–103, and Law No 03/L-199 on Courts, 22 July 2010.
[85] For a fuller account of the Iraqi High Criminal Court, see *infra* paras 9.51–9.54.
[86] CPA Order No 48, 10 December 2003, s 1(1).

No 48 of 10 December 2003 the CPA delegated to a body called the Interim Iraqi Governing Council the legislative authority formally to promulgate the statute.[87] More to the point, on 18 October 2005, the new, popularly-elected Iraqi government enacted the Law on the Iraqi High Criminal Court, which, although in substance reproducing its extant statute, renamed and regularized the court in accordance with the ban in the new Iraqi constitution on extraordinary courts. The Court is a special criminal court within the judicial system of Iraq.

3.34 The Extraordinary Chambers in the Courts of Cambodia for the Prosecution of Crimes Committed during the Period of Democratic Kampuchea (ECCC)—while often referred to as 'hybrid', 'mixed' or 'internationalized' courts on account of their composition, jurisdiction *ratione materiae*, and applicable law—are once more formally municipal criminal courts.[88] As their name makes clear, they are special chambers 'established in the existing court structure, namely the trial court and the supreme court', of Cambodia,[89] and the trial court and supreme court of Cambodia are established and empowered under the law of Cambodia.[90] Moreover, the constituent instrument of the Extraordinary Chambers themselves, namely the Law on the Establishment of Extraordinary Chambers in the Courts of Cambodia for the Prosecution of Crimes Committed during the Period of Democratic Kampuchea 2001 as amended in 2004, is in both form and formal juridical quality a municipal legal instrument. The Agreement between the United Nations and the Royal Government of Cambodia concerning the Prosecution under Cambodian Law of Crimes Committed During the Period of Democratic Kampuchea 2003 does no more than provide 'the legal basis and principles and modalities for...cooperation'[91] between the UN and Cambodia in relation to trials before the ECCC.[92] The Agreement recognizes that the ECCC have the jurisdiction *ratione materiae* provided for in the Law on the Establishment of Extraordinary Chambers in the Courts of Cambodia and jurisdiction *ratione personae* over senior leaders of Democratic Kampuchea and others most responsible for the crimes specified.[93] Furthermore, the Agreement provides that it shall be implemented in Cambodia through the Law 'as adopted and amended'.[94]

3.35 The Extraordinary African Chambers in the Senegalese Courts for the Prosecution of International Crimes Committed in Chad During the Period

---

[87] Ibid. By virtue of art 48 of the Law of Administration for the State of Iraq for the Transitional Period, 8 March 2004, the existence of the Tribunal was unaffected by the dissolution of the CPA on 28 June 2004 and the transfer of governmental authority to the appointed Iraqi interim government.
[88] For a fuller account of the Extraordinary Chambers in the Courts of Cambodia, see *infra* paras 9.62–9.65.
[89] Law on the Establishment of Extraordinary Chambers in the Courts of Cambodia 2001 (as amended 2004), art 2.
[90] See Law on the Organization of the Courts 1993 (repealed) and Law on the Organization of the Courts 2014.
[91] Agreement between the United Nations and the Royal Government of Cambodia concerning the Prosecution under Cambodian Law of Crimes Committed During the Period of Democratic Kampuchea 2003, art 1.
[92] Ibid, art 1.   [93] Ibid, art 2(1).   [94] Ibid, art 2(2).

from 7 June 1982 to 1 December 1990[95] are, as their name indicates, special chambers within the criminal courts of Senegal—specifically, within the Dakar *Tribunal Régional Hors Classe* and the Dakar Court of Appeal.[96] Although article 1(3) of the Agreement between the Government of the Republic of Senegal and the African Union on the Creation of Extraordinary African Chambers in the Senegalese Courts[97] refers to the Chambers as being '[o]f an international character', the description is not intended in the formal juridical sense, *viz* as a reference to the legal order on which the Chambers formally depend for their existence and competence. The Chambers formally depend for their existence and competence on Senegalese law. First, the Dakar *Tribunal Régional Hors Classe* and the Dakar Court of Appeal are established and empowered under the law of Senegal.[98] Secondly, the constituent instrument of the four Extraordinary African Chambers within these two courts, *viz* the Statute of the Extraordinary African Chambers in the Senegalese Courts annexed to and deemed an integral part of[99] the Senegal–AU Agreement, is a legal source of the establishment and empowerment of the Chambers not in its quality as treaty law but—on ratification of the Agreement by the president of Senegal on the authority of the national assembly of Senegal, and by virtue of article 96 of the Constitution of Senegal—in its quality as part of the law of Senegal.[100] That is, while the Statute of the Extraordinary African Chambers is in form an international instrument, it is the formal source of the judicial authority of the Chambers only through the interposition of Senegalese law. The expression '[o]f an international character' in article 1(3) of the Agreement—a pointed co-option of the term used by the ECOWAS Community Court of Justice in 2010 to describe the 'special ad hoc procedure' by which Senegal, the Court held, was obliged to try Habré[101]—refers informally to the historical origin of the Chambers in the Agreement and to the provision in the Chambers' legal framework for both the involvement of the African Union (AU) in, *inter alia*, the appointment of judges and the presence on the bench of the Extraordinary African *chambre d'Assises* and *chambre d'assises d'Appel* respectively of presiding judges from other AU states.[102]

---

[95] For a fuller account of the Extraordinary African Chambers in the Senegalese Courts, see *infra* paras 9.72–9.76.

[96] See Statut des Chambres extraordinaires africaines au sein des juridictions sénégalaises pour la poursuite des crimes internationaux commis au Tchad durant la période du 7 juin 1982 au 1er décembre 1990 ('Statute of the Extraordinary African Chambers in the Senegalese Courts for the Prosecution of International Crimes Committed in Chad During the Period from 7 June 1982 to 1 December 1990'), art 2. All translations from the French are the author's.

[97] Accord entre le Gouvernement de la République du Sénégal et l'Union Africaine sur la Création de Chambres Extraordinaires Africaines au Sein des Juridictions Sénégalaises, Dakar, 24 August 2014 ('Agreement between the Government of the Republic of Senegal and the African Union on the Creation of Extraordinary African Chambers in the Senegalese Courts').

[98] See décret n° 84-1194 du 22 octobre 1984 (as amended).

[99] See Agreement on the Creation of Extraordinary African Chambers in the Senegalese Courts, art 1(5).

[100] See *infra* para 9.72.   [101] See ibid.

[102] See, in this light, the subsequent judgment of the ECOWAS Community of Court of Justice in *Habré c Sénégal*, Case No ECW/CCJ/RUL/05/13, Judgment, 5 November 2013, para 47

IV. International and Municipal Criminal Courts: A Descriptive Pluralism

3.36 The technical juridical distinction between an international criminal court and a municipal criminal court says nothing about the range of descriptive varieties of each formal category of court. The precise international or municipal legal means by which the court is established and empowered, the composition and method of appointment of its bench and in some cases prosecution, its jurisdiction *ratione materiae*, its applicable law, its rules of procedure and evidence, the domestic or foreign location of its seat, its funding arrangements, the involvement or otherwise in its workings of an international organization, and whether it is permanent or ad hoc represent just some of the variables that result in as many practical differences among international criminal courts and municipal criminal courts respectively as between the two categories.[103]

V. The Legal Significance of the Distinction Between International and Municipal Criminal Courts

3.37 The significance for the purposes of international law of the distinction between international and municipal criminal courts can be overstated. The distinction is of some international legal import, but this is little more than formal.

A. Fallacy

(i) General

3.38 It is assumed by some that the international character of a criminal court has consequences, in and of itself, for the international legal authority for the exercise by the court of its powers.[104] The assumption is mistaken. The fact that a criminal court is international does not authorize as a matter of international law its exercise of a power of which the exercise by a municipal criminal court would constitute an international wrong by the forum state. States have no greater authority under

---

(author's translation), in which 'the Court holds that the international Agreement which created the Extraordinary African Chambers and their own legal framework as determined in their Statute confers on them an international character'.

[103] The specificities of the different international and municipal criminal courts are explored elsewhere in this book. See *infra* chapters 9 and 12–14.

[104] See eg *Taylor*, Appeals Chamber Decision on Immunity (n 33), paras 41 and 52; *Prosecutor v Al Bashir*, ICC-02/05-01/09-139-Corr, Pre-Trial Chamber, Corrigendum to the Decision pursuant to Article 87(7) of the Rome Statute on the Failure by the Republic of Malawi to Comply with the Cooperation Requests Issued by the Court with Respect to the Arrest and Surrender of Omar Hassan Ahmad Al Bashir, 13 December 2011, para 36 and *Prosecutor v Al Bashir*, ICC-02/05-01/09-140-tENG, Pre-Trial Chamber, Decision pursuant to article 87(7) of the Rome Statute on the Refusal of the Republic of Chad to Comply with the Cooperation Requests Issued by the Court with Respect to the Arrest and Surrender of Omar Hassan Ahmad Al Bashir, 13 December 2011, para 13.

international law to do together what none of them may, as a matter of international law, do alone. What is relevant to the international lawfulness of an international criminal court's exercise of a given power is not the court's international character but the precise international legal basis of the court's establishment and empowerment—that is, the particular source under international law of the court's purported authority. Where this source is a bilateral or multilateral treaty to which the relevant state is party, no exercise by the court of a power vested in it can infringe that state's international legal rights. A state is free to consent to derogations from its international legal rights, and a state that becomes party to a treaty establishing and empowering an international criminal court consents thereby to the exercise by the court of the powers conferred on it by the treaty. The same goes, *mutatis mutandis*, where an international criminal court is lawfully established and empowered by way of a decision of the UN Security Council and the state is a member of the United Nations. Where the Security Council lawfully decides to create an international criminal court and to vest it with a power the exercise of which would otherwise infringe the rights of a member state,[105] the exercise of this power does not infringe those rights. By virtue of article 25 of the UN Charter, UN member states 'agree to accept...the decisions of the Security Council in accordance with the...Charter', with the consequence that a state that becomes party to the Charter is taken to consent thereby to the exercise by an international criminal court lawfully established and empowered by a decision of the Council of any power conferred on it. But where an international criminal court is established and empowered by way of a bilateral or multilateral treaty to which a state is not party, the exercise by the court of a power in derogation of that state's rights infringes those rights unless the state otherwise manifests its consent to the derogation.[106] The state, not being a party to the treaty, cannot be taken—absent consent manifest otherwise—to have consented to the exercise in derogation of its rights of the powers conferred on the court by the treaty. The fact that the court is international makes no difference. The same would be the case, *mutatis mutandis*, were the court established and empowered by Security Council decision and the state not a member of the United Nations.

(ii) Immunities

3.39 It pays specifically to dismiss the fallacy that the denial before an international criminal court of the immunities from criminal proceedings from which a state is entitled under international law to see its serving and former officials benefit before

---

[105] Recall, *supra* n 58, UN Charter, art 1(1).
[106] It is crucial to appreciate that the formulation of the *pacta tertiis* rule in art 34 of the VCLT does not adequately reflect customary international law. It is not simply that a treaty cannot create obligations or rights for third states without their consent. It is also the case that a treaty may not impinge upon the legal rights of third states without these states' consent. See eg para 2 of the commentary to draft art 30 (the eventual art 34) of the ILC's Draft Articles on the Law of Treaties, *Ybk ILC 1966*, vol II, 226 ('nor modify in any way their legal rights without their consent'); *Island of Palmas (Netherlands/United States of America)*, 2 RIAA 829, 842 (1928); A McNair, *The Law of Treaties* (Oxford: Clarendon Press, 1961), 321.

the courts of other states is per se lawful.¹⁰⁷ No state may, without the consent of the state whose official or ex-official it is, abrogate such immunities from criminal proceedings as international law, whether customary or conventional, obliges it to accord the serving and former officials of another state, and states have no greater authority under international law to do together what none of them may, as a matter of international law, do alone. The international legality of the abrogation before an international criminal court of any procedural immunity owed under international law by the states establishing and empowering the court depends on the precise international legal authority for the abrogation.¹⁰⁸

3.40 The post-Second World War prosecution by the victorious Allied powers of the major German and Japanese war criminals before the Nuremberg and Tokyo IMTs respectively was not justified under international law by the international character of the tribunals. The four Allied parties to the multilateral treaty by which the Nuremberg IMT was established and empowered in accordance with its Charter¹⁰⁹ founded their authority jointly to try the former German leaders for acts done in their official capacity both on Germany's unconditional surrender, as implicitly manifesting that state's consent to the Allies' foreshadowed¹¹⁰ trial of the remnants of its leadership, and, moreover, on the formal subjugation of the German Reich as a matter of international law (a concept known as '*debellatio*') with the consequence that the four occupying Allied powers came to wield the undoubted sovereign authority of Germany over its own former officials.¹¹¹ As for the Tokyo IMT, the Allied powers on whose behalf the proclamation establishing the Tribunal was promulgated and its Charter approved¹¹² based their authority jointly to prosecute the former Japanese leadership for acts performed in its official capacity on Japan's unconditional surrender and, indeed, on what they read as Japan's express consent in the terms of that surrender to the trial of its leaders by the Allies.¹¹³

3.41 The international legal authority to prosecute before the ICTY the former head of state of Yugoslavia, as well as former military officials from Yugoslavia, Croatia, and Bosnia-Herzegovina, for acts done in their official capacity derives from these three states' membership of the United Nations. In accordance with article 25 of the UN Charter, member states agree to accept the lawful decisions of the Security Council, and in Security Council resolution 827 (1993) the Council lawfully decided to establish an international criminal tribunal with the powers specified in the annexed statute, as adopted by decision of the Council in the same resolution¹¹⁴—a statute that makes no allowance for any immunity from prosecution by other states from which serving and former state officials may otherwise benefit as a matter of international law.¹¹⁵ The same, *mutatis mutandis*, would be capable

---

¹⁰⁷ See eg *supra* n 104.
¹⁰⁸ See also D Akande, 'International Law Immunities and the International Criminal Court' (2004) 98 *AJIL* 407, 415–19.
¹⁰⁹ Recall *supra* para 3.13.
¹¹⁰ See eg Statement on Atrocities Signed by President Roosevelt, Prime Minister Churchill and Premier Stalin, Moscow, 30 October 1943.
¹¹¹ Recall *supra* para 2.59. ¹¹² Recall *supra* para 3.15. ¹¹³ Recall ibid.
¹¹⁴ Recall *supra* para 3.23. ¹¹⁵ See, further, *infra* paras 12.30–12.32.

of justifying the prosecution of the former head of government and other former officials of Rwanda before the ICTR, although, as it is, Rwanda has never asserted any potentially relevant immunity and, through its request for the establishment of and active support for the Tribunal, can be taken to have waived any immunity from which the relevant individuals might have benefited.

3.42 In the case of the SCSL, established and empowered as it was by way of a bilateral treaty between the UN and Sierra Leone[116] in what was at root a delegation by Sierra Leone to an international criminal court of its jurisdiction to prosecute persons responsible for crimes committed in its territory, the denial before the Court to an official or ex-official of another state of the immunities from criminal proceedings owed to that state by Sierra Leone would not have been internationally lawful were it not for the consent of the only other state in actual question, namely Liberia, which gave its full support to the trial of its former head of state before the Court. *Pace* the Court itself,[117] the fact that the SCSL was an international criminal court, rather than a municipal one, made no international legal difference. Sierra Leone would not have been permitted to do in co-operation with an international organization what it was not permitted to do by itself.

3.43 What goes for the SCSL goes, *mutatis mutandis*, for the ICC, established and empowered as it is under a multilateral treaty among states in a delegation to an international criminal court by each of these states of its jurisdiction to prosecute crimes committed in its territory, on a ship or aircraft registered in that state, or by its nationals.[118] Absent the consent of the relevant third state,[119] it would be internationally unlawful to prosecute, via the joint medium of the ICC, a serving or former official of a third state if the latter would benefit under international law from immunity from prosecution before the courts of the relevant state party to the Rome Statute.[120] The issue was identified, albeit not settled, by the Court itself in a decision of 9 April 2014 by the Pre-Trial Chamber in *Al Bashir*.[121] Having gone out of its way 'to make clear that it is not disputed that under international

---

[116] Recall *supra* paras 3.18–3.19.

[117] *Taylor*, Appeals Chamber Decision on Immunity (n 33), paras 41–42 and 52. See also *infra* para 13.32.

[118] In addition, when the ICC exercises its jurisdiction on the basis of a declaration by a non-state party under art 12(3) of the Rome Statute, this represents a delegation to the Court by the declarant state of its jurisdiction to prosecute crimes committed in its territory, on board a ship or aircraft registered in that state, or by its nationals, as the case may be. See, generally, *infra* paras 14.33–14.35 and 14.43–14.46.

[119] A 'third state' is international legal terminology for a state not party to a given treaty. See VCLT, art 2(1)(*h*) ('"Third State" means a State not a party to the treaty') and arts 34–38.

[120] The relevant state party is the state party whose participation in the Rome Statute constitutes under art 12(2) the requisite precondition to the exercise by the Court of its jurisdiction. On the presumption that the accused serving or former third-state official is a national of that third state, the relevant state party in such a case will be one in whose territory or on a ship or aircraft registered in which the crime in question was allegedly committed. All of this goes equally, *mutatis mutandis*, where the precondition to the exercise of the Court's jurisdiction is fulfilled by means of a declaration under art 12(3) of the Statute.

[121] *Prosecutor v Al Bashir*, ICC-02/05-01/09-195, Pre-Trial Chamber, Decision on the Cooperation of the Democratic Republic of the Congo Regarding Omar Al-Bashir's Arrest and Surrender to the Court, 9 April 2014.

law a sitting Head of State enjoys personal immunities from criminal jurisdiction and inviolability before national courts of foreign States even when suspected of having committed one of more of the crimes that fall within the jurisdiction of the Court',[122] the Pre-Trial Chamber continued:

25. ... An exception to the personal immunities of Heads of States is explicitly provided in article 27(2) of the Statute for prosecution before an international criminal jurisdiction. According to this provision, the existence of personal immunities under international law which generally attach to the official capacity of the person 'shall not bar the Court from exercising its jurisdiction over such a person'.

26. Still, the question *sub judice* is how far reaching this provision is meant to be, and whether such an exception for lifting personal immunities applies to Heads of all States, including non-States Parties to the Statute (third States), or whether it is only confined to those States which have adhered to the Statute. Given that the Statute is a multilateral treaty governed by the rules set out in the Vienna Convention on the Law of Treaties, the Statute cannot impose obligations on third States without their consent. Thus, the exception to the exercise of the Court's jurisdiction provided in article 27(2) of the Statute should, in principle, be confined to those States Parties who have accepted it.

27. It follows that when the exercise of jurisdiction by the Court entails the prosecution of a Head of State of a non-State Party, the question of personal immunities might validly arise....

The only difference is where the UN Security Council takes a decision under chapter VII of the UN Charter to refer to the ICC a situation implicating immunities owed to a third state.[123] Here the Council envisages that, in the event that the Prosecutor opens an investigation and in turn prosecutes, any cases arising out of the situation will proceed in accordance with the Rome Statute, which expressly provides in article 27(2) that '[i]mmunities or special procedural rules which may attach to the official capacity of a person, whether under national or international law, shall not bar the Court from exercising its jurisdiction over such a person'. In other words, in deciding to refer a situation to the ICC, the Security Council decides that any persons who may eventually be prosecuted before the Court for crimes allegedly committed in the context of that situation shall not benefit from any immunity from prosecution from which the third state in question may otherwise be entitled to see such persons benefit at the hands of the states parties or relevant state party.[124] Provided that the third state is a member of the United Nations, it has undertaken in article 25 of the Charter to accept the lawful decisions of the Security Council, meaning in this context that it is taken to have consented in advance to the Council's abrogation of any immunity from prosecution by other states from which it might otherwise have the right under international law to see its officials and ex-officials benefit.

---

[122] Ibid, para 25.   [123] See, generally, *infra* para 14.45.
[124] In practice it can be expected that the Security Council will refer a situation only where the alleged crimes are committed both in the territory and by the nationals of a third state, although it is not out of the question that it might refer a situation involving crimes alleged to have been committed in the territory of a state party by officials of a third state.

3.44 Nor can one draw support for the supposed international lawfulness per se of the denial of procedural immunities before international criminal courts from two brief dicta of the ICJ in *Arrest Warrant of 11 April 2000*.[125] To say, as the Court did in response to Belgium's reliance on them in that case, that the relevant provisions of the respective statutes of the various international criminal courts are irrelevant to the question of immunities in national criminal courts[126] is not to say that immunities pose no bar to prosecution in international criminal courts. More to the point, to say, in response to the argument that immunity from the jurisdiction of national criminal courts amounts to impunity for international crimes, that an incumbent or former minister for foreign affairs may be subject to criminal proceedings in 'certain international criminal courts, where they have jurisdiction', and to cite as examples the ICTY, ICTR, and ICC,[127] is simply to acknowledge the effect of the relevant provisions of the respective statutes. It cannot be taken as a statement that this abrogation of immunities is lawful.

B. Reality

3.45 The only inherent difference between international criminal courts and municipal criminal courts of any real legal significance pertains to the formal value of their decisions[128] from the point of view of the sources of international law. Decisions of international criminal courts are formal sources of international law in their own right, being judicial decisions within the meaning of article 38(1)(*d*) of the Statute of the International Court of Justice and as such subsidiary means for the determination of international legal rules. That is, decisions of international criminal courts represent internationally authoritative, albeit not necessarily conclusive statements as to the content and, in relevant cases, existence in the first place of any treaty-based or customary international rule at issue. In contrast, decisions of municipal criminal courts on points of international law are not formal sources of international law. They constitute no more, but no less, than state practice and accompanying *opinio juris* on the part of the forum state and as such are formally capable of contributing to establishing the interpretation to be given to a treaty provision[129] or the existence and content of a rule of customary international law only to the extent that the practice and *opinio juris* of a single state, and of that particular state on that particular point, are capable of so doing.[130] Nor is there

---

[125] See eg *Taylor*, Appeals Chamber Decision on Immunity (n 33), para 50; *Al Bashir*, Pre-Trial Chamber Corrigendum to the Decision pursuant to Article 87(7) (n 104), para 33.
[126] See *Arrest Warrant of 11 April 2000 (Democratic Republic of the Congo v Belgium)*, ICJ Rep 2002, 3, 24, para 58.
[127] See ibid, 25–6, para 61.
[128] The term as used here, as throughout international law, is not limited to the *dispositif* of a judgment but encompasses the court's reasoning and dicta.
[129] See VCLT, art 31(3)(*b*).
[130] Conversely, a decision by an international criminal court on a point of municipal law can have no formal bearing on the content of that municipal law unless municipal law so provides. That is, except where stipulated by the municipal legal system in question, decisions of international criminal courts on points of municipal law are not formal sources of municipal law. (Whether the

any convincing reason why the presence of foreign judges on a municipal criminal court should make a difference in this regard.[131]

VI. The Legal Significance of the Differences among International Criminal Courts

What is ultimately of greater legal significance than the distinction between international and municipal criminal courts are the differences as to means of establishment and empowerment among international criminal courts. 3.46

One principal legal consequence of the different means of establishment and empowerment of international criminal courts—namely the permissibility of the unavailability as a bar to trial before the court of the immunity from prosecution that international law may require one state to afford a serving or former official of another—has already been discussed.[132] The denial of such immunities, pursuant to the court's statute as adopted by the UN Security Council, before an international criminal court lawfully[133] established and empowered by decision of the Council is internationally lawful, provided that any state whose official or ex-official is tried before the court is a UN member. In contrast, the denial of such immunities to an official or ex-official of a third state before an international criminal court established and empowered by treaty—be it a bilateral treaty between a state and an international organization such as the UN or a multilateral treaty among states—is an internationally unlawful act unless the third state consents to this denial, except in the case of a trial before the ICC arising out of a situation referred to the Court by the Security Council. 3.47

The other principal legal consequence of the different means of establishment and empowerment of international criminal courts relates to the obligations of states to comply with a court's requests for assistance or orders. It is no infringement of the rights of a UN member state for the Security Council to oblige that state to comply with any request for assistance or order lawfully made pursuant to a power with which an international criminal tribunal lawfully established and empowered by the Council is vested. In accordance with article 25 of the UN Charter, UN member states 'agree to...carry out the decisions of the Security Council in accordance with the...Charter', with the consequence that they are taken to have agreed in advance to comply with any request for assistance or order by an international criminal court which the Council decides that they shall carry out.[134] So, for example, it is no breach of international law for a member 3.48

---

decisions of a state's own courts represent a formal source of that state's law will also depend on the state's legal system.)

[131] It is not the case, eg, that the presence of foreign judges on the Court of Final Appeal of the Hong Kong Special Administrative Region and on the highest appellate courts of several Pacific island states transforms the formal character of decisions of these courts on points of international law.
[132] Recall *supra* paras 3.39–3.44.   [133] Recall, *supra* n 59, UN Charter, art 1(1).
[134] Moreover, in accordance with art 103 of the UN Charter, a UN member state's obligation of compliance with any such request or order, being an obligation pursuant to art 25 of the UN Charter,

state of the UN to be compelled to abide by a request for assistance or order lawfully issued by the ICTY under the power to issue requests for assistance and orders to states conferred on the Tribunal by article 29 of the ICTY Statute: in Security Council resolution 827 (1993) the Council specifically decided that 'all States shall cooperate fully with the International Tribunal and its organs' in accordance with the resolution and the Statute[135] and that consequently all states are to take any measures necessary under their municipal law to implement the resolution and the Statute, 'including the obligation of States to comply with requests for assistance or orders issued by a Trial Chamber under Article 29 of the Statute'.[136] In contrast, an international criminal court established and empowered by treaty—again, whether a bilateral treaty between a state and an international organization such as the UN or a multilateral treaty among states—cannot create obligations for a third state without that state's consent.[137] As such, no state not party to the treaty may be obliged to comply with any request for assistance or order issued by a treaty-based international criminal court unless that state has voluntarily assumed the obligation. This is reflected both in the agreement between the UN and Sierra Leone on the establishment of the SCSL and in the Rome Statute. Article 17(1) of the SCSL Agreement stipulates that Sierra Leone 'shall cooperate with all organs of the Special Court at all stages of the proceedings', while article 17(2) specifies that Sierra Leone 'shall comply without undue delay with any request for assistance by the Special Court or an order issued by the Chambers'. No state other than Sierra Leone is mentioned.[138] Similarly, the provisions of part 9 of the Rome Statute consistently distinguish between states parties, which are obliged to comply with requests from the ICC for various sorts of co-operation, and other states, which are not unless they voluntarily undertake to comply.[139] That said, nothing precludes the Security Council from obliging a UN member state not party to the Statute to comply with requests for co-operation issued to it by the ICC. The Council has done precisely this in relation to Sudan and Libya respectively. In Security Council resolution 1593 (2005), the resolution by which it referred the situation in Sudan to the Court, the Council, acting under chapter VII of the Charter, decided 'that the Government of Sudan and all other parties to the conflict in Darfur, shall cooperate fully with and provide any necessary assistance to the Court and the Prosecutor pursuant to this resolution';[140] and, likewise, in Security Council resolution 1970 (2011), by which it referred

---

prevails over its obligations under any other international agreement in the event of conflict between the two. As for a member state's obligations under non-peremptory rules of customary international law, the precedence of the state's obligations under the Charter—in accordance with the maxim *lex specialis legi generali derogat*—goes without saying.

[135] SC res 827 (1993), 25 May 1993, para 4.

[136] Ibid. See eg *Prosecutor v Blaškić*, IT-95-14, Appeals Chamber, Judgment on the Request of the Republic of Croatia for Review of the Decision of Trial Chamber II of 18 July 1997, 29 October 1997, para 26. The same goes, *mutatis mutandis*, for the ICTR. For more on states' obligations to co-operate with both, see *infra* paras 12.49–12.53.

[137] See, as consonant with customary international law, VCLT, art 34.

[138] See, further, *infra* para 13.40. [139] See, further, *infra* paras 14.79 and 14.81.

[140] SC res 1593 (2005), 31 March 2005, para 2.

the situation in Libya to the Court, the Council, again acting under chapter VII of the Charter, decided 'that the Libyan authorities shall cooperate fully with and provide any necessary assistance to the Court and the Prosecutor pursuant to this resolution'.[141] The source of this identical obligation, extraneous to the Rome Statute, is simply article 25 of the UN Charter in combination with a lawful decision of the Security Council that the UN member state shall comply with requests for co-operation from the ICC. Nor is there any reason why the Council may not oblige only a single member state[142] to comply with requests for assistance and orders issued by an international criminal court that the Council itself has established and empowered, as the Council has effectively done vis-à-vis Lebanon and the STL.[143]

VII. Conclusion

States have recourse both to international criminal courts (meaning criminal courts that formally depend for their existence and competence on international law) and to municipal criminal courts (meaning criminal courts that formally depend for their existence and competence on municipal law) for the adjudication of international crimes. The formal juridical distinction between the two types of criminal court is of less consequence than is widely assumed. More significant for the purposes of international law are the different legal bases on which international criminal courts can be established and empowered. In practical terms, furthermore, far more important are the descriptive differences as to jurisdiction, applicable law, rules of procedure and evidence, composition of the bench and its method of appointment, and so on, among international criminal courts and municipal criminal courts respectively.

3.49

Further Reading

AKANDE, D, 'International Law Immunities and the International Criminal Court' (2004) 98 *American Journal of International Law* 407

ALAMUDDIN, A, JURDI, NN and TOLBERT, D (eds), *The Special Tribunal for Lebanon. Law and Practice* (Oxford: Oxford University Press, 2014)

BOISTER, N and CRYER, R (eds), *Documents on the Tokyo International Military Tribunal. Charter, Indictment and Judgments* (Oxford: Oxford University Press, 2008)

BOISTER, N and CRYER, R, *The Tokyo International Military Tribunal: A Reappraisal* (Oxford: Oxford University Press, 2008)

---

[141] SC res 1970 (2011), 26 February 2011, para 5.
[142] See, in this regard, UN Charter, art 48(1): 'The action required to carry out the decisions of the Security Council for the maintenance of international peace and security shall be taken by all the Members of the United Nations or by some of them, as the Security Council may determine.'
[143] See SC res 1757 (2007), para 1(*a*), cross-referable with STL Agreement, art 15.

KJELDGAARD-PEDERSEN, A, 'What Defines an International Criminal Court? A Critical Assessment of "the Involvement of the International Community" as a Deciding Factor' (2015) 28 *Leiden Journal of International Law* 113

MÉGRET, F, 'A Special Tribunal for Lebanon: The UN Security Council and the Emancipation of International Criminal Justice' (2008) 21 *Leiden Journal of International Law* 485

METTRAUX, G (ed), *Perspectives on the Nuremberg Trial* (Oxford: Oxford University Press, 2008)

PART TWO

THE SUBSTANTIVE LAW OF INTERNATIONAL CRIMES

Crimes under Customary International Law

4
The Crimes

I. Introduction

The identification and definition of crimes under customary international law 4.1
are central planks of both customary international criminal law and substantive international criminal law more generally. Crimes under customary international law were the earliest subject of international criminal law in the sense of *droit international pénal* (as distinct, but not separate, from *droit pénal international*), and it is they that have formed the basis to date of the overwhelming majority of prosecutions of international crimes at both the international and national levels. It is to crimes under customary international law, moreover, that the further questions of the modes of criminal responsibility recognized by customary international law[1] and of the grounds for excluding criminal responsibility under customary international law[2] both pertain.

After dealing with preliminary matters, this chapter outlines the crimes 4.2
accepted in principle as existing under customary international law. It should be emphasized by way of caveat that it is by no means certain that the parameters of the crimes as posited by the various international criminal courts or implied by the respective jurisdictions *ratione materiae* specified in the latter's statutes accord in every detail with the present or, where relevant, past customary international legal position. Presented here is what is, what is purported or implied to be, or what is intended to become customary international law. For the far greater part, its status as *lex lata* is neither contested nor open to serious doubt. But aspects of it are more accurately viewed as *lex ferenda* or even *lex ficta*. It should also be stressed at the outset that the chapter's treatment of the material and mental elements of each offence focuses on the more general elements. The numerous specific war crimes, the range of specific crimes against humanity, and the five specific acts capable of grounding the crime of genocide each have their specific material elements, while not a few of them have specific mental elements as well. At least as regards the crimes falling within the jurisdiction *ratione materiae* of the International Criminal Court (ICC), the material elements of each of these specific heads of crime are more or less apparent on the face of the relevant provision and are elaborated on

---

[1] See *infra* chapter 5.   [2] See *infra* chapter 6.

120   *Crimes under Customary International Law*

by the ICC's 'Elements of Crimes', even if a full appreciation of each calls for closer analysis.³

II. Preliminary Matters

A. General

4.3 A crime under customary international law is an offence defined by customary (or 'general') international law which gives rise to the individual criminal responsibility of the perpetrator under customary international law itself.⁴ In other words, it is a prohibition or positive duty, incumbent on individuals, with its formal source and definition in customary international law and for the breach of which the perpetrator is punishable as a matter of customary international law.

4.4 The material sources for crimes under customary international law—that is, the documentary and other material evidence from which we derive the existence and parameters of such offences—are many and varied.⁵ Highly significant among these are any judgments, decisions, and orders (generically, 'decisions') of international criminal courts that purport to declare customary international law. Although classical international legal doctrine relegates such decisions to the status of subsidiary means for the determination of rules of customary (or other) international law,⁶ the reality in practice is that customary international criminal law

---

³ This is an analysis in respect of which the present chapter defers to other, more expert works. See, in particular and strictly in alphabetical order, K Ambos, *Treatise on International Criminal Law. Volume 2: Crimes and Sentencing* (Oxford: Oxford University Press, 2014), chapters 1–4; A Cassese and P Gaeta, *Cassese's International Criminal Law* (3rd edn, Oxford: Oxford University Press, 2013), chapters 4–8; R Cryer et al, *An Introduction to International Criminal Law and Procedure* (3rd edn, Cambridge: Cambridge University Press, 2014), chapters 10–13; G Werle and F Jessburger, *Principles of International Criminal Law* (3rd edn, Oxford: Oxford University Press, 2014), chapters 19–38.
⁴ Recall *supra* paras 2.34 and 2.36.
⁵ Major examples, the evidentiary value of which varies considerably (and, indeed, some of which is to be treated with extreme caution), include relevant municipal legislation; relevant decisions of municipal criminal courts, including the various post-Second World War national military tribunals; the Charter of the International Military Tribunal, Nuremberg ('Nuremberg Charter'), the Charter of the International Military Tribunal for the Far East ('Tokyo Charter'), and the judgments of the Tribunals, as well as GA res 95 (I), 11 December 1946, entitled 'Affirmation of the Principles of International Law recognized by the Charter of the Nürnberg Tribunal', and the International Law Commission (ILC)'s Principles of International Law Recognized in the Charter of the Nürnberg Tribunal and in the Judgment of the Tribunal, *Ybk ILC 1950*, vol II, 191 ('ILC Nürnberg Principles'); GA res 96 (I), 11 December 1946, entitled 'The crime of genocide'; the ILC's Draft Code of Crimes against the Peace and Security of Mankind with commentaries, *Ybk ILC 1996*, vol II/2, 17 ('ILC Draft Code of Crimes'); the Statute of the International Criminal Tribunal for the former Yugoslavia ('ICTY Statute'), the Statute of the International Criminal Tribunal for Rwanda ('ICTR Statute'), and the judgments, decisions, and orders of the Tribunals; the Statute of the Special Court for Sierra Leone ('SCSL Statute') and the judgments, decisions, and orders of the Special Court; the Rome Statute of the International Criminal Court ('Rome Statute'), arts 6 to 8*bis*, the *travaux préparatoires* to the Rome Statute, the 'Elements of Crimes', ICC-ASP/1/3 (part II-B) (as amended), (which 'shall assist the Court in the interpretation and application' of arts 6 to 8*bis*, as stated in art 9(1) of the Statute), and the judgments, decisions, and orders of the Court; and so on.
⁶ See Statute of the International Court of Justice, art 38(1)(*d*).

verges on a common-law system in which international criminal courts effectively make law, even if strictly and sometimes practically speaking it remains states' tacit acceptance of the former's jurisprudence as indeed consonant with customary international law which either affirms or crystallizes the formal juridical reality.[7] As for the evidentiary value of the Rome Statute of the International Criminal Court ('Rome Statute') in the identification of customary international law, it may pay to note that articles 6 to 8*bis* of the Statute, which outline the crimes within the jurisdiction of the Court, are not and do not purport to be definitive of the customary position, representing as they do partly a conservative statement of the *droit acquis*[8] and partly self-conscious progressive development.[9] It is possible that there exist or come to exist customary international crimes not found in the Rome Statute.[10] It is similarly possible that some crimes that are within the ICC's jurisdiction, as well as the precise definitions of others, do not currently reflect customary international law, although the Statute is propelling and shaping the development of customary international law in these respects, and may well come to be seen as the conclusive statement of the crimes covered by it.

4.5 The fact that a crime is a crime under customary international law does not carry with it any jurisdictional or prosecutorial obligations for states.[11] States are not obliged to ensure that crimes under customary international law are criminal under their municipal law. Equally, while it is likely that states are permitted to extend their criminal jurisdiction over crimes under customary international law on the basis of universality,[12] they are not obliged to do so, at least by customary international law. Nor does customary international law oblige states to prosecute

---

[7] It is certainly the case that some speculative or spurious statements as to the existence or content of crimes under customary international law have been rejected by states. Consider, in this regard, *Prosecutor v Ayyash* et al, STL-11-01/I/AC/R176*bis*, Appeals Chamber, Interlocutory Decision on the Applicable Law: Terrorism, Conspiracy, Homicide, Perpetration, Cumulative Charging, 16 February 2011, paras 83–113, discussed *infra* para 4.104.
[8] Take eg the restriction of the Court's jurisdiction *ratione materiae* to the crimes of genocide, crimes against humanity, war crimes, and aggression.
[9] Consider certain subspecies of crimes against humanity and war crimes, in the latter case particularly those pertaining to non-international armed conflict, as well as the definition of the crime of aggression.
[10] Note, in this regard, art 10 of the Rome Statute, specifying for the avoidance of doubt that nothing in arts 6 to 8*bis* of the Statute 'shall be interpreted as limiting or prejudicing in any way existing or developing rules of international law for purposes other than th[e] Statute'.
[11] Arguments to this effect based on Rome Statute, preamble (fourth and sixth recitals), are clutching at straws. State practice does not go close at present to establishing any customary jurisdictional or prosecutorial obligations for states in respect of crimes under customary international law. As specifically regards a putative customary obligation to punish genocide akin to the treaty obligation recognized in art 1 of the Convention on the Prevention and Punishment of the Crime of Genocide 1948 ('Genocide Convention'), it is true that the International Court of Justice (ICJ) stated in *Reservations to the Convention on the Prevention and Punishment of the Crime of Genocide, Advisory Opinion*, ICJ Rep 1951, 15, 23, that the Genocide Convention enunciates 'principles which are recognized by civilized nations as binding on States, even without any conventional obligation'. But it is more likely that the 'principles' considered customary by the ICJ relate only to the definition of genocide and certain other basic tenets of the Convention, like the unavailability of the defence of act of state to a charge of genocide, rather than to the obligations imposed on states parties by the instrument. State practice does not suggest a customary obligation to prosecute genocide.
[12] Recall *supra* paras 1.63–1.64.

B. The General Conditions for Criminal Responsibility under Customary International Law

4.6 As under national criminal justice systems, so too is it the case under customary international criminal law that the accused must be proved to have satisfied not only the requisite material elements but also the requisite mental element or elements of the offence for which he or she is tried—that is, both the so-called *actus reus* and *mens rea*—before he or she can be convicted of it.

4.7 What is required in order to satisfy the definitional material elements, or *actus reus*, of a crime under customary international law obviously depends on the crime. In particular, commission may involve the performance of proscribed conduct (that is, the doing of prohibited acts) or it may involve the omission to perform prescribed conduct (that is, the failure to do obligatory acts).[13]

4.8 When it comes to the mental element, or *mens rea*, of crimes under customary international law, as a general rule it is an essential condition of criminal responsibility that the individual have the intent to commit the requisite material elements of the offence and the knowledge of any legally relevant facts. Criminal responsibility on the basis of negligence is not a general feature of customary international criminal law, and criminal responsibility on the basis of strict liability is unknown to the field.[14] The Rome Statute and the Elements of Crimes specify the general mental element required for criminal responsibility pursuant to the Statute.[15] Both the Statute and the Elements can, with reasonable certainty, be considered declaratory of customary international law to this extent, by way of either codification or crystallization, although the situation is less clear in relation to some of the mental elements peculiar to specific offences.[16] Article 30 of the Rome Statute ('Mental element') states:

1. Unless otherwise provided, a person shall be criminally responsible and liable for punishment for a crime within the jurisdiction of the Court only if the material elements are committed with intent and knowledge.

---

[13] See, generally, *Prosecutor v Tadić*, IT-94-1-A, Appeals Chamber, Judgment, 15 July 1999, para 188; *Prosecutor v Blaškić*, IT-95-14-A, Appeals Chamber, Judgment, 29 July 2004, para 663; *Prosecutor v Kayishema and Ruzindana*, ICTR-95-1-A, Appeals Chamber, Judgment (reasons), 1 June 2001, para 187. See also *infra* para 5.13.

[14] See also *infra* para 5.10.

[15] Article 6 of the Nuremberg Charter did not expressly require any mental element as a condition of responsibility for crimes within the International Military Tribunal (IMT)'s jurisdiction, although the Tribunal did. The same went in relation to art II of Control Council Law No 10 and art 5 of the Tokyo Charter. Nor do or did the respective statutes of the ICTY, ICTR, or SCSL embody any express, overarching requirement of intentionality. It has been left to the Tribunals and Special Court to flesh out the *mens rea* of each of the offences within their respective jurisdictions and of each of the modes of criminal responsibility for those offences.

[16] Certain species and subspecies of crimes under customary international law have additional, special mental elements, as considered *infra*.

2. For the purposes of this article, a person has intent where:
   (a) In relation to conduct, that person means to engage in the conduct;
   (b) In relation to a consequence, that person means to cause that consequence or is aware that it will occur in the ordinary course of events.
3. For the purposes of this article, 'knowledge' means awareness that a circumstance exists or a consequence will occur in the ordinary course of events. 'Know' and 'knowingly' shall be construed accordingly.

The general introduction to the Elements of Crimes provides:

As stated in article 30, unless otherwise provided, a person shall be criminally responsible and liable for punishment for a crime within the jurisdiction of the Court only if the material elements are committed with intent and knowledge. Where no reference is made in the Elements of Crimes to a mental element for any particular conduct, consequence or circumstance listed, it is understood that the relevant mental element, i.e., intent, knowledge or both, set out in article 30 applies.[17]

The general introduction to the Elements of Crimes also states that the '[e]xistence of intent or knowledge can be inferred from relevant facts and circumstances'.[18]

Intent and motive are distinct issues.[19] Only intent is a formal precondition to criminal responsibility under customary international law. In other words, what matters is that individuals mean, with the necessary knowledge, to do what they do, not why they do it.

4.9

III. War Crimes

A. Terminology

The term 'war crimes' refers to those violations of international humanitarian law (also known as the laws of armed conflict or, in the past, the laws of war) that give rise to the individual criminal responsibility of the perpetrator under international

4.10

---

[17] Elements of Crimes, general introduction, para 2. The phrase 'unless otherwise provided' in article 30 of the Rome Statute and in the general introduction to the Elements of Crimes would seem to be a reference to the mental element necessary for command and other superior responsibility, as recognized in article 28(a)(i) and (b)(i) respectively of the Rome Statute. See *infra* paras 5.102–5.108.

[18] Elements of Crimes, general introduction, para 3. Paragraph 4 of the general introduction further stipulates that, '[w]ith respect to mental elements associated with elements involving value judgement, such as those using the terms "inhumane" or "severe", it is not necessary that the perpetrator personally completed a particular value judgement, unless otherwise indicated'. In other words, the qualification of defined conduct as 'inhumane' or 'severe' is objective, not subjective.

[19] See eg *Tadić*, Appeals Chamber Judgment (n 13), para 269; *Prosecutor v Jelisić*, IT-95-10-A, Appeals Chamber, Judgment, 5 July 2001, para 106; *Prosecutor v Krnojelac*, IT-97-25-A, Appeals Chamber, Judgment, 17 September 2003, paras 100–102; *Prosecutor v Kvočka* et al, IT-98-30/1-A, Appeals Chamber, Judgment, 28 February 2005, para 106; *Prosecutor v Stakić*, IT-97-24-A, Appeals Chamber, Judgment, 22 March 2006, para 45.

law, whether customary or conventional.[20] In terms of war crimes under customary international law, the label encompasses both so-called 'violations of the laws and customs of war'[21] and the customary analogues of certain violations of the 1949 Geneva Conventions and their Additional Protocols.[22]

4.11 'War' has been replaced by 'armed conflict' in the lexicon of international humanitarian law, even if the terms 'war crimes'[23] and 'violations of the laws or [sic] customs of war'[24] are still commonly used by way of shorthand. The Rome Statute, however, speaks in more modern terms of 'violations of the laws and customs applicable in...armed conflict',[25] while the SCSL Statute refers to 'violations of international humanitarian law'.[26]

B. Evolution

(i) 'Violations of the laws and customs of war'

(a) International armed conflict

4.12 The waging of war being the exercise par excellence of sovereign authority, the corollary of the principle of sovereign equality reflected in the maxim *par in parem non habet imperium* rendered inconceivable the idea that one sovereign could regulate by his own law the belligerent acts of the military forces of an enemy sovereign, and *vice versa*. If the regulation of warfare were considered desirable by the community of European sovereigns, and it was,[27] it could be done only through recourse to the '*jus gentium*', or law of nations, recognized as the sole legal fetter on the conduct of sovereigns *inter se*. So it was that states came to regulate interstate warfare by means of rules of customary international law. Violations of these rules were remediable by a variety of means, one of them conceded among states being the punishment of captured enemy servicemen for at least the more condemnable violations of what became known as 'the laws and customs of war' and at least when the impugned acts were committed against the punishing state's servicemen or civilians. (Whether the criminal responsibility of the guilty individual arose under the law of nations itself or simply under municipal law in pursuance of the substantive rules of the laws and customs of war was impossible to tell and, indeed, the distinction would have been considered meaningless.)[28] These laws and customs of war were eventually codified,

---

[20] The older literature uses the term 'war crimes' to encompass both punishable violations of the international laws of war and acts of unprivileged belligerency—such as spying and what would now be called direct participation in hostilities by civilians—punishable under national law alone. Modern usage restricts the label to the former.

[21] Known in the past as 'violations of the laws and usages of war', these correspond in practice to those violations of the customary rules reflected in the 1907 Hague Regulations that give rise to individual criminal responsibility under customary international law, along with several novel customary war crimes. See *infra* paras 4.12–4.19.

[22] See eg Rome Statute, art 8.   [23] See eg ibid.   [24] See eg ICTY Statute, art 3.
[25] Rome Statute, art 8(2)(b) and (e).   [26] SCSL Statute, art 4.
[27] See also S Szurek, 'Historique. La formation du droit international pénal' in H Ascensio, E Decaux, and A Pellet (eds), *Droit international pénal* (2nd edn, Paris: Pedone, 2012) 21, 29, para 28.
[28] Recall *supra* para 2.55.

first in 1899 and later in the Regulations respecting the Law and Customs of War on Land annexed to the Convention respecting the Law and Customs of War on Land 1907 ('1907 Hague Regulations' and '1907 Hague Convention IV' respectively). The latter were considered for the most part to be declaratory at the time of the laws and customs of war. Where they were not, they have long been acknowledged as having emerged since as authoritative statements of customary international law.

But not every violation of the laws and customs of war was and is a customary war crime. Some rules gave and give rise on breach to state responsibility alone. Historically, precisely which rules resulted on breach in individual criminal responsibility depended on the forum of prosecution, and the inventory of such crimes was not necessarily the same from state to state, although there was a rough consistency. This practice on the part of municipal military tribunals contributed to the position under customary international law, as avowedly or implicitly reflected in the statutes of, and applied by, the various past and present international criminal courts;[29] and the practice of these international criminal courts has developed and refined the customary position, feeding back in turn into national practice.

4.13

Those violations of the rules codified in the 1907 Hague Regulations constituting war crimes under customary international law no longer comprise an exhaustive list of the violations of the laws and customs applicable in armed conflict that give rise as a customary matter to the individual criminal responsibility of the perpetrator. An example of a war crime resulting from the violation of a law or custom of war not found in the 1907 Hague Regulations is rape, recognized as a war crime only relatively recently.[30] Another is conscripting or enlisting children

4.14

---

[29] For the earliest international attempt to identify those violations of the laws and customs of war giving rise to individual criminal responsibility, see the list prepared by Sub-Commission III, on the Responsibility for the Violation of the Laws and Customs of War, of the 1919 Commission on Responsibilities of the Preliminary Peace Conference of Paris, in United Nations War Crimes Commission, *History of the United Nations War Crimes Commission and the Development of the Law of War* (London: UNWCC, 1948), 34–5. For the list of customary war crimes falling within the jurisdiction of the Nuremberg IMT, see Nuremberg Charter, art 6(*b*), which was not intended to be exhaustive ('Such violations shall include, but not be limited to...'). See also ILC Nürnberg Principles, principle VI. On the other hand, note the curious reference in Tokyo Charter, art 5(*b*) to '[c]onventional' war crimes. For the violations of the laws and customs of war falling within the jurisdiction of the ICTY, see ICTY Statute, art 3 (again, not intended as an exhaustive list, the relevant violations being stated to 'include, but not be limited to' those mentioned). As regards 'violations of the laws and customs applicable in international armed conflict' within the jurisdiction of the ICC, see the avowedly exhaustive list found in Rome Statute, art 8(2)(*b*). See also, subsequently, the shorter list in SCSL Statute, art 4, which was applicable to international and non-international armed conflict without distinction, in accordance with *Prosecutor v Norman* et al, SCSL-04-14-AR72(E), Appeals Chamber, Decision on Preliminary Motion on Lack of Jurisdiction Ratione Materiae: Nature of the Armed Conflict, 25 May 2004, para 30. The more limited list in the SCSL Statute reflects simply the more limited range of offences that took place in the conflict in Sierra Leone.

[30] See *Prosecutor v Furundžija*, IT-95-17/1, Trial Chamber, Judgment, 10 December 1998, paras 165–169 and 173. See also, previously and for what it is worth, ILC Draft Code of Crimes, art 20(*d*) ('outrages upon personal dignity in violation of international humanitarian law'—a cryptic reference probably to 1907 Hague Regulations, art 46—'in particular humiliating and degrading treatment, rape, enforced prostitution and any form of indecent assault'). See also, subsequently

under 15 years of age into armed forces or armed groups or using them to participate actively in hostilities.[31]

4.15 There is no conclusive list of the violations of the laws and customs applicable in international armed conflict that constitute war crimes. It may well be that the question is resolved over time through states' general acceptance, as both customary and a *numerus clausus*, of the 'serious violations of the laws and customs applicable in international armed conflict' enumerated in article 8(2)(*b*) of the Rome Statute, as from time to time amended. The list exhibits a general consistency with the criminal violations of the laws and customs of war identified by the ICTY, and, by dint of sheer convenience, is likely to be looked to increasingly by even those states that do not replicate article 8(2)(*b*) of the Rome Statute in their municipal criminal law.

(b) Non-international armed conflict

4.16 The classical laws and customs of war applied as a formal matter only to wars between states, now termed international armed conflicts, although they could be rendered applicable to civil wars by means of a legal device known as recognition of belligerency. Some inroads were made into this position during the Spanish Civil War of 1936–39. More significantly, between 1949 and 1995, civil wars, by then termed non-international armed conflicts, were made subject to a limited degree of treaty-based international legal regulation via article 3 common to all four of the 1949 Geneva Conventions ('common article 3') and the provisions of the Protocol Additional to the Geneva Conventions of 12 August 1949, and relating to the Protection of Victims of Non-International Armed Conflicts 1977 ('Additional Protocol II'). But none of these developments implicated individual criminal responsibility under international law, let alone under customary international law.

4.17 A seismic shift in the recognition of rules of customary international law applicable in non-international armed conflict and giving rise under customary international law to the individual criminal responsibility of government and insurgent forces alike came in the ICTY Appeals Chamber's 1995 interlocutory decision on jurisdiction in *Tadić*.[32] The Appeals Chamber held not only that certain customary international rules applicable to non-international armed conflict had developed but that their violation gave rise to the individual criminal responsibility of the perpetrator under customary international law.[33] The rules cited, while not identical in every respect to the rules governing international armed conflict,[34] were

---

and more persuasively, Rome Statute, art 8(2)(*b*)(xxii) ('rape, sexual slavery, enforced prostitution, forced pregnancy...enforced sterilization, or any other form of sexual violence also constituting a grave breach of the Geneva Conventions').

[31] See Rome Statute, art 8(*b*)(xxvi); SCSL Statute, art 4(*c*); *Prosecutor v Norman (Fofana intervening)*, SCSL-2003-04-14-AR72(E), Appeals Chamber, Decision on Preliminary Motion Based on Lack of Jurisdiction, 31 May 2004, endorsed in *Prosecutor v Brima* et al, SCSL-2004-16-A, Appeals Chamber, Judgment, 22 February 2008, para 296.

[32] See *Prosecutor v Tadić*, IT-94-1, Appeals Chamber, Decision on the Defence Motion for Interlocutory Appeal on Jurisdiction, 2 October 1995, paras 96–137.

[33] See especially ibid, para 134.   [34] See ibid, para 126.

taken to 'cover such areas as protection of civilians from hostilities, in particular from indiscriminate attacks, protection of civilian objects, in particular cultural property, protection of those who do not (or no longer) take active part in hostilities, as well as prohibition of means of warfare proscribed in international armed conflicts and ban of [sic] certain methods of conducting hostilities'.[35] The justification offered for this sweeping conclusion amounted in the final analysis to little more than a robust teleological assertion in the Nuremberg vein,[36] while the examples of state practice cited by the Appeals Chamber were highly ambivalent.[37] In the final analysis, while there was evidence at the time to support the existence of some, though perhaps not all of the customary rules of non-international armed conflict asserted by the ICTY, there was scant state practice to suggest that their violation gave rise in each case to individual criminal responsibility under customary international law.

But whatever the limitations of the reasoning in *Tadić*, states soon showed themselves prepared to accept the criminalization under international law of a considerable range of acts committed in non-international armed conflict. Article 8(2)(*e*) of the Rome Statute, concluded less than three years later, embodies a sizeable list of 'violations of the laws and customs applicable in armed conflicts not of an international character' (including rape[38] and forcibly enlisting or conscripting children under 15 years of age[39]), although this list is less extensive than the list relating to international armed conflict.[40] This is an aspect of the ICC's jurisdiction *ratione materiae* which is recognized as having at the time represented progressive development, rather than codification, of substantive customary international law.[41] But the Rome Statute is forcing the pace of state practice and *opinio juris* in this regard, in that national laws enacted to take advantage of the Statute's principle of complementarity[42] are consistently giving effect to the list of war crimes found in article 8(2)(*e*) as if they constituted customary international law.[43] Moreover, the case law of the ICTY, ICTR, and SCSL has repeatedly relied, sometimes dubiously, on the relevant provisions of the Rome Statute as evidence of the customary

4.18

---

[35] Ibid, para 127. [36] See ibid, paras 128–129. [37] See ibid, paras 131–136.
[38] See Rome Statute, art 8(2)(*e*)(vi). [39] See ibid, art 8(2)(*e*)(vii).
[40] Note that resolution RC/Res.5 of 10 June 2010, adopted at the first Review Conference of the Rome Statute, amends the Statute—subject to the customary international rules on the amendment of treaties—by inserting new sub-subparas (xiii), (xiv), and (xv), on the use of certain weapons in non-international armed conflict, into art 8(2)(*e*).
[41] It is worth noting for the avoidance of doubt that the Court need not have recourse to customary international law when exercising its jurisdiction *ratione materiae*. In accordance with Rome Statute, art 21(1)(*a*), it is to apply '[i]n the first place' the Statute and only '[i]n the second place, where appropriate', freestanding international law. The necessary consequence in cases where there exists no freestanding customary or applicable conventional law is that the Rome Statute in effect creates substantive crimes applicable in relation to individuals within its jurisdiction. See, in this light, *Prosecutor v Lubanga*, ICC-01/04-01/06-803-tEN, Pre-Trial Chamber, Decision on the Confirmation of Charges, 29 January 2007, paras 302–303. See also *infra* paras 14.57–14.59.
[42] See *infra* paras 14.60–14.76.
[43] See also the smaller list of serious violations of international humanitarian law drawn from the Rome Statute and included in SCSL Statute, art 4, applicable to international and non-international armed conflict alike.

position. In short, customary international law is being made in the Rome Statute's image. In this light, *Tadić* has become for war crimes in non-international armed conflict what Nuremberg was to war crimes in general, namely a law-catalysing or even lawmaking judgment.

4.19 As to the precise violations of the laws and customs of war that give rise in non-international armed conflict to individual criminal responsibility under customary international law, what has been said in relation to international armed conflict[44] is applicable *mutatis mutandis*. In the long run, it may be that article 8(2)(*e*) of the Rome Statute, as from time to time amended, is taken to represent a definitive statement of the 'serious violations of the laws and customs applicable in armed conflicts not of an international character' that constitute customary war crimes.

(ii) Violations of the Geneva Conventions as customary war crimes

(a) Grave breaches

4.20 The four 1949 Geneva Conventions contain near-identical provisions[45] for the punishment[46] of individuals who commit or order to be committed specified particularly serious violations—in the terminology of the Conventions, 'grave breaches'—of the respective Conventions. The inventory of grave breaches is supplemented by the enumeration of further such breaches, punishable via the obligations in respect of grave breaches laid down in the Conventions, in the Protocol Additional to the Geneva Conventions of 12 August 1949, and relating to the Protection of Victims of International Armed Conflicts 1977 ('Additional Protocol I').[47] The question for present purposes, however, is whether grave breaches of the 1949 Geneva Conventions and of Additional Protocol I have counterparts in customary international law.[48] In other words, the question is

---

[44] Recall *supra* para 4.15.
[45] See Convention for the Amelioration of the Condition of the Wounded and Sick in Armed Forces in the Field 1949 ('1949 Geneva Convention I'), arts 49 and 50; Convention for the Amelioration of the Condition of Wounded, Sick and Shipwrecked Members of Armed Forces at Sea 1949 ('1949 Geneva Convention II'), arts 50 and 51; Convention relative to the Treatment of Prisoners of War 1949 ('1949 Geneva Convention III'), arts 129 and 130; Convention relative to the Protection of Civilian Persons in Time of War 1949 ('1949 Geneva Convention IV'), arts 146 and 147.
[46] The relevant provisions of the 1949 Geneva Conventions oblige states parties to criminalize grave breaches of the Conventions under their municipal law, to provide for universal jurisdiction over such breaches, and to prosecute or surrender to a state party that will persons suspected of having committed such breaches. (They further oblige states parties to search for persons suspected of having committed such breaches.) The grave breaches provisions are silent, however, as to individual criminal responsibility under the respective conventions themselves. Article 85(5) of Protocol Additional to the Geneva Conventions of 12 August 1949, and relating to the Protection of Victims of International Armed Conflicts 1977 ('Additional Protocol I'), which states that, '[w]ithout prejudice to the application of the Conventions and th[e] Protocol, grave breaches of these instruments shall be regarded as war crimes', appears an attempt to clarify that such responsibility does arise. See *infra* para 7.8.
[47] See Additional Protocol I, art 85.
[48] The question is without regard to whether grave breaches give rise or not to individual criminal responsibility under treaty—that is, under the Conventions and Additional Protocol I themselves. In this regard, see *infra* para 7.8. The possible absence of individual criminal responsibility under treaty would not formally prejudice any customary development.

whether there exist as a matter of customary international law rules corresponding in content to the relevant provisions of the 1949 Geneva Conventions and Additional Protocol I and giving rise to the individual criminal responsibility of the perpetrator under customary international law in the event of their violation in a manner paralleling a grave breach.[49]

4.21 It had been acknowledged for some time that most of the rules embodied in the four 1949 Geneva Conventions, but less so those in Additional Protocol I, enjoyed a distinct, parallel existence under customary international law. Whether, however, customary international law equally provided for the individual criminal responsibility of persons who committed or ordered to be committed the sorts of violations of these rules deemed, for the purposes of the Conventions, 'grave breaches' was less clear.

4.22 In 1993, jurisdiction over grave breaches of the 1949 Geneva Conventions, although not of Additional Protocol I,[50] was vested in the ICTY via article 2 of its Statute; and in his report on the ICTY Statute to the Security Council,[51] the UN Secretary-General explained that 'the application of the principle *nullum crimen sine lege* requires that the [ICTY] should apply rules of international humanitarian law which are beyond doubt part of customary law so that the problem of adherence of some but not all States to specific conventions does not arise'.[52] As specifically regards grave breaches as war crimes under customary international law, the Secretary-General stated:

37. The Geneva Conventions [...] provide the core of the customary law applicable in international armed conflicts. [...]
38. Each Convention contains a provision listing the particularly serious violations that qualify as 'grave breaches' or war crimes. Persons committing or ordering grave breaches are subject to trial and punishment. [...]
39. The Security Council has reaffirmed on several occasions that persons who commit or order the commission of grave breaches of the 1949 Geneva Conventions in the territory of the former Yugoslavia are individually responsible for such breaches [...]

Although none of what the Secretary-General said compelled the conclusion that specified violations of the customary analogues of the provisions of the 1949 Geneva Conventions gave rise as a matter of customary international law to the individual criminal responsibility of the author of the violation, and while the

---

[49] Note that the question is not whether the obligations in respect of grave breaches undertaken by states parties to the 1949 Geneva Conventions and Additional Protocol I are similarly customary. The present inquiry is restricted to the existence under customary international law of war crimes corresponding to those designated as grave breaches of the Conventions and Protocol.

[50] Strictly speaking, those violations of Additional Protocol I giving rise to individual criminal responsibility are deemed to be grave breaches of the 1949 Geneva Conventions, with the consequence that it is through the latter that states parties to Additional Protocol I—which must, as a condition of participation in the Protocol, be parties also to the Conventions—are obliged to repress such violations. The term 'grave breaches of Additional Protocol I' is used merely by way of shorthand.

[51] See *infra* para 12.3.

[52] *Report of the Secretary-General pursuant to paragraph 2 of Security Council resolution 808 (1993)*, UN doc S/25704 (3 May 1993), para 34.

matter was not free from doubt, the assertion that what were referred to by way of shorthand as 'grave breaches of the Geneva Conventions'[53] constituted war crimes under customary international law was not objected to by any member of the Security Council, and was not considered remarkable. In the event, the ICTY has exercised its jurisdiction over grave breaches of the 1949 Geneva Conventions on the understanding that they comprise war crimes under customary international law.

4.23 Five years after the Security Council adopted the ICTY Statute, when states vested the ICC with jurisdiction over war crimes, they included among such crimes grave breaches of the 1949 Geneva Conventions.[54] Although this was not in and of itself conclusive of these states' belief in the customary status of grave breaches, given that the ICC may apply '[i]n the second place, where appropriate, applicable treaties',[55] it is widely understood that grave breaches are included in article 8(2)(*a*) of the Rome Statute first and foremost in their quality as war crimes under customary international law.

4.24 As for the various grave breaches of Additional Protocol I, modified versions of nearly all of these were included within the jurisdiction of the ICC as 'violations of the laws and customs applicable in international armed conflict'[56]—that is, avowedly as war crimes under customary international law. To an extent this may have represented progressive development, rather than codification, of customary international law.[57] But the legislative practice of many states parties to the Rome Statute is again consolidating the claims of these crimes to customary status.[58]

(b) Violations of common article 3 and of 1977 Additional Protocol II

4.25 Not every violation of the 1949 Geneva Conventions and their 1977 Additional Protocols is deemed a grave breach within the meaning of the Conventions. Most notably, violations of common article 3 of the 1949 Conventions, which sketches a small number of minimum standards applicable in non-international armed conflict, are not included within the grave breaches regime. Nor does Additional Protocol II, which 'develops and supplements Article 3',[59] contain grave breaches provisions.[60] The question, however, is whether customary international law

---

[53] These are really violations of customary international humanitarian law that correspond in substance to grave breaches of the Geneva Conventions.
[54] See Rome Statute, art 8(2)(*a*).   [55] Ibid, art 21(1)(*a*).   [56] Ibid, art 8(2)(*b*).
[57] See eg *Prosecutor v Kordić and Čerkez*, IT-95-14/2-A, Appeals Chamber, Judgment, 17 December 2004, paras 66–67.
[58] See also SCSL Statute, art 4(*a*).   [59] Additional Protocol II, art 1(1).
[60] In other words, while both common article 3 and Additional Protocol II lay down rules applicable as a matter of treaty law to the conduct of non-international armed conflict, states parties are not obliged to criminalize breaches of these rules as a matter of their municipal law, let alone provide for universal jurisdiction over such breaches or prosecute or extradite persons suspected of them. At the same time, municipal criminalization of such breaches and provision for an otherwise exorbitant jurisdiction over them are lawful means of implementing the obligation imposed on states parties to the 1949 Geneva Conventions to 'take measures necessary for the suppression of all acts contrary to the provisions of the [Conventions] other than the grave breaches'. (See 1949 Geneva Convention I, art 49; 1949 Geneva Convention II, art 50; 1949 Geneva Convention III, art 129; 1949 Geneva Convention IV, art 146.) As for individual criminal responsibility under the respective treaties themselves, the Conventions, in respect of common article 3, and Additional Protocol II are silent on the

recognizes individual criminal responsibility for violations of such customary equivalents of common article 3 and of the provisions of Additional Protocol II as may exist.

In 1986, in the *Nicaragua* case, the International Court of Justice (ICJ) held that the rules embodied in common article 3 had emerged as separate, parallel rules of customary international law,[61] a finding endorsed nine years later by the Appeals Chamber of the ICTY in its interlocutory decision in *Tadić*.[62] The Appeals Chamber further held that 'the core of Additional Protocol II'[63] could 'now be regarded as declaratory of existing rules or as having crystallized emerging rules of customary law'.[64] Moreover, and more to the point, the Appeals Chamber came to the conclusion—contrary to that expressed by the UN Secretary-General in his report to the Security Council on the ICTR Statute[65]—'that customary international law imposes criminal responsibility for serious violations of common Article 3, as supplemented by other general principles and rules on the protection of victims of internal armed conflict',[66] the latter seemingly a reference to the provisions of Additional Protocol II.[67] It defined a 'serious' violation as 'a breach of a rule protecting important values, and [which] must involve grave consequences for the victim'.[68] The ICTY's finding and its definition of a serious violation was subsequently endorsed by the ICTR,[69] which exercises jurisdiction over 'serious violations of Article 3 common to the Geneva Conventions of 12 August 1949 [...] and of Additional Protocol II thereto' pursuant to article 4 of its statute. The same was the case

4.26

---

question. None of this, however, has any formal bearing on whether customary international law recognizes individual criminal responsibility for violations of such customary equivalents of common article 3 and of the provisions of Additional Protocol II as may exist.

[61] See *Military and Paramilitary Activities in and Against Nicaragua (Nicaragua v United States of America), Merits, Judgment*, ICJ Rep 1986, 3, 114, para 218.

[62] See *Tadić*, Appeals Chamber Decision on Jurisdiction (n 32), paras 98 and 102.

[63] Ibid, para 98.

[64] Ibid, para 117. Also considered customary, ibid, para 98, was art 19 of the Convention for the Protection of Cultural Property in the Event of Armed Conflict 1954.

[65] See *Report of the Secretary-General pursuant to paragraph 5 of Security Council resolution 955 (1994)*, UN doc S/1995/134 (13 February 1995), para 12, where the Secretary-General explained after the event to the Security Council that, when adopting the ICTR Statute, it had 'elected to take a more expansive approach to the choice of the applicable law than the one underlying the statute of the Yugoslav Tribunal, and included within the subject-matter jurisdiction of the Rwanda Tribunal international instruments regardless of whether they were considered part of customary international law or whether they ha[d] customarily entailed the individual criminal responsibility of the perpetrator of the crime'. 'Article 4 of the statute', he continued, 'includes violations of Additional Protocol II, which, as a whole, has not yet been universally recognized as part of customary international law, and for the first time criminalizes common article 3 of the four Geneva Conventions'.

[66] *Tadić*, Appeals Chamber Decision on Jurisdiction (n 32), para 134.

[67] Indeed, recall *supra* para 4.20 that the Tribunal held the customary law of war crimes applicable in non-international armed conflict to go beyond the rules laid down in common article 3 and Additional Protocol II.

[68] *Tadić*, Appeals Chamber Decision on Jurisdiction (n 32), para 94.

[69] See *Prosecutor v Akayesu*, ICTR-96-4, Trial Chamber, Judgment, 2 September 1998, para 615, 'both with respect to serious violations of Common Article 3 and of Additional Protocol II'. See also ibid, para 616, endorsing the ICTY's definition of 'serious'.

for the Special Court for Sierra Leone, which exercised an identical jurisdiction *ratione materiae* in accordance with article 3 of its statute.[70]

4.27 Article 8(2)(*c*) of the Rome Statute vests the ICC with jurisdiction over 'serious violations of article 3 common to the four Geneva Conventions' as a *sui generis* species of war crime, subspecies of which are enumerated exhaustively in article 8(2)(*c*)(i) to (iv). Article 8(2)(*e*) of the Statute includes as 'violations of the laws and customs applicable in armed conflicts not of an international character' war crimes derived from Additional Protocol II. Again, this is generally recognized as representing more progressive development than codification, but again the Statute is shaping state practice and *opinio juris* in this respect.

C. Conditions of Responsibility

(i) Material elements

4.28 The existence of an armed conflict, whether international or non-international, is a legal precondition to the commission of a war crime. A useful definition of an 'armed conflict', a term not defined in the various international legal instruments in which it is found, was provided by the Appeals Chamber of the ICTY in its 1995 interlocutory decision in *Tadić*, where the Chamber declared that 'an armed conflict exists whenever there is a resort to armed force between States or protracted armed violence between governmental authorities and organized armed groups or between such groups within a State'.[71] Of note in this regard is that the requisite threshold of violence varies as between resort to armed force between states, known as 'international armed conflict', and armed violence within a state between governmental authorities and organized armed groups or among such groups, known as 'non-international armed conflict' or 'armed conflict not of an international character'. Any resort to armed force between states constitutes an international armed conflict. In contrast, as indicated in the Appeals Chamber's statement and as subsequently affirmed in article 8(2)(*f*) of the Rome Statute, armed violence within a state between governmental authorities and organized armed groups or among such groups must be 'protracted' before it can be considered an armed conflict.[72] In the words of article 8(2)(*d*) and (*f*) of the Rome Statute, the customary law of war crimes applicable to non-international armed conflict 'does not

---

[70] In *Norman* et al, Appeals Chamber Decision on Lack of Jurisdiction Ratione Materiae (n 29), para 24, the SCSL Appeals Chamber held there to be 'no doubt that the norms embodied in Article 3 of the Statute form part of customary international law'.

[71] See *Tadić*, Appeals Chamber Decision on Jurisdiction (n 32), para 70. This was endorsed in *Prosecutor v Bemba*, ICC-01/05-01/08-424, Pre-Trial Chamber, Decision pursuant to Article 61(7)(*a*) and (*b*) of the Rome Statute on the Charges of the Prosecutor against Jean-Pierre Bemba Gombo, 15 June 2009, para 229; *Prosecutor v Lubanga*, ICC-01/04-01/06-2842, Trial Chamber, Judgment pursuant to Article 74 of the Statute, 14 March 2012, para 535.

[72] Rome Statute, art 8(2)(*f*), second sentence, actually says that art 8(2)(*e*) 'applies to armed conflicts that take place in the territory of a State when there is protracted armed conflict between governmental authorities and organized armed groups or between such groups'. The reference to 'protracted armed conflict' must be to 'protracted armed violence' if the sentence is to avoid circularity.

apply to situations of internal disturbances and tensions, such as riots, isolated or sporadic acts of violence or other acts of a similar nature'. Discerning the dividing line in any instance can be a difficult task of factual appreciation.

4.29 The legal characterization of certain complex armed conflicts as either international or non-international is a live, hotly contested, and complicated issue[73] which it is not proposed to deal with here. The following discussion proceeds on the premise that the appropriate legal characterization has been undertaken and that the armed conflict—or, depending on the approach adopted, perhaps the theatre or incident of the armed conflict in which the impugned conduct occurs—is either international or non-international.

4.30 While the existence of an armed conflict is a necessary legal criterion for the commission of a war crime, it is not a sufficient one. In order for conduct to qualify as a war crime, there must exist some 'nexus' between the conduct and the conflict, in the terminology of the ICTY and ICTR.[74] That is, the impugned conduct must be 'closely related' to the armed conflict,[75] meaning that the existence of the armed conflict must, at a minimum, play 'a substantial part in the perpetrator's ability to commit [the crime], his decision to commit it, the manner in which it was committed or the purpose for which it was committed'.[76] In the same vein, the Elements of Crimes requires with respect to each species of war crime found in article 8 of the Rome Statute not only that the impugned conduct take place 'in the context of' an armed conflict but that it be 'associated with' that conflict[77]—a requirement referred to by various Pre-Trial Chambers, borrowing from the ICTY and ICTR, as the 'nexus' requirement.[78] Such a nexus or association will be self-evident in most cases, but a few may turn on the issue.

---

[73] See eg E Wilmshurst (ed), *International Law and the Classification of Conflicts* (Oxford: Oxford University Press, 2012).

[74] See *Prosecutor v Akayesu*, ICTR-96-4, Appeals Chamber, Judgment, 1 June 2001, para 444; *Prosecutor v Rutaganda*, ICTR-96-3-A, Appeals Chamber, Judgment, 26 May 2003, paras 569–570; *Stakić*, Appeals Chamber Judgment (n 19), para 342; *Prosecutor v Setako*, ICTR-04-81-A, Appeals Chamber, Judgment, 28 September 2011, para 246. See also, not dissimilarly, *Prosecutor v Fofana*, SCSL-2004-14-AR72(E), Appeals Chamber, Decision on Preliminary Motion on Lack of Jurisdiction Materiae [sic]: Nature of the Armed Conflict, 25 May 2004, para 25 ('related to the armed conflict').

[75] *Tadić*, Appeals Chamber Decision on Jurisdiction (n 32), para 70; *Prosecutor v Kunarac* et al, IT-96-23 and IT-96-23/1-A, Appeals Chamber, Judgment, 12 June 2002, para 55; *Rutaganda*, Appeals Chamber Judgment (n 74), paras 569–570; *Stakić*, Appeals Chamber Judgment (n 19), para 342; *Setako*, Appeals Chamber Judgment (n 74), para 249.

[76] *Kunarac* et al, Appeals Chamber Judgment (n 75), para 58. See also *Rutaganda*, Appeals Chamber Judgment (n 74), paras 569–570; *Stakić*, Appeals Chamber Judgment (n 19), para 343; *Setako*, Appeals Chamber Judgment (n 74), para 249; *Prosecutor v Taylor*, SCSL-03-01-T, Trial Chamber, Judgment, 18 May 2012, paras 563 and 566. Various ICC Pre-Trial Chambers have adopted this formulation. See eg *Prosecutor v Katanga and Ngudjolo*, ICC-01/04-01/07-717, Pre-Trial Chamber, Decision on the Confirmation of Charges, 30 September 2008, para 380 (PTC I); *Situation in the Republic of Côte d'Ivoire*, ICC-02/11-14, Pre-Trial Chamber, Decision Pursuant to Article 15 of the Rome Statute on the Authorisation of an Investigation into the Situation in the Republic of Côte d'Ivoire, 3 October 2011, para 150 (PTC III).

[77] See Elements of Crimes, art 8(2), generally.

[78] See eg *Katanga and Ngudjolo*, Pre-Trial Chamber Decision on Confirmation of Charges (n 76), section III(C), heading (PTC I); *Situation in the Republic of Côte d'Ivoire*, Pre-Trial Chamber Decision on Authorisation of Investigation (n 76), section V(B)(2)(c), heading (PTC III).

134   *Crimes under Customary International Law*

4.31   War crimes under customary international law were originally conceived of in the context of hostilities between the regular armed forces of states. But customary war crimes can now equally arise in the context of international armed conflict between the regular armed forces of a state and certain irregular armed forces in another state[79] or between the regular armed forces of a state and the armed forces of a national liberation movement,[80] as well as in the context of non-international armed conflicts between the regular armed forces of a state and the armed forces of an insurgent group or between or among non-state groups.[81] As such, membership of the regular armed forces of a state is clearly no prerequisite for responsibility for a war crime under customary international law. It suffices that the accused belong to the armed forces, regular or irregular, of one of the belligerent parties.[82]

4.32   Civilians too can be held responsible today[83] for war crimes under customary international law.[84] In order for this to happen, they need not be linked, formally or informally, to the military forces of a state or of a non-state armed group, let alone 'mandated and expected, as public officials or agents or persons otherwise holding public authority or *de facto* representing the [g]overnment, to support or fulfil the war efforts'.[85] Cases from the ICTR, as well as from the various national military tribunals established after the Second World War[86] and from other national courts,[87] indicate that, given the right facts, any civilian can be held responsible

---

[79] See eg 1949 Geneva Convention III, art 4.
[80] See Additional Protocol I, art 1(4), deeming such armed conflicts to be international.
[81] See Rome Statute, art 8(2)(*f*).
[82] See *Akayesu*, Trial Chamber Judgment (n 69), para 631.
[83] Although the concept of a war crime and, indeed, of the international laws of war was originally premised on the want of a common sovereign inherent in the mutual opposition of two or more sovereigns' armed forces, such abstract formalist considerations have long been supplemented, if not supplanted, by pragmatic humanitarian ones.
[84] See the cases cited *infra*. To the same effect, the Elements of Crimes for article 8(2) of the Rome Statute mention no requirement that the perpetrator of a war crime be a member of any regular or irregular armed forces or have some *de jure* or *de facto* mandate in respect of such forces.
[85] *Akayesu*, Appeals Chamber Judgment (n 74), para 443, referring to violations of common article 3 of the Geneva Conventions as customary war crimes, although the Appeals Chamber's conclusion was not, in the final analysis, based on reasoning limited to common article 3. The quotation comes from *Akayesu*, Trial Chamber Judgment (n 69), para 631, whose statement of the law in this regard the Appeals Chamber overturned, thereby also rejecting the circumscribed view of the customary position taken in *Prosecutor v Kayishema and Ruzindana*, ICTR-95-1-T, Trial Chamber, Judgment and Sentence, 21 May 1999, paras 175–176 (stating, para 175, that '[i]f individuals do not belong to the armed forces, they could bear...criminal responsibility only when there is a link between them and the armed forces') and *Prosecutor v Musema*, ICTR-96-13, Trial Chamber, Judgment, 27 January 2000, paras 265–275.
[86] See eg *Heyer and Six Others (The Essen Lynching Case)*, 1 LRTWC 88 (British Military Court, Essen 1945); *Klein and Six Others (The Hadamar Trial)*, 1 LRTWC 46 (US Military Commission, Wiesbaden 1945); *Tesch and Two Others (The Zyklon B Case)*, 1 LRTWC 93 (British Military Court, Hamburg 1946).
[87] See eg the cases of Consolata (Sister Gertrude) Mukangango and Julienne (Sister Maria Kisito) Mukabutera, convicted of serious violations of Additional Protocol II by the Brussels *Cour d'assises* on 8 June 2001 for their role in the massacre of more than 7,600 persons at the Sovu convent in Butare, Rwanda in 1994; and the cases of Alphonse Higaniro, managing director of a matchstick factory, and Vincent Ntezimana, President of the Association of Academic Personnel at the University of Butare, convicted in the same proceedings on analogous counts but in relation to different events in 1994. See also *Van Anraat*, Hague Court of Appeal, 9 May 2009, ILDC 753 (NL 2009), in which a Dutch

for participation in a customary war crime, including for its actual commission.[88] The determinative question as regards 'ordinary' civilian perpetrators is not their status as civilians but whether the impugned conduct bears the requisite nexus to the armed conflict.[89]

4.33 Its commission 'as part of a plan or policy or as part of a large-scale commission of such crimes', as mentioned in article 8(1) of the Rome Statute, is not a definitional requirement of a customary war crime. These words are purely for the purposes of the Statute and, motivated by a pragmatic concern for the Court's caseload, serve merely as guidance to the Prosecutor to pursue only the more serious instances of those war crimes within the Court's jurisdiction.[90]

4.34 It ought to go without saying but may nonetheless pay to underline that, in order to constitute a violation of the laws and customs of war punishable as a war crime, the conduct must first violate a rule of the laws and customs of war, a body of customary international law taken to apply to states and individuals alike.[91] This is indicated in article 8(2) of the Rome Statute, subparagraph (*b*) of which vests the Court with jurisdiction *ratione materiae* over serious violations of the laws and customs applicable in international armed conflict 'within the established framework of international law' and subparagraph (*e*) of which does the same in relation to non-international armed conflicts 'within the established framework of international law'.

4.35 Similarly, to be punishable under customary international law as a grave or other breach of the 1949 Geneva Conventions, the conduct must, in the words of article 8(2)(*a*) of the Rome Statute, be against 'persons or property protected under the provisions of the relevant Geneva Convention'[92] or must, in the words of article 8(2)(*c*), constitute a 'serious violation[ ] of article 3 common to the four Geneva Conventions'. To be more precise, the conduct must have

---

businessman was convicted of complicity in violations of the laws and customs of war for supplying chemicals used in chemical weapons to the regime of Saddam Hussein in Iraq.

[88] Nor is there any 'public official' requirement in relation specifically to torture as a customary war crime, whether as a grave breach of the Geneva Conventions or a serious violation of common article 3. No such requirement is stipulated in the Element of Crimes to art 8(2)(*a*)(ii) or 8(2)(*c*)(i) of the Rome Statute. Moreover, in *Kunarac* et al, Appeals Chamber Judgment (n 75), para 148, the ICTY Appeals Chamber took the view that 'the public official requirement is not a requirement under customary international law in relation to the criminal responsibility of an individual for torture outside of the framework of the Torture Convention'. See also *Kvočka* et al, Appeals Chamber Judgment (n 19), para 284; *Prosecutor v Semanza*, ICTR-97-20-A, Appeals Chamber, Judgment, 20 May 2005, paras 248 and 286. For the 'public official' requirement under the Convention against Torture and Other Cruel, Inhuman or Degrading Treatment or Punishment 1984 ('Torture Convention'), see *infra* paras 7.118 and 7.120.

[89] See, in this context, *Kononov v Latvia* [GC] (Merits and Just Satisfaction), no 36376/04, ECHR 2010, para 210, citation omitted: 'While in 1944 a nexus with an international armed conflict was required to prosecute acts as war crimes, that did not mean that only armed forces personnel or nationals of a belligerent State could be so accused. The relevant nexus was a direct connection between the alleged crime and the international armed conflict so that the alleged crime had to be an act in furtherance of war objectives.'

[90] No such requirement appears in the Elements of Crimes to art 8.

[91] But recall from *supra* paras 4.13, 4.15, and 4.19 that not every violation of the laws and customs of war is a war crime.

[92] See also Elements of Crimes, art 8(2)(*a*), generally.

been against persons or property protected under the customary versions of the provisions of the relevant Geneva Convention or must constitute a serious violation of the customary equivalent of common article 3. The distinction is more than formal, since, at least as developed by the ICTY and ICTR, the scope of application *ratione materiae* of the customary analogues of the provisions of the Geneva Conventions is not necessarily the same as that of their treaty-based counterparts.[93]

(ii) Mental elements

4.36   To be responsible for a war crime, the accused must intend to perform the act or acts specified as material elements and must do so with the relevant knowledge,[94] the latter in most cases meaning the 'awareness that a circumstance exists'.[95]

4.37   When it comes to the circumstance or material element *sine qua non* of war crimes, namely the existence of an armed conflict,[96] the accompanying mental element required is that the accused 'was aware of factual circumstances that established the existence of an armed conflict'.[97] In other words, '[t]here is no requirement for a legal evaluation by the perpetrator as to the existence of an armed conflict'.[98] As to the distinction between international and non-international armed conflicts, the Elements of Crimes for the war crimes enumerated in article 8 of the Rome Statute does not require an 'awareness by the perpetrator of the facts that established the character of the conflict as international or non-international'[99] or, *a fortiori*, of any legal evaluation as to the 'character as international or non-international' of the armed conflict established by factual circumstances of which the accused was aware.[100] All that is required is the awareness on the part of the accused of the factual circumstances that established the existence of an armed conflict.[101] The ICTY, in contrast, demands the awareness by the perpetrator of the factual circumstances establishing the character of the conflict as international or non-international.[102]

---

[93] See *Tadić*, Appeals Chamber Judgment (n 13), paras 164–169, as endorsed in *Prosecutor v Aleksovski*, IT-95-14/1, Appeals Chamber, Judgment, 24 March 2000, paras 151–152 and *Prosecutor v Delalić* et al ('*Čelebići*'), IT-96-21, Appeals Chamber, Judgment, 20 February 2001, paras 73 and 81–84. (Note that '*Delalić* et al' became '*Mucić* et al' on the acquittal of the accused Delalić.) See also *Tadić*, Appeals Chamber Decision on Jurisdiction (n 32), para 102 and *Čelebići*, Appeals Chamber Judgment (*supra*), paras 135, 147, and 150.
[94] Recall *supra* para 4.8.   [95] Rome Statute, art 30(3).   [96] Recall *supra* para 4.28.
[97] Elements of Crimes, art 8(2), generally. See also *Prosecutor v Naletilić and Martinović*, IT-98-34-A, Appeals Chamber, Judgment, 3 May 2006, para 119. See too *Lubanga*, Trial Chamber Judgment (n 71), paras 1016 and 1018, stating that the accused must be aware of the link between these factual circumstances and his or her conduct.
[98] Elements of Crimes, art 8, introduction. See also *Naletilić and Martinović*, Appeals Chamber Judgment (n 97), para 119. Putting it another way, there is no need to prove that the accused knew that there was an armed conflict, as made clear in *Lubanga*, Trial Chamber Judgment (n 71), para 1016.
[99] Elements of Crimes, art 8, introduction.   [100] Ibid.   [101] Ibid.
[102] See *Kordić and Čerkez*, Appeals Chamber Judgment (n 57), para 311; *Naletilić and Martinović*, Appeals Chamber Judgment (n 97), paras 113–121.

As regards grave breaches of the Geneva Conventions as customary war crimes, 4.38
the requisite mental element attaching to the material requirement that the person
or property against which the conduct was directed be protected by a customary
analogue to the relevant Geneva Convention is that '[t]he perpetrator was aware of
the factual circumstances that established that protected status'.[103]

IV. Crimes Against Humanity

A. Evolution

(i) First World War

The atrocities committed by Turkey against its own subjects, chiefly Armenians, 4.39
during the First World War shocked the conscience of the Allied and Associated
Powers to the extent that they resolved to punish those responsible. But these
outrages were committed by aliens against aliens on alien territory, without threatening in any tangible sense the essential national interests of any of the victorious
Powers, and so fell beyond the prescriptive criminal jurisdiction of their respective bodies of ordinary municipal law. Nor did any rule of international law, as
it then stood, forbid a state from wantonly killing its own nationals. As a result,
it was considered expedient by some representatives of the victorious Allied and
Associated Powers to recognize a new species of international crime to be prosecuted before an international 'high tribunal'.

In response, Sub-Commission III, on the Responsibility for the Violation of the 4.40
Laws and Customs of War, of the Commission on the Authors of the War and on
Enforcement of Penalties of the Preliminary Peace Conference in Paris proposed
in 1919 a category of offences against international law applicable to conduct on a
state's own territory against its own nationals. It referred to this category as 'crimes
against the laws of humanity', the reference to 'the laws of humanity' being drawn
from the 'Martens clause' in the preamble (ninth recital) to Convention concerning the Laws and Customs of War on Land 1899 ('1899 Hague Convention II')
and in the preamble (eighth recital) to 1907 Hague Convention IV,[104] where the
word 'humanity' is used in the sense of 'humaneness'—that is, humane conduct or

---

[103] Elements of Crimes, art 8(2)(*a*), generally. When it comes to the serious violations of common article 3 punishable under Rome Statute, art 8(2)(*c*), the requisite material element is not framed in the Elements of Crimes by reference to common article 3 itself; rather, what is said to be required is that the person or persons against whom the act was perpetrated 'were either *hors de combat*, or were civilians, medical personnel or religious personnel taking no active part in the hostilities'. See Elements of Crimes, art 8(2)(*c*), generally. This being the case, the corresponding mental element is said, ibid, to be that the accused 'was aware of the factual circumstances that established this status'.

[104] In the latter version, the Martens clause reads: 'Until a more complete code of the laws of war has been issued, the High Contracting Parties deem it expedient to declare that, in cases not included in the Regulations adopted by them, the inhabitants and the belligerents remain under the protection and the rule of the principles of the law of nations, as they result from the usages established among civilized peoples, from the laws of humanity, and the dictates of the public conscience.'

behaviour worthy of human beings—rather than in the sense of 'humankind'.[105] But the Sub-Commission's proposal was criticized by the US delegation on the ground of the novelty of this species of offence and the uncertainty and fluidity of the standards of humanity,[106] and the Sub-Commission's recommendations were not put into effect.[107]

(ii) Second World War

4.41 The atrocities committed by Turkey during the First World War were soon eclipsed by those committed by Nazi Germany against civilians in the Reich, both before and during the War, as well as against civilians in the various occupied territories, in both cases primarily against Jews and Roma. In response, article 6(c) of the Charter of the International Military Tribunal at Nuremberg embodied a category of crimes, distinct from war crimes, applicable to condemnable acts perpetrated against civilians and labelled 'crimes against humanity',

> namely, murder, extermination, enslavement, deportation, and other inhumane acts committed against any civilian population, before or during the war, or persecution on political, racial or religious grounds in execution of or in connection with any crime within the jurisdiction of the Tribunal, whether or not in violation of the domestic law of the country where perpetrated.[108]

Such crimes could in principle be committed in peacetime as well as in war. In the event, the IMT found most of the Nuremberg defendants guilty of crimes against humanity.

4.42 Concerns were expressed during the drafting of the Nuremberg Charter that crimes against humanity were a novelty under international law and, as such, violated the principle *nullum crimen sine lege*. By way of response, article 6(c) of the Charter required those crimes against humanity within the Tribunal's jurisdiction, whether committed before or during the War, to have been committed 'in execution of or in connection with any crime within the jurisdiction of the Tribunal'.[109] In short, no defendant was to be convicted solely for crimes against humanity.

4.43 In the event, as regards the persecution, repression, and murder of Jews and other civilians in the Reich prior to the outbreak of the War, the IMT ruled that,

---

[105] Even before Sub-Commission III's report, a statement of 28 May 1915 by the governments of France, UK, and Russia had condemned Turkish massacres of Armenians as 'crimes against humanity and civilisation'. See United Nations War Crimes Commission (n 29), 35.

[106] See ibid, 36–7.

[107] This went equally for the Sub-Commission's recommendations in relation to war crimes.

[108] In the original text of art 6(c) of the Charter, a semi-colon, rather than a comma, separated 'during the war' and 'or persecution'. But the text was amended by way of special protocol later in 1945. See International Military Tribunal, *Nazi Conspiracy and Aggression* (Washington, DC: US Government Printing Office, 1946), vol 1, 11–12.

[109] For the applicability of the rider to both limbs of art 6(c), see Judgment of the International Military Tribunal for the Trial of German Major War Criminals, Nuremberg, 30 September and 1 October 1946, Misc No 12 (1946), Cmd 6964, reproduced (1947) 41 *AJIL* 172 ('Nuremberg judgment'), 249.

'revolting and horrible as many of these crimes were, it ha[d] not been satisfactorily proved that they were done in execution of, or in connection with, any [crime within the jurisdiction of the Tribunal]'.[110] As such, they were not crimes against humanity within the meaning of the Charter. In contrast, 'from the beginning of the war in 1939 War Crimes were committed on a vast scale, which were also Crimes against Humanity; and insofar as the inhumane acts charged in the Indictment, and committed after the beginning of the war, did not constitute War Crimes, they were all committed in execution of, or in connection with, the aggressive war, and therefore constituted Crimes against Humanity'.[111]

4.44 Insofar as the crimes against humanity for which the defendants were convicted also constituted war crimes, article 6(c) of the Charter did not result in a substantive denial of justice. But it is a different story when it comes to those crimes against humanity committed solely in execution of, or in connection with, the aggressive war, given the similarly questionable relationship between crimes against peace and the principle *nullum crimen sine lege*.

4.45 By way of contrast with their US counterparts, the military tribunals established in the British zone of occupied Germany pursuant to the Royal Warrant of 1945[112] did not prosecute persons for crimes against humanity. It is also well accepted that paragraph 2 of article 7 of the European Convention on Human Rights (ECHR), concluded in 1950, was included in response to concerns that paragraph 1—which stipulates that '[n]o one shall be held guilty of any criminal offence on account of any act or omission which did not constitute a criminal offence under national or international law at the time when it was committed'—might have resulted in the setting free of those persons spared execution on conviction in the wake of the War of crimes against humanity and might have stymied further trials for such crimes. Article 7(2) of the ECHR provides that the guarantee in article 7(1) 'shall not prejudice the trial and punishment of any person for any act or omission which, at the time when it was committed, was criminal according to the general principles of law recognised by civilised nations'.

4.46 Despite lingering doubts, the concept and content of crimes against humanity was implicitly endorsed by the new UN General Assembly in its resolution 95 (I) of 11 December 1946, entitled 'Affirmation of the Principles of International Law recognized by the Charter of the Nürnberg Tribunal', and was explicitly endorsed in 1950 in the ILC's Principles of International Law Recognized in the Charter of the Nürnberg Tribunal and in the Judgment of the Tribunal ('Nürnberg Principles').[113]

(iii) Subsequent developments

4.47 The customary international law of crimes against humanity has developed further since the ILC's Nürnberg Principles. In article I(I) of the International Convention

---

[110] Ibid. [111] Ibid.
[112] Recall *supra* para 3.30 and see *infra* para 9.43 n 85.   [113] *Supra* n 5.

on the Suppression and Punishment of the Crime of Apartheid ('Apartheid Convention'), adopted in contentious circumstances by the UN General Assembly in resolution 3068 (XVIII) of 30 November 1973,[114] the states parties 'declare that apartheid is a crime against humanity'. For what it is worth, a list of crimes against humanity, deemed 'crimes against the peace and security of mankind', was included in 1996 in the ILC's Draft Code of Crimes against the Peace and Security of Mankind.[115] More significantly, crimes against humanity were included within the respective jurisdictions *ratione materiae*, albeit with variations here and there in their chapeau elements and enumerated species, of the ICTY (article 5), ICTR (article 3), SCSL (article 2), and ICC (article 7).

4.48 In a progressive development rapidly accepted as customary, rape—when committed as part of a widespread or systematic attack on a civilian population—is included as a crime against humanity in the statutes of the various international criminal courts.[116] Article 7(1)(g) of the Rome Statute goes further to include as crimes against humanity 'sexual slavery, enforced prostitution, forced pregnancy, enforced sterilization, or any other form of sexual violence of comparable gravity', the term 'forced pregnancy' being defined in article 7(2)(f). For its part, the Appeals Chamber of the SCSL held that forced marriage is not subsumed within the crime of sexual slavery and indeed is not predominantly a sexual crime;[117] rather, the Chamber consider forced marriage to constitute an 'other inhumane act' within the meaning of article 2(i) of the SCSL Statute.[118]

4.49 Article 7(1)(i) and (j) of the Rome Statute embody as crimes against humanity enforced disappearance of persons and the crime of apartheid respectively, as respectively defined in article 7(2)(i) and (h). The customary status of these offences as crimes against humanity is unclear. It is not insignificant, however, that, in addition to the statement relating to apartheid in article I(1) of the Apartheid Convention, article 5 of the International Convention for the Protection of Persons against Enforced Disappearance ('Enforced Disappearance Convention'), adopted without a vote by way of General Assembly resolution 61/177 of 20 December 2006,[119] declares—in what reflects a misunderstanding of the general material elements of crimes against humanity—that the 'widespread or systematic practice of enforced disappearance constitutes a crime against humanity as defined in applicable international law'.[120]

---

[114] See *infra* paras 7.11 and 7.111–7.116.   [115] *Supra* n 5.
[116] See ICTY Statute, art 5(g); ICTR Statute, art 3(g); SCSL Statute, art 2(g); Rome Statute, art 7(1)(g). See also ILC Draft Code of Crimes, art 18(j), encompassing 'enforced prostitution and other forms of sexual abuse'. But cf, as regards customary international law during the period 1975–79, Case File/Dossier No 001/18-07-2007-ECCC/SC ('*Duch*'), Supreme Court Chamber, Appeal Judgment, 3 February 2012, paras 179–180 and 213.
[117] *Brima* et al, Appeals Chamber Judgment (n 31), para 195.
[118] Ibid, para 202. The equivalent provision of the Rome Statute is art 7(1)(k).
[119] See *infra* para 7.124.
[120] A correct statement of the law would be that enforced disappearance, when 'committed as part of a widespread or systematic attack' on a civilian population, constitutes a crime against humanity. The act of enforced disappearance need not itself be widespread or systematic. See *infra* paras 7.14 and 7.124–7.127 for more. See also, this time not incorrectly, International Convention for the Protection

Article 5(*i*) of the ICTY Statute, article 3(*i*) of the ICTR Statute, article 2(*i*) of 4.50
the SCSL Statute, and article 7(1)(*k*) of the Rome Statute, following the Nuremberg
and Tokyo Charters,[121] all vest the relevant court with jurisdiction over a residual
category of 'other inhumane acts'—the inhumanity of a crime against humanity
being of its essence—or, as specified in article 7(1)(*k*) of the Rome Statute, '[o]ther
inhumane acts of a similar character [to the preceding acts listed in article 7(1)]
intentionally causing great suffering, or serious injury to body or to mental or
physical health'. The ICTY Appeals Chamber was of the view in *Stakić* that the
category of 'other inhumane acts' was 'part of customary international law',[122]
although this says nothing as to precisely what acts fall, as a matter of customary
international law, within this category.

B. Conditions of Responsibility

(i) Material elements

The first defining characteristic of a crime against humanity is that it is commit- 4.51
ted as part of an attack against a civilian population. An 'attack' in this context is
not limited to the use of armed force but encompasses, in the words of the ICTY
Appeals Chamber, 'any mistreatment of the civilian population' or, more specifically, 'a course of conduct involving the commission of acts of violence'.[123] This
formulation is substantially in line with article 7(2)(*a*) of the Rome Statute, which
defines 'attack' as found in the chapeau to article 7(1) to mean 'a course of conduct
involving the multiple commission of acts referred to in paragraph 1', *viz* murder,
extermination, enslavement, etc,[124] and with paragraph 3 of the introduction to
the Elements of Crimes for article 7, which provides that '[t]he acts need not
constitute a military attack'. The civilian population against which the attack is
directed need not be in the territory of a foreign state, let alone in occupied territory, as indicated by the reference to 'any' civilian population in the statutes of
the various past and present international criminal courts.[125] When it comes to

---

of Persons against Enforced Disappearance 2006 ('Enforced Disappearance Convention'), preamble
(fifth recital), stating that enforced disappearance constitutes a crime against humanity 'in certain
circumstances defined in international law'.

[121] See Nuremberg Charter, art 6(*c*); Tokyo Charter, art 5(*c*). See also Control Council Law No 10,
art II(1)(*c*); ILC Draft Code of Crimes, art 18(*k*) ('other inhumane acts which severely damage physical or mental integrity, health or human dignity, such as mutilation and severe bodily harm').

[122] *Stakić*, Appeals Chamber Judgment (n 19), para 315.

[123] *Kunarac* et al, Appeals Chamber Judgment (n 75), paras 86 and 89 respectively. See also *Kordić
and Čerkez*, Appeals Chamber Judgment (n 57), para 666; *Prosecutor v Nahimana* et al, ICTR-99-
52-A, Appeals Chamber, Judgment, 28 November 2007, paras 916 and 918.

[124] To the extent that art 7(1) of the Rome Statute, as elaborated on by art 7(2)(*a*), provides that
the acts of violence or mistreatment as part of which a crime against humanity takes place must themselves correspond to one or more of the species of crime against humanity enumerated in art 7(1),
a requirement reiterated *mutatis mutandis* in the context of the ICTR Statute in *Nahimana* et al,
Appeals Chamber Judgment (n 123), para 918, the distinction is probably one without a difference,
especially given the residual species of 'other inhumane acts' found in art 7(1)(*k*).

[125] See Nuremberg Charter, art 6(*c*); ICTY Statute, art 5; ICTR Statute, art 3; SCSL Statute, art
2; Rome Statute, art 7(1).

the 'civilian' aspect of a civilian population, the ICTY Appeals Chamber has held that the meaning to be accorded to 'civilian' for the purposes of crimes against humanity is the same as that accorded by the customary international law of armed conflict, as reflected in article 50 of Additional Protocol I, with the result that those endowed with combatant status—*viz* members of the armed forces (including members of militias and volunteer corps forming part of such forces) and of certain organized resistance groups—cannot be considered civilians, even when *hors de combat*.[126] As for the notion of a 'population', the ICTY Appeals Chamber has explained that 'the use of the word "population" does not mean that the entire population of the geographical entity in which the attack is taking place must have been subjected to that attack'; rather, '[i]t is sufficient to show that enough individuals were targeted in the course of the attack, or that they were targeted in such a way... that the attack was in fact directed against a civilian "population", rather than against a limited and randomly selected number of individuals'.[127] Nor is it necessary that every member of the population attacked be a civilian; instead, it is possible for a population as a whole to be considered civilian even if individuals in its midst are combatants, whether or not they are *hors de combat*, although the relative proportions will be determinative.[128]

4.52   While, in order to qualify as a crime against humanity, the specific act impugned must be committed as part of an attack against a civilian population, the impugned act itself need not be against a civilian, but can, for example, be against a combatant *hors de combat*.[129]

4.53   The ICTR Statute is alone to date among the constituent instruments of international criminal courts[130] in stipulating, in article 3, that the attack on the civilian population be 'on national, political, ethnic, racial or religious grounds'. The ICTR Appeals Chamber has emphasized,[131] endorsing the view of the ICTY Appeals Chamber,[132] that—with the exception of the specific crime against humanity of persecution[133]—discrimination is not a requirement of a customary crime against humanity.

---

[126] *Blaškić*, Appeals Chamber Judgment (n 13), paras 110–116. See also *Prosecutor v Martić*, IT-95-11-A, Appeals Chamber Judgment, 8 October 2008, paras 291–302; *Prosecutor v Brima* et al, SCSL-2004-16-T, Trial Chamber, Judgment, 20 June 2007, para 219.

[127] *Kunarac* et al, Appeals Chamber Judgment (n 75), para 90.

[128] See *Blaškić*, Appeals Chamber Judgment (n 13), paras 113 and 115 (although note that whether the soldiers are on leave is in fact immaterial); *Kordić and Čerkez*, Appeals Chamber Judgment (n 57), para 97 cross-referenced with para 50; *Prosecutor v Galić*, IT-98-29-A, Appeals Chamber, Judgment, 30 November 2006, para 144; *Prosecutor v Mrkšić and Šljivančanin*, IT-95-13/1-A, Appeals Chamber, Judgment, 5 May 2009, paras 31 and 32.

[129] *Martić*, Appeals Chamber Judgment (n 126), paras 306–314. See also *Mrkšić and Šljivančanin*, Appeals Chamber Judgment (n 128), paras 29 and 32.

[130] But see also, at the national level, Law on the Establishment of Extraordinary Chambers in the Courts of Cambodia for the Prosecution of Crimes Committed during the Period of Democratic Kampuchea (as amended), art 5. See *infra* para 9.64.

[131] *Akayesu*, Appeals Chamber Judgment (n 74), paras 464 and 466.

[132] *Tadić*, Appeals Chamber Judgment (n 13), para 305.

[133] For persecution on the foregoing or similar grounds as a species of crime against humanity, see Nuremberg Charter, art 6(c); Tokyo Charter, art 5(c); ICTY Statute, art 5(h); SCSL Statute, art 2(h); Rome Statute, art 7(1)(h); ILC Draft Code of Crimes, art 18(e).

The Crimes 143

4.54 A second general definitional requirement of a crime against humanity[134] is that the attack against a civilian population, as part of which the crime is committed, must be 'widespread or systematic'.[135] The two criteria are in the alternative, as is obvious from the disjunctive 'or' between them.[136] As for what these terms mean, the ICTY Appeals Chamber has explained, unnecessarily and not altogether helpfully, that 'widespread' imports 'the large-scale nature of the attack and the number of victims', while 'systematic' refers to 'the organised nature of the acts of violence and the improbability of their random occurrence'.[137] It is not self-evident what the Appeals Chamber intends by the phrase 'large-scale nature', at least as used in apparent contradistinction to 'the number of victims', although the connotation would appear to be geographical.

4.55 Only the attack of which the accused's conduct forms part, and not the accused's conduct itself, need be widespread or systematic. In other words, 'all other conditions being met, a single or relatively limited number of acts on [the accused's] part would qualify as a crime against humanity, unless those acts may be said to be isolated or random'.[138] In the same vein, provided that it forms part of a widespread or systematic attack, and leaving aside the specific crime against humanity of extermination, the accused's conduct need not have more than a single victim.[139]

4.56 A state of armed conflict is not a legal precondition to the commission of a crime against humanity.[140] That is, a crime against humanity can be committed in time of peace. *A fortiori*, if a crime against humanity is indeed committed in the context of armed conflict, it is immaterial whether the conflict is international or non-international and whether the crime against humanity has a nexus to it.

4.57 To be responsible for a crime against humanity, an individual need not be a government official or agent,[141] and even less a member of the armed forces of one of the belligerents.

---

[134] This second requirement is intended, but fails, to mark a point of difference between crimes against humanity and serious municipal crimes.
[135] ICTR Statute, art 3; SCSL Statute, art 2; Rome Statute, art 7(1); ILC Draft Code of Crimes, art 18 ('committed in a systematic manner or on a large scale'). The requirement is not found in Nuremberg Charter, art 6(*c*), Tokyo Charter, art 5(*c*), or ICTY Statute, art 5.
[136] See *Kunarac* et al, Appeals Chamber Judgment (n 75), paras 93 and 97; *Prosecutor v Ntakirutimana*, ICTR-96-10-A and ICTR-96-17-A, Appeals Chamber, 13 December 2004, para 516 note 883, the latter holding that the use of the word '*et*' ('and') in the French text of the ICTR Statute is a translation error.
[137] *Kunarac* et al, Appeals Chamber Judgment (n 75), para 94.   [138] Ibid, para 96.
[139] See eg *Nahimana* et al, Appeals Chamber Judgment (n 123), para 924.
[140] See Nuremberg Charter, art 6(*c*); Tokyo Charter, art 5(*c*); ICTR Statute, art 3; SCSL Statute, art 2; Rome Statute, art 7(1); ILC Draft Code of Crimes, art 18 and especially para 6 of commentary thereto. While art 5 of the ICTY Statute makes the existence of an armed conflict, whether international or non-international, a condition of a crime against humanity for the purposes of the Tribunal's jurisdiction, it was recognized in *Report of the Secretary-General pursuant to paragraph 2 of Security Council resolution 808 (1993)* (n 52), para 47, that customary international law was not so restrictive. Neither the Apartheid Convention nor the Enforced Disappearance Convention requires that the crime defined therein, declared in the text to be a crime against humanity (in the latter case, at least in certain circumstances), be committed in armed conflict.
[141] This goes equally for the specific crime against humanity of torture. See eg Rome Statute, art 7(2)(*e*), defining 'torture' for the purposes of the crime against humanity of torture embodied in article 7(1)(*f*) to mean simply 'the intentional infliction of severe pain or suffering, whether physical or

4.58   There is debate as to whether customary international law requires that crimes against humanity be committed in pursuance of some sort of policy. The earlier jurisprudence of the trial chambers of the ICTY and ICTR suggested that this was the case, but the ICTY Appeals Chamber later rejected this, holding that 'the existence of a policy or plan may be evidentially relevant, but it is not a legal element of the crime'.[142] In contrast, article 7(2)(*a*) of the Rome Statute defines the phrase 'attack directed against any civilian population' to refer to a course of conduct 'pursuant to or in furtherance of a State or organizational policy to commit such attack'.

4.59   As to what is meant in article 7(2)(*a*) of the Rome Statute by an 'organizational policy', an ICC Pre-Trial Chamber has held—and, from the point of view of a straightforward application of the customary rules of treaty interpretation, rightly—that the term 'organizational' is not limited to organizations linked to a state but extends to non-state actors[143] and is not limited to 'state-like' organizations.[144] A policy pursued by a private criminal organization, for example, could fall within article 7(2)(*a*).[145]

(ii) Mental elements

4.60   The *mens rea* required for a crime against humanity is the intent to commit the specific act—be it murder, extermination, enslavement, etc[146]—accompanied by knowledge of the attack on the civilian population and knowledge that the act comprises part of that attack.[147] In this regard, while the chapeau to article 7(1) of the Rome Statute requires simply 'knowledge of the attack', by which is meant the 'widespread or systematic attack directed against any civilian population', the Elements of Crimes for article 7 of the Statute explains

---

mental, upon a person in the custody or under the control of the accused' (with an exception being for pain or suffering 'arising only from, inherent in or incidental to, lawful sanctions'). Nor do the Elements of Crimes for art 7(1)(*f*) contain any 'public official' requirement. See also *Kunarac* et al, Appeals Chamber Judgment (n 75), para 148; *Semanza*, Appeals Chamber Judgment (n 88), para 248 and 286. For the 'public official' requirement under the Torture Convention, see *infra* paras 7.118 and 7.120. In this light, recall *supra* para 4.32 n 88.

[142] *Kunarac* et al, Appeals Chamber Judgment (n 75), para 98, citation omitted. The Appeals Chamber pointed in a footnote to a considerable body of jurisprudence to this effect. See also, among numerous others, *Semanza*, Appeals Chamber Judgment (n 88), para 274.

[143] *Situation in the Republic of Kenya*, ICC-01/09-19-Corr, Pre-Trial Chamber, Decision Pursuant to Article 15 of the Rome Statute on the Authorization of an Investigation into the Situation in the Republic of Kenya, 31 March 2010, para 92.

[144] Ibid, para 90.   [145] Ibid. But cf, *contra* and unconvincingly, ibid, diss op Kaul.

[146] See eg the express reference to the intent to commit the underlying act in Rome Statute, art 7(2)(*b*), (*e*), and (*g*). Some specific crimes against humanity have additional requirements as to *mens rea*. The crimes against humanity found in art 7(1)(*b*), (*f*), and (*i*) of the Rome Statute, as defined in art 7(2)(*b*), (*f*), and (*i*) respectively, are crimes of specific intent (*dolus specialis*), as is art 7(1)(*k*)'s residual category of '[o]ther inhumane acts of a similar character intentionally causing great suffering or serious injury to body or to mental or physical health'.

[147] See *Blaškić*, Appeals Chamber Judgment (n 13), paras 124 and 126; *Tadić*, Appeals Chamber Judgment (n 13), para 248; *Kunarac* et al, Appeals Chamber Judgment (n 75), paras 99 and 102–103; *Kordić and Čerkez*, Appeals Chamber Judgment (n 57), paras 99–100.

that this means that the perpetrator 'knew that the conduct was part of or intended the conduct to be part of a widespread or systematic attack against a civilian population'.[148] The Elements states that this 'should not be interpreted as requiring proof that the perpetrator had knowledge of all the characteristics of the attack or the precise details of the plan or policy of the State or organization'; rather, it continues, '[i]n the case of an emerging widespread or systematic attack against a civilian population', the mental element for crimes against humanity 'is satisfied if the perpetrator intended to further such an attack'.[149]

4.61 The accused need not share the purpose or goal behind the attack.[150] Indeed, the motives of the accused for taking part in the attack are irrelevant. A crime against humanity may be committed for purely personal reasons.[151] All that counts in terms of *mens rea* is that the accused intended to commit the impugned act and knew that it formed or intended that it form part of a widespread or systematic attack against a civilian population. That said, the fact that the accused committed the impugned act for motives purely personal may indicate a lack of awareness that the act formed part of such an attack.[152]

4.62 It is similarly irrelevant whether the accused intends to direct the impugned act solely against its victim or victims, rather than against the civilian population against which the attack is directed. 'It is the attack, not the acts of the accused, which must be directed against the target population and the accused need only know that his acts are part thereof.'[153]

4.63 In general, crimes against humanity do not require a discriminatory intent.[154]

V. The Crime of Genocide

A. Evolution

4.64 The customary international crime of genocide, a term coined in 1944 by the Polish lawyer and academic Raphael Lemkin,[155] was prosecuted before the

---

[148] Elements of Crimes, art 7, generally.
[149] Ibid, art 7, introduction. See, similarly, *Kunarac* et al, Appeals Chamber Judgment (n 75), para 102.
[150] *Kunarac* et al, Appeals Chamber Judgment (n 75), para 103; *Blaškić*, Appeals Chamber Judgment (n 13), para 124.
[151] *Tadić*, Appeals Chamber Judgment (n 13), paras 248 and 252; *Kunarac* et al, Appeals Chamber Judgment (n 75), para 103; *Blaškić*, Appeals Chamber Judgment (n 13), para 124.
[152] *Kunarac* et al, Appeals Chamber Judgment (n 75), para 103; *Blaškić*, Appeals Chamber Judgment (n 13), para 124; *Kordić and Čerkez*, Appeals Chamber Judgment (n 57), para 99.
[153] *Kunarac* et al, Appeals Chamber Judgment (n 75), para 103. See also *Blaškić*, Appeals Chamber Judgment (n 13), para 124.
[154] See eg *Tadić*, Appeals Chamber Judgment (n 13), paras 273–305. But a discriminatory intent is required for the specific crime against humanity of persecution.
[155] See R Lemkin, *Axis Rule in Occupied Europe* (Washington, DC: Carnegie Endowment for International Peace, 1944), chapter IX ('Genocide').

Nuremberg IMT not as a crime by that name but as a species of crime against humanity, *viz* extermination of a civilian population, within the meaning of article 6(*c*) of the Nuremberg Charter.

4.65 In resolution 96 (I) of 11 December 1946, entitled 'The crime of genocide', the UN General Assembly 'affirm[ed]' that genocide was a crime—and implicitly a crime in its own right, since the label 'crime against humanity' was not used—under customary international law. In turn, the contracting parties to the Convention on the Prevention and Punishment of the Crime of Genocide 1948 ('Genocide Convention'), approved by the General Assembly on 9 December 1948,[156] 'confirm[ed]' in article I that genocide was a crime under international law. Article I, allied to the preamble's reference to General Assembly resolution 96 (I), amounted to further recognition by states that genocide was a crime in its own right under customary international law.

4.66 Article II of the Genocide Convention defines genocide to mean

> any of the following acts committed with intent to destroy, in whole or in part, a national, ethnical [*sic*], racial or religious group, as such:
> (*a*) Killing members of the group;
> (*b*) Causing serious bodily or mental harm to members of the group;
> (*c*) Deliberately inflicting on the group conditions of life calculated to bring about its physical destruction in whole or in part;
> (*d*) Imposing measures intended to prevent births within the group;
> (*e*) Forcibly transferring children of the group to another group.

It is the group dimension of its *mens rea*—the 'intent to destroy, in whole or in part, a national, ethnical [*sic*], racial or religious group, as such'—that it is the essence of the crime of genocide.

4.67 It is the customary international crime of genocide as defined in article II of the Genocide Convention over which all the relevant modern international criminal courts have been vested with jurisdiction *ratione materiae*,[157] and no formal attempt has ever been made at the international level to use a different definition of the crime. In short, the customary definition of the crime of genocide corresponds precisely to the definition contained in article II of the Genocide Convention, and this definition is set in metaphorical stone.

B. Conditions of Responsibility

(i) Material elements

4.68 What is required by customary and conventional international law to ground criminal responsibility for genocide is the intent to destroy, in whole or in part, one of the specified groups as such, not the group's actual destruction, total or

---

[156] GA res 260 A (III), 9 December 1948.
[157] See ICTY Statute, art 4(2); ICTR Statute, art 2(2); Rome Statute, art 6. See also ILC Draft Code of Crimes, art 17.

partial. In other words, provided that the accused commits one of acts enumerated in article II(*a*) to (*e*) of the Genocide Convention with the requisite *mens rea*, a single victim will suffice for conviction of the crime of genocide.¹⁵⁸

To ground criminal responsibility for the crime of genocide, the victim or victims of the impugned act must belong to one of the groups specified in the chapeau to article II of the Genocide Convention¹⁵⁹ or the accused must believe that they do.¹⁶⁰ 4.69

Article I of the Genocide Convention specifies that genocide is a crime under international law 'whether committed in time of peace or in time of war'. The existence of an armed conflict is not a material condition of the crime of genocide. 4.70

There is no requirement that the perpetrator of the crime of genocide be a state official or agent, and even less a member of the armed forces of a belligerent party. 4.71

The existence of some sort of agreement, plan, or policy is not an essential element of the crime of genocide,¹⁶¹ although it may be evidentially useful in helping to establish the requisite intent to destroy the relevant group in whole or in part.¹⁶² 4.72

The acts specified in article II(*a*) to (*e*) of the Genocide Convention which, if committed with the requisite intent, ground responsibility for the crime of genocide are exhaustive. That is, even if committed with genocidal intent, no acts other than those enumerated in article II(*a*) to (*e*) can give rise to responsibility under international law for the crime of genocide. 4.73

The acts enumerated in article II(*a*) to (*e*) of the Genocide Convention encompass only those aimed at the physical or biological destruction of the group in question. What has been referred to loosely as 'cultural genocide' does not fall within the ambit of the crime of genocide as embodied in customary and conventional international law.¹⁶³ At the same time, '[t]he destruction of culture may 4.74

---

¹⁵⁸ See also N Robinson, *The Genocide Convention* (New York: Institute of Jewish Affairs, 1960), 58; Y Dinstein, 'International Criminal Law' (1985) 20 *Israel LR* 206, 212.

¹⁵⁹ *Nahimana* et al, Appeals Chamber Judgment (n 123), para 496. See also Elements of Crimes, art 6(*a*) to (*e*), element 2, as applied in *Prosecutor v Al Bashir*, ICC-02/05-01/09-3, Pre-Trial Chamber, Decision on the Prosecution's Application for a Warrant of Arrest against Omar Hassan Ahmad Al Bashir, 4 March 2009, para 134 and *Prosecutor v Al Bashir*, ICC-02/05-01/09-94, Pre-Trial Chamber, Second Decision on the Prosecution's Application for a Warrant of Arrest against Omar Hassan Ahmad Al Bashir, 12 July 2010, paras 10–12.

¹⁶⁰ *Nahimana* et al Appeals Chamber Judgment (n 123), para 496; *Stakić*, Appeals Chamber Judgment (n 19), para 25.

¹⁶¹ *Jelisić*, Appeals Chamber Judgment (n 19), para 48; *Prosecutor v Simba*, ICTR-01-76-A, Appeals Chamber, Judgment, 27 November 2007, para 260; *Semanza*, Appeals Chamber Judgment (n 88), para 260; *Prosecutor v Nchamihigo*, ICTR-2001-63-A, Appeals Chamber, Judgment, 18 March 2010, para 363.

¹⁶² *Jelisić*, Appeals Chamber Judgment (n 19), para 48.

¹⁶³ *Prosecutor v Krstić*, IT-98-33-A, Appeals Chamber, Judgment, 19 April 2004, para 25, going on to affirm, para 26, as having 'correctly identified the governing legal principle', *Prosecutor v Krstić*, IT-98-33-T, Trial Chamber, Judgment, 2 August 2001, para 580; *Application of the Convention on the Prevention and Punishment of the Crime of Genocide (Bosnia and Herzegovina v Serbia and Montenegro), Merits, Judgment*, ICJ Rep 2007, 43, 185–6, para 344. Although forms of cultural genocide had featured in drafts of the Genocide Convention, the concept was rejected by the Sixth Committee of the General Assembly, which prepared the final text of the Convention as adopted by the Assembly in plenary. See also para 12 of the commentary to art 17 of the ILC Draft Code of Crimes.

serve evidentially to confirm an intent, to be gathered from other circumstances, to destroy the group as such'.[164] Not dissimilarly, forcible transfer, displacement, or deportation of persons, including the practice of 'ethnic cleansing', 'does not constitute in and of itself a genocidal act'.[165] In other words, 'displacement is not equivalent to destruction'.[166] Again, however, forcible transfer and the like may provide evidence of genocidal intent.[167] Moreover, there is no reason why certain instances of the forcible transfer of a group, such as a forced death-march, undertaken with a view to the destruction of all or some of the group, rather than its mere displacement, could not be characterized under article II(*c*) of the Genocide Convention as '[d]eliberately inflicting on the group conditions of life calculated to bring about its physical destruction in whole or in part'.[168] Indeed, a footnote to the Elements of Crimes for article 6(*c*) of the Rome Statute, corresponding to article II(*c*) of the Genocide Convention, states that '[t]he term "conditions of life" may include, but is not necessarily restricted to, deliberate deprivation of resources indispensable for survival, such as food or medical services, or systematic expulsion from homes'.[169]

4.75   Torture and 'non-fatal physical violence that causes disfigurement or serious injury to the external or internal organs',[170] along with rape,[171] have been called 'quintessential examples' of 'serious bodily...harm' within the meaning of article II(*b*) of the Genocide Convention. As for 'serious...mental harm', the phrase has been taken to mean 'more than minor or temporary impairment of mental faculties such as the infliction of strong fear or terror, intimidation or threat'.[172] Many of the sorts of acts that one might expect to be prosecuted under the rubric of genocide will qualify as both serious bodily harm and serious mental harm. For its part, a footnote to the relevant element of the Elements of Crimes to article 6(*b*) of the Rome Statute, which grants the ICC jurisdiction *ratione materiae* over the genocidal acts referred to in article II(*b*) of the Genocide Convention, explains that

---

[164] *Krstić*, Appeals Chamber Judgment (n 163), partial diss op Shahabuddeen, para 53, endorsing *Krstić*, Trial Chamber Judgment (n 163), para 580; *Application of the Genocide Convention* (n 163), 186, para 344.

[165] *Krstić*, Appeals Chamber Judgment (n 163), para 33; *Prosecutor v Blagojević and Jokić*, IT-02-60-A, Appeals Chamber, Judgment, 9 May 2007, para 123. See also *Application of the Genocide Convention* (n 163), 122–3, para 190; *Al Bashir*, Pre-Trial Chamber Decision on Arrest Warrant (n 159), para 144. Again, a proposal to include measures of this sort within the definition of genocide was rejected by the drafters of the Genocide Convention.

[166] *Blagojević and Jokić*, Appeals Chamber Judgment (n 165), para 123 note 337.

[167] *Krstić*, Appeals Chamber Judgment (n 163), para 33; *Blagojević and Jokić*, Appeals Chamber Judgment (n 165), para 123; *Application of the Genocide Convention* (n 163), 123, para 190.

[168] *Application of the Genocide Convention* (n 163), 123, para 190. See also, similarly, *Al Bashir*, Pre-Trial Chamber Decision on Arrest Warrant (n 159), para 145.

[169] Elements of Crimes, art 6(*c*), element 1 note 4.

[170] *Prosecutor v Seromba*, ICTR-2001-66-A, Appeals Chamber, Judgment, 12 March 2008, paras 46 and 48; *Prosecutor v Karadžić*, IT-95-5/18-AR98bis.1, Appeals Chamber, Rule 98*bis* Judgment, 11 July 2013, para 33.

[171] *Seromba*, Appeals Chamber Judgment (n 170), para 46; *Karadžić*, Appeals Chamber Rule 98*bis* Judgment (n 170), para 33. See also *Seromba*, Appeals Chamber Judgment (n 170), para 48, citing rape as an example of 'the heinous crimes that obviously constitute serious bodily or mental harm'.

[172] *Seromba*, Appeals Chamber Judgment (n 170), para 46.

conduct falling within the provision 'may include, but is not necessarily restricted to, acts of torture, rape, sexual violence or inhuman or degrading treatment'.[173] It has been said that, to support a conviction for genocide, the bodily or mental harm inflicted on members of a group must be of such a serious nature as to threaten the group's destruction in whole or in part.[174] Whether the last statement accords with customary international law is open to question, although it may find some purchase before the ICC, given the 'contextual element' specified in the Elements of Crimes on genocide.[175]

4.76 It was held by an ICTR Trial Chamber in *Akayesu*, in a ruling not challenged on appeal, that in certain cases the organized practice of rape can further qualify as a measure intended to prevent births within the group within the meaning of article II(*d*) of the Genocide Convention.[176]

4.77 The Elements of Crimes add a further material condition to the exercise by the ICC of the jurisdiction over the crime of genocide granted it by articles 5(*a*) and 6(*a*) to (*e*) of the Rome Statute, the latter reproducing verbatim, *mutatis mutandis*,[177] article II(*a*) to (*e*) of the Genocide Convention. The final element for each of article 6(*a*) to (*e*) requires that the conduct 'took place in the context of a manifest pattern of similar conduct directed against [the relevant] group or was conduct that could itself effect such destruction'. The introduction to the section of the Elements dealing with genocide elaborates on the condition, explaining that '[t]he term "in the context of" would include the initial acts in an emerging pattern' and that '[t]he term "manifest" is an objective qualification'.[178] This further material element of the crime of genocide does not reflect customary international law, a point emphasized by the ICTY Appeals Chamber in *Krstić*.[179] It is said to have been inserted into the Elements to circumvent the theoretical possibility that 'isolated hate crimes' might fall within the ICC's jurisdiction *ratione materiae* over the crime of genocide, debasing the latter's normative currency[180]—an ill-considered

---

[173] Elements of Crimes, art 6(*b*), element 1 note 3.
[174] *Seromba*, Appeals Chamber Judgment (n 170), para 46.
[175] See *infra* para 4.77. In this regard, see *Al Bashir*, Pre-Trial Chamber Decision on Arrest Warrant (n 159), para 124: 'In the view of the Majority, according to this contextual element, the crime of genocide is only completed when the relevant conduct presents a concrete threat to the existence of the targeted group, or a part thereof. In other words, the protection offered by the penal norm defining the crime of genocide...is only triggered when the threat against the existence of the targeted group, or part thereof, becomes concrete and real, as opposed to just being latent or hypothetical.'
[176] *Akayesu*, Trial Chamber Judgment (n 69), paras 507–508.
[177] The chapeau's words 'In the present Convention, genocide means...' become 'For the purpose of this Statute, "genocide" means...'.
[178] Elements of crimes, art 8, introduction, paras 1 and 2 respectively. For the elaboration, ibid, para 3, of the requisite mental element attaching to this material condition, see *infra* para 4.86.
[179] See *Krstić*, Appeals Chamber Judgment (n 163), para 224. Nor, for that matter, does the requirement reflect the Rome Statute, although a majority of the Pre-Trial Chamber in *Al Bashir* twice accepted the more limited proposition—in principle deeply dubious, even if in practice not necessarily so—that there was no 'irreconcilable contradiction', meaning that the additional, contextual element was 'not per se contrary to article 6 of the Statute'. See *Al Bashir*, Pre-Trial Chamber Decision on Arrest Warrant (n 159), paras 132 and 133 respectively, as affirmed in *Al Bashir*, Pre-Trial Chamber Second Decision on Arrest Warrant (n 159), para 13.
[180] Cryer *et al* (n 4), 218.

rationale, given that such crimes would still likely fail the 'gravity' criterion of admissibility in article 17(1)(*d*) of the Rome Statute, making their investigation and prosecution by the Prosecutor,[181] let alone their entertainment by a Chamber, improbable in the extreme. In practice, this additional element is unlikely to make much of a difference, if any. But from the point of view of legal principle it is utterly misguided.

(ii) Mental elements

4.78   Genocide is a crime of 'specific intent' or '*dolus specialis*'. In other words, it requires that the accused have the intention, at point of commission[182] of the relevant act, to achieve a given result, rather than—or, more accurately, in addition to—the intention merely to commit the act. This requisite specific intent is formulated in the chapeau to article II of the Genocide Convention as the 'intent to destroy, in whole or in part, a national, ethnical [*sic*], racial or religious group, as such'.

4.79   The specific groups referred to in the chapeau to article II of the Genocide Convention—*viz* 'national, ethnical [*sic*], racial or religious' groups—are exhaustive.[183] The inclusion of further categories, especially political groups, was rejected by states when drafting the Genocide Convention and has been rejected time and again since, including during the drafting of the Rome Statute.[184] Furthermore, the group in question must be defined positively, by reference to a common identity of a national, ethnic, racial or religious character, not negatively, by reference to the lack of a particular national, etc identity.[185] In *Stakić*, for example, the ICTY Appeals Chamber held that, for the purposes of the crime of genocide, the accused's killing of Bosnian Muslims had to be considered separately from their killing of Bosnian Croats. The two could not be lumped together to comprise the putative genocide of 'non-Serbs'.[186]

4.80   It scarcely needs saying that the qualification 'as such' connotes that the accused's intent must be to destroy the national, ethnic, racial or religious group in its quality as that national, ethnic, racial or religious group. It is not enough to intend to destroy members of the group only in their capacity as specific or random individuals. In the words of the ICTR Appeals Chamber, '[t]he term "as such" has the *effet utile* of drawing a clear distinction between mass murder and crimes in which the perpetrator targets a specific group because of its nationality, race, ethnicity or

---

[181] See, in this regard, Rome Statute, art 53(1)(*b*) and (2)(*b*). See also ibid, art 53(2)(*c*). See too *infra* paras 14.21–14.22.

[182] It is not necessary that the accused form the specific intent prior to embarking on the commission of the act. It suffices that he or she has the requisite intent at point of commission. See *Simba*, Appeals Chamber Judgment (n 161), para 266.

[183] See eg *Al Bashir*, Pre-Trial Chamber Decision on Arrest Warrant (n 159), paras 134–137.

[184] See, similarly, *Nahimana* et al, Appeals Chamber Judgment (n 123), para 496.

[185] *Stakić*, Appeals Chamber Judgment (n 19), paras 20–28; *Application of the Genocide Convention* (n 163), 124–6, paras 193–196, referring, para 193, to the words 'as such' in support of the conclusion that the relevant group must be defined positively; *Al Bashir*, Pre-Trial Chamber Decision on Arrest Warrant (n 159), para 135.

[186] See *Stakić*, Appeals Chamber Judgment (n 19), paras 20–28.

religion'.¹⁸⁷ But the destruction of the group in its quality as that group need not be the perpetrator's sole intention.¹⁸⁸

The reference to the intent to destroy a group 'in part' is to at least a substantial part of that group, significant enough for its destruction to have an impact on the group as a whole.¹⁸⁹ This requirement of 'substantiality', described as an 'essential starting point' in ascertaining an intent to destroy a group in part, is 'critical' and to be given priority.¹⁹⁰ At the same time, the intent may be to destroy the group only within a geographically-limited area,¹⁹¹ since the opportunity available to the perpetrator is a significant consideration.¹⁹² But this criterion of 'opportunity' must be weighed against 'the first and essential factor of substantiality', so that '[i]t may be that the opportunity available to the alleged perpetrator is so limited that the substantiality criterion is not met'.¹⁹³ Numbers alone, however, are 'not in all cases the ending point of the inquiry' into the existence of the requisite intent.¹⁹⁴ Qualitative factors may be taken into account. In *Krstić*, the ICTY Appeals Chamber, in a statement later endorsed by the ICJ in *Application of the Convention on the Prevention and Punishment of the Crime of Genocide*,¹⁹⁵ explained that the 'prominence within the group' of the part targeted 'can be a useful consideration', so that, '[i]f a specific part of the group is emblematic of the overall group, or is essential to its survival, that may support a finding that the part qualifies as substantial'.¹⁹⁶ In the foregoing light, the ICJ summed up the criteria for an intention to destroy a group 'in part' as 'substantiality (the primary requirement), relevant geographic factors and the associated opportunity available to the perpetrators, and emblematic or qualitative factors',¹⁹⁷ although the Court stressed that these criteria are not exhaustive.¹⁹⁸

4.81

---

¹⁸⁷ *Prosecutor v Niyitegeka*, ICTR-96-14-A, Appeals Chamber, Judgment, 9 July 2004, para 53.
¹⁸⁸ Ibid; *Ntakirutimana*, Appeals Chamber Judgment (n 136), paras 304 and 363. Moreover, in accordance with the distinction, *supra* para 4.9, between intent and motive, the accused's motives—that is, why he or she intends to destroy the group in whole or in part—are irrelevant. See *Jelisić*, Appeals Chamber Judgment (n 19), para 49; *Kayishema and Ruzindana*, Appeals Chamber Judgment (n 13), para 161; *Stakić*, Appeals Chamber Judgment (n 19), para 45.
¹⁸⁹ *Krstić*, Appeals Chamber Judgment (n 163), paras 8 and 12; *Application of the Genocide Convention* (n 163), para 198; *Karadžić*, Appeals Chamber Rule 98*bis* Judgment (n 170), para 66; *Al Bashir*, Pre-Trial Chamber Decision on Arrest Warrant (n 159), para 146.
¹⁹⁰ *Application of the Genocide Convention* (n 163), 127, paras 200 and 201.
¹⁹¹ Ibid, 126, para 199; *Al Bashir*, Pre-Trial Chamber Decision on Arrest Warrant (n 159), para 146.
¹⁹² *Krstić*, Appeals Chamber Judgment (n 163), para 13; *Application of the Genocide Convention* (n 163), 126–7, para 199; *Al Bashir*, Pre-Trial Chamber Decision on Arrest Warrant (n 159), para 146.
¹⁹³ *Application of the Genocide Convention* (n 163), 127, para 199; *Al Bashir*, Pre-Trial Chamber Decision on Arrest Warrant (n 163), para 146.
¹⁹⁴ *Krstić*, Appeals Chamber Judgment (n 163), para 12; *Karadžić*, Appeals Chamber Rule 98*bis* Judgment (n 170), para 66.
¹⁹⁵ *Application of the Genocide Convention* (n 163), 127, para 200. See also *Al Bashir*, Pre-Trial Chamber Decision on Arrest Warrant (n 159), para 146.
¹⁹⁶ *Krstić*, Appeals Chamber Judgment (n 163), para 12; *Karadžić*, Appeals Chamber Rule 98*bis* Judgment (n 170), para 66; *Al Bashir*, Pre-Trial Chamber Decision on Arrest Warrant (n 159), para 146.
¹⁹⁷ *Application of the Genocide Convention* (n 163), 166, para 296.
¹⁹⁸ *Krstić*, Appeals Chamber Judgment (n 163), para 14; *Application of the Genocide Convention* (n 163), 127, para 201.

4.82   In *Jelisić*, a Trial Chamber of the ICTY rejected the prosecution's submission 'that an accused need not *seek* the destruction in whole or in part of a group' but rather 'that it suffices that he *knows* that his acts will inevitably, or even only probably, result in the destruction of the group in question'.[199] The Trial Chamber recalled[200] the conclusion of the Trial Chamber of the ICTR in *Akayesu* that 'an accused could not be found guilty of genocide if he himself did not share the goal of destroying in part or in whole a group even if he knew that he was contributing to or through his acts might be contributing to the partial or total destruction of a group'.[201] The Appeals Chamber in *Jelisić* affirmed that the specific intent needed for genocide 'requires that the perpetrator...seeks to achieve the destruction, in whole or in part, of a national, ethnical, racial or religious group, as such'.[202] But this view as to the precise content of the specific intent required for genocide, insofar as it excludes the accused's knowledge that the acts will inevitably result in the destruction of the relevant group, sits uneasily alongside article 30(2)(*b*) of the Rome Statute, which states that a person has the necessary intent within the meaning of the Statute where, in relation to a consequence, that person means to cause that consequence 'or is aware that it will occur in the ordinary course of events'. At the same time, the test of the latter manifestation of *mens rea*—which is known as 'oblique intention' or '*dolus directus* in the second degree'—is seemingly a strict one. A Pre-Trial Chamber of the ICC, as endorsed by a Trial Chamber, has held the latter to require that the accused 'was at least aware that, in the ordinary course of events, the occurrence...was a virtually certain consequence'.[203] In other words, so-called '*dolus eventualis*' or 'advertent recklessness' as to a mere likelihood, let alone a mere possibility, is insufficient.

4.83   Reflecting the general principle laid down in the general introduction to the ICC's Elements of Crimes,[204] the ICTY Appeals Chamber in *Jelisić* observed that proof of specific intent in the context of genocide 'may, in the absence of direct explicit evidence, be inferred from a number of facts and circumstances, such as the general context, the perpetration of other culpable acts systematically directed against the same group, the scale of atrocities committed, the systematic targeting

---

[199] *Prosecutor v Jelisić*, IT-95-10-T, Trial Chamber, Judgment, 14 December 1999, para 85, original emphasis.
[200] Ibid, para 86.
[201] *Akayesu*, Trial Chamber Judgment (n 69), para 485. See also ibid, paras 544–547.
[202] *Jelisić*, Appeals Chamber Judgment (n 19), para 46. Prior to the Appeals Chamber's judgment in *Jelisić*, the Prosecutor in *Krstić*, Trial Chamber Judgment (n 163), para 569, had rerun the argument rejected by the Trial Chamber in *Jelisić*, alleging that the requirement of genocidal intent was satisfied if 'the accused consciously desired his acts to result in the destruction, in whole or in part, of the group, as such; or he knew his acts were destroying, in whole or in part, the group, as such; or he knew that the likely consequence of his acts would be to destroy, in whole or in part, the group, as such'. The Trial Chamber in *Krstić*, in a judgment delivered a month after the Appeals Chamber's judgment in *Jelisić* but which seems not to take the latter into account, left the question open as a matter of law, but, para 571, original emphasis, 'adhere[d] to the characterisation of genocide which encompasses only acts committed with the *goal* of destroying all or part of a group'.
[203] *Bemba*, Pre-Trial Chamber Decision Pursuant to Article 61(7)(*a*) and (*b*) (n 71), para 369, endorsed in *Lubanga*, Trial Chamber Judgment (n 71), para 1011.
[204] Elements of Crimes, general introduction, para 3.

of victims on account of their membership of a particular group, or the repetition of destructive and discriminatory acts'.[205] At the same time, in *Application of the Convention on the Prevention and Punishment of the Crime of Genocide*, the ICJ cautioned that '[g]reat care must be taken in finding in the facts a sufficiently clear manifestation of [the requisite specific] intent'.[206] The Court did not agree with the contention 'that the very pattern of the atrocities committed over many communities, over a lengthy period, focused on Bosnian Muslims and also Croats, demonstrate[d] the necessary intent'.[207] It explained that '[t]he *dolus specialis*, the specific intent to destroy the group in whole or in part, has to be convincingly shown by reference to particular circumstances, unless a general plan to that end can be convincingly demonstrated to exist'; and, the Court continued, 'for a pattern of conduct to be accepted as evidence of its existence, it would have to be such that it could only point to the existence of such intent'.[208] In the language of the ICTY and ICTR Appeals Chambers, the existence of the requisite specific intent would have to be 'the only reasonable inference'[209] or, synonymously, 'the only reasonable conclusion', since if another conclusion could reasonably be reached on the evidence guilt beyond reasonable doubt has not been established.[210]

The ICTY Appeals Chamber has stressed that, when assessing evidence of genocidal intent, a 'compartmentalised mode of analysis' is to be avoided.[211] That is, '[r]ather than considering separately whether an accused intended to destroy a protected group through each of the relevant genocidal acts' of which he or she is accused, the court 'should consider whether all of the evidence, taken together, demonstrates a genocidal mental state'.[212]

4.84

---

[205] *Jelisić*, Appeals Chamber Judgment (n 19), para 47. See also *Krstić*, Appeals Chamber Judgment (n 163), para 34; *Stakić*, Appeals Chamber Judgment (n 19), para 219; *Karadžić*, Appeals Chamber Rule 98*bis* Judgment (n 170), paras 80, 83, 95, and 99; *Rutaganda*, Appeals Chamber Judgment (n 74), paras 525 and 528; *Prosecutor v Gacumbitsi*, ICTR-2001-64-A, Appeals Chamber, Judgment, 7 July 2006, paras 40–41; *Semanza*, Appeals Chamber Judgment (n 88), para 262; *Seromba*, Appeals Chamber Judgment (n 170), para 176; *Nahimana* et al, Appeals Chamber Judgment (n 123), para 524; *Kayishema and Ruzindana*, Appeals Chamber Judgment (n 13), para 159; *Simba*, Appeals Chamber Judgment (n 161), para 264; *Prosecutor v Hategekimana*, ICTR-0-55B-A, Appeals Chamber, Judgment, 8 May 2012, para 133; *Prosecutor v Mugenzi and Mugiraneza*, ICTR-99-50-A, Appeals Chamber, Judgment, 4 February 2013, para 88.
[206] *Application of the Genocide Convention* (n 163), 122, para 189.
[207] Ibid, 196–7, para 373. [208] Ibid, 197, para 373.
[209] *Krstić*, Appeals Chamber Judgment (n 163), para 41; *Prosecutor v Vasiljević*, IT-98-32-A, Appeals Chamber, Judgment, 25 February 2004, para 120; *Nahimana* et al, Appeals Chamber Judgment (n 123), para 896; *Mugenzi and Mugiraneza*, Appeals Chamber Judgment (n 205), para 88.
[210] *Čelebići*, Appeals Chamber Judgment (n 93), para 458; *Prosecutor v Ntagerura* et al, ICTR-99-46-A, Appeals Chamber, Judgment, 7 July 2006, para 306; *Prosecutor v Bagosora and Nsengiyumva*, ICTR-98-41-A, Appeals Chamber, Judgment, 14 December 2011, para 515; *Mugenzi and Mugiraneza*, Appeals Chamber Judgment (n 205), para 136.
[211] *Stakić*, Appeals Chamber Judgment (n 19), para 55; *Karadžić*, Appeals Chamber Rule 98*bis* Judgment (n 170), para 56.
[212] *Karadžić*, Appeals Chamber Rule 98*bis* Judgment (n 170), para 56, paraphrasing *Stakić*, Appeals Chamber Judgment (n 19), para 55. This does not take away from the need to assess whether the accused had the requisite specific intent at the point of commission of each discrete genocidal act. Rather, it suggests the evidentiary approach by which the court is to ascertain whether at the point of commission of each act the accused had the requisite intent.

4.85 In addition to the specific intent required of every manifestation of the crime of genocide, each of the specific acts capable of grounding criminal responsibility for genocide must be committed with intent and knowledge. Two of these acts, namely deliberately inflicting on the group conditions of life calculated to bring about its physical destruction in whole or in part, as per article II (*c*) of the Genocide Convention, and imposing measures intended to prevent births within the group, as per article II (*d*), impose an additional, particular requirement of specific intent.

4.86 The mental element that the Elements of Crimes requires to accompany its idiosyncratic 'contextual' material element is an open question. The Elements state:

> Notwithstanding the normal requirement for a mental element provided for in article 30 [of the Rome Statute], and recognizing that knowledge of the circumstances will usually be addressed in proving genocidal intent, the appropriate requirement, if any, for a mental element regarding this circumstance will need to be decided by the Court on a case-by-case basis.[213]

It remains to be seen what is made of this.

VI. The Crime of Aggression

A. Evolution

4.87 Of all the crimes under customary international law, the crime of aggression has proved the most controversial and difficult, at least since the advent of the UN Charter. There is widespread acceptance that such an international crime is recognized as a customary matter. The real question is its definition. A definition of the crime of aggression has now been agreed for the purposes of the crime's potential prosecution before the ICC.[214] But there is little cause to suggest that this definition currently enjoys the status of *lex lata*.

4.88 Article 6(*a*) of the Nuremberg Charter granted the Nuremberg Tribunal jurisdiction *ratione materiae* over 'crimes against peace', defined as the 'planning, preparation, initiation or waging of a war of aggression, or a war in violation of international treaties, agreements or assurances, or participation in a common plan or conspiracy for the accomplishment of any of the foregoing'. A near-verbatim[215] version of the same crime fell within the jurisdiction *ratione materiae* of the Tokyo Tribunal by virtue of article 5(*a*) of its Charter. Although the offence was controversial, both in its ascription to individuals of criminal responsibility under international law for acts of state and in its novelty, the Nuremberg IMT convicted several of the major German war criminals for what the Tribunal called 'the supreme international crime';[216] and while crimes against peace were even more

---

[213] Elements of Crimes, art 6, introduction, subpara (*c*).
[214] For the conditions precedent to the Court's eventual exercise of jurisdiction over the offence, see *infra* para 14.30.
[215] Tokyo Charter, art 5(*a*) speaks of 'a declared or undeclared war of aggression'.
[216] Nuremberg judgment (n 109), 186.

controversial at Tokyo, the Tribunal similarly entered convictions for them. The UN General Assembly affirmed the principles of international law recognized in the Nuremberg Charter in its resolution 95 (I) of 11 December 1946, and both the existence and definition of crimes against peace were explicitly endorsed in 1950 in principle VI of the ILC's Nürnberg Principles.

4.89 Agreement on past principle, however, was one thing. Defining for the new era of the United Nations what, in implicit reference to article 39 of the UN Charter, was henceforth to be called the 'crime of aggression' turned out to be another. In its resolution 897 (IX) of 4 December 1954, the General Assembly postponed further discussion of the ILC's work on what was then entitled the Draft Code of Offences Against the Peace and Security of Mankind pending receipt of 'a detailed report on the question of defining aggression and a draft definition of aggression'[217] from a special committee established for the purpose pursuant to the same resolution. By the time the General Assembly invited the ILC in 1981 to resume its work on what would soon be styled the Draft Code of Crimes Against the Peace and Security of Mankind,[218] the Assembly had adopted, by way of annex to resolution 3314 (XXIX) of 14 December 1974, a definition of aggression (by which was meant an act of aggression by a state, as distinct from a crime of aggression by an individual), which it called to the attention of the Security Council 'as guidance in determining, in accordance with the Charter, the existence of an act of aggression'.[219] When the ILC eventually adopted its shambolic and poorly-received Draft Code, draft article 16's definition of the crime of aggression comprised the pithy statement that '[a]n individual who, as leader or organizer, actively participates in or orders the planning, preparation, initiation or waging of aggression committed by a State shall be responsible for a crime of aggression'.

4.90 As for the Rome Statute, article 5(*d*) vests the ICC with jurisdiction *ratione materiae* over the crime of aggression. As originally adopted in 1998, article 5(*d*) was numbered article 5(1)(*d*), after which there followed an article 5(2), which provided that the ICC was to exercise jurisdiction over the crime of aggression only 'once a provision [was] adopted in accordance with articles 121 and 123 defining the crime of aggression and setting out the conditions under which the Court shall exercise jurisdiction with respect to this crime'; and it was widely assumed that, despite efforts towards a definition of the crime of aggression, this was how things would remain for the foreseeable future.[220] But, to the surprise even perhaps of the participants, the Review Conference held by the Assembly of States Parties to the Rome Statute in Kampala in 2010, negotiating on the basis of the patient work over the years of the Special Working Group on the Crime of Aggression, succeeded in adopting a definition of the crime of aggression, as well as modalities for the Court's exercise of jurisdiction over the crime.[221] The states parties agreed

---

[217] GA res 897 (IX), 4 December 1954, preamble (second recital).
[218] See GA res 36/106, 10 December 1981.
[219] GA res 3314 (XXIX), 14 December 1974, para 4.   [220] See *infra* para 14.30.
[221] See resolution RC/Res.6, 11 June 2010, para 1. See also *infra* paras 14.30, 14.34 n 72, and 14.35.

as a consequence to the deletion of article 5(2) of the Statute, thereby paving the way, at least in principle, for the Court's future exercise of its jurisdiction *ratione materiae* over the crime of aggression as defined in the new article 8*bis* ('Crime of aggression') adopted by the Review Conference.[222] The definition of the crime of aggression posited in article 8*bis* is supplemented by Elements of Crimes and by understandings 6 and 7 of the 'Understandings regarding the amendments to the Rome Statute of the International Criminal Court on the Crime of Aggression', both adopted by way of and annexed to the resolution by which article 8*bis* itself was adopted.[223] The understandings are to be considered an instrument made by one or more parties to the Statute in connection with its conclusion—or, more precisely, with the conclusion of amendments to it—and accepted by the other parties as an instrument related to the treaty, within the meaning of article 31(2)(*b*) of the Vienna Convention on the Law of Treaties 1969 (VCLT).[224] As such, they form part of the context in which, in accordance with article 31(1) of the VCLT, article 8*bis* is to be interpreted.

4.91 It would be rash to suggest that the definition of the crime of aggression in article 8*bis* of the Rome Statute, as elaborated on by the Elements of Crimes and understandings 6 and 7, is consonant with present customary international law.[225] That said, no serious alternative definition presents itself, with the consequence that, should any definition of the crime aggression ever emerge as *lex lata*, it is likely to bear a close resemblance to the Statute's version, even if the drafting of the latter is in crucial parts obscure.

B. Conditions of Responsibility

(i) Material elements

4.92 Article 8*bis* of the Rome Statute is framed around the conceptual and textual distinction between a crime of aggression, as defined in article 8*bis*(1) and comprising conduct by an individual for which that individual bears criminal responsibility under the Statute,[226] and an act of aggression, as defined in article 8*bis*(2) and comprising conduct by a state. An individual commits a crime of

---

[222] See res RC/Res.6, Annex I, para 2.
[223] See res RC/Res.6, paras 2 and 3 and Annexes II and III respectively. See *infra* paras 4.98 and 4.100 for the texts of understandings 6 and 7 respectively.
[224] Were it not for the fact that more states have become parties to the Rome Statute since the Review Conference, the 'understandings' could have been considered agreements relating to the Statute made between all the parties in connection with its conclusion—or, to be precise, with the conclusion of amendments to it—within the meaning of VCLT, art 31(2)(*a*).
[225] Recall, in this regard, Rome Statute, art 10, *supra* para 4.4 n 10. See also understanding 4 on the amendments on the crime of aggression, RC/Res.6, Annex III, which states: 'It is understood that the amendments that address the definition of the act of aggression and the crime of aggression do so for the purpose of this Statute only. The amendments shall, in accordance with article 10 of the Rome Statute, not be interpreted as limiting or prejudicing in any way existing or developing rules of international law for purposes other than this Statute.'
[226] For the effectively substantive nature of the ostensibly jurisdictional provisions of articles 6 to 8*bis* of the Rome Statute, see *infra* para 14.59.

aggression when that individual plays a specified role in an act of aggression of a particular quality.

4.93 As defined in article 8*bis*(2) of the Statute, an act of aggression means, in general terms, 'the use of armed force by a State against the sovereignty, territorial integrity or political independence of another State, or in any other manner inconsistent with the Charter of the United Nations'. This general statement is elaborated on in the succeeding sentence. This second sentence of article 8*bis*(2) provides that '[a]ny of the following acts, regardless of a declaration of war, shall, in accordance with United Nations General Assembly resolution 3314 (XXIX) of 14 December 1974, qualify as an act of aggression', before listing, in subparagraphs (*a*) to (*g*), seven distinct acts by a state[227]—drawn from General Assembly resolution 3314 (XXIX)—deemed to amount to an act of aggression within the meaning of article 8*bis* of the Statute.

4.94 As defined in article 8*bis*(1) of the Statute, a crime of aggression means 'the planning, preparation, initiation or execution, by a person in a position effectively to exercise control over or to direct the political or military action of a State, of an act of aggression which, by its character, gravity and scale, constitutes a manifest violation of the Charter of the United Nations'. That is, the crime of aggression comprises certain conduct by persons in certain positions in relation to certain acts of aggression by states.

4.95 The conduct constitutive of a crime of aggression is, as made clear in article 8*bis*(1) and underlined in the Elements of Crimes,[228] the planning, preparation, initiation or execution of an act of aggression of a particular quality by a state. The terms 'planning', 'preparation', 'initiation', and 'execution' are not defined in article 8*bis* or elsewhere in the Rome Statute. 'Planning' in this context is a form of commission of the offence, rather than an accessorial mode of responsibility for it.[229]

4.96 To be responsible for a crime of aggression, an individual must, again as specified in article 8*bis*(1) and reiterated in the Elements of Crimes,[230] be 'in a position

---

[227] These are: '(*a*) The invasion or attack by the armed forces of a State of the territory of another State, or any military occupation, however temporary, resulting from such invasion or attack, or any annexation by the use of force of the territory of another State or part thereof; (*b*) Bombardment by the armed forces of a State against the territory of another State or the use of any weapons by a State against the territory of another State; (*c*) The blockade of the ports or coasts of a State by the armed forces of another State; (*d*) An attack by the armed forces of a State on the land, sea or air forces, or marine and air fleets of another State; (*e*) The use of armed forces of one State which are within the territory of another State with the agreement of the receiving State, in contravention of the conditions provided for in the agreement or any extension of their presence in such territory beyond the termination of the agreement; (*f*) The action of a State in allowing its territory, which it has placed at the disposal of another State, to be used by that other State for perpetrating an act of aggression against a third State; (*g*) The sending by or on behalf of a State of armed bands, groups, irregulars or mercenaries, which carry out acts of armed force against another State of such gravity as to amount to the acts listed above, or its substantial involvement therein.' Elements of Crimes, art 8*bis*, introduction, para 1, reiterates that 'any of the acts referred to in article 8*bis*, paragraph 2, qualif[ies] as an act of aggression'.
[228] See Elements of Crimes, art 8*bis*, element 1.
[229] For 'planning' as a mode of accessorial responsibility, see *infra* paras 5.49–5.54.
[230] See Elements of Crimes, art 8*bis*, element 2.

effectively to exercise control over or to direct the political or military action of' the state that commits the act of aggression. In other words, the crime of aggression is what has been referred to as a 'leadership' crime. A humble functionary or foot-soldier cannot commit a crime of aggression. At the same time, the emphasis is on the individual's effective capacity to exercise control or direction, which suggests that the formal position occupied by the individual is not determinative and that whether or not he or she is in the requisite position can be decided only on a case-by-case basis.[231] As to the semantic distinction, if any, between 'to exercise control' and 'to direct', the former suggests a more arm's-length relationship between the individual and the political or military action of the state than the latter, which implies a hands-on role. Either sort of relationship, however, suffices. Article 8*bis*(1) is explicit, moreover, in specifying that the capacity to exercise control or to direct may pertain to either the political action or the military action of the state. Finally, a footnote to the Elements of Crime for article 8*bis* explains *ex abundante cautela* that more than one person may be in a position effectively to exercise control over or to direct the political or military action of the state that commits the act of aggression.[232]

4.97 Not every act of aggression within the meaning of article 8*bis*(2) can give rise to the crime of aggression. Article 8*bis*(1)'s definition of the crime of aggression requires that the act of aggression constitute a 'manifest' violation of the UN Charter, the implied reference being to article 2(4) of the Charter.[233] The Elements of Crimes to article 8*bis* make it clear that '[t]he term "manifest" is an objective qualification'.[234]

4.98 The ordinary meaning of the adjective 'manifest' is 'obvious', 'clear-cut', 'self-evident', 'flagrant' or the like. In ordinary usage, an act of aggression that constituted a 'manifest' violation[235] of the UN Charter would be an act of aggression that, on no reasonable reading of the law and facts, could be anything other than a violation of article 2(4) of the Charter. But article 8*bis*(1) of the Rome Statute, as reiterated in the Elements of Crimes and in understandings 6 and 7, specifies that it is 'by its character, gravity and scale' that an act of aggression is to be considered a 'manifest' violation of the Charter. The focus is seemingly on the seriousness, rather than the plainness, of the violation, a semantic oddity underlined in understanding 6, which reads:

> It is understood that aggression is the most serious and dangerous form of the illegal use of force; and that a determination whether an act of aggression has been committed requires consideration of all the circumstances of each particular case, including the gravity of the

---

[231] Compare, in this regard, the 'effective control' test applied in the context of command and other superior responsibility, as outlined *infra* paras 5.104–5.108.

[232] Elements of Crimes, art 8*bis*, element 2 note 1.

[233] Article 2(4) of the Charter prohibits the use of armed force by one UN member state against another except in the lawful exercise of the inherent right of individual or collective self-defence or if authorized by the Security Council under art 42 of the Charter.

[234] Elements of Crimes, art 8*bis*, introduction, para 3.

[235] See also, with shame-faced apologies to Arabic-speakers, the French (*'une violation manifeste'*) and Spanish (*'una violación manifiesta'*) texts of article 8*bis*(1).

acts concerned and their consequences, in accordance with the Charter of the United Nations.

In short, article 8*bis*(1), as elaborated on in the Elements of Crimes and the understandings, appears to give a special meaning to the word 'manifest',[236] a meaning more akin to 'serious'.

It is not clear for the purposes of article 8*bis*(1) how the terms 'gravity' and 'scale' are to be differentiated from each other, although the former would seem to go to the consequences of the act of aggression and the latter to its execution, for example whether it involves a full-scale land invasion, the frequency and intensity of any artillery, missile or aerial strikes, the ordnance deployed, and the like. Nor is it apparent how the 'gravity' and 'scale' of an act of aggression are to be distinguished from its 'character', for the reason that it is not apparent what is supposed to be meant by the last, which may or may not relate, for example, to the pertinent species of act of aggression, as enumerated in subparagraphs (*a*) to (*g*) of article 8*bis*(2), to the plainness or otherwise of the violation of article 2(4) of the UN Charter, and so on. 4.99

To complicate matters further, understanding 7 provides: 4.100

It is understood that in establishing whether an act of aggression constitutes a manifest violation of the Charter of the United Nations, the three components of character, gravity and scale must be sufficient to justify a 'manifest' determination. No one component can be significant enough to satisfy the manifest standard by itself.

Putting it another way, the three components of 'character', 'gravity', and 'scale' must—as per the text of article 8*bis*(1) itself, the Elements of Crimes to article 8*bis*,[237] and the first sentence of understanding 7—together be sufficient to justify characterizing an act of aggression as a 'manifest' violation of the UN Charter, but, as per the second sentence of understanding 7, only two of these factors need actually be taken into account.

(ii) Mental elements

In order to incur responsibility for the crime of aggression, the perpetrator must intend to plan, prepare, initiate or execute, as the case may be, an act of aggression in the knowledge, first, 'of the factual circumstances that established that such a use of armed force was inconsistent with the Charter of the United Nations' and, secondly, 'of the factual circumstances that established...a manifest violation of the Charter of the United Nations'.[238] It is not necessary that the perpetrator make a legal evaluation either as to whether the use of armed force was inconsistent with the UN Charter or 'as to the "manifest" nature of the violation of the Charter'.[239] 4.101

---

[236] See VCLT, art 31(4). [237] Elements of Crimes, art 8*bis*, element 5.
[238] Ibid, elements 4 and 6 respectively.
[239] Ibid, introduction, paras 2 and 4 respectively.

VII. Other Crimes?

4.102 It is obviously possible in principle that there currently exist crimes under customary international law other than war crimes, crimes against humanity, the crime of genocide, and the crime of aggression. But the existence *de lege lata* of any such crimes is simply unclear.

4.103 Perhaps the most realistic candidate for joining the ranks of crimes under customary international law is torture as defined in the Convention against Torture and Other Cruel, Inhuman or Degrading Treatment or Punishment 1984 ('Torture Convention')—that is, torture beyond the confines both of the 1949 Geneva Conventions and of the chapeau requirements for a crime against humanity.[240] Another is slavery, as defined in article 1(1) of the Slavery Convention 1926 and article 6(1) of the Supplementary Slavery Convention 1956.[241]

4.104 It has been held by the Appeals Chamber of the Special Tribunal for Lebanon that terrorism is a crime under customary international law.[242] The claim is unconvincing, based as it is on an overdetermined reading of the evidence that takes liberties with the requirement for *opinio juris* in the formation of rules of customary international law.

VIII. A Hierarchy of Gravity?

4.105 In *Stakić*, the ICTY Appeals Chamber—referring to the comparative gravity of the first three offences over which the Tribunal enjoys jurisdiction, *viz* the crime of genocide, crimes against humanity, and war crimes—stated that, as an inherent matter, 'there is no hierarchy [among] the crimes within the jurisdiction of the Tribunal',[243] a position it reiterated in *Mrkšić and Šljivančanin*.[244] Similarly, in *Kayishema and Ruzindana*, the ICTR Appeals Chamber observed that 'there is no hierarchy of crimes under the Statute', with the consequence that 'all of the crimes specified therein are...capable of attracting the same sentence', adding that '[t]he actual sentence imposed depends, of course, upon the evaluation of the various factors referred to in the Statute and the Rules'.[245] In its subsequent judgment in *Nahimana* et al, the ICTR Appeals Chamber cited its ICTY counterpart in *Stakić* to reiterate that 'there is no pre-established hierarchy between crimes within the jurisdiction of the Tribunal' and that 'international criminal law does not formally identify categories of offences',[246] a statement affirmed in turn in

---

[240] See *infra* paras 7.118–7.122. [241] See *infra* paras 7.34–7.36.
[242] See *Ayyash* et al (n 7), paras 83–113.
[243] *Stakić*, Appeals Chamber Judgment (n 19), para 375.
[244] *Mrkšić and Šljivančanin*, Appeals Chamber Judgment (n 128), para 375.
[245] *Kayishema and Ruzindana*, Appeals Chamber Judgment (n 13), para 367.
[246] *Nahimana* et al, Appeals Chamber Judgment (n 123), para 1060, references omitted, citing *Stakić*, Appeals Chamber Judgment (n 19), para 375.

Bikindi.²⁴⁷ In sum, as far as the ICTY and ICTR are concerned, the customary crime of genocide, customary crimes against humanity, and customary war crimes are of equal intrinsic seriousness. All other things being equal, the same conduct should attract the same sentence whether prosecuted under customary international law as the crime of genocide, a crime against humanity or a war crime. The gravity of an offence is always a function of the specific conduct alleged in a specific case,²⁴⁸ not of its formal legal characterization.²⁴⁹

It is not clear if this will be the position of the ICC. It is at least arguable that article 33(2) of the Rome Statute, in accordance with which orders to commit genocide and crimes against humanity are deemed manifestly unlawful with the consequence that the defence of superior orders is unavailable in respect of them,²⁵⁰ indicates a difference in gravity between these two crimes, on the one hand, and war crimes, on the other. Some might seek to draw the same conclusion from the transitional opt-out provision in respect of war crimes in article 124.²⁵¹ But a more persuasive explanation for article 33(2) is that an order to commit genocide or a crime against humanity is manifestly unlawful not because these crimes are inherently graver but because they have nothing to do with fighting the opposing armed forces. By the same token, an order to commit a war crime against civilians ought to be manifestly unlawful for the purposes of article 33(1)(c) of the Statute. As for article 124, this was inserted—possibly unnecessarily, given article 8(1)—to allay the fears of some western states that individual soldiers on UN peacekeeping missions at the date of the Statute's entry into force might find themselves facing war crimes charges in the ICC not in relation to the sort of systemic conduct associated with crimes against humanity and genocide but in respect of isolated and comparatively minor acts—acts which, not on account of being characterized as war crimes but simply on account of their specific nature, were of a lesser gravity. No differentiation in maximum sentence among the crimes within the Court's jurisdiction is specified in the Statute (although this is of little help, given that no maximum sentence is specified for any of the crimes within the Court's jurisdiction). On the other hand, the Pre-Trial Chamber in *Al Bashir* supported its conclusion on the additional, contextual element posited in the Element of Crimes in relation to genocide²⁵² by reference to the *soi-disant* 'traditional consideration of the crime of genocide as the "crime of crimes"'.²⁵³ It

4.106

---

²⁴⁷ See *Prosecutor v Bikindi*, ICTR-01-72-A, Appeals Chamber, Judgment, 18 March 2010, para 145.
²⁴⁸ See, in this regard, *Nahimana* et al, Appeals Chamber Judgment (n 123), para 1060, reference omitted: '[I]t is obvious that, in concrete terms, some criminal behaviours are more serious than others.... [T]he effective gravity of the offences committed is the deciding factor in the determination of the sentence...'
²⁴⁹ In this light, the all-too-common reference to genocide as 'the crimes of crimes' should be considered as no more than an ill-considered and misleading slogan. See, to the same effect, *Stakić*, Appeals Chamber Judgment (n 19), para 375; *Mrkšić and Šljivančanin*, Appeals Chamber Judgment (n 128), para 375; *Kayishema and Ruzindana*, Appeals Chamber Judgment (n 13), para 367.
²⁵⁰ See *infra* para 6.34   ²⁵¹ See *infra* para 14.31.
²⁵² Recall *supra* para 4.77 n 179.
²⁵³ *Al Bashir*, Pre-Trial Chamber Decision on Arrest Warrant (n 159), para 133.

remains to be seen whether such woolly thinking becomes entrenched. If it does, it further remains to be seen how 'the crime of crimes' compares in terms of supposed intrinsic gravity to what the Nuremberg IMT characterized as 'the supreme international crime',[254] namely the crime of aggression.

IX. Conclusion

4.107 Even if talk of 'core crimes' is as descriptively open to question as it is juridically misconceived,[255] there is no doubting that crimes under customary international law represent a large and highly significant part of international criminal law. This being the case, knowledge of at least their central definitional elements, both material and mental, is essential to a full appreciation of the field.

4.108 The fact, however, that the accused's conduct has satisfied the material and mental elements of the offence does not mean that conviction is inevitable. The criminal responsibility that he or she *prima facie* bears may be excluded in reliance on one of the grounds for excluding responsibility recognized under customary international criminal law. Putting it in plain terms, a defence may be available to him or her. Defences to criminal responsibility under customary international law are the subject of chapter 6 of this book.

4.109 It may equally be that an individual does not go about physically killing, torturing or raping anyone but, rather, orders others to do so, assists others in doing so enters into a plan for others to do so, fails to prevent others from doing so or fails to punish others for having done so. In such cases, the basic material and mental elements of the various crimes under customary international law will be insufficient to expose that person to customary international criminal responsibility. A more sophisticated conceptual and technical legal framework will be required. This framework, based on the notion of 'modes' of responsibility, is the subject of the next chapter.

Further Reading

ABI-SAAB, G and ABI-SAAB, R-M, 'Les crimes de guerre' in H Ascensio, E Decaux, and A Pellet (eds), *Droit international pénal* (2nd edn, Paris: Pedone, 2012), 141

AKANDE, D, 'What Exactly Was Agreed at Kampala on the Crime of Aggression?' (http://www.ejiltalk.org/what-exactly-was-agreed-in-kampala-on-the-crime-of-aggression/)

AKHAVAN, P, *Reducing Genocide to Law. Definition, Meaning, and the Ultimate Crime* (Cambridge: Cambridge University Press, 2012)

AMBOS, K, 'The Crime of Aggression after Kampala' (2010) 53 *German Yearbook of International Law* 463

AMBOS, K, *Treatise on International Criminal Law. Volume 2: Crimes and Sentencing* (Oxford: Oxford University Press, 2014), chapters 1–4

---

[254] Recall *supra* para 4.88.   [255] Recall *supra* paras 2.38–2.40.

BARRIGA, S and GROVER, L, 'A Historic Breakthrough on the Crime of Aggression' (2011) 105 *American Journal of International Law* 517

BEHRENS, P, 'Genocide and the Question of Motives' (2012) 10 *Journal of International Criminal Justice* 501

BERTRAND, C, 'Le crime d'agression' in H Ascensio, E Decaux, and A Pellet (eds), *Droit international pénal* (2nd edn, Paris: Pedone, 2012), 163

BETTATI, M, 'Les crimes contre l'humanité' in H ASCENSIO, E DECAUX, and A PELLET (eds), *Droit international pénal* (2nd edn, Paris: Pedone, 2012), 103

BLOKKER, N and KREẞ, C, 'A Consensus Agreement on the Crime of Aggression: Impressions from Kampala' (2010) 23 *Leiden Journal of International Law* 889

BORDA, AZ, 'A Formal Approach to Article 38(1)(d) of the ICJ Statute from the Perspective of the International Criminal Courts and Tribunals' (2013) 24 *European Journal of International Law* 649

CASSESE, A, 'The Nexus Requirement for War Crimes' (2012) 10 *Journal of International Criminal Justice* 1395

CASSESE, A and GAETA, P, *Cassese's International Criminal Law* (3rd edn, Oxford: Oxford University Press, 2013), chapters 4–8

CRYER, R, 'The Definitions of International Crimes in the *Al Bashir* Arrest Warrant Decision' (2009) 7 *Journal of International Criminal Justice* 283

CRYER, R, 'International Criminal Tribunals and the Sources of International Law: Antonio Cassese's Contribution to the Canon' (2012) 10 *Journal of International Criminal Justice* 1045

CRYER, R, FRIMAN, H, ROBINSON, D and WILMSHURST, E, *An Introduction to International Criminal Law and Procedure* (3rd edn, Cambridge: Cambridge University Press, 2014), chapters 10–13

CULLEN, A, *The Concept of Non-International Armed Conflict in International Law* (Cambridge: Cambridge University Press, 2010)

DE FROUVILLE, O, *Droit international pénal. Sources, Incriminations, Responsabilité* (Paris: Pedone, 2012), part II

DÖRMANN, K, *Elements of War Crimes under the Rome Statute of the International Criminal Court* (Cambridge: Cambridge University Press, 2003)

DUNGEL, J, 'Defining Victims of Crimes against Humanity: *Martić* and the International Criminal Court' (2009) 22 *Leiden Journal of International Law* 727

EDEN, P, 'The Role of the Rome Statute in the Criminalization of Apartheid' (2014) 12 *Journal of International Criminal Justice* 171

FAN, M, 'Custom, General Principles and the Great Architect Cassese' (2012) 10 *Journal of International Criminal Justice* 1063

FINNIN, S, 'Mental Elements under Article 30 of the Rome Statute of the International Criminal Court: A Comparative Analysis' (2012) 61 *International and Comparative Law Quarterly* 325

GAETA, P (ed), *The UN Genocide Convention: A Commentary* (Oxford: Oxford University Press, 2009), chapters 4–6

GROVER, L, 'A Call to Arms: Fundamental Dilemmas Confronting the Interpretation of Crimes in the Rome Statute of the International Criminal Court' (2010) 21 *European Journal of International Law* 543

HALLING, M, 'Push the Envelope—Watch It Bend: Removing the Policy Requirement and Extending Crimes against Humanity' (2010) 23 *Leiden Journal of International Law* 827

HAPPOLD, M, 'International Humanitarian Law, War Criminality and Child Recruitment: The Special Court for Sierra Leone's Decision in Prosecutor v Samuel Hinga Norman' (2005) 18 *Leiden Journal of International Law* 283

HENCKAERTS, J-M, 'Civil War, Custom and Cassese' (2012) 10 *Journal of International Criminal Justice* 1095

KIRSCH, P, 'Two Kinds of Wrong: On the Context Element of Crimes against Humanity' (2009) 22 *Leiden Journal of International Law* 525

KREß, C, 'The Crime of Genocide and Contextual Elements: A Comment on the ICC Pre-Trial Chamber's Decision in the *Al Bashir* Case' (2009) 7 *Journal of International Criminal Justice* 1

KREß, C, 'Nullum crimen sine lege', in *Max Planck Encyclopedia of Public International Law* (online)

KREß, C, 'On the Outer Limits of Crimes against Humanity: The Concept of Organization within the Policy Requirement: Some Reflections on the March 2010 ICC Kenya Decision' (2010) 23 *Leiden Journal of International Law* 855

KREß, C and VON HOLTZENDORFF, L, 'The Kampala Compromise on the Crime of Aggression' (2010) 8 *Journal of International Criminal Justice* 1179

McDOUGALL, C, *The Crime of Aggression under the Rome Statute of the International Criminal Court* (Cambridge: Cambridge University Press, 2013)

MILANOVIĆ, M, 'Aggression and Legality: Custom in Kampala' (2012) 10 *Journal of International Criminal Justice* 165

OOSTERVELD, V and GARRAWAY, C, 'The Elements of Genocide' in RS Lee and H Friman (eds), *The International Criminal Court: Elements of Crimes and Rules of Procedure and Evidence* (Ardsley, NY: Transnational Publishers, 2001), 41

RITTER VON FEUERBACH, PJA, 'The Foundations of Criminal Law and the *Nullum Crimen* Principle' (2007) 5 *Journal of International Criminal Justice* 1005

SASSÒLI, M, 'Humanitarian Law and International Criminal Law' in A CASSESE (ed), *The Oxford Companion to International Criminal Justice* (Oxford: Oxford University Press 2009), 111

SAUL, B, 'Legislating from a Radical Hague: the United Nations Special Tribunal for Lebanon Invents an International Crime of Transnational Terrorism' (2011) 24 *Leiden Journal of International Law* 677

SCHABAS, W, *Genocide in International Law. The Crime of Crimes* (2nd edn, Cambridge: Cambridge University Press, 2009)

SCHABAS, W, *The International Criminal Court. A Commentary on the Rome Statute* (Oxford: Oxford University Press, 2010), 101–272

SCHABAS, W, 'Le génocide' in H Ascensio, E Decaux, and A Pellet (eds), *Droit international pénal* (2nd edn, Paris: Pedone, 2012), 125

SCHEFFER, D, 'The Complex Crime of Aggression under the Rome Statute' (2010) 23 *Leiden Journal of International Law* 897

SCHWARZENBERGER, G, 'The Judgment of Nuremberg' (1946–47) 21 *Tulane Law Review* 329

SELLARS, K, *'Crimes against Peace' and International Law* (Cambridge: Cambridge University Press, 2013)

SERTIS, P, 'War Crimes during Armed Conflicts at Sea' in ED Papastavridis and KN Trapp (eds), *La criminalité en mer/Crimes at Sea* (Leiden: Martinus Nijhoff, 2014), 523

SHAHABUDDEEN, M, 'Does the Principle of Legality Stand in the Way of Progressive Development of Law?' (2004) 2 *Journal of International Criminal Justice* 1007

SIMMA, B and PAULUS, A, 'Le rôle relatif des différentes sources du droit international pénal' in H Ascensio, E Decaux, and A Pellet (eds), *Droit international pénal* (2nd edn, Paris: Pedone, 2012), 67

Sivakumaran, S, *The Law of Non-International Armed Conflict* (Oxford: Oxford University Press, 2012)

Smith, A, 'Child Recruitment and the Special Court for Sierra Leone' (2004) 2 *Journal of International Criminal Justice* 1141

Szpak, A, 'National, Ethnic, Racial, and Religious Groups Protected against Genocide in the Jurisprudence of the ad hoc International Criminal Tribunals' (2012) 23 *European Journal of International Law* 155

Szurek, S, 'Historique. La formation du droit international pénal' in H Ascensio, E Decaux, and A Pellet (eds), *Droit international pénal* (2nd edn, Paris: Pedone, 2012), 21

van der Wilt, H, 'War Crimes and the Requirement of a Nexus with an Armed Conflict' (2012) 10 *Journal of International Criminal Justice* 1113

Van Schaack, B, 'Crimen Sine Lege: Judicial Lawmaking at the Intersection of Law and Morals' (2008) 97 *Georgetown Law Journal* 119

Von Liszt, F, 'The Rationale for the *Nullum Crimen* Principle' (2007) 5 *Journal of International Criminal Justice* 1009

Weigend, T, '"In General a Principle of Justice": The Debate on the "Crime against Peace" in the Wake of the Nuremberg Judgment' (2012) 10 *Journal of International Criminal Justice* 41

Werle, G and Burghardt, B, 'Do Crimes Against Humanity Require the Participation of a State or a "State-like" Organization?' (2012) 10 *Journal of International Criminal Justice* 1151

Werle, G and Jessburger, F, *Principles of International Criminal Law* (3rd edn, Oxford: Oxford University Press, 2014), chapters 19–38

Wilmshurst, E (ed), *International Law and the Classification of Conflicts* (Oxford: Oxford University Press, 2012)

5
Modes of Responsibility

I. Introduction

5.1　In the major national criminal justice traditions, criminal responsibility attaches not just to those who pull the trigger, wield the blade or rifle the safe but also to those who encourage, direct, assist, agree on the plan with or perhaps just fail to report them. The same is true under customary international criminal law, where the collective and often organizational context of many instances of internationally criminal conduct lends particular practical significance to criminal responsibility on bases other than physical perpetration. Where to draw the line, however, between varying degrees of culpability has proved a complicated and controversial business at the international level.

5.2　This chapter examines the multiple bases or 'modes' of criminal responsibility under customary international law. Like the previous chapter[1] but even more so, it comes with the qualification that its treatment under the rubric 'crimes under customary international law' of the detailed ins and outs—as suggested by the statutes and statements of the different international criminal courts—of the various forms of criminal responsibility should not be taken to indicate that each and every element presently accords, or will ever accord, with customary international law. Many, perhaps most do, but others represent no more than candidates for customary status. Secondly, and again like the previous chapter, the focus in this chapter is on the more general aspects of the law, actual or purported.[2]

---

[1] Recall *supra* para 4.2.

[2] For other, more specialist works in this regard, see, in alphabetical order, K Ambos, *Treatise on International Criminal Law. Volume 1: Foundations and General Part* (Oxford: Oxford University Press, 2013), chapters 3–7; A Cassese and P Gaeta, *Cassese's International Criminal Law* (3rd edn, Oxford: Oxford University Press, 2013), chapters 9–11; R Cryer *et al*, *An Introduction to International Criminal Law and Procedure* (3rd edn, Cambridge: Cambridge University Press, 2014), chapter 15; E van Sliedregt, *Individual Criminal Responsibility in International Law* (Oxford: Oxford University Press, 2012); G Werle and F Jessburger, *Principles of International Criminal Law* (3rd edn, Oxford: Oxford University Press, 2014), chapters 11, 12, and 15.

II. Preliminary Matters

A. General

5.3 The various bases or 'modes' of criminal responsibility under customary international law are where public international law meets comparative law. They have mostly been drawn from 'general principles of [criminal] law recognised by civilised nations', in the words of article 38(1)(c) of the Statute of the International Court of Justice (ICJ), although in time the relevant principles have become or at least are alleged to have become customary international law. Many of these principles reflect an attempt to straddle the various national criminal justice traditions, in particular the civil law and the common law.

5.4 The modes of criminal responsibility cognizable under customary international law have been developed to date exclusively in the context of war crimes, crimes against humanity, genocide, and, at Nuremberg, crimes against peace. It remains to be seen to what extent the principles so far elaborated are applicable to such other crimes under customary international law as may currently exist or emerge in the future and, in the absence of *lex specialis*, to treaty crimes.

5.5 Although no provision to this effect is found in any of the statutes of the various international criminal courts, the sentencing practice of at least the International Criminal Tribunal for the former Yugoslavia (ICTY), the International Criminal Tribunal for Rwanda (ICTR), and the International Criminal Court (ICC) has to date given effect to the distinction drawn in sentencing under the law and practice of many national criminal justice systems between criminal responsibility as principal (that is, for committing the crime) and accessorial[3] criminal responsibility (that is, for contributing in some way to the commission of the crime, to the avoidance of its detection or to the perpetrator's evasion of arrest). All other things being equal, these international criminal courts have so far adopted the position that criminal responsibility as principal merits more severe punishment that criminal responsibility as accessory. A contrasting approach was taken by the Special Court for Sierra Leone (SCSL).[4] Moreover, whether the foregoing remains the practice of the ICC remains to be seen.[5] There are persuasive arguments to the effect that, while the distinction between principal and accessory may have its uses, there is no necessary reason why it should dictate sentencing practice—that is, why criminal

---

[3] The term is used here in its broadest possible sense.
[4] See *Prosecutor v Taylor*, SCSL-03-01-A, Appeals Chamber, Judgment, 26 September 2013, para 670.
[5] See, in this regard, *Prosecutor v Katanga*, ICC-01/04-01/07-3436, Trial Chamber, Jugement rendu en application de l'article 74 du Statut, 7 March 2014, paras 1386–1387; *Prosecutor v Lubanga*, ICC-01/04-01/06-2842, Trial Chamber, Judgment pursuant to Article 74 of the Statute, 14 March 2012, sep op Fulford, paras 8–9; *Prosecutor v Ngudjolo*, ICC-01/04-02/12-4, Trial Chamber, Judgment pursuant to Art 74 of the Statute—Concurring Opinion of Judge Christine Van den Wyngaert, 18 December 2012, paras 22–29.

168   *Crimes under Customary International Law*

responsibility as principal need always, *ceteris paribus,* attract a stiffer sentence than criminal responsibility as accessory.

5.6   The existence under customary international law of different modes of criminal responsibility means, it ought to go without saying, that multiple persons can be held responsible in respect of a single crime, each of them potentially on a different basis.[6]

5.7   An evidentiary caveat is in order regarding the jurisprudence of the ICC to date on modes of responsibility. While statements on point are not hard to find, none as yet come from the Appeals Chamber, relatively few emanate from what are only the three trial judgments to have been handed down at time of writing, and two trial judges have explicitly distanced themselves from a controversial doctrine applied by respective majorities in two of these cases.[7] The overwhelmingly greater part of pertinent statements so far come from Pre-Trial Chambers, in decisions on the issuance of arrest warrants, decisions on the authorization of investigations *proprio motu,* and decisions on the confirmation of charges.[8] This is not a firm basis on which to suggest a *jurisprudence constante.* While such decisions have their juridical value, that value is to an extent provisional.

5.8   The ICC's 'Elements of Crimes' elaborate only on the commission of the crimes and species thereof enumerated in articles 6 to 8*bis* of the Rome Statute of the International Criminal Court ('Rome Statute')—in other words, only on the definitional elements of each crime, satisfaction of which results in the perpetrator's criminal responsibility on the basis of commission or, synonymously, as principal. The Elements do not expand on the various other bases on which criminal responsibility for an offence may arise in respect of a crime within the Court's jurisdiction.

B. The Mental Elements in General

5.9   It is not only with respect to the most basic mode of criminal responsibility known to customary international law, namely commission, that the accused must be proved to have satisfied both the requisite material elements and the requisite mental element or elements—both the so-called *actus reus* and *mens rea*—before he or she can be convicted. Each of the different modes of criminal responsibility under customary international law has, in addition to its distinctive *actus reus,* a requisite and distinctive accompanying *mens rea.*[9]

5.10   It will be recalled[10] that, as a general rule, an essential condition for criminal responsibility under customary international law is a mental element, or *mens*

---

[6] This self-evident proposition was underscored in *Prosecutor v Kunarac* et al, IT-96-23 & IT-96-23/1, Trial Chamber, Judgment, 22 February 2001, para 390.
[7] See *infra* para 5.47.
[8] For details as to these different procedural stages, see *infra* paras 14.20–14.23.
[9] See, explicitly, *Prosecutor v Vasiljević*, IT-98-32-A, Appeals Chamber, Judgment, 25 February 2004, para 102; *Prosecutor v Brđanin*, IT-99-36-A, Appeals Chamber, Decision on Interlocutory Appeal, 19 March 2004, para 5.
[10] See *supra* para 4.8.

rea, amounting to intent to commit the requisite material elements of the mode of criminal responsibility in question accompanied by knowledge of any legally-relevant facts.[11] Criminal responsibility on the basis of negligence is not a general feature of customary international criminal law, and criminal responsibility on the basis of strict liability is unknown to the field. As defined in article 30(2)(*a*) and (*b*) respectively of the Rome Statute, 'intent' signifies, in relation to conduct, meaning to engage in the conduct and, in relation to a consequence, meaning to cause that consequence or being aware that it will occur in the ordinary course of events. As defined in article 30(3) of the Rome Statute, 'knowledge' signifies awareness that a circumstance exists or that a consequence will occur in the ordinary course of events. As indicated in the Elements of Crimes, the existence of intent or knowledge can be inferred from relevant facts and circumstances.[12]

It will also be recalled[13] that intent and motive are distinct issues.[14] Only intent is a formal precondition to criminal responsibility under customary international law. In other words, what matters is that individuals mean, with the necessary knowledge, to do what they do, not why they do it.

5.11

III. Commission

The respective statutes of the ICTY, ICTR, SCSL, and ICC all make express reference to criminal responsibility on the basis of the commission of the crime.[15]

5.12

A. Basic Form

As a mode of criminal responsibility, the 'commission' of a crime refers to the engagement in behaviour that, all other material elements being equal, satisfies the definitional material elements of the offence. What is required to satisfy these definitional material elements will obviously depend on the offence.[16] In particular, commission may involve the performance of proscribed conduct (that is, the doing of prohibited acts) or it may involve the omission to perform prescribed conduct (that is, the failure to do obligatory acts).[17] If the perpetrator not only satisfies the

5.13

---

[11] See eg Rome Statute, art 30(1).
[12] Elements of Crimes, ICC-ASP/1/3 (part II-B) (as amended), general introduction, para 3.
[13] See *supra* para 4.9.
[14] See eg *Prosecutor v Tadić*, IT-94-1-A, Appeals Chamber, Judgment, 15 July 1999, para 269; *Prosecutor v Jelisić*, IT-95-10-A, Appeals Chamber, Judgment, 5 July 2001, para 106; *Prosecutor v Krnojelac*, IT-97-25-A, Appeals Chamber, Judgment, 17 September 2003, paras 100–102; *Prosecutor v Kvočka* et al, IT-98-30/1-A, Appeals Chamber, Judgment, 28 February 2005, para 106; *Prosecutor v Stakić*, IT-97-24-A, Appeals Chamber, Judgment, 22 March 2006, para 45.
[15] See Statute of the International Criminal Tribunal for the former Yugoslavia ('ICTY Statute'), art 7(1); Statute of the International Criminal Tribunal for Rwanda ('ICTR Statute'), art 6(1); Statute of the Special Court for Sierra Leone ('SCSL Statute'), art 6(1); Rome Statute, art 25(3)(*a*).
[16] Recall *supra* para 4.7.
[17] See, generally, *Tadić*, Appeals Chamber Judgment (n 14), para 188; *Prosecutor v Blaškić*, IT-95-14-A, Appeals Chamber, Judgment, 29 July 2004, para 663; *Prosecutor v Kayishema and Ruzindana*, ICTR-95-1-A, Appeals Chamber, Judgment (reasons), 1 June 2001, para 187.

definitional material elements of the offence but does so with the requisite intent and knowledge, he or she will be criminally responsible for the offence on the basis of commission.

B. Joint Criminal Enterprise before the ICTY, ICTR, and SCSL

(i) Outline

5.14 The ICTY, ICTR, and SCSL have all recognized as implicit in the notion of 'commission' in articles 7(1), 6(1), and 6(1) of their respective statutes, and as part of customary international law, criminal responsibility for participation in a 'joint criminal enterprise' (JCE) to commit or resulting in the commission of a crime.[18] But although each of these organs considers participation in a joint criminal enterprise to comprise a form of commission of the crime (or, in the terminology of national criminal law, to give rise to criminal responsibility as principal), the gist of responsibility on the basis of participation in a joint criminal enterprise is that a participant in such an enterprise 'need not physically commit any part of the *actus reus* of the crime involved'.[19] Nor, for that matter, need a participant in a joint criminal enterprise be physically present when and where the crime is being committed.[20]

5.15 Joint criminal enterprise comes in three forms.[21] The first (known as 'JCE I' or JCE in its 'basic' form) is where a number of persons participate in the furtherance

---

[18] See eg *Tadić*, Appeals Chamber Judgment (n 14), paras 185–229; *Prosecutor v Milutinović et al*, IT-99-37-AR72, Appeals Chamber, Decision on Dragoljub Ojdanić's Motion Challenging Jurisdiction—Joint Criminal Enterprise, 21 May 2003, para 20. (Note that '*Milutinović* et al' became '*Šainović* et al' on the acquittal of the original eponymous accused.) The availability under the SCSL Statute of responsibility on the basis of participation in a joint criminal enterprise was taken as read in *Prosecutor v Brima et al*, SCSL-2004-16-A, Appeals Chamber, Judgment, 22 February 2008, paras 72–87. JCE is distinct from conspiracy and from organizational liability. See *Milutinović et al*, Appeals Chamber Decision on Joint Criminal Enterprise (n 18), paras 23 and 25–26; *Prosecutor v Krajišnik*, IT-00-39-A, Appeals Chamber, Judgment, 17 March 2009, para 659; *Prosecutor v Sesay et al*, SCSL-04-15-A, Appeals Chamber, Judgment, 26 October 2009, para 397.

[19] *Kvočka et al*, Appeals Chamber Judgment (n 14), para 112. See also ibid, para 99; *Tadić*, Appeals Chamber Judgment (n 14), para 192; *Prosecutor v Brđanin*, IT-99-36-A, Appeals Chamber, Judgment, 3 April 2007, para 427; *Vasiljević*, Appeals Chamber Judgment (n 9), paras 100 and 119.

[20] *Krnojelac*, Appeals Chamber Judgment (n 14), para 81; *Kvočka et al*, Appeals Chamber Judgment (n 14), para 112; *Prosecutor v Simba*, ICTR-01-76-A, Appeals Chamber, Judgment, 27 November 2007, para 296.

[21] See eg *Tadić*, Appeals Chamber Judgment (n 14), paras 196, 202–203, and 204; *Krnojelac*, Appeals Chamber Judgment (n 14), para 30; *Vasiljević*, Appeals Chamber Judgment (n 9), paras 97–99 and 119; *Kvočka et al*, Appeals Chamber Judgment (n 14), paras 82–83 and 86; *Prosecutor v Ntakirutimana*, ICTR-96-10-A and ICTR-96-17-A, Appeals Chamber, Judgment, 13 December 2004, paras 463–465. For the requisite *mens rea* for each form of JCE, see *infra* paras 5.23–5.25. The terminology adopted by the various trial and appellate chambers in relation to responsibility on the basis of participation in a joint criminal enterprise has not always been clear or consistent. The words 'plan', 'purpose', 'design', and 'enterprise' are sometimes used interchangeably, risking conceptual confusion. Ideally, what is agreed on is referred to as the 'plan' (or the 'purpose' or 'design'), while the combined endeavours of all those involved in the formulation and execution of this plan (or purpose or design)—that is, the sum of the respective contributions of the various participants, from the plan's inception and formulation to all acts in furtherance of its realization—would be referred to as the 'joint criminal enterprise' or, for short, the 'enterprise'.

of a common plan—that is, a plan to which each of these persons is privy—to commit a crime, all sharing the intent to commit that crime, and the crime is committed. The second type ('JCE II' or JCE in its 'systemic' form), a variant of the first, is the so-called 'concentration camp' case, where there exists an organized system to commit a crime, a system in which the accused voluntarily participates with the intention of furthering it and of the nature of which he or she is aware, and the crime is committed. The third type ('JCE III' or JCE in its 'extended' form) is where a number of persons participate in the furtherance of a common plan to commit a crime, sharing the intent to commit that crime, but where the crime in the event committed is a different one, albeit one that was a natural and foreseeable consequence of effecting the plan. In this last scenario, a participant in the joint criminal enterprise may be held responsible for the crime committed where he or she willingly took the risk of its occurrence.

5.16 Responsibility for participation in a joint criminal enterprise is a form of responsibility relevant to all crimes within the jurisdiction of the ICTY and ICTR, genocide included.[22] The applicability of the doctrine of joint criminal enterprise to genocide was considered to reflect customary international law by 1992 in *Rwamakuba*,[23] where the Appeals Chamber of the ICTR held that, although it was 'not clear whether the drafters [of the Genocide Convention] viewed criminal responsibility through intentional participation in a common plan as a form of commission of genocide, complicity in genocide, or conspiracy to commit genocide', the Convention's *travaux préparatoires* provided 'strong evidence' for the view that the drafting states were seeking to impose responsibility under one or other of these rubrics for conduct amounting to participation in a joint criminal enterprise, as was held criminal in certain post-Second World War cases.[24]

(ii) Material elements

5.17 There are three material preconditions to criminal responsibility on the basis of participation in a joint criminal enterprise.[25] First, there must, self-evidently, be a 'plurality of persons'.[26] Next, there must exist a common plan[27] among these

---

[22] *Tadić*, Appeals Chamber Judgment (n 14), para 188; *Brđanin*, Appeals Chamber Decision on Interlocutory Appeal (n 9), paras 5–10; *Stakić*, Appeals Chamber Judgment (n 14), para 38; *Prosecutor v Rwamakuba*, ICTR-98-44-AR72.4, Appeals Chamber, Decision on Interlocutory Appeal regarding Application of Joint Criminal Enterprise to the Crime of Genocide, 22 October 2004, paras 13–14. For its part, the SCSL did not enjoy jurisdiction *ratione materiae* over the crime of genocide.
[23] *Rwamakuba*, Appeals Chamber Decision on Interlocutory Appeal (n 22), paras 14 and 31.
[24] Ibid, para 28.
[25] See *Tadić*, Appeals Chamber Judgment (n 14), para 227; *Prosecutor v Furundžija*, IT-95-17/1-A, Appeals Chamber, Judgment, 21 July 2000, para 119; *Krnojelac*, Appeals Chamber Judgment (n 14), paras 31 and 97; *Vasiljević*, Appeals Chamber Judgment (n 9), paras 100 and 109; *Kvočka* et al, Appeals Chamber Judgment (n 14), paras 96 and 117–118; *Stakić*, Appeals Chamber Judgment (n 14), para 64; *Brđanin*, Appeals Chamber Judgment (n 19), para 364; *Ntakirutimana*, Appeals Chamber Judgment (n 21), para 466; *Prosecutor v Munyakazi*, ICTR-97-36A-A, Appeals Chamber, Judgment, 28 September 2011, para 160; *Brima* et al, Appeals Chamber Judgment (n 18), para 75.
[26] *Tadić*, Appeals Chamber Judgment (n 14), para 227. See also eg *Vasiljević*, Appeals Chamber Judgment (n 9), para 100; *Kvočka* et al, Appeals Chamber Judgment (n 14), para 116.
[27] In the case of JCE II, the common plan takes the form of a common organized system.

persons the realization of which involves the commission of a crime. Finally, the accused must participate in some way in the furtherance of this common plan. Crucially, this participation need not itself involve the commission of a crime.[28]

5.18   It is not necessary that the objective of the common plan be a crime, as long as a crime is the planned means of achieving this objective.[29]

5.19   The participants in the joint criminal enterprise 'need not be organized in a military, political or administrative structure'.[30] Nor is there any need for the common plan to have been 'previously arranged or formulated'; rather, it may 'materialize extemporaneously'.[31]

5.20   It is not necessary to have been involved in the formulation of the common plan to be held criminally responsible on the basis of participation in a joint criminal enterprise. All that is required is that the accused participate in some way in the furtherance of a plan to which he or she is privy.[32]

5.21   It is not a condition of the criminal responsibility of the participants in a joint criminal enterprise that the physical perpetrator of the crime be party to the enterprise. Rather, each of the participants in the joint criminal enterprise may be responsible for a crime where one or more participants orders or otherwise uses a third party to commit the crime, provided that the crime is within the contemplation of, or is a natural and foreseeable consequence of effecting, the participants' common plan.[33] Indeed, there is no need for any direct contact between one or more participants in the joint criminal enterprise and the physical perpetrator of the crime. The participants may be responsible for a crime on the basis of their

---

[28] *Tadić*, Appeals Chamber Judgment (n 14), para 227; *Brđanin*, Appeals Chamber Judgment (n 19), paras 427 and 431; *Kvočka* et al, Appeals Chamber Judgment (n 14), para 99; *Vasiljević*, Appeals Chamber Judgment (n 9), para 100; *Krajišnik*, Appeals Chamber Judgment (n 18), para 695; *Prosecutor v Šainović* et al, IT-05-87-A, Appeals Chamber, Judgment, 23 January 2014, para 985; *Sesay* et al, Appeals Chamber Judgment (n 18), para 611.

[29] See *Brima* et al, Appeals Chamber Judgment (n 18), paras 76 and 80. See also *Tadić*, Appeals Chamber Judgment (n 14), para 227(ii) ('The existence of a common plan, design or purpose which amounts to or involves the commission of a crime provided for in the Statute.'); *Sesay* et al, Appeals Chamber Judgment (n 18), paras 106 and 294–296. See also Rome Statute, art 25(3)(*d*) ('where such ... purpose involves the commission of a crime within the jurisdiction of the Court'), although art 25(3)(*d*) does not treat criminal responsibility for acting with a common criminal purpose as commission of the offence.

[30] *Tadić*, Appeals Chamber Judgment (n 14), para 227.

[31] Ibid. See also *Vasiljević*, Appeals Chamber Judgement (n 9), para 100; *Stakić*, Appeals Chamber Judgment (n 14), para 64; *Brđanin*, Appeals Chamber Judgment (n 19), para 418; *Šainović* et al, Appeals Chamber Judgment (n 28), para 609.

[32] *Simba*, Appeals Chamber Judgment (n 20), para 250. See also *Tadić*, Appeals Chamber Judgment (n 14), paras 196 and 227; *Brđanin*, Appeals Chamber Judgment (n 19), para 430; *Kayishema and Ruzindana*, Appeals Chamber Judgment (n 17), para 193; *Ntakirutimana*, Appeals Chamber Judgment (n 21), para 466; *Rwamakuba*, Appeals Chamber Decision on Interlocutory Appeal (n 22), para 25; *Sesay* et al, Appeals Chamber Judgment (n 18), paras 1034 and 1063 ('[T]he manner in which the members of the JCE interact and cooperate can take as many forms as conceived by the participants to pursue the realisation of their shared common criminal purpose.'). This participation must, of course, be accompanied by the requisite *mens rea*.

[33] *Brđanin*, Appeals Chamber Judgment (n 19), paras 410–414; *Prosecutor v Martić*, IT-95-11-A, Appeals Chamber, Judgment, 8 October 2008, para 168; *Krajišnik*, Appeals Chamber Judgment (n 18), paras 225–226; *Prosecutor v Karadžić*, IT-95-5/18-AR98*bis*.1, Appeals Chamber, Rule 98*bis* Judgment, 11 July 2013, para 79; *Sesay* et al, Appeals Chamber Judgment (n 18), paras 398–400.

participation in the joint criminal enterprise where an instruction by one or more of them to commit a crime within the contemplation of, or a natural and foreseeable consequence of effecting, their common plan passes through multiple pairs of hands.[34]

5.22 In terms of causation, an accused will incur criminal responsibility on the basis of participation in a joint criminal enterprise only if his or her contribution to the enterprise is significant.[35] But 'significant' does not necessarily mean substantial.[36] *A fortiori*, the accused's contribution need not be a *conditio sine qua non* of the commission of the crime.[37] At the same time, the ICTY Appeals Chamber has sought to emphasize that 'not every type of conduct would amount to a significant enough contribution to the crime for this to create criminal liability'.[38]

(iii) Mental elements

5.23 The mental element required for criminal responsibility on the basis of participation in a joint criminal enterprise varies according to the type of joint criminal enterprise, as follows.[39] JCE I demands the intent that the crime envisaged in the common plan be committed and the intent to participate in the relevant way in the furtherance of the plan.[40] JCE II calls for knowledge of the system of ill-treatment and the intent to participate in the relevant way in the furtherance of this system.[41] JCE III requires the intent to participate in the relevant way in the furtherance of the plan, the foreseeability of the commission of the crime that was in the event committed, and the willing taking of the risk that the crime would be

---

[34] *Brđanin*, Appeals Chamber Judgment (n 19), para 419.
[35] Ibid, paras 427, 430, and 432; *Krajišnik*, Appeals Chamber Judgment (n 18), para 662; *Šainović* et al, Appeals Chamber Judgment (n 28), para 988; *Simba*, Appeals Chamber Judgment (n 20), para 303; *Sesay* et al, Appeals Chamber Judgment (n 18), para 401.
[36] *Brđanin*, Appeals Chamber Judgment (n 19), para 430; *Kvočka* et al, Appeals Chamber Judgment (n 14), para 97; *Simba*, Appeals Chamber Judgment (n 20), para 303.
[37] *Brđanin*, Appeals Chamber Judgment (n 19), para 430; *Kvočka* et al, Appeals Chamber Judgment (n 14), para 98; *Simba*, Appeals Chamber Judgment (n 20), para 303; *Sesay* et al, Appeals Chamber Judgment (n 14), para 401.
[38] *Brđanin*, Appeals Chamber Judgment (n 19), para 427.
[39] See *Tadić*, Appeals Chamber Judgment (n 14), para 228; *Krnojelac*, Appeals Chamber Judgment (n 14), para 32; *Vasiljević*, Appeals Chamber Judgment (n 9), para 101; *Ntakirutimana*, Appeals Chamber Judgment (n 21), para 467; *Stakić*, Appeals Chamber Judgment (n 14), para 65; *Sesay* et al, Appeals Chamber Judgment (n 18), paras 474–475.
[40] *Tadić*, Appeals Chamber Judgment (n 14), para 228; *Brđanin*, Appeals Chamber Judgment (n 19), para 365; *Šainović* et al, Appeals Chamber Judgment (n 28), para 1470; *Munyakazi*, Appeals Chamber Judgment (n 25), para 160. The ICTY Appeals Chamber emphasized in *Šainović* et al, Appeals Chamber Judgment (n 28), para 1470, that what is required is the actual intention that the crime be committed, not just the crime's foreseeability. But cf *Sesay* et al, Appeals Chamber Judgment (n 18), paras 294–297, 305, 467–468, 471–475, and 481–493 and, *contra*, ibid, diss op Fisher, paras 1, 3, 5–28, and 42–45.
[41] *Tadić*, Appeals Chamber Judgment (n 14), para 228; *Brđanin*, Appeals Chamber Judgment (n 19), para 365. The *mens rea* of the first two forms of common purpose was elided in *Kvočka* et al, Appeals Chamber Judgment (n 14), para 110, where the ICTY stated that 'participants in a basic or systemic form of joint criminal enterprise must be shown to share the required intent of the principal perpetrators'.

committed.⁴² The idea that the accused willingly took the risk of the commission of a foreseeable crime is also known as *dolus eventualis*.

5.24   The *mens rea* for JCE III—that is, for responsibility, on the basis of participation in joint criminal enterprise, for a crime other than that agreed on in the common plan—was discussed in *Kvočka* et al, where the Appeals Chamber of the ICTY, affirming that 'an accused may be responsible for crimes committed beyond the common purpose of the...joint criminal enterprise, if they were a natural and foreseeable consequence thereof', 'emphasized that this question must be assessed in relation to the knowledge of a particular accused'.⁴³ In other words, an accused may be responsible for a crime other than that agreed on in the common plan only if he or she 'had sufficient knowledge such that the additional crimes were a natural and foreseeable consequence to him [or her]'.⁴⁴ In other words, the standard is not objective, *viz* negligence-based, but subjective.

5.25   The standard of foreseeability is that of possibility, not probability. That is, the accused must have foreseen only the possibility that the relevant crime beyond the scope of the plan might be committed, rather than the probability that it would be.⁴⁵

5.26   In *Brđanin*, the ICTY Appeals Chamber sought to dispel the notion that criminal responsibility for genocide on the basis of JCE III was incompatible with the specific intent required for the crime of genocide. The Appeals Chamber drew a distinction in this regard between the intent required for criminal responsibility for genocide on the basis of physical commission of one of the acts constitutive of the crime and the intent required for criminal responsibility for genocide on the basis of participation in a joint criminal enterprise of the third, 'extended' type.⁴⁶ For the latter, the Appeals Chamber stated, what needs to be shown is not that the accused intended to destroy a specified group in whole or in part but rather that it was reasonably foreseeable to the accused that an act constitutive of genocide would be committed in the execution of the common plan and that it would be committed with the intent to destroy a specified group in whole or in part.⁴⁷ The

---

⁴² *Tadić*, Appeals Chamber Judgment (n 14), para 228; *Brđanin*, Appeals Chamber Judgment (n 19), para 365.

⁴³ *Kvočka* et al, Appeals Chamber Judgment (n 14), para 86. The Appeals Chamber continued, ibid, emphasis omitted: 'This is particularly important in relation to the systemic form of joint criminal enterprise, which may involve a large number of participants performing distant and distinct roles. What is natural and foreseeable to one person participating in a systemic joint criminal enterprise might not be natural and foreseeable to another, depending on the information available to them.' The potentially confusing reference to 'the systemic form of joint criminal enterprise', which one might think is to JCE II, is to JCE III in circumstances where the joint criminal enterprise is manifest in a large-scale organization.

⁴⁴ Ibid.

⁴⁵ *Prosecutor v Karadžić*, IT-95-5/18-AR72.4, Appeals Chamber, Decision on Prosecution's Motion Appealing Trial Chamber's Decision on JCE III Foreseeability, 25 June 2009, paras 13–18; *Prosecutor v Gotovina and Markač*, IT-06-90-A, Appeals Chamber, Judgment, 16 November 2012, para 90; *Šainović* et al, Appeals Chamber Judgment (n 28), paras 1061, 1272, 1525, 1538, and 1557–1558; *Prosecutor v Đorđević*, IT-05-87/1-A, Appeals Chamber, Judgment, 27 January 2014, para 907.

⁴⁶ See *Brđanin*, Appeals Chamber Decision on Interlocutory Appeal (n 9), paras 5–10.

⁴⁷ Ibid, para 6. See also *Stakić*, Appeals Chamber Judgment (n 14), para 38; *Đorđević*, Appeals Chamber Judgment (n 45), para 77. But cf *Prosecutor v Ayyash* et al, STL-11-01/I/AC/R176bis,

Modes of Responsibility

argument is not compelling, given that JCE as understood by the ICTY is itself a form of commission.

(iv) Reception

The doctrine of joint criminal enterprise has proved highly controversial, especially in its 'extended' form, *viz* JCE III. 5.27

For a start, the argument that joint criminal enterprise is implicit in the notion of commission in the ICTY, ICTR, and SCSL statutes smacks of special pleading. The doctrine finds no acknowledgement whatsoever in the UN Secretary-General's report to the Security Council which accompanied the draft ICTY Statute, the Appeal's Chamber suggestion to the contrary in *Tadić*[48] being based on a quotation drawn from a discussion of a wholly different question. 5.28

Next, at least when it comes to JCE III, the alleged basis of the doctrine in pre-existing customary international law is distinctly debatable. For its part, in *Ieng Thirith, Ieng Sary and Khieu Samphan*, the Pre-Trial Chamber of the Extraordinary Chambers in the Courts of Cambodia (ECCC), while having 'no doubt that JCE I and JCE II were recognized forms of responsibility in customary international law at the time relevant for [the case before the Chamber]',[49] namely 1975, concluded that 'the authorities relied on by *Tadić* in relation to the extended form of JCE (JCE III)...do not provide sufficient evidence of consistent state practice and *opinio juris* at the time relevant to [the case before the Chamber]'[50]—in other words, did not constitute 'a sufficiently firm basis to conclude that JCE III formed part of customary international law' in 1975.[51] The ECCC Pre-Trial Chamber's conclusion was affirmed by the Trial Chamber.[52] 5.29

The requisite material elements of JCE are even more contentious. The comparative ease with which they are satisfied, particularly in the absence of any requirement that the accused's participation in the joint criminal enterprise have a substantial effect on the commission of the crime, leaves the doctrine—despite strenuous judicial assertions to the contrary[53]—looking only marginally better than guilt by association, causing it to be satirically labelled 'Just Convict Everyone'. This is especially so when JCE is applied to large-scale networks of loosely connected individuals, a practice upheld by the ICTY Appeals Chamber in *Brđanin* as not inappropriate.[54] The perceived permissiveness of the doctrine led to 5.30

Appeals Chamber, Interlocutory Decision on the Applicable Law: Terrorism, Conspiracy, Homicide, Perpetration, Cumulative Charging, 16 February 2011, paras 248–249.

[48] *Tadić*, Appeals Chamber Judgment (n 9), para 190.
[49] Criminal Case File No 002-19-09-2007-ECCC/OCIJ (PTC 35, 37, 38 & 39) (*Ieng Thirith* et al), Pre-Trial Chamber, Decision on the Appeals Against the Co-Investigative Judges' Order on Joint Criminal Enterprise (JCE), 20 May 2010, para 69.
[50] Ibid, para 77.   [51] Ibid, para 83.
[52] Case File/Dossier No 002/19-09-2007/ECCC/TC (*Nuon Chea* et al), Trial Chamber, Decision on the Applicability of Joint Criminal Enterprise, 12 September 2011, paras 29, 35, and 38.
[53] See eg *Brđanin*, Appeals Chamber Judgment (n 19), para 426; *Martić*, Appeals Chamber Judgment (n 33), para 172; *Sesay* et al, Appeals Chamber Judgment (n 18), para 317.
[54] *Brđanin*, Appeals Chamber Judgment (n 19), paras 424–425.

the emergence in at least the ICTY of a prosecutorial practice of pleading JCE in cases where other modes of responsibility, such as planning, instigating, ordering, aiding and abetting, or even command or other superior responsibility, might have been more appropriate. The issue in all of this is less whether individuals should be held responsible at all on the basis of JCE than whether they should be considered on this basis to have 'committed' the crime in question—that is, whether they should be criminally responsible as principals, as the doctrine of JCE developed by the ICTY, ICTR, and SCSL would have it, or whether accessorial liability and its attendant lesser penalty would be a fairer reflection of their moral culpability. The latter is the approach taken in those municipal legal systems that recognize a cognate doctrine.

5.31   Judge Schomburg, a trenchant critic of the concept of joint criminal enterprise as developed by the ICTY and ICTR, argued during his time at the Tribunals for the distinct concepts, derived from German criminal-law theory, of 'co-perpetration' and 'indirect perpetration'.[55] But, regardless of the theoretical merits or otherwise of Judge Schomburg's approach, neither Appeals Chamber had or has any intention of overturning its jurisprudence on point. Indeed, the ICTY Appeals Chamber held in *Stakić* that co-perpetration found no support in customary international law.[56]

5.32   It is worth noting, however, subsequent developments at the ICTR. In *Gacumbitsi*, a majority of the ICTR Appeals Chamber held in the context of mass killings amounting to genocide that the notion of commission was not limited to the act of killing—that is, to direct and physical perpetration of the crime—but could encompass other acts of direct participation, including the acts of the accused in that case, who had been present at the crime scene to direct and supervise the massacre and who had personally directed the Hutu and Tutsi refugees to separate so that the latter could be killed.[57] The accused's contribution went beyond ordering or instigating, being 'as much an integral part of the genocide as were the killings which it enabled'. The reasoning in *Gacumbitsi* was reiterated by the Appeals Chamber in *Seromba*,[58] in which the accused's actions in approving a decision to destroy a church full of people, in confirming to the bulldozer's driver that the church should be destroyed, and in advising the driver

---

[55] See *Prosecutor v Stakić*, IT-97-24-T, Trial Chamber, Judgment, 31 July 2003, paras 438–442; *Prosecutor v Simić*, IT-95-9-A, Appeals Chamber, Judgment, 28 November 2006, diss op Schomberg, paras 12–23; *Prosecutor v Gacumbitsi*, ICTR-2001-64-A, Appeals Chamber, Judgment, 7 July 2006, sep op Schomburg, paras 16–23; *Martić*, Appeals Chamber Judgment (n 33), sep op Schomburg.

[56] *Stakić*, Appeals Chamber Judgment (n 14), para 62. See, similarly, *Prosecutor v Milutinović* et al, IT-05-87-PT, Trial Chamber, Decision on Ojdanić's Motion Challenging Jurisdiction: Indirect Co-perpetration, 22 March 2006, para 40, referring to both co-perpetration and indirect co-perpetration. Note that while the term 'co-perpetration' is found in *Tadić*, Appeals Chamber Judgment (n 14) and subsequent cases, it is used there to refer to responsibility on the basis of JCE.

[57] *Gacumbitsi*, Appeals Chamber Judgment (n 55), paras 60–61.

[58] *Prosecutor v Seromba*, ICTR-2001-66-A, Appeals Chamber, Judgment, 12 March 2008, paras 161 and 171–172. See also *Prosecutor v Kalimanzira*, ICTR-05-98-A, Appeals Chamber, Judgment, 20 October 2010, para 219; *Munyakazi*, Appeals Chamber Judgment (n 25), paras 135–136. In addition, the decision in *Gacumbitsi* was extended in *Seromba*, Appeals Chamber Judgment (n 58), para 190, to the crime against humanity of extermination.

as to the fragile side of the church amounted to committing, rather than aiding and abetting, genocide. It is not easy to discern the difference between this extended notion of commission and the concepts of co-perpetration and indirect perpetration.

D. Co-Perpetration, Indirect Perpetration, and Indirect Co-Perpetration before the ICC

Article 25(3)(*a*) of the Rome Statute specifies that criminal responsibility arises where the accused commits a crime 'whether as an individual, jointly with another or through another person, regardless of whether that other person is criminally responsible'. Out of these words the various Pre-Trial and Trial Chambers—while rejecting the doctrine of joint criminal enterprise applied by the ICTY, ICTR, and SCSL, at least insofar as this treats JCE as a form of commission[59]—have fashioned sub-modes of criminal responsibility as complicated and almost as controversial as JCE. These various species of commission, or 'perpetration', reflect the same German criminal-law theory and terminology as that relied on by Judge Schomburg in the ICTY and ICTR.[60] As for the vocabulary of 'perpetration', what article 25(3)(*a*) of the Rome Statute describes as commission jointly with another person is known as 'co-perpetration' and sometimes 'direct co-perpetration'; commission through another person is labelled 'indirect perpetration'; and commission jointly with another person and through another person is referred to as 'indirect co-perpetration'.   5.33

(i) Co-perpetration

In its basic form, commission of a crime jointly with another is straightforward. Where more than one person machine-guns down or thrusts the knife into or beats and robs the victim, both or all are held criminally responsible as principals for the offence—that is, for each committing all of the material elements of the crime with the requisite intent and knowledge.   5.34

The ICC, however, has gone further to apply the idea of commission 'jointly with another' to more complex criminal enterprises. At the same time, when faced with an individual acting in furtherance of a common plan to commit or involving the commission of crimes within the ICC's jurisdiction, the various Pre-Trial and Trial Chambers have declined to impose criminal responsibility under article 25(3)(*a*) of the Rome Statute—that is, criminal responsibility for commission or, synonymously, as principal—for any contribution to the furtherance of the common plan deemed significant, as would be the case under JCE. The Pre-Trial and Trial Chambers have preferred instead a model of 'co-perpetration' based on   5.35

---

[59] Cf, on the other hand, criminal responsibility under Rome Statute, art 25(3)(*d*), for contributing to the commission or attempted commission of a crime by a group of persons acting with a common purpose.

[60] Recall *supra* para 5.31.

'joint control over the crime by reason of the essential nature of the various contributions to the commission of the crime'.[61] The essence of this approach is that the accused will be held responsible for commission of the crime only if the task assigned to and performed by him or her in furtherance of the common plan was essential to the commission of the crime—that is, if the accused had the power to frustrate the commission of the crime by not performing the task assigned to him or her.[62]

(a) **Material elements**

5.36 Criminal responsibility on the basis of co-perpetration as understood by the ICC requires the existence of an agreement or common plan between two or more persons[63] which, if implemented, will result in the commission of a crime.[64] The agreement need not be explicit but may instead be inferred from circumstantial evidence.[65] Nor need it be 'specifically directed at the commission of a crime',[66] either in its objective or in its execution, although it must, at a minimum, include 'a critical element of criminality', in the sense that 'its implementation embodies a sufficient risk that, in the ordinary course of events, a crime will be committed'.[67]

5.37 Individuals may be held criminally responsible on the basis of co-perpetration only if the task or tasks assigned to them or assumed by them in furtherance of the

---

[61] *Prosecutor v Lubanga*, ICC-01/04-01/06-803-tEN, Pre-Trial Chamber, Decision on the Confirmation of Charges, 29 January 2007, para 341; *Prosecutor v Katanga and Ngudjolo*, ICC-01/04-01/07-717, Pre-Trial Chamber, Decision on the Confirmation of the Charges, 30 September 2008, para 488. See also *Prosecutor v Al Bashir*, ICC-02/05-01/09-3, Pre-Trial Chamber, Decision on the Prosecution's Application for a Warrant of Arrest against Omar Hassan Ahmad Al Bashir, 4 March 2009, para 210; *Prosecutor v Bemba*, ICC-01/05-01/08-424, Pre-Trial Chamber, Decision pursuant to Article 61(7)(a) and (b) of the Rome Statute on the Charges of the Prosecutor against Jean-Pierre Bemba Gombo, 15 June 2009, paras 347–348; *Prosecutor v Abu Garda*, ICC-02/05-02/09-243-Red, Pre-Trial Chamber, Decision on the Confirmation of Charges, 8 February 2010, para 153; *Prosecutor v Banda and Jerbo*, ICC-02/05-03/09-121-Corr-Red, Pre-Trial Chamber, Corrigendum of [sic] the 'Decision on the Confirmation of Charges', 7 March 2011, para 126.
[62] See *infra* para 5.37.
[63] *Lubanga*, Trial Chamber Judgment (n 5), paras 981 and 1018; *Lubanga*, Pre-Trial Chamber Decision on Confirmation of Charges (n 61), para 343; *Katanga and Ngudjolo*, Pre-Trial Chamber Decision on Confirmation of Charges (n 61), para 522; *Bemba*, Pre-Trial Chamber Decision on Charges (n 61), para 350; *Prosecutor v Muthaura* et al, ICC-01/09-02/11-382-Red, Pre-Trial Chamber, Decision on the Confirmation of Charges pursuant to Article 61(7)(a) and (b) of the Rome Statute, 23 January 2012, para 297; *Prosecutor v Ruto* et al, ICC-01/09-01/11-373, Pre-Trial Chamber, Decision on the Confirmation of Charges Pursuant to Article 61(7)(a) and (b) of the Rome Statute, 23 January 2012, para 292; *Prosecutor v Mudacumura*, ICC-01/04-01/12-1-Red, Pre-Trial Chamber, Decision on the Prosecutor's Application under Article 58, 13 July 2012, para 60; *Prosecutor v Ntaganda*, ICC-01/04-02/06-309, Pre-Trial Chamber, Decision Pursuant to Article 61(7)(a) and (b) of the Rome Statute on the Charges of the Prosecutor Against Bosco Ntaganda, 9 June 2014, para 104.
[64] *Lubanga*, Trial Chamber Judgment (n 5), paras 1006 and 1018.
[65] Ibid, para 988; *Lubanga*, Pre-Trial Chamber Decision on Confirmation of Charges (n 61), para 345; *Katanga and Ngudjolo*, Pre-Trial Chamber Decision on Confirmation of Charges (n 61), para 523.
[66] *Lubanga*, Trial Chamber Judgment (n 7), para 984; *Lubanga*, Pre-Trial Chamber Decision on Confirmation of Charges (n 61), para 344.
[67] *Lubanga*, Trial Chamber Judgment (n 7), para 987. See also ibid, para 984.

common plan are 'essential' to the commission of the crime[68]—in other words, only if these individuals 'have the power to frustrate the commission of the crime by not performing their tasks'.[69] This is the gist of co-perpetration as opposed to JCE, based as the former is on joint control over the crime. What is required is that the accused 'provided an essential contribution to the common plan that resulted in the commission of the relevant crime'.[70]

Criminal responsibility on the basis of co-perpetration is 'not limited to those who physically carry out the objective [*viz* material] elements of the offence, but also include(s) those who, in spite of being removed from the scene of the crime, control or mastermind its commission because they decide whether and how the offence will be committed'.[71] That is, the accused need not commit any of the material elements of the offence or be present at the scene of the crime to be held responsible as co-perpetrator.[72] 5.38

(b) Mental elements

To be criminally responsible on the basis of co-perpetration, a form of commission, the accused must satisfy the definitional mental elements of the crime for which he or she is tried.[73] That is, except where otherwise provided, he or she must engage in the relevant conduct with intent and knowledge, as defined in article 30(2) and (3) of the Rome Statute.[74] This signifies that the accused must mean the 5.39

---

[68] Ibid, paras 999–1000, 1006, and 1018; *Lubanga*, Pre-Trial Chamber Decision on Confirmation of Charges (n 61), para 347; *Katanga and Ngudjolo*, Pre-Trial Chamber Decision on Confirmation of Charges (n 61), paras 524–526; *Bemba*, Pre-Trial Chamber Decision on Charges (n 61), para 350; *Banda and Jerbo*, Pre-Trial Chamber Corrigendum of [*sic*] Decision on Confirmation of Charges (n 61), para 136; *Abu Garda*, Pre-Trial Chamber Decision on Confirmation of Charges (n 61), para 153; *Ruto* et al, Pre-Trial Chamber Decision on Confirmation of Charges (n 63), para 292; *Muthaura* et al, Pre-Trial Chamber Decision on Confirmation of Charges (n 63), paras 297 and 401; *Ntaganda*, Pre-Trial Chamber Decision on Charges of Prosecutor (n 63), para 104.

[69] *Lubanga*, Pre-Trial Chamber Decision on Confirmation of Charges (n 61), para 347; *Katanga and Ngudjolo*, Pre-Trial Chamber Decision on Confirmation of Charges (n 61), para 525; *Banda and Jerbo*, Pre-Trial Chamber Corrigendum of [*sic*] Decision on Confirmation of Charges (n 61), para 136.

[70] *Lubanga*, Trial Chamber Judgment (n 7), para 1006.

[71] Ibid, para 1003; *Katanga*, Trial Chamber Judgment (n 5), para 1393. *Lubanga*, Pre-Trial Chamber Decision on Confirmation of Charges (n 61), para 330; *Katanga and Ngudjolo*, Pre-Trial Chamber Decision on Confirmation of Charges (n 61), para 485; *Abu Garda*, Pre-Trial Chamber Decision on Confirmation of Charges (n 61), para 152.

[72] *Lubanga*, Trial Chamber Judgment (n 7), paras 1003 and 1005. See also ibid, para 1004, emphasis omitted: 'Those who commit a crime jointly include, *inter alia*, those who assist in formulating the relevant strategy or plan, become involved in directing or controlling other participants or determine the roles of those involved in the offence. This conclusion makes it unnecessary for the prosecution to establish a direct or physical link between the accused's contribution and the commission of the crimes.'

[73] *Lubanga*, Pre-Trial Chamber Decision on Confirmation of Charges (n 61), para 349; *Katanga and Ngudjolo*, Pre-Trial Chamber Decision on Confirmation of Charges (n 61), para 527; *Bemba*, Pre-Trial Chamber Decision on Charges (n 61), para 351; *Banda and Jerbo*, Pre-Trial Chamber Corrigendum of [*sic*] Decision on Confirmation of Charges (n 61), paras 150–151; *Muthaura* et al, Pre-Trial Chamber Decision on Confirmation of Charges (n 63), para 297; *Ruto* et al, Pre-Trial Chamber Decision on Confirmation of Charges (n 63), para 333; *Ntaganda*, Pre-Trial Chamber Decision on Charges of Prosecutor (n 63), para 121.

[74] Recall *supra* para 5.10.

crime to occur as a consequence of the implementation of the common plan or must be aware that it will occur in the ordinary course of events.[75] In contrast to the position under JCE III, criminal responsibility for co-perpetration cannot arise merely on the basis of willingly taking the risk that a crime will occur (that is, on the basis of *dolus eventualis*).[76]

5.40   In addition, the accused must be aware that he or she is making an essential contribution to the implementation of the common plan.[77]

5.41   Although several Pre-Trial Chambers have specified a further mental element, namely that the accused and the other co-perpetrators 'must all be mutually aware of the risk that implementing their common plan may result in the realisation of the objective [*viz* material] elements of the crime' and 'must all mutually accept such a result',[78] this element has not been picked up by a Trial Chamber to date, making its status uncertain.

(ii) Indirect perpetration

5.42   Article 25(3)(*a*) speaks also of commission of a crime 'through another person, regardless of whether that other person is criminally responsible'. The ICC refers in this context to 'indirect perpetration', a doctrine of criminal responsibility on the basis of commission—that is, responsibility as principal—which, like its 'direct' counterpart, is founded on the notion of control over the crime.[79] The gist of criminal responsibility on the basis of indirect perpetration is that an individual may be held responsible for the commission of a crime physically perpetrated by another or others—that is, may be held responsible as principal—if he or she has the power to decide if and how the crime is committed.[80]

5.43   To be held criminally responsible on the basis of indirect perpetration for committing a crime whose material elements are performed by another or others, the

---

[75] *Lubanga*, Trial Chamber Judgment (n 7), paras 1011, 1013, and 1018; *Bemba*, Pre-Trial Chamber Decision on Charges (n 61), paras 356–359 and 369; *Banda and Jerbo*, Pre-Trial Chamber Corrigendum of [*sic*] Decision on Confirmation of Charges (n 61), para 153.

[76] *Lubanga*, Trial Chamber Judgment (n 7), para 1011; *Lubanga*, Pre-Trial Chamber Decision on Confirmation of Charges (n 61), paras 364–369; *Bemba*, Pre-Trial Chamber Decision on Charges (n 61), paras 360 and 369; *Ruto* et al, Pre-Trial Chamber Decision on Confirmation of Charges (n 63), para 336.

[77] *Lubanga*, Trial Chamber Judgment (n 7), paras 1013 and 1018; *Lubanga*, Pre-Trial Chamber Decision on Confirmation of Charges (n 61), para 367; *Katanga and Ngudjolo*, Pre-Trial Chamber Decision on Confirmation of Charges (n 61), paras 538; *Bemba*, Pre-Trial Chamber Decision on Charges (n 61), paras 351 and 371; *Banda and Jerbo*, Pre-Trial Chamber Corrigendum of [*sic*] Decision on Confirmation of Charges (n 61), para 160; *Muthaura* et al, Pre-Trial Chamber Decision on Confirmation of Charges (n 63), paras 297; *Ruto* et al, Pre-Trial Chamber Decision on Confirmation of Charges (n 63), para 333; *Ntaganda*, Pre-Trial Chamber Decision on Charges of Prosecutor (n 63), para 104.

[78] *Lubanga*, Pre-Trial Chamber Decision on Confirmation of Charges (n 61), para 361. See also subsequent Pre-Trial Chamber decisions.

[79] See *Katanga*, Trial Chamber Judgment (n 7), paras 1396 and 1399; *Katanga and Ngudjolo*, Pre-Trial Chamber Decision on Confirmation of Charges (n 61), paras 486 and 494.

[80] *Katanga*, Trial Chamber Judgment (n 7), para 1396; *Katanga and Ngudjolo*, Pre-Trial Chamber Decision on Confirmation of Charges (n 61), para 518.

accused must exercise control over the crime.[81] There is a number of ways in which such control might be exercised, and whether such control is exercised is always a question of fact to be determined on a case-by-case basis.[82]

5.44 The classic case of indirect perpetration is where one person controls the will of another,[83] reducing the second to an instrument of his or her own will, and uses that other to commit the material elements of the crime. This may occur where the first brings to bear on the second what amounts in law to duress in order to force that other to commit a crime.[84] In such a case, the first person may be held responsible for the crime as principal—that is, for committing the crime, rather for instigating, soliciting, inducing or ordering the crime or on the basis of some other form of accessorial responsibility.[85]

5.45 In a bold move, the ICC has further held that an accused may be considered to exercise control over a crime physically perpetrated by others where he or she occupies a position at the head of an 'organized and hierarchical power structure'[86] whereby those at the top can be guaranteed that an order from them to commit the material elements of the crime will be carried out.[87] In such a situation, control over the organization can be equated with control over crimes physically perpetrated by its members.[88] A precondition to criminal responsibility on the basis of indirect perpetration via control over an organization is what has been referred to as 'functional automatism',[89] meaning that the organization must be one in which the orders of its superiors are automatically carried out, if necessary by substituting personnel who refuse to comply with those who will.[90] In other words, the nature and structural dynamic of the organization must guarantee, independently of the identity of the organization's members, the control exercised by its superiors over the crime.[91] But while the existence of such an organization is a precondition, it is

---

[81] *Katanga*, Trial Chamber Judgment (n 7), para 1399; *Bemba*, Pre-Trial Chamber Decision on Charges (n 61), para 347; *Muthaura* et al, Pre-Trial Chamber Decision on Confirmation of Charges (n 63), para 296.

[82] *Katanga*, Trial Chamber Judgment (n 7), paras 1401 and 1406.

[83] See ibid, para 1401; *Lubanga*, Pre-Trial Chamber Decision on Confirmation of Charges (n 61), para 332; *Katanga and Ngudjolo*, Pre-Trial Chamber Decision on Confirmation of Charges (n 61), paras 488 and 495–499; *Abu Garda*, Pre-Trial Chamber Decision on Confirmation of Charges (n 61), para 153.

[84] For the defence of duress under customary international law, see *infra* paras 6.20–6.23.

[85] See eg *Katanga*, Trial Chamber Judgment (n 7), para 1402; *Katanga and Ngudjolo*, Pre-Trial Chamber Decision on Confirmation of Charges (n 61), paras 495 and 498.

[86] *Katanga*, Trial Chamber Judgment (n 7), para 1410. See also *Muthaura* et al, Pre-Trial Chamber Decision on Confirmation of Charges (n 63), para 297; *Ruto* et al, Pre-Trial Chamber Decision on Confirmation of Charges (n 63), para 292; *Ntaganda*, Pre-Trial Chamber Decision on Charges of Prosecutor (n 63), para 104.

[87] See *Katanga*, Trial Chamber Judgment (n 7), paras 1403–1412; *Katanga and Ngudjolo*, Pre-Trial Chamber Decision on Confirmation of Charges (n 61), paras 498–510. As acknowledged by the Trial Chamber, ibid, para 1404, this theory of indirect perpetration on the basis of organizational control ('*Organisationsherrschaft*') is drawn from the writings of the German penal theorist Claus Roxin.

[88] *Katanga*, Trial Chamber Judgment (n 7), para 1405.   [89] Ibid, para 1408.

[90] Ibid; *Katanga and Ngudjolo*, Pre-Trial Chamber Decision on Confirmation of Charges (n 6), para 512; *Muthaura* et al, Pre-Trial Chamber Decision on Confirmation of Charges (n 63), para 297; *Ruto* et al, Pre-Trial Chamber Decision on Confirmation of Charges (n 63), para 292; *Ntaganda*, Pre-Trial Chamber Decision on Charges of Prosecutor (n 63), para 104.

[91] *Katanga*, Trial Chamber Judgment (n 7), para 1409. As explained ibid, para 1410, the standard of proof demanded in this regard is especially demanding. In *Al Bashir*, Pre-Trial Chamber Decision

also necessary for the accused actually to exercise such control, meaning that he or she must direct at least a part of the organization to commit the material elements of the crime, not leaving it to a subordinate to decide whether or not to execute the directive.[92]

(iii) Indirect co-perpetration

5.46 According to the ICC, co-perpetration and indirect perpetration can be combined to give 'indirect co-perpetration'. Indirect co-perpetration is where one of the persons party to an agreement or common plan, having control over the crime by virtue of the assignment or undertaking of an essential task, performs that essential task through another person whose will he or she controls or through an organization that he or she controls.[93] The Court has held that, although article 25(3)(*a*) of the Rome Statute speaks disjunctively of commission 'jointly with another or through another person', the disjunctive here is a 'weak or inclusive' one, which can be taken to mean 'either the one or the other, and possibly both'.[94]

(iv) Reception

5.47 Not all of the judges at the ICC have rushed to embrace the 'control over the crime' approach to article 25(3)(*a*) of the Rome Statute, while the more specific doctrines of indirect perpetration through control over an organization and of indirect co-perpetration have met with even stronger judicial reservations. In the *Lubanga* trial Judge Fulford firmly distanced himself from both the broad approach and the specific doctrines, while Judge Van den Wyngaert did the same in the *Ngudjolo* trial,[95] for a variety of reasons including an insistence on orthodox principles of treaty interpretation, a resistance to the transplantation of a

---

on Arrest Warrant (n 61), para 216, the Pre-Trial Chamber found 'reasonable grounds to believe that Omar Al Bashir and the other high-ranking Sudanese political and military leaders directed the branches of the "apparatus" of the State of Sudan that they led, in a coordinated manner, in order to jointly implement the common plan'. In other words, the Pre-Trial Chamber applied the concept of indirect perpetration through control over an organization to the 'organization' represented by 'the "apparatus" of the State of Sudan'—a strikingly permissive approach to the structural dynamics of the relevant organization.

[92] *Katanga*, Trial Chamber Judgment (n 7), paras 1411–1412. See also *Katanga and Ngudjolo*, Pre-Trial Chamber Decision on Confirmation of Charges (n 61), para 514–518; *Muthaura* et al, Pre-Trial Chamber Decision on Confirmation of Charges (n 63), para 297; *Ruto* et al, Pre-Trial Chamber Decision on Confirmation of Charges (n 63), para 292; *Ntaganda*, Pre-Trial Chamber Decision on Charges of Prosecutor (n 63), para 104.
[93] See *Katanga and Ngudjolo*, Pre-Trial Chamber Decision on Confirmation of Charges (n 61), paras 491–493; *Al Bashir*, Pre-Trial Chamber Decision on Arrest Warrant (n 61), para 213; *Abu Garda*, Pre-Trial Chamber Decision on Confirmation of Charges (n 61), para 154.
[94] *Katanga and Ngudjolo*, Pre-Trial Chamber Decision on Confirmation of Charges (n 61), para 491, emphasis omitted; *Abu Garda*, Pre-Trial Chamber Decision on Confirmation of Charges (n 61), para 156.
[95] See *Lubanga*, Trial Chamber Judgment (n 7), sep op Fulford, and *Ngudjolo*, Trial Chamber Judgment (n 7), conc op Van den Wyngaert, respectively.

model of criminal responsibility derived from the criminal justice tradition of a single state, and criticism of the perceived elision of an essential contribution to the implementation of the common plan and an essential contribution to the commission of the crime.

It remains to be seen what the ICC Appeals Chamber makes of the 'control over the crime' theory and its various permutations. It is too early at present to suggest that what the Pre-Trial Chambers and Trial Chambers have done to date with article 25(3)(*a*) of the Rome Statute is how the Court will continue to apply the provision, and it would be ludicrous to claim that their approach currently represents customary international law. 5.48

IV. Planning

ICTY Statute, article 7(1), ICTR Statute, article 6(1), and SCSL Statute, article 6(1) all provide that a person who plans a crime referred to in the relevant statute shall be criminally responsible for that crime. The concept of planning a crime is not included *eo nomine* in article 23(3) of the Rome Statute, the provision on principles of criminal responsibility, although it is possible that cognate notions could be considered under subparagraphs (*c*) and especially (*d*) of the article. 5.49

As regards the crime of aggression, planning an act of aggression which constitutes a manifest violation of the UN Charter is a form of commission. That is, it is one of the ways of committing the crime specified in the definitional material elements themselves,[96] rather than an accessorial mode of responsibility. It does not, as such, represent criminal responsibility under the mode of responsibility known as 'planning'.[97] It remains to be seen, however, whether recourse is had to the jurisprudence on planning as an accessorial mode of responsibility in the adjudication of planning as commission of the crime of aggression. 5.50

A. Material Elements

The *actus reus* of 'planning' requires that 'one or more persons design the criminal conduct constituting one or more...crimes that are later perpetrated'.[98] The accused need not be the originator of the plan.[99] 'Planning' a crime does not mean 5.51

---

[96] Recall *supra* paras 4.94–4.95.
[97] See *infra* para 5.101 for more on the modes of responsibility for the crime aggression.
[98] *Prosecutor v Kordić and Čerkez*, IT-95-14/2-A, Appeals Chamber, Judgment, 17 December 2004, para 26. See also *Prosecutor v Milošević (Dragomir)*, IT-98-29/1-A, Appeals Chamber, Judgment, 12 November 2009, para 268; *Prosecutor v Nahimana* et al, ICTR-99-52-A, Appeals Chamber, Judgment, 28 November 2007, para 479; *Brima* et al, Appeals Chamber Judgment (n 18), para 301; *Taylor*, Appeals Chamber Judgment (n 3), para 494. It is not necessary that the accused be physically present at the scene of the crime, as stated for the avoidance of doubt in *Prosecutor v Boškoski and Tarčulovski*, IT-04-82-A, Appeals Chamber, Judgment, 19 May 2010, para 125.
[99] *Boškoski and Tarčulovski*, Appeals Chamber Judgment (n 98), para 154 n 418; *Taylor*, Appeals Chamber Judgment (n 3), para 494.

that the crime need be the objective of the envisaged acts or omissions; rather, it is sufficient that the accused planned for the crime to be perpetrated in the execution of any relevant objective.[100]

5.52 In the specific context of crimes against humanity, which must be committed as part of a widespread or systematic attack, culpable planning may occur prior to the commencement of the attack.[101]

5.53 As to causation, '[i]t is sufficient to demonstrate that the planning was a factor substantially contributing to [the] criminal conduct'.[102]

B. Mental Elements

5.54 The *mens rea* for criminal responsibility on the basis of planning is direct intent to plan the commission of the crime[103] or awareness of the substantial likelihood that a crime will be committed in the execution of the plan.[104]

V. Instigation

5.55 ICTY Statute, article 7(1), ICTR Statute, article 6(1), and SCSL Statute, article 6(1) each provide that a person who instigates a crime referred to in the relevant statute shall be criminally responsible for that crime. As with planning, instigation is not mentioned as such in article 25(3) of the Rome Statute, although arguably cognate concepts are found in subparagraph (*b*) of the provision.[105]

---

[100] *Taylor*, Appeals Chamber Judgment (n 3), para 494 n 1478.
[101] *Nahimana* et al, Appeals Chamber Judgment (n 98), para 934.
[102] *Kordić and Čerkez*, Appeals Chamber Judgment (n 98), para 26, citations omitted. See also *Krajišnik*, Appeals Chamber Judgment (n 18), para 662; *Brima* et al, Appeals Chamber Judgment (n 18), para 301; *Nahimana* et al, Appeals Chamber Judgment (n 98), paras 479 and 492; *Sesay* et al, Appeals Chamber Judgment (n 18), para 687. The French version of the judgment uses the expression 'un élément determinant', but the English version uses the phrase 'factor substantially contributing to', and it is the English version that is authoritative, as explained in *Nahimana* et al, Appeals Chamber Judgment (n 98), para 479 n 1157.
[103] *Kordić and Čerkez*, Appeals Chamber Judgment (n 98), para 29; *Milošević (Dragomir)*, Appeals Chamber Judgment (n 98), para 268; *Boškoski and Tarčulovski*, Appeals Chamber Judgment (n 98), para 68; *Krajišnik*, Appeals Chamber Judgment (n 18), para 662; *Nahimana* et al, Appeals Chamber Judgment (n 98), para 479; *Brima* et al, Appeals Chamber Judgment (n 18), para 301; *Taylor*, Appeals Chamber Judgment (n 3), para 494.
[104] *Kordić and Čerkez*, Appeals Chamber Judgment (n 98), para 31; *Milošević (Dragomir)*, Appeals Chamber Judgment (n 98), para 268; *Boškoski and Tarčulovski*, Appeals Chamber Judgment (n 98), paras 68 and 174; *Krajišnik*, Appeals Chamber Judgment (n 18), para 662; *Nahimana* et al, Appeals Chamber Judgment (n 98), para 479; *Brima* et al, Appeals Chamber Judgment (n 18), para 301; *Taylor*, Appeals Chamber Judgment (n 3), para 494.
[105] See, in this regard, *Ntaganda*, Pre-Trial Chamber Decision on Charges of Prosecutor (n 63), para 153 n 625, citing ICTY case law on instigation by way of elaboration of the concept of 'inducing' a crime found in Rome Statute, art 25(3)(*b*); *Prosecutor v Gbagbo*, ICC-02/11-01/11-656-Red, Pre-Trial Chamber, Decision on the Confirmation of Charges against Laurent Gbagbo, 12 June 2014, para 243, treating the modes of responsibility in Rome Statute, art 25(3)(*b*), as forms of instigation.

A. Material Elements

'Instigation', as a mode of criminal responsibility, means 'to prompt another person to commit an offence'.[106] It is not necessary that the accused be physically present at the scene of the crime.[107] 5.56

It has been held that instigation by omission is possible.[108] The suggestion does not seem to accord with the ordinary meaning of the term. 5.57

As with planning a crime against humanity, acts of instigation of a crime against humanity may occur before the commencement of the widespread or systematic attack.[109] 5.58

In terms of causation, it is not necessary to prove that the crime would not have been perpetrated without the involvement of the accused; rather, as with planning, it is sufficient to demonstrate that the instigation was a factor substantially contributing to the conduct of the person who committed the crime.[110] 5.59

B. Mental Elements

The *mens rea* for responsibility on the basis of instigation is direct intent to instigate the commission of the crime[111] or awareness of the substantial likelihood that a crime will be committed in the execution of what is instigated.[112] 5.60

---

[106] *Kordić and Čerkez*, Appeals Chamber Judgment (n 98), para 27; *Prosecutor v Ndindabahizi*, ICTR-01-71-A, Appeals Chamber, Judgment, 16 January 2007, para 117; *Nahimana* et al, Appeals Chamber Judgment (n 98), para 480; *Prosecutor v Karera*, ICTR-01-74-A, Appeals Chamber, Judgment, 2 February 2009, para 317; *Prosecutor v Nchamihigo*, ICTR-2001-63-A, Appeals Chamber, Judgment, 18 March 2010, paras 188 and 230.

[107] *Boškoski and Tarčulovski*, Appeals Chamber Judgment (n 98), para 125; *Nahimana* et al, Appeals Chamber Judgment (n 98), para 660.

[108] See *Nahimana* et al, Appeals Chamber Judgment (n 3), para 589, as implicitly upholding *Prosecutor v Taylor*, SCSL-03-01-T, Trial Chamber, Judgment, 18 May 2012, para 472. See also *Prosecutor v Blaškić*, IT-95-14-T, Trial Chamber, Judgment, 3 March 2000, paras 280 and 337; *Prosecutor v Galić*, IT-98-29-T, Trial Chamber, Judgment, 5 December 2003, para 168; *Prosecutor v Brđanin*, IT-99-36-T, Trial Chamber, Judgment, 1 September 2004, para 269.

[109] *Nahimana* et al, Appeals Chamber Judgment (n 98), para 934.

[110] *Kordić and Čerkez*, Appeals Chamber Judgment (n 98), para 27; *Krajišnik*, Appeals Chamber Judgment (n 18), para 662; *Ndindabahizi*, Appeals Chamber Judgment (n 106), para 117; *Gacumbitsi*, Appeals Chamber Judgment (n 55), paras 107 and 129; *Nahimana* et al, Appeals Chamber Judgment (n 98), paras 480, 502, 660, and 678; *Karera*, Appeals Chamber Judgment (n 106), para 317; *Nchamihigo*, Appeals Chamber Judgment (n 106), paras 118 and 230; *Prosecutor v Fofana and Kondewa*, SCSL-04-14-A, Appeals Chamber, Judgment, 28 May 2008, paras 52 and 84 ('substantial effect'); *Taylor*, Appeals Chamber Judgment (n 3), para 589 ('substantial effect'). As made clear *ex abundante cautela* in *Ndindabahizi*, Appeals Chamber Judgment (n 106), para 117, instigation is not an inchoate crime; rather, it requires that the crime instigated take place. At the same time, criminal responsibility on the basis of instigation does not require that the specific principal perpetrators be identified. See *Karera*, Appeals Chamber Judgment (n 106), para 318; *Nchamihigo*, Appeals Chamber Judgment (n 106), para 230; *Boškoski and Tarčulovski*, Appeals Chamber Judgment (n 98), para 75.

[111] *Kordić and Čerkez*, Appeals Chamber Judgment (n 98), para 29; *Boškoski and Tarčulovski*, Appeals Chamber Judgment (n 98), para 68; *Nahimana* et al, Appeals Chamber Judgment (n 98), para 480; *Nchamihigo*, Appeals Chamber Judgment (n 106), para 61; *Taylor*, Appeals Chamber Judgment (n 3), para 589.

[112] *Kordić and Čerkez*, Appeals Chamber Judgment (n 98), para 32; *Boškoski and Tarčulovski*, Appeals Chamber Judgment (n 98), paras 68 and 174; *Nahimana* et al, Appeals Chamber Judgment

5.61   It has been held that, where the crime instigated is genocide, criminal responsibility on the basis of instigation requires that the instigator have the specific intent to destroy the relevant group as such in whole or in part.¹¹³

VI. Ordering

5.62   The respective statutes of the ICTY, ICTR, SCSL, and ICC recognize criminal responsibility for ordering the commission of a crime.¹¹⁴ Criminal responsibility for ordering the commission of a crime is to be distinguished from criminal responsibility under the doctrine of command and other superior responsibility.¹¹⁵

A. Material Elements

5.63   Ordering the commission of a crime means that 'a person in a position of *de jure* or *de facto* authority instructs another person to commit [the] crime'.¹¹⁶ A formal

---

(n 98), para 480; *Nchamihigo*, Appeals Chamber Judgment (n 106), para 61; *Taylor*, Appeals Chamber Judgment (n 3), para 589 ('awareness of a substantial likelihood that his acts would have an effect on the commission of the crime').

¹¹³ *Nchamihigo*, Appeals Chamber Judgment (n 106), para 61, citing *Seromba*, Appeals Chamber Judgment (n 58), para 175.

¹¹⁴ ICTY Statute, art 7(1); ICTR Statute, art 6(1); SCSL Statute, art 6(1); Rome Statute, art 25(3)(*b*). The last extends responsibility on this basis to ordering the commission of a crime which, in the event, is merely attempted.

¹¹⁵ For the latter, see ICTY Statute, art 7(3); ICTR Statute, art 6(3); SCSL Statute, art 6(3); Rome Statute, art 28. See also *infra* paras 5.102–5.118. The distinction between ordering and command responsibility, first drawn in the landmark case of *United States v Yamashita*, 13 ILR 255 (US Military Commission, Manila 1945), was emphasized in *Blaškić*, Appeals Chamber Judgment (n 17), paras 90–91; *Kordić and Čerkez*, Appeals Chamber Judgment (n 98), para 34; *Prosecutor v Kamuhanda*, ICTR-99-54A-A, Appeals Chamber, Judgment, 19 September 2005, para 75; *Seromba*, Appeals Chamber Judgment (n 58), para 201. Where responsibility is made out on the basis of both ordering and command or other superior responsibility, the ICTY and ICTR have held that a conviction should be entered under the former, with the accused's superior position being taken into account in sentencing as an aggravating factor. See, among many others, *Prosecutor v Aleksovski*, IT-95-14/1, Appeals Chamber, Judgment, 24 March 2000, para 183; *Prosecutor v Delalić et al* ('*Čelebići*'), IT-96-21, Appeals Chamber, Judgment, 20 February 2001 (subsequently styled '*Mucić* et al' on the acquittal of the accused Delalić), para 745; *Prosecutor v Kajelijeli*, ICTR-98-44A-A, Appeals Chamber, Judgment, 23 May 2005, para 82; *Nahimana* et al, Appeals Chamber Judgment (n 98), para 487.

¹¹⁶ *Milošević (Dragomir)*, Appeals Chamber Judgment (n 98), para 290. See also eg *Kordić and Čerkez*, Appeals Chamber Judgment (n 98), para 28; *Krajišnik*, Appeals Chamber Judgment (n 18), para 662; *Nahimana* et al, Appeals Chamber Judgment (n 98), para 481; *Karera*, Appeals Chamber Judgment (n 106), para 211; *Sesay* et al, Appeals Chamber Judgment (n 18), para 164. See, similarly, *Mudacumura*, Pre-Trial Chamber, Decision on Prosecutor's Application under Article 58 (n 63), para 63; *Ntaganda*, Pre-Trial Chamber on Charges of Prosecutor (n 63), para 145; *Gbagbo*, Pre-Trial Chamber on Confirmation of Charges (n 105), para 244. As indicated in *Prosecutor v Galić*, IT-98-29-A, Appeals Chamber, Judgment, 30 November 2006, para 176, an accused cannot be held criminally responsible on the basis of ordering for omitting to give an order. See also, again eg, *Milošević (Dragomir)*, Appeals Chamber Judgment (n 98), para 267; *Prosecutor v Bagosora and Nsengiyumva*, ICTR-98-41-A, Appeals Chamber, Judgment, 14 December 2011, para 277; *Sesay* et al, Appeals Chamber Judgment (n 18), para 164. On the other hand, it is possible for the superior to order an omission. See *Blaškić*, Appeals Chamber Judgment (n 17), para 42; *Kordić and Čerkez*, Appeals Chamber Judgment (n 98), para 30; *Nahimana* et al, Appeals Chamber Judgment (n 98),

superior–subordinate relationship between the accused and the person who commits the crime is unnecessary.[117] An informal relationship of even a temporary nature can suffice,[118] although where the relationship is informal there must be 'proof of a position of authority on the part of the accused that would compel another person to commit a crime' on the accused's order,[119] which by definition is a question of fact.[120] On the other hand, where a relationship of *de jure* authority does exist, it is not a condition of criminal responsibility on the basis of ordering a crime—in contrast to the situation as regards command and other superior responsibility—that the superior exert effective control over the subordinate.[121] Mere *de jure* authority can be sufficient. Nor is there any requirement that the order be given in writing or in any particular form[122] or that the accused be physically present at the scene of the crime.[123]

The accused need not give the order directly to the principal, *viz* the physical perpetrator.[124] Criminal responsibility on the basis of ordering a crime may arise where the accused issues, passes down or otherwise transmits the order.[125] In such a situation, provided the mental elements of the mode of responsibility are met, an intermediary who passes the order on down the chain of command to the physical perpetrator may also be held responsible for ordering the crime.[126]

5.64

---

para 481; *Karera*, Appeals Chamber Judgment (n 106), para 211; *Prosecutor v Renzaho*, ICTR-97-31-A, Appeals Chamber, Judgment, 1 April 2011, para 315; *Taylor*, Appeals Chamber Judgment (n 3), para 589.

[117] See eg *Kordić and Čerkez*, Appeals Chamber Judgment (n 98), para 28; *Galić*, Appeals Chamber Judgment (n 116), para 176; *Prosecutor v Semanza*, ICTR-97-20-A, Appeals Chamber, Judgment, 20 May 2005, para 361; *Kamuhanda*, Appeals Chamber Judgment (n 115), para 75; *Sesay* et al, Appeals Chamber Judgment (n 18), para 164.

[118] *Semanza*, Appeals Chamber Judgment (n 117), para 363; *Prosecutor v Setako*, ICTR-04-81-A, Appeals Chamber, Judgment, 28 September 2011, para 240.

[119] *Boškoski and Tarčulovski*, Appeals Chamber Judgment (n 98), para 164; *Semanza*, Appeals Chamber Judgment (n 117), para 361; *Karera*, Appeals Chamber Judgment (n 106), para 211.

[120] *Semanza*, Appeals Chamber Judgment (n 117), para 363; *Setako*, Appeals Chamber Judgment (n 118), para 240.

[121] *Seromba*, Appeals Chamber Judgment (n 58), para 202; *Kamuhanda*, Appeals Chamber Judgment (n 115), para 75.

[122] *Kamuhanda*, Appeals Chamber Judgment (n 115), para 76. As made clear ibid, the existence of an order may be proved by circumstantial evidence. See also *Boškoski and Tarčulovski*, Appeals Chamber Judgment (n 98), para 160; *Galić*, Appeals Chamber Judgment (n 116), paras 171 and 178; *Kamuhanda*, Appeals Chamber Judgment (n 115), para 76; *Prosecutor v Ndindiliyimana* et al, ICTR-00-56-A, Appeals Chamber, Judgment, 1 February 2014, para 291; *Sesay* et al, Appeals Chamber Judgment (n 18), para 164.

[123] *Milošević (Dragomir)*, Appeals Chamber Judgment (n 98), para 290; *Boškoski and Tarculovski*, Appeals Chamber Judgment (n 98), para 125.

[124] *Prosecutor v Kordić and Čerkez*, IT-95-14/2, Trial Chamber, Judgment, 26 February 2001, para 388; *Blaškić*, Trial Chamber Judgment (n 108), para 282; *Prosecutor v Taylor*, SCSL-03-01-T, Trial Chamber, Judgment, 18 May 2012, para 476, as upheld by implication in *Taylor*, Appeals Chamber Judgment (n 3), para 589.

[125] *Prosecutor v Milutinović* et al, IT-05-87-T, Trial Chamber, Judgment, 26 February 2009, vol 1, para 87; *Taylor*, Trial Chamber Judgment, (n 124), para 476, as upheld by implication in *Taylor*, Appeals Chamber Judgment (n 3), para 589.

[126] *Milutinović* et al, Trial Chamber Judgment (n 125), vol 1, para 87; *Taylor*, Trial Chamber Judgment (n 125), para 476, as upheld by implication in *Taylor*, Appeals Chamber Judgment (n 3), para 589.

5.65   When it comes to causation, the order must have a 'direct and substantial effect' on the commission of the crime.[127] Again, it is unnecessary to show that the crime would not have been committed but for the order.[128]

B. Mental Elements

5.66   The *mens rea* for responsibility on the basis of ordering is twofold, namely direct intent to order the commission of the crime[129] and either awareness of the substantial likelihood that a crime will be committed in the execution of the order, as per the ICTY and ICTR,[130] or awareness that a crime will occur in the ordinary course of events, as per the Rome Statute.[131]

VII. Soliciting or Inducing

5.67   Article 25(3)(*b*) of the Rome Statute speaks, in addition to ordering, of an accused who 'solicits or induces' the commission of a crime.[132] It has been held that the only difference between ordering, on the one hand, and soliciting and inducing, on the other, is that the latter does not require a relationship of authority.[133]

VIII. Aiding and Abetting

5.68   The ICTY, ICTR, SCSL, and ICC statutes respectively recognize criminal responsibility for aiding and abetting the commission of a crime.[134] The

---

[127] See eg *Kayishema and Ruzindana*, Appeals Chamber Judgment (n 17), para 186; *Kamuhanda*, Appeals Chamber Judgment (n 55), para 75. But cf, referring to 'a direct effect', *Mudacumura*, Pre-Trial Chamber, Decision on Prosecutor's Application under Article 58 (n 63), para 63; *Ntaganda*, Pre-Trial Chamber Decision on Charges of Prosecutor (n 63), para 145; *Gbagbo*, Pre-Trial Chamber Decision on Confirmation of Charges (n 105), para 244.
[128] *Prosecutor v Strugar*, IT-01-42-T, Trial Chamber, Judgment, 31 January 2005, para 332; *Milutinović* et al, Trial Chamber Judgment (n 125), vol 1, para 88; *Taylor*, Trial Chamber Judgment (n 124), para 477.
[129] *Kordić and Čerkez*, Appeals Chamber Judgment (n 98), para 29; *Prosecutor v Ntagerura* et al, ICTR-99-46-A, Appeals Chamber, Judgment, 7 July 2006, para 365.
[130] See eg *Blaškić*, Appeals Chamber Judgment (n 17), para 42; *Kordić and Čerkez*, Appeals Chamber Judgment (n 98), para 30; *Nahimana* et al, Appeals Chamber Judgment (n 98), para 481; *Karera*, Appeals Chamber Judgment (n 106), para 211.
[131] See Rome Statute, art 30(2)(*b*) and (3). See also *Ntaganda*, Pre-Trial Chamber Decision on Charges of Prosecutor (n 63), para 145; *Gbagbo*, Pre-Trial Chamber Decision on Confirmation of Charges (n 105), para 244.
[132] As with ordering, Rome Statute, art 25(3)(*b*) extends responsibility on this basis to soliciting or inducing the commission of a crime which, in the event, is merely attempted.
[133] *Gbagbo*, Pre-Trial Chamber Decision on Confirmation of Charges (n 105), para 243.
[134] Rome Statute, art 25(3)(*c*) speaks in more detail of an accused who, '[f]or the purpose of facilitating the commission of...a crime, aids, abets or otherwise assists in its commission or its attempted commission, including providing the means for its commission'.

elements of aiding and abetting have in recent years proved one of the more hotly debated if unlikely controversies regarding the modes of criminal responsibility under customary international law.

A. Material Elements

Aiding and abetting involves acts or omissions[135] which 'assist, encourage or lend moral support to' the crime's commission.[136] Tacit encouragement or approval of the crime can suffice.[137] The conduct constituting the aiding and abetting can occur before, during, or after the commission of the crime and in a different place from the crime.[138] In principle it is unnecessary for the principal perpetrator to be aware of the aider and abettor's contribution,[139] although where this contribution takes the form of encouragement or moral support the principal's unawareness of it will affect the question of causation.[140] 5.69

Criminal responsibility may arise on the basis of aiding and abetting by omission where an individual fails to discharge a legal duty and, by this failure, assists, encourages or lends moral support to the commission of a crime.[141] In such cases, 5.70

---

[135] See eg *Ntagerura* et al, Appeals Chamber Judgment (n 129), para 370; *Nahimana* et al, Appeals Chamber Judgment (n 98), para 482; *Prosecutor v Mrkšić and Šljivančanin*, IT-95-13/1-A, Appeals Chamber, Judgment, 5 May 2009, paras 81 and 134–135; *Gotovina and Markač*, Appeals Chamber Judgment (n 45), para 127. See also *infra* para 5.70.

[136] *Tadić*, Appeals Chamber Judgment (n 14), para 229. See also eg *Aleksovski*, Appeals Chamber Judgment (n 115), paras 162–163; *Čelebići*, Appeals Chamber Judgment (n 115), para 352; *Vasiljević*, Appeals Chamber Judgment (n 9), para 102; *Ntagerura* et al, Appeals Chamber Judgment (n 129), para 370; *Nahimana* et al, Appeals Chamber Judgment (n 98), para 482; *Karera*, Appeals Chamber Judgment (n 106), para 321; *Seromba*, Appeals Chamber Judgment (n 58), paras 44, 47, and 139. See also *Fofana and Kondewa*, Appeals Chamber Judgment (n 110), para 72. As made clear in some of these cases *ex abundante cautela*, no plan or agreement is required for responsibility on the basis of aiding and abetting, in contradistinction to the situation under JCE (and, it might be added, under co-perpetration before the ICC).

[137] *Brđanin*, Appeals Chamber Judgment (n 19), paras 273 and 277 (referring to the 'silent spectator'); *Šainović* et al, Appeals Chamber Judgment (n 28), para 1687; *Prosecutor v Muvunyi*, ICTR-2000-55A-A, Appeals Chamber, Judgment, 29 August 2008, para 80; *Kayishema and Ruzindana*, Appeals Chamber Judgment (n 17), paras 201–202 (referring to the 'approving spectator'); *Prosecutor v Ndahimana*, ICTR-01-68-A, Appeals Chamber, Judgment, 16 December 2013, para 147; *Kalimanzira*, Appeals Chamber Judgment (n 58), para 74; *Sesay* et al, Appeals Chamber Judgment (n 18), para 541. As made clear in *Brđanin*, Appeals Chamber Judgment (n 19), para 273, aiding and betting by tacit encouragement or approval is not the same as aiding and abetting by omission.

[138] See eg *Čelebići*, Appeals Chamber Judgment (n 115), para 352; *Simić*, Appeals Chamber Judgment (n 55), para 85; *Ntagerura* et al, Appeals Chamber Judgment (n 129), para 372; *Fofana and Kondewa*, Appeals Chamber Judgment (n 110), para 72. Like other modes of accessorial responsibility, aiding and abetting a crime against humanity can take place prior to the commencement of the attack of which such crimes must form part, as per *Nahimana* et al, Appeals Chamber Judgment (n 98), para 934. Recall, in this regard, *supra* para 5.52.

[139] *Tadić*, Appeals Chamber Judgment (n 14), para 229; *Vasiljević*, Appeals Chamber Judgment (n 9), para 102; *Kalimanzira*, Appeals Chamber Judgment (n 58), para 87.

[140] See *Brđanin*, Appeals Chamber Judgment (n 19), paras 273.

[141] *Šainović* et al, Appeals Chamber Judgment (n 28), para 1677; *Mrkšić and Šljivančanin*, Appeals Chamber Judgment (n 135), paras 134, 146, and 200; *Prosecutor v Orić*, IT-03-68-A, Appeals

5.71 As to causation, the provision of assistance, encouragement or moral support, including by omission, must have a substantial effect on the commission of the crime.[143] It need not, however, be a *conditio sine qua non* of that commission.[144]

5.72 The controversy over criminal responsibility for aiding and abetting has centred on whether there exists under customary international law the further material condition that the accused's acts or omissions be 'specifically directed'[145] towards assisting, encouraging or lending moral support to the commission of the relevant crime by the principal. The question is whether it is sufficient that the accused—knowing, as per the requisite *mens rea*,[146] that his or her assistance, etc will assist, etc in the commission of the relevant crime—provide assistance to the principal's activities, only some of which may be criminal, and that this assistance have a substantial effect on the commission of the crime or whether the accused must provide the assistance specifically for the purpose of assisting in the commission of the crime. The ICTY Appeals Chamber denied that

---

Chamber, Judgment, 3 July 2008, para 43. See also eg *Brđanin*, Appeals Chamber Judgment, para 274 (n 19); *Galić*, Appeals Chamber Judgment (n 116), para 175; *Ntagerura* et al, Appeals Chamber Judgment (n 129), para 334.

[142] *Šainović* et al, Appeals Chamber Judgment (n 28), para 1677; *Mrkšić and Šljivančanin*, Appeals Chamber Judgment (n 135), para 154. See also *Ntagerura* et al, Appeals Chamber Judgment (n 129), para 335.

[143] See eg *Tadić*, Appeals Chamber Judgment (n 14), para 229; *Aleksovski*, Appeals Chamber Judgment (n 115), para 162; *Čelebići*, Appeals Chamber Judgment (n 115), para 352; *Vasiljević*, Appeals Chamber Judgment (n 9), para 102; *Karera*, Appeals Chamber Judgment (n 106), para 321; *Nahimana* et al, Appeal Chamber Judgment (n 98), para 482; *Kalimanzira*, Appeals Chamber Judgment (n 58) para 74; *Seromba*, Appeals Chamber Judgment (n 58), paras 44 and 139; *Fofana and Kondewa*, Appeals Chamber Judgment (n 110), para 71; *Taylor*, Appeals Chamber Judgment (n 3), para 481.

[144] *Blaškić*, Appeals Chamber Judgment (n 17), para 48; *Simić*, Appeals Chamber Judgment (n 55), para 85; *Prosecutor v Blagojević and Jokić*, IT-02-60-A, Appeals Chamber, Judgment, 9 May 2007, para 134; *Kalimanzira*, Appeals Chamber Judgment (n 58), para 86; *Prosecutor v Ntawukulilyayo*, ICTR-05-82-A, Appeals Chamber, Judgment, 14 December 2011, para 214. See also, stating that there is no need for a cause-and-effect relationship between the conduct of the aider and abettor and the commission of the crime, *Mrkšić and Šljivančanin*, Appeals Chamber Judgment (n 135), para 81; *Prosecutor v Rukundo*, ICTR-2000-70-A, Appeals Chamber, Judgment, 20 October 2010, para 52; *Ndahimana*, Appeals Chamber Judgment (n 137), para 147. The requirement that the aiding and abetting have a substantial effect on the commission of the crime raises the question of how the former may occur after the latter, as has consistently been held to be the case. An example might be where the accused assures or arranges with the principal beforehand that he or she will help out, eg by assisting in the getaway or by covering up the crime, and this assurance or arrangement has a substantial effect on the commission of the crime by the principal. But in such a situation it is arguable that the aiding and abetting consists of the assurance or arrangement prior to the crime's commission. See, along these lines, *Prosecutor v Blagojević and Jokić*, IT-02-60-T, Trial Chamber, Judgment, 17 January 2005, para 731.

[145] The expression is found in *Tadić*, Appeals Chamber Judgment (n 14), para 229 and *Vasiljević*, Appeals Chamber Judgment (n 9), para 102.

[146] See *infra* paras 5.73–5.77.

'specific direction' was a material element of aiding and abetting in *Mrkšić and Šljivančanin*,¹⁴⁷ as affirmed in *Lukić and Lukić*,¹⁴⁸ before insisting on the requirement in *Perišić*,¹⁴⁹ from which the SCSL Appeals Chamber begged to differ in *Taylor*,¹⁵⁰ only for the ICTY Appeals Chamber in *Šainović*—less than a year after a differently configured bench had acquitted the accused in *Perišić* on precisely this ground—to reject 'specific direction' as a material element of aiding and abetting under customary international law.¹⁵¹ The upshot is that there is no such requirement.

B. Mental Element

To be responsible for aiding and abetting a crime, the aider and abettor must know that his or her acts will assist in the commission of the crime.¹⁵² For its part, however, the Appeals Chamber of the SCSL consistently relaxed this requirement by demanding that the aider and abettor either knew or 'was aware of the substantial likelihood' that his or her acts would assist in the commission of the crime.¹⁵³ This less demanding statement of the *mens rea* of aiding and abetting finds no support in the case law of other international criminal courts.

5.73

According to the case law of the ICTY and ICTR, knowledge that the acts will assist in the commission of the crime is sufficient. In other words, according to the Tribunals, there is no requirement that the accused have intended to provide assistance or, at a minimum, have accepted such assistance as a foreseeable consequence of his or her conduct.¹⁵⁴ In contrast, as stressed by the Pre-Trial Chamber in *Mbarushimana*,¹⁵⁵ article 25(3)(c) of the Rome Statute speaks of an accused who 'for the purpose of facilitating the commission of...a crime' aids, abets or

5.74

---

¹⁴⁷ See *Mrkšić and Šljivančanin*, Appeals Chamber Judgment (n 135), para 159.
¹⁴⁸ See *Prosecutor v Lukić and Lukić*, IT-98-32/1-A, Appeals Chamber, Judgment, 4 December 2012, para 424.
¹⁴⁹ See *Prosecutor v Perišić*, IT-04-81-A, Appeals Chamber, Judgment, 28 February 2013, paras 36–40.
¹⁵⁰ *Taylor*, Appeals Chamber Judgment (n 14), paras 471–481 and 486.
¹⁵¹ *Šainović* et al, Appeals Chamber Judgment (n 28), paras 1649–1650. The Prosecutor's subsequent motion for reconsideration of the Appeals Chamber's decision in *Perišić* was rejected by the Appeals Chamber in *Prosecutor v Perišić*, IT-04-81-A, Appeals Chamber, Decision on Motion for Reconsideration, 20 March 2014.
¹⁵² See eg *Tadić*, Appeals Chamber Judgment (n 14), para 229; *Aleksovski*, Appeals Chamber Judgment (n 115), para 162; *Brđanin*, Appeals Chamber Judgment (n 19), para 484; *Šainović* et al, Appeals Chamber Judgment (n 28), para 1760; *Ntagerura* et al, Appeals Chamber Judgment (n 129), para 370; *Nahimana* et al, Appeals Chamber Judgment (n 98), para 482; *Ntawukulilyayo*, Appeals Chamber Judgment (n 144), para 222; *Kalimanzira*, Appeals Chamber Judgment (n 58), para 86.
¹⁵³ *Brima* et al, Appeals Chamber Judgment (n 18), paras 242–243; *Fofana and Kondewa*, Appeals Chamber Judgment (n 110), para 366; *Sesay* et al, Appeals Chamber Judgment (n 18), para 546; *Taylor*, Appeals Chamber Judgment (n 3), paras 437–438.
¹⁵⁴ *Blaškić*, Appeals Chamber Judgment (n 17), para 49; *Vasiljević*, Appeals Chamber Judgment (n 9), para 102. Again, this is a point of distinction between aiding and abetting and JCE. See eg *Tadić*, Appeals Chamber Judgment (n 14), para 229; *Krnojelac*, Appeals Chamber Judgment (n 14), para 33.
¹⁵⁵ *Prosecutor v Mbarushimana*, ICC-01/04-01/10-465-Red, Pre-Trial Chamber, Decision on the Confirmation of Charges, 16 December 2011, paras 274, 281, and 289.

otherwise assists in its commission or its attempted commission. The Pre-Trial Chamber took this to signify that mere knowledge that the acts will assist in the commission of the crime is insufficient for responsibility under article 25(3)(c) for aiding and abetting, what is required being intent that the acts will assist, in the sense of meaning that the acts will assist.[156]

5.75   It is unnecessary that the aider and abettor know the precise crime to be committed by the principal. As long as he or she is aware that one of a number of crimes will probably be committed, and as long as one of those crimes is in fact committed, he or she satisfies the *mens rea* of aiding and abetting.[157] At the same time, an aider and abettor must have knowledge of the essential elements of the crime committed by the principal.[158] What this means will depend on the facts of the case, including on the scale of the crimes and the type of assistance provided.[159]

5.76   It follows from the requirement that the aider and abettor have knowledge of the essential elements of the crime committed by the principal that, when it comes to crimes of specific intent, the aider and abettor must have knowledge of the principal's specific intent.[160] But the aider and abettor need not share that specific intent,[161] even in the context of genocide.[162]

5.77   The *mens rea* requirements for aiding and abetting by omission are the same as for aiding and abetting by a positive act.[163]

---

[156] Ibid.

[157] See eg *Blaškić*, Appeals Chamber Judgment (n 17), para 50; *Simić*, Appeals Chamber Judgment (n 55), para 86; *Šainović* et al, Appeals Chamber Judgment (n 28), para 1772; *Nahimana* et al, Appeals Chamber Judgment (n 98), para 482; *Brima* et al, Appeals Chamber Judgment (n 18), paras 242–243; *Fofana and Kondewa*, Appeals Chamber Judgment (n 110), para 366.

[158] See eg *Aleksovski*, Appeals Chamber Judgment (n 115), para 162; *Brđanin*, Appeals Chamber Judgment (n 19), para 484; *Šainović* et al, Appeals Chamber Judgment (n 28), para 1772; *Nahimana* et al, Appeals Chamber Judgment (n 98), para 482; *Karera*, Appeals Chamber Judgment (n 106), para 321; *Brima* et al, Appeals Chamber Judgment (n 18), para 244.

[159] *Šainović* et al, Appeals Chamber Judgment (n 28), para 1773.

[160] See eg *Krnojelac*, Appeals Chamber Judgment (n 14), para 52; *Prosecutor v Krstić*, IT-98-33-A, Appeals Chamber, Judgment, 19 April 2004, para 140; *Simić*, Appeals Chamber Judgment (n 55), para 86; *Ntakirutimana*, Appeals Chamber Judgment (n 98), paras 500–501; *Ntawukulilyayo*, Appeals Chamber Judgment (n 144), para 222; *Kalimanzira*, Appeals Chamber Judgment (n 58), para 86; *Fofana and Kondewa*, Appeals Chamber Judgment (n 110), para 367.

[161] See eg *Krnojelac*, Appeals Chamber Judgment (n 14), para 52; *Krstić*, Appeals Chamber Judgment (n 160), para 140; *Simić*, Appeals Chamber Judgment (n 55), para 86; *Ntakirutimana*, Appeals Chamber Judgment (n 21), paras 364 and 501; *Ntawukulilyayo*, Appeals Chamber Judgment (n 144), para 222; *Seromba*, Appeals Chamber Judgment (n 58), para 56; *Fofana and Kondewa*, Appeals Chamber Judgment (n 110), para 367. It was further held in *Krstić*, Appeals Chamber Judgment (n 160), para 143, as affirmed in *Brđanin*, Appeals Chamber Judgment (n 19), para 355, that a person may be held responsible for aiding and abetting a crime of specific intent even where the principal perpetrators have not been tried or identified.

[162] *Krstić*, Appeals Chamber Judgment (n 160), para 140; *Ntakirutimana*, Appeals Chamber Judgment (n 21), paras 500–501; *Ntawukulilyayo*, Appeals Chamber Judgment (n 144), para 222; *Kalimanzira*, Appeals Chamber Judgment (n 58), para 89 n 241; *Seromba*, Appeals Chamber Judgment (n 58), para 56.

[163] *Mrkšić and Šljivančanin*, Appeals Chamber Judgment (n 135), para 146; *Orić*, Appeals Chamber Judgment (n 141), para 43.

IX. Contribution to a Crime Committed or Attempted by a Group of Persons Acting with a Common Purpose

Criminal responsibility for contributing to the commission or attempted commission of a crime, including genocide, by a group of persons acting with a common purpose is a mode of responsibility found in article 25(3)(*d*) of the Rome Statute, where—in contrast to joint criminal enterprise or, synonymously, 'common purpose' as conceived of by the ICTY, ICTR, and SCSL—it is a form of accessorial liability, not a form of commission. In accordance with article 25(3)(*d*) of the Statute, a person shall be criminally responsible for a crime within the ICC's jurisdiction if he or she '[i]n any other way contributes to the commission or attempted commission of such a crime by a group of persons acting with a common purpose' where the contribution, which 'shall be intentional', is 'made with the aim of furthering the criminal activity or criminal purpose of the group, where such activity or purpose involves the commission of a crime within the jurisdiction of the Court', as per sub-subparagraph (i), or, as per sub-subparagraph (ii), is 'made in the knowledge of the intention of the group to commit the crime'. The prefatory phrase '[i]n any other way' at the start of article 25(3)(*d*) refers to the various contributions to the commission of a crime within the Court's jurisdiction falling within article 25(3)(*a*), (*b*), and (*c*) respectively. In other words, the contribution to the crime covered by article 25(3)(*d*) is one not covered by article 25(3)(*a*) to (*c*).[164] 5.78

The key distinction in terms of their elements as between responsibility on the basis of JCE, as developed by the ICTY, ICTR, and SCSL, and responsibility under article 25(3)(*d*) of the Rome Statute is that, whereas the former requires the accused to be party to the common plan, the latter does not.[165] The key distinctions in terms of their elements as between responsibility on the basis of co-perpetration, as developed by the ICC, and responsibility under article 25(3)(*d*) of the Rome Statute is that the former requires the accused to be party to the common plan and to make an essential contribution to the commission of the crime, while the latter does not require the accused to be party to the common plan or to make more than a significant contribution to the commission (or attempted commission) of the crime. The more fundamental, conceptual distinction between JCE and co-perpetration, on the one hand, and responsibility under article 25(3)(*d*) of the Rome Statute, on the other, is that both the former are considered manifestations of responsibility for commission of the crime, *viz* 5.79

---

[164] For gratuitous confirmation of this textual truism, see eg *Mbarushimana*, Pre-Trial Chamber Decision on Confirmation of Charges (n 155), para 269 n 640 and para 278; *Muthaura* et al, Decision on Confirmation of Charges (n 63), para 421; *Ruto* et al, Decision on Confirmation of Charges (n 63), para 351; *Ntaganda*, Decision on Charges of Prosecutor (n 63), para 158.
[165] See eg *Mbarushimana*, Pre-Trial Chamber Decision on Confirmation of Charges (n 155), para 282; *Katanga*, Trial Chamber Judgment (n 7), para 1619.

responsibility as principal, whereas the latter is a form of accessorial responsibility, *viz* responsibility as accomplice.

A. Material Elements

5.80 In order for criminal responsibility to arise under article 25(3)(*d*) of the Rome Statute, there must exist an 'agreement or common plan among two or more persons'.[166] Just as in the context of co-perpetration,[167] this agreement or common plan, which need not be explicit but can be inferred from circumstantial evidence,[168] and which need not be pre-existing but may arise spontaneously,[169] must involve 'an element of criminality', although it 'does not need to be specifically directed at the commission of a crime',[170] either in its objective or in its execution.[171] In the subsequent light of the more demanding formulation posited by the Trial Chamber in *Lubanga*, this requirement should be read as one of 'a critical element of criminality', meaning that the implementation of the agreement or common plan 'embodies a sufficient risk that, in the ordinary course of events, a crime will be committed'.[172]

5.81 Responsibility can arise under article 25(3)(*d*) of the Rome Statute 'irrespective of whether the person is or is not a member of the group acting with a common purpose'.[173]

5.82 The contribution can take the form of material assistance, for example through the supply of weapons, or moral assistance, such as encouragement.[174]

5.83 Responsibility can be incurred under article 25(3)(*d*) of the Rome Statute for contributing to the commission of a crime after the crime has been committed, provided that the contribution was agreed on by the accused

---

[166] *Mbarushimana*, Pre-Trial Chamber Decision on Confirmation of Charges (n 155), para 271. The Pre-Trial Chamber derived this requirement, which the Chamber, ibid, considered 'functionally identical to the statutory requirement of article 25(3)(*d*) of the Statute that there be a "group of persons acting with a common purpose"', from the material elements of co-perpetration under art 25(3)(*a*) of the Rome Statute. For its part, the Trial Chamber in *Katanga*, Trial Chamber Judgment (n 7), para 1625, preferred to look by way of analogy to cognate concepts developed by the ICTY and ICTR in relation to JCE. It stressed that, while the existence of a 'common plan' provided evidence of a 'common purpose' within the meaning of art 25(3)(*d*), it was not strictly legally necessary. Especially given that the Pre-Trial Chamber in *Mbarushimana*, Pre-Trial Chamber Decision on Confirmation of Charges (n 155), para 271, also spoke of an 'agreement', the distinction between the two overall formulations appears one without a difference.
[167] Recall *supra* para 5.36.
[168] *Mbarushimana*, Pre-Trial Chamber Decision on Confirmation of Charges (n 155), para 271; *Katanga*, Trial Chamber Judgment (n 7), para 1626.
[169] *Katanga*, Trial Chamber Judgment (n 7), para 1626.
[170] *Mbarushimana*, Pre-Trial Chamber Decision on Confirmation of Charges (n 155), para 271.
[171] *Katanga*, Trial Chamber Judgment (n 7), para 1627.
[172] *Lubanga*, Trial Chamber Judgment (n 7), para 987. See also ibid, para 984; *Katanga*, Trial Chamber Judgment (n 7), para 1627. It was stated, ibid, that the crime need not be one within the jurisdiction of the ICC, but it is not clear that this is correct.
[173] *Mbarushimana*, Pre-Trial Chamber Decision on Confirmation of Charges (n 155), para 275. See also *Katanga*, Trial Chamber Judgment (n 7), para 1631.
[174] See also *Katanga*, Trial Chamber Judgment (n 7), para 1635.

and the group acting with a common purpose prior to the commission of the crime.[175]

5.84 It has been held that the contribution made to the commission or attempted commission of a crime by a group acting with a common purpose 'cannot just be any contribution'[176] but must instead be 'significant'.[177] By this the Trial Chamber in *Katanga* meant 'of a nature to influence the commission of the crime', explaining that 'conduct that had no effect or impact on the commission of the crime could consequently not be considered sufficient and to constitute a contribution in the sense of article 25(3)(c) of the Statute'.[178] At the same time, in contrast to the situation in relation to co-perpetration, the contribution need not be essential.[179] That is, the commission of the crime need not depend or be conditional upon the contribution.[180] Rather, the contribution can be considered significant if it has an influence on the occurrence of the crime, the manner of its commission or both.[181]

B. Mental Elements

5.85 The requirement in article 25(3)(b) of the Rome Statute that the contribution to the commission of a crime by a group acting with a common purpose be intentional has a twofold significance. First, the accused must intend to engage in the conduct that amounts to the contribution.[182] That is, the acts constituting the contribution must be conscious and deliberate.[183] Secondly, the accused must 'be at least aware that his or her conduct contributes to the activities of the group of persons for whose crimes he or she is alleged to bear responsibility'.[184] The requirement of intentionality does not mean, however, that the accused must share the intention of the group to commit the crime.[185]

5.86 Unlike in relation to co-perpetration,[186] which is a form of commission, it is unnecessary for responsibility on the basis of contributing to the commission of a crime by a group acting with a common purpose that the accused satisfy the mental elements of the crimes with which he or she is charged.[187] What is needed is one of the subjective states specified in either article 25(3)(d)(i) or 25(3)(d)(ii) of the Rome Statute, namely that the accused either intended to further the criminal

---

[175] *Mbarushimana*, Pre-Trial Chamber Decision on Confirmation of Charges (n 155), para 287.
[176] Ibid, para 283.
[177] Ibid, paras 283 and 285; *Katanga*, Trial Chamber Judgment (n 7), paras 1620 and 1632.
[178] *Katanga*, Trial Chamber Judgment (n 7), paras 1620 and 1632.
[179] *Mbarushimana*, Pre-Trial Chamber Decision on Confirmation of Charges (n 155), para 279.
[180] *Katanga*, Trial Chamber Judgment (n 7), para 1633.   [181] Ibid.
[182] *Mbarushimana*, Pre-Trial Chamber Decision on Confirmation of Charges (n 155), para 288; *Katanga*, Trial Chamber Judgment (n 7), paras 1638–1639.
[183] *Katanga*, Trial Chamber Judgment (n 7), para 1638.
[184] *Mbarushimana*, Pre-Trial Chamber Decision on Confirmation of Charges (n 155), para 288. See also *Katanga*, Trial Chamber Judgment (n 7), para 1639.
[185] *Katanga*, Trial Chamber Judgment (n 7), para 1638.   [186] Recall *supra* para 5.39.
[187] *Mbarushimana*, Pre-Trial Chamber Decision on Confirmation of Charges (n 155), para 289.

activity or criminal purpose of the group, where this activity or purpose involves the commission of a crime within the jurisdiction of the ICC, or knew of the intention of the group to commit the crime.[188] In the second case, knowledge of a general criminal intent on the part of the group is insufficient; rather, the accused must know that the group intends to commit the specific crime with which he or she is charged.[189]

X. Specific Modes of Responsibility for the Crime of Genocide

5.87 Article III of the Genocide Convention, as consonant with customary international law, specifies that '[t]he following acts shall be punishable':

(*a*) Genocide [*viz* responsibility for the crime on the basis of commission];
(*b*) Conspiracy to commit genocide;
(*c*) Direct and public incitement to commit genocide;
(*d*) Attempt to commit genocide;
(*e*) Complicity in genocide.

The text of article III of the Convention is reproduced in article 4(3) of the ICTY Statute and article 2(3) of the ICTR Statute. The Rome Statute, in contrast, makes special provision for the modes of criminal responsibility for genocide only in respect of direct and public incitement to commit genocide, as referred to in article 25(3)(*e*). The remaining specific bases of criminal responsibility for genocide are subsumed into the general principles of criminal responsibility laid down in the other subparagraphs of article 25(3) of the Statute.[190] It remains to be seen what effect, if any, this has on customary international law, although it should be emphasized that the various chambers have underlined in other areas, and correctly, that what they are called on to apply first and, in the event of conflict, to the exclusion of customary international law is the Statute.[191]

5.88 Conspiracy to commit genocide, direct and public incitement to commit genocide, and attempt to commit genocide are all inchoate offences.[192] That is, criminal responsibility may arise on these bases despite the fact—and, in the case of attempt, by definitional virtue of the fact—that any envisaged principal perpetrator does not ultimately commit the crime of genocide.

---

[188] Ibid.   [189] *Katanga*, Trial Chamber Judgment (n 7), para 1642.
[190] Responsibility for the crime of genocide is also possible on the basis of command or other superior responsibility, as provided for in Rome Statute, art 28. See *infra* paras 5.102–5.118.
[191] See *infra* para 14.58.
[192] *Nahimana* et al, Appeals Chamber Judgment (n 98), paras 678 (direct and public incitement) and 720 (conspiracy, direct and public incitement, and attempt); *Prosecutor v Gatete*, ICTR-00-61-A, Appeals Chamber, Judgment, 9 October 2012, para 262 (conspiracy).

A. Conspiracy to Commit Genocide

Conspiracy to commit genocide, as embodied in customary international law and reflected in article III(*b*) of the Genocide Convention, comprises an agreement by two or more persons to commit the crime of genocide.[193] The *actus reus* is being party to the agreement.[194] This does not require the accused to have taken part in the formation of the agreement; rather, criminal responsibility may arise on the basis of conspiracy where the accused joins the agreement at any point prior to the commission of the offence.[195] Any attempt at exoneration on the ground of withdrawal from the agreement requires 'affirmative and contemporaneous evidence' of the accused's withdrawal.[196] As with any other element of a crime, the existence of the agreement may be proved by circumstantial evidence, but such existence must represent the only reasonable inference.[197] As to *mens rea*, criminal responsibility for conspiracy to commit genocide requires the specific intent required for the commission of genocide, namely the intent to destroy one of the specified groups in whole or in part.[198]

5.89

B. Direct and Public Incitement to Commit Genocide

Criminal responsibility arises for direct and public incitement to commit genocide, within the meaning of customary international law and article III(*c*) of the Genocide Convention, when—perhaps unsurprisingly—an individual directly and publicly incites others to commit genocide and intends directly and publicly to incite others to commit genocide.[199]

5.90

(i) Material elements

The word 'public' in 'public incitement to commit genocide' has been interpreted to refer to 'the general public' ('*le public au sens large*'), as distinct from smaller

5.91

---

[193] *Seromba*, Appeals Chamber Judgment (n 58), para 218; *Ntagerura*, Appeals Chamber Judgment (n 129), para 92; *Nahimana* et al, Appeals Chamber Judgment (n 98), para 894.
[194] *Seromba*, Appeals Chamber Judgment (n 58), paras 218 and 221; *Ntagerura*, Appeals Chamber Judgment (n 129), para 92; *Nahimana* et al, Appeals Chamber Judgment (n 98), paras 894 and 896; *Gatete*, Appeals Chamber Judgment (n 192), para 260.
[195] *Prosecutor v Popović* et al, IT-05-88-T, Trial Chamber, Judgment, 10 June 2010, para 872; *Prosecutor v Tolimir*, IT-05-88/2-T, Trial Chamber, Judgment, 12 December 2012, para 785. Nor, as per ibid, is a co-conspirator who becomes party to the agreement after its formation to be treated as less culpable for the purposes of sentencing.
[196] *Tolimir*, Trial Chamber Judgment (n 195), para 785.
[197] *Seromba*, Appeals Chamber Judgment (n 58), para 221; *Nahimana* et al, Appeals Chamber Judgment (n 98), para 896. See also ibid, para 898.
[198] *Nahimana* et al, Appeals Chamber Judgment (n 98), para 894. Recall, in this regard, *supra* paras 4.66 and 4.78–4.85.
[199] *Nahimana* et al, Appeals Chamber Judgment (n 98), para 677; *Kalimanzira*, Appeals Chamber Judgment (n 58), para 155; *Prosecutor v Mugenzi and Mugiraneza*, ICTR-99-50-A, Appeals Chamber, Judgment, 4 February 2013, para 135 (intent).

groups of individuals.²⁰⁰ The sorts of acts amounting to the *actus reus* of direct and public incitement to commit genocide include 'speeches made to large, fully public assemblies, messages disseminated by the media, and communications made through a public address system over a broad public area'.²⁰¹ The distinction is with private incitement to commit genocide and with instigation to commit genocide.²⁰²

5.92 There is a distinction between direct and public incitement to commit genocide and hate speech in general. The latter may incite discrimination and even violence, but unless it incites the commission of the crime of genocide within the meaning of article II of the Genocide Convention and customary international law, it cannot constitute direct and public incitement to commit genocide as understood by article III(*c*) of the Convention and customary international law.²⁰³

5.93 A communication which is ambiguous, in that it may or may not call on others to commit the crime of genocide, cannot be said beyond reasonable doubt to constitute 'direct' incitement to genocide.²⁰⁴ In this regard, however, what is to be considered is not simply the objective meaning of the words but 'the meaning of the words used in the specific context'²⁰⁵—that is, the communication 'as understood by its intended audience'.²⁰⁶ Ascertaining the 'true message' of the communication involves a consideration of the culture in which the communication is made and the nuances of the language in which it is made.²⁰⁷ It is not the case 'that only discourse explicitly calling for extermination, or discourse that is entirely unambiguous for all types of audiences, can justify a conviction for direct and public incitement to commit genocide'.²⁰⁸ In deciding whether the communication amounts to direct and public incitement to commit genocide, 'it does not matter that the message may appear ambiguous to another audience or in another context'.²⁰⁹ A speech, for example, 'containing no explicit appeal to commit genocide, or which appear[s] ambiguous, [may] still constitute[] direct incitement to commit genocide in a particular context'.²¹⁰ Ultimately, however, if the message 'is still ambiguous, even when considered in its context', criminal responsibility for direct and public incitement to commit genocide may not be ascribed to the message's disseminator.²¹¹

---

²⁰⁰ See *Nahimana* et al, Appeals Chamber Judgment (n 98), para 862; *Kalimanzira*, Appeals Chamber Judgment (n 58), paras 155–156.
²⁰¹ *Kalimanzira*, Appeals Chamber Judgment (n 58), para 156.
²⁰² See *Nahimana* et al, Appeals Chamber Judgment (n 98), para 679, explaining that instigating another to commit genocide need not be direct and public; *Prosecutor v Akayesu*, ICTR-96-4, Appeals Chamber, Judgment, 1 June 2001, paras 478–482; *Kalimanzira*, Appeals Chamber Judgment (n 58), para 158.
²⁰³ *Nahimana* et al, Appeals Chamber Judgment (n 98), paras 692–693.
²⁰⁴ Ibid, para 701.
²⁰⁵ Ibid. See also ibid, paras 711, 713 (recognizing that 'the political or community affiliation of the author of a speech may be regarded as a contextual element which can assist in its interpretation'), and 715.
²⁰⁶ Ibid, para 700. See also ibid, para 711.   ²⁰⁷ Ibid, para 700.
²⁰⁸ Ibid, para 702.   ²⁰⁹ Ibid, para 701.   ²¹⁰ Ibid, para 703.
²¹¹ Ibid, para 701.

Since direct and public incitement to commit genocide is an inchoate 5.94
offence, it is complete once the acts constituting the incitement are over. It does
not extend forward in time to the completion of any act of genocide incited
by it.[212]

Direct and public incitement to commit genocide, being an inchoate offence, 5.95
by definition grounds responsibility in and of itself, without the need for any
element of causation.[213]

(ii) Mental elements

The necessary intent directly and publicly to incite genocide presupposes that 5.96
the perpetrator possesses the specific intent for genocide,[214] namely the intent to
destroy one of the specified groups in whole or in part.

C. Complicity in Genocide

In *Krstić*, the ICTY Appeals Chamber held that complicity in genocide, as pro- 5.97
vided for in article III(*e*) of the Genocide Convention, 'may encompass conduct broader than that of aiding and abetting'[215]—in other words, that criminal
responsibility for complicity in genocide may arise under material conditions less
restrictive than those governing responsibility for aiding and abetting the same
crime. The assertion was seemingly endorsed in *Ntakirutimana*, where the ICTR
Appeals Chamber, citing *Krstić*, held that complicity in genocide 'encompasses
aiding and abetting'[216] and, conversely, that 'aiding and abetting constitutes a
form of complicity'.[217] The suggestion that complicity in genocide is a broader
notion than aiding and abetting genocide is, however, open to doubt, given that
the Rome Statute appears to treat the former as having been subsumed into the
latter under article 25(3)(*c*).

As to the *mens rea* required for complicity in genocide, the ICJ stated in 5.98
*Application of the Convention on the Prevention and Punishment of the Crime
of Genocide* that a person cannot be held responsible for complicity in genocide unless he or she knew of the specific intent of the principal perpetrator.[218]
But the Court expressly left open the more controversial question whether the
accomplice must share that specific intent. The latter was touched on in *Krstić*,

---

[212] Ibid, para 723.
[213] This is in contrast to instigating another to commit genocide. Instigation must make a sub-stantial, albeit not decisive, contribution to the commission of genocide by a principal. See *Nahimana et al*, Appeals Chamber Judgment (n 98), para 678 and recall *supra* para 5.59.
[214] Ibid, para 677; *Mugenzi and Mugiraneza*, Appeals Chamber Judgment (n 199), para 135.
[215] *Krstić*, Appeals Chamber Judgment (n 160), para 139.
[216] *Ntakirutimana*, Appeals Chamber Judgment (n 21), para 371, citing *Krstić*, Appeals Chamber Judgment (n 160), paras 138 and 139.
[217] *Ntakirutimana*, Appeals Chamber Judgment (n 21), para 500.
[218] *Application of the Convention on the Prevention and Punishment of the Crime of Genocide (Bosnia and Herzegovina v Serbia and Montenegro), Merits, Judgment*, ICJ Rep 2007, 43, 218, para 421.

where the ICTY Appeals Chamber, having held that aiding and abetting the crime of genocide requires merely knowledge on the part of the aider and abettor of the specific intent of the principal perpetrator,[219] noted, without deciding the issue, that 'there is authority to suggest that complicity in genocide, where it prohibits conduct broader than aiding and abetting, requires proof that the accomplice had the specific intent to destroy a protected group'.[220] In the later case of *Semanza*, the ICTR Appeals Chamber read this non-committal statement in *Krstić* and its own subsequent reference to it in *Ntakirutimana*[221] as a conclusion and affirmation to the effect that where complicity in genocide overlaps with aiding and abetting genocide all that is required of the aider and abettor is knowledge of the principal's specific intent, whereas acts of complicity beyond the scope of aiding and abetting require that the accomplice possess the specific intent of genocide.[222]

XI. Attempt

5.99 The statutes of the ICTY, ICTR, and SCSL make no general provision for the inchoate offence of attempt to commit one of the crimes within their respective jurisdictions, although the first two recognize the specific offence of attempt to commit genocide as embodied in article III(*d*) of the Genocide Convention and customary international law.[223] In this light, Trial Chambers of both the ICTY and ICTR have held that an individual may be held criminally responsible under the relevant statutes only if the offence is consummated.[224]

5.100 In contrast, article 25(3)(*f*) of the Rome Statute recognizes the criminal responsibility of a person who attempts to commit a crime 'by taking action that commences its execution by means of a substantial step', provided that the failure to consummate the crime is a consequence of 'circumstances independent of the person's intentions'.[225] Article 25(3)(*f*) adds, conversely, that 'a person who abandons the effort to commit the crime or otherwise prevents the completion of the crime shall not be liable for punishment under [the Rome] Statute for the attempt to commit that crime if that person completely and voluntarily gave up the criminal purpose'. As elaborated on by the Pre-Trial Chamber in *Banda and Jerbo*, responsibility on the basis of attempt 'requires that, in the ordinary

---

[219] *Krstić*, Appeals Chamber Judgment (n 160), paras 140–141. See also, subsequently, *Ntakirutimana*, Appeals Chamber Judgment (n 21), paras 500–501.
[220] *Krstić*, Appeals Chamber Judgment (n 160), para 142.
[221] *Ntakirutimana*, Appeals Chamber Judgment (n 21), para 500.
[222] See *Semanza*, Appeals Chamber Judgment (n 117), paras 316 and 369.
[223] Recall *supra* paras 5.87–5.88.
[224] See *Prosecutor v Rutaganda*, ICTR-96-3-T, Trial Chamber, Judgment, 6 December 1999, para 34; *Prosecutor v Akayesu*, ICTR-96-4-T, Trial Chamber, Judgment, 2 September 1998, para 473; *Prosecutor v Krnojelac*, IT-97-25-T, Trial Chamber, Judgment, 15 March 2002, para 432 note 1292.
[225] Note also the role played by attempt in the modes of accessorial responsibility recognized in art 25(3)(*b*) to (*d*) of the Rome Statute.

course of events, the perpetrator's conduct [would] have resulted in the crime being completed, had circumstances outside the perpetrator's control not intervened'.[226] As to the *mens rea*, the intent required for criminal responsibility for attempt is the intent required for criminal responsibility for commission of the crime attempted.[227]

XII. Modes of Responsibility and the Crime of Aggression

It will be recalled[228] that to be responsible for the crime of aggression an individual must, as specified in article 8*bis*(1) of the Rome Statute and reiterated in the Elements of Crimes,[229] be 'in a position effectively to exercise control over or to direct the political or military action of' the state that commits the act of aggression. In acknowledgement of this, article 25(3)*bis* of the Statute, a consequential amendment in relation to the crime of aggression, stipulates that the provisions of article 25 shall apply only in respect of 'persons in a position effectively to exercise control over or to direct the political or military action of a State'.

5.101

XIII. Command and Other Superior Responsibility

Superiors may be held criminally responsible under customary international law in relation to crimes committed by their subordinates when they fail to prevent or punish them. This mode of responsibility, recognized in the specific form of command responsibility at the end of the Second World War[230] and reflected in more general terms in the respective statutes of the ICTY, ICTR, SCSL, and ICC,[231] is a manifestation of criminal responsibility for omission.

5.102

The ICTY Appeals Chamber has held that command and other superior responsibility may arise in respect of a subordinate's criminal responsibility on any basis, and not just for the commission of a crime.[232] In other words, according to the ICTY, a commander or other superior may be held responsible for failure to

5.103

---

[226] *Banda and Jerbo*, Pre-Trial Chamber Corrigendum of [*sic*] Decision on Confirmation of Charges (n 61), para 96.
[227] *Katanga and Ngudjolo*, Pre-Trial Chamber Decision on Confirmation of Charges (n 61), para 460; *Banda and Jerbo*, Pre-Trial Chamber Corrigendum of [*sic*] Decision on Confirmation of Charges (n 61), para 106.
[228] See *supra* para 4.96.   [229] See Elements of Crimes, art 8*bis*(1), element 2.
[230] See *Yamashita* (n 115).
[231] See ICTY Statute, art 7(3) ('superior'); ICTR Statute, art 6(3) ('superior'); SCSL Statute, art 6(3) ('superior'); Rome Statute, art 28(*a*) ('military commander or person effectively acting as a military commander') and (*b*) ('superior'). The negative wording of the ICTY, ICTR, and SCSL statutes in this regard is not legally significant.
[232] See *Blagojević and Jokić*, Appeals Chamber Judgment (n 144), para 280; *Orić*, Appeals Chamber Judgment (n 141), para 21; *Bagosora and Nsengiyumva*, Appeals Chamber Judgment (n 116), para 232; *Nahimana* et al, Appeals Chamber Judgment (n 98), paras 485–486.

prevent or punish a subordinate's aiding and abetting of a crime, a subordinate's participation in a joint criminal enterprise, and so on.

A. Material Elements

5.104   The doctrine of superior responsibility acknowledged in the ICTY, ICTR, and SCSL statutes is not limited to military commanders but can extend to 'political leaders and other civilian superiors in positions of authority'.[233] The Rome Statute is explicitly to this effect, dealing with military commanders in article 28(*a*) and civilian superiors in article 28(*b*).

5.105   Command and other superior responsibility is not limited to *de jure* commanders and civilian superiors. The ICTY, ICTR, and SCSL Appeals Chambers have held that 'a commander or superior is...one who possesses the power or authority in either a *de jure* or a *de facto* form to prevent a subordinate's crime or to punish the perpetrators of the crime after the crime is committed'.[234] Effective control, rather than formal titles, is the touchstone of command and other superior responsibility.[235] In other words, '[a]s long as a superior has effective control over subordinates, to the extent that he can prevent them from committing crimes or punish them after they committed the crimes, he would be held responsible for the commission of the crimes if he failed to exercise such abilities of control'.[236] Again, the Rome Statute is expressly to this effect, speaking in article 25(*a*) of 'a military commander or person effectively acting as a military commander' and in article 25(*b*) of 'superior and subordinate relationships' other than military commanders and their equivalents where the person exercises 'effective authority and control'.

5.106   Conversely, *de jure* commanders and civilian superiors cannot be found guilty on the basis of command and other superior responsibility respectively unless they exercise effective control, 'although a court may presume that possession of such power *prima facie* results in effective control unless proof to the contrary is produced'.[237] In this light, and relying for support on the post-Second World

---

[233] *Čelebići*, Appeals Chamber Judgment (n 115), para 195. See also eg *Aleksovski*, Appeals Chamber Judgment (n 115), para 76; *Kajelijeli*, Appeals Chamber Judgment (n 115), para 85; *Prosecutor v Bagilishema*, ICTR-95-1A-A, Appeals Chamber, Judgment, 3 July 2002, paras 50–51; *Brima* et al, Appeals Chamber Judgment (n 18), para 257.

[234] *Čelebići*, Appeals Chamber Judgment (n 115), para 192. See also eg *Prosecutor v Halilović*, IT-01-48-A, Appeals Chamber, Judgment, 16 October 2007, para 59; *Kajelijeli*, Appeals Chamber Judgment (n 115), paras 85–86; *Bagilishema*, Appeals Chamber Judgment (n 233), para 50; *Brima* et al, Appeals Chamber Judgment (n 18), paras 257 and 289; *Sesay* et al, Appeals Chamber Judgment (n 18), para 849.

[235] *Čelebići*, Appeals Chamber Judgment (n 115), paras 196–197 and 256. See also eg *Bagilishema*, Appeals Chamber Judgment (n 233), paras 50–51; *Gacumbitsi*, Appeals Chamber Judgment (n 55), para 144; *Brima* et al, Appeals Chamber Judgment (n 18), para 257; *Fofana and Kondewa*, Appeals Chamber Judgment (n 18), para 175.

[236] *Čelebići*, Appeals Chamber Judgment (n 115), para 198. See also eg *Halilović*, Appeals Chamber Judgment (n 234), paras 59–60; *Kamuhanda*, Appeals Chamber Judgment (n 115), para 75; *Bagilishema*, Appeals Chamber Judgment (n 233), paras 50–51; *Brima* et al, Appeals Chamber Judgment (n 18), paras 257 and 289.

[237] *Čelebići*, Appeals Chamber Judgment (n 115), para 197. See also eg *Prosecutor v Hadžihasanović and Kubura*, IT-01-47-A, Appeals Chamber, Judgment, 22 April 2008, paras 20–21; *Nahimana* et al,

War 'High Command case',²³⁸ the ICTY Appeals Chamber held in *Halilović* that 'criminal responsibility does not attach to a military official merely on the basis of his "over-all command"',²³⁹ with the result that a chief of staff whose duties were 'exclusively operational'²⁴⁰ could not be found guilty on the basis of command responsibility. For its part, the Rome Statute refers in article 28(*a*) to 'forces under his or her effective command and control, or effective authority and control as the case may be', and in article 28(*b*) to 'subordinates under his or her effective authority and control'.

The ICTR Appeals Chamber has held that the effective control that must be established in respect of a civilian superior is not necessarily the same as that exercised by a military commander.²⁴¹ 5.107

The indicators of effective control are a question more of fact than of law,²⁴² and as such can be determined only on a case-by-case basis.²⁴³ 5.108

The responsibility of commanders and other superiors for failure to prevent or punish the crimes of those under their effective command and control or effective authority and control, as the case may be, is not strict. Rather, what is required of commanders and other superiors is that they take 'all necessary and reasonable measures within [their] power', in the words of article 28(*a*)(ii) and (*b*)(iii) of the Rome Statute.²⁴⁴ 5.109

Like the indicators of effective control, the measures necessary and reasonable to prevent or punish a subordinate's commission of a crime are a question more of fact than of law, and may vary from case to case.²⁴⁵ It cannot be excluded, for example, that disciplinary, rather than penal, measures may suffice to discharge a commander's responsibility to punish.²⁴⁶ Equally, it may be that the duty to punish is discharged 5.110

Appeals Chamber Judgment (n 98), para 625; *Prosecutor v Ntabukeze*, ICTR-98-41A-A, Appeals Chamber, Judgment, 8 May 2012, para 169.

²³⁸ *United States v von Leeb* et al ('High Command case'), 12 LRTWC 72 (USMT Nuremberg 1948).
²³⁹ *Halilović*, Appeals Chamber Judgment (n 234), para 214.
²⁴⁰ Ibid, paras 212 and 213, quoting *von Leeb* et al (n 238).
²⁴¹ *Bagilishema*, Appeals Chamber Judgment (n 233), paras 52 and 55; *Kajelijeli*, Appeals Chamber Judgment (n 115), para 87; *Nahimana* et al, Appeals Chamber Judgment (n 98), paras 605 and 785.
²⁴² See eg *Aleksovski*, Appeals Chamber Judgment (n 115), paras 73–74; *Blaškić*, Appeals Chamber Judgment (n 17), para 69; *Ntagerura* et al, Appeals Chamber Judgment (n 129), para 341; *Prosecutor v Bizimungu*, ICTR-00-56B-A, Appeals Chamber, Judgment, 30 June 2014, para 115; *Bemba*, Pre-Trial Chamber Decision on Charges (n 61), para 416.
²⁴³ *Nahimana* et al, Appeals Chamber Judgment (n 98), para 685; *Bagilishema*, Appeals Chamber Judgment (n 233), para 51; *Bemba*, Pre-Trial Chamber Decision on Charges (n 61), para 416.
²⁴⁴ See also *Blaškić*, Appeals Chamber Judgment (n 17), para 484; *Orić*, Appeals Chamber Judgment (n 141), para 18; *Halilović*, Appeals Chamber Judgment (n 234), para 59; *Gotovina and Markač*, Appeals Chamber Judgment (n 45), para 128; *Nahimana* et al, Appeals Chamber Judgment (n 98), para 484; *Gacumbitsi*, Appeals Chamber Judgment (n 55), para 143; *Sesay* et al, Appeals Chamber Judgment (n 18), paras 502 and 842.
²⁴⁵ See eg *Aleksovksi*, Appeals Chamber Judgment (n 115), paras 73–74; *Čelebići*, Appeals Chamber Judgment (n 115), para 206; *Blaškić*, Appeals Chamber Judgment (n 17), para 72; *Halilović*, Appeals Chamber Judgment (n 234), paras 63–64; *Hadžihasanović and Kubura*, Appeals Chamber Judgment (n 237), para 33; *Orić*, Appeals Chamber Judgment (n 141), para 177; *Boškoski and Tarčulovski*, Appeals Chamber Judgment (n 98), para 230; *Bagosora*, Appeals Chamber Judgment (n 116), para 672; *Bemba*, Pre-Trial Chamber Decision on Charges (n 61), para 443.
²⁴⁶ See *Hadžihasanović and Kubura*, Appeals Chamber Judgment (n 237), para 33, 142, and 154.

204 *Crimes under Customary International Law*

by filing a report to the competent authorities,[247] at least where the report is likely to trigger an investigation or disciplinary or criminal proceedings,[248] although 'if… the superior knows that the appropriate authorities are not functioning or if he knows that a report was likely to trigger an investigation that was sham, such a report would not be sufficient to fulfil the obligation to punish offending subordinates'.[249] It all depends on the circumstances.

5.111   In the case of a commander or other superior's failure to prevent a subordinate's commission of a crime, the ICTY Appeals Chamber has held that it is not necessary to establish a causal link between the failure to prevent and the commission of the crime.[250] But under article 28 of the Rome Statute, a commander or other superior may be held responsible for crimes committed by subordinates only if this commission occurs 'as a result of his or her failure to exercise control properly' over those subordinates.[251] That said, the Pre-Trial Chamber in *Bemba* held that causation in this connection is not to be assessed by reference to a 'but for' test, since, 'contrary to the visible and material effect of a positive act, the effect of an omission cannot be empirically determined with certainty'; rather, all that is required is that the commander or superior's omission increase the risk of the commission of the crimes in question.[252]

5.112   As regards a commander or other superior's criminal responsibility for failure punish a subordinate's commission of a crime,[253] the Appeals Chamber of the ICTY held by the narrowest of margins[254] in *Hadžihasanović* that a commander or other superior could not be held responsible for failure to punish crimes which took place before he or she had assumed command or authority over the subordinate.[255] The decision, which as a matter of logic is baseless, was reached on the ground that customary international law did not clearly indicate the contrary.[256] Subsequently, the Trial Chamber in *Orić* considered it immaterial for the purposes of responsibility for failure to punish whether the commander had assumed control over the subordinate at the time the latter committed the crime but felt bound to follow *Hadžihasanović*,[257] a decision upheld on appeal,[258] where the Appeals

---

[247] See *Boškoski and Tarčulovski*, Appeals Chamber Judgment (n 98), paras 230 and 234; *Hadžihasanović and Kubura*, Appeals Chamber Judgment (n 237), para 154; *Halilović*, Appeals Chamber Judgment (n 234), para 182; *Bemba*, Pre-Trial Chamber Decision on Charges of Prosecutor (n 61), para 440.
[248] *Boškoski and Tarčulovski*, Appeals Chamber Judgment (n 98), para 231.
[249] Ibid, para 234.
[250] *Blaškić*, Appeals Chamber Judgment (n 17), para 77; *Hadžihasanović and Kubura*, Appeals Chamber Judgment (n 237), paras 38–40.
[251] Rome Statute, art 28(*a*) and (*b*).
[252] *Bemba*, Pre-Trial Chamber Decision on Charges (n 61), para 425.
[253] Responsibility on this basis was considered in *Blaškić*, Appeals Chamber Judgment (n 17), para 85, to reflect customary international law.
[254] The Appeals Chamber split 3:2, Judges Shahabbuddeen and Hunt dissenting.
[255] *Prosecutor v Hadžihasanović* et al, IT-01-47-AR72, Appeals Chamber, Decision on Interlocutory Appeal Challenging Jurisdiction in Relation to Command Responsibility, 16 July 2003, para 51.
[256] For the Appeals Chamber's consideration of the evidence, see ibid, paras 44–50 and 52–56.
[257] *Prosecutor v Orić*, IT-03-68-T, Trial Chamber, Judgment, 30 June 2006, para 335.
[258] *Orić*, Appeals Chamber Judgment (n 141), para 165.

Chamber itself declined, again by the narrowest of margins,[259] to reconsider *Hadžihasanović*.[260] This position was maintained in *Halilović*[261] and *Perišić*[262] and by the ICTR Appeals Chamber in *Bizimungu*.[263]

Responsibility for failure to punish is complicated for the purposes of the Rome Statute by the requirement in article 28 that the subordinate's crime be committed 'as a result of [the commander's or other superior's] failure to exercise control properly'. One way of looking at this would be to say that failure to submit a matter to the competent authorities for investigation and prosecution results in criminal responsibility under article 28 of the Statute only if it leads to the commission of further or future crimes, and that it is by reference to these further or future crimes, not to the past ones, that the commander's responsibility is measured. But this seems odd, not least because it effectively abolishes the distinction between failure to prevent and failure to punish. An alternative way of reading article 28 would be to say, as has one Pre-Trial Chamber of the ICC,[264] that the requirement of causality applies only in relation to failure to prevent. 5.113

B. Mental Element

The ICTY, ICTR, and SCSL statutes recognize the criminal responsibility of a superior if he or she 'knew or had reason to know' that a subordinate was about to commit or had committed crimes.[265] The formulation 'had reason to know' is not the same as 'should have known'. A superior may not be held criminally responsible under the respective statutes for failing to acquire the relevant knowledge.[266] A superior may be convicted on the basis of superior responsibility 'only if information was available to him which would have put him on notice of offences committed by subordinates'.[267] In short, superior responsibility under the ICTY, 5.114

---

[259] The Appeals Chamber once more split 3:2, Judges Liu and Schomburg dissenting.
[260] *Orić*, Appeals Chamber Judgment (n 141), para 167.
[261] *Halilović*, Appeals Chamber Judgment (n 234), para 67.
[262] *Perišić*, Appeals Chamber Judgment (n 149), para 87.
[263] *Bizimungu*, Appeals Chamber Judgment (n 242), paras 292 and 369–370.
[264] See *Bemba*, Pre-Trial Chamber Decision on Charges (n 61), para 424.
[265] See, generally, *Čelebići*, Appeals Chamber Judgment (n 115), paras 216–241. See also eg *Blaškić*, Appeals Chamber Judgment (n 17), para 62; *Orić*, Appeals Chamber Judgment (n 141), para 18; *Bagilishema*, Appeals Chamber Judgment (n 233), para 28; *Nahimana* et al, Appeals Chamber Judgment (n 98), paras 484, 791, and 839; *Gacumbitsi*, Appeals Chamber Judgment (n 55), para 143; *Sesay* et al, Appeals Chamber Judgment (n 18), paras 842 and 873; *Fofana* et al, Appeals Chamber Judgment (n 110), para 371.
[266] See *Čelebići*, Appeals Chamber Judgment (n 115), para 226; *Blaškić*, Appeals Chamber Judgment (n 17), paras 62–63.
[267] *Čelebići*, Appeals Chamber Judgment (n 115), para 241. See also *Krnojelac*, Appeals Chamber Judgment (n 14), paras 151 and 154; *Blaškić*, Appeals Chamber Judgment (n 17), para 62; *Bagilishema*, Appeals Chamber Judgment (n 233), paras 28, 33, and 42; *Sesay* et al, Appeals Chamber Judgment (n 18), paras 852–853. As to the requisite level of specificity of the superior's knowledge, see eg *Čelebići*, Appeals Chamber Judgment (n 115), para 238; *Krnojelac*, Appeals Chamber Judgment (n 14), para 155. But cf *Ntabakuze*, Appeals Chamber Judgment (n 237), paras 245–250; *Bizimungu*, Appeals Chamber Judgment (n 241), paras 199 and 312. See too *Ntabakuze*, Appeals Chamber Judgment (n 237), joint dec Pocar and Liu, para 1.

ICTR, and SCSL statutes does not represent the imposition of criminal responsibility on the basis of negligence.[268]

5.115 In contrast, article 28(*a*)(i) of the Rome Statute, which uses the phrase 'should have known', embodies a negligence standard in relation to military commanders.[269] But the mental element required by article 28(*b*)(i) of the Statute in respect of other superiors is that the superior 'either knew, or consciously disregarded information which clearly indicated, that the subordinates were committing or about to commit' crimes within the meaning of the Statute.[270]

5.116 A commander or other superior need not know the precise identity of the subordinates who perpetrate the crimes in order to incur command or other superior responsibility.[271] The existence of these subordinates must, however, be proved.[272]

C. The Question of Fair Labelling

5.117 It is arguable that command and other superior responsibility as manifest in the statutes of the ICTY, ICTR, SCSL, and ICC treat as one and the same what are actually three functionally and morally distinct heads of criminal responsibility. The first, namely responsibility for failure to prevent in circumstances where the commander or other superior actually knew of his or her subordinates' offences, could be considered on a functional and moral par with responsibility for aiding and abetting those offences. In this light, it is argued, it does not seem unfair that the commander or other superior should be held responsible for those offences as such, in the same way that the aider and abettor would be. But the second and third heads—namely responsibility for failure to prevent in circumstances where the commander should have known of, or the other superior consciously disregarded, information which clearly indicated those offences, along with responsibility for failure to punish—could be seen to represent no more than the failure to acquit one's duties as a commander or other superior.[273] In these contexts, so the argument goes, it seems less fair to hold the commander or other superior responsible for the offences as such, rather than for the distinct, specific, and respective offences of failure to prevent and failure to punish offences within the jurisdiction of the Court. While it could be argued that any difference between failure to prevent when in possession of actual knowledge, on the one hand, and failure to prevent when not and failure to punish, on the other, can adequately be reflected in differential sentencing, it is said that a lighter sentence does not efface the stigma attached to a conviction for genocide as such, for a

---

[268] *Bagilishema*, Appeals Chamber Judgment (n 233), paras 34–35; *Čelebići*, Appeals Chamber Judgment (n 115), para 226; *Blaškić*, Appeals Chamber Judgment (n 17), para 62.
[269] *Bemba*, Pre-Trial Chamber Decision on Charges (n 61), para 432.
[270] See eg ibid, paras 432–434.
[271] *Blagojević and Jokić*, Appeals Chamber Judgment (n 144), para 287; *Bagosora*, Appeals Chamber Judgment (n 116), para 674; *Renzaho*, Appeals Chamber Judgment (n 116), paras 64 and 116; *Sesay* et al, Appeals Chamber Judgment (n 18), para 851.
[272] *Orić*, Appeals Chamber Judgment (n 141), para 35.
[273] See, in this light, *Bemba*, Pre-Trial Chamber Decision on Charges (n 61), para 405.

crime against humanity as such or for a war crime as such. The concern in both cases is for 'fair labelling'.[274]

In *Kononov v Latvia*, a Grand Chamber of the European Court of Human Rights understood command responsibility for failure to prevent the commission of crimes 'to be a mode of criminal liability for dereliction of a superior's duty to control, rather than one based on vicarious liability for the acts of others'.[275]

5.118

XIV. Conclusion

The modes of criminal responsibility under customary international law, whether settled or otherwise, are a detailed and at times complicated business, but perhaps no more so than their counterparts in the various national criminal justice traditions. Any attempt to reduce to cut-and-dry rules the almost-irreducible complexity of human action and inaction and the even more bewildering universe of human volition, conscious and unconscious, is arguably condemned to look like a less coherent version of the *Allgemeines Landrecht für die Preußischen Staaten*. All told, in spite of controversy, prevarication, and error, those tasked with ascertaining, applying, and, where appropriate, developing this area of international law have done not too bad a job under trying circumstances.[276]

5.119

Further Reading

AMBOS, K, 'The *Fujimori* Judgment: A President's Responsibility for Crimes Against Humanity as Indirect Perpetrator by Virtue of an Organized Power Apparatus' (2011) 9 *Journal of International Criminal Justice* 137

AMBOS, K, 'Joint Criminal Enterprise and Command Responsibility' (2007) 5 *Journal of International Criminal Justice* 159

AMBOS, K, *Treatise on International Criminal Law. Volume 1: Foundations and General Part* (Oxford: Oxford University Press, 2013), chapters 3–7

AMBOS, K, 'A Workshop, a Symposium and the *Katanga* Trial Judgment of 7 March 2014' (2014) 12 *Journal of International Criminal Justice* 219

BOAS, G, BISCHOFF, JL and REID, NL, *International Criminal Law Practitioner Library, Volume 1: Forms of Responsibility in International Criminal Law* (Cambridge: Cambridge University Press, 2008)

BONAFÉ, BI, 'Finding a Proper Role for Command Responsibility' (2007) 5 *Journal of International Criminal Justice* 599

CASSESE, A, 'Black Letter Lawyering v. Constructive Interpretation: The *Vasiljević* Case' (2004) 2 *Journal of International Criminal Justice* 265

---

[274] But cf *Hadžihasanović and Kubura*, Appeals Chamber Judgment (n 237), para 39, quoting *Prosecutor v Halilović*, IT-01-48-T, Trial Chamber, Judgment, 16 November 2005, para 78.

[275] *Kononov v Latvia* [GC] (Merits and Just Satisfaction), no 36376/04, ECHR 2010, para 211.

[276] Thankfully, too, there is a cohort of excellent scholars working on these topics, many of whose works are cited in the 'Further Reading' section of this chapter.

Cassese, A, 'The Proper Limits of Individual Responsibility under the Doctrine of Joint Criminal Enterprise' (2007) 5 *Journal of International Criminal Justice* 109

Cassese, A and Gaeta, P, *Cassese's International Criminal Law* (3rd edn, Oxford: Oxford University Press, 2013), chapters 9–11

Cryer, R, 'Imputation and Complicity in Common Law States: A (Partial) View from England and Wales' (2014) 12 *Journal of International Criminal Justice* 267

Cryer, R, Friman, H, Robinson, D and Wilmshurst, E, *An Introduction to International Criminal Law and Procedure* (3rd edn, Cambridge: Cambridge University Press, 2014), chapter 15

de Frouville, O, *Droit international pénal. Sources, Incriminations, Responsabilité* (Paris: Pedone, 2012), part III, chapter 1

DeFalco, R, 'Contextualizing *Actus Reus* under Article 25(3)(*d*) of the ICC Statute. Thresholds of Contribution' (2013) 11 *Journal of International Criminal Justice* 715

Farhang, C, 'Point of No Return: Joint Criminal Enterprise in *Brđanin*' (2010) 23 *Leiden Journal of International Law* 137

Finnin, S, *Elements of Accessorial Modes of Liability: Articles 25(3)(b) and (c) of the Rome Statute of the International Criminal Court* (Dordrecht: Martinus Nijhoff, 2012)

Finnin, S, 'Mental Elements under Article 30 of the Rome Statute of the International Criminal Court: A Comparative Analysis' (2012) 61 *International and Comparative Law Quarterly* 325

Fletcher, GP, 'New Court, Old *Dogmatik*' (2011) 9 *Journal of International Criminal Justice* 179

Fletcher, GP, 'The Theory of Criminal Liability and International Criminal Law' (2012) 10 *Journal of International Criminal Justice* 1025

Guilfoyle, D, 'Responsibility for Collective Atrocities: Fair Labelling and Approaches to Commission in International Criminal Law' (2011) 64 *Current Legal Problems* 255

Gustafson, K, 'The Requirement of an "Express Agreement" for Joint Criminal Enterprise Liability: A Critique of *Brđanin*' (2007) 5 *Journal of International Criminal Justice* 134

Harrendorf, S, 'How Can Criminology Contribute to an Explanation of International Crimes?' (2014) 12 *Journal of International Criminal Justice* 231

Levine, MJD, 'The Doctrine of Command Responsibility and Its Application to Superior Civilian Leadership: Does the International Criminal Court Have the Correct Standard?' (2007) 193 *Military Law Review* 52

Manacorda, S, *Imputazione collettiva e responsabilità personale. Uno studio sui paradigmi ascrittivi nel diritto penale internazionale* (Torino: Giappichelli, 2008)

Manacorda, S and Meloni, C, 'Indirect Perpetration *versus* Joint Criminal Enterprise: Concurring Approaches in the Practice of International Criminal Law?' (2011) 9 *Journal of International Criminal Justice* 159

Martinez, JS, 'Understanding *Mens Rea* in Command Responsibility: From *Yamashita* to *Blaškić* and Beyond' (2007) 5 *Journal of International Criminal Justice* 638

Meloni, C, 'Command Responsibility: Mode of Liability for the Crimes of Subordinates or Separate Offence of the Superior?' (2007) 5 *Journal of International Criminal Justice* 619

Mettraux, G, *International Crimes and the* Ad Hoc *Tribunals* (Oxford: Oxford University Press, 2005), chapters 16, 20, and 21

Murmann, U, 'Problems of Causation with Regard to (Potential) Actions of Multiple Protagonists' (2014) 12 *Journal of International Criminal Justice* 283

Nerlich, V, 'Superior Responsibility under Article 28 ICC Statute: For What Exactly Is the Superior Held Responsible?' (2007) 5 *Journal of International Criminal Justice* 665

OHLIN, J, 'Searching for the *Hinterman*: In Praise of Subjective Theories of Imputation' (2014) 12 *Journal of International Criminal Justice* 325

OHLIN, J, 'Second-Order Linking Principles: Combining Vertical and Horizontal Modes of Liability' (2012) 25 *Leiden Journal of International Law* 771

OHLIN, J, 'Three Conceptual Problems with the Doctrine of Joint Criminal Enterprise' (2007) 5 *Journal of International Criminal Justice* 69

OHLIN, J, VAN SLIEDREGT, E and WEIGEND, T, 'Assessing the Control-Theory' (2013) 26 *Leiden Journal of International Law* 725

POWLES, S, 'Joint Criminal Enterprise: Criminal Liability by Prosecutorial Ingenuity and Judicial Creativity?' (2004) 2 *Journal of International Criminal Justice* 606

ROXIN, C, 'Crimes as Part of Organized Power Structures' (2011) 9 *Journal of International Criminal Justice* 193

SANDER, B, 'Unravelling the Confusion Concerning Successor Superior Responsibility in the ICTY Jurisprudence' (2010) 23 *Leiden Journal of International Law* 105

SCHABAS, W, *The International Criminal Court. A Commentary on the Rome Statute* (Oxford: Oxford University Press, 2010), 421–42

SIVAKUMARAN, S, 'Command Responsibility in Irregular Groups' (2012) 10 *Journal of International Criminal Justice* 1129

STEWART, J, 'The End of "Modes of Liability" for International Crimes' (2012) 25 *Leiden Journal of International Law* 165

STEWART, J, 'Overdetermined Atrocities' (2012) 10 *Journal of International Criminal Justice* 1189

STUCKENBERG, C-F, 'Problems of "Subjective Imputation" in Domestic and International Criminal Law' (2014) 12 *Journal of International Criminal Justice* 311

VAN DER WILT, H, 'Joint Criminal Enterprise: Possibilities and Limitations' (2007) 5 *Journal of International Criminal Justice* 91

VAN SLIEDREGT, E, 'The Curious Case of International Criminal Liability' (2012) 10 *Journal of International Criminal Justice* 1171

VAN SLIEDREGT, E, *Individual Criminal Responsibility in International Law* (Oxford: Oxford University Press, 2012)

VAN SLIEDREGT, E, 'Joint Criminal Enterprise as a Pathway for Convicting Individuals for Genocide' (2007) 5 *Journal of International Criminal Justice* 184

VEST, H, 'Problems of Participation—Unitarian, Differentiated Approach, or Something Else?' (2014) 12 *Journal of International Criminal Justice* 295

WEIGEND, T, 'Perpetration through an Organization: The Unexpected Career of a German Legal Concept' (2011) 9 *Journal of International Criminal Justice* 91

WEIGEND, T, 'Problems of Attribution in International Criminal Law: A German Perspective' (2014) 12 *Journal of International Criminal Justice* 253

WERLE, G, 'Individual Criminal Responsibility in Article 25 ICC Statute' (2007) 5 *Journal of International Criminal Justice* 953

WERLE, G and JESSBURGER, F, *Principles of International Criminal Law* (3rd edn, Oxford: Oxford University Press, 2014), chapters 11, 12, and 15

YANEV, L and KOOIJMANS, T, 'Divided Minds in the *Lubanga* Trial Judgment: A Case against the Joint Control Theory' (2013) 13 *International Criminal Law Review* 789

ZORZI GIUSTINIANI, F, 'Stretching the Boundaries of Commission Liability. The ICTR Appeal Judgment in *Seromba*' (2008) 6 *Journal of International Criminal Justice* 783

6
Grounds for Excluding Responsibility

I. Introduction

6.1 Customary international criminal law recognizes a range of general grounds for the exclusion of criminal responsibility, known more commonly as defences, by which is meant complete defences—in other words, pleas that result in the acquittal of the accused of the charge to which the defence relates.[1] As with the bases of inculpation, the bases of exculpation under customary international criminal law draw heavily on general principles of law found in the various national criminal justice traditions; and as with the bases of inculpation, the tendency has been to proceed as if these general exculpatory principles have been transmuted into customary international law.

6.2 There are as many possible defences to criminal responsibility under customary international law as there are material and mental elements of the various crimes and alibis. In this light, the International Criminal Court (ICC)'s 'Elements of Crimes' note that '[g]rounds for excluding criminal responsibility or the absence thereof are generally not specified in the elements of crimes listed under each crime'.[2] At the same time, customary international criminal law recognizes some general defences, on which this chapter focuses. Equally, several general defences have been rejected by the various international and municipal courts that have tried customary international crimes, although some of these have been admitted as pleas in mitigation of punishment—that is, as grounds for the reduction of sentence on conviction. These rejected defences are examined in this chapter as well.

II. Preliminary Matters

6.3 Neither the Charter of the International Military Tribunal, Nuremberg ('Nuremberg Charter') or Charter of the International Military Tribunal for the Far East ('Tokyo Charter') nor the respective statutes of the International Criminal Tribunal for the former Yugoslavia (ICTY), the International Criminal Tribunal

---

[1] In this regard, international criminal law draws no formal distinction between justifications (*faits justicatifs*) and excuses (*faits excusatoires*).
[2] Elements of Crimes, ICC-ASP/1/3 (part II-B) (as amended), general introduction, para 5.

for Rwanda (ICTR) or the Special Court for Sierra Leone (SCSL) makes express provision for the exclusion of criminal responsibility in respect of the offences within the jurisdiction of the relevant court. But the possibility of exculpation is a general principle of criminal law recognized by all national criminal justice systems,[3] and it is reflected in the jurisprudence of these international criminal courts.[4]

6.4 Paragraph 1 of article 31 ('Grounds for excluding criminal responsibility') of the Rome Statute of the International Criminal Court ('Rome Statute')[5] acknowledges four general grounds for excluding criminal responsibility in respect of crimes within the jurisdiction of the ICC, namely mental incapacity; intoxication; self-defence, defence of others, and defence of certain property; and duress. Article 30(3) adds that 'the Court may consider a ground for excluding criminal responsibility other than those referred to in paragraph 1 where such a ground is derived from applicable law as set forth in article 21',[6] the reference to the Court's applicable law being implicitly, in this context, primarily to customary international law.[7]

6.5 In addition to the bases of exculpation laid down in article 31, article 32 of the Rome Statute ('Mistake of fact or mistake of law') states in paragraph 1 that '[a] mistake of fact shall be a ground for excluding criminal responsibility only if it negates the mental element required by the crime'. Paragraph 2 of article 31 provides that '[a] mistake of law as to whether a particular type of conduct is a crime within the jurisdiction of the Court shall not be a ground for excluding criminal responsibility', but adds that '[a] mistake of law may, however, be a ground for excluding criminal responsibility if it negates the mental element required by such a crime, or as provided for in article 33'.

6.6 In turn, article 33 of the Rome Statute ('Superior orders and prescription of law') specifies in paragraph 1:

The fact that a crime within the jurisdiction of the Court has been committed by a person pursuant to an order of a Government or of a superior, whether military or civilian, shall not relieve that person of criminal responsibility unless:
(a) The person was under a legal obligation to obey orders of the Government or the superior in question;
(b) The person did not know that the order was unlawful; and
(c) The order was not manifestly unlawful.

---

[3] See eg *Prosecutor v Kordić and Čerkez*, IT-95-14/2-T, Trial Chamber, Judgment, 26 February 2001, para 449.
[4] See also eg the International Law Commission (ILC)'s Draft Code of Crimes against the Peace and Security of Mankind with commentaries, *Ybk ILC 1996*, vol II/2, 17 ('ILC Draft Code of Crimes'), art 14 ('Defences'): 'The competent court shall determine the admissibility of defences in accordance with the general principles of law, in the light of the character of each crime.'
[5] Article 31(2) of the Rome Statute provides that the Court 'shall determine the applicability of the grounds for excluding criminal responsibility provided for in [the] Statute to the case before it'.
[6] Article 30(3) continues: 'The procedures relating to the consideration of such a ground shall be provided for in the Rules of Procedure and Evidence.' These procedures are laid down in the ICC's Rules of Procedure and Evidence (ICC RPE), ICC-ASP/1/3 (part II-A) (as amended), rule 80.
[7] For the ICC's applicable law, see *infra* para 14.57.

6.7 Paragraph 2 of the provision adds that, for the purposes of article 33, orders to commit genocide or crimes against humanity 'are manifestly unlawful'.

6.7 It is difficult to say whether these provisions accord in all their specifics with customary international law. That said, as with the definitions of the crimes themselves[8] and the modes of responsibility, they are probably shaping custom in their image.

6.8 Grounds for excluding individual criminal responsibility under international law are to be distinguished at all times from circumstances precluding wrongfulness under the law of state responsibility.[9]

III. Accepted Defences

A. Mental Incapacity

6.9 The ICTY Appeals Chamber stated in *Čelebići* that the 'lack of mental capacity', which the Chamber equated with a plea of insanity, was, 'if successful', 'a complete defence to a charge'.[10] Citing the famous *M'Naghten* rules of English criminal law, the Chamber considered the defence of lack of mental capacity available if at the time of the offence the accused 'was labouring under such a defect of reason, from disease of the mind, as not to know the nature and quality of his act or, if he did know it, that he did not know that what he was doing was wrong'.[11]

6.10 The defence of mental incapacity is embodied in article 31(1)(a) of the Rome Statute, which provides that the accused shall not be held criminally responsible if, at the time of the impugned conduct, he or she 'suffers from a mental disease or defect that destroys that person's capacity to appreciate the unlawfulness or nature of his or her conduct, or capacity to control his or her conduct to conform to the requirements of law'.[12] The archaic reference to a mental 'disease' is to what we would today call mental 'illness'. The term covers a wide range of medically-recognized psychiatric conditions, both permanent and transient. Indeed, the ICTY Appeals Chamber in *Čelebići* thought the defence embodied in article 31(1)(a) of the Rome Statute to be 'akin to the defence of insanity'.[13] That said, given the reference not only to 'mental disease' but also to '[mental] defect', the defence would appear to extend beyond insanity to embrace other

---

[8] Recall *supra* para 4.4.
[9] For the latter, see the ILC's Articles on Responsibility of States for Internationally Wrongful Acts, annexed to GA res 56/83, 12 December 2001 ('Articles on Responsibility of States'), Part One, Chapter V. See particularly in this regard Articles on Responsibility of States, art 58 ('Individual responsibility'): 'These articles are without prejudice to any question of the individual responsibility under international law of any person acting on behalf of a State.'
[10] *Prosecutor v Delalić* et al ('*Čelebići*'), IT-96-21-A, Appeals Chamber, Judgment, 20 February 2001, para 582, emphasis omitted. (Note that '*Delalić* et al' became '*Mucić* et al' on the acquittal of the accused Delalić.)
[11] Ibid.
[12] In addition to constituting a defence, mental incapacity can constitute a ground for postponement or stay of proceedings and for vitiating the formal validity of a guilty plea.
[13] *Čelebići*, Appeals Chamber Judgment (n 10), para 587.

grounds of incapacity such as mental disability, whether congenital or acquired and whether permanent or temporary. In light of the further reference to the incapacity to control one's conduct,[14] the defence would appear to encompass states of automatism.

6.11 As posited in article 31(1)(*a*) of the Rome Statute, the defence is permitted if it vitiates either the requisite mental element of the offence (that is, if it 'destroys [the accused]'s capacity to appreciate the unlawfulness or nature of his or her conduct') or the voluntariness of the accused's conduct (that is, his or her 'capacity to control his or her conduct to conform to the requirements of law'). In short, the defence seeks to obviate criminal responsibility on the basis of strict liability.

6.12 No provision has been made to date in the statutes or rules of the respective international criminal courts for the commission to a secure psychiatric facility of persons who escape criminal responsibility on account of a lack of mental capacity brought about by mental illness.[15]

6.13 What was formerly rule 67(A)(ii)(*b*)[16] of the ICTY's Rules of Procedure and Evidence (ICTY RPE) provided that 'the defence shall notify the Prosecutor of its intent to offer... any special defence, including that of diminished or lack of mental responsibility'. Pointing to this provision, the defence argued before the Appeals Chamber in *Čelebići* that the ICTY Statute recognized a defence of diminished responsibility. In response, the Chamber, noting that the Statute contained no express defence of diminished responsibility, held that rule 67(A)(ii)(*b*)'s description of diminished mental responsibility as a 'special defence' was insufficient to constitute it as such, since article 15 of the Statute, the source of the judges' power to adopt rules of procedure and evidence, did not encompass a power to adopt rules creating new defences.[17] Rule 67(A)(ii)(*b*) was held to refer to diminished mental responsibility as a mitigating circumstance.[18] The Appeals Chamber then considered whether 'a "special defence" of diminished responsibility [was] known to international law', relying, 'in the absence of reference to such a defence in established customary or conventional law', on 'the general principles of law recognised by all nations'.[19] Pointing to, *inter alia*, the fact that article 31(1)(*a*) of the Rome Statute 'requires the destruction of (and not merely the impairment [of]) the defendant's capacity',[20] the Appeals Chamber concluded that 'the relevant general principle of law upon which, in effect, both the common law and the civil law systems have acted is that the defendant's diminished mental responsibility is relevant to the sentence to be imposed and is not a defence leading to an acquittal

---

[14] Cf, in this regard, *Prosecutor v Delalić* et al ('*Čelebići*'), IT-96-21-T, Trial Chamber, Judgment, 16 November 1998, para 1156.
[15] But see the ICC's Regulations of the Court, ICC-BD/01-01-04 (as amended), reg 103(6), on persons detained by the Court, which provides for 'the detention of mentally ill persons and for those who suffer from serious psychiatric conditions'. Regulation 103(6) states that, by order of the Chamber, 'a detained person who is determined to be mentally ill or who suffers from a serious psychiatric condition may be transferred to a specialized institution for appropriate treatment'.
[16] The relevant provision is now ICTY RPE, rule 67(B)(i)(*b*).
[17] *Čelebići*, Appeals Chamber Judgment (n 10), para 583.   [18] Ibid, para 590.
[19] Ibid, para 583.   [20] Ibid, para 587.

in the true sense'.²¹ This approach is the one taken in rule 145(2)(*a*)(i) of the ICC's Rules of Procedure and Evidence (ICC RPE), which provides that, in sentencing, the Court shall, as appropriate, take into account in mitigation 'circumstances falling short of constituting grounds for exclusion of criminal responsibility, such as substantially diminished mental capacity'.

B. Intoxication

6.14 The defence of intoxication, found in numerous national criminal justice systems, is embodied in article 31(1)(*b*) of the Rome Statute, which provides that a person shall not be held criminally responsible if, at the time of the relevant conduct, '[t]he person is in a state of intoxication that destroys that person's capacity to appreciate the unlawfulness or nature of his or her conduct, or capacity to control his or her conduct to conform to the requirements of law'. Like mental incapacity, the defence of intoxication seeks to obviate the imposition of criminal responsibility on the basis of strict liability, vitiating criminal responsibility if it negates the requisite mental element of an offence or the requisite voluntariness of the accused's conduct. But the defence laid down in article 31(1)(*b*) is unavailable if 'the person has become voluntarily intoxicated under such circumstances that the person knew, or disregarded the risk, that, as a result of the intoxication, he or she was likely to engage in conduct constituting a crime within the jurisdiction of the Court'.

C. Self-Defence, Defence of Others, and Defence of Certain Property

6.15 All national criminal justice systems recognize self-defence as a ground for excluding criminal responsibility. Many also recognize defence of others, and some recognize defence of at least certain property.

6.16 Drawing on the jurisprudence of several post-Second World War national military tribunals, the United Nations War Crimes Commission (UNWCC) concluded that '[a] plea of self-defence may be successfully put forward, in suitable circumstances, in war crimes trials as in trials held under municipal law'.²²

6.17 Article 31(1)(*c*) of the Rome Statute embodies the defence of self-defence, defence of others, and defence of specified property, stating that a person shall not be held criminally responsible if, at the time of the conduct in question,

> [t]he person acts reasonably to defend himself or herself or another person or, in the case of war crimes, property which is essential for the survival of the person or another person or

---

²¹ Ibid, para 590. See also the post-Second World War case of *Gerbsch*, 13 LRTWC 131, 132 (1948), where the Special Court in Amsterdam treated as a mitigating circumstance the fact that 'the accused's "mental faculties were defective and underdeveloped" at the time of the crimes as well as at that of the trial'.

²² 15 LRTWC 177. See also ILC Draft Code of Crimes, art 14, commentary, paras 7 and 8.

property which is essential for accomplishing a military mission, against an imminent and unlawful use of force in a manner proportionate to the degree of danger to the person or the other person or property protected.[23]

As is apparent, article 31(1)(c) distinguishes between the exclusion of responsibility for genocide, crimes against humanity, and aggression and the exclusion of responsibility for war crimes, in that defence of property is accepted as a ground for excluding criminal responsibility only for war crimes. Preconditions to the availability of the defence are that any acts performed in self-defence, defence of others or defence of specified property be reasonable, be directed against an imminent and unlawful use of force, and be proportionate to the degree of danger to the accused or to the other person or persons or the property sought to be protected. These cumulative conditions reflect the requirements of the analogous defence recognized by the major national criminal justice systems. Whether the use of force against which the impugned act is directed is imminent and unlawful and whether the act is proportionate to the danger are both to be assessed objectively.

6.18 A plea of self-defence, defence of others or defence of property is unlikely to succeed in relation to most crimes within the jurisdiction of the ICC. It is difficult to imagine how it could successfully be argued that, for example, killing members of a national, ethnic, racial or religious group with an intent to destroy that group in whole or in part[24] or murder committed as part of a widespread or systematic attack directed against a civilian population[25] or employing asphyxiating, poisonous or other gases[26] could ever be a reasonable and proportionate response to an imminent and unlawful use of force. But the defence has a role to play in the context of some war crimes.

6.19 Article 31(1)(c) of the Rome Statute adds that '[t]he fact that the person was involved in a defensive operation conducted by forces shall not in itself constitute a ground for excluding criminal responsibility under this subparagraph'. The provision reflects the fundamental principle of international humanitarian law, reiterated in the preamble to 1977 Protocol I Additional to the 1949 Geneva Conventions ('Additional Protocol I'), that the reasons for which a conflict is fought, and indeed the reasons for which any individual engagement in that conflict is fought, are immaterial to the application of the laws of armed conflict. The *jus in bello* binds both sides without distinction. This principle was endorsed by the ICTY Appeals Chamber in *Kordić*, where, rejecting the invocation of the defence by an accused who fought for a non-state armed group, the Chamber 'recall[ed] that whether an attack was...defensive or offensive is from a legal

---

[23] The provision was considered declaratory of customary international law by an ICTY Trial Chamber in *Kordić and Čerkez*, Trial Chamber Judgment (n 3), para 451, although whether this is true of all of its specifics is open to doubt.
[24] See Rome Statute, art 6(*a*).   [25] See ibid, art 7(1)(*a*).
[26] See ibid, art 8(2)(*b*)(xviii).

point of view irrelevant', the only issue being 'whether the way the military action was carried out was criminal or not'.[27]

D. Duress

6.20 The defence of duress constitutes a classic point of difference between deontological and consequentialist ethics. Perhaps in reflection of this, it has enjoyed a chequered history in international criminal law, as it has in some national criminal justice systems.

6.21 Duress was accepted as a complete defence by some post-Second World War national military tribunals. Others accepted it only as a mitigating circumstance.[28]

6.22 As for the ICTY, the Trial Chamber in *Erdemović* accepted that physical and moral duress leading to the accused's fear for his own life and for that of his wife and child could, in principle, constitute a complete defence,[29] although the requirements to be met were 'particularly strict'.[30] The Chamber noted that duress had been accepted as a complete defence after the Second World War in cases where '(*a*) the act charged was done to avoid an immediate danger both serious and irreparable; (*b*) there was no adequate means of escape; (*c*) the remedy was not disproportionate to the evil'.[31] The test laid down in (*a*) and (*b*) was, in essence, whether a moral choice was possible,[32] and a person could be considered deprived of moral choice in the face of an imminent threat of death or serious bodily harm.[33] None of these statements of principle was challenged or disturbed on appeal.[34] What was, however, at issue on appeal in *Erdemović* was whether duress could constitute a complete defence to a crime against humanity or war crime involving the killing of what was referred to as an 'innocent person', by which was meant a civilian or a person *hors de combat*. A majority of the Appeals

---

[27] *Prosecutor v Kordić and Čerkez*, IT-95-14/2-A, Appeals Chamber, Judgment, 17 December 2004, para 812. These statements were reaffirmed in *Prosecutor v Martić*, IT-95-11-A, Appeals Chamber, Judgment, 8 October 2008, para 268; *Prosecutor v Boškoski and Tarčulovski*, IT-04-82-A, Appeals Chamber, Judgment, 19 May 2010, paras 31, 44, 51, and 172; and *Prosecutor v Đorđević*, IT-05-87/1-A, Appeals Chamber, Judgment, 27 January 2014, para 93 note 289. See also *Prosecutor v Šainović* et al, IT-05-87-A, Appeals Chamber, Judgment, 23 January 2014, para 1662.

[28] See, generally, 15 LRTWC 170–5; ILC Draft Code of Crimes, art 14, commentary, para 10.

[29] *Prosecutor v Erdemović*, IT-96-22-T, Trial Chamber, Sentencing Judgment (No 1), 29 November 1996, para 14.

[30] *Erdemović*, Trial Chamber Sentencing Judgment (No 1) (n 29), para 19.

[31] Ibid, para 17, implicitly adopting the summary of the post-Second World War jurisprudence offered by the UNWCC at 15 LRTWC 174, as reproduced in ILC Draft Code of Crimes, art 14, commentary, para 10.

[32] *Erdemović*, Trial Chamber Sentencing Judgment (No 1) (n 29), paras 18 and 19, citing *In re Ohlendorf* ('Einsatzgruppen case'), quoted at 15 LRTWC 174 (USMT Nuremberg 1948), *United States v Krauch* et al ('IG Farben case'), 10 LRTWC 54, 54 and 57 (USMT Nuremberg 1948), and *United States v von Leeb* et al ('High Command case'), 12 LRTWC 72 (USMT Nuremberg 1948).

[33] *Erdemović*, Trial Chamber Sentencing Judgment (No 1) (n 29), para 18, citing *von Leeb* et al (n 32).

[34] See, generally, *Prosecutor v Erdemović*, IT-96-22-A, Appeals Chamber, Judgment, 7 October 1997.

Chamber concluded that it could not but that it could be considered in mitigation of punishment.[35]

6.23 Duress is recognized as a complete defence to criminal responsibility in article 31(1)(d) of the Rome Statute, which does not rule out reliance on duress as a defence to the killing of an 'innocent person'. But the availability of the defence is subject to strict conditions. The first is that there be 'a threat of imminent death or of continuing or imminent serious bodily harm against that person or another person'. As indicated in article 31(1)(d)(i) and (ii), such threat may either be made by other persons or constituted by other circumstances beyond that person's control. The test of imminence is objective, as it is in relation to self-defence. Next, the conduct of the accused in avoidance of this threat must be necessary and reasonable, these again being objective standards. Finally, the accused must 'not intend to cause a greater harm than the one sought to be avoided'. This last standard is expressly subjective, in contrast to the test for the proportionality of an act in self-defence.

6.24 The defence of duress is sometimes referred to as the defence of 'necessity', and the term 'extreme necessity' is occasionally used where the accused purports to have committed the offence in order to prevent a harm other than that posed by a threat to himself or herself or to his or her immediate family. Extreme necessity was pleaded before the Appeals Chamber of the ICTY in *Aleksovski*; but, since the plea had not been raised at trial, the Appeals Chamber 'consider[ed] it unnecessary to dwell on whether necessity constitutes a defence under international law [and] whether it is the same as the defence of duress'.[36] Article 31 of the Rome Statute would seem to provide a negative answer to the first of these questions, requiring as it does 'a threat of imminent death or of continuing or imminent serious bodily harm against that person or another person'. Moreover, given that military necessity is no defence,[37] it is hard to see how and why extreme necessity could or should be.[38]

6.25 Duress is to be distinguished from the plea of superior orders, even if 'often the same factual circumstances engage both notions'.[39] That said, the existence of an order may be relevant when determining whether duress is made out on the facts.[40]

E. Mistake of Fact or Law

6.26 Many national criminal justice systems recognize mistake of legally significant fact as a defence to criminal responsibility. Not many, in contrast, recognize the defence

---

[35] See *Erdemović*, Appeals Chamber Judgment (n 34), sep op McDonald and Vorah, paras 88–89 (after extended analysis, paras 40–87), and diss op Li, paras 5, 8, and 12. But cf ibid, diss op Cassese, paras 11–49 and diss op Stephen, paras 23–68, expressly concurring with each other.
[36] *Prosecutor v Aleksovski*, IT-95-14/1, Appeals Chamber, Judgment, 24 March 2000, para 55. See also, similarly, *Prosecutor v Blagojević and Jokić*, IT-02-60-A, Appeals Chamber, Judgment, 9 May 2007, para 202 n 526.
[37] See *infra* paras 6.37–6.38.
[38] At the same time, the defence of duress and, were it to exist separately, the defence of necessity are both to be distinguished from the plea of military necessity.
[39] *Erdemović*, Appeals Chamber Sentencing Judgment (n 34), sep op McDonald and Vorah, para 34, reiterated in *Prosecutor v Bralo*, IT-95-17-A, Appeals Chamber, Judgment on Sentencing Appeal, 2 April 2007, para 22.
[40] *Erdemović*, Appeals Chamber Sentencing Judgment (n 34), sep op McDonald and Vorah, paras 35 and 36. See, generally, 15 LRTWC 155–8 and 170–5.

of mistake or ignorance of law. To this latter extent, most national criminal justice systems impose criminal responsibility on the basis of a form of strict liability. The reason for this is pragmatic. If the criminal courts insisted on everyone's correct knowledge of the criminal law as a condition of criminal responsibility, the only people in prison would be criminal lawyers. In short, one rationale for the rule of law, namely the maintenance of social order, trumps the other, *viz* natural justice based on fair warning to the individual, the overall justification being the ultimate avoidability of strict liability through familiarization with the law.

6.27   On the basis of the jurisprudence of the post-Second World War national military tribunals, the UNWCC concluded that '[a] mistake of fact... may constitute a defence in war crime[s] trials'.[41] The UNWCC noted too in the same jurisprudence 'some tendency to recognise that an alleged war criminal cannot be expected to have been quite as well aware of the provision[s] of international law as of those of his own municipal law',[42] a perhaps-specious explanation for a certain preparedness to allow the defence of mistake or ignorance of law.

6.28   Article 32 of the Rome Statute recognizes, in an oblique manner, both mistake of fact and mistake of law as grounds for excluding responsibility for crimes within the jurisdiction of the ICC if such a mistake negates the mental element required by the crime. Article 32(1) states that a mistake of fact 'shall be a ground for excluding criminal responsibility only if it negates the mental element required by the crime', the insertion of the word 'only' being intended to emphasize the restrictive availability of the defence. The second sentence of article 32(2) provides that a mistake of law 'may... be a ground for excluding criminal responsibility if it negates the mental element required by... a crime, or as provided for in article 33'.[43] In turn, article 33 deals with the defence of superior orders, with the precise reference in article 32(2) being to article 33(1)(*b*), the requirement that, in order to establish the defence of superior orders, the accused must not have known that the order was unlawful. What this second limb of the second sentence of article 32(2) means is that, to establish the defence of superior orders, it is unnecessary—in contrast to the situation with respect to any other mistake of law—that the accused's ignorance as to the unlawfulness of the order negate the *mens rea* of the offence.

6.29   As with the defences of mental incapacity and intoxication, the availability of the defences of mistake of fact and mistake of law seek to avoid the imposition of criminal responsibility on the basis of strict liability. The first sentence of article 32(2) specifies, however, that '[a] mistake of law as to whether a particular type of conduct is a crime within the jurisdiction of the Court shall not be a ground for excluding

---

[41] 15 LRTWC 184.   [42] 15 LRTWC 182.

[43] For its part, the Pre-Trial Chamber in *Prosecutor v Lubanga*, ICC-01/04-01/06-803-tEN, Pre-Trial Chamber, Decision on the Confirmation of Charges, 29 January 2007, para 316, stated that, 'absent a plea under article 33 of the Statute, the defence of mistake of law can succeed under article 32 only if [the accused] was unaware of a normative objective element of the crime as a result of not realising its social significance (its everyday meaning)'. The everyday meaning of this statement is a mystery, although the Chamber's citation of Eser suggests that the reference is to what is called the 'layman's parallel evaluation test'.

criminal responsibility'.[44] To this extent, a form of strict liability is imposed, for the pragmatic reasons mentioned.[45]

F. Superior Orders

One of the most controversial and inconsistently accepted defences to criminal responsibility under international law has been the plea that the accused's internationally criminal conduct was mandated by an order from his or her government or from a superior, the latter usually military but equally possibly civilian. 6.30

Prior to the Second World War, the status of the plea of superior orders varied among national military tribunals and was unclear as a matter of customary international law. Where accepted, the defence tended to overlap with the substantive defence of act of state. After the War, article II(4)(b) of Control Council Law No 10[46] proclaimed that '[t]he fact that any person acted pursuant to the order of his Government or of a superior does not free him from responsibility for a crime, but may be considered in mitigation'. In the light of this and '[t]he general upshot of a large number of decisions' of post-War municipal courts, the UNWCC concluded that the accused could not rely on the plea of superior orders as constituting a complete defence, although the plea could be considered in mitigation of punishment.[47] 6.31

As for international criminal courts, article 8 of the Nuremberg Charter provided that '[t]he fact that the defendant acted pursuant to the order of his Government or of a superior shall not free him from responsibility, but may be considered in mitigation of punishment if the Tribunal determine that justice so requires'.[48] In its judgment, however, the Nuremberg Tribunal muddied the waters by conflating the defence of superior orders and the distinct defence of duress. After recalling the rejection of the former in article 8 of its Charter, the Tribunal added that '[t]he true test, which is found in varying degrees in the criminal law of most nations, is not the existence of the order, but whether moral choice was in fact possible'.[49] In short, the Tribunal effectively recognized, contradicting article 8 6.32

---

[44] This was emphasized in *Lubanga*, Pre-Trial Chamber Decision on Confirmation of Charges (n 43), para 305, where the Pre-Trial Chamber rejected what amounted to an argument that the defence of mistake of law within the meaning of art 32(2) of the Rome Statute encompassed the accused's unawareness that his conduct entailed criminal responsibility under the Statute. See also *Prosecutor v Brima* et al, SCSL-2004-16-A, Appeals Chamber, Judgment, 22 February 2008, para 296.
[45] Recall *supra* para 6.26.
[46] Law No 10 (20 December 1945) of the Allied Control Council for Germany ('Control Council Law No 10').
[47] See 15 LRTWC 158–9 and, more generally, ibid, 157–60. See also UNWCC, *History of the United Nations War Crimes Commission and the Development of the Law of War* (London: UNWCC, 1948), 274–88; H Lauterpacht, 'The Law of Nations and the Punishment of War Crimes' (1944) 21 *BYIL* 58, 69–74; H Kelsen, *Principles of International Law* (2nd edn, RW Tucker ed, New York: Rinehart and Winston 1966), 152–3.
[48] See also Tokyo Charter, art 6.
[49] Judgment of the International Military Tribunal for the Trial of German Major War Criminals, Nuremberg, 30 September and 1 October 1946, Misc No 12 (1946), Cmd 6964, reproduced (1947) 41 *AJIL* 172 ('Nuremberg judgment'), 221.

of its Charter, that superior orders could, after all, constitute a complete defence in certain circumstances. For its subsequent part, the International Law Commission (ILC), after divisive debate in which certain members similarly elided the separate defences of superior orders and duress, reproduced the Tribunal's words in principle IV of its Principles of International Law Recognized in the Charter of the Nürnberg Tribunal and in the Judgment of the Tribunal,[50] which stated that '[t]he fact that a person acted pursuant to [an] order of his Government or of a superior does not relieve him from responsibility under international law, provided a moral choice was in fact possible to him'.

6.33 Article 7(4) of the ICTY Statute ignores the gloss placed on article 8 of the Nuremberg Charter by the Tribunal and ILC, providing, in terms almost identical to those of the Charter, that '[t]he fact that an accused person acted pursuant to an order of a Government or of a superior shall not relieve him of criminal responsibility, but may be considered in mitigation of punishment if the International Tribunal determines that justice so requires'. The respective statutes of the ICTR and SCSL reproduce this provision nearly verbatim, *mutatis mutandis*.[51]

6.34 In contrast, article 33(1) of the Rome Statute does recognize, under certain conditions and by way of a negative statement subject to exceptions, the defence of superior orders. The first condition, laid down in subparagraph (*a*), is that obedience to the order must have been prescribed by law—that is, the accused must have been under a municipal legal obligation, and not simply permitted by municipal law, to obey the orders of the government or of the superior in question. Next, in accordance with subparagraph (*b*), the accused must not have known that the order was internationally unlawful. Knowledge in this context is actual, *viz* subjective.[52] Finally, as per subparagraph (*c*), the order must not have been manifestly—in other words, objectively and plainly—internationally unlawful. Article 33(2) elaborates on article 33(1)(*c*) by deeming orders to commit genocide or crimes against humanity manifestly internationally unlawful. As a result, superior orders are a potential defence only to war crimes and, insofar as it is factually conceivable, aggression.

6.35 Even in terms of war crimes, there would seem to be limited practical scope for the defence of superior orders, as distinct from duress, in relation to members of regular armed forces instructed in the laws of armed conflict. The international unlawfulness of a superior order contrary to international law could be expected, in such a context, to be manifest.

6.36 The acceptance in the Rome Statute of the defence, albeit restricted, of superior orders is not the result of a reversion to Kelsenian ideas of the impermissibility of individual criminal responsibility under customary international law for acts of state.[53] Rather, article 33 of the Rome Statute reflects, first, the traditional concern

---

[50] Principles of International Law Recognized in the Charter of the Nürnberg Tribunal and in the Judgment of the Tribunal, *Ybk ILC 1950*, vol II, 191 ('ILC Nürnberg Principles').
[51] See ICTR Statute, art 6(4); SCSL Statute, art 6(4). See also ILC Draft Code of Crimes, art 11.
[52] Recall, in this regard, the second limb of Rome Statute, art 32(2).
[53] Recall *supra* para 2.71. The Court's jurisdiction *ratione materiae* over the crime of aggression, art 27(1)'s rejection of official capacity as a substantive defence, and the rider to art 31(1)(*c*) in respect of

of military lawyers[54] that the blanket denial of the defence of superior orders has the potential to undermine the military discipline on which depends, *inter alia* and perhaps paradoxically, compliance with the laws of armed conflict; and, secondly, a certain 'sympathy...with the predicament of the soldier who is...subject to two possibly conflicting jurisdictions'.[55]

IV. Rejected Defences

A. Military Necessity

Although the post-Second World War jurisprudence on point is not wholly consistent,[56] it is clear that military necessity does not constitute a defence to criminal responsibility under customary international law. In the words of *List*, '[m]ilitary necessity or expediency do not justify a violation of positive rules'; rather, '[t]he rules of International Law must be followed even if it results in the loss of a battle or even a war'.[57] The defence of military necessity was further rejected by the ICTY Appeals Chamber, in the specific context of the targeting of civilians and civilian objects, in *Blaškić*[58] and in *Kordić*, the latter stating that 'the prohibition against attacking civilians and civilian objects may not be derogated from because of military necessity'.[59]

6.37

While no defence of military necessity exists under customary international law, certain prohibitions governing the conduct of hostilities make allowance, as a feature of the primary rule, for considerations of military necessity, with the result that, should a genuine situation of military necessity be established on the facts, no criminal responsibility arises in the first place. Examples include the war crimes reflected in article 8(2)(*a*)(iv) (extensive destruction and appropriation of property not justified by military necessity and carried out unlawfully and wantonly) and article 8(2)(*b*)(xiii) (destroying or seizing the enemy's property unless such destruction or seizure be imperatively demanded by the necessities of war) of the Rome Statute.

6.38

---

the exercise of a state's right of self-defence all run counter to the suggestion that art 33's defence of superior orders is premised on a belief that an individual may not be held criminally responsible for acts performed as an organ of state. See *supra* paras 4.90–4.101, *infra* paras 6.41 and 14.42, and *supra* para 6.19 respectively.

[54] But cf post-Second World War German military lawyers.
[55] Lauterpacht (n 47), 71.   [56] See 15 LRTWC 175–6.
[57] *United States v List and others* ('Hostages Trial'), 8 LRTWC 34, 66–7 (USMT Nuremberg 1949).
[58] *Prosecutor v Blaškić*, IT-95-14-A, Appeals Chamber, Judgment, 29 July 2004, para 109.
[59] *Kordić and Čerkez*, Appeals Chamber Judgment (n 27), para 54 (as corrected in *Prosecutor v Kordić and Čerkez*, IT-95-14/2-A, Appeals Chamber, Corrigendum to Judgment of 17 December 2004, 26 January 2005). Both *Blaškić* and *Kordić* were endorsed and relied on in this respect in *Prosecutor v Galić*, IT-98-29-A, Appeals Chamber, Judgment, 30 November 2006, para 130 and *Prosecutor v Strugar*, IT-01-42-A, Appeals Chamber, Judgment, 17 July 2008, paras 275 and 330. See also *Prosecutor v Fofana and Kondewa*, SCSL-04-14-A, Appeals Chamber, Judgment, 28 May 2008, para 247 and *Prosecutor v Katanga*, ICC-01/04-01/07-3436, Trial Chamber, Jugement rendu en application de l'article 74 du Statut, 7 March 2014, para 800.

B. *Tu quoque*

6.39 The plea of *tu quoque* ('you too')—in other words, the accused's attempt to justify or excuse his or her crimes by reference to the prior or subsequent commission of such crimes by opposing forces—has been rejected by the ICTY Appeals Chamber.[60]

6.40 An argument seemingly based on the related principle *inadimplenti non est adimplendum*—that a party is excused from fulfilling an obligation towards another by that other's failure to fulfil its own obligation towards the first—was similarly rejected in *Martić*, where the ICTY Appeals Chamber held that the accused, charged with deliberately targeting civilians in a missile attack, could not benefit from the fact that the opposing party had allegedly not taken the precautions against the effect of attacks prescribed in article 58 of Additional Protocol I.[61]

C. Official Capacity

6.41 The constituent instruments of all the international criminal courts to date have expressly excluded the substantive defence that the impugned conduct constituted, in legal terms, an act of state and not of the individual accused. Article 7 of the Nuremberg Charter provided that '[t]he official position of defendants, whether as Heads of State or responsible officials in Government departments, shall not be considered as freeing them from responsibility or mitigating punishment'.[62] Article 7(2) of the ICTY Statute, article 6(2) of the ICTR Statute, and article 6(2) of the SCSL Statute provide that '[t]he official position of any accused person, whether as Head of State or Government or as a responsible Government official, shall not relieve such person of criminal responsibility nor mitigate punishment'.[63] For its part, paragraph 1 of article 27 ('Irrelevance of official capacity') of the Rome Statute provides:

This Statute shall apply equally to all persons without any distinction based on official capacity. In particular, official capacity as a Head of State or Government, a member of a Government or parliament, an elected representative or a government official shall in no case exempt a person from criminal responsibility under this Statute, nor shall it, in and of itself, constitute a ground for reduction of sentence.

These provisions all represent the rejection of the asserted non-responsibility of individuals for acts of state.

---

[60] See *Prosecutor v Kunarac* et al, IT-96-23 & IT-96-23/1-A, Appeals Chamber, Judgment, 12 June 2002, para 87; *Martić*, Appeals Chamber Judgment (n 27), para 111; *Prosecutor v Milošević (Dragomir)*, IT-98-29/1-A, Appeals Chamber, Judgment, 12 November 2009, para 250; *Prosecutor v Kupreškić*, IT-95-16, Trial Chamber, Judgment, 14 January 2000, paras 515–520 and 765, citing, para 516, *von Leeb* et al (n 32).

[61] *Martić*, Appeals Chamber Judgment (n 27), para 270.

[62] Recall *supra* para 2.70. See also ILC Nürnberg Principles, principle III; Tokyo Charter, art 6 (an omnibus provision where reference to mitigation of punishment would seem to apply only to superior orders).

[63] Recall *supra* paras 12.30 and 13.31 respectively.

V. Mitigating Circumstances

It is a general principle of law applied by international criminal courts and reflected in article 15 of the ILC's Draft Code of Crimes against the Peace and Security of Mankind that, '[i]n passing sentence, the court shall, where appropriate, take into account extenuating circumstances'. Mitigation of punishment was not embodied in general terms in the Nuremberg Charter or Tokyo Charter, but article 8 of the former and article 6 of the latter specifically permitted the consideration of superior orders in mitigation. Common rule 101(B)(ii) of the respective RPE of the ICTY, ICTR, and SCSL instructs the Trial Chamber to take into account at sentencing 'any mitigating circumstances'. Rule 145(2)(*a*) of the ICC RPE directs the Court to take into account mitigating circumstances such as '[t]he circumstances falling short of constituting grounds for exclusion of criminal responsibility, such as substantially diminished mental capacity or duress'.[64]

6.42

Some of the extenuating or, synonymously, mitigating circumstances classically taken into consideration by national military courts and international criminal courts relate to the impugned conduct itself,[65] others to the circumstances of the convict at time of commission,[66] and others still to the convict's subsequent conduct.[67]

6.43

The ICTY Appeals Chamber held in *Kvočka* that voluntary intoxication is not a mitigating circumstance, although forced or coerced intoxication could be.[68]

6.44

Article 7(4) of the ICTY Statute, article 6(4) of the ICTR Statute, and article 6(4) of the SCSL Statute specifically permit consideration of superior orders in mitigation of punishment. In *Mrđa*, however, a Trial Chamber of the ICTY held that 'the orders were so manifestly unlawful that [the convict] must have been well aware that they violated the most elementary laws of war and the basic dictates of humanity', concluding that '[t]he fact that he obeyed such orders, as opposed to acting on his own initiative, does not merit mitigation of punishment'.[69] Similarly,

6.45

---

[64] For diminished mental capacity as a mitigating circumstance, see also 15 LRTWC 185; *Čelebići*, Appeals Chamber Judgment (n 10), paras 580–590; *Prosecutor v Todorović*, IT-95-9/1-S, Trial Chamber, Sentencing Judgment, 31 July 2001, paras 93–95. For duress as a mitigating circumstance, see also 15 LRTWC 170–5; *Prosecutor v Erdemović*, IT-96-22-T*bis*, Trial Chamber, Sentencing Judgment, 5 March 1998 (on remission to Trial Chamber), para 17; *Prosecutor v Vasiljević*, IT-98-32-T, Trial Chamber, Judgment, 29 November 2002, para 107; *Prosecutor v Češić*, IT-95-10/1-S, Trial Chamber, Sentencing Judgment, 11 March 2004, para 97; *Prosecutor v Mrđa*, IT-02-59-S, Trial Chamber, Sentencing Judgment, 31 March 2004, para 66; *Prosecutor v Kvočka* et al, IT-98-30/1-A, Appeals Chamber, Judgment, 28 February 2005, para 645; *Prosecutor v Rutaganira*, ICTR-95-1C-T, Trial Chamber, Judgment and Sentence, 14 March 2005, paras 161–162; *Prosecutor v Bizimungu* et al, ICTR-99-50-T, Trial Chamber, Judgment and Sentence, 30 September 2011, para 2018; *Prosecutor v Sesay* et al, SCSL-04-15-A, Appeals Chamber, Judgment, 26 October 2009, paras 1256 and 1279–1280.

[65] Examples include lack of malice and the convict's relatively minor degree of participation.

[66] Examples include superior orders and duress, where not full defences, and the convict's youth and impressionability.

[67] Examples include remorse, co-operation with the court or tribunal, and pleading guilty.

[68] See *Kvočka* et al, Appeals Chamber Judgment (n 64), para 707.

[69] *Prosecutor v Mrđa*, IT-02-59-S, Trial Chamber, Sentencing Judgment, 31 March 2004, para 67.

the Military Court of Rome held in *Hass and Priebke* that superior orders could not be considered in mitigation when the orders were manifestly unlawful.[70]

6.46 The fact that the convict was avowedly motivated by what the court might consider meritorious political motives, for example the defence of a constitutional government against insurgents, cannot be considered in mitigation of punishment.[71]

6.47 The fact that an accused may benefit from an amnesty under national law has no bearing whatsoever on his or her sentence before an international criminal court, since the latter cannot be bound by any such national measure.[72]

VI. Conclusion

6.48 Defences to criminal responsibility under customary international law are the least developed aspect of substantive international criminal law, at least when it comes to the case law.[73] The discourse of international criminal law has historically shown a preference for inculpation over exculpation, with shibboleths like 'the fight against impunity' almost presupposing the guilt of those accused, formally or in the court of popular opinion, of international crimes. Indeed, it is telling that the Rome Statute should be the first constituent instrument of an international criminal court to provide expressly for, rather than expressly to deny, the availability of specific grounds for excluding criminal responsibility. It remains to be seen whether the Statute's provisions on defences see much action. If they do, it can only be hoped that as much intellectual and moral investment goes into developing a customary international law of defences to customary international crimes as has gone into the definitions of the crimes themselves and the modes of responsibility.

Further Reading

AMBOS, K, 'Other Grounds for Excluding Criminal Responsibility' in A Cassese, P Gaeta, and JWD Jones (eds), *The Rome Statute of the International Criminal Court: A Commentary. Volume I* (Oxford: Oxford University Press, 2002), 1003

---

[70] *Hass and Priebke*, Military Court of Rome, 22 July 1997.
[71] See *Prosecutor v Fofana and Kondewa*, SCSL-04-14-A, Appeals Chamber, Judgment, 28 May 2008, paras 530–535, quoting, para 533, *Kordić and Čerkez*, Appeals Chamber Judgment (n 27), para 1082.
[72] See *Prosecutor v Boškoski and Tarčulovski*, IT-04-82-A, Appeals Chamber, Judgment, 19 May 2010, para 220. See also *Prosecutor v Sesay* et al, SCSL-04-15-T, Trial Chamber, Sentencing Judgment, 8 April 2009, para 253; *Prosecutor v Brima* et al, SCSL-04-16-T, Trial Chamber, Sentencing Judgment, 19 July 2007, para 138.
[73] There is a rich vein of scholarly work on defences to international criminal responsibility, much of it coming out of the continental tradition of penal theory (with some honourable common-law exceptions). See *infra* 'Further Reading' for a selection.

AMBOS, K, *Treatise on International Criminal Law. Volume 1: Foundations and General Part* (Oxford: Oxford University Press, 2013), chapter 8

CASSESE, A, 'Justifications and Excuses in International Criminal Law' in A Cassese, P Gaeta, and JWD Jones (eds), *The Rome Statute of the International Criminal Court: A Commentary. Volume I* (Oxford: Oxford University Press, 2002), 951

CASSESE, A and GAETA, P, *Cassese's International Criminal Law* (3rd edn, Oxford: Oxford University Press, 2013), chapters 12 and 13

CRYER, R, FRIMAN, H, ROBINSON, D, and WILMSHURST, E, *An Introduction to International Criminal Law and Procedure* (3rd edn, Cambridge: Cambridge University Press, 2014), chapter 16

DE FROUVILLE, O, *Droit international pénal. Sources, Incriminations, Responsabilité* (Paris: Pedone, 2012), part III, chapter 2

DINSTEIN, Y, *The Defence of 'Superior Orders' in International Law* (Leyden: Sijthoff, 1965)

ESER, A, 'Article 31' in O Triffterer (ed), *Commentary on the Rome Statute of the International Criminal Court. Observers' Notes, Article by Article* (2nd edn, Munich: CH Beck/Hart, 2008), 863

ESER, A, 'Mental Elements—Mistake of Fact and Mistake of Law' in A Cassese, P Gaeta, and JWD Jones (eds), *The Rome Statute of the International Criminal Court: A Commentary. Volume I* (Oxford: Oxford University Press, 2002), 889

GAETA, P, 'The Defence of Superior Orders: The Statute of the International Criminal Court versus Customary International Law' (1999) 10 *European Journal of International Law* 172

HELLER, KJ, 'Mistake of Legal Element, the Common Law, and Article 32 of the Rome Statute: A Critical Analysis' (2008) 6 *Journal of International Criminal Justice* 419

HELLER, KJ, 'What Happens to the Acquitted?' (2008) 21 *Leiden Journal of International Law* 663

KRUG, P, 'The Emerging Mental Incapacity Defense in International Criminal Law: Some Initial Questions of Implementation' (2000) 94 *American Journal of International Law* 317

MCCOUBREY, H, 'From Nuremberg to Rome: Restoring the Defence of Superior Orders' (2001) 50 *International and Comparative Law Quarterly* 386

SCHABAS, W, *The International Criminal Court. A Commentary on the Rome Statute* (Oxford: Oxford University Press, 2010), 480–514

TRIFFTERER, O, 'Article 32' in O Triffterer (ed), *Commentary on the Rome Statute of the International Criminal Court. Observers' Notes, Article by Article* (2nd edn, Munich: CH Beck/Hart, 2008), 895

TRIFFTERER, O, 'Article 33' in O Triffterer (ed), *Commentary on the Rome Statute of the International Criminal Court. Observers' Notes, Article by Article* (2nd edn, Munich: CH Beck/Hart, 2008), 915

UNITED NATIONS WAR CRIMES COMMISSION, *History of the United Nations War Crimes Commission and the Development of the Law of War* (London: UNWCC, 1948), 274–88

VAN DER WILT, H, 'Justifications and Excuses in International Criminal Law: An Assessment of the Case-Law of the ICTY' in B Swart, A Zahar, and G Sluiter (eds), *The Legacy of the International Criminal Tribunal for the Former Yugoslavia* (Oxford: Oxford University Press, 2011), 275

VAN SLIEDREGT, E, *Individual Criminal Responsibility in International Law* (Oxford: Oxford University Press, 2012)

WEIGEND, T, 'Kill or Be Killed: Another Look at *Erdemović*' (2012) 10 *Journal of International Criminal Justice* 1219

WERLE, G and JESSBURGER, F, *Principles of International Criminal Law* (3rd edn, Oxford: Oxford University Press, 2014), chapter 13

ZIMMERMANN, A, 'Superior Orders' in A Cassese, P Gaeta, and JWD Jones (eds), *The Rome Statute of the International Criminal Court: A Commentary. Volume I* (Oxford: Oxford University Press, 2002), 957

Treaty Crimes

7
The Crimes and Their Modes of Responsibility

I. Introduction

A considerable number and variety of international crimes are provided for by way of multilateral treaty.[1] The object and purpose of nearly all[2] of these treaties is the more effective suppression of the conduct the subject of the treaty[3] through the undertaking by the states parties of a range of obligations relating to their national criminal justice systems—obligations of municipal criminalization, provision for appropriate penalties, extension of jurisdiction, prosecution or extradition, and so on. Together these obligations are designed 'to prevent alleged perpetrators...from going unpunished, by ensuring that they cannot find refuge in any State party'.[4]   7.1

The present chapter first examines the formal and mostly academic distinction between crimes under treaty and crimes pursuant to treaty,[5] then considers in brief who is bound by the former—that is, for which individuals the conduct the subject of the treaty constitutes an offence giving rise to criminal responsibility under international law. The remainder of the chapter sketches the background to and scope of application *ratione materiae* of each of the international criminal conventions before outlining the essentials of the various   7.2

---

[1] The focus of this chapter and the next is restricted in two respects. First, both chapters examine in detail only multilateral treaties participation in which is open, at least potentially, to all states. They do not deal directly with regional treaties. Secondly, both chapters examine only multilateral treaties concluded after 1945. They do not consider earlier treaties providing for international crimes, on account mostly of the effective superseding of these treaties by more modern ones.

[2] A notable exception is the Rome Statute of the International Criminal Court ('Rome Statute'), the object and purpose of which is the establishment and functioning of a permanent international criminal court and which provides in this connection for certain crimes against the administration of the Court's justice.

[3] See also N Boister, *An Introduction to Transnational Criminal Law* (Oxford: Oxford University Press, 2012), 20 and 78. Indeed, the treaties in question are commonly referred to as 'suppression conventions'.

[4] *Questions relating to the Obligation to Prosecute or Extradite (Belgium v Senegal), Judgment*, ICJ Rep 2012, 422, 461, para 120. See also ibid, 455, para 91; JH Burgers and H Danelius, *The United Nations Convention Against Torture: A Handbook on the Convention Against Torture and Other Cruel, Inhuman or Degrading Treatment or Punishment* (Dordrecht/London: Martinus Nijhoff, 1988), 1 and 131.

[5] For an explanation of the terminology, recall *supra* para 2.35.

crimes and the modes of responsibility other than commission specified in relation to them.[6]

II. Conceptual Issues

A. Crimes under Treaty and Crimes pursuant to Treaty

7.3 Although the position is unclear in many cases, some treaties in the field of international criminal law appear to establish crimes under international law—that is, offences, defined by international law, which give rise to the individual criminal responsibility of the perpetrator as a matter of international law itself. These offences are referred to here as crimes under treaty. Other treaties unambiguously establish crimes pursuant to international law, by which is meant that they oblige states parties to criminalize specified conduct as a matter of their municipal law without providing for individual criminal responsibility for such conduct under international law. These offences are referred to here as crimes pursuant to treaty.

7.4 While the term 'crimes under treaty' is convenient shorthand, individual criminal responsibility for such crimes actually arises by virtue of a secondary rule of customary international law which provides, as a consequence of the perpetrator's breach of a treaty obligation binding on individuals and penal in character, for that perpetrator's criminal responsibility under international law.[7]

7.5 Those treaties that do appear to create crimes under international law also oblige states parties to criminalize the relevant conduct as a matter of municipal law, so that to this extent there is no difference between the two types of treaty crime. Indeed, more generally, the formal distinction between crimes under treaty and crimes pursuant to treaty is of very little practical consequence.[8] The obligations typically undertaken by states parties are the same whatever the formal juridical characterization of the offence. To this extent, what immediately follows is a sterile exercise.

(i) Crimes under treaty

(a) Crimes under or pursuant to treaty?

7.6 There are many treaty crimes the characterization of which as crimes under treaty or crimes pursuant to treaty can be no more than a matter of speculation, although it is at least arguable that they represent crimes under treaty.

---

[6] The obligations undertaken by states parties to the treaties in question are the focus *infra* of chapter 8. The obligation of municipal criminalization, however, is per force alluded to in the present chapter.

[7] See also Y Dinstein, 'International Criminal Law' (1985) 20 *Israel LR* 206, 207: 'Ordinarily, State responsibility is expressed in the genesis of a new obligation of reparation... [I]ndividual responsibility means subjection to criminal sanctions. When an individual human being contravenes an international duty binding him directly, he commits and international offence...'.

[8] Recall *supra* para 2.15. In addition, both crimes under treaty and crimes pursuant to treaty can through the usual process of formation of customary international law, emerge as independent, parallel crimes under customary international law—that is, as customary prohibitions or positive obligations on individuals giving rise in the event of breach to the criminal responsibility of those individuals under international law.

Article 1 of the Convention for the Suppression of Unlawful Seizure of Aircraft   7.7
1970 ('Hague Convention') provides that '[a]ny person who [performs specified acts] commits an offence (herein after referred to as "the offence")'. Article 1(1) and (2) of the Convention for the Suppression of Unlawful Acts against the Safety of Civilian Aircraft 1971 ('Montreal Convention')[9]—to which both article 3 of the Convention for the Suppression of Unlawful Acts against the Safety of Maritime Navigation 1988 ('SUA Convention') and article 2 of the Protocol for the Suppression of Unlawful Acts against the Safety of Fixed Platforms Located on the Continental Shelf 1988 ('SUA Protocol') are akin—state that '[a]ny person commits an offence if he [performs specified acts]'. The same formula is found in gender-neutral language in article 1(1) to (3) of the Hague Convention as amended by the Protocol supplementary to the Convention for the Suppression of Unlawful Seizure of Aircraft 2010 ('Beijing Protocol') and article 1(1) to (4) of the Convention on the Suppression of Unlawful Acts relating to International Civil Aviation 2010 ('Beijing Convention'), which read, variously, 'Any person commits an offence if that person [performs specified acts]' or 'Any person also commits an offence if that person [performs specified acts]'. For its part, article 2 of the Convention against the Recruitment, Use, Financing and Training of Mercenaries 1989 ('Mercenaries Convention') specifies that '[a]ny person who [performs specified acts], as defined in article 1 of the…Convention, commits an offence for the purposes of the Convention'. Not dissimilarly, article 1(1) of the Convention against the Taking of Hostages 1979 ('Hostages Convention') stipulates that '[a]ny person who [performs specified acts] commits the offence of taking hostages ("hostage-taking") within the meaning of th[e] Convention'. Finally, article 2(1) of the Convention for the Suppression of Terrorist Bombings 1997 ('Terrorist Bombings Convention') states that '[a]ny person commits an offence within the meaning of this Convention if that person [performs specified acts]', this phrasing being mirrored, *mutatis mutandis*, in article 15(1) of the Second Protocol to the 1954 Hague Convention for the Protection of Cultural Property in the Event of Armed Conflict 1999 ('Second Hague Protocol'), article 2(1) of the Convention for the Suppression of the Financing of Terrorism 1999 ('Financing of Terrorism Convention'), article 2(1) of the Convention for the Suppression of Acts of Nuclear Terrorism 2005 ('Nuclear Terrorism Convention'), article 3(1) of the Convention for the Suppression of Unlawful Acts against the Safety of Maritime Navigation 2005 ('2005 SUA Convention'),[10] and articles 2*bis* and 2*ter* of the Protocol for the Suppression of Unlawful Acts against the Safety of Fixed Platforms Located on the Continental Shelf 2005 ('2005

---

[9] See also Montreal Convention as amended by Protocol for the Suppression of Unlawful Acts of Violence at Airports serving International Civil Aviation 1988 ('Montreal Convention as amended by Montreal Protocol'), art 1(1)*bis*.
[10] The Convention for the Suppression of Unlawful Acts against the Safety of Maritime Navigation 2005 is the name given to the Convention for the Suppression of Unlawful Acts against the Safety of Maritime Navigation 1988 as amended by the Protocol of 2005 to the Convention for the Suppression of Unlawful Acts against the Safety of Maritime Navigation.

SUA Protocol').[11] It could be maintained that all of these provisions establish offences, defined by international law, which give rise to individual criminal responsibility under international law itself. 'Any person who [performs specified acts] commits an offence' and 'Any person commits an offence if he [performs specified acts]' are the archetypal formulae by which crimes are created in the various municipal legislative traditions, and it is natural to suppose, as one supposes in respect of municipal legislation, that the offence recognized in the relevant treaty provision is an offence against the legal order of which the treaty itself constitutes a source, namely international law. But the argument is less persuasive in relation to those provisions which speak of an offence 'within the meaning of' or 'for the purposes of' the relevant convention. The latter wording suggests not the creation of a substantive offence under the treaty—to which, in addition, the treaty's obligations of municipal criminalization, imposition of appropriate penalties, extension of jurisdiction, and prosecution or extradition relate—but the positing of a purely nominal or hypothetical defined 'offence' for the sole purpose of serving, by way of cross-reference, as the object of these various obligations. In turn, the seeming haphazardness of this drafting distinction[12] undermines the significance to be attached to the former wording as well. In the final analysis, it is uncertain whether these provisions give rise to individual criminal responsibility under international law itself or whether the criminal responsibility of perpetrators of the defined offences is a function solely of the municipal law enacted by a state party in accordance with the treaty's obligation of municipal criminalization. The latter seems more likely.

7.8   It is similarly unclear whether grave breaches of the 1949 Geneva Conventions[13] and of 1977 Additional Protocol I[14]—the 'breaches' being of the substantive provisions of the Conventions and of the Protocol, with the elements of any grave breach combining the relevant substantive treaty provision with further material

---

[11] The Protocol for the Suppression of Unlawful Acts against the Safety of Fixed Platforms Located on the Continental Shelf 2005 is the name given to the Protocol for the Suppression of Unlawful Acts against the Safety of Fixed Platforms Located on the Continental Shelf 1988 as amended by the Protocol of 2005 to the Protocol for the Suppression of Unlawful Acts against the Safety of Fixed Platforms Located on the Continental Shelf.

[12] For example, while art 2 of the Mercenaries Convention states that '[a]ny person who [performs specified acts] commits an offence for the purposes of the Convention', art 4 states that '[a]n offence is committed by any person who [performs specified acts]'. Similarly, art 2(1) of the Nuclear Terrorism Convention provides that '[a]ny person commits an offence within the meaning of this Convention' if that person performs certain acts, but art 2(2), (3), and (4) each provide that '[a]ny person also commits an offence' if that person performs certain other acts. See also Financing of Terrorism Convention, art 2(1) and (5); 2005 SUA Convention, art 3(1) and (2); 2005 SUA Protocol, arts 2*bis* and 2*ter*, on the one hand, and art 2(1) and (2), on the other.

[13] See Convention for the Amelioration of the Condition of the Wounded and Sick in Armed Forces in the Field 1949 ('1949 Geneva Convention I'); Convention for the Amelioration of the Condition of Wounded, Sick and Shipwrecked Members of Armed Forces at Sea 1949 ('1949 Geneva Convention II'); Convention relative to the Treatment of Prisoners of War 1949 ('1949 Geneva Convention III'); and Convention relative to the Protection of Civilian Persons in Time of War 1949 ('1949 Geneva Convention IV').

[14] Protocol Additional to the Geneva Conventions of 12 August 1949, and relating to the Protection of Victims of International Armed Conflicts 1977 ('Additional Protocol I').

and mental elements drawn from the relevant 'grave breaches' provision[15]—give rise, in their quality as treaty crimes, to individual criminal responsibility under international law itself or solely under any municipal law enacted by a state party in accordance with its treaty obligation of municipal criminalization. On the one hand, the grave breaches provisions of the Conventions[16] nowhere provide expressly for individual criminal responsibility under international law. They merely oblige states parties to criminalize the breaches defined therein under their respective municipal laws.[17] On the other hand, it could be argued that, in the idiosyncratic tradition of the international law of armed conflict, the relevant substantive prescriptions of the Conventions and of Additional Protocol I bind individuals as much as states,[18] with a secondary rule of customary international law providing on their breach, in the context of individuals, for individual criminal responsibility under international law itself.[19] Indeed, it could be said in this latter light that article 85(5) of Additional Protocol I is merely declaratory of the consensus of states parties to the Conventions and Additional Protocol I itself when it provides that grave breaches of these instruments 'shall be regarded as war crimes', a statement that seems to suggest, even if its import is by no means certain, that grave breaches give rise to individual criminal responsibility under international law.[20] In the end,

---

[15] See eg 1949 Geneva Convention I, art 50: 'Grave breaches to which the preceding Article relates shall be those involving any of the following acts, if committed against persons or property protected by the Convention: wilful killing, torture or inhuman treatment, including biological experiments, wilfully causing great suffering or serious injury to body or health, and extensive destruction or appropriation of property, not justified by military necessity and carried out unlawfully and wantonly.' See also, similarly, 1949 Geneva Convention II, art 51; 1949 Geneva Convention III, art 130; 1949 Geneva Convention IV, art 147. See too Additional Protocol I, arts 11 and 85(2) to (4).

[16] Note that, in accordance with art 85(1) of Additional Protocol I, obligations under the grave breaches provisions of the 1949 Geneva Conventions apply equally to grave breaches of Additional Protocol I.

[17] See 1949 Geneva Convention I, art 49; 1949 Geneva Convention II, art 50; 1949 Geneva Convention III, art 129; 1949 Geneva Convention IV, art 146. States parties are also obliged to legislate for effective penalties for, and to extend universal jurisdiction over, grave breaches, to search for those suspected of committing or ordering them, and to prosecute or extradite such persons.

[18] See eg C Greenwood, 'Historical Development and Legal Basis' in D Fleck (ed), *The Handbook of International Humanitarian Law* (2nd edn, Oxford: Oxford University Press, 2008), 1, 39, para 134; ME O'Connell, 'Historical Development and Legal Basis' in D Fleck (ed), *The Handbook of International Humanitarian Law* (3rd edn, Oxford: Oxford University Press, 2013), 1, 38, para 135. Indeed, the very notion that an individual can commit a breach, grave or otherwise, of the Conventions implies that, in addition to binding the high contracting parties, the Conventions bind individuals directly, an observation also made by R Cryer, 'The Doctrinal Foundations of International Criminalization' in MC Bassiouni (ed), *International Criminal Law. Volume I: Sources, Subjects, and Contents* (3rd edn, Leiden: Martinus Nijhoff, 2008), 107, 111.

[19] See eg Dinstein (n 7), 207. The same argument could be made in relation to those breaches of the 1949 Geneva Conventions and of Additional Protocol I not deemed 'grave breaches', in relation to breaches of the Protocol Additional to the Geneva Conventions of 12 August 1949, and relating to the Protection of Victims of Non-International Armed Conflicts 1977 ('Additional Protocol II'), and in relation to those violations of the Convention for the Protection of Cultural Property in the Event of Armed Conflict 1954 ('1954 Hague Convention') and of the Second Hague Protocol not deemed 'serious violations' by the latter.

[20] Although the term 'war crimes' is used in some quarters to refer equally to the punishment of violations of the laws of armed conflict under municipal law, such an interpretation of art 85(5) of

however, the correct categorization of grave breaches of the Geneva Conventions and of Additional Protocol I in their quality as treaty crimes is an open question.[21] The same goes, for the same reasons,[22] for the 'serious violations' of the Second Hague Protocol, being those acts specified in article 15(1)(*a*) to (*e*) of the Protocol when committed in violation of the substantive provisions of the Protocol or of the Convention for the Protection of Cultural Property in the Event of Armed Conflict 1954 ('1954 Hague Convention').

(b) Crimes under treaty or under customary international law?

7.9   Two crimes under international law that are each the subject of a multilateral treaty for their suppression may constitute crimes under treaty and crimes under customary international law alike or solely the latter. The position is uncertain.

7.10   The contracting parties to the Convention on the Prevention and Punishment of the Crime of Genocide 1948 ('Genocide Convention'), '[h]aving considered the declaration made by the General Assembly of the United Nations in its resolution 96 (I) dated 11 December 1946 that genocide is a crime under international law',[23] 'confirm' in article I that genocide, as defined in article II of the Convention, 'is a crime under international law'.[24] The preambular reference to General Assembly resolution 96 (I), the verb 'confirm' in article I, and the term 'crime under international law' in both article I and General Assembly resolution 96 (I)—which at the time clearly meant a crime under customary international law—all indicate that the gist of the statement in article I of the Convention is that genocide, as defined in the Convention, is a pre-existing crime under customary international law. In other words, article I of the Genocide Convention does not purport to create a crime under treaty distinct in its formal source from the crime of genocide under customary international law but, rather, claims simply

---

Additional Protocol I would render the provision redundant, given the obligation already undertaken by states parties to the 1949 Geneva Conventions and Additional Protocol I to criminalize grave breaches under their municipal law.

[21] Compare eg both D Akande, 'Sources of International Criminal Law' in A Cassese (ed), *The Oxford Companion to International Criminal Justice* (Oxford: Oxford University Press, 2009) 41, 48 and Cryer (n 18), 110–11, suggesting that the grave breaches are crimes under treaty, with M Milanović, 'Is the Rome Statute Binding on Individuals? (And Why We Should Care)' (2011) 9 *JICJ* 25, 42 (the quotation from a single delegate, the popularity of whose view among 'various delegates' cannot be established either way on the face of the record, not justifying the assertion, ibid, that the 'better view', *viz* 'that these provisions do not directly bind individuals', 'is supported by the Conventions' *travaux*').

[22] The only difference in this regard between grave breaches of the 1949 Geneva Conventions and 'serious violations' of the Second Hague Protocol is that the latter are nowhere explicitly characterized as war crimes.

[23] Genocide Convention, preamble (first recital).

[24] More fully, the contracting parties 'confirm that genocide...is a crime under international law which they undertake to prevent and to punish'. But given that the General Assembly declares (or, more precisely, 'affirms') in resolution 96 (I) that genocide is a crime under international law without undertaking as such to prevent and punish it, what the contracting parties to the Genocide Convention must be taken to 'confirm' in article I is that genocide is a crime under international law, the undertaking to prevent and punish this crime appearing for the first time in the Convention itself.

to confirm the existence of the customary version of the crime.[25] All this said, it is by no means unreasonable to suggest that the effect of article I of the Genocide Convention is to posit a crime of genocide under treaty formally distinct from the crime of genocide under customary international law the existence of which the provision avowedly confirms.[26]

7.11 The states parties to the Convention on the Suppression and Punishment of the Crime of Apartheid 1973 ('Apartheid Convention')—'[o]bserving that, in the Convention on the Prevention and Punishment of the Crime of Genocide, certain acts which may also be qualified as acts of apartheid constitute a crime under international law'; '[o]bserving that, in the Convention on the Non-Applicability of Statutory Limitations to War Crimes and Crimes against Humanity, "inhuman acts resulting from the policy of apartheid" are qualified as crimes against humanity'; and '[o]bserving that the General Assembly of the United Nations has adopted a number of resolutions in which the policies and practices of apartheid are condemned as a crime against humanity'[27]—'declare' in article I(1) 'that apartheid is a crime against humanity', thereby necessarily implying that the crime of apartheid, as defined in article II of the Convention, entails individual criminal responsibility under international law. In article III, the states parties specify that '[i]nternational criminal responsibility shall apply' to a range of modes of responsibility in connection with the offence. The preambular reference to a 'crime under international law', which at the time still implied a crime under customary international law; the use in the preamble and article I(1) of the term 'crime against humanity', crimes against humanity being to that point a purely customary phenomenon; and the employment in article I(1) of the word 'declare', a verb characteristic of assertions of customary international law, all suggest that article I(1) of the Apartheid Convention does not purport to posit a crime under treaty but merely asserts that apartheid is a pre-existing crime under customary international law.[28] Again, however, it is not implausible to suggest that the effect of article I(1) of the Apartheid Convention is to posit a crime of apartheid under treaty formally distinct from the crime of apartheid under customary international law whose existence the provision claims no more than to declare.[29]

---

[25] In this light, the Genocide Convention is purely adjectival, bringing to bear a range of treaty obligations of prevention and punishment, both general and specific, with a view—to borrow from the preamble (third recital) to the Convention—to 'liberat[ing] mankind' from the 'odious scourge' of the existing customary crime of genocide through the 'international co-operation...required'.

[26] See eg, suggesting that the Genocide Convention creates a treaty crime of genocide, Dinstein (n 7), 213–14 and Akande (n 21), 48. Given the possibility that the Genocide Convention creates a treaty crime of genocide and the fact that, whatever the formal source of the crime of genocide under international law the subject of the Convention, the Convention entails a range of obligations for states parties in relation to that crime, this book treats genocide as if it were both a crime under customary international law and a crime under treaty.

[27] Apartheid Convention, preamble (fifth, sixth, and seventh recitals), the reference being to the Convention on the Non-Applicability of Statutory Limitations to War Crimes and Crimes against Humanity 1968.

[28] In this light, the Convention's object and purpose is, in the words of the preamble (ninth recital), to 'make it possible to take more effective measures at the international and national levels with a view to the suppression and punishment of the crime of apartheid'.

[29] Since it is possible that the Apartheid Convention creates a treaty crime of apartheid and since, whatever the formal source under international law of the crime of apartheid the subject of the

(c) A *sui generis* case

7.12 Article 70(1) of the Rome Statute of the International Criminal Court ('Rome Statute') vests the ICC with jurisdiction over six 'offences against its administration of justice',[30] while article 70(3) provides that, '[i]n the event of conviction, the Court may impose a term of imprisonment not exceeding five years, or a fine in accordance with the Rules of Procedure and Evidence, or both'. Since it stands to reason that the offences in question are offences against the legal order of which the Statute, a treaty, itself constitutes a source, namely international law,[31] and since none of these offences existed prior to the Statute under either customary international law or other treaty, the effect of article 70(1) is to create a species of crime under treaty—that is, to establish treaty-based offences giving rise to individual criminal responsibility under international law itself.

(ii) Crimes pursuant to treaty

7.13 Many multilateral treaties are unambiguous in establishing crimes pursuant to treaty, meaning that they oblige states parties to criminalize specified conduct as a matter of their municipal law without providing explicitly or implicitly for individual criminal responsibility for such conduct under international law. Nowhere do these treaties use the formula 'Any person who [performs specified acts] commits an offence' or 'Any person commits an offence if he [performs specified acts]', whether with or without the rider 'within the meaning of' or 'for the purposes of' the relevant convention, and nowhere do they speak of 'crimes under international law', let alone stipulate that '[i]nternational criminal responsibility shall apply' to specified acts. The treaties in question are the Supplementary Convention on the Abolition of Slavery, the Slave Trade, and Institutions and Practices Similar

---

Convention, the Convention entails a range of obligations for states parties in respect of that crime, this book treats apartheid as if it were both a crime against humanity under customary international law and a crime in its own right under treaty.

[30] Article 70(1) of the Rome Statute reads:

The Court shall have jurisdiction over the following offences against its administration of justice when committed intentionally:
(a) Giving false testimony when under an obligation pursuant to article 69, paragraph 1, to tell the truth;
(b) Presenting evidence that the party knows is false or forged;
(c) Corruptly influencing a witness, obstructing or interfering with the attendance or testimony of a witness, retaliating against a witness for giving testimony or destroying, tampering with or interfering with the collection of evidence;
(d) Impeding, intimidating or corruptly influencing an official of the Court for the purpose of forcing or persuading the official not to perform, or to perform improperly, his or her duties;
(e) Retaliating against an official of the Court on account of duties performed by that or another official;
(f) Soliciting or accepting a bribe as an official of the Court in connection with his or her official duties.

[31] As it is, municipal law as such forms no part of the Court's applicable law as outlined in art 21 of the Rome Statute.

to Slavery 1956 ('Supplementary Slavery Convention');[32] the Convention on the Prevention and Punishment of Crimes against Internationally Protected Persons, including Diplomatic Agents 1973 ('Internationally Protected Persons Convention');[33] the Convention on the Physical Protection of Nuclear Material 1979 ('Nuclear Material Convention');[34] the Convention against Torture and Other Cruel, Inhuman or Degrading Treatment or Punishment 1984 ('Torture Convention');[35] the United Nations Convention against Illicit Traffic in Narcotic Drugs and Psychotropic Substances 1988 ('Illicit Traffic Convention');[36] the Convention on the Safety of United Nations and Associated Personnel 1994 ('UN and Associated Personnel Convention');[37] the OECD Convention on Combating Bribery of Foreign Public Officials in International Business Transactions 1997 ('OECD Bribery Convention');[38] the Convention against Transnational Organized Crime 2000 ('Organized Crime Convention'),[39] along with its Protocol to Prevent, Suppress and Punish Trafficking in Persons, Especially Women and Children 2000 ('Trafficking in Persons Protocol'),[40] its Protocol against the Smuggling of Migrants by Land, Sea and Air 2000 ('Smuggling of Migrants Protocol'),[41] and its Protocol against the Illicit Manufacturing of and Trafficking in Firearms, Their Parts and

---

[32] Articles 3(1), 5, and 6(1) of the Supplementary Slavery Convention stipulate that each of a variety of specified acts in relation to slavery, the slave trade, and institutions and practices similar to slavery 'shall be a criminal offence under the laws of the States Parties to this Convention', with relevant terms such as 'slavery' being defined in art 7.

[33] The Internationally Protected Persons Convention provides in art 2(1) that the intentional commission of a range of acts against an internationally protected person 'shall be made by each State Party a crime under its internal law', the definition of an 'internationally protected person' being found in art 1(1).

[34] After defining relevant terms in art 1, the Nuclear Material Convention specifies in art 7(1) that the intentional commission of a variety of acts in relation to nuclear material 'shall be made a punishable offence by each State Party under its national law'.

[35] Article 1(1) of the Torture Convention defines the term 'torture' for the purposes of the Convention, and art 4(1) obliges each state party to 'ensure that all acts of torture are offences under its criminal law'.

[36] Article 1 of the Illicit Traffic Convention defines relevant terms, while art 3(1) and (2) provide that each state party 'shall adopt such measures as may be necessary to establish as criminal offences under its domestic law, when committed intentionally', a range of acts.

[37] After defining relevant terms in art 1, the UN and Associated Personnel Convention provides in art 9(1) that the intentional commission of enumerated acts against United Nations or associated personnel 'shall be made by each state party a crime under its national law'.

[38] Article 1(1) of the OECD Bribery Convention states that each party 'shall take such measures as may be necessary to establish that it is a criminal offence under its law for any person intentionally' to commit a range of acts, with the definitions of relevant terms being given in art 1(4).

[39] Article 2 of the Organized Crime Convention defines relevant terms, while arts 5, 6, 8, and 23 specify that each state party 'shall adopt such legislative and other measures as may be necessary to establish as criminal offences, when committed intentionally', a raft of acts.

[40] The term 'trafficking in persons' is defined in art 3 of the Trafficking in Persons Protocol, while art 5(1) obliges states parties to 'adopt such legislative and other measures as may be necessary to establish as criminal offences the conduct set forth in article 3 of th[e] Protocol, when committed intentionally'.

[41] Article 3 of the Smuggling of Migrants Protocol defines relevant terms, including 'smuggling of migrants', and art 6(1) obliges states parties to 'adopt such legislative and other measures as may be necessary to establish as criminal offences, when committed intentionally and in order to obtain, directly or indirectly, a financial or other material benefit', a range of acts in relation to the smuggling of migrants.

Components and Ammunition 2001 ('Firearms Protocol');[42] the Convention on the Physical Protection of Nuclear Material and Nuclear Facilities 2005 ('Nuclear Material and Facilities Convention');[43] the Optional Protocol to the Convention on the Rights of the Child on the Sale of Children, Child Prostitution and Child Pornography 2005 ('Children Protocol');[44] and the United Nations Convention against Corruption 2003 ('Corruption Convention').[45]

7.14   More complicated is the Convention for the Protection of All Persons from Enforced Disappearance 2006 ('Enforced Disappearance Convention'). On the one hand, the Convention follows the pattern of those conventions, and in particular the Torture Convention, that provide for crimes pursuant to treaty, first defining the term 'enforced disappearance' in article 2 and subsequently stipulating in article 4 that each state party 'shall take the necessary measures to ensure that enforced disappearance constitutes an offence under its criminal law'. On the other hand, having stated in the fifth recital of the preamble that enforced disappearance 'constitutes…, in certain circumstances defined in international law, a crime against humanity', the Convention provides in article 5 that 'the widespread or systematic practice of enforced disappearance constitutes a crime against humanity as defined in applicable international law and shall attract the consequences provided for under such applicable international law'. It is sufficiently clear, however, especially given article 5's references to 'applicable international law' and the preambular allusion to 'certain circumstances defined in international law', that article 5 is intended to be merely declaratory of existing customary international law.[46] It is not intended to create, nor does it have the effect of creating, a crime under treaty. As for the bald and more enigmatic preambular statement that enforced disappearance 'constitutes a crime',[47] the rest of the relevant

---

[42] Article 3 of the Firearms Protocol defines relevant terms, including 'illicit manufacturing' and 'illicit trafficking', and art 5(1) obliges states parties to 'adopt such legislative and other measures as may be necessary to establish as criminal offences …, when committed intentionally', certain acts, among them illicit manufacturing of firearms, their parts and components, and ammunition, as well as illicit trafficking in firearms, their parts and components, and ammunition.

[43] The Convention on the Physical Protection of Nuclear Material and Nuclear Facilities 2005 is the name given to the Convention on the Physical Protection of Nuclear Material as amended by the Amendment of 2005 to the Convention on the Physical Protection of Nuclear Material. After defining relevant terms in art 1, the Nuclear Material and Facilities Convention specifies in art 7(1) that the intentional commission of a variety of acts in relation to nuclear material 'shall be made a punishable offence by each State Party under its national law'.

[44] Article 3(1) of the Children Protocol provides that each state party 'shall ensure that, as a minimum, the following acts and activities are fully covered under its criminal or penal law' before specifying a range of activities cross-referable to the definitions given in art 2.

[45] In accordance with arts 15 to 25 of the Corruption Convention, each state party is obliged to adopt or to consider adopting 'such legislative and other measures as may be necessary to establish as criminal offences, when committed intentionally', a wide range of corrupt and related acts, the definitions of relevant terms being found in art 2.

[46] Recall, however, from *supra* para 4.55, that the more accurate statement of customary international law would be that enforced disappearance, when committed as part of a widespread or systematic attack against a civilian population, constitutes a crime against humanity. That is, provided it forms part of a widespread or systematic attack against a civilian population, a single act of enforced disappearance can constitute a crime against humanity.

[47] See also the reference in Enforced Disappearance Convention, preamble (sixth recital), to 'the crime of enforced disappearance'.

recital (again, the fifth), *viz* 'and, in certain circumstances defined in international law, a crime against humanity', with its pointed positioning of the reference to international law, strongly suggests that the reference to enforced disappearance as a crime *tout court* is merely rhetorical. In sum, the Convention does not create a crime under international law. It provides for a crime pursuant to treaty and no more.

B. Who is Bound by a Crime under Treaty?

In its purely international legal character (that is, independently of its existence once enacted, as required, into the municipal criminal law of the respective states parties), a crime under treaty amounts to an international penal obligation directly binding on individuals. Which individuals are bound by this obligation—be it solely the nationals of the states parties or additionally anyone who performs the proscribed conduct on the territory of a state party or against one of its nationals, etc—is a function of which individuals the states parties explicitly or implicitly purport to bind.[48] To date, no treaty positing or possibly positing a crime under treaty specifies the crime's scope of application *ratione personae* as a matter of international law—that is, which individuals are bound by the international penal obligation posited in the treaty; and the crimes against the administration of justice enumerated in article 70(1) of the Rome Statute are alone so far in clearly implying a scope of application *ratione personae*.[49]

7.15

It could be argued that the presumptive scope of application *ratione personae* of a crime under treaty in its international character is coextensive with the bases of jurisdiction to prescribe expressly mandated or permitted by the treaty; but it is not self-evident why what the states parties mandate or even permit regarding the scope of application *ratione personae* of the crime in its quality as a crime under their respective municipal laws should be the same as what they intend regarding its scope of application *ratione personae* as a crime under international law. The alternative is that the presumptive scope of application *ratione personae* of a crime under treaty in its quality as a crime under international law is the most plenary scope permitted to the states parties by customary international law. The argument would be that positing an international crime is a sovereign act of lawmaking by the states parties and that the most logical presumption is that, unless otherwise indicated, those states parties collectively assert their sovereignty to the fullest extent allowed by international law. The practical consequence of the second approach would be that the presumptive scope of application *ratione personae* of a crime under treaty in its quality as a crime under international law would depend on the nature of the crime. Some crimes under treaty would bind the nationals of the states parties and anyone who performed the proscribed conduct on the

7.16

---

[48] Recall *supra* para 2.82. Note that who is bound and who may permissibly be bound by a crime under treaty are two separate questions.
[49] The penal obligations effectively posited in art 70(1) of the Rome Statute bind, potentially retroactively, any individual over which the Court may, in accordance with the Statute, exercise its jurisdiction in a given case. See *infra* para 14.59.

territory of a state party, on a ship on the high seas flagged to a state party, or while serving in the armed forces of a state party. Insofar as other crimes under treaty threatened the fundamental interests of states parties, they would bind anyone anywhere; and the latter would go, *mutatis mutandis*, insofar as further crimes under treaty represented serious offences against the person and the victim was, at the time of the offence, a national of a state party.

7.17   Ultimately there is no clear answer to who is bound by a crime under treaty in its quality as a crime under international law, although the second alternative is perhaps marginally more persuasive.

III. The Crimes in Outline

7.18   The material elements of treaty crimes in their most basic mode of responsibility, *viz* commission, obviously vary with the definition of the crime posited in the treaty. As for the requisite mental element, some treaty crimes expressly require intent and/or knowledge, while others are silent, leaving it to the states parties to specify the necessary *mens rea*. As it is, even when intent and/or knowledge are specified, it is up to the state parties to flesh out these generic concepts for the purposes of their municipal law. Indeed, it is for the states parties to elaborate too such aspects of the material elements of the offence as are not sufficiently specified in the treaty to permit application by their courts. This element of leeway is suggested in many of the conventions by the formulation of the obligation of municipal criminalization as one pertaining to the 'unlawful' commission of the stated conduct, the term being referable, with tolerable circularity, to the municipal law of each state party.[50]

7.19   Each international criminal convention makes specific provision for modes of responsibility other than commission, among them ordering, complicity, attempt, and command responsibility. Such provision is usually sketchy, although recent conventions are more detailed in this regard.[51] It is an open question whether, in an application of the canon of construction *expressio unius exclusio alterius*, the mandating by the treaty of municipal provision for certain modes of responsibility in respect of a treaty crime excludes a state party's voluntary provision for other modes. The more persuasive view is that it does not, a view supported in the relevant conventions once more by the restriction of the obligation of municipal criminalization to 'unlawful' performance of the defined conduct.

---

[50] See Boister (n 3), 126. See *infra* para 8.9 for more, where it is also explained that the words 'unlawful' and 'unlawfully' mean something different in the context of the grave breaches provisions of the 1949 Geneva Conventions.

[51] A useful innovation in this respect can be found in art 15(2) of the Second Hague Protocol, which obliges states parties to comply with general principles of international law, 'including the rules extending individual criminal responsibility to persons other than those who directly commit the act', when enacting into their municipal law the crimes provided for in the Protocol.

7.20 The following sections sketch the background to and scope of application *ratione materiae* of each[52] of the international criminal conventions before outlining the essentials of the different crimes and the modes of responsibility other than commission specified in relation to them. The various conventions are presented in groups under generic headings which, with the exception of 'war crimes', are of no formal juridical significance, being merely thematically descriptive and to an extent arbitrary.

A. War Crimes

(i) Grave breaches of the 1949 Geneva Conventions and Additional Protocol I

(a) Background

7.21 None of the earlier Geneva conventions on the laws of war[53] made provision for the punishment via criminal law of the individuals through whose acts a high contracting party breached its obligations under the convention. Nor, for that matter, did the Regulations concerning the Laws and Customs of War on Land 1907 ('Hague Regulations') or the Convention concerning the Laws and Customs of War on Land 1907 to which they were annexed.[54] But with the widespread recourse to war crimes trials in the wake of the Second World War in both Europe and the Pacific, the punishment of individual authors of breaches of the new Geneva Conventions became a drafting desideratum at the Geneva diplomatic conference of 1949. The upshot was the 'grave breaches' regime common, *mutatis mutandis*, to the four 1949 conventions, the term 'war crimes' having been avoided by the drafters on account of differences over the appropriateness of its use.[55]

7.22 By the time the Geneva diplomatic conference of 1974–77 came to draft Additional Protocol I, applicable to international armed conflict, to the 1949 Geneva Conventions, it was considered natural that provision should be made for the repression by means of criminal law of the more reprehensible breaches of the Protocol. As such, a range of 'grave breaches' of Additional Protocol I, to

---

[52] Note that the crime of genocide, dealt with in its quality as a crime under customary international law in chapters 4 and 5, is not dealt with here. To the extent that there may be a formally-distinct treaty crime of genocide, its material and mental elements and modes of responsibility are identical to those of the customary version. As for the treaty obligations of contracting parties to the Genocide Convention, they are considered in the following chapter. The same goes, *mutatis mutandis*, for the crime of piracy recognized in art 105 of the United Nations Convention on the Law of the Sea 1982, dealt with *supra* paras 1.56–1.59 in its quality as a crime pursuant to customary international law.

[53] See Convention for the Amelioration of the Condition of the Wounded in Armies in the Field 1864, Convention for the Amelioration of the Condition of the Wounded and Sick in Armies in the Field 1906, Convention for the Amelioration of the Condition of the Wounded and Sick in Armies in the Field 1929, and Convention relative to the Treatment of Prisoners of War 1929.

[54] Recall *supra* para 2.56.

[55] See JAC Gutteridge, 'The Geneva Conventions of 1949' (1949) 26 *BYIL* 294, 304–5.

which the provisions on the repression of grave breaches found in the 1949 Geneva Conventions were to apply,[56] were enumerated in the Protocol.[57]

(b) Scope of application

7.23 The grave breaches provisions of each of the 1949 Geneva Conventions apply in respect of armed conflict between two or more of the high contracting parties to the relevant Convention or between a high contracting party or high contracting parties and a state which has declared that it accepts the provisions of the Convention and applies them, a scope of application which includes situations of the partial or total occupation by one state bound by the relevant Convention of the territory of another.[58] They do not apply in respect of non-international armed conflict in the territory of a high contracting party.

7.24 The grave breaches of Additional Protocol I apply, *mutatis mutandis*, in respect of the situations to which the grave breaches of the 1949 Geneva Conventions pertain,[59] as well as in respect of armed conflicts 'in which peoples are fighting against colonial domination and alien occupation and against racist regimes in the exercise of their right to self-determination'.[60]

(c) Crimes

7.25 The grave breaches of the 1949 Geneva Conventions are enumerated in article 50 of 1949 Geneva Convention I, article 51 of 1949 Geneva Convention II, article 130 of 1949 Geneva Convention III, and article 147 of 1949 Geneva Convention IV respectively. The elements of any grave breach comprise the breach of a substantive provision of the applicable Convention and, deriving from the applicable 'grave breaches' provision, both a further material element, such as killing, torture or extensive destruction of property not justified by military necessity, and an explicit or implicit mental element amounting to intent and knowledge.[61] The words 'unlawful' and 'unlawfully' found in the provisions mean 'in violation of the relevant provisions of the [Convention]', to borrow the more precise formulation of Additional Protocol I.[62]

---

[56] Additional Protocol I supplements the obligations of repression in the grave breaches provisions of the Conventions with the obligations laid down in arts 86 to 89 of the Protocol and the International Fact-Finding Commission established under art 90.

[57] In contrast, Additional Protocol II, applicable to non-international armed conflict, to the 1949 Geneva Conventions contains no grave breaches provisions.

[58] See art 2 common to the four 1949 Geneva Conventions.

[59] Additional Protocol I, art 1(3).   [60] Ibid, art 1(4).

[61] Recall *supra* para 7.8. An express requirement of intent is seen in the terms 'wilful killing', 'wilfully causing great suffering or serious injury to body or health', 'wilfully depriving a protected person of the rights of fair and regular trial', and 'extensive destruction or appropriation of property...carried out...wantonly' in the grave breaches provisions, while a requirement of intent is considered implicit in concepts such as torture and inhuman treatment, deportation, transfer and confinement of a person, compelling a person to serve in the armed forces of a hostile Power, and taking hostages. Note that the material and mental elements outlined *supra* chapter 4 in relation to grave breaches of the 1949 Geneva Conventions as crimes under customary international law are referable equally to grave breaches as treaty crimes. As such, there is no need to elaborate further on the content of the latter.

[62] Additional Protocol I, art 85(3), chapeau. See also ibid, art 85(4) ('in violation of the Conventions or the Protocol').

7.26 The grave breaches of Additional Protocol I are outlined in articles 11 and 85(2) to (4) of the Protocol. The grave breaches provided for in article 11 involve wilfully subjecting persons in the power of a Party other than the one on which they depend to unjustified medical procedures which seriously endanger their physical or mental health or integrity. Article 85(2) deems as grave breaches of the Protocol acts defined as grave breaches of the 1949 Geneva Conventions when committed against specified persons, units or transports protected by the Protocol. Article 85(3) lists as grave breaches of the Protocol a range of wilful acts in violation of a substantive provision of the Protocol on the condition that they cause death or serious injury to body or health. All of these acts involve attacks, with the exception of the perfidious use of the distinctive emblem of the Conventions and Protocol or of other protective signs recognized by either, which is recognized as a grave breach of the Protocol in article 85(3)(f). Lastly, article 85(4) characterizes as grave breaches of the Protocol, without any requirement as to resultant death or injury, a variety of wilful acts in violation of one of the Conventions or of the Protocol, among them deportation or transfer of all or part of the population of occupied territory, apartheid, certain attacks against cultural property, and depriving specified persons of the rights of fair and regular trial.

(d) Modes of responsibility

7.27 The four 1949 Geneva Conventions make only the sketchiest provision for modes of criminal responsibility in respect of grave breaches. What is explicit is that the high contracting parties must criminalize both commission and ordering the commission of a grave breach.[63] Beyond this, the common definition of a grave breach as 'involving' any of the specified acts[64] appears to leave it to the high contracting parties to impose criminal responsibility for grave breaches on whatever other bases they see fit.

7.28 The obligation under the Conventions to criminalize the commission and the ordering of the commission of grave breaches applies, via article 85(1) of Additional Protocol I, to grave breaches of the Protocol. In addition, the high contracting parties are required in effect to provide for command responsibility in respect of grave breaches of the Protocol.[65]

(ii) Serious violations of the 1999 Second Hague Protocol

(a) Background

7.29 The 1954 Hague Convention, dealing with the protection of cultural property in armed conflict, makes only weak provision for the repression via criminal law of breaches of the Convention. The high contracting parties undertake in article

---

[63] See 1949 Geneva Convention I, art 49; 1949 Geneva Convention II, art 50; 1949 Geneva Convention III, art 129; 1949 Geneva Convention IV, art 146.
[64] See 1949 Geneva Convention I, art 50; 1949 Geneva Convention II, art 51; 1949 Geneva Convention III, art 130; 1949 Geneva Convention IV, art 147.
[65] See Additional Protocol I, arts 86 and 87.

28 'to take, within the framework of their ordinary criminal jurisdiction, all necessary steps to prosecute and impose penal or disciplinary sanctions upon those persons, of whatever nationality, who commit or order to be committed a breach of the...Convention'. The option of disciplinary sanctions, such as dishonourable discharge from the armed forces or the forfeiture of pay, makes it clear that criminal prosecution is not mandatory. This, along with article 28's impressionistic approach to the establishment of national jurisdiction, the absence from the article of mention of extradition or mutual legal assistance, and the desire to see criminalized the more reprehensible breaches of the substantive provisions of the Second Hague Protocol led the drafters of the Protocol, concluded in 1999, to dedicate an entire chapter, chapter 4 ('Criminal Responsibility and Jurisdiction'), to what are referred to as 'serious violations' of the Protocol.

(b) Scope of application

7.30 Although the substantive provisions of the 1954 Hague Convention prohibiting, unless imperative military necessity requires, acts of hostility against and certain uses of cultural property and prohibiting absolutely the theft, pillage, misappropriation or vandalism of cultural property and reprisals against it apply as much during non-international as during international armed conflict, the latter including belligerent occupation, it is unclear whether article 28's obligation to repress breaches does too.[66] In contrast, not only the substantive provisions of the Second Hague Protocol but also the penal machinery of its chapter 4 apply to international and non-international armed conflict without distinction.[67] That is, the serious violations of the Protocol apply both in respect of armed conflict between two or more states parties to the Protocol, which must also be high contracting parties to the 1954 Hague Convention,[68] or between a state party or states parties and a state which has declared that it accepts the provisions of the Protocol and applies them, including in both cases situations of belligerent occupation,[69] and in respect of 'an armed conflict not of an international character, occurring within the territory of one of the [States Parties to the Protocol]'.[70]

7.31 The 'cultural property' to which, 'irrespective of origin or ownership',[71] both the 1954 Hague Convention and the Second Hague Protocol apply comprises, in accordance with article 1(a) of the Convention, 'movable or immovable cultural property of great importance to the cultural heritage of every people'[72]—that is, cultural property of great importance to the national cultural heritage of each

---

[66] See 1954 Hague Convention, art 19(1). For a more detailed discussion, see R O'Keefe, 'Protection of Cultural Property under International Criminal Law' (2010) 11 *Melb JIL* 339, 360.
[67] See Second Hague Protocol, arts 3(1) and 22(1).   [68] See ibid, arts 40–42.
[69] See ibid, art 3(1) cross-referenced with 1954 Hague Convention, art 18.
[70] Second Hague Protocol, art 22(1).   [71] 1954 Hague Convention, art 1 (chapeau).
[72] 1954 Hague Convention, art 1(a) continues 'such as monuments of architecture, art or history, whether religious or secular; archaeological sites; groups of buildings which, as a whole, are of historical or artistic interest; works of art; manuscripts, books and other objects of artistic, historical or archaeological interest; as well as scientific collections and important collections of books or archives or of reproductions of the property defined above'.

respective high contracting party, as determined by that party; in accordance with article 1(*b*), buildings whose 'main and effective purpose' is to preserve or exhibit, and refuges intended to shelter in the event of armed conflict, movable cultural property as defined in article 1(*a*);[73] and, in accordance with article 1(*c*), centres containing a large amount of cultural property as defined in article 1(*a*) and (*b*), known under the Convention as 'centres containing monuments'.[74] In the practice of the parties, the total immovable cultural property to which the 1954 Hague Convention and the Second Hague Protocol apply is generally in the order of tens of thousands of items in the territory of each party, while the few figures available for movable cultural property tentatively point to the contents of a hundred to a few hundred museums, art galleries, libraries, and archives per party.[75] Two of the offences provided for in the Second Hague Protocol apply, however, only in respect of the much more restrictive selection of cultural property protected by the regime of 'enhanced protection' established under chapter 3 of the Protocol, as included in the 'List of Cultural Property under Enhanced Protection' provided for in the Protocol.[76]

(c) **Crimes**
The serious violations of the Second Hague Protocol comprise those acts specified in article 15(1)(*a*) to (*e*) of the Protocol when committed intentionally[77] and in violation of the substantive provisions of the Protocol or Convention, namely making cultural property under enhanced protection the object of attack; using cultural property under enhanced protection or its immediate surroundings in support of military action; extensive destruction or appropriation of cultural property protected under the Convention and the Protocol; making cultural property protected under the Convention and Protocol the object of attack; and theft, pillage or misappropriation of, or acts of vandalism directed against, cultural property protected under the Convention.[78]

7.32

(d) **Modes of responsibility**
The Second Hague Protocol is unique in providing that, when giving effect to its obligation 'to adopt such measures as may be necessary to establish as offences

7.33

---

[73] The first limb of art 1(*b*) of the 1954 Hague Convention gives as examples of the buildings in question 'museums, large libraries and depositories of archives'.
[74] That the Second Hague Protocol applies to the same 'cultural property' as the 1954 Hague Convention itself is made clear in Second Hague Protocol, art 1(*b*).
[75] For a more detailed account, see R O'Keefe, 'Protection of Cultural Property' in D Fleck (ed), *The Handbook of International Humanitarian Law* (3rd edn, Oxford: Oxford University Press, 2013), 425, 428–30, para 901.
[76] See Second Hague Protocol, arts 1(*h*), 11, and 27(1)(*b*).
[77] It is unclear whether intent in this context implies knowledge simply that the property is a 'monument of architecture, art or history, whether religious or secular', an archaeological site, or any other sort of movable or immovable property referred to in article 1 of the Convention or, instead, knowledge that the property is protected by the Convention, is protected by the Convention and the Protocol, or has been placed under enhanced protection, as the case may be.
[78] For a more detailed elaboration, see O'Keefe (n 66), 372–5.

under its domestic law the offences set forth in the [instrument]', a state party 'shall comply...with the rules extending individual criminal responsibility to persons other than those who directly commit the act'.[79] In other words, states parties are obliged to provide under their municipal law for criminal responsibility in respect of serious violations of the Second Hague Protocol on the grounds, *viz* according to the modes of responsibility, recognized by customary international law. What these grounds might be remains the question.[80]

B. Crimes Relating to Slavery

(i) Background

7.34 The Slavery Convention 1926[81]—while obliging high contracting parties, in respect of territories under their sovereignty, jurisdiction, protection, suzerainty or tutelage, to prevent and suppress the slave trade and to bring about the complete abolition of slavery in all its forms—does not explicitly oblige them to enact penal laws to this end.[82] In 1956, therefore, states concluded the Supplementary Slavery Convention,[83] which provides for four treaty crimes pertaining to slavery, the slave trade, and institutions and practices similar to slavery.

(ii) Crimes

7.35 Article 3(1), on the slave trade, of the Supplementary Slavery Convention stipulates that '[t]he act of conveying...slaves from one country to another by whatever means of transport' shall be a criminal offence under the laws of the states parties. The term 'slave' is defined in article 7(*a*), by cross-reference to the term 'slavery' in the same provision, in effect as a person 'over whom any or all of the powers attaching to the right of ownership are exercised'. Next, article 5 provides that 'the act of mutilating, branding or otherwise marking a slave or a person

---

[79] Second Hague Protocol, art 15(2). The wording is infelicitous, in that states parties cannot be said to 'comply' with the rules providing for the different modes of individual criminal responsibility under customary international law. These rules create no obligations for states. But the import of the formulation is clear.

[80] For an indication, see *supra* chapter 5.

[81] Slavery Convention 1926 as amended by the Protocol amending the Slavery Convention 1953 ('Slavery Convention'). The amendments simply transfer to the United Nations the functions formerly performed in relation to the Convention by the League of Nations.

[82] Article 6 of the Slavery Convention does, however, provide: 'Those of the High Contracting Parties whose laws do not at present make adequate provision for the punishment of infractions of laws and regulations enacted with a view to giving effect to the purposes of the present Convention undertake to adopt the necessary measures in order that severe penalties may be imposed in respect of such infractions.' But the article, while premised on the enactment of laws and regulations for giving effect to the Convention's purposes, does not as such require such enactment.

[83] In the sixth preambular recital to the Supplementary Slavery Convention, the states parties declare that they have 'decided...that the Convention of 1926, which remains operative, should...be augmented by the conclusion of a supplementary convention designed to intensify national as well as international efforts towards the abolition of slavery, the slave trade and institutions and practices similar to slavery'.

of servile status in order to indicate his status, or as a punishment, or for any other reason' shall be a criminal offence under the laws of the states parties. The expression 'a person of servile status' means, as per article 7(*b*), 'a person in the condition or status resulting from any of the institutions or practices mentioned in article 1' of the Supplementary Slavery Convention. The institutions and practices mentioned in article 1 of the Convention comprise debt bondage, serfdom, various institutions or practices according to which women are effectively treated as chattels, and the handing over of a person under the age of 18 by a parent or guardian for the purpose of the exploitation of that person or of his or her labour,[84] in each case 'whether or not they are covered by the definition of slavery contained in article 1 of the Slavery Convention'.[85] Thirdly, article 6(1) of the Convention requires that '[t]he act of enslaving another person or of inducing another person to give himself or a person dependent upon him into slavery' be a criminal offence under the states parties' laws. 'Slavery' is defined, expressly reproducing the definition of 'slavery' in article 1(1) of the Slavery Convention, as 'the status or condition of a person over whom any or all of the powers attaching to the right of ownership are exercised'. Finally, article 6(2) specifies that the obligation in article 6(1) shall apply further to 'the act of inducing another person to place himself or a person dependent upon him into the servile status resulting from any of the institutions or practices mentioned in article 1'.[86] None of the offences provided for in the Supplementary Slavery Convention specifies the requisite *mens rea*.

7.36 There is debate over whether the definition of 'slavery' in article 1(1) of the Slavery Convention, as restated in article 7(*a*) of the Supplementary Slavery Convention and relied on for the purposes of the crime provided for in article 6(1) of the latter, is restricted to the exercise over a person of the formal right of ownership, *viz* to *de jure* slavery, sometimes referred to as 'chattel slavery', or extends to the exercise over a person of such powers as would attach to the right of ownership, in other words to *de facto* slavery. In *Siliadin v France*, the European Court of Human Rights understood article 1(1) of the Slavery Convention to apply only to 'a genuine right of legal ownership'.[87] But the distinction drawn in article 1(1) between the 'status' and the 'condition' of slavery, the expression 'the powers attaching to the right of ownership', as distinct from simply 'the right of ownership', the reference to 'any or all' of those powers, and the implication from article 1 of the Supplementary Slavery Convention that at least some of the institutions and practices mentioned in the article may be capable of being 'covered by the definition of slavery contained in article 1 of Slavery Convention' all suggest that article 1(1) of the Slavery Convention—and, as a consequence, article 6(1) of the

---

[84] Supplementary Slavery Convention, art 1(*a*), (*b*), (*c*), and (*d*) respectively.
[85] Ibid, art 1, chapeau.
[86] Article 6(2) is stated, however, to be subject to the introductory words of art 1(1), which speak of 'tak[ing] all practicable and necessary legislative and other measures to bring about progressively and as soon as possible the complete abolition or abandonment' of the institutions and practices outlined in the provision.
[87] *Siliadin v France* (Merits and Just Satisfaction), no 73316/01, ECHR 2005–VII, para 122.

Supplementary Slavery Convention—is not limited in its import to *de jure* slavery but extends, in the absence of formal ownership of a person, to the exercise over that person of such powers as would accrue to an owner. The second conclusion was seemingly the one reached by the Appeals Chamber of the ICTY in the course of its consideration of the content of the crime against humanity of enslavement in *Kunarac*;[88] was the one unambiguously reached, on the basis of some of the above arguments and more, by the High Court of Australia in *R v Tang*;[89] and was the one similarly clearly reached by the Supreme Court Chamber of the Extraordinary Chambers in the Courts of Cambodia in *Duch*.[90]

(iii) Modes of responsibility

7.37 The obligation of municipal criminalization laid down in article 3(1) of the Supplementary Slavery Convention extends to attempting to convey slaves from one country to another and to being an accessory to any such conveyance. The same goes, *mutatis mutandis*, for articles 5, 6(1), and 6(2), which further apply to being party to a conspiracy to accomplish any of the acts mentioned in the respective provisions.

C. Crimes Associated with Terrorism

7.38 Politically-motivated terrorism[91] with an international dimension is by no means only a late twentieth-century and early twenty-first-century phenomenon.[92] Nor are international legal responses to it. The League of Nations was active in this regard, adopting in 1937 a Convention for the Prevention and Punishment of Terrorism,[93] although the instrument received just a single ratification and a single accession, and never entered into force. It was not until the beginning of the

---

[88] *Prosecutor v Kunarac* et al, IT-96-23 and IT-96-23/1-A, Appeals Chamber, Judgment, 12 June 2002, para 117. See also *Prosecutor v Sesay* et al, SCSL-04-15-T, Trial Chamber, Judgment, 2 March 2009, paras 198–199; *Hadijatou Mani Koraou v Republic of Niger*, ECW/CCJ/JUD/06/08, Judgment, ECOWAS CCJ, 27 October 2008, para 77.

[89] *R v Tang*, 43 ILR 76, 88–90, paras 23–27 (Australia 2008).

[90] Case No 001/18-07-2007-ECCC/SC ('*Duch*'), Appeal Judgment, 3 February 2012, paras 153 and 155–156.

[91] The word is used here in a lay sense, neutrally, and only for want of a less controversial term of comparable convenience.

[92] The *fin de siècle* saw the rise of the phenomenon in its recognizably modern form, with the assassinations by members of the international anarchist movement of President Carnot of France in 1894, Empress Elisabeth of Austria–Hungary in 1898, King Umberto I of Italy in 1900, and US President William McKinley in 1901. The first half of the twentieth century witnessed numerous notorious terrorist incidents with an international flavour, among them the assassination in Sarajevo in 1914 of Archduke Franz Ferdinand of Austria–Hungary by Gavrilo Princip of the 'Young Bosnia' revolutionary movement; the assassination in Marseilles in 1934 of King Alexander of Yugoslavia by a representative of IMRO, a Macedonian revolutionary organization; and the bombing in 1946 of the King David Hotel in Jerusalem, where much of the British mandatory government of Palestine was based, along with the assassination in 1948 of the United Nations Mediator in Palestine, the Swede Count Bernadotte, both by Zionist extremists.

[93] League of Nations doc C.546.M383.1937.V (1937).

1970s, however, with the bursting onto the scene of a range of Palestinian armed organizations[94] and other militant nationalist[95] and extreme leftist[96] groups, that terrorist violence became the object of consistent and concerted legal efforts at the international level. Since then, international terrorist activity has been the most significant catalyst for the development of treaty-based international criminal law.

7.39 The history of the conclusion of universal conventions to suppress by means of criminal law acts associated with terrorism is a history of piecemeal, reactive measures.[97] A degree of systematic impetus has, however, been lent to the process by the work of the Ad Hoc Committee established by UN General Assembly resolution 51/210 of 17 December 1996. Moreover, the overhauls of the relevant treaties falling within their respective mandates by the International Atomic Energy Agency (IAEA) and International Maritime Organization (IMO) in 2005, the year of the General Assembly's adoption of the Nuclear Terrorism Convention, and by the International Civil Aviation Organization (ICAO) in 2010 reflect, as do the resultant texts, an effort, driven by partner states in the US-led Proliferation Security Initiative, to co-ordinate international legal responses to the perceived threat of the terrorist deployment of, in particular, weapons of mass destruction.

7.40 The various universal multilateral treaties that bear on international terrorism reflect a deliberate strategy on the part of states, in the light of persistent differences over the definition of terrorism as such,[98] to avoid the divisive consideration of ends and to focus instead on those means typically employed by terrorists, vaguely so called, on which sufficient international consensus exists as to their illegitimacy and necessity for condemnation and suppression. In the event, the relevant universal conventions deal with specific acts that over the years have formed part of the *modus operandi* of international terrorism and not with 'terrorist' acts as such.[99] Indeed, none of the existing universal conventions aimed at the suppression of such acts through criminal law uses the term 'terrorism' or 'terrorist' in defining the impugned conduct. Insofar as the words are employed in the conventions at all, it is only in the titles, not the provisions, of three of the more recent, namely the Terrorist Bombings Convention, the Financing of Terrorism Convention, and

---

[94] These included the Palestine Liberation Organization, the Palestine Liberation Front, the Popular Front for the Liberation of Palestine, the Popular Front for the Liberation of Palestine–General Command, the Popular Front for the Liberation of Palestine–External Operations, Fatah–The Revolutionary Council ('Abu Nidal Organization'), and Black September.

[95] Prominent among these were Irish republican groups, most famously the Provisional IRA, and the Basque group ETA.

[96] Examples include the Red Brigades in Italy, the Red Army Faction/Baader-Meinhof Group in West Germany, 17 November in Greece, the Japanese Red Army, and the Weather Underground Movement and Symbionese Liberation Army in the US.

[97] This was the case even with the abortive Convention for the Suppression and Punishment of Terrorism 1937, which was the product of legal efforts initiated by the League of Nations in the immediate wake of the assassination of King Alexander of Yugoslavia in 1934.

[98] See *infra* paras 7.102–7.104.

[99] This is sometimes referred to as the 'sectoral approach' to the international legal outlawry of terrorism.

the Nuclear Terrorism Convention. Nor, for that matter, do any of the conventions require that the acts to which they relate be inspired by political, ideological, philosophical or similar motives.[100] All provide for offences which, as defined in their respective texts, are capable of commission for wholly personal motives. In short, the pertinent instruments deal with international 'terrorism' only insofar as the acts the subject of them have at some point formed part of the repertoire of international terrorists, loosely speaking.

(i) Unlawful seizure of aircraft

(a) Background

7.41 The mid-1960s saw the birth of aircraft hijacking, perhaps the most iconic form of modern political violence before the advent of suicide bombing. Events at the end of the decade and the beginning of the next soon rendered it notorious.[101] By way of international legal response to these events and to the call to states in UN Security Council resolution 286 (1970) 'to take all possible legal steps to prevent further hijackings',[102] representatives of member states of ICAO adopted, on 16 December 1970, the Hague Convention.

7.42 Four decades later there emerged a consensus that the Hague Convention was in need of improvement in the face of changing needs.[103] As a result, on 10 September 2010 the member states of ICAO adopted the Beijing Protocol, one feature of which is a small expansion of the range of acts deemed offences under the Convention and their extension to aircraft 'in service', as distinct from 'in flight'. The Protocol, which is not yet in force, is designed to supplement rather than supplant the Convention,[104] so that, as among states parties to the Protocol, the Convention and the Protocol are to be read and interpreted together as a single instrument, to be known as 'the Hague Convention as amended by the Beijing Protocol 2010'.[105] Any state not a party to the Hague Convention that becomes

---

[100] But note the element of motivation, albeit not necessarily political or similar motive, in art 1(1) of the Hostages Convention.

[101] In 1969, the telegenic Palestinian militant Leila Khaled and comrades from the Popular Front for the Liberation of Palestine (PFLP) successfully hijacked a TWA airliner, flying it to Damascus, where they blew it up. On 31 March 1970, the Japanese Communist League–Red Army Faction, predecessor to the Japanese Red Army, hijacked a Japan Airlines flight in Tokyo, forcing it to fly to Seoul, South Korea, where they released the passengers before flying on to North Korea, where they freed the crew and abandoned the plane. On 6 September 1970, the PFLP successfully hijacked three airliners on the same day, but a fourth attempt was foiled, resulting in Leila Khaled's capture and detention in the UK. Two of the seized aircraft were flown to a remote desert airstrip in Jordan known as Dawson's Field, the third to Cairo. Three days later, a PFLP sympathizer hijacked another airliner and directed it to Dawson's Field. That same day the UN Security Council adopted resolution 286 (1970), 9 September 1970, in which, '[g]ravely concerned at the threat to innocent civilian lives from the hijacking of aircraft', it appealed 'for the immediate release of all passengers and crews without exception, held as a result of hijackings'. A further three days later, the PLFP, having removed all the passengers and crew and released most of the former, blew up all three jets. By the end of the month the hijackers, who threatened to kill the hostages, had secured Khaled's freedom and that of several PLFP detainees.

[102] SC res 286 (1970), 9 September 1970, para 2.

[103] See Beijing Protocol, preamble (second recital). [104] Ibid, art I.

[105] Ibid, art IX.

a party to the Protocol is deemed to become a party to the Hague Convention as amended by the Beijing Protocol.[106]

(b) Scope of application

7.43 The scope of application of the Hague Convention is not uniform as among its provisions. As a general rule, the Convention applies only if the place of take-off or the place of actual landing of the aircraft on board which the offence is committed is situated outside the territory of the aircraft's state of registration.[107] But articles 6 (the obligation to take the suspect into custody and undertake a preliminary inquiry into the facts), 7 (the obligation *aut dedere aut judicare*), 8 (details as to extradition), and 10 (the obligation to afford assistance in criminal matters) apply regardless of the place of take-off and landing, provided that the offender or alleged offender is subsequently found in the territory of a state other than the state of registration.[108] In either case, it is immaterial whether the aircraft is engaged in an international or domestic flight.[109] The Convention does not apply, however, to aircraft used in military, customs or police services.[110]

7.44 The scope of application of the Hague Convention as amended by the Beijing Protocol is almost identical to that of the Hague Convention, the difference being that to articles 6, 7, 8, and 10—which apply regardless of the place of take-off and actual landing of the aircraft if the offender or alleged offender is found in the territory of a state other than the state of registration—are added the new articles 7*bis* (fair treatment in custody), 8*bis* (exclusion of political offence exception), and 8*ter* (refusal of extradition or legal assistance where persecutory, etc).[111]

(c) Crimes

7.45 In accordance with the Hague Convention, any person commits an offence if that person, while on board an aircraft in flight, unlawfully seizes or exercises control of that aircraft by force, threat of force, or any other form of intimidation.[112] No *mens rea* is specified, although it stands to reason, given the nature of the relevant acts, that the offence is predicated on intent. An aircraft is considered to be 'in flight' within the meaning of the Convention 'at any time from the moment when all its external doors are closed following embarkation until the moment when any such door is opened for disembarkation', although, in the event of a forced landing, the flight is deemed to continue 'until the competent authorities take over the responsibility for the aircraft and for persons and property on board'.[113]

7.46 According to the Hague Convention as amended by the Beijing Protocol, any person commits an offence if that person 'unlawfully and intentionally seizes or exercises control of an aircraft in service by force or threat thereof, or by coercion, or by any other form of intimidation, or by any technological means'.[114] An

---

[106] Ibid, art XXI(2) and (3). [107] Hague Convention, art 3(3).
[108] Ibid, art 3(5). [109] Ibid, art 3(3). [110] Ibid, art 3(2).
[111] Hague Convention as amended by Beijing Protocol, art 3(5).
[112] Hague Convention, art 1(*a*). [113] Ibid, art 3(1).
[114] Hague Convention as amended by Beijing Protocol, art 1(1).

aircraft is considered to be 'in service' for the purposes of the amended Convention 'from the beginning of the pre-flight preparation of the aircraft by ground personnel or by the crew for a specific flight until twenty-four hours after landing'.[115] Again, in the case of a forced landing, the flight is deemed to continue 'until the competent authorities take over the responsibility for the aircraft and for persons and property on board'.[116] Any person also commits an offence as per the amended Convention if that person makes a threat to commit the foregoing offence or unlawfully and intentionally causes any person to receive such a threat 'under circumstances which indicate that the threat is credible'.[117]

(d) Modes of responsibility

7.47 The Hague Convention provides additionally, where the person is on board an aircraft in flight, for criminal responsibility on the bases of attempted commission and of complicity in the commission or attempted commission of the offence recognized in the Convention.[118]

7.48 As amended by the Beijing Protocol, the Hague Convention specifies a detailed array of modes of responsibility other than commission, which are applicable in respect of a greater or lesser range of the offences and other modes of responsibility for those offences provided for in the amended Convention. These comprise attempt to commit an offence, organizing or directing others to commit an offence, participation as an accomplice in an offence, unlawfully and intentionally assisting another to evade investigation, prosecution, or punishment in the knowledge that the other has committed an act constituting an offence or is wanted for prosecution for such an offence or has been sentenced for such an offence;[119] unlawfully and intentionally agreeing with one or more persons to commit an offence, provided that, if national law so requires, one of the participants in the agreement undertakes an act in furtherance of the agreement;[120] and unlawfully and intentionally contributing in any other way to the commission of one or more offences by a group of persons acting with a common purpose, either 'with the aim of furthering the general criminal activity or purpose of the group, where such activity or purpose involves the commission of an offence', or in the knowledge of the intention of the group to commit an offence.[121]

(ii) Unlawful acts relating to international civil aviation

(a) Background

7.49 In resolution 286 (1970), the Security Council called on states to take all possible legal steps to prevent not only further hijackings but also 'any other interference with international civil air travel'.[122] The following year, in light of the fact that

---

[115] Ibid, art 3(1).   [116] Ibid.   [117] Ibid, art 1(2).
[118] Hague Convention, art 1(a) and (b) respectively.
[119] Hague Convention as amended by Beijing Protocol, art 1(3)(a) to (d).
[120] Ibid, art 1(4)(a).   [121] Ibid, art 1(4)(b)(i) and (ii).
[122] SC res 286 (1970), 9 September 1970, para 2. Earlier that year the Popular Front for the Liberation of Palestine–General Command (PLFP–GC), a splinter group of the PLFP, had detonated

the Hague Convention covered only the seizure and not the sabotage of or other acts of violence against civil aircraft, representatives of the member states of ICAO adopted, on 23 September 1971, the Montreal Convention.[123]

7.50 The 1970s and 1980s saw a spate of terrorist attacks at airports around the world against persons or facilities at those airports.[124] In response, on 24 February 1988, member states of ICAO adopted the Protocol for the Suppression of Unlawful Acts of Violence at Airports serving International Civil Aviation, supplementary to the Montreal Convention ('Montreal Protocol'). The Montreal Protocol inserts into the Montreal Convention, for states parties to both, an additional offence relating to acts of violence against the facilities of, or persons or aircraft not in service at, an airport serving international civil aviation.

7.51 Twenty-two years later, in response to a range of successful, attempted, and imagined terrorist acts—among the first the attacks of 11 September 2001 against targets in the US—involving the use of, directed against, or taking place on board civil aircraft or at or against civil airports,[125] member states of ICAO adopted, on 10 September 2010, the Beijing Convention. The Beijing Convention represents an update and consolidation in a single instrument of the Montreal Convention as amended by the Montreal Protocol. The Beijing Convention encompasses a variety of acts not covered by the Montreal Convention even as amended by the Montreal Protocol, such as the use of civil aircraft for the purpose of causing death, serious bodily injury, and so on, and various acts in connection with aircraft involving biological, chemical or nuclear weapons or the like. As among states parties to both the Montreal Convention (whether or not parties as well to the Montreal Protocol) and the Beijing Convention, the Beijing Convention is to prevail.[126] In other words, the Beijing Convention, which is not yet in force, is designed to supersede the Montreal Convention, both as originally adopted and as amended by the Montreal Protocol.

(b) Scope of application

7.52 Except as regards the offence of destroying or damaging air navigation facilities, the Montreal Convention, including as amended by the Montreal Protocol, applies as a general rule only if the place of take-off or actual or intended landing of the aircraft is situated outside the territory of the aircraft's state of registration or if the offence is committed in the territory of a state other than that of the aircraft's

---

a bomb on board a Swissair flight to Tel Aviv while it was over Switzerland, destroying the aircraft and killing 41 people. The group simultaneously triggered a device on board an Austrian Airlines flight from Frankfurt to Tel Aviv, but the plane was able to make an emergency landing.

[123] The Convention should not be confused with the other, perhaps better-known 'Montreal Convention', namely the Convention for the Unification of Certain Rules for International Carriage by Air 1999.
[124] Chief among these were the assault by the Japanese Red Army at Lod airport in Tel Aviv in 1972, the 1975 bombing at LaGuardia airport in New York, the 1982 bombing of the international airport in Ankara, the 1983 bombing at Orly airport in Paris, the 1984 bombing at London Heathrow airport, the near-simultaneous attacks in 1985 at airports in Rome and Vienna and an attack later the same year at Narita airport in Tokyo, and the 1986 bombing at Seoul's Kimpo airport.
[125] See Beijing Convention, preamble (second and third recitals).   [126] Ibid, art 24.

registration.[127] But, in an exception to this rule, the Convention also applies if the offender or alleged offender is subsequently found in the territory of a state other than the state of registration of the aircraft.[128] Either way, the Convention applies irrespective of whether the aircraft is engaged in an international or domestic flight,[129] but does not apply to aircraft used in military, customs or police service.[130] As regards the offence of destroying or damaging air navigation facilities,[131] the Convention applies only if the air navigation facilities are used in international air navigation.[132]

7.53 The scope of application of the Beijing Convention is the same as that of the Montreal Convention.[133]

(c) Crimes

7.54 The Montreal Convention posits as an offence the unlawful and intentional commission of a range of acts, namely any act of violence against a person on board an aircraft in flight that is likely to endanger the safety of the aircraft; the destruction of an aircraft in service or any damage to it that renders it incapable of flight or is likely to endanger its safety in flight; the placing or causing to be placed on an aircraft in service, by any means whatsoever, of a device or substance likely to destroy the aircraft or to cause damage to it that renders it incapable of flight or is likely to endanger its safety in flight; any destruction or damage of air navigation facilities or interference with their operation that is likely to endanger the safety of aircraft in flight; and the communication of knowingly false information that endangers the safety of an aircraft in flight.[134] For the purposes of the Convention, an aircraft is considered to be in flight in the same circumstances as those recognized in the Hague Convention[135] and in service in the same circumstances as those recognized in the Hague Convention as amended by the Beijing Protocol.[136]

7.55 As amended by the Montreal Protocol, the Montreal Convention provides also for the offences—committed unlawfully and intentionally with any device, substance or weapon—of violence, causing or likely to cause serious injury or death, against a person at an airport serving international civil aviation[137] and of destruction of or serious damage to the facilities of such an airport, or of or to aircraft not in service located there, or disruption of the services of such an airport where this endangers or is likely to endanger safety at that airport.[138]

7.56 The Beijing Convention adds to the offences posited by the Montreal Convention as amended by the Montreal Protocol a series of offences involving the use of aircraft to certain ends or of specific weapons or substances against or on

---

[127] Montreal Convention, art 4(2) and (6). [128] Ibid, art 4(3) and (6).
[129] Ibid, art 4(2) and (6). [130] Ibid, art 4(1). [131] See ibid, art 1(1)(*d*).
[132] Ibid, art 4(5). [133] See Beijing Convention, art 5.
[134] Montreal Convention, art 1(1)(*a*) to (*e*). [135] Ibid, art 2(*a*). Recall *supra* para 7.45.
[136] Ibid, art 2(*a*). Recall *supra* para 7.46.
[137] Montreal Convention as amended by Montreal Protocol, art 1(1)*bis(a)*.
[138] Ibid, art 1(1)*bis(b)*.

board aircraft. It posits as an offence, where committed unlawfully and intentionally, the use of an aircraft in service for the purpose of causing death, serious bodily injury or serious damage to property or the environment; the release or discharge from an aircraft in service of any biological, chemical or nuclear weapon or explosive, radioactive or similar substances in a manner that causes or is likely to cause death, serious bodily injury or serious damage to property or the environment, and the use of the same in the same manner against or on board an aircraft in service; and the transport, causing to be transported or facilitation of the transport of the same and similar, unless this is consistent with or is for a use or activity consistent with the rights, responsibilities, and obligations of a state party to the Convention under any applicable multilateral treaty on non-proliferation to which it is a party.[139] The Beijing Convention further specifies that it is an offence to make a threat to commit the offences recognized in the Convention, with the exception of the offence of transporting, causing to be transported or facilitating the transport of specified objects on board an aircraft, or unlawfully and intentionally to cause any person to receive such a threat 'under circumstances which indicate that the threat is credible'.[140]

(d) Modes of responsibility

7.57 The Montreal Convention, including as amended by the Montreal Protocol, provides in addition for criminal responsibility on the bases of attempted commission and of complicity in the commission or attempted commission of the offences recognized in the Convention.[141]

7.58 The Beijing Convention provides for the same modes of responsibility other than commission as does the Hague Convention as amended by the Beijing Protocol.[142]

(iii) Crimes against internationally protected persons

(a) Background

7.59 By letter of 12 May 1970, the government of the Netherlands addressed to the president of the UN Security Council its concern over 'the increasing number of attacks on diplomats', asking him to bring this to the attention of members of the Security Council and the appropriate UN organs,[143] which the latter did, including by way of letter to the chairman of the International Law Commission (ILC). In 1971, at the first meeting of its twenty-third session and just over three weeks after a fatal attack on a consular officer,[144] a member of the ILC

---

[139] See Beijing Convention, art 1(1)(f) to (i).   [140] Ibid, art 1(3).
[141] Montreal Convention, art 1(2)(a) and (b) respectively.
[142] See Beijing Convention, art 1(4) and (5). Recall *supra* para 7.48.
[143] UN doc S/9789 (12 May 1970).
[144] On 1 April 1971, Monika Ertl, acting on behalf of a Bolivian revolutionary movement and using a gun supplied to her by the Italian publishing magnate Giangiacomo Feltrinelli, assassinated the Bolivian consul in Hamburg.

suggested that the Commission consider producing draft articles on such crimes as the murder, kidnapping, and assault of diplomats and other persons entitled to special protection under international law. The Commission decided that, if the General Assembly so requested, it would do so. In response, the General Assembly requested the Commission to study the question as soon as possible, in the light of comments received from member states, with a view to preparing draft articles for submission to the Assembly at the earliest date the Commission considered appropriate.[145] The Commission addressed the question the following year, and moved rapidly to the adoption of 12 provisional draft articles with commentaries, which it presented to the General Assembly for the latter to submit to governments for comments. On 14 December 1973, the Internationally Protected Persons Convention was adopted without a vote by way of annex to General Assembly resolution 3166 (XXVIII).

(b) Crimes

7.60 The Internationally Protected Persons Convention obliges states parties to criminalize under their municipal law the intentional commission of murder, kidnapping, and other attacks on the person or liberty of an internationally protected person; any violent attack on the official premises, private accommodation or means of transport of an internationally protected person that is likely to endanger the person or liberty of the internationally protected person; and threats to commit any of the foregoing.[146] The Convention defines an internationally protected person to encompass all those individuals benefiting under customary or conventional international law from inviolability of their person and liberty by virtue of their connection with a state or international organization, *viz* heads of state, heads of government, and ministers for foreign affairs, whenever any of these is in a foreign state, as well as accompanying members of their family;[147] and any representative or official of a state or any official or other agent of an intergovernmental organization 'who, at the time when and in the place where a crime against him, his official premises, his private accommodation or his means of transport is committed, is entitled pursuant to international law to special protection from any attack on his person, freedom or dignity', as well as members of that person's family forming part of his or her household.[148]

(c) Modes of responsibility

7.61 The Convention requires states parties to criminalize not only the commission of and threat to commit any of the specified attacks but also any attempt to commit such an attack and any act constituting participation as an accomplice in such an attack.[149]

---

[145] GA res 2780 III (XXVI), 3 December 1971.
[146] Internationally Protected Persons Convention, art 2(1)(*a*) to (*c*).
[147] Ibid, art 1(1)(*a*). [148] Ibid, art 1(1)(*b*). [149] Ibid, art 2(1)(*d*) and (*e*).

(iv) Hostage-taking

(a) Background

The early 1970s witnessed a series of notorious incidents of hostage-taking.[150] In December 1976, the General Assembly—gravely concerned at the increase in hostage-taking and recognizing the urgent need for further effective measures to put an end to it—established an Ad Hoc Committee on the Drafting of an International Convention against the Taking of Hostages, requesting the latter to draft such a convention at the earliest possible date.[151] In the event, it was not until three years and several infamous episodes[152] later that, on 17 December 1979, the Hostages Convention was adopted without a vote by way of annex to General Assembly resolution 34/146.

7.62

(b) Scope of application

The Hostages Convention does not apply where, cumulatively, the offence is committed within a single state, the hostage and the alleged offender are nationals of that state, and the alleged offender is found in the territory of that state.[153] In

7.63

---

[150] During the Olympic Games in Munich in 1972, members of the Palestinian militant group 'Black September' shot and killed two members of the Israeli Olympic team before taking nine others hostage in the Olympic village in support of their demand for the freeing of over 200 Palestinian and other prisoners from Israeli jails, as well as the release of Andreas Baader and Ulrike Meinhof, two of the founders of the Red Army Faction in Germany, who had trained with the PFLP. In the event, all nine hostages were killed after a rescue attempt by the German authorities. In December 1973, after killing 30 people at Rome airport, Palestinian militants took hostage five Italians and the crew of a Lufthansa airliner, which was flown to Athens, where they killed one passenger and dumped his body on the tarmac, and then on to Damascus and finally Kuwait, where they released the remaining hostages. The following year and in 1975, the Japanese Red Army was involved in three major hostage incidents, including one at the French embassy in The Hague and one co-ordinated with the seizure of the Japanese embassy in Kuwait by the PFLP. Then, on 27 June 1976, an Air France airliner with 260 people on board was hijacked en route from Tel Aviv, via Athens, to Paris, by members of the Popular Front for the Liberation of Palestine–External Operations and members of the German 'Revolutionary Cells'. It was flown to Entebbe airport outside Kampala, Uganda, where most of the non-Jewish passengers were released, leaving on board as hostages 83 Israeli and/or Jewish hostages, as well as 20 non-Jews (including the crew) who had refused the offer of release. The crisis came to an end when Israeli forces stormed the plane, killing all the hijackers with the loss of the lives of only three hostages and one Israeli commando.

[151] GA res 31/103, 15 December 1976.

[152] On 13 October 1977, however, Arab militants hijacked a Lufthansa airliner en route to Frankfurt, demanding *inter alia* the release from Stammheim prison of the four surviving leaders of the German Red Army Faction. The plane was flown to Rome, then on to Larnaca, Dubai, and Aden, where the captain was convicted on board by a hastily convened 'revolutionary tribunal' and executed and his body dumped on the runway. When the plane eventually landed in Mogadishu, Somalia, it was stormed by a special unit of the German police, who secured the release of all the hostages unharmed. When the news broke in Germany, the kidnappers of Hanns Martin Schleyer, the president of the German employers' association taken hostage over a month before by persons also demanding the release of the Stammheim inmates, was shot dead. Next, in March 1978, Aldo Moro, former Prime Minister of Italy and leading Christian Democrat, was taken hostage in Rome by the Red Brigades. Despite an appeal for his release by Pope Paul VI, he was executed 55 days later. Finally, on 4 November 1979, demonstrators stormed the US embassy in Tehran, as well as the US consulates in Tabriz and Shiraz, taking hostage the diplomatic and consular staff and setting in train a crisis that would last for 444 days, ending with the release of the hostages within minutes of President Carter's departure from office.

[153] Hostages Convention, art 13.

addition, insofar as the 1949 Geneva Conventions or their Additional Protocols I and II are applicable to a particular act of hostage-taking, and insofar as states parties to the Hostages Convention are bound under the Geneva Conventions or Additional Protocols to prosecute or hand over the hostage-taker, the Hostages Convention does not apply to an act of hostage-taking committed in the course of an armed conflict covered by the applicable Geneva Convention or Protocol.[154]

(c) Crimes

7.64 The Hostages Convention defines as the offence of 'hostage-taking' within the meaning of the Convention the seizure or detention and threat to kill, to injure or to continue to detain another person ('the hostage') in order to compel a third party, in the form of a state, intergovernmental organization, natural or juridical person, or group of persons, to do or abstain from doing any act as an explicit or implicit condition of the release of the hostage.[155]

(d) Modes of responsibility

7.65 In addition to the commission of hostage-taking, the Convention deems as an offence for its purposes the attempt to commit an act of hostage-taking and the participation as an accomplice in the commission or attempted commission of an act of hostage-taking.[156]

(v) Crimes relating to the physical protection of nuclear material and facilities

(a) Background

7.66 In response to persistent concerns relating to the security of nuclear material used for peaceful purposes while in use, storage or transit, on 26 October 1979 states, under the auspices of the IAEA, adopted the Nuclear Material Convention. Unlike preceding multilateral treaties in the field of international criminal law, the Convention is not concerned solely with penal measures, embodying as it also does a range of more regulatory obligations for states parties. Penal measures are nonetheless a central element of the instrument.

7.67 From the early 1990s, concern grew over the theft of nuclear material from reactors, laboratories, and military sites in parts of the former Soviet Union, the fear being that criminal networks might acquire enriched uranium or plutonium for sale to so-called 'rogue' states or terrorist groups. A decade later, the uncovering of a well-established clandestine traffic in nuclear technology centring on the Pakistani nuclear scientist Abdul Qadeer Khan, along with reports of the disappearance of radioactive material from insecure nuclear facilities in central and west Africa and

---

[154] Ibid, art 12. In practice, the reference to 'the Additional Protocols' can embrace only Additional Protocol I, since Additional Protocol II, which contains no grave breaches provisions, does not require the high contracting parties to prosecute or hand over a hostage-taker.
[155] Hostages Convention, art 1(1).   [156] Ibid, art 1(2)(*a*) and (*b*).

anxieties over a potential terrorist attack on a nuclear reactor, crystallized the determination to improve the Nuclear Material Convention, including by expanding the range of offences for which it provided.[157] The upshot was the Amendment to the Convention on the Physical Protection of Nuclear Material agreed in Vienna on 8 July 2005 under the aegis of the IAEA. The Convention and the Amendment are to be read together as a single instrument called the Convention on the Physical Protection of Nuclear Material and Nuclear Facilities 2005 ('Nuclear Material and Facilities Convention').[158] The Amendment, and hence the Nuclear Material and Facilities Convention, is yet to enter into force.

(b) Scope of application

7.68 The criminal-law provisions of the Nuclear Material Convention apply to nuclear material used for peaceful purposes 'while in international nuclear transport'[159] and while in domestic use, storage and transport.[160] The term 'nuclear material' is defined, by reference to chemical criteria, to encompass certain isotopes of plutonium and uranium and material containing them.[161] The expression 'international nuclear transport' is defined to mean 'the carriage of a consignment of nuclear material by any means of transportation intended to go beyond the territory of the State where the shipment originates beginning with the departure from a facility of a shipper in that State and ending with the arrival at a facility of the receiver within the State of ultimate destination'.[162]

7.69 The criminal-law provisions of the Nuclear Material and Facilities Convention apply to nuclear material used for peaceful purposes that is in use, storage or transport, as well as to nuclear facilities used for peaceful purposes.[163] The Convention does not apply to nuclear material used or retained for military purposes or to any nuclear facility containing such material.[164] A 'nuclear facility' refers to 'a facility (including associated buildings and equipment) in which nuclear material is produced, processed, used, handled, stored or disposed of, if damage to or interference with such a facility could lead to the release of significant amounts of radiation or radioactive material'.[165] The Convention further specifies:

The activities of armed forces during an armed conflict, as those terms are understood under international humanitarian law, which are governed by that law, are not governed by this Convention, and the activities undertaken by the military forces of a State in the exercise of their official duties, inasmuch as they are governed by other rules of international law, are not governed by this Convention.[166]

The term 'armed forces', as understood under international humanitarian law, is not limited to the armed forces of the government of a state, while 'the activities

---

[157] See Nuclear Material and Facilities Convention, preamble (seventh, eleventh, and twelfth recitals).
[158] Amendment of 2005 to the Convention on the Physical Protection of Nuclear Material, art 1.
[159] Nuclear Material Convention, art 2(1). [160] Ibid, art 2(2).
[161] See ibid, art 1(*a*) and (*b*). [162] Ibid, art 1(*c*).
[163] Nuclear Material and Facilities Convention, art 2(1). [164] Ibid, art 2(5).
[165] Ibid, art 1(*d*). [166] Ibid, art 2(4)(*b*).

undertaken by the military forces of a State in the exercise of their official duties' are not limited to armed conflict, including belligerent occupation.

(c) Crimes

7.70 The Nuclear Material Convention requires states parties to make the intentional commission of a range of acts pertaining to the transport of nuclear material offences under their municipal law, namely any receipt, possession, use, transfer, alteration, disposal or dispersal of nuclear material, without lawful authority, that causes or is likely to cause death or serious injury to any person or substantial damage to property; the theft or robbery of nuclear material; the embezzlement or fraudulent obtaining of nuclear material; any demand for nuclear material involving the threat or use of force or any other form of intimidation; and any threat to use nuclear material to cause death or serious injury to any person or substantial property damage or threat to engage in theft or robbery of nuclear material 'in order to compel a natural or legal person, international organization or State to do or refrain from doing any act'.[167]

7.71 The Nuclear Material and Facilities Convention, as well as broadening two of the crimes provided for in the Nuclear Material Convention to embrace the causing or likelihood of causing substantial damage to the environment,[168] includes a handful of new crimes, each of them requiring intent. These comprise the carrying, sending or moving of nuclear material into or out of a state without lawful authority; any act directed against or interfering with the operation of a nuclear facility where the offender intentionally causes or knows that the act is likely to cause death or serious injury or substantial damage to property or the environment by exposure to radiation or release of radioactive substances; and any threat to commit the foregoing offence to cause death or serious injury or substantial damage to property or the environment or to compel a natural or legal person, international organization or state to do or refrain from doing any act.[169]

(d) Modes of responsibility

7.72 With the exception of demands and threats in respect of nuclear material, those acts the object of the Nuclear Material Convention's obligation of municipal criminalization must be rendered punishable on the basis of attempt as well.[170] Any act of 'participation' in any of the specified offences, including in the offence of attempt to commit such an offence, must also be criminalized under a state party's municipal law.[171] The reference to 'participation', as distinct from 'participation as an accomplice' as found in many other conventions, is vague. It would seem to be up to each state party to decide for itself whether the term encompasses only complicity or also, for example, and depending on a state party's criminal law,

---

[167] Nuclear Material Convention, art 7(1)(*a*) to (*e*).
[168] See Nuclear Material and Facilities Convention, art 7(1)(*a*) and (*g*)(i), first limb.
[169] Ibid, art 7(1)(*d*), (*e*), and (*g*). An exception to the offence in art 7(1)(*e*) exists where the act is undertaken in conformity with the national law of the state party in whose territory the nuclear facility is situated.
[170] Nuclear Material Convention, art 7(1)(*f*). [171] Ibid, art 7(1)(*g*).

conspiracy and participation in a joint criminal enterprise (at least where the latter is not considered a form of commission).

The Nuclear Material and Facilities Convention specifies, in addition to commission, attempt, and 'participation', criminal responsibility for organizing others to commit any offence recognized in the Convention bar a criminal demand or threat and for contributing to the commission of any of the same by a group of persons acting with a common purpose, either with the aim of furthering the criminal activity or criminal purpose of the group, where such activity or purpose involves the commission of an offence recognized in the Convention, or in the knowledge of the intention of the group to commit such an offence.[172]   7.73

(vi) Unlawful acts against the safety of maritime navigation and against the safety of fixed platforms located on the continental shelf

(a) **Background**

In 1985, members of the Palestine Liberation Front (PLF) seized the Italian cruise   7.74
liner *Achille Lauro* in the Mediterranean as it sailed from Alexandria to Port Said, demanding the release of 50 Palestinian prisoners in Israeli jails and eventually killing the wheelchair-bound US national Leon Klinghoffer, dumping his body overboard. 'Shipjacking' of this sort, along with certain other acts of maritime violence that were already raising concerns within the shipping industry, fell outside the international legal definition of piracy. As a consequence, in late 1985, the UN General Assembly requested the International Maritime Organization (IMO) 'to study the problem of terrorism aboard or against ships with a view to making recommendations on appropriate measures'.[173] In November 1986, Austria, Egypt, and Italy (the last two states having been directly touched by the *Achille Lauro* affair)[174] formally proposed that the IMO draft a convention on the suppression of relevant acts against the safety of maritime navigation. Less than 18 months later, on 10 March 1988, IMO member states meeting in Rome adopted the SUA Convention.[175] The significance of the SUA Convention lies not just in its role, in practice rather limited, in the suppression of terrorist acts at sea but in its potential utility in suppressing not only acts of maritime depredation that, chiefly on account of their occurrence within territorial waters, do not fall within the definition of piracy *jure gentium* but also acts of piracy itself.

---

[172] Nuclear Material and Facilities Convention, art 7(1)(*j*) and (*k*).
[173] GA res 40/61, 9 December 1985, para 13, as recalled in SUA Convention, preamble (tenth recital).
[174] In addition to their connection to the vessel and its fateful voyage, Egypt and Italy were involved, in different ways, in the resolution of the affair. After a negotiated resolution to the hostage stand-off which resulted in an Egyptian commercial airliner taking off for Tunisia with the hijackers and other PLF figures on-board, US fighter aircraft forced the plane to land in Italy, where the hijackers were prosecuted.
[175] 'SUA', standing as it does for 'Suppression of Unlawful Acts', is not a particularly revealing acronym, although it seems to have become entrenched.

7.75 Concluded at the same time as the SUA Convention was the SUA Protocol, aimed at combating chiefly the seizure of oil and gas rigs and the commission of acts of violence against them or persons on them. The Protocol is parasitic upon the SUA Convention, rendering applicable to the crimes it sets forth the criminal-law articles of the Convention bar that mandating prescriptive jurisdiction,[176] for which it makes it own provision.[177]

7.76 In 2005, concerns akin to those that led to the adoption the same year by the UN General Assembly of the Nuclear Terrorism Convention, along with a more general desire to update and improve the workings of the SUA Convention, motivated IMO member states to adopt the Protocol of 2005 to the SUA Convention, which is to be read together with the Convention as a single instrument known as the Convention for the Suppression of Unlawful Acts against the Safety of Maritime Navigation 2005 ('2005 SUA Convention'). The 2005 SUA Convention extends to, *inter alia*, the maritime use and transport of weapons of mass destruction and the maritime transport of clandestine nuclear material and technology.

7.77 At the same conference at which they adopted the Protocol of 2005 to the SUA Convention, member states of IMO adopted the Protocol of 2005 to the Protocol for the Suppression of Unlawful Acts against the Safety of Fixed Platforms Located on the Continental Shelf, which is to be read together with the SUA Protocol as a single instrument called the Protocol for the Suppression of Unlawful Acts against the Safety of Fixed Platforms Located on the Continental Shelf 2005 ('2005 SUA Protocol'). The 2005 SUA Protocol bears the same relation, *mutatis mutandis*, to the 2005 SUA Convention as the SUA Protocol bears to the SUA Convention.[178] The 2005 SUA Protocol extends to, *inter alia*, the use of weapons of mass destruction against or on a fixed platform as defined in the Protocol.

(b) Scope of application

7.78 As a general rule, the SUA Convention applies only if the ship to which the offence pertains is navigating or is scheduled to navigate into, through or from the waters beyond the outer limit of the territorial sea of a single state (whether or not it navigates into, through or from the territorial sea of another state) or beyond the lateral limits of that state's territorial sea with adjacent states.[179] But, by way of exception, the Convention also applies when the offender or alleged offender is found in the territory of a state party other than the state in whose territorial sea the ship was navigating or was scheduled to navigate.[180] The term 'ship' is defined for the purposes of the Convention to mean 'a vessel of any type whatsoever not permanently attached to the sea-bed, including dynamically supported craft, submersibles, or any other floating craft'.[181] The Convention does not apply, however, to warships,

---

[176] See SUA Protocol, art 1(1) and (2).   [177] See ibid, art 3.
[178] See 2005 SUA Protocol, art 1(1).
[179] SUA Convention, art 4(1). The relevant state need not be party to the Convention, as indicated by the distinction between the word 'State' in art 4(1) and the term 'State Party' in art 4(2).
[180] Ibid, art 4(2).
[181] Ibid, art 1. Dynamically-supported craft include hovercraft and hydrofoils.

ships owned or operated by a state when being used as naval auxiliaries or for customs or police purposes, or ships withdrawn from navigation or laid up.[182]

7.79 The provisions of the SUA Convention applicable, *mutatis mutandis*, to the offences on board or against fixed platforms set forth in the SUA Protocol apply to these offences only, as a general rule, if the fixed platform is located on a state's continental shelf.[183] The exception is where the offender or alleged offender is subsequently found in the territory of a state party other than the coastal state in question, in which case the relevant provisions of the Convention apply, *mutatis mutandis*, to the offences in the Protocol even if the fixed platform was located in the coastal state's internal waters or territorial sea.[184] The term 'fixed platform' as used in the Protocol means 'an artificial island, installation or structure permanently attached to the sea-bed for the purpose of exploration or exploitation of resources or for other economic purposes'.[185]

7.80 The scope of application of the 2005 SUA Convention is the same as that of the SUA Convention. The 2005 SUA Convention specifies, however, that it does not apply to 'the activities of armed forces during an armed conflict, as those terms are understood under international humanitarian law, which are governed by that law', or to activities undertaken by the military forces of a state in the exercise of their official duties, inasmuch as they are governed by other rules of international law.[186] The term 'armed forces', as understood under international humanitarian law, is not limited to the armed forces of the government of a state, while 'the activities undertaken by the military forces of a State in the exercise of their official duties' are not limited to armed conflict, including belligerent occupation.[187]

7.81 The provisions of the 2005 SUA Convention applicable, *mutatis mutandis*, to the offences on board or against fixed platforms set forth in the 2005 SUA Protocol apply to these offences only, as a general rule, if the fixed platform is located on a state's continental shelf,[188] although the relevant provisions further apply in respect of fixed platforms located in a coastal state's internal waters or territorial sea in the event that the offender or alleged offender is subsequently found in the territory of a state party other than the coastal state.[189] The term 'fixed platform' is used in the 2005 SUA Protocol in the same way as in the SUA Protocol.[190] The 'carve-out' in the 2005 SUA Convention in respect of any activities of armed forces during an armed conflict that are governed by international humanitarian law and of any activities undertaken by the military forces of a state in the exercise of their official duties that are governed by other rules of international law applies equally to the 2005 SUA Protocol.[191]

---

[182] Ibid, art 2(1). Article 2(2) specifies for the avoidance of doubt that nothing in the Convention affects the immunities of warships and other government ships operated for non-commercial purposes.
[183] SUA Protocol, art 1(1).   [184] Ibid, art 1(2).
[185] Ibid, art 1(3). The most common form of fixed platform is an oil or gas rig.
[186] 2005 SUA Convention, art 2*bis*(2).   [187] Recall *supra* para 7.69.
[188] 2005 SUA Protocol, art 1(1).   [189] Ibid, art 1(2).   [190] Ibid, art 1(3).
[191] See ibid, art 1(1), cross-referenced with 2005 SUA Convention, art 2*bis*(2).

(c) Crimes

7.82 The SUA Convention posits as offences a range of acts when committed unlawfully and intentionally,[192] these being the seizure of or exercise of control over a ship by force, threat of force, or any other form of intimidation; any act of violence against a person on board a ship that is likely to endanger the safe navigation of the ship; the destruction of a ship or any damage to it or its cargo that is likely to endanger its safe navigation; the placing or causing to be placed on a ship, by any means whatsoever, of a device or substance likely to destroy it or to cause damage to it or its cargo that endangers or is likely to endanger its safe navigation; any destruction of, serious damage to or serious interference with the operation of maritime navigational facilities that is likely to endanger the safe navigation of a ship; the communication of knowingly false information that endangers the safe navigation of a ship; injury to or the killing of any person in connection with the commission or attempted commission of any of the foregoing offences;[193] and any threat, with or without condition, to commit the second, third or fifth of the foregoing offences if that threat is aimed at compelling a physical or juridical person to do or refrain from doing any act and is likely to endanger the safe navigation of the ship or, as regards maritime navigational facilities, a ship.[194] The first of these offences is capable of encompassing acts that would equally qualify as piracy.

7.83 The 2005 SUA Convention contains a raft of new offences supplementary to those found in the SUA Convention.[195] First, it declares as offences within the meaning of the Convention—if committed unlawfully and intentionally and 'when the purpose of the act, by its nature or context, is to intimidate a population, or to compel a government or an international organization to do or abstain from doing any act'—the use against or on or the discharge from a ship of any explosive, any radioactive material or any biological chemical or nuclear weapon in a manner causing or likely to cause death or serious injury or damage; the discharge from a ship of any other hazardous or noxious substance in a quantity or concentration causing or likely to cause death or serious injury or damage; the use of a ship in a manner causing death or serious injury or damage; and the threat, with or without condition, to commit one of the foregoing offences.[196] Next, the Convention posits as an offence the unlawful and intentional transport on board a ship of the sorts of substances the transport of which on board an aircraft is an offence according to the Beijing Convention.[197] Lastly, the 2005

---

[192] Although the preamble (twelfth recital) to the SUA Convention notes that such acts of a ship's crew as are subject to 'normal shipboard discipline' are 'outside the purview of th[e] Convention', it is not clear whether, and unlikely that, this statement could remove from the scope of the Convention acts satisfying the elements of the crimes provided for in art 3.

[193] SUA Convention, art 3(1)(*a*) to (*g*).

[194] Ibid, art 3(2)(*c*), explicitly leaving the requirement or otherwise of a condition to national law.

[195] In addition, the 2005 SUA Convention moves to art 3*quater(a)* the offence found in SUA Convention, art 3(1)(*g*) of injuring or killing a person in connection with the actual or attempted commission of any of the offences in the Convention.

[196] 2005 SUA Convention, art 3*bis*(1)(*a*)(i) to (iv), the last explicitly leaving the requirement or otherwise of a condition to national law.

[197] Ibid, art 3*bis*(1)(*b*) and (2). Recall *supra* para 7.56.

SUA Convention makes it an offence unlawfully, intentionally, and with the intention of assisting the person to evade prosecution to transport a person on board a ship in the knowledge that the person has committed an offence within the meaning of the Convention or an offence set forth in any treaty listed in the Convention's Annex.[198]

7.84 The SUA Protocol declares as offences, when committed unlawfully and intentionally, the seizure of or exercise of control over a fixed platform by force, threat of force, or any other form of intimidation; any act of violence against a person on board a fixed platform that is likely to endanger the safety of the platform; destruction of a fixed platform or any damage to it that is likely to endanger its safety; placing or causing to be placed on a fixed platform, by any means whatsoever, a device or substance likely to destroy it or endanger its safety; injuring or killing any person in connection with the commission or attempted commission of any of the foregoing offences;[199] and any threat, with or without condition, to commit the second or third of the foregoing offences if that threat is aimed at compelling a physical or juridical person to do or refrain from doing any act and is likely to endanger the safety of the fixed platform.[200]

7.85 The 2005 SUA Protocol includes as offences supplementary to those found in the SUA Protocol[201] the unlawful and intentional commission vis-à-vis a fixed platform, 'when the purpose of the act, by its nature or context, is to intimidate a population, or to compel a government or an international organization to do or abstain from doing any act', of the acts deemed criminal under the same conditions vis-à-vis ships by the 2005 SUA Convention.[202]

(d) Modes of responsibility

7.86 The SUA Convention provides for criminal responsibility in respect of the offences set out therein on the basis not only of commission but also of attempt and of abetting or otherwise being an accomplice to the commission of an offence.[203]

7.87 The 2005 SUA Convention specifies an array of modes of responsibility other than commission, which apply in respect of a greater or lesser range of the offences provided for in the Convention. These comprise attempt to commit an offence, participation as an accomplice in an offence, organizing or directing others to commit an offence, and contributing in any other way to the commission of one or more offences by a group of persons acting with a common purpose, either

---

[198] Ibid, art 3*ter*. These treaties are currently the Hague Convention, the Montreal Convention, the Internationally Protected Persons Convention, the Hostages Convention, the Nuclear Material Convention, the Montreal Protocol, the SUA Protocol, the Terrorist Bombings Convention, and the Financing of Terrorism Convention.
[199] SUA Protocol, art 2(1)(*a*) to (*e*).
[200] Ibid, art 2(2)(*c*), explicitly leaving the requirement or otherwise of a condition to national law.
[201] In addition, the 2005 SUA Protocol moves to art 2*ter*(*a*) the offence found in SUA Protocol, art 2(1)(*e*) of injuring or killing a person in connection with the actual or attempted commission of any of the offences in the Convention.
[202] 2005 SUA Protocol, art 2*bis*. Recall *supra* para 7.83.
[203] SUA Convention, art 3(2)(*a*) and (*b*) respectively.

with the aim of furthering the criminal activity or criminal purpose of the group, where such activity or purpose involves the commission of an offence set forth in the Convention, or in the knowledge of the intention of the group to commit such an offence.[204]

7.88 The SUA Protocol provides for criminal responsibility in respect of the relevant offences on the bases, in addition to that of commission, of attempt and of abetting or otherwise being an accomplice.[205]

7.89 The 2005 SUA Protocol stipulates the same modes of responsibility as the 2005 SUA Convention.[206]

(vii) Terrorist bombings

(a) Background

7.90 The 1980s and early 1990s saw a grisly procession, across a range of states, of terrorist bombings of public buildings, often premises occupied by foreign governments or nationals.[207] In response, by way of resolution 51/210 of 17 December 1996, the UN General Assembly established an Ad Hoc Committee 'to elaborate an international convention for the suppression of terrorist bombings'.[208] The Committee worked quickly, and not even a year later the Terrorist Bombings Convention was adopted without a vote by way of annex to General Assembly resolution 52/164 of 15 December 1997.

(b) Scope of application

7.91 With the exception of the provisions on mutual assistance, fair treatment, and prevention of the relevant offences, the Terrorist Bombings Convention does not apply where, cumulatively, the offence is committed within a single state, the alleged offender and victims are nationals of that state, the alleged offender is found in the territory of that state, and no other state enjoys prescriptive jurisdiction on any of the bases specified in the Convention bar universal jurisdiction.[209] In addition, the Convention was the first to specify that '[t]he activities of armed forces during an armed conflict, as those terms are understood under international humanitarian law, which are governed by that law, are not governed by this Convention, and the activities undertaken by the military forces of a State in the exercise of their official duties, inasmuch as they are governed by other rules of international law, are not governed by this Convention'.[210] Unlike, however, the later Nuclear Materials and Facilities Convention, the 2005 SUA Convention, and the 2005 SUA Protocol, the Terrorist Bombings Conventions defines the term 'military forces of a State', stating it to refer to 'the armed forces

---

[204] 2005 SUA Convention, art 3*quater(b)* to (*e*).
[205] SUA Protocol, art 2(2)(*a*) and (*b*) respectively.   [206] 2005 SUA Protocol, art 2*bis*.
[207] The final straw was seen at least by western states to come in 1996, when the Khobar Towers, a US military barracks in Dahran, Saudi Arabia was bombed, causing the deaths of many US servicemen.
[208] GA res 51/210, 17 December 1996, para 9.
[209] Terrorist Bombings Convention, art 3.
[210] Ibid, art 9(2). See also ibid, preamble (final recital) and recall *supra* para 7.69.

of a State which are organized, trained and equipped under its internal law for the primary purpose of national defence or security, and persons acting in support of those armed forces who are under their formal command, control and responsibility'.[211]

(c) Crimes

The Terrorist Bombings Convention defines as an offence within the meaning of the Convention the unlawful and intentional delivery, placing, discharge or detonation of an explosive or other lethal device in, into or against a place of public use, a state or government facility, a public transportation system or an infrastructure facility either with the intent to cause death or serious bodily injury or with the intent to cause extensive destruction of such a place, facility or system, where such destruction results in or is likely to result in major economic loss.[212] The terms 'explosive or other lethal device', 'place of public use', 'state or government facility', 'public transportation system', and 'infrastructure facility' are all defined in article 1 of the Convention. 7.92

(d) Modes of responsibility

The Terrorist Bombings Convention provides additionally for criminal responsibility on the basis of attempt to commit an offence recognized in the Convention; participation as an accomplice in the commission or attempted commission of such an offence; organizing or directing others to commit or to attempt to commit such an offence; and contributing in any other way to the commission or attempted commission of such an offence by a group of persons acting with a common purpose, either with the aim of furthering 'the general criminal activity or purpose' of the group or in the knowledge of the intention of the group to commit or attempt to commit an offence.[213] 7.93

(viii) *Financing of terrorism*

(a) Background

On 7 August 1998, the US embassies in Nairobi, Kenya and Dar-es-Salaam, Tanzania were bombed, causing over 200 deaths and 4,000 injuries, mostly of locals. Suspicion centred on the involvement of the millionaire former Saudi national Osama bin Laden. In response, and given widespread recognition of the role played by transnational financial networks in the sponsorship of terrorist acts, the UN General Assembly instructed the Ad Hoc Committee established two years previously in resolution 51/210 to 'elaborate a draft international convention for the suppression of terrorist financing'.[214] On 9 December 1999, on the basis of the Committee's work, the General Assembly adopted without a vote 7.94

---

[211] Ibid, art 1(4).   [212] Ibid, art 2(1)(*a*) and (*b*).
[213] Ibid, art 2(2) and (3)(*a*), (*b*), and (*c*).
[214] GA res 53/108, 8 December 1998, para 11. The Security Council condemned the attacks in SC res 1189 (1998), 13 August 1998.

the Financing of Terrorism Convention, annexed to General Assembly resolution 54/109.

(b) Scope of application

7.95 With the exception of the provisions on mutual assistance, fair treatment, and prevention of the offences in question, the Financing of Terrorism Convention does not apply where, cumulatively, the offence is committed within a single state, the alleged offender is a national of that state and is present in the territory of that state, and no other state enjoys prescriptive jurisdiction on any of the bases specified in the Convention bar universal jurisdiction.[215]

(c) Crimes

7.96 The Financing of Terrorism Convention states that a person commits an offence within the meaning of the Convention if that person 'by any means, directly or indirectly, unlawfully and wilfully, provides or collects funds with the intention that they should be used or in the knowledge that they are to be used, in full or in part, in order to carry out' one of two sorts of act.[216] The first is an act constituting an offence within the scope of and as defined in one of the treaties listed in the Convention's annex,[217] these being at present the other 'anti-terrorist' conventions and protocols concluded between 1970 and 1997. The other comprises any other act 'intended to cause death or serious bodily injury to a civilian, or to any other person not taking an active part in the hostilities in a situation of armed conflict, when the purpose of such act, by its nature or context, is to intimidate a population, or to compel a government or an international organization to do or to abstain from doing any act'.[218] It is unnecessary that the funds are actually used to carry out a specified offence.[219] The terms 'funds', 'state or governmental facility', and 'proceeds' are defined in article 1 of the Convention.

(d) Modes of responsibility

7.97 The Financing of Terrorism Convention provides additionally for criminal responsibility on the basis of attempt to commit an offence set forth in the Convention; participation as an accomplice in such an offence or attempted offence; organizing or directing others to commit or attempt to commit such an offence; and intentionally contributing in any other way to the commission or attempted commission of one or more such offences by a group of persons acting with a common purpose, either with the aim of furthering the general criminal activity or purpose of the group, where such activity or purpose involves the commission of such an offence, or in the knowledge of the intention of the group to commit such an offence.[220]

---

[215] Financing of Terrorism Convention, art 3.   [216] Ibid, art 2(1), chapeau.
[217] Ibid, art 2(1)(*a*). Optional provision is made in art 2(2) for states parties to the Convention that are not or cease to be parties to the listed conventions.
[218] Ibid, art 2(1)(*b*).   [219] Ibid, art 2(3).
[220] Ibid, art 2(4) and (5)(*a*), (*b*), and (*c*).

(ix) Nuclear terrorism

(a) Background

In the mid-1990s there grew concern, fed by reports of the unregulated circulation of nuclear material,[221] that a terrorist group might assemble and detonate a nuclear device or a conventional device capable of dispersing radioactive material (a so-called 'dirty bomb'), with major loss of life and contamination of the urban and natural environment. In response, the UN General Assembly, in resolution 51/210 of 17 December 1996, instructed the Ad Hoc Committee established in the same resolution to elaborate, after its preparation of a convention on terrorist bombings, a convention for the suppression of acts of nuclear terrorism.[222] Eventually, on 13 April 2005, basing itself on the Committee's work, the General Assembly adopted without a vote the Nuclear Terrorism Convention by way of annex to General Assembly resolution 59/290.

7.98

(b) Scope of application

With the exception of the provisions on prevention, fair treatment, and mutual assistance, the Nuclear Terrorism Convention does not apply where, cumulatively, the offence is committed within a single state, the alleged offender and the victims are nationals of that state, the alleged offender is found in the territory of that state, and no other state enjoys prescriptive jurisdiction on any of the bases specified in the Convention bar universal jurisdiction.[223] In addition, the Convention makes clear that '[t]he activities of armed forces during an armed conflict, as those terms are understood under international humanitarian law, which are governed by that law, are not governed by this Convention, and the activities undertaken by the military forces of a State in the exercise of their official duties, inasmuch as they are governed by other rules of international law, are not governed by this Convention'.[224] The term 'military forces of a State' is defined the same way as in the Terrorist Bombings Convention.[225]

7.99

(c) Crimes

The Nuclear Terrorism Convention makes it an offence within the meaning of the Convention for a person unlawfully and intentionally to possess radioactive material or to make or possess a 'device' (meaning a nuclear explosive device or a device for the dispersal of radioactive material or the emission of radiation) with the intent to cause death or serious bodily injury or substantial damage to property or the environment; unlawfully and intentionally to use in any way radioactive material or a device or to use or damage a nuclear facility in a manner which releases or risks the release of radioactive material, with the intent to cause death or serious bodily injury or substantial damage to property or the environment or

7.100

---

[221] Recall *supra* para 7.67.   [222] GA res 51/210, 17 December 1996, para 9.
[223] Nuclear Terrorism Convention, art 3.   [224] Ibid, art 4(2).
[225] See ibid, art 1(6) and recall *supra* para 7.91. See also ibid, preamble (final recital).

with the intent to compel a natural or legal person, an international organization or a state to do or refrain from doing any act; to threaten, 'under circumstances which indicate the credibility of the threat', to commit the immediately preceding offence; or unlawfully and intentionally to demand radioactive material, a device or a nuclear facility by threat, under circumstances which indicate the credibility of the threat, or by use of force.[226]

(d) Modes of responsibility

7.101 The Convention provides additionally for criminal responsibility on the same bases as provided for in the Financing of Terrorism Convention.[227]

(x) Terrorism per se?

(a) Background

7.102 Apart from the League of Nations' abortive Convention for the Prevention and Punishment of Terrorism,[228] efforts to conclude an international penal convention aimed at suppressing terrorism as such have to date foundered.

7.103 In 1972, in the wake of the taking hostage and killing of Israeli athletes at the 1972 Munich Olympics by the Palestinian group 'Black September', the UN General Assembly established an Ad Hoc Committee on International Terrorism, one of whose assigned tasks was the elaboration of a general international criminal convention dealing with terrorism.[229] But the various delegates to the Committee never reached agreement on a text. The biggest stumbling block was the definition to be given to the term 'terrorism'.[230] Many states sought to draw a distinction between terrorism, which was to be condemned, and the legitimate and lawful struggle of peoples, especially national liberation movements, against colonial and racist regimes and alien domination.[231] There was also a marked difference over whether 'terrorism' involved by definition conduct by non-state actors or whether conduct by state organs (as distinct from state support for terrorism committed by non-state actors) could come under the rubric.[232] Neither issue had been contemplated when the League of Nations adopted its Convention for the Prevention and Punishment of Terrorism.[233] While the ideological tide began to turn in the

---

[226] Ibid, art 2(1)(*a*) and (*b*) and (2)(*a*) and (*b*).
[227] See ibid, art 2(3) and (4)(*a*), (*b*), and (*c*) and recall *supra* para 7.97.
[228] Recall *supra* para 7.38.   [229] See GA res 3034 (XXVII), 18 December 1972, para 9.
[230] Another obstacle came in the form of differences over the relative priority to be accorded to what might be called, on the one hand, symptomatic measures (that is, measures to suppress 'terrorist' acts) and, on the other, diagnostic and therapeutic measures (*viz* measures to address the causes of terrorism).
[231] No state condoned political violence against itself. It was only when directed against certain other states that such violence was considered justifiable.
[232] It was certain first-world states that proponents of the latter position had in mind.
[233] Article 1(2) of the League's convention, to be read in conjunction with art 2's enumerated crimes of violence, provided a general definition of 'acts of terrorism', *viz* 'criminal acts directed against a State and intended or calculated to create a state of terror in the minds of particular persons, or a group of persons or the general public'.

late 1980s, still no consensus on the precise legal meaning of the term 'terrorism' was reached.[234]

(b) Draft comprehensive convention on international terrorism

In late 1998, the UN General Assembly decided that the Ad Hoc Committee established under General Assembly resolution 51/210 should consider, 'on a priority basis, the elaboration of a comprehensive convention on international terrorism'.[235] But if the polemic that characterized the debate in the 1970s and 1980s has been consigned to history, the work of the Ad Hoc Committee towards a comprehensive convention on international terrorism remains stymied by controversy over the definition to be given to the term 'terrorism' or, more precisely, over the limits to be placed on the scope of application of any definition and, as a consequence, of any eventual convention.

7.104

Progress has been made by the Ad Hoc Committee on defining the bare acts which, all other things being equal, constitute terrorism. The current text of article 2(1) of the draft comprehensive convention on international terrorism reads:

7.105

Any person commits an offence within the meaning of the present Convention if that person, by any means, unlawfully and intentionally, causes:
(a) Death or serious bodily injury to any person; or
(b) Serious damage to public or private property, including a place of public use, a State or government facility, a public transportation system, an infrastructure facility or the environment; or
(c) Damage to property, places, facilities, or systems referred to in paragraph 1(b) of this article, resulting or likely to result in major economic loss,
when the purpose of the conduct, by its nature or context, is to intimidate a population, or to compel a Government or an international organization to do or to abstain from doing any act.[236]

This provision, which combines aspects of the crimes in the Terrorist Bombings Convention with the purposive element in article 2(1)(b) of the Financing of

---

[234] International terrorism was not, despite its earlier consideration, included in the ILC's Draft Code of Crimes against the Peace and Security of Mankind, *Ybk ILC 1996*, vol II/2, 17, para 50. Reasons for this included the difficulty of its definition, as well as the fact that it was not a crime under customary international law. Nor, again in spite of its serious consideration, was international terrorism included in the Rome Statute as a crime within the jurisdiction of the ICC. The main reason was once more the problem of defining the offence, in particular whether it included acts committed in the context of a struggle for self-determination by a people under colonial and other foreign domination. Indeed, in the fifth recital of the preamble to resolution E of the Rome Conference, Final Act of the United Nations Diplomatic Conference of Plenipotentiaries on the Establishment of an International Criminal Court, UN doc A/CONF.183/10, 17 July 1998, Annex I, the delegations to the Conference regretted 'that no generally acceptable definition of the crimes of terrorism and drug crimes could be agreed upon' for inclusion within the jurisdiction of the Court.

[235] GA res 53/108, 8 December 1998, para 11. See also GA res 54/110, 9 December 1999, paras 12 and 13; GA res 56/88, 12 December 2001, paras 16 ('as a matter of urgency') and 17.

[236] *Report of the Ad Hoc Committee established by General Assembly resolution 51/210 of 17 December 1996, Sixth session (28 January–1 February 2002)*, UN doc A/57/37 (2002), Annex II.

272   *Treaty Crimes*

Terrorism Convention, remains acceptable to the various delegations to the Ad Hoc Committee.

7.106   But agreement on the material elements of an offence of terrorism as such provides little cause for excitement, since debate over the divisive questions whether to distinguish between terrorist acts and acts in furtherance of a people's right to self-determination and whether organs of a state are capable of committing terrorism has simply shifted to article 3 [18], dealing with the scope of application of the proposed convention and containing contested exclusion clauses. Two rival texts lie at the heart of current discussions. In one corner is the text circulated by the co-ordinator of informal contacts with the delegations in 2007 and pushed by what might loosely be called western states, which reads in relevant part:

2. The activities of armed forces during an armed conflict, as those terms are understood under international humanitarian law, which are governed by that law, are not governed by this Convention.
3. The activities undertaken by the military forces of a State in the exercise of their official duties, inasmuch as they are governed by other rules of international law, are not governed by this Convention.
[...]
5. This Convention is without prejudice to the rules of international law applicable in armed conflict, in particular those rules applicable to acts lawful under international humanitarian law.[237]

Paragraphs 2 and 3 correspond verbatim to the 'carve-out' found in the Nuclear Material and Facilities Convention,[238] the 2005 SUA Convention,[239] the Terrorist Bombings Convention,[240] and the Nuclear Terrorism Convention.[241] The reference in paragraph 2 to 'armed conflict' would include belligerent occupation, an aspect of international armed conflict. In the other corner is the text proposed by member states of the Organization of the Islamic Conference (now the Organization of Islamic Cooperation) in 2002, which provides in relevant part:

2. The activities of the parties during an armed conflict, including in situations of foreign occupation, as those terms are understood in international humanitarian law, which are governed by that law, are not governed by this Convention.
3. The activities undertaken by the military forces of a State in the exercise of their official duties, inasmuch as they are in conformity with international law, are not governed by this Convention.[242]

---

[237] *Report of the* Ad Hoc *Committee established by General Assembly resolution 51/210 of 17 December 1996, Eleventh session (5, 6 and 15 February 2007)*, UN doc A/62/37 (2007), Annex, para 14 (numbered art 18), now reflected in art 3 [18] as proposed by the Bureau of the Ad Hoc Committee for discussion at the Committee's sixteenth session, *Report of the* Ad Hoc *Committee established by General Assembly resolution 51/210 of 17 December 1996, Sixteenth session (8 to 12 April 2013)*, UN doc A/68/37 (2013), Annex II, 16.
[238] Nuclear Material and Facilities Convention, art 2(4)(*b*). Recall *supra* para 7.69.
[239] 2005 SUA Convention, art 2*bis*(2). Recall *supra* para 7.80.
[240] Terrorist Bombings Convention, art 9(2). Recall *supra* para 7.91.
[241] Nuclear Terrorism Convention, art 4(2). Recall *supra* para 7.99.
[242] *Report of the* Ad Hoc *Committee established by General Assembly resolution 51/210 of 17 December 1996, Sixth session* (n 236), Annex IV. It may be worth noting that while the Arab Convention for

The difference is twofold and, despite appearances, significant, and reflects at the level of technical legal drafting the principled and to an extent ideological debate that has persisted since the early 1970s.

First, the reference to 'armed forces' in paragraph 2 of the text circulated by 7.107 the co-ordinator of informal contacts, while possibly encompassing more than the armed forces of a state and dissident armed forces, would not extend at its very broadest beyond armed units of those organized resistance movements, recognized national liberation movements, and organized opposition groups that are established along military lines, under a command responsible for the conduct of its subordinates, subject to a system of military discipline, and, possibly, conducting their operations in accordance with international humanitarian law. In contrast, the term 'the parties' in paragraph 2 of the second text would extend to, *inter alia*, any party—regardless of the formality or military character of its organization or its subscription to international humanitarian law—to the sort of international armed conflict recognized in article 1(4) of Additional Protocol I, namely 'armed conflicts in which peoples are fighting against colonial domination and alien occupation and against racist régimes in the exercise of their right of self-determination'. Since the activities of any party to an armed conflict, including of civilians taking direct part in hostilities on the side of any such party, are governed—although not necessarily permitted, let alone privileged—by international humanitarian law, the OIC draft would exclude from the scope of the crime of terrorism posited in article 2 of the draft comprehensive convention suicide bombings, missile attacks, and other acts of violence against civilians and civilian objects by any group or individual fighting in support of a people's right to self-determination.

Secondly, under the draft of paragraph 3 circulated by the co-ordinator of 7.108 informal contacts, the activities undertaken by the military forces of a state in the exercise of their official duties—an expression encompassing not only activities undertaken during armed conflict, including belligerent occupation, but also law enforcement, crowd control, and other activities undertaken outside armed conflict—need only be governed by rules of international law other than international humanitarian law, the implied reference being to rules of international human rights law, in order to be excluded from the scope of the draft comprehensive convention on international terrorism. They need not be permitted by such rules for the convention not to apply to them. In short, a breach by a state of international human rights law which might otherwise constitute, on the

---

the Suppression of Terrorism 1998, the Convention of the Organization of the Islamic Conference on Combating International Terrorism 1999, and the Organization of African Unity (now African Union) Convention on the Prevention and Combating of Terrorism 1999 all provide general definitions of terrorism, they all exclude from its scope acts in furtherance of a people's struggle for self-determination. See Arab Convention for the Suppression of Terrorism, arts 1(2) and 2(*a*), the latter adding, however, that '[t]his provision shall not apply to any act prejudicing the territorial integrity of any Arab State'; Convention of the Organization of the Islamic Conference on Combating International Terrorism, arts 1(2) and 2(*a*); Organization of African Unity Convention on the Prevention and Combating of Terrorism, arts 1(3) and 3(1).

part of a member of that state's military forces, the crime of terrorism recognized in article 2 of the convention remains simply a breach of international human rights law and not also a criminal act of terrorism as per the convention. In contrast, under the OIC text of paragraph 3, activities undertaken by the military forces of a state in the exercise of their official duties must be in conformity with international law—be it international human rights law or, in what appears an attempt to posit *lex specialis* to the *lex generalis* of paragraph 2, international humanitarian law—in order to be excluded from the scope of the crime of terrorism in article 2 of the convention. In other words, to the extent that it falls within the definition of the crime of terrorism laid down in article 2, a state's breach of international human rights law or even international humanitarian law via the activities of its military forces can also qualify as a criminal act of terrorism in accordance with the convention. In short, according to the OIC text, organs of a state can commit terrorism.

7.109 The Ad Hoc Committee remains deadlocked over these issues, and it is hard to foresee agreement being reached until the concrete situation that forms the subtext to the OIC's position—namely the question of the Occupied Palestinian Territory,[243] with the attendant actions of, on the one hand, Palestinian armed groups other than the official military forces of the Palestinian Authority and, on the other, the Israel Defence Forces—is resolved. 'Non-western' states were prepared to agree to exclusion clauses formulated in the same terms as the 'western' text of paragraphs 2 and 3 of article 3 [18] of the draft comprehensive convention on international terrorism when the treaty crimes at stake involved ships, nuclear material and facilities, and nuclear terrorism more generally, none of them still or ever part of the *modus operandi* of the relevant actors; and they were perhaps wrong-footed during the drafting process when the first such exclusion clauses were included in 1997 in the Terrorist Bombings Convention. These same states now seem to have drawn a line in the sand.

D. Crimes Associated with Political Repression

7.110 Three of the treaty crimes created from among the plethora of conventions in the field of international criminal law relate to acts classically associated with repressive governmental regimes. Each represents the international criminalization of acts which, when committed by states, already constituted violations of internationally-guaranteed human rights.[244]

---

[243] In *Legal Consequences of the Construction of a Wall in the Occupied Palestinian Territory, Advisory Opinion*, ICJ Rep 2004, 136, 182–3, para 118, the ICJ affirmed that the Palestinians constitute a people with a right to self-determination.
[244] The international human rights heritage of two of the crimes, torture and enforced disappearance, is reflected in the establishment under the relevant conventions of respective monitoring bodies, namely the Committee against Torture and the Committee on Enforced Disappearances.

(i) Apartheid

(a) Background

7.111 The official policy of systematic racial discrimination practised from 1948 by successive National Party governments in South Africa and known in Afrikaans as *'apartheid'* ('apartness'), along with its extension to South African-administered South West Africa (Namibia), had from the start been the object of condemnation within the United Nations, a condemnation that became more vociferous and insistent as the process of decolonization unfolded across Africa. To apartheid as such was added from 1965 onwards similar racist practices under the white minority government of the putative breakaway state of Rhodesia. Policies and practices of this sort violated a raft of provisions of the International Convention on the Elimination of All Forms of Racial Discrimination 1965, as well as of the International Covenant on Civil and Political Rights 1966 and the International Covenant on Economic, Social and Cultural Rights 1966. Moreover, in resolution 2202A (XXI) of 16 December 1966, the UN General Assembly had already '[c]ondemn[ed] the policies of apartheid practised by the Government of South Africa as a crime against humanity',[245] a characterization reaffirmed in relation to 'inhuman acts resulting from the policy of apartheid' in article 1(*b*) of the Convention on the Non-Applicability of Statutory Limitations to War Crimes and Crimes against Humanity 1968.[246] Intending, however, to 'make it possible to take more effective measures at the international and national levels with a view to the suppression and punishment of the crime of apartheid', on 30 November 1973 the General Assembly adopted by way of annex to General Assembly resolution 3068 (XXVIII)—by a margin of 91 votes in favour, 4 against, and 26 abstentions—the Apartheid Convention.

(b) Crimes

7.112 The crime of apartheid provided for in the Apartheid Convention is not limited to acts in furtherance of apartheid as such—that is, to acts undertaken pursuant to the governmental policy of systematic racial discrimination in place in South Africa between 1948 and 1994 and extended to South West Africa (Namibia). Precisely what else it does extend to, however, is complicated by ambiguous drafting. The chapeau to article II of the Convention reads:

For the purpose of the present Convention, the term 'the crime of apartheid', which shall include similar policies and practices of racial segregation and discrimination as practised in southern Africa, shall apply to the following inhuman acts committed for the purpose of establishing and maintaining domination by one racial group of persons over any other racial group of persons and systematically oppressing them...

---

[245] GA res 2202A (XXI), 16 December 1966, para 1. The resolution was adopted by a margin of 84:2:13.
[246] The Convention was adopted by a margin of 56:7:36 by way of annex to GA res 2391 (XXIII), 25 November 1968.

The relative clause pertaining to 'similar policies and practices of racial segregation and discrimination as practised in southern Africa' could be taken to indicate that, leaving aside apartheid as such, the 'inhuman acts' enumerated in the following paragraphs and subparagraphs of article II qualify as the treaty crime of apartheid only insofar as they take place 'in southern Africa', a term referable to Rhodesia and probably also to what were then the Portuguese colonies of Angola and Mozambique. But the principal clause is formulated in general terms, stating as it does that the term 'the crime of apartheid' applies to the succeeding enumerated acts when committed for the purpose of establishing and maintaining domination 'by one racial group of persons over any other racial group of persons' and systematically oppressing the latter. In the final analysis, despite the canon of treaty interpretation militating against textual redundancy, the better reading is that the relative clause is no more than parenthetically descriptive, not limiting the generality of the principal clause given that the greater (*viz* acts committed for the purpose of establishing and maintaining domination and systematic oppression by 'one racial group' of 'any other racial group') includes the lesser (*viz* policies and practices of racial segregation and discrimination as practised in southern Africa). In other words, any of the acts enumerated in article II constitutes the crime of apartheid if 'committed for the purpose of establishing and maintaining domination by one racial group of persons over any other racial group of persons and systematically oppressing them'.[247]

7.113 Article III of the Apartheid Convention stipulates that criminal responsibility is incurred for the crime of apartheid 'irrespective of the motive involved'. In this respect, the concept of motive cannot be the same as 'the purpose of establishing and maintaining domination by one racial group of persons over any other racial group of persons and systematically oppressing them', for which an act enumerated in article II of the Convention must be committed in order to qualify as the crime of apartheid. Motive within the meaning of article III of the Convention must refer to the reason why an individual who commits one of the specified acts seeks to establish and maintain the domination and systematic oppression by one racial group of another. Such motives might include a sense of racial superiority, economic self-interest or fear. Whatever the motive, however, article III declares it to be irrelevant to criminal responsibility for article II's crime of apartheid.

7.114 Article III makes it clear that the crime of apartheid is not limited to state actors, referred to in the provision as 'representatives of the State'. Responsibility for the crime of apartheid can be incurred by private parties as well, be they 'members of organizations and institutions' or unaffiliated individuals.

7.115 The acts which, when combined with the chapeau requirement of purpose, constitute the treaty crime of apartheid are fivefold, with several of these themselves encompassing several distinct acts and a few having elements in common

---

[247] See also J Dugard, '*L'apartheid*' in H Ascensio, E Decaux, and A Pellet (eds), *Droit international pénal* (2nd edn, Paris: Pedone, 2012), 197, 199–200, paras 7–11.

with the crime of genocide. The acts comprise the denial to a member or members of a racial group of the right to life and liberty of person through murder, through the infliction of serious bodily or mental harm or subjection to torture or cruel, inhuman or degrading treatment or punishment, or through arbitrary arrest and illegal imprisonment; deliberate imposition on a racial group of living conditions calculated to cause its physical destruction in whole or in part; legislative and other measures 'calculated to prevent a racial group...from participation in the political, social, economic and cultural life of the country and the deliberate creation of conditions preventing the full development of such a group'; legislative and other measures 'designed to divide the population along racial lines by the creation of separate reserves and ghettos for the members of a racial group or groups, the prohibition of mixed marriages among members of various racial groups, [or] the expropriation of landed property belonging to a racial group...or to members thereof'; exploitation of the labour of a racial group; and 'persecution of organizations and persons, by depriving them of fundamental rights and freedoms, because they oppose apartheid'.[248]

(c) **Modes of responsibility**

The Apartheid Convention provides for responsibility not only for committing but also for 'participat[ing]' in, directly inciting, conspiring in, directly abetting, encouraging, and co-operating in the commission of the crime of apartheid.[249] It is unclear precisely what is meant by 'participat[ion] in' the crime.[250]

7.116

(ii) Torture

(a) **Background**

Acts of torture attributable to a state have been prohibited under international human rights law, both universal and regional, since its inception and from even earlier, in the context of armed conflict, under international humanitarian law. In 1975, moreover, the UN General Assembly adopted a Declaration on the Protection of All Persons from Being Subjected to Torture and Other Cruel, Inhuman or Degrading Treatment or Punishment, which contained a definition of torture and declared that each state was to ensure that acts of torture, so defined, were offences under its criminal law.[251] It was not until 1984,[252] however, that UN member states, '[d]esiring to make more effective the struggle against torture...throughout the world'[253] by creating a 'conventional mechanism aimed at preventing suspects from escaping the consequences of

7.117

---

[248] Apartheid Convention, art 2(*a*) to (*f*).   [249] Ibid, art 3.
[250] Recall *supra* para 7.72.
[251] See GA res 3452 (XXX), 9 December 1975, Annex, arts 1 and 6.
[252] For a detailed account of the drafting of the Torture Convention, see Burgers and Danelius (n 4), 31–113.
[253] Torture Convention, preamble (sixth recital). See, similarly, the preamble (third and final recitals) to GA res 32/62, 8 December 1977, the resolution in which the General Assembly requested the Commission on Human Rights to draft a convention against torture and other cruel, inhuman or degrading treatment or punishment.

their criminal responsibility',[254] adopted without a vote, by way of annex to General Assembly resolution 39/46 of 10 December 1984, the Torture Convention.

(b) Crime

7.118 States parties to the Torture Convention are obliged to establish as an offence under their criminal law the following, defined in article 1(1) as 'torture' for the purposes of the Convention:

> any act by which severe pain or suffering, whether physical or mental, is intentionally inflicted on a person for such purposes as obtaining from him or a third person information or a confession, punishing him for an act he or a third person has committed or is suspected of having committed, or intimidating or coercing him or a third person, or for any reason based on discrimination of any kind, when such pain or suffering is inflicted by or at the instigation of or with the consent or acquiescence of a public official or other person acting in an official capacity.

Article 1(1) further specifies that torture, as understood in the Convention, does not include pain or suffering 'arising only from, inherent in, or incidental to lawful sanctions', the reference being chiefly to corporal and capital punishment, although the language is capable of embracing, for example, mental suffering arising from incarceration. Whether the lawfulness of a sanction is a question purely of the municipal law of the sanctioning state or also of international human rights law and, where relevant, international humanitarian law remains contested.[255]

7.119 The requisite notion of 'severe' pain or suffering is a question of factual appreciation in each case.[256] Provided that any pain or suffering inflicted can reasonably[257] be qualified as 'severe' according to the ordinary meaning to be given to the term,[258] the criterion is met. Attempts conclusively to list *a priori* what sorts of pain and suffering are to be characterized as either severe or not represent an unwarranted gloss on the text of article 1(1).[259] Moreover, understandings of severity can change over time.[260]

---

[254] *Obligation to Prosecute or Extradite* (n 4), 455, para 91. See also ibid, 461, para 120; Burgers and Danelius (n 4), 1 and 131; M Nowak and E McArthur, *The United Nations Convention Against Torture: A Commentary* (Oxford: Oxford University Press, 2008), 8.

[255] See Burgers and Danelius (n 4), 121–2; Nowak and McArthur (n 254), 79–84, paras 120–127.

[256] See eg *Selmouni v France* [GC] (Merits and Just Satisfaction), no 25803/94, ECHR 1999-V, para 100, referring to the notion of severity in Torture Convention, art 1(1).

[257] In accordance with the customary international rule on the application of treaties codified in art 26 of the Vienna Convention on the Law of Treaties 1969 ('VCLT'), a treaty must be applied in good faith. As explained by the ICJ in *Gabčíkovo-Nagymaros Project (Hungary/Slovakia), Judgment*, ICJ Rep 1997, 7, 79, para 142, the requirement of good faith obliges the parties to apply the treaty 'in a reasonable way and in such a manner that its purpose can be realized'. See, not dissimilarly, *Whaling in the Antarctic (Australia v Japan: New Zealand intervening), Judgment*, 31 March 2014, paras 61 and 67.

[258] See VCLT, art 31(1).

[259] 'Interpretation must be based above all on the text of the treaty', in the words of the ICJ in *Territorial Dispute (Libya/Chad), Judgment*, ICJ Rep 1994, 6, 22, para 41. See, in this regard, the sensible approach taken in Human Rights Committee, *General Comment No. 20: Article 7*, UN doc CCPR/C/20 (10 March 1992), para 4, in relation to the prohibition on torture under international human rights law.

[260] See eg *Selmouni v France* (n 256), para 101.

It is commonly said that, to qualify as the crime of torture pursuant to the 7.120
Torture Convention, the person inflicting the pain and suffering must be a public,
viz state, official. This is inaccurate. As article 1(1) of the Convention makes clear,
pain and suffering inflicted not only by but also 'at the instigation of or with the
consent or acquiescence of' a public official satisfies the definition of the treaty
crime of torture. In other words, private individuals who inflict severe pain or suffering on a person for a purpose or reason stipulated in article 1(1) may be criminally responsible for the crime of torture provided that they act at the instigation,
with the consent, or with the acquiescence of a state official.[261] 'Consent' would
appear to suggest express prior permission and 'acquiescence' tacit prior permission
or manifest subsequent toleration.

In *Elmi v Australia*, an individual communication focusing on the obligation of 7.121
non-refoulement in article 3 of the Torture Convention, the Committee Against
Torture took the view that, where a state is without a government, a member of
a faction which, '*de facto*,... exercise[s] certain prerogatives that are comparable
to those normally exercised by... governments' can be considered 'a public official or other person acting in an official capacity' within the meaning of article
1 of the Torture Convention.[262] The Committee stressed in the later *HMHI v
Australia*, in which it distinguished *Elmi* on the facts, that its finding in *Elmi* as to
'groups exercising quasi-governmental authority' was restricted to 'the exceptional
circumstance of state authority that was wholly lacking'.[263] But notwithstanding what the Committee reiterated was 'the exceptional situation in *Elmi*',[264]
the Committee's view is open to doubt. Even more doubtful is the ruling in the
English criminal case of *R v Zardad (Faryadi)* that, even where there exists a government within a state, the expression 'a public official or other person acting in
an official capacity' in article 1 of the Torture Convention can extend to 'people
who are acting for an entity which has acquired *de facto* effective control over an
area of a country and is exercising governmental or quasi-governmental functions
in that area'.[265]

Article 1(1) of the Convention specifies that, to fall within the definition of the 7.122
crime of torture, pain and suffering must be inflicted for a particular purpose (that
is, to secure a particular end) or for a discriminatory reason (that is, on account
of some quality of the victim). The purposes listed are illustrative, as indicated by
the words 'for such purposes as', although, to be treated as sufficient for the crime
of torture, any other purpose must fall within the ordinary meaning of the word
'torture' and accord with the *ejusdem generis* canon of construction.[266] As for the

---

[261] See also Nowak and McArthur (n 254), 77, para 116, detailing the drafting history of this element of art 1(1) of the Torture Convention.
[262] UN Committee against Torture, *Elmi v Australia*, UN doc CAT/C/22/D/120/1998 (25 May
1999), para 6.5.
[263] UN Committee against Torture, *HMHI v Australia*, UN doc CAT/C/28/D/177/2001 (22
January 2003), para 6.4.
[264] Ibid.   [265] *R v Zardad (Faryadi)*, ILDC 95 (UK 2004), para 38.
[266] As to the latter, see also Burgers and Danelius (n 4), 118; Nowak and McArthur (n 254), 69,
para 97.

alternative requirement of a discriminatory reason, the text of article 1(1) states that any such reason and discrimination of any kind will both do.

(c) Modes of responsibility

7.123 The Torture Convention specifies criminal responsibility on the bases of commission, attempt, complicity, and participation.[267] Again, the concept of 'participation' is somewhat obscure,[268] although in the present context it clearly denotes something other than complicity, as is mentioned in its own right. The term would seem capable of accommodating both common-law notions of conspiracy and joint enterprise and approximate civil-law concepts.

(iii) Enforced disappearance

(a) Background

7.124 The practice of 'enforced disappearance', prevalent under the various military regimes in power in South and Central America during the 1970s and 1980s, represents a gross violation of the rights to liberty and ultimately to life as guaranteed by international human rights law, a point underlined by the UN General Assembly in 1992 in adopting the Declaration on the Protection of All Persons from Enforced Disappearance.[269] In 2006, '[d]etermined to prevent enforced disappearances and to combat impunity for [the practice]',[270] which it recognized as a crime,[271] the General Assembly adopted without a vote, by way of annex to resolution 61/177, the Enforced Disappearance Convention.

(b) Crime

7.125 States parties to the Enforced Disappearance Convention are obliged to establish as an offence under their criminal law the following, defined in article 2 as 'enforced disappearance' for the purposes of the Convention:

> the arrest, detention, abduction or any other form of deprivation of liberty by agents of the State or by persons or groups acting with the authorization, support or acquiescence of the State, followed by a refusal to acknowledge the deprivation of liberty or by concealment of the fate or whereabouts of the disappeared person, which place such a person outside the protection of the law.

Article 5 adds that '[t]he widespread or systematic practice of enforced disappearance constitutes a crime against humanity as defined in applicable international law'. Article 5 is not in fact correct as a statement of 'applicable international law', according to which an act—and, according to the Rome Statute, the act specifically of enforced disappearance—constitutes a crime against humanity not if practised in a widespread or systematic fashion but if it is committed as part of a widespread

---

[267] Torture Convention, art 4(1). [268] Recall *supra* paras 7.72 and 7.116.
[269] GA res 47/133, 18 December 1992.
[270] Enforced Disappearance Convention, preamble (sixth recital).
[271] Ibid, preamble (fifth and sixth recitals).

or systematic attack.²⁷² Only the attack of which the accused's conduct forms part, and not the accused's conduct itself, need be widespread or systematic—in other words, 'all other conditions being met, a single or relatively limited number of acts on [the accused's] part would qualify as a crime against humanity, unless those acts may be said to be isolated or random'.²⁷³ But be that as it may. What is clear from article 2's definition of 'enforced disappearance' is that a single instance of enforced disappearance suffices for the purposes of the treaty crime of enforced disappearance pursuant to the Enforced Disappearance Convention.

(c) **Modes of responsibility**

The Enforced Disappearance Convention specifies criminal responsibility on the basis of, 'at least', the commission of the crime; ordering, soliciting or inducing the commission of the crime; attempt to commit the crime; complicity in (*viz* being an accomplice to) the crime; participation in the crime; and superior responsibility for the crime.²⁷⁴ The concept of 'participation' is once more opaque, although, as under the Torture Convention, goes beyond complicity.²⁷⁵ 7.126

The conditions for superior responsibility under the Convention are set out in article 6(1)(*b*) and reproduce verbatim, *mutatis mutandis*, article 28(*b*) of the Rome Statute, which applies to superiors other than military commanders and persons effectively acting as military commanders. The cumulative conditions in article 6(1)(*b*) of the Convention are that the superior '[k]new, or consciously disregarded information which clearly indicated, that subordinates under his or her effective authority and control were committing or about to commit a crime of enforced disappearance'; '[e]xercised effective responsibility for and control over activities which were concerned with the crime of enforced disappearance'; and '[f]ailed to take all necessary and reasonable measures within his or her power to prevent or repress the commission of an enforced disappearance or to submit the matter to the competent authorities for investigation and prosecution'.²⁷⁶ For its part, article 6(1)(*c*) of the Convention specifies that article 6(1)(*b*) 'is without prejudice to the higher standards of responsibility applicable under relevant international law to a military commander or to a person effectively acting as a military commander'. It is unclear what the intended, let alone actual import of article 6(1)(*c*) is. The provision may have been included merely to stress *ex abundante cautela* that the standard of diligence demanded by the Convention of a *de jure* or *de facto* military commander, as a 'superior' within the meaning of article 6(1)(*b*), does nothing to affect the standard of diligence demanded of a *de jure* or *de facto* military commander—whether generally or in specific relation to the crime 7.127

---

²⁷² As made clear in the chapeau to art 7(1) of the Rome Statute and as provided for under customary international law, the attack must be against a civilian population.
²⁷³ *Kunarac* et al, Appeals Chamber Judgment (n 88), para 96. Recall *supra* paras 4.55 and 7.14 n 46.
²⁷⁴ Enforced Disappearance Convention, art 6(1)(*a*) and (*b*).
²⁷⁵ Recall *supra* paras 7.72, 7.116, and 7.123.
²⁷⁶ Enforced Disappearance Convention, art 6(1)(*b*)(i), (ii), and (iii).

against humanity of enforced disappearance is also unclear, albeit of no practical significance—for the purposes of customary international law or, to the extent that there may be a difference, the Rome Statute. Alternatively, article 6(1)(c) may be designed to indicate that a 'superior' for the purposes of article 6(1)(b) of the Convention does not include a *de jure* or *de facto* military commander, the standard of diligence demanded of whom by the Convention comports with 'the higher standards of responsibility applicable under relevant international law'.

(iv) Crimes relating to mercenarism

(a) Background

7.128 The role of mercenarism in suppressing the legitimate exercise of the inalienable right of peoples to self-determination[277] had been of concern to the UN General Assembly since at least the beginning of the 1960s, when Belgian and other foreign 'soldiers of fortune' fought on the side of Moïse Tshombe and his attempted secession of the province of Katanga from the newly-independent Republic of the Congo (Kinshasa). This concern became more acute as mercenaries from around the globe descended on the self-declared state of Rhodesia after 1965 to fight for the white minority regime in its 'bush war' aimed at preventing the exercise by the black majority of its right to self-determination. The part subsequently played in the 1970s and 1980s by foreign mercenaries, among them many white South Africans, in support of guerrilla wars waged against the governments of the independent southern African states of Angola and Mozambique, as well as the contemporaneous serial *coup d'étatisme* of the notorious French mercenary Bob Denard in the Comoros, kept the topic of mercenarism on the General Assembly's agenda, leading eventually to the adoption without a vote of the Mercenaries Convention, by way of annex to General Assembly resolution 44/34 of 4 December 1989. Interest in the Mercenaries Convention has revived in recent years with the rise to prominence in theatres of armed conflict of so-called 'private security companies', although whether individuals employed by such a company constitute mercenaries within the meaning of the Convention is not a question amenable to a single answer.

(b) Scope of application

7.129 The term 'mercenary' is defined in article 1 of the Mercenaries Convention in bifurcated fashion. Paragraph 1 deals with mercenaries recruited to fight in an armed conflict. Paragraph 2 deals, insofar as they are not already covered by paragraph 1,[278] with mercenaries recruited for the purpose of participating in a 'concerted act of violence' aimed at either overthrowing a government or otherwise undermining the constitutional order of a state or at undermining the territorial integrity of a state.

---

[277] See, in this regard, Mercenaries Convention, preamble (second recital) and art 5(1).
[278] See ibid, art 1(2), chapeau '(in any other situation)'.

In accordance with the cumulative criteria laid down in article 1(1)(*a*) to (*e*), a 7.130
mercenary is any person who is specially recruited locally or abroad to fight in an
armed conflict; is motivated to take part in the hostilities 'essentially by the desire
for private gain and, in fact, is promised, by or on behalf of a party to the conflict,
material compensation substantially in excess of that promised or paid to combatants of similar rank and functions in the armed forces of that party';[279] is neither
a national of a party to the conflict nor a resident of territory controlled by a party
to the conflict; is not a member of the armed forces of a party to the conflict; and
has not been sent by a state which is not a party to the conflict on official duty as a
member of its armed forces. This narrow definition excludes from mercenary status
foreign members of, for example, the French and Spanish Foreign Legions and the
Ghurka units of the UK and Indian armed forces.

In accordance with the cumulative conditions in article 1(2)(*a*) to (*e*), a mer- 7.131
cenary is any person who, in any other situation, is specially recruited locally or
abroad for the purpose of participating in a concerted act of violence aimed at
either overthrowing a government or otherwise undermining the constitutional
order of a state or at undermining the territorial integrity of a state; is motivated
to take part therein 'essentially by the desire for significant private gain and is
prompted by the promise or payment of material compensation';[280] is neither a
national nor resident of the state against which such an act is directed; has not been
sent by a state on official duty; and is not a member of the armed forces of the state
on whose territory the act is undertaken.

(c) Crimes

The Mercenaries Convention recognizes for the purposes of the Convention what 7.132
are essentially two offences, one targeting supply and demand, the other the acts
of the mercenaries themselves. First, it is an offence for any person to recruit, use,
finance or train mercenaries.[281] Secondly, it is an offence for a mercenary to participate directly in hostilities, where the context is an armed conflict as per article
1(1), or in a concerted act of violence, where the context, as per article 1(2), is an
act of this sort aimed at overthrowing a government or otherwise undermining
the constitutional order of a state or at undermining the territorial integrity of
a state.[282] It is not an offence for the purposes of the Convention merely to be a
mercenary. Although the *mens rea* for neither offence is specified, both presuppose
intent.

(d) Modes of responsibility

The Convention provides for criminal responsibility on the basis, in addition to 7.133
commission, of attempt to commit one of the offences set forth in the Convention
and of complicity in the commission or attempted commission of any such
offence.[283]

---

[279] Ibid, art 1(1)(*b*).   [280] Ibid, art 1(2)(*b*).   [281] Ibid, art 2.
[282] Ibid, art 3(1).   [283] Ibid, art 4(*a*) and (*b*).

E. Crimes Relating to or Associated with Organized Crime

7.134 Second in number only to those associated with terrorism are the universal multilateral treaties providing for offences relating to or associated with organized crime. Starting with the illicit traffic in narcotics, which states had long sought to suppress through internationally-mandated co-operation in criminal matters,[284] international criminal law now embodies six instruments targeting either organized crime as such or activities characteristically associated with it.

(i) Illicit traffic in narcotic drugs and psychotropic substances

(a) Background

7.135 By the 1980s it had become evident to UN member states that existing multilateral treaties, and in particular their criminal-law provisions, were insufficient to suppress the illicit traffic in drugs, which was viewed as a rapidly-growing threat to public health and order and the sovereignty and security of states,[285] the latter not least in that the illegal drug trade 'supported or generated other serious forms of organized crime'.[286] The issue was considered urgent, and in 1984 the General Assembly requested the UN's Commission on Narcotic Drugs to prepare, as a matter of priority, a convention on the illicit traffic in drugs to complement the extant instruments.[287] It would not be until 20 December 1988,[288] however, that states adopted the Illicit Traffic Convention.

(b) Crimes

7.136 The Illicit Traffic Convention provides for a plethora of detailed offences,[289] some of them the object of a strict obligation of municipal criminalization, some of them requiring municipal criminalization only insofar as this is in conformity with the constitutional principles and 'basic concepts' of a state party's legal system.[290] Insofar as some of these offences require knowledge, intent or purpose, the Convention specifies that this may be inferred from

---

[284] See, *inter alia*, Convention for the Suppression of the Illicit Traffic in Dangerous Drugs 1936.

[285] See Illicit Traffic Convention, preamble (first, third, thirteenth, and fourteenth recitals); United Nations, *Commentary on the United Nations Convention against Illicit Traffic in Narcotic Drugs and Psychotropic Substances Done at Vienna on 20 December 1988* (New York: United Nations, 1998), UN doc E/CN.7/590 (1998), 1–2, paras 1–5. The main existing treaties were the Single Convention on Narcotic Drugs 1961, the Single Convention on Narcotic Drugs as amended by the Protocol amending the Single Convention on Narcotic Drugs 1972, and the Convention on Psychotropic Substances 1971.

[286] United Nations (n 285), 1, para 2. The concern is reflected in Illicit Traffic Convention, preamble (third and fifth recitals) and art 3(5)(*a*) and (*b*).

[287] See GA res 39/141, 14 December 1984. Consider also GA res 39/142, 14 December 1984 and GA res 39/143, 14 December 1984.

[288] For a concise account of the drafting of the Illicit Traffic Convention and the General Assembly's frustration with its rate of progress, see United Nations (n 285), 4–11, paras 9–25.

[289] See, generally, ibid, 48–85, paras 3.1–3.101.

[290] For the latter species of obligation of municipal criminalization, see Illicit Traffic Convention, art 3(1)(*b*) and (2). See also *infra* para 8.11.

objective factual circumstances.²⁹¹ All relevant terms are defined in article 1 of the Convention.

7.137 The offences the object of the Convention's strict obligation of municipal criminalization are essentially of two sorts, both requiring intent. Five offences pertain to the production or cultivation and distribution of narcotic drugs and psychotropic substances, in two instances contrary to the existing conventions on these matters.²⁹² A second pair of offences relates to the laundering of property derived from any of the foregoing offences.²⁹³ The term 'property' is defined for the purposes of the Convention as 'assets of every kind, whether corporeal or incorporeal, movable or immovable, tangible or intangible, and legal documents or instruments evidencing title to, or interest in, such assets'.²⁹⁴

7.138 The offences the object of the Convention's conditional obligation of municipal criminalization are divided into two groups. The first group comprises the knowing acquisition, possession or use of property derived from one or more of the foregoing offences and the knowing possession of specified equipment, materials or substances used in or for the illicit cultivation, production or manufacture of narcotic drugs or psychotropic substances.²⁹⁵ The second group comprises a lone offence, to which, unlike the first group and the other offences provided for in the Convention, the instrument's other criminal-law obligations—of extension of jurisdiction, of confiscation, of extradition or where relevant prosecution, of mutual legal assistance, and so on—do not apply. This unique offence is the intentional possession, purchase or cultivation of narcotic drugs or psychotropic substances contrary to the existing conventions on these matters.²⁹⁶

(c) Modes of responsibility

7.139 Beyond commission, the modes of responsibility specified in the Convention are the object only of the conditional obligation of municipal criminalization. These further modes comprise publicly inciting or inducing others, by any means, to commit any of the offences set forth in the Convention or to use narcotic drugs or psychotropic substances illicitly; participation in the commission of any such offence; association or conspiracy to commit any such offence; attempt to commit any such offence; and aiding, abetting, facilitating or²⁹⁷ counselling the commission of any such offence.²⁹⁸ The concept of 'participation' in this context must be something other than, on the one hand, association or conspiracy and, on the other, aiding, abetting, facilitating or counselling.²⁹⁹

---

²⁹¹ Illicit Traffic Convention, art 3(3).
²⁹² See ibid, art 3(1)(*a*)(i) to (v). The 'Table I and Table II' mentioned ibid, art 3(1)(*a*)(iv), are tables of substances frequently used in the illicit manufacture of narcotic drugs or psychotropic substances. The tables are compiled and maintained as per ibid, arts 12 and 21(*e*).
²⁹³ See ibid, art 3(1)(*b*)(i) and (ii).   ²⁹⁴ See ibid, art 1(*q*).
²⁹⁵ Ibid, art 3(1)(*c*)(i) and (ii).   ²⁹⁶ Ibid, art 3(2).
²⁹⁷ The text uses 'and', but the relationship between the terms seems as a logical matter to be disjunctive, as it expressly is in the later art 5(1)(*b*) of the Organized Crime Convention, the drafters of which based many of the provisions on those of the Illicit Traffic Convention.
²⁹⁸ Illicit Traffic Convention, art 3(1)(*c*)(i) and (ii) and (2).
²⁹⁹ Compare *supra* paras 7.72, 7.116, 7.123, and 7.126.

(ii) Transnational organized crime

(a) Background

7.140 The concern over the increasing power and globalization of organized crime that informed efforts towards the Illicit Traffic Convention intensified in the 1990s, becoming acute when states identified 'growing links between transnational organized crime and terrorist crimes'.[300] A series of staging-posts eventually led to a decision of the UN General Assembly to establish an open-ended intergovernmental ad hoc committee for the purpose of elaborating a convention against transnational organized crime.[301] The work of the Ad Hoc Committee on the Elaboration of a Convention against Transnational Organized Crime proceeded quickly, and as early as 15 November 2000 the General Assembly adopted without a vote, by way of annex to General Assembly resolution 55/25, the Organized Crime Convention.[302] Adopted along with the Convention were two optional protocols, to which a third was added in 2001.[303] The Convention was opened for signature not long afterwards at a ceremony in Palermo, Italy, leading to its occasional labelling as the 'Palermo Convention'.[304]

(b) Scope of application

7.141 The scope of application of the Organized Crime Convention is not a straightforward matter. On the one hand, the Convention is said in article 3(1) to apply, except as otherwise stated in the instrument, to the prevention, investigation, and prosecution of the offences laid down in articles 5, 6, 8, and 23 and of 'serious crime' as defined in the Convention only 'where the offence is transnational in nature and involves an organized criminal group'. Article 3(2) elaborates that an offence is considered 'transnational in nature' within the meaning of the Convention if it satisfies any one of four criteria, namely that it is committed in more than one state; is committed in one state but a substantial part of its preparation, planning, direction or control takes place in another; is committed in one state but involves an organized criminal group that engages in criminal activities in more than one state; or is committed in one state but has substantial effects in another.[305] On the other hand, article 34(2), to which article 3(1)'s words 'except as otherwise stated' are directed, specifies that the offences laid down in

---

[300] GA res 55/25, 15 November 2000, preamble (eighth recital).
[301] See GA res 53/111, 9 December 1998. For details as to the background to the Organized Crime Convention, see United Nations Office on Drugs and Crime, Travaux préparatoires *of the negotiations for the elaboration of the United Nations Convention against Transnational Organized Crime and the Protocols thereto* (New York: United Nations, 2006), ix–xxvi and 1–315; D McClean, *Transnational Organized Crime. A Commentary on the UN Convention and its Protocols* (Oxford: Oxford University Press, 2007), 1–13.
[302] See GA res 55/25, 15 November 2000, Annex I.
[303] Each of these three protocols is considered separately *infra*.
[304] The name 'Palermo Convention' seems to have fallen victim to the mania for acronyms, with the Convention now frequently referred to as 'UNCTOC' or, more sonorously but less logically, 'UNTOC'.
[305] Organized Crime Convention, art 3(2)(*a*) to (*d*).

articles 5, 6, 8, and 23 'shall be established in the domestic law of each State Party independently of the transnational nature or the involvement of an organized criminal group as described in article 3, paragraph 1, of [the] Convention, except to the extent that article 5 of [the Convention] would require the involvement of an organized criminal group'. In other words, article 3(1) does not superimpose on the offences in articles 5, 6, 8, and 23 as defined on the face of the four provisions additional material elements of transnationality and the involvement of an organized criminal group,[306] the two conditions that otherwise obtain for the Convention's application; but to the extent that the offence defined in article 5 requires on its face the involvement of an organized criminal group, such involvement remains required for that offence. The upshot of the combined operation of articles 3(1) and 34(2) is that states parties to the Convention must ensure that the offences provided for on the face of articles 5, 6, 8, and 23 are offences under their municipal law but that the Convention's remaining obligations in relation to the prevention, investigation, and prosecution of these offences and of 'serious crime' as defined in the Convention arise only insofar as the offence in question is transnational in nature, within the meaning of article 3(2), and involves an organized criminal group.

7.142 'Serious crime' is defined for the purposes of the Convention as conduct constituting an offence punishable by a maximum deprivation of liberty of at least four years or a more serious penalty.[307] An 'organized criminal group' is defined to mean 'a structured group of three or more persons, existing for a period of time and acting in concert with the aim of committing one or more serious crimes or offences established in accordance with the Convention, in order to obtain, directly or indirectly, a financial or other material benefit'.[308] In turn, a 'structured group' is defined as 'a group that is not randomly formed for the immediate commission of an offence and that does not need to have formally defined roles for its members, continuity of its membership or a developed structure'.[309]

(c) Crimes
7.143 The Organized Crime Convention provides for four distinct heads of offence, some of these being themselves divided into separate offences. These are participation in an organized criminal group (article 5), laundering of the proceeds of crime (article 6), corruption (article 8[310]), and obstruction of justice (article 23).[311]

---

[306] See also Ad Hoc Committee on the Elaboration of a Convention against Transnational Organized Crime, *Report of the* Ad Hoc *Committee on the Elaboration of a Convention against Transnational Organized Crime on the work of its first to eleventh sessions, Addendum: Interpretative notes for the official records (travaux préparatoires) of the negotiation of the United Nations Convention against Transnational Organized Crime and the Protocols thereto*, UN doc A/55/383/Add.1 (3 November 2000), para 59.
[307] Organized Crime Convention, art 2(*b*).   [308] Ibid, art 2(*a*).
[309] Ibid, art 2(*c*).
[310] This offence is discussed *infra* paras 7.179–7.184, in the section on crimes relating to corruption.
[311] On arts 5, 6, and 23 of the Organized Crime Convention generally, see also McClean (n 301), 59–91 and 255–8.

7.144   The offence of participation in an organized criminal group defined in article 5 of the Convention is less an offence in its own right than a set of specified modes of responsibility applicable in certain contexts in respect of 'serious crimes' provided for independently under a state party's municipal law. The offence has two limbs, the first of these limbs being similarly divided into two, both requiring intent. First, each state party is obliged to establish as municipal criminal offences, 'distinct from those involving the attempt or completion of the criminal activity', either or both of two things, namely, on the one hand, agreeing with one or more persons to commit a serious crime as defined in the Convention 'for a purpose relating directly or indirectly to the obtaining of a financial or other material benefit' and, if this is required by the state party's municipal law, involving an act undertaken by one of the participants in furtherance of the agreement or involving an organized criminal group as defined in the Convention; and, on the other hand, conduct, 'with knowledge of either the aim and general criminal activity of an organized criminal group or its intention to commit the crimes in question', constituting the taking of an active part in criminal activities of the organized criminal group or[312] other activities of the group in the knowledge that this participation will contribute to the achievement of the group's aim.[313] Secondly, each state party is obliged to establish as criminal offences acts of organizing, directing, aiding, abetting, facilitating or counselling the commission of a serious crime involving an organized criminal group.[314] Insofar as knowledge, intent, aim, purpose or agreement is required for any of the foregoing offences, it may be inferred, according to the Convention, from objective factual circumstances.[315]

7.145   When it comes to the offence in article 6 of the laundering of the proceeds of crime, the Convention distinguishes between offences the object of a strict obligation of municipal criminalization, albeit 'in accordance with fundamental principles of [a state party's] domestic law',[316] and offences requiring municipal criminalization only insofar as this is in conformity with 'the basic concepts' of a state party's legal system[317] (and even then in accordance with fundamental principles of its domestic law). Both require intent.[318] First, in an echo of the Illicit Traffic Convention,[319] states parties must criminalize the conversion or transfer of property, in the knowledge that such property is the proceeds of crime, 'for the purpose of concealing or disguising the illicit origin of the crime or of helping any person who is involved in the commission of the predicate offence to evade the legal consequences of his or her actions'; and they must criminalize the concealment or disguise 'of the true nature, source, location, disposition, movement or ownership of or rights with respect to' property in the

---

[312] Neither 'or' nor 'and' appears in the text, but the relationship would appear as a logical matter to be disjunctive.
[313] Organized Crime Convention, art 5(1)(*a*)(i) and (ii). See also the further elaboration ibid, art 5(3).
[314] Ibid, art 5(1)(*b*).   [315] Ibid, art 5(2).
[316] Ibid, art 6(1), chapeau. See also *infra* para 8.11.
[317] Ibid, art 6(1)(*b*). See also *infra* para 8.11.
[318] Ibid, art 6(1), chapeau. See also *infra* para 8.11.
[319] See Illicit Traffic Convention, art 3(1)(*b*)(ii).

knowledge that such property is the proceeds of crime.[320] 'Property' is defined as under the Illicit Traffic Convention,[321] while 'proceeds of crime' means 'any property derived from or obtained, directly or indirectly, through the commission of an offence'.[322] Secondly, unless this is contrary to basic concepts of their respective legal systems, states parties must criminalize the acquisition, possession or use of property in the knowledge, at the time of receipt, that it is the proceeds of crime.[323] Again, knowledge, intent or purpose may be inferred from objective factual circumstances.[324]

As for the offence of obstruction of justice provide for in article 23, states parties must establish as criminal offences, when committed intentionally, a range of acts vis-à-vis, on the one hand, witnesses and others producing evidence and, on the other, justice or law enforcement officials in relation to the commission of offences covered by the Convention, the reference encompassing both the offences established pursuant to articles 5, 6, and 8 of the Convention and the serious crimes to which article 5 relates. As regards witnesses, what must be criminalized is both the use of physical force, threats or intimidation and the promise, offering or giving of an undue advantage, in each case to induce false testimony or to interfere in the giving of testimony or the production of evidence.[325] As regards justice or law enforcement officials, what must be criminalized under article 23 is only the use of physical force, threats or intimidation to interfere with the exercise of their official duties.[326] The intentional promise, offering or giving to public officials of an undue advantage in order that they act or refrain from acting in the exercise of their official duties is already the object of an obligation of municipal criminalization in accordance with article 8(1)(a).

7.146

(d) Modes of responsibility

The offence of participation in an organized criminal group in article 5 is, as previously observed,[327] really a variety of obligatory modes of responsibility applicable in certain contexts in relation to serious crimes under municipal law, while no mode of responsibility other than commission is specified in relation to the offence of obstruction of justice in article 23. As for the offence in article 6 of laundering the proceeds of crime, states parties must provide, unless this is contrary to basic concepts of their respective legal systems, for criminal responsibility on the additional bases of participation in the offence, association or conspiracy to commit the offence, attempt to commit the offence, and aiding, abetting, facilitating or[328] counselling the commission of the offence.[329]

7.147

---

[320] Organized Crime Convention, art 6(1)(a)(i) and (ii). The term 'predicate offence' is defined ibid, art 2(h) to mean simply 'any offence as a result of which proceeds have been generated that may become the subject of an offence as defined in article 6'. See also the further elaboration in ibid, art 6(2)(c) and (e).
[321] Ibid, art 2(d) and *supra* para 7.136.   [322] Ibid, art 2(e).   [323] Ibid, art 6(1)(b).
[324] Ibid, art 6(2)(f).   [325] Ibid, art 23(a).   [326] Ibid, art 23(b).
[327] Recall *supra* para 7.142.
[328] The text uses 'and', but the relationship between the terms seems as a logical matter to be disjunctive, as it expressly is in Organized Crime Convention, art 5(1)(b).
[329] Ibid, art 6(1)(b)(ii).

(iii) *Trafficking in persons*

(a) Background

7.148 The traffic in persons, or at least in women and children, has long been a matter of international legal regulation,[330] in part penal—from the quaintly-entitled[331] International Agreement for the Suppression of the White Slave Traffic 1904 and the International Convention for the Suppression of the White Slave Traffic 1910 to the International Convention for the Suppression of Traffic in Women and Children 1921 and the International Convention for the Suppression of the Traffic in Women of Full Age 1933, both concluded under the aegis of the League of Nations, as well as the Convention for the Suppression of the Traffic in Persons and of the Exploitation of the Prostitution of Others 1950 and article 6 of the Convention for the Elimination of All Forms of Discrimination against Women 1979. By the 1990s, however, the concern was that the existing international instruments were inadequate to prevent and punish people-trafficking, which by then had become a lucrative trade for organized criminal groups, and to protect its victims.[332] In the event, the General Assembly requested the Ad Hoc Committee on the Elaboration of a Convention against Transnational Organized Crime to discuss the elaboration of an international instrument to counter the traffic in women and children.[333] The resultant Trafficking in Persons Protocol, broadened to encompass all trafficking in persons and prepared at speed, was adopted by the General Assembly at the same time as, and in the form of an optional protocol to, the Organized Crime Convention.[334]

7.149 As its full title indicates, the Trafficking in Persons Protocol supplements the Organized Crime Convention, the provisions of which apply, *mutatis mutandis*, to the Protocol unless otherwise stated. The offences laid down in the Protocol are deemed to be offences established in accordance with the Convention. The two instruments are to be interpreted together.[335]

(b) Scope of application

7.150 The scope of application of the Trafficking in Persons Protocol is even less straightforward a matter than that of the Organized Crime Convention.[336] In accordance with article 4 of the Protocol, akin to article 3(1) of the Convention, the Protocol applies, except as otherwise stated in the instrument, to the prevention, investigation, and prosecution of the offences specified in the Convention 'where those offences are transnational in nature and involve an organized criminal group'. All relevant terms, including the notion of an offence as 'transnational in nature',

---

[330] Indeed, the UN collection *Multilateral Treaties deposited with the Secretary-General* features a discrete chapter, chapter VII, entitled 'Traffic in Persons'.
[331] The word 'racist' is perhaps more accurate.
[332] See eg Trafficking in Persons Protocol, preamble.
[333] See GA res 53/111, 9 December 1998. For the background to and drafting of the Trafficking in Persons Protocol, see United Nations Office on Drugs and Crime (n 301), ix–xxvi and 317–447; McClean (n 301), 18–21.
[334] See GA res 55/25, 15 November 2000, Annex II.
[335] Trafficking in Persons Protocol, art 1.   [336] Recall *supra* paras 7.140–7.141.

The Crimes and Their Modes of Responsibility 291

are to be defined as per the Convention, the provisions of which apply, *mutatis mutandis*, to the Protocol unless otherwise stated.[337] No provision equivalent to article 34(2) of the Convention is found in the Protocol; but since the provisions of the Convention apply, *mutatis mutandis*, to the Protocol unless otherwise stated, and since the offences established pursuant to the Protocol are to be regarded as offences established pursuant to the Convention, article 34(2) of the Convention—dealing with the scope of application specifically of the obligations of municipal criminalization found in articles 5, 6, 8, and 23 of the Convention—applies, *mutatis mutandis*, to the Protocol. The consequence is that, despite article 4 of the Protocol, the twin conditions of transnationality and the involvement of an organized criminal group are not to be considered additional material elements of the offences defined in article 3 of the Protocol, which states parties are obliged to criminalize, pursuant to article 5 of the Protocol, according to their unadorned terms. The limitation stipulated in article 4 of the Protocol applies only to the remaining obligations specified in the Protocol and in the Convention as applicable to the Protocol.[338]

(c) **Crime**

Article 5 of the Trafficking in Persons Protocol obliges states parties to establish as a criminal offence under their municipal law the intentional commission of the acts specified in article 3. Article 3(*a*) defines trafficking in persons as

7.151

the recruitment, transportation, transfer, harbouring or receipt of persons, by means of the threat or use of force or other forms of coercion, of abduction, of fraud, of deception, of the abuse of power or of a position of vulnerability or of the giving or receiving of payments or benefits to achieve the consent of a person having control over another person, for the purpose of exploitation.

The provision explains that the notion of 'exploitation' is to be taken to include, 'at a minimum, the exploitation of the prostitution of others or other forms of sexual exploitation, forced labour or services, slavery or practices similar to slavery, servitude or the removal of organs'. Article 3(*b*) elaborates that the consent of a victim of trafficking in persons to the intended exploitation is to be considered irrelevant where any of the foregoing means have been used. Conversely, article 3(*c*) stipulates that the recruitment, transportation, transfer, harbouring or receipt of a child for the purposes of exploitation, a child being defined in article 3(*d*) as any person under 18, is to be regarded as 'trafficking in persons' for the purposes of the Protocol even if it does not involve any of the means cited.[339]

The essential differences between trafficking in persons, as falling within the Trafficking in Persons Protocol, and the smuggling of migrants, as covered by the second optional protocol to the Organized Crime Convention,[340] are twofold,

7.152

---

[337] Trafficking in Persons Protocol, art 1(2). Recall *supra* para 7.148.
[338] See also McClean (n 301), 330.   [339] See, generally, ibid, 315–29 and 331–3.
[340] See *infra* paras 7.153–7.160.

namely that the former necessarily involves the exercise of control over and exploitation of persons and the latter necessarily involves the procurement of illegal entry into a state.

(d) Modes of responsibility

7.153 The Protocol obliges a state party to criminalize not only the commission of trafficking in persons but also participating as an accomplice in the commission of the same, organizing or directing others to commit the same, and, provided that this comports with 'the basic concepts of its legal system', attempting to commit the same.[341]

(iv) Smuggling of migrants

(a) Background

7.154 Rising concern over the large-scale smuggling of migrants led the General Assembly to request the Ad Hoc Committee on the Elaboration of a Convention against Transnational Organized Crime, in addition to its development of a convention against transnational organized crime and its possible development of an instrument to counter the traffic in women and children, to discuss the elaboration of an international instrument to combat the phenomenon.[342] The outcome was the Smuggling of Migrants Protocol, which was adopted by the General Assembly along with, and in the form of a further optional protocol to, the Organized Crime Convention.[343]

7.155 The Smuggling of Migrants Protocol bears the same relation, *mutatis mutandis*, to the Organized Crime Convention as the Trafficking in Persons Protocol does.[344]

7.156 As its full title makes clear, the Smuggling of Migrants Protocol applies regardless of whether the smuggling is by land, sea or air.

(b) Scope of application

7.157 The Smuggling of Migrants Protocol has the same scope of application, *mutatis mutandis*, as the Trafficking in Persons Protocol.[345]

(c) Crimes

7.158 Article 6(1) of the Smuggling of Migrants Protocol obliges states parties to criminalize three distinct offences when committed intentionally and in order to obtain, directly or indirectly, a financial or other material benefit.[346] The

---

[341] Trafficking in Persons Protocol, art 5(2)(*b*), (*c*), and (*a*) respectively.
[342] See GA res 53/111, 9 December 1998. For the background to and drafting of the Smuggling of Migrants Protocol, see United Nations Office on Drugs and Crime (n 301), ix–xxvi and 449–578; McClean (n 301), 21–6.
[343] See GA res 55/25, 15 November 2000, Annex II.
[344] See Smuggling of Migrants Protocol, art 1 and *supra* para 7.148.
[345] Recall *supra* para 7.149. Articles 4, 3, and 6 of the Smuggling of Migrants Protocol are to the Protocol what arts 4, 3, and 5 of the Trafficking in Persons Protocol are to that Protocol.
[346] See, generally, McClean (n 301), 379–85 and 390–5.

first offence is the smuggling of migrants, defined in article 3(*a*) of the Protocol to mean 'the procurement, in order to obtain, directly or indirectly, a financial or other material benefit, of the illegal entry of a person into a State Party of which the person is not a national or a permanent resident'. In turn, article 3(*b*) defines 'illegal entry' to mean 'crossing borders without complying with the necessary requirements for legal entry into the receiving State'. The second offence, which must be committed for the purpose of enabling the smuggling of migrants, is the production of a fraudulent travel or identity document or the procurement, provision or possession of the same. A 'fraudulent travel or identity document' is defined in article 3(*c*) to mean any travel or identity document 'that has been falsely made or altered in some material way by anyone other than a person or agency lawfully authorized to make or issue the travel or identity document on behalf of a State'; that has been improperly issued or obtained through misrepresentation, corruption or duress or in any other unlawful manner; or that is being used by a person other than the rightful holder. The third offence provided for in article 6 is enabling, via the immediately foregoing or any other illegal means, a person who is not a national or a permanent resident to remain in a state without complying with the necessary requirements for remaining in the state.

7.159 The essential differences between the smuggling of migrants, as covered by the Smuggling of Migrants Protocol, and trafficking in persons, as falling within the Trafficking in Persons Protocol, are twofold, namely that the former necessarily involves the procurement of illegal entry into a state and the latter necessarily involves the exercise of control over and exploitation of persons.[347]

(d) Modes of responsibility

7.160 The Protocol obliges a state party to criminalize not only the commission of the offences set forth in the Protocol but also participating as an accomplice in the commission of the same, although in the case of procuring, providing or possessing a fraudulent travel or identity document a state party's obligation is subject to 'the basic concepts of its legal system'; organizing or directing others to commit any of the offences set forth in the Protocol; and, provided that this comports with 'the basic concepts of its legal system', attempting to commit the same.[348]

(v) *Illicit manufacture of and trafficking in firearms and related items*

(a) Background

7.161 Longstanding efforts to stem the illicit trade in small arms fed into the request by the General Assembly to the Ad Hoc Committee on the Elaboration of a Convention against Transnational Organized Crime to consider elaborating a

---

[347] Recall *supra* para 7.151.
[348] Smuggling of Migrants Protocol, art 5(6)(*b*), (*c*), and (*a*) respectively.

fourth instrument, on the illicit manufacture and trafficking of firearms. Work on the instrument was not completed in time for its adoption alongside the Convention and its two other protocols, so that it was not until 31 May 2001 that the Firearms Protocol was adopted without a vote as an annex to General Assembly resolution 55/255.[349] The Protocol is not to be confused with the Arms Trade Treaty adopted by the General Assembly in 2013.[350]

7.162 The Firearms Protocol bears the same relation, *mutatis mutandis*, to the Organized Crime Convention as the Trafficking in Persons Protocol and Smuggling of Migrants Protocol do.[351]

(b) Scope of application

7.163 The Firearms Protocol has the same scope of application, *mutatis mutandis*, as the Trafficking in Persons Protocol and the Smuggling of Migrants Protocol.[352]

7.164 The Firearms Protocol does not apply to state-to-state transactions or to state transfers of firearms 'in cases where the application of the Protocol would prejudice the right of a State Party to take action in the interest of national security consistent with the Charter of the United Nations'.

(c) Crimes

7.165 Article 5(1) of the Firearms Protocol obliges states parties to establish as criminal offences three acts.[353] The first is the illicit manufacturing of firearms, their parts and components, and ammunition, the terms 'firearm', 'parts and components', and 'ammunition' being defined in article 3.[354] As for 'illicit manufacturing', article 3(*d*) defines this to mean the manufacturing or assembly of firearms, their parts and components, and ammunition, in one of three contexts, namely from parts and components that are illicitly trafficked, without a licence or authorization from a competent authority of the state party where the manufacture or assembly takes place, or without marking the firearms at the time of manufacture as required by article 8. The second act to be criminalized by states parties is the illicit trafficking in firearms, their parts and components, and ammunition. Illicit trafficking is defined in article 3(*e*) as

> the import, export, acquisition, sale, delivery, movement or transfer of firearms, their parts and components and ammunition from or across the territory of one State Party to that of another State Party if any one of the States Parties concerned does not authorize it in accordance with the terms of [the Firearms] Protocol or if the firearms are not marked in accordance with article 8 of [the] Protocol...

---

[349] For the background to and drafting of the Firearms Protocol, see United Nations Office on Drugs and Crime (n 301), ix–xxvi and 579–737; McClean (n 301), 26–9.

[350] See GA res 67/234 B, 2 April 2013, adopted 154:3:23, adopting UN doc A/CONF.217/2013/L.3, Annex.

[351] Firearms Protocol, art 1 and *supra* paras 7.148 and 7.154.

[352] Recall *supra* paras 7.149 and 7.156. Articles 4(1), 3, and 4 of the Firearms Protocol are to the Protocol what arts 4, 3, and 5 of the Trafficking in Persons Protocol are to that Protocol.

[353] See, generally, McClean (n 301), 454–61 and 465–7.

[354] Firearms Protocol, art 5(1)(*a*), cross-referable to art 3(*a*), (*b*), and (*c*) respectively.

(d) Modes of responsibility

In addition to commission of the offences set forth in the Protocol, 'organizing, directing, aiding, abetting, facilitating or counselling the commission of an offence', as well as, subject to the 'basic concepts' of a state party's legal system, attempting to commit or participating as an accomplice in an offence, must be rendered criminal in accordance with the Protocol.[355]

7.166

(vi) Sale of children, child prostitution, and child pornography

(a) Background

On top of longstanding concerns over the sale of children, in particular for forced labour, the rapid growth of the internet and with it the massive market in online pornography led in the mid-1990s to the acute exacerbation of fears over the sexual exploitation of children that had already been prevalent since the boom in sex tourism and predatory North–South paedophilia over the preceding two decades. Similar anxieties were already reflected in articles 32 to 36 of the Convention on the Rights of the Child 1989 and in the Programme of Action for the Prevention of the Sale of Children, Child Prostitution and Child Pornography adopted by the UN Commission on Human Rights in 1992.[356] In 1996, the First World Congress against Commercial Sexual Exploitation of Children, held in Stockholm, agreed a Declaration and Agenda for Action in which, recognizing the role played by '[c]riminals and criminal networks' who 'take part in procuring and channelling vulnerable children toward commercial sexual exploitation and in perpetuating such exploitation', the states represented at the Congress made a political undertaking to '[c]riminalise the commercial sexual exploitation of children, as well as other forms of sexual exploitation of children, and condemn and penalise all those offenders involved, whether local or foreign'.[357] In 1999, the International Conference on Combating Child Pornography on the Internet, hosted in Vienna, called for 'the worldwide criminalization of the production, distribution, exportation, transmission, importation, intentional possession and advertising of child pornography'.[358] Finally, '[c]onsidering that, in order further to achieve the purposes of the Convention on the Rights of the Child and the implementation of

7.167

---

[355] Ibid, art 5(2)(b) and (a) respectively.
[356] UN Commission on Human Rights, *Programmes of Action for the Prevention of the Sale of Children, Child Prostitution and Child Pornography and for the Elimination of the Exploitation of Child Labour*, UN doc E/CN.4/RES/1992/74 (5 March 1992), Annex. The Programme of Action is recalled in Children Protocol, preamble (eleventh recital).
[357] First World Congress against Commercial Sexual Exploitation of Children, 'Stockholm Declaration', 31 August 1996, paras 7 and 12 respectively. The Declaration and accompanying Agenda for Action are recalled in Children Protocol, preamble (eleventh recital).
[358] Children Protocol, preamble (sixth recital).

its provisions, . . . it would be appropriate to extend the measures that States Parties should undertake in order to guarantee the protection of the child from the sale of children, child prostitution and child pornography', the UN General Assembly adopted without a vote, by way of annex to resolution 54/263 of 25 May 2000, the Children Protocol.[359] Despite its constituting a protocol to a human rights treaty, the Children Protocol is a classic international criminal convention.

7.168   Participation in the Children Protocol is open to any state party or signatory to the Convention on the Rights of the Child.[360]

(b) Crimes

7.169   In accordance with article 3(1) of the Children Protocol, each state party must ensure that three heads of offence, at a minimum, 'are fully covered under its criminal or penal law, whether such offences are committed domestically or transnationally or on an individual or organized basis'. The first head, as specified in article 3(1)(*a*), relates to acts and activities 'in the context of sale of children', with article 2(*a*) defining 'sale of children' to mean 'any act or transaction whereby a child is transferred by any person or group of persons to another for remuneration or any other consideration'. The relevant offences in this context comprise offering, delivering or accepting, by whatever means, a child for the purpose of, variously, his or her sexual exploitation, the transfer of his or her organs for profit, or his or her engagement in forced labour;[361] and improperly inducing consent, as an intermediary, for the adoption of a child in violation of applicable international legal instruments on adoption.[362] The next head of offence, in article 3(1)(*b*), comprises offering, obtaining, procuring or providing a child for child prostitution, the term 'child prostitution' being defined in article 2(*b*) to mean 'the use of a child in sexual activities for remuneration or any other form of consideration'. Finally, article 3(1)(*c*) recognizes the offence of producing, distributing, disseminating, importing, exporting, offering, selling or possessing 'for the above purposes' child pornography, which is defined in article 2(*c*) to mean 'any representation, by whatever means, of a child engaged in real or simulated explicit sexual activities or any representation of the sexual parts of a child for primarily sexual purposes'. It is not self-evident to which purposes the phrase 'the above purposes' refers. The only purposes mentioned in article 3(1) of the Protocol are those in article 3(1)(*a*), namely the respective purposes of the sexual exploitation of a child, the transfer of a child's organs for profit, and the engagement of a child in forced labour; but while the first of these might make vague sense by way of cross-reference, the remaining two do not. The only way of making sense of the phrase is to read 'above' as 'foregoing' or 'preceding', a licence perhaps justified by the appearance in the original text of the words 'producing, distributing, disseminating, importing, exporting, offering, selling' in the line above the words 'or possessing for the above purposes'. In

---

[359] See GA res 54/263, 25 May 2000, Annex II.   [360] Children Protocol, art 13.
[361] Ibid, art 3(1)(*a*)(i).   [362] Ibid, art 3(1)(*a*)(ii).

this light, what states parties are obliged to criminalize in accordance with article 3(1)(*c*) of the Children Protocol is the production, distribution, dissemination, import, export, offer or sale of child pornography, as well as the possession of child pornography for the purpose, variously, of its production, distribution, dissemination, import, export, offer or sale.

No *mens rea* is specified in article 3(1). This is a question for each state party. 7.170

(c) Modes of responsibility

Apart from criminalizing the commission of the offences laid down in article 3(1) of the Children Protocol, states parties are obliged, '[s]ubject to the provisions of [their] national law', to criminalize attempts to commit and complicity or 'participation' in the commission of these offences.[363] 7.171

F. Crimes Relating to Corrupt Practices

Provision is made in three non-regional multilateral treaties for the criminalization of what can be referred to broadly as corrupt practices. The treaties in question are the OECD Bribery Convention, concluded under the auspices of the Organization for Economic Co-operation and Development (OECD); the Organized Crime Convention, specifically article 8; and the Corruption Convention. There is a degree of overlap among the three.[364] 7.172

(i) OECD Bribery Convention

(a) Background

The origins of the OECD Bribery Convention[365] lie in the US's Foreign Corrupt Practices Act 1977 (FCPA), which outlawed the bribery of a foreign public official for the purpose of obtaining or retaining business for or with, or directing business to, any person. Realizing that the FCPA placed US corporations at a competitive disadvantage, at least as narrowly conceived,[366] the US pushed for the conclusion of a universal multilateral treaty against corruption under the aegis of the UN's Economic and Social Council, a project which ground to a halt, at least for the then-foreseeable future, at the beginning of the 1980s. As a substitute, in 1989 the US requested the Paris-based OECD to pursue the idea of a convention against bribery of foreign public officials. The eventual upshot, passing via a recommendation of the OECD Council of 7.173

---

[363] Ibid, art 3(2). For the concept of 'participation', see *supra* paras 7.72, 7.116, 7.123, 7.126, and 7.139.
[364] It makes practical sense for this reason to outline the various crimes by convention, rather than by subject-matter.
[365] For the origins of the OECD Bribery Convention, see M Pieth, 'Introduction' in M Pieth, LA Low, and N Bonucci (eds), *The OECD Convention on Bribery. A Commentary* (Cambridge: Cambridge University Press, 2014), 3, 8–22.
[366] See Pieth (n 365), 11.

1994 on bribery in international business transactions and a revised version of the same in May 1997,[367] was the OECD Bribery Convention, adopted on 21 November 1997.

7.174   The OECD Bribery Convention was open for signature by OECD member states and by those non-member states invited to become full participants in the OECD Working Group on Bribery in International Business Transactions. It is open to accession by non-signatory states that are either OECD members or full participants in the Working Group on Bribery in International Business Transactions or any successor to it.[368]

(b) Crime

7.175   The OECD Bribery Convention provides for a single, somewhat convoluted offence, referred to in the Convention as 'bribery of a foreign public official'.[369] In accordance with article 1(1), each state party must make it criminal for anyone

> intentionally to offer, promise or give any undue pecuniary or other advantage, whether directly or through intermediaries, to a foreign public official, for that official or for a third party, in order that the official act or refrain from acting in relation to the performance of official duties, in order to obtain or retain business or other improper advantage in the conduct of international business.

The term 'foreign public official' is defined in article 1(4)(*a*) to mean

> any person holding a legislative, administrative or judicial office of a foreign country, whether appointed or elected; any person exercising a public function for a foreign country, including for a public agency or public enterprise; and any official or agent of a public international organisation.

The term 'foreign country' is said in article 1(4)(*b*) to embrace all levels and subdivisions of government, from national to local. It is not limited to states, but includes instead 'any organised foreign area or entity, such as an autonomous territory or a separate customs territory',[370] examples being Taiwan, the north of Cyprus, Hong Kong, and non-self-governing territories possessed of responsible government. The foreignness of the country is in relation to the state party obliged

---

[367] Recommendation of the Council on Bribery in International Business Transactions, 27 May 1994, OECD doc C(94)75/FINAL and Revised Recommendation of the Council on Combating Bribery in International Business Transactions, 23 May 1997, OECD doc C(97)123/FINAL, respectively. (The extant recommendation is now the Recommendation of the Council for Further Combating Bribery of Foreign Public Officials in International Business Transactions, 26 November 2009, OECD doc C(2009)159/REV1/FINAL, as amended by C/(2010)19.)

[368] OECD Bribery Convention, art 13.

[369] Ibid, art 1(3). See, generally, Commentaries on the Convention on Combating Bribery of Foreign Public Officials in International Business Transactions (adopted by the Negotiating Conference on 21 November 1997) in OECD, *Convention on Combating Bribery of Foreign Public Officials in International Business Transactions and Related Documents* (Paris: OECD Publishing, 2011), paras 3–19; Pieth (n 365), 30–4; I Zerbes, 'Article 1. The Offence of Bribery of Foreign Public Officials' in M Pieth, LA Low, and N Bonucci (eds), *The OECD Convention on Bribery. A Commentary* (Cambridge: Cambridge University Press, 2014), 59.

[370] Commentaries on the Convention on Combating Bribery (n 369), para 18.

in accordance with article 1(1) to criminalize the conduct. That is, the OECD Bribery Convention does not cover the bribery of a state party's own public officials.[371] As for the inclusion of officials and agents of public international organizations within the definition of a 'foreign public official', this stretches the word 'foreign' beyond its ordinary meaning, but be that as it may.[372] The expression 'act or refrain from acting in relation to the performance of official duties' is said in article 1(4)(c) to encompass any use of the public official's position, whether or not it falls within the official's authorized competence.

7.176 The offence set forth in article 1(1) of the OECD Bribery Convention applies, as the text makes plain, only in the context of the conduct of international business. The Convention provides no definition of the term 'international business'. The 'international' element is seemingly provided by the actual or prospective involvement of a company or other commercial entity or an individual of the nationality of one state—this being the company or other commercial entity or individual on whose behalf the person alleged to have offered, promised or given the bribe acted—in business in another state or organized area or entity. In other words, the Convention does not apply in the context of business conducted or sought by a legal or natural person in the state of that person's nationality. Conversely, the Convention does apply in the context of business conducted or sought by a legal or natural person in a state other than the state of that person's nationality, even if the alleged offender is a national of the first state. As for 'business', the ordinary meaning of the word is capable of encompassing any commercial dealings.

7.177 The offence laid down in article 1(1) of the Convention covers only the offer, promise or giving of a bribe to a public official—what is sometimes referred to as 'active' bribery. It does not encompass the solicitation or receipt of a bribe by any such official,[373] sometimes referred to as 'passive' bribery.

7.178 Nothing in article 1(1) of the Convention requires that the offer, promise or giving of the bribe be a *conditio sine qua non* of the obtaining or retention by the commercial interest in question of business or other improper advantage in the conduct of business in the foreign country. All that article 1(1) demands is that the bribe be offered, promised or given with a view to obtaining or retaining the business, etc. It may well be that the offer, promise or giving of the bribe makes no difference, in that the commercial interest on behalf of which the bribe is offered, promised or given does not in fact obtain or retain the business, etc or would have obtained or retained the business, etc in any event.[374] Indeed, it may be that any bribe offered, promised or given is not accepted by the foreign public official.

---

[371] See also Pieth (n 365), 33; Zerbes (n 369), 69.
[372] See, in this regard, VCLT, art 31(4), which provides that a special meaning shall be given to a treaty term if it is established that the parties so intended.
[373] See also Commentaries on the Convention on Combating Bribery (n 369), para 1; Pieth (n 365), 31–2; Zerbes (n 369), 67–8.
[374] See eg Commentaries on the Convention on Combating Bribery (n 369), para 4.

(c) Modes of responsibility

7.179 Article 1(2) of the OECD Bribery Convention obliges states parties to provide for criminal responsibility for 'complicity in, including incitement, aiding and abetting, or authorisation of' bribery of a foreign public official.

(ii) Organized Crime Convention

(a) Background

7.180 Although initial efforts within the UN to draft a universal convention on corruption foundered,[375] the problem of corruption remained of interest to the Economic and Social Council and the General Assembly. In 1996, the General Assembly adopted the United Nations Declaration against Corruption and Bribery in International Commercial Transactions[376] and an International Code of Conduct for Public Officials.[377] Three years later, the Assembly— '[n]oting the corrosive effect that corruption has on democracy, development, the rule of law and economic activity'; '[r]ecognizing that corruption is a primary tool of organized crime in its efforts, often conducted on an international basis, to subvert Governments and legitimate commerce'; and '[d]rawing attention to the increasing number of regional conventions and other regional instruments recently developed to fight corruption'[378]—directed the Ad Hoc Committee on the Elaboration of a Convention against Transnational Organized Crime[379] to incorporate into the draft convention under preparation 'measures against corruption linked to organized crime, including provisions regarding the sanctioning of acts of corruption involving public officials'.[380] The upshot was the offences laid down in the Organized Crime Convention in article 8 ('Criminalization of corruption'), which were inspired by article 1(1) of the OECD Bribery Convention and by provisions in the Inter-American Convention Against Corruption 1996[381] and the Council of Europe's Criminal Law Convention on Corruption 1999.[382]

(b) Scope of application

7.181 The exception to article 3(1) of the Organized Crime Convention provided for in article 34(2) makes it clear that states parties must criminalize the conduct defined in article 8 regardless of whether it is transnational in nature or involves an organized criminal group.[383]

---

[375] See *supra* para 7.172.
[376] GA res 51/191, 16 December 1996, Annex.
[377] GA res 51/59, 12 December 1996, Annex.
[378] GA res 54/128, 17 December 1999, preamble (first to third recitals).
[379] Recall GA res 53/111, 9 December 1998.
[380] GA res 54/128, 17 December 1999, para 5.
[381] See Inter-American Convention Against Corruption 1996, arts VI and VII.
[382] Criminal Law Convention on Corruption 1999, arts 2–11.
[383] Recall *supra* para 7.140.

(c) Crimes

In contrast to article 1(1) of the OECD Bribery Convention, article 8(1) of the 7.182
Organized Crime Convention obliges states parties to criminalize both so-called
'active' and 'passive' bribery and to do so regardless of whether such acts are committed in the conduct of international business or, indeed, of business. On the
other hand, and again in contrast to the OECD Bribery Convention, the offences
the object of article 8(1)'s strict obligation of municipal criminalization relate only
to a state party's own officials, although article 8(2) contains an undertaking to
consider criminalizing 'active' and 'passive' bribery of foreign public officials and
international civil servants.

Article 8(1)(*a*) of the Organized Crime Convention specifies as a crime the 7.183
intentional 'promise, offering or giving to a public official, directly or indirectly, of
an undue advantage, for the official himself or herself or another person or entity,
in order that the official act or refrain from acting in the exercise of his or her official duties'. Article 8(1)(*b*) lays down the crime of the intentional 'solicitation or
acceptance by a public official, directly or indirectly, of an undue advantage, for the
official himself or herself or another person or entity, in order that the official act
or refrain from acting in the exercise of his or her official duties'. The term 'public
official' is defined in article 8(4), by way of *renvoi* to national law, as 'a public official or a person who provides a public service as defined in the domestic law and
as applied in the criminal law of the State Party in which the person in question
performs the function'. Nothing on the face of article 8(1) or article 8(4) restricts
the term 'public official' to a public official of the state party obliged in accordance
with article 8(1) to criminalize the relevant conduct; but article 8(1) must be read
in the context of article 8(2), in accordance with which states parties must consider criminalizing 'conduct referred to in [article 8(1)] involving a foreign public
official or international civil servant', the necessary implication *a contrario* being
that article 8(1) does not extend to the 'active' or 'passive' bribery of such persons.

In addition to the obligation to consider criminalizing the 'active' or 'passive' 7.184
bribery of foreign public officials and international civil servants, article 8(2) of
the Organized Crime Convention imposes an obligation to consider criminalizing
'other forms of corruption'.

(d) Modes of responsibility

State parties must criminalize participation as an accomplice in any offence provided for in municipal law pursuant to article 8.[384] 7.185

(iii) Corruption Convention

(a) Background

In the same resolution of 1999 in which it directed the Ad Hoc Committee on the 7.186
Elaboration of a Convention against Transnational Organized Crime to incorporate

---
[384] Organized Crime Convention, art 8(3).

measures against corruption into the draft convention,[385] the General Assembly requested the Committee 'to explore the desirability of an international instrument against corruption, either ancillary to or independent of the Convention [against Transnational Organized Crime], to be developed after the finalization of the Convention and [its] three additional instruments'.[386] The following year, '[r]ecognizing that an effective international legal instrument against corruption, independent of the United Nations Convention against Transnational Organized Crime, [was] desirable', the Assembly decided to establish an ad hoc committee for the negotiation of such an instrument at the Vienna headquarters of the United Nations Centre for International Crime Prevention of the United Nations Office for Drug Control and Crime Prevention.[387] The Ad Hoc Committee for the Negotiation of a Convention against Corruption commenced work in January 2002, and in only seven sessions[388] produced the Corruption Convention, adopted by way of annex to General Assembly resolution 58/4 of 31 October 2003.

(b) Crimes

7.187 Chapter III ('Criminalization and law enforcement') of the Corruption Convention embodies an array of treaty crimes pertaining to corruption, each of them requiring intent. Some of these crimes are the object of a strict obligation of municipal criminalization, while states parties are obliged only to consider criminalizing others. In either case, insofar as knowledge, intent or purpose is required as an element of an offence specified in the Convention, it may be inferred from objective factual circumstances.[389]

7.188 Article 15(*a*) and (*b*) of the Corruption Convention require the criminalization of exactly the same offences of 'active' and 'passive' bribery of a state party's own public officials as provided for in article 8(1)(*a*) and (*b*) of the Organized Crime Convention.[390] Just as in accordance with article 8(1)(*a*) and (*b*) of the Organized Crime Convention, the acts specified in article 15(*a*) and (*b*) of the Corruption Convention shall constitute offences irrespective of whether they are committed in the conduct of international business or of business *tout court*. The term 'public official' is defined in article 2(*a*) of the Corruption Convention to mean

> (i) any person holding a legislative, executive, administrative or judicial office of a State Party, whether appointed or elected, whether permanent or temporary, whether paid or unpaid, irrespective of that person's seniority; (ii) any other person who performs a public function, including for a public agency or public enterprise, or provides a public service, as defined in the domestic law of the State Party and as applied in the pertinent area of law

---

[385] Recall *supra* para 7.179.
[386] GA res 54/128, 17 December 1999, para 6. For the background to the Corruption Convention, see United Nations Office on Drugs and Crime, Travaux préparatoires *of the negotiations for the elaboration of the United Nations Convention against Corruption* (New York: United Nations, 2010), xii–xlii.
[387] GA res 55/61, 4 December 2000, paras 1 and 7 respectively.
[388] For the drafting of the Convention, see, generally, United Nations Office on Drugs and Crime (n 386).
[389] Corruption Convention, art 28.   [390] Recall *supra* paras 7.181–7.182.

of that State Party; (iii) any other person defined as a 'public official' in the domestic law of a State Party.[391]

That article 15 of the Corruption Convention relates strictly to a state party's own officials is made manifest when the provision is read in the light of article 16, which deals with the bribery of foreign public officials and the officials of public international organizations.

7.189 Article 16(1) of the Corruption Convention obliges states parties to criminalize what, in near-verbatim terms, is the offence of bribery of a foreign public official or official of a public international organization found in article 1(1) of the OECD Bribery Convention.[392] 'Foreign public official' is defined in article 2(*b*) of the Corruption Convention to mean 'any person holding a legislative, executive, administrative or judicial office of a foreign country, whether appointed or elected; and any person exercising a public function for a foreign country, including for a public agency or public enterprise'. 'Official of a public international organization' is stated in article 2(*c*) to mean 'an international civil servant or any person who is authorized by such an organization to act on behalf of that organization'. As with article 1(1) of the OECD Bribery Convention, the offence laid down in article 16(1) of the Corruption Convention applies, as the text makes plain, only in the context of the conduct of international business, a term for which, like the OECD Convention, the Corruption Convention provides no definition.

7.190 Article 17(1) of the Corruption Convention imposes a strict obligation of municipal criminalization in respect of the offence of 'embezzlement, misappropriation or other diversion by a public official for his or her benefit or for the benefit of another person or entity, of any property, public or private funds or securities or any other thing of value entrusted to the public official by virtue of his or her position'. 'Property' is defined as under the Illicit Traffic Convention and Organized Crime Convention.[393]

7.191 Article 23(1) of the Corruption Convention provides, in terms identical to those of article 6 of the Organized Crime Convention,[394] for offences connected with the laundering of the proceeds of crime. The term 'proceeds of crime' is defined as under the Organized Crime Convention.[395]

7.192 In accordance with article 25 of the Corruption Convention, states parties must criminalize the same offences of obstruction of justice as laid down in article 23 of the Organized Crime Convention.[396]

---

[391] The provision continues, however, that, 'for the purpose of some specific measures contained in chapter II of th[e] Convention, "public official" may mean any person who performs a public function or provides a public service as defined in the domestic law of the State Party and as applied in the pertinent area of law of that State Party'. The qualification is irrelevant to the crimes specified in chapter III of the Corruption Convention.
[392] Recall *supra* paras 7.174–7.177.
[393] See Corruption Convention, art 2(*d*) and recall *supra* paras 7.136 and 7.144.
[394] Recall *supra* para 7.144.
[395] See Corruption Convention, art 2(*e*) and recall *supra* para 7.144.
[396] Recall *supra* para 7.145.

7.193   Additionally, the Corruption Convention obliges states parties to consider criminalizing the solicitation or acceptance of a bribe by a foreign public official or an official of a public international organization, irrespective of any link with the conduct of international or any other business; 'active' and 'passive' trading in influence; abuse of functions or position; illicit enrichment; 'active' and 'passive' bribery in the private sector; embezzlement of property in the private sector; and 'the concealment or continued retention of property when the person involved knows that such property is the result of any of the offences established in accordance with th[e] Convention'.[397]

(c) Modes of responsibility

7.194   States parties to the Corruption Convention must criminalize, in accordance with their municipal law, 'participation in any capacity such as an accomplice, assistant or instigator' in an offence established pursuant to the Convention.[398]

7.195   The Corruption Convention makes specific provision for modes of responsibility in relation to the offences of laundering of the proceeds of crime set forth in article 23. Article 23(1)(*b*)(ii) stipulates that, subject to 'the basic concepts of its legal system', a state party must impose criminal responsibility for any offence established pursuant to article 23 of the Convention on the bases, variously, of participation in any such offence; association or conspiracy to commit any such offence; attempt to commit any such offence; and of aiding, abetting, facilitating or[399] counselling the commission of any such offence.[400]

G. Crimes Against the Safety of United Nations and Associated Personnel

(i) Background

7.196   A string of fatal attacks against UN military and civilian personnel in the early 1990s led the UN General Assembly to decide in late 1993 to establish an ad hoc committee to elaborate a convention on the safety and security of UN and associated personnel.[401] Progress was swift, and on 9 December 1994 the General Assembly adopted the UN and Associated Personnel Convention.[402]

---

[397] See Corruption Convention, arts 16(2), 18, 19, 20, 21, 22, and 24 respectively.

[398] Ibid, art 27(1). Although the statement is of no practical value as a matter of public international law, states parties may—rather than must—provide additionally, in accordance with article 27(2) and (3) of the Convention, for criminal responsibility on the basis of attempt and preparation respectively.

[399] The text uses 'and', but the relationship between the terms seems as a logical matter to be disjunctive, as it expressly is in Organized Crime Convention, art 5(1)(*b*).

[400] Corruption Convention, art 23(1)(*b*)(ii) is modelled on Organized Crime Convention, art 6(1)(*b*)(ii), which in turn is modelled on, although deviates slightly from, Illicit Traffic Convention, art 3(1)(*c*)(iv). Recall *supra* paras 7.138 and 7.146.

[401] See GA res 47/83, 9 December 1993.

[402] See GA res 49/59, 9 December 1994, adopted without a vote.

7.197   The later emergence of a consensus that the scope of application of the UN and Associated Personnel Convention was too narrow[403]—specifically in its effective, albeit not formal exclusion of UN operations conducted for the purpose of delivering humanitarian, political or development assistance in peacebuilding or emergency humanitarian assistance[404]—led eventually to the General Assembly's adoption on 8 December 2005 of the Optional Protocol to the Convention on the Safety of United Nations and Associated Personnel ('UN and Associated Personnel Protocol').[405] The Protocol supplements the Convention, and, as among states parties to both, the Convention and Protocol are to be read as a single instrument.[406]

(ii) Scope of application

7.198   The scope of application of the UN and Associated Personnel Convention was the major sticking point during negotiations leading to the treaty's adoption. The result was an unhappy compromise over the range of UN operations in respect of which the Convention applies.

7.199   Article 2(1) of the UN and Associated Personnel Convention provides that the Convention applies in respect of 'United Nations and associated personnel and United Nations operations' as defined in article 1. Article 1(*a*) defines 'United Nations personnel' to encompass both persons engaged or deployed by the UN Secretary-General as members of the military, police or civilian components of a 'United Nations operation' and other officials and experts, when on mission, of the UN, its specialized agencies or the IAEA 'who are present in an official capacity in the area where a United Nations operation is being conducted'.[407] 'Associated personnel' is defined in article 1(*b*) of the Convention to mean as follows:

(i)   Persons assigned by a Government or an intergovernmental organization with the agreement of the competent organ of the United Nations,
(ii) Persons engaged by the Secretary-General of the United Nations or by a specialized agency or by the International Atomic Energy Agency,
(iii) Persons deployed by a humanitarian non-governmental organization or agency under an agreement with the Secretary-General of the United Nations or with a specialized agency or with the International Atomic Energy Agency,

to carry out activities in support of the fulfilment of the mandate of a United Nations operation...

---

[403] See especially UN Secretary-General, *Scope of legal protection under the Convention on the Safety of United Nations and Associated Personnel. Report of the Secretary-General*, UN doc A/55/637 (21 November 2000).
[404] Optional Protocol to the Convention on the Safety of United Nations and Associated Personnel 2005 ('UN and Associated Personnel Protocol'), preamble (third recital).
[405] GA res 60/42, 8 December 2005.
[406] UN and Associated Personnel Protocol, art I.
[407] UN and Associated Personnel Convention, art 1(*a*)(i) and (ii) respectively.

The rub is the definition of a 'United Nations operation' laid down in article 1(*c*), which reads:

'United Nations operation' means an operation established by the competent organ of the United Nations in accordance with the Charter of the United Nations and conducted under United Nations authority and control:
(i) Where the operation is for the purpose of maintaining or restoring international peace and security; or
(ii) Where the Security Council or the General Assembly has declared, for the purposes of this Convention, that there exists an exceptional risk to the safety of the personnel participating in the operation…

Article 1(*c*), in particular article 1(*c*)(i), must be read in the light of article 2(2) of the Convention, which specifies that the Convention does not apply to a United Nations operation 'authorized by the Security Council as an enforcement action under Chapter VII of the Charter of the United Nations in which any of the personnel are engaged as combatants against organized armed forces and to which the law of international armed conflict applies'. In sum, the UN and Associated Personnel Convention applies in respect of two alternative categories of operation: first, and automatically, in respect of operations established by the competent UN organ for the purpose of maintaining and restoring international peace and security and conducted under UN authority and control, unless the operation is a chapter VII enforcement operation in which any of the personnel are engaged as combatants against organized armed forces and to which the law of international armed conflict applies; secondly, to other operations established by the competent organ of the United Nations and conducted under United Nations authority and control, but only in the event that the Security Council or General Assembly declares that there exists an exceptional risk to the safety of the personnel participating in the operation. The first situation covers any non-combat 'blue helmet' operation authorized by the Security Council under chapter VII of the UN Charter[408] and, despite some debate over the issue, almost certainly traditional 'blue helmet' peacekeeping operations authorized by either the Security Council or, in accordance with the 'Uniting for Peace' resolution,[409] the General Assembly and deployed with the consent of the host state without the need for recourse by the Security Council to its coercive powers under chapter VII.[410] Excluded from the scope of the Convention are UN combat operations authorized under chapter VII as an enforcement action; UN-authorized operations conducted under national authority and control; and UN-authorized operations, conducted under UN authority and control, established for a purpose other than the maintenance of international peace and security, unless the Security Council or General Assembly declares that there exists an exceptional risk to the safety of the personnel participating in the operation.

---

[408] UN operations under chapter VII of the Charter are by definition for the purpose of maintaining or restoring international peace and security.
[409] GA res 377 A (V), 3 November 1950.
[410] The non-invocation of chapter VII does not take away from the fact that such operations are for the purpose of maintaining or restoring international peace and security.

As it has transpired, neither the Security Council nor the General Assembly 7.200
has ever declared, for the purposes of article 1(*c*)(ii) of the UN and Associated
Personnel Convention, the existence of an exceptional risk to the safety of personnel participating in a UN-authorized and UN-conducted operation. As a result,
the Convention had by the early 2000s never applied in respect of any such operation established other than for the maintenance of international peace and security.
At the same time, UN and associated personnel had been attacked in precisely this
context. The chief aim of the UN and Associated Personnel Protocol is to remedy
this inadequacy by extending the automatic application of the Convention to such
situations.

As among states parties to both the Convention and the Protocol, the 7.201
Convention applies in respect of all operations other than—and in addition to—
those specified in article 1(*c*) of the Convention where such operations are established by a competent UN organ in accordance with the Charter and conducted
under UN authority and control for the purpose of delivering humanitarian,
political or development assistance in peacebuilding or emergency humanitarian assistance.[411] It does not apply, however, in respect of any permanent UN
office, such as the headquarters of the Organization or of its specialized agencies,
established under an agreement with the UN.[412] Moreover, in accordance with
article II(3) of the Protocol, a host state party may declare, prior to the deployment of the operation, that it will not apply the Convention to a UN operation
established to deliver emergency humanitarian assistance for the sole purpose of
responding to a natural disaster.

(iii) Crimes

The UN and Associated Personnel Convention obliges states parties to criminal- 7.202
ize the murder, kidnapping or other attack on the person or liberty of any United
Nations or associated personnel; any violent attack on the official premises, private
accommodation or means of transportation of United Nations or associated personnel that is likely to endanger their person or liberty; and a threat to commit any
of the foregoing acts 'with the objective of compelling a physical or juridical person
to do or to refrain from doing any act'.[413]

(iv) Modes of responsibility

The states parties to the UN and Associated Personnel Convention must criminal- 7.203
ize not only the commission of the crimes set forth in the Convention but also
any attempt to commit any such crime and any act constituting participation as

---

[411] UN and Associated Personnel Protocol, art II(1)(*a*) and (*b*). None of the relevant terms is defined in the Protocol.
[412] Ibid, art II(2).
[413] UN and Associated Personnel Convention, art 9(1)(*a*) to (*c*) respectively.

an accomplice in any such crime, in an attempt to commit any such crime, or in organizing or ordering others to commit any such crime.[414]

IV. Conclusion

7.204　Treaty crimes tend to be viewed as the poor relation of customary international crimes, a perception manifest in and reinforced by juridically meaningless and factually misleading talk of 'core crimes' and a seeming fixation on international criminal tribunals as the forum of choice for the prosecution of international crimes. The upshot is that the material and mental elements of the overwhelming majority of international crimes—those, or at least most of those, provided for by treaty—are rarely the focus of sustained scholarly attention.[415] This is despite the fact that, for every instance of the crime of aggression, countless more internationally criminal acts of drug trafficking, organized crime, trafficking in persons, smuggling of migrants, bribery of foreign public officials, and corruption, not to mention of torture and enforced disappearance and of maritime depredation, are perpetrated. It is also in spite of the fact that, at the universal level alone, no fewer than nine multilateral treaties posit what in all but formal definition are international crimes of terrorism. It can only be hoped that the valuable efforts already undertaken by some to remedy this situation inspire further in-depth interest in this 'other' part of the substantive law of international crimes.

Further Reading

ALLAIN, J, 'The Definition of Slavery in International Law' (2009) 52 *Howard Law Journal* 239

ALLAIN, J (ed), *The Legal Understanding of Slavery: From the Historical to the Contemporary* (Oxford: Oxford University Press, 2012)

AMBOS, K, *Treatise on International Criminal Law. Volume 2: Crimes and Sentencing* (Oxford: Oxford University Press, 2014), chapter 5

BOISTER, N, *An Introduction to Transnational Criminal Law* (Oxford: Oxford University Press, 2012), chapters 3–11

BOISTER, N, *Penal Aspects of the UN Drug Conventions* (The Hague: Kluwer, 2001)

BOISTER, N and CURRIE, RJ (eds), *Routledge Handbook of Transnational Criminal Law* (Abingdon: Routledge, 2015)

BOURLOYANNIS-VRAILAS, M-C, 'The Convention on the Safety of United Nations and Associated Personnel' (1995) 44 *International and Comparative Law Quarterly* 560

BURGERS, JH and DANELIUS, H, *The United Nations Convention Against Torture: A Handbook on the Convention Against Torture and Other Cruel, Inhuman or Degrading Treatment or Punishment* (Dordrecht/London: Martinus Nijhoff, 1988)

---

[414] Ibid, art 9(1)(*d*) and (*e*).
[415] Leading the honourable exceptions in this regard is Neil Boister. See eg Boister (n 3) and N Boister and RJ Currie (eds), *Routledge Handbook of Transnational Criminal Law* (Abingdon: Routledge, 2015).

CHERIEF, H, 'La pénalisation de la prolifération maritime des armes de destruction massive' in ED Papastavridis and KN Trapp (eds), *La criminalité en mer/Crimes at Sea* (Leiden: Martinus Nijhoff, 2014), 485

Commentaries on the Convention on Combating Bribery of Foreign Public Officials in International Business Transactions (adopted by the Negotiating Conference on 21 November 1997) in OECD, *Convention on Combating Bribery of Foreign Public Officials in International Business Transactions and Related Documents* (Paris: OECD Publishing, 2011)

DECAUX, E and DE FROUVILLE, O (eds), *La Convention pour la protection des toutes les personnes contre les disparitions forcées* (Brussels: Bruylant, 2009)

DUGARD, J, 'L'apartheid' in H Ascensio, E Decaux, and A Pellet (eds), *Droit international pénal* (2nd edn, Paris: Pedone, 2012), 197

FRIEDRICHS, J, 'Defining the International Public Enemy: The Political Struggle behind the Legal Debate on International Terrorism' (2006) 19 *Leiden Journal of International Law* 69

GALLAGHER, AT, *The International Law of Human Trafficking* (Cambridge: Cambridge University Press, 2012)

GALLAGHER, AT and DAVID, F, *The International Law of Migrant Smuggling* (Cambridge: Cambridge University Press, 2014)

KLEIN, P, 'Le droit international à l'épreuve du terrorisme' (2006) 321 *Recueil des cours* 203

LE BŒUF, R, 'Les disparitions forcées' in H Ascensio, E Decaux, and A Pellet (eds), *Droit international pénal* (2nd edn, Paris: Pedone, 2012) 233

LLEWELLYN, H, 'The Optional Protocol to the 1994 Convention on the Safety of United Nations and Associated Personnel' (2006) 55 *International and Comparative Law Quarterly* 718

MCCLEAN, D, *Transnational Organized Crime. A Commentary on the UN Convention and its Protocols* (Oxford: Oxford University Press, 2007)

MARSTON, G, 'Early Attempts to Suppress Terrorism: The Terrorism and International Criminal Court Conventions of 1937' (2002) 73 *British Year Book of International Law* 293

NOWAK, M and MCARTHUR, E, *The United Nations Convention Against Torture: A Commentary* (Oxford: Oxford University Press, 2008)

O'KEEFE, R, 'Protection of Cultural Property under International Criminal Law' (2010) 11 *Melbourne Journal of International Law* 339

PICTET, J, *The Geneva Conventions of 12 August 1949, Commentary IV: Geneva Convention relative to the Protection of Civilian Persons in Time of War* (Geneva: International Committee of the Red Cross, 1958)

PIETH, M, 'Criminalizing the Financing of Terrorism' (2006) 4 *Journal of International Criminal Justice* 1074

PIETH, M, LOW, LA, and BONUCCI, N (eds), *The OECD Convention on Bribery. A Commentary* (Cambridge: Cambridge University Press, 2014)

SANDOZ, Y, SWINARSKI, C, and ZIMMERMANN, B, *Commentary on the Additional Protocols of 8 June 1977 to the Geneva Conventions of 12 August 1949* (Geneva: ICRC/Martinus Nijhoff, 1987)

SAUL, B, *Defining Terrorism in International Law* (Oxford: Oxford University Press, 2006)

TREVES, T, 'La Convention de 1989 sur les mercenaires' (1990) 36 *Annuaire français de droit international* 520

UNITED NATIONS, *Commentary on the United Nations Convention against Illicit Traffic in Narcotic Drugs and Psychotropic Substances Done at Vienna on 20 December 1988* (New York: United Nations, 1998), UN doc E/CN.7/590 (1998)

UNITED NATIONS OFFICE ON DRUGS AND CRIME, Travaux préparatoires *of the negotiations for the elaboration of the United Nations Convention against Corruption* (New York: United Nations, 2010)

UNITED NATIONS OFFICE ON DRUGS AND CRIME, Travaux préparatoires *of the negotiations for the elaboration of the United Nations Convention against Transnational Organized Crime and the Protocols thereto* (New York: United Nations, 2006)

WEBB, P, 'The United Nations Convention Against Corruption: Global Achievement or Missed Opportunity?' (2005) 8 *Journal of International Economic Law* 191

WITTEN, SM, 'The International Convention for the Suppression of Terrorist Bombings' (1998) 92 *American Journal of International Law* 774

WOOD, MC, 'The Convention on the Prevention and Punishment of Crimes against Internationally Protected Persons, including Diplomatic Agents' (1974) 23 *International and Comparative Law Quarterly* 791

8
The Obligations and Rights of States Parties

I. Introduction

The object and purpose of nearly all of the multilateral treaties that provide for international crimes[1] is the more effective suppression of the conduct the subject of the treaty[2] through the undertaking by the states parties of a range of obligations relating to their national criminal justice systems—obligations of municipal criminalization, provision for appropriate penalties, extension of jurisdiction, prosecution or extradition, and so on. Together these obligations are designed 'to prevent alleged perpetrators…from going unpunished, by ensuring that they cannot find refuge in any State party'.[3] These obligations are the focus of the present chapter,[4] which looks first at the obligations common to all or most of the relevant treaties before turning to the more significant of the obligations found in only some or one of them.

A state party's municipal law, including its constitution, or the insufficiency thereof provide no justification or excuse, as a matter of international law, for the state party's non-compliance with a treaty obligation incumbent on it.[5] A corollary is that a state which undertakes treaty obligations 'is bound to make in its legislation such modifications as may be necessary to ensure the fulfilment of the obligations undertaken'.[6]

8.1

8.2

---

[1] Recall from *supra* para 7.1 n 2 the exception of the Rome Statute of the International Criminal Court ('Rome Statute'). Recall also the limitations on the scope of chapter 7 outlined *supra* para 7.1 n 1. The same limitations apply to the present chapter.

[2] See also N Boister, *An Introduction to Transnational Criminal Law* (Oxford: Oxford University Press, 2012), 20 and 78. Indeed, the treaties in question are commonly referred to as 'suppression conventions'.

[3] *Questions relating to the Obligation to Prosecute or Extradite (Belgium v Senegal), Judgment*, ICJ Rep 2012, 422, 461, para 120. See also ibid, 455, para 91; JH Burgers and H Danelius, *The United Nations Convention Against Torture: A Handbook on the Convention Against Torture and Other Cruel, Inhuman or Degrading Treatment or Punishment* (Dordrecht/London: Martinus Nijhoff, 1988), 1 and 131.

[4] The crimes themselves are the focus of *supra* chapter 7.

[5] This principle, first articulated judicially in the *Alabama Claims Arbitration (United States of America/United Kingdom)*, 1 Moore Int Arb 653, 656 (1872), is reflected in the specific context of treaty obligations in art 27 of the Vienna Convention on the Law of Treaties 1969 ('VCLT'), which the ICJ held in *Obligation to Prosecute or Extradite* (n 3), 460, para 113, to reflect customary international law.

[6] *Exchange of Greek and Turkish Populations, Advisory Opinion*, PCIJ Rep Ser B No 10 (1925), 20.

8.3　A state party's non-compliance with a treaty obligation results in state responsibility, meaning the state party's delictual responsibility under international law. Such responsibility, which does not affect the state party's continuing obligation of compliance with the treaty obligation,[7] imposes on that state secondary obligations to cease its non-compliance, if this is continuing, to offer assurances and guarantees of non-repetition, if circumstances so require, and to make full reparation for any injury caused by its non-compliance.[8] In *Obligation to Prosecute or Extradite*, the International Court of Justice (ICJ) held that the obligations undertaken by states parties to the Convention against Torture and Other Cruel, Inhuman or Degrading Treatment or Punishment 1984 ('Torture Convention') are obligations *erga omnes partes*,[9] meaning that 'any State party to the Convention may invoke the responsibility of another State party'.[10] That is, any state party to the Torture Convention enjoys standing to demand that a state party which fails to comply with any of its obligations under the Convention cease its non-compliance, offering appropriate assurances and guarantees of non-repetition if circumstances so require, and make reparation to any injured state or to the beneficiaries of the obligation breached.[11] The reasoning relied on by the Court to reach this conclusion is equally applicable to all other international criminal conventions.

8.4　It is an axiom of international law that treaties cannot create obligations for states not parties to them, known in the terminology of the law of treaties as 'third states', without those states' consent.[12] Putting it another way, the various multilateral treaties providing for international crimes bind only states parties to them.

8.5　Both crimes under treaty and crimes pursuant to treaty can, through the usual process of formation of customary international law, emerge as independent, parallel crimes under customary international law. This does not necessarily mean, however, that the range of obligations binding on states parties to the treaty in question become customary too. Indeed, where to date treaty crimes have emerged as crimes under customary international law, there is no indication that the obligations of municipal criminalization, the fixing of appropriate penalties, extension of jurisdiction, and so on, have become binding as a matter of customary international law on all states.[13]

---

[7] Articles on Responsibility of States for Internationally Wrongful Acts, GA res 56/83, 12 December 2001, Annex ('Articles on Responsibility of States'), art 29.

[8] Ibid, arts 30 and 31.　　[9] *Obligation to Prosecute or Extradite* (n 3), 449, para 68.

[10] Ibid, 450, para 69.　　[11] See Articles on Responsibility of States, art 48(2).

[12] VCLT, art 34, as consonant—as far as it goes (see *infra* n 52)—with customary international law. See also VCLT, art 2(1)(h) ('"Third State" means a State not a party to the treaty').

[13] A question perhaps remains over the crime of genocide 'confirmed' in art 1 of the Convention on the Prevention and Punishment of the Crime of Genocide 1948 ('Genocide Convention'), given the ICJ's statement in *Reservations to the Convention on the Prevention and Punishment of the Crime of Genocide, Advisory Opinion*, ICJ Rep 1951, 15, 23, as subsequently reiterated, that the Genocide Convention enunciates 'principles which are recognized by civilized nations as binding on States, even without any conventional obligation'. But state practice strongly suggests that the situation with respect to genocide is ultimately no different.

II. Characteristic Obligations

A. Municipal Criminalization

Each international criminal treaty obliges the states parties to it to criminalize 8.6
specified conduct under their municipal law. Some treaties do this by means of a
provision that elides the technically distinct obligations of municipal criminalization and imposition of appropriate or effective penalties,[14] while others tease apart
criminalization as such[15] and the penalty to attach.

---

[14] See Supplementary Convention on the Abolition of Slavery, the Slave Trade, and Institutions and Practices Similar to Slavery 1956 ('Supplementary Slavery Convention'), arts 3(1), 5, and 6(1) and (2); Genocide Convention, art 5; Convention for the Amelioration of the Condition of the Wounded and Sick in Armed Forces in the Field 1949 ('1949 Geneva Convention I'), art 49; Convention for the Amelioration of the Condition of Wounded, Sick and Shipwrecked Members of Armed Forces at Sea 1949 ('1949 Geneva Convention II'), art 50; Convention relative to the Treatment of Prisoners of War 1949 ('1949 Geneva Convention III'), art 129; Convention relative to the Protection of Civilian Persons in Time of War 1949 ('1949 Geneva Convention IV'), art 146; Convention for the Suppression of Unlawful Seizure of Aircraft 1970 ('Hague Convention'), art 2; Convention for the Suppression of Unlawful Seizure of Aircraft as amended by the Protocol supplementary to Convention for the Suppression of Unlawful Seizure of Aircraft 2010 ('Hague Convention as amended by Beijing Protocol'), art 2; Convention for the Suppression of Unlawful Acts against the Safety of Civilian Aircraft 1971 ('Montreal Convention'), art 3; International Convention on the Suppression and Punishment of the Crime of Apartheid 1973 ('Apartheid Convention'), art IV; International Convention against the Taking of Hostages 1979 ('Hostages Convention'), art 2; Convention for the Suppression of Unlawful Acts against the Safety of Maritime Navigation 1988 ('SUA Convention'), art 5; Convention for the Suppression of Unlawful Acts against the Safety of Maritime Navigation 2005 (being the Convention for the Suppression of Unlawful Acts against the Safety of Maritime Navigation 1988 as amended by the Protocol of 2005 to the Convention for the Suppression of Unlawful Acts against the Safety of Maritime Navigation) ('2005 SUA Convention'), art 5; Convention on the Suppression of Unlawful Acts relating to International Civil Aviation 2010 ('Beijing Convention'), art 3.

[15] See Convention on the Prevention and Punishment of Crimes against Internationally Protected Persons, including Diplomatic Agents 1973 ('Internationally Protected Persons Convention'), art 2(1); Convention on the Physical Protection of Nuclear Material 1979 ('Nuclear Material Convention'), art 7(1); Convention against Torture and Other Cruel, Inhuman or Degrading Treatment or Punishment 1984 ('Torture Convention'), art 4(1); Convention against Illicit Traffic in Narcotic Drugs and Psychotropic Substances 1988 ('Illicit Traffic Convention'), art 3(1); International Convention against the Recruitment, Use, Financing and Training of Mercenaries 1989 ('Mercenaries Convention'), art 5(1); Convention on the Safety of United Nations and Associated Personnel 1994 ('UN and Associated Personnel Convention'), art 9(1); Convention on Combating Bribery of Foreign Public Officials in International Business Transactions 1997 ('OECD Bribery Convention'), art 1(1); Second Protocol to the Hague Convention of 1954 for the Protection of Cultural Property in the Event of Armed Conflict 1999 ('Second Hague Protocol'), art 15(2); International Convention for the Suppression of Terrorist Bombings 1997 ('Terrorist Bombings Convention'), art 4(*a*); International Convention for the Suppression of the Financing of Terrorism 1999 ('Financing of Terrorism Convention'), art 4(*a*); Optional Protocol to the Convention on the Rights of the Child on the Sale of Children, Child Prostitution and Child Pornography 2000 ('Children Protocol'), art 3(1); United Nations Convention against Transnational Organized Crime 2000 ('Organized Crime Convention'), arts 5, 6, 8, and 23; Protocol to Prevent, Suppress and Punish Trafficking in Persons, Especially Women and Children, supplementing the United Nations Convention against Transnational Organized Crime 2000 ('Trafficking in Persons Protocol'), art 5; Protocol against the Smuggling of Migrants by Land, Sea and Air, supplementing the United Nations Convention against Transnational Organized Crime

8.7 The wording of the respective provisions does not oblige states parties to enact a specific offence corresponding verbatim to the offence provided for in the treaty. As borne out in the subsequent practice of states parties, reliance, where feasible and appropriate, on more general existing crimes is permissible.[16] As long as the conduct specified in the treaty is punishable under the state party's criminal law, the obligation of municipal criminalization has been acquitted.[17] For example, article V of the Convention on the Prevention and Punishment of the Crime of Genocide 1948 ('Genocide Convention') states:

> The Contracting Parties undertake to enact... the necessary legislation to give effect to the provisions of the present Convention...

The word 'necessary' and the phrase 'to give effect to' suggest that reliance on existing statute or common law which does the trick, so to speak, is a permissible means of acquitting the relevant obligation. The grave breaches provisions

---

2000 ('Smuggling of Migrants Protocol'), art 6(1) and (2); Protocol against the Illicit Manufacturing of and Trafficking in Firearms, Their Parts and Components and Ammunition, supplementing the United Nations Convention against Transnational Organized Crime 2001 ('Firearms Protocol'), art 5(1) and (2); United Nations Convention against Corruption 2003 ('Corruption Convention'), arts 15–18, 23, 25, and 27; Convention on the Physical Protection of Nuclear Material and Nuclear Facilities (being the Convention on the Physical Protection of Nuclear Material as amended by the Amendment to the Convention on the Physical Protection of Nuclear Material 2005) ('Nuclear Material and Facilities Convention'), art 7(1); International Convention for the Suppression of Acts of Nuclear Terrorism 2005 ('Nuclear Terrorism Convention'), art 5(*a*); International Convention for the Protection of All Persons from Enforced Disappearance 2006 ('Enforced Disappearance Convention'), art 4.

[16] It is by no means uncommon for states parties to rely on existing crimes for the implementation of the obligation of municipal criminalization under at least certain treaties, a practice acquiesced in by the other states parties. This is the case even under the most directly-worded provisions, namely arts 3(1), 5, 6(1), and 6(2) of the Supplementary Slavery Convention, which all provide that the act in question 'shall be a criminal offence under the laws of the states parties'.

[17] See eg Commentaries on the Convention on Combating Bribery of Foreign Public Officials in International Business Transactions (adopted by the Negotiating Conference on 21 November 1997), para 3, in OECD, *Convention on Combating Bribery of Foreign Public Officials in International Business Transactions and Related Documents* (Paris: OECD Publishing, 2011) 14, 14; D McClean, *Transnational Organized Crime. A Commentary on the UN Convention and its Protocols* (Oxford: Oxford University Press, 2007), 67, by implication. For their part, as regards the Torture Convention, Burgers and Danelius (n 3), 129, state: 'Article 4 [of the Torture Convention] does not mean that there must be a specific, separate offence corresponding to torture under article 1 of the convention'. Similarly, M Nowak and E McArthur, *The United Nations Convention Against Torture: A Commentary* (Oxford: Oxford University Press, 2008) state, 233, para 14, that 'the Convention does not oblige States parties to include a specific, separate offence in national criminal law' and, 230, para 1, that it is 'not a strict legal requirement... that States parties fully incorporate the definition of Article 1... into their domestic criminal code'. After surveying the practice of the Committee Against Torture (CAT), and citing especially UN docs CAT/C/CR/30/6, para 6 and CAT/C/CR/29/5, para 6(*a*), the authors conclude, ibid, 239, para 27: 'Based on these findings of the Committee, Article 4 does not explicitly require that the Convention definition of torture be reproduced *verbatim* in national criminal legislation. Rather, States must include a definition of torture which makes torture punishable in national legislation which covers the elements set out in the Convention definition.' See also ibid, 249, para 49, where the authors reiterate that 'the Committee does not go as far as requiring that Article 1 must be reproduced *verbatim* in domestic criminal law'. (As it is, CAT it is not a judicial body vested by the states parties to the Torture Convention with the power authoritatively to interpret the text.)

of the four 1949 Geneva Conventions[18] are even clearer in this regard. They provide:

The High Contracting Parties undertake to enact any legislation necessary to provide effective penal sanctions for... any of the grave breaches of the present Convention...

More recent provisions, such as article 15(2) of the Second Protocol to the Hague Convention of 1954 for the Protection of Cultural Property in the Event of Armed Conflict 1999 ('Second Hague Protocol'), are also sufficiently clear:

Each Party shall adopt such measures as may be necessary to establish as offences under its domestic law the offences set forth in this article...

For their part, the United Nations Convention against Illicit Traffic in Narcotic Drugs and Psychotropic Substances 1988 ('Illicit Traffic Convention'), the United Nations Convention against Transnational Organized Crime 2000 ('Organized Crime Convention'), and the United Nations Convention against Corruption 2003 ('Corruption Convention') are explicit:

Nothing contained in this Convention shall affect the principle that the description of the offences established in accordance with this Convention... is reserved to the domestic law of a State Party and that such offences shall be prosecuted and punished in accordance with that law.[19]

What goes for existing crimes goes equally for crimes of sufficient scope enacted later.

At the same time, reliance on a more general statutory or common-law crime which does not cover all conduct encompassed by the definition of the relevant treaty crime will constitute a breach of the state party's obligation of municipal criminalization.[20] 8.8

Many of the conventions oblige states parties to criminalize the 'unlawful' commission of the relevant conduct.[21] The implication is that it is for the municipal law of 8.9

---

[18] 1949 Geneva Convention I, art 49; 1949 Geneva Convention II, art 50; 1949 Geneva Convention III, art 129; 1949 Geneva Convention IV, art 146.

[19] Illicit Traffic Convention, art 3(11); Organized Crime Convention, art 11(6); Corruption Convention, art 30(9). A similar provision is found in early international criminal conventions. See Convention for the Suppression of the Illicit Traffic in Dangerous Drugs 1936 ('Dangerous Drugs Convention'), art 15 ('The present Convention does not affect the principle that the offences referred to in Articles 2 and 5 shall in each country be defined, prosecuted and punished in conformity with the general rules of its domestic law.'); International Convention for the Suppression of Counterfeiting Currency 1929 ('Counterfeiting Convention'), art 18 ('The present Convention does not affect the principle that the offences referred to in Article 3 should in each country, without ever being allowed impunity, be defined, prosecuted and punished in conformity with the general rules of its domestic law.')

[20] See also Burgers and Danelius (n 3), 129, concluding that, 'whatever solution is adopted, the criminal law must cover all cases falling within the definition in article 1 of the Convention'; Nowak and McArthur (n 17), 239, para 27, stating that states parties must ensure that national criminal law 'covers the elements set out in the Convention definition'. For this reason, as highlighted in Nowak and McArthur (n 17), 233–8, paras 13–26, 240, para 33, and 249, para 49, CAT recommends that states parties to the Torture Convention adopt legislation which mirrors art 1.

[21] See Hague Convention, art 1(*a*); Hague Convention as amended by Beijing Protocol, art 1(1), (2)(*a*), and (3)(*d*); Montreal Convention, art 1(1) and Montreal Convention as amended by

each state party to flesh out any material and mental elements of the offence as are not sufficiently specified in the convention to permit their application by the state party's courts.[22] The word simply makes explicit what is already apparent from the formulation of the obligation of municipal criminalization. The exception in this regard is the grave breaches regime of the 1949 Geneva Conventions, where the words 'unlawful' and 'unlawfully'[23] mean 'in violation of the relevant provisions of the [Convention]', to borrow the more precise formulation of Additional Protocol I.[24]

8.10   Each convention obliges states parties to criminalize specified modes of responsibility for the offence other than commission, among them variously ordering, complicity, attempt, and command responsibility. Such provision is usually sketchy, although recent conventions are more detailed in this regard.[25] It is an open question whether, in an application of the canon of construction *expressio unius exclusio alterius*, the mandating by the treaty of municipal provision for certain modes of responsibility in respect of a treaty crime excludes a state party's voluntary provision for other modes in respect of that crime. The more persuasive view is that it does not, a view supported again in many conventions by the restriction of the obligation of municipal criminalization to 'unlawful' performance of the defined conduct.

8.11   In a few instances, the obligation of municipal criminalization is said to be subject to a state party's constitutional principles and/or 'the basic concepts of its legal system' or 'the fundamental principles of its legal system'.[26] The legal effect of this safeguard clause is, in a reversal of the situation under general international law, to relieve a state party of the relevant obligation should its municipal law not permit compliance with it.[27] Such a clause is to be distinguished from the formulations 'in

the Protocol for the Suppression of Unlawful Acts of Violence at Airports serving International Civil Aviation 1988 ('Montreal Convention as amended by Montreal Protocol'), art 1(1)*bis*; SUA Convention, art 3(1); Protocol for the Suppression of Unlawful Acts against the Safety of Fixed Platforms Located on the Continental Shelf 1988 ('SUA Protocol'), art 2(1); Terrorist Bombings Convention, art 2(1); Financing of Terrorism Convention, art 2(1); 2005 SUA Convention, arts 3(1), 3*bis*(1), 3*ter*, and 3*quater*(*a*); Protocol for the Suppression of Unlawful Acts against the Safety of Fixed Platforms Located on the Continental Shelf 2005 (being the Protocol for the Suppression of Unlawful Acts against the Safety of Fixed Platforms Located on the Continental Shelf 1988 as amended by the Protocol of 2005 to the Protocol for the Suppression of Unlawful Acts against the Safety of Fixed Platforms Located on the Continental Shelf) ('2005 SUA Protocol'), arts 2(1), 2*bis*, and 2*ter*(*a*); Nuclear Terrorism Convention, arts 2(1) and 2(2)(*b*); Beijing Convention, art 1(1), (2), (3)(*b*), and (4)(*d*).

[22] See Boister (n 2), 126.
[23] 1949 Geneva Convention I, art 50; 1949 Geneva Convention II, art 51; 1949 Geneva Convention III, art 130; 1949 Geneva Convention IV, art 147.
[24] Protocol Additional to the Geneva Conventions of 12 August 1949, and relating to the Protection of Victims of International Armed Conflicts 1977 ('Additional Protocol I'), art 85(3), chapeau. See also ibid, art 85(4) ('in violation of the Conventions or the Protocol').
[25] A useful innovation in this respect can be found in art 15(2) of the Second Hague Protocol, which obliges states parties to comply with general principles of international law, 'including the rules extending individual criminal responsibility to persons other than those who directly commit the act', when enacting into their municipal law the crimes provided for in the Protocol.
[26] See Illicit Traffic Convention, art 3(1)(*c*) and (2); Organized Crime Convention, art 6(1)(*b*); Smuggling of Migrants Protocol, art 6(2)(*a*) and (*b*) and (3); Firearms Protocol, art 5(2)(*a*); Corruption Convention, arts 20, 23(1)(*b*), and 26(2).
[27] Consider also, in a variation on the theme, Organized Crime Convention, art 6(2)(*e*) and Corruption Convention, art 23(2)(*e*), which read: 'If required by fundamental principles of the

accordance with fundamental principles of its domestic law',[28] 'in accordance with its domestic law',[29] 'consistent with its legal system',[30] and 'consistent with its legal principles',[31] all of which serve merely to emphasize, usually *ex abundante cautela*, that a state party enjoys a measure of discretion as to precisely how it gives effect to its obligations under the provision in question.[32]

8.12 None of the international criminal conventions specifies that a given defence or given defences must be available to the crime in question, and in general it is understood that the availability or otherwise of defences to treaty crimes is a matter for the law of each state party,[33] provided that the scope of any defence is not such as effectively to decriminalize the conduct that the states parties are obliged to criminalize.[34] This discretion is made explicit in the Illicit Traffic Convention, the Organized Crime Convention, and the Corruption Convention, which each provide that nothing in the convention 'shall affect the principle that the description...of the applicable legal defences...is reserved to the domestic law of a State Party'.[35] That defences to treaty crimes may in principle be pleaded under municipal law is similarly implied once more by the reference in the obligation of municipal criminalization to 'unlawful' performance of the impugned conduct. But a handful of conventions prohibit the availability of specific defences to the relevant crimes.[36]

8.13 Although the gist of the Rome Statute of the International Criminal Court ('Rome Statute'), unlike that of the main corpus of multilateral treaties in the field of international criminal law, is not the undertaking by states parties of obligations in relation to their national criminal justice systems, article 70(4)(*a*) of the Statute nonetheless obliges each state party to 'extend its criminal laws penalizing offences against the integrity of its own investigative or judicial process to offences against the administration of justice referred to in [article 70(1)]'.

8.14 Certain provisions of the Organized Crime Convention and Corruption Convention oblige states parties to 'consider adopting'[37] legislation to make certain conduct an offence under their municipal law.

---

domestic law of a State Party, it may be provided that the offences set forth in...this article do not apply to the persons who committed the predicate offence'.

[28] Organized Crime Convention, art 6(1); Corruption Convention, art 23(1).
[29] Corruption Convention, art 27(1), (2), and (3).
[30] Illicit Traffic Convention, art 3(9).   [31] Corruption Convention, art 26(1).
[32] See eg McClean (n 17), 77.   [33] See also Boister (n 2), 125 and 128.
[34] If deliberate, such subversion of the relevant offence by a state party would amount to a failure to fulfil in good faith the obligation of municipal criminalization.
[35] Illicit Traffic Convention, art 3(11); Organized Crime Convention, art 11(6); Corruption Convention, art 30(9). A similar provision is found in early international criminal conventions. See Dangerous Drugs Convention, art 15 ('The present Convention does not affect the principle that the offences referred to in Articles 2 and 5 shall in each country be defined, prosecuted and punished in conformity with the general rules of its domestic law.'); Counterfeiting Convention, art 18 ('The present Convention does not affect the principle that the offences referred to in Article 3 should in each country, without ever being allowed impunity, be defined, prosecuted and punished in conformity with the general rules of its domestic law.')
[36] See *infra* paras 8.78–8.80.
[37] Organized Crime Convention, art 8(2); Corruption Convention, arts 16(2), 18–22, and 24.

B. Provision for Appropriate Penalties

8.15 A second obligation, linked to the obligation of municipal criminalization, undertaken by states parties to most of the international criminal conventions is that of making the offence in question punishable by appropriate penalties which take into account its grave nature.[38] The conventions concluded under the auspices of the International Civil Aviation Organization (ICAO) speak, to equivalent effect, of 'severe' penalties.[39] An analogous obligation to provide 'effective' penalties is found in the Genocide Convention[40] and in the four 1949 Geneva Conventions,[41] while the Convention on Combating Bribery of Foreign Public Officials in International Business Transactions 1997 ('OECD Bribery Convention') requires 'effective, proportionate and dissuasive' criminal penalties.[42] It should go without saying that the word 'effective' does not impose an obligation of result.

8.16 It is left to each state party to determine, within the bounds of good faith,[43] what an 'appropriate', 'severe' or 'effective' penalty is,[44] although the Illicit Traffic Convention provides the examples of 'imprisonment or other forms of deprivation of liberty, pecuniary sanctions and confiscation'.[45] Only statutory provision for a manifestly insufficient penalty will constitute a breach of the relevant obligation. For its part, the OECD Bribery Convention specifies that the range of penalties available for the offence of bribery of a foreign public official 'shall be comparable to that applicable to the bribery of the Party's own public officials'.[46]

8.17 Reliance on a more general statutory or common-law crime, whether existing or enacted later, to render punishable a treaty crime would violate a state party's obligation to make the offence punishable by penalties that reflect its gravity if the punishment attaching to the crime were inappropriately mild.

8.18 The Illicit Traffic Convention and the Protocol against the Smuggling of Migrants by Land, Sea and Air to the United Nations Convention against Transnational Organized Crime 2000 ('Smuggling of Migrants Protocol') oblige states parties

---

[38] See Hostages Convention, art 2; Internationally Protected Persons Convention, art 2(2); Nuclear Material Convention, art 7(2); Torture Convention, art 4(2); Illicit Traffic Convention, art 3(4)(*a*); SUA Convention, art 5; Mercenaries Convention, art 5(3); UN and Associated Personnel Convention, art 9(2); Terrorist Bombings Convention, art 4(*b*); Financing of Terrorism Convention, art 4(*b*); Children Protocol, art 3(3); Organized Crime Convention, art 11(1); Corruption Convention, art 30(1); Nuclear Material and Facilities Convention, art 7(2); Nuclear Terrorism Convention, art 5(*b*); 2005 SUA Convention, art 5; Enforced Disappearance Convention, art 7(1).

[39] See Hague Convention, art 2; Hague Convention as amended by Beijing Protocol, art 2; Montreal Convention, art 3; Beijing Convention, art 3. As Nowak and McArthur (n 17), 249, para 50, correctly point out, there is no substantive difference between this second formulation and the first.

[40] See Genocide Convention, art V.

[41] See 1949 Geneva Convention I, art 49; 1949 Geneva Convention II, art 50; 1949 Geneva Convention III, art 129; 1949 Geneva Convention IV, art 146.

[42] OECD Bribery Convention, art 3(1). See also ibid, art 8(2) ('effective, proportionate and dissuasive civil, administrative or criminal sanctions'); Corruption Convention, art 26(4) ('effective, proportionate and dissuasive criminal or non-criminal sanctions').

[43] See VCLT, art 26.

[44] See Burgers and Danelius (n 3), 129; Nowak and McArthur (n 17), 230, para 2 and 239–42, paras 28–36; Boister (n 2), 130–1.

[45] Illicit Traffic Convention, art 3(4)(*a*). [46] OECD Bribery Convention, art 3(1).

to treat certain factors pertaining to the commission of the crime as aggravating circumstances,[47] while the International Convention for the Protection of All Persons from Enforced Disappearance 2006 ('Enforced Disappearance Convention') permits a state party to treat certain factors as such.[48] The Enforced Disappearance Convention also permits a state to treat certain factors as mitigating circumstances.[49]

The Illicit Traffic Convention, the Organized Crime Convention, and the Corruption Convention oblige states parties to take into account the seriousness of the offence in question and, in accordance with the first, the seriousness of any aggravating circumstances 'when considering the eventuality of early release or parole of persons convicted of [the pertinent] offences'.[50] 8.19

C. Establishment of Jurisdiction

The various international criminal conventions oblige or, in some instances, permit states parties to take measures necessary to enable them to exercise their respective national criminal jurisdictions over the specified offence on a variety of bases. The obligation to establish jurisdiction over an offence is to be distinguished from the obligation to prosecute or extradite suspected offenders found in a state party's territory.[51] The former refers to a state party's obligation to empower its criminal courts to try the offence on the jurisdictional bases stipulated. 8.20

A treaty's stipulation or authorization of the provision by states parties for specific heads of prescriptive jurisdiction raises the question of the *pacta tertiis* rule, since a treaty may not infringe the international legal rights of third states[52] and none of the relevant treaty provisions expressly restricts the scope of the obligation or permission to provide for specific heads of jurisdiction to situations where the alleged offender is a national of a state party. The answer to the question is as follows. The *pacta tertiis* rule is not violated by the prosecution for a treaty 8.21

---

[47] See Illicit Traffic Convention, art 3(5); Smuggling of Migrants Protocol, art 6(3).
[48] See Enforced Disappearance Convention, art 7(2)(*b*). It is hard to see why states parties need permission to do this.
[49] See ibid, art 7(2)(*a*). Again, the need for such a provision is not obvious.
[50] Illicit Traffic Convention, art 3(7); Organized Crime Convention, art 11(4); Corruption Convention, art 30(5).
[51] See also eg *Arrest Warrant of 11 April 2000 (Democratic Republic of the Congo v Belgium)*, ICJ Rep 2002, 3, 173–5, paras 59–62 (diss op Van den Wyngaert); United Nations, *Commentary on the United Nations Convention against Illicit Traffic in Narcotic Drugs and Psychotropic Substances Done at Vienna on 20 December 1988* (New York: United Nations, 1998), UN doc E/CN.7/590 (1998), 100, para 4.2.
[52] Recall *supra* para 3.37 n 105 that the formulation of the *pacta tertiis* rule in art 34 of the VCLT does not adequately reflect customary international law. It is not simply that a treaty cannot create obligations or rights for third states without their consent. It is also the case that a treaty may not impinge upon the legal rights of third states without these states' consent. See eg para 2 of the commentary to draft art 30 (the eventual art 34) of the ILC's Draft Articles on the Law of Treaties, *Ybk ILC 1966*, vol II, 226 ('nor modify in any way their legal rights without their consent'); *Island of Palmas (Netherlands/United States of America)*, 2 RIAA 829, 842 (1928); A McNair, *The Law of Treaties* (Oxford: Clarendon Press, 1961), 321.

crime of a national of a third state before the courts of a state party in cases where the crime is alleged to have taken place on the state party's territory or on a ship on the high seas flagged to the state party or on board an aircraft in flight registered in the state party; where the crime is alleged to have taken place while the accused was serving in the armed forces of the state party; as regards at least serious offences against the person, where the victim of the alleged crime was a national of the state party at the time of alleged commission; where the alleged crime was directed against a sufficiently vital interest of the state party or had sufficiently direct and substantial effects within its territory; or where the conduct for which the alleged offender is prosecuted would under customary international law constitute the crime of genocide, a crime against humanity, a war crime, the crime of aggression or some other crime under customary international law. In other words, as long as the treaty-based head of jurisdiction relied on as the basis of the court's competence is one recognized by customary international law in respect of the conduct for which the alleged offender is prosecuted, the international legal situation is in essence no different than in relation to the prosecution of any other offence under the law of the forum state. The international legal complexion changes, however, where the treaty-based head of jurisdiction relied on is not one recognized by customary international law in respect of the conduct in question. This is the case in respect of most treaty crimes as regards the exercise of universal jurisdiction over third-state nationals. Such exercise will be internationally unlawful.[53]

8.22   In the immediately foregoing light, the customary rule of treaty interpretation reflected in article 31(3)(c) of the Vienna Convention on the Law of Treaties 1969 ('VCLT')[54] furnishes a ground for arguing that a treaty-based obligation or permission to establish over an offence a prescriptive jurisdiction exorbitant as a matter of customary international law is to be read down to extend only to where the alleged offender is a national of a state party. An alternative outcome, justified by reference to the same rule of treaty interpretation, would be to read down the typically-accompanying obligation to prosecute or extradite alleged offenders[55] so that it extends only to those cases where the jurisdictional basis for prosecution or extradition is internationally lawful.

8.23   Unique to date in this regard is article 16(2)(b) of the Second Hague Protocol, which specifies that the Protocol imposes no obligation to establish jurisdiction over nationals of a state not party to the Protocol, a 'carve-out' which is further

---

[53] See also A Cassese, 'Is the Bell Tolling for Universality? A Plea for a Sensible Notion of Universal Jurisdiction' (2003) 1 *JICJ* 589, 594; D Akande, 'The Jurisdiction of the International Criminal Court over Nationals of Non-Parties: Legal Basis and Limits' (2003) 1 *JICJ* 618, 623; V Lowe and C Staker, 'Jurisdiction', in MD Evans (ed), *International Law* (3rd edn, Oxford: Oxford University Press, 2010), 313, 328.

[54] VCLT, art 31(3)(c) requires, in the interpretation of a treaty provision, the taking into account of any other relevant rules of international law applicable in the relations between the states parties. This requirement was considered consonant with customary international law in, *inter alia*, *Certain Questions of Mutual Assistance in Criminal Matters (Djibouti v France), Judgment*, ICJ Rep 2008, 177, 219, para 112.

[55] See *infra* paras 8.48–8.57.

stated to apply to members of the armed forces of non-states parties. The provision is without prejudice to a state party's voluntary provision for jurisdiction in respect of the offences specified in the Protocol over the nationals and service personnel of non-states parties.

In obliging or permitting states parties to establish prescriptive jurisdiction on a variety of bases over the same offence, the international criminal conventions foreshadow instances of concurrent jurisdiction. None of the conventions mandates a hierarchy among the multiple heads of jurisdiction it provides for,[56] although the Convention for the Suppression of Unlawful Acts against the Safety of Maritime Navigation 1988 as amended by its Protocol of 2005 ('2005 SUA Convention') establishes a priority as between the prescriptive criminal jurisdiction of the flag state and any prescriptive jurisdiction potentially enjoyed by a state that arrests the vessel with the flag state's consent.[57] Some of the more recent conventions make provision among states parties enjoying concurrent jurisdiction for consultation and efforts towards coordination in the exercise of jurisdiction.[58]

8.24

(i) Miscellaneous jurisdictional bases

All bar one of the relevant conventions oblige states parties to establish jurisdiction over the offence on the basis of territoriality.[59] It is significant in this regard that, as a matter of international law, a state's territory includes its territorial

8.25

---

[56] See also Boister (n 2), 152–3. See also, in relation to specific conventions, United Nations (n 51), 101, para 4.4; Nowak and McArthur (n 17), 317, paras 163 and 165, according to whom the drafters of the Torture Convention expressly rejected the imposition of a hierarchy among the concurrent jurisdictions provided for in the Convention.

[57] See 2005 SUA Convention, art 8*bis*(8).

[58] See OECD Bribery Convention, art 4(3) ('When more than one Party has jurisdiction over an alleged offence described in this Convention, the Parties involved shall, at the request of one of them, consult with a view to determining the most appropriate jurisdiction for prosecution.'); Financing of Terrorism Convention, art 7(5) ('When more than one State Party claims jurisdiction over the offences set forth in [the Convention], the relevant States Parties shall strive to co-ordinate their actions appropriately...'); Organized Crime Convention, art 15(5) ('If a State Party exercising its jurisdiction under paragraph 1 or 2 of this article has been notified, or has otherwise learned, that any other States Parties are conducting an investigation, prosecution or judicial proceeding in respect of the same conduct, the competent authorities of those States Parties shall, as appropriate, consult one another with a view to coordinating their actions.'); Corruption Convention, art 42(5) (ditto).

[59] See Hague Convention as amended by Beijing Protocol, art 4(1)(*a*); Montreal Convention, art 5(1)(*a*); Internationally Protected Persons Convention, art 3(1)(*a*); Hostages Convention, art 5(1)(*a*); Nuclear Material Convention, art 8(1)(*a*); Torture Convention, art 5(1)(*a*); SUA Convention, art 6(1)(*b*) (with explicit reference to territorial sea); Illicit Traffic Convention, art 4(1)(*a*)(i); Mercenaries Convention, art 9(1)(*a*); UN and Associated Personnel Convention, art 10(1)(*a*); OECD Bribery Convention, art 4(1); Terrorist Bombings Convention, art 6(1)(*a*); Second Hague Protocol, art 16(1)(*a*); Financing of Terrorism Convention, art 7(1)(*a*); Children Protocol, art 4(1); Organized Crime Convention, art 15(1)(*a*); Corruption Convention, art 42(1)(*a*); Nuclear Material and Facilities Convention, art 8(1)(*a*); Nuclear Terrorism Convention, art 9(1)(*a*); 2005 SUA Convention, art 6(1)(*b*) (with explicit reference to territorial sea); Enforced Disappearance Convention, art 9(1)(*a*); Beijing Convention, art 8(1)(*a*). See also Rome Statute, art 70(4)(*a*). An obligation to provide for territorial jurisdiction is also implicit in Genocide Convention, art VI, as pointed out in *Arrest Warrant* (n 51), 71, para 27 (joint sep op Higgins, Kooijmans, and Buergenthal).

sea and superjacent airspace. In most contexts, provision for territorial jurisdiction will involve no legislative measures on the part of states parties above and beyond the criminalization of the offence, but the situation may be different as regards jurisdiction in respect of the state's territorial sea and superjacent airspace.[60]

8.26 The Protocol for the Suppression of Unlawful Acts against the Safety of Fixed Platforms Located on the Continental Shelf 1988 ('SUA Protocol') and the Protocol for the Suppression of Unlawful Acts against the Safety of Fixed Platforms Located on the Continental Shelf 2005 ('2005 SUA Protocol') mandate the extension of a state party's jurisdiction to cover specified offences taking place on a fixed platform located on the state party's continental shelf.[61]

8.27 Extraterritorial jurisdiction over the offence on the basis of nationality is mandated by a host of conventions,[62] while the same jurisdiction is permitted—in what is no more than a restatement of the position under customary international law—by four further instruments.[63] In many civil-law states, provision for nationality jurisdiction, like provision for territorial jurisdiction, will flow automatically from criminalization, but the position is different in other states, especially in those of the common-law tradition. For its part, the OECD Bribery Convention provides that '[e]ach Party which has jurisdiction to prosecute its nationals for offences committed abroad shall take such measures as may be necessary to establish its jurisdiction to do so in respect of the bribery of a foreign public official, according to the same principles'.[64]

8.28 Extraterritorial jurisdiction over non-nationals on the basis of the protective principle is mandated in relation to the crimes specified in the Convention on the Prevention and Punishment of Crimes against Internationally Protected Persons, including Diplomatic Agents 1973 ('Internationally Protected Persons Convention')[65] and is permitted by the International Convention for the Suppression of Terrorist Bombings 1997 ('Terrorist Bombings Convention'), the International Convention for the Suppression of the Financing of Terrorism 1999 ('Financing of Terrorism Convention'), and the International Convention

---

[60] See also United Nations (n 51), 104–5, para 4.15; Nowak and McArthur (n 17), 309, para 145.

[61] SUA Protocol, art 3(1)(*a*); 2005 SUA Protocol, art 3(1)(*a*).

[62] See Hague Convention as amended by Beijing Protocol, art 4(1)(*e*); Internationally Protected Persons Convention, art 3(1)(*b*); Hostages Convention, art 5(1)(*b*); Nuclear Material Convention, art 8(1)(*b*); Torture Convention, art 5(1)(*b*); SUA Convention, art 6(1)(*c*); SUA Protocol, art 3(1)(*b*); Mercenaries Convention, art 9(1)(*b*); UN and Associated Personnel Convention, art 10(1)(*b*); Terrorist Bombings Convention, art 6(1)(*c*); Second Hague Protocol, art 16(1)(*b*); Financing of Terrorism Convention, art 7(1)(*c*); Nuclear Material and Facilities Convention, art 8(1)(*b*); Nuclear Terrorism Convention, art 9(1)(*c*); 2005 SUA Convention, art 6(1)(*c*); Enforced Disappearance Convention, art 9(1)(*b*); Beijing Convention, art 8(1)(*e*). See also Rome Statute, art 70(4)(*a*).

[63] Illicit Traffic Convention, art 4(2)(*a*)(ii) (along with jurisdiction on the basis of residency); Children Protocol, art 4(2)(*a*) (ditto); Organized Crime Convention, art 15(2)(*b*); Corruption Convention, art 42(2)(*b*).

[64] OECD Bribery Convention, art 4(2).

[65] Internationally Protected Persons Convention, art 3(1)(*c*), referring to an offence 'committed against an internationally protected person...who enjoys his status as such by virtue of functions which he exercises on behalf of that State'.

for the Suppression of Acts of Nuclear Terrorism 2005 ('Nuclear Terrorism Convention').[66] Similarly, a range of conventions variously mandate or permit what can be characterized as the assertion of the protective principle in relation to offences committed 'in order' or 'in an attempt' 'to compel [a state party] to do or abstain from doing any act'.[67]

Extraterritorial jurisdiction over non-nationals on the basis of passive personality is permitted by a clutch of conventions.[68] No convention to date obliges states parties to provide for passive personality jurisdiction. 8.29

Most international criminal conventions mandate the establishment of jurisdiction over offences taking place on an aircraft registered in or a ship flying the flag of the relevant state party.[69] Further mandatory jurisdictional rules with respect to offences on board aircraft are laid down in the conventions concluded under the aegis of ICAO.[70] In addition, the assertion of jurisdiction over specified offences on board an aircraft operated by the government of the state party in question is permitted by the Terrorist Bombings Convention, the Financing of Terrorism Convention, and the Nuclear Terrorism Convention.[71] 8.30

Provision for a variant of passive personality jurisdiction is mandated by the Convention for the Suppression of Unlawful Seizure of Aircraft as amended by the Protocol supplementary to Convention for the Suppression of Unlawful Seizure of Aircraft 2010 ('Hague Convention as amended by Beijing Protocol'), the Convention for the Suppression of Unlawful Acts against the Safety of Civilian 8.31

---

[66] Terrorist Bombings Convention, art 6(2)(b), referring to an offence 'committed against a State or government facility of that State abroad, including an embassy or other diplomatic or consular premises of that State'; Financing of Terrorism Convention, art 7(2)(b) (ditto); Nuclear Terrorism Convention, art 9(2)(b) (ditto).

[67] See Hostages Convention, art 5(1)(c) (mandatory); SUA Convention, art 6(2)(c) (permissive); SUA Protocol, art 3(2)(c) (permissive); UN and Associated Personnel Convention, art 10(2)(c) (permissive); Terrorist Bombings Convention, art 6(2)(d) (permissive); Financing of Terrorism Convention, art 7(2)(c) (permissive); Nuclear Terrorism Convention, art 9(2)(d) (permissive); 2005 SUA Convention, art 6(2)(c) (permissive); 2005 SUA Protocol, art 3(2)(c) (permissive).

[68] See Hague Convention as amended by Beijing Protocol, art 4(2)(a); Hostages Convention, art 5(1)(d); Torture Convention, art 5(1)(c); SUA Convention, art 6(2)(b); SUA Protocol, art 3(2)(b); UN and Associated Personnel Convention, art 10(2)(b); Terrorist Bombings Convention, art 6(2)(a); Financing of Terrorism Convention, art 7(2)(a); Children Protocol, art 4(2)(b); Organized Crime Convention, art 15(2)(b); Corruption Convention, art 42(2)(a); Nuclear Terrorism Convention, art 9(2)(a); 2005 SUA Convention, art 6(2)(b); 2005 SUA Protocol, art 3(2)(b); Enforced Disappearance Convention, art 9(1)(c); Beijing Convention, art 8(2)(a).

[69] See Hague Convention, art 4(1)(a) (aircraft only); Hague Convention as amended by Beijing Protocol, art 4(1)(b) (aircraft only); Montreal Convention, art 5(1)(b) (aircraft only); Internationally Protected Persons Convention, art 3(1)(a); Hostages Convention, art 5(1)(a); Nuclear Material Convention, art 8(1)(a); Torture Convention, art 5(1)(a); SUA Convention, art 6(1)(a) (ships only); Illicit Traffic Convention, art 4(1)(a)(ii); Mercenaries Convention, art 9(1)(a); UN and Associated Personnel Convention, art 10(1)(a); Terrorist Bombings Convention, art 6(1)(b); Financing of Terrorism Convention, art 7(1)(b); Children Protocol, art 4(1); Organized Crime Convention, art 15(1)(b); Corruption Convention, art 42(1)(b); Nuclear Material and Facilities Convention, art 8(1)(a); Nuclear Terrorism Convention, art 9(1)(b); 2005 SUA Convention, art 6(1)(a) (ships only); Enforced Disappearance Convention, art 9(1)(a); Beijing Convention, art 8(1)(b) (aircraft only).

[70] See Hague Convention, art 4(1)(b) and (c); Montreal Convention, art 5(1)(c) and (d); Beijing Convention, art 8(1)(c) and (d).

[71] Terrorist Bombings Convention, art 6(2)(e); Financing of Terrorism Convention, art 7(2)(e); Nuclear Terrorism Convention, art 9(2)(e).

Aircraft 1971 ('Montreal Convention'), and the Convention on the Suppression of Unlawful Acts relating to International Civil Aviation 2010 ('Beijing Convention') in respect of offences committed against an aircraft registered in the relevant state party[72] and by the Convention for the Suppression of Unlawful Acts against the Safety of Maritime Navigation 1988 ('SUA Convention') and the 2005 SUA Convention in respect of offences against ships flying the flag of the state party.[73]

8.32 A form of the effects doctrine is invoked by some conventions to permit extraterritorial jurisdiction over offences committed by non-nationals.[74]

8.33 Several conventions permit the assertion of extraterritorial jurisdiction over offences committed by stateless persons habitually resident in the state party in question.[75]

(ii) Universal jurisdiction

8.34 The establishment over the relevant offence of prescriptive jurisdiction on the basis of universality is mandated by the great majority of the conventions in the field of international criminal law[76] and permitted by others.[77]

8.35 It is worth emphasizing for the avoidance of doubt that universal jurisdiction properly so called can be as much a function of a treaty provision, be it mandatory or merely permissive, as of customary international law. In this regard, the common casual characterization of universal jurisdiction as the authority under international law of 'all' states or 'any' or 'every' state to criminalize given acts is misleading. All the term 'universal jurisdiction' means is prescriptive jurisdiction, or equally the authority under international law to establish prescriptive

---

[72] See Hague Convention as amended by Beijing Protocol, art 4(1)(*b*); Montreal Convention, art 5(1)(*b*); Beijing Convention, art 8(1)(*b*).

[73] See SUA Convention, art 6(1)(*a*); 2005 SUA Convention, art 6(1)(*a*).

[74] See Illicit Traffic Convention, art 3(1)(*c*)(iv); Financing of Terrorism Convention, art 7(2)(*a*); Organized Crime Convention, art 15(2)(*c*).

[75] See Hague Convention as amended by Beijing Protocol, art 4(2)(*b*); Hostages Convention, art 5(1)(*b*); SUA Convention, art 6(2)(*a*); SUA Protocol, art 3(2)(*a*); Mercenaries Convention, art 9(1)(*b*); UN and Associated Personnel Convention, art 10(2)(*a*); Terrorist Bombings Convention, art 6(2)(*c*); Financing of Terrorism Convention, art 7(2)(*d*); Organized Crime Convention, art 15(2)(*b*); Corruption Convention, art 42(2)(*b*); Nuclear Terrorism Convention, art 9(2)(*c*); 2005 SUA Convention, art 6(2)(*a*); 2005 SUA Protocol, art 3(2)(*a*); Beijing Convention, art 8(2)(*b*).

[76] See 1949 Geneva Convention I, art 49; 1949 Geneva Convention II, art 50; 1949 Geneva Convention III, art 129; 1949 Geneva Convention IV, art 146; Hague Convention, art 4(2); Hague Convention as amended by Beijing Protocol, art 4(3); Montreal Convention, art 5(2); Internationally Protected Persons Convention, art 3(2); Hostages Convention, art 5(2); Nuclear Material Convention, art 8(2); Torture Convention, art 5(2); SUA Convention, art 6(4); SUA Protocol, art 3(4); Mercenaries Convention, art 9(2); UN and Associated Personnel Convention, art 10(4); Second Hague Protocol, art 16(1)(*c*) (in relation to only some offences provided for in the Protocol); Terrorist Bombings Convention, art 6(4); Financing of Terrorism Convention, art 7(4); Children Protocol, art 4(3); Nuclear Material and Facilities Convention, art 8(2); Nuclear Terrorism Convention, art 9(4); 2005 SUA Convention, art 6(4); 2005 SUA Protocol, art 3(4); Enforced Disappearance Convention, art 9(2); Beijing Convention, art 8(3).

[77] See Apartheid Convention, art V; Illicit Traffic Convention, art 4(2)(*b*); Organized Crime Convention, art 15(4); Corruption Convention, art 42(4).

jurisdiction, in the absence of any other internationally-accepted jurisdictional nexus.[78] The authority under international law to establish prescriptive jurisdiction in the absence of any other internationally-accepted jurisdictional nexus may, by virtue of customary international law, be vested in all states as against nationals of all states or it may be the preserve of states parties to a treaty and only as against nationals of other states parties.[79]

8.36 Pursuant to the most common version of the pertinent provision, each state party undertakes to 'take such measures as may be necessary to establish its jurisdiction over the offences [in question] in cases where the alleged offender is present in its territory', without any requirement that these offences take place on the territory of that state or that the alleged offender or the victim be one of its nationals. The effect of this provision, as alluded to by the ICJ in *Obligation to Prosecute or Extradite*,[80] is to oblige states parties to enact legislation, where necessary, asserting universal prescriptive jurisdiction over the relevant offences.[81] The rider as to the alleged offender's presence in the jurisdiction prevents the provision from giving rise to an obligation on states parties to empower their courts to try an accused *in absentia*, an obligation which would in practice prevent the many states that insist on trial *in personam* from becoming parties to the treaty.

8.37 The standard formulation of the universality provision speaks of a state party's obligation to take such measures as may be necessary to establish jurisdiction over the relevant offences in cases where the alleged offender is present in its territory 'and it does not extradite him'. The final words in no way restrict the scope of a state party's obligation to assert over the offences what is universal prescriptive jurisdiction pure and simple—that is, to deem the specified conduct criminal at point of commission in the absence of any other recognized nexus. The contingent circumstances of a state party's subsequent exercise, *viz* enforcement, of a prescriptive jurisdiction provided for by it can logically have no effect on the extent of the latter to begin with and thereby on the extent of any treaty obligation to provide for it. The reference to extradition is no more than an allusion, and a misleading one at that,[82] to the distinct obligation *aut dedere aut judicare* found in the same conventions.

---

[78] In this light, the term 'quasi-universal jurisdiction' sometimes used in the literature to refer to universal jurisdiction mandated or permitted by treaty is both misbegotten and meaningless.
[79] See also eg Lowe and Staker (n 53), 328; R Cryer *et al*, *An Introduction to International Criminal Law and Procedure* (3rd edn, Cambridge: Cambridge University Press, 2014), 331.
[80] *Obligation to Prosecute or Extradite* (n 3), 451, paras 74 and 75, 453, para 84, 455, para 91, and 461, para 119.
[81] Judge Higgins, Kooijmans, and Buergenthal's characterization of such provisions in *Arrest Warrant* (n 51) as 'obligatory territorial jurisdiction over persons, albeit in relation to acts committed elsewhere' (ibid, 75, para 41) or 'a territorial jurisdiction over persons for extraterritorial events' (ibid, 75, para 42) not only mistakenly conflates jurisdiction to prescribe and jurisdiction to enforce but, as regards the former, is a little absurd. An assertion of prescriptive jurisdiction over conduct that takes place outside the territory of the prescriptive state is, regardless of how it is enforced, an assertion of extraterritorial jurisdiction, as Judge Loder noted in *The SS 'Lotus'*, PCIJ Rep Ser A No 10 (1927), 35 (diss op Loder).
[82] See *infra* paras 8.54–8.55.

8.38 The four 1949 Geneva Conventions also oblige states parties to empower their courts to try grave breaches of the Conventions on the basis of universality, utilizing a common provision which elides the obligation to provide for universal jurisdiction with the obligation to prosecute. The provision reads in relevant part:

> Each High Contracting Party shall be under the obligation to…bring [persons alleged to have committed, or to have ordered to be committed, such grave breaches], regardless of their nationality, before its own courts.[83]

The explicit immateriality of the nationality of the suspect and the implicit immateriality of the place of commission of the offence, the nationality of the victim, and so on add up to make this, *inter alia*, an obligation to assert universal jurisdiction.[84]

8.39 The obligation to establish jurisdiction 'when the aircraft on board which the offence is committed lands in its territory with the alleged offender still on board', as found in the conventions concluded under the auspices of ICAO,[85] is a form of mandatory universal jurisdiction.[86]

8.40 Article VI of the Genocide Convention neither mandates nor expressly permits universal jurisdiction over the crime of genocide. Equally, however, as the ICJ made clear in *Application of the Convention on the Prevention and Punishment of the Crime of Genocide*, article VI 'certainly does not prohibit States, with respect to genocide, from conferring jurisdiction on their criminal courts based on criteria other than where the crime was committed which are compatible with international law, in particular the nationality of the accused'.[87] For its part, the European Court of Human Rights held in *Jorgić v Germany* that the conclusion arrived at by the German courts that the Genocide Convention did not exclude the exercise

---

[83] 1949 Geneva Convention I, art 49; 1949 Geneva Convention II, art 50; 1949 Geneva Convention III, art 129; 1949 Geneva Convention IV, art 146.

[84] In *Arrest Warrant* (n 51), two judges denied that the grave breaches provisions of the Geneva Conventions contain any jurisdictional provision. See ibid, 38, para 6 and 44, para 17 (sep op Guillaume) and 56, para 7 (dec Ranjeva). Others appeared to cast doubts. See ibid, 71–2, para 31 (joint sep op Higgins, Kooijmans, and Buergenthal). But others still affirmed that the grave breaches provisions mandate universal jurisdiction. See ibid, 122, para 65 (sep op Bula-Bula) and 173–4, para 59 (diss op Van den Wyngaert). In the final analysis, state practice makes it clear and the *travaux préparatoires* confirm that the grave breaches provisions of the 1949 Geneva Conventions do indeed provide for mandatory universal jurisdiction. See, in this regard, R O'Keefe, 'The Grave Breaches Regime and Universal Jurisdiction' (2009) 7 *JICJ* 811, 814–15.

[85] See Hague Convention, art 4(1)(*b*); Hague Convention as amended by Beijing Protocol, art 4(1)(*c*); Montreal Convention, art 5(1)(*c*); Beijing Convention, art 8(1)(*c*).

[86] To the extent that the offence of hijacking could be considered to continue until the hijacker relinquishes control of the aircraft, such jurisdiction could also be considered a manifestation of objective territoriality. See Boister (n 2), 139. The same argument could not plausibly be made in relation to aircraft sabotage.

[87] *Application of the Convention for the Prevention and Punishment of the Crime of Genocide (Bosnia and Herzegovina v Serbia and Montenegro), Judgment*, ICJ Rep 2007, 43, 227, para 442. See, similarly, *Attorney-General for Israel v Eichmann*, 36 ILR 5, 18, para 25 (Israel (DC Jerusalem) 1961). It is worth recalling in this regard that universal jurisdiction over genocide is most likely permitted by customary international law.

of extraterritorial jurisdiction, including universal jurisdiction, by the contracting parties 'must be considered as reasonable (and indeed convincing)'.[88]

The exercise of universal jurisdiction over—and *a fortiori* the municipal criminalization of—those breaches of the 1949 Geneva Conventions (including of common article 3) and of their 1977 Additional Protocols (including of Additional Protocol II) not classified as grave breaches is arguably a permissible implementation of the obligation imposed on states parties by the grave breaches provisions to 'take measures necessary for the suppression of all acts contrary to the provisions of the present Convention other than the grave breaches defined in the following Article'.[89] The same goes, *mutatis mutandis*, in relation to article 28 of the Hague Convention for the Protection of Cultural Property in the Event of Armed Conflict 1954 and article 21 of its Second Protocol. 8.41

(iii) Residual jurisdictional bases

The great majority of the international criminal conventions include a residual provision to the following effect: 8.42

This Convention does not exclude any criminal jurisdiction exercised in accordance with national law.[90]

It is unclear whether such a clause effectively constitutes an agreement among the states parties that the exercise over the relevant offences of literally any head of prescriptive jurisdiction provided for in national law is to be considered permissible as among the states parties[91]—but not mandatory, in contrast to those heads of jurisdiction specified as such in the convention—or whether its purpose is no more than to spell out *ex abundante cautela* that the convention's requirement or express

---

[88] *Jorgić v Germany*, 148 ILR 234, 259, para 68 (ECtHR 2007).
[89] 1949 Geneva Convention I, art 49; 1949 Geneva Convention II, art 50; 1949 Geneva Convention III, art 129; 1949 Geneva Convention IV, art 146. See also T Meron, 'International Criminalization of Internal Atrocities' (1995) 89 *AJIL* 554, 568–71.
[90] Hague Convention, art 4(3); Hague Convention as amended by Beijing Protocol, art 4(4). See also Montreal Convention, art 5(3); Internationally Protected Persons Convention, art 3(3); Hostages Convention, art 5(3); Nuclear Material Convention, art 8(3); Torture Convention, art 5(3); SUA Convention, art 6(5); SUA Protocol, art 3(5); Illicit Traffic Convention, art 4(3); Mercenaries Convention, art 9(3); UN and Associated Personnel Convention, art 10(5); Terrorist Bombings Convention, art 6(5); Children Protocol, art 4(4); Nuclear Material and Facilities Convention, art 8(3); Nuclear Terrorism Convention, art 9(5); 2005 SUA Convention, art 6(5); 2005 SUA Protocol, art 3(5); Enforced Disappearance Convention, art 9(3); Beijing Convention, art 8(4).
[91] In *Arrest Warrant* (n 51), 174–5, para 61 (diss op Van den Wyngaert), Judge ad hoc Van den Wyngaert expressed the view that a provision to this effect does not exclude the exercise of universal jurisdiction over the offences in question (although this conclusion was predicated on her affirmation, at least in principle, of the *Lotus* presumption). Nowak and McArthur (n 17), 327, para 183, take the same view in specific relation to art 5(3) of the Torture Convention, claiming support in the intention of the drafters (but citing no evidence and admitting earlier that the provision 'did not give rise to any substantive discussions' in the Human Rights Commission or General Assembly). See too Burgers and Danelius (n 3), 133. For a concordant municipal judicial implication that such provisions permit literally any criminal jurisdiction exercised in accordance with national law, see *United States v Rezaq*, ILDC 1391 (US 1998), para 34.

authorization of certain heads of prescriptive jurisdiction is without prejudice to the international lawfulness of the exercise under national law of any other head as may otherwise be internationally lawful, be it permitted by customary international law or mandated or permitted by a different treaty.[92] The ordinary meaning of the word 'any'[93] and the object and purpose of the various conventions suggest the former, and the *pacta tertiis* principle does nothing to militate against such a reading,[94] keeping in mind that any otherwise-exorbitant jurisdiction authorized in effect by the provision would be lawful only *inter se*. In the end, however, little if anything hangs on the difference, given that every convention in which such a provision is found either obliges or permits states parties to exercise the most plenary of all heads of prescriptive jurisdiction, namely universal jurisdiction.

8.43 The text of the provision is no clearer as formulated in three of the more recent treaties, which state:

> Without prejudice to norms of general international law, this Convention does not exclude the exercise of any criminal jurisdiction established by a State Party in accordance with its domestic law.[95]

The specification that the provision is without prejudice to norms of general, *viz* customary, international law could be taken to imply *a contrario* that the convention does not exclude as among the states parties such exercises of criminal jurisdiction in accordance with domestic law as would be exorbitant as a matter of general international law. But, allowing for a degree of imprecise drafting, the same specification might equally be taken to import that what the convention does not exclude are only such exercises of criminal jurisdiction in accordance with domestic law as also accord with general international law. The practical difference is again negligible. Moreover, a wholly different reading is suggested by the *travaux préparatoires* to the Organized Crime Convention, which point to the insertion of the 'without prejudice' clause as a means of underlining *ex abundante cautela* that the provision in no way permits a state party to enforce its law in the territory of another state party.[96]

---

[92] See eg United Nations (n 51), 116, para 4.40. It is possible too that the provision is geared towards the lawfulness as much of the exercise, in the sense of the method of enforcement, of the underlying prescriptive jurisdiction as of the prescriptive jurisdiction itself. That is, a collateral purpose of the provision may be to clarify, *ex abundante cautela*, that the convention's mandating or express permitting of universal prescriptive jurisdiction in cases where the alleged offender is present in a state party's territory is without prejudice to the international lawfulness of the provision under a state party's law for the exercise *in absentia* of universal jurisdiction over the offence. See, in this regard, Nowak and McArthur (n 17), 327, para 183.

[93] The expression 'any criminal jurisdiction' is not, however, to be taken to include jurisdiction to enforce. The context lent to the words by the immediately preceding paragraphs of the same article makes it abundantly clear that the reference to 'criminal jurisdiction' is to jurisdiction to prescribe alone.

[94] The *pacta tertiis* rule would constitute a rule of international law applicable among the states parties within the meaning of VCLT, art 31(3)(c).

[95] Organized Crime Convention, art 15(6); Corruption Convention, art 42(6); Financing of Terrorism Convention, art 7(6) (inserting 'the' before 'norms').

[96] See UN doc A/AC.254/4/Rev.4, 20 note 102. The point is already made in Organized Crime Convention, art 4(2).

8.44 For its part, article 16(2)(*a*) of the Second Hague Protocol, pertaining to the war crimes (or 'serious violations') provided for in chapter 4 of the Protocol, reads:

[T]his Protocol does not preclude...the exercise of jurisdiction under national and international law that may be applicable, or affect the exercise of jurisdiction under customary international law...

The additional reference to the exercise of jurisdiction 'under...international law that may be applicable' is seemingly to jurisdiction established in accordance with some other relevant treaty provision, such as the grave breaches provisions of Additional Protocol I to the extent that they overlap with the subject-matter of the Protocol,[97] or in accordance with the customary international law of war crimes. The stipulation that the Protocol does not 'affect the exercise of jurisdiction under customary international law' appears to be another way of saying that the Protocol is without prejudice to the customary international rules on jurisdiction to prescribe—the 'norms of general international law' referred to in other conventions.[98]

(iv) Jurisdiction exercised by an international criminal court

8.45 The Genocide Convention and the International Convention on the Suppression and Punishment of the Crime of Apartheid 1973 ('Apartheid Convention') both make express provision for trial of the relevant offence by an international criminal court. Article VI of the Genocide Convention, stated in mandatory terms, reads:

Persons charged with genocide...shall be tried by a competent tribunal of the State in the territory of which the act was committed, or by such international penal tribunal as may have jurisdiction with respect to those contracting Parties which shall have accepted its jurisdiction.

The ICJ has held that article VI's reference to an 'international penal tribunal' whose jurisdiction relevant contracting parties 'have accepted' extends to an international criminal tribunal established pursuant to a resolution of the UN Security Council adopted under chapter VII of the UN Charter whose jurisdiction those contracting parties are obliged to accept and with which they are obliged to co-operate by virtue of the resolution or some other rule of international law.[99] For its part, article V of the Apartheid Convention, stated in permissive terms, reads:

Persons charged with [*apartheid*] may be tried by a competent tribunal of any State Party to the Convention which may acquire jurisdiction over the person of the accused or by an international penal tribunal having jurisdiction with respect to those States Parties which shall have accepted its jurisdiction.

---

[97] See Additional Protocol I, art 85(4)(*d*).   [98] See *supra* para 8.43.
[99] *Application of the Genocide Convention* (n 87), 227–8, paras 445–446. For more on art VI of the Genocide Convention, see *infra* para 8.57.

It is worth recalling that the ICC enjoys jurisdiction *ratione materiae* over the crimes of both genocide, pursuant to articles 5 and 6 of the Rome Statute, and *apartheid*, pursuant to articles 5 and 7(1)(*j*), in the latter instance when the offence satisfies the chapeau requirements of a crime against humanity.

D. Taking into Custody and Making a Preliminary Inquiry

8.46 The majority of the international criminal conventions contain provisions or a provision to the following effect:

> 1. Upon being satisfied, after an examination of information available to it, that the circumstances so warrant, any State Party in whose territory a person alleged to have committed any offence referred to in article 4 is present shall take him into custody or take other legal measures to ensure his presence. The custody and other legal measures shall be as provided in the law of that State but may be continued only for such time as is necessary to enable any criminal or extradition proceedings to be instituted.
> 2. Such State shall immediately make a preliminary inquiry into the facts.[100]

Some of the conventions place the obligations in the opposite, more logical order,[101] others contain no obligation to make a preliminary inquiry into the facts,[102] and others still both omit the obligation of a preliminary inquiry and tie the obligation to assume custody to a request for extradition.[103] Most of the conventions complement the obligation to take alleged offenders into custody and to make a preliminary inquiry into the facts with obligations to assist those in custody in communicating immediately with an appropriate representative of their state of nationality (or, in the case of stateless persons, of habitual residence) and to notify and report to relevant states.[104]

---

[100] Torture Convention, art 6(1) and (2). See also Hague Convention, art 6(1) and (2); Hague Convention as amended by Beijing Protocol, art 6(1) and (2); Montreal Convention, art 6(1) and (2); Hostages Convention, art 6(1); SUA Convention, art 7(1) and (2); Mercenaries Convention, art 10(1); Terrorist Bombings Convention, art 7(1) and (2); Financing of Terrorism Convention, art 9(1) and (2); Nuclear Terrorism Convention, art 10(1) and (2); 2005 SUA Convention, art 7(1) and (2); Enforced Disappearance Convention, art 10(1) and (2); Beijing Convention, art 9(1) and (2).

[101] See Terrorist Bombings Convention, art 7(1) and (2); Financing of Terrorism Convention, art 9(1) and (2); Nuclear Terrorism Convention, art 10(1) and (2).

[102] See Internationally Protected Persons Convention, art 6(1); Nuclear Material Convention, art 9; UN and Associated Personnel Convention, art 13(1); Nuclear Material and Facilities Convention, art 9.

[103] See Illicit Traffic Convention, art 6(8); Organized Crime Convention, art 16(9); Corruption Convention, art 44(10).

[104] See Hague Convention, art 6(3) and (4); Hague Convention as amended by Beijing Protocol, art 6(3) and (4); Montreal Convention, art 6(3) and (4); Internationally Protected Persons Convention, art 6(1) and (2); Hostages Convention, art 6(2), (3), and (6); Torture Convention, art 6(3) and (4); Nuclear Material Convention, art 9; SUA Convention, art 7(3) and (5); Mercenaries Convention, art 10(2), (3), and (5); UN and Associated Personnel Convention, art 13(2); Terrorist Bombings Convention, art 7(3) and (6); Financing of Terrorism Convention, art 9(3) and (6); Nuclear Terrorism Convention, art 10(3) and (6); SUA Convention, art 7(3) and (5); Enforced Disappearance Convention, art 10(2) and (3); Beijing Convention, art 9(3) and (4).

8.47 The nature and content of the preliminary inquiry into the facts required of states parties by article 6(2) of the Torture Convention (and, by implication, by all cognate provisions) was elaborated on by the ICJ in *Questions regarding the Obligation to Prosecute or Extradite*. The Court explained that this preliminary inquiry, 'conducted by those authorities which have the task of drawing up a case file and collecting facts and evidence', 'is intended, like any inquiry carried out by the competent authorities, to corroborate or not the suspicions regarding the person in question'.[105] Although 'the choice of means for conducting the inquiry remains in the hands of the States Parties',[106] co-operation is to be sought, where relevant, from the state in whose territory the crime is alleged to have been committed and from any other state where complaints in relation to the case have been filed.[107] As to the precise point at which a state party must 'immediately make a preliminary inquiry into the facts', in the words of the provision, this is 'as soon as the suspect is identified in the territory of the State'[108] or, putting it another way, as soon as a state party has reason to suspect a person in its territory of being responsible for the crime in question.[109]

E. Prosecution or Extradition (*aut dedere aut judicare*)

8.48 Most of the international criminal conventions impose on states parties—usually by way of a single provision,[110] in two cases by way of two[111]—obligations to the following effect:

The Contracting State in the territory of which the alleged offender is found shall, if it does not extradite him, be obliged, without exception whatsoever and whether or not the offence was committed in its territory, to submit the case to its competent authorities for the purpose of prosecution. Those authorities shall take their decision in the same manner as in the case of any ordinary offence of a serious nature under the law of that State.[112]

This is commonly referred to as the obligation to prosecute or extradite (*aut dedere aut judicare*, literally 'to hand over or to adjudge') suspected offenders. But it is

---

[105] *Obligation to Prosecute or Extradite* (n 3), 453, para 83. As noted by the Court, ibid, the evidence 'may consist of documents or witness statements relating to the events at issue and to the suspect's possible involvement in the matter concerned'.
[106] Ibid, 454, para 86.   [107] Ibid, 453, para 83.   [108] Ibid, 454, para 86.
[109] Ibid, para 88.
[110] See Hague Convention, art 7; Hague Convention as amended by Beijing Protocol, art 7; Montreal Convention, art 7; Internationally Protected Persons Convention, art 7; Hostages Convention, art 8(1); Nuclear Material Convention, art 10; SUA Convention, art 10(1); Mercenaries Convention, art 12; UN and Associated Personnel Convention, art 14; Terrorist Bombings Convention, art 8(1); Financing of Terrorism Convention, art 10(1); Nuclear Material and Facilities Convention, art 10; Nuclear Terrorism Convention, art 11(1); 2005 SUA Convention, art 10(1); Beijing Convention, art 10.
[111] See Torture Convention, art 7(1) and (2); Enforced Disappearance Convention, art 11(1) and (2).
[112] Hague Convention, art 7. See also Second Hague Protocol, art 17(1), omitting the second sentence. See too, in more basic form, 1949 Geneva Convention I, art 49; 1949 Geneva Convention II, art 50; 1949 Geneva Convention III, art 129; 1949 Geneva Convention IV, art 146.

more precisely an obligation on states parties, should they not extradite a suspected offender, to submit the case to their prosecuting authorities with a view to prosecution.

8.49 In *Obligation to Prosecute or Extradite*, the ICJ explained as follows the relationship between the prosecution and extradition limbs of the standard formulation of the obligation *aut dedere aut judicare*:

> [T]he choice between extradition or submission for prosecution, pursuant to the Convention, does not mean that the two alternatives are to be given the same weight. Extradition is an option offered to the State by the Convention, whereas prosecution is an international obligation under the Convention, the violation of which is a wrongful act engaging the responsibility of the State.[113]

In other words, the custodial state's obligation is to prosecute, but it may relieve itself of this obligation by extraditing the suspect to a state willing and able to prosecute.[114] This relationship between the limbs of the provision has two consequences. First, the custodial state's obligation to submit a case to its prosecuting authorities with a view to prosecution is not dependent on its prior receipt and refusal of a request for the suspect's extradition.[115] Rather, the obligation to prosecute arises in all circumstances where the custodial state does not extradite the suspect, including where no request for the suspect's extradition has been received.[116] Secondly, extradition being no more than an option open to the custodial state, the latter's internationally wrongful failure to prosecute an alleged offender present in its territory does not give rise to an obligation to extradite that person to a state that will prosecute. This is clear from the ICJ's decision in *Obligation to Prosecute or Extradite*, insofar as Senegal, whose responsibility under the Torture Convention was engaged by its failure to prosecute Hissène Habré, was not ordered to extradite him to Belgium, which had requested his extradition; rather, the Court ordered Senegal, 'without further delay, [to] submit the case of Mr Hissène Habré to its competent authorities for the purpose of prosecution, if it does not extradite him'.[117]

8.50 As provided for in the Organized Crime Convention and the Corruption Convention, the obligation *aut dedere aut judicare*, contained in a paragraph of an article entitled 'Extradition', is more circumscribed. It reads:

> A State Party in whose territory an alleged offender is found, if it does not extradite such person in respect of an offence to which this article applies solely on the ground that he or she is one of its nationals, shall, at the request of the State Party seeking extradition, be obliged to submit the case without undue delay to its competent authorities for the purpose of prosecution. Those authorities shall take their decision and conduct their

---

[113] *Obligation to Prosecute or Extradite* (n 3), 456, para 95.   [114] Ibid.
[115] But cf the obligation as formulated in OECD Bribery Convention, art 10(3); Organized Crime Convention, art 16(10); Corruption Convention, art 44(11). Consider also, less clearly, Illicit Traffic Convention, art 6(9).
[116] *Obligation to Prosecute or Extradite* (n 3), 456, para 94.
[117] Ibid, 463, para 122(6). See also ibid, 461, para 121.

proceedings in the same manner as in the case of any other offence of a grave nature under the domestic law of that State Party. The States Parties concerned shall cooperate with each other, in particular on procedural and evidentiary aspects, to ensure the efficiency of such prosecution.[118]

The provision has its origins in a more complicated provision in the Illicit Traffic Convention, which does not limit the residual obligation of prosecution to where the state party seeking extradition requests.[119] For its part, the OECD Bribery Convention provides more simply that '[a] Party which declines a request to extradite a person for bribery of a foreign public official solely on the ground that the person is its national shall submit the case to its competent authorities for the purpose of prosecution'.[120] A seemingly weaker version of the analogous provision is found in the Optional Protocol to the Convention on the Rights of the Child on the Sale of Children, Child Prostitution and Child Pornography 2000 ('Children Protocol'), which obliges a state party, on refusal of an extradition request on the basis of the nationality of the alleged offender, to 'take suitable measures' to submit the case to its competent authorities for the purpose of prosecution.[121] Under all these conventions, prosecution is not an obligation in its own right, of which the custodial state may relieve itself via extradition; rather, the obligation to prosecute is triggered only by a refusal to extradite, and in the case of the three more recent conventions it applies only in respect of nationals of the custodial state party. At the same time, the Illicit Traffic Convention, the Organized Crime Convention, and the Corruption Convention all contain a provision to the following effect:

Each State Party shall endeavour to ensure that any discretionary legal powers under its domestic law relating to the prosecution of persons for offences established in accordance with this Convention are exercised to maximise the effectiveness of law enforcement measures in respect of those offences and with due regard to the need to deter the commission of such offences.[122]

Article 5 of the OECD Bribery Convention, after stating that the '[i]nvestigation and prosecution of the bribery of a foreign public official shall be subject to the applicable rules and principles of each Party', provides more pointedly that such investigation and prosecution 'shall not be influenced by considerations of national economic interest, the potential effect upon relations with another State or the identity of the natural or legal persons involved'.

8.51 What is referred to by way of shorthand as the obligation to 'prosecute' is really, as is apparent on the face of the relevant provision, an obligation on a state party in whose territory a suspect is present to submit the case to its prosecuting authorities

---

[118] Organized Crime Convention, art 16(10); Corruption Convention, art 44(11).
[119] See Illicit Traffic Convention, art 6(9).   [120] OECD Bribery Convention, art 10(3).
[121] Children Protocol, art 5(5).
[122] Illicit Traffic Convention, art 3(6); Organized Crime Convention, art 11(2); Corruption Convention, art 30(3).

with a view to prosecution. As the second sentence of the provision makes clear, the obligation does not require that those authorities, in the absence of a satisfactory case, proceed to trial. The point was underlined four decades ago by the International Law Commission (ILC):

> As the article is drafted, it is clear that no obligation is created thereunder to punish or to conduct a trial. The obligation of the State where the alleged offender is present will have been fulfilled once it has submitted the case to its competent authorities... for the purpose of prosecution. It will be up to those authorities to decide whether to prosecute or not, subject to the normal requirement of treaty law that the decision be taken in good faith in the light of all the circumstances involved. The obligation of the State party in such case will be fulfilled under the article even if the decision which those authorities may take is not to commence criminal trial proceedings.[123]

The point was reiterated by the ICJ in *Obligation to Prosecute or Extradite*:

> The obligation to submit the case to the competent authorities for the purpose of prosecution... was formulated in such a way as to leave it to those authorities to decide whether or not to initiate proceedings, thus respecting the independence of States parties' judicial systems.[124]

The Court emphasized that '[t]he obligation to submit the case to the competent authorities... may or may not result in the institution of proceedings, in the light of the evidence before them, relating to the charges against the suspect'.[125]

8.52 The option of extradition to a state which has made an extradition request is exercisable, according to the ICJ, only 'on the condition that [the extradition] is to a state which has jurisdiction in some capacity... to prosecute and try' the suspect.[126] More specifically, the Court, referring to the Torture Convention, spoke of a state with jurisdiction 'pursuant to Article 5 of the Convention',[127] *viz* the article mandating various bases of jurisdiction, the implication being that a state party may extradite a suspect only to another state party. Although there is no indication of the latter condition on the face of the standard *aut dedere aut judicare* formulation,[128] which says simply 'if it does not extradite

---

[123] *Ybk ILC 1972*, vol II, 318. See also International Law Commission, *Report on the work of its fifty-eighth session (1 May to 9 June and 3 July to 11 August 2006)*, UN doc A/61/10 (2006), 396, para 221.
[124] *Obligation to Prosecute or Extradite* (n 3), 455, para 90. See too Burgers and Danelius (n 3), 138; Nowak and McArthur (n 17), 361–2, paras 61–62; United Nations (n 51), 168–9, para 6.37. The formulation might additionally be seen as safeguarding the presumption of the suspect's innocence.
[125] *Obligation to Prosecute or Extradite* (n 3), 456, para 94.   [126] Ibid, 461, para 120.
[127] Ibid.
[128] But cf, speaking of 'hand[ing]... over for trial to another High Contracting Party concerned', 1949 Geneva Convention I, art 49; 1949 Geneva Convention II, art 50; 1949 Geneva Convention III, art 129; 1949 Geneva Convention IV, art 146. Each of these provisions specifies that the high contracting party to which a person is surrendered must have made out a *prima facie* case and that surrender shall be 'in accordance with the provisions of [the surrendering party's] legislation'.

[the suspect]',[129] the interpretative context provided by related provisions points to it.[130] An exception in this respect is the Enforced Disappearance Convention.[131]

8.53 As to the timeframe within which a state party to a treaty containing the obligation *aut dedere aut judicare* must, if it does not extradite the suspect, submit the case to its authorities for the purpose of prosecution, the ICJ stated in *Obligation to Prosecute or Extradite*:

> 114. While Article 7, paragraph 1, of the Convention does not contain any indication as to the time frame for performance of the obligation for which it provides, it is necessarily implicit in the text that it must be implemented within a reasonable time, in a manner compatible with the object and purpose of the Convention.
>
> 115. The Court considers that the obligation on a State to prosecute, provided for in Article 7, paragraph 1, of the Convention, is intended to allow the fulfilment of the Convention's object and purpose, which is 'to make more effective the struggle against torture' (Preamble to the Convention). It is for that reason that proceedings should be undertaken without delay.

The Court later spoke of taking all measures necessary for the implementation of the obligation 'as soon as possible'.[132]

8.54 Although the obligation *aut dedere aut judicare* and the notion of prescriptive jurisdiction are frequently conflated,[133] they are conceptually distinct. It is true that

---

[129] But see Organized Crime Convention, art 16(10); Corruption Convention, art 44(11).

[130] Paragraph 2 of art 5 of the Torture Convention, mandating provision for universal jurisdiction, speaks of 'where the alleged offender is present in any territory under [a state party's] jurisdiction and it does not extradite him pursuant to article 8 to any of the States mentioned in paragraph 1 of this article', paragraph 1 in turn providing that '[e]ach State Party' shall take such measures as may be necessary to establish its jurisdiction over the crime of torture on a range of prescriptive bases other than universal jurisdiction. Article 8 of the Torture Convention makes provision for extradition of alleged offenders from one state party to another. See also, analogously, Hague Convention, arts 4(2) and 8; Hague Convention as amended by Beijing Protocol, arts 4(2) and 8; Montreal Convention, arts 5(2) and 8; Internationally Protected Persons Convention, arts 3(2) and 8; Hostages Convention, art 5(2); Nuclear Material Convention, arts 8(2) and 11; Mercenaries Convention, art 9(2). See also, explicitly, Illicit Traffic Convention, art 4(2)(*b*) ('another Party'); SUA Convention, art 6(4) ('States Parties'); SUA Protocol, art 3(4) ('States Parties'); UN and Associated Personnel Convention, arts 10(4) ('States Parties') and 15; Terrorist Bombings Convention, art 6(4) ('States Parties'); Financing of Terrorism Convention, art 7(4) ('States Parties'); Nuclear Terrorism Convention, art 9(4) ('States Parties'); 2005 SUA Convention, art 6(4) ('States Parties'); 2005 SUA Protocol, art 3(4) ('States Parties'); Beijing Convention, arts 8(3) ('States Parties') and 12.

[131] Enforced Disappearance Convention, arts 9(2) ('unless it extradites or surrenders him or her to another State in accordance with its international obligations') and 11 ('The State Party in the territory under whose jurisdiction a person alleged to have committed an offence of enforced disappearance is found shall, if it does not extradite that person or surrender him or her to another State in accordance with its international obligations or surrender him or her to an international criminal tribunal whose jurisdiction it has recognized, submit the case to its competent authorities for the purpose of prosecution.')

[132] *Obligation to Prosecute or Extradite* (n 3), 460, para 117.

[133] See eg, most egregiously, *Arrest Warrant* (n 51), 24–5, para 59 and 'Universal Criminal Jurisdiction with Respect to the Crime of Genocide, Crimes against Humanity and War Crimes' (Resolution III of the Cracow session of the Institut de droit international), in Institut de droit international, *Annuaire de l'IDI*, vol 71, part II, 297, para 2. But cf *Arrest Warrant* (n 51), 173–5, paras 59–62 (diss op Van den Wyngaert).

the obligation to prosecute presupposes the existence of an underlying jurisdiction and could, in the absence of separate provision for jurisdiction, be taken to confer it, as is the case pursuant to the grave breaches provisions of the 1949 Geneva Conventions. But the point is that, except for the 1949 Geneva Conventions, the various international criminal conventions lay down separate obligations in respect of, on the one hand, prosecution and, on the other, the prescriptive jurisdiction on which such prosecution is based.[134]

8.55   A particularly common manifestation of the foregoing conflation concerns the obligation *aut dedere aut judicare* and universal prescriptive jurisdiction.[135] The two are not inherently connected.[136] The obligation to prosecute or extradite is applicable as much when the underlying prescriptive jurisdiction is founded on territoriality, nationality, the protective principle, passive personality, etc, as when it is founded on universality.[137]

8.56   It is doubtful whether the '*dedere*' limb of the standard obligation *aut dedere aut judicare* is satisfied by surrendering the suspect to an international criminal court with jurisdiction over the alleged crime.[138] Surrender to an international criminal court does not constitute extradition.[139] Moreover, while surrender to a competent international criminal court would seemingly be consonant with the object

---

[134] See also Burgers and Danelius (n 3), 136; Nowak and McArthur (n 17), 351, para 21.

[135] See eg *Preliminary report on the obligation to extradite or prosecute ('aut dedere aut judicare') by Mr Zdsislaw Galicki, Special Rapporteur*, UN doc A/CN.4/571 (7 June 2006). The ILC decided to include the topic of the obligation to extradite or prosecute ('*aut dedere aut judicare*') in its programme of work in 2005. Work on the topic has proved a debacle.

[136] It may well be that the historical origins of the two are linked, but they are now conceptually distinct. It is also true that the option of extradition is alluded to in the standard formulation of the obligation to provide for universal jurisdiction. See *supra* para 8.37. But the point remains that the obligation *aut dedere aut judicare* applies to the exercise as much of other heads of prescriptive jurisdiction as of universality.

[137] See, in this light, International Law Commission, *Report on the work of its fifty-eighth session* (n 123), 397–8, para 226: 'A general preference was expressed for drawing a clear distinction between the concepts of the obligation to extradite or prosecute and that of universal criminal jurisdiction. It was recalled that the Commission had decided to focus on the former and not the latter, even if for some crimes the two concepts existed simultaneously. It was pointed out that the topic did not necessarily require a study in extraterritorial criminal jurisdiction.' See also, more recently, International Law Commission, *Report of the International Law Commission, Sixty-fourth session (7 May–1 June and 2 July–3 August 2012)*, UN doc A/67/10, 118, para 214: 'It was considered appropriate for the Commission to delink the topic from universal jurisdiction insofar as the obligation to extradite or prosecute did not depend on universal jurisdiction.'

[138] But cf, at least as regards the *aut dedere aut judicare* obligation in the grave breaches of the 1949 Geneva Conventions, J Pictet, *The Geneva Conventions of 12 August 1949, Commentary IV: Geneva Convention relative to the Protection of Civilian Persons in Time of War* (Geneva: International Committee of the Red Cross, 1958), 593, arguing on the basis of *Final Record of the Diplomatic Conference of Geneva 1949* (Berne: Federal Political Department, 1950), vol II-B, 114–15, that the common provision 'does not exclude handing over the accused to an international criminal court whose competence has been recognized by the Contracting Parties'. But nothing of the sort appears in the *travaux préparatoires* cited by Pictet, and, more to the point, it is hard to see how such a position could be reconcilable with the text.

[139] See eg Rome Statute, art 102; *Naletilić v Croatia*, 121 ILR 209 (ECtHR 2000); *Prosecutor v Mejakić*, IT-02-65-AR11*bis*, Appeals Chamber, Decision on Joint Defence Appeal against Decision on Referral under Rule 11*bis*, 7 April 2006, para 31, as affirmed in *Prosecutor v Ljubičić*, IT-00-41-AR11*bis*.1, Appeals Chamber, Decision on Appeal against Decision on Referral under Rule 11*bis*, 4 July 2006, para 8.

and purpose of the treaties in question,[140] which is to promote the repression of the relevant crimes, the object and purpose of a treaty, in the light of which the ordinary meaning of the terms in context must be read, cannot be used in effect to amend the treaty's express provisions. In this light, article 11(1) of the Enforced Disappearance Convention, which includes in its '*dedere*' limb the option 'or surrender him or her to an international criminal court whose jurisdiction it has recognized',[141] is a sensible innovation. On the other hand, there is scope for arguing that surrendering the suspect to a competent international criminal court for prosecution acquits the '*judicare*' limb of the obligation *aut dedere aut judicare*, insofar as the state party could be said to delegate to the international tribunal its prosecution of the case.[142]

Article VI of the Genocide Convention[143] has been interpreted by the ICJ as pertaining as much to prosecution and surrender of suspects as to jurisdiction over them, with the Court construing the provision as an undertaking by a contracting party to try persons alleged to have committed genocide in its territory or, in these and other cases, to hand suspects over for trial by a competent international criminal tribunal whose jurisdiction it has accepted.[144] Moreover, the Court has held that, if there exists an international criminal tribunal competent to try the crime of genocide in the relevant case, article VI of the Genocide Convention obliges those contracting parties that have accepted its jurisdiction to co-operate with it.[145] This in turn implies that these contracting parties 'will arrest persons accused of genocide who are in their territory—even if the crime of which they are accused was committed outside it—and, failing prosecution of them in the parties' own courts, that they will hand them over for trial by the competent international tribunal'.[146] In contrast, the permissive formulation

8.57

---

[140] In practice, additionally, it is hard to imagine another state objecting to such surrender, unless perhaps there existed a choice between surrender to the ICC and extradition pursuant to a request by a state party to the treaty in question that was not also a state party to the Rome Statute.

[141] Recall, in this regard, Rome Statute, art 7(1)(*i*), which includes enforced disappearance committed as part of a widespread or systematic attack against a civilian population as a crime against humanity within the jurisdiction of the ICC.

[142] Consider, in this light, *Prosecutor v Katanga and Ngudjolo*, ICC-01/04-01/07-1497, Appeals Chamber, Judgment on the Appeal of Mr Germain Katanga against the Oral Decision of Trial Chamber II of 12 June 2009 on the Admissibility of the Case, 25 September 2009, para 83, as affirmed in *Prosecutor v Bemba*, ICC-01/05-01/08-962, Appeals Chamber, Judgment on the appeal of Mr Jean-Pierre Bemba Gombo against the decision of Trial Chamber III of 24 June 2010 entitled 'Decision on the Admissibility and Abuse of Process Challenges', 19 October 2010, para 74, in which a decision by a state with custody of the suspect to surrender that suspect to the ICC for prosecution was held not to constitute a decision not to prosecute within the meaning of article 17(1)(*b*) of the Rome Statute.

[143] Recall *supra* para 8.45.

[144] See *Application of the Genocide Convention* (n 87), 226–7, paras 439–443 and 229, paras 449–450.

[145] Ibid, 227, para 443. See also ibid, 227–8, para 446. Recall in this regard the Court's ruling, ibid, 227–8, paras 445–446, that art VI's reference to an 'international penal tribunal' whose jurisdiction relevant contracting parties 'have accepted' extends to an international criminal tribunal established pursuant to a resolution of the UN Security Council adopted under chapter VII of the UN Charter whose jurisdiction those contracting parties are obliged to accept and with which they are obliged to co-operate by virtue of the resolution or some other rule of international law.

[146] Ibid, 227, para 443.

of article V of the Apartheid Convention[147] is more obviously strictly jurisdictional, creating for states parties neither an obligation to prosecute persons suspected of the crime of apartheid, wherever allegedly committed, nor to surrender them to a competent international criminal tribunal whose jurisdiction they have accepted.

F. Details as to Extradition

8.58 Nearly all of the international criminal conventions contain a suite of provisions relating to the technicalities of extradition between states parties in respect of the offence the subject of the convention.[148] These provisions stipulate, first, that the offence shall be deemed to be included as an extraditable offence in any existing extradition treaty between states parties and, secondly, that states parties shall include the offence as an extraditable offence in every extradition treaty subsequently concluded between them.[149] Next, provision is made in the event that a state party which conditions the availability of extradition on the existence of an extradition treaty between it and the requesting state receives an extradition request in respect of the offence from a state party with which it has no treaty. The conventions specify in this regard that the requested state party may at its option consider the convention as the legal basis for extradition in respect of the offence.[150] This permissive rule—while unnecessary as a matter of public international law, since a state is always at liberty to disregard a self-imposed restraint—is designed to facilitate extradition in proceedings in certain jurisdictions.[151] As

---

[147] Recall *supra* para 8.45.
[148] See also, much more basically, Additional Protocol I, art 88(2) and (3).
[149] See Hague Convention, art 8(1); Hague Convention as amended by Beijing Protocol, art 8(1); Montreal Convention, art 8(1); Internationally Protected Persons Convention, art 8(1); Hostages Convention, art 10(1); Torture Convention, art 8(1); Illicit Traffic Convention, art 6(2); Nuclear Material Convention, art 11(1); SUA Convention, art 11(1); Mercenaries Convention, art 15(1); UN and Associated Personnel Convention, art 15(1); Terrorist Bombings Convention, art 9(1); Financing of Terrorism Convention, art 11(1); Second Hague Protocol, art 18(1); Children Protocol, art 5(1); Organized Crime Convention, art 16(3); Corruption Convention, art 44(4); Nuclear Material and Facilities Convention, art 11(1); Nuclear Terrorism Convention, art 13(1); 2005 SUA Convention, art 11(1); Enforced Disappearance Convention, art 13(2) and (3); Beijing Convention, art 12(1). See also OECD Bribery Convention, art 10(1), omitting second obligation.
[150] See Hague Convention, art 8(2); Hague Convention as amended by Beijing Protocol, art 8(2); Montreal Convention, art 8(2); Internationally Protected Persons Convention, art 8(2); Hostages Convention, art 10(2); Torture Convention, art 8(2); Illicit Traffic Convention, art 6(3); Nuclear Material Convention, art 11(2); SUA Convention, art 11(2); Mercenaries Convention, art 15(2); UN and Associated Personnel Convention, art 15(2); OECD Bribery Convention, art 10(2); Terrorist Bombings Convention, art 9(2); Financing of Terrorism Convention, art 11(2); Second Hague Protocol, art 18(2); Children Protocol, art 5(2); Organized Crime Convention, art 16(4); Corruption Convention, art 44(5); Nuclear Material and Facilities Convention, art 11(2); Nuclear Terrorism Convention, art 13(2); SUA Convention, art 11(2); Enforced Disappearance Convention, art 13(4); Beijing Convention, art 12(2).
[151] The provision usually adds that extradition 'shall be subject to the conditions provided by the law of the requested State'. See also, referring to 'the law of the requested State Party or by applicable extradition treaties', Illicit Traffic Convention, art 6(5); Organized Crime Convention, art 16(7); Enforced Disappearance Convention, art 13(6); Corruption Convention, art 44(8). See too, almost identically, OECD Bribery Convention, art 10(4).

regards states parties which do not condition the availability of extradition on the existence of an extradition treaty, the conventions oblige them to recognize the offence as an extraditable offence between themselves.[152] Next, many of the conventions mandate that, for the purpose of extradition between states parties in respect of the offence, the offence shall be treated as if it had been committed not only where it was in fact committed but also in the territories of those states parties that would enjoy jurisdiction on any basis obliged by the convention bar universality.[153] Finally, some of the conventions contain a catch-all provision to the effect that all extradition treaties and arrangements between states parties with regard to the offence the subject of the convention shall be deemed to be modified as between the states parties to the extent that they are incompatible with the convention.[154]

8.59 Several conventions oblige states parties not to give effect to the political offence exception to extradition in respect of the crime in question. The first sentence of article VII of the Genocide Convention provides that the various manifestations of the crime of genocide 'shall not be considered as political crimes for the purpose of extradition', while the second sentence states that the contracting parties 'pledge themselves in such cases to grant extradition in accordance with their laws and treaties in force'. Article XI of the Apartheid Convention is to the same effect. The more recent conventions provide:

None of the offences set forth in [this Convention] shall be regarded, for the purposes of extradition..., as a political offence or as an offence connected with a political offence or as an offence inspired by political motives. Accordingly, a request for

---

[152] See Hague Convention, art 8(3); Hague Convention as amended by Beijing Protocol, art 8(3); Montreal Convention, art 8(3); Internationally Protected Persons Convention, art 8(3); Hostages Convention, art 10(3); Torture Convention, art 8(3); Illicit Traffic Convention, art 6(4); Nuclear Material Convention, art 11(3); SUA Convention, art 11(3); Mercenaries Convention, art 15(3); UN and Associated Personnel Convention, art 15(3); Terrorist Bombings Convention, art 9(3); Financing of Terrorism Convention, art 11(3); Second Hague Protocol, art 18(3); Children Protocol, art 5(3); Organized Crime Convention, art 16(6); Corruption Convention, art 44(7); Nuclear Material and Facilities Convention, art 11(3); Nuclear Terrorism Convention, art 13(3); 2005 SUA Convention, art 11(3); Enforced Disappearance Convention, art 13(5); Beijing Convention, art 12(3). The provision in question usually adds the rider 'subject to the conditions provided by the law of the requested State'. Recall also, *supra* n 147, Illicit Traffic Convention, art 6(5); Organized Crime Convention, art 16(7); Enforced Disappearance Convention, art 13(6); Corruption Convention, art 44(8).
[153] See Hague Convention, art 8(4); Hague Convention as amended by Beijing Protocol, art 8(4); Montreal Convention, art 8(4); Internationally Protected Persons Convention, art 8(4); Hostages Convention, art 10(4); Torture Convention, art 8(4); Nuclear Material Convention, art 11(4); SUA Convention, art 11(4); Mercenaries Convention, art 15(4); UN and Associated Personnel Convention, art 15(4); Terrorist Bombings Convention, art 9(4); Financing of Terrorism Convention, art 11(4); Second Hague Protocol, art 18(4); Children Protocol, art 5(4); Nuclear Material and Facilities Convention, art 11(4); Nuclear Terrorism Convention, art 13(4); 2005 SUA Convention, art 11(4); Beijing Convention, art 12(4). The provision does not require that such states parties have actually established jurisdiction.
[154] See SUA Convention, art 11(7); Terrorist Bombings Convention, art 9(5); Financing of Terrorism Convention, art 11(5); Nuclear Terrorism Convention, art 13(5); 2005 SUA Convention, art 11(7); Beijing Convention, art 12(5). For municipal interpretation and application of art 9(5) of the Terrorist Bombings Convention, see *Lariz Iriondo*, ILDC 125 (AR 2005) (Argentina).

extradition...based on such an offence may not be refused on the sole ground that it concerns a political offence or an offence connected with a political offence or an offence inspired by political motives.[155]

A corresponding provision is found in the current text of the draft comprehensive convention on international terrorism.[156]

8.60 The Organized Crime Convention and the Corruption Convention specify that states parties may not refuse a request for extradition on the sole ground, otherwise applicable under the extradition law of some jurisdictions, that the offence is also considered to involve fiscal matters.[157]

8.61 The more recent[158] international criminal conventions include in relation to extradition an identical safeguard clause, as follows:

Nothing in this Convention shall be interpreted as imposing an obligation to extradite...if the requested State Party has substantial grounds for believing that the request for extradition for offences set forth in [this Convention]...has been made for the purpose of prosecuting or punishing a person on account of that person's race, religion, nationality, ethnic origin or political opinion or that compliance with the request would cause prejudice to that person's position for any of these reasons.[159]

A corresponding provision is found in the current text of the draft comprehensive convention on international terrorism.[160]

---

[155] Hague Convention as amended by Beijing Protocol, art 8*bis*; Terrorist Bombings Convention, art 11; Second Hague Protocol, art 20(1); Financing of Terrorism Convention, art 14; Nuclear Material and Facilities Convention, art 11A; Nuclear Terrorism Convention, art 15; 2005 SUA Convention, art 11*bis*; Enforced Disappearance Convention, art 13(1); Beijing Convention, art 13. See, similarly, Illicit Traffic Convention, art 3(10), stating, however, that the non-treatment of the offences in question as political offences or politically motivated is without prejudice to 'the constitutional limitations and the fundamental domestic law' of the states parties. See also the even more limited stipulation in Corruption Convention, art 44(4), which provides that, in the event that a state party uses the Convention itself as the legal basis for extradition and insofar as its own law so permits, the offences established in accordance with the Convention shall not be considered political offences.

[156] The provision appears as art 16 [14] in the text of the preamble and arts 1, 2, and 4 to 27 of the draft comprehensive convention on international terrorism prepared by the Bureau of the Ad Hoc Committee established by General Assembly resolution 51/210 of 17 December 1996 for discussion at the Committee's sixteenth session, *Report of the Ad Hoc Committee established by General Assembly resolution 51/210 of 17 December 1996, Sixteenth session (8 to 12 April 2013)*, UN doc A/68/37 (2013), Annex I.

[157] Organized Crime Convention, art 15(16); Corruption Convention, art 44(16). See, similarly, Illicit Traffic Convention, art 3(10), with the same limitation as *supra* n 155 with respect to 'the constitutional limitations and the fundamental domestic law' of the states parties. The earliest example of the making of provision to this effect is the Optional Protocol to the International Convention for the Suppression of Counterfeiting Currency 1929, deeming the offences in art 3 of Convention 'ordinary offences', a characterization that would equally circumvent the political offence exception.

[158] But see also, very similarly, Illicit Traffic Convention, art 6(6).

[159] Hague Convention as amended by Beijing Protocol, art 8*ter*; Terrorist Bombings Convention, art 12; Second Hague Protocol, art 20(2); Financing of Terrorism Convention, art 15; Organized Crime Convention, art 16(14); Corruption Convention, art 44(15); Nuclear Material and Facilities Convention, art 11B; Nuclear Terrorism Convention, art 16; 2005 SUA Convention, art 11*ter*; Enforced Disappearance Convention, art 13(7); Beijing Convention, art 14.

[160] See art 17 [15] of the text prepared by the Bureau for discussion at the Committee's sixteenth session, *Report of the Ad Hoc Committee, Sixteenth session* (n 156), Annex I.

G. Mutual Assistance in Criminal Matters

Almost every international criminal convention contains a provision to the effect 8.62
that the states parties are to afford each other 'the greatest measure of assistance' in
connection with criminal proceedings brought in respect of the offence or offences
provided for in the convention, with some specifying *ex abundante cautela* that
such assistance shall include the supply of evidence necessary for the proceedings
and that the undertaking encompasses the investigation stage and extradition proceedings.[161] Many of the conventions indicate at the same time that this obligation is not to affect obligations under applicable treaties on mutual assistance in
criminal matters.[162]

Some of the conventions embody a rule of speciality in relation to mutual assis- 8.63
tance in criminal matters, providing that the requesting state party shall not, without the prior consent of the requested state party, transmit or use information or
evidence furnished by the latter for investigations, prosecutions or proceedings
other than those stated in the request.[163] Two of these instruments exempt exculpatory material from the rule.[164]

---

[161] Hague Convention, art 10(1); Hague Convention as amended by Beijing Protocol, art 10(1); Montreal Convention, art 11(1); Internationally Protected Persons Convention, art 10(1); Additional Protocol I, art 88(1); Hostages Convention, art 11(1); Nuclear Material Convention, art 13(1); Torture Convention, art 9(1); Illicit Traffic Convention, art 7(1); SUA Convention, art 12(1); Mercenaries Convention, art 13(1); UN and Associated Personnel Convention, art 16(1); Terrorist Bombings Convention, art 10(1); OECD Bribery Convention, art 9(1); Financing of Terrorism Convention, art 12(1); Second Hague Protocol, art 19(1); Children Protocol, art 6(1); Organized Crime Convention, art 18(1); Corruption Convention, art 46(1); Nuclear Material and Facilities Convention, art 13(1); Nuclear Terrorism Convention, art 14(1); 2005 SUA Convention, art 12(1); Enforced Disappearance Convention, art 14(1); Beijing Convention, art 17(1). The relevant provision usually specifies that the law of the requested state is to apply in all cases. But cf—specifying conformity with 'any treaties or other arrangements on mutual legal assistance' as may exist between the relevant states parties or, in their absence, in accordance with the domestic law of those states parties—SUA Convention, art 12(2); Terrorist Bombings Convention, art 10(2); Financing of Terrorism Convention, art 12(5); Second Hague Protocol, art 19(2); Children Protocol, art 6(2); Nuclear Terrorism Convention, art 14(2); Beijing Convention, art 17(2). Cf also Torture Convention, art 9(2), omitting the fallback reference to domestic law; OECD Bribery Convention, art 9(1) ('to the fullest extent possible under [the requested state party's] laws and relevant treaties and arrangements'); Organized Crime Convention, art 18(2) ('to the fullest extent possible under relevant laws, treaties, agreements and arrangements of the requested State Party'); Corruption Convention, art 46(2) (ditto); Enforced Disappearance Convention, art 14(2) ('subject to the conditions provided for by the domestic law of the requested State Party or by applicable treaties on mutual assistance, including, in particular, the conditions in relation to the grounds upon which the requested State Party may refuse to grant mutual legal assistance or may make it subject to conditions').

[162] Hague Convention, art 10(2); Hague Convention as amended by Beijing Protocol, art 10(2); Montreal Convention, art 11(2); Internationally Protected Persons Convention, art 10(2); Additional Protocol I, art 88(3); Hostages Convention, art 11(2); Nuclear Material Convention, art 13(2); Illicit Traffic Convention, art 7(6); Mercenaries Convention, art 13(2); UN and Associated Personnel Convention, art 16(2); Organized Crime Convention, art 18(6); Corruption Convention, art 46(6); Nuclear Material and Facilities Convention, art 13(2); 2005 SUA Convention, art 12(2).

[163] See Illicit Traffic Convention, art 7(12); Financing of Terrorism Convention, art 12(3); Organized Crime Convention, art 18(19); Corruption Convention, art 46(19).

[164] See Organized Crime Convention, art 18(19); Corruption Convention, art 46(19).

8.64   With the exception of the Genocide Convention and the Apartheid Convention, which make no provision whatsoever in relation to mutual assistance in criminal matters, those conventions which specify that none of the offences set forth in the convention are to be regarded as a political offence, etc for the purpose of extradition state the same in relation to such assistance, a request for which is not to be refused on the ground that it concerns a political offence, etc.[165] The current text of the draft comprehensive convention on international terrorism also refers in this context to mutual assistance in criminal matters.[166]

8.65   The Illicit Traffic Convention, the OECD Bribery Convention, the Financing of Terrorism Convention, the Organized Crime Convention, and the Corruption Convention—all of which pertain to offences necessarily or usually with a financial aspect—stipulate that a request for assistance in criminal matters in relation to the offences set forth in the convention is not to be refused on the ground of bank secrecy.[167] The last two further provide that assistance shall not be refused solely on the ground that the offence is considered to involve fiscal matters.[168]

8.66   The human rights safeguard clause as found in most of the more recent conventions is stated to apply also to mutual assistance in criminal matters.[169]

III. Some Specific Obligations

A. Prevention of the Crime

(i) Genocide

8.67   Article I of the Genocide Convention imposes on the contracting parties an obligation to prevent the crime of genocide recognized in the Convention. In *Application of the Convention for the Prevention and Punishment of the Crime of Genocide*, the ICJ held that article I was 'not to be read merely as an introduction to later express

---

[165] See Hague Convention as amended by Beijing Protocol, art 8*bis*; Terrorist Bombings Convention, art 11; Second Hague Protocol, art 20(1); Financing of Terrorism Convention, art 14; Nuclear Material and Facilities Convention, art 11A; Nuclear Terrorism Convention, art 15; 2005 SUA Convention, art 11*bis*; Enforced Disappearance Convention, art 13(1); Beijing Convention, art 13. See also, similarly, Illicit Traffic Convention, art 3(10), subject to the 'without prejudice' clause considered *supra* n 155.

[166] See art 16 [14] of the text prepared by the Bureau for discussion at the Committee's sixteenth session, *Report of the* Ad Hoc *Committee, Sixteenth session* (n 156), Annex I.

[167] Illicit Traffic Convention, art 7(5); OECD Bribery Convention, art 9(3); Financing of Terrorism Convention, art 12(2); Organized Crime Convention, art 18(8); Corruption Convention, art 46(8). Note, however, the grounds for refusal specifically permitted by Illicit Traffic Convention, art 7(15); Organized Crime Convention, art 18(21); Corruption Convention, art 46(21).

[168] Organized Crime Convention, art 18(22); Corruption Convention, art 46(22). See also, similarly, Illicit Traffic Convention, art 3(10), subject to the 'without prejudice' clause considered *supra* n 155.

[169] See Hague Convention as amended by Beijing Protocol, art 8*ter*; Terrorist Bombings Convention, art 12; Second Hague Protocol, art 20(2); Financing of Terrorism Convention, art 15; Nuclear Material and Facilities Convention, art 11B; Nuclear Terrorism Convention, art 16; 2005 SUA Convention, art 11*ter*; Beijing Convention, art 14.

references to legislation, prosecution and extradition' but, rather, 'creates obligations distinct from those which appear in the subsequent Articles'.[170] In short, pursuant to article I, 'the Contracting Parties have a direct obligation to prevent genocide'.[171] The content of this obligation, moreover, goes beyond the specific measure cited in article XIII of the Convention, which provides that any contracting party 'may call upon the competent organs of the United Nations to take such action under the Charter of the United Nations as they consider appropriate for the prevention... of acts of genocide'.[172]

8.68 The obligation to prevent the crime of genocide is distinct from a contracting party's concomitant obligation under article I of the Genocide Convention to punish the crime of genocide,[173] even if it may be 'true that one of the most effective ways of preventing criminal acts, in general, is to provide penalties for persons committing such acts, and to impose those penalties effectively on those who commit the acts one is trying to prevent'.[174]

8.69 The obligation to prevent the crime of genocide laid down in article I of the Genocide Convention is an obligation of conduct, not result.[175] In the words of the ICJ in *Application of the Convention for the Prevention and Punishment of the Crime of Genocide*, it is not 'an obligation to succeed, whatever the circumstances, in preventing the commission of genocide'[176] but, rather, is an obligation 'to employ all means reasonably available to [a contracting party], so as to prevent genocide so far as possible'.[177] A contracting party will have breached article I of the Genocide Convention if it 'manifestly failed to take all measures to prevent genocide which were within its power, and which might have contributed to preventing the genocide'—in other words, if it manifestly failed to exercise 'due diligence' to prevent the crime of genocide:[178]

[A] State's obligation to prevent [the crime of genocide], and the corresponding duty to act, arise at the instant that the State learns of, or should normally have learned of, the existence of a serious risk that genocide will be committed. From that moment onwards, if the State has available to it means likely to have a deterrent effect on those suspected of preparing genocide, or reasonably suspected of harbouring specific intent (*dolus specialis*), it is under a duty to make such use of these means as the circumstances permit.[179]

---

[170] *Application of the Genocide Convention* (n 87), 111, para 162.
[171] Ibid, 113, para 165.
[172] Ibid, 220, para 427. Nor, ibid, does calling on the competent UN organs relieve contracting parties 'to take such action as they can to prevent genocide from occurring, while respecting the United Nations Charter and any decisions that may have been taken by its competent organs'.
[173] Ibid, 219–20, paras 425 and 427.   [174] Ibid, 219, para 426.
[175] Ibid, 221, para 430.   [176] Ibid.   [177] Ibid.
[178] Ibid. The Court speaks, ibid, 223, para 432, of contracting parties' obligation 'to do their best to ensure that... acts [of genocide] do not occur'.
[179] Ibid, 222, para 431. As to the level of knowledge sufficient to trigger the obligation, the Court explains, ibid, 223, para 432: '[A] State may be found to have violated its obligation to prevent even though it had no certainty, at the time when it should have acted, but failed to do so, that genocide was about to be committed or was under way; for it to incur responsibility on this basis it is enough that the State was aware, or should normally have been aware, of the serious danger that acts of genocide would be committed.'

The precise content of the obligation will depend on a range of factors, most notably the contracting party's 'capacity to influence effectively the action of persons likely to commit, or already committing, genocide'.[180] It is irrelevant, however, to a finding of responsibility for breach of article I of the Genocide Convention whether the deployment by a contracting party of 'all means reasonably at its disposal' would in fact have prevented the commission of the crime of genocide.[181] At the same time, a contracting party can breach the obligation of prevention laid down in article I only if genocide is in fact committed.[182]

8.70   Article I of the Genocide Convention does not permit contracting parties to intervene forcibly in another state to prevent the crime of genocide without the authorization of the UN Security Council. Article I must be interpreted in the light of other rules of international law binding on the parties to the Genocide Convention,[183] with the result that the provision's obligation to prevent the crime of genocide is not be read to encompass measures of prevention involving a violation of the prohibition on the unlawful use of interstate force laid down in article 2(4) of the UN Charter, to which all contracting parties to the Genocide Convention are also parties, and customary international law. As it is, even were article I interpreted more expansively, article 103 of the UN Charter provides that, in the event of conflict between UN member states' obligations under the Charter and their obligations under other international agreements, their Charter obligations prevail, with the consequence that the prohibition on the use of interstate force laid down in article 2(4) of the Charter would trump to the extent of the inconsistency the Genocide Convention's obligation to prevent the crime of genocide. That contracting parties may not intervene forcibly in another state to prevent genocide unless authorized to do so by the Security Council is reflected *a contrario* in article VIII of the Genocide Convention, which provides that any contracting party 'may call upon the competent organs of the United Nations to take such action under the Charter of the United Nations as they consider appropriate for the prevention and suppression of acts of genocide'. It is also implicit in the ICJ's reference in *Application of the Convention on the Prevention and Punishment of the Crime of Genocide* to the obligation to prevent genocide 'while respecting the United Nations Charter',[184] as well as in the Court's explanation

---

[180] Ibid, 221, para 430. The Court elaborates, ibid: 'This capacity itself depends, among other things, on the geographical distance of the State concerned from the scene of the events, and on the strength of the political links, as well as links of all other kinds, between the authorities of that State and the main actors in the events.'

[181] Ibid. See also ibid, 233, para 461 ('The obligation to prevent the commission of the crime of genocide is imposed by the Genocide Convention on any State party which, in a given situation, has it in its power to contribute to restraining in any degree the commission of genocide.') Whether the steps that the contracting party could reasonably have taken would actually have prevented the commission of the crime of genocide is, however, relevant to the question of reparation for breach of article I's obligation of prevention, as explained by the Court, ibid, 233–4, para 462. In the context of reparation, the question, ibid, 234, para 462, 'is whether there is a sufficiently direct and certain causal nexus between the wrongful act, the [contracting party]'s breach of the obligation to prevent genocide, and the injury suffered..., consisting of all damage of any type, material or moral, caused by the acts of genocide'.

[182] Ibid, 221–2, para 431.   [183] See VCLT, art 31(3)(*c*).

[184] *Application of the Genocide Convention* (n 87), 220, para 427.

that the capacity of a contacting party to influence effectively persons likely to commit or already committing genocide 'must...be assessed by [*inter alia*] legal criteria, since it is clear that every State may only act within the limits permitted by international law'.[185]

8.71 In *Application of the Convention on the Prevention and Punishment of the Crime of Genocide*, the ICJ derived from article I of the Genocide Convention an implicit prohibition on the commission of genocide by contracting parties themselves[186] (that is, by means of conduct attributable to them)[187] and not just by individuals (whether or not the conduct of those individuals is attributable to a contracting party). The Court reasoned that this implicit prohibition 'follows, first, from the fact that the Article categorizes genocide as "a crime under international law"', by which the Court meant that, 'by agreeing to such a categorization, the States parties must logically be undertaking not to commit the act so described';[188] and, secondly, 'from the expressly stated obligation to prevent the commission of acts of genocide', since in the Court's view it 'would be paradoxical if States were...under an obligation to prevent, so far as within their power, commission of genocide by persons over whom they have a certain influence, but were not forbidden to commit such acts through their own organs, or persons over whom they have such firm control that their conduct is attributable to the State concerned under international law'.[189] Stressing, however, that international law does not recognize the criminal responsibility of states, the Court held that the commission of genocide by a contracting party contrary to article I of the Genocide Convention results only in that state's delictual responsibility.[190] The Court's conclusion and reasoning are fundamentally flawed.[191] First, if the term 'crime under international law' used in article I refers to an international legal prohibition binding on individuals the breach of which gives rise to the individual criminal responsibility of the perpetrator under international law, and if, as the Court underlines,[192] individual criminal responsibility under international law and state responsibility are conceptually distinct, it is impossible to see how by recognizing a crime under international law a state undertakes not to commit the impugned conduct itself. The problem is compounded by the semantic and juridical oddity of the Court's position that the commission of something labelled a 'crime' should result in delictual, not criminal, responsibility.[193] Similarly, while reasoning along the lines of the Court's

---

[185] Ibid, 221, para 430. [186] See ibid, 113–14, paras 166–7 and 118–19, para 179.
[187] Ibid, 114, para 167. [188] Ibid, 113, para 166. [189] Ibid.
[190] Ibid, 114, para 167 and 115, para 170.
[191] A variety of other criticisms can be levelled at the Court's conclusion and reasoning. For a selection from the six judges who disagreed with the Court's analysis, see ibid, 279–82, paras 1–4 (joint dec Shi and Koroma), 297–308, paras 38–72 (sep op Owada), 333–45, paras 41–61 (sep op Tomka), 370–1 (dec Skotnikov), and 551–4, paras 126–129 (sep op Kreća).
[192] Ibid, 116, para 173.
[193] See also ibid, 371 (dec Skotnikov). It is certainly not the case under the major national legal systems that a criminal prohibition is per se alternatively remediable as a tort. Conduct amounting to a crime often amounts additionally and coincidentally to a tort, but a crime is not *ipso facto* substitutable by a tort.

second argument may have force generally, it does not where what a contracting party undertakes in article I to prevent is expressly characterized as a 'crime under international law' and is referred to in the provision only as such (and not, *pace* the Court, as 'acts' of genocide).[194] A state cannot incur criminal responsibility, as the Court itself acknowledges, and there is no sound reason why something called a crime should result instead in delictual responsibility.

(ii) Others

8.72 The Genocide Convention is not the only multilateral treaty in which the states parties undertake to prevent a treaty crime.[195] But the precise content of the obligation of prevention varies according to the wording of the relevant provision. The ICJ did not purport in *Application of the Convention on the Prevention and Punishment of the Crime of Genocide* to lay down 'a general jurisprudence applicable to all cases where a treaty . . . includes an obligation for States to prevent certain acts'.[196] At the same time, to the extent that the wording of the relevant provision does not contradict it, what the Court says in its judgment is not without relevance.

8.73 In accordance with article 2(1) of the Torture Convention, each state party 'shall take effective legislative, administrative, judicial or other measures to prevent acts[197] of torture in any territory under its jurisdiction', the term 'torture' being defined in article 1(1) of the Convention. The Committee against Torture has emphasized that article 2's obligation to take effective measures to prevent acts of torture goes beyond implementation of the specific measures required by the succeeding articles of the Convention[198]—in other words, that the obligation is a freestanding one. In terms of the content of this obligation, the Committee takes the view that a failure adequately to punish torture amounts to a failure to prevent it.[199] More significantly, the Committee appears to treat an act of torture attributable to a state party as *ipso facto* a breach by that state party of its

---

[194] Ibid, 113, para 166.
[195] In addition, states parties to the Apartheid Convention undertake in art IV(*a*) to adopt any legislative or other measures necessary to prevent not the crime of apartheid itself but rather 'any encouragement of the crime of apartheid'.
[196] *Application of the Genocide Convention* (n 87), 220, para 429.
[197] Since any crime of torture as exists pursuant to the Convention will be dependent for its juridical existence on a state party's implementation of the obligation in art 4 of municipal criminalization, and since a state party might seek to circumvent its obligation of prevention under art 2(1) by refraining from criminalizing torture as required by art 4, the reference in art 2 is to 'acts', not 'the crime', of torture. Note that a state party is further obliged, by virtue of art 16 of the Torture Convention, to prevent in any territory under its jurisdiction 'other acts of cruel, inhuman or degrading treatment or punishment which do not amount to torture as defined in article 1, when such acts are committed by or at the instigation of or with the acquiescence of a public official or other person acting in an official capacity'.
[198] See eg Committee against Torture, *General Comment No 2: Implementation of article 2 by States parties*, UN doc CAT/C/GC/2 (24 January 2008), paras 1 and 25.
[199] See Nowak and McArthur (n 17), 109, para 42 and 113–14, paras 51–52. See also, by implication, Committee against Torture (n 198), paras 2 and 7.

obligation to prevent torture,[200] effectively crafting out of article 2(1) an obligation on states parties not to commit torture[201] which is not found *expressis verbis* in the Convention.[202] To the extent, however, that 'torture' is defined in article 1(1) of the Convention to include acts inflicted by private parties with the consent or acquiescence of a public official or other person acting in an official capacity, the Committee appears to apply a standard of due diligence, so that a state party will be responsible for a breach of article 2(1) in this context only 'where State authorities or others acting in [an] official capacity know or have reasonable grounds to believe that acts of torture or ill-treatment are being committed by... private actors' and those officials or others fail to do what is within their power to prevent such acts.[203]

Article 10(1) of the Montreal Convention and article 16(1) of the Beijing Convention provide that states parties 'shall, in accordance with international and national law, endeavour to take all practicable measures for the purpose of preventing the offences set forth in Article 1'. For its part, article 4 of the Internationally Protected Persons Convention reads: 8.74

States Parties shall co-operate in the prevention of the crimes set forth in [the] Convention, particularly by:
(*a*) taking all practicable measures to prevent preparations in their respective territories for the commission of those crimes within or outside their territories;
(*b*) exchanging information and co-ordinating the taking of administrative and other measures as appropriate to prevent the commission of those crimes.

The provision is reproduced almost verbatim in article 13(1) of the SUA Convention, article 13(1) of the 2005 SUA Convention, and article 11 of the Convention on the Safety of United Nations and Associated Personnel 1994 ('UN and Associated Personnel Convention'), in fuller form in article 4 of the International Convention against the Taking of Hostages 1979 ('Hostages Convention') and article 6 of the International Convention against the Recruitment, Use, Financing and Training of Mercenaries 1989 ('Mercenaries Convention'), and in much fuller form in article 15 of the Terrorist Bombings Convention and article 7 of the Nuclear Terrorism Convention. For its part, article 8*bis* of the 2005 SUA Convention provides in paragraph 1 that states parties 'shall co-operate to the fullest extent possible to prevent and suppress unlawful acts covered by th[e] Convention, in conformity with international law, and shall respond to requests pursuant to this article as expeditiously as possible', before elaborating a detailed regime among states parties for the consensual boarding of ships flagged to another state party.

---

[200] In other words, where the act of torture is attributable to a state party, the Committee appears to treat art 2(1)'s obligation to prevent torture as an obligation of result.
[201] See Nowak and McArthur (n 17), 107–8, para 40 and 111–12, paras 48–49 and the practice of the Committee cited therein. See also Committee against Torture (n 198), para 17.
[202] On the absence from the Torture Convention of an explicit prohibition on the commission of acts of torture by a state party, see Nowak and McArthur (n 17), 107, para 40 and 111, para 46.
[203] Committee against Torture (n 198), para 18.

B. Punishment of the Crime

8.75 The contracting parties to the Genocide Convention undertake in article I not only to prevent but also to punish the crime of genocide. It is not clear, however, whether the latter obligation goes beyond a contracting party's specific obligation under article VI of the Convention to try persons alleged to have committed genocide in its territory or, in these and other cases, to hand suspects over for trial by a competent international criminal tribunal whose jurisdiction it has accepted.[204] What does seem clear is that a contracting party's breach of article VI constitutes *ipso facto* a breach also of article I's obligation to punish the crime of genocide.[205]

8.76 The states parties to the Apartheid Convention are obliged by article IV(*a*) '[t]o adopt any legislative or other measures necessary... to punish persons guilty of that crime'. The provision's context, in particular the jurisdictional authorization granted to states parties in article V, indicates that the legislative measures necessary to punish persons guilty of the crime of apartheid presuppose the legislative measures necessary to prosecute persons suspected of being guilty of the crime.

C. Searching for Suspects

8.77 The grave breaches provisions of the 1949 Geneva Conventions, as supplemented by Additional Protocol I, uniquely provide:

> Each High Contracting Party shall be under the obligation to search for persons alleged to have committed, or to have ordered to be committed, such grave breaches...[206]

The ICRC commentary to this common provision explains that the obligation is limited to situations where 'a Contracting Party realizes that there is on its territory a person who has committed such a breach',[207] a construction with which contracting parties appear to agree. In other words, there is neither a rolling obligation to search for persons alleged to have committed a grave breach nor an obligation to search abroad.[208]

---

[204] See *Application of the Genocide Convention* (n 87), 226–7, paras 439–443 and 229, paras 449–450, where the question is complicated by the Court's characterization of the applicant's submission as going to both art I and, implicitly, art VI. For a contracting party's obligation, pursuant to art VI of the Genocide Convention, to co-operate with a competent international criminal tribunal whose jurisdiction it has accepted, see *supra* para 8.57.

[205] See *Application of the Genocide Convention* (n 87), 226–7, paras 439–443 and 229, paras 449–450.

[206] 1949 Geneva Convention I, art 49; 1949 Geneva Convention II, art 50; 1949 Geneva Convention III, art 129; 1949 Geneva Convention IV, art 146.

[207] Pictet (n 138), 593. See also *Arrest Warrant* (n 51), 44, para 17 (sep op Guillaume), 72, para 32 (joint sep op Higgins, Kooijmans, and Buergenthal), 93, para 7 (sep op Rezek), and 123, para 70 (sep op Bula-Bula).

[208] As it is, any search conducted by a state in another state's territory would require the consent of the territorial state.

D. Exclusion of Specific Defences

While none of the international criminal conventions provides for defences to the crimes set forth in the convention, a few prohibit states parties from permitting reliance by an individual on a particular defence or defences to those crimes.

8.78

Article 2(3) of the Torture Convention provides that '[a]n order from a superior officer or a public authority may not be invoked as a justification [for] torture'.[209] The provision prohibits a state party from permitting the invocation by an individual of the defence of superior orders so as to obviate criminal responsibility for the crime of torture provided for in the Convention.[210] The reference to the invocation of superior orders as a justification would seem not to rule out reliance on superior orders as a mitigating circumstance, as would be permitted by customary international law.[211] The Enforced Disappearance Convention contains the same provision, *mutatis mutandis*.[212]

8.79

Hand in hand with the exclusion in some more recent[213] conventions of the possibility of reliance on the political offence exception as a bar to extradition or assistance in criminal matters has gone the exclusion of political and similar motivations as possible defences to criminal responsibility. The Terrorist Bombings Convention, the Financing of Terrorism Convention, and the Nuclear Terrorism Convention provide:

8.80

> Each State Party shall adopt such measures as may be necessary, including, where appropriate, domestic legislation, to ensure that criminal acts within the scope of this Convention,

---

[209] For its part, art 2(2) of the Torture Convention reads: 'No exceptional circumstances whatsoever, whether a state of war or a threat or war, internal political instability or any other public emergency, may be invoked as a justification [for] torture.' Article 2(2) relates, however, not to individual criminal responsibility but to state responsibility, ruling out reliance by a state party, in respect of its obligations under the Convention with regard to torture, on some unspecified form of derogation in time of public emergency (even if derogation is not a 'justification' as such, but, subject to strict conditions, renders obligations inapplicable *a priori*) or on necessity as a circumstance precluding wrongfulness. See also Nowak and McArthur (n 17), 120–1, paras 62 and 65. The provision is somewhat curious, given that the Torture Convention does not prohibit states parties *expressis verbis* from committing torture. But art 2(1) obliges states parties to prevent torture, and, as explained *supra* para 8.73, this is applied, as it was perhaps intended to be applied, in such a way that an act of torture attributable to a state party is *ipso facto* a breach by that state party of its obligation to prevent torture. In short, art 2(2) is not redundant. That the equivalent of art 2(2) of the Torture Convention applies to state responsibility and not individual criminal responsibility is seen clearly in the Enforced Disappearance Convention, where art 1(2) ('No exceptional circumstances whatsoever, whether a state of war or a threat of war, internal political instability or any other public emergency, may be invoked as a justification for enforced disappearance.') follows the statement in art 1(1) that '[n]o one shall be subjected to enforced disappearance', while art 6(2) ('No order or instruction from any public authority, civilian, military or other, may be invoked to justify an offence of enforced disappearance.'), the equivalent of art 2(3) of the Torture Convention, is found in the same article as, and immediately after, the obligation of municipal criminalization of enforced disappearance.

[210] The defence of superior orders is probably better seen as an excuse, rather than a justification, but the distinction is immaterial for the purposes of international criminal law.

[211] In this last regard, consider VCLT, art 31(3)(c). See also Burgers and Danelius (n 3), 124; Nowak and McArthur (n 17), 125, para 72.

[212] See Enforced Disappearance Convention, art 6(2).

[213] See also, previously and not dissimilarly, Apartheid Convention, art III (chapeau) ('International criminal responsibility shall apply, irrespective of the motive involved, to...').

350   *Treaty Crimes*

in particular where they are intended to provoke a state of terror in the general public or in a group of persons or particular persons, are under no circumstances justifiable by considerations of a political, philosophical, ideological, racial, ethnic, religious or other similar nature...[214]

The same provision appears in the current text of the draft comprehensive convention on international terrorism.[215]

E. Corporate Liability

8.81 A range of conventions oblige states parties to provide for the legal liability of corporate entities in respect of the commission of one of the crimes set forth in the convention by a person responsible for the management or control of the entity, a liability which may but need not be criminal. Article 5 of the Financing of Terrorism Convention and article 5*bis* of the 2005 SUA Convention provide:

> 1. Each State Party, in accordance with its domestic legal principles, shall take the necessary measures to enable a legal entity located in its territory or organized under its laws to be held liable when a person responsible for the management or control of that legal entity has, in that capacity, committed an offence set forth in article 2. Such liability may be criminal, civil or administrative.
> 2. Such liability is incurred without prejudice to the criminal liability of individuals having committed the offences.
> 3. Each State Party shall ensure, in particular, that legal entities liable in accordance with paragraph 1 above are subject to effective, proportionate and dissuasive criminal, civil or administrative sanctions. Such sanctions may include monetary sanctions.

These provisions are reproduced verbatim in the current text of the draft comprehensive convention on international terrorism,[216] article 10(1) to (4) of the Organized Crime Convention and article 26(1) to (4) of the Corruption Convention are closely analogous, although do not specify that the entity need be located in a state party's territory or organized under its laws, while article 3(4) of the Children Protocol embodies a version of the first paragraph. Article 2 of the OECD Bribery Convention provides more sparingly that each state party 'shall take measures as may be necessary, in accordance with its legal principles, to establish the liability of legal persons for the bribery of a foreign public official', similarly not stipulating that such liability be criminal.[217] The related article 3(2) of the Convention states that, '[i]n the event that, under the legal system of a

---

[214] See Terrorist Bombings Convention, art 5; Financing of Terrorism Convention, art 6; Nuclear Terrorism Convention, art 6.
[215] See art 7 [5] of the text prepared by the Bureau for discussion at the Committee's sixteenth session, *Report of the* Ad Hoc *Committee, Sixteenth session* (n 156), Annex I.
[216] See art 11 [9] of the text prepared by the Bureau for discussion at the Committee's sixteenth session, *Report of the* Ad Hoc *Committee, Sixteenth session* (n 156), Annex I.
[217] See also Commentaries on the Convention on Combating Bribery (n 17), para 20: 'In the event that, under the legal system of a Party, criminal responsibility is not applicable to legal persons, that Party shall not be required to establish such criminal responsibility.'

Party, criminal responsibility is not applicable to legal persons, that Party shall ensure that legal persons shall be subject to effective, proportionate and dissuasive non-criminal sanctions, including monetary sanctions, for bribery of foreign public officials'.

In both article 2*bis*(1) of the Hague Convention as amended by the Beijing Protocol and article 4(1) of the Beijing Convention, the word 'shall' as found in paragraph 1 of the more common formulation outlined above[218] is replaced by 'may', rendering the provision merely permissive and therefore redundant, since states do not need leave to provide for corporate liability under their municipal law. As for article 2*bis*(3) of the amended Hague Convention and article 4(3) of the Beijing Convention, these read: **8.82**

> If a State Party takes the necessary measures to make a legal entity liable in accordance with paragraph 1 of this Article, it shall endeavour to ensure that the applicable criminal, civil or administrative sanctions are effective, proportionate and dissuasive. Such sanctions may include monetary sanctions.

In short, as found in the two major ICAO instruments, the article posits no more than what might be considered best practice.

F. Issues of Enforcement

(i) Jurisdiction to prescribe not implying jurisdiction to enforce

A variety of international criminal conventions contain provisions inserted *ex abundante cautela* which are intended to make it clear that the obligations on a state party to criminalize and to empower its courts to exercise adjudicative competence over specified conduct performed extraterritorially does not imply a right, let alone an obligation, on the part of that state party to exercise in respect of that conduct powers of criminal-law enforcement in the territory of another state party.[219] Article 2 of the Illicit Traffic Convention, the pioneering provision to this effect, states in relevant part: **8.83**

> 2. The Parties shall carry out their obligations under this Convention in a manner consistent with the principles of sovereign equality and territorial integrity of States and that of non-intervention in the domestic affairs of other States.
> 3. A Party shall not undertake in the territory of another Party the exercise of jurisdiction and performance of functions which are exclusively reserved for the authorities of that other Party by its domestic law.

The two paragraphs are reproduced almost verbatim in the Terrorist Bombings Convention, the Financing of Terrorism Convention, the Organized Crime

---

[218] See *supra* para 8.81.
[219] See eg United Nations (n 51), 45, para 2.17 and 47, para 2.22. *A fortiori*, the relevant conventional provisions on the assertion of extraterritorial prescriptive jurisdiction do not authorize a state party to exercise powers of criminal-law enforcement in the territory of a non-state party.

352   *Treaty Crimes*

Convention, the Corruption Convention, and the Nuclear Terrorism Convention,[220] as well as in the current text of the draft international convention on international terrorism.[221] Article 9 of the SUA Convention, unchanged in article 9 of the 2005 SUA Convention, performs an analogous function in relation to jurisdiction to enforce at sea, providing that nothing in the convention 'shall affect in any way the rules of international law pertaining to the competence of States to exercise investigative or enforcement jurisdiction on board ships not flying their flag'. For its part, article 13 of the Hostages Convention, included in response to the Israeli rescue operation at Entebbe[222] and alluding to the use of interstate force contrary to article 2(4) of the UN Charter, stipulates that nothing in the convention 'shall be construed as justifying the violation of the territorial integrity or political independence of a State in contravention of the Charter of the United Nations'.

(ii) Enforcement at sea

8.84 The Illicit Traffic Convention and the 2005 SUA Convention establish respective regimes, subject at all times to the authorization of the flag-state party, for the boarding by the authorities of one state party of a ship on the high seas flagged to another, when those authorities have reasonable grounds to believe that the ship or a person on board has been, is or is about to be involved in the commission of an offence set forth in the convention, as well as for the detention of the ship, cargo, and persons on board when evidence of such an offence is found.[223] The 2005 SUA Convention specifies for the avoidance of doubt that the boarding state's exercise of enforcement powers in relation to the ship does not affect the right of the flag state to exercise its jurisdiction both to prescribe and to enforce over the detained ship, cargo or other items and persons on board, 'including by way of seizure, forfeiture, arrest and prosecution', although it remains open to the flag state to consent to the exercise of such jurisdiction by any state enjoying prescriptive jurisdiction under the convention.[224] Both conventions emphasize that any

---

[220] See Terrorist Bombings Convention, arts 17 and 18; Financing of Terrorism Convention, arts 20 and 22; Organized Crime Convention, art 4(1) and (2); Corruption Convention, art 4(1) and (2); Nuclear Terrorism Convention, arts 21 and 22.

[221] See arts 21 [20] and 22 of the text prepared by the Bureau for discussion at the Committee's sixteenth session, *Report of the* Ad Hoc *Committee, Sixteenth session* (n 156), Annex I.

[222] Recall *supra* para 7.62 n 150.

[223] See Illicit Traffic Convention, art 17; 2005 SUA Convention, art 8*bis*. See also United Nations Convention on the Law of the Sea 1982, art 108(2) (*re* illicit traffic in narcotic drugs and psychotropic substances). Article 17(4) of the Illicit Traffic Convention, reproduced in more precise form in article 8*bis*(10)(*d*) of the 2005 SUA Convention, specifies that the authorized action 'shall be carried out only by warships or military aircraft, or other ships or aircraft clearly marked and identifiable as being on government service and authorized to that effect'. The Council of Europe has sought to specify details as to the implementation of art 17 of the Illicit Traffic Convention as among those of its member states that are parties to the latter convention in its Agreement on Illicit Traffic by Sea, implementing art 17 of the United Nations Convention against Illicit Traffic in Narcotic Drugs and Psychotropic Substances 1995.

[224] 2005 SUA Convention, art 8*bis*(8).

action taken in accordance with the relevant provision must 'take due account of the need not to interfere with or affect the rights and obligations and the exercise of jurisdiction of coastal States in accordance with the international law of the sea'.[225] The 2005 SUA Convention adds, for the further avoidance of doubt, that the convention's boarding regime 'does not apply to or limit boarding of ships conducted by any State Party in accordance with international law, seaward of any State's territorial sea, including boardings based upon the right of visit, the rendering of assistance to persons, ships and property in distress or peril, or an authorization from the flag State to take law enforcement or other action'.[226]

(iii) Detention of UN and associated personnel

Article 8 of the UN and Associated Personnel Convention regulates the exercise of enforcement jurisdiction over United Nations and associated personnel captured or detained by a state party, providing:

8.85

> Except as otherwise provided in an applicable status-of-forces agreement, if United Nations or associated personnel are captured or detained in the course of the performance of their duties and their identification has been established, they shall not be subjected to interrogation and they shall be promptly released and returned to United Nations or other appropriate authorities.

The later article III ('Duty of a State Party with respect to article 8 of the Convention') of the Optional Protocol to the Convention on the Safety of United Nations and Associated Personnel 2005 elaborates:

> The duty of a State Party to this Protocol with respect to the application of article 8 of the Convention to United Nations operations defined in article II of this Protocol shall be without prejudice to its right to take action in the exercise of its national jurisdiction over any United Nations or associated personnel who violates the laws and regulations of that State, provided that such action is not in violation of any other international law obligation of the State Party.

Article III of the Optional Protocol has its origins in states parties' disenchantment with article 8 of the Convention in light of the implication of UN and associated personnel in sex-trafficking and sexual abuse in the course of their operations, especially in west Africa.

(iv) Transfer of proceedings

Article 21 of the Organized Crime Convention and article 47 of the Corruption Convention provide:

8.86

> States Parties shall consider the possibility of transferring to one another proceedings for the prosecution of an offence covered by this Convention in cases where such transfer

---

[225] Illicit Traffic Convention, art 17(11); 2005 SUA Convention, art 8*bis*(10)(*c*)(i).
[226] 2005 SUA Convention, art 8*bis*(11).

is considered to be in the interests of the proper administration of justice, in particular in cases where several jurisdictions are involved, with a view to concentrating the prosecution.

Article 8 of the Illicit Traffic Convention represents a more basic version of the same.

(v) Confiscation and seizure

8.87 The Illicit Traffic Convention, the OECD Bribery Convention, the Organized Crime Convention, the Children Protocol, and the Corruption Convention all make provision, in varying degrees of detail, for the obligatory confiscation and/or seizure of the proceeds of the relevant offences,[227] while the last makes additional provision for the mandatory freezing of the same.[228]

IV. Conclusion

8.88 Whether the many universal multilateral treaties for the suppression of international crimes achieve their aim is anyone's guess. It is doubtful whether criminological research—of which precious little, if any, exists on the effect of the various international criminal conventions—could provide an answer either way. States nonetheless seem to think that the conclusion of and participation in such treaties is a worthwhile endeavour, perhaps if only to be seen to be doing something about what they view as the reprehensible conduct addressed by each treaty. In this light, it is not unlikely that they will continue to conclude such treaties.

Further Reading

BOISTER, N, *An Introduction to Transnational Criminal Law* (Oxford: Oxford University Press, 2012), chapters 11–19, 21, and 22

BOISTER, N and CURRIE, RJ (eds), *Routledge Handbook of Transnational Criminal Law* (Abingdon: Routledge, 2015)

BURGERS, JH and DANELIUS, H, *The United Nations Convention Against Torture: A Handbook on the Convention Against Torture and Other Cruel, Inhuman or Degrading Treatment or Punishment* (Dordrecht/London: Martinus Nijhoff, 1988)

CHEAH, WL, 'Extradition and Mutual Legal Assistance in the Prosecution of Serious Municipal Crimes: A Comparative and Critical Analysis of Applicable Legal Frameworks' in ED Papastavridis and KN Trapp (eds), *La criminalité en mer/Crimes at Sea* (Leiden: Martinus Nijhoff, 2014), 311

---

[227] See Illicit Traffic Convention, art 5; OECD Bribery Convention, art 3(3) ('or property the value of which corresponds to that of such proceeds...[or] monetary sanctions of comparable effect'); Organized Crime Convention, arts 12 and 13; Children Protocol, art 7; Corruption Convention, art 31.
[228] See Corruption Convention, art 31.

Commentaries on the Convention on Combating Bribery of Foreign Public Officials in International Business Transactions (adopted by the Negotiating Conference on 21 November 1997) in OECD, *Convention on Combating Bribery of Foreign Public Officials in International Business Transactions and Related Documents* (Paris: OECD Publishing, 2011)

Decaux, E and de Frouville, O (eds), *La Convention pour la protection des toutes les personnes contre les disparitions forcées* (Bruxelles: Bruylant, 2009)

Gaeta, P (ed), *The UN Genocide Convention—A Commentary* (Oxford: Oxford University Press, 2009)

Guilfoyle, D, *Shipping Interdiction and the Law of the Sea* (Cambridge: Cambridge University Press, 2009)

Klein, N, *Maritime Security and the Law of the Sea* (Oxford: Oxford University Press, 2011)

Kreß, C, 'Reflections on the *Iudicare* Limb of the Grave Breaches Regime' (2009) 7 *Journal of International Criminal Justice* 789

McClean, D, *Transnational Organized Crime. A Commentary on the UN Convention and its Protocols* (Oxford: Oxford University Press, 2007)

Nowak, M and McArthur, E, *The United Nations Convention Against Torture: A Commentary* (Oxford: Oxford University Press, 2008)

O'Keefe, R, 'The Grave Breaches Regime and Universal Jurisdiction' (2009) 7 *Journal of International Criminal Justice* 811

Pictet, J, *The Geneva Conventions of 12 August 1949, Commentary IV: Geneva Convention relative to the Protection of Civilian Persons in Time of War* (Geneva: International Committee of the Red Cross, 1958)

Pieth, M, Low, LA, and Bonucci, N (eds), *The OECD Convention on Bribery. A Commentary* (2nd edn, Cambridge: Cambridge University Press, 2014)

Tams, C, Berster, L, and Schiffbauer, B (eds), *Convention on the Prevention and Punishment of the Crime of Genocide. A Commentary* (Oxford: Hart Publishing, 2013)

United Nations, *Commentary on the United Nations Convention against Illicit Traffic in Narcotic Drugs and Psychotropic Substances Done at Vienna on 20 December 1988* (New York: United Nations, 1998), UN doc E/CN.7/590 (1998)

United Nations Office on Drugs and Crime, Travaux préparatoires *of the negotiations for the elaboration of the United Nations Convention against Corruption* (New York: United Nations, 2010)

United Nations Office on Drugs and Crime, Travaux préparatoires *of the negotiations for the elaboration of the United Nations Convention against Transnational Organized Crime and the Protocols thereto* (New York: United Nations, 2006)

PART THREE

THE SUPPRESSION OF INTERNATIONAL CRIMES

Municipal Law and Courts

9

Substantive Law, Jurisdiction, Prosecution, and Courts

I. Introduction

Notwithstanding the intellectual energy and material and human resources expended on them, international courts play only a limited and selective role in the adjudication of international crimes. (Practical constraints are such that it could hardly be otherwise.) It is to national criminal justice authorities that, exceptional events aside, the greater part of the task of suppressing international crimes can be expected to fall. Indeed, it is to the municipal suppression of international crimes that the multiplicity of international criminal conventions are directed, and it is to municipal criminal justice that the Rome Statute of the International Criminal Court ('Rome Statute') gives first bite of the investigative and prosecutorial cherries.[1] This being the case, it makes sense to examine how international crimes play out in municipal law and courts.

9.1

The first[2] steps in any such examination are to consider how, as a technical matter, states give effect in their respective bodies of municipal criminal law and criminal procedure to the substantive law of international crimes and to the jurisdiction over such crimes permitted or mandated by international law, and what international law may say about aspects of this; to consider technical, principled, and pragmatic questions relating to, specifically, the prosecution of international crimes at the national level; and to consider the sorts of criminal courts to which states entrust the municipal adjudication of international crimes. These are the functions of the present chapter. In all these respects, it is possible, by and large, to speak only in terms of tendencies. Precisely how international criminal law is implemented in a particular municipal legal order will depend on the municipal legal order in question. At the same time, it is possible to give examples of patterns.

9.2

---

[1] See *infra* paras 14.60–14.76 for the notion of 'complementarity'—in practice a set of rules governing the admissibility of cases before the International Criminal Court (ICC)—embodied in the Rome Statute.

[2] For subsequent steps, see *infra* chapters 10 and 11.

II. Substantive Law and Jurisdiction

9.3 If a state wishes or is obliged by treaty to provide for the suppression of an international crime or crimes through the machinery of its criminal justice system, the first thing it must do is to ensure that the specified conduct is criminal as a matter of its municipal law and that its courts are competent in desired or mandated instances to adjudicate upon its alleged commission. It may also wish or be obliged to consider the municipal provision or denial of certain defences in cases of international crimes. All this throws up technical questions of municipal law, as well as questions of international law and legal policy.

A. Criminalization and Extension of Jurisdiction

(i) A variety of techniques

9.4 There is a variety of techniques by which a state may render punishable under its criminal law and triable by its criminal courts crimes under or pursuant to customary or conventional international law.

9.5 The provisions relied on may be existing and general. In terms of the definition of and penalty attaching to the offence, the state may rely on common crimes, such as murder, assault, robbery, and so on, already found in the criminal code or other penal statute or, in some states, in the common law.[3] In terms of jurisdiction over the offence, the state may rely on generic grants of adjudicative competence, such as on the basis of nationality or passive personality, extant in the criminal code, code of criminal procedure or other penal statute.

9.6 Equally, a state may choose to enact legislation relating specifically to a given international crime or species of international crime, such as war crimes, in terms both of definition and penalty and of jurisdiction. In turn, specific statutory enactment in relation to international crimes can be done one of two ways. It can be done on an ad hoc basis, via the passage each time of legislation, whether free-standing or in the form of amending legislation to the criminal code and perhaps too the code of criminal procedure. It can also be done via the one-off passage of a statutory provision that provides for the direct applicability of any international crime or species of international crime as exists under customary international law or under or pursuant to any treaty to which the state is or may in future become

---

[3] In *Munyeshyaka*, 127 ILR 134, 137–8 (France 1998), the French Court of Cassation (Criminal Chamber) held that French law did not require that an accused be charged with the most serious crime possible on the facts. In that case, owing to the procedural incompetence of the French criminal courts over the complainants' allegations of genocide committed by a Rwandan national in Rwanda, the accused's acts were formally characterized instead as the crime of torture within the meaning of the Convention against Torture and Other Cruel, Inhuman or Degrading Treatment or Punishment 1984 ('Torture Convention'), over which the French courts did enjoy jurisdiction, specifically on the basis of universality. The same reasoning would logically apply to the characterization of an international crime as a common crime, and the law of many states would accord with French law on this point.

party. An example of the latter is Canada's Crimes Against Humanity and War Crimes Act 2000. Sections 4(1)(c) and 6(1)(c) of the Act, applicable respectively to crimes committed in and outside Canada, provide that every person who commits a war crime is guilty of an indictable offence. Sections 4(3) and 6(3) provide identical definitions of the term 'war crime' as used in sections 4(1)(c) and 6(1)(c) respectively, stating:

'war crime' means an act or omission committed during an armed conflict that, at the time and in the place of its commission, constitutes a war crime according to customary international law or conventional international law applicable to armed conflicts, whether or not it constitutes a contravention of the law in force at the time and in the place of its commission.

The term 'conventional international law' in sections 4(3) and 6(3) is defined in section 2(1) of the Act to refer to any convention, treaty or other international agreement

(a) that is in force and to which Canada is a party; or
(b) that is in force and the provisions of which Canada has agreed to accept and apply in an armed conflict in which it is involved.

The upshot of this suite of provisions is that any time Canada becomes a party to a treaty on the law of armed conflict which provides for individual criminal responsibility, or any time Canada agrees to accept and apply such a treaty in an armed conflict in which it is involved, and any time a war crime emerges under customary international law, that war crime, wherever and by whomever it is committed, constitutes an indictable offence under Canadian law.[4] Another example is article 18 clause 2 of the US's Uniform Code of Military Justice (UCMJ), which reads:

General courts-martial...have jurisdiction to try any person who by the law of war is subject to trial by a military tribunal and may adjudge any punishment permitted by the law of war.

The term 'law of war' as used in article 18 clause 2 is not limited to customary international law. Rather, the provision grants the US general courts-martial jurisdiction to try war crimes both under customary international law and pursuant to treaties to which the US is party. The practical consequence of the provision is therefore the same as under the Canadian legislation, even if under article 18 clause 2 of the UCMJ the crimes are given municipal effect solely by means of a grant of jurisdiction over offences determined and defined by *renvoi* to international law, rather than by enactment into the substantive criminal law of the US.[5]

---

[4] For an application of the Act, see *The Queen v Munyaneza (Désiré)*, ILDC 1339 (CA 2009) (Canada).

[5] In addition to the jurisdiction granted by art 18 cl 2, art 18 cl 1 of the UCMJ grants the US general courts-martial jurisdiction to try persons subject to the UCMJ for any offence made punishable by it. (Violations of the laws and customs of war, grave breaches of the Geneva Conventions, and so on, are not embodied as such in the UCMJ.) The range of persons subject to the UCMJ is spelled out in art 2(a), and comprises members of the US armed forces and a host of related personnel, as well as prisoners of war in the custody of the US armed forces. In practice, a person subject to the

9.7   It is not uncommon for states to rely on an existing common crime, found in the criminal code or at common law, for the definition of the crime and the fixing of its penalty and on a specific legislative provision for the relevant jurisdictional element. An example is the UK's War Crimes Act 1991, section 1(1) of which reads:

[P]roceedings for murder, manslaughter or culpable homicide may be brought against a person in the United Kingdom irrespective of his nationality at the time of the alleged offence if that offence—
(a) was committed during the period beginning with 1st September 1939 and ending with 5th June 1945 in a place which at the time was part of Germany or under German occupation; and
(b) constituted a violation of the laws and customs of war.

The result is that any customary war crime committed in the German Reich or in German-occupied Europe during the Second World War that amounts under existing English law to murder, manslaughter or culpable homicide is punishable as such, regardless of the nationality of the offender, in the UK.[6] Another example is the crime of torture in France avowedly pursuant to the Convention against Torture and Other Cruel, Inhuman or Degrading Treatment or Punishment 1984 ('Torture Convention').[7] Article 222-1 of the French Penal Code, a venerable provision dating back through various iterations to the original Penal Code of Napoleonic times,[8] provides:

Subjecting a person to torture or to acts of barbarity is punishable by... imprisonment.

Next, article 689-1 of the Code of Criminal Procedure states:

In application of the international conventions referred to in the following articles, any person who, outside the territory of the Republic, commits one of the crimes enumerated in those articles may, if present in France, be prosecuted and adjudged by the French courts.

In turn, article 689-2 provides:

In application of the Convention against Torture and Other Cruel, Inhuman or Degrading Treatment or Punishment, adopted in New York on 10 December 1984, any person who commits torture within the meaning of article 1 of the Convention may be prosecuted and adjudged in accordance with the conditions laid down in article 689-1.

In short, articles 689-1 and 689-2 of the Code of Criminal Procedure grant the French courts universal jurisdiction, as mandated by the Torture Convention,[9]

UCMJ accused of a war crime will not be tried for a war crime, pursuant to art 18 cl 2, but rather for an analogous common crime found in subchapter X of the UCMJ, such as murder (as per UCMJ, art 118) or manslaughter (as per UCMJ, art 119).

[6] For the only conviction under the Act, see *R v Sawoniuk*, Central Criminal Court, 1 April 1999, upheld on appeal in *R v Sawoniuk (Anthony)* [2000] Cr App R 220 (UK).
[7] The following translations are the author's.   [8] See Code Napoléon, art 421-1.
[9] Recall *supra* para 8.34 n 76.

over the crime of torture, as known to French law, in article 222-1 of the Penal Code.¹⁰

A provision commonly found in national criminal codes or codes of criminal procedure stipulates that any offence in the criminal code is of such ambit or, to the same end, that the criminal courts enjoy such jurisdiction as is mandated by any treaty to which the state is party or perhaps even just signatory.¹¹ Depending on the content of the criminal code, this statement of substantive ambit or grant of adjudicative competence will combine either with a municipal version of the relevant treaty crime or with an analogous common crime to give effect to the state party's obligation to provide for various heads of extraterritorial jurisdiction over the conduct specified in the treaty. 9.8

(ii) The permissibility of reliance on common crimes

The various international criminal conventions do not oblige states parties to enact specific offences corresponding verbatim to the offences provided for in the convention. Reliance on existing provisions, where feasible and appropriate, is permissible. As long as the conduct specified as criminal by the convention is punishable, the obligation of municipal criminalization has been acquitted. At the same time, reliance on a common crime that does not cover all conduct encompassed by the definition of the treaty crime would constitute a breach of the obligation of municipal criminalization. Similarly, if the punishment attaching to the common crime is inappropriately mild, reliance on that crime for the prosecution of a treaty crime would violate the obligation to render the impugned conduct punishable by penalties that reflect the offence's gravity.¹² 9.9

---

¹⁰ For an application of the Act, see *Munyeshyaka* (n 3). See, similarly, *Bosnia-Herzegovina Genocide case* ('*Kusljić*'), 131 ILR 274 (2001) and *Sokolović*, ILDC 56 (DE 2001) (Germany), involving convictions for the common crime of murder under the German Criminal Code on a universal jurisdictional basis furnished by section 6(9) of the Criminal Code ('German criminal law shall...apply, regardless of the law of the locality where they are committed, to...offences which on the basis of an international agreement binding on the Federal Republic of Germany must be prosecuted even though committed abroad') and arts 146 and 147 of the Convention relative to the Protection of Civilian Persons in Time of War 1949 ('Fourth Geneva Convention'); *Shantou Municipal People's Prosecutor v Naim (Atan)*, ILDC 1161 (CN 2003) (China), involving a conviction for the common crime of robbery under the Criminal Code of the People's Republic of China (PRC) on a universal jurisdictional basis furnished by art 9 of the Criminal Code ('This Code is applicable to the crimes specified in international treaties to which the PRC is a signatory or party and over which the PRC exercises criminal jurisdiction in accordance with its treaty obligations.') and arts 3(1)(*a*) and 6(4) of the Convention for the Suppression of Unlawful Acts against the Safety of Maritime Navigation 1988 ('SUA Convention').

¹¹ Recall, *supra* n 10, Criminal Code (Germany), art 6(9) and Criminal Code (PRC), art 9. See also eg Code of Criminal Procedure (Belgium), art 12*bis*; Criminal Code (Denmark), art 8; Penal Code (El Salvador), art 10; Criminal Code (Ethiopia), art 17(1)(*a*); Courts Act 1993 (Ghana), art 56(4)(*n*); Penal Code (Guatemala), art 5(4); Islamic Penal Code (Iran), art 9; Penal Code (Japan), art 4-2; Criminal Code (Russia), art 12(3); Organic Law on the Judiciary (Spain), art 23(4)(*p*); Criminal Code (Switzerland), art 6(1).

¹² Recall *supra* paras 8.7–8.8.

9.10　When it comes to crimes under customary international law, international law does not require their municipal criminalization,[13] with the result that a state cannot breach any international obligation by virtue of its legislation or lack of legislation in this regard.

(iii) The question of divergence in scope

(a) As between international and national law

9.11　The point as to definitional insufficiency in relation to treaty crimes[14] is not limited to reliance on common crimes for municipal criminalization. It applies equally to any municipal definition of a treaty crime. That is, a municipal version of a treaty crime which does not cover all conduct falling within the treaty's definition of the offence will constitute a breach of the state party's obligation of municipal criminalization.

9.12　The converse—namely an over-inclusive municipal definition of an international crime, be it a treaty crime or a crime under customary international law—also has potential to create problems, and probably more so. A state asserting universal jurisdiction over an international crime enacted into its law, whether pursuant to a treaty obligation or as permitted by customary international law, might define the crime more broadly than international law does. To the extent of the overbreadth, the municipal version will be wholly municipal in provenance, with the result that, to the extent again of the overbreadth, the state will be exercising an exorbitant jurisdiction. This was traditionally a sensitive issue in the context of the definition of piracy, especially when in the nineteenth century the UK began to suppress the high-seas slave trade pursuant to municipal legislation defining it as piracy. It is for this reason that the reference is traditionally to 'piracy *jure gentium*'.[15] Similar problems plague the question of retroactivity in relation to crimes under customary international law. If any municipal legislation under which an accused is tried that was not in force when the relevant customary international crime was committed is to satisfy a strict application of the *nullum crimen* principle,[16] it must define the crime in the same way that the latter was defined under customary international law at the time of its commission.[17]

(b) As among different bodies of national law

9.13　International criminal conventions commonly oblige states parties to render conduct criminal under their municipal law if that conduct is committed

---

[13] Recall *supra* para 4.5. That said, reliance on common crimes for the prosecution of crimes under customary international law may raise issues before certain international criminal courts. See *infra* paras 12.40 and 12.44–12.45.

[14] Recall *supra* para 9.9.

[15] See eg *The SS 'Lotus'*, PCIJ Rep Ser A No 10 (1927), 70 (diss op Moore).

[16] But cf the broader understanding of the *nullum crimen* principle, encompassing acts criminal according to the general principles of law recognised by civilized nations, as embodied in art 15(2) of the International Covenant on Civil and Political Rights 1966 (ICCPR) and art 7(2) of the European Convention on Human Rights 1950 (ECHR).

[17] See, generally, *Polyukhovich v Commonwealth of Australia*, 91 ILR 1, 41–51 (Brennan J) (Australia 1991).

intentionally. But none of the relevant conventions defines intent, and the concept can vary from state to state. The same goes in relation to modes of responsibility such as attempt, complicity, and 'participation',[18] to which some of the conventions oblige states parties to give effect. The upshot in both cases is that conduct punishable in one state party pursuant to the convention will not necessarily be punishable in another.

9.14 The point has a resonance beyond the context of the conventional obligation of municipal criminalization.[19] As a more general matter, given the variation among municipal bodies of criminal law when it comes to general principles of imposing responsibility, it is commonly the case that an individual convicted of an international crime in one state on the basis of given conduct could not be prosecuted for, let alone convicted of, that crime in another state on the basis of the same conduct.[20] To an extent this 'margin of appreciation' is built into the system,[21] especially when a state party's obligation is to render the specified conduct criminal 'in accordance with fundamental principles of its domestic law', 'in accordance with its domestic law', 'consistent with its legal system', and 'consistent with its legal principles'.[22] This is doubly so when the obligation of municipal criminalization is expressly subject to a state party's constitutional principles, 'the basic concepts of its legal system' or 'the fundamental principles of its legal system'.[23]

B. Defences

9.15 It may be that a state party, when enacting a treaty crime into its municipal law, enacts a defence to that crime not found in the treaty defining it or at least treats as applicable to that crime the defences laid down in the general part of its criminal code or at common law.[24] The provision of specifically municipal defences to treaty crimes appears not, in general, to be internationally unlawful. The treaty obligation to render the specified conduct a crime under municipal law is not violated when a state party, in addition to enacting the offence, enacts

---

[18] For the last, recall *supra* paras 7.72, 7.116, 7.123, 7.126, 7.139, and 7.171.

[19] The varying national parameters of the material and mental elements of crimes pose questions once more before certain international criminal courts.

[20] See also N Boister, *An Introduction to Transnational Criminal Law* (Oxford: Oxford University Press, 2012), 125–6. For one municipal legal approach to the question, see the International Criminal Court (UK) Act 2001, ss 50(1), (2) and (5), 51, 52, 55, 56(1), 65, and 66(3) and (4). Equivalent provisions are found in the International Criminal Court (Scotland) Act 2001.

[21] Consider also the issue of variation in penalties. See Boister (n 20), 130–1. For more on the broader question of principle, see *infra* paras 9.20–9.21.

[22] Recall *supra* para 8.11.   [23] Recall ibid.

[24] An example of the latter was seen in *R v Abdul-Hussain (Mustafa Shakir)*, Court of Appeal (Criminal Division), 17 December 1998 (UK), noted [1999] *Crim L Rev* 570, as endorsed on point in *R v Safi (Ali Ahmed)* [2003] EWCA Crim 1809, Court of Appeal (Criminal Division), 6 June 2003 (UK), noted (2003) 74 *BYIL* 471, where the English courts held that a defence of duress was in principle available, on the usual grounds, to a charge of hijacking under s 1 of the Aviation Security Act 1982 (UK), which incorporates the offences provided for in the Convention for the Suppression of Unlawful Seizure of Aircraft 1970. See also the example in Boister (n 20), 128.

or at least permits municipal defences to it. Nor does the '*judicare*' limb of the standard conventional obligation *aut dedere aut judicare* impose on a state party anything more than a duty to 'submit [relevant cases] to its competent authorities for the purpose of prosecution'. It does not oblige a state party to impose responsibility on persons accused of the relevant treaty crime. The United Nations Convention against Illicit Traffic in Narcotic Drugs and Psychotropic Substances 1988, the United Nations Convention against Transnational Organized Crime 2000, and the United Nations Convention against Corruption 2003 are explicit in this regard, each stating that '[n]othing contained in this Convention shall affect the principle that the description...of the applicable legal defences [to the offences established in accordance with this Convention] or other legal principles controlling the lawfulness of conduct is reserved to the domestic law of a State Party and that such offences shall be prosecuted and punished in accordance with that law'.[25]

9.16 The international legal complexion is different in those rare cases where a convention defining an international crime expressly excludes a particular defence.[26] Consider, for example, section 134 of the UK's Criminal Justice Act 1988 ('CJA 1988'), which enacts into municipal law the offence of torture within the meaning of the Torture Convention. Subsections 1 to 3 of section 134 of the CJA 1988 criminalize torture in a manner consonant with the definition of the offence in article 1 of the Convention. But subsection 4 of section 134 provides:

> It shall be a defence for a person charged with an offence under this section in respect of any conduct of his to prove that he had lawful authority, justification or excuse for that conduct.

The provision appears to allow for the defence of superior orders, reliance on which is expressly excluded by article 2(3) of the Convention, which states that

---

[25] United Nations Convention against Illicit Traffic in Narcotic Drugs and Psychotropic Substances 1988, art 3(11); United Nations Convention against Transnational Organized Crime 2000, art 11(6); United Nations Convention against Corruption 2003, art 30(9). A similar provision is found in early international criminal conventions. See Convention for the Suppression of the Illicit Traffic in Dangerous Drugs 1936, art 15 ('The present Convention does not affect the principle that the offences referred to in Articles 2 and 5 shall in each country be defined, prosecuted and punished in conformity with the general rules of its domestic law.'); International Convention for the Suppression of Counterfeiting Currency 1929, art 18 ('The present Convention does not affect the principle that the offences referred to in Article 3 should in each country, without ever being allowed impunity, be defined, prosecuted and punished in conformity with the general rules of its domestic law.')

[26] In addition to art 2(3) of the Torture Convention and the analogous art 6(2) of the International Convention for the Protection of All Persons from Enforced Disappearance 2006 ('Enforced Disappearance Convention'), see art 5 of the International Convention for the Suppression of Terrorist Bombings 1997, art 6 of the International Convention for the Suppression of the Financing of Terrorism 1999, and art 6 of the International Convention for the Suppression of Acts of Nuclear Terrorism 2005, all of which provide that each state party 'shall adopt such measures as may be necessary, including, where appropriate, domestic legislation, to ensure that criminal acts within the scope of this Convention, in particular where they are intended to provoke a state of terror in the general public or in a group of persons or particular persons, are under no circumstances justifiable by considerations of a political, philosophical, ideological, racial, ethnic, religious or other similar nature'. Recall *supra* paras 8.78–8.80.

'[a]n order from a superior officer or a public authority may not be invoked as a justification [for] torture'.[27] For its part, article 4(1) of the Torture Convention obliges each state party to 'ensure that all acts of torture are offences under its municipal law', the definition of torture for the purposes of this obligation being that laid down in article 1(1). Subsections 1 to 3 of section 134 of the CJA 1988 do precisely this. The apparent provision in section 134(4) for the defence of superior orders does not as such violate the obligation undertaken by the UK in article 4(1) of the Convention. Nor does the '*judicare*' limb of article 7(1)'s obligation *aut dedere aut judicare* oblige the UK actually to impose responsibility on persons accused of torture within the meaning of the Convention. But an acquittal by an English, Scots or Northern Irish criminal court based on section 134(4) of the CJA 1988 would breach the stipulation in article 2(3) of the Torture Convention that superior orders 'may not be invoked' as a justification for torture.

It may also be that a state recognizes in its municipal criminal law defences to crimes under customary international law not recognized by customary international law itself. This is unambiguously lawful. Since customary international law imposes no obligation on states to punish customary international crimes,[28] it cannot exclude the applicability of specific defences to such crimes. 9.17

The converse of the above situations is also possible. It may be that a state does not permit the invocation before its criminal courts of a defence to an internationally-derived crime in circumstances where international law would recognize the defence. Since the various international criminal conventions do not provide for defences, this possibility is limited to crimes under customary international law, and it does not appear to be internationally unlawful. Consider, for example, the UK's International Criminal Court (UK) Act 2001. The Act contains no specific defences, leaving the question of exculpation in respect of the crimes of genocide, crimes against humanity, and war crimes to 'the principles of the law of England and Wales', in the words of section 56(1). For its part, English criminal law does not recognize duress of circumstance (known in English law as 'necessity') as a defence to murder. But the defence, as now embodied in article 31(1)(*d*)(ii) of the Rome Statute,[29] is possibly recognized by customary international law. No rule of customary international law renders the municipal denial of such a defence unlawful, since customary international law does not oblige states to give effect to defences recognized by it.[30] It is perhaps, however, arguable that the exercise of universal jurisdiction over a crime under customary international law coupled with the inadmissibility of a defence available under customary international law adds up to the assumption 9.18

---

[27] See also, *mutatis mutandis*, Enforced Disappearance Convention, art 6(2).
[28] Recall *supra* para 4.5.   [29] Recall *supra* para 6.23.
[30] Nor does international human rights law stipulate the availability of specific defences, as long as the deprivation of the accused's liberty is in accordance with such procedures as are established by law and he or she receives a fair trial.

of an exorbitant jurisdiction. The same argument, *mutatis mutandis*, could be made in relation to retroactivity.[31]

9.19   One approach to the question is found in section 11 of Canada's Crimes Against Humanity and War Crimes Act, which states:

> In proceedings for an offence under any of sections 4 to 7, the accused may, subject to sections 12 to 14 and to subsection 607(6) of the Criminal Code, rely on any justification, excuse or defence available under the laws of Canada or under international law at the time of the alleged offence or at the time of the proceedings.

Section 13 excludes the defence of prescription of law otherwise available to crimes under Canadian law. Section 14 excludes the defence of superior orders.

C. Mutual Recognition or Harmonization?

9.20   One might ask whether divergence between international and municipal law and among different bodies of municipal law is necessarily a problem for international criminal law, provided that international obligations are fulfilled and international prohibitions observed. It could with reason be argued that, as long as international minimum standards are observed, it is better to tolerate national variation in order to facilitate and thereby encourage national implementation of international criminal law.[32] On the other hand, one might legitimately take the view that this encouragement comes at the cost of international criminal law's universality and with it fairness as among individuals responsible for identical conduct.[33] That is, one might insist on identical national standards. This is the familiar debate between mutual recognition and harmonization, viewed here through the prism of international criminal law.

9.21   Even if, however, one were to argue for harmonization, the question how it could be achieved remains. A uniform international criminal code is scarcely a realistic, let alone feasible prospect.

III. Prosecution

9.22   Ensuring that internationally-specified conduct is criminal under municipal law and within the procedural competence of the municipal courts are together one thing. Actually prosecuting persons suspected of the crime is another. Prosecution

---

[31] Both the assumption by Australia of an exorbitant prescriptive jurisdiction and the problem of retroactive criminalization were thought by Brennan, Deane, and Gaudron JJ (dissenting) of the High Court of Australia in *Polyukhovich* (n 17) to vitiate Australia's War Crimes (Amendment) Act 1995.
[32] See eg F Mégret, 'In Defense of Hybridity: Towards a Representational Theory of International Criminal Justice' (2005) 38 *Cornell ILJ* 725. For the argument that, as it is, the various international criminal conventions are having a 'harmonizing impact', see Boister (n 20), 126–30.
[33] See eg Mégret (n 32), 735–6: 'Although international criminal law is clearly fully compatible with some measure of national margin of appreciation, the credibility of the law will be affected by major contradictions.'

raises the question of the municipal implementation of the obligation *aut dedere aut judicare*. In addition, it is usually only with a decision to prosecute that controversy erupts over a state's provision for universal prescriptive jurisdiction, a controversy which tends to be all the greater when prosecution is pursued *in absentia*. Both issues will now be examined.

A. *Aut dedere aut judicare*

9.23 It is difficult to see how the treaty obligation *aut dedere aut judicare* can be implemented by means of legislation in any national criminal justice system that guarantees the independence of the prosecuting authorities (who in many states, moreover, are judicial in character, with the attendant implications for judicial independence).

9.24 But the obligation *aut dedere aut judicare* is perhaps amenable to breach via legislation. Take, for example, the UK's CJA 1988, section 135 of which—referable to the crime of torture within the meaning of article 1 of the Torture Convention, enacted into municipal law via section 134 of the Act—provides that proceedings under section 134 may be commenced only by or with the consent of the Attorney General. This was included in the Act as a filter for frivolous or otherwise unmeritorious claims.[34] Article 7(1) and (2) of the Torture Convention, however, read:

1. The State Party in territory under whose jurisdiction a person alleged to have committed any offence referred to in article 4 is found shall, in the cases contemplated in article 5, if it does not extradite him, submit the case to its competent authorities for the purpose of prosecution.
2. These authorities shall take their decision in the same manner as in the case of any ordinary offence of a serious nature under the law of that State. . . .

It is distinctly arguable that section 135 of the CJA 1988 results in the breach of the first sentence of article 7(2) of the Torture Convention.

B. Prosecution on the Basis of Universal Jurisdiction

(i) *In general*

9.25 The more accurate conclusion is that war crimes, crimes against humanity, and genocide are punishable as a matter of customary international law on the basis of universality.[35] Moreover, a host of international criminal conventions oblige states parties to provide for universal jurisdiction over the relevant crimes and, when an alleged perpetrator is present within their territory, to submit the case to the prosecuting authorities for the purpose of prosecution if they do not extradite the

---

[34] Section 70(2) of the International Criminal Court (UK) Act inserted a similar provision, s 1A(3), into the UK's Geneva Conventions Act 1957.
[35] Recall *supra* para 1.63.

372   *Municipal Law and Courts*

individual to a state that will.[36] Notwithstanding this, some states—most notably China, Israel, the US, and especially and most vociferously Rwanda and the states of the African Union (AU) *en bloc*—have objected to the exercise of this jurisdiction by prosecuting authorities in European states, especially Belgium, France, and Spain.

9.26 In 2008, the AU took the issue of what it has repeatedly condemned as 'the abuse of universal jurisdiction'[37] to the AU–EU Ministerial Troika,[38] which agreed to establish a technical ad hoc expert group to clarify the legal issues and to report to the following Troika meeting.[39] The experts duly reported,[40] to little obvious avail.

9.27 Remaining unsatisfied, the group of African states, via Tanzania, took the matter to the UN General Assembly in 2009. Since then, the more diplomatically entitled question of the 'scope and application of the principle of universal jurisdiction' has been the subject of four reports compiled by the Secretary-General on the basis of information and observations submitted by member states;[41] has been annually debated—for want of a better word for set-piece and often verbatim reiteration of *a priori* positions—in the Assembly's Sixth, *viz* Legal, Committee, which each year since 2010 has further convened a working group 'to undertake a thorough discussion of the scope and application of universal jurisdiction';[42] and has been the subject of annual resolutions of the General Assembly in plenary.[43] Little has so far come of all this, beyond a common view 'that the legitimacy and credibility of the use of universal jurisdiction are best ensured by its responsible and judicious application consistent with international law'.[44]

9.28 In the midst of these developments, the report of the United Nations Fact-Finding Mission on the Gaza Conflict ('Goldstone report')[45] 'support[ed] the reliance on universal jurisdiction as an avenue for States to investigate violations of grave breach provisions of the Geneva Convention of 1949, prevent impunity

---

[36] Recall *supra* paras 8.34–8.39 and 8.48–8.56.

[37] See AU Assembly Decision on the Report of the Commission on the Abuse of the Principle of Universal Jurisdiction, AU doc Decision Assembly/AU/Dec 199(XI), 1 July 2008; AU Assembly Decision on the Implementation of the Assembly Decision on the Abuse of the Principle of Universal Jurisdiction, AU doc Decision Assembly/AU/Dec 213(XII), 3 February 2009; AU Assembly Decision on the Abuse of the Principle of Universal Jurisdiction, AU doc Decision Assembly/AU/Dec 243(XIII) Rev.1, 3 July 2009; and all subsequent, identically-entitled resolutions.

[38] See AU–EU Ministerial Troika, 10th meeting, 16 September 2008 (Brussels), and 11th meeting, 20–21 November 2008 (Addis Ababa).

[39] See AU–EU Ministerial Troika, 11th meeting, joint communiqué, 21 November 2008, doc 1698/08.

[40] See *AU–EU Technical* Ad hoc *Expert Group on the Principle of Universal Jurisdiction: Report*, Council of the European Union doc 8672/1/09 REV 1 (16 April 2009).

[41] See UN docs A/65/181 (29 July 2010), A/66/93 (20 June 2011) and A/66/93/Add.1 (16 August 2011), A/67/116 (28 June 2012), and A/68/113 (26 June 2013).

[42] GA res 65/33, 6 December 2010, para 2; GA res 66/103, 9 December 2011, para 2; GA res 67/98, 14 December 2012, para 2; GA res 68/117, 16 December 2013, para 2.

[43] See *supra* n 42. See also, previously, GA res 64/117, 16 December 2009.

[44] GA res 65/33, preamble (fourth recital); GA res 66/103, preamble (fifth recital); GA res 67/98, preamble (fifth recital); GA res 68/117, preamble (fifth recital).

[45] *Report of the United Nations Fact-Finding Mission on the Gaza Conflict*, UN doc A/HRC/12/48 (25 September 2009) ('Goldstone report'). The report's recommendations were endorsed by the UN Human Rights Council in HRC res S-12/1 B, 16 October 2009, para 3 and by the UN General Assembly in GA res 64/10, 5 November 2009, para 1.

and promote international accountability'; 'recommend[ed] that the States parties to the Geneva Conventions of 1949 should start criminal investigations in national courts, using universal jurisdiction, where there is sufficient evidence of the commission of grave breaches of the Geneva Conventions of 1949' by Israel and the Palestinian authorities in Gaza; and further recommended that, '[w]here so warranted following investigation, alleged perpetrators should be arrested and prosecuted in accordance with internationally recognized standards of justice'.[46]

When the state practice is analysed closely, the controversy relates less to universal criminal jurisdiction per se than to the exercise of such jurisdiction, and indeed of any jurisdiction, over the serving and former officials of foreign states. The exercise of universal jurisdiction over private parties accused of international crimes has not provoked outcry—indeed, quite the opposite. The main legal complaint by aggrieved states is that targeted officials are entitled, in their view, to immunity from the criminal jurisdiction of foreign states even in respect of allegations of international crimes.[47] In other words, insofar as the controversy is one of international law rather than geopolitics, what is billed as a debate over universal jurisdiction is really mostly an argument over the scope of the immunities from criminal jurisdiction from which foreign state officials benefit under international law. 9.29

To the extent that the controversy is geopolitical, the claim by African states that they are selectively targeted by biased European prosecutors is unsupported by the data.[48] 9.30

(ii) In absentia

Correctly analysed, whether prosecution *in absentia* on the basis of universal jurisdiction is permissible under international law implicates two distinct questions, namely whether jurisdiction to prescribe criminal laws on the basis of universality 9.31

---

[46] Goldstone report (n 45), paras 1857 and 1975(*a*).
[47] See eg, *inter alia*, UN doc A/C.6/64/SR.12 (25 November 2009), 3, paras 14–15 (Tunisia, on behalf of the African group of states), 4, paras 20–21 (Iran, on behalf of the Movement of Non-Aligned Countries), 6, para 35 (Swaziland), 7, para 44 (South Africa), 8, para 49 (China), 14, paras 93–94 (Sudan), 16, para 101 (Tunisia); UN doc A/C.6/64/SR.13 (24 November 2009), 2, para 1 (Indonesia), 2, para 2 (Iran), 4, para 14 (Russia), 8, para 47 (Ethiopia); UN doc A/C.6/65/SR.10 (3 November 2010), 9, para 55 (Iran, on behalf of the Movement of Non-Aligned Countries), 10, para 59 (Malawi, on behalf of the African group of states), 11, para 69 (Egypt); UN doc A/C.6/65/SR.11 (14 January 2011), 2, para 1 (Libya), 4, para 19 (Senegal), 5, para 25 (China), 5, para 26 (Algeria), 6, para 32 (Democratic Republic of the Congo), 6, para 34 (Cuba), 8, para 46 (Vietnam), 9, para 57 (Russia), 10, para 66 (Ghana); UN doc A/C.6/65/SR.12 (10 November 2010), 4, para 20 (Venezuela), 4, paras 22–23 (Sudan); UN doc A/C.6/66/SR.13 (30 November 2011), 2, paras 1, 2, and 4 (Sri Lanka), 2, para 5 (China), 3, paras 8–9 (South Africa), 6, para 30 (Burkina Faso), 8, paras 44–45 (Iran), 9; UN doc A/C.6/67/SR.13 (24 December 2012), 2, para 2 (Angola), 2, para 4 (South Africa), 2, para 6 (Mozambique), 4, para 17 (Bangladesh), 4, paras 18–19 (Sri Lanka); UN doc A/C.6/68/SR.12 (20 December 2013), 12, paras 73–74 (Egypt, on behalf of the African group of states); UN doc A/C.6/68/SR.13 (6 January 2014), 11, para 65 (Rwanda); UN doc A/C.6/68/SR.14 (6 January 2014), 5, para 23 (Equatorial Guinea), 6, para 29 (Lesotho).
[48] See eg *AU–EU Expert Group Report* (n 40), paras 26 and 40–41.

is internationally lawful and whether the enforcement of criminal laws *in absentia* is internationally lawful.[49] The answer to the second question is yes, as noted by Judges Higgins, Kooijmans, and Buergenthal in their joint separate opinion in *Arrest Warrant*:

> Some [national] jurisdictions provide for trial *in absentia*; others do not. If it is said that a person must be within the jurisdiction at the time of the trial itself, that may be a prudent guarantee for the right of fair trial but has little to do with bases of jurisdiction recognized under international law.[50]

The upshot is that, if universal jurisdiction to prescribe criminal laws is internationally lawful in a given instance, so too is so-called 'universal jurisdiction *in absentia*', *viz* the enforcement *in absentia* of universal prescriptive jurisdiction.[51]

9.32 The foregoing remains the case, all other things being equal,[52] when the universal jurisdiction exercised is treaty-based, rather than customary. The view that the exercise *in absentia* of a universal prescriptive jurisdiction mandated by treaty is impermissible, as put forward by President Guillaume, Judge Ranjeva, and Judge ad hoc Bula-Bula in their respective separate opinions and declarations in *Arrest Warrant*,[53] is incorrect. It is true that the most common version of the treaty obligation to enact legislation, where necessary, asserting universal jurisdiction over the offences in question requires a state party to 'take such measures as may be necessary to establish its jurisdiction over the offences in cases where the alleged offender is present in its territory'.[54] Similarly, the standard treaty obligation *aut dedere aut judicare* speaks of a state party 'in the territory of which the alleged offender is found'.[55] So too the obligation on a high contracting party to bring before its courts or to surrender to a state that will persons alleged to have committed grave breaches of the 1949 Geneva Conventions presupposes the suspect's territorial presence. But to conclude from these formulations that the prosecution *in absentia* of the universal jurisdiction obliged by the treaty is prohibited is to confuse what is not mandatory with what is impermissible. The rider or presupposition as to the suspect's presence in the territory prevents these

---

[49] Recall *supra* para 1.55.
[50] *Arrest Warrant of 11 April 2000 (Democratic Republic of the Congo v Belgium)*, ICJ Rep 2002, 3, 79–80, para 56.
[51] See also ibid, 169–73, paras 52–58 (diss op Van den Wyngaert). See too B Stern, 'À Propos de la Compétence Universelle...', in E Yakpo and T Boumedra (eds), *Liber Amicorum Judge Mohammed Bedjaoui* (The Hague: Kluwer, 1999), 735, 750 and 752 (limiting her conclusion to investigation and the issuance of a warrant); G de la Pradelle, 'La compétence universelle' in H Ascensio, E Decaux, and A Pellet (eds), *Droit international pénal* (2nd edn, Paris: Pedone, 2012), 1007, 1017–18, para 27 (somewhat guardedly); M. Henzelin, 'La compétence pénale universelle. Une question non résolue par l'Arrêt Yerodia' (2002) 106 *RGDIP* 819, 846–53 (seemingly limiting his conclusion à la Stern). But cf, *contra*, L Reydams, *Universal Jurisdiction. International and Municipal Legal Perspectives* (Oxford: Oxford University Press, 2003), 55.
[52] Recall, as regards third states, *supra* para 8.21.
[53] See *Arrest Warrant* (n 50), 39–40, para 9 (sep op Guillaume), 56–7, para 7 (dec Ranjeva), and 124–5, para 75 (sep op Bula-Bula), all in specific relation to so-called 'universal jurisdiction *in absentia*' pursuant to the grave breaches provisions of the Fourth Geneva Convention.
[54] Recall *supra* para 8.36.   [55] Recall *supra* para 8.48.

provisions from giving rise to obligations on states parties to empower their courts to try an accused *in absentia* and to prosecute on this basis, obligations which would in practice prevent the many states that insist on trial *in personam* from becoming parties to the treaty. The territorial limitation serves as a lowest common denominator designed to encourage maximum participation in the treaties.[56] As regards, moreover, the option of extradition under the obligation *aut dedere aut judicare*, a state obviously cannot extradite a person over whom it does not have custody. Most of these points were made by Judges Higgins, Kooijmans, and Buergenthal[57] and by Judge ad hoc Van den Wyngaert[58] in *Arrest Warrant*. In sum, the question of the international permissibility of the exercise *in absentia* of a treaty-mandated universal jurisdiction comes down to whether, as a general matter, the issuance of an arrest warrant *in absentia* and trial *in absentia* are internationally lawful or not—and they are.

(iii) *Voluntary restrictions on prosecution on the basis of universal jurisdiction*

Aware of the diplomatic sensitivities aroused by universal jurisdiction, many states whose courts enjoy competence on this basis over international crimes have put in place restrictions on the exercise of such jurisdiction.[59] It is common, for example, for municipal law to require that the alleged offender or alleged victim have, subsequent to the event, become a national or resident of the forum state. By no means an infrequent municipal precondition to the exercise of universal jurisdiction in states which otherwise permit criminal proceedings *in absentia* is that an alleged offender be present in the forum state's territory before the prosecuting authorities initiate proceedings against him or her. Some national legislation requires that the attorney-general or the equivalent authorize prosecutions for offences over which the courts enjoy universal jurisdiction. Where statute imposes no such requirements, the courts of some states have nonetheless demanded a sufficient concrete link between the forum and either the suspect or the victim.

9.33

IV. Adjudication[60]

When it comes to the adjudication of international crimes at the national level, states have recourse to a range of different sorts of criminal courts, some of them

9.34

---

[56] See also H Ascensio, 'Are Spanish Courts Backing Down on Universality? The Supreme Tribunal's Decision in *Guatemalan Generals*' (2003) 1 *JICJ* 690, 700.

[57] *Arrest Warrant* (n 50), 80, para 57 (joint sep op Higgins, Kooijmans, and Buergenthal).

[58] Ibid, 170, para 54 and 175, para 62 (diss op Van den Wyngaert).

[59] For examples of the following municipal restrictions, see *AU–EU Expert Group Report* (n 40), paras 18 and 24. In addition, see the amendments to art 23 of the Organic Law on the Judiciary (Spain) effected via Organic Law 1/2014, 13 March 2014, BOE-A-2014-2709.

[60] This section deals only with fora for trial—that is, with formal judicial enforcement of criminal law. It does not consider alternative justice mechanisms such as truth and reconciliation commissions, Rwanda's *gacaca* courts, and so on.

of general jurisdiction, some of them of special. In this regard, international law is unprescriptive. As long as any applicable international criminal treaty obligations are acquitted and any applicable standards under conventional and customary international human rights law are met, states are at liberty to decide the precise characteristics of any municipal criminal court relied on for the trial of an international crime.

9.35 As will be seen, it may on occasion be that a state tries a civilian for an international crime in a military court. Trying civilians in military courts is not per se offensive to international human rights standards. It depends on the court's mode of establishment, its composition, and its rules of procedure and evidence. Many military courts are established by law, within the meaning of international human rights law; are staffed by professional judges, whether full-time military personnel or reservists; and accord all the fair trial guarantees demanded by international law. Others are kangaroo courts. That the trial of a civilian in a military court is not in itself a violation of the internationally-guaranteed right to fair trial is made clear in the UN Human Rights Committee's General Comment No 32, on article 14 of the International Covenant on Civil and Political Rights 1966 ('ICCPR'),[61] although the Committee cautions that '[t]rials of civilians by military or special courts should be exceptional, i.e. limited to cases where the State party can show that resorting to such trials is necessary and justified by objective and serious reasons'.[62] The European Court of Human Rights takes a similar line in relation to the right to fair trial secured by article 6 of the Convention for the Protection of Human Rights and Fundamental Freedoms 1950 ('European Convention on Human Rights'), as seen in *Ergin v Turkey (No 6)*.[63] In explaining, however, that '[t]he power of military criminal justice should not extend to civilians unless there are compelling reasons justifying such a situation, and if so only on a clear and foreseeable legal basis', the Court stipulates that '[t]he existence of such reasons must be substantiated in each specific case', stressing that '[i]t is not sufficient for the national legislation to allocate certain categories of offence to military courts *in abstracto*'.[64] (It is perhaps telling that *Ergin* itself involved trial by a military criminal court in the context of a domestic insurgency, rather than more generally.) For its part, however, the Inter-American Court of Human Rights flatly rejects the trial of civilians in military criminal courts.[65]

---

[61] See Human Rights Committee, *General Comment No 32 (Article 14: Right to equality before courts and tribunals and to a fair trial)*, UN doc CCPR/C/GC/32 (23 August 2007), para 22.
[62] Ibid, references omitted. The last sentence continues 'and where with regard to the specific class of individuals and offences at issue the regular civilian courts are unable to undertake the trials'. This final condition does not seem to accord with state practice.
[63] (2006) 47 EHRR 829, paras 42–44.   [64] Ibid, para 47.
[65] See eg *Castillo Petruzzi v Peru*, Inter-Am Ct HR (Ser C) No 52 (1999), paras 128–129; *Durand and Ugarte v Peru*, Inter-Am Ct HR (Ser C) No 68 (2000), para 117; *Cantoral Benavides v Peru*, Inter-Am Ct HR (Ser C) No 69 (2000), paras 112–113. In *Radilla Pacheco v Mexico (Preliminary Objections, Merits, Reparations and Costs)*, Inter-Am Ct HR (Ser C) No 209, para 272, as reiterated on several occasions, the Court stated: 'In a democratic State of law, the military criminal jurisdiction shall have a restrictive and exceptional scope and be directed toward the protection of special juridical interests, related to the tasks characteristic of the military forces. Therefore...only active soldiers shall be prosecuted within the military jurisdiction for the perpetration of crimes or offenses that based on their own nature threaten the juridical rights of the military order itself.'

A. Municipal Criminal Courts of General Jurisdiction

When international crimes are tried in municipal courts, it is most common for these courts to be criminal courts of general jurisdiction, in the sense of jurisdiction *ratione materiae* not specifically over international crimes and jurisdiction *ratione loci* and *personae* of the usual scope. Nor is any special organizational provision usually made within such courts for the adjudication of international crimes. In Kosovo, however, cases in the ordinary courts implicating, among other offences, certain international crimes have been and may be assigned on an ad hoc basis, by an international appointee, to specially-constituted panels within the ordinary criminal courts in which foreign judges are in the majority. 9.36

(i) *The ordinary criminal courts and the regular military courts*

By and large international crimes are tried in the forum state's ordinary criminal courts, proceeding according to the ordinary criminal procedure of that state and applying its ordinary substantive criminal law, which may or may not include offences deriving from international law. Alternatively, alongside their ordinary (or 'civil', meaning civilian) criminal courts, most states have a system of regular military courts, frequently known as courts-martial, of general criminal jurisdiction *ratione materiae*, to which service personnel, often including captured hostile combatants, and sometimes also civilians, including and perhaps uniquely foreigners, are answerable.[66] Depending on the state and on the crime, a military court might apply the forum state's ordinary criminal law; the forum state's military criminal law, embodying a range of common crimes such as murder, assault, rape, and robbery, military offences such as disobedience of orders, desertion, mutiny, and aiding the enemy, and perhaps also offences deriving from international law; or the laws and customs of war, as derived from international law. Whether a person charged with an international crime is tried before an ordinary criminal court or a military criminal court depends on the state and on the crime. These days, most states try all international crimes other than war crimes in the ordinary criminal courts. But a divergence of practice is apparent when it comes to war crimes. Some states try all those accused of war crimes, even service personnel, in the ordinary criminal courts. At the other end of the spectrum, some states try all those accused of war crimes, even civilians, in military courts. In the middle, some states try civilians accused of war crimes in the ordinary criminal courts and service personnel accused of the same in military courts.[67] 9.37

In 2011, Croatia designated the county courts of Osijek, Rijeka, Split, and Zagreb as exclusively competent to hear trials in Croatia for crimes within the 9.38

---

[66] Note that, in terms of the material sources of customary international law, the case law of military courts constitutes state practice, just like the case law of the ordinary criminal courts of a state.
[67] For its part, the US has a complicated system of overlapping competences as between the courts-martial and the ordinary criminal courts and as between the courts-martial and military commissions.

jurisdiction of the International Criminal Court (ICC).[68] But this is simply a matter of venue. The four designated courts remain both formally and in practice courts of general criminal jurisdiction *ratione materiae*. It is merely that they alone among Croatian courts may entertain first-instance proceedings for war crimes, crimes against humanity, and genocide, which they do as only one part of a normal criminal caseload.

9.39   Kenya, with international assistance, has constructed a special courthouse in Shanzu, a suburb of Mombasa, for trying piracy cases. Similar court buildings are under construction in the Seychelles, Mauritius, and the region of Puntland in Somalia. These are no more than purpose-built trial facilities to enable the ordinary criminal courts to process piracy cases more expeditiously and effectively. These so-called 'piracy courts' are not formal divisions, sections or even panels within the criminal courts. Even less do they enjoy jurisdiction *ratione materiae* only over piracy.[69]

(ii) 'Regulation 64' panels and EULEX panels within the courts of Kosovo

9.40   After the provisional replacement in 1999 in the erstwhile province of Kosovo of the governmental authority of the Federal Republic of Yugoslavia with that of the United Nations Mission in Kosovo (UNMIK),[70] UNMIK—in which '[a]ll legislative and executive authority with respect to Kosovo, including the administration of the judiciary, [was] vested'[71]—bore the burden of ensuring the effective functioning of the territory's criminal justice system.[72] The task

---

[68] See art 1 of Law NN 55/11, 6 May 2011, amending art 12 of Law NN 175/03 on the Implementation of the Statute of the International Criminal Court and the Prosecution of Crimes against the International Law of War and Humanitarian Law 2003 (as corrected). Former art 12(2) of the original Law on the Implementation of the Statute of the International Criminal Court gave jurisdiction to other Croatian courts as well. The ICTY, proceeding under rule 11*bis* of its Rules of Procedure and Evidence, has transferred one case, involving two indictees, to the Croatian authorities for the purpose of prosecution. See *Prosecutor v Ademi and Norac*, IT-04-78-PT, Referral Bench, Decision for Referral to the Authorities of the Republic of Croatia pursuant to Rule 11*bis*, 14 September 2005.

[69] The Shanzu Law Courts, as they are known, are used for other high-security cases as well, such as the trial of members of the militant group Al-Shabaab.

[70] See SC res 1244 (1999), 10 June 1999.

[71] UNMIK reg 1999/1, 25 July 1999 (as amended), s 1(1). In further accordance with s 1(1), this authority was to be exercised by the Special Representative of the Secretary-General.

[72] In accordance with s 3 of UNMIK regulation 1999/1, the laws applicable in the territory of Kosovo prior to 24 March 1999, among them the Criminal Code of the Socialist Federal Republic of Yugoslavia, continued to apply in Kosovo insofar as they did not conflict with international human rights standards, the fulfilment of UNMIK's mandate or any other regulation promulgated by UNMIK. Section 3 of UNMIK regulation 1999/1 was repealed by UNMIK regulation 1999/25, 15 December 1999, consequent upon the promulgation of UNMIK regulation 1999/24, 15 December 1999. In accordance with s 1 of UNMIK regulation 1999/24, the law applicable in Kosovo comprised, in addition to UNMIK regulations and their subsidiary instruments, the law that applied in Kosovo on 22 March 1989, before the rescission of Kosovo's autonomous status within the Socialist Republic of Serbia, then a constituent republic of the Socialist Federal Republic of Yugoslavia. This law included the Criminal Code of the Socialist Autonomous Province of Kosovo. On 6 July 2003, by way of UNMIK regulation 2003/25, UNMIK promulgated a Provisional Criminal Code of Kosovo, which entered into force on 6 April 2004.

was rendered more difficult by the flight of ethnic Serbian judges and prosecutors, the refusal to serve of those that remained, and the inexperience of their Albanian Kosovar counterparts. The problem was most acute in Mitrovica. To remedy the shortage of experienced judicial and prosecutorial personnel there, to improve local professional standards, and to seek to guarantee the independence and impartiality of the local criminal justice system in the face of threats of violence and attempts at corruption, particularly in cases involving allegations of war crimes and crimes against humanity and organized criminal activity, the Special Representative of the UN Secretary-General promulgated UNMIK regulation 2000/6, which granted him the power to appoint foreign judges and prosecutors to the District Court of Mitrovica and to other courts and prosecutors' offices within the former court's territorial jurisdiction.[73] These 'international' judges and prosecutors were vested with the authority to fulfil all the functions of local judges and prosecutors, including to select and take charge of new and pending criminal cases and investigations.[74] Pursuant to UNMIK regulation 2000/34 of a few months later, what applied to the District Court of Mitrovica was extended to all prosecutors' offices and courts, including the Supreme Court, throughout Kosovo.[75] When these moves proved insufficient, the Secretary-General's Special Representative promulgated UNMIK regulation 2000/64, which empowered him, at any stage in given criminal proceedings, not only to replace a local judge or prosecutor with an international one for the purpose of the proceedings or to designate a new venue for the proceedings but also, if desired, to constitute for the purpose of the proceedings a panel (known as a 'regulation 64' panel) of three judges, of which two, including the presiding judge, were to be international.[76] In practice it was to 'regulation 64' panels that proceedings in respect of war crimes, crimes against humanity, and genocide alleged to have been committed in the territory of Kosovo during the events of 1998–99 were subsequently assigned, although such panels also tried other cases of a controversial nature, in particular those involving organized crime. The panels were not an unqualified success.

9.41 In 2008, UNMIK's judicial and prosecutorial mandate was handed over to the European Union Rule of Law Mission in Kosovo (EULEX).[77] 'Regulation 64' panels were replaced by analogous panels of EULEX judges assigned to the proceedings by the President of the Assembly of EULEX judges, in accordance

---

[73] UNMIK reg 2000/6, 15 February 2000, s 1(1).   [74] Ibid, ss 1(2) and (3).
[75] UNMIK reg 2000/34, 27 May 2000, s 1.
[76] UNMIK reg 2000/64, 15 December 2000, ss 1 and 2. The jurisdiction *ratione materiae* of the criminal courts of Kosovo, including of 'regulation 64' panels within them, remained general, their jurisdiction *ratione loci* and *personae* remained as it was, and the criminal procedure ordinarily followed in Kosovo remained applicable.
[77] See UN doc S/PRST/2008/24 (26 November 2008). For the EU's part, see Council Joint Action 2008/124/CFSP of 4 February 2008 on the European Union Rule of Law Mission in Kosovo, EULEX KOSOVO, OJ L 42/92, 16.2.2008 and Council Decision 2012/291/CFSP of 5 June 2012 amending and extending Council Joint Action 2008/124/CFSP of 4 February 2008 on the European Union Rule of Law Mission in Kosovo, EULEX KOSOVO, OJ L 146/46, 6.6.2012.

with legislation enacted by the Assembly of Kosovo.[78] The cases dealt with by EULEX judges now relate more to organized criminal activity such as trafficking in persons than to war crimes and crimes against humanity.[79] On 23 April 2014, the Assembly of Kosovo voted in favour of an extension of EULEX's mandate until June 2016.

B. Municipal Criminal Courts of Special Jurisdiction

9.42   There also exist municipal criminal courts[80] with special jurisdiction in respect of international crimes, in the sense of jurisdiction *ratione materiae*, be it *de jure* or *de facto*, specifically over given international crimes and sometimes wider-than-usual jurisdiction *ratione loci* and *personae* in relation to the same. Such courts come in any number of varieties.[81] They may be specially-designated panels, sections, chambers or divisions within the ordinary criminal courts or they may be special courts as such. In terms of their creation, to date they have been established, variously, by the forum state alone,[82] as would usually be the case with a municipal criminal court; by the forum state pursuant to a treaty of co-operation with an international organization; by an international territorial administration with legislative power in respect of the territory; by occupying powers; and by a local body appointed by occupying powers. In terms of personnel, such courts may be staffed by local judges and prosecutors appointed by the forum state alone, as one might expect with a municipal criminal court, or by a mix of local and foreign judges and prosecutors appointed by the forum state alone, by the forum state and another entity together, or by another entity alone.

(i) Special military courts

9.43   There may be instances in which a state has recourse to special municipal military courts, outside the regular system of courts-martial, for the trial of certain international crimes. The US, for example, has long had occasion to rely on ad hoc military commissions for the wartime prosecution of foreign nationals accused of

---

[78] See Law No 03/L-053 on the Jurisdiction, Case Selection and Case Allocation of EULEX Judges and Prosecutors in Kosovo, 13 March 2008, arts 2–4, especially arts 3.7 and 4.7. There is also a scheme of EULEX prosecutors. See, in this latter connection, Law No 03/L-052 on the Special Prosecution Office in the Republic of Kosovo, 13 March 2008, art 16.

[79] See Provisional Criminal Code of Kosovo, art 139, incorporating verbatim the definition of 'trafficking in persons' found in art 3(*a*) of the Protocol to Prevent, Suppress and Punish Trafficking in Persons, Especially Women and Children 2000, supplementary to the United Nations Convention against Transnational Organized Crime 2000.

[80] Unless otherwise specified or clear from the context, reference here to 'courts' should be taken to include reference to panels, sections, divisions, and chambers within courts as such.

[81] What makes each of these criminal courts a municipal court is that, as a formal juridical matter, each derives its existence and competence from the municipal legal order of the forum state (which, in the case of courts established by an occupying power exercising legislative authority over the territory, is in one sense the occupying state and another sense the occupied state).

[82] In some cases this has been with outside financial and technical assistance.

violations of the laws and customs of war.[83] Not dissimilarly, a variety of states created special municipal military courts in the European, Asian, and Pacific theatres in the course and in the wake of the Second World War, in both occupied territory and their own, for the trial of persons accused of war crimes and, in some cases, crimes against humanity and/or crimes against peace.[84]

(ii) Special panels in the District Court of Dili and Court of Appeal of East Timor

In 1999, in the wake of the authorized deployment of a multinational force to restore peace and security in East Timor[85] and of Indonesia's agreement to withdraw from the territory, the UN Security Council established the United Nations Transitional Administration in East Timor (UNTAET) and empowered it 'to exercise all legislative and executive authority, including the administration of justice'.[86] In the exercise of UNTAET's municipal legislative authority, the Transitional Administrator vested the District Court of Dili, a court of general jurisdiction *ratione materiae*,[87] with exclusive jurisdiction to try 'serious crimes'—namely genocide, war crimes, crimes against humanity, torture, murder, and sexual offences—committed between 1 January and 25 October 1999.[88] In other words, the District Court of Dili alone among the first-instance courts of East Timor was competent to adjudicate, as one strand of its more plenary jurisdiction, the specified crimes. As well as being a designation of exclusive venue, the measure amounted to a grant to the District Court of Dili of a jurisdiction *ratione materiae*

9.44

---

[83] See eg the Second World War military commissions referred to at 15 LRTWC 30, among them the US Military Commission at Manila which heard *In re Yamashita*, 13 ILR 255 (1945). See also the provision made in 10 USC §§948a–950t ('Military Commissions Act 2009') for 'the use of military commissions to try alien unprivileged enemy belligerents for violations of the law of war and other offenses triable by military commission', in the words of 10 USC §948b(*a*).

[84] See the special military courts referred to at 15 LRTWC 28–48, among them the various British military courts established in Asia and occupied Germany pursuant to the Royal Warrant of 14 June 1945, Army Order 81/1945 (18 June 1945); the Australian military courts established in Darwin, Hong Kong, Labuan, Manus Island, Morotai, Rabaul, Singapore, and Wewak pursuant to the War Crimes Act 1945 (Cth); the special military tribunals established by China for the trial of alleged war criminals pursuant to its Law of 24 October 1946 governing the Trial of War Criminals, as noted 14 LRTWC 152–60; and the US military tribunals established in occupied Germany pursuant to Ordinance No 7 of the Military Government of the United States Zone of Germany (18 October 1946). As to the municipal character of the military criminal courts and tribunals established by the US, the UK, and France in their respective zones of occupied Germany, recall *supra* para 3.29.

[85] See SC res 1264 (1999), 15 September 1999.

[86] SC res 1272 (1999), 25 October 1999, para 1. See, pursuant to this, UNTAET reg 1999/1, 27 November 1999, s 1.1, by which '[a]ll legislative and executive authority with respect to East Timor, including the administration of the judiciary, [was] vested in UNTAET', to be exercised by the Transitional Administrator, and s 1.2, in accordance with which the Transitional Administrator was empowered to 'appoint any person to perform functions in the civil administration in East Timor, including the judiciary'.

[87] See UNTAET reg 2000/11, 6 March 2000, s 6. In accordance with s 3.1 of UNTAET reg 1999/1, the applicable law of the East Timorese courts remained, as a general rule, the law in force prior to 25 October 1999.

[88] UNTAET reg 2000/11, ss 10.1 and 10.2.

over genocide, war crimes, crimes against humanity, and torture not enjoyed by the other district courts of East Timor, insofar as the crimes over which the district courts otherwise enjoyed jurisdiction did not encompass these offences. The Transitional Administrator further specified, in an exception to the usually district-specific jurisdiction *ratione loci* of the district courts, that for a transitional period the District Court of Dili was to enjoy jurisdiction over the entire territory of East Timor.[89] In addition, the Transitional Administrator in East Timor granted himself the power to establish, after consultation with the Court Presidency, special panels within the District Court of Dili 'with the expertise to exercise [the] exclusive jurisdiction vested in the court'.[90] These panels were to be composed of both East Timorese and 'international' judges.[91] Appeal from a special panel continued to lie, as with any appeal from the district courts, to the Court of Appeal of East Timor,[92] but appeals involving 'serious crimes' were to be heard by a panel, again established by the Transitional Administrator after consultation, 'with the expertise to hear and decide such appeals' and composed of both East Timorese and international judges.[93]

9.45   Three months later, the Transitional Administrator established the envisaged special panels in both the District Court of Dili and the Court of Appeal, vesting them with exclusive jurisdiction—vis-à-vis not only the other district courts of East Timor but also the District Court of Dili generally—over the serious criminal offences previously specified,[94] with genocide, crimes against humanity, and war crimes being defined as per articles 6, 7, and 8 respectively of the Rome Statute and torture being defined as in article 1 of the Torture Convention.[95] The modes of criminal responsibility, the *mens rea*, and the defences accepted and rejected largely mirrored those in the Rome Statute.[96] In cases involving genocide, war crimes, crimes against humanity, and torture, the panels' jurisdiction was without regard to whether the offence was committed outside East Timor or by or against a non-East Timorese citizen.[97] Moreover, insofar as any of the serious criminal offences over which the panels enjoyed jurisdiction *ratione materiae* was committed in the territory of East Timor, the panels were to enjoy jurisdiction *ratione loci* regardless of the judicial district where the offence was committed.[98] Official capacity was deemed irrelevant, as per the Rome Statute, both to substantive responsibility and, in the case of procedural immunities, to

---

[89] Ibid, s 7.3.
[90] Ibid, s 10.3. The President of the Court of Appeal was substituted for the Presidency of the District Court of Dili by way of s 9.3 of UNTAET reg 2001/25, 14 September 2001.
[91] Ibid.   [92] Ibid, s 14.2.   [93] Ibid, art 15.5.
[94] UNTAET reg 2000/15, 6 June 2000, s 1.
[95] Ibid, ss 4–7. In relation to torture, s 7.3 of UNTAET reg 2000/15 reproduces art 2(2) of the Torture Convention, providing that '[n]o exceptional circumstances whatsoever, whether a state of war or a threat of war, internal political instability or any other public emergency, may be invoked as a justification [for] torture.'
[96] UNTAET reg 2000/15, ss 14–21. One exception was command and superior responsibility, which was provided for as per ICTY Statute, art 7(3) and ICTR Statute, art 6(3). Recall *supra* paras 5.102–5.116. The other was the defence of superior orders, which was excluded as a complete defence as per ICTY Statute, art 7(4) and ICTR Statute, art 6(4).
[97] UNTAET reg 2000/15, ss 2.1 and 2.2.   [98] Ibid, s 2.5.

amenability to the exercise of jurisdiction,[99] the latter implicating international law in the case of the Indonesian military and police. Prosecution of genocide, war crimes, crimes against humanity, and torture was not subject to statutory limitation.[100] As for the panels' applicable law, where appropriate this was to comprise, in addition to the ordinary criminal law in force in East Timor,[101] 'applicable treaties and recognised principles and norms of international law, including the established principles of the international law of armed conflict'.[102] As regards the panels' composition, both those in the District Court of Dili and those in the Court of Appeal were to feature two international judges and one East Timorese judge.[103]

The special panels continued to operate on the independence of Timor-Leste on 20 May 2002.[104] They conducted 55 trials in total. Twenty-four persons pleaded guilty, 84 were convicted, and four were acquitted. The special panels stopped operating in 2005.[105] The process was not without its flaws.[106] 9.46

(iii) Ad hoc human rights courts in the Central Jakarta District Court and other Indonesian human rights courts

By way of Act 26 of 2000 concerning Human Rights Courts ('Act 26/2000'), Indonesia made provision for the establishment of 'human rights courts', vesting them with exclusive[107] jurisdiction *ratione materiae* 'to hear and rule on cases of gross violations of human rights',[108] the term being defined to 'include' (in reality, to comprise), first, the crime of genocide and, secondly, crimes against humanity.[109] A 'human rights court'[110] within the meaning of the Act is 'a special court within the context of a court of general jurisdiction',[111] the relevant courts of general 9.47

---

[99] UNTAET reg 2000/15, s 15.   [100] Ibid, s 17.1.
[101] Confusion was engendered in this regard by the eccentric decision of the Court of Appeal of East Timor in *Prosecutor v Armando dos Santos*, Case No 16/2001, 15 July 2003, that the ordinary criminal law in force was Portuguese, not Indonesian. Legislation was enacted on 8 October 2003 to make clear that this was not the case.
[102] UNTAET reg 2000/15, s 3.1(*b*). The applicable criminal procedure was that of the Transitional Rules of Criminal Procedure promulgated in UNTAET reg 2000/30, 25 September 2000, and subsequently repromulgated in revised form in UNTAET reg 2001/25.
[103] UNTAET reg 2000/15, s 22.
[104] See, in this regard, Constitution of the Democratic Republic of Timor-Leste, ss 163(1) and 165.
[105] See *Report to the Secretary-General of the Commission of Experts to Review the Prosecution of Serious Violations of Human Rights in Timor-Leste (then East Timor) in 1999*, UN doc S/2005/458 (15 July 2005), Annex II, 32, para 120. For the various judgments, see http://wcsc.berkeley.edu/east-timor/east-timor-2/.
[106] See, generally, C Reiger and M Wierda, *The Serious Crimes Process in Timor-Leste: In Retrospect* (New York: International Center for Transitional Justice, 2006).
[107] See Act 26 of 2000 concerning Human Rights Courts ('Act 26/2000'), art 27(1).
[108] Ibid, art 4.   [109] Ibid, art 7(*a*) and (*b*) respectively.
[110] The term is defined in art 1(3) of Act 26/2000 as 'a court dealing specifically with gross violations of human rights', while art 4 states that a human rights court is competent to hear and rule on cases of gross violations of human rights. In other words, the jurisdiction *ratione materiae* of such courts is limited to the crime of genocide and crimes against humanity.
[111] Ibid, art 2.

jurisdiction being the district courts in either district or municipal capitals and each district court in the Special District of Jakarta.[112] The establishment of human rights courts in four specific judicial districts, namely Central Jakarta, Surabaya, Medan, and Makassar, was supposed to have commenced from the date of the Act's entry into force.[113] At last report the only human rights court actually to have been established was the one in Makassar (South Sulawesi), which has tried two individuals accused in relation to events in Abepura (Papua) in late 2000. The bench of a human rights court is composed of two judges from that court alongside three ad hoc judges,[114] the latter of whom need not be practising judges[115] and are appointed by the head of state on the recommendation of the chief justice of the Supreme Court of Indonesia.[116] Appeal, like any appeal from the Indonesian district courts, lies to the High Court or Supreme Court.[117] The applicable criminal procedure is, unless otherwise specified, the criminal procedure ordinarily followed in the districts courts of Indonesia,[118] and the Act mandates awards of restitution, compensation, and rehabilitation to the victims of gross violations of human rights or their beneficiaries.[119]

9.48 As regards the jurisdiction *ratione materiae* of Indonesia's human rights courts, the crime of genocide is defined for the purposes of the Act effectively as per the definition in article II of the Convention on the Prevention and Punishment of the Crime of Genocide 1948 ('Genocide Convention') and article 6 of the Rome Statute,[120] while crimes against humanity are defined by close reference to article 7(1), without article 7(2), of the Rome Statute.[121] Apart from command and superior responsibility, which are provided for in terms taken from article 28 of the Rome Statute,[122] the Act does not as such specify modes of responsibility, although it does specify penalties for attempt and conspiracy to commit, as well as aiding and abetting the commission of, the offences laid down in the Act.[123] The Law stipulates that neither offence is subject to statutory limitation.[124] The jurisdiction *ratione loci* of human rights courts extends beyond the territory of Indonesia in cases where the accused is an Indonesian national,[125] while persons under the age of 18 at the time of the alleged commission of the offence are excluded from such courts'

---

[112] Ibid, art 3. [113] Ibid, art 45(1). [114] Ibid, art 27(2).
[115] See ibid, art 29. [116] Ibid, art 28(1). [117] See ibid, arts 32 and 33.
[118] Ibid, art 10. [119] Ibid, art 35(1).
[120] See ibid, art 8. The one *de minimis* difference between the text of the chapeau to art 8 of Act 26/2000—at least as it is translated into English on the website of the Asian Legal Resource Centre (ALRC)—and the text of the chapeau to art II of the Convention on the Prevention and Punishment of the Crime of Genocide 1948 ('Genocide Convention') is the insertion in the former, after the word 'destroy', of the synonymous alternative 'or exterminate'. See http://hrli.alrc.net/mainfile.php/indonleg/132/. But this may be no more than translator's licence.
[121] Act 26/2000, art 9. The two substantive differences are that the chapeau to art 9 of Act 26/2000 does not mention knowledge of the attack and that the acts constitutive of the various species of crime against humanity under the Act do not include the residual category of 'other inhumane acts' found in art 7(1)(k) of the Rome Statute. What other differences there are between the chapeau to art 9 of Act 26/2000 as translated into English on the ALRC website and the chapeau to art 7(1) of the Rome Statute would appear to be no more than a function of translation.
[122] Act 26/2000, art 42. [123] Ibid, art 41.
[124] Ibid, art 46. [125] Ibid, art 5.

jurisdiction *ratione personae*.[126] As for the jurisdiction *ratione temporis* of human rights courts, it is implicit that this extends only from the date of entry into force of Act 26/2000,[127] this being the Act's date of enactment on 23 November 2000. For the adjudication of gross violations of human rights allegedly committed prior to the Act's entry into force, Act 26/2000 makes provision for the establishment—by presidential decree, on parliamentary recommendation—of ad hoc human rights courts 'for particular incidents', these again being 'within the context of a court of general jurisdiction'[128] and proceeding in accordance with the Act.[129]

On 24 April 2001, on a recommendation of 21 March 2001 by the Indonesian parliament, President Wahid of Indonesia issued a decree establishing two ad hoc human rights court in the Central Jakarta District Court, one in relation to the events of 1999 in East Timor and another in relation to the 1984 Tanjung Priok massacre in Jakarta.[130] But the temporal jurisdiction of the court for East Timor reached back under this decree only to the date of the independence referendum in the territory on 30 August 1999,[131] thereby excluding from the court's competence a range of serious crimes allegedly committed by Indonesian military personnel from early April 1999 onwards. Under renewed international criticism, new Indonesian president Megawati Sukarnoputri issued an amending decree, both widening and focusing the court's jurisdiction *ratione temporis*, which now encompassed the months of April and September 1999 (but nothing in between),[132] and limiting its jurisdiction *ratione loci* to the cities of Dili, Liquiçá, and Suai.[133]

9.49

Of the mere 34 individuals in total prosecuted before the Ad Hoc Human Rights Court for East Timor in the Central Jakarta District Court, the Ad Hoc Human Rights Court for Tanjung Priok in the Central Jakarta District Court, and the Human Rights Court in the Makassar District Court, all have been acquitted. Of these, 18 had their convictions at trial overturned on appeal to the Supreme Court.[134] There is widespread consensus that, despite the efforts of certain committed trial judges, the proceedings—from the bringing of cases and framing of indictments to the conduct of the prosecution to the role of the Supreme Court—have been inconsistent with an intention to bring suspects and accused to justice.[135]

9.50

---

[126] Ibid, art 6. [127] The implication is drawn from ibid, arts 43(1) and 47(1).
[128] Ibid, art 43, quotes from art 43(2) and (3) respectively. [129] Ibid, art 44.
[130] See Presidential Decree No 53/2001 establishing an Ad Hoc Human Rights Court at the Central Jakarta District Court, 23 April 2001, issued 24 April 2001.
[131] Ibid, art 2.
[132] Presidential Decree No 96/2001 amending Presidential Decree No 53/2001 establishing an Ad Hoc Human Rights Court at the Central Jakarta District Court, 1 August 2001, issued 2 August 2001, art 1. International crimes are alleged to have been committed between April and September 1999. No international crimes are alleged to have been committed after late September 1999, when the Australian-led International Force for East Timor (INTERFET) arrived in the territory.
[133] Presidential Decree No 96/2001, art 1.
[134] International Center for Transitional Justice and KontraS, *Derailed: Transitional Justice in Indonesia Since the Fall of Soeharto* (March 2011), 39.
[135] See eg ibid, 49–51; S Linton, 'Unravelling the First Three Trials at Indonesia's Ad Hoc Court for Human Rights Violations in East Timor' (2004) 17 *LJIL* 303; P Burgess, 'De Facto Amnesty? The Example of Post-Soeharto Indonesia' in F Lessa and LA Payne (eds), *Amnesty in the Age of Human Rights Accountability: Comparative and International Perspectives* (Cambridge: Cambridge University Press, 2012), 263.

(iv) Iraqi High Criminal Court

9.51   On 10 December 2003, the Coalition Provisional Authority (CPA), the organ through which the various states in belligerent occupation of Iraq governed the territory, promulgated Order No 48, formally delegating to the Interim Iraqi Governing Council the municipal legislative authority to promulgate in turn a statute 'to establish an Iraqi Special Tribunal... to try Iraqi nationals or residents of Iraq accused of genocide, crimes against humanity, war crimes or violations of certain Iraqi laws'[136]—that is, to try the most senior figures of the defeated Baath regime. The 'proposed provisions'[137] of the statute, drafted by CPA lawyers in consultation with Iraqi stakeholders and annexed to Order No 48, were duly promulgated the same day by the Governing Council. By virtue of a transitional law,[138] the existence of the Tribunal was unaffected by the dissolution of the CPA on 28 June 2004 and the transfer of governmental authority to the appointed Iraqi Interim Government. Finally, on 18 October 2005, the new, popularly-elected Iraqi government enacted the Law on the Iraqi High Criminal Court (also known as the Supreme Iraqi Criminal Tribunal or, less accurately but more commonly in English, the Iraqi High Tribunal), which, while regularizing and renaming the court, in substance reproduced its extant statute.

9.52   The Iraqi High Criminal Court is a special criminal court within the judicial system of Iraq. Comprising investigating judges, trial chambers, an appeals chamber, and a prosecutor, it is composed entirely of Iraqi nationals, although unexercised provision is made for the appointment of foreign judges.[139] The president of the Court may appoint non-Iraqi experts to advise on international law and on the relevant practice of other courts, both municipal and international.[140] Similarly, the chief investigating judge and the chief prosecutor may appoint non-Iraqi experts to assist in investigation and prosecution.[141] The applicable rules of procedure and evidence are both the Iraqi code of criminal procedure and special rules appended to the Law.[142]

9.53   The Court is vested[143] with what is effectively exclusive[144] jurisdiction *ratione materiae* to try genocide, crimes against humanity, and war crimes, and with concurrent[145] jurisdiction *ratione materiae* over several crimes under Iraqi law, among them what is in essence the crime of aggression committed against another Arab state; jurisdiction *ratione personae* over natural persons of Iraqi nationality or residency; jurisdiction *ratione loci* over the territory of both Iraq and foreign states; and jurisdiction *ratione temporis* over the period between 17 July 1968, the date of the revolution that brought the Baath party to power in Iraq, and 1 May 2003, the date deemed to mark the close of active hostilities in the invasion

---

[136] CPA Order No 48, 10 December 2003, s 1(1).   [137] Ibid.
[138] See Law of Administration for the State of Iraq for the Transitional Period, 8 March 2004, art 48.
[139] Law on the Iraqi High Criminal Court 2005, arts 28 and 3(5).   [140] Ibid, art 7(2).
[141] Ibid, arts 8(9) and 9(7) respectively.   [142] Ibid, art 16.
[143] See ibid, arts 1(2) and 11–14.   [144] See ibid, art 29(2).
[145] See ibid, art 29(1).

and occupation of Iraq by Coalition forces and with this the end of the Baath government. The definition of the crime of genocide is taken from article II of the Genocide Convention,[146] to which Iraq acceded on 20 January 1959. The provisions on crimes against humanity and war crimes reproduce almost verbatim the corresponding provisions of the Rome Statute,[147] potentially raising issues as to retroactivity. The Law expressly permits recourse to decisions of international criminal courts and tribunals as aids to the interpretation of the provisions on genocide, crimes against humanity, and war crimes.[148] The provision on modes of responsibility is similarly taken virtually word-for-word from the Rome Statute,[149] although separate provision is made, as per article III of the Genocide Convention, for modes of responsibility in respect of genocide.[150] The defences available are those under Iraqi criminal law, albeit interpreted consistently with both the Law and Iraq's international legal obligations in respect of crimes within the Court's jurisdiction.[151] Superior orders are specifically excluded as a complete defence.[152] Official capacity is irrelevant to substantive criminal responsibility, and no procedural immunities are available as bars to prosecution,[153] although the latter does not implicate international law given that the relevant officials are all Iraqi. The crimes within the Court's jurisdiction are not subject to statutory limitation,[154] and no pardon granted prior to the Law's entry into force applies to them.[155] The Law makes no express provision for the Court's applicable law, although it is clear by implication from various provisions that this is both the Law itself and the more general provisions of Iraqi criminal law.

9.54 The Iraqi High Criminal Court has convicted numerous members of the former Baath regime of genocide, crimes against humanity, and war crimes, sentencing some of them, most notably Saddam Hussein and Ali Hassan Al-Majid ('Chemical Ali'), to death by hanging.[156] Proceedings before the Court have been beset by controversy.

(v) War Crimes Chambers of the High Court and Appeals Court in Belgrade

9.55 In June 2003, the Republic of Serbia[157] designated the High Court in Belgrade, a court of general jurisdiction *ratione materiae*, as having what was implicitly exclusive jurisdiction among first-instance courts in Serbia to try the offences of genocide, crimes against humanity, war crimes, and aggression, as embodied

---

[146] See ibid, art 11(1).
[147] See ibid, arts 12 and 13. Article 12(1) does not include apartheid among the possible acts constitutive of a crime against humanity.
[148] Ibid, art 17(3).   [149] See ibid, art 15(2).   [150] See ibid, art 11(2).
[151] Ibid, art 17(1) and (3).   [152] Ibid, art 17(5).   [153] Ibid, art 15(3).
[154] Ibid, art 17(4).   [155] Ibid, art 17(6).
[156] For unofficial translations of the 'Anfal' and 'Dujail' trial and cassation judgments, see http://law.case.edu/grotian-moment-blog/index.asp?t=1.
[157] At this point the Republic of Serbia was one of the constituent republics of the State Union of Serbia and Montenegro. From 2006 it was a state in its own right.

in the Serbian Criminal Code, as well as the offences within the jurisdiction of the International Criminal Tribunal for the former Yugoslavia (ICTY)[158] and the offence, as also recognized in the Serbian Criminal Code, of aiding and abetting an offender after commission, when such offences, regardless of the nationality of the alleged offender or victim, were committed in the territory of the former Socialist Federal Republic of Yugoslavia.[159] It simultaneously designated the Appeals Court in Belgrade as having implicitly exclusive jurisdiction over appeals in respect of the same.[160] As well as relating to venue, these measures amounted to grants both of a jurisdiction *ratione materiae* additional to that otherwise enjoyed by the various circuits of the Serbian High Court and Appeals Court, insofar as the offences within the jurisdiction of the ICTY did not as such fall within these courts' jurisdiction, and of a wider-than-usual jurisdiction *ratione loci* and *personae*, to the extent that the jurisdiction of these courts may not have run to extraterritorial acts by and against non-nationals.

9.56   Pursuant to the same legislation, Serbia, with international assistance, established a War Crimes Chamber within the High Court in Belgrade and a corresponding War Crimes Chamber within the Appeals Court in Belgrade for the purpose of exercising the exclusive jurisdiction granted to these courts over the specified offences.[161] As well as hearing cases initiated by the Office of the War Crimes Prosecutor created under the same legislation,[162] the War Crimes Chambers were to receive cases transferred from the ICTY, pursuant to rule 11*bis* of the latter's amended Rules of Procedure and Evidence, as part of the Tribunal's completion strategy.[163]

9.57   To 13 February 2014, 70 persons had been finally convicted and 32 finally acquitted by the War Crimes Chambers.[164] The ICTY has handed over many files to the Serbian authorities for possible trial before the War Crimes Chamber of the High Court in Belgrade, and under rule 11*bis* of its Rules of Procedure and

---

[158] This substantive duplication of subject-matter jurisdiction was to facilitate the transfer of cases from the International Criminal Tribunal for the former Yugoslavia (ICTY).

[159] Law on the Organisation and Competences of Government Authorities in War Crimes Proceedings 2003 (as amended), arts 2, 3, and 9.

[160] Ibid.

[161] Ibid, arts 10 and 10a. In accordance with art 13, unless otherwise provided the provisions of the Serbian Code of Criminal Procedure applicable to cases involving organized crime apply in the War Crimes Chambers both at first instance and on appeal, as do, where not inconsistent with this, the more general provisions of the Code of Criminal Procedure. As made clear for the avoidance of doubt in art 14, this is so as much in cases transferred to the War Crimes Chamber of the Higher Court by the ICTY as in those initiated by the Office of the War Crimes Prosecutor in Belgrade. Appeal from the War Crimes Chamber of the Appeals Court in Belgrade continues to lie to the Supreme Court of Cassation, while constitutional challenges relating to trials before the War Crimes Chamber of the High Court in Belgrade may be pursued before the Constitutional Court.

[162] See ibid, art 4.

[163] For details as to the ICTY's completion strategy and rule 11*bis* of its Rules of Procedure and Evidence, see *infra* paras 12.6 and 12.38–12.41.

[164] See the official summary provided by the Office of the War Crimes Prosecutor of the Republic of Serbia, http://www.tuzilastvorz.org.rs/html_trz/predmeti_eng.htm. See also, generally, Republic of Serbia, Office of the War Crimes Prosecutor, *Serbia on Its Way Towards Justice and Reconciliation: Office of the War Crimes Prosecutor, 10 Years Later* (Belgrade: 2013).

Evidence has transferred one case to the same authorities.¹⁶⁵ The Tribunal has also provided technical assistance to the Serbian prosecutorial and judicial authorities.

(vi) *War crimes sections of the Criminal and Appellate Divisions of the Court of Bosnia and Herzegovina*

The Court of Bosnia and Herzegovina has three divisions, *viz* Criminal, Administrative, and Appellate.¹⁶⁶ In turn, the Criminal Division has three sections, namely Section I (War Crimes), Section II (Organized Crime, Economic Crime, and Corruption), and Section III (all other crimes within the jurisdiction of the Court).¹⁶⁷ Section I of the Appellate Division is given over to appeals from Section I (War Crimes) of the Criminal Division, while Section II of the Appellate Division has responsibility for appeals from Section II (Organized Crime, Economic Crime, and Corruption) of the Criminal Division. 9.58

Section I (War Crimes) of the Criminal Division of the Court of Bosnia and Herzegovina was instituted in 2004,¹⁶⁸ at the instigation of the High Representative for Bosnia and Herzegovina¹⁶⁹ and with international assistance, with a view to, *inter alia*, the receipt of cases transferred from the ICTY, as part of the Tribunal's completion strategy, pursuant to rule 11*bis* of its amended Rules of Procedure and Evidence¹⁷⁰ and of files on suspects not indicted to that point by the Tribunal. Like the other sections of the Criminal Division, the War Crimes Section formally retains jurisdiction *ratione materiae* over all crimes in the Criminal Code and other laws of Bosnia and Herzegovina, as well as over certain crimes of the respective territorial-political entities of Bosnia and Herzegovina and certain other criminal matters.¹⁷¹ As 9.59

---

¹⁶⁵ See *Prosecutor v Kovačević*, IT-01-42/2-1, Referral Bench, Decision on Referral of Case Pursuant to Rule 11*bis* with Confidential and Partly *Ex Parte* Annexes, 17 November 2006.
¹⁶⁶ Law on the Court of Bosnia and Herzegovina 2000 (as amended), art 19(2).
¹⁶⁷ Ibid, art 24(1).
¹⁶⁸ See Law on the Amendments to the Law on the Court of Bosnia and Herzegovina, *Official Gazette* No 61/04, art 8.
¹⁶⁹ The High Representative for Bosnia and Herzegovina is an international appointee charged with ensuring the implementation, on behalf of an international and interagency body called the Peace Implementation Council, of the civilian component of the Dayton Peace Agreement, which brought an end in 1995 to the wars in the former Yugoslavia.
¹⁷⁰ See also Law on the Transfer of Cases from the International Criminal Tribunal for the former Yugoslavia to the Prosecutor's Offices of Bosnia and Herzegovina and the Use of Evidence Collected by the International Criminal Tribunal for the former Yugoslavia in Proceedings before the Courts of Bosnia and Herzegovina 2004 (as amended). In the preamble (eleventh recital) to SC res 1503 (2003), 28 August 2003, the UN Security Council noted 'that an essential prerequisite to achieving the objectives of the ICTY Completion Strategy is the expeditious establishment under the auspices of the High Representative and early functioning of a special chamber within the State Court of Bosnia and Herzegovina (the "War Crimes Chamber") and the subsequent referral by the ICTY of cases of lower- or intermediate-rank accused to the Chamber'. The so-called 'War Crimes Chamber' is actually the War Crimes Sections of the Criminal and Appellate Divisions of the Court of Bosnia and Herzegovina.
¹⁷¹ See Law on the Court of Bosnia and Herzegovina, art 13. One of the other criminal matters within the jurisdiction *ratione materiae* of the Criminal Division is specified in art 13(3)(*b*), which reads: 'The Court shall further be competent to issue practice directions on the application of the substantive criminal law of Bosnia and Herzegovina falling within the competence of the Court on

390   *Municipal Law and Courts*

a matter of administrative practice, however, it is assigned only cases of war crimes, crimes against humanity, and genocide.

9.60   Organizationally, the distinguishing feature of Sections I and II of the Criminal Division and Sections I and II of the Appellate Division used to be that international judges could be appointed to them.[172] This practice was instituted in 2003 by the High Representative for Bosnia and Herzegovina in respect of what was then the Special Panels for Organized Crime, Economic Crime, and Corruption within the Criminal Division and Appellate Division respectively,[173] with the High Representative himself appointing such judges. In 2004, the facility for the appointment of international judges was extended for a transitional period to the newly-created Sections I and II of the Criminal Division and Appellate Division respectively.[174] Under this later dispensation, the High Representative appointed international judges on the joint recommendation of the President of the Court and the President of the High Judicial and Prosecutorial Council of Bosnia and Herzegovina. With the end of the transition period in 2012, international judges no longer sit on the Court.

9.61   The War Crimes Sections of the Criminal and Appellate Divisions of the Court of Bosnia and Herzegovina have prosecuted many persons accused of responsibility for war crimes, crimes against humanity, and genocide committed during the war in Bosnia and Herzegovina.[175] The ICTY has handed over numerous files to the Bosnian authorities for possible trial before the War Crimes Section of the Criminal Division, has transferred six cases, involving ten indictees, to the same authorities for trial,[176] and has provided considerable technical assistance. But a judgment of the Grand Chamber of the European Court of Human Rights relating to the War Crimes Sections' applicable law,[177] along with the judgment's application by the Constitutional Court of Bosnia and Herzegovina,[178] have recently created problems.

---

genocide, crimes against humanity, war crimes and violations of the laws and practices of warfare and individual criminal responsibility related to those crimes, *ex officio* or on the request by any court of the Entities or of the Brčko District of Bosnia and Herzegovina.'

[172] In *Prosecutor v Stanković*, IT-96-23/2-PT, Referral Bench, Decision on Referral of Case under Rule 11*bis*, 17 May 2005, para 26, the ICTY rightly held that the presence of international judges on the bench of the War Crimes Sections of the Criminal and Appellate Divisions of the Court of Bosnia and Herzegovina did not make the Court any less a 'national' court. Having been 'established pursuant to the statutory law of Bosnia and Herzegovina', the Court was 'thus a court of Bosnia and Herzegovina, a "national court"'.

[173] See Decision No 97/03 of the High Representative enacting the Law re-amending the Law on the Court of Bosnia and Herzegovina, 24 January 2003, *Official Gazette* No 3/03, art 12.

[174] See Law on the Court of Bosnia and Herzegovina, art 65(2) and (4).

[175] For details of the various cases, see the official website of the Court of Bosnia and Herzegovina, http://www.sudbih.gov.ba/?jezik=e.

[176] See *Prosecutor v Stanković*, IT-96-23/2; *Prosecutor v Janković*, IT-96-23/2; *Prosecutor v Mejakić, Gruban, Fuštar and Knežević*, IT-02-65; *Prosecutor v Ljubičić*, IT-00-41; *Prosecutor v Todović and Rašević*, IT-97-25/1; *Prosecutor v Trbić*, IT-05-88/1.

[177] See *Maktouf and Damjanović v Bosnia and Herzegovina* [GC] (Merits and Just Satisfaction), nos 2312/08 & 34179/08, ECHR 2013.

[178] See *Damjanović*, Case No AP 325/08, Decision on Admissibility and Merits, Constitutional Court of Bosnia and Herzegovina, 27 September 2013; *Đukić*, Case No AP 5161/10, Decision on Admissibility and Merits, Constitutional Court of Bosnia and Herzegovina, 23 January 2014.

(vii) Extraordinary Chambers in the Courts of Cambodia

In 1997, after a coup d'état by co-prime minister Hun Sen, the government of Cambodia requested the assistance of the UN in prosecuting the former leadership of the Khmer Rouge regime which from 1975 to 1979 killed approximately two million people, a quarter of the population of what was then styled 'Democratic Kampuchea'. There ensued from 1999 protracted negotiations, which collapsed in 2002 over the independence and impartiality of the municipal trial mechanism envisaged in the Law on the Establishment of Extraordinary Chambers in the Courts of Cambodia for the Prosecution of Crimes Committed during the Period of Democratic Kampuchea promulgated by Cambodia in 2001.[179] At the request, however, of the UN General Assembly,[180] which at the same time emphasized the need to ensure 'international standards of justice, fairness and due process of law' and 'the impartiality, independence and credibility of the process, in particular with regard to the status and work of the judges and prosecutors',[181] the UN Secretary-General resumed negotiations with the government of Cambodia. So it was that, on 6 June 2003, in terms earlier approved in draft form by the General Assembly,[182] the UN and Cambodia concluded an Agreement concerning the Prosecution under Cambodian Law of Crimes Committed During the Period of Democratic Kampuchea, which provides 'the legal basis and principles and modalities for...cooperation'[183] between the two parties in relation to the trial before 'Extraordinary Chambers within the existing court structure of Cambodia'[184] of 'senior leaders of Democratic Kampuchea and those who were most responsible for the crimes and serious violations of Cambodian penal law, international humanitarian law and custom, and international conventions recognized by Cambodia, that were committed during the period from 17 April 1975 to 6 January 1979'.[185] The Agreement recognizes that the Extraordinary Chambers have the jurisdiction *ratione materiae* provided for in the Law on the Establishment of Extraordinary Chambers in the Courts of Cambodia and jurisdiction *ratione personae* over senior leaders of Democratic Kampuchea and others most responsible for the crimes specified.[186] On 19 October 2004, Cambodia ratified the Agreement. On 27 October 2004, it enacted legislation to amend the Law[187] so as to bring the latter into line with the terms of the Agreement.[188] The

9.62

---

[179] Reach Kram No NS/RKM/0801/12, 10 August 2001.
[180] See GA res 57/228A, 18 December 2002, para 1.
[181] Ibid, paras 4 and 5. See also, previously, GA res 56/169, 19 December 2001, part IV, para 2.
[182] See GA res 228B, 13 May 2003, para 1.
[183] Agreement between the United Nations and the Royal Government of Cambodia concerning the Prosecution under Cambodian Law of Crimes Committed During the Period of Democratic Kampuchea 2003, art 1.
[184] Ibid, preamble (fourth recital). [185] Ibid, art 1. [186] Ibid, art 2(1).
[187] See Reach Kram No NS/RKM/1004/006, 27 October 2004.
[188] See Law on the Establishment of Extraordinary Chambers in the Courts of Cambodia for the Prosecution of Crimes Committed during the Period of Democratic Kampuchea (as amended), http://www.eccc.gov.kh/sites/default/files/legal-documents/KR_Law_as_amended_27_Oct_2004_Eng.pdf.

392   *Municipal Law and Courts*

Agreement provides that it shall be implemented in Cambodia through the Law 'as adopted and amended'.[189]

9.63   The Extraordinary Chambers in the Courts of Cambodia (ECCC) are precisely that, namely special chambers 'established in the existing court structure, namely the trial court and the supreme court', of Cambodia, specifically for the purpose of adjudging the criminal responsibility of 'senior leaders of Democratic Kampuchea and those who were most responsible for the crimes and serious violations of Cambodian laws related to crimes, international humanitarian law and custom, and international conventions recognized by Cambodia, that were committed during the period from 17 April 1975 to 6 January 1979'.[190] Located in Phnom Penh,[191] they 'shall automatically dissolve following the definitive conclusion of [the] proceedings'.[192] The Trial Chamber comprises five judges, of whom three (including the president) are Cambodian and two foreign.[193] The Supreme Court Chamber, which serves as both appellate chamber and final instance, is composed of seven judges, four (among them the president) Cambodian and three foreign.[194] The preparation of indictments and the conduct of trials fall to two co-prosecutors, one Cambodian and one foreign,[195] while the conduct of investigations falls to co-investigating judges, one Cambodian and one foreign.[196] All judges, co-prosecutors, and co-investigating judges are appointed by Cambodia's Supreme Council of the Magistracy, in the case of the foreigners on the nomination of the UN Secretary-General.[197] They are to be independent, not accepting or seeking instructions from any government or other source,[198] and are assisted by both Cambodian and foreign staff[199] under the supervision of an Office of Administration with a Cambodian director and foreign deputy director.[200] The applicable criminal procedure is—in addition to specific provisions contained in the Law[201]—the ordinary criminal procedure of Cambodia, supplemented and interpreted where necessary by reference to 'procedural rules established at the international level'.[202] This amalgam of procedural rules has been consolidated by the ECCC themselves into what are called their Internal Rules.[203] More generally, the Law requires the Trial Chamber to ensure that trials are fair and expeditious and are conducted in accordance with international standards of justice, fairness, and due process of law, as guaranteed by articles 14 and 15 of the ICCPR.[204] Cambodian criminal procedure and, as a result, the

---

[189] Agreement between the United Nations and the Royal Government of Cambodia, art 2(2). Conversely and confusingly, art 47*bis* of the Law itself provides that the Agreement, following its ratification by Cambodia, 'shall apply as law within the Kingdom of Cambodia'.
[190] Law on the Establishment of Extraordinary Chambers in the Courts of Cambodia (as amended), art 2.
[191] Ibid, art 43.   [192] Ibid, art 47.   [193] Ibid, art 9.   [194] Ibid.
[195] Ibid, art 16.   [196] Ibid, art 23.   [197] Ibid, arts 11, 18, and 26.
[198] Ibid, arts 10, 19, and 25.   [199] Ibid, arts 13, 22, and 28.   [200] Ibid, art 30.
[201] See ibid, arts 23–24 and 33–39.
[202] Ibid, arts 20, 23, 33. See also Agreement between the United Nations and the Royal Government of Cambodia, art 12(1).
[203] See ECCC Internal Rules (rev.8), 3 August 2011.
[204] Law on the Establishment of Extraordinary Chambers in the Courts of Cambodia (as amended), art 33. See also ibid, art 35.

Chambers' Internal Rules permit civil party (*partie civile*) proceedings and claims for reparation.

9.64 The ECCC enjoy jurisdiction *ratione materiae* over a range of serious municipal crimes and international crimes, although in each case only insofar as they were committed during the period from 17 April 1975 to 6 January 1979.[205] The international crimes in question comprise genocide, crimes against humanity, grave breaches of the 1949 Geneva Conventions, the destruction of cultural property in armed conflict contrary to the 1954 Hague Convention for the Protection of Cultural Property in the Event of Armed Conflict, and crimes against the internationally protected persons specified in the Vienna Convention on Diplomatic Relations 1961 ('VCDR').[206] The Law's definitions of the first three—at least as translated into English—differ from the international definitions insofar as what under the international definitions represent enumerations of the several acts constitutive of each generic offence are formulated in the Law as mere illustrations, being preceded in the chapeau to each offence by the words 'such as',[207] although as applied this has proved a distinction without a difference. Apart from this, genocide is defined strictly in accordance with article II of the Genocide Convention,[208] with political groups being excluded from the list of groups encompassed by the requisite specific intent. Crimes against humanity are defined along the lines of article 3 of the Statute of the International Criminal Tribunal for Rwanda,[209] with the attack in question needing to be on national, political, ethnic, racial or religious grounds and no connection to armed conflict, let alone to a war crime or crime against peace, being required.[210] The serious municipal crimes within the Extraordinary Chambers' jurisdiction are homicide, torture, and religious persecution, all as provided for in the 1956 Cambodian Penal Code.[211] Apart from commission[212] and particular modes of responsibility in respect of the crime of genocide,[213] the modes of responsibility specified comprise planning, instigation, ordering, aiding and abetting, and superior responsibility,[214] the last as provided for in the ICTY and ICTR

---

[205] See ibid, arts 3–8.
[206] The provision in respect of crimes against persons required to be protected by the Vienna Convention on Diplomatic Relations ('VCDR') raises an issue as to retroactivity, given that the VCDR does not bind individuals, let alone provide for individual criminal responsibility under international law. But none of the accused has been indicted under this head.
[207] See Law on the Establishment of Extraordinary Chambers in the Courts of Cambodia (as amended), chapeaux to arts 4, 5, and 6 respectively.
[208] Ibid, art 4.
[209] The issues of retroactivity potentially raised thereby, in particular in relation to certain species of crimes against humanity, were examined in Case File/Dossier No 001/18-07-2007-ECCC/SC ('*Duch*'), Supreme Court Chamber, Appeal Judgment, 3 February 2012, paras 98–280.
[210] Law on the Establishment of Extraordinary Chambers in the Courts of Cambodia (as amended), art 5.
[211] Ibid, art 3.
[212] As regards joint criminal enterprise before the ECCC, see Criminal Case File No 002-19-09-2007-ECCC/OCIJ (PTC 35, 37, 38 & 39) (*Ieng Thirith, Ieng Sary & Khieu Samphan*), Pre-Trial Chamber, Decision on the Appeals Against the Co-Investigative Judges Order on Joint Criminal Enterprise (JCE), 20 May 2010.
[213] See the text immediately *infra*.
[214] Law on the Establishment of Extraordinary Chambers in the Courts of Cambodia (as amended), art 29.

statutes.[215] The modes of responsibility provided for in relation to genocide, which are supplementary to the generally-applicable modes, comprise attempt, conspiracy, and 'participation', the latter seemingly representing the equivalent under Cambodian law of complicity.[216] The former position or rank of the accused neither relieves them of responsibility nor mitigates punishment,[217] although where former Cambodian officials are tried by a Cambodian court this does not implicate international law, while superior orders are rejected as a complete defence.[218] The crime of genocide and crimes against humanity are excluded from statutory limitation by the Law,[219] which also stipulates that the government of Cambodia shall not request amnesty or pardon for persons investigated for or convicted of the offences within the ECCC's jurisdiction.[220] No provision stipulates the ECCC's applicable law, but the Supreme Court Chamber has held this to be international law, both customary and conventional, as it stood and insofar as it bound the accused during the period 1975–79, along with the relevant provisions of Cambodia's 1956 Penal Code.[221] When it comes to the ECCC's jurisdiction *ratione personae*, the Supreme Court Chamber has ruled that, while the Chambers have jurisdiction only over Khmer Rouge officials, the expressions 'senior leaders' and 'most responsible' represent no more than guides to investigative and prosecutorial policy, rather than formal limits on the Chambers' competence in respect of given persons.[222]

9.65 Only five indictees have been brought before the ECCC. One case, that of Kaing Guek Eav (alias 'Duch'), former chairman of the notorious S-21 detention centre (or 'Tuol Sleng'), has been completed, with the Supreme Court Chamber sentencing the convict to life imprisonment after the Trial Chamber, having found him guilty of a variety of crimes against humanity and grave breaches of the Geneva Conventions and sentenced him to only 35 years' imprisonment on account of mitigating circumstances, reduced his sentence by a further five years in view of his prior illegal detention, and reduced the time he was actually to spend in prison by reference to time already spent.[223] Proceedings against Ieng Sary (alias 'Van') were terminated in 2013 on the death of the accused.[224] His co-accused, Ieng Thirith (alias 'Phea'), was declared unfit to stand trial in 2012 on account of dementia, although placed under judicial supervision.[225] On 7 August 2014, the

---

[215] Recall *supra*, paras 5.102–5.116.
[216] Law on the Establishment of Extraordinary Chambers in the Courts of Cambodia (as amended), art 4. No provision is made for direct and public incitement to commit genocide.
[217] Ibid, art 29.   [218] Ibid.   [219] Ibid, arts 3 and 4.
[220] Ibid, art 40. Article 40 adds that '[t]he scope of any amnesty or pardon that may have been granted prior to the enactment of this Law is a matter to be decided by the Extraordinary Chambers'. The reference is to the royal pardon granted by King Sihanouk to Ieng Sary (alias 'Van') in respect of his 1979 conviction for genocide and the royal amnesty from further prosecution granted to the same.
[221] '*Duch*', Appeal Judgment (n 209), para 92.   [222] Ibid, para 79.
[223] See '*Duch*', Appeal Judgment (n 209) and Case File/Dossier No 001/18-07-2007/ECCC/TC ('*Duch*'), Trial Chamber, Trial Judgment, 26 July 2010.
[224] See Case File/Dossier No 002/19-09-2007/ECCC/TC (*Ieng Sary*), Trial Chamber, Termination of the Proceedings against the Accused Ieng Sary, 14 March 2013.
[225] See Case File/Dossier No 002/19-09-2007-ECCC-SC (16) (*Ieng Thirith*), Supreme Court Chamber, Decision on Immediate Appeal against the Trial Chamber's Order to Unconditionally Release the Accused Ieng Thirith, 14 December 2012.

Substantive Law, Jurisdiction, Prosecution, and Courts 395

Trial Chamber convicted Nuon Chea (alias 'Brother Number Two') and Khieu Samphan (alias 'Hem') of crimes against humanity, and sentenced them both to life imprisonment.²²⁶ Two suspects whose identities remain confidential are under investigation in two further cases. Proceedings before the ECCC have been the subject of controversy, much of it over the doubtful impartiality of some of the Cambodian personnel.

(viii) International Crimes Division of the High Court of Uganda

In 2008, in pursuance of the Juba Agreement on Accountability and Reconciliation concluded in 2007 between the government of Uganda and the Lord's Resistance Army/Movement, the chief justice of Uganda created within the High Court of Uganda, separate from the High Court's existing Criminal Division, a special War Crimes Division, which in 2011 was renamed the International Crimes Division.²²⁷ The International Crimes Division enjoys jurisdiction *ratione materiae* over genocide, crimes against humanity, war crimes, terrorism, human trafficking, piracy, 'and any other international crimes as may be provided for under the Penal Code Act, the Geneva Conventions Act, the International Criminal Court Act or under any other penal enactment'.²²⁸ Its substantive applicable law is Uganda's Penal Code Act 1950 (as amended), Geneva Conventions Act 1964, and International Criminal Court Act 2010, and its rules of procedure and evidence are those otherwise applicable to criminal trials in Uganda.²²⁹   **9.66**

To date, the International Crimes Division has embarked on only a single trial, that of Lord's Resistance Army commander Thomas Kwoyelo, who is charged with multiple offences under the Geneva Conventions Act and, in the alternative, the Penal Code Act.   **9.67**

(ix) International Crimes Tribunals, Bangladesh

In 1973, two years after the bloodbath that triggered and accompanied the secession of East Pakistan from Pakistan and the former's emergence as the independent state of Bangladesh, the parliament of Bangladesh enacted the International Crimes (Tribunals) Act 1973. The aim was the establishment, through subsequent delegated legislation, of special municipal criminal tribunals to try and punish persons, regardless of their nationality, accused of committing, of attempting or conspiring to commit, or of abetting, complicity in, failure to prevent or   **9.68**

---

²²⁶ See Case File/Dossier No 002/19-09-2007/ECCC/TC (E313) (*Nuon Chea and Khieu Samphan*), Trial Chamber, Judgment, 7 August 2014.
²²⁷ Appeal from the International Crimes Division, like appeal from any other division of the High Court, lies to the Court of Appeal of Uganda, while recourse to the Constitutional Court is also available.
²²⁸ The High Court (International Crimes Division) Practice Directions 2011, para 6(1), legislative citations omitted. Reference is to Uganda's Penal Code Act 1950, Geneva Conventions Act 1964, and International Criminal Court Act 2010.
²²⁹ The High Court (International Crimes Division) Practice Directions 2011, para 8(1).

command responsibility for the commission of crimes against humanity, crimes against peace, the crime of genocide, violations of the laws and customs of war (*sub nom* war crimes), violations of the 1949 Geneva Conventions or 'any other crimes under international law' in the territory of Bangladesh, whether before or after the commencement of the Act.[230] It was not until 2009, however, and after the passage of amendments to the Act[231] to bring it into line with what were considered to be contemporary international standards, that the International Crimes Tribunal (ICT) was established in Dhaka with a view to prosecuting persons alleged to bear criminal responsibility for the atrocities of 1971. In 2012, the Bangladeshi government established a second ICT pursuant to the Act.[232] Further amendments to the Act were passed that same year and again in 2013,[233] including provision for trial *in absentia*[234] and retroactive provision for the prosecution of organizations.[235]

9.69 What are known as ICT-1 and ICT-2 are special criminal tribunals within the judicial system of Bangladesh, staffed entirely by Bangladeshi personnel appointed by the Bangladeshi government. They operate according to special Rules of Procedure adopted by the ICT in 2010 and special, non-technical rules of evidence provided for in the Act.[236] Appeals from convictions and from acquittals and sentencing are available to the Appellate Division of the Supreme Court of Bangladesh.[237]

9.70 While no provision of the International Crimes (Tribunals) Act specifies the ICTs' applicable law, it is clear that the latter is the Act itself[238] and the Rules of Procedure. As regards the ICTs' jurisdiction *ratione materiae*,[239] to the extent that this has not been amended since the passage of the Act in 1973 no issue of retroactivity arises. There are, however, at least two problems regarding whether, in either their formulation or their application to the facts, some of the stated offences were crimes under international law[240] when the Act was passed. First, in an obvious deviation from customary international law both past and present, political groups are included in the Act among the groups whose destruction as such, in whole or in part, comprises the specific intent characteristic of the crime of genocide.[241]

---

[230] International Crimes (Tribunals) Act 1973, ss 3 and 4, quote from s 3(2)(*f*).
[231] See International Crimes (Tribunals) (Amendment) Act 2009.
[232] See International Crimes (Tribunals) Act, s 6(1) and *Gazette* of 22 March 2012.
[233] See International Crimes (Tribunals) (Amendment) Act 2012 and International Crimes (Tribunals) (Amendment) Act 2013.
[234] International Crimes (Tribunals) (Amendment) Act 2012, s 2, inserting International Crimes (Tribunals) Act, s 10A.
[235] International Crimes (Tribunals) (Amendment) Act 2013, s 2, amending International Crimes (Tribunals) Act, s 3(1).
[236] See International Crimes (Tribunals) Act, ss 19 and 22 and *Gazette* of 17 July 2010. In accordance with s 23 of the International Crimes (Tribunals) Act, neither the Criminal Procedure Code 1898 (as amended) nor the Evidence Act 1872 (as amended) applies to proceedings before the ICTs.
[237] International Crimes (Tribunals) Act, ss 21(1) and (2).
[238] In this regard, s 26 provides that the provisions of the Act 'shall have effect notwithstanding anything inconsistent therewith contained in any other law for the time being in force'.
[239] See International Crimes (Tribunals) Act, s 3(2).
[240] There is a separate issue as to whether they were crimes under the municipal law in force in East Pakistan/Bangladesh during the events of 1971.
[241] See International Crimes (Tribunals) Act, s 3(2)(*c*), chapeau.

Secondly, insofar as any armed conflict as existed in the territory of the former East Pakistan prior to its emergence under international law as the state of Bangladesh may be better characterized as non-international, it is doubtful whether individual criminal responsibility could have arisen under the customary international law of the day for acts therein.

Nine of the persons indicted to date by the ICTs have been leaders or associates of the Jamaat-e-Islami party that opposed the secession of East Pakistan in 1971, while the two remaining indictees have been leaders of the Bangladesh National Party opposed to the ruling Awami League. Ten persons have been tried to date, some *in absentia*. All have been convicted of some or all crimes charged, with most being sentenced to death by hanging.[242] Serious concerns have been raised as to the impartiality of the proceedings.

9.71

(x) *Extraordinary African Chambers in the Senegalese courts*

On 20 March 2001, the Senegalese Court of Cassation ruled that, for want of legislative implementation, the Senegalese courts lacked the competence to prosecute the former dictator of Chad Hissène Habré—against whom a civil-party complaint had been lodged in Dakar, where he lived—on the basis of the universal jurisdiction mandated by article 5(2) of the Torture Convention, to which Senegal was party. In 2005, Habré was indicted in Belgium, which circulated an international warrant for his arrest and requested his extradition from Senegal. But the Senegalese courts declared themselves incompetent to consider the request. In May 2006, the Committee against Torture concluded that Senegal stood in breach of articles 5(2) and 7(1) of the Torture Convention for its failure to vest its courts with universal jurisdiction over torture and its failure to prosecute Habré.[243] Two months later, on the recommendation of a Commission of Eminent African Jurists established by it earlier that year,[244] the Assembly of the African Union (AU) conferred on Senegal a 'mandate' to try Habré 'in the name of Africa'.[245] Senegal amended its legislation with a hypothetical view to the prosecution of Habré, who in response argued before the Community Court of Justice of the Economic Community of West African States (ECOWAS) that his right not to be subject to the retroactive application of criminal law would thereby be violated.[246] In a bizarre judgment, the Community Court of

9.72

---

[242] For the various judgments, see http://www.ict-bd.org/ict1/judgments.php and http://www.ict-bd.org/ict2/judgments.php.

[243] *Guengueng* et al *v Senegal*, Communication No 181/2001, 17 May 2006, UN doc CAT/C/36/D/181/2001 (19 May 2006).

[244] The jurists recommended the adoption of an 'African option' for the resolution of the Habré controversy, and considered both that Senegal was the state 'best suited' to try Habré, since it was bound by international law to do so, and that Chad should co-operate with it to this end. See *Report of the Committee of Eminent African Jurists on the Case of Hissène Habré* (June 2006), 4, paras 27, 29, and 30 respectively.

[245] Decision Assembly/AU/Dec.127 (VII), para 5(ii).

[246] See also, similarly, *Yogogombaye v Senegal*, Judgment, African Court of Human and Peoples' Rights, 15 December 2009 (dismissed for lack of jurisdiction).

Justice ruled in late 2010 that any trial of Habré in Senegal was to be by way of a 'special ad hoc procedure of an international character',[247] a modality subsequently endorsed by the AU,[248] although initially resisted by Senegal. On 31 January 2012, a meeting of AU heads of state and government requested the AU Commission and, *inter alia*, the government of Senegal to consider practical modalities for, and the financial implications of, 'the expeditious trial of Hissène Habré'.[249] Just over six months later, in its judgment in the case brought against Senegal by Belgium in February 2009, the International Court of Justice (ICJ)—holding Senegal in breach of its obligations under articles 6(2) and 7(1) of the Torture Convention—ruled that the latter, in the event that it did not extradite Habré, was obliged to submit the case to its competent authorities for the purpose of prosecution.[250] Eventually, on 22 August 2012, the Agreement between the Government of the Republic of Senegal and the African Union on the Creation of Extraordinary African Chambers in the Senegalese Courts was concluded with a view to the establishment and functioning, pursuant to cooperation between Senegal and the AU, of 'Extraordinary African Chambers in the Senegalese courts for the prosecution of international crimes committed in Chad between 7 June 1982 and 1 December 1990'.[251] The composition of and legal framework for the envisaged chambers were to be determined by the annexed statute, which was stated to form an integral part of the Agreement,[252] and by the laws of Senegal.[253] By way of article 1(2) of the Agreement, Senegal undertook to enact the necessary legislative and related measures for the creation, 'within the judicial system of Senegal', of the Extraordinary African Chambers; and on 19 December 2012, the National Assembly of Senegal adopted Law No 2012-25, promulgated by the president on 28 December 2012, 'authorizing the President of the Republic to ratify the Agreement between the Government of the Republic of Senegal and the African Union on the Creation of Extraordinary African Chambers in the Senegalese Courts'.[254] On its ratification by the president, the Agreement, including the annexed Statute of the Extraordinary African Chambers in the Senegalese Courts for the Prosecution of International Crimes Committed in Chad During

---

[247] *Habré v Senegal*, Case No ECW/CCJ/APP/07/08, Judgment, ECOWAS Community Court of Justice, 18 November 2010, para 61.
[248] Decision Assembly/AU/Dec.340 (XVI).
[249] Decision Assembly/AU/Dec.401 (XVIII), para 5.
[250] *Questions relating to the Obligation to Prosecute or Extradite (Belgium v Senegal), Judgment*, ICJ Rep 2012, 422, 463, para 122.
[251] Accord entre le Gouvernement de la République du Sénégal et l'Union Africaine sur la Création de Chambres Extraordinaires Africaines au Sein des Juridictions Sénégalaises, Dakar, 24 August 2014 ('Agreement between the Government of the Republic of Senegal and the African Union on the Creation of Extraordinary African Chambers in the Senegalese Courts'), preamble (fifth recital). All translations from the French are the author's.
[252] Ibid, art 1(5). [253] Ibid, art 2.
[254] Loi no 2012-25 autorisant le Président de la République à ratifier l'Accord entre le Gouvernement de la République du Sénégal et l'Union africaine sur la création de Chambres extraordinaires africaines au sein des juridictions sénégalaises ('Law no 2012-25 authorizing the President of the Republic to ratify the Agreement between the Government of the Republic of Senegal and the African Union on the Creation of Extraordinary African Chambers in the Senegalese Courts'), 28 December 2012.

the Period from 7 June 1982 to 1 December 1990,[255] assumed force of municipal law in Senegal, in accordance with article 96 of the Senegalese constitution.[256]

The Extraordinary African Chambers in the Senegalese Courts are, as the name suggests, special chambers within the criminal courts of Senegal tasked, in the words of article 1 of their Statute, 'with the prosecution by the Republic of Senegal of international crimes committed in Chad between 7 June 1982 and 1 December 1990'. They will cease to exist once the relevant decisions have been definitively rendered.[257] They consist of an Extraordinary African *chambre d'instruction* in the Dakar *Tribunal Régional Hors Classe* and an Extraordinary African *chambre d'accusation, chambre d'Assises*, and *chambre d'assises d'Appel* respectively at the Dakar Court of Appeal.[258] They have jurisdiction 'to prosecute and adjudge the person or persons most responsible for crimes and serious violations of international law, international custom, and international conventions ratified by Chad, committed on the territory of Chad during the period from 7 June 1982 to 1 December 1990'.[259] The bench of the Extraordinary African *chambre d'instruction* is composed exclusively of Senegalese judges, four of them sitting *juges d'instruction* and two of them stand-ins appointed by the president of the AU Commission on the nomination of the Senegalese minister of justice.[260] The Extraordinary African *chambre d'accusation* is made up of four judges in total, all of them again Senegalese, three of them sitting judges and one of them a stand-in appointed by the president of the AU Commission on the nomination of the Senegalese minister of justice.[261] Both the Extraordinary African *chambre d'Assises* and the Extraordinary African *chambre d'assises d'Appel* consist of two sitting Senegalese judges, two stand-in Senegalese judges appointed by the president of the AU Commission on the nomination of the Senegalese minister of justice, and a president from another AU member state the method of whose appointment is not specified.[262] The chief prosecutor and three assistant prosecutors are all Senegalese and are appointed by the president of the AU Commission on the nomination of the Senegalese minister of

9.73

---

[255] Statut des Chambres extraordinaires africaines au sein des juridictions sénégalaises pour la poursuite des crimes internationaux commis au Tchad durant la période du 7 juin 1982 au 1 décembre 1990 ('Statute of the Extraordinary African Chambers in the Senegalese Courts for the Prosecution of International Crimes Committed in Chad During the Period from 7 June 1982 to 1 December 1990').

[256] See also art 98 of the Constitution of the Republic of Senegal, in accordance with which treaties or other international agreements, duly ratified or approved and subsequently published, enjoy a status within the Senegalese legal order superior to that of legislation.

[257] Statute of the Extraordinary African Chambers in the Senegalese Courts, art 37(1).

[258] Ibid, art 2.

[259] Ibid, art 3(1). See also Agreement on the Creation of Extraordinary African Chambers in the Senegalese Courts, art 1(1), referring additionally to international conventions ratified by Senegal. Article 3(2) of the Statute permits the Chambers to focus on 'the most serious crimes falling within their jurisdiction'.

[260] Statute of the Extraordinary African Chambers in the Senegalese Courts, art 11(1). The judges of all of the chambers must have spent at least ten years as a judge, in accordance with art 11(5) of the Statute. The same provision requires that the presidents of the Extraordinary African *chambre d'Assises* and *chambre d'assises d'Appel* respectively must additionally meet the conditions laid down in their respective states for the exercise of high judicial office.

[261] Ibid, art 11(2).   [262] Ibid, art 11(3) and (4).

justice.²⁶³ The applicable criminal procedure is provided for in the Statute, in the first instance, and, failing this, in the Senegalese code of criminal procedure.²⁶⁴ A catalogue of rights of the accused drawn from article 14 of the ICCPR is provided for in article 21 of the Statute. The Statute expressly provides for the participation of victims in proceedings as civil parties (*parties civiles*).²⁶⁵ Where not regulated by the Statute, such participation is regulated by the Senegalese code of criminal procedure.²⁶⁶ Without prejudice to the rights of victims under Senegalese law more generally or international law, the Statute makes provision for reparations for victims in the form of restitution, compensation, and rehabilitation.²⁶⁷ The Chambers may order that reparation in the form of compensation is to be disbursed from the trust fund for victims established under the Statute.²⁶⁸ The trust fund, which may itself direct reparations to victims either individually or collectively, and whether or not they have taken part in proceedings before the Chambers, is to be funded by voluntary contributions from foreign governments, international institutions, nongovernmental organizations or other any source willing to lend support to victims of international crimes committed in Chad during Habré's time in power.²⁶⁹

9.74　　The Extraordinary African Chambers in the Senegalese Courts enjoy jurisdiction *ratione materiae* over the crimes of genocide, crimes against humanity, war crimes, and torture.²⁷⁰ The first is defined as per article II of the Genocide Convention, except that 'wilful homicide' is substituted for 'murder'; the definition of crimes against humanity has many elements in common with, but varies from, that in article 7(1) of the Rome Statute; the war crimes within the Chambers' jurisdiction comprise what are effectively, albeit not expressly, grave breaches of the 1949 Geneva Conventions, along with serious violations of article 3 common to the same and of 1977 Additional Protocol II; and the definition of torture combines the texts of articles 1(1) and 2(3) of the Torture Convention.²⁷¹ The provisions on modes of responsibility, official capacity, superior responsibility, and superior orders track closely those in the ICTY and ICTR statutes.²⁷² The crimes within the jurisdiction of the Chambers are declared to be imprescriptible, and no amnesty granted to a person within the Chambers' jurisdiction poses a bar to prosecution.²⁷³ The Statute contains a detailed provision on *non bis in idem* which, in addition to applying to the Chambers *mutatis mutandis* the rules applicable to the ICC in article 20(1) and (3) of the Rome Statute, purports to prohibit the trial before another court of anyone previously convicted or acquitted by the Chambers—a prohibition capable of binding effect only insofar as it applies to Senegal in respect of subsequent trial before another Senegalese court.²⁷⁴ The Chambers' applicable law

---

²⁶³ Ibid, art 12(1). In accordance with art 12(2) of the Statute, all must have at least ten years' professional experience and, specifically, considerable experience of criminal investigations and prosecutions.
²⁶⁴ Ibid, art 17(1).　　²⁶⁵ Ibid, art 14.　　²⁶⁶ Ibid, art 14(5).
²⁶⁷ See ibid, art 27(1) and (4).　　²⁶⁸ See ibid, art 27(2).　　²⁶⁹ Ibid, art 28.
²⁷⁰ See ibid, arts 4–8.
²⁷¹ See ibid, art 5, especially subpara (*a*), and arts 6, 7, and 8 respectively.
²⁷² See ibid, art 10(2) to (5) respectively.　　²⁷³ Ibid, arts 9 and 20 respectively.
²⁷⁴ See ibid, art 19(1) and (3) and art 19(2) respectively. For art 20 of the Rome Statute, see *infra* paras 14.77–14.78.

is stated to be the Statute and, in circumstances not foreshadowed in the Statute, Senegalese law.[275] No specific provision is made for the Chambers' jurisdiction *ratione personae*. The general reference to their jurisdiction in article 3(1) of the Statute refers to 'the person or persons most responsible' for the crimes in question, with the consequence that the trial of former key figures of the Habré regime in Chad other than Habré himself is not ruled out.

9.75 In an implicit reference to Belgian judicial efforts aimed at the prosecution of Hissène Habré, the Extraordinary African Chambers are directed to take all measures necessary for 'judicial cooperation, the receipt and the use, where needed, of the results of investigations carried out by the judicial authorities of other States in respect of the crimes referred to' in the Statute.[276] The Chambers are authorized to request the transfer to them of any criminal proceedings and, in this context, to treat as valid transcripts and any evidence established by the competent authorities of the requested state.[277]

9.76 On 13 August 2013, Hissène Habré was committed for trial by a *juge d'instruction* of the Extraordinary African *chambre d'instruction* of the Dakar *Tribunal Régional Hors Classe*. On 5 November 2013, in response to a request by Habré for the indication of provisional measures to compel Senegal to halt investigations and proceedings against him, among other things, the ECOWAS Community Court of Justice ruled that *prima facie* it lacked jurisdiction over the merits of the case and that, as a result, it was not in a position to order provisional measures.[278] Investigations and pre-trial consideration of applications to participate as civil parties in the proceedings before the Extraordinary African Chambers continue.

(xi) Kosovo International Crimes Tribunal

9.77 On 23 April 2014, the Assembly of Kosovo voted in favour of the establishment in cooperation with the EU of a special municipal criminal tribunal for the investigation and possible prosecution of a range of international crimes, relating in particular to the treatment of persons in detention over the period 1999–2000 and the subsequent harvesting and trafficking of some detainees' organs, for which senior members of the Kosovo Liberation Army and later of the government of Kosovo are alleged to bear responsibility. The vote follows a January 2011 report of the Committee on Legal Affairs and Human Rights of the Parliamentary Assembly of the Council of Europe[279] and a follow-up investigation by a Special Investigative Task Force (SITF) established in September 2011 under the authority of EULEX. While details of the tribunal are yet to be finalized, it has been reported that the

---

[275] Statute of the Extraordinary African Chambers in the Senegalese Courts, art 16.
[276] Ibid, art 18(1).   [277] Ibid, art 18(2).
[278] See *Habré c Sénégal*, Case No ECW/CCJ/RUL/05/13, Judgment, ECOWAS Community Court of Justice, 5 November 2013.
[279] Parliamentary Assembly, Council of Europe, Committee on Legal Affairs and Human Rights, *Inhuman treatment of people and illicit trafficking in human organs in Kosovo. Report*, doc 12462 (7 January 2011).

court will be established under the law of Kosovo and formally headquartered in Kosovo but will be staffed entirely by 'international' judges and prosecutors and undertake most of its work in the Netherlands.

V. Conclusion

9.78 The lion's share of the legal suppression of international crimes will, for the foreseeable future, fall to national criminal justice systems. National criminal justice genuinely pursued bars the exercise of jurisdiction by the ICC over the crimes within the Court's purview, which are limited anyway to genocide, crimes against humanity, war crimes, and aggression (the exercise of jurisdiction over the last facing additional hurdles); and, with the winding down of the ICTY, International Criminal Tribunal for Rwanda (ICTR), and Special Court for Sierra Leone (SCSL) and the expensive, vaguely embarrassing spectacle of the Special Tribunal for Lebanon (STL), states seemingly have little appetite for the further creation of ad hoc international criminal courts. Nor, for that matter, does the ICC have the resources and capacity to try more than a few persons at any time. As it is, the many and varied international criminal conventions oblige states parties to submit cases to their competent criminal justice authorities for the purpose of prosecution or to extradite the suspect to a state that will and can.

9.79 All this said, the prosecution of international crimes at the municipal level can face legal obstacles both international and municipal. Where the suspect or accused is a serving or former official of a foreign state, questions of international and municipal law may arise as to immunity from prosecution and inviolability from measures of constraint. It may also be the case that prosecution is barred by a statute of limitations or amnesty. It is on these legal obstacles that the following two chapters focus.

Further Reading

ALDYKIEWICZ, JE and CORN, GS, 'Authority to Court-Martial Non-US Military Personnel for Serious Violations of International Humanitarian Law Committed During Internal Armed Conflicts' (2001) 167 *Military Law Review* 74

BEKOU, O, 'Crimes at Crossroads. Incorporating International Crimes at the National Level' (2012) 10 *Journal of International Criminal Justice* 677

BOISTER, N, *An Introduction to Transnational Criminal Law* (Oxford: Oxford University Press, 2012), chapter 11

BURGERS, JH and DANELIUS, H, *The United Nations Convention against Torture: A Handbook on the Convention against Torture and Other Cruel, Inhuman or Degrading Treatment or Punishment* (Dordrecht/London: Martinus Nijhoff, 1988)

BURGESS, P, 'De Facto Amnesty? The Example of Post-Soeharto Indonesia' in F Lessa and LA Payne (eds), *Amnesty in the Age of Human Rights Accountability: Comparative and International Perspectives* (Cambridge: Cambridge University Press, 2012), 263

CHEHTMAN, A, 'Developing Bosnia and Herzegovina's Capacity to Process War Crimes Cases: Critical Notes on a "Success Story"' (2011) 9 *Journal of International Criminal Justice* 547

CLARK, P, *The Gacaca Courts, Post-Genocide Justice and Reconciliation in Rwanda* (Cambridge: Cambridge University Press, 2010)

CRYER, R, *Prosecuting International Crimes. Selectivity and the International Criminal Law Regime* (Cambridge: Cambridge University Press, 2005), 167–84

DEHN, JC, 'The Hamdan Case and the Application of a Municipal Offence. The Common Law Origins of "Murder in Violation of the Law of War"' (2009) 7 *Journal of International Criminal Justice* 63

GARDNER, M, 'Piracy Prosecutions in National Courts' (2012) 10 *Journal of International Criminal Justice* 797

GUILFOYLE, D, 'Prosecuting Somali Pirates: A Critical Evaluation of the Options' (2012) 10 *Journal of International Criminal Justice* 767

HELLER, KJ, *The Nuremberg Military Tribunals and the Origins of International Criminal Law* (Oxford: Oxford University Press, 2011)

HELLER, KJ and SIMPSON, G (eds), *The Hidden Histories of War Crimes Trials* (Oxford: Oxford University Press, 2013)

HOVEN, E, 'Civil Party Participation in Trials of Mass Crimes: A Qualitative Study at the Extraordinary Chambers in the Courts of Cambodia' (2014) 12 *Journal of International Criminal Justice* 81

KEMP, S, 'Guatemala Prosecutes former President Ríos Montt: New Perspectives on Genocide and Domestic Criminal Justice' (2014) 12 *Journal of International Criminal Justice* 133

LAFONTAINE, F, 'Universal Jurisdiction—The Realistic Utopia' (2012) 10 *Journal of International Criminal Justice* 1277

LINTON, S (ed), *Hong Kong's War Crimes Trials* (Oxford: Oxford University Press, 2013)

LINTON, S, 'Unravelling the First Three Trials at Indonesia's Ad Hoc Court for Human Rights Violations in East Timor' (2004) 17 *Leiden Journal of International Law* 303

McDONALD, A, 'Bosnia's War Crimes Chamber and the Challenges of an Opening and Closure' in J Doria, H-P Gasser, and MC Bassiouni (eds), *The Legal Regime of the International Criminal Court. Essays in Honour of Professor Igor Blishchenko* (Leiden: Martinus Nijhoff, 2009), 297

METTRAUX, G, 'A Little-known Case from the American Civil War: The War Crimes Trial of Major General John H Gee' (2010) 8 *Journal of International Criminal Justice* 1059

METTRAUX, G, 'The 2005 Revision of the Statute of the Iraqi Special Tribunal' (2007) 5 *Journal of International Criminal Justice* 287

NOWAK, M and McARTHUR, E, *The United Nations Convention Against Torture: A Commentary* (Oxford: Oxford University Press, 2008)

OKADA, E, 'The Australian Trials of Class B and C War Crimes Suspects, 1945–51' (2009) 16 *Australian International Law Journal* 47

RASIAH, N, "The Court-martial of Corporal Payne and Others and the Future Landscape of International Criminal Justice' (2009) 7 *Journal of International Criminal Justice* 177

REIGER, C and WIERDA, M, *The Serious Crimes Process in Timor-Leste: In Retrospect* (New York: International Center for Transitional Justice, 2006)

REPUBLIC OF SERBIA, OFFICE OF THE WAR CRIMES PROSECUTOR, *Serbia on Its Way Towards Justice and Reconciliation: Office of the War Crimes Prosecutor, 10 Years Later* (Belgrade: 2013)

ROGERS, APV, 'The Use of Military Courts to Try Suspects' (2002) 51 *International and Comparative Law Quarterly* 967

ROGERS, APV, 'War Crimes Trials under the Royal Warrant: British Practice 1945–1949' (1990) 39 *International and Comparative Law Quarterly* 780

ROSE, C, 'The UK Bribery Act 2010 and Accompanying Guidance: Belated Implementation of the OECD Anti-Bribery Convention' (2012) 61 *International and Comparative Law Quarterly* 485

SISSONS, M and BASSIN, AS, 'Was the *Dujail* Trial Fair?' (2007) 5 *Journal of International Criminal Justice* 272

STEGMILLER, I, 'Legal Developments in Civil Party Participation at the Extraordinary Chambers in the Courts of Cambodia' (2014) 27 *Leiden Journal of International Law* 465

TIBA, FK, 'The *Mengistu* Genocide Trial in Ethiopia' (2007) 5 *Journal of International Criminal Justice* 513

TOTANI, Y, *Justice in Asia and the Pacific Region, 1945–1952. Allied War Crimes Prosecutions* (Cambridge: Cambridge University Press, 2015)

WILLIAMS, S, 'The Extraordinary African Chambers in the Senegalese Courts: An African Solution to an African Problem?' (2013) 11 *Journal of International Criminal Justice* 1139

10
Immunity and Inviolability

I. Introduction

Just because a state enjoys jurisdiction under international law (and, *a fortiori*, just because its courts enjoy jurisdiction under municipal law) over a given individual in respect of a given act does not necessarily mean as a matter of international law that it may exercise it. The individual may benefit as a matter of international law from immunity from the criminal process of that state by virtue of his position or her performance of the act as an official of a foreign state.[1] In other words, it may be as a matter of international law that—on account of his current office in or posting on behalf of a foreign state or on account of her having performed the impugned act in her capacity as a foreign-state official—the individual may not be prosecuted, subjected to extradition proceedings or compelled to testify in the courts of the forum state. The same individual may also benefit under international law from inviolability from measures of physical constraint in the state in question, by which is meant that he or she may not lawfully be arrested, detained or required to submit to search by that state. 10.1

After introducing the key concepts, this chapter outlines and analyses the scope of the immunity from foreign criminal jurisdiction and the inviolability from foreign measures of physical constraint—both generally and in relation to allegations of international crimes—from which, in relevant cases, a state is entitled under international law to see its serving and former officials benefit. The term 'state official' is used throughout to refer to any individual who represents the state or exercises state functions.[2] 10.2

---

[1] This chapter does not deal with the separate but related questions of the jurisdictional immunities owed by states in respect of the administrative, technical, and service staff of foreign missions and posts and in respect of the private servants and family of members of such missions and posts. Nor does it consider the jurisdictional immunities owed by states in respect of the officials of international organizations.

[2] See draft art 2(*e*) of the draft articles on immunity of State officials from foreign criminal jurisdiction provisionally adopted on 15 July 2014 by the Drafting Committee of the International Law Commission, UN doc A/CN.4/L.850 (15 July 2014): '"State official" means any individual who represents the State or who exercises State functions.'

II. General

10.3 A state (known as the 'forum state') owes all other states an obligation under international law to ensure in varying circumstances that its courts do not entertain criminal proceedings, in the form of either prosecution or proceedings for extradition, against the serving and former officials of those other states and do not compel such persons to testify in criminal proceedings against anyone. That is, the forum state may be obliged by international law to accord immunity from its criminal jurisdiction to the officials and ex-officials of foreign states. There are circumstances too in which a state owes all other states an obligation under international law to ensure that its authorities do not take measures of physical constraint, in the form of arrest, detention, search, and so on, against those other states' serving officials. In other words, a state may be obliged by international law to ensure the inviolability of the officials (but not ex-officials) of foreign states.[3]

10.4 Insofar as international law regulates the grant of immunity and inviolability to serving and former state officials, it does so only in respect of the serving and former officials of foreign states. Whether the forum state accords immunity from the process of its criminal courts and inviolability from measures of physical constraint to its own officials and ex-officials is a matter for that state.[4]

10.5 Even if individuals may be their beneficiaries, the various immunities from criminal jurisdiction and the inviolability that a state may be obliged by international law to accord to the officials and ex-officials of a foreign state are owed to the foreign state itself. Serving and former officials of a foreign state enjoy no individual right under international law to immunity from criminal process or to inviolability from measures of physical constraint.

10.6 It is open to a foreign state to waive any immunity from criminal jurisdiction and inviolability from measures of physical constraint from which it may be entitled under international law to see its serving and former officials benefit. That is, it may choose to permit another state to prosecute its officials or ex-officials, to subject them to extradition proceedings, to compel them to testify or to subject them to measures of physical constraint.

10.7 Both immunity and inviolability are procedural, not substantive, bars.[5] In other words, those foreign state officials who benefit from immunity and, in

---

[3] A state's obligation to afford inviolability to certain foreign state officials has implications beyond the context of measures of physical constraint, but these further implications are beyond the scope of this chapter.

[4] More precisely, it is a matter for that state as far as the international rules on procedural immunity are concerned. There may be questions to be answered under international human rights law. See also United Nations Convention against Corruption 2003, art 30(2): 'Each State party shall take such measures as may be necessary to establish or maintain, in accordance with its legal system and constitutional principles, an appropriate balance between any immunities or jurisdictional privileges accorded to its public officials for the performance of their functions and the possibility, when necessary, of effectively investigating, prosecuting and adjudicating offences established in accordance with this Convention.'

[5] See eg *Arrest Warrant of 11 April 2000 (Democratic Republic of the Congo v Belgium)*, ICJ Rep 2002, 3, 25, para 60. See also, in relation to civil proceedings, *Jurisdictional Immunities of the State (Germany v Italy: Greece intervening), Judgment*, ICJ Rep 2012, 99, 124, para 58 and 140, para 93; *Al-Adsani v United Kingdom*, 123 ILR 24, 38, para 48 (ECtHR (GC) 2001).

relevant cases, inviolability remain bound by the law of the forum state insofar as it may apply to them. It is simply that they cannot be brought to book for its breach as long as the immunity and, in relevant cases, the inviolability is available to them. Putting it in international legal terms, any obligation on a state to accord immunity or inviolability is without prejudice to its enjoyment of the underlying jurisdiction to prescribe and to enforce, even if it may bar their exercise in a given case. Should a foreign state choose to waive the immunity or inviolability from which it is entitled to see its serving and former officials benefit, any applicable municipal law, which has always bound the official in question, may be enforced.

It is 'a generally recognized principle', which states are 'under an obligation to respect', that 'questions of immunity are...preliminary issues which must be expeditiously decided *in limine litis*'.[6] That is, the availability or otherwise of immunity, at least from prosecution or extradition proceedings, must be determined 'at the outset of the proceedings, before consideration of the merits'.[7]   10.8

The immunities from criminal jurisdiction that one state is obliged by international law to accord the serving or former officials of a foreign state fall into two essential categories. The first comprises immunities *ratione personae* (also known as personal immunities or, more appropriately,[8] status immunities), which require the barring of any form of criminal proceedings—be it pre-trial or trial proceedings or extradition proceedings—against the holders of certain foreign-state offices or posts for the duration of their term of office or their posting. The same immunity requires the barring of any judicial order to give evidence as a witness for the same period. The archetype of this first species of immunity is the immunity from the criminal jurisdiction of the receiving[9] and any transit[10] state's courts from which the sending[11] state's diplomatic agents benefit as a matter of customary and conventional international law for the duration of their posting. Of equivalent scope is the customary and conventional immunity from the criminal jurisdiction of the receiving and any transit state's courts from which the representatives of a state in a special mission and members of the mission's diplomatic staff benefit, as well as the immunity from the criminal jurisdiction of the host[12] and any transit state's courts   10.9

---

[6] *Difference Relating to Immunity from Legal Process of a Special Rapporteur of the Commission on Human Rights, Advisory Opinion*, ICJ Rep 1999, 62, 88, para 63. See also, recalling and applying the ICJ's dictum, *A v Ministère public de la Confédération, B and C*, Swiss Federal Criminal Court, 25 July 2012, para 5.2 ('*Nezzar*').

[7] *Jurisdictional Immunities* (n 5), 145, para 106. See also ibid, 136, para 82.

[8] The adjective 'personal' can be misleading in this context, since the immunity is for the benefit of the individual as office-holder and is owed not to that individual but to the state of which he or she is an official.

[9] The 'receiving' state is the state in which a foreign diplomatic agent, etc is posted or to which a special mission is sent.

[10] A 'transit' state is any state through which a foreign diplomatic agent, etc passes while travelling directly, in either direction, between the territory of the sending state and the territory of the receiving state.

[11] The 'sending' state is the state that the foreign diplomatic agent, etc represents.

[12] The 'host' state is the state in which an international organization is headquartered or otherwise has an office.

from which the representatives of member states to the principal and subsidiary organs of the UN and to conferences convened by it, along with certain officials posted to a state's permanent mission to certain international organizations, all benefit. Other, uncodified immunities *ratione personae* are the immunity to be accorded to a foreign state's serving head of state, the immunity to be accorded to a foreign state's serving head of government, and the immunity to be accorded to a foreign state's serving minister for foreign affairs. The second category of immunities under international law comprises immunities *ratione materiae* (also known as subject-matter immunities or, less desirably,[13] 'functional' immunities), which prohibit criminal proceedings in respect of certain subject-matter against serving and former officials of a foreign state and any order to give evidence as a witness on the same subject-matter. The chief example of this species of immunity is state immunity (also known as sovereign or foreign sovereign immunity), which in its uncodified criminal context requires the barring of any form of criminal proceedings and any order to give evidence against any serving or former official of a foreign state in respect of acts performed in an official capacity. Other, codified examples are the immunity from the criminal jurisdiction of the receiving and any transit state's courts from which serving and former consular officers[14] benefit in respect of acts performed in the exercise of their consular functions; the immunity from the criminal jurisdiction of the host and any transit state's courts from which the serving and former representatives of member states at meetings organized by a UN specialized agency benefit in respect of acts performed in their official capacity; and the immunity from the criminal jurisdiction of the former receiving or host state's courts that continues to accrue to the advantage of former diplomatic agents, etc.[15]

10.10   In 2007, the International Law Commission (ILC) decided to include the topic of the immunity of state officials from foreign criminal jurisdiction in its current programme of work. The topic encompasses both immunity *ratione personae* and immunity *ratione materiae*,[16] and appears to extend to inviolability from measures

---

[13] The adjective 'functional' could be taken to suggest that the rationale for such immunity is merely the facilitation of the functions of the state officials in question. But as regards state immunity, the chief immunity *ratione materiae*, the facilitation of an official's duties is no more than a collateral, albeit important practical benefit, the principled *raison d'être* for the immunity being far more abstract, namely the corollary of the sovereign equality of states summed up in the maxim *par in parem non habet imperium*. See *infra* paras 10.48–10.49. In contrast, the facilitation of the official's job is of the essence of immunity *ratione personae*. See *infra* paras 10.20 and 10.34.

[14] Unless otherwise specified, the term 'consular officer' is used throughout this chapter to refer to both career consular officers and honorary consular officers.

[15] For the relationship between these other, codified immunities *ratione materiae* and the uncodified rules of state immunity from criminal jurisdiction, see *infra* paras 10.45 and 10.92.

[16] The ILC's current work on the immunity of state officials from foreign criminal jurisdiction does not encompass special rules governing aspects of the issue. See draft art 1(2) of the draft articles on immunity of State officials from foreign criminal jurisdiction provisionally adopted so far by the Commission, *Report of the International Law Commission, Sixty-fifth session (6 May–7 June and 8 July–9 August 2013)*, UN doc A/68/10 (2013), 51, para 48. Chief among these special rules—in their qualities both as treaty rules and, where relevant, as rules of customary international law—are those immunities stipulated in a treaty, in particular diplomatic immunity and inviolability, as regulated by the Vienna Convention on Diplomatic Relations 1961 ('VCDR'); consular immunity and quasi-inviolability, as

of physical constraint. Work has not progressed very far to date, and what value it has at this stage lies less in and of itself than in the state practice it has precipitated in the form of delegations' reactions to it in the course of the annual consideration of the work of the ILC by the Sixth (*viz* Legal) Committee of the UN General Assembly.

III. The Content of Immunity and Inviolability

Immunity from jurisdiction relates to amenability to judicial process, while inviolability pertains to subjection to measures of physical constraint or other interference.[17] At its simplest, the forum state's international legal obligation to accord foreign state officials immunity from its criminal jurisdiction is an obligation to ensure that they are not prosecuted, subjected to judicial proceedings for their extradition or compelled to give evidence in criminal proceedings against whomever, either at all or in respect of certain acts;[18] and, at its simplest, the forum state's international legal obligation to accord foreign state officials inviolability is an obligation to ensure that they are not arrested, detained or subjected to search.[19] The question is what more immunity and inviolability require, both jointly and severally. 10.11

In *Arrest Warrant of 11 April 2000*, the International Court of Justice (ICJ), speaking in the specific context of immunity *ratione personae*, asserted that 'immunity and...inviolability protect the individual concerned against any act of authority of another State which would hinder him or her in the performance of his or her duties'.[20] This potentially very far-reaching statement was reiterated and applied to a head of state in *Certain Questions of Mutual Assistance in Criminal Matters*,[21] where the Court continued that 'the determining factor in 10.12

---

governed by the Vienna Convention on Consular Relations 1963 ('VCCR'); the immunity and inviolability of the representatives of a state in a special mission and of members of the mission's diplomatic staff, as regulated by the Convention on Special Missions 1969 ('CSM'); the immunity and inviolability of the representatives of member states to the principal and subsidiary organs of the UN and to conferences convened by it, as found in the Convention on the Privileges and Immunities of the United Nations 1946 ('CPIUN'); the immunity and inviolability of the representatives of member states to meetings organized by a UN specialized agency, as provided for in the Convention on the Privileges and Immunities of the Specialized Agencies 1947 ('CPISA'); the immunity and inviolability of the head and members of a state's permanent mission to an international organization of a universal character, as recognized in the Vienna Convention on the Representation of States in their Relations with International Organizations of a Universal Character 1975 ('VCRS') (not in force); and any immunity and inviolability specified in a status of forces agreement, status of mission agreement or the like.

[17] See eg *Immunity of State officials from foreign criminal jurisdiction. Memorandum by the Secretariat*, UN doc A/CN.4/596 (31 March 2008), 18, para 15.

[18] Throughout this chapter, the word 'acts' is intended to encompass omissions.

[19] See eg the provisions of the various codification conventions cited *infra* paras 10.25, 10.29, and 10.30.

[20] *Arrest Warrant* (n 5), 22, para 54.

[21] See *Certain Questions of Mutual Assistance in Criminal Matters (Djibouti v France), Judgment*, ICJ Rep 2008, 177, 237, para 170.

assessing whether or not there has been an attack on the immunity'—by which was meant both the immunity from jurisdiction and the inviolability[22]—'of the Head of State lies in the subjection of the latter to a constraining act of authority'.[23]

10.13 The ICJ's statements and rulings in *Arrest Warrant* and *Certain Questions of Mutual Assistance* form the backbone of discussion of the content of immunity from foreign criminal jurisdiction and inviolability from foreign measures of physical constraint in the background study on the immunity of state officials from foreign criminal jurisdiction prepared for the ILC by the UN Secretariat,[24] in the reports so far of the ILC's special rapporteurs on the topic,[25] and in the Sixth Committee to date.[26] At the same time, both the generality of the Court's formulations and the specificities of the cases it has been called on to adjudicate have meant that, although its statements are treated as central to the debate, their 'full effect... on national laws providing for the prosecution of foreign State officials remains unclear'.[27]

10.14 Additionally, although the ICJ has indicated, albeit in very general terms, what is prohibited by immunity from criminal jurisdiction and inviolability from measures of physical constraint when taken together, its reluctance in *Arrest Warrant* to specify what was implicated by immunity from jurisdiction and inviolability respectively has sowed the seeds of uncertainty. When it came in that case to whether the mere issue and international circulation of a warrant for the arrest of a state official—as distinct from, on the one hand, the official's prosecution and trial and, on the other, his or her actual arrest—was an issue going to immunity from jurisdiction or to inviolability or to both, the Court hedged it bets. It concluded that the issue of the arrest warrant by the Belgian prosecuting authorities 'failed to respect the immunity of [the] Minister and, more particularly, infringed the immunity from criminal jurisdiction and the inviolability then enjoyed by him under international law';[28] that the circulation of the warrant by Belgium 'failed to respect the immunity of the incumbent Minister for Foreign Affairs of the Congo and, more particularly, infringed the immunity from criminal jurisdiction and the inviolability then enjoyed by him under international law';[29] and that 'the issue and circulation of the arrest warrant of 11 April 2000 by the Belgian authorities failed to respect the immunity of the incumbent Minister for Foreign Affairs of the Congo and, more particularly, infringed the immunity from criminal jurisdiction and the inviolability then enjoyed by [him] under international law'.[30]

---

[22] See the immediately preceding sentence, ibid, where the Court, quoting from *Arrest Warrant* (n 5), 22, para 54, refers more comprehensively to the '"full immunity from criminal jurisdiction and inviolability" which protects [the head of state] "against any act of authority of another State which would hinder him or her in the performance of his or her duties"'.

[23] *Certain Questions of Mutual Assistance* (n 21), 237, para 170.

[24] See *Secretariat Memorandum* (n 17), 151–3, paras 235–236 and 155–61, paras 240–245.

[25] See *Second report on immunity of State officials from foreign criminal jurisdiction by Roman Anatolevitch Kolodkin, Special Rapporteur*, UN doc A/CN.4/631 (10 June 2010), 22–7, paras 40–51.

[26] See eg UN doc A/C.6/66/SR.26 (7 December 2011), 5, para 17 (Switzerland).

[27] *Secretariat Memorandum* (n 17), 158–61, paras 242–245.

[28] *Arrest Warrant* (n 5), 29, para 70. [29] Ibid, 30, para 71. [30] Ibid, 31, para 75.

The Court similarly went on to find in the *dispositif* that 'the issue... of the arrest warrant of 11 April 2000, and its international circulation, constituted violations of a legal obligation of the Kingdom of Belgium towards the Democratic Republic of the Congo, in that they failed to respect the immunity from criminal jurisdiction and the inviolability which the incumbent Minister for Foreign Affairs of the Democratic Republic of the Congo enjoyed under international law'.[31] Insofar as a serving state official may benefit under international law from both immunity *ratione personae* and, as appears invariably to accompany it, inviolability, the question of the line between the two concepts is academic. Insofar, however, as a serving or former state official may benefit from only immunity *ratione materiae*, and to the extent that it remains uncertain whether immunity *ratione materiae* is accompanied in its application to individuals by their inviolability, the problem is of practical significance. The UN Secretariat, highlighting the dissenting opinion in *Arrest Warrant* of Judge ad hoc Van den Wyngaert,[32] noted the imprecision attendant upon the Court's omnibus references to 'immunity from jurisdiction and inviolability',[33] although the ILC's first special rapporteur was less attuned to this nuance.[34] The better view is that the issue and circulation of an arrest warrant goes to immunity from criminal jurisdiction, rather than to inviolability, the latter being a question, in the words of the ILC in the diplomatic context, of 'measures that would amount to direct coercion'[35]—that is, of what the UN Secretariat has referred to as trespass to the person.[36]

In contrast, the ICJ was tolerably clear in *Certain Questions of Mutual Assistance* in treating a summons to appear as a witness as going to immunity from jurisdiction, rather than inviolability.[37] This is correct.[38] For example, article 31, paragraph 2 of the Vienna Convention on Diplomatic Relations 1961 ('VCDR'), which provides that '[a] diplomatic agent is not obliged to give evidence as a witness', appears in article 31 alongside provisions dealing with the immunity of a diplomatic agent from the criminal and civil jurisdiction of the receiving state (paragraph 1) and from measures of execution in that state (paragraph 3), as well as a provision specifying that the immunity of a diplomatic agent from the jurisdiction of the receiving state 'does not exempt him from [that] jurisdiction' (paragraph 4). Conversely, no prohibition on compelling a diplomat to give evidence as a witness is found in article 29 of the VCDR, which states in its first sentence that '[t]he person of a diplomatic agent shall be inviolable' and in its second that a diplomatic agent 'shall not be liable to any form of arrest or

10.15

---

[31] Ibid, 33, para 78(2).   [32] See ibid, 179, para 75 (diss op Van den Wyngaert).
[33] See *Secretariat Memorandum* (n 17), 151–2, para 235.
[34] See *Second report Kolodkin* (n 25), 22–3, para 40.
[35] Paragraph 1 of commentary to draft art 27 of the ILC's Draft Articles on Diplomatic Intercourse and Immunities, *Ybk ILC 1958*, vol II, 89, 97. Draft art 27 became VCDR, art 29.
[36] *Secretariat Memorandum* (n 17), 18, para 15.
[37] See *Certain Questions of Mutual Assistance* (n 21), 237, para 171 and 240, para 179.
[38] In addition to the provisions of the VCDR cited in the following text, see *infra* the provisions of the other codification conventions on privileges and immunities.

detention'.³⁹ In the event, applying its concept of a 'constraining act of authority', the ICJ ruled in *Certain Questions of Mutual Assistance* that a foreign criminal court's issuance, in relation to a state official, of a summons to appear as a witness did not violate the immunity from jurisdiction owed in respect of that official when the summons represented not a measure of compulsion but merely an invitation to testify that the official could freely accept or decline.[40] This was *a fortiori* the case as regards a summons that expressly sought the official's consent.[41] Conversely, a criminal court's issuance against a foreign state official of a binding summons to appear as a witness or *subpoena ad testificandum* would violate any obligation incumbent on the forum state to accord the foreign official immunity from criminal jurisdiction.

10.16   Differing views have been expressed in the context of the ILC's work as to whether the ICJ's reliance in *Certain Questions of Mutual Assistance* on the notion of 'a constraining act of authority' would mean that the mere opening of a criminal investigation into the acts of a foreign state official would violate the immunity from jurisdiction owed in respect of that individual.[42] The more common and sounder view is that it would not.[43]

10.17   When it comes to inviolability, the ICJ held in *United States Diplomatic and Consular Staff in Tehran* that the observance of the obligation to ensure inviolability does not mean that a beneficiary of inviolability 'caught in the act of committing an assault or other offence may not, on occasion, be briefly arrested by the police of the receiving State in order to prevent the commission of the particular crime'.[44]

IV. Immunity *Ratione Personae* and Inviolability

A. Preface

10.18   Over and above the immunity *ratione materiae* from foreign criminal jurisdiction from which all serving and former state officials benefit under customary international law by virtue, and therefore in respect, of their performance of acts on behalf of the state,[45] certain state officials benefit under international

---

[39] That said, para 9 of the commentary to draft art 29 (the eventual VCDR, art 31) of the ILC's Draft Articles on Diplomatic Intercourse and Immunities (n 35), 98, explains that immunity from being obliged to give evidence as a witness 'derives from the diplomatic agent's inviolability'.
[40] See *Certain Questions of Mutual Assistance* (n 21), 237, para 171.
[41] See ibid, 240, para 179.
[42] Compare eg *Secretariat Memorandum* (n 17), 158–61, paras 242–245 with *Second report Kolodkin* (n 25), 23–5, paras 41–43 and UN doc A/C.6/66/SR.26 (n 20), 5, para 17 (Switzerland).
[43] But cf *Re Honecker*, 80 ILR 365, 366 (Federal Republic of Germany 1984).
[44] *United States Diplomatic and Consular Staff in Tehran (United States of America v Islamic Republic of Iran), Judgment*, ICJ Rep 1980, 3, 40, para 86. See also para 1 of the commentary to draft art 27 (eventually VCDR, art 29) of the ILC's Draft Articles on Diplomatic Intercourse and Immunities (n 35), 97.
[45] See *infra* section V. The various immunities *ratione personae* do not oust immunity *ratione materiae*. Rather, those state officers who benefit from immunity *ratione personae* continue during their term of office to benefit in tandem under customary international law from immunity

Immunity and Inviolability 413

law from immunity from foreign criminal jurisdiction by virtue, and therefore for the duration, of their particular office or posting—that is, from what is called immunity *ratione personae*, a.k.a. personal or status immunity. Since immunity *ratione personae* accrues to its beneficiaries on account of their occupation of a given office or post, and not on account of their performance of given acts, it serves for their term of office or their posting to bar both foreign criminal proceedings against them and any order to give evidence directed towards them regardless of whether the conduct the subject of the proceedings or order was performed by them in an official or private capacity or, for that matter, during or before their term of office or their posting. By the same token, since immunity *ratione personae* accrues by virtue of the office or post, its beneficiaries cease to benefit from it once they leave office or cease to be posted to the forum state.[46]

10.19 The beneficiaries under international law of immunity *ratione personae* tend also to benefit, for their term of office or their posting, from inviolability from foreign measures of physical constraint.

10.20 The rationale for immunity *ratione personae* and inviolability is different from that for the species of immunity *ratione materiae* known as state immunity. Whereas state immunity is a logical corollary of the sovereign equality of states which in principle undergirds international law,[47] immunity *ratione personae* and inviolability are based on purely pragmatic considerations, requiring the barring of criminal proceedings against their beneficiaries—as explained by the ICJ in *Arrest Warrant*—in order 'to ensure the effective performance of their functions on behalf of their respective States'.[48]

10.21 Immunity *ratione personae* and inviolability can both be waived by the state that the official serves.

10.22 When the holders of an office or post attracting immunity *ratione personae* vacate that office or leave that post, they do not lose all immunity from the criminal jurisdiction of the forum state. Rather, they continue to benefit under international law from immunity *ratione materiae* in respect of acts performed in their official capacity.[49]

10.23 Some species of immunity *ratione personae* from foreign criminal jurisdiction and inviolability from foreign measures of physical constraint have been codified

---

ratione materiae in respect of acts performed by them in an official capacity. The immunity *ratione materiae* will go mostly unnoticed for the duration of their office, since the greater (the immunity *ratione personae*) subsumes in effect the lesser (the immunity *ratione materiae*). In the words of Y Dinstein, 'Diplomatic Immunity from Jurisdiction *Ratione Materiae*' (1966) 15 *ICLQ* 76, 79, the customary immunity *ratione materiae* which benefits those state officers entitled in addition to personal immunity is, for their period of office, 'eclipsed by the shadow of the personal immunity'. But for situations in which this immunity *ratione materiae* will be determinative, see *infra* nn 54, 58, 60, and 61.

[46] See eg draft art 4(1) and (2) of the draft articles on immunity of State officials provisionally adopted so far (n 16).
[47] See *infra* para 10.48.   [48] *Arrest Warrant* (n 5), 21, para 53.
[49] See *infra* paras 10.55–10.56 and 10.97–10.100. See also the 'without prejudice' clause in draft art 4(3) of the draft articles on immunity of State officials provisionally adopted so far (n 16).

in multilateral treaties. Others remain creatures of customary international law alone.

B. Beneficiaries

(i) Diplomatic agents

10.24　The first codified species of immunity *ratione personae* is the immunity of a serving diplomatic agent[50] from the criminal process of the receiving state and transit states. In accordance with the customary international rule reflected in article 31(1) of the VCDR, foreign diplomatic agents benefit, for the duration of their posting,[51] from immunity from the criminal jurisdiction of the state to which they are accredited.[52] This immunity encompasses both proceedings and measures of compulsion such as binding summonses to appear, with article 31(2) of the VCDR specifying that a diplomatic agent 'is not obliged to give evidence as a witness'.[53] As per the customary rule encapsulated in article 40(1) of the VCDR, this immunity is opposable to transit states. No state other than the receiving state and transit states is obliged to accord a foreign diplomatic agent immunity *ratione personae* from the jurisdiction of its criminal courts.[54]

10.25　In addition to immunity *ratione personae* from criminal jurisdiction, foreign diplomatic agents benefit in the receiving state and any transit states, pursuant to articles 29 and 40(1) of the VCDR and customary international law, from inviolability from any form of arrest or detention.[55] As with immunity *ratione personae*, no other state is required to ensure the inviolability of a foreign diplomatic agent.

10.26　As per the customary position codified in article 39(2) of the VCDR, foreign diplomatic agents cease to enjoy immunity *ratione personae* and inviolability in the receiving state once their posting has come to an end and they quit the territory of

---

[50] The term is used as per VCDR, art 1(*e*).

[51] The precise temporal scope of this immunity *ratione personae* and its concomitant inviolability is specified in VCDR, art 39(1) and (2).

[52] In accordance, however, with art 9(1) of the VCDR, the receiving state may declare a foreign diplomatic agent *persona non grata* with the result that the sending state must recall the individual or terminate his or her functions with the mission. In accordance with the general rule laid down in art 39(2) of the VCDR, such a declaration does not abrogate the immunity or inviolability of the diplomat agent while the latter remains present in the territory of the receiving state, unless he or she does not quit the territory within a reasonable period.

[53] This and any analogous immunity from the obligation to give evidence as a witness applies as much to proceedings against a third party as to proceedings against the beneficiary of the immunity. In short, the immunity is from any obligation to give evidence as a witness.

[54] But all states are obliged to accord a foreign diplomatic agent the same immunity *ratione materiae* from which all serving and former foreign state officials benefit under customary international law in respect of acts performed by them in an official capacity. See eg *Re P (No 2)*, 114 ILR 485, 495–6 (UK 1998). See also *Preliminary report on immunity of State officials from foreign criminal jurisdiction by Roman Anatolevitch Kolodkin, Special Rapporteur*, UN doc A/CN.4/601 (29 May 2008), 50, para 99.

[55] The ICJ recognized the customary character of the inviolability of foreign diplomatic agents in *United States Diplomatic and Consular Staff in Tehran* (n 44), 31, para 62.

Immunity and Inviolability 415

that state, although they continue to benefit from both immunity *ratione personae* and inviolability in any transit state through which they pass en route back to the sending state.[56]

Article 32(1) of the VCDR and customary international law provide that any immunity from criminal jurisdiction and inviolability from which a foreign diplomatic agent may benefit can be waived by the sending state. As per article 32(2), such waiver must be express.

10.27

(ii) Certain members of special missions, etc

The immunity *ratione personae* and inviolability of a range of other state officials whose posts or short-term tasks place them on a conceptual par with diplomatic agents are codified in a range of conventions and almost certainly reflect customary international law.

10.28

The immunity *ratione personae* and inviolability of the representatives of a state in a special mission and the members of the mission's diplomatic staff are stipulated in the Convention on Special Missions 1969 ('CSM').[57] A 'special mission' is defined in article 1(*a*) of the CSM as 'a temporary mission, representing the State, which is sent by one State to another State with the consent of the latter for the purpose of dealing with it on specific questions or of performing in relation to it a specific task'. Article 31(1) of the CSM provides that the representatives of the sending state in a special mission and the members of the mission's diplomatic staff shall enjoy immunity from the criminal jurisdiction of the receiving state, while article 31(3) specifies that the same persons may not be obliged to give evidence as a witness. In addition, in accordance with article 29 of the CSM, the person of a representative of a state in a special mission and of a member of the diplomatic staff of the mission shall be inviolable, making them not liable to any form of arrest or detention. Article 42(1) extends the obligation to accord immunity *ratione personae* from criminal jurisdiction and inviolability from measures of physical constraint to transit states.[58] The temporal scope of this immunity *ratione personae* and inviolability is akin to that of the immunity *ratione personae* and inviolability of a diplomatic agent.[59] As recognized in article 41(1), the immunity and inviolability from which state representatives in a special mission and members of the mission's diplomatic staff benefit may be waived by the sending state. As per article 41(2), such waiver must be express.

10.29

---

[56] See *infra* para 10.98 for the immunity *ratione materiae* of an individual formerly accredited as a diplomatic agent to the forum state.

[57] For definitions of all relevant terms, see CSM, art 1. For the analogous immunity *ratione personae* from the criminal jurisdiction of the receiving state from which an ad hoc envoy charged with a special mission benefits as a matter of customary international law, see eg *Tabatabai*, 80 ILR 388, 419–20 (Federal Republic of Germany 1984).

[58] For the position of other states, recall, *mutatis mutandis, supra* n 54.

[59] See CSM, art 43(1) and (2) and recall *supra* para 10.25. For the immunity *ratione materiae* of persons no longer serving as representatives of a state in a special mission or as members of the diplomatic staff of the mission, see *infra* para 10.99.

10.30 Analogous immunities *ratione personae* from criminal jurisdiction and inviolability from measures of physical constraint are specified in relation to the representatives of member states to the principal and subsidiary organs of the UN and to conferences convened by it, as regulated by the Convention on the Privileges and Immunities of the United Nations 1946 ('CPIUN'),[60] and in relation to the heads and members of states' permanent missions to certain international organizations, as set out in the Vienna Convention on the Representation of States in their Relations with International Organizations of a Universal Character 1975 ('VCRS')[61] (not in force). As regards waiver, article IV, section 14 of the CPIUN provides:

> Privileges and immunities are accorded to the representatives of Members not for the personal benefit of the individuals themselves, but in order to safeguard the independent exercise of their functions in connection with the United Nations. Consequently a Member not only has the right but is under a duty to waive the immunity of its representative in any case where in the opinion of the Member the immunity would impede the course of justice, and it can be waived without prejudice to the purpose for which the immunity is accorded.

Whether the duty of waiver imposed on member states in relevant cases makes a difference in practice is open to doubt.

(iii) Heads of state

10.31 The least contentious of the uncodified species of immunity *ratione personae* is the immunity from criminal process that the forum state must accord a serving head of a foreign state. For the duration of their term of office, heads of state benefit under customary international law from immunity from foreign criminal jurisdiction,[62] an immunity that encompasses immunity from any obligation to give evidence;[63] and whereas the immunity *ratione personae* of diplomatic agents and those most

---

[60] See CPIUN, art IV, ss 11(*a*) and (*g*) and 14. While s 11(*a*) provides for immunity *ratione materiae* from the criminal jurisdiction of the host state and transit states 'in respect of words spoken or written and all acts done by [such representatives] in their capacity as representatives', s 11(*g*) stipulates that such representatives benefit additionally from the immunity *ratione personae* enjoyed by what are referred to as 'diplomatic envoys'. It is generally accepted that the effect of s 11(*g*) is to extend to representatives of member states to the principal and subsidiary organs of the UN and to conferences convened by it the immunity *ratione personae* from which diplomatic agents benefit, as now codified in VCDR, arts 31 and 40(1). See eg *United Nations Juridical Yearbook 1976*, 224, 227, and the civil case of *Tachiona v Mugabe*, ILDC 1090 (US 2004), paras 29–31. For the position of states other than the host and transit states, recall, *mutatis mutandis, supra* n 54. For the immunity *ratione materiae* of persons no longer serving in such capacities, see *infra* para 10.99.

[61] See VCRS, arts 28, 30(1) and (3), and 31(1) and (2). For the position of states other than the host and transit states, recall, *mutatis mutandis, supra* n 54. For the immunity *ratione materiae* of persons no longer serving in such capacities, see *infra* para 10.99.

[62] *Arrest Warrant* (n 5), 21, para 51; *Certain Questions of Mutual Assistance* (n 21), 236–7, para 170 and 238, para 173. See also draft arts 3 and 4 of the draft articles on immunity of State officials provisionally adopted so far (n 16).

[63] *Certain Questions of Mutual Assistance* (n 21), 237, para 171, by necessary implication.

like them is opposable only to the receiving state and any transit state, the immunity *ratione personae* of the head of a foreign state is opposable to all states. Heads of state equally benefit as a customary international matter, for the same period and in the same states, from inviolability from measures of physical constraint.[64] When heads of state are present in the territory of another state, their enjoyment of immunity and inviolability is without regard to whether their visit is official or private.[65] Both immunity *ratione personae* and inviolability cease to enure in the event that the head of state ceases to be head of state.[66] Both may be waived by the state of which they are head.

The original rationale for the immunity *ratione personae* and inviolability of heads of foreign states was the same as that for state (a.k.a. 'foreign sovereign') immunity, from which it was indistinguishable and, indeed, to which it gave rise, namely sovereign equality.[67] Today, however, the immunity *ratione personae* accruing to the benefit of heads of foreign states is rationalized by reference to the same pragmatic considerations that explain diplomatic immunity.[68] 10.32

(iv) Others

Prior to the ICJ's judgment in *Arrest Warrant*, serving diplomats and heads of state were alone in being incontrovertibly the beneficiaries under customary international law of immunity *ratione personae* from foreign criminal jurisdiction and from foreign judicial measures to compel their giving evidence as a witness, as well as of inviolability from foreign measures of physical constraint such as arrest and detention. In contrast, the position of serving heads of government and, even more so, of serving ministers for foreign affairs was uncertain. There was some evidence to suggest that they too benefited from immunity *ratione personae* and from inviolability,[69] but this was slight and ambivalent.[70] Against the normative background of a state's jurisdiction within its own territory to enforce its criminal law in the absence of a positive rule of international law compelling its abstention, it was perhaps more plausible that these latter two officers of state, and particularly ministers for foreign affairs, benefited only from the immunity *ratione materiae* from foreign 10.33

---

[64] Ibid, 238, paras 173–174.
[65] *Arrest Warrant* (n 5), 22, para 55, by necessary implication.
[66] For the immunity *ratione materiae* of a former head of state, see *infra* para 10.97.
[67] See *infra* para 10.48.
[68] *Arrest Warrant* (n 5), 20–2, paras 51–55, by necessary implication. See also *Re Honecker* (n 43), 366.
[69] See eg CSM, art 21(2): 'The Head of the Government, the Minister for Foreign Affairs and other persons of high rank, when they take part in a special mission of the sending State, shall enjoy in the receiving State or in a third State, in addition to what is granted by the present Convention, the facilities, privileges and immunities accorded by international law.' See also, *mutatis mutandis*, VCRS, art 50(2).
[70] First, neither CSM, art 21(2) nor VCRS, art 50(2) presupposes that the 'immunities accorded by international law' to heads of government and ministers for foreign affairs comprise immunity *ratione personae* from criminal jurisdiction and inviolability or, for that matter, are identical in content. Secondly, and more basically, whether either provision accords with customary international law is unclear.

10.34 In *Arrest Warrant*, however, the ICJ ruled that a serving minister for foreign affairs was entitled to immunity *ratione personae* from foreign criminal jurisdiction and to inviolability from foreign measures of physical constraint.[71] The Court presented its conclusion as one of customary international law,[72] but it adduced no state practice or *opinio juris* in support. Instead it argued teleologically. The immunities that as a matter of customary international law protected ministers for foreign affairs did so, the Court reasoned, 'to ensure the effective performance of their functions on behalf of their respective States'.[73] 'In the performance of these functions', the Court continued, a minister for foreign affairs 'is frequently required to travel internationally, and thus must be in a position freely to do so whenever the need should arise'.[74] '[A]ccordingly', the Court concluded, 'the functions of a Minister for Foreign Affairs are such that, throughout the duration of his or her office, he or she when abroad enjoys full immunity from criminal jurisdiction and inviolability'.[75] This immunity and inviolability for the duration of minister's term of office are without regard, the Court specified, to the capacity, be it official or private, in which the impugned acts were performed or, indeed, to whether they were performed during or prior to that term of office.[76] Nor, according to the Court, can any distinction be drawn between official and private visits to foreign states.[77]

criminal jurisdiction from which any state official benefits under customary international law in respect of acts performed in an official capacity.

10.35 The ICJ noted in *Arrest Warrant* that it was called on to address the immunity and inviolability only of a minister for foreign affairs.[78] At the same time, it alluded to the implicitly-cognate immunities from which, *inter alia*, heads of government were protected by international law;[79] and it highlighted in passing the analogous representative capacities under international law of a minister for foreign affairs and a head of government, both being taken, like the head of state, to speak for the state solely by virtue of their office.[80] Nor did the Court say that other officers of state did not benefit from immunity *ratione personae* and from inviolability. Indeed, it considered it 'firmly established' that 'certain holders of high-ranking office in a State', of which the head of state, head of government, and minister for foreign affairs were cited as examples, 'enjoy immunities from jurisdiction in other States'.[81] But the Court subsequently specified in *Certain Questions of Mutual Assistance*, without explanation beyond remarking that neither was a diplomat or on a special mission, that at least two officers of state, namely a senior prosecuting magistrate (*procureur de la République*) and the head of national security, do not benefit under customary international law from immunity *ratione personae* from foreign criminal jurisdiction.[82]

---

[71] *Arrest Warrant* (n 5), 22, para 54. [72] See ibid, 21, paras 52–53.
[73] Ibid, 21, para 53.   [74] Ibid.   [75] Ibid, 22, para 54.
[76] Ibid, 22, para 55. In short, immunity and inviolability enured *ratione personae*.
[77] Ibid.   [78] Ibid, 21, para 51.   [79] See ibid, 21, para 51.
[80] See ibid, 21, para 53.   [81] Ibid, 21, para 51.
[82] *Certain Questions of Mutual Assistance* (n 21), 243–4, para 194.

Immunity and Inviolability 419

The ICJ's ruling in *Arrest Warrant* on the minister for foreign affairs and its heavy-handed hint in the same case as to the head of government have already proved instrumental in the development of the law. It now seems generally taken as read that both these officers of state are the beneficiaries under customary international law of immunity *ratione personae* from foreign criminal jurisdiction and of inviolability from foreign measures of physical constraint. In Belgium, where *Arrest Warrant* originated, the Court of Cassation held the year after the ICJ's judgment that customary international law 'prohibits heads of...Government from being the subject of proceedings before the criminal courts of foreign States'.[83] In Italy, the Court of Cassation has stated *obiter* that heads of government and ministers for foreign affairs 'clearly' benefit under customary international law from immunity *ratione personae* from foreign criminal jurisdiction and personal inviolability.[84] The UN Secretariat, in its study on the immunity of state officials for the ILC, described the ICJ's judgment in *Arrest Warrant* as 'an authoritative assessment of the state of customary international law with respect to the immunity *ratione personae* of the minister for foreign affairs, which could be used, *mutatis mutandis*, to justify the immunity of the incumbent head of Government'.[85] As for the ILC itself, while not every member of the Commission has been convinced that the ICJ's decision as to ministers for foreign affairs had 'a firm basis in customary international law',[86] there has been 'broad agreement',[87] strongly informed by the Court's judgment in *Arrest Warrant*, that immunity *ratione personae* is enjoyed not only by heads of state but also by heads of government and ministers for foreign affairs.[88] This position is reflected in a draft article provisionally adopted by the Commission at its most recent session.[89] It is a position unanimously endorsed by states in discussions in the Sixth Committee.[90]

10.36

---

[83] *Re Sharon and Yaron*, 127 ILR 110, 123 (2003). The subsequently-inserted art 1*bis* of the Preliminary Title of Chapter I of the Belgian Code of Criminal Procedure provides for the immunity of 'heads of state, heads of government, and ministers for foreign affairs during the period when they exercise their function', to the extent that this is 'in conformity with international law'.
[84] *Italy v Djukanović*, ILDC 74 (IT 2004), para 10.
[85] *Secretariat Memorandum* (n 17), 78, para 121.
[86] *International Law Commission. Report on the work of its sixtieth session (5 May to 6 June and 7 July to 8 August 2008)*, UN doc A/63/10 (2008), 334, para 290. See also *Report of the International Law Commission. Sixty-third session (26 April–3 June and 4 July–12 August 2011)*, UN doc A/66/10 (2011), 225, para 132; *Report of the International Law Commission. Sixty-fourth session (7 May–1 June and 2 July–3 August 2012)*, UN doc A/67/10, 99 (2012), para 115.
[87] *Report ILC sixtieth session* (n 86), 339, para 307.
[88] See also *Preliminary report Kolodkin* (n 54), 58, para 111; *Second report Kolodkin* (n 25), 4, para 7(*j*) and 20, para 35; *Preliminary report on immunity of State officials prepared by Ms Concepción Escobar Hernández, Special Rapporteur*, UN doc A/CN.4/654 (31 May 2012), 8, para 33 and 14, para 63; *Second report on the immunity of State officials from foreign criminal jurisdiction by Concepción Escobar Hernández, Special Rapporteur*, UN doc A/CN.4/661 (4 April 2013), 18–19, para 58; *Report ILC sixty-fourth session* (n 86), 100, para 116.
[89] See draft arts 3 and 4 of the draft articles on immunity of State officials provisionally adopted so far (n 16).
[90] See A/C.6/68/SR.19 (13 November 2013), 17, para 89 (special rapporteur). See also, previously, *Preliminary report Escobar* (n 88), 10, para 44; *Report of the International Law Commission on the work of its sixty-third session (2011): Topical summary of the discussion held in the Sixth Committee of the General Assembly during its sixty-sixth session, prepared by the Secretariat*, UN doc A/CN.4/650 (20 January 2012), 4, para 6; *Report of the International Law Commission on the work of its sixty-third*

10.37 The ICJ's policy-based approach to identifying the state officials that benefit as a putative matter of customary international law from immunity *ratione personae* and inviolability has also proved influential. The English magistrates' courts have twice relied on the ICJ's approach to recognize the ersatz customary international immunity *ratione personae* from criminal jurisdiction of a visiting minister for defence,[91] a reliance and outcome mirrored in dicta from the Swiss Federal Criminal Court[92] and in the position accepted in the abstract by the senior prosecuting magistrate of the Paris Court of Appeal.[93] One English magistrates' court has done and found the same in respect of a visiting minister for commerce and international trade.[94] The ICJ's reasoning in *Arrest Warrant* has similarly framed the debate within the ILC and the Sixth Committee as to which, if any, other state officials enjoy immunity *ratione personae* from foreign criminal jurisdiction.[95]

10.38 At the same time, the ICJ's reference in *Arrest Warrant* to holders of 'high-ranking office' and its repeated assimilation of ministers for foreign affairs to heads of state and heads of government has been taken as a cue by most that the beneficiaries under customary international law of immunity *ratione personae* from criminal jurisdiction and of inviolability are relatively few. For its part, a Divisional Court of the High Court of England and Wales—recalling the ICJ's statements in both *Arrest Warrant* and *Certain Questions of Mutual Assistance*,[96] considering 'of note' the Court's ruling in the latter as to the head of national security,[97] highlighting Special Rapporteur Kolodkin's reference to a 'narrow circle' of high-ranking officials,[98] and believing that the Court's words in *Arrest Warrant* implied that in order to fall within this circle 'it must be possible to attach to the individual in question a similar status' to that of a head of state or head of government, these two office-holders being 'the paradigm of those entitled to such immunity'[99]—has held that the head of the executive office of the national security council of a foreign state is not entitled to immunity *ratione personae* from criminal jurisdiction.[100] More generally, the Swiss Federal Criminal Court has recalled that, '[i]n the Yerodia case, the ICJ specified that it was high-ranking representatives who benefit'

and sixty-fifth sessions: Topical summary of the discussion held in the Sixth Committee of the General Assembly during its sixty-eighth session, prepared by the Secretariat, UN doc A/CN.4/666, (23 January 2014), 7, para 23.

[91] *Re Mofaz*, 128 ILR 709, 711–12 (2004), mistakenly referring throughout to 'State immunity'; *Re Barak*, City of Westminster Magistrates' Court, 29 September 2009, unreported.

[92] See *Nezzar* (n 6), para 5.4.2.

[93] Procureur Général (Cour d'Appel de Paris), correspondence reference 2007/09216/SGE, 28 February 2008. The case ultimately implicated the immunity *ratione materiae* of a former US Secretary of Defense, but the public prosecutor relied on *Arrest Warrant*, and indeed on the practice of the UK magistrates' courts, to assert that a serving Secretary of Defense would be entitled to the immunity *ratione personae* recognized by the ICJ.

[94] *Re Bo Xilai*, 128 ILR 713, 714 (2005).

[95] As regards the ILC, see eg *Preliminary report Kolodkin* (n 54), 60–3, paras 117–121; *Report ILC sixtieth session* (n 86), 334, para 290; *Report ILC sixty-fourth session* (n 86), 100, para 116. As regards the Sixth Committee, see *supra* n 90 and *infra* nn 103 and 105.

[96] *Khurts Bat v Investigating Judge of the German Federal Court*, 147 ILR 633, 652–3, paras 56–58 (2011).

[97] Ibid, 653, para 58.   [98] Ibid, 653, para 59.   [99] Ibid.   [100] Ibid, 653, para 61.

Immunity and Inviolability 421

from immunity *ratione personae*.[101] Similarly, the talk within the ILC[102] and the Sixth Committee[103] in the context of the former's work on the immunity of state officials has consistently been of 'high-ranking', 'high-level', and 'senior' officials and posts, with reference being made repeatedly to the ICJ's judgments in *Arrest Warrant* and *Certain Questions of Mutual Assistance*.

10.39 In the end, precisely which state officials can be taken to satisfy both the functional criterion and the apparent criterion of rank relied on by the ICJ will come down, like all questions of customary international law, to a weighing of the practice, including verbal practice, and *opinio juris* of states. The draft article on point provisionally adopted by the ILC (whose work on the immunity of state officials from foreign criminal jurisdiction does not deal with diplomatic and similar codified heads of immunity *ratione personae*) limits the availability of immunity *ratione personae* to serving heads of state, heads of government, and ministers for foreign affairs;[104] but the divided reaction to this in the Sixth Committee[105] indicates that a consensus is yet to emerge among states as to the beneficiaries under customary international law of immunity *ratione personae* from foreign criminal jurisdiction.

C. The Scope of Immunity *Ratione Personae* and Inviolability

(i) In general

10.40 The immunity *ratione personae* from foreign criminal jurisdiction from which serving diplomatic agents, certain members of special missions, etc, heads of state, heads of government, and ministers for foreign affairs benefit under international

---

[101] *Nezzar* (n 6), para 5.3.1, author's translation. The reference to 'the Yerodia case' is to *Arrest Warrant*, Abdoulaye Yerodia Ndombasi being the name of the Congolese Minister for Foreign Affairs at the centre of the case.
[102] See eg *Preliminary report Kolodkin* (n 54), 43, para 90; *Report ILC sixtieth session* (n 86), 334, para 290; *Second report Kolodkin* (n 25), 20–1, paras 35 and 37; *Preliminary report Escobar* (n 88), 8, para 33 and 14, para 62.
[103] See eg *Report of the International Law Commission on the work of its sixtieth session (2008): Topical summary of the discussion held in the Sixth Committee of the General Assembly during its sixty-third session, prepared by the Secretariat*, UN doc A/CN.4/606 (21 January 2009), 20, paras 102–3; *Topical summary Sixth Committee sixty-sixth session* (n 90), 4, para 6; *Report of the International Law Commission on the work of its sixty-third and sixty-fourth sessions: Topical summary of the discussion held in the Sixth Committee of the General Assembly during its sixty-seventh session, prepared by the Secretariat*, UN doc A/CN.4/657 (18 January 2013), 8–9, para 30; *Topical summary Sixth Committee sixty-eighth session* (n 90), 7, para 23.
[104] See draft arts 3 and 4 of the draft articles on immunity of State officials provisionally adopted so far (n 16). See also paras 8 to 12 of the draft commentary to draft art 3 as provisionally adopted by the Commission at its sixty-fifth session, *Report ILC sixty-fifth session* (n 13), 62–5, paras 8–12.
[105] See *Topical summary Sixth Committee sixty-eighth session* (n 90), 7, para 23; UN doc A/C.6/68/SR.17 (8 November 2013), 12, paras 58–59 (Switzerland), 14, para 77 (Singapore), 19, paras 115–116 (France); UN doc A/C.6/68/SR.18 (15 November 2013), 3, para 9 (Belarus), 5, para 20 (UK), 13, para 71 (Germany), 15, para 84 (Chile); UN doc A/C.6/68/SR.19 (13 November 2013), 4, para 15 (Poland), 5, para 20 (India), 9, para 42 (Israel), 10–11, paras 48–50 (Russia), 12, para 59 (China), 14–15, paras 74–75 (Iran). See also, previously, *Topical summary Sixth Committee sixty-seventh session* (n 103), 8–9, paras 30–31.

law is stated in absolute terms.[106] For the duration of their term of office or posting, individuals occupying these offices or posts may not lawfully be subjected to any foreign criminal proceedings whatsoever, regardless of the subject-matter of the charges.[107] Since this immunity enures *ratione personae, viz* by virtue solely of the individual's occupation of the relevant office or post, it is immaterial too whether the crimes charged are alleged to have been committed in a private capacity or even before the office-holder or post-holder assumed office or took up the post. As regards heads of state, heads of government, and ministers for foreign affairs, it is further immaterial, according to the ICJ, whether they are present in the forum state—if they are, indeed, present in the forum state—on an official or private visit.[108] Similarly, the beneficiaries of immunity *ratione personae* may not as a matter of international law be compelled, for the duration of their office or posting, to appear or otherwise give evidence as a witness on any subject-matter whatsoever in foreign criminal proceedings.[109] And what goes for immunity *ratione personae* from foreign criminal jurisdiction goes equally, *mutatis mutandis*, for inviolability from foreign measures of physical constraint.[110] In short, immunity *ratione personae* and its concomitant inviolability amount to what the ICJ has called 'full immunity from criminal jurisdiction and inviolability'.[111]

(ii) *Immunity* ratione personae, *inviolability, and allegations of international crimes*

10.41   Controversy has surrounded whether the forum state is obliged by international law to bar criminal proceedings in its courts when a foreign state official who would otherwise benefit from immunity *ratione personae* is charged with an international crime. The conclusion to be drawn from state practice and international jurisprudence is that the various immunities *ratione personae* undoubtedly pose a bar as a matter of international law to prosecution in a foreign court for an international crime. In other words, both treaty-based and customary immunity *ratione personae* remain absolute, no customary exception being made for allegations of international crimes. The same goes, *mutatis mutandis*, for inviolability. As it is, it is plain that none of the treaty provisions stipulating immunity *ratione personae* from foreign criminal jurisdiction and inviolability from foreign measures of physical constraint contains an exception in respect of allegations of international crimes, and as among states parties these provisions constitute *lex specialis* to the *lex generalis* of customary international law.

---

[106] See VCDR, art 31(1); CSM, art 31(1); CPIUN, art IV, ss 11(*a*) and (*g*); VCRS, art 30(1); *Arrest Warrant* (n 5), 22, para 54.
[107] This contrasts with the position in relation to civil proceedings, where minor exceptions to immunity are recognized.
[108] *Arrest Warrant* (n 5), 22, para 55.
[109] See VCDR, art 31(3); CSM, art 31(3); VCRS, art 30(3); *Certain Questions of Mutual Assistance* (n 21), 237, para 171, by necessary implication.
[110] See VCDR, art 29; CSM, art 29; CPIUN, art IV, ss 11(*a*); VCRS, art 28; *Arrest Warrant* (n 5), 22, para 54; *Certain Questions of Mutual Assistance* (n 21), 238, paras 173–174.
[111] *Arrest Warrant* (n 5), 22, para 54.

Prior to *Arrest Warrant*, the embryonic state practice of direct relevance was 10.42
mixed, although the tendency was to uphold immunity *ratione personae* in the
face of charges of international crimes. On the one hand, Belgium had abrogated
by statute what were otherwise internationally-recognized immunities from criminal jurisdiction, both *ratione personae* and *ratione materiae*, in proceedings alleging war crimes, crimes against humanity, and genocide.[112] On the other hand,
the Spanish courts had dismissed on immunity grounds three separate private
applications for the prosecution for international crimes of a serving head of a
foreign state;[113] four of the UK's law lords had remarked *obiter* in *Pinochet (No 3)*
that a serving head of state would benefit from immunity *ratione personae* as a
bar to prosecution in a foreign court for the crime of torture embodied in the
Convention against Torture and Other Cruel, Inhuman or Degrading Treatment
or Punishment 1984 ('Torture Convention');[114] the French Court of Cassation
had upheld the immunity *ratione personae* of a serving head of a foreign state in
private criminal proceedings alleging the offence of aircraft sabotage provided
for in the Convention for the Suppression of Unlawful Acts against the Safety of
Civilian Aircraft 1971;[115] and in 2001 the Danish prosecuting authorities had
rejected a private application for the prosecution of a foreign ambassador alleged
to have been responsible in a former capacity for the crime of torture within the
meaning of the Torture Convention.[116]

What was at issue before the ICJ in *Arrest Warrant* was whether an exception 10.43
existed under customary international law to immunity *ratione personae* from
foreign criminal jurisdiction and to inviolability from foreign measures of physical constraint when the allegations against the state official were of war crimes
and crimes against humanity. Having, avowedly, 'carefully examined State practice, including national legislation and those few decisions of national higher
courts, such as the House of Lords or the French Court of Cassation', the Court
declared itself 'unable to deduce from this practice that there exists under customary international law any form of exception to the rule according immunity
from criminal jurisdiction and inviolability to incumbent Ministers for Foreign
Affairs...where they are suspected of having committed war crimes and crimes
against humanity'.[117] The Court added:

[A]lthough various international conventions on the prevention and punishment of certain
serious crimes impose on States obligations of prosecution or extradition [and] requir[e]

---

[112] See Law of 16 June 1993 on the punishment of grave breaches of the Geneva Conventions of 12 August 1949 and their Additional Protocols I and II of 18 June 1977, as amended by the Law of 10 February 1999 on the punishment of grave breaches of international humanitarian law, art 5(3).

[113] See *Hassan II*, Audiencia Nacional (Central Examining Magistrate No 5), 23 December 1998; *Obiang Nguema* et al, Audiencia Nacional (Central Examining Magistrate No 5), 23 December 1998; *Castro*, Audiencia Nacional (Plenary), 4 March 1999.

[114] See *R v Bow Street Metropolitan Stipendiary Magistrate, ex parte Pinochet Ugarte (No 3)*, 119 ILR 135, 197–8 (Lord Hope), 220 (Lord Saville), 231 (Lord Millett), and 243 (Lord Phillips) (UK 1999), the last referring to all crimes subject to treaty-based mandatory universal jurisdiction.

[115] See *Gaddafi*, 125 ILR 490, 509 (2001).

[116] See J Hartmann, 'The Gillon Affair' (2005) 54 *ICLQ* 745.

[117] *Arrest Warrant* (n 5), 24, para 58.

them to extend their criminal jurisdiction, [this] in no way affects immunities under customary international law, including those of Ministers for Foreign Affairs.[118]

Such immunities, the Court stressed, 'remain opposable before the courts of a foreign State, even where those courts exercise such a jurisdiction under these conventions'.[119]

10.44   The ICJ's outright rejection in *Arrest Warrant* of an exception to immunity *ratione personae* from foreign criminal jurisdiction in relation to war crimes and crimes against humanity, even where, as in relation to the grave breaches of the Geneva Conventions at issue in the case, states parties to a treaty are obliged both to extend extraterritorial jurisdiction over a specified offence and to submit to their authorities for the purpose of prosecution or to extradite persons suspected of its commission, has been seminal. In the wake of the Court's pronouncement, which, against a normative background of the availability of immunity in the absence of a positive exception, cannot be gainsaid, national courts—sometimes expressly relying on *Arrest Warrant*, sometimes referring unspecifically to customary international law—have uniformly barred criminal proceedings against a variety of beneficiaries and purported beneficiaries of immunity *ratione personae* in respect of a variety of international crimes. Heads of state, a head of government, ministers for defence, and a minister for international trade and development have been held immune in respect of allegations of genocide, crimes against humanity, grave breaches of the Geneva Conventions, torture as per the Torture Convention, and aircraft sabotage as per the Convention for the Suppression of Unlawful Acts against the Safety of Civilian Aircraft.[120] In addition, three magistrates' courts in the UK have upheld in the face of allegations of, variously, grave breaches and torture the immunity *ratione personae* from the criminal jurisdiction of the receiving state from which a representative of the sending state in a special mission benefits under customary international law.[121]

---

[118] Ibid, 25, para 59.   [119] Ibid.

[120] See the courts of Belgium (*Re Sharon and Yaron* (n 83), 123, involving a head of government and allegations of genocide, crimes against humanity, and grave breaches of the Fourth Geneva Convention, as well as complaints, alleging a range of international crimes, against Cuban President Fidel Castro, Iraqi President Saddam Hussein, Ivorian President Laurent Gbagbo, Mauritanian President Maaouya Ould Sid'Ahmed Taya, Rwandan President Paul Kagame, President of the Central African Republic Ange-Félix Patassé, President of the Republic of Congo Denis Sassou Nguesso, and President of the Palestinian Authority Yasser Arafat); France (complaint against President Mugabe of Zimbabwe in 2003 alleging torture); the Netherlands (*The Hague City Party and others v Netherlands*, ILDC 849 (NL 2005), involving a head of state and allegations of aggression and grave breaches of the Geneva Conventions, and a complaint against President Yudhoyono of Indonesia in 2010 alleging various international crimes); Spain (*Castro*, Audiencia Nacional (Plenary), 13 December 2007, involving a head of state and allegations of genocide, and *Rwanda*, Audiencia Nacional (Central Examining Magistrate No 4), 6 February 2008, involving a head of state and alleged aircraft sabotage); and the UK (*Tatchell v Mugabe*, 136 ILR 572 (2004), involving a head of state and alleged torture, *Re Mofaz* (n 91), involving a minister for defence and alleged grave breaches of the Fourth Geneva Convention, *Re Barak* (n 91), ditto, and *Re Bo Xilai* (n 94), 714, involving a minister for overseas trade and development and alleged torture).

[121] See *Re Bo Xilai* (n 94), 714–15 (allegations of torture); *Re Barak* (n 91) (allegations of grave breaches); *Re Gorbachev*, City of Westminster Magistrates' Court (Daphne Wickham, Deputy Senior District Judge), 30 March 2011, unreported (allegations of torture).

For its part, in its study on the immunity of state officials from foreign criminal jurisdiction, the UN Secretariat referred to the view 'prominently held by the International Court of Justice in the *Arrest Warrant* case' as 'the majority view'.[122] Similarly, the ILC's first special rapporteur spoke unhesitatingly of 'the prevailing view... upheld by the International Court of Justice in the *Arrest Warrant* and *Certain Matters of Mutual Assistance in Criminal Matters* cases',[123] and, while not every member of the Commission has proved happy with the first special rapporteur's 'strict *lex lata* perspective',[124] few have denied the *lex lata* outright.[125] In their reactions to date to the ILC's work, only a handful of governments have demurred from the Court's position.[126] Finally, in a decision of 9 April 2014 in the *Al Bashir* case, a Pre-Trial Chamber of the International Criminal Court (ICC) acknowledged in passing that 'it is not disputed that under international law a sitting Head of State enjoys personal immunities from criminal jurisdiction and inviolability before national courts of foreign States even when suspected of having committed one of more of the crimes that fall within the jurisdiction of the Court'.[127]

V. Immunity *Ratione Materiae*

Apart from the immunity *ratione personae*, customary or conventional, that serves to shield a small number of state officials from foreign criminal jurisdiction for the duration of their office or posting, there exist under international law various species of immunity *ratione materiae* that, as a rule, prohibit the forum state from exercising its criminal jurisdiction over serving or former foreign-state officials, as the case may be, in respect of acts performed by them in their capacity as state officials. The *lex generalis* in this regard is represented by the uncodified customary international law of state immunity from foreign criminal jurisdiction, which

10.45

---

[122] *Secretariat Memorandum* (n 17), 58, para 92.
[123] *Second report Kolodkin* (n 25), 30, para 55. See also *Third report on immunity of State officials from foreign criminal jurisdiction by Roman Anatolevitch Kolodkin, Special Rapporteur*, UN doc A/CN.4/646 (24 May 2011), 27, para 45, in relation to the Court's rejection of arguments based on treaties mandating universal jurisdiction and *aut dedere aut judicare*.
[124] *Report ILC sixty-third session* (n 86), 221, para 118. See also, generally, ibid, 221–4, paras 117–131 and 233, para 178.
[125] See eg *Report ILC sixty-fourth session* (n 86), 100, para 117: 'The occasional mention that there may be exceptions to immunity from foreign criminal jurisdiction for persons enjoying immunity *ratione personae* was questioned by some members as having no basis in customary international law.'
[126] Indeed, see *Topical summary Sixth Committee sixty-sixth session* (n 90), 4–5, para 10: 'While some delegations believed that immunity ought not be invoked for grave crimes under international law, and in particular with regard to immunity *ratione materiae*, other delegations noted that there did not seem to be any evidence in customary law to support the existence of exceptions to immunity. It was particularly noted that immunity *ratione personae* was absolute, including with regard to grave crimes.'
[127] *Prosecutor v Al Bashir*, ICC-02/05-01/09-195, Pre-Trial Chamber, Decision on the Cooperation of the Democratic Republic of the Congo Regarding Omar Al-Bashir's Arrest and Surrender to the Court, 9 April 2014, para 25.

applies to every serving and former state official in respect of acts performed by them in their official capacity. In addition, there exists a number of treaty-based species of immunity *ratione materiae* which, although in origin and essence simply codifications of the then-prevailing rules on state immunity from foreign criminal jurisdiction, constitute, in their quality as treaty-law, *lex specialis* among states parties to the treaty in question, even if their content—leaving aside possible customary exceptions to state immunity in the criminal context—remains prima facie the same as the *lex generalis*. Insofar as a serving or former state official is not the subject of any applicable treaty-based species of immunity *ratione materiae*, he or she benefits only from the customary law of state immunity from foreign criminal jurisdiction. Like immunity *ratione personae*, all species of immunity *ratione materiae* are owed, as a matter of international law, to the state of which the individual beneficiary is or was an official, and can therefore be waived by that state.

A. State Immunity

10.46 While absolute immunity *ratione personae* from foreign criminal jurisdiction extends under international law to only a small number of serving state officials, a less expansive immunity *ratione materiae* covers all serving as well as former state officials in respect of acts performed by them in their official capacity.[128]

10.47 At the level of abstract principle, the ICJ implied in both *Certain Questions of Mutual Assistance*[129] and *Jurisdictional Immunities of the State*[130] that the immunity *ratione materiae* from foreign criminal jurisdiction from which all serving and former state officials benefit under customary international law is, in conceptual terms, a manifestation of state immunity[131]—that is, a function of the immunity from the jurisdiction of the courts of another state of the official's state itself (of which the official, when acting in that capacity, comprises an organ)[132] and, as such, based on the corollary of the sovereign equality of states summed up in the maxim *par in parem non habet imperium*. The Appeals Chamber of the International Criminal Tribunal for the former Yugoslavia (ICTY) implied the same in *Blaškić*.[133] This characterization, which is in line with the orthodox understanding of state officials' immunity *ratione materiae* from foreign

[128] For the relationship between immunity *ratione personae* and immunity *ratione materiae*, recall *supra* n 45.
[129] See *Certain Questions of Mutual Assistance* (n 21), 242, para 188 and 243, paras 191 and 193.
[130] See *Jurisdictional Immunities* (n 5), 139, para 91.
[131] See also G Buzzini, 'Lights and Shadows of Immunities and Inviolability of State Officials in International Law: Some Comments on the *Djibouti v France* Case' (2009) 22 *LJIL* 455.
[132] See Articles on Responsibility of States for Internationally Wrongful Acts, GA res 56/83, 12 December 2001, Annex ('Articles on Responsibility of States'), art 4(1).
[133] See *Prosecutor v Blaškić*, IT-95-14, Appeals Chamber, Judgment on the Request of the Republic of Croatia for Review of the Decision of Trial Chamber II of 18 July 1997, 29 October 1997, para 41.

criminal jurisdiction,[134] renders at least formally untenable the suggestion[135] that so-called 'functional immunity' from foreign criminal jurisdiction is a *sui generis* species of immunity. The Court's characterization was adopted by the ILC's first special rapporteur on the immunity of state officials from foreign criminal jurisdiction,[136] and has not been disputed by states in their consideration of the ILC's work in the Sixth Committee.[137]

(i) Background

The quasi-metaphysical quality known as sovereignty (in early modern terminology, '*suprema potestas*' or 'supreme power') means having no power superior by right to oneself; and if by definition each sovereign, *viz* each person or polity possessed of sovereignty, need yield to no other power, each sovereign must by definition be equal. For one sovereign to subject another to the process of his or her or its courts would necessarily be to deny that equality—or, putting it another

10.48

---

[134] See eg *Pinochet (No 3)* (n 114); *Agent judiciare du Trésor c Malta Maritime Authority et Camel X*, Cour de cassation (Chambre criminelle), 23 November 2004, no 04-84.265 and *Association des familles des victimes du 'Joola'*, Cour de cassation (Chambre criminelle), no 09-84818, *Bull crim* (2010), no 9 (France); *Adamov (Evgeny) v Federal Office of Justice*, ILDC 339 (CH 2005), para 3.4.2 (Switzerland); *Lozano (Mario Luiz)* ('Calipari case'), ILDC 1085 (IT 2008), para 5 (Italy). See also J Crawford, *Brownlie's Principles of Public International Law* (8th edn, Oxford: Oxford University Press, 2012), 499; P Daillier, M Forteau, and A Pellet, *Droit international public* (8th edn, Paris: LGDJ, 2009), paras 289–290; E David, *Éléments de Droit International Pénal et Européen* (Brussels: Bruylant, 2009), 58 ('[L]'immunité des agents étatiques n'est qu'une application du principe de l'immunité des Etats'); E Decaux and L Trigeaud, 'Les immunités pénales des agents de l'État et des organisations internationales' in H Ascensio, E Decaux, and A Pellet (eds), *Droit international pénal* (2nd edn, Paris: Pedone, 2012) 545, 558–9, paras 38–40. Consider also Rome Statute of the International Criminal Court ('Rome Statute'), art 98(1), referring in the criminal context to 'the State . . . immunity of a person . . . of a third State'. The same is the case as regards civil actions against state officials. See eg United Nations Convention on Jurisdictional Immunities of States and Their Property 2004 ('UN Convention on State Immunity'), art 2(1)(*b*)(iv), defining 'State' for the purposes of the Convention to encompass 'representatives of the State acting in that capacity'. See also *Jones* et al *v United Kingdom* (Merits and Just Satisfaction), nos 34356/06 & 40528/06, ECHR 2014, para 200 ('the immunity which is applied in a case against State officials remains "State" immunity') and—having referred at para 202 to *Second report Kolodkin* (n 25), on the immunity *ratione materiae* of state officials from foreign criminal jurisdiction—para 204 ('The weight of authority at international and national level therefore appears to support the proposition that State immunity in principle offers individual employees or officers of a foreign State protection in respect of acts undertaken on behalf of the State under the same cloak as protects the State itself.')

[135] See eg A Cassese, 'When May Senior State Officials be Tried for International Crimes? Some Comments on the *Congo v Belgium* Case' (2002) 13 *EJIL* 853, 862; N Ronzitti, 'L'immunità funzionale degli organi stranieri dalla giurisdizione penale: Il caso *Calipari*' (2008) 91 *RDI* 1033, 1039; R Van Alebeek, *The Immunity of States and Their Officials in International Criminal Law and International Human Rights Law* (Oxford: Oxford University Press, 2008), chapter 3; D Akande and S Shah, 'Immunities of State Officials, International Crimes, and Foreign Domestic Courts' (2011) 21 *EJIL* 815, 826–7.

[136] See *Second report Kolodkin* (n 25), 12–13, para 23.

[137] For explicit endorsement, see UN docs A/C.6/66/SR.26 (7 December 2011), 3, para 7 (Norway, on behalf of the Nordic countries) and A/C.6/68/SR.17 (8 November 2013), 8, para 34 (Norway, on behalf of the Nordic countries). See also UN doc A/C.6/66/SR.27 (8 December 2011), 4, para 23 (Sri Lanka) ('sovereign immunity'); UN doc A/C.6/67/SR.22 (4 December 2012), 6, para 31 (UK).

way, would by definition be to deny the other's sovereignty by assuming power over it. It would be a contradiction in terms. *Par in parem non habet imperium* ('An equal has no authority over an equal'), in the words of the old maxim. According, then, to the classical doctrine of sovereign immunity, the person of the sovereign was absolutely immune from the jurisdiction of the courts of another sovereign; and in time the doctrine—which would become known in most quarters as state immunity—came to apply more broadly to the sovereign entity of the state, both as such and in the respective guises of its government, the various departments of that government, its agencies and instrumentalities, its individual officials, and its property.

10.49 But as states and their various emanations came to engage more and more in a wide range of activities of a commercial or otherwise quotidian nature, the absolute immunity accorded them in foreign courts from mundane civil proceedings in respect of, for example, contracts for the sale of goods, commercial debts, and contracts of employment came increasingly to be perceived as a source of injustice. In response, the law of most states came by the 1990s to embody in the context of civil proceedings a restrictive doctrine of state immunity, according to which a state in its various manifestations is immune from suit in another state's courts only in respect of acts performed by it in the exercise of sovereign authority (so-called '*acta jure imperii*'), by which is meant inherently sovereign acts or, putting it another way, acts that a state alone can perform, as distinct from acts which, although performed by the state, are of a nature such that any private person could perform them (or '*acta jure gestionis*'). The restrictive doctrine of state immunity from civil proceedings is now part of contemporary customary international law. The conceptual underpinnings of the international law of state immunity remain nonetheless unchanged. For sovereignty to be made subject to the power of another remains an oxymoron, the only difference being that, whereas under the absolute doctrine of state immunity sovereignty was considered manifest in the defendant state per se, under the restrictive doctrine the defendant state is treated as the embodiment of sovereignty only in respect of acts which a state alone can perform. In this light, state or sovereign immunity can be thought of as always having been accorded to the state and its various emanations *ratione materiae*—that is, by virtue of the subject-matter in question, that subject-matter being sovereignty itself.

10.50 The doctrine of restrictive state immunity which now prevails in the civil context is reflected in the United Nations Convention on Jurisdictional Immunities of States and Their Property 2004 ('UN Convention on State Immunity', not yet in force), annexed along with a set of 'understandings' to General Assembly resolution 59/38 of 2 December 2004, and recognized as being consonant for the most part with customary international law.

10.51 In its application to individual state officials, the doctrine of absolute state immunity meant that such officials, both serving and former, benefited from immunity from the jurisdiction of foreign courts in respect of all acts performed by them in their official (or, synonymously, public) capacity. That is, as long as the acts the subject of the suit or prosecution were done by them in their capacity as an organ of the state, current and former state officials were covered by the immunity from foreign proceedings to which the state was entitled. Conduct performed in their official capacity was treated as if it were the state's conduct, the state's conduct was by definition a manifestation of sovereignty, and sovereignty could not be subjected to the power of another. Conversely, serving and former state officials could be made to answer in a foreign court for their private acts, *viz* any acts performed by them not in their capacity as organs of state, which *a fortiori* included acts performed prior to the assumption of their position.[138]

Today, in the context of civil proceedings, the modern doctrine of restrictive state immunity means that serving and former officials—who, as far as state immunity goes, cannot be covered by any greater immunity under international law than that to which the state as such is entitled—benefit from immunity from the jurisdiction of foreign courts only in respect of those acts performed by them in their official capacity which can be characterized as exercises of sovereign authority (*acta jure imperii*). They may, conversely, be subject to foreign civil proceedings in respect of acts which, although performed by them in their official capacity, are of their nature such that a private person could have performed them (*acta jure gestionis*) and, *a fortiori*, in respect of acts performed by them in a private capacity. That is, as far as the international law of state immunity[139] from civil proceedings is concerned, state officials who do in their official capacity what a private person could have done are treated the same as state officials acting in their private capacity. Neither is entitled to state immunity in respect of the relevant conduct; and as a consequence both may end up personally liable for that conduct under the municipal law applied by the foreign court. Whether—in the event that a foreign court does hold them liable for *acta jure gestionis* performed in the course of their employment—state officials are entitled to indemnification by the state of which they are or were an official will depend on the municipal law of the employer state. 10.52

The question, however, is what the contemporary law of state immunity says in relation to criminal proceedings against foreign state officials and ex-officials. There is a 'general understanding', with which the General Assembly has expressed its agreement,[140] that the UN Convention on State Immunity does not apply to criminal proceedings; and, as it is, its provisions are manifestly not directed towards them. As for relevant state practice, there exists precious little of this. 10.53

It might be thought to stand to reason that, just as in civil proceedings, serving and former state officials benefit today from immunity from the criminal jurisdiction of foreign courts not in respect of all acts performed by them in their official capacity but only in respect of those of their acts performed in an official capacity that can be characterized as exercises of sovereign authority. But the problem is how to distinguish in the criminal context between official and 10.54

---

[138] This marks the difference between immunity *ratione personae* and absolute immunity *ratione materiae*.

[139] The situation is different under the rules on attribution of conduct to a state in the context of state responsibility, where the sole relevant question is whether the official performed the impugned act as an organ of the state—in other words, in an official capacity.

[140] See GA res 59/38, 2 December 2004, para 2.

inherently sovereign acts, in respect of which state immunity would serve to bar proceedings against a foreign state official, and official acts of a nature such that private persons could perform them (as distinct from acts in fact performed in a private capacity). In the civil context, the abstract distinction has been rendered concrete over the years via the general recognition of a set of exceptions to a foreign state's immunity from proceedings framed in every case bar one around an understanding of the essentially commercial nature of a state's non-sovereign conduct.[141] In the criminal context, no such set of accepted exceptions has emerged to the otherwise absolute immunity from jurisdiction from which foreign state officials have traditionally benefited in respect of acts performed by them in their official capacity, and it is not obvious what such exceptions might in principle be. Instead, when it comes to state practice,[142] those few municipal courts that have had to grapple with the immunity *ratione materiae* from criminal proceedings owed under international law in respect of a foreign state official or ex-official have tended to speak of immunity from criminal jurisdiction in respect of acts performed in an official capacity or, synonymously but less desirably, in respect of official acts.[143] As for the ICJ, in a brief dictum in *Arrest Warrant* it spoke, conversely, of the unavailability to the accused of immunity *ratione materiae* from foreign criminal jurisdiction in respect of acts performed 'in a private capacity',[144] the implication *a contrario* being that such immunity extends, at least prima facie, to all acts performed by the accused in a public, *viz* official, capacity.[145] The same was similarly implied in *Certain Questions of Mutual Assistance*, where the Court 'observe[d] that it ha[d] not been "concretely verified" before it that the acts which were the subject of the summonses as *témoins assistés* issued by France were indeed acts within the scope of [the relevant officials'] duties as organs of State'.[146] For his part, the ILC's first special rapporteur on the immunity of state officials from foreign criminal jurisdiction expressly concluded that the immunity *ratione materiae*, or state immunity, from foreign criminal jurisdiction from which a serving or former state official benefits is not restricted by reference to the distinction between *acta jure imperii* and *acta jure gestionis*,[147] and there appears to have been no dissent from this position either within the Commission or, more

---

[141] See eg UN Convention on State Immunity, Part III.

[142] It is worth noting that, although the various codification conventions considered *infra* regulate the immunity *ratione materiae*—in essence, the state immunity—available to former diplomatic agents, consular officers, and so on, they remain uninstructive on point, since they were all concluded while, as a matter of customary international law, the doctrine of absolute state immunity, according to which a serving or former state official enjoyed immunity *ratione materiae* in respect of all acts performed in an official capacity, prevailed even in respect of civil proceedings.

[143] See the cases mentioned *infra*. But cf *Adamov* (n 134), para 3.4.2, by way of obiter dictum (Switzerland), and *Lozano* (n 134), para 5 (Italy).

[144] *Arrest Warrant* (n 5), 25, para 61.

[145] Consider also the implication *a contrario* from the Court's explanation in *Arrest Warrant* (n 5), 22, para 55, that, in relation to the immunity *ratione personae* from foreign criminal jurisdiction of a serving minister for foreign affairs, 'no distinction can be drawn between acts performed...in an "official" capacity, and those claimed to have been performed in a "private capacity"'.

[146] *Certain Questions of Mutual Assistance* (n 21), 243, para 191. See also ibid, 244, para 196.

[147] *Second report Kolodkin* (n 25), 16, para 28 and 58, para 94(*e*).

significantly, within the Sixth Committee of the General Assembly. In short, it would appear that, as a general rule, as argued by the ILC's first special rapporteur, state officials, serving and former, are entitled under customary international law to immunity from foreign criminal jurisdiction 'in respect of acts performed in an official capacity'.[148]

(ii) In general

(a) Basics

10.55 Serving and former state officials benefit under customary international law from immunity from foreign criminal proceedings in respect of acts performed by them in their official capacity. In other words, they may not be prosecuted or subjected to extradition proceedings in a foreign court if the subject-matter of the charges or of the alleged offences in respect of which extradition is requested is conduct performed by them in their capacity as a state official. Equally, serving and former state officials may not be compelled to testify as a witness in foreign criminal proceedings if the subject-matter of the testimony is conduct performed by them in their official capacity.

10.56 It is worth emphasizing that even when state officials no longer occupy the position in the context of which they performed given acts, they continue to benefit under customary international law from immunity *ratione materiae* in respect of those acts. Although they themselves may no longer be state officials at all or may occupy a different position within the machinery of state, the character of the acts as acts performed in an official capacity remains unchanged, and it is by virtue and in respect of such acts that the individual benefits from state immunity from foreign criminal jurisdiction.

10.57 State immunity inheres in the state itself, and a state, via its government, may waive any state immunity which might otherwise serve to shield one of its serving or former officials from the criminal jurisdiction of a foreign court.

10.58 It is unclear whether it is necessary as a matter of customary international law for the state of which the individual is or was an official to invoke its immunity on the individual's behalf in proceedings before a foreign criminal court. In *Certain Questions of Mutual Assistance*, the ICJ remarked in the context of immunity *ratione materiae* that 'the State which seeks to claim immunity for one of its State organs', including one of its officials, 'is expected to notify the authorities of the other State concerned', so as to 'allow the court of the forum State to ensure that it does not fail to respect any entitlement to immunity and ... thereby

---

[148] Ibid, 58, para 94(*b*). The first special rapporteur's conclusion has been implicitly adopted by the second. See *Preliminary report Escobar* (n 88), 15, para 65; *Second report Escobar* (n 88), 16, para 50; *Third report on the immunity of State officials from foreign criminal jurisdiction by Concepción Escobar Hernández, Special Rapporteur*, UN doc A/CN.4/673 (2 June 2014), 6, para 12(*b*). See also International Law Commission, Sixty-sixth session, Immunity of State Officials from Foreign Criminal Jurisdiction, Statement of the Chairman of the Drafting Committee, Mr Gilberto Vergne Saboia, 25 July 2014, 6 ('It is widely acknowledged that State officials enjoy immunity *ratione materiae* for official acts or for acts performed in an official capacity.').

engage the responsibility of that State'.¹⁴⁹ While the ILC's first special rapporteur on the immunity of state officials from foreign criminal jurisdiction elevated what the Court characterized as an expectation into a rule of law,¹⁵⁰ states have taken the view in the Sixth Committee that 'whether the immunity of State officials other than Heads of State, Heads of Government and foreign ministers ha[s] to be claimed actively by the officials' home State' is 'a question that deserve[s] further consideration'.¹⁵¹ From the point of view of legal principle, the assertion of any such formal requirement is of dubious merit, at least when considered in the light of the position in respect of civil proceedings, where it is unnecessary for the state to claim immunity on behalf of one of its officials and where, indeed, the forum state is obliged to consider the question of state immunity *proprio motu*, if necessary.¹⁵²

10.59 It is uncertain whether the serving state officials who benefit, as regards foreign criminal jurisdiction, only from immunity *ratione materiae* under customary international law also benefit as a customary matter from any degree of inviolability from foreign measures of physical constraint. What meagre state practice there is admits of no conclusion. It is true that career consular officers, whose immunity *ratione materiae* from the criminal jurisdiction of the receiving state and transit states is at root a manifestation of state immunity,¹⁵³ enjoy an attenuated form of inviolability,¹⁵⁴ but this is on account of the sorts of pragmatic considerations that motivate the full inviolability of diplomatic agents, heads of state, and the like. What is clear is that no former state official of any stamp enjoys any measure of personal inviolability.

(b) 'Acts performed in an official capacity'

10.60 The availability to a serving or former state official of immunity *ratione materiae* from foreign criminal jurisdiction turns on whether the impugned act was 'performed in an official capacity'. There is little municipal judicial practice directly on point. Guidance can be looked for, however, in municipal case law on cognate immunities *ratione materiae*, such as the treaty-based immunity *ratione materiae* from foreign criminal jurisdiction of serving and former consular officers,¹⁵⁵ former diplomatic agents,¹⁵⁶ former representatives of a state in a special mission and former members of the mission's diplomatic staff,¹⁵⁷ and so on, although the express formulation of the various treaty provisions may on occasion make a

---

¹⁴⁹ *Certain Questions of Mutual Assistance* (n 21), 244, para 196.
¹⁵⁰ See *Third report Kolodkin* (n 123), 8–9, paras 16–18. See also *Re Gorbachev* (n 121).
¹⁵¹ *Topical summary Sixth Committee sixty-third session* (n 87), 19, para 97.
¹⁵² See eg UN Convention on State Immunity, art 6(1).
¹⁵³ See *infra* para 10.92, especially n 277.   ¹⁵⁴ See *infra* para 10.95.
¹⁵⁵ See VCCR, arts 43(1) ('acts performed in the exercise of consular functions'), 44(3) ('matters connected with the exercise of their functions'), and 53(4) ('acts performed...in the exercise of his functions'). See further *infra* paras 10.93–10.94.
¹⁵⁶ See VCDR, art 39(2) ('acts performed...in the exercise of his functions as a member of the mission'). See further *infra* para 10.98.
¹⁵⁷ See CSM, art 43(2) ('acts performed...in the exercise of his functions'). See further *infra* para 10.99.

difference.¹⁵⁸ One can look also to the municipal case law on the immunity *ratione materiae* of serving and former state officials from foreign civil proceedings insofar as this case law examines, as a first step in the analysis, whether the act the subject of the proceedings was performed in an official capacity.¹⁵⁹ In addition, in *Certain Questions of Mutual Assistance in Criminal Matters*, the ICJ appeared to signal by implication¹⁶⁰ that the question whether, for the purposes of immunity *ratione materiae* from foreign criminal jurisdiction, a serving or former state official can be said to have acted in his or her official capacity is at least at a basic level the same as the question whether, for the purposes of the attribution of conduct to a state in the context of the law of state responsibility, an individual occupying the position of an organ of the state within the meaning of article 4(1) of the Articles on Responsibility of States for Internationally Wrongful Acts ('Articles on Responsibility of States') can be said to have acted in his or her capacity as an organ of the state.¹⁶¹ This approach whereby the law relating to the immunity *ratione materiae* from foreign criminal jurisdiction of serving and former state officials draws upon the rules governing the attribution to a state of the conduct of persons considered organs of the state was adopted and applied by the ILC's first special rapporteur on the immunity of state officials from foreign criminal jurisdiction,¹⁶² and its gist has found favour with nearly all of the delegations that have had cause to refer to it in the Sixth Committee.¹⁶³ While it is to be employed with a degree of circumspection,¹⁶⁴ the approach is essentially sound.¹⁶⁵

---

¹⁵⁸ See *infra* para 10.92. Consider eg the reliance in the context of consular immunity on the specific wording of arts 5(*m*) and 43(1) of the VCCR in *General Prosecutor at the Court of Appeals of Milan v Adler* ('Abu Omar case'), ILDC 1960 (IT 2012), para 23.4 (Italy).

¹⁵⁹ Recall eg, reflecting customary international law on point, UN Convention on State Immunity, art 2(1)(*b*)(iv), defining 'State' for the purposes of the Convention to encompass 'representatives of the State acting in that capacity'. Insofar as the case law on civil jurisdiction asks additionally whether the act was one *jure imperii* or *jure gestionis* or, alternatively but to the same effect, falls within one of the enumerated exceptions to state immunity provided for in the applicable municipal statute, this is to be factored out in the criminal context. See *supra* para 10.54 and *infra* para 10.61.

¹⁶⁰ See *Certain Questions of Mutual Assistance* (n 21), 243, para 191 and 244, para 196.

¹⁶¹ Consider also *Blaškić* (n 133), para 41, responding to the arguments recalled ibid, para 39; *Former Syrian Ambassador to the German Democratic Republic*, 115 ILR 595, 605, citations omitted (Germany 1997) ('According to Article 39(2), second sentence, of the VCDR, diplomatic immunity for official acts continues to exist after the termination of the diplomat's position. What is to be understood as an official act follows from the purpose of this rule: The official acts of diplomats are attributable to the sending state. Judicial proceedings against [former] diplomats come, in their effects, close to proceedings against the sending State. Continuing diplomatic immunity for official acts thus serves to protect the sending State itself.... The complainant acted in the exercise of his official functions as a member of the mission, within the meaning of Article 39(2), second sentence, of the VCDR, because he is charged with an omission that lay within the sphere of his responsibility as ambassador, and which is to that extent attributable to the sending State.'). See too, in the civil context, *Jones v Ministry of the Interior of the Kingdom of Saudi Arabia*, 129 ILR 629, 718–19, para 12 (Lord Bingham) and 742–3, paras 74–79 (Lord Hoffmann) (UK 2006).

¹⁶² *Second report Kolodkin* (n 25), 12–16, paras 23–27, especially 14, para 24. See also *Secretariat Memorandum* (n 17), 102, para 156.

¹⁶³ See UN doc A/C.6/66/SR.26 (7 December 2011), 3, para 8 (Norway, on behalf of the Nordic countries); UN doc A/C.6/66/SR.27 (8 December 2011), 10, para 71 (Portugal); UN doc A/C.6/67/SR.20 (7 December 2012), 18, para 111 (Austria); UN doc A/C.6/67/SR.21 (4 December 2012), 6, para 29 (Belarus), 12, para 60 (Republic of the Congo), 15, para 83 (Portugal); UN doc A/C.6/67/SR.22 (4 December 2012), 13, para 82 (Italy).

¹⁶⁴ See also UN doc A/C.6/66/SR.26, 3, para 8 (Norway, on behalf of the Nordic countries).

¹⁶⁵ See also Buzzini (n 131), 465–6.

10.61   Whether the act was performed in an official rather than a private capacity is not the same as whether the act was an act *jure imperii* rather than *jure gestionis*. In other words, it is not necessary to ask, as it is in relation to civil proceedings against a serving or former state official or any other organ of state, whether the act was inherently sovereign in character, meaning the sort of thing that only a state can do rather than the sort of thing a private person could have done.[166] It pays to reiterate[167] that the distinction between acts *jure imperii* and acts *jure gestionis* is inapplicable in the criminal context, where the question is the more straightforward, logically prior one as to whether state officials perform the relevant acts in their capacity as state officials or in their capacity as private persons.

10.62   Equally, the question to be asked as regards prosecution and extradition is not whether the crime as such was committed in an official capacity. Framing the inquiry this way is to have impermissible regard to the merits of the case in order to determine the prior, procedural question of the accused's immunity from the proceedings.[168] Rather, as with immunity *ratione materiae* from civil jurisdiction (*mutatis mutandis*),[169] the question is whether the bare acts alleged to have been performed by the official, rather than the alleged acts as legally characterized by the prosecution, were performed in an official capacity—that is, whether the killing, rather than the murder, crime against humanity or genocide, or whether the appropriation of property, rather than the theft or pillage, was done in an official capacity.

10.63   Whether the act was performed in an official capacity is a descriptive, not normative inquiry. The question is not whether the official acted in some notionally proper official capacity as measured by the standards of the public policy of the forum state or international public policy. One asks simply whether the official acted in what was in fact an official capacity, meaning in the exercise of actual, rather than ideal, state authority.[170]

10.64   Analogy with the customary international rules on the attribution to a state of the acts of organs of the state codified in articles 4 and 7 of the Articles on Responsibility of States suggests that the notion of state authority relevant to the question of official capacity for immunity *ratione materiae* from criminal proceedings is not limited to actual authority but extends to mere 'colour of authority'.[171]

---

[166] As codified, this question amounts to asking whether one of the enumerated exceptions to the prima facie availability of state immunity applies, although it is worth noting that the exception in relation to acts causing death or personal injury, etc in the forum state does not correspond to the *jure imperii*/*jure gestionis* distinction.

[167] Recall *supra* para 10.54.   [168] Recall *supra* para 10.8.

[169] See *infra* para 10.86.

[170] But cf, implicitly, *Pinochet*, 119 ILR 345, 349 (Belgium 1998); *R v Bow Street Metropolitan Stipendiary Magistrate, ex parte Pinochet Ugarte (No 1)*, 119 ILR 50 (UK 1998). Note that *Pinochet (No 1)* was subsequently annulled in *R v Bow Street Metropolitan Stipendiary Magistrate, ex parte Pinochet Ugarte (No 2)*, 119 ILR 112 (UK 1999), with the result that it cannot be counted for the purposes of state practice.

[171] See *Armed Activities on the Territory of the Congo (Democratic Republic of the Congo v Uganda), Judgment*, ICJ Rep 2005, 168, 242, para 214. See also the international cases cited in paras 5 to 7 of the commentary to art 7 of the Articles on Responsibility of States, *Ybk ILC 2001*, vol II/2, 31, 46, as well as the text of para 13 of the commentary to art 4 of the Articles on Responsibility of States, ibid, 42, which

In other words, as accepted by the ILC in relation to the immunity *ratione materiae* from foreign criminal jurisdiction of consular officers and employees,[172] as argued by the ILC's first special rapporteur on the immunity of state officials from foreign criminal jurisdiction,[173] and as emphasized by the UK's House of Lords in *R v Bow Street Metropolitan Stipendiary Magistrate, ex parte Pinochet Ugarte (No 3)*,[174] one of the few cases directly on point, the fact that officials act in excess of authority or instructions contrary to instructions or contrary to the general law, including the criminal law, of the state of which they are officials does not of itself mean that their acts are not performed in an official capacity.[175] Only 'where the conduct is so removed from the scope of their official functions that it should be assimilated to that of private individuals, not attributable to the State',[176] will the *ultra vires* acts of state officials be deemed to have been performed in a private capacity. The acts of state officials 'purportedly or apparently carrying out their official functions'[177] remain acts performed in an official capacity. It is for this reason that it is preferable to avoid paraphrases such as 'in the exercise of duty',[178]

---

reads in relevant part: 'A particular problem is to determine whether a person who is a State organ acts in that capacity. It is irrelevant for this purpose that the person concerned may have had ulterior or improper motives or may be abusing public power. Where such a person acts in an apparently official capacity, or under colour of authority, the actions in question will be attributable to the State. The distinction between unauthorized conduct of a State organ and purely private conduct has been clearly drawn in international arbitral decisions.... The case of purely private conduct should not be confused with that of an organ functioning as such but acting *ultra vires* or in breach of the rules governing its operation. In this latter case, the organ is nevertheless acting in the name of the State: this principle is affirmed in article 7.'

[172] See paras 2 and 3 of the commentary to draft art 43 of the ILC's Draft Articles on Consular Relations, *Ybk ILC 1961*, vol II, 92, 117, the provision which became art 43 of the VCCR and specified that '[m]embers of the consulate shall not be amenable to the jurisdiction of the judicial or administrative authorities of the receiving State in respect of acts performed in the exercise of consular functions'. Paragraphs 2 and 3 of the commentary state in relevant part: 'The rule that, in respect of acts performed by them in the exercise of their functions (official acts) members of the consulate are not amenable to the jurisdiction of the judicial and administrative authorities of the receiving State, is part of customary international law. This exemption represents an immunity which the sending State is recognized as possessing in respect of acts which are those of a sovereign State.... In the opinion of some members of the Commission, the article should have provided that only official acts within the limits of the consular powers enjoy immunity from jurisdiction. The Commission was unable to accept this view.' But cf *Adler* (n 158), para 23.5.

[173] See *Second report Kolodkin* (n 25), 15–19, paras 27 and 29–31.

[174] See *Pinochet (No 3)* (n 114), 154–5 (Lord Browne-Wilkinson), 169 (Lord Goff), 194–5 (Lord Hope), 224 (Lord Millett).

[175] See also, as regards immunity *ratione materiae* from civil proceedings, *Jones v Saudi Arabia* (n 161), 718–19, para 12 (Lord Bingham) and 742–3, paras 74–79 (Lord Hoffmann); *Jaffe v Miller*, 95 ILR 446, 460 (Canada 1993). But cf *contra* the cases cited in *Secretariat Memorandum* (n 17), 104, para 159 note 452. It ought to go without saying that it is immaterial for the purposes of immunity from foreign criminal jurisdiction whether the act was allegedly contrary to the criminal law of the forum state, as opposed to the state served by the official. Were this not so, there would be no point in discussing immunity from foreign criminal jurisdiction in the first place.

[176] Paragraph 7 of commentary to art 7 of Articles on Responsibility of States (n 171), 46.

[177] Paragraph 8 of commentary to art 7 of Articles on Responsibility of States (n 171), 46.

[178] It is for this reason that case law under art VII(3)(*a*)(ii) of the Agreement between the Parties to the North Atlantic Treaty regarding the Status of their Forces 1951 ('NATO SOFA') and its analogues, dealing with jurisdiction over 'offences arising out of any act or omission done in the performance of official duty', is not necessarily a reliable guide to the content of the notion of an act performed 'in an official capacity'.

'within the scope of [the officials'] duties as organs of state',[179] 'in the discharge of their mandate',[180] and even 'official acts', all of which, while perhaps not intended to connote a meaning different from 'in an official capacity', are prone to mislead.

10.65   A question arguably arises in the context of abuse of authority as to the significance of the purpose or motive of the act. It is one thing to consider an abuse of state authority as nonetheless an act performed in an official capacity if the motive for the abuse is the official's furtherance of the perceived interests of the state. It is arguably something else to consider an abuse of authority as an act performed in an official capacity when its motive is purely or perhaps even just predominantly personal.[181] Nonetheless, under the customary rules on the attribution of conduct for the purposes of state responsibility, motive is immaterial. An act may be for an ulterior personal purpose and still be attributable to the state as an act of an organ of the state acting in that capacity, provided that the act was purportedly or apparently an exercise of state authority.[182] For his part, the ILC's first special rapporteur on the immunity of state officials took the firm view, based on a strict identity between the principles applicable to attribution and those applicable to state immunity, that what counts as an act of a state organ acting in that capacity for the purposes of the former counts *ipso facto* as an act performed in an official capacity for the purposes of the latter, with the corollary that the 'classification of the conduct of an official as official conduct does not depend on the motives of the person'.[183] Ultimately, although a teleological distinction between the two contexts has an instinctive attraction, legal principle militates in favour of the special rapporteur's approach.[184]

10.66   If acting under orders or instructions, pursuant to established state policy or otherwise with official sanction, a state official is *ipso facto* acting in an official capacity.[185] This is so, following from the above, even if the order, instruction, policy or other sanction was itself *ultra vires* or unlawful.[186]

---

[179] *Certain Questions of Mutual Assistance* (n 21), 243, para 141.

[180] Draft art 3(*d*) proposed by the ILC's second special rapporteur on the immunity of state officials from foreign criminal jurisdiction, *Second report Escobar* (n 88), 17, para 53.

[181] Indeed, one or two old cases in semi-cognate immunity contexts suggest the second approach, considering such acts to have been performed in a personal capacity.

[182] Recall *supra* nn 171 and 176, especially *Mallén v United States of America*, 4 RIAA 173, 177, paras 7–9 (Mexico–US General Claims Commission 1927), involving the attribution of an exercise of state authority by way of 'mere pretext for taking private vengeance' (ibid, 177, para 8).

[183] *Second report Kolodkin* (n 25), 15, para 27.

[184] See also Buzzini (n 131), 465–6. As it is, it pays to bear in mind that a state may always waive any immunity from foreign criminal jurisdiction from which one of its officials or former officials would stand to benefit.

[185] See *Former Syrian Ambassador* (n 161), 606; *Re P (No 2)* (n 54), 495–6. See also the 'Bingham' affair (1858), in A McNair (ed), *International Law Opinions, Selected and Annotated, Volume I: Peace* (Cambridge: Cambridge University Press, 1956), 196, 197.

[186] In this way, the availability under customary international law of immunity *ratione materiae* from foreign criminal process does not correspond to the availability or otherwise under customary international law of the substantive defence of superior orders.

10.67 The fact that state officials are seconded or otherwise deployed outside their usual line of duty[187] does not necessarily mean that they are not acting in an official capacity. If they are deployed as a servant of the state—that is, in the employment and under the instructions of the state—and are acting in that capacity at the relevant time, their acts will be performed in an official capacity.

10.68 No rule of international law requires the forum state to treat as conclusive a declaration by another state that an official of the latter acted with official sanction. It is a matter for the municipal law of each state to determine the evidentiary weight to be given to such a declaration.

10.69 Ultimately whether an act is to be considered one 'performed in an official capacity' will depend on the facts of each case. It is not a question amenable to detailed prescriptive statements. Discerning the line between an official's official and private capacities can be a subtle task of factual appreciation, although it can also be made more complicated than it need be.

(iii) An exception for unconsensual presence and alleged commission in forum state?

10.70 The ILC's first special rapporteur on the immunity of state officials asserted that there existed as a matter of customary international law one exception to the immunity *ratione materiae* of state officials from foreign criminal jurisdiction. He described as a 'special case', in respect of which 'there are sufficient grounds to talk of an absence of immunity', the exercise of criminal jurisdiction over a serving or former official of a foreign state 'by a state in whose territory an alleged crime has taken place, [where] this state has not given its consent to the performance in its territory of the activity which led to the crime and to the presence in its territory of the foreign official who committed [that] crime'.[188] This putative exception has since been applied by a Divisional Court of the High Court of England and Wales,[189] but its basis in positive customary international law is open to question, given the paucity of the relevant practice and the opacity of the attendant *opinio juris*.[190] Whether it finds wider traction remains to be seen.

---

[187] Take eg military personnel deployed on a private ship as a vessel protection detachment (VPD).
[188] *Second report Kolodkin* (n 25), 59–60, para 94(*p*).
[189] See *Khurts Bat* (n 96), 662, para 96 and 663, para 99. Note the misapplication of the putative exception by the English court, which looked to whether the defendant to the extradition proceedings was alleged to have committed the crime, etc in German territory, rather than in the territory of the UK, the forum state. For more, see R O'Keefe, '*Khurts Bat v Investigating Judge of the German Federal Court*' (2011) 82 *BYIL* 564. It is unclear whether the putative exception is the basis on which the German Federal Prosecutor asserted that no immunity was available in the same case.
[190] None of the practice cited by the special rapporteur is judicial. It consists, rather, of states' not asserting immunity in given cases to prevent the prosecution in a foreign court of one or more of their officials. The problem is that there is any number of plausible non-legal reasons why a state would elect not to claim immunity from prosecution on behalf of an official charged with a crime alleged to have been committed in the course of a clandestine operation in the territory of another, perhaps friendly state.

(iv) State immunity and allegations of international crimes

10.71 The affording of immunity *ratione materiae* to serving and former foreign state officials alleged to have committed international crimes in their official capacity has been challenged in recent times. Whether international law requires the forum state to grant immunity *ratione materiae* to a foreign state official or ex-official accused of, or the subject of a request for extradition in relation to, an international crime is at present unclear. Weighing several pointed dicta from the ICJ and a sparse body of state practice, on the one hand, against a competing sparse body of state practice, on the other, the empirically more persuasive conclusion is that there currently exists no exception to state immunity from foreign criminal jurisdiction in relation to allegations of either international crimes per se or any specific international crime. For what it is worth, such an outcome would be supported by legal argument from first principles.

(a) Positive law

10.72 Prior to the celebrated *Pinochet* case in the late 1990s, state immunity had never been asserted or otherwise raised in municipal proceedings against foreigners in respect of crimes derived from international law. Notably, it had not been asserted or raised in trials in military tribunals, such as the trials for war crimes and, in the case of US tribunals, crimes against humanity after the Second World War. But these facts cannot be taken to indicate general agreement among states that state immunity would not have been available in such cases. For a start, in the immediate wake of the Second World War there existed no autochthonous German[191] or Japanese governments capable of claiming state immunity to the benefit of their former officials. As it was, moreover, at least the prosecutions of German ex-officials before the respective Allied military tribunals in occupied Germany did not, technically speaking, implicate state immunity, since the four Allied powers declared themselves to be exercising the sovereign authority of the subjugated German state,[192] which was obviously not barred by international law from trying its own former officials in respect of acts performed by them in an official capacity. To the hypothetical extent, furthermore, that there might otherwise have been an obligation on the forum state to raise the issue of state immunity *proprio motu* in the war crimes trials in other states at the end of the War,[193] Germany and Japan's respective unconditional surrenders were taken to imply consent to whatever post-War measures the victorious Powers might take against the defeated regimes. When it came to later prosecutions and extradition proceedings in foreign courts in respect of war crimes and crimes against humanity, these all involved persons

---

[191] Indeed, after the subjugation of Germany, the sovereign power of the government of Germany was vested in the four occupying Powers, and these Powers obviously did not invoke immunity *ratione materiae* as a potential bar to proceedings against German ex-officials.
[192] Recall *supra* para 2.59.
[193] Recall from *supra* para 10.58 that whether the forum state is obliged to raise the issue of immunity *ratione materiae* on a *proprio motu* basis remains a matter of debate in the context of criminal proceedings.

accused of committing crimes on behalf of Axis states during the Second World War, and the governments of those states or of their successors were either happy to see such people tried abroad or were themselves seeking the latter's extradition for trial back home.[194] In sum, the relevant state practice before the late 1990s was ambivalent at very best.

10.73 There was, nonetheless, a sprinkling of perhaps not wholly irrelevant international and municipal judicial dicta of a progressive nature. The International Military Tribunal (IMT) at Nuremberg stated boldly that '[h]e who violates the laws of war cannot obtain immunity while acting in pursuance of the authority of the State, if the State in authorizing action moves outside its competence under international law'.[195] But the assertion was in fact made in relation to the plea of act of state, the putative defence—commonly referred to at the time as an immunity, albeit a substantive, not merely procedural one—that the defendant was not criminally responsible in the first place for acts performed in an official capacity. Substantive responsibility does not presuppose procedural amenability; and state immunity, which was not invoked before the Tribunal, was inapplicable anyway for the reason for which it was inapplicable before the respective military tribunals of the four occupying Powers.[196] Subsequently, in *Attorney-General of the Government of Israel v Adolf Eichmann*, even though procedural immunity was not pleaded, the District Court of Jerusalem referred to article IV of the Convention on the Prevention and Punishment of the Crime of Genocide 1948 ('Genocide Convention') as providing for 'the absence of immunity from criminal liability of rulers and public officials',[197] the reference to 'criminal liability' again indicating that that the 'immunity' spoken of was, strictly speaking, substantive. Finally, it was asserted wholly *obiter* by the Appeals Chamber of the ICTY in *Blaškić* that 'those responsible for [war crimes, crimes against humanity, and genocide] cannot invoke immunity from national...jurisdiction even if they perpetrated such crimes while acting in their official capacity'.[198]

---

[194] In *Government of Israel v Adolf Eichmann*, 36 ILR 5 (Israel 1961 and 1962) and in the 'Ivan the Terrible' cases, *viz Demjanjuk v Petrovsky*, 79 ILR 534 (US 1985) and *State of Israel v John (Ivan) Demianiuk*, digested (1988) 18 *Israel Ybk HR* 229 (Israel 1988), the accused/defendant, a former German state official and a former member of a local SS unit in occupied Ukraine respectively, did not raise state immunity, presumably on the basis of its guaranteed waiver by Germany, the foreign state in whose service both had acted. See, similarly, *In Re Koch*, 30 ILR 496 (Poland 1959); *Barbie*, 78 ILR 124, 100 ILR 330 (France 1983, 1984, 1985, and 1988); *Polyukhovich v Commonwealth of Australia*, 91 ILR 1 (Australia 1991); *Hass and Priebke*, Military Court of Rome, 22 July 1997/Military Court of Appeal, 7 March 1998/Court of Cassation, 16 November 1998 (Italy). In *R v Finta*, 82 ILR 424, 98 ILR 520 (Canada 1989 and 1992), the foreign state (Hungary) actively assisted the prosecution. In the extradition case of *Artukovic v Rison*, 79 ILR 383 (US 1985 and 1986), it was the foreign state itself (Yugoslavia, as successor to the pro-Nazi Croatian state established during the Second World War) that sought the accused's surrender on war crimes charges. See, similarly, *Kroeger v Swiss Federal Prosecutor's Office*, 72 ILR 606 (Switzerland 1966, West Germany requesting); *Re Federal Republic of Germany and Rauca*, 88 ILR 277 (Canada 1983, West Germany requesting).

[195] International Military Tribunal (Nuremberg), Judgment and Sentences, reproduced (1947) 41 *AJIL* 172, 221.

[196] Recall *supra* para 10.72.   [197] *Eichmann* (n 194), 35, para 21 (DC Jerusalem).

[198] *Blaškić* (n 133), para 41.

10.74   The matter came to a head in 1999 in *Pinochet (No 3)*, where the majority came to the conclusion that state immunity did not attach to the treaty crime of torture—that is, to torture within the meaning, and prosecuted in pursuance, of the Torture Convention. Lords Browne-Wilkinson and Hutton held that the international crime of torture, as defined in article 1(1) of the Torture Convention, could never be considered an 'official function'.[199] Lords Millet and Saville held that the international crime of torture, as defined in article 1(1) of Torture Convention, could not attract immunity, even though it was an 'official function'.[200] Lords Hope and Phillips reached their respective conclusions via idiosyncratic routes, but they, along with Lord Goff in dissent, expressly rejected the argument that the crime of torture as defined in the Torture Convention could never be an official function.[201] The ratio, therefore, was that favoured by Lords Millet and Saville.[202] The reasoning runs as follows: serving and former state officials benefit under customary international law from immunity from foreign criminal proceedings in respect of acts performed in the exercise of their official functions; torture is defined in article 1(1) of the Torture Convention in such a way that only state officials can commit it; article 5(2) of the Convention mandates the establishment of universal jurisdiction over the offence, and article 7(1) obliges states parties to submit to their relevant authorities for prosecution or to extradite those persons in their custody suspected of torture as defined in the Convention; *ergo*, even if those suspected of torture are state officials otherwise entitled to state immunity, the Convention's definition of torture combined with the mandatory universal jurisdiction and the obligation *aut dedere aut judicare* that the Convention imposes must be taken to mean that state immunity cannot attach to torture within the meaning of the Convention.[203] In short, the ratio of *Pinochet (No 3)* was restricted to the crime of torture specifically within the meaning of, and prosecuted in pursuance of, the Torture Convention. Indeed, their Lordships 'doubt[ed] whether, before the coming into force of the Torture Convention, the existence of the international crime of torture...was enough to justify the conclusion that the organisation of state torture could not rank for immunity purposes as performance of an official function'.[204] In other words, contrary to journalistic and some academic and judicial suggestion,

---

[199]   See *Pinochet (No 3)* (n 114), 153–7 (Lord Browne-Wilkinson), 204 and 215–17 (Lord Hutton).
[200]   See ibid, 220–1 (Lord Saville), 231–2 (Lord Millet).
[201]   See ibid, 194–5 ('unsound in principle') (Lord Hope), 166 ('contrary to principle and authority, and indeed contrary to common sense') and 169 (Lord Goff), 244 (Lord Phillips).
[202]   That this is the ratio of *Pinochet (No 3)* was affirmed in *Jones v Saudi Arabia* (n 161), 723–4, para 19 (Lord Bingham), 743, para 81 and 744, para 83 (Lord Hoffmann).
[203]   Recall, however, *supra* para 7.120, that is not in fact true that torture as defined in art 1(1) of the Torture Convention can be committed only by a state official. Note too that three of the lords in *Pinochet (No 3)* were at pains to emphasize that the situation was not one of implied waiver. See *Pinochet (No 3)* (n 114), 201 (Lord Hope), 216–17 (Lord Hutton), and 231–2 (Lord Millet). Rather, as these lords saw it, immunity simply did not arise in the first place. This reasoning was forced on them by s 2(2) of the State Immunity Act 1978 (UK), in accordance with which a foreign state's prior submission to the jurisdiction of the UK courts must be by written agreement.
[204]   *Pinochet (No 3)* (n 114), 156 (Lord Browne-Wilkinson). See also ibid, 165 (Lord Goff), 195–6 (Lord Hope), 219 (Lord Saville).

Pinochet (No 3) did not assert the unavailability of state immunity in respect of international crimes generally. Misconception, however, achieved more purchase than the truth. The respective judgments of Lords Browne-Wilkinson and Hutton in *Pinochet (No 3)*, along with the far broader ratio of the Lords' quashed decision in *Pinochet (No 1)*,[205] gave rise to the frequently-heard argument that international crimes could never be an 'official function' with the result that prosecution in respect of such crimes could not be barred by the plea of state immunity.

While *Pinochet (No 3)* was restricted in its reasoning to the crime of torture pursuant to the Torture Convention, the subsequent Dutch case of *Bouterse*[206] involved allegations not only of torture within the meaning of the Torture Convention but also of war crimes and crimes against humanity. The reasoning of the Court of Appeal of Amsterdam,[207] which set aside the state immunity otherwise enjoyed by a former head of state, seemed to go considerably beyond *Pinochet (No 3)* in stating that 'the commission of very grave criminal offences of this kind cannot be regarded as part of the official duties of a head of state'.[208] The Court's unhelpfully brief statement appears to assert the unavailability of state immunity in respect of international crimes as such, and not just torture prosecuted pursuant to the Torture Convention.

10.75

For its part, Belgium had statutorily abrogated all immunities in respect of genocide, crimes against humanity, and war crimes in the legislation at the centre of the *Arrest Warrant* case.[209]

10.76

Whether state immunity was available in respect of international crimes did not, in the event, fall to be decided by the ICJ in *Arrest Warrant* in 2002. But the Court, in a gratuitous and no doubt carefully conceived dictum, went out of its way to refer to the scope of the immunity from foreign criminal jurisdiction from which a former minister for foreign affairs benefits under international law, explaining:

10.77

Provided that it has jurisdiction under international law, a court of one State may try a former Minister for Foreign Affairs of another State in respect of acts committed prior or subsequent to his or her period of office, as well as in respect of acts committed during that period of office in a private capacity.[210]

---

[205] *Pinochet (No 1)* (n 170).
[206] *Wijngaarde et al v Bouterse*, Court of Appeal of Amsterdam, 20 November 2000 (2000) 3 YIHL 677.
[207] The decision was overturned on appeal but on other grounds.
[208] *Bouterse* (n 206), para 4.2.
[209] Recall *supra* para 10.42. The legislation was repealed in August 2003, even if many of its provisions—but not the provision abrogating immunity—have been re-enacted into the criminal code. As it was, the Belgian Court of Cassation had held in February 2003 in *Re Sharon and Yaron* (n 83), 124, that the repealed Act did not exclude immunities available under customary international law. The current article in the Belgian Code of Criminal Procedure (Preliminary Title, Chapter I, art 1*bis*) effectively provides for state immunity '[i]n conformity with international law', which cleverly begs the question.
[210] *Arrest Warrant* (n 5), 25, para 61.

In this way the Court appears by implication to reject the argument that immunity *ratione materiae* is unavailable under customary international law as a procedural bar to the prosecution in a foreign court of a serving or former state official for an international crime allegedly committed by that official in anything other than a private capacity. This rejection goes hand-in-hand with the Court's earlier pronouncement in which it stresses that, 'although various international conventions on the prevention and punishment of certain serious crimes impose on States obligations of prosecution or extradition [and] require[e] them to extend their criminal jurisdiction', this 'in no way affects immunities under customary international law, including those of Ministers for Foreign Affairs', which 'remain opposable before the courts of a foreign State, even where those courts exercise such a jurisdiction under these conventions'[211]—the reference to 'immunities under customary international law' being pointedly general, not restricted to the immunity *ratione personae* of a serving minister for foreign affairs at immediate issue in the case. Both statements are directed squarely at *Pinochet (No 3)*. Additionally, the Court's considered reference to the unavailability of residual immunity *ratione materiae* in respect of acts performed 'in a private capacity'— rather than to the continuing existence of immunity in respect of acts performed in an official capacity or 'official acts', both of which might have been read down to exclude acts under mere colour of officialdom—takes careful aim at the broader ratio of the Lords' quashed decision in *Pinochet (No 1)*, as made popular by activists and as effectively relied on by the Court of Appeal of Amsterdam in *Bouterse* when it stated that 'the commission of very grave criminal offences of this kind' (in that case torture within the meaning of the Torture Convention, war crimes, and crimes against humanity) 'cannot be regarded as part of the official duties of a head of state'.[212]

10.78 The ICJ's implicit rejection of an exception to the immunity *ratione materiae* from foreign criminal proceedings of a serving or former state official in respect of either international crimes generally or treaty crimes subject to the obligations to establish universal jurisdiction and to prosecute or extradite has proved influential. In 2005, basing his decision expressly on *Arrest Warrant* (although seeming to conflate immunity *ratione personae* and immunity *ratione materiae*), the German federal prosecutor refused to open an investigation into allegations of crimes against humanity committed in office by the former head of state of China, arguing that the ICJ's judgment, which the prosecutor said dealt with both present and former ministers for foreign affairs, affirmed 'a well recognized rule in international law grant[ing] immunity from criminal prosecution by other states to present and former heads of government and heads of state', even 'if these officials are prosecuted for international crimes'.[213] Similarly, in late 2007, the prosecuting magistrate of the *Tribunal de Grande Instance* of Paris announced that he would not investigate

---

[211] Ibid, 25, para 59. Recall *supra* para 10.43. [212] *Bouterse* (n 206), 687–8, para. 4.2.
[213] Generalbundesanwalt beim Bundesgerichsthof, correspondence reference 3 ARP 654/03–2, 26 June 2005, para I, translation from Amnesty International, *Germany: End Impunity Through Universal Jurisdiction* ('No Safe Haven' Series No 3), EUR 23/003/2008, 72.

a complaint filed with him alleging that former US Secretary of Defense Donald Rumsfeld had ordered and authorized torture. He stated:

[T]he Ministry of Foreign Affairs has indicated that, applying the rules of customary international law, as affirmed by the International Court of Justice, the immunity from criminal jurisdiction of heads of State and of government and of ministers for foreign affairs continues to subsist, after their office comes to an end, in respect of acts performed in their official capacity and that, as former Secretary of Defense, Mr Rumsfeld should benefit by extension from the same immunity in respect of acts performed in the exercise of his office.[214]

The senior prosecuting magistrate of the Paris Court of Appeal rejected a challenge to the dismissal of the complaint, emphasizing that the ICJ had indicated in *Arrest Warrant* that the immunity of high-ranking officers of state was lost on completion of their term of office only in respect of acts performed before or after their term of office and in respect of acts performed while in office that were unrelated to that office.[215]

10.79 But not all relevant actors have taken the ICJ's dictum in *Arrest Warrant* to exclude without exception the abrogation of the immunity *ratione materiae* of a serving or former foreign state official in the face of prosecution for an international crime. In 2008, the Italian Court of Cassation held in *Lozano*, without even alluding to the ICJ's dictum in *Arrest Warrant*, that state immunity poses no bar to prosecution for those international crimes, such as the war crimes alleged in that case, which are said to violate norms of *jus cogens*.[216] In 2009, the Institut de droit international, in its resolution entitled 'Immunity from Jurisdiction of the State and of Persons Who Act on Behalf of the State in case of International Crimes', posited in article III(1) that '[n]o immunity from jurisdiction other than personal immunity in accordance with international law applies with regard to international crimes'.[217] In 2012, the Swiss Federal Criminal Court in *A v Ministère public de la Confédération* ('*Nezzar*'), while acknowledging the Court's words in *Arrest Warrant* on the immunity of a former minister for foreign affairs, preferred—in addition to taking a rose-tinted view of responses to the work of the ILC's first special rapporteur on the immunity of state officials[218]—to recall, with striking creativity, that, '[i]n the same judgment, the ICJ equally underlined that the immunity from jurisdiction that a serving minister for foreign affairs enjoys does not mean that he benefits from impunity in respect of crimes he may have committed, whatever their gravity'.[219] The Federal Criminal Court went on to abrogate the immunity *ratione materiae* of a former

---

[214] Procureur de la République (Tribunal de Grande Instance de Paris, Cour d'Appel de Paris), correspondence reference AS/2007/3350/A4/JCM/FC/ALM, 16 November 2007, author's translation.
[215] See Procureur Général (Cour d'Appel de Paris), correspondence reference 2007/09216/SGE, 28 February 2008.
[216] See *Lozano* (n 134), para 6. The Court of Cassation eventually upheld immunity *ratione materiae* on other grounds.
[217] Institut de droit international, 'Resolution on the Immunity from Jurisdiction of the State and of Persons Who Act on Behalf of the State in case of International Crimes' (2009) 73 *Annuaire de l'IDI* 226.
[218] See *Nezzar* (n 6), para 5.3.6.   [219] Ibid, para 5.3.3.

minister of defence of a foreign state in respect of allegations of war crimes,[220] although the ratio of the decision seems ultimately premised not on customary international law but on the Court's somewhat overdetermined reading of an official statement by Swiss legislators when enacting into Swiss law the crimes within the jurisdiction of the ICC.[221] As for statements in the Sixth Committee, Belgium declared its view in 2011 'that *de lege lata*, crimes that violated international treaties or international customary law gave rise to exclusion from immunity *ratione materiae*';[222] Peru asserted the same year that '[a]cts that constituted grave crimes under international law clearly could not be considered official functions covered by immunity *ratione materiae*', with the result that 'no immunity could be invoked in respect of such acts';[223] Singapore stated, again in 2011, that 'existing sources of international law certainly provided for exceptions' as regards 'the question of which crimes were or should be excluded from immunity *ratione materiae*';[224] and the Italian delegation argued in 2012 that immunity *ratione materiae* was unavailable in respect of alleged international crimes.[225] Austria and the Netherlands have argued for the same position *de lege ferenda*.[226]

10.80   In implicit response to *Lozano* and like reasoning in the criminal context, the ICJ in *Jurisdictional Immunities*—while posting the formal caveat that it was 'addressing only the immunity of the State itself from the jurisdiction of courts of other States', since 'the question whether, and if so to what extent, immunity might apply in criminal proceedings against an official of the State [was] not in issue' in the case[227]—recalled:

In *Arrest Warrant*, the Court held, albeit without express reference to the concept of *jus cogens*, that the fact that a Minister for Foreign Affairs was accused of criminal violations of

---

[220] See ibid, paras 5.4.3 and 5.5.
[221] See ibid, para 5.4.3, where the Federal Criminal Court recalls the official statement that the law was intended 'to ensure the unwavering repression' of genocide, crimes against humanity, and war crimes. This led the Court to reason, ibid, author's translation: '[I]t would be contradictory and pointless if at the same time, on the one hand, one were to affirm the desire to combat these grave violations of humanity's fundamental values and, on the other, if one were to concede a broad interpretation of the rules of functional immunity (*ratione materiae*) to the benefit of former rulers or officials, the concrete result of which would be to prevent, *ab initio*, any opening of an investigation.... Such a situation would be paradoxical, and the criminal-law policy that the legislator wanted to implement would be destined to remain a dead letter in nearly every case. This is not what [the legislator] wanted. It flows from this in the present case that the applicant ought not to benefit from any immunity *ratione materiae*.'
[222] UN doc A/C.6/66/SR.26 (7 December 2011), 14, para 67. See also ibid, para 69; UN doc A/C.6/67/SR.22 (4 December 2012), 7, para 44.
[223] UN doc A/C.6/66/SR.26, 13, para 63 (Peru).
[224] UN doc A/C.6/66/SR.28 (2 December 2011), 6, para 30.
[225] UN doc A/C.6/67/SR.22, 13, paras 82–83.
[226] See A/C.6/66/SR.26, 16, para 79 (Austria); UN docs A/C.6/66/SR.28, 11, para 59 and A/C.6/68/SR.18 (15 November 2013), 7, para 33 (Netherlands). See also, not dissimilarly, UN docs A/C.6/66/SR.27 (8 December 2011), 11, para 74 and A/C.6/67/SR.21 (4 December 2012), 15, para 85 (Portugal), speaking of immunity per se; UN docs A/C.6/66/SR.27 (8 December 2011), 12–13, para 86 and A/C.6/67/SR.22 (4 December 2012), 9–10, para 59 (New Zealand); UN doc A/C.6/68/SR.18 (15 November 2013), 18, para 98 (Greece), speaking of immunity per se.
[227] The distinction was one of the reasons the Court in *Jurisdictional Immunities* (n 5), 137–8, para 87, considered irrelevant the House of Lords' decision in *Pinochet (No 3)* (n 114), the other being that the decision turned on the wording of the Torture Convention.

rules which undoubtedly possess the character of *jus cogens* did not deprive the Democratic Republic of the Congo of the entitlement which it possessed as a matter of customary international law to demand immunity on his behalf.[228]

More generally, although again speaking directly of the immunity from civil proceedings of the state sued as such, the Court highlighted in *Jurisdictional Immunities* a perceived fatal flaw in what it characterized as gravity-based normative arguments against the availability of immunity from foreign jurisdiction, namely that such arguments are premised on a consideration of the merits of the case, whereas the barring of consideration of the merits is the essence of immunity.[229]

10.81 Although it obviously remains to be seen, it is unlikely that a preponderance of national courts and other relevant actors will fail to recognize as a blanket dismissal of *jus cogens*-based arguments against immunity from foreign criminal jurisdiction the ICJ's characterization in *Jurisdictional Immunities* of its earlier decision in *Arrest Warrant*.[230] It is true that *Arrest Warrant* itself pertained to immunity *ratione personae*; but it is significant that the Court relied on it in *Jurisdictional Immunities* to dismiss *jus cogens*-based arguments against state immunity (with the immediate context of civil proceedings against the state *eo nomine* representing no more than a formal distinction). Indeed, the ILC's second special rapporteur on immunity of state officials from foreign criminal jurisdiction indicated in her preliminary report that the Court's judgment in *Jurisdictional Immunities* 'deserves special consideration because [of] some of its methodological elements', 'whose potential implications for the immunity of State officials from foreign criminal jurisdiction the Commission should consider'.[231] Members of the Commission agreed.[232]

10.82 In a range of other relevant post-*Pinochet* cases, the state of which the accused or the person the object of the extradition request was a serving or former official has not claimed immunity *ratione materiae* on his behalf, either because the foreign government at the time of the proceedings has been of a very different political persuasion from that in whose service the then-official acted or

---

[228] *Jurisdictional Immunities* (n 5), 141, para 95, reference omitted. The UK House of Lords, in the civil case of *Jones v Saudi Arabia* (n 161), 726–7, para 24 (Lord Bingham) and, more clearly, 734, paras 48–49 (Lord Hoffmann), had already read *Arrest Warrant* as a denial of the *a priori* logic that deemed jurisdictional immunity incompatible with *jus cogens*.

[229] *Jurisdictional Immunities* (n 5), 136, para 82. For the full quotation, see below, text accompanying n 238.

[230] That said, six months after the ICJ's judgment in *Jurisdictional Immunities*, the Swiss Federal Criminal Court in *Nezzar* (n 6), especially paras 5.3.4, 5.3.5, and 5.4.3, referring in passing to the putative *jus cogens* status of the international criminal prohibitions in question, denied immunity *ratione materiae* to a former minister for defence of a foreign state accused of war crimes. But the decision of the Swiss minister challenged before the Federal Criminal Court predates the ICJ's judgment, as do all the pleadings in the challenge bar the *réplique* (two days after the ICJ's judgment) and the *duplique* (two months later), neither of which could by that point have incorporated the ICJ's jurisprudence. See *Nezzar* (n 6), paras F to H.

[231] *Preliminary report Escobar* (n 88), 11, para 49.

[232] See *Report ILC sixty-fourth session* (n 86), 96, para 100, 97–8, para 106, and 101–2, paras 127–131.

because the proceedings were conducted *in absentia* and not recognized by the foreign state.²³³

10.83 For what it is worth, the ILC's first special rapporteur on the immunity of state officials came to the firm conclusion in 2010 that state immunity continued as a matter of customary international law to bar the prosecution of a foreign state official in respect of acts performed in an official capacity even when the allegation was of an international crime.²³⁴ Only Belgium, Italy, Peru, and Singapore are to date on record in the Sixth Committee as having suggested otherwise.²³⁵ While most other states have said nothing as to current customary international law on point, China, France, and Russia have explicitly maintained that no exception to immunity *ratione materiae* exists in respect of allegations of international crimes.²³⁶

10.84 In sum, whether customary international law presently requires the forum state to afford immunity *ratione materiae* to a foreign state official or former official accused of, or the subject of a request for extradition in respect of, an international crime remains an open question. The position of the ICJ appears to be that it does—in other words, that no exception for allegations of international crimes or of any specific international crime exists to the immunity *ratione materiae* from criminal jurisdiction that a state owes other states in respect of those other states' officials and ex-officials; there is some state practice to support this view; and while the import of the silence on point of the great majority of states is difficult to gauge, it is hard to imagine that this silence reflects a groundswell of opposition to the continuing availability of immunity in this regard.

---

²³³ See the cases cited ibid, 44–6, paras 69–70. See also *Ould Dah*, Assize Court of Gard, 1 July 2005 (France), involving trial and judgment *in absentia*. As regards the original, stymied Senegalese prosecution of Hissène Habré for the crime of torture provided for in the Torture Convention, Belgium's subsequent request for Habré's extradition, and Habré's prospective prosecution before the Extraordinary African Chambers in the Senegalese Courts, Chad, the state of which Habré was formerly head, had waived any immunity *ratione materiae* from which the accused might have benefited. See *Questions relating to the Obligation to Prosecute or Extradite (Belgium v Senegal)*, Judgment, ICJ Rep 2012, 422, 432, para 20, referring to a letter from the Chadian minister of justice citing the decision of the Sovereign National Conference, N'Djamena, 15 January–7 April 1993, officially to lift 'all immunity from legal process' which might otherwise have served to bar proceedings against the former president. As for the Italian proceedings in *Milde*, Military Tribunal of La Spezia, 10 October 2006, which centred on internationally criminal conduct by a German soldier in Italy during the Second World War, Germany did not invoke immunity *ratione materiae* to shield its former official from prosecution, although it did plead state immunity in the linked civil proceedings in the same case. Nor did the accused Milde himself claim immunity, aware as he no doubt was that Germany would have waived it.

²³⁴ *Second report Kolodkin* (n 25), 56, para 90.   ²³⁵ See *supra* nn 221–224.
²³⁶ See UN docs A/C.6/66/SR.27 (8 December 2011), 3, para 10 and A/C.6/67/SR.21 (4 December 2012), 14, paras 76–77 (China); UN doc A/C.6/66/SR.20 (23 November 2011), 8, para 43 (France); UN docs A/C.6/66/SR.27 (8 December 2011), 10, para 66 and A/C.6/68/SR.19 (13 November 2013), 10, para 44 (Russia). Consider also, more generally, UN doc A/C.6/66/SR.26 (7 December 2011), 5, para 14 (Switzerland); UN doc A/C.6/66/SR.28 (2 December 2011), 10, para 51 (Kenya); UN docs A/C.6/67/SR.22 (4 December 2012), 14, para 86 and A/C.6/68/SR.19 (13 November 2013), 7, para 29 (Cuba); UN doc A/C.6/66/SR.19 (22 November 2011), 8, para 43 (Niger).

(b) Legal arguments from first principles

10.85 Various legal arguments from first principles have been made against the availability to a serving or former state official of immunity *ratione materiae* from foreign criminal jurisdiction when the prosecution or request for extradition alleges an international crime. None of these arguments is convincing. Three suffer from a common logical vice, while all have their further, specific flaws.

10.86 The fatal flaw in all normative arguments, whether based on legal principle or humanitarian policy, against the availability of immunity, whether *ratione materiae* or *ratione personae*, as a bar to foreign criminal proceedings in respect of allegations of international crimes is that they are premised on the outcome of adjudication on the merits, whereas the barring of adjudication on the merits is the essence of immunity. That is, all such arguments presuppose the legal characterization of the alleged conduct as wrongful, specifically criminal; the legal wrongfulness of the alleged conduct is a question for determination on the merits; and the determination of the merits of the case is precisely what procedural immunity exists to prevent.[237] The ICJ highlighted this 'logical problem'[238] in *Jurisdictional Immunities*, albeit in relation to civil proceedings against the state sued as such, saying:

> Immunity from jurisdiction is...necessarily preliminary in nature. Consequently a national court is required to determine whether or not a foreign State is entitled to immunity as a matter of international law before it can hear the merits of the case brought before it and before the facts have been established. If immunity were to be dependent upon the State actually having committed a serious violation of international human rights law or the law of armed conflict, then it would become necessary for the national court to hold an enquiry into the merits in order to determine whether it had jurisdiction. If, on the other hand, the mere allegation that the State had committed such wrongful acts were to be sufficient to deprive the State of its entitlement to immunity, immunity could, in effect, be negated simply by skilful construction of the claim.[239]

Instructive contrasts can be drawn in this regard with the customary exceptions to state immunity from foreign civil proceedings, an immunity encompassing the immunity from suit of serving and former state officials in respect of acts performed in their official capacity.[240] None of these exceptions presupposes the legal wrongfulness of the facts alleged. For example, the 'commercial transaction' exception[241] posits merely that the alleged state conduct the subject of the proceedings arose out of a commercial transaction, rather than that it constituted a breach of contract, a tort or some other municipal private-law wrong. Equally, what is known in some quarters

---

[237] This is not to suggest that normative arguments against immunity presume guilt. In their most carefully framed form, such arguments claim no more than that procedural immunity poses no bar to proceedings in respect of allegations of international crimes, as distinct from proceedings in respect of international crimes. But in the final analysis the only difference between the two formulations is that the former does not prejudge proof to the requisite standard of the facts alleged. Incipient in even the more sophisticated formulation is still the presumption that the alleged facts, if proved, disclose unlawful conduct.

[238] *Jurisdictional Immunities* (n 5), 136, para 82.   [239] Ibid, 136, para 82.
[240] See eg UN Convention on State Immunity, Part III.   [241] See eg ibid, art 10.

as the 'territorial tort' or 'domestic tort' exception[242] is in fact without regard to the possible legal characterization of the state's alleged conduct as tortious. The exception pertains, rather, to proceedings relating to compensation for death or personal injury or for damage to or loss of tangible property caused by the defendant state's alleged act or omission in the forum state. Also instructive are the few exceptions to immunity *ratione personae* from civil proceedings recognized in the various conventions, which relate not to legal wrongs as such but simply to actions relating to private immovable property, to succession, to professional or commercial activity, and to vehicular accidents, in each case when the official in question acts in a private capacity.[243] Finally, it is also worth contrasting normative arguments regarding allegations of international crimes with the putative exception to immunity *ratione materiae* from criminal proceedings in respect of alleged criminal conduct by a foreign state official in the territory of the forum state when the forum state has consented neither to the activity allegedly leading to the offence nor to the presence in its territory of the accused official.[244] The purported exception is predicated not on the criminality of the alleged activity but merely on the alleged performance of that activity in the forum state's territory absent the twofold consent of the forum state.

10.87 As for the not-infrequent assertion that an international crime can never be an act performed in an official capacity, its additional shortcoming beyond its presumption as to the merits is that it mistakenly treats as a normative question what is purely a descriptive exercise. It pays to reiterate[245] that, for the purpose of immunity *ratione materiae* under international law, an act is to be considered as performed in an official capacity if it is performed in the actual exercise of state authority. The propriety or desirability of this exercise is immaterial to immunity.[246]

10.88 The popular claim that state immunity poses no bar under international law to the prosecution of serving or former state officials for crimes under customary international law in violation of *jus cogens* likewise has a particular weakness beyond its premise as to the merits. Even were one to accept the doubtful proposition that international prohibitions binding solely on individuals can be norms of *jus cogens*,[247] the status of a prohibition as one of *jus cogens* goes to its applicability in the first place, not to the consequences of its breach, at least insofar as one is not talking of article 41 of the Articles on Responsibility of States.[248] To say that a prohibition under customary international law is non-derogable—meaning that under no circumstances may it be set aside, explicitly or by implication, as inapplicable to a legal or, hypothetically, natural person to which or whom it otherwise applies—is to say nothing about the availability of a legal forum,[249] let alone a

---

[242] See eg ibid, art 12.
[243] See VCDR, art 31(1)(*a*) to (*c*); CSM, art 31(2)(*a*) to (*d*); VCRS, art 30(1)(*a*) to (*c*).
[244] Recall *supra* para 10.70.   [245] Recall *supra* para 10.63.
[246] See, in this regard, A/C.6/67/SR.21 (4 December 2012), 14, para 77 (China).
[247] Recall *supra* paras 2.79–2.81.
[248] See the limited parameters of Articles on Responsibility of States, arts 40 and 41.
[249] See eg *Armed Activities on the Territory of the Congo (New Application: 2002) (Democratic Republic of the Congo v Rwanda), Jurisdiction and Admissibility, Judgment*, ICJ Rep 2006, 6, 32, para 64 and 52, para 125.

municipal legal forum,[250] for adjudging responsibility, least of all responsibility under municipal law, for its breach. This was made clear, with none-too-subtle allusion to municipal criminal jurisdiction, in the ICJ's judgment in *Jurisdictional Immunities*.[251] The Court stated:

Assuming for this purpose that the rules of the law of armed conflict which prohibit the murder of civilians in occupied territory, the deportation of civilian inhabitants to slave labour and the deportation of prisoners of war to slave labour are rules of *jus cogens*, there is no conflict between those rules and the rules on State immunity. The two sets of rules address different matters.[252]

'To the extent that it is argued that no rule which is not of the status of *jus cogens* may be applied if to do so would hinder the enforcement of a *jus cogens* rule, even in the absence of a direct conflict', the Court saw 'no basis for such a proposition':[253]

A *jus cogens* rule is one from which no derogation is permitted but the rules which determine the scope and extent of jurisdiction and when that jurisdiction may be exercised do not derogate from those substantive rules which possess *jus cogens* status, nor is there anything inherent in the concept of *jus cogens* which would require their modification or would displace their application.[254]

The Court recalled that it had taken this approach in two cases of its own, including *Arrest Warrant*, 'notwithstanding that the effect was that a means by which a *jus cogens* rule might be enforced was rendered unavailable':[255]

In *Arrest Warrant*, albeit without express reference to the concept of *jus cogens*, the fact that a Minister for Foreign Affairs was accused of criminal violations of rules which undoubtedly possess the character of *jus cogens* did not deprive the Democratic Republic of the Congo of the entitlement which it possessed as a matter of customary international law to demand immunity on his behalf.[256]

Nor could an argument against state immunity be mounted on the back of article 41 of the Articles on Responsibility of States:

The rules of State immunity are procedural in character and are confined to determining whether or not the courts of one State may exercise jurisdiction in respect of another State. They do not bear upon the question whether the conduct in respect of which the proceedings are brought was lawful or unlawful.... [R]ecognizing the immunity of a foreign State in accordance with international law does not amount to recognizing as lawful a situation

---

[250] See eg *Jones v Saudi Arabia* (n 161), 726–7, para 24 (Lord Bingham), 732, paras 44–45 and 734, para 49 (Lord Hoffmann).
[251] Subsequently, in *Jones v United Kingdom* (n 134), the European Court of Human Rights (Fourth Section) considered the ICJ's judgment in *Jurisdictional Immunities* (n 5) to be 'authoritative as regards the content of customary international law' when it concluded that 'no *jus cogens* exception to State immunity had yet crystallised'.
[252] *Jurisdictional Immunities* (n 5), 140, para 93. [253] Ibid, 141, para 95.
[254] Ibid.
[255] Ibid. The other case was *Armed Activities (New Application: 2002)* (n 249).
[256] *Jurisdictional Immunities* (n 5), 141, para 95.

created by the breach of a *jus cogens* rule, or rendering aid or assistance in maintaining that situation, and so cannot contravene the principle in Article 41 of the International Law Commission's Articles on State Responsibility.[257]

Although the Court was at pains to emphasize in *Jurisdictional Immunities* that it was 'addressing only the immunity of the State itself from the [civil] jurisdiction of courts of other States', since 'the question whether, and if so to what extent, immunity might apply in criminal proceedings against an official of the State [was] not in issue' in the case,[258] its account of its decision in *Arrest Warrant* and its bringing of this account within its systematic rebuttal of *jus cogens*-based arguments against state immunity have obvious implications for these arguments in the criminal context as well.

10.89 Just as flawed, both in its dependence on a prefiguring of the merits and more especially, is the sophisticated argument that state immunity cannot serve to bar municipal criminal proceedings against serving or former state officials accused of crimes under customary international law because the international prohibition at issue binds only the individual official, not the state, rendering the latter incapable of being the 'real' or 'proper' defendant to the proceedings, as the law of state immunity is said to demand.[259] As to its especial flaws, the argument, even on its own terms, confuses the attributability to the state of the conduct of the official—the sole relevant question—with the subsequent, immaterial question of the applicability to the state of the relevant primary rule of international law. Insofar as analogy with the secondary rules of international law codified in articles 4 and 7 of the Articles on Responsibility of States and case law pertaining to them can be considered useful guides to what constitutes an act performed in an official capacity under the law of state immunity, all that is necessary for the availability to a serving or former state official of immunity *ratione materiae* from foreign criminal jurisdiction is that the official's act be attributable to the state. That the international prohibition indirectly implicated by municipal prosecution for a crime under customary international law does not and cannot bind that state is beside the point. Putting it simply, the international law of immunity *ratione materiae* from foreign criminal jurisdiction does not demand that the state be capable of committing in any formal sense the international crime alleged. All it says is that, for the procedural purposes of the international rules on immunity from foreign jurisdiction, the alleged crime is to be treated as if it were[260] the state that committed it. The state's commission of the alleged crime is purely notional,

---

[257] Ibid, 140, para 93. For the further rejection in the criminal context, distinguishing between substance and procedure, of the relevance of *jus cogens* to immunity from municipal jurisdiction, see UN doc A/C.6/SR.26 (7 December 2011), 17, para 86 (Germany).
[258] Recall, in this regard, *supra* n 227.
[259] See eg Van Alebeek (n 135), chapter 5; Z Douglas, 'State Immunity for the Acts of State Officials' (2011) 82 *BYIL* 281; A Sanger, 'Immunity of State Officials from the Criminal Jurisdiction of a Foreign State' (2013) 62 *ICLQ* 193.
[260] In the words of the German Federal Constitutional Court in *Former Syrian Ambassador* (n 161), 605, foreign judicial proceedings against former diplomats 'come, in their effects, close to' proceedings against the sending state.

not formally juridical. As it is, even if the capacity to be the bearer of the relevant obligation were somehow relevant to immunity *ratione materiae*, the applicable substantive law is not international law but the municipal criminal law of the forum state. That is, whatever its ultimate source in customary international law, the crime with which a serving or former state official will be charged in any foreign prosecution will be one under the law of the forum state.[261] The international prohibition from which it derives and whether a state can be bound by it are neither here nor there.

When it comes to the argument, accepted by Lords Browne-Wilkinson and Hutton in *Pinochet (No 3)*, that a treaty crime can never be an 'official act' if it is defined in such a way that it can be committed only by a state official and is the focus of obligations to establish universal jurisdiction and to prosecute or extradite,[262] the absurdity of an act by definition official never being official should be self-evident.[263] 10.90

More coherent is the claim, the ratio of *Pinochet (No 3)*,[264] that a treaty crime both committed by definition by a state official and subject to the twin obligations of universal jurisdiction and prosecution or extradition cannot give rise, without depriving the treaty of effect, to immunity *ratione materiae* from foreign prosecution—at least insofar as not only the forum state but also the state of which the accused is or was an official are parties to the treaty. But even this argument, which, while the most limited in scope,[265] is the best of the arguments against immunity *ratione materiae* in the criminal context, is by no means watertight. First, although their Lordships strenuously denied that this was the case in *Pinochet (No 3)*,[266] the argument is in substance based on an implied waiver of immunity by the state of the accused, and it is extremely likely that a state's waiver of an immunity that would otherwise serve to shield one of its officials from foreign proceedings must, as a matter of customary international law, be express. This is certainly the 10.91

---

[261] In this regard, moreover, it is not beyond the realm of possibility that, under the municipal law of the forum state, corporate entities such as a foreign state may be capable of criminal responsibility in addition to the criminal responsibility of any of their serving or former officials.

[262] Recall *supra* para 10.74. The argument is capable of applying—and even then not really (see immediately *infra*)—only to the offences of torture pursuant to the Torture Convention and enforced disappearance pursuant to the International Convention for the Protection of All Persons from Enforced Disappearance 2006 ('Enforced Disappearance Convention'), these being the only two treaty crimes defined the relevant way. Recall, however, *supra* para 7.120, that is not in fact true that torture as defined in art 1(1) of the Torture Convention can be committed only by a state official. The same goes, *mutatis mutandis*, for the definition of enforced disappearance in art 2 of the Enforced Disappearance Convention.

[263] For the same point, see *Jones v Saudi Arabia* (n 161), 724, para 19 (Lord Bingham), 743, para 81 and 744, para 83 (Lord Hoffmann). Indeed, in *Jones v United Kingdom* (n 134), para 206, the European Court of Human Rights held that the definition of torture in art 1 of the Torture Convention 'appears to lend support to the argument that acts of torture can be committed in an "official capacity" for the purposes of State immunity'.

[264] Recall *supra* para 10.74.

[265] This argument, like the immediately preceding one, can apply, and even then only with a measure of creative licence, only to the offences of torture pursuant to the Torture Convention and enforced disappearance pursuant to the Enforced Disappearance Convention.

[266] Recall *supra* n 203.

requirement in the various codifications of immunity, both *ratione materiae* and *ratione personae*, from foreign jurisdiction, both criminal and civil.[267] Secondly, even on the argument's own terms, it is simply not the case that any relevant treaty would be deprived of effect by the availability of immunity *ratione materiae* as a bar to foreign prosecution on the jurisdictional basis of universality. The internal logic of any such treaty might just as easily, and more plausibly, be premised on the express waiver by the state of which the accused is or was an official of any immunity *ratione materiae* that might otherwise serve to bar the accused's prosecution in a foreign state party's courts.[268] Moreover,[269] the forum (*viz* custodial) state and the state of nationality of the suspect, which can be expected in almost all cases to be the state of which the accused is or was an official, must both be parties to the treaty if the former's exercise in accordance with the treaty of an otherwise exorbitant universal jurisdiction is to be lawful;[270] and this being so, the state of nationality of the suspect will be treaty-bound to criminalize and to empower its courts to try the offence in question on the basis of, *inter alia*, nationality, and to prosecute on this basis should it obtain custody of the suspect.[271] In this light, the obligation to assert universal jurisdiction and the obligation *aut dedere aut judicare* are not deprived of effect by the continuing availability to state officials and ex-officials of immunity *ratione materiae* as a bar to prosecution for the offence in question in the courts of a foreign state party. Rather, given the international unlawfulness of prosecuting the serving or former officials of foreign states for acts performed in their official capacity, the forum state will be obliged to extradite the suspect to a state party that is both permitted by international law and willing to prosecute,[272] in other words the state of nationality, which in turn will be treaty-bound to prosecute the suspect. (Insofar as the forum state's exercise of criminal jurisdiction over the suspect for the purposes of extradition would itself be an otherwise-impermissible abrogation of immunity, the state parties must be taken to have waived the immunity *ratione materiae* from which their serving and former officials would otherwise benefit;[273] but this waiver would extend only to extradition proceedings, not to prosecution, and only to proceedings with a view to extradition to the state of which the suspect is or was an official.) Thirdly and finally, despite the heroic attempts in *Pinochet (No 3)* to distinguish the two, it is ultimately not apparent why the logic of inconsistency-cum-ineffectiveness should mean that no immunity *ratione materiae* arises in respect of the offence but that, as four of their Lordships held,[274] such immunity *ratione personae* from which state

---

[267] See VCDR, art 32(2); CSM, art 41(2); VCRS, art 31(2); VCCR, art 45(2).
[268] See also *Pinochet (No 3)* (n 114), 171 (Lord Goff).
[269] For an argument to the same effect as that made here, see *Third report Kolodkin* (n 123), 28, para 48.
[270] Recall *supra* para 8.21.   [271] Recall *supra* paras 8.27 and 8.48–8.56 respectively.
[272] Recall *supra* para 8.52.
[273] Alternatively, in the waiver-free language of *Pinochet (No 3)* (n 114), immunity *ratione materiae* cannot arise in the first place to the extent of the extradition proceedings.
[274] Recall *supra* n 114. See also JH Burgers and H Danelius, *The United Nations Convention Against Torture: A Handbook on the Convention Against Torture and Other Cruel, Inhuman or Degrading Treatment or Punishment* (Dordrecht/London: Martinus Nijhoff, 1988), 131.

officials might benefit by virtue of their office or post continues to bar their prosecution for the same offence in the courts of a foreign state party.[275] If only state officials can commit the offence that is subject to the obligations of universal jurisdiction and *aut dedere aut judicare*, and if it is only by virtue of being a state official that immunity *ratione personae* enures to the benefit of the accused, this would seem as convincing an argument—which is to say not very convincing—for saying that no immunity can arise as the argument based on the fact that the offence was allegedly committed in an official capacity.

B. Treaty-based Species of Immunity *Ratione Materiae*

10.92 A range of particular serving and former state officials enjoy treaty-based species of immunity *ratione materiae* from foreign criminal jurisdiction over and above the customary immunity *ratione materiae* from foreign criminal jurisdiction, *viz* state immunity, from which they otherwise benefit under customary international law in respect of acts performed in their official capacity. All of these codified immunities *ratione materiae* are best seen in origin and essence as instantiations of the immunity *ratione materiae*, or state immunity, from which any serving or former state official benefits.[276] What distinguishes them formally, however, from the state immunity from foreign criminal jurisdiction from which they historically derive is that they are now embodied in treaty form. These treaty-based species of immunity *ratione materiae* from foreign criminal jurisdiction therefore constitute *lex specialis* to the *lex generalis* of customary state immunity from foreign criminal jurisdiction. What this means is that they are to be applied over any otherwise applicable rule of state immunity in the event and to the extent of any inconsistency. The significance of this in practice is twofold. First, and most obviously, close attention must be paid to the precise wording of each relevant provision. Secondly, insofar as any exceptions may exist or emerge in future as a matter of customary international law to the state immunity from foreign criminal jurisdiction from which the general body of serving and former state officials benefit, these exceptions would not limit any unencumbered treaty-based immunity *ratione materiae* applicable among states parties to the treaty in question[277] unless the express wording of the provision in question provides scope for this.

---

[275] See also *Pinochet (No 3)* (n 114), 171 (Lord Goff).

[276] See *infra* para 10.94, including n 290. See also *Pinochet (No 3)* (n 114), 153 (Lord Browne-Wilkinson) ('[U]nder article 39(2) [of the VCDR] the ambassador, like any other official of the state, enjoys immunity in relation to his official acts done while he was an official.'), 223 (Lord Millett) ('Immunity *ratione materiae*... operates to prevent the official and governmental acts of one state from being called into question in proceedings before the courts of another.... It is available to former heads of state and heads of diplomatic missions, and any one whose conduct in the exercise of the authority of the state is afterwards called into question, whether he acted as head of government, government minister, military commander or chief of police, or subordinate public official.')

[277] In the context of civil proceedings, these other immunities *ratione materiae* are now clearly wider than state immunity as such, the restrictive doctrine of which has subsequently come to represent customary international law and is reflected in the UN Convention on State Immunity.

(i) Serving and former consular officers

10.93 The immunity from the criminal jurisdiction of the receiving state and any transit states from which consular officers, by which is meant both career consular officers and honorary consular officers, benefit under the Vienna Convention on Consular Relations 1963 ('VCCR') and customary international law is an immunity *ratione materiae*. In accordance with article 43(1)[278] of the VCCR, serving consular officers are not amenable to the criminal jurisdiction of the receiving state 'in respect of acts performed in the exercise of consular functions'. As the ILC has made clear, this immunity extends to *ultra vires* acts.[279] Article 44(3)[280] specifies that members of a consular post, which includes consular officers, may not be obliged 'to give evidence concerning matters connected with the exercise of their functions or to produce official correspondence and documents relating thereto'. As for transit states, article 54(1) renders opposable to them the immunity from jurisdiction of career consular officers alone.[281] For its part, article 53(4)[282] of the VCCR indicates that, once their functions as members of the consular post have come to an end, consular officers continue to enjoy immunity from the criminal jurisdiction of the receiving[283] state 'with respect to acts performed...in the exercise of [their] functions'. As per article 45(1), the sending state may waive any immunity from which members of its consular posts would otherwise benefit. In the criminal context, this waiver must always be express, as stated in article 45(2).

10.94 Whether the immunity *ratione materiae* of a serving or former consular officer from foreign criminal jurisdiction extends to acts falling outside the enumeration of 'consular functions' in article 5 of the VCCR is a difficult question.[284] Clarity is not fostered in this regard by the divergence in wording between article 43(1) of the VCCR, on the immunity of a serving consular officer in respect of 'acts performed in the exercise of consular functions', and article 53(4), on the immunity of a former consular officer in respect of 'acts performed by a consular officer...in the exercise of his functions'. Given the presumption that a term is to bear a single meaning throughout a treaty, a presumption reinforced where the treaty expressly defines the term, article 43(1) could be read to suggest that the scope of a serving consular officer's immunity from criminal jurisdiction is to be circumscribed by

---

[278] See also VCCR, art 58(2), specifying that art 43 is applicable as much to honorary as to career consular officers.
[279] Recall *supra* n 172.
[280] See also VCCR, art 58(2), specifying that art 44(3) is applicable to honorary consular officers as well.
[281] For the similar situation as regards other members of a consular post, see VCCR, art 54(2). That art 54 of the VCCR is inapplicable to honorary consular officers is indicated by its omission from art 58(2).
[282] See also VCCR, art 58(2), specifying that art 53, like art 44(3), is applicable to honorary consular officers as well.
[283] Once the functions of consular officers have come to an end and the latter have returned to the sending state, there can be no such thing as a transit state.
[284] The question is not the same as whether the immunity *ratione materiae* of a serving or former consular officer from foreign criminal jurisdiction extends to *ultra vires* acts—that is, to acts beyond the scope of the consular officer's authority under the law of the sending state or beyond the scope of or contrary to instructions given to him or her by a superior.

the *numerus clausus* of 'consular functions' specified in article 5—in other words, that consular officers enjoy immunity from jurisdiction only in respect of such acts as fall within the scope of the 'consular functions' listed in article 5. Particularly significant in this context are article 5(*a*), which speaks of 'protecting in the receiving State the interests of the sending State...within the limits permitted by international law', although the implication from the ILC's commentary is that the reference to the 'limits permitted by international law' is to the prohibition on interference in the internal affairs of the receiving state;[285] and article 5(*m*), which refers to 'any other functions entrusted to a consular post by the sending State which are not prohibited by the laws and regulations of the receiving State or to which no objection is taken by the receiving State or which are referred to in the international agreements in force between the sending State and the receiving State'. Article 53(4), in contrast, appears to indicate that the immunity from criminal jurisdiction of former consular officers extends to any functions, in the sense of responsibilities or tasks, assigned to them or otherwise sanctioned in the course of their job as consular officers. For its part, however, the logic of immunity *ratione materiae* dictates that the scope of the immunities recognized respectively in articles 43(1) and 53(4) be the same—in other words, that 'consular functions' and 'his functions' mean the same thing. In this connection, one might note that the presumption in favour of according a term a single meaning throughout a treaty is no more than a presumption, defeasible via the operation of the rules of treaty interpretation; that a cardinal principle of the 'golden rule' of treaty interpretation is that a term must be interpreted in context;[286] that the context of a term includes the remaining text of the treaty,[287] *viz* its other provisions; and that the term 'consular functions' could be read quite naturally to mean 'functions as a consul' or 'functions as a consular officer', an expression meaning the same as 'his functions', while it would be less natural to construe the term 'his functions' as 'his execution of consular functions as enumerated in article 5'. These cumulative considerations militate in favour of interpreting 'consular functions' as found in article 43(1) to mean 'his functions [as a consular officer]'—in other words, to read article 43(1) as according consular officers immunity from criminal jurisdiction in respect of any acts performed by them in their capacity, *viz* their actual capacity, as consular officers, rather than in their exercise as consular officers of such functions as article 5 lists as 'consular functions'.[288] The *travaux préparatoires* confirm[289] this reading of article 43(1). In the commentary to draft article 43 of its Draft Articles on Consular Relations, which became article 43(1) of the VCCR, the ILC states:

The rule that, in respect of acts performed by them in the exercise of their functions (official acts) members of the consulate are not amenable to the jurisdiction of the

---

[285] See para 7 of the commentary to draft art 5 of the ILC's Draft Articles on Consular Relations (n 172), 96.
[286] VCLT, art 31(1).   [287] VCLT, art 31(2), chapeau.
[288] But cf *Adler* (n 158), para 23.4. It might be noted that *Adler* should have proceeded by reference to art 54(3) of the VCCR, rather than art 43(1), since the individuals tried *in absentia* were no longer consular officers.
[289] See VCLT, art 32.

judicial and administrative authorities of the receiving State... represents an immunity which the sending State is recognized as possessing in respect of acts which are those of a sovereign State.[290]

The significance of this statement is twofold. First, it suggests that the immunity from jurisdiction of serving and former consular officers is in substance a manifestation of state immunity, and it will be recalled that, in the criminal context, state immunity is accorded in respect of all acts performed in an official capacity, meaning all acts performed in the actual exercise of state authority. Secondly, and as a corollary of the foregoing, the ILC paraphrases 'acts performed in the exercise of consular functions', as found in both draft article 43 and the eventual article 43(1) of the VCCR, as 'acts performed by them in the exercise of their functions (official acts)'.

10.95 The immunity *ratione materiae* from criminal jurisdiction of career consular officers[291] is accompanied by an attenuated form of inviolability from measures of physical constraint.[292] In those cases in which they may be subject to the criminal jurisdiction of the receiving state or a transit state, namely in respect of acts performed during their posting in their private capacity or prior to their posting, article 41(1) of the VCCR dictates that career consular officers may not be arrested or detained pending trial, 'except in the case of a grave crime and pursuant to a decision by the competent judicial authority'. Article 41(2) specifies that, except in the case of a grave crime, consular officers shall not be committed to prison 'or be liable to any other form of restriction on their personal freedom save in execution of a judicial decision of final effect'. Except in the case of a grave crime, any proceedings instituted against a career consular officer must be conducted, as per article 41(3), 'in a manner which will hamper the exercise of consular functions as little as possible'. The inviolability enjoyed by career consular officers comes to an end with the end of their posting and their return to the sending state.

(ii) Serving and former representatives of member states at meetings organized by a UN specialized agency

10.96 In accordance with article V, section 13(*a*) of the Convention on the Privileges and Immunities of the Specialized Agencies 1947 ('CPISA'), representatives of member states at meetings organized by a UN specialized agency—examples of the latter being the FAO, the ILO, the IMF, UNESCO, UNICEF, the WHO, and

---

[290] Paragraph 2 of commentary to draft art 43 of the Draft Articles on Consular Relations (n 172), 117. Draft art 43 reads: 'Members of the consulate shall not be amenable to the jurisdiction of the judicial or administrative authorities of the receiving State in respect of acts performed in the exercise of consular functions.'
[291] That the rule does not apply to honorary consular officers is indicated by the omission of art 41 of the VCCR from art 58(2).
[292] The ICJ recognized the customary character of the inviolability of career consular officers in *United States Diplomatic and Consular Staff in Tehran* (n 44), 31, para 62.

the World Bank—benefit in the host state and any transit states from immunity from criminal jurisdiction 'in respect of words spoken or written and all acts done by them in their official capacity', as well as from full inviolability from arrest and detention. The immunity from criminal jurisdiction, but not the inviolability, enjoyed by such individuals continues to be opposable to the host[293] state after their functions have come to end 'in respect of words spoken or written and all acts done by them in discharging their duties', in the words of article V, section 14. Any available immunity and inviolability may be waived by the sending state, in accordance with article V, section 16. Indeed, the same provision stipulates that the sending state 'is under a duty to waive the immunity of its representatives in any case where, in the opinion of the member, the immunity would impede the course of justice, and where it can be waived without prejudice to the purpose for which the immunity is accorded'.[294]

(iii) Certain former beneficiaries of immunity ratione personae

10.97 The beneficiaries for the duration of their postings of treaty-based species of immunity *ratione personae*—namely diplomatic agents, the relevant members of a special mission, the representatives of member states to the principal and subsidiary organs of the UN and to conferences convened by it, and the heads and members of states' permanent missions to relevant international organizations—benefit after their posting has come to an end to treaty-based species of immunity *ratione materiae* in respect of acts performed in their former capacity. In contrast, the beneficiaries of a purely customary immunity *ratione personae*—namely heads of state, heads of government, ministers for foreign affairs, and possibly certain other senior state officials—benefit after they leave office only from the immunity *ratione materiae*, or state immunity, from foreign criminal jurisdiction from which the general body of former state officials continues to benefit under customary international law in respect of acts performed in an official capacity.[295] To the extent that the respective contents of the treaty-based and customary regimes of immunity *ratione materiae* are prima facie identical, the distinction is one without a difference. But should any customary exceptions exist or emerge to the uncodified immunity *ratione materiae*, viz state immunity, from foreign criminal jurisdiction from which the general body of former state officials benefit in respect of acts performed in their official capacity, such exceptions, while restricting the scope of the customary immunity *ratione materiae* enjoyed by a former head of state, etc, would not serve to restrict the enjoyment by a former diplomatic agent, etc of the pertinent treaty-based immunity *ratione materiae*.

---

[293] Recall, *mutatis mutandis*, *supra* n 283.   [294] Recall, in this regard, *supra* para 10.30.
[295] See eg *Pinochet (No 3)* (n 114), generally, and especially 153–4 (Lord Browne-Wilkinson), 223 (Lord Millett), 240 (Lord Phillips) ('While a head of state is serving, his status ensures him immunity. Once he is out of office, he is in the same position as any other state official and any immunity will be based upon the nature of the subject matter of the litigation.'). See also *Secretariat Memorandum* (n 17), 112–13, paras 170–173; *Preliminary report Kolodkin* (n 54), 38, paras 80–82, 41–2, para 88.

10.98   Article 39(2) of the VCDR provides that a diplomat agent formerly accredited to the forum state continues to benefit from immunity from its criminal jurisdiction in respect of acts 'performed... in the exercise of his functions as a member of the mission'. Again, the meaning of the key phrase is the same, *mutatis mutandis*, as the phrase 'performed in an official capacity' for the purposes of the law of state immunity.[296] As explained by the German Federal Constitutional Court, 'it is irrelevant whether the conduct... fulfilled diplomatic functions in the sense of Article 3 of the VCDR'.[297] It is similarly irrelevant whether the act was *ultra vires*. Just as with the immunity *ratione personae* of a serving diplomatic agent, the immunity *ratione materiae* of a former diplomatic agent may be waived by the sending state, although any such waiver must be express.[298]

10.99   Equivalent immunities *ratione materiae* serve to shield from the criminal jurisdiction of the erstwhile receiving or host state the former representatives of a state in a special mission and the former members of the mission's diplomatic staff;[299] former representatives of member states to the principal and subsidiary organs of the UN and to conferences convened by it;[300] and former heads and members of states' permanent missions to relevant international organizations.[301]

10.100   None of the beneficiaries of treaty-based immunity *ratione materiae* continues to enjoy inviolability from measures of physical constraint once their posting has come to an end and they return to the sending state.

VI. Conclusion

10.101   The question of the immunity of serving and former state officials from foreign criminal jurisdiction may appear to be in a state of flux, especially as regards proceedings alleging international crimes. But appearance can belie reality. The fundamental rules are tolerably clear.

10.102   Aside from the treaty-based recipients of immunity *ratione personae* and inviolability, such as diplomatic agents and their analogues, it is beyond doubt that the 'troika' of the head of state, the head of government, and the minister for foreign affairs benefits while in office under customary international law from absolute immunity from the criminal jurisdiction of foreign states, including in respect of allegations of international crimes, and from absolute inviolability from foreign measures of physical constraint. It may be that a very small number of other

---

[296] Recall *supra* paras 10.60–10.69.
[297] *Former Syrian Ambassador* (n 161), 607, citation omitted.
[298] Recall VCDR, art 32(1) and (2).
[299] See CSM, art 43(2) ('acts performed... in the exercise of his functions') and art 41(1) and (2).
[300] See CPIUN, art IV, s 12 ('words spoken or written and all acts done by them in discharging their duties'), cross-referable to ibid, s 11(*a*) ('words spoken or written and all acts done by them in their capacity as representatives'), and art IV, s 14 (containing the duty to waive cited *supra* para 10.30).
[301] See VCRS, art 38(2) ('acts performed... in the exercise of his functions as a member of the mission') and art 31(1) and (2).

high-ranking state officials do too, although it is more likely that the issue of their immunity from criminal jurisdiction while on strictly public visits to foreign states will be resolved at a practical level via the conventional and probably also customary immunity *ratione personae* owed in relation to the representatives of a state in a special mission.

As regards immunity *ratione materiae*, and again leaving aside its treaty-based recipients (of whom consuls and representatives of member states at meetings organized by UN specialized agencies additionally enjoy inviolability, attenuated and full respectively, for the duration of their posting), all serving and former state officials benefit under customary international law from immunity from the criminal jurisdiction of foreign states in respect of acts performed in their official capacity, a descriptive concept which in all likelihood can embrace, whatever their motive, *ultra vires* acts and even acts criminal under the law of the official's state. When it comes to the controversial question whether this customary immunity *ratione materiae* extends to proceedings alleging international crimes, it is crucial not to substitute the wishful thinking of various scholars, certain members of the ILC, and a handful of states for positive customary international law, which at present appears to continue to support the upholding of immunity *ratione materiae* in the face of allegations of internationally criminal conduct, a position vigorously supported as a matter of principle by powerful states such as China and Russia and tacitly endorsed by others less keen to put it so bluntly. Nor, despite the uncritical assumption of not a few commentators and domestic judges, is any consistent trend away from this position discernible. The slight state practice in this direction is counterbalanced by state practice to the opposite effect, while the ICJ has thrown its considerable weight behind the maintenance of the *status quo ante*.

10.103

The outcome of the ILC's current work on the immunity of state officials from foreign criminal jurisdiction remains to be seen. The second special rapporteur on the topic is of a different stamp from the first. But this does not mean that what in all likelihood is the silent majority of the Commission's members and, far more significantly, of states will be unhorsed on the road to Damascus.

10.104

Further Reading

Akande, D and Shah, S, 'Immunities of State Officials, International Crimes, and Foreign Domestic Courts' (2010) 21 *European Journal of International Law* 815

Buzzini, G, 'Lights and Shadows of Immunities and Inviolability of State Officials in International Law: Some Comments on the *Djibouti v France* Case' (2009) 22 *Leiden Journal of International Law* 455

Denza, E, *Diplomatic Law. Commentary on the Vienna Convention on Diplomatic Relations* (3rd edn, Oxford: Oxford University Press, 2008)

Dinstein, Y, 'Diplomatic Immunity from Jurisdiction *Ratione Materiae*' (1966) 15 *International and Comparative Law Quarterly* 76

Foakes, J, *The Position of Heads of State and Senior Officials in International Law* (Oxford: Oxford University Press, 2014)

Fox, H and Webb, P, *The Law of State Immunity* (3rd edn, Oxford: Oxford University Press, 2013), chapters 18 and 19

Hartmann, J, 'The Gillon Affair' (2005) 54 *International and Comparative Law Quarterly* 745

Institut de droit international, 'Resolution on the Immunity from Jurisdiction of the State and of Persons Who Act on Behalf of the State in case of International Crimes' (2009) 73 *Annuaire de l'Institut de droit international* 226

Jia, BB, 'The Immunity of State Officials for International Crimes Revisited' (2012) 10 *Journal of International Criminal Justice* 1303

Lee, LT and Quigley, J, *Consular Law and Practice* (3rd edn, Oxford: Oxford University Press, 2008)

McLachlan, C, '*Pinochet* Revisited' (2002) 51 *International and Comparative Law Quarterly* 959

O'Keefe, R, 'Jurisdictional Immunities' in C Tams and J Sloan (eds), *The Development of International Law by the International Court of Justice* (Oxford: Oxford University Press, 2013), 107

O'Keefe, R, '*Khurts Bat v Investigating Judge of the German Federal Court*' (2011) 82 *British Yearbook of International Law* 564

Van Alebeek, R, *The Immunity of States and Their Officials in International Criminal Law and International Human Rights Law* (Oxford: Oxford University Press, 2008)

Watts, A, 'The Legal Position in International Law of Heads of State, Heads of Governments and Foreign Ministers' (1994) 247 *Recueil des Cours* 9

Wickremasinghe, C, 'Immunities Enjoyed by Officials of States and International Organizations' in M Evans (ed), *International Law* (3rd edn, Oxford: Oxford University Press, 2010), 380

Wood, M, 'The Immunity of Official Visitors' (2012) 16 *Max Planck Yearbook of United Nations Law* 35

Wuerth, I, '*Pinochet*'s Legacy Reassessed' (2012) 106 *American Journal of International Law* 731

11

Statutory Limitation and Amnesty

I. Introduction

Many national criminal justice systems have laws, commonly known as statutes of limitations,[1] barring the prosecution of crimes after the passage of a set period, such as 20 or 30 years from alleged commission—a phenomenon also known as prescription. It has also been the practice in many states emerging from military or other authoritarian rule, internal armed conflict or serious political unrest to provide for amnesty in respect of at least certain politically-motivated crimes alleged to have been committed during the relevant era—that is, to bar the prosecution or even to provide retroactively for the substantive non-responsibility of persons suspected of certain offences over that time.[2] There is additionally the more recent phenomenon, pioneered in post-apartheid South Africa, of the so-called 'truth and reconciliation' commission (TRC), which usually provides for amnesty in respect of at least certain politically-motivated crimes on the condition that the alleged perpetrators confess, repent, and seek the forgiveness of victims or their families, failure to do which, or to do so genuinely, results in the application of the usual processes of the criminal justice system.

11.1

Both statutory limitation and amnesty, the latter with or without a TRC, raise questions of both international criminal law and general international law[3] when the crime subject to limitation or amnesty is an international crime. The present chapter focuses on these questions, which are essentially twofold—first, whether the state that provides for limited or total impunity in respect of an international crime breaches any obligation it may have under international criminal law or general international law; and, secondly, whether any rule of international criminal law or general international law prohibits a state from prosecuting an alleged perpetrator of an international crime covered by another state's statute of limitations or amnesty.

11.2

---

[1] Reference is also made to statutes of 'limitation', in the singular.
[2] The practice of the early release from prison of persons convicted of certain offences is sometimes also referred to as 'amnesty'. While this practice has at least the potential to implicate certain rules of international law, specifically in the field of human rights, it will not be considered here. The same goes, *mutatis mutandis*, for the practices of pardoning convicted offenders and of according certain state officials for the duration of their office immunity *ratione personae* from the criminal process of the state of which they are officials.
[3] The term 'general international law' is used throughout this chapter to refer not to customary international law as such (to which the term usually refers) but simply to the general corpus of international law beyond the confines of international criminal law.

II. The State Providing for Statutory Limitation or Amnesty

11.3 Whether a state is precluded by international law from providing for statutory limitation or amnesty in respect of all or some international crimes implicates both international criminal law and general international law. Each will be examined in turn. It is crucial to bear in mind, however, that the fact that a state's provision for statutory limitation or amnesty in respect of an international crime may not be prohibited by international criminal law or general international law does not mean that it is not prohibited by international law at all. It may be that international human rights law prohibits it. There are equally situations in which both international criminal law and international human rights law prohibit statutory limitation or amnesty in respect of the same international crime.[4] But while international human rights law is an essential element of the bigger picture, it falls outside the scope of this book.

A. International Criminal Law

11.4 International criminal law has no implications for a state's provision of statutory limitation or amnesty in respect of crimes of a purely municipal provenance.[5] But the permissibility under this body of law of statutes of limitations and amnesties in respect of crimes originating in international law is less straightforward. The first stage of the inquiry is whether there exist any rules of international criminal law, conventional or customary, which expressly prohibit a state from giving effect, in respect of all or specific international crimes, to an otherwise-applicable statute of limitations or amnesty. The second stage is whether, failing this, any such prohibition can be derived from more general obligations under international criminal law.

(i) Express rules

(a) Statutory limitation

11.5 International law itself knows no limitation period in respect of international crimes.[6] The question, however, is whether international law, in the form of either treaty or custom, expressly prohibits states from laying down their own limitation periods in respect of all or specific international crimes. The answer is that neither treaty nor custom expressly prohibits statutory limitation of the prosecution of international crimes per se but that three treaties prohibit

---

[4] Insofar as international human rights law is relevant to statutory limitation or amnesty of an international crime, it is in the latter's quality not as an international crime per se but either as a municipal crime or as an act attributable to the state that is itself a breach of an international human rights obligation binding on that state.

[5] International human rights law, in contrast, imposes relevant obligations in this regard.

[6] See eg the more circumscribed finding to this effect in *Kononov v Latvia* [GC] (Merits and Just Satisfaction), no 36376/04, ECHR 2010, para 232.

statutory limitation of the prosecution of war crimes and crimes against humanity, the latter defined so as to include genocide. As for customary international law on the second point, while the matter is not beyond doubt and the situation arguably fluid, it is likely at present that no settled rule prohibits statutory limitation of the prosecution of war crimes, crimes against humanity, and genocide.

(a) Treaty

11.6 A sole universal multilateral treaty expressly obliges states parties, of which there are only 54, not to provide for statutory limitation of the prosecution of specific international crimes. Article 1 of the Convention on the Non-Applicability of Statutory Limitations to War Crimes and Crimes Against Humanity 1968, adopted by way of annex to UN General Assembly resolution 2391 (XXIII) of 26 November 1968, provides that no statutory limitation shall apply to war crimes or crimes against humanity, the latter being taken to include genocide.

11.7 Article 29 of the Rome Statute of the International Criminal Court ('Rome Statute') stipulates that '[t]he crimes within the jurisdiction of the Court shall not be subject to any statute of limitations'. The provision is perhaps ambiguous on its face. But the fact that the Statute does not oblige states parties to criminalize the crimes within the Court's jurisdiction, as well as the applicability strictly to the Court itself of the provisions found alongside article 29 in Part 3 of the Statute, indicate that article 29 applies only to prosecution and trial by the International Criminal Court (ICC), and this would appear to be how states parties to the Statute read it.[7]

11.8 The Committee against Torture (CAT) recommended in 2006 that France make the crime of torture within the meaning of the Convention against Torture and Other Cruel, Inhuman or Degrading Treatment or Punishment 1984 ('Torture Convention') imprescriptible.[8] But it gave no indication of the basis in the text of the Convention for its purely hortatory statement,[9] which is unsurprising, given that the Convention contains no express prohibition on statutory limitation in relation to the crime of torture for which it provides. Subsequently, in its *General Comment No 2*, the Committee implied that 'impediments which preclude or indicate unwillingness to provide prompt and fair prosecution and

---

[7] See also *infra* para 14.50. For the effect of statutes of limitations and amnesties on the exercise of jurisdiction by the ICC itself, see *infra* paras 14.48 and 14.51.

[8] See UN doc CAT/C/FRA/CO/3 (3 April 2006), para 5.

[9] In addition, in its *General Comment No 3 (2012): Implementation of article 14 by States parties*, UN doc CAT/C/GC/3 (13 December 2012), para 40, the Committee against Torture states that, '[o]n account of the continuous nature of the effects of torture, statutes of limitations should not be applicable as these deprive victims of the redress, compensation, and rehabilitation due to them'. But the reference here is to statutes of limitations barring civil actions for the recovery of damages in respect of torture. See, similarly, *OR, MM & MS v Argentina*, Decision on Admissibility, UN doc A/45/44 (1990), 111, where the Committee stated that Argentina's amnesty laws were contrary to the 'spirit and purpose' of the Torture Convention and urged Argentina not to leave victims without a remedy.

punishment of perpetrators of torture or ill-treatment' violate article 2(2) of the Torture Convention. But all that article 2(2) says is that '[n]o exceptional circumstances whatsoever, whether a state of war or a threat of war, internal political instability or any other public emergency, may be invoked as a justification of torture',[10] and in this regard—even leaving aside that article 2(2) applies only to torture and not also to other ill-treatment—the Committee's suggestion betrays a fundamental confusion between a decision not to prosecute and the invocation of a justification for torture.

11.9   Other universal treaties providing for international crimes regulate but do not prohibit a state party's provision for statutory limitation in relation to the crime or crimes specified in the treaty. The Convention for the Protection of All Persons from Enforced Disappearance 2006—article 5 of which declares that 'the widespread or systematic practice of enforced disappearance constitutes a crime against humanity as defined in applicable international law and shall attract the consequences provided for under such applicable international law'—provides in article 8(1), expressly 'without prejudice to article 5':

A State Party which applies a statute of limitations in respect of enforced disappearance shall take the necessary measures to ensure that the term of limitation for criminal proceedings:
(*a*) Is of long duration and is proportionate to the extreme seriousness of this offence;
(*b*) Commences from the moment when the offence of enforced disappearance ceases, taking into account its continuous nature.[11]

The reference in article 8(1) to the 'continuous nature' of the offence of enforced disappearance is to the common characterization of the crime as ongoing 'as long as the perpetrators continue to conceal the fate and the whereabouts of persons who have disappeared and these facts remain unclarified', in the words of article 17 of the Declaration on the Protection of All Persons from Enforced Disappearance adopted by the General Assembly in 1992.[12] Not dissimilarly, although subject to 'appropriateness', article 29 of the United Nations Convention against Corruption 2003 provides:

Each State Party shall, where appropriate, establish under its domestic law a long statute of limitations period in which to commence proceedings for any offence established in accordance with this Convention and establish a longer statute of limitations period or provide for the suspension of the statute of limitations where the alleged offender has evaded the administration of justice.

The article builds on the closely-analogous rule, which lacks the provision for suspension of the statute of limitations, found in article 3(8) of the United

---

[10] Committee against Torture, *General Comment No 2: Implementation of article 2 by States parties*, UN doc CAT/C/GC/2 (24 January 2008), para 5.
[11] Article 8(2) adds that each state party 'shall guarantee the right of victims of enforced disappearance to an effective remedy during the term of limitation'.
[12] GA res 47/133, 18 December 1992. See also eg *Rodríguez (Miguel Ángel Solís)*, CA Santiago, 5 January 2004 (Chile).

Nations Convention against Illicit Traffic in Narcotic Drugs and Psychotropic Substances 1988 and restated in article 11(5) of the United Nations Convention against Transnational Organized Crime 2000. For its part, article 6 of the OECD Convention on Combating Bribery of Foreign Public Officials in International Business Transactions 1997 states that '[a]ny statute of limitations applicable to the offence of bribery of a foreign public official shall allow an adequate period of time for the investigation and prosecution of this offence'.

As for regional treaties, the seven contracting states to the European Convention on the Non-Applicability of Statutory Limitation to Crimes against Humanity and War Crimes 1974, concluded under the aegis of the Council of Europe, undertake not to apply statutory limitation to the prosecution of 'the crimes against humanity specified in the Convention on the Prevention and Punishment of the Crime of Genocide'[13] or, 'when the specific violation under consideration is of a particularly grave character by reason either of its factual and intentional elements or of the extent of its foreseeable consequences', to the prosecution of war crimes, defined to include both grave breaches of the 1949 Geneva Conventions and such comparable customary war crimes as existed when the Convention entered into force.[14] It is further open to contracting states to extend this obligation, via a declaration under article 6, to 'any other violation of a rule or custom of international law which may hereafter be established and which the Contracting State concerned considers... as being of a comparable nature to those [previously] referred to'.[15] 11.10

As among the 12 member states of the International Conference on the Great Lakes region,[16] the Protocol for the Prevention and Punishment of the Crime of Genocide, War Crimes and Crimes Against Humanity and All Forms of Discrimination 2006, in which the states parties undertake to prevent and punish genocide, war crimes and crimes against humanity,[17] provides in article 11 ('Statutory Limitation') that '[t]he prosecution of persons alleged to have committed the crime of genocide, war crimes, and crimes against humanity, shall not be limited by time'. 11.11

(β) Customary international law
Customary international law does not expressly prohibit a state from providing for statutory limitation in respect of international crimes as such. As for war crimes, 11.12

---

[13] European Convention on the Non-Applicability of Statutory Limitation to Crimes against Humanity and War Crimes 1974, art 1(1).
[14] Ibid, art 1(2). It is not clear whether the entry into force referred to is the Convention's initial entry into force, namely 27 June 2003, or its entry into force for a given contracting state.
[15] Ibid, art 1(3). The word 'hereafter' would seem to refer to the date of the Convention's conclusion, namely 25 January 1974. The Netherlands has made a declaration under art 6 extending the obligation in art 1 of the Convention to grave breaches of 1977 Additional Protocol I.
[16] These are Angola, Burundi, Central African Republic, Republic of Congo, Democratic Republic of the Congo, Kenya, Uganda, Rwanda, Republic of South Sudan, Sudan, Tanzania, and Zambia.
[17] See Protocol for the Prevention and Punishment of the Crime of Genocide, War Crimes and Crimes Against Humanity and All Forms of Discrimination 2006, art 8.

crimes against humanity, and genocide, the relevant state practice and, in particular, the opacity of the associated *opinio juris* provide an insufficient basis on which to conclude categorically that customary international law expressly prohibits a state at present from time-barring the prosecution of these offences, although the claim is not unarguable.

11.13 Article II(5) of Law No 10 (20 December 1945) of the Allied Control Council for Germany ('Control Council Law No 10') on the trial of persons suspected of crimes against peace, war crimes, and crimes against humanity before the respective municipal military tribunals of the four Allied Powers in occupation of Germany—exercising, as they saw it, the sovereign authority of Germany itself[18]—stated:

> In any trial or prosecution for a crime herein referred to, the accused shall not be entitled to the benefits of any statute of limitation in relation to the period 30 January 1933 to 1 July 1945...

There is no indication, however, that the four Powers saw this unavailability of statutory limitation as reflective of an obligation under customary international law. Nor was it suggested by more than two states[19] when the UN General Assembly adopted the Convention on the Non-Applicability of Statutory Limitations to War Crimes and Crimes Against Humanity[20] that the fundamental rule embodied in the Convention was declaratory of custom. Nonetheless, in its judgment of 1997 in *Hass and Priebke*, the Military Court of Rome concluded:

> [I]t can be seen that the Convention adopted by the United Nations General Assembly by way of resolution 2391 (XXIII) of 26 November 1968 solemnly affirmed as a matter of international law the principle of the imprescriptibility of war crimes and crimes against humanity; that this act by the United Nations clearly represents the culmination of a slow but continuous progress at the international level... towards the more effective suppression of violations of the laws and customs of war; and that within this body of law the principle of the imprescriptibility of war crimes and crimes against humanity enjoys

---

[18] Recall *supra* para 2.59.

[19] See UN doc A/C.3/SR.1518 (17 November 1967), para 5 (Bulgaria); UN doc A/C.3/SR.1514 (14 November 1967), paras 37–39 and UN doc A/C.3/SR.1567 (10 October 1968), para 22 (Czechoslovakia).

[20] The Convention was adopted by a margin of only 56:7:36. The voting patterns for GA resolutions 2583 (XXIV) of 15 December 1969, 2712 (XXV) of 15 December 1970, and 2840 (XXVI) of 18 December 1971, all of which invite states that have not done so to become parties to the Convention and two of which express the hope that states that were unable to vote for the adoption of the Convention will refrain from action running counter to its main purposes, also reveal a degree of division. This division related in part to the inclusion of 'inhuman acts resulting from the policy of apartheid' within art 1(*b*)'s understanding of crimes against humanity and in part to the availability of statutory limitation as a general principle of certain states' criminal law. As for the fact that the Convention has a mere 54 states parties, this has no formal bearing on whether the rules posited in it have since come to reflect customary international law. It is also worth keeping in mind that common-law states tend not to impose limitation periods in the first place for crimes or at least for crimes of a certain gravity. This perhaps makes the participation of such states in the Convention inherently less likely.

the objective character of 'jus cogens' insofar as it contributes to the protection of the collective interests of international society.[21]

The Court's assertions are wildly optimistic,[22] and the existence of the European Convention on the Non-Applicability of Statutory Limitations to War Crimes and Crimes Against Humanity does nothing to change this. For their part, the Basic Principles and Guidelines on the Right to a Remedy and Reparation for Victims of Gross Violations of International Human Rights Law and Serious Violations of International Humanitarian Law, adopted by the UN General Assembly in 2005,[23] state that, '[w]here so provided for in an applicable treaty or contained in other international legal obligations, statutes of limitations shall not apply to gross violations of international human rights law and serious violations of international humanitarian law which constitute crimes under international law'.[24] But the reference to 'other international legal obligations' simply begs the question.

In terms of contemporary legislative practice, quite a few states whose criminal justice systems embody statutory limitation periods disapply such statutes in cases of either war crimes or crimes against humanity (the latter often defined to encompass genocide) or both;[25] and, where this is not the case, some national courts have ruled that customary international law compels such disapplication.[26] But the tendency is not overwhelming. Moreover, many of the states in question are parties to the Convention on the Non-Applicability of Statutory Limitations to War Crimes and Crimes Against Humanity, and whether what practice of non-states parties there is stems from a conviction that customary international law requires it is often hard to tell. As for the statutes of special municipal courts vested with jurisdiction over international crimes, article 17(4) of the Law on the Iraqi High Criminal Court, taken directly from the statute drafted for what was then the Iraqi Special Tribunal by the Coalition Provisional Authority in 2003, provides that the crimes over which the Tribunal is granted jurisdiction in articles 11 to 14, *viz* genocide, crimes against humanity, war crimes, and certain crimes against Iraqi law, 'shall not be subject to any statute of limitations'. In contrast, the Law on the Establishment

11.14

---

[21] *Hass and Priebke*, Military Court of Rome, 22 July 1997, para 1.1.14(*d*).
[22] All the same, the decision of the Military Court of Rome was upheld by the Military Court of Appeal on 7 March 1998 and by the Italian Court of Cassation on 16 November 1998.
[23] Recall *supra* n 4.
[24] Basic Principles and Guidelines on the Right to a Remedy and Reparation for Victims of Gross Violations of International Human Rights Law and Serious Violations of International Humanitarian Law, GA res 60/147, 16 December 2005, para 6.
[25] See eg J-M Henckaerts and L Doswald-Beck (eds), *Customary International Humanitarian Law. Volume II: Practice. Part 2* (Cambridge: Cambridge University Press, 2005), 4047–52. See also art 8 of Belgium's Law of 16 June 1993 as amended by the Law of 23 April 2003 on the repression of serious violations of international humanitarian law and art 144*ter* of the Judicial Code.
[26] See *Pinochet*, 119 ILR 345, 357–8 (Belgium 1998); *Pinto (Victor Raúl) v Relatives of Tomás Rojas*, ILDC 1093 (CL 2007), paras 30–31 (Chile). See also, by way of *obiter dictum*, *Fujimori v Attorney-General*, ILDC 1516 (PE 2009), para 711 (Peru).

of Extraordinary Chambers in the Courts of Cambodia for the Prosecution of Crimes Committed During the Period of Democratic Kampuchea, as amended in 2004, stipulates only that genocide and crimes against humanity shall not be subject to any statute of limitations.[27] It is silent on—and, in accordance with the canon of construction *expressio unius exclusio alterius*, would therefore seem to permit—the availability of statutory limitation as regards grave breaches of the Geneva Conventions, destruction of cultural property contrary to the Hague Convention on the Protection of Cultural Property in the Event of Armed Conflict 1954 ('1954 Hague Convention'), and crimes against internationally protected persons contrary to the Vienna Convention on Diplomatic Relations 1961 ('VCDR').[28] For its part, the Statute of the Extraordinary African Chambers in the Senegalese Courts provides that the crimes within the Chambers' jurisdiction, namely genocide, crimes against humanity, war crimes, and torture, are imprescriptible.[29]

11.15   When it comes to the practice of the UN, as distinct from its member states, UNTAET regulation 2000/15 of 6 June 2000, promulgated by the UN Transitional Authority for East Timor and providing for special panels within the District Court of Dili for the prosecution of serious crimes, provides in section 17.1 that genocide, crimes against humanity, war crimes, and torture may not be subject to any statute of limitations.

(b) **Amnesty**

11.16   No treaty expressly prohibits a state from granting amnesty in relation to international crimes generally or specific international crimes, and it is difficult to conclude that customary international law does so either, although the second proposition is not untenable when it comes to war crimes and crimes against humanity, the latter defined to embrace genocide.

(a) Treaty

11.17   Article 6(5) of 1977 Additional Protocol II to the 1949 Geneva Conventions, applicable to non-international armed conflict, states:

At the end of hostilities, the authorities in power shall endeavour to grant the broadest possible amnesty to persons who have participated in the armed conflict, or those deprived

---

[27] See Law on the Establishment of Extraordinary Chambers in the Courts of Cambodia for the Prosecution of Crimes Committed During the Period of Democratic Kampuchea (as amended), arts 4 and 5.

[28] See ibid, arts 6–8.

[29] Statut des Chambres extraordinaires africaines au sein des juridictions sénégalaises pour la poursuite des crimes internationaux commis au Tchad durant la période du 7 juin 1982 au 1 décembre 1990 ('Statute of the Extraordinary African Chambers in the Senegalese Courts for the Prosecution of International Crimes Committed in Chad During the Period from 7 June 1982 to 1 December 1990'), art 9 (author's translation). See, in this connection, *Habré c Sénégal*, Case No ECW/CCJ/RUL/05/13, Judgment, 5 November 2013, para 43 (author's translation), for a fleeting reference, wholly *obiter*, by the Community Court of Justice of the Economic Community of West African States (ECOWAS) to the international crimes within the jurisdiction of the Extraordinary African Chambers as being 'considered grave, punishable and imprescriptible by the law of nations'.

of their liberty for reasons related to the armed conflict, whether they are interned or detained.

It is generally accepted, however, that article 6(5) refers to the grant of amnesty to former insurgents for purely municipal offences founded on mere participation in hostilities, such as treason, or on homicide, wounding, destruction of property, and the like carried out as an ordinary and internationally-lawful incident of hostilities.[30]

In its *General Comment No 2*, the Committee against Torture referred specifically to amnesties as one of the 'impediments which preclude or indicate unwillingness to provide prompt and fair prosecution and punishment of perpetrators of torture or ill-treatment' that the Committee considered a violation of article 2(2) of the Convention.[31] Again, however, the Committee confuses a decision not to prosecute with the invocation of a justification for torture.[32]   11.18

(β) Customary international law
No rule of customary international law expressly prohibits the amnesty of international crimes as such, and state practice is too inconsistent and the accompanying *opinio juris* too hard to discern to justify the confident conclusion at present that any such rule expressly prohibits amnesty in respect of war crimes, crimes against humanity, and genocide, even if the latter is not out of the question.   11.19

In paragraph III of the Declaration of Amnesty[33] annexed to the Treaty of Lausanne 1923, the British Empire, France, Greece, Italy, Japan, Romania, and Turkey provided for '[f]ull and complete amnesty... for all crimes or offences committed during the [period 1 August 1914 to 20 November 1922] which were evidently connected with the political events which have taken place during that period'. That is, they provided for amnesty in respect of, *inter alia*, violations of the laws and customs of war and, more significantly, atrocities against civilian populations committed in connection with the First World War and the subsequent Greco-Turkish War. In contrast, article II(5) of Control Council Law No 10 (1945) stated that '[no] amnesty granted under the Nazi regime [shall] be admitted as a bar to trial or punishment', although there is nothing to suggest that the Four Powers saw the unavailability of amnesty for war crimes and crimes against humanity as a requirement of customary international law.   11.20

---

[30] See eg J-M Henckaerts and L Doswald-Beck (eds), *Customary International Humanitarian Law. Volume I: Rules* (Cambridge: Cambridge University Press, 2005), 612; UK Ministry of Defence, *The Manual of the Law of Armed Conflict* (Oxford: Oxford University Press, 2004), 403, para 15.42 n 97; D Fleck (ed), *The Handbook of International Humanitarian Law* (3rd edn, Oxford: Oxford University Press, 2013), 609. See also *The Massacres of El Mozote and Nearby Places v El Salvador*, Judgment, 25 October 2012, Inter-Am Ct HR (Ser C), para 286; *Pinto* (n 26), para 20. But cf *Azanian People's Organization (AZAPO) v President of the Republic of South Africa*, 131 ILR 492, 511–12, para 30 (South Africa 1996).
[31] Recall *supra* n 9.   [32] Recall *supra* para 11.8.
[33] Lausanne, 24 July 1923, 28 LNTS 145.

11.21 There are many, more recent instances of provision by states for blanket amnesty capable of extending to international crimes.[34] There are also numerous examples to the contrary,[35] and some municipal courts have held that customary international law prohibits amnesty in respect of either or both crimes against humanity[36] and war crimes.[37]

11.22 Although the non-binding Declaration on the Protection of All Persons from Enforced Disappearance, adopted by the UN General Assembly in 1992, provides that persons who have committed or are alleged to have committed the crime of enforced disappearance 'shall not benefit from any special amnesty law or similar measures that might have the effect of exempting them from any criminal proceedings or sanction',[38] the binding Convention on the Protection of All Persons from Enforced Disappearance, concluded by the General Assembly 14 years later, contains no provision on amnesty in respect of the crime of enforced disappearance. Quite simply, no agreement could be reached to this effect.[39] Not dissimilarly, Security Council resolutions tend to avoid the language of binding legal obligation

---

[34] L Mallinder, 'Can Amnesties and International Justice be Reconciled?' (2007) 1 *IJTJ* 208, 214, puts at 24 the number of amnesties since 1999 alone that extend to international crimes. By way of example, Uganda, in its Amnesty Act 2000, granted a blanket amnesty, capable of covering international crimes, to any member of the Lord's Resistance Army or any other insurgent who surrendered. (The Amnesty (Amendment) Act 2006 authorizes the Minister of Internal Affairs to certify named individuals as ineligible for amnesty, but such certification requires parliamentary approval for its effect, an approval the Ugandan parliament has been reluctant to give.) In *Thomas Kwoyelo, alias Latoni v Uganda*, Constitutional Court of Uganda, 22 September 2011 (available at http://www.icrc.org/ihl-nat), in dismissing the Ugandan Attorney-General's submission, *contra proferentem*, that 'the blanket amnesty which is granted under the Amnesty Act is in violation of Uganda's international law obligations' (ibid, thirteenth unnumbered page), the Constitutional Court of Uganda observed that it had 'not come across any uniform international standards or practices which prohibit states from granting amnesty' (ibid, seventeenth unnumbered page). For other examples, see Henckaerts and Doswald Beck (n 25), 4018–27; M Freeman, *Necessary Evils: Amnesties and the Search for Justice* (Cambridge: Cambridge University Press, 2011); F Lessa and LA Payne (eds), *Amnesty in the Age of Human Rights Accountability: Comparative and International Perspectives* (Cambridge: Cambridge University Press, 2012); F Lessa *et al*, 'Persistent or Eroding Impunity? The Divergent Effects of Legal Challenges to Amnesty Laws for Past Human Rights Violations' (2014) 47 *Israel LR* 105.

[35] Mallinder (n 34), 214, puts the figure at 29. In addition to those discussed *infra* para 11.23, see eg art VI ('Amnesty') of the Agreement on Refugees and Displaced Persons annexed to the General Framework Agreement for Peace in Bosnia and Herzegovina, UN doc A/50/790–S/1995/999 (30 November 1995), Attachment, Annex 7, excluding from the scope of amnesty crimes within the jurisdiction of the ICTY; Constitution of Ethiopia (1994), art 28(1), denying organs of state the power to grant amnesty in respect of crimes against humanity. It is also worth recalling the substance of the government of Uganda's position in *Kwoyelo* (n 34), as reiterated in an interview later given by the Director of Public Prosecutions, that 'amnesty is inapplicable to international crimes'. See SMH Nouwen, *Complementarity in the Line of Fire. The Catalysing Effect of the International Criminal Court in Uganda and Sudan* (Cambridge: Cambridge University Press, 2013), 217.

[36] See *Office of the Prosecutor v Priebke*, ILDC 1599 (AR 1995), paras 4 and 5, *Chile v Arancibia Clavel*, ILDC 1082 (AR 2004), paras 28 and 32, and *Riveros v Office of the Public Prosecutor*, ILDC 1084 (AR 2007), para 28 (Argentina); *Pinochet* (n 26), 358 (Belgium).

[37] See *Pinto* (n 26), para 30.

[38] Declaration on the Protection of All Persons from Enforced Disappearance, para 18.

[39] The absence of such a provision is without prejudice, however, to any consequences which may flow from art 5's characterization of widespread or systematic enforced disappearance (or, as it should be, enforced disappearance committed as part of a widespread or systematic attack against a civilian population) as a crime against humanity.

when referring to amnesty for international crimes. For example, Security Council resolution 1325 (2000) emphasizes the 'responsibility' of states to prosecute those responsible for genocide, crimes against humanity, and war crimes, and stresses the 'need' to exclude these crimes, 'where feasible', from amnesty provisions.[40] Likewise, Security Council resolution 1820 (2008), noting that rape and other forms of sexual violence can constitute a war crime, a crime against humanity, and a material element of the crime of genocide, stresses the 'need' for the exclusion of crimes of sexual violence from amnesty provisions adopted in the context of conflict-resolution processes.[41]

The consistent practice of the UN Secretariat when brokering or sponsoring peace agreements and when undertaking to lend states assistance with transitional justice is to insist on the exclusion of amnesty for international crimes.[42] For example, article III of the Comprehensive Agreement on Human Rights of 29 March 1994 between the Government of Guatemala and the *Unidad Revolucionaria Nacional Guatemalteca*, brokered by the Organization, provides that the Guatemalan government 'shall not sponsor the adoption of legislative or any other type of measures designed to prevent the prosecution and punishment of persons responsible for human rights violations'; and pursuant to this, in accordance with section 8 of Guatemala's National Reconciliation Law 1996, the amnesty granted to those who participated in the civil war does not extend to 'crimes of genocide, torture and enforced disappearances, as well as those crimes for which a statute of limitations does not apply or those for which extinction of criminal responsibility cannot be admitted in accordance with Guatemalan internal legislation or international treaties ratified by Guatemala'. In a similar vein, although the peace agreement signed between the government of Sierra Leone and the RUF in Lomé, Togo, on 7 July 1999 ('Lomé Agreement' or 'Lomé Accord')[43] contains amnesty provisions in respect of crimes committed during the civil war in Sierra Leone, the preamble to Security Council resolution 1315 (2000) recalls 'that the Special Representative

11.23

---

[40] SC res 1325 (2000), 31 October 2000, para 11. The formula 'responsibility [to do something]'—as opposed to 'obligation [to do something]', 'duty [to do something]' or the classic 'shall [do something]', and as opposed to 'responsibility [for having done something]', the latter being international legal terminology for 'liability [for having done something]'—is standard diplomatic code within UN organs and specialized agencies for denoting something other than an international legal obligation. Compare eg the *soi-disant* 'responsibility to protect'.

[41] SC res 1820 (2008), 19 June 2008, para 4.

[42] See eg *The rule of law and transitional justice in conflict and post-conflict societies: Report of the Secretary-General*, UN doc S/2004/616 (23 August 2004), 5, para 10 and *The rule of law and transitional justice in conflict and post-conflict societies: Report of the Secretary-General*, UN doc S/2001/634 (12 October 2011), 5, para 12. See also the practice of the UN High Commissioner for Refugees (UNHCR) in relation to art 3(c) of the Quadripartite Agreement on Voluntary Return of Refugees and Displaced Persons concluded on 4 April 1994 among UNCHR, Russia, and the Abkhaz and Georgian sides to the conflict in Georgia; and the policy of the UN High Commissioner for Human Rights (UNHCHR) as stated in Office of the United Nations High Commissioner for Human Rights, *Rule-of-Law Tools for Post-Conflict States: Amnesties* (New York/Geneva: United Nations, 2009), UN doc HR/PUB/09/01.

[43] UN doc S/1999/777. The Lomé Agreement was reaffirmed at a meeting of ECOWAS, the UN, the government of Sierra Leone, and the RUF held in Abuja, Nigeria, on 2 May 2001.

of the Secretary-General appended to his signature of the Lomé Agreement a statement that the United Nations holds the understanding that the amnesty provisions of the Agreement shall not apply to international crimes of genocide, crimes against humanity, war crimes and other serious violations of international humanitarian law'.[44] The UN's understanding of the Lomé Agreement is reflected in article 10 ('Amnesty') of the Statute of the Special Court for Sierra Leone,[45] established pursuant to the Agreement of 16 January 2002 between the United Nations and the Government of Sierra Leone on the Establishment of a Special Court for Sierra Leone. Article 10 states that '[a]n amnesty granted to any person falling within the jurisdiction of the Special Court in respect of the crimes referred to in articles 2 to 4 of the present Statute shall not be a bar to prosecution'.[46] Explaining the arrangement to the Security Council, the report of the Secretary-General on the establishment of a Special Court for Sierra Leone (SCSL) states:

> While recognizing that amnesty is an accepted legal concept and a gesture of peace and reconciliation at the end of a civil war or an internal armed conflict, the United Nations has consistently maintained the position that amnesty cannot be granted in respect of international crimes, such as genocide, crimes against humanity or other serious violations of international humanitarian law.[47]

The Secretary-General characterizes article 10 of the SCSL Statute as 'the denial of legal effect to the amnesty granted at Lomé, to the extent of its illegality under international law'.[48] For its part, article 11 ('Amnesty') of the Agreement of 6 June 2003 between the United Nations and the Royal Government of Cambodia concerning the Prosecution under Cambodian Law of Crimes committed during the Period of Democratic Kampuchea, the treaty which paved the way for co-operation between the UN and the Extraordinary Chambers in the Courts of Cambodia for the Prosecution of Crimes Committed During the Period of Democratic Kampuchea, provides that the government of Cambodia 'shall not request an amnesty...for any persons who may be investigated for...crimes referred to in the present Agreement'.[49] The crimes referred to in the agreement

---

[44] SC res 1315 (2000), 14 August 2000, preamble (sixth recital).
[45] While commonly referred to as a 'mixed' criminal tribunal, the SCSL is formally an international criminal court, so that it would not have been bound by any Sierra Leonean amnesty law anyway. See *supra* paras 3.18–3.20 and *infra* para 13.6.
[46] Likewise, in art 16 ('Amnesty') of the Agreement between the United Nations and the Lebanese Republic on the establishment of a Special Tribunal for Lebanon (STL), 23 January/6 February 2007, annexed to SC res 1757 (2007), 30 May 2007, the government of Lebanon undertakes not to grant amnesty to any person for any crime falling within the jurisdiction of the STL, an international criminal court. The provision further specifies that any amnesty already so granted shall not pose a bar to prosecution. The latter is backed up by art 6 ('Amnesty') of the Statute of the Tribunal, attached to the Agreement. These provisions, however, are not directly relevant to the present inquiry, since the Tribunal does not enjoy jurisdiction over international crimes.
[47] *Report of the Secretary-General on the establishment of a Special Court for Sierra Leone*, UN doc S/2000/915 (4 October 2000), para 22.
[48] Ibid, para 24.
[49] Article 11(1) also prohibits the Cambodian government from requesting a pardon for persons convicted of any such crime. Article 11(2) states: 'This provision is based upon a declaration by the Royal Government of Cambodia that until now, with regard to matters covered in the law,

comprise, in addition to certain serious municipal crimes, the crime of genocide, crimes against humanity, grave breaches of the Geneva Conventions, and, by reference to the relevant Cambodian statute, the destruction of cultural property contrary to the 1954 Hague Convention and crimes against internationally protected persons contrary to the VCDR. By way of final example,[50] the parties to the AU and UN-brokered Doha Document for Peace in Darfur 2011 agree in article 60 that 'war crimes, crimes against humanity, crimes of genocide, crimes of sexual violence, and gross violations of human rights and humanitarian law shall not be included in the scope of application of the amnesty [to be granted in accordance with the provision]'.[51] With all these examples, however, it pays to bear in mind that the practice of the UN Secretariat is not to be equated with the practice and *opinio juris* of the UN's member states and, moreover, that what a state does as the price of UN involvement in a peace process need not reflect

---

there has been only one case, dated 14 September 1996, when a pardon was granted to only one person with regard to a 1979 conviction on the charge of genocide. The United Nations and the Royal Government of Cambodia agree that the scope of this pardon is a matter to be decided by the Extraordinary Chambers.' The Extraordinary Chambers are part of the municipal criminal courts of Cambodia. See *supra* paras 3.34 and 9.62–9.63.

[50] In addition to the examples in the text, consider the following. First, while art 8(1)(*b*) of Protocol I to the Arusha Peace and Reconciliation Agreement for Burundi, 28 August 2000, to which the UN Secretary-General was one of the many signatories, provides that the transitional National Assembly 'may pass a law or laws providing a framework for granting an amnesty consistent with international law for such political crimes as it or the National Truth and Reconciliation Commission may find appropriate', para 1 of art 18 ('Combating impunity during the transition') of Protocol II states that, in accordance with Protocol I to the Agreement, 'the transitional Government shall request the establishment of an International Judicial Commission of Inquiry which will investigate acts of genocide, war crimes and other crimes against humanity and report thereon to the Security Council of the United Nations'. The reference to Protocol I is to para 10 of art 6 ('Principles and measures relating to genocide, war crimes and other crimes against humanity') of that instrument. In art 6(1) of Protocol I, the parties to the agreement undertake to combat 'the impunity of crimes', and art 6(11) provides for a request by the government of Burundi 'for the establishment by the United Nations Security Council of an international criminal tribunal to try and punish those responsible should the findings of the [International Judicial Commission's] report point to the existence of acts of genocide, war crimes and other crimes against humanity'. Secondly, art VII(5) of the Annex to the Linas-Marcoussis Agreement of 23 January 2003 between the warring factions in Côte d'Ivoire, on the monitoring committee for which sat a special representative of the Secretary-General, provides: 'The Government of National Reconciliation will take the necessary steps to ensure the release and amnesty of all military personnel detained on charges of threatening State security and will extend the benefit of these measures to soldiers living in exile. The amnesty law will under no circumstances mean that those having committed serious economic violations and serious violations of human rights and international humanitarian law will go unpunished.' The Linas-Marcoussis Agreement, which was unsuccessful in bringing to an end the conflict in Côte d'Ivoire, was followed by the similarly fruitless, ECOWAS-brokered Ouagadougou Political Agreement, 4 March 2007, contained in UN doc S/2007/144 (13 March 2007), art 6(3) ('Amnesty law') of which extended the scope of a 2003 amnesty law but maintained an exception in relation to 'economic crimes, war crimes and crimes against humanity'. Thirdly, on 26 July 2007 a spokesperson for the Secretary-General announced that the UN would boycott a commission set up jointly by Indonesia and Timor-Leste to promote reconciliation between their peoples unless it was precluded from recommending amnesty for, *inter alia*, crimes against humanity. It was stated that 'the Organization cannot endorse or condone amnesties for genocide, crimes against humanity, war crimes or gross violations of human rights, nor should it do anything that might foster them'. See UN doc SG/SM/11101 (26 July 2007).

[51] For the circumstances leading to the insertion of this clause, see Nouwen (n 35), 318–19.

11.24 In the end, as things presently stand, and despite the assertion of Judge Robertson of the SCSL in *Kondewa* that customary international law 'invalidates [*sic*] amnesties offered under any circumstances to persons most responsible' for crimes against humanity (taken to include genocide and 'widespread torture') and 'the worst war crimes',[52] it is unclear whether there exists an express customary international prohibition to this effect. Certainly no such prohibition exists in respect of international crimes per se.

(ii) Derivation from other rules

11.25 The current likely absence of any express rules—apart from those on statutory limitation in the one universal and two regional multilateral treaties[53]—rendering impermissible statutes of limitations and amnesties in respect of international crimes does not mean that such a prohibition cannot be derived from other rules of international criminal law. If one proceeds this way, the international legality of statutory limitation and amnesty for international crimes depends on the type of international crime, and even on the particular international crime, in question.

11.26 Some commentators point in this connection to the sixth recital of the preamble to the Rome Statute, in which states parties recall 'that it is the duty of every State to exercise its criminal jurisdiction over those responsible for international crimes'. But this vague prefatory recollection is an insufficient hook on which to hang an argument that either the Statute itself or customary international law prohibits statutes of limitations or amnesties in respect of the crimes within the Court's jurisdiction.

11.27 As regards crimes under customary international law, given that their prosecution is not mandatory, a state does not—absent any express prohibition—breach international law by providing for their statutory limitation or amnesty.

11.28 As for treaty crimes subject to the conventional obligation *aut dedere aut judicare*, at least in its standard formulation, the international lawfulness of statutes of limitations, on the one hand, and of amnesties, on the other, tends in practice to differ, although in principle need not. In this regard, it pays to recall that, in accordance with the '*judicare*' limb of the usual wording of the obligation *aut dedere aut judicare*, a state party is required not to prosecute as such but, rather, to submit the case to its competent authorities for the purpose of prosecution and to ensure that these authorities take the decision whether or not to prosecute 'in the same manner as in the case of any ordinary offence of a serious nature under the law of that State'.[54] When it comes to amnesty, its grant will tend to be incompatible with this

---

[52] *Prosecutor v Kondewa*, SCSL-2004-14-AR72(E), Appeals Chamber, Decision on Lack of Jurisdiction/Abuse of Process: Amnesty Provided by Lomé Accord, 25 May 2004, sep op Robertson, para 51.

[53] Recall *supra* paras 11.6 and 11.10 respectively.   [54] Recall *supra* paras 8.48 and 8.51.

framing of the obligation *aut dedere aut judicare*,⁵⁵ although for reasons more complicated than the glib one usually asserted, namely that there is an obligation to prosecute.⁵⁶ In practice, when an amnesty is in place, the state will simply not submit cases of the relevant offence to its authorities for prosecution, in clear breach of its treaty obligation to do so. In the event that it does go through the motions of submitting a case, things are more nuanced, although ultimately no less unlawful in most conceivable instances. The key is that politically-inspired amnesties tend in practice to apply only to crimes allegedly committed in connection with the past political or military situation, leaving any other alleged commission of the same offence open to prosecution. This differentiation violates the state's obligation to ensure that its authorities take the decision whether or not to prosecute in the same manner as in the case of any ordinary offence of a serious nature under the law of that state. When it comes, in contrast, to statutes of limitations, these usually apply across the board to crimes allegedly committed for whatever reason, so that it cannot usually be said that a decision not to prosecute a statute-barred treaty crime is taken in a manner different from the case of any ordinary offence of a serious nature under the law of the state in question. As long as the state submits the offence to its authorities for the purpose of prosecution, it does not fall foul of the obligation *aut dedere aut judicare*. The difference, however, between amnesty and statutory limitation disappears—at least where in both cases the state goes to the trouble of submitting the case to its competent authorities for the purpose of prosecution—in the event that the state, albeit it for the purpose of barring the prosecution of crimes committed in a specific context, enacts a general amnesty, applicable to all crimes of commensurate seriousness committed, for whatever purpose, over a given period.

In the specific case of the treaty crime of genocide, the obligation to punish the offence in article I of the Convention on the Prevention and Punishment of the Crime of Genocide 1948 would seem to render internationally unlawful both its statutory limitation and amnesty.⁵⁷

11.29

---

⁵⁵ Contrast, possibly, the vaguer formulation in the grave breaches provisions of the 1949 Geneva Conventions. Consider, in this regard, the rejection by the Constitutional Court of Uganda in *Kwoyelo v Uganda* (n 34), seventeenth unnumbered page, of the government's argument (ibid, twelfth to thirteenth unnumbered pages) that amnesty was incompatible with the grave breaches provisions of the Conventions. But cf Criminal Case File No 002/19-09-2007-ECCC/OCIJ (PTC 75) (*Ieng Sary*), Pre-Trial Chamber, Decision on Ieng Sary's Appeal against the Closing Order, 11 April 2011, para 201; *Marguš v Croatia* [GC] (Merits and Just Satisfaction), no 4455/10, ECHR 2014, para 132.

⁵⁶ See eg *Prosecutor v Kallon & Kamara*, SCSL-2004-15-AR72(E) & SCSL-2004-16-AR72(E), Appeals Chamber, Decision on Challenge to Jurisdiction: Lomé Accord Amnesty, 13 March 2004, para 73; *Ieng Sary*, Pre-Trial Chamber Decision on Ieng Sary's Appeal against the Closing Order (n 55), para 201; *Marguš* (n 55), para 132; *Pinto* (n 26), paras 16–17; DF Orentlicher, 'Settling Accounts: The Duty to Prosecute Human Rights Violations of a Prior Regime' (1991) 100 *Yale LJ* 2537, 2566–7.

⁵⁷ See also *Ieng Sary*, Pre-Trial Chamber Decision on Ieng Sary's Appeal against the Closing Order (n 55), para 201. Consider in the same light the undertaking to punish genocide, war crimes, and crimes against humanity in art 8 of the Great Lakes Pact's Protocol for the Prevention and Punishment of the Crime of Genocide, War Crimes and Crimes Against Humanity and All Forms of Discrimination.

B. General International Law

11.30   It is often said that the status of a given international criminal prohibition as a norm of *jus cogens* means that any municipal statute of limitations or amnesty in respect of that crime is internationally unlawful.[58] But even leaving aside whether, as a conceptual matter, international criminal prohibitions are capable of constituting *jus cogens*,[59] the hypothetical peremptory status of an international criminal prohibition has no logical implications for the international legality of a statute of limitations or amnesty in respect of that crime. The non-derogability of an international criminal prohibition would mean that under no circumstances could it permissibly be set aside, explicitly or by implication, as inapplicable *ex ante* to an individual to whom it would otherwise apply. Non-derogability would not necessitate that a state in all circumstances prosecute alleged breaches of an applicable prohibition. To say that prosecution is time-barred or barred by an amnesty or even to say *ex post* that an individual is not criminally responsible is not to say that the proscription did not bind the individual to begin with. In this regard, the reasoning relied on by the ICJ in *Jurisdictional Immunities of the State* to dismiss *jus cogens*-based arguments for the abrogation of procedural immunity is applicable, *mutatis mutandis*, to statutory limitation and amnesty, particularly insofar as the Court recast its decision in *Arrest Warrant* on immunity from prosecution for international crimes as a rejection of the argument that the putative peremptory character of an international criminal prohibition makes a difference.[60]

11.31   Many international crimes can, when committed by a state official, additionally constitute violations of international human rights law for which the state in question will be internationally responsible. Similarly, independently of the parallel international criminal prohibitions, states bear conventional and customary obligations under international humanitarian law, conventional and customary obligations not to commit acts of genocide, and a customary obligation not to commit acts of aggression,[61] breach of any of which results in state responsibility. Insofar as a state's responsibility imposes a secondary obligation on it to make reparation for any injury caused by its breach, it may be that an appropriate modality of reparation, particularly in respect of any breach of international human rights law, international humanitarian law, the prohibition on state genocide, and the prohibition on acts of aggression amounting in parallel to an international crime, is satisfaction in the form of the prosecution of the state official or officials whose attributable act or acts constituted the breach.[62] Were an obligation to afford satisfaction in the

---

[58] See eg *Prosecutor v Furundžija*, IT-95-17/1, Trial Chamber, Judgment, 10 December 1998, paras 155 (amnesty) and 157 (statute of limitations), in relation to the prohibition on torture.

[59] Recall *supra* paras 2.79–2.81.

[60] Recall *supra* para 10.89, discussing *Jurisdictional Immunities of the State (Germany v Italy: Greece intervening), Judgment*, ICJ Rep 2012, 99.

[61] Recall *supra* para 2.77.

[62] See Articles on Responsibility of States for Internationally Wrongful Acts, GA res 56/83, 12 December 2001, Annex ('Articles on Responsibility of States'), art 37, especially art 37(2), speaking of 'another appropriate modality'. As outlined in para 5 of the ILC's commentary to art 37, *Ybk ILC*

form of prosecution to arise, the responsible state could not evade it by pointing to a statute of limitations or amnesty applicable under the municipal law of that state.[63] It would be obliged by international law to prosecute regardless.

III. Foreign Prosecuting States

International law does not prohibit the prosecution of an international crime statute-barred or amnestied in one state by any foreign state with concurrent prescriptive jurisdiction over that crime. The exercise by a state of a prescriptive jurisdiction authorized by international law, whether customary or conventional, cannot constitute a violation of the customary international prohibition on a state's intervention in the domestic affairs of another. This is doubly so where both states are parties to a convention obliging the extension of jurisdiction over the crime and the prosecution, failing extradition, of persons suspected of its commission.[64] In the latter case, the foreign state will be treaty-bound, failing extradition, to prosecute. Nor does such prosecution violate the principle *ne bis in idem* guaranteed by international human rights law, which applies only in respect of offences for which a person has already been convicted or acquitted and only to proceedings within the same state.[65] As for municipal law, it is self-evident that the courts of one state are not bound by the legislation of another state. 11.32

There is a variety of state practice to the above effect (although not all of it[66] referable to what international law may say on the matter). In the *Pinochet* proceedings commenced in 1998, Spain sought Senator Pinochet's arrest pursuant to the Torture Convention despite the amnesty he enjoyed in Chile, where the criminal acts of torture were alleged to have taken place. The UK government, which initiated proceedings for Senator Pinochet's extradition on receipt of Spain's request, was equally content to ignore the Chilean amnesty. In 2002, in the case of *Ould Dah*,[67] involving allegations of torture in Mauritania by an officer in the Mauritanian army, the French Court of Cassation held that a Mauritanian amnesty law was inapplicable in the French criminal courts, since it would deprive of all substance the jurisdiction granted them by articles 689-1 and 689-2 of the Code of Criminal Procedure, which gave effect to the universal jurisdiction mandated by the Torture Convention. In 2007, in the case of *Public Prosecutor v F*, the District 11.33

2001, vol II/2, 106, one such modality may be 'penal action against the individuals whose conduct caused the internationally wrongful act'.

[63] See, among many others, *Alabama Claims Arbitration (United States of America/United Kingdom)*, 1 Moore Int Arb 653, 656 (1872).
[64] But cf *R v Bow Street Metropolitan Stipendiary Magistrate, ex parte Pinochet Ugarte (No 1)*, 119 ILR 50, 90–3 (Lord Lloyd, wrongly (UK 1998). Note that *Pinochet (No 1)* was subsequently annulled in *R v Bow Street Metropolitan Stipendiary Magistrate, ex parte Pinochet Ugarte (No 2)*, 119 ILR 112 (UK 1999), with the result that it cannot be counted for the purposes of state practice.
[65] Recall *supra* para 1.72.
[66] See eg *South Africa v Basson*, ILDC 494 (ZA 2005), paras 239–46 (South Africa).
[67] *Ould Dah*, no 6228, Court of Cassation, 23 October 2002 (France).

Court of The Hague ruled that the prosecution of an Afghan for the war crime of torture was not barred by an amnesty in Afghanistan.[68] For its part, the Statute of the Extraordinary African Chambers in the Senegalese Courts, which regulates the investigation and prosecution of the former dictator of Chad Hissène Habré before the Extraordinary African Chambers of the Dakar *Tribunal Régional Hors Classe* and the Dakar Court of Appeal in respect of crimes committed in Chad between 7 June 1982 and 1 December 1990, provides that any amnesty granted to a person within the jurisdiction of the Chambers in respect of the crimes of genocide, crimes against humanity, war crimes, and torture shall not pose a bar to prosecution.[69]

11.34 The international permissibility of the prosecution by a state with concurrent prescriptive jurisdiction over it of an international crime statute-barred or amnestied in another state has been affirmed by international courts. In *Ould Dah v France*, declaring inadmissible the convict's complaint under the European Convention on Human Rights (ECHR) in relation to France's ignoring of the Mauritian amnesty in the *Ould Dah* proceedings, the European Court of Human Rights noted 'that international law does not preclude a person who has benefited from an amnesty [from] being tried in his or her originating State from being tried by another State'.[70] The point had previously been emphasized by the Appeals Chamber of the Special Court for Sierra Leone.[71]

IV. Conclusion

11.35 International law may well be only one factor in any state's decision whether to provide for statutory limitation or amnesty in respect of the prosecution of alleged international crimes. Particularly as regards amnesty in the context of democratic transitions from tyranny or conflict to the rule of law and peace, societies engage in complex calculations and trade-offs in seeking to overcome the past and secure the future.

11.36 In terms of the relevant international law, to a consideration of international criminal law and general international law needs to be added, in the case of the state providing for limitation or amnesty, an examination of what international human rights law may demand.

11.37 In the case of foreign states, international law does not oblige them to defer to a statute of limitations or amnesty enacted in another state. Indeed, when it comes to international crimes subject to the obligation *aut dedere aut judicare*, it may well oblige them not to.

---

[68] *Public Prosecutor v F*, ILDC 797 (NL 2007), para 34 (Netherlands).
[69] Statute of the Extraordinary African Chambers in the Senegalese Courts, art 20.
[70] *Ould Dah v France* (dec), no 13113/03, ECHR 2009, 17.
[71] *Kallon & Kamara*, Decision on Challenge to Jurisdiction: Lomé Accord Amnesty (n 56), para 67; *Prosecutor v Gbao*, SCSL-2004-15-AR72(E), Appeals Chamber, Decision on Preliminary Motion on the Invalidity of the Agreement between the United Nations and the Government of Sierra Leone on the Establishment of the Special Court, 25 May 2004, para 8.

Further Reading

BURKE-WHITE, WW, 'Reframing Impunity: Applying Liberal International Law Theory to an Analysis of Amnesty Legislation' (2001) 42 *Harvard International Law Journal* 467

DU BOIS-PEDAIN, A, *Transitional Amnesty in South Africa* (Cambridge: Cambridge University Press, 2007)

FREEMAN, M, *Necessary Evils: Amnesties and the Search for Justice* (Cambridge: Cambridge University Press, 2011)

FREEMAN, M and PENSKY, M, 'The Amnesty Controversy in International Law' in F Lessa and LA Payne (eds), *Amnesty in the Age of Human Rights Accountability: Comparative and International Perspectives* (Cambridge: Cambridge University Press, 2012), 42

KOK, RA, *Statutory Limitations in International Criminal Law* (The Hague: TMC Asser Press, 2007)

KREICKER, H, 'Statute of Limitations' in A Cassese (ed), *The Oxford Companion to International Criminal Justice* (Oxford: Oxford University Press, 2009), 522

LAFONTAINE, F, 'No Amnesty or Statute of Limitation for Enforced Disappearances: The Sandoval Case before the Supreme Court of Chile' (2005) 3 *Journal of International Criminal Justice* 469

LESSA, F and PAYNE, LA (eds), *Amnesty in the Age of Human Rights Accountability: Comparative and International Perspectives* (Cambridge: Cambridge University Press, 2012)

LESSA, F, OLSEN, TD, PAYNE, LA, PEREIRA, G, and REITER, A, 'Persistent or Eroding Impunity? The Divergent Effects of Legal Challenges to Amnesty Laws for Past Human Rights Violations' (2014) 47 *Israel Law Review* 105

MALLINDER, L, *Amnesty, Human Rights and Political Transitions: Bridging the Peace and Justice Divide* (Oxford: Hart Publishing, 2008)

MALLINDER, L, 'Can Amnesties and International Justice be Reconciled?' (2007) 1 *International Journal of Transitional Justice* 208

ORENTLICHER, DF, 'Settling Accounts: The Duty to Prosecute Human Rights Violations of a Prior Regime' (1991) 100 *Yale Law Journal* 2537

O'SHEA, AG, 'Truth and Reconciliation Commission' in R Wolfrum (ed), *Max Planck Encyclopedia of Public International Law* (2012), volume X, 106

SEIBERT-FOHR, A, 'Amnesties' in R Wolfrum (ed), *Max Planck Encyclopedia of Public International Law* (2012), volume I, 358

SEIBERT-FOHR, A, *Prosecuting Serious Human Rights Violations* (Oxford: Oxford University Press, 2009)

STAHN, C, 'Accommodating Individual Criminal Responsibility and National Reconciliation: The UN Truth Commission for East Timor' (2001) 95 *American Journal of International Law* 952

International Criminal Courts

12

The International Criminal Tribunals for the Former Yugoslavia and Rwanda and Their Residual Mechanism

I. Introduction

The International Criminal Tribunal for the former Yugoslavia (ICTY) and the International Criminal Tribunal for Rwanda (ICTR), the first international criminal courts since Nuremberg and Tokyo, are established and empowered on a wholly different international legal basis from their post-Second World War predecessors, namely by way of a decision taken by the United Nations Security Council under chapter VII ('Action with respect to Threats to the Peace, Breaches of the Peace, and Acts of Aggression') of the Charter of the United Nations. In this way they represent a novel exercise in international criminal justice and, indeed, of the Security Council's chapter VII powers. This exercise has withstood challenge, legal, political, and logistical, and has generally proved an unexpected success.   12.1

Although their successor judicial body, the International Residual Mechanism for Criminal Tribunals or, as it is more commonly known, the Mechanism for International Criminal Tribunals (MICT), is up and running and the Tribunals themselves are in what was previously scheduled to be their final year of operation, the ICTY and ICTR continue to merit consideration from an institutional perspective as paradigms of one formal and technical model for the adjudication of international crimes by an international criminal court.   12.2

II. General

A. Establishment, Envisaged Closure, and the Mechanism for International Criminal Tribunals

In mid-1991, armed conflict broke out in the territory of the Socialist Federal Republic of Yugoslavia (SFRY). By mid-1992, after the dissolution of the SFRY into five successor states and the shifting of the focus of the fighting to Bosnia-Herzegovina, the conflict had become notorious for the practice of 'ethnic cleansing', for systematic sexual violence, for the inhumane treatment of detainees,   12.3

and for the premeditated destruction of historical and religious sites. By way of response, in Security Council resolution 780 (1992) of 6 October 1992, the United Nations Security Council requested the UN Secretary-General to establish a commission of experts to report to him on evidence of grave breaches of the 1949 Geneva Conventions and other violations of international humanitarian law committed in the territory of the former Yugoslavia. On the strength of the commission's report, the Security Council decided in resolution 808 (1993) of 22 February 1993 to establish 'an international tribunal... for the prosecution of persons responsible for serious violations of international humanitarian law committed in the territory of the former Yugoslavia since 1991', and requested the Secretary-General to submit to the Council as soon as possible a report 'on all aspects of [the] matter'.[1] The Secretary-General's report, drafted by the UN Secretariat and reflecting comments received by states, recommended that the tribunal, a draft statute for which was included in the report, be created under chapter VII of the UN Charter. So it was that in Security Council resolution 827 (1993) of 25 May 1993 the Security Council, determining that the situation in the former Yugoslavia continued to constitute a threat to international peace and security and acting under chapter VII of the UN Charter, approved the Secretary-General's report and decided 'to establish an international tribunal for the sole purpose of prosecuting persons responsible for serious violations of international humanitarian law committed in the territory of the former Yugoslavia between 1 January 1991 and a date to be determined by the Security Council upon the restoration of peace and to this end to adopt the Statute of the International Tribunal' annexed to the Secretary-General's report ('ICTY Statute').[2] It further decided in the same resolution that all states were to 'cooperate fully with the International Tribunal and its organs', in accordance with the resolution and the Statute of the Tribunal, and that consequently all states were to take any measures necessary under their domestic law to implement the resolution and the Statute, 'including the obligation of States to comply with requests for assistance or orders issued by a Trial Chamber under Article 29 of the Statute'.[3]

12.4   Over a 100-day period between 6 April 1994, when an aircraft carrying the Rwandan president Juvénal Habyarimana was shot down near the capital Kigali, and 4 July 1994, when Kigali fell to the rebel army of the Rwandan Patriotic Front (RPF), Hutu extremists in the central African state of Rwanda, with the co-operation of elements of the populace, murdered up to one million Tutsi and moderate Hutu in a systematic and pre-meditated campaign of genocide. On 17 May 1994, in Security Council resolution 918 (1994), the UN Security Council determined that the situation in Rwanda constituted a threat to peace and security in the region. It subsequently requested the Secretary-General to establish a commission of experts to report on 'evidence of grave violations of international humanitarian law committed in the territory of Rwanda, including... evidence

---

[1] SC res 808 (1993), 22 February 1993, paras 1 and 2 respectively.
[2] SC res 827 (1993), 25 May 1993, para 2.   [3] Ibid, para 4.

of possible acts of genocide', and to report within four months on the findings of the Commission, recommending further steps.⁴ Having subsequently been requested by the new government of Rwanda to establish an international tribunal to punish those responsible for atrocities, the Security Council, acting under chapter VII of the UN Charter, decided in Security Council resolution 955 (1994) of 8 November 1994 'to establish an international tribunal for the sole purpose of prosecuting persons responsible for genocide and other serious violations of international humanitarian law committed in the territory of Rwanda and Rwandan citizens responsible for genocide and other such violations committed in the territory of neighbouring states, between 1 January 1994 and 31 December 1994' and to this end to adopt the Statute of the International Criminal Tribunal for Rwanda ('ICTY Statute') annexed to the resolution.⁵ It further decided in the same resolution that all states were obliged to 'cooperate fully with the International Tribunal and its organs', in accordance with the resolution and the Statute of the Tribunal, and that consequently all states were to take any measures necessary under their domestic law to implement the resolution and the Statute, 'including the obligation of States to comply with requests for assistance or orders issued by a Trial Chamber under Article 28 of the Statute'.⁶

12.5 In his report to the Security Council on the then-proposed ICTY and in a subsequent report on the already-established ICTR, the UN Secretary-General outlined the two main benefits of establishing the Tribunals by way of Security Council decision under chapter VII of the Charter. One was speed. While the Secretary-General acknowledged that a treaty would be the preferable way to proceed 'in the normal course of events', such an approach had 'the disadvantage of requiring considerable time to establish an instrument and then to achieve the required number of ratifications for entry into force';⁷ and although, of the political organs of the UN, the General Assembly was more representative than the Security Council, the involvement of the former was 'not reconcilable with the urgency expressed by the Security Council'.⁸ In contrast, establishment by the Council under chapter VII was 'expeditious'.⁹ The second benefit was efficacy. A treaty might not be ratified by 'those States which should be parties to [it] if it is to be truly effective',¹⁰ whereas all UN member states 'would be under a binding obligation to take whatever action is required to carry out a decision taken as an enforcement measure under Chapter VII'.¹¹ As specifically regards the ICTR, 'establishment...under Chapter VII, notwithstanding the request received from the Government of Rwanda, was necessary to ensure not only the cooperation of

---

⁴ SC res 935 (1994), 1 July 1994, paras 1 and 3.
⁵ SC res 955 (1994), 8 November 1994, para 1.   ⁶ Ibid, para 2.
⁷ *Report of the Secretary-General pursuant to paragraph 2 of Security Council resolution 808 (1993)*, UN doc S/25704 (3 May 1993), para 20.
⁸ Ibid, para 21.
⁹ Ibid, para 23. See also *Report of the Secretary-General pursuant to paragraph 5 of Security Council resolution 955 (1994)*, UN doc S/1995/143 (13 February 1995), para 6.
¹⁰ *Report of the Secretary-General pursuant to Security Council resolution 808 (1993)* (n 7), para 20.
¹¹ Ibid, para 23.

Rwanda throughout the life-span of the Tribunal, but the cooperation of all States in whose territory persons alleged to have committed serious violations of international humanitarian law and acts of genocide in Rwanda might be situated'.[12]

12.6   Neither the ICTY nor the ICTR was intended to be permanent, and by 2003 the US, wary of an open-ended financial commitment, was looking to wind them down by the end of the decade. In response to pressure from the Security Council, the Tribunals adopted 'completion strategies', which, in addition to the appointment of a purpose-dedicated Prosecutor to the ICTR, involved the appointment and assignment to specific cases of '*ad litem*' judges, supplementary to the permanent judges of each Tribunal, in order to increase the work-rate; the referral, courtesy of the insertion into the Tribunals' respective Rules of Procedure and Evidence (RPE) of rule 11*bis*,[13] of numerous middle-ranking cases, involving both persons under investigation and persons indicted by the Tribunal, to national prosecution authorities and courts in the former Yugoslavia[14] and eventually to Rwanda; assistance in the building of prosecutorial and judicial capacity in these institutions; and the passing of evidence onto them.

12.7   In recognition, however, of the likelihood that a considerable number of cases would trickle on for some time, of the need for ongoing supervision of the enforcement of sentences and of the protection of victims and witnesses, and of a range of other issues militating in favour of the maintenance of the Tribunals' jurisdiction in some form, the Security Council, acting under chapter VII of the Charter, decided in Security Council resolution 1966 (2010) of 22 December 2010 to establish the 'International Residual Mechanism for Criminal Tribunals', now referred to as the Mechanism for International Criminal Tribunals (MICT or 'the Mechanism'), and to adopt the statute of the Mechanism ('MICT Statute') annexed to the resolution.[15] The MICT is a bare-bones, maximally cost-effective ad hoc international criminal tribunal, with branches in The Hague and Arusha,[16] which, as also decided in Security Council resolution 1966 (2010), 'continue[s] the jurisdiction, rights and obligations and essential functions' of the ICTY and ICTR,[17] although at present this jurisdiction overlaps with those of the ICTY and ICTR themselves, which continue to hear any trial or appellate proceedings pending at the date of commencement of the relevant branch of the MICT's functions. Echoing resolutions 827 (1993)

---

[12] *Report of the Secretary-General pursuant to Security Council resolution 955 (1994)* (n 9), para 6.
[13] See *infra* paras 12.38–12.41.   [14] Recall *supra* paras 9.38 and 9.55–9.61.
[15] SC res 1966 (2010), 22 December 2010, para 1, referring to Statute of the International Residual Mechanism for Criminal Tribunals, ibid, Annex 1 ('MICT Statute'). In accordance with ibid, para 17, establishment of the MICT is for an initial period of four years, to be followed, on completion each time of a review of the progress of the Mechanism's work, by periods of two years, unless the Council decides otherwise. In ibid, para 2, the Council further decided that 'the provisions of [the] resolution and the Statutes of the Mechanism and of the ICTY and ICTR shall be subject to the transitional arrangements set out in Annex 2 of [the] resolution'.
[16] MICT Statute, art 3. As regards the Arusha branch, see Agreement between the United Nations and the United Republic of Tanzania concerning the Headquarters of the International Residual Mechanism for Criminal Tribunals 2013.
[17] SC res 1966 (2010), para 2. See also MICT Statute, art 1(1).

and 955 (1994), the Security Council further decided in resolution 1966 (2010) that all states are obliged 'to cooperate fully with the Mechanism', in accordance with the resolution and the Statute of the Mechanism, and that consequently all states are to take any measures necessary under their domestic law to implement the resolution and the Statute, 'including the obligation of States to comply with requests for assistance or orders issued by the Mechanism pursuant to its Statute'.[18] In the same resolution, the Security Council requested the ICTY and ICTR 'to take all possible measures to expeditiously complete all their remaining work...no later than 31 December 2014, to prepare their closure and to ensure a smooth transition to the Mechanism, including through advance teams in each of the Tribunals'.[19] As per paragraph 1 of Security Council resolution 1966 (2010), the MICT assumed its mandate vis-à-vis the ICTR on 1 July 2012 and vis-à-vis the ICTY on 1 July 2013.

There is no chance that the 31 December 2014 deadline set by the Security Council for the completion by the ICTY and ICTR of their work will be met, with the result that both Tribunals will remain functional for some time yet. 12.8

B. Basic Facts

The ICTY has had its seat and continues to sit in The Hague, the Netherlands,[20] 12.9 pursuant to a headquarters agreement with the Netherlands.[21] Its basic legal instruments are its Statute, adopted and amended by the Security Council, and its RPE, adopted and amended by the Tribunal's judges.[22] It has three Trial Chambers and an Appeals Chamber.[23] It has a Prosecutor, backed by an Office of the Prosecutor, who acts 'independently as a separate organ' of the Tribunal and who 'shall not seek or receive instructions from any Government or from any other source'.[24] The Tribunal has its own detention unit, in Scheveningen, The Hague, where the accused remain from arrival to the conclusion of appellate proceedings. As made clear in the Dutch legislation implementing the agreement, the Netherlands has transferred to the ICTY its jurisdiction to hear applications for release from the Tribunal's detention. These and other provisions mean that the Netherlands 'has nothing to do with' the detention of suspects and accused by the ICTY.[25] Even less are trial and appellate proceedings before the Tribunal attributable to the Netherlands under the law of

---

[18] SC res 1966 (2010), para 9.   [19] Ibid, para 3.   [20] ICTY Statute, art 31.
[21] Agreement between the United Nations and the Kingdom of the Netherlands Concerning the Headquarters of the International Tribunal for the Prosecution of Persons Responsible for Serious Violations of International Humanitarian Law Committed in the Territory of the Former Yugoslavia Since 1991, The Hague, 29 July 1994 (as amended) ('ICTY HQ Agreement').
[22] See ICTY Statute, art 15 and ICTY Rules of Procedure and Evidence, UN doc IT/32/Rev.49 (22 May 2013).
[23] ICTY Statute, art 11(*a*).   [24] Ibid, art 16(2).
[25] *Slobodan Milošević v International Criminal Tribunal for the former Yugoslavia and State of the Netherlands*, Hague District Court, 26 February 2002, 41 ILM 1310 (2002), para 5.1. See, similarly, *Slobodan Milošević v State of the Netherlands*, Hague District Court, 31 August 2001, 41 ILM 86 (2002), para 3.15.

state responsibility.²⁶ Those convicted serve their sentences in one of the 17 European states that have concluded either general or ad hoc agreements to this effect with the Tribunal.

12.10 The ICTR has had its seat and continues to sit in Arusha, Tanzania,²⁷ pursuant to a headquarters agreement with Tanzania.²⁸ Its Statute, adopted and amended by the Security Council, is almost identical to that of the ICTY, except for the Tribunal's jurisdiction *ratione materiae, loci* and *temporis*. Its RPE, adopted and amended by the judges,²⁹ are based on the original version of the ICTY RPE and remain substantially similar to them. The Tribunal's structure is the same as that of the ICTY.³⁰ Until August 2003, the ICTY Prosecutor and the ICTR Prosecutor were one and the same person, but the amendment of article 15 of the ICTR Statute saw the appointment to the Tribunal of its own Prosecutor. Like the ICTY, the ICTR has a detention facility. Sentences are served either in Rwanda or in one of the six other states, three of them European, that have signed agreements to this effect with the Tribunal.

12.11 The ICTY and the ICTR, as well as the MICT, constitute subsidiary organs of the Security Council within the meaning of article 29 of the UN Charter.³¹ As a consequence, all three report to the Council,³² and the Council enjoys—and, in the case of the ICTY and ICTR, has repeatedly exercised—the power to amend their respective statutes.

12.12 The respective statutes and RPE of the ICTY and ICTR embody a range of due process rights for accused and suspects. Article 21 of the ICTY Statute and article 20 of the ICTR Statute, which reproduce virtually verbatim the text of article 14 of the International Covenant on Civil and Political Rights (ICCPR),

---

²⁶ See *Galić v Netherlands* (dec), no 22617/07, ECHR 2009; *Blagojević v Netherlands* (dec), no 49032/07, ECHR 2009.
²⁷ The seat of the ICTR is not specified in the ICTR Statute, since its location had not been settled at the time the Security Council adopted the Statute. See, in this regard, *Report of the Secretary-General pursuant to Security Council resolution 955 (1994)* (n 9), para 40: 'The Rwandan Ambassador reiterated his Government's position that the seat of the Tribunal should be located in Kigali for the moral and educational value that its presence there would have for the local population. In a spirit of compromise and cooperation, however, he indicated that his Government would raise no objection to the seat of the Tribunal being established in a location easily accessible to Rwanda in a neighbouring State.' For his part, the Secretary-General noted, ibid, para 43: '[I]n the atmosphere now prevailing in Rwanda, there are serious security risks in bringing into the country leaders of the previous regime alleged to have committed acts of genocide to stand trial before the International Tribunal.'
²⁸ Agreement between the United Nations and the United Republic of Tanzania concerning the Headquarters of the International Tribunal for Rwanda, Dar es Salaam, 31 August 1995 ('ICTR HQ Agreement').
²⁹ See ICTR Statute, art 14 and ICTR Rules of Procedure and Evidence (last amended 10 April 2013) ('ICTR RPE').
³⁰ See ICTY Statute, art 10(*a*).
³¹ See *Report of the Secretary-General pursuant to Security Council resolution 808 (1993)* (n 7), para 28 and ICTY HQ Agreement, preamble (second recital); *Report of the Secretary-General pursuant to Security Council resolution 955 (1994)* (n 9), para 8 and ICTR HQ Agreement, preamble (second recital).
³² See, explicitly, MICT Statute, art 32(2), providing that the President and Prosecutor 'shall submit six-monthly reports to the Security Council on the progress of the work of the Mechanism'. In accordance with ICTY Statute, art 33, ICTR Statute, art 32, and MICT Statute, art 32(1), an annual report is to be submitted both to the Security Council and to the General Assembly.

secure to the accused the classic internationally-recognized procedural guarantees. These are buttressed by article 20(1) of the ICTY Statute and article 19(1) of the ICTR Statute, which state that Trial Chambers 'shall ensure that a trial is fair and expeditious and that proceedings are conducted...with full respect for the rights of the accused'.[33] Article 18(3) of the ICTY Statute, article 17(3) of the ICTR Statute, and rule 42 of the respective ICTY and ICTR RPE provide for rights of suspects during investigation.[34] These rights are reproduced in the MICT Statute and RPE.[35] In its judgment of 2000 in *Naletilić v Croatia*, the European Court of Human Rights (Fourth Section) held that, 'in view of the content of its Statute and Rules of Procedure, [the ICTY] offers all the necessary guarantees including those of impartiality and independence'.[36] The same could be said of the ICTR and MICT.

12.13 The ICTY and ICTR Statutes and RPE make provision for the protection and support of witnesses and victims. Article 20(1) of the ICTY Statute and article 19(1) of the ICTR Statute require Trial Chambers to ensure that trial proceedings are conducted with due regard for the protection of victims and witnesses, while article 22 of the former and article 21 of the latter require the Tribunal to provide for the same in its RPE, with special mention being made of the conduct of in camera proceedings and the protection of the victim's identity. In turn, the RPE of each Tribunal specify in considerable detail the measures that may be ordered for the protection of victims and witnesses.[37] In accordance with rule 34 of the respective RPE, a Victims and Witnesses Section was set up within each Tribunal under the authority of the Registry, with a mandate to recommend protective measures and provide counselling and support, especially in cases of rape and sexual assault. All these provisions are reproduced, *mutatis mutandis*, in the MICT Statute and RPE.[38]

12.14 The ICTY, ICTR, and MICT are funded out of the regular budget of the UN in accordance with article 17 of the Charter.[39] At their peaks in 2008–2009, the gross budgets of the ICTY and ICTR were US $376.2 million and US $305.4 million respectively, which represented a large proportion of the overall annual budget of the UN.

---

[33] See also ICTY Statute, art 20(2) and ICTR Statute, art 19(2), providing that a Trial Chamber shall satisfy itself at the commencement of trial that the rights of the accused are respected; ICTY Statute, art 20(3) and ICTR Statute, art 19(3), providing that hearings shall in general be public; and rule 62(A)(i) of the respective RPE, requiring the Trial Chamber or Judge, on the initial appearance of the accused, to 'satisfy itself, himself or herself that the right of the accused to counsel is respected'.

[34] See also rules 43 ('Recording Questioning of Suspects') and 63 ('Questioning of the Accused') of the respective RPE.

[35] See MICT Statute, arts 16(3), 18(1) and (3), and 19, as well as MICT Rules of Procedure and Evidence, UN doc MICT/1 (8 June 2012) ('MICT RPE'), rules 40, 41, 64(A)(i), and 66.

[36] *Naletilić v Croatia*, 121 ILR 209, 212 (ECtHR 2000). The ECtHR's conclusion was endorsed by the Hague District Court the following year in *Milošević v Netherlands* (n 25), para 3.4.

[37] See rules 69, 75, and 79(A)(ii) of the respective RPE.

[38] See MICT Statute, arts 18(1) and 20 and MICT RPE, rules 32, 75, 86, and 93(A)(ii).

[39] See ICTY Statute, art 32, ICTR Statute, art 30, and MICT Statute, art 30.

C. Cases

12.15   Neither Tribunal, and especially the ICTY, had many cases at first. But with the initiation of arrests by SFOR in Bosnia-Herzegovina[40] and changed political circumstances in the countries of the former Yugoslavia, the ICTY amassed a packed docket. In total it indicted 161 individuals, none of whom remains at large. Proceedings before the Tribunal against the great majority of indictees have been completed, while 13 cases have been transferred to national authorities. The ICTR witnessed a similar steep rise in its activity over the years. It indicted 98 individuals, although two indictments were later withdrawn. Ten cases in all have been transferred to national authorities, eight to Rwanda and two to France. Nine of its indictees remain at large, all bar three of whose cases have been transferred to Rwanda, with the remaining three slated to be tried before the MICT in the event of their capture.

12.16   Cases in both the ICTY and ICTR have long proceeded and continue to proceed at a snail's pace. This is for a range of reasons, some of which have changed over time and not all of them the fault of any of the organs of the Tribunals. A single trial can take several and, in some cases, many years.

D. The Functions of the Mechanism for International Criminal Tribunals

12.17   The function of the MICT, as succinctly stated in article 2 of its Statute, is to 'continue the functions of the ICTY and of the ICTR, as set out in the present Statute ("residual functions"), during the period of its operation'. The main residual functions are severalfold. First, the MICT is to conduct any trial or appellate proceedings of persons indicted by the ICTY or ICTR that were not pending before the relevant Tribunal at the date of the commencement of operation of the relevant branch of the MICT insofar as the case has not been transferred to national authorities.[41] In terms of trial, this means that, barring unforeseen retrials, only three persons stand to be tried before the MICT for genocide, crimes against humanity, or war crimes, and only in the event that they are captured, namely Félicien Kabuga, Protais Mpiranya, and Augustin Bizimana, all of whom remain at large. In terms of appellate proceedings, it means that the MICT will hear appeals in the cases at trial before the ICTY or ICTR at the date of the commencement of operation of the relevant branch of the MICT. Secondly, the MICT is to conduct any trials and appeals of persons indicted by the MICT for contempt of, or for knowingly and wilfully giving false testimony before, the Tribunals or the MICT itself.[42] Thirdly, the MICT is to deal with issues arising in relation to the enforcement of sentences of persons convicted by the ICTY or ICTR.[43] Fourthly, the

---

[40] See *infra* paras 12.54–12.55.   [41] See MICT Statute, art 1(2) and (3).
[42] See ibid, art 1(4).
[43] See ibid, art 25(2). The MICT has the same mandate in respect of the enforcement of sentences imposed by the MICT itself.

MICT has responsibilities in relation to the ongoing protection and support of victims and witnesses who testified before the ICTY or ICTR.[44] Finally, the MICT is to manage the archives of the two Tribunals, a task encompassing the preservation of, and regulation of access to, these materials,[45] which remain the property of the UN.[46]

III. Legality of Establishment

The first accused before the ICTY challenged the Tribunal's jurisdiction by alleging that the Tribunal's creation was *ultra vires* the Security Council's powers under the UN Charter. His argument was essentially that the armed conflict in the former Yugoslavia, being as he saw it a non-international armed conflict, could not lawfully be characterized by the Council as a threat to the peace within the meaning of article 39 of the Charter; that, even if it could be, the Security Council was not authorized to take any measures at its discretion with a view to maintaining the peace but was bound to choose among those expressly provided for in articles 41 and 42 of the Charter; and that the establishment of an international criminal tribunal was not only absent from the measures cited in articles 41 and 42 but was also of a different nature from these measures.[47]

12.18

In response,[48] the Appeals Chamber held, first, that a '"threat to the peace" is more of a political concept' than one amenable to legal determination, although 'the determination that there exists such a threat is not a totally unfettered discretion, as it has to remain, at the very least, within the limits of the Purposes and Principles of the Charter'.[49] In relation to the facts of the case before it, the Tribunal concluded that the practice of the Security Council evidenced 'a common understanding, manifested by the "subsequent practice" of the membership of the United Nations at large, that the "threat to the peace" of Article 39 may include, as one of its species, internal armed conflicts'.[50] Next, the Appeals Chamber held that, once the Security Council determines under article 39 that a particular situation poses a threat to the peace, it enjoys 'a very wide margin of discretion' under the provision 'to choose the appropriate course of action and to evaluate the suitability of the measures chosen, as well as their potential contribution to the restoration or maintenance of peace',[51] although its 'very broad and exceptional powers' had to be channelled through either article 41 or article 42.[52] As a non-forcible measure, the establishment of a tribunal was

12.19

---

[44] See ibid, art 20. Again, this mandate extends to its victims and witnesses who testify before the MICT itself.
[45] See ibid, art 27(2).   [46] Ibid, art 27(1).
[47] See *Prosecutor v Tadić*, IT-94-1, Appeals Chamber, Decision on Interlocutory Motion on Jurisdiction, 2 October 1995, para 27.
[48] As a preliminary determination, the Appeals Chamber held, ibid, paras 19 and 22, that the ICTY enjoyed inherent jurisdiction to rule on the validity of its own jurisdiction and that, in the exercise of this jurisdiction, it was not barred from reviewing the lawfulness of Security Council action.
[49] Ibid, para 30.   [50] Ibid.   [51] Ibid, para 32.   [52] Ibid, para 31.

prima facie pursuant to article 41, and in this regard the Council was not limited in its choice of non-forcible measures to those specifically mentioned in article 41, these being 'merely illustrative examples which obviously do not exclude other measures' not involving the use of force.⁵³ Nor did the wording or logic of article 41 require the Council to act through member states; rather, action by the Organization itself was permissible.⁵⁴ As for the argument that the Security Council, not being an organ endowed with judicial powers, could not delegate the exercise of such powers to a subsidiary organ, this represented a 'fundamental misunderstanding' of the Council's act.⁵⁵ The Council had not delegated to the ICTY the exercise of any of its powers; rather, the establishment of the Tribunal was itself an exercise by the Council of its undoubted powers with respect to the maintenance and restoration of peace and security, being as it was a measure calculated to maintain or restore peace in the former Yugoslavia.⁵⁶ Finally, as to whether the establishment of a judicial organ was an appropriate and effective means of achieving the objective of restoring the peace, article 39, the Appeals Chamber averred, 'leaves the choice of means and their evaluation to the Security Council, which enjoys wide discretionary powers in this regard; and it could not have been otherwise, as such a choice involves political evaluation of highly complex and dynamic situations'.⁵⁷ In sum, the ICTY was lawfully established under chapter VII of the UN Charter.⁵⁸ This ruling has been affirmed in other cases before the Tribunal.⁵⁹

12.20   What goes for the ICTY in all these respects goes also for the ICTR.⁶⁰

---

⁵³ Ibid, para 35, emphasis omitted.   ⁵⁴ Ibid, paras 35–36.   ⁵⁵ Ibid, para 37.
⁵⁶ Ibid, para 38.   ⁵⁷ Ibid, para 39.
⁵⁸ The accused in *Tadić* argued additionally that the ICTY was not 'established by law' within the meaning of the right to fair trial guaranteed at the international level by art 14 of the ICCPR. The Appeals Chamber, however, was not satisfied that this guarantee was applicable to proceedings before an international court. One aspect of it, namely that courts must be established by a legislature and not by executive decree, could not be translated to the international setting, and especially not to the UN, where there was no clear-cut division of judicial, legislative, and executive functions among the various organs. Nor did the fact that the Organization has no legislature mean that the UN as a whole was incapable of establishing a court without an amendment to the Charter. It did 'not follow from the fact that the United Nations has no legislature that the Security Council is not empowered to set up this International Tribunal if it is acting pursuant to an authority found within its constitution, the United Nations Charter'; and, as already made clear, the Appeals Chamber was 'of the view that the Security Council was endowed with the power to create th[e] International Tribunal as a measure under Chapter VII in the light of its determination that there exists a threat to the peace'. See ibid, para 44.
⁵⁹ See *Prosecutor v Milošević (Slobodan)*, IT-02-54, Trial Chamber, Decision on Preliminary Motions, 8 November 2001, para 7; *Prosecutor v Šešelj*, IT-03-67-PT, Trial Chamber, Decision on Motion by Vojislav Šešelj Challenging Jurisdiction and Form of Indictment, 26 May 2004, para 12; *Prosecutor v Milutinović* et al, IT-99-37-AR72.2, Appeals Chamber, Reasons for Decision Dismissing Interlocutory Appeal concerning Jurisdiction over the territory of Kosovo, 8 June 2004, 4; *Prosecutor v Tolimir*, IT-05-88/2-PT, Trial Chamber, Decision on Preliminary Motions on the Indictment pursuant to Rule 72 of the Rules, 14 December 2007, para 29. See, similarly, *Milošević v Netherlands* (n 25), para 3.3.
⁶⁰ See *Prosecutor v Kanyabashi*, ICTR-96-15-T, Trial Chamber, Decision on the Defence Motion on Jurisdiction, 18 June 1997, paras 17–29; *Prosecutor v Ntakirutimana*, ICTR-96-10-A & ICTR-96-17-A, Appeals Chamber, Judgment, 13 December 2004, paras 398–399.

IV. Jurisdiction

A. Existence

The competence of the ICTY is spelled out in general terms in article 1 of the ICTY Statute, which provides that the Tribunal 'shall have the power to prosecute persons responsible for serious violations of international humanitarian law committed in the territory of the former Yugoslavia since 1991 in accordance with the provisions of the... Statute'. Article 1 of the ICTR Statute states that the Tribunal 'shall have the power to prosecute persons responsible for serious violations of international humanitarian law committed in the territory of Rwanda and Rwandan citizens responsible for such violations committed in the territory of neighbouring States between 1 January 1994 and 31 December 1994, in accordance with the provisions of... Statute'. As for the MICT, article 1(1) of its Statute provides in relevant part that the Mechanism 'shall continue the material, territorial, temporal and personal jurisdiction of the ICTY and the ICTR as set out in Articles 1 to 8 of the ICTY Statute and Articles 1 to 7 of the ICTR Statute'. 12.21

(i) Jurisdiction ratione materiae *(subject-matter jurisdiction)*

The jurisdiction *ratione materiae*, or subject-matter jurisdiction, of the ICTY differs from that of the ICTR, since the facts giving rise to the establishment of each Tribunal differ. The ICTY has jurisdiction over grave breaches of the 1949 Geneva Conventions (article 2), violations of the laws and customs of war (article 3), genocide (article 4), and crimes against humanity (article 5). The ICTR has jurisdiction over genocide (article 2), crimes against humanity (article 3), and violations of article 3 common to the Geneva Conventions and of Additional Protocol II (article 4). In accordance with article 1(1) of the MICT Statute, the MICT enjoys both respective jurisdictions *ratione materiae*. 12.22

Neither the ICTY Statute nor the ICTR Statute contains any express statement as to the Tribunal's applicable law, as distinct from its jurisdiction *ratione materiae*.[61] Taking their lead as they did from the Nuremberg Charter, where the question of applicable law was deliberately passed over, the Statutes conflate jurisdiction *ratione materiae* and applicable law. But the Secretary-General, in his report to the Security Council prior to the establishment of the ICTY, indicated 12.23

---

[61] Jurisdiction *ratione materiae* is a question of procedural competence. It is the question of what subject-matters the court is empowered to entertain—here, what crimes the Tribunal can adjudicate. Applicable law is a substantive question. It is the question of what body or bodies of rules the court is empowered to look to when adjudicating upon the subject-matters it entertains—here, whether the Tribunal is to apply international law, municipal law, or both; if international law, whether customary international law, treaties, general principles of law recognized by civilized nations, judicial decisions and the writings of eminent publicists, or all of them, and whether only international criminal law or perhaps also international human rights law, where relevant.

that the latter would apply international law, asserting that the Tribunal would have no call to apply municipal law except in sentencing;[62] and in practice, while both the ICTY and ICTR have referred to municipal law to seek to affirm that a perhaps-controversial application of international law did not violate the principle of legality,[63] neither has founded any crime within its jurisdiction on Yugoslav or Rwandan law, as the case may be. As for which formal sources of international law the Tribunals apply, the Secretary-General stated in his report on the proposed ICTY that 'the application of the principle *nullum crimen sine lege* requires that the [ICTY] should apply rules of international humanitarian law which are beyond any doubt part of customary law so that the problem of adherence of some but not all States to specific conventions does not arise'.[64] But in practice this has not been the case. In *Tadić*, the ICTY Appeals Chamber held that 'the rule must be customary in nature or, if it belongs to treaty law, the required conditions must be met'.[65] As for what these 'required conditions' were, the Appeals Chamber, emphasizing that 'the only reason behind the stated purpose of the drafters that the International Tribunal should apply customary international law was to avoid violating the principle of *nullum crimen sine lege* in the event that a party to the conflict did not adhere to a specific treaty', held it to follow that, in addition to customary international law, the Tribunal was authorized to apply any treaty that 'was unquestionably binding on the parties at the time of the alleged offence' and 'was not in conflict with or derogating from peremptory norms of international law'.[66] The Appeals Chamber concluded 'that, in general, such agreements fall within [the ICTY's] jurisdiction under Article 3 of the Statute'.[67] Nor have the classic multilateral standard-setting treaties been the only international agreements looked to by the ICTY to ground war crimes within its jurisdiction. In *Blaškić*, for example, a bilateral agreement signed between Croatia and Bosnia-Herzegovina under the auspices of the ICRC was considered an international agreement capable of founding a crime under article 3 of the ICTY Statute.[68] As for the ICTR, the Secretary-General explained after the event to the Security Council that the Council had 'elected to take a more expansive approach to the choice of the applicable law than the one underlying the statute of the Yugoslav Tribunal, and included within the subject-matter jurisdiction of the Rwanda Tribunal international instruments regardless of whether they were

---

[62] In the latter regard, see the second sentence of ICTY Statute, art 24(1) and ICTR Statute, art 23(1) ('In determining the terms of imprisonment, the Trial Chambers shall have recourse to the general practice regarding prison sentences in the courts of the former Yugoslavia/Rwanda.')

[63] See eg *Prosecutor v Kayishema and Ruzindana*, ICTR-95-1-T, Trial Chamber, Judgment, 21 May 1999, para 157.

[64] *Report of the Secretary-General pursuant to Security Council resolution 808 (1993)* (n 7), para 34. The reference is to the states of the former Yugoslavia.

[65] *Tadić*, Appeals Chamber Decision on Jurisdiction (n 47), para 94.

[66] Ibid, para 143, citations omitted.

[67] Ibid, para 144. This ruling has been applied by both Tribunals. See eg *Prosecutor v Kordić and Čerkez*, IT-95-14/2-A, Appeals Chamber Judgment, 17 December 2004, paras 41–46; *Prosecutor v Galić*, IT-98-29-A, Appeals Chamber, Judgment, 30 November 2006, paras 81 and 85; *Prosecutor v Kayishema and Ruzindana*, Trial Chamber Judgment (n 63), para 156.

[68] *Prosecutor v Blaškić*, Trial Chamber, Judgment, 3 March 2000, para 172.

considered part of customary international law or whether they ha[d] customarily entailed the individual criminal responsibility of the perpetrator of the crime'.[69] 'Article 4 of the statute', he continued, 'includes violations of Additional Protocol II, which, as a whole, has not yet been universally recognized as part of customary international law, and for the first time criminalizes common article 3 of the four Geneva Conventions'.[70] Nor have solely agreements been looked to by the ICTR to underpin crimes within its jurisdiction. In *Kayishema and Ruzindana*, an announcement by the RPF to the ICRC that it considered itself bound by the rules of international humanitarian law left 'no doubt that persons responsible for the breaches of these international instruments during the events in the Rwandan territories in 1994 could be subject to prosecution'.[71]

(ii) Jurisdiction ratione personae *(personal jurisdiction)*

The ICTY and ICTR, and therefore the MICT,[72] have jurisdiction over natural persons.[73] As made clear in the Secretary-General's report on the ICTY, this is to the exclusion of juridical persons, such as organizations.[74]   12.24

The ICTY and ICTR's jurisdiction over natural persons pertains only to the living. The Tribunals cease to enjoy jurisdiction *ratione personae*, even in relation to an appeal, on the death of the accused or the convict.[75]   12.25

(iii) Jurisdiction ratione temporis *(temporal jurisdiction)*

Article 8 of the ICTY Statute provides that the temporal jurisdiction of the ICTY 'shall extend to a period beginning on 1 January 1991'. Security Council resolution 827 (1993), pursuant to which the Security Council established the ICTY, referred to the prosecution of serious violations of international humanitarian law committed in the territory of the former Yugoslavia 'between 1 January 1991 and a date to be determined by the Security Council upon the restoration of peace'.   12.26

---

[69] *Report of the Secretary-General pursuant to Security Council resolution 955 (1994)* (n 9), para 12.
[70] Ibid. The Secretary-General added, however, ibid, note 8: 'Although the question of whether common article 3 entails the individual responsibility of the perpetrator of the crime is still debatable, some of the crimes included therein, when committed against the civilian population, also constitute crimes against humanity and as such are customarily recognized as entailing the criminal responsibility of the individual.'
[71] *Kayishema and Ruzindana*, Trial Chamber Judgment (n 63), para 157.
[72] MICT Statute, art 1(1).   [73] ICTY Statute, art 6 and ICTY Statute, art 5.
[74] *Report of the Secretary-General pursuant to Security Council resolution 808 (1993)* (n 7), para 50.
[75] *Prosecutor v Delić*, IT-04-83-A, Appeals Chamber, Decision on the Outcome of the Proceedings, 29 June 2010, paras 6 and 8; *Prosecutor v Rutaganda*, ICTR-96-03-R68, Appeals Chamber, Decision on Rutaganda's Pending Motions, 27 October 2010; *Prosecutor v Popović* et al, IT-05-88-A, Appeals Chamber, Decision Terminating Appellate Proceedings in Relation to Milan Gvero, 7 March 2013, para 5. Where a convict dies between conviction at trial and judgment on appeal, the trial judgment, insofar as it relates to the deceased, is considered final, as made clear in *Delić*, Appeals Chamber Decision on the Outcome, para 15 and *Popović*, Appeals Chamber Decision Terminating Appellate Proceedings, para 6. Nor do the deceased's counsel or next-of-kin have standing to seek review of the trial judgment, as made clear in *Prosecutor v Delić*, IT-04-83-R.1, Appeals Chamber, Decision on Defence Motion for Review, 17 December 2013.

But in the event the Security Council never determined any such date. As a result, 'the Tribunal's temporal jurisdiction is open-ended'.[76] Nothing in the MICT Statute, in accordance with article 1(1) of which the ICTY's temporal jurisdiction is 'continue[d]' under the Mechanism, alters this.

12.27 In contrast, in accordance with article 7 of ICTR Statute, the temporal jurisdiction of the ICTR 'shall extend to a period beginning on 1 January 1994 and ending on 31 December 1994'.[77] This limitation did not, however, prevent the Trial Chamber in *Nahimana, Barayagwiza and Ngeze* from exercising jurisdiction over the offences of conspiracy to commit genocide and direct and public incitement to commit genocide in circumstances where the conspiracy was hatched among the accused and some of the incitement took place before 1994 (since both modes of participation in genocide were to be considered as continuing until the completion of the acts contemplated, *viz* the physical acts of genocide, which took place in 1994) or from admitting evidence of acts prior to 1994 which went towards proving acts in 1994.[78] On appeal, the Appeals Chamber overturned the first ruling, holding that the Statute's *travaux préparatoires* and the principle of strict construction of criminal provisions made it clear that the Tribunal enjoyed jurisdiction to convict the accused 'only where all of the elements required to be shown in order to establish his guilt were present in 1994'.[79] The existence of continuing conduct was no exception to this rule.[80] On the other hand, the Appeals Chamber considered it 'well established that the provisions of the Statute on the temporal jurisdiction of the Tribunal do not preclude the admission of evidence on events prior to 1994, if the Chamber deems such evidence relevant and of probative value [as per RPE, rule 89(C)] and there is no compelling reason to exclude it'.[81] The temporal jurisdiction enjoyed by the ICTR is now enjoyed also by the MICT, as per article 1(1) of the latter's Statute.

(iv) *Jurisdiction* ratione loci *(territorial jurisdiction)*

12.28 Article 8 of the ICTY Statute provides that the territorial jurisdiction of the Tribunal 'shall extend to the territory of the former Socialist Federal Republic

---

[76] *Prosecutor v Boškoski and Tarčulovski*, IT-04-82-AR72.1, Appeals Chamber, Decision on Interlocutory Appeal on Jurisdiction, 22 July 2005, para 10.

[77] See, in this regard, *Report of the Secretary-General pursuant to Security Council resolution 955 (1994)* (n 9), para 14: 'Although the crash of the aircraft carrying the Presidents of Rwanda and Burundi on 6 April 1994 is considered to be the event that triggered the civil war and the acts of genocide that followed, the Council decided that the temporal jurisdiction of the Tribunal would commence on 1 January 1994, in order to capture the planning stage of the crimes.'

[78] See *Prosecutor v Nahimana, Barayagwiza and Ngeze*, ICTR-99-52-T, Trial Chamber, Judgment, 3 December 2003, paras 100–104, 1017, and 1044.

[79] *Prosecutor v Nahimana, Barayagwiza and Ngeze*, ICTR-99-52-A, Appeals Chamber, Judgment, 28 November 2007, para 313.

[80] Ibid, para 317. As it was, the offence of direct and public incitement to commit genocide was held not to be a continuing crime, as per ibid, para 723. The Appeals Chamber was not obliged to rule in this respect on conspiracy to commit genocide.

[81] Ibid, paras 315 and 319, citing, *inter alia, Prosecutor v Simba*, ICTR-01-76-AR72.2, Appeals Chamber, Decision on Interlocutory Appeal Regarding Temporal Jurisdiction, 29 July 2004.

of Yugoslavia, including its land surface, airspace and territorial waters'. On a plain reading of this provision, the ICTY Appeals Chamber was able to hold that the Tribunal enjoyed jurisdiction *ratione loci* not only in relation to those parts of the territory of the former Socialist Federal Republic of Yugoslavia that had been embroiled in armed conflict when the Tribunal was established but also in relation to both Kosovo[82] and Macedonia.[83] In addition, the express reference in article 8 to airspace gave the Prosecutor jurisdiction to investigate allegations of war crimes by NATO in its 1999 bombing campaign over what was then the Federal Republic of Yugoslavia.[84] The MICT inherits this jurisdiction *ratione loci*.

Article 7 of the ICTR Statute states that the Tribunal's territorial jurisdiction 'shall extend to the territory of Rwanda including its land surface and airspace as well as to the territory of neighbouring States in respect of serious violations of international humanitarian law committed by Rwandan citizens'. As explained by the UN Secretary-General, '[i]n extending the territorial jurisdiction of the Tribunal beyond the territorial bounds of Rwanda, the Council envisaged mainly the refugee camps in Zaire [now the Democratic Republic of the Congo (DRC)] and other neighbouring countries in which serious violations of international humanitarian law are alleged to have been committed in connection with the conflict in Rwanda'.[85] The second limb of article 7 has never been relied on. Both limbs nonetheless pass to the MICT.

12.29

B. Exercise

(i) Immunity

Neither the ICTY nor the ICTR is barred from exercising its jurisdiction over the accused by the customary international rules on state immunity, head-of-state immunity, head-of-government immunity or any other species of procedural immunity, whether *ratione materiae* or *ratione personae*, in accordance with which a state is obliged to ensure that its courts refrain from exercising jurisdiction over the serving or former officials of another. Most fundamentally, no provision of either Statute provides that the Tribunal is bound to respect such immunities, with the result that the Tribunal's jurisdiction over the accused, as otherwise authorized by the Statute, remains unfettered. In addition, article 7(2) of the ICTY Statute and article 6(2) of the ICTR Statute state identically that '[t]he official position of any accused person, whether as Head of State or Government or as a responsible Government official, shall not relieve such

12.30

---

[82] *Milutinović* et al, Appeals Chamber Reasons for Decision (n 59).
[83] *Boškoski and Tarčulovski*, Appeals Chamber Decision on Jurisdiction (n 76), para 10.
[84] See *Final Report to the Prosecutor by the Committee Established to Review the NATO Bombing Campaign Against the Federal Republic of Yugoslavia* (2000).
[85] *Report of the Secretary-General pursuant to Security Council resolution 955 (1994)* (n 9), para 13.

person of criminal responsibility nor mitigate punishment'; and although article 7 of the Nuremberg Charter, of which article 7(2) of the ICTY Statute and article 6(2) of the ICTR Statute are near-verbatim restatements, was in fact directed at criminal responsibility as such, having been inserted to deny the substantive defence of act of state, rather than jurisdictional immunity, article 7(2) of the ICTY Statute and article 6(2) of the ICTR Statute have been consistently read as abrogating—insofar as abrogation might be thought necessary, given that nowhere is either Tribunal directed in the first place to give effect to these—all potentially-relevant immunities.[86] The same situation applies in relation to the MICT by virtue of article 1(1) of its Statute.

12.31 Whether this undoubtedly effective unavailability of immunities from jurisdiction is internationally lawful is a distinct question, to which the answer is that it undoubtedly is.[87] Its legal basis is the establishment of each Tribunal, in response to a threat to the peace, by way of a Security Council decision under chapter VII of the Charter. In accordance with article 1(1) of the Charter, the UN is not obliged to act in conformity with the principles of international law when taking 'effective collective measures for the prevention and removal of threats to the peace'. Nor is any UN member state in a legal position to object to this, given that, in article 25 of the Charter, 'Members of the United Nations agree to accept...the decisions of the Security Council in accordance with the...Charter'. As regards the ICTR, moreover, Rwanda, not least in requesting the establishment of the Tribunal to begin with, manifestly waived any immunity to which it would have been entitled to see its ex-officials benefit.

12.32 While none of the accused in The Hague or Arusha has been a head of state or head of government at the time of prosecution, at the time of his alleged or proven crimes one was a head of state,[88] one was a head of government,[89] and many were state officials of some form acting in that capacity.

(ii) Remedial discretion

12.33 In *Barayagwiza*, the Appeals Chamber of the ICTR held that the Tribunal was permitted to decline to exercise its jurisdiction over an individual 'where to exercise that jurisdiction in light of serious and egregious violations of the accused's rights would prove detrimental to the [Tribunal]'s integrity'.[90] The Appeals Chamber of the ICTY endorsed this proposition in *Nikolić (Dragan)*, where it stated that 'certain human rights violations are of such a serious nature that they

---

[86] Pointing to this provision, the Secretary-General stated in *Report of the Secretary-General pursuant to Security Council resolution 808 (1993)* (n 7), para 55, that 'a plea of head of State immunity...will not constitute a defence', even if he too seems to have conflated substantive and procedural immunity.

[87] Recall *supra* paras 3.37 and 3.40.

[88] Slobodan Milošević was the head of state of the Federal Republic of Yugoslavia from 1997 to 2000.

[89] Jean Kambanda was prime minister of Rwanda during the genocide of 1994.

[90] *Prosecutor v Barayagwiza*, ICTR-97-19, Appeals Chamber, Decision, 3 November 1999, para 74. See also ibid, para 112.

require that the exercise of jurisdiction be declined'.[91] The Appeals Chamber emphasized, however, that such a case would be 'exceptional' and that the remedy of setting aside jurisdiction would 'usually be disproportionate', observing that the 'correct balance must...be struck between the fundamental rights of the accused and the essential interests of the international community in the prosecution of persons charged with serious violations of international [criminal] law'.[92]

V. Relationship to National Criminal Jurisdictions

A. Concurrency

In accordance with article 9(1) of the ICTY Statute and article 8(1) of the ICTR Statute, the ICTY and ICTR enjoy concurrent jurisdiction with national courts to prosecute persons for acts within their jurisdiction. In the words of the Secretary General's report on the ICTY, in establishing the Tribunal 'it was not the intention of the Security Council to preclude or prevent the exercise of jurisdiction by national courts with respect to such acts'.[93] 'Indeed', the report continues, 'national courts should be encouraged to exercise their jurisdiction in accordance with their relevant national laws and procedures'.[94] This jurisdictional concurrency is maintained under the MICT, as per article 5(1) of the latter's Statute. 12.34

The concurrency of the Tribunals' jurisdiction with that of national jurisdictions raises the question of which jurisdiction, the international or national, is to prevail in the event of competition between them and of possible double jeopardy. Both questions are answered in the statutes of the ICTY, ICTR, and MICT. 12.35

B. Primacy

(i) General

In accordance with article 9(2) of the ICTY Statute and article 8(2) of the ICTR Statute, each Tribunal enjoys primacy over national courts. This means, in the words of these provisions, that at any stage of the proceedings both the ICTY and ICTR 'may formally request national courts to defer' to their competence—that is, to halt national investigations or proceedings in favour of investigations and proceedings in the relevant international tribunal.[95] Such a request is binding by virtue of the obligation to comply with requests issued 12.36

---

[91] *Prosecutor v Nikolić (Dragan)*, IT-94-2-AR73, Appeals Chamber, Decision on Interlocutory Appeal considering Legality of Arrest, 5 June 2003, para 30.
[92] Ibid.
[93] *Report of the Secretary-General pursuant to Security Council resolution 808 (1993)* (n 7), para 64.
[94] Ibid.   [95] This primacy is fleshed out in rules 8–13 of the Tribunals' respective RPE.

by a Trial Chamber laid down in article 29(1) of the ICTY Statute and article 28(1) of the ICTR Statute, the sources of the binding force of which are Security Council resolutions 827 (1993) and 955 (1994) respectively and article 25 of the UN Charter. The MICT enjoys the same primacy, in accordance with article 5(2) of its Statute.[96]

12.37 The first accused before the ICTY, Tadić, had been the subject of a successful request for deferral made in 1994 to Germany, where he was under investigation. He argued before the ICTY that the Tribunal's primacy was a violation of the sovereignty of Bosnia-Herzegovina, pointing to article 2(7) of the UN Charter, which states that nothing in the Charter 'shall authorize the United Nations to intervene in matters which are essentially within the domestic jurisdiction of any state'. He neglected, however, to cite the next limb of article 2(7), which states that 'this principle shall not prejudice the application of enforcement measures under Chapter VII'—a clause relied on by the Appeals Chamber in rejecting his submission.[97]

(ii) Rule 11bis

12.38 Neither the ICTY nor the ICTR is obliged to exercise its primacy over national courts. On the contrary, rule 11*bis* of their respective RPE provides that the Tribunal may refer one of its own cases back to the authorities of a state.[98] Recourse to rule 11*bis*, which was part of the Tribunals' 'completion strategies' and which there is no further cause to invoke, was required only in relation to persons actually indicted by the Tribunal. Cases merely under investigation could be referred without judicial authorization.

---

[96] A request under art 5(2) of the MICT Statute for deferral of national proceedings is binding on UN member states in accordance with art 28(1) of the Statute and, ultimately, SC res 1966 (2010), para 9 and UN Charter, art 25.

[97] *Tadić*, Appeals Chamber Decision on Jurisdiction (n 47), para 56. The Appeals Chamber also rejected the accused's argument that the ICTY's primacy over national courts amounted to a violation of the principle *jus de non evocando*, a feature of many national constitutions which prohibits the government from establishing extraordinary courts in times of unrest to try political offences, usually without the fair trial guarantees applicable in the ordinary criminal courts. The principle was held, ibid, paras 62–63, to have no application in the context of an international criminal tribunal established by the Security Council. Nor, as made clear ibid, para 62, were any rights of the accused 'thereby infringed or threatened; quite to the contrary, they [were] all specifically spelt out and protected under the Statute of the International Tribunal'. See also *Prosecutor v Kanyabashi*, ICTR-96-15-T, Trial Chamber, Decision on the Defence Motion of Jurisdiction, 18 June 1997, paras 30–32.

[98] The accused in *Stanković* argued that the Tribunal did not have the power to refer his case to a national court as rule 11*bis*, inserted into the Statute by the Tribunal's judges, was *ultra vires* the ICTY Statute—in other words, that the Security Council had not conferred this power on the Tribunal. The Appeals Chamber dismissed the challenge. See *Prosecutor v Stanković*, IT-96-23/2-AR11*bis*.1, Appeals Chamber, Decision on Rule 11*bis* Referral, 1 September 2005, paras 14–16. See also *Prosecutor v Mejakić* et al, IT-02-65-AR11*bis*.1, Appeals Chamber, Decision on Joint Defence Appeal against Decision on Referral under Rule 11*bis*, 7 April 2006, paras 15–17. But the Tribunal had no power to order a state to accept a transferred case, as made in clear in *Stanković*, Appeals Chamber Decision on Rule 11*bis* Referral, para 40.

What was transferred by way of rule 11*bis* was the case, not necessarily the person of the accused. The accused may already have been in detention in the state to which transfer was requested[99] or may still have been at large.[100] **12.39**

Rule 11*bis* decisions required the Referral Bench (ICTY) or Trial Chamber (ICTR) to scrutinize the municipal criminal law, procedure, and practice, in the broadest sense, of the state to which referral was proposed, in order to ascertain that the accused could in fact be tried there and that an appropriate punishment would be available. As regards criminalization and punishment of the alleged conduct, it was held in *Bagaragaza*, partly by analogy with the rule *non bis in idem* specified in article 9(2)(*a*) of the ICTR Statute,[101] that referral to a national court under rule 11*bis* was not permitted where the alleged conduct would be tried as an ordinary municipal crime (or 'common' crime).[102] **12.40**

Attempts by some accused to resist transfer of their case to a national jurisdiction on the ground that a given extradition treaty or provision of national law did not permit it were rightly dismissed by the ICTY.[103] **12.41**

A version of rule 11*bis* is found in article 6(2) to (6) of the MICT Statute. Article 6(1) of the Statute provides that the MICT 'shall have the power, and shall undertake every effort', to refer to national jurisdictions cases involving persons indicted by the ICTY or ICTR who are not among the most senior leaders suspected of being most responsible for crimes within the jurisdiction of the Mechanism.[104] Provision for such referral was considered prudent when the MICT Statute was adopted in late 2010, when efforts to refer certain cases from the ICTR to Rwanda were ongoing. These cases have since been successfully referred, meaning that reliance for this purpose on article 6(2) is not envisaged. Article 6(1), however, also grants the MICT the power to refer to national jurisdictions cases involving persons indicted for contempt of, or for knowingly and wilfully giving false testimony before, the Tribunals or MICT.[105] Referral of such cases is not to be ruled out. **12.42**

(iii) Non bis in idem

It is a general principle of criminal law common to most national criminal justice traditions that a person shall not be tried twice for the same offence. The **12.43**

---

[99] See eg the case of Wenceslas Munyeshyaka, who was in custody in France, and the case of Michel Bagaragaza, who was in detention in the Netherlands.
[100] See eg the cases of Fulgence Kayishema, Charles Sikubwabo, Phénéas Munyarugarama, Aloys Ndimbati, Charles Ryandikayo, and Ladislas Ntaganzwa.
[101] See *infra* para 12.44–12.45.
[102] *Prosecutor v Bagaragaza*, ICTR-05-86-AR11*bis*, Appeals Chamber, Decision on Rule 11*bis* Appeal, 30 August 2006, paras 16–18. Consider also *Tadić*, Appeals Chamber Decision on Jurisdiction (n 47), para 58.
[103] See *Mejakić*, Appeals Chamber Decision on Referral (n 98), para 31; *Prosecutor v Ljubičić*, IT-00-41-AR11*bis*.1, Appeals Chamber, Decision on Appeal against Decision on Referral under Rule 11*bis*, 4 July 2006, para 8.
[104] MICT Statute, art 6(1), cross-referenced with ibid, art 1(3) and, in turn, ibid, art 1(2).
[105] Ibid, art 6(1), cross-referenced with ibid, art 1(4).

principle—often referred to as the prohibition on 'double jeopardy', and reflected in the common law in the pleas of *autrefois acquit* and *autrefois convict*—tends to go in international law by the Latin label *non bis in idem* or, introducing an implied subjunctive mood, *ne bis in idem*. As regards criminal proceedings in municipal tribunals, the principle is guaranteed by the rule stipulated in article 14(7) of the ICCPR. The prohibition has a particular resonance in the context of trial by an international criminal tribunal enjoying jurisdiction concurrent with that of national courts, where there is the factual possibility that an accused before the international tribunal may have already faced trial in a national court in respect of the same acts, and *vice versa*.

12.44　Article 10 of the ICTY Statute and article 9 of the ICTR Statute make identical provision, *mutatis mutandis*, in respect of the rule *non bis in idem*.[106] Paragraph 1 of each, dealing with trial at the national level after trial by the relevant Tribunal, stipulates that no person shall be tried before a national court 'for acts constituting serious violations of international humanitarian law under the…Statute for which he or she has already been tried by the…Tribunal'. The binding force for states of this common provision derives from the obligation to comply with requests from a Trial Chamber stipulated in article 29 of the ICTY Statute and article 28 of the ICTR Statute respectively, as backed by Security Council resolutions 827 (1993) and 955 (1994) respectively and article 25 of the UN Charter. Paragraph 2 common to article 10 of the ICTY Statute and article 9 of the ICTR Statute, dealing with the converse scenario, bars subsequent trial before the Tribunal 'for acts constituting serious violations of international humanitarian law' unless, as per subparagraph (*a*), 'the act for which he or she was tried [by the national court] was characterized as an ordinary crime' or, as per subparagraph (*b*), 'the national court proceedings were not impartial or independent, were designed to shield the accused from international criminal responsibility, or the case was not diligently prosecuted'. Paragraph 3 of both provisions, referable to the exceptions to *non bis in idem* recognized in paragraph 2(*a*) and (*b*), adds that, '[i]n considering the penalty to be imposed on a person convicted of a crime under the present Statute, the International Tribunal shall take into account the extent to which any penalty imposed by a national court on the same person for the same act has already been served'. Article 7 of the MICT Statute is in terms identical, *mutatis mutandis*, to those of article 10 of the ICTY Statute and article 9 of the ICTR Statute, with the prohibition in paragraph 1 encompassing persons tried by the ICTY, the ICTR or the MICT.

12.45　Paragraph 2(*a*) common to article 10 of the ICTY Statute, article 9 of the ICTR Statute, and article 7 of the MICT Statute represents a significant point of distinction between the prohibition on double jeopardy at the international level as embodied in these three statutes and the prohibition as embodied in article 20(3) of the Rome Statute.[107]

---

[106] See also rule 13 of the respective RPE.　　[107] See *infra* para 14.78.

VI. Relationship to the International Court of Justice

The ICTY and ICTR, on the one hand, and the International Court of Justice (ICJ), on the other, do different things. The former determine individual criminal responsibility through prosecutions brought and conducted by an organ of the relevant Tribunal itself on behalf of all UN member states. The latter determines state responsibility through one state's suit against another.[108] There is nonetheless the possibility that the Tribunals and the ICJ might deal with related subject-matters, whether factual, legal or both,[109] which raises the question of their relationship, given that the former are judicial organs of the United Nations, albeit judicial organs created as subsidiary organs of the Security Council, while the latter is characterized in article 92 of the UN Charter as 'the principal judicial organ of the United Nations'. 12.46

Despite the language of article 92 of the Charter, there is no hierarchy between the ICJ, on the one hand, and the ICTY and ICTR, on the other. The ICTY and ICTR are not bound by the rulings of the ICJ on points of law.[110] Indeed, there is no formal relationship at all between them. Nor has comity been understood to dictate that the ICTY and ICTR take their legal lead, where relevant, from the ICJ. Notoriously, the ICTY in the Appeals Chamber judgment in *Tadić* declined to apply the test for state control over irregular forces laid down by the ICJ in the *Nicaragua* case, although strictly speaking a different legal point was at issue in each case.[111] In *Kvočka*, moreover, the ICTY Appeals Chamber refused the accused's motion for either the suspension of any decision on questions pending before the ICJ in the case of *Application of the Convention on the Prevention and Punishment of the Crime of Genocide* or a ruling that the ICTY would not decide on the same legal and factual questions.[112] But this is not to say that the ICTY and ICTR have completely ignored the judgments of the ICJ (or, indeed, of other international courts and tribunals). In *Čelebići*, the ICTY Appeals Chamber, quoting from the separate opinion of Judge Shahabuddeen in the ICTR Appeals Chamber judgment in *Semanza*,[113] stated that it would 'necessarily take into 12.47

---

[108] The ICJ also provides advisory opinions for UN organs and specialized agencies.

[109] See, most notably, the ICJ cases on the application of the Genocide Convention between Bosnia-Herzegovina and Serbia and Montenegro and between Croatia and Serbia.

[110] See eg *Prosecutor v Delalić* et al ('*Čelebići*'), IT-96-21-A, Appeals Chamber, Judgment, 20 February 2001, para 24 and *Prosecutor v Kvočka* et al, IT-98-30/1, Appeals Chamber, Decision on Interlocutory Appeal by the Accused Zoran Zigić against the Decision of Trial Chamber I dated 5 December 2000, 25 May 2001, paras 16–18.

[111] *Prosecutor v Tadić*, IT-94-1-A, Appeals Chamber, Judgment, 15 July 1999, paras 115–145. The ruling was upheld in *Prosecutor v Aleksovski*, IT-95-14/1-A, Appeals Chamber, Judgment, 24 March 2000, para 134 and *Čelebići*, Appeals Chamber Judgment (n 110), paras 23–26.

[112] See *Kvočka*, Appeals Chamber Decision on Interlocutory Appeal by Zoran Zigić (n 110).

[113] The Appeals Chamber 'agree[d] that "so far as international law is concerned, the operation of the desiderata of consistency, stability, and predictability does not stop at the frontiers of the Tribunal"', and acknowledged that it could not 'behave as if the general state of the law in the international community whose interests it serves is none of its concern'. See *Čelebići*, Appeals Chamber Judgment (n 110), para 24, quoting *Prosecutor v Semanza*, ICTR-97-20-A, Appeals Chamber, Judgment, 31 May 2000, sep op Shahabuddeen, para 25.

consideration other decisions of international courts'.[114] Similarly, in *Kvočka*, the ICTY Appeals Chamber noted that 'decisions of the International Court of Justice addressing general questions of international law are of the utmost significance' and that it would consider such decisions.[115] In both cases, however, the Tribunal emphasized its own competence and underlined its freedom to come to different findings and conclusions.

12.48 As for the converse, the ICJ is equally not bound by findings of fact or law made by the ICTY or ICTR. But again this is not to say that it will not take them into account where relevant. Indeed, in *Application of the Convention on the Prevention and Punishment of the Crime of Genocide*, the ICJ stated that it 'should in principle accept as highly persuasive relevant findings of fact made by the [ICTY] at trial, unless of course they have been upset on appeal'.[116] 'For the same reasons', the Court continued, 'any evaluation by the Tribunal based on the facts as so found, for instance about the existence of the required intent, is also entitled to due weight'.[117] Later, the Court declared that it 'attache[d] the utmost importance to the factual and legal findings made by the ICTY in ruling on the criminal liability of the accused before it', and reiterated that it '[took] fullest account of the ICTY's trial and appellate judgments dealing with the events underlying the dispute'.[118] It distinguished such findings, however, from 'positions adopted by the ICTY on issues of general international law which do not lie within the specific purview of its jurisdiction and, moreover, the resolution of which is not always necessary for deciding the criminal cases before it'.[119] In the latter light, the Court had no hesitation in following its own *Nicaragua* jurisprudence and rejecting the test of state control over irregular forces laid down for the purposes of the ICTY in *Tadić*.

VII. Co-operation with the Tribunals

A. General

12.49 It will be recalled that Security Council resolutions 827 (1993) and 855 (1994) oblige UN member states to 'co-operate fully' with the relevant Tribunal, with special reference being made in the first to article 29 of the ICTY Statute and in the second to article 28 of the ICTR Statute. In short, requests for assistance and orders issued to UN member states by the ICTY under article 29 of its Statute and by the ICTR under article 28 of its Statute are binding. The same goes for requests and orders issued to UN member states by the MICT under article 28 of its Statute, given the obligation on UN member states 'to cooperate fully with the Mechanism' laid down in Security Council resolution 1966 (2010). As recalled

---

[114] *Čelebići*, Appeals Chamber Judgment (n 110), para 24.
[115] *Kvočka*, Appeals Chamber Decision on Interlocutory Appeal by Zoran Žigić (n 110), para 18.
[116] *Application of the Convention on the Prevention and Punishment of the Crime of Genocide (Bosnia and Herzegovina v Serbia and Montenegro), Merits, Judgment*, ICJ Rep 2007, 43, 134, para 223.
[117] Ibid.   [118] Ibid, 209, para 403.   [119] Ibid.

in *Blaškić*, the binding force for UN member states of requests and orders issued by the ICTY, and by the same token by the ICTR and MICT, 'derives from the provisions of Chapter VII and Article 25 of the United Nations Charter and from the Security Council resolution adopted pursuant to those provisions'.[120] Neither the Tribunals nor the MICT, however, has the power to enforce the orders they direct to states or to sanction states for failure to co-operate.[121] Both tasks fall to the Security Council.[122]

Article 29 of the ICTY Statute and, *mutatis mutandis*, article 28 of the ICTR Statute provide: **12.50**

1. States shall co-operate with the International Tribunal in the investigation and prosecution of persons accused of committing serious violations of international humanitarian law.
2. States shall comply without undue delay with any request for assistance or an order issued by a Trial Chamber, including, but not limited to:
   (*a*) The identification and location of persons;
   (*b*) The taking of testimony and the production of evidence;
   (*c*) The service of documents;
   (*d*) The arrest or detention of persons;
   (*e*) The surrender or the transfer of the accused to the International Tribunal.[123]

These obligations are supported by, *inter alia*, rule 7*bis* of the ICTY and ICTR RPE respectively, pursuant to which the president of the relevant Tribunal shall notify the Security Council in cases where a state has failed to comply with a request for assistance or order.

Article 28(1) and (2) of the MICT Statute are in terms almost identical to those of article 29 of the ICTY Statute and article 28 of the ICTR Statute, although the general obligation of co-operation in paragraph 1 extends to the investigation and prosecution of persons accused of contempt of, or knowingly and wilfully giving false testimony before, the Tribunals or the MICT.[124] Article 28 of the MICT Statute also features a paragraph 3 relating to certain requests to the MICT for assistance.[125]   **12.51**

In *Blaškić*, the Appeals Chamber of the ICTY held that, in addition to its power to request or order states to take measures in relation to individuals within their   **12.52**

---

[120] *Prosecutor v Blaškić*, IT-95-14, Appeals Chamber, Judgment on the Request of the Republic of Croatia for Review of the Decision of Trial Chamber II of 18 July 1997, 29 October 1997, para 26.
[121] See eg ibid, paras 25 and 33.   [122] See eg ibid, para 33.
[123] See also rules 54–61 ('Orders and Warrants') and 66–70 ('Production of Evidence') of the respective RPE.
[124] Rather than referring to 'persons accused of committing serious violations of international humanitarian law', art 28(1) of the MICT Statute speaks of 'persons covered by Article 1 of this Statute'. Article 1(4) of the MICT Statute deals with persons indicted for contempt and for knowingly and willingly giving false testimony.
[125] MICT Statute, art 28(3) reads: 'The Mechanism shall respond to requests for assistance from national authorities in relation to investigation, prosecution and trial of those responsible for serious violations of international humanitarian law in the countries of former Yugoslavia and Rwanda, including, where appropriate, providing assistance in tracking fugitives whose cases have been referred to national authorities by the ICTY, the ICTR, or the Mechanism.'

jurisdiction, it enjoyed the power directly to subpoena—that is, to issue a binding order under threat of penal sanction—individuals acting in their private capacity to appear before the Tribunal as a witness, to produce a document or the like.[126] The sanctions available to the Tribunal in relation to an individual's non-compliance with a binding order were held to include both an inherent power to hold the individual in contempt of the Tribunal and the contempt power conferred by rule 77 of the ICTY RPE.[127]

12.53   As emphasized by the Appeals Chamber of the ICTY[128] and by the European Court of Human Rights,[129] surrender to the Tribunals is not extradition.

B. Special Forcible Measures

12.54   In accordance with the General Framework Agreement for Peace in Bosnia and Herzegovina 1995 ('Dayton Agreement'), the states parties, *viz* Bosnia-Herzegovina, Croatia, and the Federal Republic of Yugoslavia (now the separate successor states of Montenegro and Serbia), are obliged to 'cooperate fully with all entities involved in implementation' of the Agreement, including those 'authorized by the United Nations Security Council, pursuant to the obligation of all Parties to cooperate in the investigation and prosecution of war crimes and other violations of international humanitarian law'.[130] This obligation is restated in article X of Annex 1-A to the Agreement, which refers explicitly to the ICTY. Pursuant also to Annex 1-A, the states parties invite the Security Council 'to authorize Member states or regional organizations and arrangements to establish the IFOR [a multinational military Implementation Force] acting under Chapter VII of the United Nations Charter'.[131] They further express their understanding and agreement that 'IFOR shall have the right...to monitor and help ensure compliance by all parties with this Annex'[132] and that 'the IFOR Commander shall have the authority...to do all that the commander judges necessary and proper, including the use of military force,...to carry out [these and other] responsibilities'.[133] In furtherance of the Dayton Agreement, the Security Council, determining that the situation in the region continued to constitute a threat to international peace and security and acting under chapter VII of the Charter, adopted resolution 1031 (1995), which recognized that the states parties to the Dayton Agreement were obliged to co-operate fully with all entities involved in its implementation, expressly mentioning the ICTY, and

---

[126] *Blaškić*, Appeals Chamber Judgment on the Request of Croatia (n 120), paras 47–48 and 56 and disposition.
[127] Ibid, para 59 and disposition. See, in particular, ICTY RPE, rule 77(A)(iii), empowering the ICTY to hold in contempt of the Tribunal a person who knowingly, wilfully, and without just excuse fails to comply with an order to attend before or produce documents before a Chamber.
[128] See *Mejakić*, Appeals Chamber Decision on Referral (n 98), para 31; *Ljubičić*, Appeals Chamber Decision on Referral (n 103), para 8.
[129] *Naletilić v Croatia* (n 36).   [130] Dayton Agreement, art IX.
[131] Ibid, Annex 1-A, art VI(1). See also ibid, art I(1)(*a*).
[132] Ibid, art VI(2)(*a*).   [133] Ibid, art VI(5).

that they had in particular 'authorized the multinational force... to take such actions as required, including the use of necessary force, to ensure compliance with Annex 1-A of the Peace Agreement'.[134] The resolution went on to authorize UN member states to establish IFOR 'in order to fulfil the role specified in Annex 1-A' of the Dayton Agreement[135] and 'to take all necessary measures to effect the implementation of and to ensure compliance with Annex 1-A of the Agreement'.[136] It stressed that the states parties were to be subject to 'such enforcement action by IFOR as may be necessary to ensure implementation of th[e] Annex', and took note 'that the parties ha[d] consented to IFOR's taking such actions'.[137] Security Council resolution 1088 (1996), also adopted under chapter VII of the Charter, subsequently provided in relation to IFOR's legal successor, SFOR (a multinational Stabilization Force), what resolution 1031 (1995) had for IFOR.[138]

12.55 By a resolution of 16 December 1995, the North Atlantic Council, NATO's decision-making body, 'having regard to the United Nations Security Council Resolution 827, the United Nations Security Council Resolution 1031, and Annex 1-A of the General Framework Agreement for Peace in Bosnia and Herzegovina', provided that 'IFOR should detain any persons indicted by the International Criminal Tribunal who come into contact with IFOR in its execution of assigned tasks, in order to assure the transfer of those persons to the International Criminal Tribunal'. In 1997, in a robust application of their mandate, SFOR elements began actively to arrest indictees and to transfer them to the custody of the ICTY. Before its winding up in December 2005, SFOR succeeded in arresting and transferring to The Hague 23 persons indicted by the ICTY. It killed two further persons who resisted arrest. Its involvement in the capture of indictees marked a turning point in the ICTY's fortunes.

VIII. Conclusion

12.56 The histories of the ICTY and ICTR are remarkable. Created arguably as little more than a way for the Security Council, or certain members of it, to be seen to be doing something about the horrors of the ongoing wars in the former Yugoslavia, the ICTY has ended up prosecuting or handing over to others to prosecute all bar an unindicted or dead few of the foremost political and military parties to international crimes perpetrated during the conflicts. The ICTR, established again perhaps more out of guilt than expectation, has, with only nine of its indictees still at large, been a similar statistical triumph. But the achievements of the two Tribunals are not to be measured only quantitatively. Without their judgments over the past two decades it would remain hard to talk plausibly of a corpus

---

[134] SC res 1031 (1995), 15 December 1995, para 5. [135] Ibid, para 14.
[136] Ibid, para 15. [137] Ibid.
[138] See SC res 1088 (1996), 12 December 1996, paras 7, 18, and 19.

12.57 of customary international criminal law, and the contributions of at least their Appeals Chambers to this corpus have by and large been sound.

None of this is to suggest that the ICTY and ICTR have got everything right. Whatever the many reasons, it is simply unacceptable, and from many angles, that any trial should last as long as most have done before the Tribunals. It has also to be said that certain lines of the Appeals Chambers' *jurisprudence constante* are eminently contestable. But even these failings have proved salutary insofar as other international criminal courts, as well as certain municipal criminal courts trying international crimes, have learned from the ICTY and ICTR's mistakes. It is to be hoped that something remains to be learned from their and the MICT's successes.

Further Reading

ACQUAVIVA, G, 'Was a Residual Mechanism for International Criminal Tribunals Really Necessary?' (2011) 9 *Journal of International Criminal Justice* 789

CLARK, JN, 'The ICTY and Reconciliation in Croatia' (2012) 10 *Journal of International Criminal Justice* 397

DEL MAR, K, 'Weight of Evidence Generated through Intra-Institutional Fact-finding before the International Court of Justice' (2011) 2 *Journal of International Dispute Settlement* 293

DENIS, C, 'Critical Overview of the "Residual Functions" of the Mechanism and its Date of Commencement (including Transitional Arrangements)' (2011) 9 *Journal of International Criminal Justice* 819

EL ZEIDY, MM, 'From Primacy to Complementarity and Backwards: (Re)-Visiting Rule 11 *bis* of the Ad Hoc Tribunals' (2008) 57 *International and Comparative Law Quarterly* 403

GRADONI, L, '"You Will Receive a Fair Trial Elsewhere": The Ad Hoc International Criminal Tribunals Acting as Human Rights Jurisdictions' (2007) 54 *Netherlands International Law Review* 1

JOHNSON, LD, 'Closing an International Criminal Tribunal While Maintaining International Human Rights Standards and Excluding Impunity' (2005) 99 *American Journal of International Law* 158

KLARIN, M, 'The Impact of the ICTY Trials on Public Opinion in the Former Yugoslavia' (2009) 7 *Journal of International Criminal Justice* 89

KUTNJAK IVKOVICH, S and HAGAN, J, *Reclaiming Justice: The International Criminal Tribunal for the Former Yugoslavia and Local Courts* (New York: Oxford University Press, 2011)

METTRAUX, G, *International Crimes and the* Ad Hoc *Tribunals* (Oxford: Oxford University Press, 2005), chapters 1 and 2

MUNDIS, D, 'The Judicial Effects of the "Completion Strategies" on the Ad Hoc International Criminal Tribunals' (2005) 99 *American Journal of International Law* 142

ORIE, AMM, '*Stare decisis* in the ICTY Appeal System? Successor Responsibility in the Hadžihasanović Case' (2012) 10 *Journal of International Criminal Justice* 625

POND, E, *Endgame in the Balkans: Regime Change, European Style* (Washington, DC: Brookings Institution, 2006)

RAAB, D, 'Evaluating the ICTY and its Completion Strategy. Efforts to Achieve Accountability for War Crimes and their Tribunals' (2005) 3 *Journal of International Criminal Justice* 82

Ryngaert, C, 'State Cooperation with the International Criminal Tribunal for Rwanda' (2013) 13 *International Criminal Law Review* 125

Sarooshi, D, 'The Powers of the United Nations International Criminal Tribunals' (1998) 2 *Max Planck Yearbook of United Nations Law* 141

Schabas, W, *The UN International Criminal Tribunals. The Former Yugoslavia, Rwanda and Sierra Leone* (Cambridge: Cambridge University Press, 2006)

Shahabuddeen, M, *International Criminal Justice at the Yugoslav Tribunal: A Judge's Recollection* (Oxford: Oxford University Press, 2012)

Stroh, D, 'State Cooperation with the International Criminal Tribunals for the Former Yugoslavia and Rwanda' (2001) 5 *Max Planck Yearbook of United Nations Law* 249

Swart, B, Zahar, A, and Sluiter, G (eds), *The Legacy of the International Criminal Tribunal for the Former Yugoslavia* (Oxford: Oxford University Press, 2012)

Wayde Pittman, T, 'The Road to the Establishment of the International Residual Mechanism for Criminal Tribunals: From Completion to Continuation' (2011) 9 *Journal of International Criminal Justice* 797

Zacklin, R, 'Some Major Problems in the Drafting of the ICTY Statute' (2004) 2 *Journal of International Criminal Justice* 361

13

The Special Court for Sierra Leone and Residual Special Court for Sierra Leone

I. Introduction

13.1 The Special Court for Sierra Leone (SCSL) is to date the only international criminal court to have been established and empowered by means of a bilateral treaty between a state and an international organization, unless one counts separately its historical successor in the form of the Residual Special Court for Sierra Leone (RSCSL).[1] It is also the only international criminal court so far to have enjoyed subject-matter jurisdiction over both international and municipal crimes, even if in the event it never exercised its jurisdiction over the latter, and to have had its seat not just in the state where the events within its jurisdiction took place but at the invitation of that state; and it was the first to have had on its bench a combination of 'international' and 'national' judges. In all these ways the SCSL—while established after its equally experimental antecedents, the International Criminal Tribunal for the former Yugoslavia (ICTY) and the International Criminal Tribunal for Rwanda (ICTR)—was also an experiment in international criminal justice. In many ways this experiment too was a success.

13.2 The SCSL represents a first for international criminal justice in another way too. Whereas the closure of the International Military Tribunal (IMT) at Nuremberg and the IMT for the Far East at Tokyo left nothing by way of unfinished judicial business, and whereas the ICTY and the ICTR currently function alongside their 'Residual Mechanism', the SCSL is the only international criminal court to date both to have closed and to have seen its remaining work transferred to a successor judicial body.

13.3 Although the SCSL no longer exists, and although the work of the RSCSL is expected to be comparatively mundane, both—like the ICTY, ICTR, and the Mechanism for International Criminal Tribunals (MICT)—merit consideration

---

[1] Recall, *supra* para 3.24, that the Special Tribunal for Lebanon (STL), an international criminal court intended to have been established by means of a bilateral treaty between the UN and Lebanon, was eventually established by way of Security Council resolution 1757 (2007), 30 May 2007. Recall also, *supra* paras 3.34–3.35, 9.62–9.65, and 9.72–9.76, that the Extraordinary Chambers in the Courts of Cambodia and the Extraordinary African Chambers in the Senegalese Courts, each of which is the subject of a bilateral treaty between an international organization and a state, are municipal, not international, criminal courts.

from an institutional angle as exemplars of one formal and technical model for the adjudication of international (and factually-related municipal) crimes by way of an international criminal court and on account of some more general questions of international law posed, albeit not always convincingly answered, by their activities.

II. General

A. Establishment, Closure, and the Residual Special Court for Sierra Leone

Throughout the 1990s, the West African state of Sierra Leone was ravaged by a civil war notorious for the horrors visited on the civilian population. On 31 July 2000, the Secretary-General of the United Nations reported to the Security Council that the President of Sierra Leone had requested UN assistance in setting up a court to try senior members of the rebel Revolutionary United Front (RUF) 'for crimes against the people of Sierra Leone and for the taking of United Nations peacekeepers as hostages'.[2] In response, in resolution 1315 (2000) of 14 August 2000, the Security Council, recognizing 'the desire of the Government of Sierra Leone for assistance from the United Nations in establishing a strong and credible court that [would] meet the objectives of bringing justice and ensuring lasting peace' and reiterating that the situation in Sierra Leone constituted a threat to international peace and security, requested the Secretary-General 'to negotiate an agreement with the Government of Sierra Leone to create an independent special court' consistent with the resolution; recommended that 'the subject matter jurisdiction of the special court should include...crimes against humanity, war crimes and other serious violations of international humanitarian law, as well as crimes under relevant Sierra Leonean law committed within the territory of Sierra Leone'; recommended further that 'the special court should have personal jurisdiction over persons who bear the greatest responsibility for the commission of the crimes referred to'; and emphasized 'the importance of ensuring the impartiality, independence and credibility of the process, in particular with regard to the status of the judges and the prosecutors'.[3] The Security Council also requested the Secretary-General to submit to it a report on the establishment of the special court, including recommendations. The Secretary-General's subsequent report recommended 'a treaty-based sui generis court of mixed jurisdiction and composition', established pursuant to an agreement between the UN and the government of Sierra Leone.[4] The upshot in January 2002 was an Agreement between the

13.4

---

[2] *Fifth Report on the United Nations Mission in Sierra Leone*, UN doc S/2000/751 (31 July 2000), 2, para 9. For the letter from the president of Sierra Leone, dated 12 June 2000, see UN doc S/2000/786 (10 August 2000).
[3] SC res 1315 (2000), 14 August 2000, paras 1–4 respectively.
[4] *Report of the Secretary-General on the establishment of a Special Court for Sierra Leone*, UN doc S/2000/915 (4 October 2000), 3, para 9.

United Nations and the Government of Sierra Leone on the Establishment of a Special Court for Sierra Leone ('SCSL Agreement'),[5] with annexed Statute of the Special Court for Sierra Leone ('SCSL Statute'), entered into on behalf of the UN by a representative of the Secretary-General. The Security Council welcomed the Agreement in the preamble to Security Council resolution 1400 (2002) of 28 March 2002. The SCSL Agreement entered into force on 12 April 2002, and the SCSL officially commenced work on 1 July 2002.

13.5 The SCSL, like the ICTY and ICTR, was not intended to be permanent. Its last business was completed in the second half of 2013, and on 2 December 2013 the UN and Sierra Leone officially closed it,[6] with its premises being handed over to the latter. Its essential remaining functions[7] are now performed by an entity called the Residual Special Court for Sierra Leone (RSCSL), established pursuant to an August 2010 Agreement between the United Nations and the Government of Sierra Leone on the Establishment of a Residual Special Court for Sierra Leone ('RSCSL Agreement'), which entered into force on 2 October 2012 and to which is annexed the Statute of the Residual Special Court for Sierra Leone ('RSCSL Statute').[8] The RSCSL, a stripped-down, maximally cost-efficient version of the SCSL designed 'to carry out th[os]e functions of the Special Court for Sierra Leone that must continue after the closure of the Special Court', is deemed, subject to the RSCSL Agreement and RSCSL Statute, 'to continue the jurisdiction, functions, rights and obligations of the Special Court'.[9] It officially commenced work on 1 January 2014.

B. Basic Facts

13.6 As recognized by the Appeals Chamber of the SCSL[10] and by the Supreme Court of Sierra Leone,[11] the SCSL was an international criminal court.[12] The same goes

---

[5] Agreement between the United Nations and the Government of Sierra Leone on the Establishment of a Special Court for Sierra Leone, Freetown, 16 January 2002 ('SCSL Agreement'), with annexed Statute of the Special Court for Sierra Leone ('SCSL Statute').

[6] See, in this connection, SCSL Agreement, art 23, envisaging the termination of the Agreement by agreement of the parties on completion of the SCSL's judicial activities.

[7] See *infra* paras 13.18–13.19.

[8] See Agreement between the United Nations and the Government of Sierra Leone on the Establishment of a Residual Special Court for Sierra Leone, Freetown, 11 August 2010 ('RSCSL Agreement'), with annexed Statute of the Residual Special Court for Sierra Leone ('RSCSL Statute'). The Statute forms an integral part of the Agreement, in accordance with RSCSL Agreement, art 1(2).

[9] See RSCSL Agreement, art 1(1) and (3) respectively. Consider also RSCSL Statute, arts 1–6.

[10] *Prosecutor v Kallon and Kamara (Fofana and Gbao intervening)*, SCSL-2004-15-AR72(E) and SCSL-2004-16-AR72(E), Appeals Chamber, Decision on Challenge to Jurisdiction: Lomé Accord Amnesty, 13 March 2004, paras 86 and 88; *Prosecutor v Kallon, Norman and Kamara (Fofana intervening)*, SCSL-2004-15-AR72(E), SCSL-2004-14-AR72(E) and SCSL-2004-16-AR72(E), Appeals Chamber, Decision on Constitutionality and Lack of Jurisdiction, 13 March 2004, paras 55 and 71; *Prosecutor v Taylor*, SCSL-03-01-I, Appeals Chamber, Decision on Immunity from Jurisdiction, 31 May 2004, para 42.

[11] *Sesay, Kondewa and Fofana v President of the Special Court and Others*, SC No 1/2003, Supreme Court of Sierra Leone, 14 October 2005, 13–16.

[12] For details, recall *supra* paras 3.17–3.20.

for the RSCSL. The SCSL did not formally depend nor does the RSCSL formally depend for its establishment or judicial powers on the municipal law of Sierra Leone or any other state. The SCSL formally derived its existence and competence directly from the SCSL Agreement and annexed SCSL Statute, while the RSCSL formally derives its existence and competence directly from the RSCSL Agreement and annexed RSCSL Statute. Conversely, the SCSL was not an organ of the state of Sierra Leone, hence the name 'Special' Court. In accordance with Sierra Leone's Special Court Agreement 2002 (Ratification) Act 2002, the Special Court did 'not form part of the Judiciary of Sierra Leone'[13] and offences prosecuted before the Special Court were 'not prosecuted in the name of the Republic of Sierra Leone'.[14]

The SCSL is often referred to as a 'mixed' or 'hybrid' criminal tribunal. The informal label[15] describes the Special Court's jurisdiction *ratione materiae* and the composition of its bench.[16] The SCSL enjoyed jurisdiction *ratione materiae* over both international crimes and crimes under Sierra Leonean law.[17] Each of the two Trial Chambers comprised one judge appointed by the government of Sierra Leone and two appointed by the UN Secretary-General on nominations from states, especially states of the Economic Community of West African States (ECOWAS) and the Commonwealth, with the Appeals Chamber arranged 2:3.[18] The government of Sierra Leone and the Secretary-General consulted on the appointment of judges.[19] There was no requirement that judges appointed by the government of Sierra Leone be nationals of Sierra Leone, and many were not. In appointment to the roster of judges of the RSCSL, 'particular account' is to be taken of the

13.7

---

[13] Special Court Agreement 2002 (Ratification) Act 2002, s 11(1). That the SCSL existed outside the judicial system of Sierra Leone was affirmed by the Appeals Chamber in *Kallon, Norman and Kamara (Fofana intervening)*, Appeals Chamber Decision on Constitutionality and Lack of Jurisdiction (n 10), para 49.

[14] Special Court Agreement 2002 (Ratification) Act 2002, s 13.

[15] Recall, *supra* paras 3.6–3.9, that the characterization is not a formal juridical one. See also *Kallon and Kamara (Fofana and Gbao intervening)*, Appeals Chamber Decision on Challenge to Jurisdiction: Lomé Accord Amnesty (n 10), para 85 ('[The Special Court] is described as "hybrid" or of "mixed jurisdiction" because of the nature of the laws it is empowered to apply. Its description as hybrid should not be understood as denoting that it is part of two or more legal systems.'); *Prosecutor v Kondewa*, SCSL-2004-14-AR72(E), Appeals Chamber, Decision on Preliminary Motion on Lack of Jurisdiction: Establishment of Special Court Violates Constitution of Sierra Leone, 25 May 2004, sep op Robertson, para 17 ('[T]he word "hybrid" that has crept into many academic commentaries as an adjectival description of the Special Court should not be taken literally.... The Special Court... is the creation of international law.... [It] derives no juristic authority from national law and does not operate in any sense as a national court subject to the Constitution of Sierra Leone.')

[16] Recall, in this light, *Report of the Secretary-General on the establishment of a Special Court for Sierra Leone* (n 4), 3, para 9 ('a treaty-based... court of mixed jurisdiction and composition').

[17] See SCSL Statute, arts 2–5. See also now RSCSL Statute, arts 2–5. For details, see *infra* paras 13.23–13.27.

[18] SCSL Agreement, art 2(2) and SCSL Statute, art 12(1). For the varied but essentially similar arrangement with respect to the RSCSL, see RSCSL Statute, arts 11 and 13. Security Council resolution 1315 (2000) had floated whether the SCSL might share an Appeals Chamber with the ICTY and ICTR, but the idea was rejected as 'legally unsound and practically not feasible, without incurring unacceptably high administrative and financial costs', in the words of *Report of the Secretary-General on the establishment of a Special Court for Sierra Leone* (n 4), 8, para 40.

[19] SCSL Agreement, art 2(3).

experience of former judges of the SCSL, the ICTY, the ICTR, the Extraordinary Chambers in the Courts of Cambodia (ECCC), the International Criminal Court (ICC), and the STL.[20]

13.8 The SCSL's seat was in Freetown, Sierra Leone, where it sat for the most part, pursuant to a headquarters agreement with Sierra Leone.[21] But the SCSL Agreement[22] and the Special Court's Rules of Procedure and Evidence (RPE)[23] provided for the Court's sitting away from its seat and, indeed, outside Sierra Leone, as happened in the case against the former president of Liberia, Charles Taylor, both trial and appellate proceedings in which were held in the facilities of the ICC in The Hague.[24] The SCSL also sat briefly in Kigali, Rwanda, in 2012, in the Kigali office of the ICTR, during a contempt trial involving the convicts Kamara and Kanu, who are serving their sentences in Mpanga prison there.[25] The RSCSL is stated to have its principal seat in Freetown, but is currently operating from what is referred to as an interim seat in The Hague, maintaining only a sub-office in Freetown for witness and victim protection and support until the UN and Sierra Leone agree otherwise.[26] The RSCSL may meet away from its seat 'if it considers it necessary for the efficient exercise of its functions',[27] and the RPE direct the president of the Residual Special Court to 'carry out his or her functions remotely', 'in as far as possible', and to be present at the Court's seat 'only as necessary'.[28]

13.9 The principal legal instruments governing the operation of the SCSL were its Statute,[29] attached to and declared to form an integral part of the SCSL Agreement, and its RPE.[30] The RPE of the ICTR at the time of the establishment of the SCSL were deemed applicable *mutatis mutandis* to the latter,[31] although the judges of

---

[20] RSCSL Statute, art 11(3).
[21] Headquarters Agreement between the Republic of Sierra Leone and the Special Court for Sierra Leone, Freetown, 21 October 2003.
[22] SCSL Agreement, art 10. (Note that the provision refers to the seat of the SCSL as simply 'in Sierra Leone.')
[23] SCSL RPE, rule 4.
[24] Owing to security concerns in relation to Freetown, where Taylor's trial would in the ordinary course of events have been held, the president of Liberia requested the trial's transfer to The Hague. Letters were exchanged between the Special Court and the Kingdom of the Netherlands; a memorandum of understanding was agreed between the Special Court and the International Criminal Court (ICC); the UN Security Council, acting under chapter VII of the UN Charter, adopted Security Council resolution 1688 (2006) of 16 June 2006, which mandated the transfer of Taylor, who was to remain under the exclusive jurisdiction of the Special Court, to the ICC's facilities in The Hague; and the president of the Special Court, pursuant to rule 4 of the RPE, both authorized a Trial Chamber of the Special Court to exercise its functions in The Hague and ordered the accused to be transferred there. Taylor was transferred to the ICC detention unit on 20 June 2006.
[25] See *Independent Counsel v Bangura* et al, SCSL-2011-02-T, President, Authorisation pursuant to Rule 4, 29 June 2012.
[26] RSCSL Statute, art 10. [27] Ibid. See also RSCSL RPE, rule 4(B).
[28] RSCSL RPE, rule 4(A).
[29] SCSL Agreement, art 1(2) and SCSL Statute, chapeau provision. See also RSCSL Agreement, art 1(2) and RSCSL Statute, chapeau provision.
[30] See now also RSCSL Rules of Procedure and Evidence (RPE) (as amended 4 December 2013), as provided for in RSCSL Statute, art 16.
[31] SCSL Statute, art 14(1).

The Special Court for Sierra Leone and Residual Special Court 515

the SCSL as a whole were empowered to amend them.³² The RPE were amended 14 times, for the last time on 31 May 2012.

In a departure from the common-law tradition of the Sierra Leone courts, the SCSL had, as an organ of the Court, an independent Prosecutor. The Prosecutor was appointed by the UN Secretary-General, in consultation with the government of Sierra Leone.³³ 13.10

The Statute of the SCSL stated that the judges of the Appeals Chamber were to be 'guided by the decisions of the Appeals Chamber of the International Tribunals for the former Yugoslavia and for Rwanda'.³⁴ At the same time, the Appeals Chamber emphasized that it was not bound by the decisions of the ICTY and ICTR Appeals Chambers, being required to refer to them for guidance, not to follow them.³⁵ When it came to the interpretation and application of the laws of Sierra Leone, the judges of the Appeals Chamber were to be guided by the decisions of the Supreme Court of Sierra Leone.³⁶ 13.11

Sentences handed down by the SCSL were intended to be served in Sierra Leone,³⁷ but the alternative provision made in the Statute for imprisonment in a third state³⁸ has been relied on in light of unsatisfactory prison conditions in Sierra Leone. The only SCSL convicts to date to be detained in Sierra Leone are those convicted of contempt, and these have been detained not within the ordinary Sierra Leone prison system but in the former SCSL detention facility, which was transferred to the jurisdiction of Sierra Leone along with the Freetown courthouse complex.³⁹ 13.12

The SCSL Statute and RPE provided for a range of due-process rights for accused and suspects modelled on equivalent provisions in the statutes and RPE of the ICTY and ICTR respectively.⁴⁰ These rights are reproduced in the Statute and RPE of the RSCSL.⁴¹ 13.13

The SCSL RPE made provision for measures of protection and support for witnesses and victims.⁴² Pursuant to the Statute and the RPE, a Witnesses and 13.14

---

³² Ibid, art 14(2).
³³ SCSL Agreement, art 3(1) and SCSL Statute, art 15(3). See also now RSCSL Statute, art 14(1).
³⁴ SCSL Statute, art 20(3). See now RSCSL Statute, art 21(3), adding to the Appeals Chambers of the ICTY and ICTR respectively the Appeals Chamber of the SCSL.
³⁵ *Prosecutor v Norman, Fofana and Kondewa*, SCSL-2004-14-T, Appeals Chamber, Decision on Interlocutory Appeals against Trial Chamber Decision refusing to Subpoena the President of Sierra Leone, 11 September 2006, para 13; *Prosecutor v Taylor*, SCSL-03-01-A, Appeals Chamber, Judgment, 26 September 2013, paras 352 and 472.
³⁶ SCSL Statute, art 20(3). See now RSCSL Statute, art 21(3).
³⁷ See SCSL Statute, art 22, stating that sentences 'shall' be served in Sierra Leone. But cf now RSCSL Statute, art 23(1), stating that sentences 'may' be served in Sierra Leone.
³⁸ See ibid. See also *infra* para 13.13.
³⁹ See, in this connection, Supplementary Agreement between the Special Court for Sierra Leone and the Government of the Republic of Sierra Leone on the Enforcement of Sentences for Contempt of the Special Court for Sierra Leone, Freetown, 26 March 2013 and Memorandum of Understanding between the Special Court for Sierra Leone and Government of the Republic of Sierra Leone, Freetown, 13 August 2013. One of these convicts has since been granted early release.
⁴⁰ See SCSL Statute, art 17 and SCSL RPE, arts 26*bis*, 42, 43, 60, 61(i), and 63. Recall, in this regard, *supra* para 12.12.
⁴¹ See RSCSL Statute, art 17 and RSCSL RPE, arts 26*bis*, 42, 43, 60, 61(i), and 63.
⁴² See especially SCSL RPE, rules 69 and 75.

Victims Section was set up within the Special Court's Registry with functions relating to protective measures and security arrangements, as well as to counselling and other appropriate assistance, for witnesses, victims, 'and others who [were] at risk on account of testimony given by such witnesses'.[43] The continuing protection and support of witnesses and victims is one of the *raisons d'être* of the RSCSL, and is the current function of the Residual Special Court's sub-office in Freetown.[44]

13.15 The SCSL was supposed to be funded by 'voluntary contributions from the international community',[45] with the result that its financial situation was consistently parlous. The UN gave it four 'subvention grants' over the years to bail it out.[46] The RSCSL is also supposed to be funded by voluntary contributions, although the RSCSL Agreement permits the UN and Sierra Leone and the RSCSL's oversight committee to 'explore alternative means of financing'.[47]

C. Cases

13.16 The SCSL indicted 13 individuals in total. Proceedings were consolidated into four cases, one dealing with former senior members of an armed group known as the Armed Forces Revolutionary Council (AFRC), one with senior members of a militia calling itself the Civil Defence Forces (CDF), one with senior members of the rebel army known as the Revolutionary United Front (RUF), and one with Charles Taylor, former president of Liberia. One indictee, RUF battlefield commander Sam Bockarie, died before arrest; another, RUF leader Foday Sankoh, died before standing trial; and a third, senior CDF figure Sam Hinga Norman, died between the close of trial proceedings and the handing down of judgment. One indictee, former AFRC chairman Johnny Paul Koroma, officially remains a fugitive from justice, although reports have suggested that he may be dead.

13.17 On 20 June 2007, the SCSL handed down its first verdicts, with a Trial Chamber convicting three former leaders of the AFRC of a range of offences.[48] The Appeals Chamber delivered its judgment in the case on 22 February 2008, upholding sentences of 50 years' imprisonment for Alex Tamba Brima, 45 years for Ibrahim Bazzy Kamara, and 50 years for Santigie Borbor Kanu.[49] On 2 August 2007, a

---

[43] SCSL Statute, art 16(4). See also SCSL RPE, rule 34.
[44] See RSCSL Statute, arts 1(1) and 18, RSCSL Agreement, art 6, and RSCSL RPE, rules 34, 69, and 75. See also *infra* para 13.18.
[45] SCSL Agreement, art 6.
[46] See, in this regard, ibid, providing that, '[s]hould voluntary funds be insufficient for the Court to implement its mandate, the Secretary-General and the Security Council shall explore alternative means of financing the Special Court'.
[47] RSCSL Agreement, art 3.
[48] See *Prosecutor v Brima, Kamara and Kanu*, SCSL-04-16-T, Trial Chamber Judgment, 20 June 2007. See also *Prosecutor v Brima, Kamara and Kanu*, SCSL-04-16-T, Trial Chamber, Sentencing Judgment, 19 July 2007.
[49] See *Prosecutor v Brima, Kamara and Kanu*, SCSL-04-16-A, Appeals Chamber, Judgment, 22 February 2008.

Trial Chamber convicted two former leaders of the CDF of various offences.[50] The Appeals Chamber delivered its judgment in the case on 28 May 2008, upholding certain convictions, overturning others and substituting new ones, and increasing the sentences imposed from six to 15 years' imprisonment for Moinina Fofana and from eight to 20 years for Allieu Kondewa.[51] On 25 February 2009, in the last substantive trial to be heard by the SCSL in Sierra Leone, three former leading members of the RUF were convicted on charges of war crimes and crimes against humanity.[52] On 26 October 2009, the Appeals Chamber delivered its judgment in the case, overturning certain convictions but allowing certain prosecution appeals, and upholding sentences of 52 years' imprisonment for Issa Hassan Sesay, 40 years for Morris Kallon, and 25 years for Augustine Gbao.[53] All eight convicts were transferred to Rwanda to serve their sentences.[54] Fofana has since been granted early release by the president of the RSCSL.[55] On 26 April 2012, Charles Taylor was convicted of a range of war crimes and crimes against humanity,[56] and on 30 May 2012 he was sentenced to 50 years' imprisonment.[57] The Appeals Chamber upheld his conviction and sentence on 26 September 2013.[58] Taylor is imprisoned in the UK,[59] but has applied to the RSCSL for termination of the enforcement of his sentence there and for transfer to Rwanda. The SCSL also convicted a number of persons of contempt of court.

D. The Functions of the Residual Special Court for Sierra Leone

The functions of the RSCSL are spelled out in article 1(1) of its Statute, which, referring to those functions of the SCSL that must continue to be performed after the closure of the SCSL,[60] provides that the RSCSL shall

13.18

maintain, preserve and manage its archives, including the archives of the Special Court; provide for witness and victim protection and support; respond for requests for access to

---

[50] See *Prosecutor v Fofana and Kondewa*, SCSL-04-14-T, Trial Chamber, Judgment, 2 August 2007. See also *Fofana and Kondewa*, SCSL-04-14-T, Trial Chamber, Judgment on the Sentencing of Moinina Fofana and Allieu Kondewa, 9 October 2007.
[51] See *Prosecutor v Fofana and Kondewa*, SCSL-04-14-A, Appeals Chamber, Judgment, 28 May 2008.
[52] See *Prosecutor v Sesay, Kallon and Gbao*, SCSL-04-15-T, Trial Chamber, Judgment, 2 March 2009. See also *Sesay, Kallon and Gbao*, SCSL-04-15-T, Trial Chamber, Sentencing Judgment, 8 April 2009.
[53] See *Prosecutor v Sesay, Kallon and Gbao*, SCSL-04-15-A, Appeals Chamber, Judgment, 26 October 2009.
[54] See, in this connection, Amended Agreement between the Special Court for Sierra Leone and the Government of the Republic of Rwanda on the Enforcement of Sentences of the Special Court for Sierra Leone, Kigali, 18 March 2009.
[55] See *Prosecutor v Fofana and Kondewa*, SCSL-04-14-ES-836, President, Decision of the President on Application for Early Release, 11 August 2014.
[56] See *Prosecutor v Taylor*, SCSL-03-01-T, Trial Chamber, Judgment, 18 May 2012 (written judgment).
[57] See *Prosecutor v Taylor*, SCSL-03-01-T, Trial Chamber, Sentencing Judgment, 30 May 2012.
[58] See *Taylor*, Appeals Chamber Judgment (n 35).
[59] See, in this connection, Agreement between the Special Court for Sierra Leone and the Government of the United Kingdom of Great Britain and Northern Ireland on the Enforcement of Sentences of the Special Court for Sierra Leone, London, 9 July 2007.
[60] See also SCSL Agreement, art 1(1).

evidence by national prosecution authorities; supervise enforcement of sentences; review convictions and acquittals; conduct contempt of court proceedings; provide defence counsel and legal aid for the conduct of proceedings before the Residual Special Court; respond to requests from national authorities with respect to claims for compensation; and prevent double jeopardy.

The protection and support of victims and witnesses who appeared before the SCSL (and of those who appear before the RSCSL) and of others who are at risk on account of testimony given by witnesses and victims is given special mention in article 18 of the RSCSL Statute, while ownership and management of the archives of the SCSL is specifically dealt with in article 7 of the RSCSL Agreement.

13.19   Article 1(2) of the RSCSL Statute makes it clear that 'the Residual Special Court shall have the power to prosecute the remaining fugitive Special Court indictee if his case has not been referred to a competent national jurisdiction, and to prosecute any cases resulting from review of convictions and acquittals'. At the same time, article 7(1) of the RSCSL Statute provides that the Residual Special Court 'shall have power, and shall undertake every effort, to refer the case of the remaining fugitive Special Court indictee to a competent national jurisdiction for investigation and prosecution'. Article 7(2) specifies that, after referral, the RSCSL 'shall monitor the case through cooperation with international or [sic] regional organizations'. Article 7(3) empowers the RSCSL to revoke the referral only if, first, the national jurisdiction 'is unwilling or unable to prosecute the accused' or 'the national court proceedings are not impartial or independent, are designed to shield the accused from international criminal responsibility, or the case is not diligently prosecuted' and, secondly, the accused has not yet been found guilty or acquitted. Article 7 of the RSCSL Statute is fleshed out in rule 11*bis* of the RSCSL RPE. It is not realistically expected that the RSCSL will conduct any substantive trials or appeals.

III. Legality of Establishment

13.20   The legality of the establishment of the SCSL pursuant to a treaty, to which its statute was annexed, between Sierra Leone and the United Nations, with the latter represented by a delegate of the Secretary-General, was challenged before the SCSL in *Fofana*.[61] The accused argued essentially[62] that the creation of the SCSL was, for a range of reasons, *ultra vires* the UN Charter. The Appeals Chamber rejected the argument. It held, first, that whether or not the Security Council was entitled to delegate to the Secretary-General, via Security Council

---

[61] *Prosecutor v Fofana*, SCSL-2004-14-AR72(E), Appeals Chamber, Decision on Preliminary Motion on Lack of Jurisdiction Materiae [sic]: Illegal Delegation of Powers by the United Nations, 25 May 2004. See also *Prosecutor v Gbao*, SCSL-2004-15-AR72(E), Appeals Chamber, Decision on Preliminary Motion on the Invalidity of the Agreement between the United Nations and the Government of Sierra Leone on the Establishment of the Special Court, 25 May 2004, para 5.

[62] The argument constantly changed.

resolution 1315 (2000), its power to enter into the SCSL Agreement as a collective measure for the maintenance of international peace and security was not, as the accused alleged, at issue. No delegation of power was needed, since article 98 of the Charter, among others, made it clear that the Secretary-General—being, as head of the UN Secretariat, an executive organ of the Organization—was authorized and bound to perform such functions as were entrusted to him by the Security Council, and in this case was simply performing such functions.[63] The Appeals Chamber next held that the establishment of an international criminal tribunal by way of agreement with a state was a measure within the wide discretion granted to the Security Council under article 24(1) of the Charter to maintain international peace and security and that, since the Council was not acting coercively, it was immaterial whether this measure had been taken under chapter VII or not.[64] Finally, in response to an argument based on articles 22 and 23 of the SCSL Agreement—which required the agreement of Sierra Leone to the amendment or termination of the Agreement—that the Security Council had acted unlawfully in creating a subsidiary organ beyond its control, the Appeals Chamber highlighted not only the control exercised by the Council, via the Secretary-General, by means of the Court's Management Committee[65] but also the ultimate power of the Council to take coercive measures binding on Sierra Leone in the event that the latter did not agree to amendment or termination.[66] A more obvious reply to the last of the accused's submissions might have been that the SCSL was not a subsidiary organ of the Security Council in the first place.

IV. Jurisdiction

A. Existence

The competence of the SCSL was spelled out in general terms in article 1(1) of its Statute, which stated that, except as provided for in article 1(2), the Court had 'the power to prosecute persons who bear the greatest responsibility for serious violations of international humanitarian law and Sierra Leonean law committed in the territory of Sierra Leone since 30 November 1996, including those leaders who, in committing such crimes, have threatened the establishment of and

13.21

---

[63] *Fofana*, Appeals Chamber Decision on Preliminary Motion on Lack of Jurisdiction Materiae (n 61), para 16.
[64] Ibid, paras 18–21. Although pointing to the Security Council's determination in SC resolution 1315 (2000) that the situation in Sierra Leone continued to pose a threat to international peace and security, the SCSL did not make a finding as to under which article of the Charter the Council was acting when requesting the Secretary-General to enter into an agreement with the government of Sierra Leone.
[65] The Committee was established pursuant to art 7 of the SCSL Agreement.
[66] *Fofana*, Appeals Chamber Decision on Preliminary Motion on Lack of Jurisdiction Materiae (n 61), paras 22–29. See also the separate opinion of Judge Robertson, citing *Prosecutor v Tadić*, IT-94-1, Appeals Chamber, Decision on Interlocutory Motion on Jurisdiction, 2 October 1995.

implementation of the peace process in Sierra Leone'. Article 1(2) of the RSCSL Statute restates this general competence for the purposes of the Residual Special Court, albeit dropping the reference to those leaders who threatened the peace process.

13.22   Special provision was made in the SCSL Statute in respect of 'transgressions' by peacekeepers and related personnel present in Sierra Leone pursuant to the status of mission agreement in force between the UN and Sierra Leone or to agreements between Sierra Leone and other governments or regional organizations or with the consent of the government of Sierra Leone. The reference was implicitly to reports of criminal acts that were current at the time of the negotiation of the Agreement and Statute. In accordance with article 1(2) of the Statute, such 'transgressions' remained within the 'primary jurisdiction' of the sending state. But article 1(3) added that, in the event that the sending state was 'unwilling or unable genuinely to carry out an investigation or prosecution', the SCSL was empowered, 'if authorized by the Security Council on the proposal of any State, [to] exercise jurisdiction over such persons'. The last never happened, and article 1(2) and (3) of the SCSL Statute are not reproduced in the RSCSL Statute.

(i) Jurisdiction ratione materiae (subject-matter jurisdiction)

13.23   The SCSL enjoyed jurisdiction over crimes against humanity, in accordance with article 2 of the SCSL Statute; violations of article 3 common to the Geneva Conventions and of Additional Protocol II to the Geneva Conventions, as per article 3 of the Statute; certain other serious violations of international humanitarian law specified in article 4 of the Statute; and certain crimes under Sierra Leonean law specified in article 5. The same jurisdiction *ratione materiae* is conferred on the RSCSL by articles 2 to 5 of the RSCSL Statute.

13.24   As with the ICTY and ICTR, the Statute of the SCSL elided the distinct questions of jurisdiction *ratione materiae* and applicable law, at least under articles 2 to 4.[67] But the Secretary-General specified in his report to the Security Council on the establishment of the SCSL that the Special Court's 'applicable law includes international as well as Sierra Leonean law',[68] while stating that '[t]he subject-matter jurisdiction of the Special Court comprises crimes under international humanitarian law and Sierra Leonean law'.[69] The elision of jurisdiction *ratione materiae* and applicable law was remedied in 2004 with the adoption of rule 72*bis* ('General Provisions on Applicable Law') of the SCSL RPE, which provided:

The applicable laws [*sic*] of the Special Court include:
(i) the Statute, the Agreement [between Sierra Leone and the UN], and the Rules;
(ii) where appropriate, other applicable treaties and the principles and rules of international customary law;

---

[67] Article 5 spoke explicitly of 'crimes under Sierra Leonean law'.
[68] *Report of the Secretary-General on the establishment of a Special Court for Sierra Leone* (n 4), 3, para 9.
[69] Ibid, para 12.

(iii) general principles of law derived from national laws of legal systems of the world including, as appropriate, the national laws of the Republic of Sierra Leone, provided that those principles are not inconsistent with the Statute, the Agreement and with international customary law and internationally recognized norms and standards.

The reference in subparagraph (iii) to the laws of Sierra Leone was solely as a source of general principles of law. In other words, provision for recourse to the law of Sierra Leone as such, which would be necessary in order for the Court to exercise the jurisdiction granted it in article 5 and which would tally with the Secretary-General's report, was omitted.[70] The omission reflected the Prosecutor's eventual decision not to indict anyone under article 5 of the Statute. Rule 72*bis* is reproduced, *mutatis mutandis*, in rule 72*bis* of the RSCSL's RPE.

Insofar as the SCSL had jurisdiction over international crimes, the Secretary-General stated in his report that the crimes within the Special Court's jurisdiction were considered customary.[71] As with the ICTY and ICTR, the concern was for the principle *nullum crimen sine lege*. In the event, the SCSL stuck to an insistence on the customary character of the crime at time of commission.[72]

13.25

Article 4 of the SCSL Statute vested the Special Court with jurisdiction over only three 'other serious violations of international humanitarian law', namely intentionally directing attacks against the civilian population as such or against individual civilians not taking direct part in hostilities, as per subparagraph (*a*); intentionally directing attacks against 'personnel, installations, material, units or vehicles involved in a humanitarian assistance or peacekeeping mission in accordance with the Charter of the United Nations', as long as they qualify for protection as civilians or civilian objects, as per subparagraph (*b*); and conscripting or enlisting children under the age of 15 years into armed forces or groups or using them to participate actively in hostilities, as per subparagraph (*c*). Conscription, enlistment or use of child soldiers was held by the Appeals Chamber to be a war crime under customary international law at the time of the commission of the relevant acts in Sierra Leone.[73]

13.26

---

[70] It is worth noting, however, the odd word 'include' in the chapeau.
[71] *Report of the Secretary-General on the establishment of a Special Court for Sierra Leone* (n 4), 3, para 12.
[72] See eg *Kallon, Norman and Kamara (Fofana intervening)*, Appeals Chamber Decision on Constitutionality and Lack of Jurisdiction (n 10), paras 80–82; *Prosecutor v Norman (Fofana intervening)*, SCSL-2003-04-14-AR72(E), Appeals Chamber, Decision on Preliminary Motion Based on Lack of Jurisdiction (Child Recruitment), 31 May 2004, para 25. See also *Sesay, Kallon & Gbao*, Appeals Chamber Judgment (n 53), paras 888–891, where the Appeals Chamber noted (para 888, citations omitted) that 'the principle of *nullum crimen sine lege* does not impede the development of the law through the interpretation and clarification of the elements of a particular crime, but it does preclude the creation of a new criminal offence by defining a crime that was previously undefined or "interpreting existing law beyond the reasonable limits of acceptable clarification"'.
[73] See *Norman (Fofana intervening)*, Appeals Chamber Decision on Preliminary Motion Based on Lack of Jurisdiction (Child Recruitment) (n 72) (majority); *Brima, Kamara and Kanu*, Appeals Chamber Judgment (n 49), para 296; *Fofana and Kondewa*, Appeals Chamber Judgment (n 51), para 139; *Sesay, Kallon & Gbao*, Appeals Chamber Judgment (n 53), para 923.

13.27   The crimes under Sierra Leonean law listed in article 5 of the SCSL Statute comprised, in subparagraph (*a*), offences under the Prevention of Cruelty to Children Act 1926 relating to the abuse of girls and, in subparagraph (*b*), offences under the Malicious Damage Act 1861 relating to wanton destruction of property. As explained in the Secretary-General's report, recourse was had to Sierra Leonean law in article 5 of the SCSL Statute to cover 'cases where a specific situation or an aspect of it was considered to be either unregulated or inadequately regulated under international law'.[74] Although no-one was indicted by the SCSL Prosecutor under article 5, the provision is reproduced, *mutatis mutandis*, in article 5 of the RSCSL Statute.

(ii) *Jurisdiction* ratione personae, ratione temporis, *and* ratione loci *(personal, temporal, and territorial jurisdiction)*

13.28   As stated in article 1(1) of the SCSL Statute, the Special Court enjoyed jurisdiction over 'persons who bear the greatest responsibility for serious violations of international humanitarian law and Sierra Leonean law committed in the territory of Sierra Leone since 30 November 1996'. As made clear in the Secretary-General's report, the qualification 'most responsible' was to be seen not as a formal limitation on the jurisdiction *ratione personae* of the SCSL 'but as a guidance to the Prosecutor in the adoption of a prosecution strategy and in making decisions to prosecute in individual cases'.[75] This was reiterated in *Brima, Kamara and Kanu*, where it was held that the phrase merely 'guide[d] the Prosecutor in the exercise of his prosecutorial discretion'.[76] The phrase is reproduced in article 1(2) of the RSCSL Statute, which goes on to state, for the avoidance of doubt, that 'the Residual Special Court shall have the power to prosecute the remaining fugitive Special Court indictee if his case has not been referred to a competent national jurisdiction, and to prosecute any cases resulting from review of convictions and acquittals'.[77]

13.29   Article 7(1) of the SCSL Statute denied the Special Court jurisdiction *ratione personae* over any person who was under the age of 15 at the time of the alleged commission of the crime. The issue of juvenile offenders was the subject of starkly opposing views during the negotiation of the Agreement and Statute, with the government and popular opinion in Sierra Leone wishing to see the SCSL hold accountable child soldiers as young as 12 at the time of alleged commission and non-governmental organizations opposing the prosecution of anyone under 18 at the time of alleged commission. The result lay midway between these two poles.[78]

---

[74] *Report of the Secretary-General on the establishment of a Special Court for Sierra Leone* (n 4), 5, para 19.
[75] See ibid, 7, para 30.
[76] *Brima, Kamara and Kanu*, Appeals Chamber Judgment (n 49), para 282.
[77] Recall *supra* para 3.17.
[78] See *Report of the Secretary-General on the establishment of a Special Court for Sierra Leone* (n 4), 7–8, paras 32–38.

In the event, no person under the age of 18 at the time of alleged commission was prosecuted, and the provision is not reproduced in the RSCSL Statute.

Like the ICTY,[79] the SCSL held that it ceased to enjoy jurisdiction *ratione personae* on the death of the accused, with the consequence that, even where the accused died after the close of trial proceedings (but before the handing down of judgment), the trial was terminated.[80]

13.30

B. Exercise

(i) Immunity

Article 6(2) of the SCSL Statute stated that '[t]he official position of any accused persons, whether as Head of State or Government or as a responsible government official, shall not relieve such person of criminal responsibility nor mitigate punishment'. Although the provision, which derives historically from the Nuremberg Charter, referred to criminal responsibility, rather than to procedural amenity to prosecution, it was taken to abrogate all immunities from jurisdiction from which state officials—a term intended in the provision to extend to persons who were officials at the time of alleged commission—might otherwise have been taken to benefit before the SCSL.[81] The provision is reproduced in article 6(2) of the RSCSL Statute.

13.31

The abrogation of immunities before the SCSL was at issue in *Taylor*.[82] At the time of his indictment and the circulation of an arrest warrant for him, the accused[83] was the head of state of Liberia. He argued that the indictment and circulation of the arrest warrant was a violation of the immunity *ratione personae* to which he was entitled even in respect of allegations of international crimes, as per the International Court of Justice (ICJ) in *Arrest Warrant*. But the Appeals Chamber held that the accused was not entitled to immunity before the SCSL. Observing that the Special Court 'cannot ignore whatever the Statute directs or permits or empowers it to do unless such provisions are void as being in conflict with a peremptory norm of general international law',[84] the Appeals Chamber concluded that the Statute's abrogation of head-of-state immunity was not in conflict with any such norm.[85] Finding that the SCSL was an international criminal tribunal[86] 'with all that implies for the question of immunity for a serving Head

13.32

---

[79] Recall *supra* para 12.25.

[80] See *Prosecutor v Norman, Fofana and Kondewa*, SCSL-04-14-T, Trial Chamber, Decision on Registrar's Submission of Evidence of Death of Accused Samuel Hinga Norman and Consequential Issues, 21 May 2007, paras 13 and 18.

[81] As it is, and as with the ICTY and ICTR, no article of the SCSL's Statute provided in the first place that the Special Court was bound by such immunities, leaving unaffected the latter's jurisdiction over the accused and the crime.

[82] *Taylor*, Appeals Chamber Decision on Immunity from Jurisdiction (n 10).

[83] Charles Taylor was neither then nor at the time of the application by which he challenged the SCSL's exercise of jurisdiction in the custody of the SCSL or even in Sierra Leone.

[84] *Taylor*, Appeals Chamber Decision on Immunity from Jurisdiction (n 10), para 43.

[85] Ibid, para 53.   [86] Ibid, paras 41 and 42.

of State',[87] the Appeals Chamber held that 'the principle seems now established that the sovereign equality of states does not prevent a Head of State from being prosecuted before an international criminal tribunal or court'.[88] The last link in the chain of reasoning is flawed. While it is true that the SCSL is an international criminal tribunal, this does not, *pace* the Court, have any necessary implications for the immunity of a head of state.[89] The question must be whether the Security Council can be said to have established the SCSL pursuant to a decision taken under chapter VII of the Charter—a decision which, as a measure taken under chapter VII, could permissibly derogate from rules of international law otherwise applicable between states and which, insofar as it were a decision of the Security Council, member states would be obliged to accept.[90] In answering this question, the Appeals Chamber's assertion (which, as it is, is dubious)[91] that 'it was clear that the power of the Security Council to enter into an agreement for the establishment of the court was derived from the Charter of the United Nations both in regard to the general purposes of the United Nations as expressed in Article 1 of the Charter and the specific powers of the Security Council in Articles 39 and 41'[92] is nothing to the point. What matters is solely whether the Security Council adopted the SCSL Statute, which denies to the accused the benefit of immunity from jurisdiction, pursuant to a decision taken under chapter VII of the Charter, and the answer is that it did not. It never adopted the SCSL Statute at all,[93] let alone by way of a decision under chapter VII. All this said, head-of-state immunity is not a norm of *jus cogens* such as might have invalidated the SCSL Statute, which clearly granted the Special Court the power to disregard any procedural immunity from which, by virtue of their official position, the accused might have benefited under international law.[94]

(ii) Amnesty

13.33 The peace agreement signed between the government of Sierra Leone and the RUF at Lomé, Togo, on 7 July 1999 ('Lomé Agreement' or 'Lomé Accord')[95] contains amnesty provisions in respect of crimes committed during the civil war in Sierra Leone. But Security Council resolution 1315 (2000) recalls 'that the

---

[87] Ibid, para 41. [88] Ibid, para 52.
[89] Recall *supra* paras 3.38–3.43, especially para 3.41. [90] Recall *supra* para 3.40.
[91] Nowhere in Security Council resolution 1315 (2000), by which the Security Council requested the Secretary-General to enter into an agreement with the government of Sierra Leone to create the SCSL, does the Council state that it is acting under chapter VII of the Charter. Indeed, given that it was not acting coercively, it is hard to see why it would be doing so.
[92] *Taylor*, Appeals Chamber Decision on Immunity from Jurisdiction (n 10), para 37.
[93] The Security Council merely 'welcomed the Agreement', in SC res 1400 (2002), 28 March 2002, preamble (tenth recital).
[94] In the event, after his departure from power, Liberia consented to Taylor's arrest and prosecution before the SCSL.
[95] UN doc S/1999/777 (12 July 1999), Annex. The Lomé Agreement was reaffirmed at a meeting of ECOWAS, the UN, the government of Sierra Leone, and the RUF held at Abuja, Nigeria, on 2 May 2001.

Special Representative of the Secretary-General appended to his signature of the Lomé Agreement a statement that the United Nations holds the understanding that the amnesty provisions of the Agreement shall not apply to international crimes of genocide, crimes against humanity, war crimes and other serious violations of international humanitarian law'.[96] In his report to the Security Council, the Secretary-General stated that, '[w]hile recognizing that amnesty is an accepted legal concept and a gesture of peace and reconciliation at the end of a civil war or an internal armed conflict, the United Nations has consistently maintained the position that amnesty cannot be granted in respect of international crimes, such as genocide, crimes against humanity or other serious violations of international humanitarian law'.[97] He also recalled the disclaimer that his special representative was instructed to append to his signature of the Lomé Accord and the reference to it in Security Council resolution 1315 (2000).[98] The UN's stated understanding of the Lomé Accord was accepted by the government of Sierra Leone and was reflected in article 10 ('Amnesty') of the SCSL Statute, which stated that '[a]n amnesty granted to any person falling within the jurisdiction of the Special Court in respect of the crimes referred to in articles 2 to 4 of the present Statute shall not be a bar to prosecution'.[99] The provision is reproduced, *mutatis mutandis*, in article 10 ('Amnesty') of the RSCSL Statute.

13.34   The SCSL's exercise of jurisdiction despite the Lomé Accord amnesty was unsuccessfully challenged in *Kallon and Kamara (Fofana and Gbao intervening)*. The gist of the Appeals Chamber's decision was that the Lomé Accord was not a treaty, so that, whatever effect it may have had on prosecutions in the municipal courts of Sierra Leone, it could not bar the exercise by an international criminal court such as the SCSL of a jurisdiction granted it under its statute.[100] The reasoning is more than a little odd. Even if the Lomé Accord were a treaty, it is difficult to see how it could deprive the SCSL of its jurisdiction, since the Special Court itself was not a party to the Accord and, even if it were, the Accord would still not necessarily trump the Special Court's Statute.

---

[96] SC res 1315 (2000), preamble (fifth recital).
[97] *Report of the Secretary-General on the establishment of a Special Court for Sierra Leone* (n 4), 5, para 22, citation omitted.
[98] Ibid, para 23.
[99] Article 10 of the SCSL Statute made no reference to art 5 of the Statute, meaning that the Lomé Accord did constitute a bar to the prosecution of the crimes under Sierra Leonean law mentioned in art 5 of the Statute.
[100] *Kallon and Kamara (Fofana and Gbao intervening)*, Appeals Chamber Decision on Challenge to Jurisdiction: Lomé Accord Amnesty (n 10), para 86. That the Lomé Accord did not bar the SCSL's exercise of its jurisdiction under the Statute was affirmed in *Prosecutor v Kondewa*, SCSL-2004-14-AR72(E), Appeals Chamber, Decision on Lack of Jurisdiction/Abuse of Process: Amnesty Provided by the Lomé Accord, 25 May 2004; *Prosecutor v Kanu*, SCSL-2004-16-AR72(E), Appeals Chamber, Decision on Motion Challenging Jurisdiction and Raising Objections Based on Abuse of Process, 25 May 2004; *Prosecutor v Fofana*, SCSL-04-14-AR72(E), Appeals Chamber, Decision on Preliminary Motion on Lack of Jurisdiction: Illegal Delegation of Jurisdiction by Sierra Leone, 25 May 2004; and *Gbao*, Appeals Chamber Decision on Preliminary Motion on the Invalidity of the Agreement (n 61).

V. Relationship to the Courts of Sierra Leone

13.35 In accordance with article 8(1) of the SCSL Statute, the SCSL and the courts of Sierra Leone enjoyed concurrent jurisdiction. In other words, the fact that the Special Court enjoyed jurisdiction over a given crime and a given person did not in itself deprive the criminal courts of Sierra Leone of any jurisdiction that they may also have enjoyed over the same crime and the same person. This concurrency is maintained as between the RSCSL and the Sierra Leonean courts.[101]

13.36 Article 8(2) of the SCSL Statute, however, provided further that the SCSL enjoyed primacy over the courts of Sierra Leone. Article 8(2) empowered the SCSL formally to request a Sierra Leonean court to defer to its competence; and by virtue of article 17(2) of the SCSL Agreement, Sierra Leone was obliged to 'comply without undue delay with any request for assistance by the Special Court', including, as per subparagraph (*d*), with a request for the transfer of an indictee to the Court. As made clear by the Secretary-General, this primacy did not extend to the courts of third states.[102] A corresponding relationship of primacy exists between the RSCSL and the courts of Sierra Leone, in accordance with article 8(2) of the RSCSL Statute and article 11(*d*) of the RSCSL Agreement.

13.37 Article 9 of the SCSL Statute embodied and article 9 of the RSCSL Statute embodies a *non bis in idem* provision identical, *mutatis mutandis*, to that in the ICTY and ICTR Statutes.[103]

13.38 The relationship between the SCSL and the Truth and Reconciliation Commission (TRC) established in Sierra Leone was a contentious issue, with something of a 'turf war' breaking out between the two.[104]

---

[101] See RSCSL Statute, art 8(1).

[102] *Report of the Secretary-General on the establishment of a Special Court for Sierra Leone* (n 4), 3, para 10. See also *Kallon, Norman and Kamara (Fofana intervening)*, Appeals Chamber Decision on Constitutionality and Lack of Jurisdiction (n 10), para 69.

[103] Recall *supra* paras 12.43–12.45. See also SCSL RPE, rule 13: 'When the President receives reliable information to show that criminal proceedings have been instituted against a person before a court of any State for acts for which that person has already been tried by the Special Court, he shall issue a reasoned order or request to such court seeking permanent discontinuance of its proceedings. If that court fails to do so, the President may take appropriate action.' In the case of third states, any request issued by the President was non-binding. See now the identical RSCSL RPE, rule 13.

[104] See eg *Prosecutor v Norman*, SCSL-2003-08-PT, President, Decision on Appeal by the Truth and Reconciliation Commission for Sierra Leone ('TRC' or 'the Commission') and Chief Samuel Hinga Norman JP against the Decision of His Lordship Mr Justice Bankole Thompson delivered on 30 October 2003 to Deny the TRC's Request to Hold a Public Hearing with Chief Samuel Hinga Norman JP, 28 November 2003; *Prosecutor v Gbao*, SCSL-2004-15-PT, Acting President, Decision on Appeal by the Truth and Reconciliation Commission ('TRC') and Accused against the Decision of Judge Bankole Thompson delivered on 3 November 2003 to Deny the TRC's Request to Hold a Public Hearing with Augustine Gbao, 7 May 2004.

VI. Co-operation with the Special Court

In accordance with article 17(1) of the SCSL Agreement, Sierra Leone was obliged to 'cooperate with all organs of the Special Court at all stages of the proceedings', in particular by facilitating the Prosecutor's access to sites, persons, and relevant documents required for an investigation. Article 17(2) of the Agreement elaborated, providing that Sierra Leone was to 'comply without undue delay with any request for assistance by the Special Court or an order issued by the Chambers', including, but not limited to, those for the identification and location of persons, service of documents, arrest or detention of persons, and transfer of an indictee to the Court.[105] Article 17 of the SCSL Agreement is reproduced, *mutatis mutandis*, in article 11 of the RSCSL Agreement.

13.39

By way of contrast with this and with the position in relation to the ICTY and ICTR, third states were under no obligation to co-operate with the SCSL. As made clear by the Secretary-General, the Special Court 'lack[ed] the power to request the surrender of an accused from any third State and to induce the compliance of its authorities with any such request'.[106] The Secretary-General added that, '[i]n examining measures to enhance the deterrent powers of the Special Court, the Security Council may wish to consider endowing it with Chapter VII powers for the specific purpose of requesting the surrender of an accused from outside the jurisdiction of the Court'.[107] The Security Council was never minded to do so.[108] The fact, however, that third states were not legally obliged to cooperate with the SCSL did not bar the latter from inviting them to provide assistance, as made clear in rule 8(C) of the Special Court's RPE.[109]

13.40

---

[105] With the exception of Charles Taylor, all arrested indictees were arrested in Sierra Leone by the Sierra Leonean authorities.

[106] *Report of the Secretary-General on the establishment of a Special Court for Sierra Leone* (n 4), 3, para 10. The fact that the SCSL had no power to order a state other than Sierra Leone to surrender an accused to the Court is in part why Charles Taylor, indicted by the Special Court in 2003, was able to remain at large in exile in Nigeria for almost three years. In the event, however, on receipt of a request for extradition from the then-president of Liberia, Nigeria voluntarily apprehended Taylor and flew him to Liberia, where, in the execution of a mandate conferred on it by the Security Council (see *infra* n 108), the United Nations Mission in Liberia (UNMIL) detained him, transported him to Freetown, Sierra Leone, and, on 29 March 2006, handed him over to the SCSL.

[107] *Report of the Secretary-General on the establishment of a Special Court for Sierra Leone* (n 4), 3, para 10.

[108] That said, in SC res 1638 (2005), 11 November 2005, the Security Council, determining that Charles Taylor's return to Liberia 'would constitute an impediment to stability and a threat to the peace of Liberia and to international peace and security in the region' and acting under chapter VII of the Charter, decided that the mandate of UNMIL was to 'include the following additional element: to apprehend and detain former President Charles Taylor in the event of a return to Liberia and to transfer him or facilitate his transfer to Sierra Leone for prosecution before the Special Court for Sierra Leone'.

[109] Third states by and large acceded to invitations for assistance from the SCSL, eg in the collection of evidence.

VII. Conclusion

13.41 Whether the SCSL achieved justice, contributed to the consolidation of peace in Sierra Leone, and gave some sense of vindication to victims are questions for a different forum. As an experiment in international criminal justice in the institutional sense, however, the Special Court was more successful than not. It remains to be seen if its model of an international criminal court established and empowered by means of a treaty between an international organization and a single state proves attractive—and, in the event that it does, gets off the ground[110]—in different, future historical and societal contexts. Should it do so, the experience of the SCSL and of the RCSL may be instructive.

Further Reading

BOISTER, N, 'Failing to Get to the Heart of the Matter in Sierra Leone? The Truth Commission is Denied Unrestricted Access to Chief Hinga Norman' (2004) 2 *Journal of International Criminal Justice* 1100

CASSESE, A, 'The Special Court and International Law. The Decision Concerning the Lomé Agreement Amnesty' (2004) 2 *Journal of International Criminal Justice* 1130

CHERNOR JALLOH, C (ed), *The Sierra Leone Special Court and its Legacy. The Impact for Africa and International Criminal Law* (Cambridge: Cambridge University Press, 2014)

DONLON, F, 'The Transition of Responsibilities from the Special Court to the Residual Special Court for Sierra Leone' (2013) 11 *Journal of International Criminal Justice* 857

HAPPOLD, M, 'International Humanitarian Law, War Criminality and Child Recruitment: The Special Court for Sierra Leone's Decision in *Prosecutor v Sam Hinga Norman*' (2005) 18 *Leiden Journal of International Law* 283

MANSARAY, B and SANUSI, S, 'Residual Matters of Ad Hoc Courts and Tribunals: The SCSL Experience' (2010) 36 *Commonwealth Law Bulletin* 593

MPHEPO, T, 'The Residual Special Court for Sierra Leone. Rationale and Challenges' (2014) 14 *International Criminal Law Review* 177

NOUWEN, SMH, 'The Special Court for Sierra Leone and the Immunity of Taylor: The *Arrest Warrant* Case Continued' (2005) 18 *Leiden Journal of International Law* 645

SCHABAS, W, 'Conjoined Twins of Transitional Justice? The Sierra Leone Truth and Reconciliation Commission and the Special Court' (2004) 2 *Journal of International Criminal Justice* 1082

SCHABAS, W, *The UN International Criminal Tribunals. The Former Yugoslavia, Rwanda and Sierra Leone* (Cambridge: Cambridge University Press, 2006)

SIVAKUMARAN, S, 'War Crimes before the Special Court for Sierra Leone: Child Soldiers, Hostages, Peacekeepers and Collective Punishments' (2010) 8 *Journal of International Criminal Justice* 1009

SMITH, A, 'Child Recruitment and the Special Court for Sierra Leone' (2004) 2 *Journal of International Criminal Justice* 1141

---

[110] Recall, *supra* para 3.24, the failed establishment of the STL by this means, with recourse being had in the end to a decision of the Security Council under chapter VII of the UN Charter.

14

The International Criminal Court

I. Introduction

The only extant international criminal court to be established under a multilateral treaty among states is also the first and only permanent international criminal court, namely the International Criminal Court (ICC), which officially came into being on 1 July 2002 with the entry into force of its constituent instrument. Despite occupying the dreams of optimists for decades, the adoption of its statute in 1998 by 120 states took even its proponents by surprise. But the Court is now very much a reality, and in a relatively short period has become a significant if still by no means integral feature of the international institutional landscape.   14.1

After sketching in the background to and basic facts about the ICC, this chapter outlines the powers of the Court and the obligations and rights of states in relation to it.[1]   14.2

II. General

A. Establishment

The idea of establishing a permanent international criminal court dates from at least the 1920s, although at that time it was largely in the realm of speculation.   14.3

After the Second World War and the UN General Assembly's affirmation of the Nuremberg principles,[2] the possibility became a very real one, as reflected in article VI of the Convention on the Prevention and Punishment of the Crime of Genocide 1948 ('Genocide Convention'), which, rather than granting states parties universal jurisdiction over the crime of genocide, provides that persons charged with genocide are to be tried by a competent tribunal of the state in the territory of which the act was committed 'or by such international penal tribunal as may have jurisdiction with respect to those Contracting Parties which have accepted its jurisdiction'. In part B of General Assembly resolution 260 (III) of   14.4

---

[1] The chapter deals only fleetingly with the Court's procedure, focusing strictly on the bare essentials.
[2] Recall *supra* para 2.60.

9 December 1948, the resolution in part A of which the Genocide Convention was adopted, the General Assembly, '[c]onsidering that, in the course of development of the international community, there will be an increasing need for the development of an international judicial organ for the trial of certain crimes under international law', invited the International Law Commission (ILC) 'to consider the desirability and possibility of establishing an international judicial organ for the trial of persons charged with genocide or other crimes over which jurisdiction will be conferred upon that organ by international conventions'.[3] The ILC worked on the topic until 1954, by which time the latter had been lumped together with the question of a draft code of offences against the peace and security of mankind, which ground to a halt on the problem of the definition of the crime of aggression. That year, the General Assembly decided to postpone consideration of the question of an international criminal jurisdiction,[4] and again in 1957, and so on effectively until the late 1980s.

14.5   In the late 1980s, certain Caribbean states pushed for the revival of the idea of an international criminal court out of concern over large-scale drug-trafficking. The ILC was charged once more with developing proposals for such a court, in the context of its revived project of a draft code of crimes against the peace and security of mankind. The first topic was soon hived off from the second, and in 1994 the Commission adopted a Draft Statute for an International Criminal Court ('ILC Draft Statute').[5] The ILC Draft Statute was significantly different from that eventually adopted in Rome in 1998. First, it envisaged a wholly 'adjectival'[6] court, with draft article 20 vesting the latter with jurisdiction *ratione materiae* over a range of crimes, both customary and treaty-based, which were not defined in the Statute but, rather, whose adjudication would call for *renvoi* to 'applicable treaties and the principles and rules of general international law' and, 'to the extent applicable, any rule of national law', as specified in draft article 33. These crimes were genocide, aggression, serious violations of the laws and customs applicable in armed conflict, crimes against humanity, and 'crimes established under or pursuant to the treaty provisions listed in the Annex, which, having regard to the conduct alleged, constitute exceptionally serious crimes of international concern'. The crimes listed in the Annex were those provided for in a range of international humanitarian and international criminal conventions, including, *inter alia*, grave breaches of the 1949 Geneva Conventions, the crimes provided for in the Convention for the Suppression of Unlawful Seizure of Aircraft 1970, the crime of torture provided for in the Convention against Torture and Other Cruel, Inhuman or Degrading Treatment or Punishment 1984 ('Torture Convention'), and the crimes provided for in the United Nations

---

[3] The General Assembly also requested the ILC 'to pay attention to the possibility of establishing a Criminal Chamber of the International Court of Justice'. The ILC dispensed with this possibility.
[4] See GA res 898 (IX), 14 December 1954.
[5] Draft Statute for an International Criminal Court with commentaries, *Ybk ILC 1994*, vol II/2, ('ILC Draft Statute'), 26, para 91.
[6] See para 2 of the commentary to draft art 19 and paras 4 and 15 of the commentary to draft art 20 of the ILC Draft Statute, ibid.

Convention against Illicit Traffic in Narcotic Drugs and Psychotropic Substances 1988. Secondly, the draft Statute did not grant the Prosecutor the power to open an investigation *proprio motu*. Only the Security Council could refer a matter and only states parties could lodge a complaint, as the terminology had it.[7] Lastly, no prosecution could be brought under the Draft Statute if it arose from a matter being dealt with at the time by the Security Council under chapter VII of the UN Charter, unless the Council decided otherwise.[8] In short, the ILC Draft Statute foreshadowed a minimalist, unthreatening court, so as to facilitate, through its lack of controversy, the ease and speed of its establishment.

What happened, however, is that the Draft Statute's positive reception by states and the establishment in 1993 and 1994 respectively of the International Criminal Tribunal for the former Yugoslavia (ICTY) and the International Criminal Tribunal for Rwanda (ICTR) crystallized a diplomatic consensus in favour of a more ambitious judicial institution. By the time states gathered in Rome in 1998 for the United Nations Diplomatic Conference of Plenipotentiaries on the Establishment of an International Criminal Court, a different, more substantial, and more substantive international criminal court was envisaged, and, after much haggling, the result was the Rome Statute of the International Criminal Court ('Rome Statute'), adopted on 17 July 1998. **14.6**

The Rome Statute entered into force on 1 July 2002, on a specified day after the deposit of the sixtieth instrument of ratification, acceptance, approval or accession.[9] There are currently 122 states parties to it. The states parties meet collectively as a body established under the Statute called the Assembly of States Parties (ASP), in which each has one vote and which meets annually and in further, special sessions 'when circumstances so require'.[10] The ASP, which is not an organ of the Court, is charged with a range of tasks under the Statute.[11] **14.7**

Since the Rome Statute is a treaty, it may not affect the legal rights and obligations of states not parties to it, known in the terminology of the law of treaties as 'third states',[12] unless the third state in question consents.[13] In this regard, it is crucial to appreciate[14] that the formulation in article 34 of the Vienna Convention on the Law of Treaties 1969 ('VCLT') of the cardinal rule of the law of treaties *pacta tertiis nec nocent nec prosunt* does not adequately reflect customary international law. It is not simply that a treaty cannot create obligations or rights for third states **14.8**

---

[7] ILC Draft Statute, arts 21(1) and 23(1). [8] Ibid, art 23(3).
[9] See Rome Statute, art 126(1).   [10] See ibid, art 112, quote from art 12(6).
[11] These are summarized ibid, art 112(2).
[12] See Vienna Convention on the Law of Treaties 1969 ('VCLT'), art 2(1)*(h)*: '"Third State" means a State not a party to the treaty'. See also eg VCLT, Part III, Section 4, heading and arts 35–38.
[13] In the case of conferral of rights, this consent is presumed, unless a contrary indication is apparent or the treaty provides otherwise, in accordance with VCLT, art 36(1). Note that the other main consequence of the fact that the Rome Statute is a treaty is that it must be interpreted according to the customary rules on treaty interpretation reflected in the VCLT, as made clear by the Appeals Chamber on many occasions. See eg *Situation in the Democratic Republic of the Congo*, ICC-01/04-168, Appeals Chamber, Judgment on the Prosecutor's Application for Extraordinary Review of Pre-Trial Chamber I's 31 March 2006 Decision Denying Leave to Appeal, 13 July 2006, para 33.
[14] Recall *supra* para 3.37 n 105.

14.9 without their consent. It is also the case that a treaty may not impinge upon the legal rights of third states without those states' consent.[15]

14.9 The Rome Statute does not oblige states parties to criminalize as a matter of municipal law the crimes within the Court's jurisdiction, let alone exercise jurisdiction over these crimes on extraordinary bases or prosecute or extradite persons suspected of their commission.

B. Basic Facts

14.10 Unlike the International Military Tribunal (IMT) at Nuremberg, the IMT for the Far East at Tokyo, the ICTY, the ICTR, the Special Court for Sierra Leone (SCSL), and the Special Tribunal for Lebanon (STL), all of which were or are ad hoc international criminal courts, the essence of the ICC, as emphasized in the Rome Statute,[16] is that it is a permanent international criminal court.

14.11 The ICC is not a UN organ. It is not a part of the UN system at all. Rather, in the words of the preamble (ninth recital), it is an independent institution 'in relationship with the United Nations'. In accordance with article 2 of the Rome Statute, the Court has been 'brought into relationship' with the UN through a Negotiated Relationship Agreement approved by the ASP in 2004.[17] That said, the UN Security Council is acknowledged in articles 13(*b*) and 16 of the Rome Statute as having important powers in relation to the Court.

14.12 The ICC is explicitly deemed to have international legal personality, along with 'such legal capacity as may be necessary for the exercise of its functions and the fulfilment of its purposes'.[18]

14.13 The Court has its seat in The Hague, the Netherlands, pursuant to a headquarters agreement with the Netherlands,[19] although it may sit elsewhere 'whenever it considers it desirable'.[20] It may 'exercise its functions and powers' in the territory of any state party to the Rome Statute and, by special agreement, in the territory

---

[15] See eg para 2 of the commentary to draft art 30 (the eventual art 34) of the ILC's Draft Articles on the Law of Treaties, *Ybk ILC 1966*, vol II, 226 ('nor modify in any way their legal rights without their consent'); *Island of Palmas (Netherlands/United States of America)*, 2 RIAA 829, 842; A McNair, *The Law of Treaties* (Oxford: Clarendon Press, 1961), 321.

[16] See eg Rome Statute, preamble (ninth recital) and art 1.

[17] Negotiated Relationship Agreement between the International Criminal Court and the United Nations 2004, ICC doc ICC-ASP/3/Res.1.

[18] Rome Statute, art 4(1).

[19] Headquarters Agreement between the International Criminal Court and the Host State 2007, ICC doc ICC-BD/04-01-08. For the difficulties posed for the Netherlands as host state by applications for asylum by witnesses in ICC proceedings, see *Djokaba Lambi Longa v Netherlands* (dec), no 33917/12, ECHR 2012. See especially, however, ibid, para 44, holding that an individual held at the ICC detention facility in The Hague, having been transferred to the Court's custody by a state with previous custody over him, was not within the 'jurisdiction' of the Netherlands within the meaning of art 1 of the European Convention on Human Rights (ECHR).

[20] Rome Statute, art 3(1) and (3) respectively. See also ibid, art 62, as well as Rules of Procedure and Evidence, ICC doc ICC-ASP/1/3 and Corr.1), part II.A (as amended) ('ICC RPE'), rule 100 (as amended by ASP res ICC-ASP/12/Res.7, 27 November 2013, para 1). The Court currently occupies temporary premises while permanent premises are being built.

of any other state.[21] Sentences imposed by the Court are to be served in a state designated by the Court from a list of states that have indicated to it their willingness to accept sentenced persons.[22]

14.14 The principal legal instruments governing the operation of the Court are the Rome Statute, what is called the 'Elements of Crimes', and the Rules of Procedure and Evidence (RPE).[23] The Elements of Crimes,[24] adopted and amended by the ASP, are to 'assist the Court in the interpretation and application of articles 6, 7, 8 and 8*bis*' of the Statute[25]—that is, of the provisions specifying the crimes within the Court's jurisdiction. They and any amendments to them are required to be consistent with the Rome Statute.[26] The RPE, unlike the RPE of the ICTY, ICTR, SCSL, and STL, were adopted and are amended not by the judges but by the ASP,[27] although the judges are authorized in urgent cases to draft, adopt, and apply provisional RPE until these are adopted, amended or rejected at the next ordinary or special session of the ASP.[28]

14.15 The organs of the Court are the Presidency, the Court's three divisions (namely the Appeals Division, the Trial Division, and the Pre-Trial Division), the Office of the Prosecutor (OTP), and the Registry.[29] All the judges of the Appeals Division together make up the Appeals Chamber.[30] Three judges of the Trial Division make up a Trial Chamber,[31] and either three judges or a single judge of the Pre-Trial Division make up a Pre-Trial Chamber.[32] In February 2003, the ASP elected the first 18 judges to the Court. Further elections have taken place since then. In accordance with article 36(8)(*a*) of the Rome Statute, the membership of the Court—that is, the composition of its bench—responds to the need for the representation of the principal legal systems of the world, equitable geographical representation, and a fair distribution of male and female judges. In April 2003, the ASP elected the first Chief Prosecutor, Luis Moreno Ocampo, from Argentina. On the expiration of his term in 2012, Fatou Bensouda, from The Gambia, formerly the Deputy Prosecutor, was elected to replace him.

14.16 The Rome Statute makes detailed provision for the due-process rights not only of the accused[33] but also of persons during an investigation.[34] The former are modelled on article 14 of the ICCPR.

14.17 Of all the legal frameworks providing for and regulating the operation of international criminal courts, that of the ICC is the most solicitous of the interests of victims. Not only do the Rome Statute and RPE make provision, as the other regimes do, for extensive measures of protection and support for

---

[21] Rome Statute, art 4(2).   [22] Ibid, art 103(1)(*a*).
[23] See ibid, arts 1, 9, and 51, as well as art 21(1)(*a*).
[24] ICC doc ICC-ASP/1/3 (part II-B) (as amended).   [25] Rome Statute, art 9(1).
[26] Ibid, art 9(3).
[27] Ibid, art 51(1) and (2). This is in contrast to the Regulations of the Court provided for ibid, art 52. The RPE have been amended several times.
[28] Rome Statute, art 51(3).   [29] Ibid, art 34.   [30] Ibid, art 39(2)(*b*)(i).
[31] Ibid, art 39(2)(*b*)(ii).   [32] Ibid, art 39(2)(*b*)(iii).   [33] See ibid, art 67.
[34] See ibid, art 55.

both witnesses and victims,[35] including by way of the establishment within the Registry of a Victims and Witnesses Unit along the lines of those within the registries of the ICTY, ICTR, SCSL, and STL.[36] They also embody several innovations as far as international criminal courts are concerned. First, '[w]here the personal interest of the victims are affected', the Rome Statute and RPE provide for the active participation of such victims, through legal representatives where the Court considers it appropriate, 'at stages of the proceedings determined to be appropriate by the Court and in a manner which is not prejudicial to or inconsistent with the rights of the accused and a fair and impartial trial'.[37] Next, the Rome Statute and RPE authorize a Trial Chamber, on the conviction of the accused, to make an order for reparations—which may include restitution, compensation, and rehabilitation—to or in respect of victims.[38] Such an order may be made directly against the convict or may specify that reparations be made through what is called the Trust Fund for Victims.[39] Finally, as provided for in the Rome Statute and the RPE,[40] the ASP has established said Trust Fund for Victims, which is not an organ of the Court, 'for the benefit of victims of crimes within the jurisdiction of the Court, and of the families of such victims'.[41]

14.18   The ICC is funded[42] essentially from assessed contributions made by states parties, as well as by additional voluntary contributions from a range of potential

---

[35] See ibid, arts 54(1)(*b*), 57(3)(*c*), 68(1), (2), (4) and (5), 87(4), and 93(1)(*j*), as well as, *inter alia*, ICC RPE, rules 87 and 88. See also the 'general principle' in respect of victims and witnesses enunciated in rule 86 of the RPE: 'A Chamber in making any direction or order, and other organs of the Court in performing their functions under the Statute or the Rules, shall take into account the needs of all victims and witnesses in accordance with article 68, in particular, children, elderly persons, persons with disabilities and victims of sexual or gender violence.'

[36] See Rome Statute, art 43(6) and ICC RPE, rules 16–19. See also Rome Statute, art 68(5). For the ICTY, ICTR, and SCSL, recall *supra* paras 12.13 and 13.14. For the STL, see STL Statute, art 12(4) and STL Rules of Procedure and Evidence ('STL RPE'), rule 50.

[37] Rome Statute, art 68(3). See also ICC RPE, rules 89–93, and the definition of the term 'victims' in ICC RPE, rule 85. See too *Situation in the Democratic Republic of the Congo*, ICC-01/04-101-tEN-Corr, Pre-Trial Chamber, Decision on the Applications for Participation in the Proceedings of VPRS 1, VPRS 2, VPRS 3, VPRS 4, VPRS 5, and VPRS 6, 17 January 2006; *Prosecutor v Lubanga*, ICC-01/04-01/06-1432, Appeals Chamber, Judgment on the Appeals of the Prosecutor and the Defence against Trial Chamber I's Decision on Victims' Participation of 18 January 2008, 11 July 2008. The model has been taken up in STL Statute, art 17 and STL RPE, rules 86 and 87. The STL also has a special Victims' Participation Unit, as per STL RPE, rule 51.

[38] See Rome Statute, art 75 and ICC RPE, rules 94–99. See also *Prosecutor v Lubanga*, ICC-01/04-01/06-2904, Trial Chamber, Decision Establishing the Principles and Procedures To Be Applied to Reparations, 7 August 2012; *Prosecutor v Lubanga*, ICC-01/04-01/06-2953, Appeals Chamber, Decision on the Admissibility of the Appeals against Trial Chamber I's 'Decision Establishing the Principles and Procedures To Be Applied to Reparations' and Directions on the Further Conduct of Proceedings, 14 December 2012. See too ASP res ICC-ASP/10/Res.3, 20 December 2011; ASP res ICC-ASP/11/Res.7, 21 November 2012; ASP res ICC-ASP/12/Res.5, 27 November 2013. Contrast the regime of compensation for victims provided for in STL Statute, art 25.

[39] Rome Statute, art 75(2).   [40] See ibid, art 79 and ICC RPE, rule 98.

[41] Rome Statute, art 79. The mandate of the Trust Fund includes the payment of reparations to victims as ordered by a Trial Chamber on the conviction of an accused, as per ibid, art 75(2) and ICC RPE, rule 98.

[42] See Rome Statute, arts 113–118.

sources. There is also provision for the approval of funding by the UN General Assembly, especially in relation to expenses incurred as a consequence of a referral by the Security Council.

C. The Procedural Essentials

The way in which a case ends up before the ICC is very different from the procedurally straightforward route (notwithstanding the problematic practical hurdle of securing custody) followed in the ICTY, ICTR, and SCSL.[43] 14.19

To begin with, as regards the crimes specified in articles 6 (genocide), 7 (crimes against humanity), and 8 (war crimes) of the Rome Statute, the Court's exercise of its jurisdiction must be triggered by one of three means outlined in article 13 of the Statute.[44] The first of these means, as foreshadowed in article 13(*a*) and elaborated on in article 14(1), is that a state party may refer to the Prosecutor a 'situation' in which one or more crimes within the jurisdiction of the Court appears to have been committed, 'requesting the Prosecutor to investigate the situation for the purpose of determining whether one or more specific persons should be charged with the commission of such crimes'.[45] Alternatively, in accordance with article 13(*b*), the UN Security Council, acting under chapter VII of the UN Charter, may refer a situation to the Prosecutor. The third possibility, as envisaged in article 13(*c*), is that the Prosecutor may—on the basis of information received on crimes within the Court's jurisdiction and having concluded that there exists a reasonable basis on which to proceed—initiate an investigation *proprio motu, viz* without the need for the referral of a situation by a state party or the Security Council. Article 15 of the Statute stipulates, however, that the Prosecutor may open an investigation *proprio motu* only if, on her submission to a Pre-Trial Chamber of a request for authorization, the Pre-Trial Chamber authorizes the commencement of the investigation.[46] 14.20

The Prosecutor is not obliged to initiate an investigation when a situation is referred to her by a state party or the Security Council or when she otherwise receives information on crimes within the Court's jurisdiction. Article 53(1) of the Statute makes it clear that if—having evaluated the information made available to 14.21

---

[43] In these fora the Prosecutor, on the basis of information received, initiated an investigation of his or her own accord, and elected or not to prepare an indictment charging an individual with crimes under the relevant statute; a Trial Chamber or Designated Judge reviewed the indictment and, if satisfied that a *prima facie* case had been established, confirmed it and, at the request of the Prosecutor, issued a warrant for the individual's arrest, detention, surrender or transfer to the Tribunal or Court; the individual, on arrival at the Tribunal or Court, made an initial appearance before the Trial Chamber and entered a plea; and, if he or she pleaded 'not guilty', the case proceeded to trial, albeit often via myriad pre-trial motions.

[44] For the special rules relating to the crime of aggression in the event that the condition specified in arts 15*bis*(3) and 15*ter*(3) is met, see Rome Statute, arts 15*bis* and 15*ter*.

[45] Ibid, art 14(2) provides: 'As far as possible, a referral shall specify the relevant circumstances and be accompanied by such supporting documentation as is available to the State referring the situation.'

[46] See also ICC RPE, rules 46–50.

her and having considered the factors specified in subparagraphs (*a*), (*b*), and (*c*) respectively of article 53(1)[47]—the Prosecutor concludes that there is no reasonable basis on which to proceed under the Statute, she may decide against initiating an investigation.[48] The Prosecutor's evaluation of a situation or information with a view to deciding whether to initiate an investigation is known as a 'preliminary examination'.[49]

14.22 Having conducted an investigation,[50] whether pursuant to a referral of a situation or *proprio motu*, the Prosecutor is not obliged to bring a prosecution or prosecutions—that is, to apply for the issuance by a Pre-Trial Chamber of a warrant of arrest or summons to appear in respect of a specified individual.[51] As indicated in article 53(2) of the Statute, the Prosecutor may conclude, for one of the reasons stipulated in subparagraphs (*a*), (*b*), and (*c*) respectively, that there is insufficient basis for a prosecution.[52] Should, however, the Prosecutor apply and apply successfully to a Pre-Trial Chamber for the issuance of an arrest warrant or a summons to appear in relation to a named individual, what follows is referred to as a 'case'.

14.23 On the arrival of the individual at the Court, and after his or her initial appearance before a Pre-Trial Chamber,[53] the Pre-Trial Chamber must hold a hearing to confirm the charges on which the Prosecutor intends to seek trial.[54] This involves the Chamber's determining 'whether there is sufficient evidence to establish substantial grounds to believe that the person committed each of the crimes charged'.[55] Should the Pre-Trial Chamber eventually[56] so decide, only then does the case proceed to trial,[57] perhaps via various pre-trial motions.

---

[47] In accordance with subparas (*a*), (*b*), and (*c*) of article 53(1), the Prosecutor 'shall consider whether: (*a*) The information available to the Prosecutor provides a reasonable basis to believe that a crime within the jurisdiction of the Court has been or is being committed; (*b*) The case is or would be admissible under article 17; and (*c*) Taking into account the gravity of the crime and the interests of victims, there are nonetheless substantial reasons to believe that an investigation would not serve the interests of justice'. Article 53(1) adds that, in the event that the Prosecutor determines on the basis of subpara (*c*) alone that there is no reasonable basis to proceed, she must inform the Pre-Trial Chamber.
[48] Rome Statute, art 53(1). See also ICC RPE, rules 104 and 105. Such a decision is reviewable in the circumstances specified in Rome Statute, art 53(3).
[49] See eg Rome Statute, art 15(6).
[50] For the duties and powers of the Prosecutor with respect to investigations, see ibid, art 54. For the role of the Pre-Trial Chamber in relation to 'a unique investigative opportunity', see ibid, art 56.
[51] For the issuance by the Pre-Trial Chamber of a warrant of arrest or summons to appear, see ibid, art 58.
[52] Such a decision is reviewable in the circumstances specified in art 53(3). The reasons specified in art 53(2)(*a*), (*b*), and (*c*) are that: '(*a*) There is not a sufficient legal or factual basis to seek a warrant or summons under article 58; (*b*) The case is inadmissible under article 17; or (*c*) A prosecution is not in the interests of justice, taking into account all the circumstances, including the gravity of the crime, the interests of victims and the age or infirmity of the alleged perpetrator, and his or her role in the alleged crime'. Should the Prosecutor decide against prosecution, art 53(2) requires her to inform the Pre-Trial Chamber and, where a situation has been referred to her, the referring state party or the Security Council, as the case may be. See also ICC RPE, rule 106.
[53] See Rome Statute, art 60. [54] See ibid, art 61. [55] Ibid, art 61(7).
[56] See ibid, art 61(7) to (10) for the range of options. [57] See ibid, art 61(11).

D. Core Activity to Date

The Prosecutor has been referred eight situations to date, six by states parties[58] and two by the Security Council.[59] Investigations have subsequently been opened into seven of these situations, while the Prosecutor declined to open an investigation into the last.[60] In addition, the Prosecutor has twice applied for and been granted authorization to open an investigation *proprio motu*.[61]   14.24

The Court has issued arrest warrants for 26 persons on substantive counts and five more in relation to offences against the administration of justice, while a further nine summonses to appear voluntarily before the Court (one of them since replaced by an arrest warrant) have been issued. Three trials have been completed, resulting in two convictions and one acquittal, with appeals pending in all three cases. Pre-Trial Chambers have declined to confirm charges against some individuals, the Prosecutor has withdrawn the charges against another, numerous individuals for whose arrest the Court has issued warrants remain at large, three more have died since the issue of warrants for their arrest, one is in custody in Libya, and one case has been terminated on the ground that genuine proceedings in train at the national level render it inadmissible before the Court.   14.25

In addition to where investigations have subsequently been opened, as well as to the two ongoing preliminary investigations into situations referred to her,   14.26

---

[58] These are the situation concerning the Lord's Resistance Army in Uganda, referred by Uganda in December 2003 and subsequently renamed 'the situation concerning northern Uganda'; the situation in the Democratic Republic of the Congo since 1 July 2002, referred by DRC in April 2004; the situation in the Central African Republic since 1 July 2002, referred by CAR in January 2005; the situation in Mali since January 2012, referred by Mali on 13 July 2012; 'the situation on registered vessels of the Union of the Comoros, the Hellenic Republic and the Kingdom of Cambodia', referred by the Comoros on 14 May 2013 and relating to the 'Gaza Freedom Flotilla' incident; and the situation in the Central African Republic since 1 August 2012, known as 'the situation in the Central African Republic II', referred by CAR on 30 May 2014.

[59] These are the situation in Darfur, Sudan, since 1 July 2002, referred by the Security Council by way of SC res 1593 (2005), 31 March 2005, and the situation in the Libyan Arab Jamahiriya since 15 February 2011, referred by the Security Council by way of SC res 1970 (2011), 26 February 2011.

[60] On 6 November 2014, on the conclusion of her preliminary examination, the Prosecutor announced that, by reference to article 53(1)(*b*) of the Rome Statute, she was not opening an investigation into the situation on registered vessels of the Union of the Comoros, the Hellenic Republic, and the Kingdom of Cambodia. See *Situation on Registered Vessels of Comoros, Greece and Cambodia. Article 53(1) Report* (6 November 2014), concluding that, although the available information provided a reasonable basis to believe that war crimes had been committed, the crimes were not of sufficient gravity to satisfy the criterion for a case's admissibility in art 17(1)(*d*) of the Statute. As of 7 November 2014, there was no indication whether the Comoros, which referred the situation, would request review of the Prosecutor's decision in accordance with art 53(3)(*a*) of the Statute.

[61] On 31 March 2010, a Pre-Trial Chamber acceded to the Prosecutor's request to authorize his opening of an investigation *proprio motu* into the situation in Kenya regarding post-election violence there in 2007–08. On 3 October 2011, a Pre-Trial Chamber acceded to the Prosecutor's request to authorize his opening of an investigation *proprio motu* into the situation in Côte d'Ivoire since 28 November 2010, an authorization later broadened to encompass the period from 19 September 2002 to 28 November 2010.

the Prosecutor is currently conducting eight preliminary examinations,[62] and has closed three others after deciding not to proceed.[63]

III. Jurisdiction

A. Existence

14.27   In accordance with article 19(1) of the Rome Statute, '[t]he Court shall satisfy itself that it has jurisdiction in any case brought before it'. In other words, the Court is obliged to ensure that it has jurisdiction in any case before it, with the consequence that, should the suspect or accused or a state or, for that matter, the Prosecutor—all of whom may challenge the Court's jurisdiction, in accordance with article 19[64]—raise no challenge to jurisdiction, the Court must nonetheless examine the issue, *proprio motu*.

(i) Jurisdiction ratione materiae *(subject-matter jurisdiction)*

14.28   In accordance with article 12(1) of the Rome Statute, a state party to the Statute accepts the jurisdiction of the Court with respect to the crimes referred to in article 5 ('Crimes within the jurisdiction of the Court'), namely genocide, crimes against humanity, war crimes, and aggression.

14.29   The Court's subject-matter jurisdiction over genocide, crimes against humanity, and war crimes is elaborated on in detail in articles 6, 7, and 8 respectively.[65]

14.30   When it comes to aggression, a former article 5(2) provided that the Court was to exercise jurisdiction over the crime of aggression only 'once a provision [was] adopted in accordance with articles 121 and 123 defining the crime of aggression and setting out the conditions under which the Court shall exercise jurisdiction with respect to this crime'; and it was widely assumed that, despite efforts towards a definition of the crime of aggression, this was how things would remain for the foreseeable future. But a Review Conference held by the ASP in Kampala in spring 2010, having settled on a definition of the crime of aggression and on modalities for the Court's exercise of jurisdiction over it, agreed as a consequence to the deletion of this article 5(2), thereby paving the way, at least in principle, for the Court's future exercise of its jurisdiction *ratione materiae* over the crime of aggression as defined in a new article 8*bis*.[66] There remain, however, three further obstacles to the Court's actual exercise of this jurisdiction. First, the amendments to the Rome Statute relating to

---

[62] These involve information received on alleged crimes in Afghanistan, Colombia, Georgia, Guinea, Honduras, Iraq, Nigeria, and Ukraine.
[63] These involve information received on crimes alleged to have been committed by North Korean forces in the territory of, and on a vessel registered in, South Korea; in Palestine; and in Venezuela.
[64] See Rome Statute, art 19(2) and (3). Article 19(5) stipulates that a state permitted to challenge the Court's jurisdiction must do so at the earliest opportunity.
[65] Recall *supra* chapter 4.
[66] Recall *supra* para 4.90, referring to RC/Res.6, 11 June 2010.

the crime of aggression are subject to ratification by each of the states parties, in accordance with article 121(5) of the Statute, and the Court's exercise of jurisdiction over the crime is dependent on ratification of the amendments by at least 30 states parties, as specified in articles 15*bis*(2) and 15*ter*(2).[67] Secondly, as indicated in articles 15*bis*(3) and 15*ter*(3), this exercise is further contingent on a decision to be taken collectively by the states parties no earlier than 1 January 2017, meaning that in 2017 or thereafter the states parties *en masse* will have a chance to consider whether to go ahead and activate the Court's jurisdiction over aggression. Finally, as per article 15*bis*(4), a state party may—by lodging with the Registrar, prior to ratifying or accepting the relevant amendments to the Statute, a declaration that it does not accept this jurisdiction—opt out of the Court's jurisdiction over the crime of aggression where this jurisdiction results from either a state party's referral of a situation to the Prosecutor or the Prosecutor's opening of an investigation *proprio motu*.[68]

As regards war crimes, article 124 of the Rome Statute, an optional provision intended as a transitional measure, allows a state to declare that, for a period of seven years after the entry into force of the Rome Statute for that state, it does not accept the jurisdiction of the Court with respect to war crimes committed by its nationals or on its territory. A proposal to delete article 124 now that it has served its original purpose[69] was put to the Kampala Review Conference, but the delegates elected to maintain the provision in its current form.[70]

14.31

(ii) *Jurisdiction* ratione loci *and* ratione personae *(territorial and personal jurisdiction)*

No provision of the Rome Statute specifies as such the ICC's jurisdiction *ratione loci* and *ratione personae*. The questions are dealt with indirectly in article 12(2) and (3) under the rubric 'Preconditions to the exercise of jurisdiction', with article 12(2) and (3) referring in turn to article 13 ('Exercise of jurisdiction'). The preconditions in question vary depending on whether, on the one hand, a situation has been referred to the Prosecutor by a state party as per article 13(*a*) or the Prosecutor has initiated an investigation *proprio motu* as per article 13(*c*) or, on the other hand, a situation has been referred to the Court by the Security Council in accordance with article 13(*b*). In other words, when it comes to the Court's territorial and personal jurisdiction, the existence of jurisdiction in the first place is inseparable from the circumstances of its exercise.

14.32

---

[67] As of 23 November 2014, 19 states parties had ratified the amendments on the crime of aggression.

[68] In contrast, it is not open to a state party to opt out of the Court's jurisdiction over the crime of aggression where this jurisdiction results from the referral of a situation to the Prosecutor by the UN Security Council acting under chapter VII of the Charter.

[69] Article 124 was adopted to allay especially French fears that peacekeepers serving in Bosnia-Herzegovina at the time of the Statute's entry into force would be brought before the Court. France has now withdrawn its declaration, and the declaration by Colombia, the only other state party to date to have opted out of the Court's jurisdiction over war crimes, has now expired.

[70] They did, however, undertake in resolution RC/Res.4, 10 June 2010, to review the provision again during the fourteenth session of the ASP.

14.33   Article 12(2) and (3) provide:

> 2. In the case of article 13, paragraph (*a*) or (*c*), the Court may exercise its jurisdiction if one or more of the following States are Parties to this Statute or have accepted the jurisdiction of the Court in accordance with paragraph 3:
>   (*a*) The State on the territory of which the conduct in question occurred or, if the crime was committed on board a vessel or aircraft, the State of registration of that vessel or aircraft;
>   (*b*) The State of which the person accused of the crime is a national.
> 3. If the acceptance of a State which is not a Party to this Statute is required under paragraph 2, that State may, by declaration lodged with the Registrar, accept the exercise of jurisdiction by the Court with respect to the crime in question. The accepting State shall cooperate with the Court without any delay or exception in accordance with Part 9.

That is, where a situation is referred to the Court by a state party to the Rome Statute or where an investigation has been initiated by the Prosecutor *proprio motu*, the Court may exercise its jurisdiction over a crime only when the latter is alleged to have been committed either, first, on the territory of a state party or on board a vessel or aircraft registered in a state party or, secondly, by a national of a state party. In either case, however, it will suffice that the state on which the exercise of jurisdiction depends, although not a party to the Rome Statute, accepts the Court's jurisdiction with respect to the crime in question by means of a declaration lodged with the Registrar.[71] In other words, in the scenarios outlined in article 12(2) and (3), states parties to the Rome Statute and non-states

---

[71] In accordance with rule 44(2) of the ICC RPE, inserted at the insistence of the US during the post-1998 Preparatory Commission, a declaration under art 12(3) of the Statute constitutes acceptance of the Court's jurisdiction with respect to any and all crimes under the Statute that are of relevance to the situation or investigation. In other words, a state accepting the Court's jurisdiction under art 12(3) cannot limit that acceptance to crimes committed by the adversary. Rather, a declaration under the provision also brings within the Court's jurisdiction any crimes under the Statute committed on the side of the declarant government. On 18 April 2003, Côte d'Ivoire became the first non-state party to accept the exercise of jurisdiction by the Court under art 12(3) of the Statute, in its case with respect to crimes committed on its territory since 19 September 2002, an acceptance affirmed on 14 December 2010 and again on 3 May 2011. As a non-state party, it could not refer a situation to the Prosecutor, so it had to wait in the event for the Prosecutor to initiate an investigation *proprio motu* in respect of the alleged crimes. Permission for the Prosecutor to open an investigation into crimes alleged to have been committed on the territory of Côte d'Ivoire from 28 November 2010 onwards was granted by a Pre-Trial Chamber on 3 October 2011, and on 22 February 2012 this authorization was extended to crimes alleged to have been committed in Côte d'Ivoire since 19 September 2002, the date from which Côte d'Ivoire's acceptance of the Court's exercise of jurisdiction is effective. For its part, on 22 January 2009, the Palestinian National Authority (PA), acting as 'the Government of Palestine', lodged a declaration pursuant to art 12(3) of the Statute in which it accepted the jurisdiction of the Court with respect to crimes committed on 'the territory of Palestine' since 1 July 2002. Whether the declaration was valid depended on whether Palestine was to be considered a 'State' within the meaning of article 12(3) of the Statute. On 3 April 2012, the OTP eventually decided as follows: 'In interpreting and applying article 12 of the Rome Statute, the Office has assessed that it is for the relevant bodies at the United Nations or the Assembly of States Parties to make the legal determination whether Palestine qualifies as a State for the purpose of acceding to the Rome Statute and thereby enabling the exercise of jurisdiction by the Court under article 12(1). The Rome Statute provides

parties accepting the Court's exercise of jurisdiction do not assert, through the collective medium of the Court, what would in effect be universal jurisdiction. Rather, they claim collective jurisdiction only on the bases of what are effectively territoriality, the *sui generis* prescriptive jurisdiction of the state of registration of a ship or aircraft, and nationality—all of them heads of prescriptive jurisdiction accepted under customary international law as permissible in relation to all offences.[72]

14.34 The limitations imposed by article 12(2) of the Statute apply only, as the chapeau to the provision indicates, '[i]n the case of article 13, paragraph (*a*) or (*c*)'— that is, where a situation has been referred to the Prosecutor by a state party or where the Prosecutor has opened an investigation *proprio motu*. Where instead, as foreseen in paragraph (*b*) of article 13, a situation is referred to the Prosecutor by the Security Council acting under chapter VII of the UN Charter, article 12(2) poses no bar to the exercise of the Court's jurisdiction. That is, where the Security Council refers a situation, the Court may exercise its jurisdiction regardless of whether the crime in question is alleged to have been committed on the territory of, or on board a vessel or aircraft registered in, or by a national of, a state party to the Statute or a non-state party making a declaration under article 12(3).[73] In short, when the Security Council starts the ball rolling, the ICC may exercise what amounts, on the part of the states parties to the Statute, to the collective assertion of universal jurisdiction over crimes within the Court's jurisdiction. The primary justification for this is that, as article 1(1) of the UN Charter makes clear *a contrario*, the Security Council can derogate from international law when acting under chapter VII of the Charter,[74] so that it makes no legal difference if not all the crimes provided for in articles 6 to 8 of the Rome Statute give rise to universal jurisdiction under customary international law or, indeed, accord with customary international law in the first place.

14.35 Even where a situation has been referred to the Prosecutor by a state party or where the Prosecutor has opened an investigation *proprio motu*, a practical upshot of article 12(2) of the Statute is that the ICC may exercise jurisdiction over a

---

no authority for the Office of the Prosecutor to adopt a method to define the term "State" under article 12(3) which would be at variance with that established for the purpose of article 12(1).' See Office of the Prosecutor, *Situation in Palestine* (3 April 2012), para 6. Since, however, the according by the UN General Assembly, via GA res 67/19, 29 November 2012, of 'non-member observer state' status to Palestine, things have become more complicated. The Prosecutor's position is that GA res 67/19 does not retroactively validate the PA's declaration of 22 January 2009 but that Palestine could lodge a new declaration under art 12(3) or become a state party to the Rome Statute.

[72] The reason for this self-restraint was a desire on the part of the drafters to avoid complications created by the *pacta tertiis* rule of the law of treaties in the light of the controversy surrounding universal jurisdiction over crimes under customary international law. Putting it simply, states have no greater right to do together what none of them is permitted by international law to do alone, and not all states involved in drafting the Rome Statute were convinced that customary international law permitted universal jurisdiction over each and every one of the crimes within the ICC's jurisdiction. As a result, it was decided to stick to heads of prescriptive jurisdiction the assertion of which was undeniably permissible in respect of any crime.

[73] This will be the case even in relation to aggression. See Rome Statute, art 15*ter*.

[74] Recall *supra* para 3.27.

national of a state not party to the Statute, as long as the individual is alleged to have committed a crime within the Court's jurisdiction while on the territory of, or on board a vessel or aircraft registered in, a state party or a state making a declaration under article 12(3); and, equally, that the Court may exercise jurisdiction over a crime committed on the territory of a non-state party, as long as the crime is alleged to have been committed by a national of a state party or of a state making a declaration under article 12(3). Neither scenario, however, will be permissible in respect of the crime of aggression, in relation to which the conditions in article 12(2)(*a*) and article 12(2)(*b*) must be satisfied cumulatively, rather than in the alternative.[75]

14.36   As specifically regards the Court's jurisdiction *ratione personae*, paragraph 1 of article 24 ('Non-retroactivity *ratione personae*') of the Statute provides that no-one shall be criminally responsible under the Statute for conduct prior to the Statute's entry into force. This means that no-one may be convicted of a crime within the jurisdiction of the Court committed prior to 1 July 2002. This provision is the counterpart to article 11(1).[76]

14.37   Article 25(1) limits the Court's jurisdiction to natural persons. Corporations and other legal persons are not subject to its jurisdiction.

14.38   Article 26 provides that the Court has no jurisdiction over persons who were under the age of 18 at the time of alleged commission of the crime.

(iii) Jurisdiction ratione temporis *(temporal jurisdiction)*

14.39   In accordance with paragraph 1 of article 11 ('Jurisdiction *ratione temporis*') of the Rome Statute, the ICC has jurisdiction only in relation to crimes committed after the Statute's entry into force, *viz* after 1 July 2002. Furthermore, pursuant to article 11(2), where a state has become a party to the Statute after the Statute's entry into force, the Court may exercise its jurisdiction only in relation to crimes committed after the Statute's entry into force for that state, unless the state has made a declaration under article 12(3). In other words, unless the state makes a declaration under article 12(3), the Court may not rely on article 12(2)(*a*) to ground its exercise of jurisdiction if, at the time of alleged commission, the Statute was not in force for the state on whose territory, etc the crime is alleged to have been committed; and the Court may not rely on article 12(2)(*b*) to ground its exercise of jurisdiction if, at the time of alleged commission, the Statute was not in force for the state whose national is alleged to have committed the crime. By way of declaration under article 12(3), however, a state party may accept the exercise of the Court's jurisdiction over crimes alleged to have been committed on its territory, etc or by one of its nationals prior to the Statute's entry into force for that state. Article 12(3) does

---

[75] See Rome Statute, art 15*bis*(5), as provided for in resolution RC/Res.6, Annex, para 3.
[76] See *infra* para 14.39.

not, on the other hand, enable the Court to exercise jurisdiction over crimes alleged to have been committed prior to 1 July 2002, the date of the Statute's 'initial' or 'definitive' entry into force.

B. Exercise

(i) Irrelevance of official capacity

Article 27 of the Rome Statute renders the official capacity of an accused irrelevant for the purposes of trial before the ICC. In doing so, it teases apart the question of substantive responsibility, *viz* whether individuals may be held responsible for crimes within the jurisdiction of the Court in respect of conduct performed in the capacity of a state official, from the logically subsequent question of procedural amenability to prosecution, *viz* whether proceedings may be brought before the Court against a current or former state official suspected of responsibility for a crime within the Court's jurisdiction. 14.40

The fact that the official position of the accused poses no substantive or procedural bar to prosecution before the ICC does not mean that procedural adjustments may not be made in cases against at least certain serving officers of state so as to accommodate their official duties. In late 2013, in the wake of Appeals Chamber and Trial Chamber decisions in the *Ruto and Sang* and *Kenyatta* cases,[77] involving the deputy head of state and government and the head of state and government of Kenya, the ASP inserted into the RPE rule 134*quater* ('Excusal from presence at trial due to extraordinary public duties').[78] Paragraph 1 of rule 134*quater* permits an accused subject to a summons to appear (as opposed to a warrant of arrest) 'who is mandated to fulfill extraordinary public duties at the highest national level' to submit a written request to the Trial Chamber to be excused and to be represented by counsel only. Paragraph 2 directs the Trial Chamber to consider the request expeditiously and, 'if alternative measures are inadequate, [to] grant the request where it determines that it is in the interests of justice and provided that the rights of the accused are fully ensured'. The paragraph continues that the decision is to be taken 'with due regard to the subject matter of the specific hearings in question' and is subject to review at any time.[79] 14.41

---

[77] See *Prosecutor v Ruto and Sang*, ICC-01/09-02/11-1066, Appeals Chamber, Judgment on the Appeal of the Prosecutor against the Decision of Trial Chamber V(a) of 18 June 2013 entitled 'Decision on Mr Ruto's Request for Excusal from Continuous Presence at Trial', 25 October 2013, on appeal from *Prosecutor v Ruto and Sang*, ICC-01/09-02/11-777, Trial Chamber, Decision on Mr Ruto's Request for Excusal from Continuous Presence at Trial, 18 June 2013; *Prosecutor v Kenyatta*, ICC-01/09-02/11-830, Trial Chamber, Decision on Defence Request for Conditional Excusal from Continuous Presence at Trial, 18 October 2013.

[78] See ASP res ICC-ASP/12/Res.7, 27 November 2013, para 3.

[79] For an application of rule 134*quater*, see *Prosecutor v Ruto and Sang*, ICC-01/09-02/11-1186, Trial Chamber, Reasons for the Decision on Excusal from Presence at Trial under Rule 134*quater*, 18 February 2014.

(a) Substantive responsibility

14.42 Article 27(1) provides:

> This Statute shall apply equally to all persons without any distinction based on official capacity. In particular, official capacity as a Head of State or Government, a member of a Government or parliament, an elected representative or a government official shall in no case exempt a person from criminal responsibility under this Statute, nor shall it, in and of itself, constitute a ground for reduction of sentence.

The wording of the second sentence—an echo of article 8 of the Nuremberg Charter, as well as of article 7(2) of the ICTY Statute and article 6(2) of the ICTR Statute[80]—is directed towards the substantive plea of act of state, as raised but rejected at Nuremberg. Although the wording could be taken to refer to the person's capacity at the time of the proceedings before the Court, it is clear that the provision's real concern is the capacity in which the person acted when performing the conduct at issue before the Court.

(b) Procedural immunity

14.43 Article 27(2) reads:

> Immunities or special procedural rules which may attach to the official capacity of a person, whether under national or international law, shall not bar the Court from exercising its jurisdiction over such a person.

In other words, any state immunity, diplomatic immunity, head-of-state immunity, head-of-government immunity, etc from criminal proceedings that one state may owe another in respect of a serving or former official of the latter does not bar prosecution before the ICC. Nor does any subject-preclusion device such as the procedural (rather than substantive) plea of act of state familiar to Anglo–American lawyers.

14.44 The non-according of internationally-mandated procedural immunities before the ICC is uncontroversial in international legal terms as regards the officials and former officials of states parties to the Statute, since states parties, in consenting to the Court's operation in accordance with its Statute, which includes article 27, are taken to consent to this. The same goes, *mutatis mutandis*, in relation to any state not party to the Statute (or 'third state', as the international legal terminology has it)[81] that has accepted the Court's jurisdiction in respect of the crime prosecuted by way of a declaration under article 12(3).[82] But the non-recognition of immunities before the Court is problematic as a matter of international law as regards the officials and former officials of any third state that has not made a declaration under article 12(3). Such states cannot be taken to have waived any immunity

---

[80] See also, subsequently, SCSL Statute, art 6(2).

[81] Recall *supra* para 14.9, citing VCLT, art 2(1)(*h*).

[82] Laurent Gbagbo, whose case is proceeding to trial before the Court, was at the time of his alleged crimes President of Côte d'Ivoire, a state not party to the Statute, but Côte d'Ivoire has accepted the Court's jurisdiction in relation to the alleged crimes by way of a declaration under art 12(3) of the Statute.

from prosecution owed to them by other states in respect of their officials and ex-officials, who can be prosecuted before the Court in jurisdictional reliance on article 12(2)(*a*), article 12(3), or article 13(*b*) of its Statute.[83] The international legal basis for dispensing with immunities owed to third states is extremely shaky at best. The ICC is not established by a decision taken under chapter VII of the UN Charter by the UN Security Council, which is empowered to derogate from international law when taking collective measures for the maintenance of peace and security within the meaning of article 1(1) of the Charter—a derogation to which UN member states are taken by article 25 of the Charter to consent.[84] Indeed, according to the logic rightly relied on to defend the Court's assumption of jurisdiction over third-state nationals by virtue of article 12(2)(*a*), the states parties to the Statute, by empowering the Court to try crimes within its jurisdiction, are merely doing collectively what any one of them could do singly, namely punish crimes committed on its territory. This being the case, however, they conversely have no more right to do collectively what none of them could do singly, namely abrogate any procedural immunity that they may owe under international law to another state in respect of the latter's serving or former officials. The question in the final analysis must be the extent of the immunities from criminal jurisdiction that international law obliges one state to accord another in respect of the latter's serving and former officials when the charge is the crime of genocide, a crime against humanity, a war crime or the crime of aggression. In this regard, it will be recalled that, as customary international law presently stands, the various immunities *ratione personae* do indeed pose a procedural bar to the prosecution of those foreign state officials in relation to whom they are owed even when what is charged is an international crime; and it will further be recalled that the same is more likely than not the case when it comes to the immunity *ratione materiae* from prosecution from which serving and former foreign state officials benefit in respect of acts performed in their official capacity.[85] The point was acknowledged in a decision of 9 April 2014 by the Pre-Trial Chamber in *Al Bashir*.[86] Having gone out of its way 'to make clear that it is not disputed that under international law a sitting Head of State enjoys personal immunities from criminal jurisdiction and inviolability before national courts of foreign States even when suspected of having committed one of more of the crimes that fall within the jurisdiction of the Court',[87] the Pre-Trial Chamber continued:

25. ...An exception to the personal immunities of Heads of States is explicitly provided in article 27(2) of the Statute for prosecution before an international criminal

---

[83] See *supra* paras 14.33–14.35. One of the suspects targeted by an arrest warrant in relation to the situation in Darfur, Omar Al Bashir, is currently the President of Sudan, a state not party to the Rome Statute, and the impugned acts are alleged to have been performed by him in that capacity. Another, Ahmad Harun, was at the time of the alleged offences Minister of State for the Interior of Sudan and, again, is alleged to have performed the impugned acts in that capacity.

[84] Recall *supra* paras 3.40 and 3.42.   [85] Recall *supra* chapter 10.

[86] *Prosecutor v Al Bashir*, ICC-02/05-01/09-195, Pre-Trial Chamber, Decision on the Cooperation of the Democratic Republic of the Congo Regarding Omar Al-Bashir's Arrest and Surrender to the Court, 9 April 2014.

[87] Ibid, para 25.

jurisdiction. According to this provision, the existence of personal immunities under international law which generally attach to the official capacity of the person 'shall not bar the Court from exercising its jurisdiction over such a person'.

26. Still, the question *sub judice* is how far reaching this provision is meant to be, and whether such an exception for lifting personal immunities applies to Heads of all States, including non-States Parties to the Statute (third States), or whether it is only confined to those States which have adhered to the Statute. Given that the Statute is a multilateral treaty governed by the rules set out in the Vienna Convention on the Law of Treaties, the Statute cannot impose obligations on third States without their consent. Thus, the exception to the exercise of the Court's jurisdiction provided in article 27(2) of the Statute should, in principle, be confined to those States Parties who have accepted it.

27. It follows that when the exercise of jurisdiction by the Court entails the prosecution of a Head of State of a non-State Party, the question of personal immunities might validly arise...

The Pre-Trial Chamber was not, however, required to indicate what the resolution might be were the Court to be confronted squarely with the question, noting instead only that article 98(1) of the Statute was designed to obviate the contingency.[88]

14.45 The legal complexion is different, however, where the Security Council takes a decision under chapter VII of the UN Charter to refer to the ICC a situation implicating immunities owed to a third state.[89] Here—as rightly explained by the Pre-Trial Chamber in its decision of 4 March 2009 in *Al Bashir*, citing its previous decision in *Situation in Darfur, Sudan*[90]—the Security Council envisages that, in the event that the Prosecutor opens an investigation and in turn prosecutes, any cases arising out of the situation will proceed in accordance with the Rome Statute, which expressly provides in article 27(2) that such immunities as may attach to the official capacity of a person under international law shall not bar the Court from exercising its jurisdiction over such a person. In other words, in deciding to refer a situation to the ICC, the Security Council decides that any persons who may eventually be prosecuted before the Court for crimes allegedly committed in the context of that situation shall not benefit from any immunity from prosecution from which the third state in question may otherwise be entitled to see such persons benefit at the hands of the states parties or relevant state party.[91] Provided that the third state is a member of the United Nations, it has undertaken in article 25 of the Charter to accept the lawful decisions of the Security Council, meaning in this case that it is taken to have consented in

---

[88] Ibid, para 27. [89] Recall *supra* 3.43.
[90] *Prosecutor v Al Bashir*, ICC-02/05-01/09-3, Pre-Trial Chamber, Decision on the Prosecution's Application for a Warrant of Arrest against Omar Hassan Ahmad Al Bashir, 4 March 2009, para 43, citing *Situation in Darfur, Sudan*, ICC-02/05-185, Pre-Trial Chamber, Decision on Application under Rule 103, 4 February 2009, para 31.
[91] In practice it can be expected that the Security Council will refer a situation only where the crimes are alleged to have been committed both in the territory and by the nationals of a third state, although it is not out of the question that it might refer a situation involving crimes alleged to have been committed on the territory of a state party by officials of a third state.

advance to the Council's abrogation of any immunity from prosecution by other states from which it might otherwise have the right under international law to see its officials and ex-officials benefit.

To suggest that the state parties to the Rome Statute are not entitled to exercise, 14.46 by means of the ICC's exercise of jurisdiction, criminal jurisdiction over serving and, in relevant cases, former officials of third states is not to suggest that the Court would be prevented from proceeding with a case implicating any immunity that may attach to the official capacity of such a person under international law. Article 27(2) of the Statute is unambiguous; and, in accordance with its applicable law as provided for in article 21(1), the Court shall apply in the first place the Rome Statute and only in the second place, and even then only where appropriate, applicable treaties and the principles and rules of international law, such as the various treaties and customary international rules on immunities. It was in part on this basis that the Pre-Trial Chamber in *Al Bashir* concluded that 'the current position of Omar Al Bashir as Head of a state which is not a party to the Statute has no effect on the Court's jurisdiction'.[92] That said, there is a persuasive argument based on article 31(3)(c) of the VCLT[93] for reading down article 27(2) so as to restrict its application to the officials and former officials of states parties alone.

Some argue that article 27(2) of the Rome Statute goes beyond the availability 14.47 of immunities before the ICC to encompass immunities before municipal courts, the suggestion being that the provision effectively obliges states parties to the Statute not to accord immunity from criminal jurisdiction to serving or former foreign-state officials in respect of crimes within the jurisdiction of the ICC. The argument flies in the face of the text of article 27(2), which says simply and unambiguously that such immunities 'shall not bar the Court from exercising its jurisdiction'. Nor is there any persuasive indication that the states parties to the Statute give article 27(2) anything other than its ordinary meaning.[94] On the contrary, in

---

[92] *Al Bashir*, Pre-Trial Chamber Decision on Warrant of Arrest (n 90), para 41. See also ibid, paras 42–44.
[93] VCLT, art 31(3)(c) requires, in the interpretation of a treaty provision, the taking into account of any other relevant rules of international law applicable in the relations between the state parties. This requirement was considered consonant with customary international law in, *inter alia*, *Certain Questions of Mutual Assistance in Criminal Matters (Djibouti v France), Judgment*, ICJ Rep 2008, 177, 219, para 112.
[94] The study prepared by the UN Secretariat by way of background to the ILC's work on the immunity of state officials from foreign criminal jurisdiction points to only two states parties as 'exclud[ing] the application of immunities in respect of prosecution of crimes referred to in article 5 of the Rome Statute'; and, even then, it is by no means clear that the relevant legislation of the first, South Africa, has anything to do with procedural immunity, as distinct from substantive criminal responsibility, while there is no indication whether the relevant legislation of the second, Croatia, is motivated by that state's interpretation and application of article 27 of the Rome Statute. See *Immunity of State officials from foreign criminal jurisdiction. Memorandum by the Secretariat*, UN doc A/CN.4/596 (31 March 2008), 49–51, para 86, especially note 210. Consider also, in the same light, the two further examples, those of the Democratic Republic of the Congo and Niger, pointed to by the ILC's first special rapporteur on the topic in *Second report on immunity of State officials from foreign criminal jurisdiction by Roman Anatolevitch Kolodkin, Special Rapporteur*, UN doc A/CN.4/631 (10 June 2010), 48, para 74 note 202. Consider too, in this light, understanding 5 of the Understandings regarding the amendments to the Rome Statute of the International Criminal Court on the crime of aggression adopted by the Review Conference in Kampala, resolution RC/

their respective reactions to the work of the UN Secretariat and the ILC on the immunity of state officials from foreign criminal jurisdiction, none of which suggests that article 27(2) of the Statute has implications for prosecution by states parties at the national level,[95] no state has ever argued that article 27(2) has the effect suggested. In sum, in the words of the Belgian Court of Cassation in *Re Sharon and Yaron*, article 27(2) of the Statute 'does not challenge the principle of customary international criminal law relating to jurisdictional immunity where the protected person is prosecuted . . . before the national courts of a State'.[96]

(ii) Irrelevance of statutes of limitations

14.48 Article 29 of the Rome Statute states that the crimes within the jurisdiction of the Court shall not be subject to any statute of limitations. In other words, a municipal statute of limitations in respect of a crime within the jurisdiction of the ICC poses no bar to prosecution before the ICC.

14.49 The states parties to the Statute are clearly entitled under international law to ignore a statute of limitations applicable in a third state,[97] since a statute of limitations in one state cannot bind another,[98] and the states parties are merely doing through the ICC what any one of them could do individually.

14.50 Some argue that the import of article 29 extends down to the municipal level—in other words, that article 29 can be interpreted to mean that, in the event that states parties provide for prosecution before their municipal criminal courts of crimes within the jurisdiction of the ICC, they are prohibited from applying statutes of limitations to such prosecution. But the fact that the Rome Statute does not oblige states to criminalize, let alone prosecute the crimes within the jurisdiction of the Court, along with the applicability only to the Court itself of the provisions found alongside article 29 in Part 3 of the Statute, indicate persuasively that article 29 applies only to prosecution and trial by the ICC. Moreover, this would appear to be how states parties to the Statute read it.

(iii) Amnesties

14.51 The Rome Statute is silent on amnesties, since no agreement could be reached on the point at the 1998 diplomatic conference in Rome. But since no provision in the

---

Res.6, 11 June 2010, Annex III: 'It is understood that the amendments shall not be interpreted as creating the right . . . to exercise domestic jurisdiction with respect to an act of aggression committed by another State.'

[95] Indeed, the study prepared by the UN Secretariat for the ILC considers it 'generally recognized that article 27 of the Rome Statute is to be interpreted as excluding the defence of immunity before the International Criminal Court alone'. See *Immunity of State officials. Memorandum by the Secretariat* (n 94), 97, para 150.

[96] 127 ILR 110, 124 (2003).

[97] As for the states parties themselves, they obviously consent through art 29 to the irrelevance before the ICC of any statutes of limitations applicable in their own jurisdictions to crimes within the jurisdiction of the Court.

[98] Recall *supra* para 11.32.

Statute stipulates that the Court is obliged to have regard to a municipal amnesty, the Court's jurisdiction remains unfettered in this regard. Nor is there any reason why the states parties cannot provide for this in relation to an amnesty applicable in a third state,[99] given that an amnesty in one state cannot bind another state and the parties are merely exercising jointly, through the medium of the Court, the jurisdiction that they could exercise severally.

(iv) Article 16

In accordance with article 16 of the Rome Statute, no prosecution may be commenced or proceeded with under the Statute for a period of 12 months after the Security Council, 'in a resolution adopted under Chapter VII of the Charter of the United Nations, has requested the Court to that effect'. Article 16 continues that any such request 'may be renewed by the Council under the same conditions', by which is meant more accurately that, should the Council choose in the exercise of its Charter-based powers to renew any such request, no prosecution may be commenced or proceeded with for a further 12 months. 14.52

The effect of article 16 of the Statute is not to 'authorize' the Security Council to request the non-commencement or non-continuation of a prosecution by the Court. The Security Council's authority to make such a request flows from articles 39 and 41 of the UN Charter. Rather, what article 16 does is to bar the Court, including the Prosecutor as an organ of the Court, from commencing or proceeding with a prosecution on receipt of such a request—in effect, to make a 'request' to this effect from the Security Council binding on the Court. 14.53

The inclusion of article 16 in the Statute was contentious,[100] and the provision initially proved controversial in practice. In an effort to have at least those of its armed forces involved in UN operations shielded from the jurisdiction of the ICC, the US—a state not party to the Rome Statute—engaged in brinkmanship after the Statute's entry into force on 1 July 2002, threatening to pull its troops out of existing UN-established or UN-authorized operations[101] unless it had its way, a move that would have crippled these operations. In response, the Security Council adopted resolution 1422 (2002) of 12 July 2002, which reads in relevant part: 14.54

The Security Council,...
  Determining that operations established or authorized by the United Nations Security Council are deployed to maintain or restore international peace and security,
  Determining further that it is in the interests of international peace and security to facilitate Member States' ability to contribute to operations established or authorised by the United Nations Security Council,
  Acting under Chapter VII of the Charter of the United Nations,

---

[99] As for the states parties themselves, they clearly consent to the Court's exercise of jurisdiction over any crime covered in their own jurisdictions by an amnesty.

[100] It was something of a concession to the US, to allay its fears that a politically-motivated Prosecutor might seek to bring US officials and service personnel before the ICC.

[101] Examples included deployments in Bosnia-Herzegovina and Kosovo and on the Egypt–Israel border.

1. Requests, consistent with provisions of Article 16 of the Rome Statute, that the ICC, if a case arises involving current or former officials or personnel from a contributing State not a Party to the Rome Statute over acts or omissions relating to a United Nations established or authorized operation, shall for a twelve-month period starting 1 July 2002 not commence or proceed with investigation or prosecution of any such case, unless the Security Council decides otherwise;
2. Expresses the intention to renew the request in paragraph 1 under the same conditions each 1 July for further 12-month periods for as long as may be necessary;
3. Decides that Member States shall take no action inconsistent with paragraph 1 and their international obligations...

The request was renewed in identical terms in Security Council resolution 1487 (2003) of 12 June 2003, although never again.[102] Some have argued that Security Council resolution 1422 (2002) and Security Council resolution 1487 (2003) were not lawful invocations of article 16 of the Statute, suggesting that a situation must first have been referred to the Prosecutor or that she must first have initiated a preliminary examination pursuant to article 15(1) before article 16 can be deployed. The argument is a weak one.[103] The plain words of the provision indicate that '[n]o investigation...may be commenced' if the Security Council requests under chapter VII that this be so.

14.55 An attempt by Kenya, backed by the African Union (AU), to invoke article 16 to request the deferral of trial proceedings against President Uhuru Kenyatta and Deputy President William Ruto of Kenya failed on 15 November 2013 to secure enough votes in the Security Council, with seven states (including China and Russia) voting in favour and eight states (including France, the UK, and the US) abstaining.

14.56 When the Security Council referred the situation in Darfur to the ICC by way of resolution 1593 (2005) of 31 March 2005, it provided as follows, in recognition of the presence in Darfur of a mission from AU states and possibly with an eye to the potential deployment of US personnel:

The Security Council,...
Recalling article 16 of the Rome Statute under which no investigation or prosecution may be commenced or proceeded with by the International Criminal Court for a period of 12 months after a Security Council request to that effect,...
Taking note of the existence of agreements referred to in Article 98(2) of the Rome Statute,
Determining that the situation in Sudan continues to constitute a threat to international peace and security,
Acting under Chapter VII of the Charter of the United Nations,
...6. Decides that nationals, current or former officials or personnel from a contributing State outside Sudan which is not a party to the Rome Statute of the International Criminal Court shall be subject to the exclusive jurisdiction of that contributing State for all alleged

---

[102] With the US having spent its remaining political capital on the invasion of Iraq, it failed in 2004 to secure a further 12-month renewal of the request. It did not attempt any further such requests.
[103] Whether this was a proper use of art 16 is a separate question.

acts or omissions arising out of or related to operations in Sudan established or authorized by the Council or the African Union, unless such exclusive jurisdiction has been expressly waived by that contributing State…

Paragraph 6 of Security Council resolution 1593 (2005) is in terms identical, *mutatis mutandis*, to those of the earlier paragraph 7 of Security Council resolution 1497 (2003) of 1 August 2003, relating to the UN-authorized multinational force in Liberia, a resolution that made no reference to article 16 of the Rome Statute. Indeed, despite the deliberately ambiguous preambular reference to article 16 in Security Council resolution 1593 (2005), neither paragraph 6 of the resolution nor, *a fortiori*, paragraph 7 of Security Council resolution 1497 (2003) before it represented an invocation of article 16 of the Rome Statute. Neither paragraph constituted a request directed towards the Court, as envisaged in article 16. Nor, for that matter, does either mention a 12-month period. Both paragraphs, rather, represent decisions directed towards, and binding on, UN member states. What each amounts to, and this in practice explains—but, on closer analysis, does not legally justify[104]—the additional preambular reference to article 98(2) of the Rome Statute, is a sort of Security Council-mandated status of forces or status of mission arrangement, excluding the jurisdiction of all states bar the sending state over the individuals in question.

IV. Applicable Law

Unlike the earlier statutes of the ICTY and ICTR, as well as the later statute of the SCSL, the Rome Statute distinguishes between the ICC's jurisdiction *ratione materiae* and its applicable law. Article 21 ('Applicable law') of the Statute provides:

14.57

1. The Court shall apply:
   (a) In the first place, this Statute, Elements of Crimes and its Rules of Procedure and Evidence;
   (b) In the second place, where appropriate, applicable treaties and the principles and rules of international law, including the established principles of the international law of armed conflict;
   (c) Failing that, general principles of law derived by the Court from national laws of legal systems of the world including, as appropriate, the national laws of States that would normally exercise jurisdiction over the crime, provided that those principles are not inconsistent with this Statute and with international law and internationally recognized norms and standards.
2. The Court may apply principles and rules of law as interpreted in its previous decisions.

---

[104] Neither paragraph constitutes an 'agreement' within the meaning of art 98(2) of the Rome Statute, first because neither is an agreement (that is, a treaty or the like between states) at all and secondly because the effect of each is a function simply of a decision of the Security Council under chapter VII of the Charter, rather than of art 98(2) of the Rome Statute.

3. The application and interpretation of law pursuant to this article must be consistent with internationally recognized human rights, and be without any adverse distinction founded on grounds such as gender..., age, race, colour, language, religion or belief, political or other opinion, national, ethnic or social origin, wealth, birth or other status.

The reference to 'the principles and rules of international law' in article 21(1)(*b*) is to customary international law. As for article 21(1)(*c*), what this authorizes the Court to apply is general principles of law derived from national laws, not the national laws themselves. National law as such does not form part of the ICC's applicable law.

14.58 The Appeals Chamber has interpreted article 21(1) in such a way that 'recourse to other sources of law is possible only if there is a lacuna in the Statute or the Rules of Procedure and Evidence'.[105] In other words, in the case of the Statute, the Court may apply other applicable treaties and customary international law (and, failing that, general principles of law derived from national law) only in the event that the Statute leaves a gap that cannot be remedied through recourse to the rules on treaty interpretation codified in the VCLT.[106]

14.59 The fact that the Court must, where no gap exists, apply the Statute to the exclusion of freestanding treaty or customary international law might be thought to raise concerns as to the conformity of at least some potential ICC prosecutions with the principle *nullum crimen sine lege*, given the doubt whether every aspect of the Court's jurisdiction *ratione materiae* detailed in the Statute conforms to customary international law[107] or at the very least to potentially applicable treaty.[108] Such concerns, however, tend to miss the point that articles 6, 7, 8, and 8*bis*, while ostensibly merely jurisdictional, in effect posit substantive law—that is, in practice they criminalize the commission by individuals within the Court's jurisdiction of the crimes over which

---

[105] *Prosecutor v Ruto and Sang*, ICC-01/09-01/11-1598, Appeals Chamber, Judgment on the Appeals against the Decision of Trial Chamber V(a) of 17 April 2014 entitled "Decision on Prosecutor's Application for Witness Summonses and resulting Request for State Party Cooperation", 9 October 2014, para 105. See also *Al Bashir*, Pre-Trial Chamber Decision on Warrant of Arrest (n 90), para 44; *Prosecutor v Katanga*, ICC-01/04-01/07-3436, Trial Chamber, Jugement rendu en application de l'article 74 du Statut, 7 March 2014, para 1395; *Prosecutor v Katanga and Ngudjolo*, ICC-01/04-01/07-717, Pre-Trial Chamber, Decision on the Confirmation of Charges, 30 September 2008, para 508; *Prosecutor v Ruto* et al, ICC-01/09-01/11-373, Pre-Trial Chamber, Decision on the Confirmation of Charges Pursuant to Article 61(7)(*a*) and (*b*) of the Rome Statute, 23 January 2012, para 289.

[106] *Ruto and Sang*, Appeals Chamber Judgment on Witness Summonses and State Party Cooperation (n 105), para 105 (implicitly); *Al Bashir*, Pre-Trial Chamber Decision on Warrant of Arrest (n 90), para 44 (explicitly).

[107] On the contrary, it is apparent that the Rome Statute embodies a more than *de minimis* element of what at least in 1998 was progressive development, especially as regards some examples of war crimes (especially in non-international armed conflict), some of the species of crimes against humanity, and some of the modes of responsibility. The point has now been made abundantly clear by what at least in principle is the Court's jurisdiction *ratione materiae* over the crime of aggression.

[108] Nor would art 22 ('*Nullum crimen sine lege*') help, since para 1 of this provision merely begs the question, stating as it does that a person shall not be criminally responsible under the Statute unless the conduct in question constitutes, at the time of commission, 'a crime within the jurisdiction of the Court'.

the Court enjoys jurisdiction.[109] Textual indications of what is effectively the substantive import of the Court's jurisdiction *ratione materiae* can be found in several key provisions of the Statute. Paragraph 1 of article 22 ('*Nullum crimen sine lege*') states that a person shall not be 'criminally responsible under [the] Statute' unless the conduct in question constituted, at the time it took place, a crime within the jurisdiction of the Court, as distinct from a crime 'under international law independently of [the] Statute', in the words of article 22(3). Paragraph 1 of article 24 ('Non-retroactivity *ratione personae*') provides similarly that no person shall be 'criminally responsible under [the] Statute' for conduct prior to the Statute's entry into force. For its part, Article 20(3), on the principle *ne bis in idem*, refers to conduct 'proscribed' under articles 6, 7, and 8 of the Statute, as distinct from conduct over which the Court enjoys jurisdiction by virtue of articles 6, 7, and 8. In this light, there can, at least at first blush, be no objection that conviction pursuant to the Statute might amount to *ex post facto* criminalization. The jurisdictional provisions of the Statute have the collateral effect of laying down law binding on any individual within the Court's jurisdiction, and in accordance with article 11 the Court's jurisdiction is strictly prospective, a prospectivity buttressed by article 24. It was in essence on this basis that the Pre-Trial Chamber in *Lubanga* rejected the hypothesis[110] that prosecution before the ICC for the war crime of enlisting, conscripting, and using children under 15 years of age to participate actively in hostilities violated the principle of legality. In the Chamber's view, the relevant offences were 'defined with sufficient particularity in articles 8(2)(*b*)(xxvi) and 8(2)(*e*)(vii), 22 to 24 and 77 of the Rome Statute', which entered into force before the accused's alleged acts, 'as entailing criminal responsibility and punishable as criminal offences'.[111] The problem, however, is where prosecution comes about by sole virtue of a declaration by a non-state party under article 12(3) of the Statute, by a retrospective declaration by a state party under the same provision or by a referral by the Security Council of a situation involving crimes allegedly committed in the territory of a non-state party by nationals of a non-state party. In such cases, the Court's jurisdiction is cast over the accused only after the alleged commission of the offence. At the point of alleged commission, that person is not within the Court's jurisdiction and as a result is not in effect prohibited by the Statute from committing the offence, since he or she is neither on the territory or a national of a state party to the Statute, as required by article 12(2). In a case of

---

[109] See R O'Keefe, 'The ILC's Contribution to International Criminal Law' (2006) 49 *GYIL* 201, 248–9; M Milanović, 'Is the Rome Statute Binding on Individuals? (And Why We Should Care)' (2011) 9 *JICJ* 25; M Milanović, 'Aggression and Legality: Custom in Kampala' (2012) 10 *JICJ* 165.

[110] In the event, the accused made no submission to this effect.

[111] *Prosecutor v Lubanga*, ICC-01/04-01/06-803-tEN, Pre-Trial Chamber, Decision on the Confirmation of Charges, 29 January 2007, para 302. 'Accordingly', the Pre-Trial Chamber concluded, ibid, para 303, 'there [was] no infringement of the principle of legality if the Chamber exercise[d] its power to decide whether [the accused] ought to be committed for trial on the basis of written (*lex scripta*) pre-existing criminal norms approved by the State Parties to the Rome Statute (*lex praevia*), defining prohibited conduct and setting out the related sentence (*lex certa*)'. See also *Katanga and Ngudjolo*, Pre-Trial Chamber Decision on Confirmation of Charges (n 105), para 508, in relation to responsibility under art 25(3)(*a*) of the Rome Statute on the basis of commission through an organization controlled by the accused.

this sort, unless the offence and mode of responsibility charged were independently cognizable under customary international law or applicable treaty at point of commission, the accused faces the prospect of being convicted of an act that it was not internationally criminal for him or her to commit.

V. Relationship with National Jurisdictions

A. 'Complementarity'

14.60 In contrast to the primacy over national jurisdictions enjoyed by the ICTY and ICTR, the ICC regime is premised on the principle of 'complementarity'. The preamble's tenth recital emphasizes 'that the International Criminal Court established under this Statute shall be complementary to national jurisdictions', and article 1 provides that '[a]n International Criminal Court is hereby established...and shall be complementary to national jurisdictions'. The neologistic notion of 'complementarity' is intended to convey that the Court's jurisdiction neither trumps nor is trumped by national criminal jurisdictions. What complementarity means in practice, however, is that states are entitled to pre-empt the Court's investigation and prosecution of crimes within its jurisdiction. If a state is investigating or prosecuting a given case itself or has done so, and if it is doing or has done so genuinely, the case is rendered inadmissible before the ICC.[112] In short, rather than being truly 'complementary' to national criminal jurisdiction, the Court's jurisdiction can be trumped by it. In the words of the Appeals Chamber in *Katanga and Ngudjolo*, national criminal jurisdictions enjoy primacy over the ICC.[113]

14.61 There is no provision in the Rome Statute headed 'Complementarity'. Rather, the principle is embodied in article 17 ('Issues of admissibility') and following, and amounts to a set of rules governing the admissibility of cases before the Court. Article 17 provides:

1. Having regard to paragraph 10 of the Preamble and article 1, the Court shall determine that a case is inadmissible where:
   (a) The case is being investigated or prosecuted by a State which has jurisdiction over it, unless the State is unwilling or unable genuinely to carry out the investigation or prosecution;
   (b) The case has been investigated by a State which has jurisdiction over it and the State has decided not to prosecute the person concerned, unless the decision resulted from the unwillingness or inability of the State genuinely to prosecute;
   (c) The person concerned has already been tried for conduct which is the subject of the complaint, and a trial by the Court is not permitted under article 20, paragraph 3;
   ...

---

[112] At the same time, no state is obliged to prosecute first.
[113] *Prosecutor v Katanga and Ngudjolo*, ICC-01/04-01/07-1497, Appeals Chamber, Judgment on the Appeal of Mr Germain Katanga against the Oral Decision of Trial Chamber II of 12 June 2009 on the Admissibility of the Case, 25 September 2009, para 85.

2. In order to determine unwillingness in a particular case, the Court shall consider, having regard to the principles of due process recognized by international law, whether one or more of the following exist, as applicable:
   (a) The proceedings were or are being undertaken or the national decision was made for the purpose of shielding the person concerned from criminal responsibility for crimes within the jurisdiction of the Court referred to in article 5;
   (b) There has been an unjustified delay in the proceedings which in the circumstances is inconsistent with an intent to bring the person concerned to justice;
   (c) The proceedings were not or are not being conducted independently or impartially, and they were or are being conducted in a manner which, in the circumstances, is inconsistent with an intent to bring the person concerned to justice.
3. In order to determine inability in a particular case, the Court shall consider whether, due to a total or substantial collapse or unavailability of its national judicial system, the State is unable to obtain the accused or the necessary evidence and testimony or otherwise unable to carry out its proceedings.[114]

Article 17(1) obliges the Court, rather than simply permits it, to determine that a case is inadmissible in the circumstances enumerated in the provision. Article 17 is backed up by the procedures laid down in article 18 ('Preliminary rulings regarding admissibility') and article 19 ('Challenges to the jurisdiction of the Court or the admissibility of a case') of the Statute. Article 18 concerns admissibility at the point when the Prosecutor decides to commence an investigation into a situation referred to her by a state party in accordance with articles 13(a) and 14 or at the point when the Prosecutor wishes to initiate an investigation *proprio motu* in accordance with articles 13(c) and 15 and article 53.[115] Article 19 regulates challenges to, *inter alia*, the admissibility of a specific case. In accordance with article 19(1), the Court may—as well as in response to a challenge to admissibility—determine the question of admissibility *proprio motu*.[116]

14.62 Article 17 refers to 'a State', not to 'a State Party'. In other words, the action of states not parties to the Rome Statute can render a case inadmissible before the ICC.

14.63 Admissibility under article 17 is not a 'once and for all' decision. Since what a state is doing or has done in respect of a given case may change over time, so too may whether the case is admissible before the ICC. In the words of the Appeals Chamber in *Katanga and Ngudjolo*, 'the Statute assumes that the factual situation on the basis of which the admissibility of a case is established is not necessarily

---

[114] Note the further admissibility bar, which is not as such a question of complementarity, specified in Rome Statute, art 17(1)(d), namely that the case 'is not of sufficient gravity to justify further action by the Court'. Note also that, in addition to considering the admissibility of the case in accordance with art 53(1)(b) and (2)(b) when deciding whether to investigate and to prosecute respectively, the Prosecutor may decline, under art 53(1)(c) and (2)(c) respectively, to investigate or prosecute on the ground that, taking into account *inter alia* the gravity of the crime, prosecution would not serve or be in the interests of justice.

[115] The procedure under art 18 of the Rome Statute does not apply when the Security Council refers a situation to the Prosecutor in accordance with art 13(b).

[116] Note that, in accordance with art 19(3), the Prosecutor is not obliged to raise the issue of admissibility.

static, but ambulatory', with the result that 'a case that was originally admissible may be rendered inadmissible by a change of circumstances in the concerned States and *vice versa*'.[117] At the same time, except in exceptional circumstances, a person or state entitled to challenge the admissibility of a case under article 19 may do so only once and only prior to or at the commencement of trial.[118] Challenges to admissibility at either the commencement of trial or, exceptionally, subsequently may only be based on article 17(1)(c), which gives effect to the principle *ne bis in idem* embodied in article 20.[119] In addition, article 19(5) stipulates that a state seeking to challenge the admissibility of a case must do so 'at the earliest opportunity'.[120]

14.64   It is not infrequently said that a case is admissible under article 17 of the Statute if a state with jurisdiction over it is unwilling or unable to investigate or prosecute, which could be taken to imply that a case is inadmissible before the Court as long as a state expresses a willingness or establishes an ability to investigate or prosecute.[121] Both the statement and the implication are incorrect readings of article 17(1)(a) and (b). If the state in question is not currently investigating or prosecuting and has not previously investigated, the case is *ipso facto* admissible. In other words, where the state is and has been inactive, a putative willingness or ability to investigate or prosecute does not render the case inadmissible.[122] On the other hand, if the state is currently investigating or prosecuting the case, the question that falls to be decided, by reference to article 17(1)(a), is whether it is willing and able to do so genuinely—that is, in a genuine manner. Similarly, if the state has previously investigated but not in the event prosecuted, the question under article

---

[117] *Katanga and Ngudjolo*, Appeals Chamber Judgment on Admissibility (n 113), para 56. Note, in this regard, Rome Statute, art 18(3) and (7).
[118] Rome Statute, art 19(4).   [119] Ibid. For art 20, see *infra* paras 14.76–14.77.
[120] As explained, however, by the Appeals Chamber in *Prosecutor v Muthaura* et al, ICC-01/09-02/11-274, Appeals Chamber, Judgment on the Appeal of the Republic of Kenya against the Decision of Pre-Trial Chamber II of 30 May 2011 entitled 'Decision on the Application by the Government of Kenya Challenging the Admissibility of the Case Pursuant to Article 19(2)(b) of the Statute', 30 August 2011, para 45 and *Prosecutor v Ruto* et al, ICC-01/09-01/11-307, Appeals Chamber, Judgment on the Appeal of the Republic of Kenya against the Decision of Pre-Trial Chamber II of 30 May 2011 entitled 'Decision on the Application by the Government of Kenya Challenging the Admissibility of the Case Pursuant to Article 19(2)(b) of the Statute', 30 August 2011, para 46, art 19(5) does not mean that a state must challenge the admissibility of a case as soon as a summons to appear or, in relevant cases, an arrest warrant has been issued.
[121] Conversely, some commentators previously interpreted art 17(1)(a) and (b) to conclude that a state party may not refer a situation to the Court pursuant to art 14 unless it is unable itself to investigate or prosecute the crimes alleged to have taken place in the context of that situation. This construction, sometimes known as 'negative complementarity', flies in the face of the text of art 17(1)(a) and (b). It is even less sustainable today given what is clearly the acquiescence of the states parties to the Rome Statute in the Prosecutor's opening of investigations, on the basis each time of a 'self-referral', in relation to the situations respectively in northern Uganda, the DRC, the CAR, and Mali.
[122] The point was underlined in *Katanga and Ngudjolo*, Appeals Chamber Judgment on Admissibility (n 113), paras 1, 2, 75, and 78, as affirmed in *Prosecutor v Bemba*, ICC-01/05-01/08-962, Appeals Chamber, Judgment on the Appeal of Mr Jean-Pierre Bemba Gombo against the Decision of Trial Chamber III of 24 June 2010 entitled 'Decision on the Admissibility and Abuse of Process Challenges', 19 October 2010, para 107. See also *Muthaura*, Appeals Chamber Judgment on Admissibility (n 120), para 40; *Ruto*, Appeals Chamber Judgment on Admissibility (n 120), para 41.

17(1)(*b*) is whether the decision not to prosecute stemmed 'from an unwillingness or inability genuinely to prosecute'.¹²³ In short, it is the genuineness of the investigation or prosecution or decision whether or not to prosecute that is at issue under article 17(1)(*a*) and (*b*). Putting it another way, determining admissibility under article 17(1)(*a*) and (*b*) involves a two-stage inquiry, namely, first, whether the state in question is taking or has taken any action in relation to the case and, secondly, whether any such action is or was genuine.¹²⁴ A negative answer at either stage renders the case admissible before the Court.

A state that challenges the admissibility of a case before the ICC bears the burden of proving that the case is inadmissible. That is, it falls to the state to establish both that it is taking or has taken the requisite action and that it has done so in a genuine fashion.¹²⁵   14.65

The wording of article 17(1) focuses on an individual case before the court, rather than on the situation as a whole out of which a case has emerged. In a challenge under article 19 of the Statute to the admissibility of what has been referred to as a 'concrete' case, this is precisely how article 17(1) is applied. A challenge to admissibility pursuant to article 18, however, although involving the application of article 17(1), deals not with an individual case but with the opening of an investigation, at which point 'the contours of the likely cases will often be relatively vague because the investigations of the Prosecutor are at their initial stages'.¹²⁶ The divergence necessitates that the meaning of the word 'case' as used in article 17(1) (*a*) and (*b*) 'be understood in the context to which it is applied'.¹²⁷   14.66

When applied in the context of a challenge to a concrete case pursuant to article 19 of the Statute, what article 17(1)(*a*) and by necessary implication article 17(1)(*b*)   14.67

---

¹²³ In this second scenario, the reference to an unwillingness or inability genuinely to prosecute is, on its face, silly. Given that no prosecution has taken place, the question cannot be whether it was pursued genuinely. But the expression draws its content from art 17(2) and (3), in the context of which it makes sense. As for art 17(2) and (3) themselves, the reference respectively to 'unwillingness' and 'inability' is shorthand—unfortunate shorthand, albeit understandable from the point of view of textual economy—for 'unwillingness and inability genuinely to investigate or prosecute or to take the decision whether or not to prosecute'. Similarly unfortunate, but similarly understandable, is the use in the English-language text of art 17(2) and (3) of the term 'proceedings' to refer to both prosecution and investigation, the latter not usually being taken to fall within the notion of 'proceedings'.
¹²⁴ See eg *Katanga and Ngudjolo*, Appeals Chamber Judgment on Admissibility (n 113), para 78; *Muthaura*, Appeals Chamber Judgment on Admissibility (n 120), para 40; *Ruto*, Appeals Chamber Judgment on Admissibility (n 120), para 41; *Prosecutor v Gaddafi and Al-Senussi*, ICC-01/11-01/11-547-Red, Appeals Chamber, Judgment on the Appeal of Libya against the Decision of Pre-Trial Chamber I of 31 May 2013 entitled 'Decision on the admissibility of the case against Saif Al-Islam Gaddafi', 21 May 2014, para 213; *Prosecutor v Gaddafi and Al-Senussi*, ICC-01/11-01/11-565, Appeals Chamber, Judgment on the Appeal of Mr Abdullah Al-Senussi against the Decision of Pre-Trial Chamber I of 11 October 2013 entitled 'Decision on the admissibility of the case against Abdullah Al-Senussi', 24 July 2014, para 68.
¹²⁵ *Muthaura*, Appeals Chamber Judgment on Admissibility (n 120), para 61; *Ruto*, Appeals Chamber Judgment on Admissibility (n 120), para 62; *Gaddafi and Al-Senussi*, Appeals Chamber Judgment on Admissibility: Al-Senussi (n 124), para 166.
¹²⁶ *Muthaura*, Appeals Chamber Judgment on Admissibility (n 120), para 38; *Ruto*, Appeals Chamber Judgment on Admissibility (n 120), para 39.
¹²⁷ *Muthaura*, Appeals Chamber Judgment on Admissibility (n 120), para 38; *Ruto*, Appeals Chamber Judgment on Admissibility (n 120), para 39.

focus on is the individual and the alleged conduct,[128] the latter meaning the conduct that gives rise to criminal responsibility under the Statute.[129] What article 17(1)(*a*) and by implication article 17(1)(*b*) are taken to mean is that a national investigation or prosecution must encompass or, in the case of an investigation resulting in a decision not to prosecute, must have encompassed not only the same individual or individuals but also 'substantially the same conduct' as alleged in the case before the ICC if it is to render the latter inadmissible.[130] Putting it another way, the question is whether the case the subject of action at the national level 'sufficiently mirrors' the case before the Court.[131] The parameters of the relevant conduct from the Court's point of view are to be ascertained by reference to whichever document the Statute envisages as defining the factual allegations against the suspect or accused at the stage of the proceedings in question, be it, at the pre-trial phase, the warrant of arrest or summons to appear or, at the trial phase, the charges confirmed by the Pre-Trial Chamber.[132]

14.68   Where a suspect is alleged by the Prosecutor to bear criminal responsibility under the Statute not for the commission of a crime 'with his own hand' but through the conduct of others, for example as an indirect co-perpetrator, the conduct of these others is a necessary component of the case and, as such, must be taken into account by the Court when assessing whether an investigation at the national level renders proceedings before the Court inadmissible.[133] In other words, 'the "conduct" that defines the "case" is both that of the suspect . . . and that described in the incidents [cited in the Prosecutor's case] which is imputed to the suspect'.[134] (By 'incident' is meant 'a historical event, defined in time and place, in the course of which crimes within the jurisdiction of the Court were allegedly committed by one or more direct perpetrators'.)[135] The incidents investigated at

---

[128] *Muthaura*, Appeals Chamber Judgment on Admissibility (n 120), para 39; *Ruto*, Appeals Chamber Judgment on Admissibility (n 120), para 40; *Gaddafi and Al-Senussi*, Appeals Chamber Judgment on Admissibility: Gaddafi (n 124), paras 60 and 85; *Gaddafi and Al-Senussi*, Appeals Chamber Judgment on Admissibility: Al-Senussi (n 124), para 99.
[129] *Gaddafi and Al-Senussi*, Appeals Chamber Judgment on Admissibility: Gaddafi (n 124), paras 61 and 85; *Gaddafi and Al-Senussi*, Appeals Chamber Judgment on Admissibility: Al-Senussi (n 124), para 99.
[130] *Muthaura*, Appeals Chamber Judgment on Admissibility (n 120), paras 1 and 39; *Ruto*, Appeals Chamber Judgment on Admissibility (n 120), paras 1 and 40; *Gaddafi and Al-Senussi*, Appeals Chamber Judgment on Admissibility: Gaddafi (n 124), paras 60 and 63; *Gaddafi and Al-Senussi*, Appeals Chamber Judgment on Admissibility: Al-Senussi (n 124), paras 100 and 119.
[131] *Gaddafi and Al-Senussi*, Appeals Chamber Judgment on Admissibility: Gaddafi (n 124), paras 73 and 85; *Gaddafi and Al-Senussi*, Appeals Chamber Judgment on Admissibility: Al-Senussi (n 124), paras 100 and 119.
[132] *Muthaura*, Appeals Chamber Judgment on Admissibility (n 120), para 39; *Ruto*, Appeals Chamber Judgment on Admissibility (n 120), para 40.
[133] *Gaddafi and Al-Senussi*, Appeals Chamber Judgment on Admissibility: Gaddafi (n 124), para 62; *Gaddafi and Al-Senussi*, Appeals Chamber Judgment on Admissibility: Al-Senussi (n 124), paras 99 and 101. What goes at the national level for an investigation goes equally, by necessary implication, for a prosecution.
[134] *Gaddafi and Al-Senussi*, Appeals Chamber Judgment on Admissibility: Gaddafi (n 124), para 62. See also ibid, paras 70 and 85; *Gaddafi and Al-Senussi*, Appeals Chamber Judgment on Admissibility: Al-Senussi (n 124), para 99.
[135] *Gaddafi and Al-Senussi*, Appeals Chamber Judgment on Admissibility: Gaddafi (n 124), para 62, where the Chamber went on to stress that the exact scope of an 'incident' cannot be determined in

the national level must be substantially the same as the incidents the subject of the Prosecutor's case if the national investigation is to render the case before the Court inadmissible.[136] A large degree of overlap between the incidents covered by the national investigation and those covered by the Prosecutor's case is not essential, provided that the former include those incidents forming the crux or the most serious aspects of the case.[137] In coming to its assessment, the Court is to take into account any information provided by the investigating state as to why it is not investigating or has not investigated incidents forming part of the Prosecutor's case, as well as the impact on victims of any ruling that an investigation not covering all the incidents in the Prosecutor's case renders the proceedings before the Court inadmissible.[138]

14.69 When determining whether conduct under ongoing investigation at the national level is substantially the same as the conduct at issue in the case before the Court, there is no need for the Court to afford a measure of leeway to enable the investigation to unfold. In other words, what the Court is to examine is the conduct under investigation at that time at the national level.[139]

14.70 In order for the Court to make its assessment as to admissibility in the context of an ongoing investigation by a state, 'the contours of the case being investigated domestically... must be clear'—that is, it must be possible for the Court to compare what is being investigated at the national level with the case before the Court.[140] A lack of 'defining parameters' is 'an indication that there is no concrete case under investigation'.[141]

14.71 A state that challenges the admissibility of a case before the Court on the ground that it is investigating the same individual in respect of substantially the same conduct must provide the Court with evidence of 'a sufficient degree of specificity and probative value' as to demonstrate that it is indeed investigating the case.[142] It is insufficient 'merely to assert that investigations are ongoing'.[143] For this reason, the Appeals Chamber has taken the view, notwithstanding article 19(5), 'that a State should, as a general rule, not challenge the admissibility of a case until it is in a

---

the abstract but, rather, depends on 'all the circumstances of a case, including the context of the crimes and the overall allegations against the suspect'; *Gaddafi and Al-Senussi*, Appeals Chamber Judgment on Admissibility: Al-Senussi (n 124), para 99.

[136] *Gaddafi and Al-Senussi*, Appeals Chamber Judgment on Admissibility: Gaddafi (n 124), para 72; *Gaddafi and Al-Senussi*, Appeals Chamber Judgment on Admissibility: Al-Senussi (n 124), para 100.

[137] *Gaddafi and Al-Senussi*, Appeals Chamber Judgment on Admissibility: Gaddafi (n 124), para 72; *Gaddafi and Al-Senussi*, Appeals Chamber Judgment on Admissibility: Al-Senussi (n 124), para 100.

[138] *Gaddafi and Al-Senussi*, Appeals Chamber Judgment on Admissibility: Gaddafi (n 124), para 74.

[139] *Muthaura*, Appeals Chamber Judgment on Admissibility (n 120), para 43; *Ruto*, Appeals Chamber Judgment on Admissibility (n 120), para 44; *Gaddafi and Al-Senussi*, Appeals Chamber Judgment on Admissibility: Gaddafi (n 124), para 77.

[140] *Gaddafi and Al-Senussi*, Appeals Chamber Judgment on Admissibility: Gaddafi (n 124), para 83. See also ibid, paras 84–85.

[141] Ibid, para 83.

[142] *Muthaura*, Appeals Chamber Judgment on Admissibility (n 120), paras 2 and 61; *Ruto*, Appeals Chamber Judgment on Admissibility (n 120), paras 2 and 62.

[143] *Muthaura*, Appeals Chamber Judgment on Admissibility (n 120), paras 2 and 61; *Ruto*, Appeals Chamber Judgment on Admissibility (n 120), paras 2 and 62.

position to substantiate that challenge'.[144] As to the measures necessary to show that a state is investigating or, by the same token, has investigated the case, the Appeals Chamber has spoken of 'the taking of steps directed at ascertaining whether this individual is responsible for that conduct, for instance by interviewing witnesses or suspects, collecting documentary evidence, or carrying out forensic analyses'.[145]

14.72   The assessment whether the same conduct is the subject of investigation or prosecution at the national level or has been the subject of investigation is a question of the facts alleged at the national level, not of the legal characterization of them.[146] In particular, it is immaterial whether the conduct is characterized at the national level as an international crime or an 'ordinary' or common crime, provided that the case covers substantially the same conduct as that the subject of proceedings before the ICC.[147]

14.73   Since, in accordance with article 17(2)(c), the Court must, 'having regard to the principles of due process recognized by international law', consider whether the national proceedings 'were not or are not being conducted independently or impartially', it has been argued by some that the Court has the power to declare a case admissible under article 17(1)(a) or (b), by reason of the state's unwillingness to proceed genuinely, where the national proceedings violate to his or her detriment an individual's right to a fair trial or any cognate pre-trial rights.[148] The argument fails to take into account, as article 31(1) of the VCLT requires, the context of the words in question and the object and purpose of the Rome Statute.[149] The rest of article 17(2), an essential element of the interpretative context of article 17(2)(c), makes it clear that the gist of the paragraph as a whole—and, ultimately, of article 17(1)(a) and (b), on which it elaborates—is to allow a case to proceed before the ICC where national proceedings are or were skewed in favour, not to the detriment, of the individual; and, more specifically, article 17(2)(c) requires not only that the domestic proceedings 'were not or are not being conducted independently or impartially' but also that 'they were or are being conducted in a manner which, in the circumstances, is inconsistent with an intent to bring the person concerned to justice'—in other words, is inconsistent with an intent to see the

---

[144] *Gaddafi and Al-Senussi*, Appeals Chamber Judgment on Admissibility: Gaddafi (n 124), para 164. The Appeals Chamber continues, ibid: 'In this regard, admissibility proceedings should not be used as a mechanism or process through which a State may gradually inform the Court, over time and as its investigation progresses, as to the steps it is taking to investigate a case. Admissibility proceedings should rather only be triggered when a State is ready and able, in its view, to fully demonstrate a conflict of jurisdiction on the basis that the requirements set out in article 17 are met.'

[145] *Muthaura*, Appeals Chamber Judgment on Admissibility (n 120), paras 1 and, with slight variation, 40; *Ruto*, Appeals Chamber Judgment on Admissibility (n 120), paras 1 and, with slight variation, 41.

[146] *Gaddafi and Al-Senussi*, Appeals Chamber Judgment on Admissibility: Al-Senussi (n 124), para 119.

[147] Ibid.

[148] See eg F Gioia, 'State Sovereignty, Jurisdiction, and "Modern" International Law: The Principle of Complementarity in the International Criminal Court' (2006) 19 *LJIL* 1095, 1110–13.

[149] Note that what art 31(1) of the VCLT speaks of is the object and purpose 'of the treaty', meaning of the treaty as a whole, not—*pace* the Appeals Chamber in *Gaddafi and Al-Senussi*, Appeals Chamber Judgment on Admissibility: Al-Senussi (n 124), para 2—of the individual provision that falls to be interpreted.

person answer appropriately for any crimes that he or she may have committed. Moreover, the object and purpose of the Rome Statute, in the light of which article 19(2)(c) is to be interpreted, is to create an international criminal court, complementary to national criminal jurisdictions, for the prosecution of individuals, not a *de facto* international human rights court with a supervisory jurisdiction over the fairness of national investigations and prosecutions. The same conclusion was reached by the Appeals Chamber in *Al-Senussi*, in which the suspect had argued that the violation of his fundamental rights in Libya's extant proceedings against him rendered his case admissible before the ICC:

1. For a case to be admissible because the State is unwilling genuinely to investigate or prosecute in terms of article 17(2)(c) of the Statute, it must be shown that the proceedings were not or are not being conducted independently or impartially and that the proceedings were or are being conducted in a manner which, in the circumstances, is inconsistent with an intent to bring the person concerned to justice.
2. Taking into account the text, context and object and purpose of the provision, this determination is not one that involves an assessment of whether the due process rights of a suspect have been breached per se. In particular, the concept of proceedings 'being conducted in a manner which, in the circumstances, is inconsistent with an intent to bring the person concerned to justice' should generally be understood as referring to proceedings which will lead to a suspect evading justice, in the sense of not appropriately being tried genuinely to establish his or her criminal responsibility, in the equivalent of sham proceedings that are concerned with that person's protection.[150]

But the Appeals Chamber added:

3. However, there may be circumstances, depending on the facts of the individual case, whereby violations of the rights of the suspect are so egregious that the proceedings can no longer be regarded as being capable of providing any genuine form of justice to the suspect so that they should be deemed, in those circumstances, to be 'inconsistent with an intent to bring the person to justice'.[151]

The rider—along with the suggestion, on which it logically depends, that the very same term and, by extension, the very same provision of the treaty should 'generally' be given one meaning but in some circumstances another—is contrary to the foundational premise of treaty interpretation that there exists only a single 'correct' or authoritative interpretation of a provision. It also gives a meaning to the expression 'bring...to justice' which departs, spuriously, from its ordinary meaning. Finally, it is contrary to the object and purpose of the Rome Statute.[152]

---

[150] *Gaddafi and Al-Senussi*, Appeals Chamber Judgment on Admissibility: Al-Senussi (n 124), paras 1 and 2. See also ibid, paras 214–228 and 230–231.
[151] Ibid, para 3. See also ibid, paras 229–230.
[152] The Appeals Chamber itself implies as much, ibid, para 219: '[T]he Court was not established to be an international court of human rights, sitting in judgment over domestic legal systems to ensure that they are compliant with international standards of human rights.... [I]f the interpretation proposed by the Defence were adopted, the Court would come close to becoming an international court of human rights. A case could be admissible merely because domestic proceedings do not fully

14.74   Where a state closes an investigation in order to surrender, or after surrendering, a suspect to the ICC, this does not constitute a decision not to prosecute the person concerned within the meaning of article 17(1)(*b*), with the result that, all others things being equal, the case will be admissible before the ICC.[153]

14.75   The existence of a municipal statute of limitations or amnesty would not appear to satisfy any of the criteria of inadmissibility in article 17. In many cases subject to a time bar or amnesty, not even an investigation will take place, let alone a prosecution; and in the unlikely event that an investigation does take place but prosecution is stymied by the limitation period or amnesty, it is distinctly arguable[154] that the decision not to prosecute results from an unwillingness or inability genuinely to prosecute, within the meaning of article 17(1)(*b*) and 17(2) and (3).[155] Even the grant of amnesty as part of a *bona fide* truth and reconciliation package that includes the threat of prosecution in the event of non-co-operation would not appear to render a case inadmissible before the ICC.[156]

B. *Ne bis in idem*

14.76   The relationship between the ICC and national jurisdictions is further elaborated on in article 20 ('*Ne bis in idem*'), paragraphs 2 and 3 of which provide:

> 2. No person shall be tried by another court for a crime referred to in article 5 for which that person has already been convicted or acquitted by the Court.

respect the due process rights of a suspect. This would necessarily involve the Court passing judgment generally on the internal functioning of the domestic legal systems of States in relation to individual guarantees of due process.'

[153] See *Katanga and Ngudjolo*, Appeals Chamber Judgment on Admissibility (n 113), para 83, as affirmed in *Bemba*, Appeals Chamber Judgment on Admissibility and Abuse of Process (n 122), para 74.

[154] This was the view of the French Conseil constitutionnel in *Decision No 98-408 DC (Re Treaty Establishing the International Criminal Court)*, 125 ILR 475, 488 (1999), when it held that 'it results from the Statute that the International Criminal Court may lawfully be seized of a case simply on the basis of the application of an amnesty law or domestic rules concerning statutory limitation'.

[155] Article 17(1)(*b*) is no bar to the Court's jurisdiction if the decision not to prosecute results from an unwillingness or inability genuinely to prosecute (the word 'genuinely' in this instance being redundant, since, if no prosecution has taken place, there can be no question of prosecuting genuinely). Article 17(2)(*a*) includes within an unwillingness genuinely to prosecute a situation where the decision not to prosecute was taken for the purpose of shielding the person concerned from criminal responsibility for crimes within the jurisdiction of the Court (which is not the same as shielding them from prosecution by the Court). This is exactly what a decision not to prosecute on the basis of an amnesty, including an amnesty granted as part of a truth and reconciliation package, entails, namely shielding the person concerned from criminal responsibility for the offence in question. For its part, art 17(3) includes within an inability genuinely to prosecute the inability to carry out proceedings due to a total or partial unavailability of the national judicial system, and it is arguable the judicial system is unavailable where an amnesty bars recourse to it.

[156] Note, however, that, even if a case is admissible under art 17, it remains within the Prosecutor's discretion under art 53(1)(*c*) not to initiate an investigation in the first place if, '[t]aking into account the gravity of the crime and the interests of victims, there are nonetheless substantial reasons to believe that an investigation would not serve the interests of justice'. The Prosecutor also enjoys a discretion under art 53(2)(*c*) to conclude, after investigating a crime, that a prosecution 'is not in the interests of justice, taking into account all the circumstances, including the gravity of the crime, the interests of victims and the age or infirmity of the alleged perpetrator, and his or her role in the alleged crime'.

3. No person who has been tried by another court for conduct also proscribed under article 6, 7 or 8 shall be tried by the Court with respect to the same conduct unless the proceedings in the other court:
   (a) Were for the purpose of shielding the person concerned from criminal responsibility for crimes within the jurisdiction of the Court; or
   (b) Otherwise were not conducted independently or impartially in accordance with the norms of due process recognized by international law and were conducted in a manner which, in the circumstances, was inconsistent with an intent to bring the person concerned to justice.

Article 20(3) is cited in article 17(1)(c) as a ground for declaring a case inadmissible before the Court.

In contrast to article 10(2)(a) of the ICTY Statute and article 9(2)(a) of the ICTR Statute,[157] article 20 of the Rome Statute provides for no exception to the rule *ne bis in idem* in cases where the act for which the accused was tried at the national level 'was characterized as an ordinary crime'.[158] This was a conscious choice on the part of the drafters.[159] 14.77

VI. Co-operation with the Court

A. General

The obligations on states to co-operate with the ICC are premised on the Court's establishment by way of treaty, with what this implies as to the *pacta tertiis* rule, and not under chapter VII of the UN Charter. States not parties to the Rome Statute cannot, as a general rule, be obliged by the Statute to co-operate with the Court.[160] Nor may the obligations imposed on states parties diminish the rights of such third states. 14.78

---

[157] Recall *supra* paras 12.44–12.45.
[158] Note also in this regard Rome Statute, art 93(10)(a), in accordance with which the Court may, on request, co-operate with and provide assistance to a state party conducting an investigation into or a trial in respect of conduct which constitutes a crime within the jurisdiction of the Court 'or which constitutes a serious crime under the national law of the requesting State'.
[159] The point was emphasized in *Prosecutor v Gaddafi and Al-Senussi*, ICC-01/11-01/11-344-Red, Pre-Trial Chamber, Public Redacted Decision on the Admissibility of the Case against Saif Al-Islam Gaddafi, 31 May 2013, paras 86–87.
[160] See, in this regard, *Prosecutor v Gaddafi and Al-Senussi*, ICC-01/11-01/11-420, Pre-Trial Chamber, Decision on the Request of the Defence of Abdullah Al-Senussi To Make a Finding of Non-Cooperation by the Islamic Republic of Mauritania, and Refer the Matter to the Security Council, 28 August 2013, para 12; *Prosecutor v Al Bashir*, ICC-02/05-01/09-162, Pre-Trial Chamber, Decision Regarding Omar Al-Bashir's Potential Travel to the United States of America, 18 September 2013, para 10; *Prosecutor v Al Bashir*, ICC-02/05-01/09-164, Pre-Trial Chamber, Decision Regarding Omar Al-Bashir's Potential Travel to the Federal Republic of Ethiopia and the Kingdom of Saudi Arabia, 10 October 2013, para 7; *Prosecutor v Al Bashir*, ICC-02/05-01/09-169, Pre-Trial Chamber, Decision Regarding Omar Al-Bashir's Potential Travel to the State of Kuwait, 18 November 2013, para 7; *Prosecutor v Al Bashir*, ICC-02/05-01/09-180, Pre-Trial Chamber, Decision on the 'Prosecution's Urgent Notification of Travel in the Case of *The Prosecutor v Omar Al Bashir*', 30 January 2014, para 9; *Prosecutor v Al Bashir*, ICC-02/05-01/09-184, Pre-Trial Chamber, Decision on the 'Prosecution's Urgent Notification of Travel in the Case of *The Prosecutor v Omar Al Bashir*', 17 February 2014,

14.79 Article 86 of the Statute lays down a general obligation of co-operation for states parties, saying that 'States Parties shall, in accordance with the provisions of this Statute, co-operate fully with the Court in its investigation and prosecution of crimes within the jurisdiction of the Court'.[161] The content of this obligation is fleshed out in the remaining provisions of Part 9 of the Statute, which refer inconsistently but synonymously to both 'cooperation' and 'assistance'.

14.80 Pursuant to article 87(1) of the Statute, the Court may request co-operation from states parties. In accordance with article 87(7), failure by a state party to comply with a request for co-operation may, if it prevents the Court from exercising its functions and powers under the Statute, be the subject of a finding to this effect by the Court and of referral by it to the ASP or, where it was the Security Council that referred the situation to the Court, to the Security Council. Additionally, article 87(5) authorizes the Court to 'invite' a state not party to the Statute to provide assistance; and if a state that agrees to provide assistance fails in the event to do so, it may too be referred to the ASP or, in relevant circumstances, to the Security Council. Thirdly, article 87(6) empowers the Court to 'ask' any intergovernmental organization to provide information or documents or other forms of co-operation or assistance agreed on with the organization and within its competence and mandate.

14.81 The crucial question of the arrest and surrender of persons to the Court is regulated by article 89. Article 89(1) provides:

> The Court may transmit a request for the arrest and surrender of a person, together with the material supporting the request outlined in article 91, to any State on the territory of which that person may be found and shall request the cooperation of that State in the arrest and surrender of such a person. States Parties shall, in accordance with the provisions of this Part and the procedure under their national law, comply with requests for arrest and surrender.

The provision draws a distinction between 'any State on the territory of which [a] person may be found', as referred to in the first sentence, and 'States Parties', as referred to in the second. In other words, while the Court is authorized to request even third states to arrest and surrender a person, only states parties are obliged to comply.[162]

---

para 11; *Prosecutor v Al Bashir*, ICC-02/05-01/09-192, Pre-Trial Chamber, Decision Regarding Omar Al-Bashir's Potential Travel to the State of Kuwait, 24 March 2014, para 8; *Prosecutor v Al Bashir*, ICC-02/05-01/09-199, Pre-Trial Chamber, Decision Regarding the Visit of Omar Hassan Ahmad Al Bashir to the Federal Republic of Ethiopia, 29 April 2014, para 12; *Prosecutor v Al Bashir*, ICC-02/05-01/09-204, Pre-Trial Chamber, Decision on the 'Prosecution's Urgent Notification of Travel in the Case of *The Prosecutor v Omar Al Bashir*', 7 July 2014, para 10. The sole exception is where a third state accepts the jurisdiction of the Court over a crime by way of a declaration under art 12(3), in which case art 12(3) and rule 44(2) make it clear that the third state thereby accepts the obligations to co-operate with the Court spelled out in Part 9 of the Statute.

[161] Note that, in accordance with rule 176(2) of the RPE, it is the Registrar, not the Chamber itself, who transmits any requests for co-operation made by a Chamber.

[162] See the cases and paragraphs cited *supra* n 160. See also Rome Statute, art 59(1), obliging a state party that has received a request for arrest and surrender immediately to take steps to arrest the person in question, and the provision for provisional arrest in ibid, art 92.

14.82 The mere issuance of an arrest warrant by a Pre-Trial Chamber does not create an obligation for states parties to arrest the named individual. Rather, as per article 58(4) of the Statute, an arrest warrant serves merely as the basis on which the Court may request the arrest and surrender or the provisional arrest of the individual under articles 89(1) and 92 respectively. It is only on the transmission of such a request from the Court that the state party to which it is directed is bound to act.

14.83 Article 90 deals with the thorny issue of competition between a request from the Court for the surrender of a person under article 89 and a request from any other state for the extradition of the same person for the same conduct. Where the requesting state is a state party to the Rome Statute, the requested state must, in accordance with article 90(2) and (3), give priority to the Court's request if the Court has determined that the case is admissible. Where the requesting state is not a party to the Statute, the outcome depends on whether the requested state is under an international obligation to extradite the person to the requesting state. If it is not, the requested state must give priority to the Court's request, in accordance with article 90(4). Cases where the requested state is under 'an existing international obligation' to extradite the person to a requesting third state are governed by article 90(6), as follows:

[T]he requested State shall determine whether to surrender the person to the Court or extradite the person to the requesting State. In making its decision, the requested State shall consider all the relevant factors, including but not limited to:
(a) The respective dates of the requests;
(b) The interests of the requesting State including, where relevant, whether the crime was committed in its territory and the nationality of the victims and of the person sought; and
(c) The possibility of subsequent surrender between the Court and the requesting State.

A variation on this theme is found in article 90(7), dealing with competing requests in respect of 'conduct other than that which constitutes the crime for which the Court seeks the person's surrender'. The term 'existing' in both article 90(6) and article 90(7) means existing at the time of the Court's request, rather than at the time of the Statute's entry into force for the state party. The terms 'surrender' and 'extradition' are defined in article 102.

14.84 Article 93, the obverse of article 87, deals with the obligations of states parties in relation to requests by the Court, in connection with investigations or prosecutions, for forms of co-operation (as per the heading) or assistance (as per the text) other than arrest and surrender. Article 93(1) lists types of assistance that states parties are obliged to provide the Court should it request them, among them the identification of persons, the taking and production of evidence, the questioning of persons, and the like, rounding off the enumeration with a residual category in article 93(1)(*l*) of '[a]ny other type of assistance which is not prohibited by the law of the requested State, with a view to facilitating the investigation and prosecution of crimes within the jurisdiction of the

Court'.¹⁶³ The only general ground on which a state party may refuse a request for assistance, in whole or in part, is, in accordance with articles 93(4) and 72 of the Statute, if the request involves the production of documents or disclosure of evidence relating to that state party's national security.

14.85   In accordance with article 97 of the Statute, '[w]here a State Party receives a request under [Part 9] in relation to which it identifies problems which may impede or prevent the execution of the request, that State shall consult with the Court without delay in order to resolve the matter'. The provision includes, as one of three non-exhaustive examples of such a problem, '[t]he fact that execution of the request in its current form would require the requested State to breach a pre-existing treaty obligation undertaken with respect to another State'.

14.86   There is nothing to stop the UN Security Council from imposing obligations of co-operation with the Court on a UN member state that is not a party to the Statute. This is precisely what the Security Council did in Security Council resolution 1593 (2005) of 31 March 2005, the resolution by which it referred the situation in Darfur to the Court. Acting under chapter VII of the Charter, the Council decided in the resolution 'that the Government of Sudan...shall cooperate fully with and provide any necessary assistance to the Court and the Prosecutor pursuant to this resolution'.¹⁶⁴ Such obligations take their binding force from article 25 of the UN Charter, rather than from article 86 and following of the Rome Statute. They prevail, by virtue of article 103 of the Charter, over other treaty obligations, and *a fortiori* over any conflicting customary obligations, owed by the third-state UN member state.¹⁶⁵ Contrary, however, to the implication at an early stage of the *Al Bashir* case,¹⁶⁶ this does not mean that article 87 of the Rome Statute (or, for that matter, any other provision of the Statute) becomes binding on the third state, which does not, through the intercession of the Security Council, become a 'State Party' as per the wording of article 87 and of the other provisions of Part 9 of the Statute. As such, the Court

---

¹⁶³ In the last regard, see also Rome Statute, art 93(5). Article 93(1)(*l*) of the Statute was held by a majority of the Trial Chamber in *Prosecutor v Ruto and Sang*, ICC-01/09-01/11-1274-Corr2, Trial Chamber, Decision on Prosecutor's Application for Witness Summonses and Resulting Request for State Party Cooperation, 17 April 2014, paras 115–156, to encompass an obligation on states parties—should the Court so request and should the law of the requested state party not prohibit this—to compel the attendance before the Court of witnesses subpoenaed by the latter. On appeal, the Appeals Chamber limited its ruling to the narrower point at issue before the Trial Chamber, namely whether, on receipt of a request from the Court to the effect, a state party was obliged to compel witnesses to appear before the Court sitting *in situ* in the state party's territory or by way of video-link. Basing its decision not on art 93(1)(*l*) of the Statute, reliance on which it considered 'inapposite', but on art 93(1)(*b*), the Appeals Chamber held in *Ruto and Sang*, Appeals Chamber Judgment on Witness Summonses and State Party Cooperation (n 105), paras 2, 117, 128, and 132, that a state party was so obliged.
¹⁶⁴ SC res 1593 (2005), 31 March 2005, para 2.
¹⁶⁵ See eg *Al Bashir*, Pre-Trial Chamber Decision on Warrant of Arrest (n 90), paras 244–247; *Prosecutor v Ahmad Muhammad Harun ('Ahmad Harun') and Ali Muhammad Ali Abd-Al-Rahman ('Ali Kushayb')*, ICC-02/05-01/07-57, Pre-Trial Chamber, Decision Informing the United Nations Security Council about the Lack of Cooperation by the Republic of the Sudan, 25 May 2010, preamble (fifteenth recital).
¹⁶⁶ See *Al Bashir*, Pre-Trial Chamber Decision on Warrant of Arrest (n 90), para 248 and disposition.

may not rely on article 87(7) of the Statute in the event of the third state's failure to co-operate—a point effectively, and with striking insouciance, conceded by the Court when it later held in *Harun and Abd-Al-Rahman* that, where the Security Council imposes on a UN member state not party to the Statute an obligation to co-operate with the Court, the Court has the inherent, rather than Statute-based, power to inform the Security Council in the event that that third state fails to comply and its failure prevents the Court from executing the task entrusted to it by the Council.[167] The Court has since reiterated numerous times that, where the Security Council decides that a third state shall co-operate with the Court, the obligation of co-operation stems from the UN Charter, not from the Rome Statute.[168]

In addition to its power to issue binding requests to states parties for co-operation, the Court is empowered by article 64(6)(*b*) of its Statute to subpoena—that is, to issue a binding order under threat of penal sanction—an individual to appear as a witness before it.[169] **14.87**

B. Article 98

Of crucial relevance to requests by the Court for surrender or assistance is article 98 ('Co-operation with respect to waiver of immunity and consent to surrender'). Both paragraphs of article 98 are framed as limitations on the Court's power, barring the Court from proceeding with a request for surrender or assistance in the circumstances specified. Nothing on the face of either provision indicates that, should the Court proceed with a request notwithstanding the relevant limitation, a state party would not be bound to comply, in accordance with the terms of Part 9 of the Statute.[170] That said, it is very arguably implicit as a general principle of law that states parties are bound only by such requests for surrender or assistance from the Court as are lawful under the Statute. **14.88**

Neither article 98(1) nor article 98(2) precludes a state party with custody over a suspect from voluntarily surrendering that person to the Court in breach of any pertinent obligation it may owe a third state. Each paragraph of article 98 specifies no more than that the Court may not proceed with a request for surrender (or assistance) in the circumstances outlined. **14.89**

The fact that a case arises out of a situation referred to the Court by the UN Security Council does nothing in and of itself to alter the applicability of article **14.90**

---

[167] *Harun and Abd-Al-Rahman*, Pre-Trial Chamber Decision Informing the Security Council (n 165), preamble (seventeenth recital).
[168] See the cases and paragraphs cited *supra* n 160.
[169] *Ruto and Sang*, Appeals Chamber Judgment on Witness Summonses and State Party Cooperation (n 105), paras 1 and 113. Article 64(6)(*b*) of the Rome Statute provides that, in performing its functions prior to trial or during the course of a trial, a Trial Chamber may, as necessary, '[r]equire the attendance and testimony of witnesses and production of documents and other evidence'. The accused had argued implausibly that the word 'require' in the English-language version of the provision did not necessarily entail a power to issue a mandatory order.
[170] At the same time, recall, *supra* para 14.85, Rome Statute, art 97.

98 of the Statute. The Security Council's referral of a situation no more than sets in train the usual procedure and engage the Court's usual powers under the Statute.[171]

(i) Article 98(1)

(a) In general

14.91 Article 98(1) provides:

> The Court may not proceed with a request for surrender or assistance which would require the requested State to act inconsistently with its obligations under international law with respect to the State or diplomatic immunity of a person or property of a third State, unless the Court can first obtain the cooperation of that third State for the waiver of the immunity.

The provision makes no reference to the immunity of heads of state, heads of government, ministers for foreign affairs or any others who may benefit under customary international law or treaty from immunity *ratione personae*. It is generally accepted, however, that the reference to 'diplomatic' immunity is to be interpreted to encompass other comparable immunities recognized by customary international law and applicable treaty.[172] It is also taken as read that the reference to 'immunity' encompasses inviolability.[173] The upshot of article 98(1) is that while, in accordance with article 27 of the Statute, the procedural immunities owed under international law by one state to another in respect of the latter's officials and ex-officials pose no bar to the exercise of the Court's jurisdiction once an accused is before the Court, they may stand in the way of the person's surrender.

14.92 Article 98(1) applies only in respect of 'a person or property of a third state'. The reference to a 'third' state is—in accordance with standard international legal usage,[174] as well as elementary logic[175]—to a state not party to the Rome Statute. As regards states parties *inter se*, the immunities from foreign legal process otherwise owed under international law by one state to another in respect

---

[171] Recall *supra* para 14.46 and cases cited therein.

[172] That art 98(1) was textually capable of application to heads of state was not questioned in *Prosecutor v Al Bashir*, ICC-02/05-01/09-139-Corr, Pre-Trial Chamber, Corrigendum to the Decision pursuant to Article 87(7) of the Rome Statute on the Failure by the Republic of Malawi to Comply with the Cooperation Requests Issued by the Court with Respect to the Arrest and Surrender of Omar Hassan Ahmad Al Bashir, 13 December 2011, in *Prosecutor v Al Bashir*, ICC-02/05-01/09-140-tENG, Pre-Trial Chamber, Decision Pursuant to Article 87(7) of the Rome Statute on the Refusal of the Republic of Chad to Comply with the Cooperation Requests Issued by the Court with Respect to the Arrest and Surrender of Omar Hassan Ahmad Al Bashir, 13 December 2011, or in any of the many subsequent decisions on point in *Al Bashir*.

[173] For the use of the term 'immunity' to cover both immunity *stricto sensu* and inviolability, see eg *Arrest Warrant of 11 April 2000 (Democratic Republic of the Congo v Belgium)*, ICJ Rep 2002, 3, 29, para 70, 30, para 71, and 31, para 75.

[174] Recall *supra* para 14.9, especially n 12.

[175] The reference in art 98(1) to a 'third' state cannot, as some imply, be simply to a state other than the requested state, since such a state would constitute a 'second' state or, more idiomatically, 'another' state, the Court itself not being a state.

of the latter's serving and former officials pose no bar to the Court's request to a state party for surrender of a person to it, a request binding by virtue of article 89(1) of the Statute. This is something to which states parties mutually consent by becoming parties to the Statute, which makes no allowance as among the parties for otherwise internationally-mandated jurisdictional immunities. Nor does article 98(1) extend to the immunities from which, pursuant to treaty, the officials of international organizations may benefit.[176] The reference in article 98(1) is strictly to states.

(b) The *Al Bashir* case
Serious issues in relation to article 98(1) have arisen in the *Al Bashir* case, chiefly on account of the Court's zealous and increasingly creative persistence in legal error. 14.93

On 4 March 2009, a Pre-Trial Chamber issued a warrant for the arrest of Omar Al Bashir, the sitting head of state of Sudan, a state not party to the Rome Statute.[177] Two days later, as requested by the Pre-Trial Chamber in accordance with article 89(1) of the Statute and rule 176(2) of the RPE, the Registrar issued a request to states parties to the Statute for Bashir's arrest and surrender to the Court.[178] After the Prosecutor's successful appeal against the Pre-Trial Chamber's original decision not to authorize the inclusion in the warrant of the charge of genocide, a second warrant was issued on 2 July 2010.[179] Later that month, the Registrar issued a supplementary request to states parties for Bashir's arrest and surrender.[180] Both these requests implicate article 98(1), which is not mentioned in either request despite the Registrar's recalling numerous other provisions of the Statute, since a serving head of state is entitled to absolute immunity *ratione personae* from the criminal jurisdiction of other states and absolute inviolability from foreign measures of personal constraint.[181] 14.94

---

[176] In this regard, in relation to the UN, see Negotiated Relationship Agreement between the International Criminal Court and the United Nations, art 19: 'If the Court seeks to exercise its jurisdiction over a person who is alleged to be criminally responsible for a crime within the jurisdiction of the Court and if, in the circumstances, such person enjoys, according to the Convention on the Privileges and Immunities of the United Nations and the relevant rules of international law, any privileges and immunities as are necessary for the independent exercise of his or her work for the United Nations, the United Nations undertakes to cooperate fully with the Court and to take all necessary measures to allow the Court to exercise its jurisdiction, in particular by waiving any such privileges and immunities in accordance with the Convention on the Privileges and Immunities of the United Nations and the relevant rules of international law.'

[177] See *Prosecutor v Omar Hassan Ahmad Al Bashir ('Omar Al Bashir')*, ICC-02/05-01/09-1, Pre-Trial Chamber, Warrant of Arrest for Omar Hassan Ahmad Al Bashir, 4 March 2009, issued pursuant to *Al Bashir*, Pre-Trial Chamber Decision on Warrant of Arrest (n 90).

[178] See *Prosecutor v Al Bashir*, ICC-02/05-01/09-7, Registrar, Request to All States Parties to the Rome Statute for the Arrest and Surrender of Omar Al Bashir, 6 March 2009.

[179] See *Prosecutor v Omar Hassan Ahmad Al Bashir ('Omar Al Bashir')*, ICC-02/05-01/09-95, Pre-Trial Chamber, Second Warrant of Arrest for Omar Hassan Ahmad Al Bashir, 12 July 2010.

[180] *Prosecutor v Al Bashir*, ICC-02/05-01/09-96, Registrar, Supplementary Request to All States Parties to the Rome Statute for the Arrest and Surrender of Omar Hassan Ahmad Al Bashir, 21 July 2010.

[181] Recall *supra* paras 10.31 and 10.40–10.44.

14.95   The Court's requests were strenuously objected to by the African Union (AU), whose Assembly decided in Assembly Decision 245 (XIII) of 3 July 2009, and reiterated the following year, that 'AU Member States shall not cooperate pursuant to the provisions of Article 98 of the Rome Statute of the ICC relating to immunities, for the arrest and surrender of President Omar El Bashir of The Sudan'.[182] Notwithstanding this, in August 2010, the Pre-Trial Chamber in *Al Bashir* held that Kenya, which Bashir was scheduled to visit, had 'a clear obligation to cooperate with the Court in relation to the enforcement of [the Court's] warrants of arrest, which stems both from the United Nations Security Council Resolution 1593 (2005), whereby the United Nations Security Council "urge[d] all States and concerned regional and other international organizations to cooperate fully" with the Court, and from article 87 of the Statute of the Court, to which the Republic of Kenya is a State Party',[183] and held the same in relation to Chad.[184] Subsequently, the Pre-Trial Chamber, dropping the legally embarrassing reference to Security Council resolution 1593 (2005), requested that Kenya 'take any necessary measures to ensure that Omar Al Bashir, in the event that he visits the country, be arrested and surrendered to the Court in accordance with its obligations under the Statute';[185] requested that the Central African Republic do the same for the same reasons;[186] noted, reinstating its previous solecism, that Djibouti had 'an obligation to cooperate with the Court in relation to the enforcement of such warrants of arrest, which stems both from the United Nations Security Council Resolution 1593 (2005) whereby the United Nations Security Council "urge[d] all States and concerned regional and other international organizations to cooperate fully" with the Court, and from article 87 of the Statute of the Court, to which Djibouti is a State Party';[187] considered that Chad was bound by articles 86 and 89 of the Statute to abide by the Court's requests for co-operation in the arrest and surrender of Bashir;[188] and said the same as the last in relation to

---

[182] AU Assembly Decision 245 (XIII), 3 July 2009, para 10. See also AU Assembly Decision 296 (XV), 27 July 2010, para 5.

[183] *Prosecutor v Al Bashir*, ICC-02/05-01/09-107, Pre-Trial Chamber, Decision informing the United Nations Security Council and the Assembly of the States Parties to the Rome Statute about Omar Al-Bashir's presence in the territory of the Republic of Kenya, 27 August 2010, preamble (third recital).

[184] See, almost verbatim, *Prosecutor v Al Bashir*, ICC-02/05-01/09-109, Pre-Trial Chamber, Decision informing the United Nations Security Council and the Assembly of the States Parties to the Rome Statute about Omar Al-Bashir's recent visit to the Republic of Chad, 27 August 2010, preamble (third recital).

[185] *Prosecutor v Al Bashir*, ICC-02/05-01/09-117, Pre-Trial Chamber, Decision Requesting Observations from the Republic of Kenya, 25 October 2010, disposition.

[186] *Prosecutor v Al Bashir*, ICC-02/05-01/09-121, Pre-Trial Chamber, Demande de coopération et d'informations adressée à la République Centrafricaine, 1 December 2010, disposition.

[187] *Prosecutor v Al Bashir*, ICC-02/05-01/09-129, Pre-Trial Chamber, Decision informing the United Nations Security Council and the Assembly of the States Parties to the Rome Statute about Omar Al-Bashir's recent visit to Djibouti, 12 May 2011, preamble (third recital).

[188] *Prosecutor v Al Bashir*, ICC-02/05-01/09-132, Pre-Trial Chamber, Decision requesting Observations about Omar Al Bashir's Recent Visit to the Republic of Chad, 18 August 2011, preamble (eighth recital).

Malawi.[189] In response, the AU adopted Assembly Decision 334 (XVI) of 31 January 2011, in which it 'deeply regret[ted]' the Pre-Trial Chamber's decisions of August the previous year to inform the Security Council and the ASP of Chad and Kenya's non-co-operation, and decided that, 'by receiving President Bashir, the Republic of Chad and the Republic of Kenya were implementing various AU Assembly Decisions on the warrant of arrest issued by [the] ICC against President Bashir'.[190] The AU Assembly reaffirmed the second of these statements in Assembly Decision 366 (XVII) of 30 June 2011.[191]

14.96 On 12 December 2011, changing legal tack, the Pre-Trial Chamber held—in a decision wrongheaded on multiple grounds, not the least of them being reference in passing to 'a third State which has ratified the Statute'[192]—that states parties were obliged to co-operate with the Court with respect to the arrest and surrender of Bashir notwithstanding article 98(1) of the Statute since, as a matter of customary international law, head-of-state immunity did not serve to bar prosecution for an international crime before an international criminal court or tribunal, with the consequence that, there being no conflict between a state party's obligations of arrest and surrender under the Statute and its obligations towards third states under the customary international law of immunities, article 98(1) did not apply.[193] The following day the Pre-Trial Chamber expressly adopted this reasoning, which has the effect of excising article 98(1) from the Rome Statute, to issue an analogous decision regarding Chad.[194] In response, on 30 January 2012, the AU Assembly

reaffirm[ed] its understanding that Article 98(1) was included in the Rome Statute establishing the ICC out of recognition that the Statute is not capable of removing an immunity which international law grants to the officials of States that are not parties to the Rome Statute, and by referring the situation in Darfur to the ICC, the UN Security Council intended that the Rome Statute would be applicable, including Article 98.[195]

The Pre-Trial Chamber nonetheless effectively reiterated its decision of 12 December 2011 in an order of 15 February 2013[196] and in decisions of 22

---

[189] *Prosecutor v Al Bashir*, ICC-02/05-01/09-137, Pre-Trial Chamber, Decision requesting Observations about Omar Al Bashir's Recent Visit to Malawi, 19 October 2011, preamble (ninth recital).
[190] AU Assembly Decision 334 (XVI), 31 January 2011, paras 4 and 5 respectively.
[191] AU Assembly Decision 366 (XVII), 30 June 2011, para 5.
[192] *Al Bashir*, Pre-Trial Chamber Corrigendum to the Decision on the Failure by Malawi to Comply (n 172), para 18 (original decision 12 December 2011). The Pre-Trial Chamber made amends in *Al Bashir*, Pre-Trial Chamber Decision on the Cooperation of the Democratic Republic of the Congo (n 86), para 26, where it referred to 'non-States Parties to the Statute (third States)'.
[193] See *Al Bashir*, Pre-Trial Chamber Corrigendum to the Decision on the Failure by Malawi to Comply (n 172), paras 14–18 and 22–43.
[194] *Al Bashir*, Pre-Trial Chamber Decision on the Refusal of Chad to Comply (n 172) paras 12–14.
[195] AU Assembly Decision 397 (XVIII), 30 January 2012, para 6.
[196] See *Prosecutor v Al Bashir*, ICC-02/05-01/09-145, Pre-Trial Chamber, Order Regarding Omar Al-Bashir's Potential Visit to the Republic of Chad and to the State of Libya, 15 February 2013, para 10.

February 2013,[197] 26 March 2013,[198] 15 July 2013,[199] 5 September 2013,[200] 26 February 2014,[201] 3 March 2014,[202] and 25 March 2014.[203] For its part, the AU Assembly reaffirmed its view that Chad and Kenya, among others, were acting 'in conformity with the decisions of the Assembly and therefore should not be penalized'.[204]

14.97   The Pre-Trial Chamber's subsequent decision of 9 April 2014, however, recasts for the second time the legal basis on which the Court justifies its proceeding with requests to states parties for the arrest and surrender of the sitting head of a third state. Rather than relying on the ratio of its decision of 13 December 2011, the Pre-Trial Chamber's latest decision reasons as follows:

> [B]y issuing Resolution 1593(2005) the SC decided that the 'Government of Sudan [. . .] shall cooperate fully with and provide any necessary assistance to the Court and the Prosecutor pursuant to this resolution'. Since immunities attached to Omar Al Bashir are a procedural bar from prosecution before the Court, the cooperation envisaged in said resolution was meant to eliminate any impediment to the proceedings before the Court, including the lifting of immunities. Any other interpretation would render the SC decision requiring that Sudan 'cooperate fully' and 'provide any necessary assistance to the Court' senseless. Accordingly, the 'cooperation of that third State [Sudan] for the waiver of the immunity', as required under the last sentence of article 98(1) of the Statute, was already ensured by the language used in paragraph 2 of SC Resolution 1593 (2005). By virtue of said paragraph, the SC implicitly waived the immunities granted to Omar Al Bashir under international law and attached to his position as a Head of State. Consequently, there also exists no impediment at the horizontal level between the DRC and Sudan as regards the execution of the 2009 and 2010 Requests.[205]

The argument remains unpersuasive. It is not apparent why a decision by the Security Council that Sudan must co-operate fully with and provide any

---

[197] See *Prosecutor v Al Bashir*, ICC-02/05-01/09-147, Pre-Trial Chamber, Decision Requesting Observations on Omar Al-Bashir's Visit to the Republic of Chad, 22 February 2013.

[198] See *Prosecutor v Al Bashir*, ICC-02/05-01/09-151, Pre-Trial Chamber, Decision on the Non-Compliance of the Republic of Chad with the Cooperation Requests Issued by the Court Regarding the Arrest and Surrender of Omar Hassan Ahmad Al-Bashir, 26 March 2013.

[199] *Prosecutor v Al Bashir*, ICC-02/05-01/09-157, Pre-Trial Chamber, Decision Regarding Omar Al-Bashir's Visit to the Federal Republic of Nigeria, 15 July 2013.

[200] *Prosecutor v Al Bashir*, ICC-02/05-01/09-159, Pre-Trial Chamber, Decision on the Cooperation of the Federal Republic of Nigeria Regarding Omar Al-Bashir's Arrest and Surrender to the Court, 5 September 2013.

[201] *Prosecutor v Al Bashir*, ICC-02/05-01/09-186, Pre-Trial Chamber, Decision Regarding Omar Al-Bashir's Visit to the Democratic Republic of the Congo, 26 February 2014.

[202] See *Prosecutor v Al Bashir*, ICC-02/05-01/09-189, Pre-Trial Chamber, Decision Requesting Observations on Omar Al-Bashir's Visit to the Democratic Republic of the Congo, 3 March 2014.

[203] *Prosecutor v Al Bashir*, ICC-02/05-01/09-194, Pre-Trial Chamber, Decision Regarding Omar Al-Bashir's Potential Visit to the Republic of Chad, 25 March 2014.

[204] AU Assembly decision 482 (XXI), 26 May 2013, para 3.

[205] *Al Bashir*, Pre-Trial Chamber Decision on the Cooperation of the Democratic Republic of the Congo (n 86), para 29, citations omitted.

necessary assistance to the Court should be taken to mean that such co-operation and assistance has *ipso facto* been obtained, as article 98(1) requires in relation to a third state's waiver of immunity before the Court may proceed with a request to a state party for the surrender of a serving or former official of the third state. It would doubtless be open to the Security Council, acting under chapter VII of the UN Charter, to decide that the state party in question must surrender the person to the Court notwithstanding article 98(1) and the immunity and inviolability owed by the state party to the third state in respect of the person.[206] But the Security Council has not done this in this case. As the Pre-Trial Chamber implicitly acknowledges, article 98(1) remains applicable. As such, the Court must first obtain Sudan's co-operation for the waiver of the immunity from foreign criminal jurisdiction and inviolability from foreign measures of constraint from which it is entitled under international law to see its head of state benefit; and the fact remains that the Court has not obtained Sudan's co-operation for such a waiver. Indeed, it is yet to invite such co-operation, as provided for in article 87(5).

Even less persuasive is the Pre-Trial Chamber's argument that—since the Security Council, 'acting under Chapter VII, has implicitly lifted the immunities of Omar Al Bashir by virtue of Resolution 1593 (2005)';[207] since, by virtue of article 25 of the UN Charter, member states agree to accept and carry out the decisions of the Security Council; and since, by virtue of article 103 of the UN Charter, a member state's obligations under the Charter prevail over that state's obligations under any other international agreement—the obligation of the DRC (being the state party that refused in this instance to comply with the Pre-Trial Chamber's request for the arrest and surrender of Omar Al Bashir) to surrender Bashir to the ICC prevails over the DRC's obligation pursuant to the Constitutive Act of the African Union and Assembly Decision 245 (XIII) not to surrender Bashir.[208] The Pre-Trial Chamber's necessary implication, and innuendo,[209] that the DRC's refusal to surrender Bashir to the Court constituted, via the combined effect of Security Council resolution 1593 (2005) and article 25 of the UN Charter, a breach of an obligation arising for the DRC under the Charter is absurd.

14.98

---

[206] Recall, *supra* para 3.27, that, when acting under chapter VII of the Charter, the Security Council may take measures in derogation of the rights and obligations of member states under non-peremptory rules of international law.
[207] *Al Bashir*, Pre-Trial Chamber Decision on the Cooperation of the Democratic Republic of the Congo (n 86), para 31.
[208] See ibid, paras 30–32.
[209] See ibid, para 32: '[T]he Chamber considers that the DRC not only disregarded the 2009 and 2010 Requests related to its obligation to cooperate in the arrest and surrender of Omar Al Bashir, pursuant to articles 86 and 89 of the Statute, but also SC Resolution 1593 (2005). This course of action calls upon the SC and the Assembly of States Parties to take the necessary measures they deem appropriate.'

(ii) Article 98(2)

(a) In general

14.99 Article 98(2) reads:

> The Court may not proceed with a request for surrender which would require the requested State to act inconsistently with its obligations under international agreements pursuant to which the consent of a sending State is required to surrender a person of that State to the Court, unless the Court can first obtain the cooperation of the sending State for the giving of consent for the surrender.

Article 98(2) was designed to cater for status of forces agreements ('SOFAs'),[210] status of mission agreements ('SOMAs'),[211] and even non-military (for example, scientific) agreements that would require the consent of a sending state to the surrender to the Court of persons within its scope.[212] There is no reason, however, why it could not apply to other agreements falling within the terms of article 98(2). Whatever examples the drafters of the provision had in mind, article 98(2) is not limited to them. The ordinary meaning of the provision is general in import, extending to any international agreement that, in the unvarnished words of article 98(2), would require the consent of a sending state to the surrender to the Court of persons within its scope. Nor is there any reason why the plain words of article 98(2) would be limited to agreements entered into before the coming into force of the Rome Statute. In short, there is nothing to say that article 98(2) could not, all other things being equal, permissibly encompass international agreements concluded after 1 July 2002 that are designed specifically to prevent the surrender of certain third-state persons to the Court.

14.100 Unlike article 98(1), article 98(2) does not apply only in respect of third states—that is, as specifically regards article 98(2), in relation only to international agreements between states parties and states not parties to the Statute. Rather, the Court may not proceed with a request for surrender if this would require a state party to breach a SOFA, SOMA or cognate international agreement even with a

---

[210] Recall *supra* para 1.81. See eg Agreement between the Parties to the North Atlantic Treaty regarding the Status of their Forces 1951, art VII; Agreement Between the Republic of Bosnia and Herzegovina and the North Atlantic Treaty Organisation (NATO) Concerning the Status of NATO and its Personnel, Appendix B to Annex 1-A to the General Framework Agreement for Peace in Bosnia and Herzegovina 1995, arts 6 and 7; Agreement Between the Republic of Croatia and the North Atlantic Treaty Organisation (NATO) Concerning the Status of NATO and its Personnel, Appendix B to Annex 1-A to the General Framework Agreement for Peace in Bosnia and Herzegovina 1995, arts 6 and 7.

[211] Recall *supra* para 1.81. See eg Agreement between the Democratic Republic of East Timor and the United Nations concerning the Status of the United Nations Mission of Support in East Timor 2002, art 55(*b*); Military Technical Agreement between International Security Assistance Force (ISAF) and the Interim Administration of Afghanistan 2002, Annex A, paras 3 and 4; African Union-Sudan Status of Mission Agreement (SOMA) on the Establishment and Management of the Ceasefire Commission in the Darfur Area of The Sudan (CFC) 2004, art 62(*b*).

[212] See eg Agreement concerning Cooperation on the Civil International Space Station 1998, art 22(1) and (2)(*a*).

sending state party, unless the Court can first obtain the co-operation of the sending state party for the giving of consent for surrender.[213]

(b) 'Article 98' agreements

In a practice that has been discontinued, even if the existing instruments remain in force, the US variously and successfully invited, cajoled, and pressured[214] over a hundred states, among them states parties and signatories to the Rome Statute, into concluding with it bilateral non-surrender agreements, better known as 'article 98' agreements, the reference being to article 98(2) of the Statute, on which the agreements purport to rely for their effect. The aim of such agreements is to prevent the surrender to the ICC of any US official, employee, serviceperson or ordinary national. For example, article 2 of the US–Uzbekistan Agreement regarding the Surrender of Persons to the International Criminal Court 2002, which reflects the more-or-less standard template for 'article 98' agreements, provides:

14.101

Persons of one Party present in the territory of the other shall not, absent the expressed consent of the first Party,
(a) be surrendered or transferred by any means to the International Criminal Court for any purpose, or
(b) be surrendered or transferred by any means to any other entity or third country, or expelled to a third country, for the purpose of surrender to or transfer to the International Criminal Court.

Article 3 provides that when the US extradites, surrenders or otherwise transfers 'a person of the Republic of Uzbekistan' to a third state, it will not agree to the surrender or transfer of that person to the ICC by the third state without the express consent of Uzbekistan. Article 4 provides vice versa. The term 'persons' is defined in article 1 to mean 'current or former Government officials, employees (including contractors), or military personnel or nationals of one Party'. The reference to contractors would include local contractors, for example Uzbek nationals engaged by the US to perform in-country services, the classic case being a local interpreter. The reference to 'other nationals' would include private businesspeople, tourists, and so on.

The international lawfulness of a state party to the Rome Statute's envisaged non-surrender of a suspect to the ICC pursuant to an 'article 98' agreement with the US is contested. So too is the international legality of a state party's mere entry

14.102

---

[213] That said, it might be expected in practice that the Court would either, first, in the exercise of its powers under art 87(1)(a), request the sending state party to give its consent to surrender, a request binding on that other state party by virtue of art 93(1)(l); or, secondly, in accordance with art 89(1), issue a binding request to the sending state to surrender the individual itself.

[214] Pursuant to the American Servicemembers' Protection Act, 22 USC §§7421–7433, and the so-called 'Nethercutt Amendment' of 2005 to the annual Foreign Operations Appropriations Act, the provision by the US of assistance funds to any state party to the Rome Statute was made conditional on the conclusion of an 'article 98' agreement between that state and the US. This policy was modified by amendments to the Nethercutt amendment in the Foreign Operations Appropriations Acts of 2006 and 2008 respectively.

into such an agreement.²¹⁵ It has even been alleged that the US has acted internationally unlawfully by encouraging states parties to agree to non-surrender. In all of this, it is to be recalled that, in accordance with article 89(1) of the Rome Statute, the ICC may transmit to any state on whose territory a suspect is found requests for his or her arrest and surrender to the Court and for the state's co-operation in that arrest and surrender and that states parties to the Statute are obliged by the same provision to comply with the Court's request for arrest and surrender.

14.103   Any international legal assessment of 'article 98' agreements must focus first and foremost on the wording of article 98(2) of the Rome Statute. Article 98(2) prevents the Court from requiring a state party to surrender a 'person', a term not defined in the Statute,²¹⁶ where surrender would be inconsistent with the state party's obligations under an international agreement pursuant to which the consent of a 'sending State' is required to surrender the person to the Court. The expression 'sending State' is not defined in the Statute either, but it is a well-known term of art in international law, and refers to a state whose armed forces or police or other official or government-employed or government-contracted personnel are stationed or otherwise deployed in the territory of another state pursuant to some sort of agreement to which both states are parties. What article 98(2) means in practice, therefore, is that—because the Court may not proceed with a request for such a person—a state party to the Rome Statute can never, at least lawfully, be placed in the position of being bound by article 89(1) to surrender to the ICC a person where that person is a serviceperson, government official, government-employed or government-contracted scientist or technician, etc of another state present in the territory of the state party pursuant to an agreement with that other state. Conversely, a state party to the Statute may be requested by the Court, and therefore can be bound by article 89(1), to surrender a person in relation to whom the other state could not be considered a 'sending State' within the meaning ordinarily accorded the term in international law—that is, a person in no way 'sent' by that other state. Now, insofar as some of the government officials, employees, including contractors, and military personnel covered, in accordance with article 1, by the standard 'article 98' agreement may genuinely be considered 'sent' by the US to the territory of the relevant state party to the Rome Statute, in that they are stationed or otherwise deployed in that territory pursuant to a formal or informal agreement between the US and that state party, no breach by that state party—occasioned by its obligation of non-surrender under article 2 of the 'article 98' agreement—of the obligation of surrender embodied in article 89(1) of the Rome Statute can ever come about, at least lawfully, since the ICC may not, as stipulated in article 98(2) of the Statute, proceed with a request for their surrender. To proceed with such a request would be to require the state party to act inconsistently with its obligation under an international agreement, namely the 'article 98' agreement, pursuant to which the request

---

²¹⁵ In neither case can the same conduct by a state not party to the Statute be impugned as a matter of international law.
²¹⁶ In the absence of evidence that the states parties to the Rome Statute intended a special meaning to be given to the term 'person', the latter must be taken to bear its ordinary meaning.

of a sending state is required to surrender a person of that state to the Court. To this extent, then, there can be no international legal objection to 'article 98' agreements, since, to this extent, they cannot give rise to a breach of the Statute. But the definition of 'persons' laid down in article 1 of the standard 'article 98' agreement extends to all current or former US government officials, all US employees, including contractors, all US military personnel, and all US nationals. At least some of these—namely, many employees, including contractors; military personnel not stationed in the territory of the state party but merely engaged in armed conflict there; and garden-variety nationals, such as businesspeople and tourists—cannot plausibly be characterized as having been 'sent' by the US. As such, the Court is not forbidden by article 98(2) of the Statute from requesting their surrender. In the event of such a request, the requested state party would be bound by article 89(1) of the Statute to surrender them, and any refusal by it to do so on account of its 'article 98' agreement with the US would constitute, *prima facie*, a violation of article 89(1).[217] Ultimately, then, the international legal problem with 'article 98' agreements is not the principle but their overly broad scope as drafted.

That the legal problem with 'article 98' agreements is their scope as drafted, rather than the concept as such, seems to be the view of at least certain influential states.[218] First, there are statements to this effect in European fora. In response to the US campaign to encourage states parties and signatories to the Rome Statute to enter into 'article 98' agreements, the Council of the European Union adopted in September 2002 a set of Guiding Principles concerning Arrangements between a State Party to the Rome Statute of the International Criminal Court and the United States Regarding the Conditions to Surrender of Persons to the Court.[219]

14.104

---

[217] Some individuals not covered by art 98(2) of the Rome Statute may, however, be covered by art 98(1), which, it will be recalled, specifies that the Court may not proceed with a request for surrender or assistance which would require the requested state to act inconsistently as regards the immunities of third-state officials. In addition, the legal complexion differs when a state party in receipt of a request from the Court for a suspect's surrender has also received a request from a third state for the extradition of the same individual in respect of the conduct forming the basis of the crime for which the Court seeks his or her surrender. If, in such cases, the requested state party is under an existing international legal obligation to extradite the suspect to the requesting state, art 90(6) may permit the requested state party—depending on how 'all the relevant factors', some of them specified in art 90(6)(*a*) to (*c*), play out—to surrender the suspect to the requesting state, rather than to the Court. The same goes *mutatis mutandis*, under art 90(7), in cases where the request from the third state relates to conduct other than that which constitutes the crime for which the Court seeks the suspect's surrender. (Note that it will not, by any means, be in all cases that the requested state party's extradition obligations to the US will be relevant. For a start, the US does not have extradition arrangements with many of the states parties to the Rome Statute with which it has entered into 'article 98' agreements.) Excepting, however, the situations covered by art 98(1) and art 90(6) or 90(7), where persons covered by the standard 'article 98' agreement do not properly fall within the scope of art 98(2) of the Rome Statute a state party's refusal, by reference to such an agreement, to surrender them will constitute a breach of art 89(1) of the Statute.

[218] It is also seemingly the view of the Committee Against Torture (CAT), which, in UN doc CAT/C/GEO/CO/3 (25 July 2006), para 14, recommended that Georgia 'take all the necessary measures to review the relevant terms of those agreements which prohibit the transfer of citizens from certain States who are on Georgian territory to the International Criminal Court'. See also eg UN doc CAT/C/TGO/CO/1 (28 July 2006), para 16 (CAT to Togo).

[219] 30 September 2002, 42 ILM 240 (2003) ('Guiding Principles'). See also, in this regard, Council Common Position 2003/444/CFSP of 16 June 2003 on the International Criminal Court, OJ L 150/67, 18.6.2003, art 5(2), in accordance with which the Union and its Member States 'shall

These principles speak of the inconsistency with ICC states parties' obligations of the agreements 'as presently drafted' and, in a section entitled 'Scope of persons', indicate that '[a]ny solution should cover only persons on the territory of the requested State because they have been sent by a sending State', citing in support article 98(2) of the Rome Statute.[220] Not dissimilarly, in Parliamentary Assembly of the Council of Europe resolution 1336 (2003) of 25 June 2003, the Assembly 'consider[ed] that it is possible for bilateral exemption agreements to be construed narrowly, such as… to ensure that the scope of persons affected by the agreement is consistent with the text of Article 98(2) of the ICC Treaty'.[221] Secondly, and tellingly, other states have sought through purpose-drafted treaty provisions to prevent the surrender to the ICC of those of their military and civilian personnel falling within the proper scope of article 98(2) of the Rome Statute. Annex A ('Arrangements regarding the Status of the International Security Assistance Force') of the Military Technical Agreement concluded in January 2002 between the International Security Assistance Force (ISAF), composed of NATO personnel, and the Interim Administration of Afghanistan reads in relevant part:

> The Interim Administration agree that ISAF and supporting personnel, including associated liaison personnel, may not be surrendered to, or otherwise transferred to the custody of, an international tribunal or any other entity or State without the express consent of the contributing nation.[222]

In contradistinction to US 'article 98' agreements, the scope of this provision is limited to ISAF and supporting personnel, including associated liaison personnel—that is, to persons belonging to contingents 'sent', within the meaning ascribed to the term by international law, by the respective states contributing to ISAF. Similarly, the UN Security Council has adopted two resolutions under chapter VII of the UN Charter which, although not falling within

---

continue, as appropriate, to draw the attention of third States to the Council Conclusions of 30 September 2002 on the International Criminal Court and to the EU Guiding Principles annexed thereto, with regard to proposals for agreements or arrangements concerning conditions for the surrender of persons to the Court'. See too Statement by the Presidency on behalf of the European Union on reaffirming the EU position supporting the integrity of the Rome Statute, 27 July 2004, 11680/04 (Presse 235) P 85/04, in which it is reiterated that the EU 'cannot support bilateral Non Surrender Agreements that do not conform with the Rome Statute in the way indicated by the Guiding Principles, as endorsed by the EU with regard to these agreements', and in which the EU 'urges State Parties to the International Criminal Court negotiating bilateral Non Surrender Agreements to act in accordance with these principles'.

[220] The Guiding Principles also suggest that '[a]ny solution should take into account that some persons enjoy State or diplomatic immunity under international law', citing in support art 98(1) of the Rome Statute.

[221] Parliamentary Assembly of the Council of Europe resolution 1336 (2003), 25 June 2003, para 11. The suggestion that the definition of the term 'persons' in art 1 of the standard-form 'article 98' agreement can be interpreted so as to ensure consistency with art 98(2) of the Rome Statute is simply wishful thinking. See R O'Keefe, '"Article 98" Agreements, the Law of Treaties & the Law of State Responsibility' in M Szabó (ed), *State Responsibility and the Law of Treaties* (The Hague: Eleven Publishing, 2010), 35, 46–7.

[222] Military Technical Agreement between the ISAF and Afghanistan, Annex A, para 4 (last sentence).

article 98(2) of the Rome Statute for the reason that they are not 'international agreements',[223] could be said to reflect a belief that measures designed specifically to prevent the surrender of third-state military personnel to the Court are not per se unlawful. In Security Council resolution 1497 (2003), the Council, having authorized member states to establish a Multinational Force in Liberia, decided that

> current or former officials or personnel from a contributing State, which is not a party to the Rome Statute of the International Criminal Court, shall be subject to the exclusive jurisdiction of that contributing State for all alleged acts or omissions arising out of or related to the Multinational Force or United Nations stabilization force in Liberia, unless such exclusive jurisdiction has been expressly waived by that contributing State...[224]

When the Security Council later referred the situation in Darfur to the ICC by means of resolution 1593 (2005), it decided, '[t]aking note of the existence of agreements referred to in Article 98-2 of the Rome Statute', that

> nationals, current or former officials or personnel from a contributing State outside Sudan which is not a party to the Rome Statute of the International Criminal Court shall be subject to the exclusive jurisdiction of that contributing State for all alleged acts or omissions arising out of or related to operations in Sudan established or authorized by the Council or the African Union, unless such exclusive jurisdiction has been expressly waived by that contributing State...[225]

This second resolution is controversial in its extension to mere nationals,[226] which was probably with a view to what at the time was the possible deployment of US personnel in Sudan.

It is sometimes further claimed that the mere entry into the typical 'article 98' agreement by a state party or even a signatory to the Rome Statute is unlawful, in that it is calculated to give rise to a breach of article 89(1) by the state in question in the event of a lawful request from the ICC to that state for a suspect's surrender. The argument in the case of signatories to the Statute is based on article 18(*a*) of the VCLT, which obliges a signatory to refrain from acts that would defeat the object and purpose of the treaty. As regards states parties, the argument is more obscure,[227]

14.105

---

[223] Although neither decision of the Council creates an 'international agreement' for the purposes of art 98(2) of the Rome Statute, they are binding on UN member states by virtue of art 25 of the UN Charter, and, by virtue of art 103 of the UN Charter, the obligation thereby created prevails over the obligations of arrest and surrender to the Court imposed on states parties to the Statute by art 89(1) in the event of a hypothetical request from the Court.

[224] SC res 1497 (2003), para 7. Recall *supra* para 14.54. Mexico, France, and Germany abstained from voting.

[225] SC res 1593 (2005), para 6. Recall again *supra* para 14.56. Brazil abstained from voting.

[226] It is nonetheless without doubt a lawful exercise of the Security Council's powers under chapter VII of the UN Charter, and is binding on UN member states.

[227] *Pace* the Council of the European Union's Guiding Principles, the mere entry into an 'article 98' agreement cannot be 'inconsistent with the ICC States Parties' obligations with regard to the ICC Statute'. The Statute contains no provision prohibiting entry into such agreements, and art 89(1) is not breached unless and until a state party, in circumstances not covered by arts 90(6) and 90(7), refuses to hand over to the Court a person whose surrender the Court may, taking correct account of arts 98(2) and 98(1), request.

but the most plausible contention is that a state party to a treaty is obliged by customary international law, independently of the terms of the treaty in question, not to engage in conduct inconsistent with that treaty's object and purpose.[228] Such an obligation, said by the International Court of Justice (ICJ) to be implicit in the rule *pacta sunt servanda* codified in article 26 of the VCLT,[229] was recognized by the ICJ in the *Nicaragua* case, where it was characterized variously and synonymously as 'the obligation not to defeat the object and purpose of the treaty'[230] and the obligation to refrain from acts 'depriving'[231] or 'calculated to deprive'[232] the treaty of its object and purpose, acts 'calculated to defeat',[233] 'directed to defeating'[234] or 'tending to defeat'[235] the treaty's object and purpose, or acts 'such as to undermine the whole spirit'[236] of the treaty. The obligation identified in *Nicaragua* was arguably foreshadowed by the ICJ in a dictum in *Reservations to the Convention on the Prevention and Punishment of the Crime of Genocide*, where the Court held it to be 'a generally recognized principle that... none of the contracting parties [to a multilateral convention] is entitled to frustrate or impair, by means of unilateral decisions or particular agreements, the purpose and *raison d'être* of the convention'.[237] Even were this aspect of *Nicaragua* good law,[238] however, there would remain the more fundamental obstacle, in relation to both states parties and signatories, posed by the *prima facie* compatibility of the typical 'article 98' agreement with the object and purpose of the Rome Statute. In the words of the Statute's preamble (tenth recital) and article 1, the object and purpose of the Rome Statute is to provide for the establishment of a permanent international criminal court, with jurisdiction over the most serious crimes of international concern, which 'shall be complementary to national criminal jurisdictions'. Putting it another way, and drawing additionally on the legal embodiment of complementarity in article 17, the Statute's object and purpose is the punishment of the most serious crimes of international concern

---

[228] See eg Parliamentary Assembly of the Council of Europe resolution 1300 (2002), 25 September 2002, para 10; European Parliament resolution on the International Criminal Court (ICC), EU doc P5_TA(2002)0449, 26 September 2002, para 3.

[229] *Military and Paramilitary Activities in and against Nicaragua (Nicaragua v United States of America), Merits*, ICJ Rep 1986, 3, 135, para 270. Consider, in this light, Parliamentary Assembly of the Council of Europe resolution 1300 (2002), para 10: 'The Assembly considers that these exemption agreements are not admissible under the international law governing treaties, in particular the Vienna Conventions on the Law of Treaties, according to which states must refrain from any action which would not be consistent with the object and the purpose of a treaty.'

[230] *Nicaragua* (n 229), 138, para 276.   [231] Ibid, 136, para 271.
[232] Ibid, para 272.   [233] Ibid, 138, para 276.   [234] Ibid.
[235] Ibid, 137, para 273.   [236] Ibid, 138, para 276.
[237] *Reservations to the Convention on the Prevention and Punishment of the Crime of Genocide, Advisory Opinion*, ICJ Rep 1951, 15, 21.

[238] To the extent that it is conceived of as an obligation above and beyond those laid down in the express provisions of the treaty, the reality as a matter of customary international law of the obligation suggested by the Court in *Nicaragua* is open to doubt, since it asserts the priority of the general over the specific, positing that a state which acts in a manner not contrary to any provision of a treaty can nonetheless breach international law by acting contrary to the treaty's rationale. But it could plausibly be maintained, as the ICJ maintained in *Nicaragua* (n 229), 136, para 272, that there is a difference between conduct expressly permitted by a treaty provision, which must surely trump the instrument's object and purpose to the extent of hypothetical inconsistency, and conduct not expressly prohibited by any provision.

first at the national level, should states so desire, and only by the ICC where the mechanisms of national criminal justice have not been engaged at all or are not or have not been engaged in a genuine manner. Reference could also be made in this regard to the Statute's preambular statements that the effective prosecution of the most serious crimes of international concern must be ensured 'by taking measures at the national level' and that 'it is the duty of every State to exercise its criminal jurisdiction over those responsible for international crimes'.[239] And the point is that the preamble to the standard 'article 98' agreement[240] does its best to align such agreements with this object and purpose. It first reaffirms 'the importance of bringing to justice those who commit genocide, crimes against humanity and war crimes'. It next recalls 'that the Rome Statute of the International Criminal Court done at Rome on July 17, 1998 by the United Nations Conference of Plenipotentiaries on the Establishment of an International Criminal Court is intended to complement and not supplant national criminal jurisdiction'. It then, before finally '[b]earing in mind Article 98 of the Rome Statute', considers 'that the Parties have each expressed their intention to investigate and prosecute where appropriate acts within the jurisdiction of the International Criminal Court alleged to have been committed by their officials, employees, military personnel or other nationals'. In other words, even if one were to hold that there exists an independent obligation not to frustrate the object and purpose of a treaty, it would be difficult to argue that the standard 'article 98' agreement does so in relation to the Rome Statute. If the preamble to the agreement is to be believed, and a state's bad faith is not to be presumed, 'article 98' agreements amount to no more than complementarity in action.

14.106 In the final analysis, then, the international lawfulness or otherwise of US 'article 98' agreements with states parties to the Rome Statute is more complicated than some make out. It is very difficult to conclude that the mere entry into them is unlawful. Nor can one aver that compliance with them by states parties to the Rome Statute would be a breach of the Statute in every instance. But reliance on them to resist requests for surrender by the Court would nonetheless breach the Statute in some, perhaps many circumstances.

VII. Conclusion

14.107 It is not unfair to say that the ICC has scarcely covered itself in glory during the first 12 years of its existence. The wisdom of certain strategies and tactics pursued by the Prosecutor has been open to serious doubt, some Pre-Trial Chambers have displayed an over-inflated sense of their place in the procedural scheme established under the Statute, and not a few judges have exhibited a lamentable grasp of general international law and elementary international legal technique, as well as an over-determination to reach the result they deem necessary to 'end impunity'. Nor

---

[239] Rome Statute, preamble (fourth and sixth recitals respectively).
[240] See eg US–Uzbekistan Agreement regarding the Surrender of Persons to the International Criminal Court, preamble.

have these failings been without consequences for the Court. On the contrary, crucial prosecutorial and judicial missteps have alienated many states parties and served as a poor advertisement to third states. That said, certain Trial Chambers and the Appeals Chamber have shown impressive legal rigour and the requisite dispassion, while not a few individuals within the Office of the Prosecutor are consummate lawyers and professionals.

14.108   What is undoubtedly true is that no human institution could have lived up to the unrealistic expectations attendant upon the establishment of the Court. Grandiose claims were the order of the day, and the higher the hopes the heavier the disappointment. In this light, the experience of the Court's first decade could be viewed as a salutary dose of reality. As it is, it is too early to write off a body designed to be permanent. An eye to the *longue durée* would lend perspective.

Further Reading

AKANDE, D, 'The Effect of Security Council Resolutions and Domestic Proceedings on State Obligations to Cooperate with the ICC' (2012) 10 *Journal of International Criminal Justice* 299

AKANDE, D, 'International Law Immunities and the International Criminal Court' (2004) 98 *American Journal of International Law* 407

AKANDE, D, 'The Jurisdiction of the International Criminal Court over Nationals of Non-Parties: Legal Basis and Limits' (2003) 1 *Journal of International Criminal Justice* 618

AKANDE, D, 'The Legal Nature of the Security Council Referrals to the ICC and its Impact on Al Bashir's Immunities' (2009) 7 *Journal of International Criminal Justice* 333

APTEL, C, 'Prosecutorial Discretion at the ICC and Victims' Right to Remedy: Narrowing the Impunity Gap' (2012) 10 *Journal of International Criminal Justice* 1357

AMERICAN SOCIETY OF INTERNATIONAL LAW, 'US Policy Toward the International Criminal Court: Furthering Positive Engagement. Report of an Independent Task Force' (March 2009)

BENZING, M, 'The Complementarity Regime of the International Criminal Court: International Criminal Justice between State Sovereignty and the Fight against Impunity' (2003) 7 *Max Planck Yearbook of United Nations Law* 591

CASSESE, A and GAETA, P, *Cassese's International Criminal Law* (3rd edn, Oxford: Oxford University Press, 2013), chapter 14

CASSESE, A, GAETA, P, and JONES, JWD (eds), *The Rome Statute of the International Criminal Court: A Commentary* (Oxford: Oxford University Press, 2002), 2 vols

CERONE, JP, 'Dynamic Equilibrium: The Evolution of US Attitudes toward International Criminal Courts and Tribunals' (2007) 18 *European Journal of International Law* 227

CRYER, R, FRIMAN, H, ROBINSON, D, and WILMSHURST, E, *An Introduction to International Criminal Law and Procedure* (3rd edn, Cambridge: Cambridge University Press, 2014), chapter 8

DEEN-RACSMÁNY, Z, 'The Nationality of the Offender and the Jurisdiction of the International Criminal Court' (2001) 95 *American Journal of International Law* 606

FERNANDEZ, J and PACREAU, X (eds), *Statut de Rome de La Cour pénal internationale: Commentaire article par article* (Paris: Pedone, 2012), 2 vols

FLECK, D, 'Are Foreign Military Personnel Exempt from International Criminal Jurisdiction under Status of Forces Agreements?' (2003) 1 *Journal of International Criminal Justice* 651

GAETA, P, 'Is the Practice of "Self-Referrals" a Sound Start for the ICC?' (2004) 2 *Journal of International Criminal Justice* 949

JAIN, N, 'A Separate Law for Peacekeepers? The Clash between the Security Council and the International Criminal Court' (2005) 16 *European Journal of International Law* 239

KIRSCH, P and HOLMES, J, 'The Rome Conference on an International Criminal Court: The Negotiating Process' (1999) 93 *American Journal of International Law* 2

LEIGH, M, 'The United States and the Statute of Rome' (2001) 95 *American Journal of International Law* 124

MCCARTHY, C, *Reparations and Victim Support in the International Criminal Court* (Cambridge: Cambridge University Press, 2012)

MCCARTHY, C, 'Victim Redress and International Criminal Justice: Competing Paradigms or Compatible Forms of Justice?' (2012) 10 *Journal of International Criminal Justice* 351

MCGOLDRICK, D, ROWE, P, and DONNELLY, E (eds), *The Permanent International Criminal Court: Legal and Policy Issues* (Oxford: Hart Publishing, 2004)

MILANOVIĆ, M, 'Aggression and Legality: Custom in Kampala' (2012) 10 *Journal of International Criminal Justice* 165

MILANOVIĆ, M, 'Is the Rome Statute Binding on Individuals? (And Why We Should Care)' (2011) 9 *Journal of International Criminal Justice* 25

NERLICH, V, 'The Confirmation of Charges Procedure at the International Criminal Court: Advance or Failure?' (2012) 10 *Journal of International Criminal Justice* 1339

NOUWEN, SMH, *Complementarity in the Line of Fire. The Catalysing Effect of the International Criminal Court in Uganda and Sudan* (Cambridge: Cambridge University Press, 2013)

NOUWEN, SMH, 'Fine-tuning Complementarity' in BS Brown (ed), *Research Handbook on International Criminal Law* (Cheltenham: Edward Elgar, 2011), 206

NOUWEN, SMH, 'Legal Equality on Trial: Sovereigns and Individuals Before the International Criminal Court' (2013) 43 *Netherlands Yearbook of International Law* 151

O'KEEFE, R, '"Article 98" Agreements, the Law of Treaties & the Law of State Responsibility' in M Szabó (ed), *State Responsibility and the Law of Treaties* (The Hague: Eleven Publishing, 2010), 35

O'KEEFE, R, 'The ILC's Contribution to International Criminal Law' (2006) 49 *German Yearbook of International Law* 201

O'KEEFE, R, 'The United States and the ICC: The Force and Farce of the Legal Arguments' (2011) 24 *Cambridge Review of International Affairs* 335

PENA, M and CARAYON, G, 'Is the ICC Making the Most of Victim Participation?' (2013) 7 *International Journal of Transitional Justice* 1

RASTAN, R, 'Testing Co-operation: The International Criminal Court and National Authorities' (2008) 21 *Leiden Journal of International Law* 431

ROBINSON, D, 'Serving the Interests of Justice: Amnesties, Truth Commissions and the International Criminal Court' (2003) 14 *European Journal of International Law* 481

RONEN, Y, 'Israel, Palestine and the ICC—Territory Uncharted but not Unknown' (2014) 12 *Journal of International Criminal Justice* 7

SCHABAS, W, *The International Criminal Court: A Commentary on the Rome Statute* (Oxford: Oxford University Press, 2010)

SCHEFFER, D, 'The United States and the International Criminal Court' (1999) 93 *American Journal of International Law* 12

SEIBERT-FOHR, A, 'The Relevance of the Rome Statute of the International Criminal Court for Amnesties and Truth Commissions' (2003) 7 *Max Planck Yearbook of United Nations Law* 553

SLUITER, G, *International Criminal Adjudication and the Collection of Evidence: Obligations of States* (Antwerp/Oxford: Intersentia, 2002)

SPIGA, V, 'No Redress without Justice: Victims and International Criminal Law' (2012) 10 *Journal of International Criminal Justice* 1377

STAHN, C and EL ZEIDY, MM (eds), *The International Criminal Court and Complementarity: From Theory to Practice* (Cambridge: Cambridge University Press, 2011)

TRIFFTERER, O (ed), *Commentary on the Rome Statute of the International Criminal Court: Observers' Notes, Article by Article* (2nd edn, Munich: CH Beck/Hart, 2008)

VAN DER WILT, H, 'Bilateral Agreements between the US and States Parties to the Rome Statute' (2005) 18 *Leiden Journal of International Law* 93

WEDGWOOD, R, 'The International Criminal Court: An American View' (1999) 10 *European Journal of International Law* 93

Index

abduction without consent of territorial state, international
and international law of state responsibility 1.107, 1.108, 1.110
legality of municipal prosecution consequent upon 1.109
as violation of customary international rules on enforcement jurisdiction 1.107, 1.113
as violation of extradition treaty 1.111
as violation of international human rights law 1.112

acts of state
individual criminal responsibility under international law for 2.69–2.73, 6.36, 10.73, 12.30, 14.40, 14.42

actus reus
see also causation
as general condition of criminal responsibility
for crimes under customary international law 4.6, 4.7
for treaty crimes 7.18
implications of word 'unlawful' in definition of treaty crimes 8.9
meaning 4.6

admissibility *see* 'complementarity'; International Criminal Court

African Union (AU)
African Union–European Union Technical Ad hoc Expert Group on the Principle of Universal Jurisdiction 1.70, 9.26
and *Al-Bashir* case 14.95, 14.96, 14.98
and article 16 of Rome Statute 14.55
and Extraordinary African Chambers in the Senegalese Courts 3.35, 9.72, 9.73
peacekeeping mission in Darfur, jurisdiction over members 14.56
and universal jurisdiction 1.63, 9.25–9.27, 9.29, 9.30

aggression, crime of
see also crimes against peace
conditions of responsibility
material elements 4.92–4.100
mental elements 4.101
evolution 4.87–4.91
jurisdiction of International Criminal Court over 14.28, 14.30
modes of responsibility for 4.95, 5.50, 5.101

aiding and abetting
under customary international law
and command and other superior responsibility 5.103, 5.117
and complicity in genocide 5.97, 5.98
and crimes against humanity 5.69
and crime of genocide 5.76
and joint criminal enterprise 5.30, 5.69
material elements 5.69–5.72
mental elements 5.73–5.77
under municipal law
Act 26 of 2000 concerning Human Rights Courts (Indonesia) 9.48
International Crimes (Tribunals) Act 1973 (Bangladesh) 9.68
Law on the Establishment of Extraordinary Chambers in the Courts of Cambodia 9.64
Serbian Criminal Code 9.55
prescriptive jurisdiction in relation to 1.59
under statutes of international criminal courts 5.68
treaty crimes, as mode of responsibility for 7.86, 7.88, 7.116, 7.139, 7.144, 7.147, 7.166, 7.179, 7.195

aircraft
see also civil aviation, unlawful acts relating to, crimes of
crimes on board
jurisdiction *ratione loci* of International Criminal Court 14.33–14.35
prescriptive jurisdiction of states 1.47, 8.21, 8.30, 14.33
and piracy *jure gentium* 1.58
unlawful acts relating to, crimes of
background, definitions, etc 7.49–7.58
and individual criminal responsibility under international law 7.7
obligations of states parties 8.30, 8.31, 8.39
unlawful seizure of, crime of
background, definitions, etc 7.41–7.48
and individual criminal responsibility under international law 7.7
obligations of states parties 8.30, 8.31, 8.39

amnesty
definition 11.1
for international crimes
international legality of grant 11.3, 11.4, 11.16–11.31
international legality of ignoring by third states 11.32–11.34, 11.37
and international human rights law 11.3, 11.36

amnesty (*cont.*):
  and jurisdiction of international criminal courts
    International Criminal Court 14.51, 14.75
    Special Court for Sierra Leone 13.33–13.34
  and jurisdiction of municipal criminal courts
    Extraordinary African Chambers in the Senegalese Courts 9.74
    Extraordinary Chambers in the Courts of Cambodia 9.64
  and sentencing before international criminal courts 6.47
apartheid
  as crime against humanity under customary international law 4.47, 4.49, 4.56, 7.11, 11.13
  as grave breach of Additional Protocol I 7.26
  and jurisdiction of Iraqi High Criminal Court 9.53
  as treaty crime in own right 7.9, 7.11
  and acts of state 2.73
  background, definition, etc 7.111–7.116
  obligations and rights of states parties 1.61, 8.45, 8.57, 8.59, 8.64, 8.72, 8.76, 8.80
applicable law
  distinguished from jurisdiction *ratione materiae* 12.23
  of international criminal courts 2.15, 2.31, 3.1, 3.6, 3.7, 3.9, 3.36, 3.49
    International Criminal Court 6.4, 7.12, 14.46, 14.57–14.59
    International Criminal Tribunal for Rwanda 4.26, 12.23
    International Criminal Tribunal for the former Yugoslavia 4.26, 12.23
    International Military Tribunal, Nuremberg 2.57, 12.23
    Special Court for Sierra Leone and Residual Special Court for Sierra Leone 13.24
    Special Tribunal for Lebanon 3.25
  of municipal criminal courts 2.55, 3.1, 3.6, 3.7, 3.9, 3.36, 3.49
    Extraordinary African Chambers in the Senegalese Courts 9.74
    Extraordinary Chambers in the Courts of Cambodia 3.34, 9.64
    International Crimes Division of High Court of Uganda 9.66
    International Crimes Tribunals (Bangladesh) 9.70
    Iraqi High Criminal Court 9.53
    Special Panels in District Court of Dili and Court of Appeal of East Timor 9.44, 9.45

war crimes sections of Criminal and Appellate Divisions of Court of Bosnia and Herzegovina 9.61
appropriate penalties, treaty obligation to provide for 7.1, 8.1, 8.6, 8.15–8.19, 9.9
armed conflict
  and crime of genocide 4.70
  and crimes against humanity 4.41, 4.56
  definition and characterization 4.28, 4.29
  distinction between international and non-international 4.28, 4.29, 4.37
  exercise of enforcement jurisdiction during international 1.83–1.85
  existence of as material element of war crimes under customary international law 4.28, 4.37
  accompanying mental element 4.37
  nexus to as material element of war crimes under customary international law 4.30, 4.32
  replacement of term 'war' by 4.11
arrest 1.12, 1.13, 1.74, 1.79, 1.86, 1.91, 1.93, 1.112, 1.115, 1.116, 1.120, 1.121, 1.124, 5.5
  see also immunity of state officials from foreign criminal jurisdiction; inviolability of state officials from foreign measures of physical constraint
  apartheid, treaty crime of, definition 7.115
  enforced disappearance, treaty crime of, definition 7.125
  genocide, treaty crime of, obligation on contracting parties 8.57
  grave breaches of Geneva Conventions, treaty crimes of, obligation on contracting parties 9.28
  inviolability of foreign state officials from 10.1, 10.3, 10.11, 10.14, 10.15, 10.17, 10.25, 10.29, 10.33, 10.95, 10.96, 14.94, 14.96–14.98
  for purpose of surrender to international criminal court
    International Criminal Court 5.7, 14.22, 14.25, 14.81, 14.82, 14.84, 14.94–14.98, 14.102, 14.104
    International Criminal Tribunal for Rwanda 12.50, 14.19
    International Criminal Tribunal for the former Yugoslavia 12.15, 12.50, 12.55, 14.19
    Special Court for Sierra Leone 13.32, 13.39, 14.19
  of vessels 1.12, 1.69, 1.74, 1.115, 1.116, 1.120, 1.124, 8.24, 8.84
  warrant of 1.63, 5.7, 10.14, 14.19, 14.22, 14.25, 14.41, 14.63, 14.67, 14.82, 14.95
    for Al Bashir, Omar 14.44, 14.94–14.98
    for Habré, Hissène 9.72
    for Taylor, Charles 13.32

Index

immunity of foreign state officials from issuance and circulation of 10.14
issuance *in absentia* 9.32
'article 98' agreements 14.99–14.106
Assembly of States Parties to Rome Statute (ASP) 14.7, 14.14, 14.15, 14.30
attempt
  under international law
    crime of genocide 5.88, 5.89, 5.99
    crimes under customary international law in general 5.99–5.100
    treaty crimes 7.19, 7.37, 7.47, 7.48, 7.57, 7.61, 7.65, 7.72, 7.73, 7.82, 7.86, 7.87, 7.88, 7.93, 7.97, 7.123, 7.126, 7.133, 7.139, 7.147, 7.153, 7.160, 7.166, 7.171, 7.194, 7.195, 7.203, 8.10, 9.13,
  under municipal law
    Act 26 of 2000 concerning Human Rights Courts (Indonesia) 9.48
    International Crimes (Tribunals) Act 1973 (Bangladesh) 9.68
    Law on the Establishment of Extraordinary Chambers in the Courts of Cambodia 9.64
    prescriptive jurisdiction in relation to 1.50, 1.59
Australia
  post-Second World War military courts 9.43
aut dedere aut judicare **(obligation to prosecute or extradite)** 2.24, 7.1, 7.7, 8.1
  absence of obligation under customary international law 4.5
  absence of obligation under Rome Statute 14.9
  and amnesty 11.28, 11.37
  content of treaty obligation 8.22, 8.48–8.56, 9.15, 9.16
  distinguished from prescriptive jurisdiction 8.20, 8.54
  distinguished from universal jurisdiction 8.55
  and Geneva Conventions and Additional Protocols 4.25, 7.8
  and immunity of state officials from foreign criminal jurisdiction 10.43, 10.44, 10.74, 10.77, 10.78, 10.90, 10.91
  and international abduction without consent of territorial state 1.113
  municipal implementation of treaty obligation 9.23–9.24
  and proceedings *in absentia* 9.32
  and statutes of limitations 11.28, 11.37

Bangladesh
  International Crimes Tribunals 9.68–9.71
Bosnia and Herzegovina
  arrests by SFOR of ICTY indictees in 12.15, 12.55

war crimes sections of Criminal and Appellate Divisions of Court of 9.58–9.61
as municipal criminal court 9.60
bribery, crimes relating to 7.204
background, definitions, etc 7.12, 7.173–7.179, 7.182–7.185, 7.187, 7.188, 7.193, 7.194
'active' and 'passive' forms of bribery distinguished 7.177
and individual criminal responsibility under international law 7.13
obligations of states parties 1.69, 8.15, 8.16, 8.27, 8.50, 8.81, 11.9

Cambodia
  Extraordinary Chambers in the Courts of 3.34, 5.29, 7.36, 9.62–9.65, 11.14, 11.23, 13.1, 13.7
  as municipal criminal courts 3.34
causation
  aiding and abetting 5.69, 5.71
  command and other superior responsibility 5.111, 5.113
  direct and public incitement to commit genocide 5.95
  instigation 5.59
  joint criminal enterprise 5.22
  obligation to prevent genocide 8.69
  ordering 5.65
  planning 5.53
children
  conscripting or enlisting into armed forces or groups, war crime of 4.14, 4.18
  of a national, ethnic, racial or religious group, forcibly transferring to another group as crime of genocide 4.66
  sale or prostitution of or pornography involving, crime of
    background, definition, etc 7.167–7.171
    confiscation and seizure of proceeds 8.87
    corporate liability 8.81
    and individual criminal responsibility under international law 7.13
    obligation *aut dedere aut judicare* 8.50
  trafficking in, crime of 7.148–7.153
  use of to participate actively in hostilities, war crime of 4.14
China
  post-Second World War military tribunals 9.43
civil aviation
  see also aircraft
  unlawful acts relating to, crimes of
    background, definitions, etc 7.49–7.58
    and individual criminal responsibility under international law 7.7
    obligations of states parties 8.30, 8.31, 8.39

Coalition Provisional Authority
  (CPA) 3.33, 9.51
command and other superior responsibility
  under customary international
      law 5.102–5.103
    distinguished from ordering 5.62, 5.63
    fair labelling, question of 5.117–5.118
    and crime of genocide 5.87, 5.117
    and joint criminal enterprise 5.30
    material elements 4.96, 5.104–5.113
    mental elements 5.114–5.116
    and universal jurisdiction 1.59
  under municipal law
    Act 26 of 2000 concerning Human
        Rights Courts (Indonesia) 9.48
    International Crimes (Tribunals) Act
        1973 (Bangladesh) 9.68
    Law on the Establishment of
        Extraordinary Chambers in the
        Courts of Cambodia 9.64
    Statute of the Extraordinary African
        Chambers in the Senegalese
        Courts 9.74
    UNTAET regulation 2000/15 9.45
  under statutes of international criminal
      courts
    Rome Statute 4.8, 5.104–5.106, 5.109,
        5.111, 5.113, 5.115, 9.45, 9.48
    Statute of the International Criminal
        Tribunal for Rwanda and Statute of
        the International Criminal Tribunal
        for the former Yugoslavia 5.102,
        5.104, 5.105, 5.114, 5.117
    Statute of the Special Court for Sierra
        Leone 5.102, 5.104, 5.105, 5.114, 5.117
    Statute of the Special Tribunal for
        Lebanon 3.25
  treaty crimes, as mode of responsibility
      for 7.19, 7.28, 7.126, 7.127, 8.10
commission
  see also co-perpetration; indirect
      perpetration; joint criminal
      enterprise (JCE)
  basic form 5.13, 5.32
  'control over the crime' approach 5.35, 5.37,
      5.38, 5.42–5.48
  co-perpetration 5.31–5.41, 5.46
    and contribution to commission of a
        crime by a group of persons acting
        with a common purpose 5.79, 5.86
    indirect co-perpetration 5.33, 5.46
  indirect perpetration 5.31–5.33, 5.42–5.46
    indirect co-perpetration 5.33, 5.46
  joint criminal enterprise 5.14–5.33, 5.35,
      5.37, 5.39, 5.78–5.79
  'jointly with another or through another
      person' 5.33–5.35, 5.42
'common'/'ordinary' crimes 1.63, 1.65, 2.15,
    2.55, 8.7, 8.8, 8.17, 9.5–9.9, 9.11, 9.37,
    12.40, 12.44, 12.45, 14.72, 14.77

common purpose, contribution to a crime by
    a group of persons acting with a
  under Rome Statute
    distinguished from joint criminal
        enterprise 5.78–5.79
    material elements 5.80–5.84
    mental elements 5.85–5.86
  under Statute of the Special Tribunal for
      Lebanon 3.25
  treaty crimes, as mode of responsibility
      for 7.48, 7.73, 7.87, 7.93, 7.97
'complementarity' 4.18, 9.1,
    14.60–14.75, 14.105
  see also International Criminal Court
complicity
  in genocide 2.60, 5.16, 5.87, 5.97, 5.98
    and aiding and abetting 5.97, 5.98
  under municipal law 9.13, 9.65, 9.68
  under Statute of the Special Tribunal for
      Lebanon 3.25
  treaty crimes, as mode of responsibility
      for 7.19, 7.47, 7.57, 7.72, 7.123, 7.126,
      7.133, 7.171, 7.179, 8.10
confiscation 1.12, 1.74, 7.183, 8.16, 8.87
conspiracy
  to commit genocide 5.16, 5.87, 5.88,
      5.89, 12.27
  joint criminal enterprise distinguished
      from 5.14
  under municipal law
    Act 26 of 2000 concerning Human
        Rights Courts (Indonesia) 9.48
    International Crimes (Tribunals) Act
        1973 (Bangladesh) 9.68
    Law on the Establishment of
        Extraordinary Chambers in the
        Courts of Cambodia 9.64
    Lebanese Criminal Code 3.25
  under Nuremberg Charter 4.88
  prescriptive jurisdiction in relation
      to 1.50, 1.59
  treaty crimes, as mode of responsibility
      for 7.37, 7.72, 7.116, 7.123, 7.139,
      7.147, 7.195,
consular relations
  see also immunity of state officials from
      foreign criminal jurisdiction;
      inviolability of state officials from
      foreign measures of physical
      constraint
  consular officers/consuls 7.59, 10.9,
      10.10, 10.54, 10.59, 10.60, 10.64,
      10.93–10.95, 10.103
  consular premises/consulates 1.27,
      7.64, 8.28
contiguous zone
  enforcement jurisdiction within 1.123
continental shelf
  enforcement jurisdiction in relation
      to 1.125

Index

prescriptive jurisdiction in relation to artificial islands, installations, and structures on 1.46
unlawful acts against safety of fixed platforms located on, treaty crimes of
background, definition, etc 2.47, 7.75, 7.77, 7.79, 7.81, 7.84, 7.85, 7.88, 7.89
and individual criminal responsibility under international law 7.7
prescriptive jurisdiction of states parties 8.26
co-perpetration 5.31–5.35
and contribution to a crime by a group of persons acting with a common purpose 5.79, 5.86
indirect co-perpetration 5.33, 5.46
and joint criminal enterprise 5.31, 5.33, 5.35, 5.37, 5.39
material elements 5.36–5.38
mental elements 5.39–5.41
'**core crimes**' 2.38–2.40
corporate liability 8.81–8.82
corruption, crimes relating to 2.39, 7.204
see also bribery, crimes relating to; organized crime, transnational, crimes relating to
background, definitions, etc 7.180, 7.186–7.195
and individual criminal responsibility under international law 7.13
obligations and rights of state parties 1.69, 8.7, 8.12, 8.14, 8.19, 8.50, 8.59, 8.60, 8.65, 8.81, 8.83, 8.86, 8.87, 9.15, 10.4, 11.9
Council of Europe 1.95, 7.180, 8.84, 9.77, 11.10, 14.104
courts, criminal
distinction between international and municipal 3.1, 3.2, 3.5–3.7
basis 3.5, 3.8, 3.9
significance 3.1, 3.37–3.45
'hybrid,' 'mixed' or 'internationalized' 3.6–3.7, 3.31
international
see also International Criminal Court (ICC); International Criminal Tribunal for Rwanda (ICTR); International Criminal Tribunal for the former Yugoslavia (ICTY); International Military Tribunal, Nuremberg (Nuremberg IMT/Nuremberg Tribunal); International Military Tribunal for the Far East, Tokyo (Tokyo IMT/Tokyo Tribunal); Mechanism for International Criminal Tribunals (MICT); Special Court for Sierra Leone (SCSL); Residual Special Court for Sierra Leone (RSCSL); Special Tribunal for Lebanon (STL)

definition 3.10
differences among 3.1, 3.7, 3.9–3.11, 3.36–3.39, 3.46–3.49
legal means of establishment and empowerment 3.11–3.27
terminology 3.3–3.4
municipal
see also Australia; Bangladesh; Bosnia and Herzegovina; Cambodia; China; Croatia; East Timor; France; Indonesia; Iraq; Kenya; Kosovo; Senegal; Serbia; Uganda; United Kingdom; United States
definition 3.28
differences among 3.1, 3.28, 3.36, 3.49, 9.34
general versus special jurisdiction 9.34
legal means of establishment and empowerment 3.29–3.35
ordinary and military 9.35, 9.37–9.39, 9.43
crime
see also international crime
definition 2.4
distinguished from delict 2.6
in substance a legal obligation 2.5
crimes against humanity
under customary international law
absence of equivalent prohibition on states 2.78
and amnesty 11.16, 11.19–11.24, 11.33, 13.33
apartheid as species of 4.49
comparative gravity of 4.105–4.106
defences to 6.6, 6.7, 6.17, 6.22, 6.34
enforced disappearance as species of 4.49, 4.60
enslavement as species of 1.60, 4.41, 4.51, 4.60, 7.36
evolution 4.39–4.50
extermination as species of 4.60, 4.64
material elements 4.51–4.59
mental elements 4.60–4.63
modes of responsibility for 5.4, 5.32, 5.52, 5.58, 5.69, 5.117
'other inhumane acts' as species of 4.48, 4.50, 4.60
persecution as species of 4.53, 4.63, 5.32
rape as species of 4.48
sexual slavery, enforced prostitution, forced pregnancy, enforced sterilisation or any other form of sexual violence of comparable gravity as species of 4.48
and statutory limitation 11.5, 11.6, 11.9–11.15
torture as species of 4.57
and universal jurisdiction 1.59–1.64, 8.21, 9.25

crimes against humanity (*cont.*):
  jurisdiction of International Criminal Court
    over 4.4–4.47, 9.78, 14.28, 14.29
    apartheid 4.49, 8.45
    enforced disappearance 4.49, 4.60, 8.56
    'other inhumane acts' 4.50, 4.60
    rape, sexual slavery, enforced prostitution,
      forced pregnancy, enforced
      sterilisation or any other form
      of sexual violence of comparable
      gravity 4.48
    torture 4.57
  jurisdiction of municipal criminal
    courts over
    ad hoc human rights courts
      (Indonesia) 9.47, 9.48
    county courts of Osijek, Rijeka, Split, and
      Zagreb (Croatia) 9.38
    Extraordinary Chambers in the Courts of
      Cambodia 9.64, 9.65
    Extraordinary African Chambers in the
      Senegalese Courts 9.74
    International Crimes Division of High
      Court of Uganda 9.66
    International Crimes Tribunals
      (Bangladesh) 9.68, 9.70
    Iraqi High Criminal Court 9.51,
      9.53, 9.54
    'regulation 64' panels and EULEX
      panels within the courts of
      Kosovo 9.40, 9.41
    post-Second World War municipal
      military courts 4.45, 9.43
    Special Panels in District Court of
      Dili and Court of Appeal of East
      Timor 3.31, 9.44, 9.45
    War Crimes Chambers of High Court
      and Court of Appeal in Belgrade
      (Serbia) 9.55, 9.56
    war crimes sections of Criminal and
      Appellate Divisions of Court of
      Bosnia and Herzegovina 9.59, 9.61
  and *jus cogens* 2.79–2.81
  and term 'international humanitarian
    law' 2.8
  treaty-based species of
    apartheid 4.49, 7.11, 7.111
    enforced disappearance 4.49, 7.14, 7.124,
      7.125, 7.127
'crimes against the peace and security of
  mankind' 2.41–2.43
'crimes of international concern',
  etc 2.44–2.45
crimes pursuant to international law
  see also international crimes
  justification for use of term 2.35
  meaning of term 2.35
  as species of international crime 2.33, 2.35
  subspecies of
    crimes pursuant to customary
      international law 2.36

crimes pursuant to treaty 2.36, 7.3–7.6,
  7.13, 7.14
crimes under customary international law
  see crimes under international law;
  international crimes
crimes under international law
  see also international crimes
  as anomalous corpus of rules of public
    international law 2.50
  justification for use of term 2.34
  meaning of term 2.34, 2.49
  as species of international crime 2.33, 2.34
  subspecies of
    crimes under customary international
      law 2.36, 4.3
    crimes under treaty 2.36, 7.3–7.6,
      7.15–7.17
criminalization
  municipal
    absence of obligation in relation to crimes
      under customary international
      law 4.5, 9.10
    absence of obligation under Rome
      Statute 14.9
    of breaches of Geneva Conventions and
      Additional Protocols other than
      grave breaches 4.25, 8.41
    divergence in scope in relation to
      international crimes 9.11–9.14
    obligation in relation to treaty
      crimes 2.18, 7.1, 7.4, 7.7, 7.8, 7.18,
      7.19, 7.37, 7.72, 7.136, 7.137–7.139,
      7.145, 7.146, 7.150, 7.182, 7.187,
      7.190, 8.1, 8.5–8.15, 8.73, 8.79, 9.9,
      9.11, 9.13–9.15
    variety of techniques in relation to
      international crimes 9.4–9.8
  international 2.21–2.30
Croatia
  county courts of Osijek, Rijeka, Split, and
    Zagreb 9.38
cultural genocide 4.74
cultural property, destruction and plunder of
  in armed conflict, war crimes relating to
  background, definition, etc 2.65, 4.17, 7.8,
    7.26, 7.29–7.33, 8.7
  and individual criminal responsibility under
    international law 7.7
  obligations and rights of states parties 2.65,
    7.8, 8.7, 8.41
  jurisdiction of Extraordinary Chambers in
    the Courts of Cambodia over 9.64,
    11.14, 11.23
custody
  see also arrest; detention
  treaty obligation to take suspect into 8.46

defences
  see also duress; intoxication; mental
    incapacity; military necessity, plea
    of; mistake of fact or law, defence of;

official capacity, plea of; self-defence,
    defence of others, and defence of
    certain property, defence of; superior
    orders; *tu quoque*, plea of
  to crimes under customary international
    law 6.1–6.3, 6.7, 6.48
  distinguished from circumstances
    precluding responsibility under law
    of state responsibility 6.8
  rejected defences 6.37–6.41, 10.73, 12.30
  under municipal law 9.3, 9.15–9.19, 9.45,
    9.53, 9.64, 9.74
  to treaty crimes 8.12, 8.78–8.80, 9.16
  prohibition of availability of specific
    defences 8.12, 8.78–8.80, 9.16
detention 1.9, 1.79, 1.100, 1.114
  see also arrest; enforced disappearance, crime
    of; hostage-taking, crime of
  during international armed
    conflict 1.83–1.85
  International Criminal Court
    by Court 14.13
    power of Court to order 6.12
  International Criminal Tribunal for
    Rwanda
    power of Tribunal to order 12.50, 14.19
    by Tribunal 12.10
  International Criminal Tribunal for the
    former Yugoslavia
    power of Tribunal to order 12.50,
      14.19
    by Tribunal 12.9
  inviolability of foreign state officials
    from 10.1, 10.3, 10.11, 10.14, 10.15,
    10.17, 10.25, 10.29, 10.33, 10.95,
    10.96, 14.94, 14.96–14.98
  by SFOR of ICTY indictees 12.55
  Special Court for Sierra Leone
    power of Court to order 13.39, 14.19
    by Tribunal 13.12
  of UN and associated personnel 8.85
  of vessels 1.124, 8.84
diplomatic relations
  see also immunity of state officials from
    foreign criminal jurisdiction;
    internationally protected persons,
    crimes against; inviolability of state
    officials from foreign measures of
    physical constraint
  diplomatic controversy/sensitivities 1.28,
    1.32, 1.42, 1.63, 9.33
  diplomatic agents/diplomats 7.59, 7.60,
    10.9, 10.15, 10.24–10.29, 10.31, 10.33,
    10.35, 10.40, 10.54, 10.59, 10.60,
    10.89, 10.97, 10.98, 10.102, 10.43
  diplomatic premises/embassies 1.27, 1.78,
    7.94, 8.28
  diplomatic staff of special mission 10.9,
    10.10, 10.29, 10.60, 10.99
**direct and public incitement to commit
  genocide**

  under customary international law 5.87,
    5.88, 5.90–5.96, 12.27
double criminality *see* extradition
double jeopardy *see ne bis in idem*
due process 9.62, 9.63, 12.12, 13.13, 14.16,
  14.61, 14.73, 14.76
duress
  see also superior orders
  and indirect perpetration 5.44
  as defence
    to crimes under customary international
      law 5.44, 6.4, 6.20–6.25, 6.32, 6.35
    to crimes within jurisdiction
      of International Criminal
      Court 6.4, 6.23
    and defence of superior orders 6.25
    under English law 9.15, 9.18
    and plea of military necessity 6.24
    and plea of necessity/extreme
      necessity 6.24
  as mitigating circumstance 6.42, 6.43

East Timor
  Ad Hoc Human Rights Court for East
    Timor in Central Jakarta District
    Court (Indonesia) 9.49
  Special Panels in District Court of Dili
    and Court of Appeal of 1.63, 3.31,
    9.44–9.46, 11.15
  as municipal criminal courts 3.31
  United Nations Transitional Authority for
    East Timor (UNTAET) 1.39, 3.31,
    9.44, 11.15
**Economic Community of West African States
  (ECOWAS)** 3.35, 9.72, 9.76, 11.14,
    11.23, 13.7, 13.33
enforced disappearance, crime of 11.23
  as crime against humanity under customary
    international law 4.49, 4.60
  as crime against humanity within
    jurisdiction of International Crime
    Court 4.49, 4.60, 8.56
  as treaty crime
    background, definition, etc 4.49, 4.56,
      7.14, 7.110, 7.124–7.127, 7.204
    and individual criminal responsibility
      under international law 7.14
    obligations of states parties 8.18, 8.52,
      8.56, 8.79, 9.16, 11.9, 11.22
enslavement *see* crimes against humanity;
  slavery; slave trade
ethnic cleansing 4.74, 12.3
**European Rule of Law Mission in Kosovo
  (EULEX)** 3.32, 9.40, 9.41, 9.77
exclusive economic zone (EEZ)
  enforcement jurisdiction
    within 1.124–1.125
  prescriptive jurisdiction within
    artificial islands, installations, and
      structures 1.46
    fisheries offences 1.45

exculpation
  possibility of as a general principle of criminal law 6.3
extermination *see* crimes against humanity
extradition 1.67, 1.86, 1.92, 1.94, 7.29, 11.32, 12.41, 14.101
  see also aut dedere aut judicare (obligation to prosecute or extradite)
  competing requests
    extradition or surrender to International Criminal Court 14.83, 14.103
    extradition to one state or another 1.66
  concept 1.93
    distinguished from surrender to an international criminal court 12.53
  extradition treaties 1.95, 1.96, 1.111
  grounds for refusal by requested state, typical
    'double criminality' 1.97
    fiscal matters exception, treaty obligation not to give effect to 8.60
    political offence exception, general and treaty obligation not to give effect to 1.98, 8.59, 8.64, 8.80
    nationality of suspect/convict 1.99
  human rights safeguard clause 8.61
  and immunity of state officials from foreign criminal jurisdiction 10.1, 10.3, 10.6, 10.11, 10.55, 10.62, 10.70–10.72, 10.82, 10.84, 10.85, 10.91
  non-refoulement 1.102
  and treaty obligation in relation to mutual assistance in criminal matters 8.62
  and treaty obligation to take suspect into custody and make preliminary inquiry into facts 8.46
  provisions in international criminal conventions on technicalities of 8.58–8.61
  replacement within European Union by European arrest warrant 1.95
  restrictions on requesting state
    prohibition on onward surrender 1.101
    rule of speciality 1.100
Extraordinary African Chambers in the Senegalese Courts *see* Senegal
Extraordinary Chambers in the Courts of Cambodia *see* Cambodia

financing of terrorism *see* terrorism, financing of, crime of
firearms and related items, illicit manufacture of and trafficking in, crimes of 2.47
  see also organized crime, transnational, crimes relating to
  definition, background, etc 7.161–7.166
  and individual criminal responsibility under international law 7.13
France
  and International Military Tribunal, Nuremberg 2.59, 3.13
  post Second World War military courts 3.30, 9.43
  as municipal criminal courts 3.30
freezing of assets 8.87

Geneva Conventions, grave breaches of
  as crimes under customary international law 4.10, 4.20–4.23, 12.23
  material elements 4.28–4.33, 4.35
  mental elements 4.36–4.38
  and crime of hostage-taking 7.63
  jurisdiction of international criminal courts over
    International Criminal Court 4.23, 4.27
    International Criminal Tribunal for the former Yugoslavia 4.22, 12.22, 12.23
  jurisdiction of municipal criminal courts over
    Extraordinary Chambers in the Courts of Cambodia 9.64, 9.65, 11.14, 11.23
    Extraordinary African Chambers in the Senegalese Courts 9.74
  and *jus cogens* 2.81
  and political offence exception to extradition 1.98
  as treaty crimes 7.8, 9.28, 11.10, 14.5
  background, definitions, etc 7.18, 7.21, 7.23, 7.25, 7.27, 8.9
  and individual criminal responsibility under international law 7.7
  obligations of contracting parties 1.63, 2.65, 7.8, 8.7, 8.38, 8.54, 8.56, 8.77, 9.32, 10.44, 11.28
Geneva Conventions, grave breaches of Additional Protocol I to
  as crimes under customary international law 4.20–4.22, 4.24
  and crime of hostage-taking 7.63
  as treaty crimes 7.22, 7.24, 7.26, 7.28, 8.44, 11.10
Geneva Conventions, other violations of and violations of Additional Protocol II to 4.16, 7.8, 8.41
  as crimes under customary international law 4.25–4.27, 13.25
  material elements 4.28–4.33, 4.35
  mental elements 4.36–4.38
  and crime of hostage-taking 7.63
  jurisdiction of Extraordinary African Chambers in the Senegalese Courts over 9.74
  jurisdiction of international criminal courts over
    International Criminal Court 4.27
    International Criminal Tribunal for Rwanda 12.22, 12.23
    Special Court for Sierra Leone 13.23, 13.25

Index 593

genocide, crime of
see also aiding and abetting; attempt; complicity; conspiracy; direct and public incitement to commit genocide; instigation; joint criminal enterprise (JCE)
and amnesty 11.16, 11.19, 11.22–11.24, 11.29, 11.31, 11.33, 13.33
under customary international law
absence of obligation to prosecute, etc 4.5, 8.5
background 4.64, 4.65
comparative gravity of 1.105–1.106
defences to 6.6, 6.7, 6.17, 6.34
and Elements of Crimes 4.77, 4.86
equivalent prohibition on states 2.77
material elements 4.66–4.77
mental elements 4.66, 4.67, 4.78–4.86, 5.26
modes of responsibility for 5.4, 5.16, 5.26, 5.32, 5.61, 5.76, 5.78, 5.87–5.99, 5.117, 12.27
rape as 4.75, 4.76
torture as 4.75
and universal jurisdiction 1.59, 1.61–1.64, 8.21, 8.40, 9.25
jurisdiction of municipal criminal courts over
ad hoc human rights courts (Indonesia) 9.47, 9.48
county courts of Osijek, Rijeka, Split, and Zagreb (Croatia) 9.38
Extraordinary Chambers in the Courts of Cambodia 9.64, 9.65
Extraordinary African Chambers in the Senegalese Courts 9.74
International Crimes Division of High Court of Uganda 9.66
International Crimes Tribunals (Bangladesh) 9.68, 9.70
Iraqi High Criminal Court 9.51, 9.53, 9.54
'regulation 64' panels and EULEX panels within the courts of Kosovo 9.40
Special Panels in District Court of Dili and Court of Appeal of East Timor 3.31, 9.44, 9.45
War Crimes Chambers of High Court and Court of Appeal in Belgrade (Serbia) 9.55, 9.56
war crimes sections of Criminal and Appellate Divisions of Court of Bosnia and Herzegovina 9.59, 9.61
and *jus cogens* 2.79–2.81
and political offence exception to extradition 1.98
and statutory limitation 11.5, 11.6, 11.10–11.15, 11.29, 11.31
and term 'international humanitarian law' 2.8

treaty crime of 7.9, 7.10, 7.20
and acts of state 2.72, 10.73
background, definition, etc 4.64–4.67, 7.20, 9.48, 9.53, 9.64, 9.74, 10.73
equivalent prohibition on contracting states 2.77
modes of responsibility for 5.87, 7.20, 9.64
obligations of contracting states 8.5, 8.7, 8.15, 8.25, 8.40, 8.45, 8.57, 8.59, 8.64, 8.67–8.71, 14.4
and treaty crime of apartheid 7.115

gravity of crime
and International Criminal Court
as criterion of admissibility of case 4.77, 14.24, 14.61
as factor in Prosecutor's decision whether to initiate investigation 14.21, 14.75
as factor in Prosecutor's decision whether to bring prosecution 14.22, 14.61, 14.75
not a definitional criterion of an international crime 2.22–2.27
no inherent hierarchy of among crimes under customary international law 4.105–4.106

Habré, Hissène 9.72, 9.75, 9.76, 11.33
heads of government
see also immunity of state officials from foreign criminal jurisdiction; internationally protected persons, crimes against; inviolability of state officials from foreign measures of physical constraint
attacks on 7.60
immunity and inviolability of serving and former 3.41, 7.60, 10.9, 10.33, 10.35, 10.36, 10.38–10.40, 10.44, 10.58, 10.78, 10.92, 10.97, 10.102, 12.30, 12.32, 14.43, 14.91
individual criminal responsibility under international law for acts of state by 2.2, 6.41, 14.42
heads of state
see also immunity of state officials from foreign criminal jurisdiction; internationally protected persons, crimes against; inviolability of state officials from foreign measures of physical constraint
attacks on 1.98, 7.60
excusal from presence at trial before International Criminal Court 14.41
immunity and inviolability of serving and former 3.41–3.43, 10.9, 10.12, 10.31–10.33, 10.35, 10.36, 10.38–10.40, 10.42, 10.44, 10.58,

heads of state (*cont.*):
10.59, 10.75, 10.77, 10.78, 10.82,
10.92, 10.97, 10.102, 12.30, 12.32,
13.31, 13.32, 14.43, 14.44, 14.46,
14.91, 14.94, 14.96, 14.97
individual criminal responsibility under
international law for acts of state
by 2.2, 2.70, 6.41, 14.42
high seas
definition of 1.44
enforcement jurisdiction in relation to 1.44,
1.115, 1.119, 8.84
'hot pursuit' 1.118
piracy *jure gentium* 1.57, 1.116
transport of slaves 1.117
piracy *jure gentium*, commission
on as definitional element
1.56, 1.58
prescriptive jurisdiction in relation to 1.44,
1.45, 1.69
aircraft on surface of 1.47
collisions 1.18, 1.44
piracy *jure gentium* 1.44, 1.56–1.59
transport of slaves 1.60
hijacking *see* aircraft; civil aviation, crimes
relating to
hostage-taking, crime of
as grave breach of Geneva
Conventions 7.25, 7.63
as treaty crime in own right
background, definition, etc 7.40,
7.62–7.65
and individual criminal responsibility
under international law 7.7
obligations of states parties 8.74, 8.83
human rights *see* international human
rights law

IFOR (Implementation Force) 12.54
**illicit traffic in narcotic drugs and
psychotropic substances** *see* narcotic
drugs and psychotropic substances, illicit
traffic in, crime of
**immunity of state officials from foreign
criminal jurisdiction**
see also consular relations; diplomatic
relations; heads of government; heads
of state; inviolability of state officials
from foreign measures of physical
constraint; ministers for foreign affairs;
special missions
concept, general characteristics, and basic
content 10.1, 10.3–10.9, 10.11–10.16,
10.101, 10.104
distinguished from inviolability of state
officials from foreign measures of
physical constraint 10.3, 10.11,
10.14, 10.15
and conflation with question of universal
jurisdiction 1.63, 9.29

and conflation with substantive defence of
act of state 2.52, 2.70
definitions
'host' state 10.9
'receiving' state 10.9
'sending' state 10.9
'transit state' 10.9
immunity *ratione materiae* and immunity
ratione personae distinguished
10.9
immunity *ratione materiae*
'acts performed in an official
capacity' 10.60–10.69
and allegations of international
crimes 10.71–10.91, 10.103
and alleged commission during
unconsensual presence in forum
state 10.70
beneficiaries 10.9, 10.45, 10.46, 10.51,
10.55, 10.56, 10.92–10.100, 10.103
concept, rationale, and general aspects
and scope 10.9, 10.45–10.69
undesirability of term 'functional
immunity' 10.9
whether requiring to be invoked by
official's state 10.58
immunity *ratione personae*
and allegations of international
crimes 10.41–10.44, 10.102
beneficiaries 10.9, 10.24–10.39, 10.102
concept, general characteristics,
rationale, and basic scope 10.9,
10.18–10.23, 10.40
potentially misleading quality of term
'personal immunity' 10.9
and jurisdiction of international criminal
courts 3.39–3.44, 3.47
International Criminal Court 3.43,
14.43–14.47
International Criminal Tribunal
for Rwanda and International
Criminal Tribunal for the former
Yugoslavia 3.41, 12.30–12.32
International Military Tribunal,
Nuremberg and International
Military Tribunal for the Far East,
Tokyo 3.40
Special Court for Sierra Leone 3.42,
13.31, 13.32
and jurisdiction of specific municipal
criminal courts
Iraqi High Criminal Court 9.53
post-Second World War municipal
military courts 10.72
Special Panels in District Court of
Dili and Court of Appeal of East
Timor 9.45
and surrender to International Criminal
Court 14.88–14.92, 14.103
Al Bashir case 14.93–14.98

work of International Law Commission
  (ILC) on topic 10.10, 10.13,
  10.14–10.16, 10.36–10.39, 10.44,
  10.47, 10.54, 10.58, 10.60, 10.64,
  10.65, 10.70, 10.79, 10.81, 10.83,
  10.93, 10.94, 10.103, 10.104, 14.47
inchoate offences 1.50, 1.59, 5.59, 5.88, 5.94,
  5.95, 5.99
incitement *see* direct and public incitement to
  commit genocide
indirect perpetration 5.33, 5.42–5.45, 5.47
  indirect co-perpetration 5.33, 5.46, 5.47
individual criminal responsibility
  explicit provision for as distinguishing
    feature of international criminal
    law 2.8
  under international law 2.10, 2.12, 2.15,
    2.16, 2.17, 2.20, 2.33–2.35, 2.49,
    2.50, 2.83
    for acts of state 2.69–2.73, 6.36, 10.73,
      12.30, 14.40, 14.42
    concept 2.2
    under customary international law 2.5,
      2.10, 2.15, 2.20, 2.33, 2.36, 2.67,
      2.68, 4.3, 7.9–7.11
    evolution 2.51–2.73
    and state responsibility 2.2, 2.74–2.81
    theoretical source of binding nature
      of criminal obligations under
      international law 2.82
    under treaty 2.5, 2.15, 2.16, 2.37, 2.68,
      7.3–7.12
Indonesia
  ad hoc human rights courts 9.47–9.50
instigation
  as mode of responsibility
    for crimes under customary international
      law 1.59, 5.30, 5.32, 5.44,
      5.55–5.61, 5.91
    under Law on the Establishment of
      Extraordinary Chambers in the
      Courts of Cambodia 9.64
    for treaty crimes 7.194
  by public official
    and obligation to prevent other acts
      of cruel, inhuman or degrading
      treatment or punishment 8.73
    and treaty crime of torture 7.118, 7.120
intent *see* mens rea
**International Atomic Energy Agency
  (IAEA)** 7.39, 7.66, 7.67, 7.199
**International Civil Aviation Organization
  (ICAO)** 7.39, 7.41, 7.42, 7.49–7.51, 8.15,
  8.30, 8.39, 8.82
International Court of Justice (ICJ)
  relationship with International
    Criminal Tribunal for the former
    Yugoslavia 12.46–12.48
international crimes
  concept 2.3–2.20

definition 2.20, 2.32
  definitional misconceptions 2.21–2.31
  taxonomy and terminology 2.33–2.37
    'crimes pursuant to customary
      international law' 2.36
    'crimes pursuant to international
      law' 2.35
    'crimes pursuant to treaty' 2.36, 7.3
    'crimes under customary international
      law' 2.36, 4.3
    'crimes under international law' 2.34
    'crimes under treaty' 2.36, 7.3
    'customary international crimes' 2.37
    'treaty crimes' 2.37
International Criminal Court (ICC)
  applicable law 14.57–14.59
  Assembly of States Parties (ASP) 14.7,
    14.14, 14.15, 14.30
  establishment and empowerment 3.12, 3.13,
    14.1, 14.3–14.9
    ILC Draft Statute for an International
      Criminal Court 14.5, 14.6
  basic facts 14.10–14.18
  'complementarity' 4.18, 9.1,
    14.60–14.75, 14.105
  co-operation with 14.78–14.87
    see also African Union (AU); 'article 98'
      agreements
    and agreements with sending
      states 14.88–14.90,
      14.99–14.106
    and immunity and inviolability of officials
      of third states 14.88–14.98
  core activity to date 14.24–14.26,
    14.107, 14.108
  due process rights 14.16
  and 'complementarity' 14.73
  Elements of Crimes
    adoption and amendment 14.14
    consistency with Rome
      Statute 4.77, 14.14
    purpose 4.4, 14.14
  funding 14.18
  as an international criminal
    court 3.12, 3.13
  as only international criminal
    court to date not of an ad hoc
    character 3.4, 14.10
  jurisdiction, exercise
    admissibility 4.77, 14.60–14.75
    amnesties 14.51
    deferral 14.52–14.56
    immunity of state officials 3.43, 3.44,
      3.47, 14.40, 14.43–14.47
    preconditions to 3.43, 14.32–14.35
    statutes of limitations 14.48–14.50
  jurisdiction, existence 14.27
    see also aggression, crime of; crimes
      against humanity; genocide, crime
      of; Geneva Conventions, grave

596 *Index*

International Criminal Court (ICC) (*cont.*):
  breaches of; Geneva Conventions, other violations of and violations of Additional Protocol II to; violations of the laws and customs of war; war crimes
  jurisdiction *ratione loci* 14.32–14.35
  jurisdiction *ratione materiae* 1.60, 4.4, 4.11, 4.13, 4.18, 4.19, 4.23, 4.24, 4.27, 4.33, 4.47–4.50, 4.58, 4.67, 4.75, 4.77, 4.87–4.101, 14.28–14.31
  jurisdiction *ratione personae* 14.32–14.38
  jurisdiction *ratione temporis* 14.39
  offences against the Court's administration of justice 7.12
  organs 14.15
  procedural essentials 14.19–14.23
    confirmation of charges 14.23
    initiation of investigation 14.21
    initiation of investigation *proprio motu* 14.20, 14.21, 14.32–14.35
    preliminary examination 14.21
    referral of situation 14.20, 14.32–14.35
    request for arrest warrant or summons to appear 14.22
    prosecution 14.22
  Prosecutor/Office of the Prosecutor (OTP) 14.15, 14.20–14.27, 14.30, 14.32–14.35, 14.45, 14.53, 14.54, 14.61, 14.64, 14.66, 14.68, 14.75, 14.86, 14.94, 14.97, 14.107
  Regulations of the Court, adoption and amendment 14.15
  relationship with national jurisdictions
    'complementarity' 4.18, 9.1, 14.60–14.75, 14.105
    ne bis in idem 14.76–14.77
  relationship with United Nations 14.11
  role of United Nations Security Council 3.43, 3.48, 14.11, 14.18, 14.20, 14.21, 14.32, 14.34, 14.44, 14.45, 14.52–14.56, 14.86, 14.90, 14.95–14.98, 14.104
  Rome Statute
    see also aggression, crime of
    absence of obligations of municipal criminalization, etc on states parties 14.9
    adoption and entry into force 14.1, 14.6, 14.7
    amendments on crime of aggression 4.90, 4.91, 14.30
    as direct source of existence and competence of Court 3.13
    interpretation in accordance with customary international rules on treaty interpretation 14.8
    and *pacta tertiis* rule 3.43, 3.48, 14.8, 14.44–14.45, 14.78, 14.92
    relationship of jurisdiction *ratione materiae* to substantive customary international law 4.4, 4.8, 4.15, 4.18, 4.19, 4.23, 4.24, 4.27, 4.33, 4.49, 4.50, 4.58, 4.91
    substantive effect of jurisdiction *ratione materiae* 2.15, 14.59
  Review Conference in Kampala 4.18, 4.90, 14.30, 14.31
  Rules of Procedure and Evidence, adoption and amendment 14.14
  use of term 'court' in name 3.3
  victims and witnesses 14.10
    reparations 14.10
    Trust Fund for Victims 14.10
international criminal courts *see* courts, criminal
international criminal law
  distinguished from international human rights law 2.8
  distinguished from main body of international humanitarian law 2.8
  professed aims of viii
  scope of field as understood by book vii
international criminal procedure vii
International Criminal Tribunal for Rwanda (ICTR)
  absence from Statute of express *mens rea* requirement 4.8
  absence from Statute of express provision for defences 6.3
  applicable law 12.23
  assessment 12.56, 12.57
  basic facts 12.11–12.14
  cases 12.15, 12.16
  'completion strategy' 12.6, 12.38
  co-operation with 3.48, 12.49–12.53
  detention by 12.10
  due process rights 12.12, 12.33
  establishment and empowerment 3.22, 3.23, 3.27, 12.1, 12.4
    see also Mechanism for International Criminal Tribunals (MICT)
  ad hoc nature 12.6
  legality 3.26, 12.18–12.20
  perceived benefits of legal basis 12.5
  transition to Mechanism for International Criminal Tribunals 12.7, 12.8, 12.17
  funding 12.14
  as an international criminal court 3.22, 3.23
  jurisdiction, exercise
    immunity of state officials 3.41, 3.44, 3.47, 12.30–12.32
    remedial discretion 12.33
  jurisdiction, existence 12.21
    see also crimes against humanity; genocide, crime of; war crimes; Geneva Conventions, other

violations of and violations of
Additional Protocol II to
jurisdiction *ratione loci* 12.10, 12.29
jurisdiction *ratione materiae* 4.4, 4.26,
4.47, 4.50, 4.53, 4.54, 4.66, 4.67,
12.10, 12.22, 12.23
jurisdiction *ratione personae* 12.24, 12.25
jurisdiction *ratione temporis* 12.10, 12.27
procedural essentials 14.19
Prosecutor 12.10
relationship to International Court of
Justice 12.46–12.48
relationship to national jurisdictions
concurrency 12.34, 12.35
non bis in idem 12.43–12.45
primacy 12.36, 12.37
rule 11*bis* 12.38–12.42
relationship to United Nations 12.11
Rules of Procedure and Evidence, adoption
and amendment 12.10
Statute, adoption and
amendment 12.10, 12.11
structure 12.10
use of term 'tribunal' in title 3.3
witnesses and victims 12.13
**International Criminal Tribunal for the
former Yugoslavia (ICTY)**
absence from Statute of express *mens rea*
requirement 4.8
absence from Statute of express provision for
defences 6.3
applicable law 12.23
assessment 12.56, 12.57
basic facts 12.9, 12.11–12.14, 12.56–12.57
cases 12.15, 12.16
'completion strategy' 9.56, 9.59,
12.6, 12.38
co-operation with 3.48, 12.49–12.55
detention by 12.9
due process rights 12.12, 12.33
establishment and empowerment 3.22,
3.23, 3.27, 12.1, 12.3
see also Mechanism for International
Criminal Tribunals (MICT)
ad hoc nature 12.6
legality 3.26, 12.18, 12.19
perceived benefits of legal basis 12.5
transition to Mechanism for International
Criminal Tribunals 12.7,
12.8, 12.17
funding 12.14
as an international criminal
court 3.22, 3.23
jurisdiction, exercise
immunity of state officials 3.41, 3.44,
3.47, 12.30–12.32
remedial discretion 12.33
jurisdiction, existence 12.21
see also crimes against humanity;
genocide, crime of; war crimes;

Geneva Conventions, grave
breaches of
jurisdiction *ratione loci* 12.28
jurisdiction *ratione materiae* 4.4, 4.14,
4.15, 4.22, 4.47, 4.50, 4.56, 4.66,
4.67, 12.22, 12.23
jurisdiction *ratione personae* 12.24, 12.25
jurisdiction *ratione temporis* 12.26
procedural essentials 14.19
Prosecutor 12.9
relationship to International Court of
Justice 12.46–12.48
relationship to national jurisdictions
concurrency 12.34, 12.35
non bis in idem 12.43–12.45
primacy 12.36, 12.37
rule 11*bis* 12.38–12.42
relationship to United Nations 12.11
Rules of Procedure and Evidence, adoption
and amendment 12.9
Statute, adoption and
amendment 12.9, 12.11
structure 12.9
use of term 'tribunal' in title 3.3
witnesses and victims 12.13
international criminal tribunals *see* courts,
criminal
**international humanitarian law (law of armed
conflict/laws of war)**
'carve out' in relation to in international
criminal conventions 7.69, 7.80, 7.81,
7.91, 7.99, 7.106–7.108
and crime of genocide 2.8
and crimes against humanity 2.8, 2.78, 4.51
and defence of self-defence, defence
of others, and defence of certain
property 6.19
detention in international armed conflict
under 1.83–1.85
international criminal law distinguished
from main body of 2.8, 2.23
'other serious violations of', jurisdiction
of Special Court for Sierra Leone
over 13.23, 13.26
overlap with international criminal
law 2.8, 11.31
replacement of 'war' with 'armed conflict' in
terminology of 4.11
and torture 7.117, 7.118
and war crimes 2.8, 4.10, 4.34, 4.35, 7.8
international human rights law
and amnesty 11.3, 11.23, 11.31,
11.32, 11.36
and availability of defences under municipal
law 9.18
'carve out' in relation to in international
criminal conventions 7.108
and crimes against humanity 2.78, 4.45
and due process guarantees in statutes of
international criminal courts 12.12

international human rights law (*cont.*):
  and early release 11.1
  and extradition 1.91, 1.102
  and immunity from criminal jurisdiction of state's own officials 10.4
  and international abduction without consent of territorial state 1.108, 1.112
  and International Criminal Court
    applicable law 14.57
    'complementarity' 14.73
  international criminal law distinguished from 2.8, 2.23
  and international criminalization 2.23, 2.30
  and municipal criminalization 2.10
    prohibition on retroactive criminalization (*nullum crimen sine lege*) 2.15, 4.45
  and municipal trial 9.34
  ne bis in idem 11.32
  trial of civilians in military courts 9.35
  overlap with international criminal law 11.31
  and statutory limitation 11.3, 11.13, 11.31, 11.32, 11.36
  and treaty crimes of apartheid, torture and enforced disappearance 7.110, 7.111, 7.115, 7.117–7.119, 7.124
  and treaty crimes of sale of children, child prostitution, and child pornography 7.167

International Law Commission (ILC), work of
  on consular relations
    commentary on scope of consular immunity 10.64, 10.93, 10.94
  on crimes against internationally protected persons 7.59
    commentary on obligation *aut dedere aut judicare* 8.51
  on diplomatic intercourse and immunity
    content of immunity and inviolability of diplomatic agents 10.14, 10.15, 10.17
  on draft code of crimes against the peace and security of mankind 2.39
    definition of crime of aggression 4.89
    exclusion of crime of international terrorism 7.103
    list of crimes against humanity 4.47
    possibility of exculpation in trial for international crime 6.3
    possibility of mitigation of sentence on conviction of international crime 6.42
    use of term 'crimes against the peace and security of mankind' 2.41–2.43
    use of term 'crimes under international law' 2.34
  on draft statute for an international criminal court 2.15, 2.16, 2.31, 2.36
    exclusion from jurisdiction *ratione materiae* of crime of international terrorism 7.103
    use of term 'crimes of international concern' 2.44, 2.45
    use of term 'crimes pursuant to international law' 2.35
    use of term 'crimes under international law' 2.34, 2.35
    use of term 'international crime' 2.11
  on immunity of state officials from foreign criminal jurisdiction 10.10, 10.13, 10.103, 10.104
    consideration in Sixth Committee of United Nations General Assembly 10.10, 10.13, 10.36–10.39, 10.47, 10.54, 10.58, 10.60, 10.79, 10.83
    content of immunity and inviolability 10.13, 10.16
    immunity *ratione materiae* 10.47, 10.54, 10.58, 10.64, 10.65, 10.70, 10.79, 10.81, 10.83
    immunity *ratione personae*, beneficiaries of 10.36–10.39
    immunity *ratione personae*, scope of 10.44
    scope of work 10.10
  on Nürnberg principles 2.60, 2.61
    endorsement in commentary of individual criminal responsibility under international law 2.66
    endorsement in commentary of individual criminal responsibility under international law for acts of state 2.72
    endorsement of existence and definition of crimes against humanity 4.46, 4.47
    endorsement of existence and definition of crimes against peace 4.89
    position on defence of superior orders 6.32, 6.33
    use of term 'crimes under international law' 2.11, 2.34
  on obligation *aut dedere aut judicare* 8.55

internationally protected persons, crimes against
  as treaty crimes
    background, definition, etc 7.59–7.61
    and individual criminal responsibility under international law 7.13
    obligations of states parties 8.28, 8.74
  jurisdiction of Extraordinary Chambers in the Courts of Cambodia 9.64, 11.15, 11.23
  and Vienna Convention on Diplomatic Relations 9.64, 11.15, 11.23

International Maritime Organization (IMO) 7.39, 7.74, 7.76, 7.77

Index 599

International Military Tribunal for the Far East, Tokyo (Tokyo IMT/Tokyo Tribunal)
  absence from Charter of express *mens rea* requirement 4.8
  absence from Charter of express provision for defences 6.3
  closure 13.2
  establishment and empowerment 3.14–3.16
  as an international criminal court 3.14–3.16
  jurisdiction
    crimes against peace 4.88
    immunity from exercise 3.40
    'other inhumane acts' as species of crime against humanity 4.50
    war crimes 4.14
  mitigation of punishment 6.41, 6.42
  use of term 'tribunal' in name 3.3
International Military Tribunal, Nuremberg (Nuremberg IMT/Nuremberg Tribunal)
  absence from Charter of express *mens rea* requirement 4.8
  absence from Charter of express provision for defences 6.3
  character of applicable law 2.59, 12.23
  closure 13.2
  and defence of superior orders 6.32, 6.33
  establishment and empowerment 3.12, 3.13
  as an international criminal court 3.12, 3.13
  judgment as lawmaking 4.18
  jurisdiction
    crimes against humanity 4.41–4.44, 4.50
    crimes against peace 2.73, 4.88, 4.106, 5.4
    immunity from exercise 3.40, 10.73, 12.30, 13.31
    mitigation of punishment 6.42
    and question of individual criminal responsibility under international law 2.57–2.65
    for acts of state 2.70–2.73, 6.41, 10.73, 12.30, 13.31, 14.42
  use of term 'tribunal' in name 3.3
international refugee law
  obligation of *non-refoulement* under 1.102
International Residual Mechanism for Criminal Tribunals *see* Mechanism for International Criminal Tribunals (MICT)
intoxication
  as defence to crimes under customary international law 6.4, 6.14, 6.29
  as mitigating circumstance in sentencing for crimes under customary international law 6.44
inviolability of state officials from foreign measures of physical constraint
  see also immunity of state officials from foreign criminal jurisdiction

  and allegations of international crimes 3.43, 10.41, 10.43, 10.44, 10.102, 14.44
  beneficiaries 10.19, 10.25–10.39, 10.59, 10.95, 10.96, 10.100, 10.102, 10.103
  concept, general characteristics, and basic content 10.1, 10.3–10.7, 10.11–10.15, 10.17, 10.19–10.21, 10.23, 10.40, 10.101, 10.102, 10.104
  distinguished from immunity of state officials from foreign criminal jurisdiction 10.3, 10.11, 10.14, 10.15
  rationale 10.20
  and surrender to International Criminal Court 14.88–14.92, 14.103
  Al Bashir case 14.93–14.98
  and treaty definition of 'internationally protected person' 7.60
  and work of International Law Commission (ILC) on immunity of state officials from foreign criminal jurisdiction 10.10
Iraq
  Iraqi High Criminal Court 3.33, 9.51–9.54, 11.14
  as a municipal criminal court 3.33

joint criminal enterprise (JCE)
  concept 5.14, 5.16, 5.33
  distinguished from
    aiding and abetting 5.30, 5.69
    conspiracy 5.14
    contribution to a crime by a group of persons acting with a common purpose 5.78–5.79
  co-perpetration 5.35, 5.37, 5.39
  forms of 5.15
  material elements 5.17–5.22
  mental elements 5.23–5.26
  reception 5.27–5.32
jurisdiction, treaty obligation to establish
  see also jurisdiction, national criminal; universal jurisdiction
  concurrent jurisdiction envisaged 8.24
  as feature of international criminal conventions 7.1, 8.1, 8.20
  miscellaneous jurisdictional bases 8.25–8.33
  and *pacta tertiis* rule 8.21–8.23
  universal jurisdiction 8.34–8.41
jurisdiction, national
  concept 1.1, 1.3–1.5, 1.10, 1.13, 1.14
  distinct aspects delineated and defined 1.6–1.9, 1.11
    jurisdiction to adjudicate (adjudicative jurisdiction) 1.8
    jurisdiction to enforce (enforcement jurisdiction) 1.9
    jurisdiction to prescribe (prescriptive jurisdiction) 1.7

jurisdiction, national criminal 1.2
  customary and conventional rules
    distinguished 1.14
  distinct aspects delineated and
    defined 1.11–1.13, 1.15, 1.74
  jurisdiction to enforce (enforcement
    jurisdiction) 1.12, 1.74
  jurisdiction to prescribe (prescriptive
    jurisdiction) 1.12, 1.15
  jurisdiction to enforce (enforcement
    jurisdiction)
    see also abduction without consent of
      territorial state, international;
      extradition; mutual assistance in
      criminal matters
    at sea 1.44, 1.57, 1.115–1.125
    co-operation in enforcement in foreign
      territory 1.86–1.106
    exceptions to general rule 1.78–1.85
    general rule 1.75–1.77
    illegally or irregularly obtained
      custody 1.107–1.114
  jurisdiction to prescribe (prescriptive
    jurisdiction), general aspects of
    absence of customary international rule
      of *ne bis in idem* among concurrent
      bases 1.72, 1.73
    absence of hierarchy among concurrent
      bases under customary international
      law 1.66–1.71
    concurrent prescriptive jurisdiction,
      concept 1.23
    permissive under customary international
      law 1.24
    structure 1.16–1.22
  jurisdiction to prescribe (prescriptive
    jurisdiction), bases under customary
    international law and treaty
    see also piracy *jure gentium*; universal
      jurisdiction
    at sea 1.43–1.46, 8.26, 8.30, 14.33
    'effects' doctrine 1.49–1.51, 8.32
    foreign members of armed forces 1.48
    nationality 1.30–1.33, 8.27, 14.33
    on board aircraft 1.47, 8.30, 14.33
    passive personality 1.36–1.42, 8.29, 8.31
    'protective' principle 1.34, 1.35, 8.28
    residency 1.52–1.53, 8.33
    residual bases not prejudiced by
      treaty 8.42–8.44
    territoriality 1.25–1.29, 8.25, 14.33
    universal jurisdiction/universality
      1.54–1.65, 8.34–8.41, 9.25–9.33,
      14.33, 14.34
jus cogens
  and amnesty and statutory
    limitation 11.30
  and crimes under international
    law 2.79–2.81

and immunity of state officials
  from foreign criminal
  jurisdiction 10.79–10.81, 10.88
and powers of United Nations Security
  Council 3.27

Kenya
  detention and trial of pirates captured by
    EUNAVFOR (European Union-led
    naval force) 1.57
  Shanzu Law Courts 9.39
Kosovo
  International Crimes Tribunal 9.77
  jurisdiction *ratione loci* of ICTY over
    territory of 12.28
  'regulation 64' panels and EULEX panels
    within the courts of 9.40, 9.41
  as municipal criminal courts 3.32

Lebanon *see* Special Tribunal for
  Lebanon (STL)
limitation *see* statutory limitation

**maritime navigation, unlawful acts against
  safety of, crimes of**
  background, definitions, etc 7.74, 7.76, 7.78,
    7.80, 7.82, 7.83, 7.86, 7.87
  overlap within definition of piracy *jure
    gentium* 7.82
  and individual criminal responsibility under
    international law 7.7
  obligations of states parties 7.106, 8.24,
    8.31, 8.74, 8.81, 8.83, 8.84, 9.7
**Mechanism for International Criminal
  Tribunals (MICT)** 12.2, 13.3
  co-operation with 12.49, 12.51
  due process rights 12.12
  establishment and empowerment 3.22,
    3.33, 12.7
  functions 12.7, 12.15, 12.17
  funding 12.14
  jurisdiction, exercise 12.30
  jurisdiction, existence 12.7, 12.21, 12.22,
    12.24, 12.26–12.29
  relationship to national criminal
    jurisdictions 12.34–12.36, 12.42,
    12.44, 12.45
  relationship to United Nations 12.11
  witnesses and victims 12.13, 12.17
mens rea
  absence of express requirement of in statutes
    of international criminal courts prior to
    Rome Statute 4.8
  as general condition of criminal
    responsibility under customary
    international law 4.6
  intent and knowledge as general
    mental elements under customary
    international law 4.8, 5.10

dependent on mode of responsibility in question 5.9
implications for of word 'unlawful' in definition of treaty crimes 8.9
intent and knowledge as general mental elements under Rome Statute 4.8, 5.10
intent and motive distinguished 4.9, 5.11
meaning 4.6
provision for in relation to treaty crimes 7.18

mental incapacity
as defence to crimes under customary international law 6.4, 6.9–6.13, 6.29
automatism 6.19
diminished mental capacity as mitigating circumstance in sentencing for crimes under customary international law 6.13, 6.42

mercenarism, crimes relating to
background, definition, etc 7.128–7.133
and individual criminal responsibility under international law 7.7
obligations of states parties 8.74

migrants, smuggling of, crimes relating to 7.204
see also organized crime, transnational, crimes relating to
background, definitions, etc 7.174–7.160
distinguished from trafficking in persons 7.152, 7.159
and individual criminal responsibility under international law 7.13

military necessity, plea of
distinguished from defence of duress and plea of necessity/extreme necessity 6.24
rejection of as defence to crimes under customary international law 6.37–6.38

ministers for foreign affairs
see also immunity of state officials from foreign criminal jurisdiction; internationally protected persons, crimes against; inviolability of state officials from foreign measures of physical constraint
attacks on 7.60
immunity and inviolability of serving and former 10.9, 10.33–10.36, 10.39, 10.40, 10.97

mistake of fact or law, defence of 6.5, 6.26–6.29
and defence of superior orders 6.28

mitigating circumstances 6.42–6.47

modes of responsibility
see also aiding and abetting; attempt; command and other superior responsibility; commission; common purpose, contribution to a crime by a group of persons acting with a; complicity; conspiracy; co-perpetration; direct and public incitement to commit genocide; indirect perpetration; instigation; joint criminal enterprise; omission, criminal responsibility on basis of; ordering; participation; planning; soliciting or inducing
accessorial responsibility 4.95, 5.5, 5.30, 5.44, 5.50, 5.69, 5.78, 5.79, 5.100, 7.37
concept 5.1, 5.3
for crimes under customary international law 5.1, 5.3, 5.4, 5.6
caveat as to customary status 5.2
caveat as to relevant jurisprudence to date of International Criminal Court 5.7
distinction between principal and accessory 5.5
mens rea 5.9–5.11
for crimes under Rome Statute 5.7
not elaborated on in Elements of Crimes 5.8
under municipal law 9.13, 9.14
for treaty crimes 5.4, 7.19

mutual assistance in criminal matters
absence of obligation to afford under customary international law 1.104
concept 1.103–1.05
political offence exception 1.106
rule of speciality 8.62
exception for exculpatory material 8.62
treaty obligation to afford greatest measure of 1.105, 8.62
human rights safeguard clause 8.66
treaty obligation not to refuse request on ground of bank secrecy 8.65
treaty obligation not to give effect to political offence exception 8.64
treaty obligation not to refuse request solely on ground of fiscal matters exception 8.65

narcotic drugs and psychotropic substances, illicit traffic in, crimes relating to 7.204
background, definition, etc 7.134–7.139, 7.145, 7.190
and individual criminal responsibility under international law 7.13
obligations and rights of states parties 8.7, 8.12, 8.16, 8.18, 8.19, 8.50, 8.59, 8.60, 8.65, 8.83, 8.84, 8.86, 8.87, 9.15, 11.9

ne bis in idem/non bis in idem
as between international and municipal courts 12.43–12.45, 13.37, 14.76–14.77
functions of Residual Special Court for Sierra Leone 13.18

ne bis in idem/non bis in idem (*cont.*):
  as between municipal courts of different states 1.72, 1.73
nuclear material and facilities, physical protection of, crimes relating to
  background, definitions, etc 7.66–7.73, 7.91, 7.106
  and individual criminal responsibility under international law 7.13
nuclear terrorism *see* terrorism, nuclear, crime of
nullum crimen sine lege 1.57, 1.97, 2.15, 4.22, 4.42, 4.44, 9.12, 12.23, 13.25, 14.59
Nuremberg Tribunal *see* International Military Tribunal, Nuremberg (Nuremberg IMT/Nuremberg Tribunal)

OECD (Organization for Economic Cooperation and Development) 7.172–7.174
offence *see* crime
omission, criminal responsibility on basis of 2.5, 2.15, 4.7, 5.13
  aiding and abetting 5.69–5.72, 5.77
  command and other superior responsibility 5.102, 5.111
  instigation 5.57
  ordering 5.63
ordering
  as material element of indirect perpetration 5.45
  as material element of joint criminal enterprise 5.21
  as mode of responsibility in own right
    for crimes under customary international law 5.62–5.66
    under Law on the Establishment of Extraordinary Chambers in the Courts of Cambodia 9.63
  distinguished from command and other superior responsibility 5.62
  for treaty crimes 7.8, 7.19, 7.27–7.29, 7.126, 7.203, 8.10, 8.38, 8.77
Organization of the Islamic Conference/Organization of Islamic Cooperation 7.106
organized crime, transnational, crimes relating to 2.39, 7.204
  see also bribery, crimes relating to; corruption, crimes relating to; firearms and related items, illicit manufacture of and trafficking in, crimes of; migrants, smuggling of, crimes relating to; narcotic drugs and psychotropic substances, illicit traffic in, crimes relating to; persons, trafficking in, crimes relating to
  background, definitions, etc 7.140–7.147, 7.180–7.185

  and individual criminal responsibility under international law 7.13
  obligations and rights of states parties 1.69, 8.7, 8.12, 8.14, 8.19, 8.24, 8.43, 8.50, 8.60, 8.65, 8.81, 8.83, 8.86, 8.87, 9.15, 11.9

pacta tertiis **rule (**'*pacta tertiis nec nocent nec prosunt*'**)**
  accurate statement of rule 3.38, 8.21, 14.8
  definition of 'third state' 3.43, 8.4, 14.8
  and powers of international criminal courts 3.38–3.43, 3.47, 3.48, 13.36, 13.40
    International Criminal Court 3.43, 3.47, 3.48, 14.8, 14.33, 14.78, 14.81, 14.86, 14.92, 14.92
  and prescriptive jurisdiction on treaty basis 8.21–8.23, 8.42
participation
  as accomplice as mode of responsibility for treaty crimes 7.48, 7.61, 7.65, 7.87, 7.93, 7.97, 7.185, 7.194, 7.203
  and applicable law of Special Tribunal for Lebanon 3.25
  in an organised criminal group, crime of 7.143, 7.144, 7.147
  'participation' as mode of responsibility for treaty crimes 7.72, 7.73, 7.123, 7.126, 7.139, 7.147, 7.171, 7.195, 9.13
persons, trafficking in, crimes relating to 7.204
  see also organized crime, transnational, crimes relating to
  treaty crimes 7.148–7.153, 9.41
  distinguished from smuggling of migrants 7.152, 7.159
  and individual criminal responsibility under international law 7.13
  and EULEX panels within courts of Kosovo 9.41
  and International Crimes Division of High Court of Uganda 9.66
piracy *jure gentium*, **crime of**
  absence of individual criminal responsibility under international law for 2.10, 2.53
  capture and transfer of Somali pirates 1.57, 1.70, 1.122
  definition 1.56, 1.58
    distinguished from 'robbery at sea' 1.56
    distinguished from 'shipjacking' 7.74
    'private' ends 1.58
  exclusion from ILC Draft Statute for an International Criminal Court 2.15
  high-seas slave-trade and 1.60, 9.12
  history 1.56, 2.53
  as international crime 2.12, 2.14, 2.15, 2.53
    as crime pursuant to customary international law 7.20

jurisdiction of International Crimes
  Division of High Court of Uganda
  over 9.66
prescriptive jurisdiction over ancillary
  conduct on land 1.59
reliance on SUA Convention to
  suppress 7.74
overlap with definition of crimes against
  safety of maritime navigation 7.82
rhetorical character of label '*hostes humani
  generis*' 1.56
significance of qualifier '*jure
  gentium*' 1.56, 9.12
specification as to vessels effecting seizure of
  pirate ship 1.116
trial of in Shanzu Law Courts (Kenya) 9.39
universal jurisdiction over commission
  enforcement 1.44, 1.57, 1.116
  prescriptive 1.44, 1.56–1.59, 1.62, 1.64,
    2.10, 9.12
planning
  as form of commission of crime of
    aggression 4.94, 4.95, 4.101, 5.50
  as mode of responsibility in own right for
    crimes under customary international
    law 5.49–5.54
    crimes against humanity 5.52
  as mode of responsibility in own right
    under Law on the Establishment of
    Extraordinary Chambers in the Courts
    of Cambodia 9.63
political offence exception *see* extradition;
  mutual assistance in criminal matters
preliminary inquiry into facts, treaty
  obligation to make 8.46–8.47
prevention of crime, treaty obligation of
  genocide 8.67–8.71
    derivation of obligation on contracting
      states not to commit genocide 8.71
    precise content varying with wording of
      specific treaty provision 8.72
  torture 8.73
    derivation of obligation on states parties
      not to commit torture 8.73
  various other treaty crimes 8.74
Proliferation Security Initiative 7.39
prosecution, treaty obligation of *see aut dedere
  aut judicare* (obligation to
  prosecute or extradite)
punishment of crime, treaty obligation of
  apartheid 8.76
  genocide 8.75–8.76

rape
  as crime of genocide 4.75, 4.76
  as crime against humanity 4.48
  as war crime 4.14, 4.18
**Residual Special Court for Sierra Leone
  (RSCSL)** 13.1–13.3, 13.41
  applicable law 13.24
  composition 3.20, 13.7
  co-operation with 13.39
  due process rights 13.13
  establishment and empowerment 3.17–3.19,
    13.5, 13.6
  functions 13.8, 13.19
  funding 13.15
  as an international criminal
    court 3.20, 13.6
  jurisdiction, exercise 13.31, 13.33
  jurisdiction, existence 3.20, 13.7,
    13.21–13.23, 13.27, 13.29
  relationship to national jurisdictions 13.19,
    13.35–13.37
  seat 13.8
  witnesses and victims 13.8, 13.14, 13.18
responsibility, grounds for excluding *see*
  defences
retroactivity *see nullum crimen sine lege*
robbery at sea
  distinguished from piracy *jure gentium*
    1.56
  reliance on SUA Convention to
    suppress 7.74
  suppression within territorial sea of
    Somalia 1.122
Rwanda
  gacaca courts viii
  International Criminal Tribunal for *see*
    International Criminal Tribunal for
    Rwanda (ICTR)

seizure *see* confiscation
**self-defence, defence of others, and defence
  of certain property, defence of** 6.4,
  6.15–6.19
  jus in bello binding both sides to conflict
    without distinction 6.19
self-determination, right of peoples to
  and efforts towards comprehensive
    convention on international
    terrorism 7.103, 7.106, 7.107, 7.109
  role of mercenaries in suppressing exercise
    of 7.128
  and scope of application of Additional
    Protocol I to Geneva Conventions 7.24
Senegal
  Extraordinary African Chambers in the
    Senegalese Courts 3.35, 9.72–9.76
  as municipal criminal courts 3.35
Serbia
  former Socialist Republic of 3.32, 9.40
  War Crimes Chambers of High Court and
    Appeals Court in Belgrade 9.55–9.57
Sierra Leone
  see also Residual Special Court for Sierra
    Leone (RSCSL); Special Court for
    Sierra Leone (SCSL)

Sierra Leone (*cont.*):
  Truth and Reconciliation Commission (TRC) 13.38
slavery/enslavement
  as crime against humanity under customary international law 1.60, 4.41, 4.51, 4.60
  as crime under customary international law in own right 4.73
  sexual slavery
    as war crime under customary international law 4.14
    as crime against humanity under customary international law 4.48
  treaty crimes relating to and to institutions and practices similar to 7.13, 7.34–7.37
  definition of 'slavery' 7.36
  and individual criminal responsibility under international law 7.13
slave trade
  as crime against humanity under customary international law 1.60
  on high seas
    enforcement jurisdiction over 1.17
    prescriptive jurisdiction over 1.60, 1.62
  as treaty crime 7.13, 7.34–7.37
  and individual criminal responsibility under international law 7.13
smuggling of migrants *see* migrants, smuggling of, crimes relating to
soliciting or inducing
  as mode of responsibility
    for crimes under customary international law 5.67
    for treaty crimes 7.126
Special Court for Sierra Leone (SCSL) 13.1–13.3, 13.41
  absence from Statute of express *mens rea* requirement 4.8
  absence from Statute of express provision for defences 6.3
  applicable law 13.24
  assessment 13.41
  basic facts 13.6–13.15
  cases 13.16–13.17
  composition 3.20, 13.7
  co-operation with 13.39, 13.40
    third states 13.40
  detention by 13.12
  due process rights 13.13
  establishment and empowerment 3.17–3.19, 13.4, 13.6
  see also Residual Special Court for Sierra Leone (RSCSL)
  ad hoc character 13.5
  legality 13.20
  transition to Residual Special Court for Sierra Leone 13.5
  funding 13.15
  as an international criminal court 3.20, 13.6
  jurisdiction, exercise
    amnesty 13.33, 13.34
    immunity of state officials 13.31, 13.32
  jurisdiction, existence 3.20, 13.7, 13.21, 13.22
    see also crimes against humanity; Geneva Conventions, other violations of and violations of Additional Protocol II to; international humanitarian law; war crimes
  jurisdiction *ratione loci* 13.28
  jurisdiction *ratione materiae* 4.11, 4.14, 4.47, 4.48, 4.50, 5.16, 13.23–13.27
  jurisdiction *ratione personae* 13.28–13.30
  jurisdiction *ratione temporis* 13.28
  position on criminal responsibility as principal and as accessory 5.5
  procedural essentials 14.19
  Prosecutor 13.10
  relationship to courts of Sierra Leone 13.19
    concurrency 13.35
    non bis in idem 13.37
    primacy 13.36
    third states 13.36
  relationship with Sierra Leone Truth and Reconciliation Commission 13.38
  Rules of Procedure and Evidence, adoption and amendment 13.9
  structure 13.7, 13.10
  use of term 'court' in title 3.3
  witnesses and victims 13.14
special missions
  definition of 'special mission' 10.29
  immunity of certain members and former members from foreign criminal jurisdiction 10.9, 10.29, 10.33, 10.35, 10.40, 10.44, 10.60, 10.97, 10.99, 10.102
  excluded from scope of International Law Commission's work on immunity of state officials from foreign criminal jurisdiction 10.10
Special Tribunal for Lebanon (STL)
  absence of detailed account of in book vii
  applicable law 2.31, 3.25
  asserted existence of crime of terrorism under customary international law 4.104
  composition 3.25
  establishment and empowerment 3.24, 3.25, 3.27
  as an international criminal court 3.25
  jurisdiction *ratione materiae* 3.25, 3.25
  witnesses and victims 14.17
  use of word 'tribunal' in name 3.3

Index 605

status of forces agreements (SOFAs) 1.81,
  8.85, 10.10, 10.64, 14.56, 14.99, 14.100
status of mission agreements (SOMAs) 1.81,
  14.56, 14.99, 14.100
statutory limitation
  definition 11.1
  for international crimes
    international legality of grant 11.3–11.15,
      11.25–11.31
    international legality of ignoring by third
      states 11.32–11.34, 11.37
    and international human rights
      law 11.3, 11.36
    and jurisdiction of International Criminal
      Court 14.48–14.50, 14.75
    and jurisdiction of specific municipal
      criminal courts
      ad hoc human rights courts
        (Indonesia) 9.48
      Extraordinary Chambers in the Courts of
        Cambodia 9.64
      Iraqi High Criminal Court 9.53
      Special Panels in District Court of
        Dili and Court of Appeal of East
        Timor 9.45
superior orders
  as defence 2.71, 4.106, 6.6, 6.30–6.36,
    8.79, 10.66
  conflation with defence of duress 6.32
  and defence of mistake of law 6.28
  distinguished from defence of
    duress 6.25, 6.35
  overlap with plea of act of
    state 2.71, 6.31
  as mitigating circumstance in sentencing for
    crimes under customary international
    law 6.31–6.33, 6.42, 6.45
superior responsibility *see* command and other
  superior responsibility
surrender *see* suspects
suspects
  obligation to search for under Geneva
    Conventions 8.77
  surrender of
    see also arrest; *aut dedere aut judicare*
      (treaty obligation to prosecute or
      extradite); extradition; immunity
      of state officials from foreign
      criminal jurisdiction; International
      Criminal Court (ICC); International
      Criminal Tribunal for Rwanda
      (ICTR); International Criminal
      Tribunal for the former Yugoslavia
      (ICTY); inviolability of state officials
      from foreign measures of physical
      constraint; Special Court for Sierra
      Leone (SCSL)
    no obligation of interstate surrender under
      customary international law 1.90

surrender to an international
  criminal court and extradition
  distinguished 12.53, 14.83

Taylor, Charles 13.8, 13.16, 13.17,
  13.32, 13.40
terrorism
  see also aircraft; civil aviation, unlawful
    acts relating to, crimes of; continental
    shelf; hostage-taking, crime of;
    internationally protected persons,
    crimes against; maritime navigation,
    unlawful acts against safety of, crimes
    of; nuclear material and facilities,
    physical protection of, crimes relating
    to; terrorism, financing of, crime of;
    terrorism, nuclear, crime of; terrorist
    bombings, crimes relating to
  asserted existence as crime under customary
    international law 4.104
  treaty-based international criminal legal
    responses to 7.38–7.41, 7.102–7.109
  efforts towards comprehensive
    convention on international
    terrorism 7.104–7.109
terrorism, financing of, crime of
  background, definition, etc 7.94–7.97, 7.101,
    7.105, 7.106
  and individual criminal responsibility under
    international law 7.7
  obligations and rights of states parties 8.28,
    8.30, 8.65, 8.80, 8.81, 8.83, 9.16
  use of word 'terrorism' in treaty title 7.40
terrorism, nuclear, crime of
  background, definition,
    etc 7.98–7.101, 7.106
  and individual criminal responsibility under
    international law 7.7
  obligations and rights of states parties 8.28,
    8.30, 8.74, 8.80, 8.83, 9.16
  use of word 'terrorism' in treaty title 7.40
terrorist bombings, crime of
  background, definition *etc* 7.90–7.93,
    7.105, 7.106
  and individual criminal responsibility under
    international law 7.7
  obligations and rights of states parties 8.28,
    8.30, 8.74, 8.80, 8.83, 9.16
  use of word 'terrorist' in treaty title 7.40
third states *see pacta tertiis* rule
Timor-Leste *see* East Timor
Tokyo Tribunal *see* International Military
  Tribunal for the Far East, Tokyo (Tokyo
  IMT/Tokyo Tribunal)
torture
  as crime in own right under customary
    international law 1.63, 4.103
  as 'international crime' 2.12, 2.81
  and equivalent obligation for states 2.77

torture (*cont.*):
  as grave breach of Geneva
    Conventions 4.32, 7.8, 7.25
  jurisdiction of municipal criminal
    courts over
      Extraordinary African Chambers in the
        Senegalese Courts 9.74, 11.14
      Extraordinary Chambers in the Courts of
        Cambodia 9.64
      Special Panels in the District Court of
        Dili and Court of Appeal of East
        Timor 3.31, 9.44, 9.45, 11.15
  and *jus cogens* 2.79–2.81
  as crime of genocide 4.75
  as treaty crime of apartheid 7.115
  prohibition on/right not to be tortured
    under international human rights
    law 2.8
  'public official' requirement
    torture as crime against humanity
      under customary international
      law 4.57
    torture as treaty crime in own right 7.118,
      7.120, 10.74, 10.90
    torture as war crime under customary
      international law 4.32
  as species of crime against humanity under
    customary international law 4.57
    definition 4.57
  as treaty crime in own right 7.204
    and amnesty 11.18, 11.23, 11.24,
      11.33
    background, definition, etc 2.10, 7.110,
      7.117–7.123
    and immunity of state officials from
      foreign criminal jurisdiction 10.42,
      10.44, 10.74, 10.75, 10.77, 10.78,
      10.80, 10.82, 10.90, 10.91
    incapable of transnational
      commission 2.47
    and individual criminal responsibility
      under international law 2.10, 7.13
    as 'international crime' 2.12, 2.14
    obligations of states parties 8.3, 8.7, 8.8,
      8.24, 8.47, 8.49, 8.52, 8.53, 8.73,
      8.79, 9.16, 9.24, 9.72
    municipal legislative implementation 9.7,
      9.16, 9.24
    and statutory limitation 11.8,
      11.14, 11.15
  as war crime under customary international
    law 4.32
trafficking in persons *see* persons, trafficking
  in, crimes relating to
transfer of proceedings 8.86
'transnational' crimes 2.46–2.48
transnational organized crime *see* organized
  crime, transnational, crimes relating to

tribunals, international criminal *see* courts,
  criminal
treaty crimes
see also international crimes
  and crimes under customary international
    law 8.5
  and individual criminal responsibility under
    international law 2.36, 2.37, 7.2–7.12
  difficulty of ascertaining provision for
    under treaty 2.16, 7.6, 7.13, 7.14
  possibility of in principle under
    treaty 2.68
  technical reality of under treaty 7.4
  meaning of term 2.37
  object and purpose of relevant
    treaties 7.1, 8.1
  obligations in relation to as obligations *erga*
    omnes 8.3
  and *pacta tertiis* rule 8.4, 8.21–8.23
  scope of application *ratione personae* of
    crimes under treaty 7.15, 7.16
  as species of international crime 2.36, 2.37
  subspecies of
    crimes pursuant to treaty 2.37, 7.3, 7.5,
      7.13, 7.14
    crimes under treaty 2.37, 7.2–7.12,
      7.15, 7.16
    formal distinction of little practical
      consequence 7.5
tu quoque, plea of 6.39–6.40

Uganda
  International Crimes Division of High
    Court 9.66–9.67
United Nations and associated personnel,
  crimes against the safety of
  background, definitions, etc 7.196–7.203
  and individual criminal responsibility under
    international law 7.13
  obligations of states parties 8.74, 8.85
United Kingdom (UK)
  and International Military Tribunal,
    Nuremberg 2.59, 3.13
  post-Second World War military
    courts 3.30, 4.45, 9.43
  as municipal criminal courts 3.30
United Nations Mission in Kosovo
  (UNMIK) 3.32, 9.40, 9.41
United Nations Transitional Administration
  in East Timor (UNTAET) 1.39, 1.63,
  3.31, 9.44, 11.15
United Nations War Crimes Commission
  (UNWCC) 6.16
United States (US)
  'article 98' agreements 14.101–14.106
  and International Military Tribunal,
    Nuremberg 2.59, 3.13
  military commissions 9.37, 9.43

Index

post-Second World War military
 tribunals 3.30, 4.45, 9.43
 as municipal criminal courts 3.30
universal jurisdiction
 controversy over exercise 1.28, 1.32, 1.42,
  9.22, 9.25–9.30
 voluntary restrictions on exercise 1.28,
  1.32, 1.42, 1.53, 9.33
 definition 1.54, 8.35
  as a manifestation of prescriptive
   jurisdiction 1.54
  distinguished from treaty obligation *aut
   dedere aut judicare* 8.55
 exercise *in absentia*
  permissibility under customary
   international law 1.55, 9.31
  permissibility pursuant to
   treaty 9.31, 9.32
  term 'universal jurisdiction *in absentia*'
   disaggregated 1.55, 9.31
 municipal implementation 9.12, 9.18
 obligation/permission to establish
  pursuant to treaty 2.10, 4.20, 7.8,
  8.34–8.41, 9.25
  and third states 8.21–8.23
 permissibility under customary
  international law
  common crimes in cases of double
   criminality 1.65
  crimes under customary international
   law 1.61–1.64, 2.10, 2.20, 4.5, 8.40,
   9.25, 14.33, 14.34
  piracy *jure gentium* 1.44, 1.56–1.59, 2.10
  slavery and the slave trade 1.60
 and prescriptive jurisdiction based on
  residency 1.52
 rationale/rationalization
  for crimes under customary international
   law 1.64
  formal legal rationalization differing
   as between piracy *jure gentium*
   and crimes under customary
   international law 1.64
  functional justification same as between
   piracy *jure gentium* and crimes under
   customary international law 1.64
  for piracy *jure gentium* 1.56

victims
 support for viii, 12.7, 12.13, 12.17, 13.14,
  13.18, 14.17
 participation of in proceedings before
  International Criminal Court 14.17
 Trust Fund for Victims 14.17
violations of the laws and customs of war
 in international armed conflict
  absence of conclusive list 4.15
  evolution 2.55–2.67, 2.69–2.73,
   4.12–4.15, 4.24
  jurisdiction of international criminal
   courts over 4.11, 4.13, 4.15,
   4.34, 12.22
  material elements 4.28–4.34
  mental elements 4.36, 4.37
 in non-international armed conflict
  absence of conclusive list 4.19
  evolution 4.16–4.19
  jurisdiction of international criminal
   courts over 4.18, 4.19, 12.22
  material elements 4.28–4.34
  mental elements 4.36, 4.37
 as subset of war crimes under customary
  international law 4.10
 terminology
  'serious violations of international
   humanitarian law' 4.11
  'violations of the laws and customs
   applicable in armed conflict' 4.11
 use of term 'war' 4.11

waiver of immunity *see* immunity of state
 officials from foreign criminal
 jurisdiction
war crimes
 see also cultural property, destruction
  and plunder of in armed conflict,
  war crimes relating to; Geneva
  Conventions, grave breaches of;
  Geneva Conventions, grave breaches
  of Additional Protocol I to; Geneva
  Conventions, other violations of and
  violations of Additional Protocol II
  to; violations of the laws and
  customs of war
 under customary international law
  comparative gravity 4.105, 4.106
  evolution 4.12–4.27
  material elements 4.28–4.35
  mental elements 4.36–4.38
 explanation of term 4.10
 under treaty 4.10, 7.8
  grave breaches of Geneva Conventions
   and Additional Protocol I
   7.21–7.28
  serious violations of the 1999 Second
   Hague Protocol 7.29–7.33
 use of term 'war' 4.11
warrant of arrest *see* arrest
witnesses
 claims for asylum by in context
  of international criminal
  proceedings 14.13
 and 'complementarity' 14.71
 and immunity of state officials from foreign
  criminal jurisdiction 10.9, 10.15,
  10.24, 10.29, 10.33, 10.40, 10.55

witnesses (*cont.*):
  and mutual assistance in criminal matters 1.105
  powers of international criminal courts in relation to 12.52, 14.84, 14.87
  and states' enforcement jurisdiction 1.77
  protection and support for by international criminal courts viii, 12.7, 12.13, 12.17, 13.8, 13.14, 13.18, 14.17
  and treaty obligation to conduct a preliminary inquiry into the facts 8.47
  treaty crimes relating to
    crimes against the administration of the International Criminal Court's justice 7.12
    crimes of corruption 7.146

Yugoslavia *see* International Criminal Tribunal for the former Yugoslavia (ICTY)

Printed and bound by CPI Group (UK) Ltd, Croydon, CR0 4YY